D1274260

Library of Southern Civilization

Library of Southern Civilization
LEWIS P. SIMPSON, EDITOR

Twelve Years a Slave, by Solomon Northup
Edited by Sue Eakin and Joseph Logsdon

Bricks Without Straw, by Albion Tourgée
Edited by Otto H. Olsen

Still Rebels, Still Yankees and Other Essays
Donald Davidson

*The Diary of Edmund Ruffin
Volume I, Toward Independence:
October, 1856–April, 1861*
Edited by William Kauffman Scarborough

The Great South, by Edward King
Edited by W. Magruder Drake and Robert R. Jones

THE GREAT SOUTH

The

GREAT
SOUTH

by Edward King

Edited by W. Magruder Drake and Robert R. Jones

LOUISIANA STATE UNIVERSITY PRESS

BATON ROUGE 1972

ISBN 0–8071–0240–7
Library of Congress Catalog Card Number 72–79332
Copyright © 1972 by Louisiana State University Press
All rights reserved
Manufactured in the United States of America
Printed by Kingsport Press, Inc., Kingsport, Tennessee

814838

LIBRARY
ALMA COLLEGE
ALMA, MICHIGAN

TO
Lelia Drake
AND
R. Jefferson and Marian N. Jones
TO ALL OF WHOM THE GREAT SOUTH IS HOME.

LIBRARY
OHIO STATE
MAIN

CONTENTS

	EDITORS' INTRODUCTION	xxi
	PREFACE	lxvii
	DEDICATION	lxix
I	LOUISIANA, PAST AND PRESENT	17
II	THE FRENCH QUARTER OF NEW ORLEANS—THE REVOLUTION AND ITS EFFECTS	28
III	THE CARNIVAL—THE FRENCH MARKETS	38
IV	THE COTTON TRADE—THE NEW ORLEANS LEVEES	50
V	THE CANALS AND THE LAKE—THE AMERICAN QUARTER	59
VI	ON THE MISSISSIPPI RIVER—THE LEVEE SYSTEM—RAILROADS—THE FORT ST. PHILIP CANAL	67
VII	THE INDUSTRIES OF LOUISIANA—A SUGAR PLANTATION—THE TECHE COUNTRY	78
VIII	THE POLITICAL SITUATION IN LOUISIANA	89
IX	"HO FOR TEXAS!"—GALVESTON	99
X	A VISIT TO HOUSTON	110
XI	PICTURES FROM PRISON AND FIELD	117
XII	AUSTIN, THE TEXAN CAPITAL—POLITICS—SCHOOLS	127
XIII	THE TRUTH ABOUT TEXAS—THE JOURNEY BY STAGE TO SAN ANTONIO	137
XIV	AMONG THE OLD SPANISH MISSIONS	147
XV	THE PEARL OF THE SOUTH-WEST	157
XVI	THE PLAINS—THE CATTLE TRADE	167
XVII	DENISON—TEXAN CHARACTERISTICS	175
XVIII	THE NEW ROUTE TO THE GULF	186
XIX	THE "INDIAN TERRITORY"	197
XX	RAILROAD PIONEERING—INDIAN TYPES AND CHARACTER	204
XXI	MISSOURI—ST. LOUIS, PAST AND PRESENT	215
XXII	ST. LOUIS GERMANS AND AMERICANS—SPECULATIVE PHILOSOPHY—EDUCATION	222
XXIII	COMMERCE OF ST. LOUIS—THE NEW BRIDGE OVER THE MISSISSIPPI	230
XXIV	THE MINERAL WEALTH OF MISSOURI	237
XXV	TRADE IN ST. LOUIS—THE PRESS—KANSAS CITY—ALONG THE MISSISSIPPI —THE CAPITAL	246
XXVI	DOWN THE MISSISSIPPI FROM ST. LOUIS	257
XXVII	MEMPHIS, THE CHIEF CITY OF TENNESSEE—ITS TRADE AND CHARACTER	264
XXVIII	THE "SUPPLY" SYSTEM IN THE COTTON COUNTRY, AND ITS RESULTS—NEGRO	

	LABOR—PRESENT PLANS OF WORKING COTTON PLANTATIONS—THE BLACK MAN IN THE MISSISSIPPI VALLEY	270
XXIX	ARKANSAS—ITS RESOURCES—ITS PEOPLE—ITS POLITICS—TAXATION—THE HOT SPRINGS	278
XXX	VICKSBURG AND NATCHEZ, MISSISSIPPI—SOCIETY AND POLITICS—A LOUISIANA PARISH JURY	287
XXXI	LIFE ON COTTON PLANTATIONS	297
XXXII	MISSISSIPPI—ITS TOWNS—FINANCES—SCHOOLS—PLANTATION DIFFICULTIES	311
XXXIII	MOBILE, THE CHIEF CITY OF ALABAMA	319
XXXIV	THE RESOURCES OF ALABAMA—VISITS TO MONTGOMERY AND SELMA	328
XXXV	NORTHERN ALABAMA—THE TENNESSEE VALLEY—TRAITS OF CHARACTER—EDUCATION	339
XXXVI	THE SAND-HILL REGION—AIKEN—AUGUSTA	344
XXXVII	ATLANTA—GEORGIA POLITICS—THE FAILURE OF RECONSTRUCTION	350
XXXVIII	SAVANNAH, THE FOREST CITY—THE RAILWAY SYSTEM OF GEORGIA—MATERIAL PROGRESS OF THE STATE	358
XXXIX	GEORGIAN AGRICULTURE—"CRACKERS"—COLUMBUS—MACON—SOCIETY—ATHENS—THE COAST	371
XL	THE JOURNEY TO FLORIDA—THE PENINSULA'S HISTORY—JACKSONVILLE	377
XLI	UP THE ST. JOHN'S RIVER—TOCOI—ST. AUGUSTINE	383
XLII	ST. AUGUSTINE, FLORIDA—FORT MARION	390
XLIII	THE CLIMATE OF FLORIDA—A JOURNEY TO PALATKA	398
XLIV	ORANGE CULTURE IN FLORIDA—FERTILITY OF THE PENINSULA	402
XLV	UP THE OCLAWAHA TO SILVER SPRING	408
XLVI	THE UPPER ST. JOHN'S—INDIAN RIVER—KEY WEST—POLITICS—THE NEW CONSTITUTION	416
XLVII	SOUTH CAROLINA—PORT ROYAL—THE SEA ISLANDS—THE REVOLUTION	422
XLVIII	ON A RICE PLANTATION IN SOUTH CAROLINA	429
XLIX	CHARLESTON, SOUTH CAROLINA	438
L	THE VENICE OF AMERICA—CHARLESTON'S POLITICS—A LOVELY LOWLAND CITY—IMMIGRATION	444
LI	THE SPOLIATION OF SOUTH CAROLINA	454
LII	THE NEGROES IN ABSOLUTE POWER	460
LIII	THE LOWLANDS OF NORTH CAROLINA	466
LIV	AMONG THE SOUTHERN MOUNTAINS—JOURNEY FROM EASTERN TENNESSEE TO WESTERN NORTH CAROLINA	474
LV	ACROSS THE "SMOKY" TO WAYNESVILLE—THE MASTER CHAIN OF THE ALLEGHANIES	480
LVI	THE "SUGAR FORK" AND DRY FALLS—WHITESIDE MOUNTAIN	490
LVII	ASHEVILLE—THE FRENCH BROAD VALLEY—THE ASCENT OF MOUNT MITCHELL	503

CONTENTS   xi

LVIII   The South Carolina Mountains—Cascades and Peaks of Northern
             Georgia   515
LIX   Chattanooga, the Gateway of the South   527
LX   Lookout Mountain—The Battles Around Chattanooga—Knoxville—
             Eastern Tennessee   536
LXI   A Visit to Lynchburg in Virginia   552
LXII   In South-western Virginia—The Peaks of Otter—The Mineral Springs 561
LXIII   Among the Mountains—From Bristol to Lynchburg   569
LXIV   Petersburg—A Negro Revival Meeting   579
LXV   The Dismal Swamp—Norfolk—The Coast   588
LXVI   The Education of Negroes—The American Missionary Association—The
             Peabody Fund—The Civil Rights Bill   596
LXVII   The Hampton Normal Institute—General Armstrong's Work—Fisk
             University—Berea and Other Colleges   603
LXVIII   Negro Songs and Singers   609
LXIX   A Peep at the Past of Virginia—Jamestown—Williamsburg—Yorktown 621
LXX   Richmond—Its Trade and Character   626
LXXI   The Partition of Virginia—Reconstruction and Politics in West and
             East Virginia   639
LXXII   From Richmond to Charlottesville   647
LXXIII   From Charlottesville to Staunton, Virginia—The Shenandoah Valley
             —Lexington—The Graves of General Lee and "Stonewall" Jackson—
             From Goshen to "White Sulphur Springs"   656
LXXIV   Greenbrier White Sulphur Springs—From the "White Sulphur" to
             Kanawha Valley—The Mineral Springs Region   670
LXXV   The Kanawha Valley—Mineral Wealth of Western Virginia   681
LXXVI   Down the Ohio River—Louisville   693
LXXVII   A Visit to the Mammoth Cave   699
LXXVIII   The Trade of Louisville   707
LXXIX   Frankfort—The Blue Grass Region—Alexander's Farm—Lexington   713
LXXX   Politics in Kentucky—Mineral Resources of the State   721
LXXXI   Nashville and Middle Tennessee   726
LXXXII   A Glance at Maryland's History—Her Extent and Resources   733
LXXXIII   The Baltimore and Ohio Railroad   741
LXXXIV   The Trade of Baltimore—Its Rapid and Astonishing Growth   748
LXXXV   Baltimore and Its Institutions   757
LXXXVI   Southern Characteristics—State Pride—The Influence of Railroads—
             Poor Whites—Their Habits   771
LXXXVII   The Carrying of Weapons—Moral Character of the Negroes   777
LXXXVIII   Dialect—Forms of Expression—Diet   784

LXXXIX   IMMIGRATION—THE NEED OF CAPITAL—DIVISION OF THE NEGRO VOTE—THE
            SOUTHERN LADIES   792

XC   RAMBLES IN VIRGINIA—FREDERICKSBURG—ALEXANDRIA—MOUNT VERNON—
            ARLINGTON   795

          APPENDIX   803

          INDEX   807

ILLUSTRATIONS

AND MAPS.

PAGE.

Scene on the Oclawaha River, Florida—Frontispiece
General Map of the Southern States........... 15
Bienville, the Founder of New Orleans......... 17
The Cathedral St. Louis—New Orleans........ 18
"A blind beggar hears the rustling of her gown,
    and stretches out his trembling hand for
    alms,"............................. 19
"A black girl looks wonderingly into the holy-water
    font".. 19
The Archbishop's Palace, New Orleans........ 20
"Some aged private dwellings, rapidly decaying," 25
A brace of old Spanish Governors.—From por-
    traits owned by Hon. Charles Gayarré, of New
    Orleans...................................... 26
"And where to-day stands a fine Equestrian Statue
    of the Great General"....................... 27
"A lazy negro, recumbent in a cart"............ 29
"The negro nurses stroll on the sidewalks, chatter-
    ing in quaint French to the little children".... 30
"The interior garden, with its curious shrine".... 31
"The new Ursuline Convent, New Orleans....... 32
"And while they chatter like monkeys, even about
    politics, they gesticulate violently"........... 35
"The old French and Spanish cemeteries present
    long streets of cemented walls".............. 36
The St. Louis Hotel, New Orleans............. 37
The Carnival—"White and black join in its mas-
    querading"................................. 38
"The coming of Rex, most puissant King of Car-
    nival"...................................... 40
"The Bœuf-Gras—the fat ox—is led in the proces-
    sion"....................................... 41
"When Rex and his train enter the queer old
    streets, the balconies are crowded with spec-
    tators"..................................... 42
"The joyous, grotesque maskers appear upon the
    ball-room floor"............................. 43
"Many bright eyes are in vain endeavoring to
    pierce the disguise"......................... 45
"The French market at sunrise on Sunday morning" 46
"Passing under long, hanging rows of bananas
    and pine-apples"............................ 47
"One sees delicious types in these markets" 48
"In a long passage, between two of the market
    buildings, sits a silent Louisiana Indian wo-
    man"....................................... 49
"Stout colored women, with cackling hens dang-
    ling from their brawny hands"............... 49
"These boats, closely ranged in long rows by the
    levée"...................................... 50

PAGE.

"Whenever there is a lull in the work, they sink
    down on the cotton bales".................... 52
"Not far from the levée there is a police court,
    where they especially delight to lounge"...... 52
"The cotton thieves"............................ 55
"There is the old apple and cake woman"....... 55
"The Sicilian fruit-seller"........ 56
"At high water, the juvenile population perches on
    the beams of the wharves, and enjoys a little
    quiet fishing".............................. 57
"The polite but consequential negro policeman," 57
The St. Charles Hotel, New Orleans........... 59
The New Basin............................... 60
The old Spanish Fort......................... 60
The University of Louisiana, New Orleans..... 61
The Theatres of New Orleans.................. 61
Christ Church, New Orleans........ 62
The Canal street Fountain, New Orleans....... 62
The Charity Hospital, New Orleans............ 63
The old Maison de Santé, New Orleans........ 63
The United States Marine Hospital, New Orleans 64
Trinity Church, New Orleans.................. 64
St. Paul's Church, New Orleans............... 64
First Presbyterian Church, New Orleans....... 65
The Catholic Churches of New Orleans — St. Jo-
    seph's, St. Patrick's, Jesuit Church and School 65
The Custom-House, New Orleans.............. 66
The United States Branch Mint, New Orleans.. 66
"Sometimes the boat stops at a coaling station".. 68
"The Wasp"................................... 69
"Some tract of hopelessly irreclaimable, grotesque
    water wilderness." (From a painting by Julio.) 70
The monument on the Chalmette battle-field.... 72
Light-house, South-west Pass.................. 74
"Pilot Town," South-west Pass................. 75
"A Nickel for Daddy"......................... 77
"A cheery Chinaman".......................... 82
Sugar-cane Plantation—"The cane is cut down
    at its perfection".......................... 83
"The beautiful 'City Park,'" New Orleans...... 87
Map showing the Distribution of the Colored
    Population of the United States. (From the
    U. S. Census Reports)...................... 88
Map of the Gulf States and Arkansas.......... 89
The Supreme Court, New Orleans............. 92
The United States Barracks, New Orleans...... 93
Mechanics' Institute, New Orleans............ 95
Going to Texas............................... 99
"It is only a few steps from an oleander grove to
    the surf".................................... 102

PAGE.

"The mule-carts unloading schooners anchored lightly in the shallow waves"................ 103
"Galveston has many huge cotton-presses"...... 104
The Custom-House, Galveston................ 105
"Primitive enough is this Texan jail".......... 106
The Catholic Cathedral, Galveston............ 107
"Watch the negro fisherman as he throws his line horizonward"................................ 108
"The cotton-train is already a familiar spectacle on all the great trunk lines"................ 110
"There are some notable nooks and bluffs along the bayou"................................ 112
"The Head-quarters of the Masonic Lodges of the State"................................ 113
"The railroad depots are everywhere crowded with negroes, immigrants, tourists and speculators"................................ 113
The New Market, Houston.................... 114
"The ragged urchin with his saucy face"....... 114
"The negro on his dray, racing good-humoredly with his fellows"........................ 115
"The auctioneer's young man"................ 116
Sam Houston................................ 117
View on the Trinity River.................... 118
"We frequently passed large gangs of the convicts chopping logs in the forest by the roadside"................................ 119
"Satanta had seated himself on a pile of oakum"................................ 121
"As the train passes, the negroes gather in groups to gaze at it until it disappears in the distance"................................ 123
The State Capitol, Austin.................... 127
The State Insane Asylum, Austin.............. 128
The Texas Military Institute, Austin.......... 128
The Governor's Mansion, Austin.............. 129
The Alamo Monument, Austin................ 131
The Land Office of Texas, Austin............ 133
"The emigrant wagon is a familiar sight there".. 135
Sunning themselves—"A group of Mexicans, lounging by a wall"................... 140
"We encounter wagons drawn by oxen"........ 141
"Here and there we pass a hunter's camp"...... 143
"We pass groups of stone houses"............. 146
"The vast pile of ruins known as the San José Mission"................................ 147
The old Concepcion Mission, near San Antonio, Texas................................ 151
An old window in the San José Mission........ 155
"An umbrella and candlestick graced the christening font"................................ 155
"The comfortable country-house so long occupied by Victor Considerant"................. 156
The San Antonio River—"Its blueish current flows in a narrow but picturesque channel".. 157
The source of the San Antonio River.......... 157
San Pedro Springs—"The Germans have established their beer gardens"................. 158
"Every few rods there is a waterscape in miniature"................................ 158
"The river passes under bridges, by arbors and bath-houses"................................ 159
The Ursuline Convent, San Antonio.......... 159
St. Mary's Church, San Antonio.............. 160

PAGE.

A Mexican Hovel............................ 161
The Military Plaza, San Antonio.............. 161
"The Mexicans slowly saw and carve the great stones"................................ 162
"The elder women wash clothes by the brookside" 163
Mexican types in San Antonio.................. 164
"The remnant of the old Fort of the Alamo".... 165
"The horsemen from the plains"............... 167
"The candy and fruit merchants lazily wave their fly-brushes"................................ 168
A Mexican beggar............................ 168
"The citizens gather at San Antonio, and discuss measures of vengeance"................... 170
A Texan Cattle-Drover........................ 171
Military Head-quarters, San Antonio.......... 172
Negro Soldiers of the San Antonio Garrison... 173
Scene in a Gambling House—"Playing Keno," Denison, Texas............................ 175
"Men, drunk and sober, danced to rude music". 176
"Red Hall"................................ 178
The Public Square in Sherman, Texas......... 180
"With swine that trotted hither and yon"....... 181
Bridge over the Red River—(Missouri, Kansas and Texas Railway)........................ 182
The New Route to the Gulf.................... 186
"The Pet Conductor".......................... 188
"Charlie"................................ 188
Our Special Train............................ 189
"A stock-train from Sedalia was receiving a squealing and bellowing freight".................. 190
"The old Hospital," Fort Scott................. 191
Bridge over the Marmiton River, near Fort Scott 192
A Street in Parsons, Kansas.................... 193
A Kansas Herdsman.......................... 193
A Kansas Farm-yard.......................... 194
"The Little Grave, with the slain horses lying upon it"................................ 195
"The stone house which the graceless Kaw has turned into a stable for his pony"........... 195
"The warrior galloping across the fields "....... 196
Monument erected to the memory of Brevet-Major E. A. Ogden, near Fort Riley, Kansas 196
An Indian Territorial Mansion................ 197
A Creek Indian............................ 199
Bridge across the North Fork of the Canadian River, Indian Territory (M. K. and T. Railway) 199
An Adopted Citizen.......................... 200
An Indian Stock-Drover...................... 201
"The ball-players are fine specimens of men".. 202
A Gentleman from the Arkansas Border........ 203
Limestone Gap, Indian Territory.............. 204
"Coming in the twilight to a region where great mounds reared their whale-backed heights ".. 205
A "Terminus" Rough........................ 206
"We came to the bank of the Grand River, on a hill beyond which was the Post of Fort Gibson"................................ 206
A Negro Boy at the Ferry.................... 208
"We found the ferries obstructed by masses of floating ice"................................ 209
"They wore a prim, Shakerish costume"........ 210
A Trader among the Indians.................. 210
"The Asbury Manual Labor School," in the Creek domain................................ 211

The Toll-Bridge at Limestone Gap, Indian Territory 213

"Looking down on the St. Louis of to-day, from the high roof of the Insurance temple" 215

"Where now stands the great stone Cathedral" .. 216

The old Chouteau Mansion (as it was) 217

The St. Louis Life Insurance Company's Building 218

"In those days the houses were nearly all built of hewn logs" 218

"The crowd awaiting transportation across the stream has always been of the most cosmopolitan and motley character" 220

The Court-House, St. Louis 222

Thomas H. Benton (for thirty years United States Senator from Missouri) 223

William T. Harris, editor of the St. Louis "Journal of Speculative Philosophy" 226

The High School, St. Louis 228

Washington University, St. Louis 229

The new Post-Office and Custom-House in construction at St. Louis 230

The new Bridge over the Mississippi at St. Louis 233

View of the Caisson of the East Abutment of the St. Louis Bridge, as it appeared during construction 234

The building of the East Pier of the St. Louis Bridge 235

In the "Cut" at Iron Mountain, Missouri 237

At the Vulcan Iron Works, Carondelet 238

The Furnace, Iron Mountain, Missouri 241

The Summit of Pilot Knob, Iron County, Missouri 243

The "Tracks," Pilot Knob, Missouri 244

Map of Missouri 245

View in Shaw's Garden, St. Louis 246

Statue to Thomas H. Benton, in Lafayette Park. 247

The "Four Courts" Building, St. Louis 248

The Gratiot Street Prison, St. Louis 248

First Presbyterian Church, St. Louis 249

Christ Church, St. Louis 250

The Missouri Capitol, at Jefferson City 254

"The Cheery Minstrel" 255

The Steamer "Great Republic," a Mississippi River Boat 257

"Down the steep banks would come kaleidoscopic processions of negroes and flour barrels" 258

The Levée at Cairo, Illinois 259

An Inundated Town on the Mississippi's bank .. 260

The Pilot-House of the "Great Republic" 261

A Crevasse in the Mississippi River's Banks 262

View in the City Park at Memphis, Tennessee .. 264

The Carnival at Memphis, Tennessee—"The gorgeous pageants of the mysterious Memphi" 268

A Steamboat Torch-Basket 277

View on the Arkansas River at Little Rock 279

The Arkansas State Capitol, Little Rock 281

The Hot Springs, Arkansas 286

Vicksburg, Mississippi 287

The National Cemetery at Vicksburg, Mississippi 288

The Gamblers' Graves, Vicksburg, Mississippi. 289

Colonel Vick, of Vicksburg, Mississippi, Planter 289

Natchez-under-the-Hill, Mississippi 291

View in Brown's Garden, Natchez, Mississippi .. 292

Avenue in Brown's Garden, Natchez, Mississippi 293

A Mississippi River Steamer arriving at Natchez in the night 294

"Sah?" 296

A Cotton Wagon-Train 302

A Cotton-Steamer 304

Scene on a Cotton Plantation 307

Baton Rouge, Louisiana 309

The Red River Raft as it Was 310

Map showing the Cotton Region of the United States. (From the U. S. Census Reports.) ... 312

Map of South Carolina, Georgia, Florida and Alabama 313

The Mississippi State Capitol at Jackson 313

"At the proper seasons, one sees in the long main street of the town, lines of emigrant wagons," 314

"The negroes migrate to Louisiana and Texas in search of paying labor" 318

On the Bay Road near Mobile, Alabama 319

"Mobile Bay lay spread out before me" 320

"A negro woman fished silently in a little pool" . 321

The Custom-House, Mobile, Alabama 322

Bank of Mobile and Odd Fellows' Hall, Mobile, Alabama 323

The Marine and City Hospitals, Mobile, Ala.... 324

Trinity Church, Mobile, Alabama 324

In the City Park, Mobile—"Ebony nurse-maids flirt with their lovers" 325

In the City Park, Mobile—"Squirrels frolic with the children" 326

Barton Academy, Mobile, Alabama 326

Christ Church, Mobile, Alabama 327

The Alabama State Capitol, at Montgomery, 332

The Market-Place at Montgomery, Alabama.... 334

The Cotton-Plant 343

A Street Scene in Augusta, Georgia 344

A Bell-Tower in Augusta, Georgia 347

A Confederate Soldier's Grave, at Augusta, Ga. 348

Sunset over Atlanta, Georgia 350

The State-House, Atlanta, Georgia 353

An Up-Country Cotton-Press 357

View on the Savannah River, near Savannah, Georgia 358

General Oglethorpe, the Founder of Savannah 359

The Pulaski Monument in Savannah, Georgia. 360

A Spanish Dagger-Tree, Savannah 361

"Looking down from the bluff," Savannah 362

"The huge black ships swallowed bale after bale" 363

An old Stairway on the Levée at Savannah 364

The Custom-House at Savannah 365

View in Bonaventure Cemetery, Savannah 365

The Independent Presbyterian Church, Savannah 366

View in Forsyth Park, Savannah 367

"Forsyth park contains a massive fountain" 368

A Savannah Sergeant of Police 369

General Sherman's Head-quarters, Savannah .. 370

A pair of Georgia "Crackers" 372

The Eagle and Phœnix Cotton-Mills, Columbus, Georgia 373

PAGE.

The old Fort on Tybee Island, Georgia........ 375
Happiness.................................... 376
Moonlight over Jacksonville, Florida.......... 377
Jacksonville, on the St. John's River, Florida... 381
Residence of Mrs. Harriet Beecher Stowe, at
   Mandarin, Florida......................... 383
Green Cove Springs, on the St. John's River, Fla. 384
On the Road to St. Augustine, Florida......... 386
A Street in St. Augustine, Florida............ 387
St. Augustine, Florida—" An ancient gateway " 388
The Remains of a Citadel at Matanzas Inlet.... 391
View of Fort Marion, St. Augustine, Florida.... 392
Light-house on Anastasia Island, near St. Au-
   gustine, Florida........................... 393
View of the Entrance to Fort Marion, St. Au-
   gustine, Florida........................... 394
" The old sergeant in charge".................. 395
The Cathedral, St. Augustine, Florida........ 396
The Banana—" At Palatka, we first found the
   banana in profusion "..................... 400
" Just across the river from Palatka lies the beau-
   tiful orange grove owned by Colonel Hart "... 402
Entrance to Colonel Hart's orange grove, oppo-
   site Palatka.............................. 404
The Guardian Angel........................ 407
A Peep into a Forest on the Oclawaha........ 409
" We would brush past the trees and vines "...... 410
The " Marion " at Silver Spring............... 412
Shooting at Alligators........................ 414
View on the upper St. John's River, Florida.... 416
Sunrise at Enterprise, St. John's River, Florida. 419
A Country Cart.............................. 421
View of a Rice-field in South Carolina........ 429
Negro Cabins on a Rice Plantation........... 431
" The women were dressed in gay colors "...... 432
" With forty or fifty pounds of rice-stalks on their
   heads "........ 432
A Pair of Mule-Boots......................... 434
A " Trunk-Minder "........................... 434
Unloading the Rice-Barges.................... 435
" At the winnowing-machine "................... 436
" Aunt Bransom "—A venerable ex-slave on a
   South Carolina Rice Plantation 437
View from Fort Sumter, in Charleston Harbor.. 438
The old Charleston Post-Office............... 440
Houses on the Battery, Charleston............ 441
A Charleston Mansion........................ 442
The Spire of St. Philip's Church, Charleston.. 443
The Orphan House, Charleston............... 444
The Battery, Charleston...................... 445
The Grave of John C. Calhoun, Charleston.... 446
The Ruins of St. Finbar Cathedral, Charleston. 447
" The highways leading out of the city are all richly
   embowered in loveliest foliage ".............. 449
Magnolia Cemetery, Charleston 450
Garden in Mount Pleasant, opposite Charleston 452
Peeping Through............................ 453
A Future Politician 459
The State-House at Columbia, South Carolina.. 460
Sketches of South Carolina State Officers and
   Legislators under the Moses Administration.. 462
Iron Palmetto in the State-House Yard at Colum-
   bia 465
A Wayside Sketch............................ 473

PAGE.

" The Small Boy ".............................. 474
" The Judge "................................. 476
The Judge shows the Artist's Sketch-Book..... 479
" The family sang line by line ".................. 481
A Mountain Farmer.......................... 482
" We caught a glimpse of the symmetrical Cata-
   louche mountain "......................... 483
The Cañon of the Cata10uche as seen from
   " Bennett's "............................. 484
Mount Pisgah, Western North Carolina........ 486
The Carpenter—A Study from Waynesville Life 487
View on Pigeon River, near Waynesville....... 488
The Dry Fall of the Sugar Fork, Blue Ridge,
   North Carolina............................ 490
View near Webster, North Carolina........... 492
Lower Sugar Fork Fall, Blue Ridge, North Car-
   olina.......... 495
The Devil's Court-House, Whiteside Mountain. 499
Jonas sees the Abyss.......................... 501
Asheville, North Carolina, from " Beaucatcher
   Knob"................................... 504
View near Warm Springs, on the French Broad
   River 506
Lover's Leap, French Broad River, Western
   North Carolina........................... 508
View on the Swannanoa River, near Asheville,
   Western North Carolina..:................ 509
First Peep at Patton's......................... 510
The " Mountain House," on the way to Mount
   Mitchell's Summit........ 511
View of Mount Mitchell...................... 512
The Judge climbing Mitchell's High Peak..... 513
Signal-Station and " Mitchell's Grave," Summit
   of the Black Mountains.................... 514
The Lookers-on at the Greenville Fair......... 516
Table Mountain, South Carolina.............. 518
" Let us address de Almighty wid pra'r "......... 520
Mount Yonah, as seen from Clarksville, Geor-
   gia...................................: 521
The "Grand Chasm," Tugaloo River, Northern
   Georgia...:............................. 522
Toccoa Falls, Northern Georgia............... 524
A Mail-Carrier.............................. 526
Mission Ridge, near Chattanooga, Tennessee.. 527
Lookout Mountain, near Chattanooga, Tennessee 529
The Mineral Region in the vicinity of Chattanooga 531
Map showing Grades of Illiteracy in the United
   States. (From the U. S. Census Reports.)... 532
Map of Middle Atlantic States, southern section,
   and North Carolina........................ 533
The Rockwood Iron-Furnaces, Eastern Tenn-
   essee.................................... 533
The " John Ross House," near Chattanooga.
   Residence of one of the old Cherokee Land-
   holders.................................. 534
Catching a " Tarpin "........................ 535
View from Lookout Mountain near Chattanooga 536
Umbrella Rock, on Lookout Mountain........ 537
Looking from " Lookout Cave "............... 538
" Rock City," Lookout Mountain.............. 539
View from Wood's Redoubt, Chattanooga...... 540
On the Tennessee River, near Chattanooga.... 542
The " Suck," on the Tennessee River......... 543
A Negro Cabin on the bank of the Tennessee.. 544

PAGE.

Knoxville, Tennessee......................... 546
The East Tennessee University, Knoxville 548
At the Ætna Coal Mines..................... 550
"Down in a Coal Mine"....................... 551
The old Market at Lynchburg.. 552
The James River, at Lynchburg, Virginia...... 553
A Side Street in Lynchburg, Virginia.......... 555
Scene in a Lynchburg Tobacco Factory....... 557
"Down the steep hills every day come the country
  wagons " 558
Summoning Buyers to a Tobacco Sale......... 560
Evening on the James River—"The soft light
  which gently rested upon the lovely stream ".. 561
In the Gap of the Peaks of Otter, Virginia...... 562
The Summit of the Peak of Otter, Virginia..... 564
Blue Ridge Springs, South-western Virginia.... 566
Bristol, South-western Virginia................ 569
White Top Mountain, seen from Glade Springs 570
Making Salt, at Saltville, Virginia............. 571
Wayside Types—A Sketch from the Artist's Vir-
  ginia Sketch-Book.......................... 573
Wytheville, Virginia.......................... 574
Max Meadows, Virginia....................... 575
The Roanoke Valley, Virginia................ 576
View near Salem, Virginia.................... 577
View on the James River below Lynchburg.... 578
Appomattox Court-House—"It lies silently half-
  hidden in its groves and gardens ".......... 579
"The hackmen who shriek in your ear as you arrive
  at the depot ".............................. 581
"The 'Crater,' the chasm created by the explosion
  of the mine which the Pennsylvanians sprung
  underneath Lee's fortifications "............. 582
"The old cemetery, and ruined, ivy-mantled Bland-
  ford Church "............................. 583
"Seen from a distance, Petersburg presents the
  appearance of a lovely forest pierced here and
  there by church spires and towers " 585
A Queer Cavalier............................ 587
City Point, Virginia.......................... 588
A Peep into the Great Dismal Swamp......... 589
A Glimpse of Norfolk, Virginia............... 591
Map of the Virginia Peninsula 593
Hampton Roads............................. 594
The Ruins of the old Church at Jamestown, Vir-
  ginia..................................... 621
Statue of Lord Botetourt at Williamsburg, Vir-
  ginia..................................... 622
The old Colonial Powder Magazine at Williams-
  burg, Virginia............................. 623
The old Church of Bruton Parish—Williamsburg,
  Virginia.................................. 624
Cornwallis's Cave, near Yorktown, Virginia... 624
View of Richmond, Virginia, from the Manches-
  ter side of the James River 626
Libby Prison, Richmond, Virginia............ 627
Capitol Square, with a view of the Washington
  Monument, Richmond, Virginia............. 628
St. John's Church, Richmond, Virginia........ 629
View on the James River, Richmond, Virginia.. 630
Monument to the Confederate Dead, Richmond,
  Virginia.................................. 631
The Gallego Flouring-Mill, Richmond, Vir-
  ginia..................................... 631

PAGE.

Scene on a Tobacco Plantation—Burning a Plant
  Patch 632
Tobacco Culture—Stringing the Primings...... 633
A Tobacco Barn in Virginia.................. 633
The Old Method of Getting Tobacco to Market. 634
Getting a Tobacco Hogshead Ready for Market. 635
Scene on a Tobacco Plantation—Finding To-
  bacco Worms.............................. 636
The Tredegar Iron Works, Richmond, Virginia 637
A Water-melon Wagon 646
A Marl-bed on the Line of the Chesapeake and
  Ohio Railroad............................. 647
Earthworks on the Chickahominy, near Rich-
  mond, Virginia............................ 648
Scene at a Virginia "Corn-Shed "............. 649
Gordonsville, Virginia—"The negroes, who
  swarm day and night like bees about the
  . trains " 650
The Tomb of Thomas Jefferson, at Monticello,
  near Charlottesville, Virginia................ 651
Monticello—The Old Home of Thomas Jefferson,
  author of the Declaration of American Inde-
  pendence.................................. 652
The University of Virginia, at Charlottesville... 653
A Water-melon Feast.......................... 655
Piedmont, from the Blue Ridge................ 656
View of Staunton, Virginia.................... 657
Winchester, Virginia......................... 658
Buffalo Gap and the Iron-Furnace............ 659
Elizabeth Iron-Furnace, Virginia.............. 660
The Alum Spring, Rockbridge Alum Springs,
  Virginia.................................. 661
The Military Institute, Lexington, Virginia.... 661
Washington and Lee College, Lexington, Va. 662
Portrait of General Thomas J. Jackson, known
  as "Stonewall Jackson." (From an engraving
  owned by M. Knoedler & Co., N. Y.)........ 663
General Robert Edward Lee, born January 19,
  1801; died October 11, 1870................. 664
The Great Natural Arch, Clifton Forge, Jack-
  son's River 665
Beaver Dam Falls........................... 665
Falling Springs Falls, Virginia................ 666
Griffith's Knob, and Cow Pasture River........ 667
Clay Cut, Chesapeake and Ohio Railroad..... 668
"Mac, the Pusher "........................... 668
Jerry's Run................................. 669
Scene on the Greenbrier River in Western Vir-
  ginia..................................... 670
The Hotel and Lawn at Greenbrier White Sul-
  phur Springs, West Virginia............... 671
The Eastern Portal of Second Creek Tunnel,
  Chesapeake and Ohio Railroad.............. 672
A Mountain Ride in a Stage-Coach........... 673
Anvil Rock, Greenbrier River................ 675
A West Virginia "Countryman "............... 675
A Freighters' Camp, West Virginia........... 676
"The rude cabin built beneath the shadow of a
  huge rock " 677
"The rustic mill built of logs "................ 678
The Junction of Greenbrier and New Rivers.... 678
Descending the New River Rapids............ 679
A hard road for artists to travel.............. 680
The "Hawk's Nest," from Boulder Point...... 681

xviii

	PAGE.
Great Kanawha Falls	682
Miller's Ferry, seen from the Hawk's Nest	682
Richmond Falls, New River	683
Big Dowdy Falls, near New River	684
Whitcomb's Bowlder	685
The Inclined Plane at Cannelton	686
Fern Spring Branch, a West Virginia Mountain Stream	687
Charleston, the West Virginia Capital	688
The Hale House, Charleston	688
Rafts of Saw-Logs on a West Virginia River	689
The Snow Hill Salt Works, on the Kanawha River	690
Indian Mound, near St. Albans	690
View of Huntington and the Ohio River	691
The result of climbing a sapling—An Artist in a Fix	692
The Levée at Louisville, Kentucky	693
A familiar scene in a Louisville Street	695
A Waiter at the Galt House, Louisville, Kentucky	696
Scene in the Louisville Exposition	697
Mammoth Cave, Kentucky—The Boat Ride on Echo River	699
The Entrance to Mammoth Cave (Looking Out)	700
Mammoth Cave—In "the Devil's Arm-Chair"	702
The Mammoth Cave—"The Fat Man's Misery"	703
Mammoth Cave—"The Subterranean Album"	704
A Country Blacksmith Shop	706
The Court-House, Louisville	707
The Cathedral, Louisville	708
The Post-Office, Louisville	708
The City Hall, Louisville	709
George D. Prentice. (From a Painting in the Louisville Public Library)	710
The Colored Normal School, Louisville	710
Louisville, Kentucky, on the Ohio River, from the New Albany Heights	711
Chimney Rock, Kentucky	712
Frankfort, on the Kentucky River	713
The Ascent to Frankfort Cemetery, Kentucky	714
The Monument to Daniel Boone in the Cemetery at Frankfort, Kentucky	715
View on the Kentucky River, near Frankfort	719
Asteroid Kicks Up	717
A Souvenir of Kentucky	719
A little Adventure by the Wayside	720
"Steady"	725
The Tennessee State Capitol, at Nashville	726
View from the State Capitol, Nashville, Tennessee	727
Tomb of Ex-President Polk, Nashville, Tennessee	728
The Hermitage—General Andrew Jackson's old homestead, near Nashville, Tennessee	729
Young Tennesseans	730
The old home of Gen. Andrew Jackson, near Nashville	731
	PAGE.
Tomb of Andrew Jackson, at the "Hermitage," near Nashville	732
View from Federal Hill, Baltimore, Maryland, looking across the Basin	733
The Oldest House in Baltimore	735
Fort McHenry, Baltimore Harbor	738
Jones's Falls, Baltimore	740
Exchange Place, Baltimore, Maryland	741
The Masonic Temple, Baltimore, Maryland	742
The Shot-Tower, Baltimore, Maryland	742
Scene on the Chesapeake and Ohio Canal	743
The Blind Asylum, Baltimore, Maryland	745
The Eastern High School, Baltimore, Maryland	746
View of a Lake in Druid Hill Park, Baltimore	747
Maryland Institute, Baltimore	748
Woodberry, near Druid Hill Park	749
The new City Hall, Baltimore, Maryland	750
Lafayette Square, Baltimore, Maryland	750
The City Jail, Baltimore, Maryland	752
The Peabody Institute, Baltimore, Maryland	753
First Presbyterian Church, Baltimore	754
A Tunnel through the Alleghanies	756
Mount Vernon Square, with a view of the Washington Monument, Baltimore, Maryland	758
The Battle Monument, seen from Barnum's Hotel, Baltimore	759
The Battle Monument, Baltimore, Maryland	760
The Cathedral, Baltimore, Maryland	760
The Wildey Monument, Baltimore, Maryland	761
Entrance to Druid Hill Park, Baltimore, Maryland	761
Scene on the Canal, near Harper's Ferry	762
The Bridge at Harper's Ferry	763
View of the Railroad and River, from the Mountains at Harper's Ferry	764
Jefferson's Rock, Harper's Ferry	769
Cumberland Narrows and Mountains	767
Cumberland Viaduct, Maryland	768
Harper's Ferry, Maryland	769
Old John Cupid, a Williamsburg Herb Doctor	770
Southern Types—Come to Market	771
Southern Types—A Southern Plough Team	772
Southern Types—Negro Boys Shelling Peas	773
Southern Types—A "likely Girl" with her Baby	775
Southern Types—Catching his Breakfast	776
Southern Types—Negro Shoeblacks	777
Southern Types—A Little Unpleasantness	779
Southern Types—"Going to Church"	780
Southern Types—A Negro Constable	781
Southern Types—The Wolf and the Lamb in Politics	784
Southern Types—Two Veterans discussing the Political Situation	737
The Potomac and Washington, seen from Arlington	800
Homeward Bound	801

ACKNOWLEDGMENTS

The editors wish to acknowledge the assistance and advice of their colleagues and the administrative staff of the University of Southwestern Louisiana throughout the preparation of this new edition. We thank Mrs. Jeannine Sibille of the Laboratory of the Department of Office Administration for expeditiously coordinating the typing of two drafts of the introductory material, and Miss Morele Roy for typing the index. Special thanks are due to Professors Matthew J. Schott and Lawrence D. Rice for their constructive suggestions for improving the introduction.

We owe a particular debt of gratitude to the University of Southwestern Louisiana Foundation and the administrators of the University of Southwestern Louisiana Faculty Development Fund. The entire project would have been impossible without financial support from these two sources.

The Louisiana State University Library kindly made available its copy of the original edition of the King volume for use in reproducing the book.

EDITORS' INTRODUCTION

During the Reconstruction era, travelers flocked in unprecedented numbers to observe southern life and to record their impressions for others. They produced a multitude of travel accounts, many of which have been republished in edited versions.[1] But the most useful of these narratives has received little attention since its publication nearly a hundred years ago. Edward King's *The Great South,* the most carefully conceived and executed of the accounts, provided the widest geographical coverage and offered the most comprehensive examination of southern life and society. King's work was unquestionably the most thorough treatment of the South since Frederick Law Olmsted's analysis of the slave states in the 1850s. It is manifestly impossible to preserve or embalm a people, a region, or an era of history, but Edward King, as had Olmsted before him, achieved the next best thing in presenting a remarkably sensitive and vivid picture of the American South in an important period of its history.

King's Life and Career as Author and Journalist

In his own day, Edward King was well known as a journalist and war correspondent, and he achieved some recognition as an author of novels, poetry, short stories, and articles. His travel accounts, especially *The Great South,* were widely acclaimed and went through several editions. Today he is largely forgotten. However, King's work is remembered by two groups of scholars. Among analysts and historians of American literature, his "Great South" articles, which were published in *Scribner's Monthly* in 1873 and 1874 and which were later reorganized and expanded into this book, are referred to most frequently in connection with his discovery of George Washington Cable and the role King played in launching him on his literary career. Cable's articles and books on New Orleans and Louisiana, and the work of other southern writers of the "local color" school, helped to promote the developing spirit of nationalism of the 1870s. Furthermore some historians of the late Reconstruction period also recognize the importance of *The Great South* for its part in encouraging sectional reconciliation and promoting the "New South" movement.

King, the son of Edward and Lorinda Smith King, was born in Middle-

---

[1] Fletcher M. Green, "The South in Reconstruction, 1865–1880," in Thomas D. Clark (ed)., *The Postwar South, 1865–1900: An Era of Reconstruction and Readjustment,* Vol. I of Clark (ed.), *Travels in the New South: A Bibliography* (2 vols.; Norman: University of Oklahoma Press, 1962), 3–7, 66–67.

field, Massachusetts, on September 8, 1848.[2] His father, a Methodist clergyman, died when King was about three years old. After teaching school for several years, King's mother moved to Huntington, Massachusetts, where, about 1860, she married Samuel W. Fisher, a clergyman who later turned to schoolteaching for a time. It seems probable that King's mother began his education and his stepfather continued it for three or four years. At the age of fifteen or sixteen, King left home and worked briefly in a factory. In 1864 he began his career as a journalist, developing his skills as a reporter and writer through practical experience. After some two years with the Springfield *Daily Union,* he joined the Springfield *Republican,* working as reporter, subeditor, and editorial writer until late 1869.

The *Republican* sent King to Europe in 1867 to cover the Paris Exposition. His first book, *My Paris: French Character Sketches* (1868), was based on his experiences and observations of life in the French capital. Although later characterized as "naïvely romantic," the book was well received at the time and went through three editions by 1873.[3]

King returned to Paris in the fall of 1869 and in early October journeyed to Spain. In Valencia he and Henry M. Stanley witnessed and reported on the abortive Republican uprising, a preliminary of the Second Carlist Wars.[4] In 1870, representing the Boston *Morning Journal,* he covered the Franco-Prussian War and the subsequent events of the Commune.[5] At Frankfort,

[2] King's full name was Edward Smith King, although he apparently never used his middle name in his professional career. The best biographical sketches of King are by Robert W. Burwell, in Allen Johnson and Dumas Malone (eds.), *Dictionary of American Biography* (20 vols. and supplements; New York: Charles Scribner's Sons, 1928—), X, 387–88; Stanley J. Kunitz and Howard Haycraft (eds.), *American Authors, 1600–1900: A Biographical Dictionary of American Literature* (New York: H. W. Wilson Co., 1938), 439; and *National Cyclopaedia of American Biography* (51 vols.; New York: James T. White and Co., permanent series, to date, 1891—), XXIV, 274–75. The basic facts of King's life and the information on his writings given in the following paragraphs are, except where otherwise noted, largely drawn from these three sources. All give King's date of birth as September 8, 1848. Older reference works and obituary notices in the New York *Times,* March 29, 1896, and the Springfield *Sunday Republican,* March 29, 1896, give his birthdate as July 31, 1848. The longest contemporary account of King's life is the obituary in the Springfield *Sunday Republican.* A briefer version of this appeared in the Boston *Evening Transcript,* March 30, 1896.

[3] Kunitz and Haycraft, *American Authors, 1600–1900,* p. 439; Springfield *Sunday Republican,* March 29, 1896; King to George W. Cable, May 14, 1873 and [June, 1873], in George W. Cable Collection, Howard-Tilton Memorial Library, Tulane University. This collection contains the largest number of extant King letters, and those from King to Cable referred to hereinafter may be found there except as otherwise noted. (Dates the editors supply in brackets are deduced from other events or letters to which King refers, from the places from which the letters were written, or from other internal evidence, although these dates do not always agree with those inserted on the originals in a different handwriting.) The most complete listing of King's published works is in *A Catalog of Books Represented by the Library of Congress Printed Cards Issued to July 31, 1942* (166 vols.; Ann Arbor: Edwards Brothers Inc., 1942–46), LXXX, 421–22.

[4] Edward King, "An Expedition with Stanley," *Scribner's Monthly,* V (November, 1872), 105–12. King first met Stanley, with whom he maintained a lifelong friendship, during this trip. After their return to Paris, King, in November, 1869, saw Stanley off on the famous trip that ultimately resulted in his "finding" Livingstone in Africa. King later wrote what was basically an illustrated condensation of Stanley's *How I Found Livingstone in Central Africa,* entitled "How Stanley Found Livingstone," *Scribner's Monthly,* V (January, 1873), 298–314.

[5] None of the sources cited in footnote 2 indicate that King was in Europe by the fall of 1869. But see footnote 4 and a letter from King to William Warland Clapp, editor of the *Morning Journal,* in which he says he "sailed for Europe in 1869" and implies that he was working

where he was confined briefly by the Germans on charges of espionage, he served as a volunteer emergency nurse to the wounded, and during the street fighting of the Commune in Paris, he took custody of the bodies of Americans who were killed. King's first novel, *Kentucky's Love* (1873), and a book for boys, *Under the Red Flag* (1895), were based on his experiences in Europe in 1870 and 1871, as were several articles and one of his earliest and best poems.[6]

By the time King returned to the United States in 1871, his experience and work in France had gained him a reputation as "one of the ablest of the younger American journalists." A contemporary newspaperman referred to him as the "star correspondent and editorial writer" of the *Journal,* ranking him with Henry M. Stanley, Archibald Forbes, and other famous war correspondents of that day.[7] Thus it was not surprising that King, although only twenty-four, was selected in 1872 by Dr. Josiah Gilbert Holland, editor of *Scribner's Monthly,* to undertake a lengthy tour of the South to gather information for a series of articles. Holland had known King when both men were associated with the Springfield *Republican.* During 1873 and for much of 1874, most of King's time was taken up by the southern journeys and by rewriting, revising, and proofreading the *Scribner's* articles that resulted in *The Great South.*[8]

With work on *The Great South* nearly completed, King joined the New York *Times* in August, 1874, but in March, 1875, he returned to Europe, once again as a correspondent for the Boston *Morning Journal.*[9] King spent most of the next thirteen years abroad, making Paris his headquarters. Although representing the *Journal,* he wrote for other newspapers and periodicals.[10] On return trips to the United States, he covered the Centennial Exposition of 1876 in Philadelphia, and in early 1879 he again toured parts of the South, including Florida, Georgia, Louisiana, and Kentucky. Following the latter trip, King considered writing "one or two articles for Scribner on the Southern Question."[11] but he never fulfilled this aim. Meanwhile he traveled widely in Europe, "becoming one of the best-known men in Paris, quite the chief man of the American colony." He visited the Balkans both before and during the Russo-Turkish War of 1877–1878, accompanying the Russian

---

for that paper at the time. King to W. W. Clapp, December 21, 1872, in W. W. Clapp Papers, Houghton Library, Harvard University. Letters from King to Clapp referred to hereinafter are in this collection.

[6] The poem, "A Woman's Execution, Paris, May '71" was the first of King's writings published in *Scribner's Monthly,* II (September, 1871), 500. It was later included in his *Echoes from the Orient* (1880), and in Edmund Clarence Stedman (ed.), *An American Anthology 1787–1900* (Boston: Houghton Mifflin Co., 1900), 512. Three of the articles appeared in *Scribner's Monthly* (September and October, 1872, and March, 1873), and one in a special Christmas (1871) issue of the Boston *Journal.* Edward P. Mitchell, *Memoirs of an Editor: Fifty Years of American Journalism* (New York: Charles Scribner's Sons, 1924), 95.

[7] Paul Buck, *The Road to Reunion, 1865–1900* (Boston: Little, Brown and Co., 1937), 131; Mitchell, *Memoirs of an Editor,* 95–96.

[8] King to Cable, August 9, 1873, December 18, [1873].

[9] King to Cable [summer, 1874], October 10, 1874, and March 19, [1875].

[10] King to W. W. Clapp, January 21 and December 27, 1876; Springfield *Sunday Republican,* March 29, 1896.

[11] King to Cable, January 27, February 3, 18, 19, and March 16, 1879.

army. On a brief trip to the United States in 1883, he crossed the continent with a group of correspondents to attend the opening of the Northern Pacific Railroad.[12]

Between 1876 and King's final return to the United States in 1888, he published a wide variety of books. The first of these was *French Political Leaders* (1876), a collection of brief biographies of public men.[13] About two-thirds of King's first volume of poetry, *Echoes from the Orient* (1880), dealt with the Balkans and Turkish region, but it included some of his earlier verse on other subjects.[14] A novel, *The Gentle Savage*, whose principal character is an American Indian in a European setting, was published in 1883.[15] In 1884 King returned to the United States to supervise publication of *Europe in Calm and Storm: Twenty Years' Experiences and Reminiscences of an American Journalist* (1885).[16] This volume, which is even longer than *The Great South*, is basically a "scissors and paste" product, composed largely of King's newspaper and magazine articles describing historical events, scenery, manners, institutions, and famous persons. In a sense it is a European version of *The Great South*, although the coverage is less systematic and comprehensive, and it is based on observations made over a longer time period. In 1886 King published what was perhaps his weakest work, *The Golden Spike*, which deals with the Northwest and the opening of the Northern Pacific Railroad. *A Venetian Lover*, a narrative in blank verse and lyrics, appeared the following year.

While in Paris between 1885 and 1888, King was involved in an unsuccessful business venture and suffered heavy financial losses, apparently because of inexperience and bad judgment. Upon his return to the United States, he became an editorial writer for Albert Pulitzer's New York *Journal*. After working briefly for Peter F. Collier's *Once a Week*, he rejoined the *Journal*, serving first under John R. McLean and then, after 1895, under William Randolph Hearst. During these years King strove to repay the debts incurred in the Paris business failure, even though he had not been primarily responsible for them.[17]

In 1893 King went to Chicago to write a series of articles on the World's Fair. His best novel, *Joseph Zalmonah*, appeared the same year. *Zalmonah* graphically portrays the life of Russian immigrant Jews and the deplorable

[12] Springfield *Sunday Republican*, March 29, 1896; Mitchell, *Memoirs of an Editor*, 96, 391.

[13] This was the third volume in a series of "Brief Biographies" edited by Thomas Wentworth Higginson. It received a favorable notice in *Scribner's Monthly*, XII (May 1876), 134.

[14] The book was favorably reviewed in the *Nation*, XXXI (October 28, 1880), 312–13, which discussed King as a "new poet" and predicted a promising career for him. It has received some attention in more recent times. See Claudio Isopescu, "Le Poèt Américain Edward King et ses Inspirations Roumaines," *Buletinul Bibliotecii Română*, October, 1954.

[15] Cable, in a letter of April 13, 1883, to his wife called it "a much-praised novel." Quoted in Lucy L. Cable Biklé, *George W. Cable: His Life and Letters* (New York: Charles Scribner's Sons, 1928), 98.

[16] Springfield *Sunday Republican*, March 29, 1896. Three later editions of this book, published in 1885, 1886, and 1887, were titled *Descriptive Portraiture of Europe in Storm and Calm*. . . .

[17] Springfield *Sunday Republican*, March 29, 1896. See also Boston *Evening Transcript*, March 30, 1896.

working conditions in the sweat shops of the New York garment district. The plot is at times contrived and the writing melodramatic, but King presents a realistic picture of the labor problems and of the religious, social, and cultural customs of the Russian Jewish community. Largely ignored today, the book clearly deserves a place in the social protest and muckraking literature of the period.[18]

Besides the works mentioned above, King wrote numerous articles, short stories, and poems for newspapers and magazines in the United States, England, and France. He also contributed to or compiled tourist guides and a travel book, and he completed another volume of poetry that was never published.

King remained a bachelor and in his later years made his home in Brooklyn with his half-sister, Charlotte Fisher, and her husband, John McGhie. He was only in his forties, but suffered from asthma and Bright's disease and was not in robust health. After falling ill in March, 1896, he seemed to be recuperating, but died suddenly and unexpectedly on the twenty-seventh. He was buried in Bridgeport, Connecticut.

Characterized as reserved and "of a typical New England nature," especially with strangers, King had an engaging personality nevertheless and was always popular with fellow journalists and literary friends in Europe and America. While in Paris he founded the Stanley Club and was secretary of the *Société de Gens de Lettres*. His letters to George Washington Cable, which at times display a delightful wit, provide the best insight into King's personality, in particular his fluctuating moods of optimism and discouragement. He was personally attractive, with blond hair and a ruddy complexion (Cable referred to him as "Rosycheeks"). When the well-known portraitist George P. A. Healy painted his picture in Paris, King was stout and had a full beard, although later he wore his beard in a Vandyke style.[19]

From his youth King had had high ambitions to produce good literature, especially poetry, and he had received early encouragement from Ralph Waldo Emerson. But despite the fact that his last, unpublished book of poems may have included his best work, the judgment of some contemporaries that he was a first-rate poet would scarcely seem justified.[20] King primarily was a journalist, and most of his books were written to make money. One scholar has criticized his shallowness and "almost capricious exploitation of a variety of subjects." A fellow journalist, who had known him since 1869, deplored the fact that King did not fulfill the "brilliant promise of youth," but spent the last years of his life in routine work "on an inconspicuous New York newspaper."

[18] The book was reprinted by Gregg Press, Ridgewood, N. J., in 1968. One of King's earliest short stories, "Only Half a Woman," *Scribner's Monthly,* VII (November, 1873), 82–90, was set in the working-class district of London; although extremely sentimental, the story contained overtones of social protest.

[19] Springfield *Sunday Republican,* March 29, 1896; Mitchell, *Memoirs of an Editor,* 93, 95–96.

[20] Springfield *Sunday Republican,* March 29, 1896. The book of poetry, which was to have been published posthumously, was tentatively titled *Songs of the Sea.* The laudatory *Republican* obituary pointed out that King had begun work on "one great novel" before he died. His failure to receive wide recognition and acceptance in American literary circles was attributed to his long residence in Europe.

King's consciousness of his failure to produce work of more lasting quality is strikingly reflected in his early letters to Cable.[21]

The Great South Project: The Articles and the Book

Scribner's Monthly, which began publication in November, 1870, with Dr. Holland as editor, soon became one of the most popular and influential periodicals in the nation.[22] The success of the magazine under the direction of Holland and his able assistant, Richard Watson Gilder, with the astute financial management of Roswell Smith, was due in large part to its tone of moral uplift, its public-spirited ideals, and its dedication to the education of the public. Moreover the magazine well reflected the spirit of nationalism and reconciliation of the era. Another important factor in its success was the improved quality of its illustrations, produced by a new process developed by its art director, Alexander W. Drake.[23]

Both before and after the appearance of King's "Great South," *Scribner's Monthly* and other popular journals published descriptive accounts of the South and other sections of the country. King himself had written such articles for *Lippincott's*.[24] A two-part series on Virginia in *Scribner's* by Jedediah Hotchkiss, from which King in his later book borrowed heavily, had appeared some months before the first "Great South" article.[25] But the articles on the South that "attracted the greatest attention" were those by King. They increased the popularity of an already successful magazine, both in the United

[21] Kunitz and Haycraft, *American Authors, 1600–1900,* p. 439; King to Cable [June, 1873] and December [1873]; Mitchell, *Memoirs of an Editor,* 97. Mitchell added, "Poor King! Yet even Melville faded to a custom-house clerkship."

[22] The magazine, subtitled *An Illustrated Magazine for the People* and published by Scribner and Company, had been projected by and was owned by Holland, Roswell Smith, and Charles Scribner. It was connected with the book publishing firm of Charles Scribner's Sons only through the part ownership of Scribner, and later his son, Charles Scribner, Jr. After the younger Scribner sold his interest in 1881, *Scribner's Monthly* became *Century Magazine. Scribner's Magazine,* a different journal, was begun in 1887 by the Charles Scribner's Sons publishing house. See Arthur W. John, "A History of *Scribner's Monthly* and the *Century Illustrated Monthly Magazine,* 1870–1900" (Ph.D. dissertation, Harvard University, 1954), for an extended treatment of the founding and history of this journal; and Frank Luther Mott, *A History of American Magazines, 1865–1885* (Cambridge: Harvard University Press, 1938), 457–68, for a briefer account.

[23] In later years Holland, in accounting for the success of the magazine, gave priority to its "superb engravings and the era it introduced of improved illustrative art." Other national magazines, especially *Harper's Monthly,* had earlier used engravings to enhance their popularity and attractiveness, but *Scribner's Monthly* was the only magazine to use Drake's superior process for some years. *Scribner's Monthly,* I (November, 1870), 105–106, and XXII (June, 1881), 303; Mott, *American Magazines,* 187–90, 466; Robert Underwood Johnson, *Remembered Yesterdays* (Boston: Little, Brown and Co., 1923), 99–100; John, "A History of *Scribner's Monthly,*" 160.

[24] Mott, *American Magazines,* 398. An earlier series on the South, John Richard Dennett's "The South as It Is," had appeared in the *Nation* in 1865–1866. It has recently been reprinted in book form, edited by Henry M. Christman (London: Sidgwick and Jackson, 1965).

[25] Jed[ediah] Hotchkiss, "New Ways in the Old Dominion: The Chesapeake and Ohio Railroad," *Scribner's Monthly,* V (December, 1872), 137–60, (January, 1873), 273–93. Hotchkiss (1827–99) had been Stonewall Jackson's topographical engineer during the Civil War. In the 1870s and 1880s, he wrote several books and promotional pamphlets on the geological features, mineral resources, and railroads of Virginia.

States and England, and they typified the philosophy, features, and introduction of new literary talent that characterized *Scribner's Monthly.*[26]

Sources differ in assigning the credit for conceiving and suggesting King's tour of the South. Holland, as editor, made the final decision and selected King for the assignment. On the other hand, publisher Roswell Smith confidently risked the thirty-thousand-dollar investment in the trip, and King credited Smith with suggesting the series. In any event both Holland and Smith were interested in promoting nationalism and sectional reconciliation, and in increasing the popularity and success of the magazine.[27]

King traveled some twenty-five thousand miles by train, river and coastal steamers, stagecoach, wagon, and on horseback through every state in the South—not only the eleven former Confederate states, but also the southern or border states of Maryland, West Virginia, Kentucky, Missouri, a part of Kansas and the Indian Territory.[28]

He began his first tour in January, 1873, traveling from Baltimore to Pittsburgh and on to St. Louis. Then he went to Sedalia, Missouri, through the southeastern corner of Kansas and the Indian Territory and into Texas. From here King and his party traveled southward to Galveston and then moved on to New Orleans by mid-February. In March and April, after a trip to Mobile, he again toured parts of Texas, returning by rail to St. Louis.

In June, King went by train from St. Louis to East Tennessee, where he began his trip through the North Carolina mountains. Apparently he toured parts of eastern South Carolina, Georgia, and North Carolina before returning to New York. After spending two weeks in St. Louis, beginning July 15, he visited White Sulphur Springs, West Virginia, and there wrote several of the *Scribner's* articles. In September he was in Lynchburg and southwest Virginia; then he returned by way of Lynchburg to Petersburg. He hoped to make a quick trip to New Orleans in October but evidently was unable to do so. By mid-October he had begun a tour of North Georgia, western South Carolina, and parts of Tennessee, including Chattanooga and vicinity. He again traveled through western South Carolina on a trip from Atlanta to Charlotte in November, and some time either in late October or November he visited Charleston and Columbia. During late November and early December, he toured eastern and central Alabama, parts of Georgia, including Savannah, and Florida. On December 18 he passed through Bristol, Tennessee, on

[26] Mott, *American Magazines,* 47–48; John, "A History of *Scribner's Monthly,*" 201, 208.
[27] Washington Gladden, "Roswell Smith," *Century Illustrated Monthly Magazine,* XLIV (June, 1892), 310–13, says Smith suggested the series. The Springfield *Sunday Republican,* March 29, 1896, states that Holland selected King and Smith sent him on the tour, but Johnson, *Remembered Yesterdays,* 96–97, says that Smith originated the project, calling it "the first high note of nationalism struck by the magazine."
[28] It is impossible to trace precisely either the itinerary or chronology of King's various journeys. Other than his letters to Cable, few of his personal papers that might have shed light on the trip have survived. In addition the articles King wrote for *Scribner's Monthly* were not filed at regular intervals as dispatches to a newspaper or journal, as were the writings of some other observers of the southern scene. Indeed, King wrote some of the articles weeks or months after his visit or visits to a particular area, thus combining, especially in the book version, events and observations of different trips. See, for example, King to Cable, August 9, 1873, written from White Sulphur Springs, West Virginia; also King to Cable [June] 1873, from St. Louis, in which he refers to sending him the proof of the first Louisiana article.

his way to New York, where he remained until March, 1874. He again went to St. Louis that month, then made a steamboat trip down the Mississippi to New Orleans. From New Orleans he journeyed back through Mississippi to Memphis, then to Nashville, north into Kentucky, including Louisville, and on to Cincinnati. Another trip, in May and June of 1874, took him to parts of Virginia and Maryland.

Correlation of Trip Chronology and the Material in "Great South" Articles and Book

CHAPTERS IN BOOK	ARTICLES IN *Scribner's Monthly*	AREA OR TOPIC VISITED OR DESCRIBED	PROBABLE TIME
1–7	2nd and 3rd (Nov. and Dec., 1873); some re-arrangement and inter-mingling of material	New Orleans and other parts of Louisiana	Feb., 1873, March 1874
8	Much of this not in *Scribner's*	New Orleans and Louisiana politics	
9–16	4th and 5th (Jan. and Feb., 1874) rearranged, and in general a reversal in order in the book of material from these articles	Texas: Galveston, Houston, Austin, San Antonio	Jan., Apr., and early May, 1873
17	1st (Jul., 1873) and 5th (Feb., 1874)	Texas: Denison, Sherman	Jan. and May, 1873
18–20	1st (Jul., 1873); some rearrangement and omission of *Scribner's* material	Sedalia, Mo.; southeast Kansas; Indian Territory	Jan. and May, 1873
21–25	10th (July., 1874); pages 234–36 of book not in article	St. Louis, other parts of Missouri, including Kansas City	In St. Louis in Jan., late May to early June, and July, 1873, and March, 1874, and in other parts of area one or more times
26–30	13th (Oct., 1874)	Down the Mississippi River; Arkansas, Memphis, Vicksburg, Natchez, eastern Louisiana	March, 1874
31	Pp. 297–310 of book not in *Scribner's*; most of p. 310 is from 13th article	Cotton plantations in eastern Louisiana (across from Natchez)	March, 1874
32–33	12th (Sept., 1874) reversal in order of material of these chapters	Mississippi (and some of western Alabama); Mobile	Fall, 1873, March, 1873, possibly March, 1874

CHAPTERS IN BOOK	ARTICLES IN *Scribner's Monthly*	AREA OR TOPIC VISITED OR DESCRIBED	PROBABLE TIME
34–35	11th (Aug., 1874, latter part) but mostly 12th (Sept., 1874)	Montgomery, Selma, and northern Alabama	Mostly in fall, 1873
36–39	11th (Aug., 1874)	Eastern South Carolina, and Georgia	Early summer and fall, 1873
40–46	14th (Nov., 1874)	Various parts of Florida	Late Nov. until mid-Dec., 1873
47–52	9th (June, 1874)	South Carolina lowlands; Charleston; Columbia; South Carolina politics	Fall, 1873 and possibly summer, 1873
53	Not in *Scribner's*	Lowlands of North Carolina, including Raleigh	Possibly after leaving North Carolina mountains in early to mid-summer, 1873, or in fall, 1873
54–57	6th (March, 1874)	Eastern Tennessee and western North Carolina mountains	June, 1873
58–60	8th (May, 1874), with reversal and rearrangement of material	Various regions, modes of travel, and trips in eastern Tennessee, northern Georgia, and western South Carolina	Mostly in Oct., 1873
61–65	7th (Apr., 1874) with 2 or 3 pages of material not in King's *Scribner's* articles. (Some from Hotchkiss)	Virginia: Lynchburg to Bristol, back to Lynchburg, on to Petersburg, Norfolk and vicinity	Mostly Sept., 1873, though also in Bristol in Dec.
66–67	A little of this from parts of one or two articles on other areas	Negro education and colleges	
68	Not in *Scribner's*	Negro songs and singers	
69–75	Not in King's *Scribner's* articles. (Some drawn or condensed from Hotchkiss articles)	Virginia and West Virginia: Coastal area, Richmond, Charlottesville, the Valley; White Sulphur Springs, Kanawha Valley	King in parts of these areas at various times, including his stay at White Sulphur Springs
76–81	15th (Dec., 1874). Reversal in order of first 5 pages of article between chapters 76 and 77	Kentucky: from down the Ohio, and up from Nashville to Louisville and other areas	Various times, probably mostly late fall, 1873

CHAPTERS IN BOOK	ARTICLES IN *Scribner's Monthly*	AREA OR TOPIC VISITED OR DESCRIBED	PROBABLE TIME
82–85	King article in Apr., 1875, *Scribner's* on Baltimore "The Liverpool of America," has some material similar to parts of these chapters	Maryland, Baltimore, Harpers Ferry	May–June, 1874
86–89	Not in *Scribner's*	See chapter titles: various southern types and traits	
90	Not in *Scribner's*	Fredericksburg, Mt. Vernon, Arlington, and Alexandria	May–June, 1874

Neither the articles in *Scribner's* nor the arrangement of material by or within chapters of the book follows the tour chronologically. This is most apparent with regard to the sections dealing with King's descriptions of western and central Mississippi (chapters 30 and 32), and northern Georgia, eastern Tennessee, and northwestern South Carolina (chapters 58 through 60).[29]

It is clear that King and his party did not visit all of the areas, towns, and communities which are described or mentioned in the articles or the book. King's references to "we" or "our party," his relation of personal experiences, and his more detailed and interesting descriptions of certain places indicate that he actually visited them. On the other hand, his use of the indefinite "one," or "the observer," suggests that he obtained his information on a few areas and on historical, descriptive, or statistical topics from other sources.[30]

While Robert W. Burwell's assertion that the *Scribner's* articles "appeared in book form,"[31] is inaccurate, the statement in the preface that the "whole" of

[29] The information on King's itinerary summarized and tabulated above is derived from various letters from King to Cable, especially those of March 25, April 13, 24, May 9, 14, July 13, 22, August 9, September 6, December 18, 1873; February 4, 24, 26, and March 17, 1874. Almost all of the 1873 and 1874 letters in the Cable Collection, Tulane University, either in the heading or text, give indication of King's whereabouts or plans. Other sources for the chronology and itinerary are references in the book and in the *Scribner's* articles, and the brief summary of the King journeys on pp. 2–3 of the four-volume British edition of King's book (*The Southern States of North America* [London: Blackie and Son, 1875]). The last-named, the only summary description of the journeys the editors were able to locate, describes three trips, the first beginning "during the winter of 1872 [sic]" and continuing into 1873, a second in the spring of 1874, and a third in May and June, 1874. This summary is not entirely accurate and leaves out much of the backtracking, the trips to New York and West Virginia, and other details.

[30] For example, King relied on both Cable and the Louisiana historian Charles Gayarré for information and verification of facts about New Orleans and Louisiana, and he sent Cable portions of his articles on Louisiana to check. There is evidence that King and his party did not actually visit the Teche country of Louisiana. King to Cable, March 25, 1873, April 13, [1873], [June, 1873]; Arlin Turner, *George W. Cable: A Biography* (Durham: Duke University Press, 1956), 53–54; Grace King, *Memories of a Southern Woman of Letters* (New York: Macmillan Co., 1932), 50.

[31] Burwell in *Dictionary of American Biography*, X (1933), 387.

the *Scribner's* material was "re-written" and "re-arranged" is an exaggeration. More than 24 percent of the book had not appeared in the fifteen *Scribner's Monthly* "Great South" articles.[32] King considerably rearranged the contents of certain chapters and shifted material between chapters, adding some material from the trips made after he had written the original *Scribner's* articles. He

Material in Book Not Included in the Scribner's *"Great South" Series*

CHAPTERS IN BOOK	BOOK PAGES	TOPIC OR AREA DESCRIBED	APPROXIMATE NO. OF PAGES
8	89–98	Second trip to New Orleans—much of the material on Louisiana political situation	7
23	234–36	Mississippi River Bridge at St. Louis	3
31	295–309	Cotton plantation across the river from Natchez	14
62	561–62	Description of Natural Bridge (from Hotchkiss)	2
66–68	596–620	Education of Negroes, Negro colleges, Negro songs (some material on colleges from earlier articles)	24
69–75 65	621–92 593–95	Virginia and West Virginia. Some, especially illustrations, similar to Hotchkiss articles	74
82–85	733–70	Maryland, Baltimore, etc. Part similar to King's Apr., 1875, *Scribner's* article	38
86–89	771–94	Summary and impressions of the Negro and the South	24
90	795–802	Fredericksburg, Mt. Vernon, Arlington, etc.	8
			194

[32] Contrary to the assertions of some writers, the series began with "The New Route to the Gulf," *Scribner's Monthly*, VI (July, 1873), 257–88. It resumed with the first article on Louisiana in the initial issue of vol. VII (November, 1873), and an article appeared in each of the next thirteen issues. The series officially ended in December, 1874, as announced in the magazine. ("The 'Great South' Series of Papers," *Scribner's Monthly*, IX [December, 1874], 248.) This announcement promised additional papers on parts of the South with which the North was more familiar, as part of a new series planned for the next year on "American Life and Scenery." But the only other article by King in the magazine was one on Baltimore, "The Liverpool of America," IX (April, 1875), 681–95, part of which he used in chapters 82 through 85 of the book.

also updated some statistical data and generally improved both style and
sentence structure.[33] Nevertheless *The Great South* was too hastily written
and might have been improved by deleting portions of some articles and by
additional revising and rearranging.[34] Despite some confusing arrangement of
newly introduced chapters, the added material that summarizes and interprets
black culture and education and analyzes the southern character is quite
valuable.

The graphic illustrations are an outstanding feature of the "Great South"
articles and book, and they add significantly to the historical value of the account.[35] Most of them are from original sketches by J. Wells Champney and
carry his usual signature, "Champ," or his initials in some form.[36] The other
signatures or names that appear on most of the illustrations are those of other
artists or of the engravers who worked from the artists' original sketches. Although Champney did not accompany the *Scribner's* expedition in the late
spring and early summer of 1873 nor at all in 1874, King credits him with
more than four hundred of the sketches.[37] Much of the material added to the
text contains no illustrations, but more than fifty of the sketches in chapters
69 through 75, and a few in other chapters, had appeared in the 1872–1873
Hotchkiss articles in *Scribner's.*[38]

Like most nineteenth century journalists, King often failed to give exact
citations and proper credit to the source of his information. He used material from Hotchkiss and others without properly citing the sources, and he
was frequently inaccurate in transcribing quotations, even when he indicated
the origin. These factors, in addition to his failure to base all his conclusions on

[33] On the other hand, King at times used less picturesque language in the book than in the
articles.
[34] A notice from *Saturday Review*, XL, 407 (quoted in John Foster Kirk, *A Supplement
to Allibone's Critical Dictionary of English Literature and British and American Authors* [2
vols.; Philadelphia: J. B. Lippincott, 1896] II, 948) contends that the book "would have been
a most valuable and telling work if he [King] had taken the trouble to rewrite it."
[35] There are approximately 430 engravings in the *Scribner's* articles and 542 in the book,
although a few in the magazine do not appear in the book version. Furthermore the spacing,
arrangement, and captions frequently are different, and some of the illustrations in the book
are located at some distance from the subject matter of the text. This is especially true of
some sketches of southern types or characters used as fillers at the ends of chapters. Many
of the engravings have been used, often without credit, in both popular and scholarly works
down to the present time.
[36] For a biographical sketch of Champney, see Frederick W. Coburn, *Dictionary of American Biography*, III (1929), 610. This indicates that Champney covered much of the same
ground in Europe in the 1870s, as illustrator and reporter, as did King. Some of the editions
of King's *Europe in Storm and Calm* state on the title page that it was illustrated by Champney.
[37] *The Great South* (Hartford: American Publ. Co., 1875), ii (lxviii in the present ed.) ;
"The 'Great South' Series of Papers," *Scribner's Monthly*, IX (December, 1874), 248;
King to Cable, May 9, May 14, [June], July 22, December 18, 1873, February 4, 1874. Brief
references to several of the other artists and/or engravers, such as William Avery, Edward Bookhout, J. Arnold, J. P. Davis, F. S. King, John Minton, and W. L. Sheppard may be
found in George C. Groce and David H. Wallace (eds.), *The New York Historical Society
Dictionary of Artists in America, 1564–1860* (New Haven: Yale University Press, 1957) ; and
Mantle Fielding, *Dictionary of American Painters, Sculptors, and Engravers* (New York:
Paul A. Struck, 1945). The Champney-J. P. Davis and Champney-W. L. Sheppard sketches
are perhaps somewhat superior to the others.
[38] Referred to in footnote 25 above.

firsthand observation, may account for the comment of one critic that King was somewhat careless with facts.[39]

The "Great South" articles were popular in the North and South, as well as in England. The magazine series was a financial success from the standpoint of increasing the circulation of *Scribner's Monthly* throughout the United States and of promoting the newly established English edition abroad.[40] Editor Holland was confident that the "Great South" series had accomplished its goals. In the same issue that carried the concluding article, he noted that it was "with no ordinary pride and satisfaction that we thus record the completion of a task undertaken with the desire to enlighten our country concerning itself, and to spread before the nation the natural resources, the social condition, and the political complications" of the South.[41]

A rival magazine, the *Nation,* was less kind in its evaluation of King's reporting. It remarked that he was a "fluent rather than a statistical or weighty reporter," but admitted that he gave a clear notion of the general condition of affairs and was often "graphic and amusing." The comment concluded with the remark that this variety of illustrated article was more popular with the majority of Americans than most new novels.[42]

The book itself, on which King had begun work some months before the last of the articles appeared in the magazine,[43] was published simultaneously in the United States and England.[44] In this country southern newspapers, as well as many northern ones, were lavish in their praise of *The Great South.* The New York *Times* remarked that the author was a "close observer," and noted that both the writing and illustrations were "characteristic and truthful." The Philadelphia *Dollar Weekly* pointed out that the "pictures of negro life" were "drawn with a pencil free from partisan control." The Petersburg, Virginia, *Index and Appeal* credited King with "a sincere intention to tell the full facts as he ascertained them," adding that he was "obviously free from any of the prejudice of which malice and ignorance are the hateful parents." Other newspapers and journals commented on the value of the statistics and informa-

---

[39] For example, a quotation from Robert Somers on pp. 306–307 contains some elisions and errors. The original is on pp. 128–129 of Robert Somers, *The Southern States of North America Since the War, 1870–71,* with an introduction and index by Malcolm C. McMillan (University, Ala.: University of Albama Press, 1965.)

[40] Marion Reid Murray, "The 1870's in American Literature," *American Speech,* I (March, 1926), 325–26; John, "A History of *Scribner's Monthly,*" 201, 208.

[41] *Scribner's Monthly,* IX (December, 1874), 248–49.

[42] *Nation,* XVII (December 25, 1873), 427. A recent scholar, generally agreeing with this analysis, feels that the *Nation's* earlier series by John Richard Dennett (cited in footnote 24 above) was "more analytical and studied" than King's, but points out that the temper of the country with regard to the freedmen and national reconciliation had changed in the intervening years. Mott, *American Magazines,* 334, 464.

[43] King to Cable, three undated letters, [summer and fall, 1874].

[44] Apparently the only American edition is the one reprinted here. In England, Blackie and Son, London, published the book in 1875, in one, three, and four volumes, with the title *The Southern States of North America. . . .* The material and pagination of the introductory matter of the British editions differ slightly from the American. Also, an introductory color map and seven full-page illustrations scattered throughout the text are added. In the four-volume edition, on pages 1 through 4, there is an advertisement of the book, including the description of the trip noted in footnote 29 above. The pagination of the text of the book, which begins with page 17, is the same in all of the original editions, American and British, and has been retained in the present edition. The current publisher has added new front matter.

tion, the vivid writing, and the excellent character sketches. Critics also noted that King and the publishers had obtained facts, views, and statistics from a wide variety of individuals and sources with access to information that had been scattered or destroyed during the war.[45]

King, writing from London early in 1876, noted that the book was a "far greater" success there than in America.[46] While it received a generally favorable reception from reviewers, some of the English journals were more critical than were the American newspapers. While praising King's efforts to be fair in looking on the Negro as a brother, the *Westminster Review* scolded him, and more especially the illustrators, for "displaying a comic memory of the black man as a 'Quashee,' and a patronizing observation of him as a creature scarcely on a par with themselves, lurking in the background of all the work of their pen and brushes." But the *Review* conceded that the book's evaluation of the South's commercial and political prospects made the region attractive to prospective immigrants. In conclusion the critique strongly endorsed the book's readability and interest, observing that there was scarcely a page that was "not bright and sparkling or vividly descriptive, . . . and enlivened by some telling sketch of men or places."[47]

Of all the accounts of the postwar South that appeared in newspapers, magazines, books, and official reports, King's is generally considered, along with those by Somers, Pike, and Nordhoff, as among the "most influential of the period."[48] These works, and similar material in *Harper's, Lippincott's, Appleton's,* and the *Atlantic,* were widely read, received favorable reviews, and served to soften the northern attitude toward the South. King's and Nordhoff's accounts have been characterized as the best written in the 1870s. Reports on the South in the 1880s were far greater in quantity but of poorer quality than those of the 1870s. Enthusiasm and boosterism were by the later decade replacing analysis, and there was little new in the way of descriptive material to be added to what King and Nordhoff had said earlier.[49]

There is widespread agreement among scholars that King's journeys and "Great South" publications had important effects on the development of southern literature. Of particular importance was King's discovery of George

[45] These comments are from notices from the press in the advertisement referred to in footnote 44. There are quotations from twenty newspapers or journals, at least thirteen from the North. While they were doubtless selected and quoted for the purpose of impressing prospective purchasers of the British edition, the wide selection reflects the interest in the book in the United States.

[46] King to W. W. Clapp, January 21, 1876.

[47] *Westminster Review,* CV (January, 1876), 119–20. Many of the illustrations do present caricatures of blacks, but they do not accurately reflect King's attitudes. See pp. xli, xlix–l, liv–lviii below for an analysis of King's views. See also the comment from the *Saturday Review,* cited in footnote 34 above, which, although somewhat critical of King's writing, notes that the book was "full of information and interest."

[48] Buck, *The Road to Reunion,* 133. Reports by Carl Schurz, Benjamin Truman, and General Grant, and accounts by American journalists such as John R. Dennett, Sidney Andrews, John T. Trowbridge, and Whitelaw Reid had appeared soon after the war. A second group published after 1870, by which time the bitter feelings resulting from the war were declining and the movement for reconciliation was gaining momentum, included the writings of Robert Somers, James S. Pike, Charles Nordhoff, and King. See citation in footnote 1.

[49] Buck, *The Road to Reunion,* 133, 188; McIlwaine, *The Southern Poor-White,* 100.

Washington Cable. On his first visit to New Orleans, in February, 1873, [50] King, seeking a source of information on the region, initiated a friendship with Cable, who had done some writing for New Orleans papers, including historical sketches on the city's institutions.[51] Cable's biographers and the treatments of both King and Cable in works on American literature refer to King as Cable's "discoverer." He read the author's stories, sent or took them in person to *Scribner's,* later placed them elsewhere, and gave him frequent encouragement and advice on his writing. In effect he served as Cable's literary agent.[52]

The effect of King's "Great South" series on the development and acceptance of southern local color writing is difficult to measure. In reply to an inquiry by Fred Lewis Pattee in 1914, Cable wrote: "I cannot say that King's 'Great South' papers affected the Southern literary awakening. I think the two were merely coincidental."[53] Nevertheless twentieth century scholars maintain that the ideas and philosophy of magazines like *Scribner's Monthly* "accounted in large part for the vogue of local color in national literature." King's articles, "the first extended treatment of the South during Reconstruction to appear in the national magazine press, helped to prepare readers and editors for the literary use of Southern material."[54] Thus King's tour of the South, the *Scribner's* articles, and the book had significant effects,

[50] New Orleans *Picayune* (morning ed.), February 14, 1873, in a listing of "Arrivals at Principal Hotels," notes that both King and Champney were registered at the St. Charles Hotel, so they had apparently arrived in the city on February 13.

[51] Biklé, *George W. Cable,* 43–45; Arlin Turner, "George W. Cable's Literary Apprenticeship," *Louisiana Historical Quarterly,* XXIV (January, 1941), 5; Turner, *George W. Cable,* 51–54. See footnote 30 above for King's reliance on Cable for information on Louisiana. It seems likely that King initiated his contact and friendship with Cable for this purpose rather than, as one source puts it, that *Scribner's* sent him South as a "literary scout," (Kunitz and Haycraft, *American Authors, 1600–1900,* 439). Buck, *The Road to Renunion,* 222, implies that *Scribner's,* in pursuance of its nationalistic policy, was looking for the type of writing that Cable was doing.

[52] See the citations in footnotes 30 and 43; Arthur H. Quinn, *American Fiction: An Historical and Critical Survey* (New York: D. Appleton-Century Co., 1936), 323; Philip Butcher: *George W. Cable* (New York: Twayne Publ., Inc., 1962), 25; Fred Lewis Pattee in William Porterfield Trent, *et al* (eds.), *Cambridge History of American Literature* (4 vols.; New York: G. P. Putnam's Sons, 1917–21), III, 379. Cable, after King's death, referred to him as "my dear friend and 'discoverer,' " although King had earlier disclaimed the designation "discoverer," remarking "Cable discovered himself—and would have dawned upon the world had there never been any Great South scribes in New Orleans." The quotation from Cable is in Kjell Ekström, *George Washington Cable: A Study of His Early Life and Work* (Cambridge: Harvard University Press, 1950), 100–101; and in Biklé, *George W. Cable,* 51, from a letter Cable wrote to Mary E. Burt. (Neither source gives the date or location of the original.) King's remarks are in a letter to [Robert Underwood] Johnson, [1893], Cable Collection, Tulane University. It was through Johnson, then associate editor of *Century Magazine,* that King and Cable renewed their correspondence and acquaintanceship after a lapse of several years.

[53] Cable to Fred Lewis Pattee, quoted in Biklé, *George W. Cable,* 47. Turner, *George W. Cable,* 53, and Louis D. Rubin, Jr., *George W. Cable: The Life and Times of a Southern Heretic* (New York: Pegasus Publishers, 1969), 14, in paraphrasing this quotation make Cable's statement sound more positive than it actually was.

[54] Rubin, *George W. Cable,* 14. See also Buck, *The Road to Reunion,* 222ff., for a discussion of the promotion by *Scribner's* and other national magazines of nationalism through the publication of local color writing. Several sources consider King's discovery of Cable and the publication by *Scribner's* and other journals of the works of southern authors, the most important results of King's tour. See for example, Grace King, *Memories of a Southern Woman,* 50.

direct and indirect, on literary developments not only in the South but throughout the country.

THE COTTON KINGDOM Revisited

Fletcher M. Green, an authority on southern travel literature, has referred to King's *The Great South* as the "fullest and at the same time one of the most accurate and revealing" of the postbellum travel accounts of the South. King "saw almost everything" and was, in Green's words, "fair, unprejudiced, and impartial." Professor Green's sense of the importance of King's work is not exaggerated. Aside from Frederick Law Olmsted's *The Cotton Kingdom, The Great South* is the most comprehensive and historically significant travel account ever written about the region.[55]

There are interesting parallels between these two major treatments of the South, as well as between their authors. Both Olmsted and King were New Englanders, both had sharpened their powers of observation and gained greater intellectual maturity in traveling abroad, and both had published accounts of their European experiences before their southern journeys. In contrast to many authors of nineteenth century southern travel accounts, both Olmsted and King made lengthy journeys across the whole of the southern region; each spent more than a year visiting not only the older southern states, but also the Gulf states, the Southwest, the mountain region, and the back country. King visited the Indian Territory and several states which Olmsted did not cover in his travels.[56]

Both Olmsted and King sought to accomplish the same basic end in their treatments—the presentation of a realistic and extensive firsthand account of southern life and society. Although Olmsted treated various important aspects of the antebellum South, his primary interest was in the institution of slavery, which in his opinion was the major determinant of southern attitudes, human relations, and patterns of life. Indeed to Olmsted the South was co-equal to that territory in which slavery existed, and originally he had planned to use the overall title *Our Slave States* for his trilogy on the South. In some respects *The Great South* can be considered a sequel to Olmsted's work, for King consciously made his account a study not of the former Confederate South, but of the "States formerly under the dominion of Slavery."[57]

The South of the 1870s, of course, was a different South—one without the dominant peculiar institution of antebellum days. King was convinced that "one of the most remarkable revolutions ever recorded in history" had swept over the region, ushering in a new regime and creating a New South. It was King's purpose, as indicated in the book's preface, to present a forthright and

[55] Green, "The South in Reconstruction," 66–67. For an excellent biographical sketch of Olmsted and the best analysis of his southern travel acounts, see "Editor's Introduction" in Frederick Law Olmsted, *The Cotton Kingdom: A Traveller's Observations on Cotton and Slavery in the American Slave States,* ed., Arthur M. Schlesinger (New York: Alfred A. Knopf, 1953).

[56] *Ibid.,* xi–xiii, xvi–xx.

[57] See p. v of the one-volume British edition cited in footnote 44 above; Schlesinger, "Editor's Introduction," ix, xiv, xxi–xxii, xlvi–liv.

informed account of the material resources, the social and political condition, and the future prospects of this New South.[58]   The book is much more than simply an account of reconstruction, as it is so often labeled.   King treated the Indian Territory and four non-Confederate states which had not experienced political reconstruction.   Moreover the economic developments, tourist attractions, social organization, and numerous other aspects of the southern scene with which he dealt at length were only indirectly related to the process of reconstruction.

Whether Edward King ever read Olmsted's accounts of the South is problematic, but he clearly shared many of Olmsted's views.   Like Olmsted —and Alexis de Tocqueville before him—King believed that the institution of slavery was primarily responsible for the essential differences between Northerners and Southerners.   The dissimilarities in habits, customs, and language were not simply climatic, King argued, "they were inbred by the system and tendencies . . . so lately done away with."[59]

In King's view the impact of slavery on white Southerners had been overwhelmingly unfortunate.   That many of them lacked ambition, thrift, and enterprise seemed to be only the natural consequence of slavery.   In contrast northern and European immigrants to the South invariably appeared to be industrious and progressive.   For example, he describes northern immigrants in the frontier town of Denison, Texas, as energetic, self-reliant, and confident; the native Texan, however, "is a child of the sun; he dislikes effort; it gives him no gratification to labor in the rough ways of a new town like Denison."   In Florida enterprising Northerners dominated orange culture because the "natives of the poor class . . . [were] too idle to develop the country."[60]

Slavery had been, in King's opinion, an unprogressive system that had dwarfed the trade of cities and prevented the growth of manufacturing centers. The contrast between the effects of slavery and of free society on economic development was most pronounced along the Ohio River.   On the Ohio side, there were "large manufacturing towns, evidences of thrift, industry and investment," while across the river few of the towns were large or bustling.[61] Nothing demonstrated to King the detrimental impact of slavery so vividly as the remarkable economic progress of some areas of the South after 1865. For example, St. Louis, under free institutions, had achieved "more prosperity in ten years than under the old *regime* it would have attained in fifty." Georgia farmers, with careful fertilizing and cultivation, had doubled cotton production since the war.[62]

But slavery had not only stunted economic growth; it had also stifled the intellectual, emotional, and moral growth of the southern people.   It had relegated the black man to the status of "an article of barter"; the slave "had no identity [and] was supposed to possess little consciousness, moral or other-

[58] King, *Great South*, 1–2, 428, 776.
[59] *Ibid.*, 771; Schlesinger, "Editor's Introduction," xlvii–xlviii.
[60] King, *Great South*, 177, 403, 176–82, 218–19, 708, 713, 749, 775, 797.
[61] *Ibid.*, 694; see also 708–709, 755.   For a similar statement on economic development along the Ohio, see Alexis de Tocqueville, *Democracy in America*, ed. J. P. Mayer (Garden City: Doubleday and Co., Inc., 1969), 345–46.
[62] King, *Great South*, 218–19, 348.

wise." King was convinced that slavery had also prevented the growth of a progressive middle class. It had produced two classes in white society, the "high up and the low down," the gentleman planter and the "ruffian, brawling, ill-educated, and generally miserable poor white."[63] Moreover the system of slave labor had fostered the idea that labor itself was degrading; even the planters in many cases had been unambitious and unprogressive under the old regime. In some instances, as in northern Texas, the rich slaveowner had been "a kind of patriarchal savage, proud of his own dirt and ignorance."[64] In short, slavery had been a thoroughly regressive system.

King agreed with Olmsted's conclusion that cotton was a "cruel and ruinous monarch."[65] It was a serious mistake, King maintained, to concentrate on one staple crop, necessitating dependence on highly priced foodstuffs from the West and North. Reliance upon these coarse food supplies kept the status of the laboring man depressed, and the generally "repulsive" conditions of labor in turn discouraged white immigration. Moreover, because southern planters operated almost entirely on borrowed capital, falling prices and crop failures placed many of them in financial straits. In Alabama cotton planters suffered "savage reverses" during the early 1870s; when the crop on which they placed sole reliance failed, they found themselves penniless and starving. Hence, King wrote, "they gather up the wrecks of their fortunes, pack their Lares and Penates in an emigrant wagon or car, and doggedly work their way to Texas." The "all cotton" policy was a "foolish" and "false system."[66]

Like Olmsted, King considered the South a distinctive section with its own characteristics, although he rejected the argument of an "amiable gentleman in Savannah . . . that the people of the North and South were two distinct nations." But as had Olmsted before him, King found that the South was not a uniform, homogeneous society. The most striking impression he received was "that the inhabitants of each State have remarkably distinguishing characteristics."[67] *The Great South* is a testament to the wide diversity of the South of the 1870s. In adjustments to the revolutionary changes of the period, in economic activity and prospects, in the development of education, and particularly in the course of political reconstruction, there were minor variations and major differences from state to state and between the major subdivisions of the region.

Both Olmsted and King were American nationalists who sought to play mediatorial roles in fostering mutual understanding between the sections. While Olmsted had hoped to help prevent the breakup of the Union, King reasoned that an informative account of the South and its people would help

[63] *Ibid.*, 773, 602, 427, 346. Like many of the abolitionists in the prewar period, King erred in his assumption that antebellum southern society could be divided into upper and lower classes, with no middle class. Actually there was a large and healthy middle class in the antebellum South. Olmsted had not made the same error. For King's views of the "poor-whites" and editorial comment thereon, see below, pp. xli and note 78.

[64] *Ibid.*, 182, 90, 730, 159.   [65] Schlesinger, "Editor's Introduction," xxxiv.

[66] King, *Great South*, 270–72, 329–34, 340. The "main suffering" in Alabama occurred, King wrote (p. 331), "because the people raised but little food."

[67] *Ibid.*, 771; Schlesinger, "Editor's Introduction," xlvii–xlviii.

reunite the nation. Although he devoted considerable attention to describing distinctive southern characteristics, King thought that essentially Southerners constituted only different "types of a common nationality." In fact he expressed some disappointment in not finding "more marked peculiarities in the people of Texas," noting that in the cities of that state the visitor "sees but little variation from his own types."[68]

Reconciliation is a dominant theme throughout *The Great South*. It was King who made the oft-cited observation that the "citizens of Alabama, as a mass, are as loyal to the idea of the Union to-day as are the citizens of New York."[69] Of course there were exceptions to this generalization. In some of the rougher parts of Tennessee, Northerners were looked upon as natural enemies, and the northern visitor might encounter "occasional small spite" in several of the southern capitals. In North Carolina King found the people in some small towns "more inclined to bitterness and less reconciled to the results of the war than anywhere else in the South." Such attitudes were likely to be more common and more pronounced in the backcountry areas.[70]

Generally, however, King found the old prejudices and enmities diminishing. In Missouri the "best spirit" prevailed, and old enemies worked side by side in the upbuilding of the state. At resort areas like White Sulphur Springs, Southerners and Northerners seemed "to have forgotten their sectional bickerings, and to have come together in friendliest mood." Even in rural Alabama and Mississippi, and in the South Carolina upcountry, "something of national feeling" was developing. King closes the book with a scene in Arlington cemetery, where "now and then old soldiers, who for long years fought fiercely against each other in opposing ranks, pause in friendly converse by some grassy mound. . . ."[71] *The Great South* clearly and persuasively promoted the developing sense of national identity in postbellum America.

King's observations about numerous aspects of southern life and manners were in basic agreement with those of Olmsted. In the 1850s Olmsted had found the southern diet "abominable," and although King maintained that criticism of the southern cuisine could not be general, his evidence almost belies that conclusion.[72] In the interior of Texas, for example, the mass of people had "a hearty scorn for anything good to eat." As a group southern farmers were a "lean, ill-fed race" who subsisted primarily on "hog and hominy." In the southern mountains, he complained, "whenever by rare chance a beef steak found its way to the table, it had been remorselessly fried until not a particle of juice remained in its substance."[73] His "severest experience" with southern cooking was in an unnamed "metropolis" in northern Texas. There "a dirty cloth was laid on a dirtier table, and pork, fried to a cinder and swimming in grease hot enough to scorch the palate, was placed before the

[68] King, *Great South*, 181, 711–16; Schlesinger, "Editor's Introduction," xxvii, xxxix–xl, xliv–xlvi, xvi–xviii.

[69] King, *Great South*, 340–41.   [70] *Ibid.*, 468, 515–16, 677, 730, 341, 401.

[71] *Ibid.*, 256, 674, 401, 341, 139, 310, 515–16, 802.

[72] Schlesinger, "Editor's Introduction," xii–xiii, xix–xxi; King, *Great South*, 791. "Nowhere in the world," wrote King "is there better cookery or a richer bill of fare than that offered in Baltimore, in Charleston, in Savannah, and in New Orleans."

[73] King, *Great South*, 182–84, 421, 791.

guests. To this was presently added . . . a yellow mess of dough supposed to be biscuit, a cup of black, bitter bean-juice named coffee, and as a
crowning torture, a mustard-pot, with very watery mustard in it."[74]

As had Olmsted, King found life in parts of the South crude and unrefined.
This was true not only of frontier regions, but also of areas along the North
Carolina coast and among the mountains of Tennessee, North Carolina, and
the Virginias. In the "log-built, unkempt settlements in the interior" of
Arkansas, King noted, "morals are bad, manners [are] worse, and there are
no comforts or graces." In the remote districts of Texas one might find "more
ignorance and less idea of comfort than he would have thought possible in
America," and King observed an aspect of wild desolation about the North
Carolina lowlands. Primitive living conditions were most common among
blacks and poor whites.[75]

The lack of modern and efficient conveniences and facilities, although not
so prevalent as in the antebellum South, was also common in the New South.
In one small Texas town, King's accommodations for the night were in a
"creaking loft, over a whiskey saloon wherein a mob of drunken railroad
laborers were quarreling, and threatening, with the most outrageous profanity,
to annihilate each other." He grumbled that the ordinary backcountry road
in Virginia was "simply abominable," and that riding in an omnibus over the
wooden pavement in Memphis was "almost unendurable." Travel by rail
was generally slow and was marked in some areas by frequent delays that
would not have been tolerated in the North. King was unable to buy tickets
on the Alabama and Chattanooga railroad; "so hopeless is the embarrassment" of the railroad, he wrote, that "no one knows, or scarcely considers it
worthwhile to inquire, who owns it."[76]

King saw a great deal of ignorance, prejudice, and provincialism, particularly among the lower classes. The poor-white countrymen all through
the cotton belt were "bounded, prejudiced and ignorant of most things outside
the limits of the State"; the ignorance of this class in Alabama seemed "as
dense as that of the blacks." He found the extent of illiteracy in North Carolina, Florida, Texas, Georgia, Arkansas, and Tennessee alarming. Tennessee's illiteracy rate was the third highest in the nation; in the South as a whole,
less than half of the adults could read and write, and the percentage of illiteracy
among the white population was increasing. King's observations led him to
the conclusion that the South's lack of an educated citizenry was the "cause
of many phases of its unhappy condition."[77]

King also observed low standards of living and much poverty throughout
the South. In Montgomery County, Alabama, successive crop failures had
produced "a general complaint of poverty, much destitution, and, in some

<hr/>

[74] *Ibid.,* 183–84.
[75] Schlesinger, "Editor's Introduction," xlix, lii–lv; King, *Great South,* 283, 181–82, 467,
730, and 474–578, *passim.*
[76] King, *Great South,* 183–84, 563, 264, 365, 374–78, 426, 312. For several of Olmsted's
experiences with southern railroads and steamboats, see *The Cotton Kingdom,* 44, 72, 110.
[77] King, *Great South,* 340, 334, 420, 470, 134, 283, 356, 547, 730, 602, 775.

cases, despair." Along the South Carolina coast, there were wide belts of abandoned plantations and "deserted and bankrupt towns, . . . filled with moss-grown and rotting houses, whose owners have fled, unless too poor to get away." The "poverty" of New Orleans' formerly wealthy families forced the closing of the city's opera in the winter of 1873. But King was particularly fascinated by the large class of primitive and degraded "poor whites," whom he described as uneducated, shiftless, and childlike. The women invariably were "lean and scrawny," the men "lank and hungry." Of the thousands of people of this class who were emigrating to Arkansas and Texas, "not one had in his face a particle of color; all had the same dead, pallid complexion." There was nothing like them, King wrote, among native Americans in the North.[78]

An even higher proportion of southern blacks existed at a marginal subsistence level. Around Montgomery, Alabama, many blacks who had been discharged by planters during the hard times of the early 1870s were forced to migrate or to turn to charity. King saw "men and women . . . slouching all day, . . . living on garbage and the results of begging and predatory expeditions—a prey to any disease that comes along, and festering in ignorance." The mass of New Orleans' improvident blacks lived in cramped and unsanitary quarters, crowded together "as in all [southern] cities . . . in ill-built and badly-ventilated cabins." In the mountains of Tennessee, blacks lived "the very rudest and most incult life imaginable." He noted that "the children rolled in the dirt, and had no thoughts of school. . . . the cabin was cleanly, but primitive in all its furnishings; the round of these people's lives seemed to be sleeping and waking, with a struggle between morning and evening to get enough to put into their mouths; they had no thoughts of thrift or progress."[79]

King, as had Olmsted, discovered that violence was pervasive in southern life. Although the northern impression that most southern men carried weapons and used them on slight provocation was exaggerated, it was true that large numbers of Southerners habitually carried weapons and used them freely. The worse phase of the southern character, King felt, was an unwillingness to resort to judicial settlement of disputes. In the Deep South especially, a "class of so-called gentlemen" frequently employed the revolver when offended, and the courts often did not deal with such men with sufficient sternness.[80]

There was also legal and officially sanctioned violence in the South. In Texas convict laborers, employed "like galley slaves," were systematically overworked. King's observation of the "abject, cowering mass of black and

[78] *Ibid.*, 331, 341, 451, 35, 318, 340, 420–21, 371–72, 515, 283, 774–75, 346, 99. King, like many other Northerners, used "poor-white" as a "term of remarkable elasticity" to "reconcile the poverty of the South with the national faith in opportunity and boundless progress." Northerners viewed these Southerners as backward people and tended to greatly exaggerate their numbers. C. Vann Woodward, *Origins of the New South, 1877–1913* (Baton Rouge: Louisiana State University Press, 1951), 109–10, 176–77.

[79] King, *Great South*, 542–43, 330, 341, 45–46; also 740, 793.

[80] Schlesinger, "Editor's Introduction," xlix–i; King, *Great South*, 777, 138–39, 289, 317.

white humanity" of a Texan convict train clung like a "horrid nightmare" in
his memory. Some of the Texas jails were throwbacks to the "barbarities of
the Middle Ages." Unfortunately, King reported, the Democratic Party in
the South was not always the party of law and order. Democratic leaders were
inflammatory and Democratic legislatures were prone to repeal progressive
legislation passed by Republican lawmakers; for instance, the redemption of
Texas and Arkansas increased the number of misdeeds in those states.[81]

King was of the opinion that most of the violence was committed by
"the rougher whites." Desperadoes and border ruffians, whose chief amusement was "coarse and bestial intoxication," committed numerous outrages
against persons and property in the frontier areas of Texas, Missouri, and
Arkansas. But it was not only on the undeveloped frontier that violence was
common. Among the lower classes generally, quarrels grew into deep-seated
feuds which often ended fatally. Such violence was pronounced in the mountain regions of Tennessee and the backcountry of Kentucky, where ignorance
and lawlessness were prevalent. Violence against blacks was particularly common in the backcountry. In Kentucky ruffians "took 'niggers' from their
houses and whipped them on most trivial provocation." Indeed, concluded
King, "the rural Caucasian has a kind of subdued thirst for negro gore, which,
when once really awakened, is not readily appeased."[82]

Although the similarities between *The Cotton Kingdom* and *The Great
South* are numerous, there are also important differences. *The Great South*
is a considerably larger volume with broader geographical coverage. Descriptive and travelogue material, historical commentary, and original illustrations
are integral features of *The Great South,* but not of *The Cotton Kingdom.*
But there is a more fundamental difference between the two volumes. Unlike
Olmsted's, King's treatment does not offer a circumstantial, day-by-day account of common life in the South nor a rich collection of pin-point character
sketches of Southerners. King was an analytical journalist as well as a reporter, and his *Great South* presents an informative and evaluative overview of
the South from his perspective, leaving much less to the judgment of the reader
than does *The Cotton Kingdom.*[83]

The differences in the accounts reflect the different circumstances and
times in which the authors observed the South. Olmsted made most of his
journeys on horseback, usually alone, and as a consequence he met all sorts of
Southerners and shared in their everyday lives. King, on the other hand,
usually traveled with a fair-sized staff; his accommodations were generally
arranged in advance, and they were always the best available. Except for his
trips through the backcountry of the southern mountains and the Texas frontier, which he made on horseback and by stagecoach, he traveled mostly by
rail or steamboat. On the Mississippi he used the famed steamer *Robert E. Lee*
and also the *Great Republic,* which he described as "literally a floating

[81] King, *Great South,* 118–22, 778. King also observed (p. 727) "gangs of negro convicts
. . . working at street and wall making" near the Tennessee Capitol in Nashville.
[82] *Ibid.,* 372, 777, 121, 252, 283, 730, 715.
[83] Schlesinger, "Editor's Introduction," xii, xvi–xvii, xxiv–xxv, xxxi, liii.

palace." In Texas and the Indian Territory, special trains were placed at his disposal. Hence, he saw less of common life than Olmsted had. King did attempt to meet and talk with people representing as broad a spectrum of southern society as possible, but because of his mode of travel and his keen interest in economic and political developments, he made extended contacts most often with persons of the established order—planters, politicians, and businessmen.[84]

Another significant difference between these two classic "Yankee" accounts of southern life has been their acceptance and use by the reading public and by professional scholars. *The Cotton Kingdom* was reissued numerous times in the 1860s, and it has since appeared in a number of edited and annotated reprints. Southern historians, while disagreeing over the import of Olmsted's work, almost universally accept it as a classic source on the antebellum South.[85] In contrast *The Great South* has remained in relative obscurity since its publication in four formats in 1875. There has been no edited reissue of the work, and only in recent years have two unedited reproductions been published.

Although southern historians such as Willie Lee Rose, C. Vann Woodward, and Charles E. Wynes have effectively used *The Great South* in their studies,[86] scholars have not generally turned to King's account as a major primary source. Many of the more significant studies of reconstruction and the New South, including important bibliographical and historiographical works, make no mention of *The Great South*.[87] Of the historians who have cited King's work, some have distorted his conclusions in their attempts to generalize about a region in which he found great diversity. For example, King never claimed, as one historian states, that "Southerners were as loyal to the idea of the Union as were any citizens of New York." Moreover, in light of the evidence King presents to the contrary, it is misleading to use his work to support the unqualified generalization that Mississippi whites were convinced of the unreliability of Negro labor. But the contention that King found a generally drab, gloomy, and hopeless South, where there was "little inclination toward industrial organization and progress," is the most serious misin-

---

[84] *Ibid.,* xvi, xviii–xxi ; King, *Great South,* I, 139–46, 475, 258, 261, 305, 118, 188.

[85] Schlesinger, "Editor's Introduction," ix, xlvi–xlvii. Olmsted's careers both as a critic of the South and as a famous landscape architect have been the subjects of monographic studies.

[86] Willie Lee Rose, *Rehearsal for Reconstruction: The Port Royal Experiment* (New York: Random House, Inc., 1967), 378–79, 398; Woodward, *Origins of the New South,* 109, 111, 162; Charles E. Wynes, *Race Relations in Virginia, 1870–1902* (Charlottesville: University of Virginia Press, 1961), 7, 27, 71. Also see Harvey Wish (ed.), *Reconstruction in the South, 1865–1877* . . . (New York: Farrar, Straus & Giroux, 1965), 183–87; Vernon Lane Wharton, *The Negro in Mississippi, 1865–1890* (New York: Harper and Row, Publ., 1965), 49, 177; Buck, *The Road to Reunion,* 130–33, 151, 188, 222.

[87] See, for example, William A. Dunning, *Reconstruction, Political and Economic, 1865–1877* (New York: Harper and Row, Publ., 1962) ; Kenneth M. Stampp, *The Era of Reconstruction, 1865–1877* (New York: Random House, 1967); John Samuel Ezell, *The South Since 1865* (New York: Macmillan Co., 1963) ; Arthur S. Link and Rembert W. Patrick (eds.), *Writing Southern History: Essays in Historiography in Honor of Fletcher M. Green* (Baton Rouge: Louisiana State University Press, 1965). Dunning does mention *The Great South* in a bibliographical note.

terpretation because it runs directly counter to the central theme of *The Great South*.[88]

The Promise of the New South

The Great South is not only an invaluable account of the New South of the 1870s; it is also a period piece of Gilded Age America, reflecting the confidence, optimism, and exuberance that characterized the postbellum period. The 1870s were the early years of what Carl Degler has called the Age of the Economic Revolution, and it is not surprising that King's primary concern was with southern economic resources and activities and the region's potential for economic development. King's unbounded faith in the efficacy of public education in overcoming the social ills of the South, and his confidence that economic growth would invariably improve the human condition also reflect Gilded Age ideas. That *The Great South* contains extremely little on southern literature and art is indicative not only of the paucity of southern activity and achievement in these areas, but also of Gilded Age America's preoccupation with material progress.[89]

Edward King's New South of the 1870s differed markedly from Olmsted's Old South of the 1850s. Olmsted had found a region that was primarily and overwhelmingly rural. Transportation facilities were crude and accommodations poor; the cities, except for a few major centers, were uninteresting communities with unpaved streets and undeveloped commercial resources.[90] Twenty years later railroads crisscrossed the South, connecting nearly all the major cities and many of the small towns, and King was able to visit most of the region in relatively comfortable rail or water accommodations. Moreover the South was no longer so predominantly rural. Although a majority of Southerners were still country dwellers, increasing numbers of them were being attracted to the developing urban areas of the region.

The Great South fully treats urbanization in the South. Nearly half of the chapters focus on southern cities and towns, and portions of other chapters deal with urban matters. King dealt with the cities of each state, from the "little city" of Asheville, North Carolina, with a population of 2,500, to the South's largest city, St. Louis, a "cosmopolitan capital" of more than 310,000 people. In King's view the cities were the most dynamic areas of the South; they were the centers of industrial, commercial, educational, intellectual, and promotional activity. On the other hand, the rural portions of Arkansas, Alabama, Mis-

[88] John Hope Franklin, *Reconstruction: After the Civil War* (Chicago, 1961), 199 (See p. xxxix, n.69, above.); Wharton, *The Negro in Mississippi*, 48–49; Thomas D. Clark and Albert D. Kirwan, *The South Since Appomattox* (New York: Oxford University Press, 1967), 136–37. Also see Woodward, *Origins of the New South*, 111, 162; Richard Hofstadter, William Miller, and Daniel Aaron, *The United States: The History of a Republic* (Englewood Cliffs: Prentice-Hall, Inc., 1967), 458.

[89] See Carl Degler, *The Age of the Economic Revolution, 1876–1900* (Glenview, Ill.: Scott, Foresman and Company, 1967); and H. Wayne Morgan (ed.), *The Gilded Age: A Reappraisal* (Syracuse: Syracuse University Press, 1963).

[90] Schlesinger, "Editor's Introduction," liii–liv, xlix.

sissippi, and the coastal plain of the Carolinas were the most unprogressive areas of the region.[91]

King thought the recent development of southern cities had been phenomenal. For example, Dallas was growing "like an enchanted castle in a fairy tale," and Kansas City was a "young colossus" that seemed "to have sprung out of the ground by magic." Older cities like St. Louis and Baltimore were experiencing "astonishingly rapid growth," and Atlanta was emerging from the ashes of war into "a new, vigorous, awkwardly alert city." Such developments were characteristic of every part of the South. Even in isolated and sparsely settled Arkansas, the handsome city of Little Rock was undergoing "wonderful growth."[92]

However, urban development in the South was not a story of unrelieved progress. In the entire state of Mississippi, there were "but half-a-dozen towns of considerable size," the largest being economically depressed Vicksburg, a town of fifteen thousand people. Mobile, Alabama, with thirty-five thousand inhabitants, was "tranquil and free from commercial bustle." King found "no activity" in the city, commenting that it was "as still as one of those ancient fishing villages on the Massachusetts coast when the fishermen are away." In Beaufort, South Carolina, a "silence as of the grave reigned everywhere," and in other towns of the state King discovered a pervading sense of "complete prostration, dejection, stagnation." Many of the towns in Virginia, North Carolina, and the cotton belt of Alabama were experiencing little if any growth.[93]

But in King's view, the stagnation and lack of progress in such towns were atypical. As a whole he thought southern urban development vigorous and impressive. Indeed he tended to overestimate the rate of urbanization and the prospects for future growth. For instance, he accepted the exaggerated claim that the population of St. Louis was 450,000, and his prediction that the city would have a million inhabitants within a generation was wide of its mark. The same holds true for his forecast that Columbus, Georgia, would "one day rival Lowell or Manchester" as an industrial city. Even more rashly King expressed confidence that New Braunfels, Texas, and Wedverton, Maryland, would become extensive manufacturing centers, and that Strasburg, Virginia, would one day be a "place of great importance."[94]

King also predicted that Asheville, Jacksonville, Chattanooga, Birmingham, and Charleston (West Virginia) would become major urban centers. When he visited these places in 1873, they were actually small towns, none with a population of more than twelve thousand; some had been mere villages at the close of the war and Birmingham had not been founded until 1869. Yet his

[91] King, *Great South*, 505, 218–19, 255, 279–85, 344, 424–37, 466–77, and sections on cities, *passim*. See also Buck, *The Road to Reunion*, 184–86.

[92] King, *Great South*, 125, 251, 239, 244, 741, 350, 281–82.

[93] *Ibid.*, 313, 287–88, 322, 426, 468, 797, 330–31, 342.

[94] *Ibid.*, 218–19, 255, 373, 145, 739, 801. St. Louis had indeed grown very rapidly in the 1860s, with population increasing from 160,773 to 310,864. The growth rate slowed in the 1870s, then picked up in the 1880s. In 1880 the population was 350,518; in 1890 it was 451,-770. The city's peak population was 856,796 in 1950.

long-range projections for these cities were essentially accurate.[95] Despite his excessive optimism and extravagant language, King was a keen observer and perceptive analyst. Although his treatment of urban development was sometimes faulty in detail, one conclusion is clearly justified from the weight of his evidence. The urban revolution was under way in the South in the early 1870s, even as it was in the North.

King recognized that a concomitant to urban development, at the same time dependent upon the growth of cities and in turn stimulating that growth, was commercial and industrial activity. Nearly every area of the South was experiencing a significant surge in trade and business in the early 1870s. The rapid increase in the production of cotton, especially in the Gulf states, was the single most important factor in that growth. King observed "vast masses of bales" stacked on the New Orleans levee, and in Texas he found that the cotton train was a familiar sight on the great trunk lines. Cotton was a key product in the trade of nearly every southern state, and across the entire lower South it was the main staple of commerce. In the upper South, tobacco products were the major items of trade. Aside from cotton and tobacco, such products as flour, lumber, coal, liquor, dry goods, meat products, and other provisions formed the basis for southern commerce.[96]

Although King observed a great deal of industrial development, progress was most impressive in two industries. Iron furnaces, foundries, and rolling mills were in operation in a dozen communities across the South, but the manufacture of iron was concentrated in two areas, Missouri and the three-state region around Chattanooga, Tennessee. There was "nothing else so wonderful . . . in the South or South-West," King thought, as the development of iron works around St. Louis. Although the amazing growth of iron production had largely come since the end of the war, Missouri was ready by the early 1870s to "enter as a formidable competitor upon one of the greatest industrial fields in the world"; the state, King wrote, would become the "England of tomorrow." In the Chattanooga area, iron furnaces were reportedly producing pig iron more cheaply than anywhere else in the country, and industrialists were confident that the region would soon rival Pittsburgh in iron manufacturing. Progress was so rapid that King feared that the great beauty of Chattanooga's surroundings would "some day be hidden by the smoke from the five hundred chimneys which will be erected in honor of the god Iron."[97]

The other major southern industry was cotton textiles. Cotton factories had sprung up in such widely scattered cities as Houston, New Orleans, Petersburg, Nashville, and Charlotte. A dozen prosperous factories in middle and northern Alabama regularly paid large dividends, 20 percent reputedly being "not uncommon." But the greatest activity in cotton manufacturing was in the sand-hill region extending from Aiken, South Carolina, to Augusta, Georgia. Augusta and Graniteville, South Carolina, had developed extensive factories; the Augusta mills had thousands of spindles and hundreds of looms in operation, and the Graniteville mills annually produced eight million yards

[95] *Ibid.,* 505, 380–82, 530–32, 336–38, 688–91.
[96] *Ibid.,* 49–58, 103–14, 266–67, 322–23, 347–48, 365–66, 438–39, and sections on cities, *passim.*
[97] *Ibid.,* 238–39, 244, 240–43, 532, 533–35.

of cloth. Graniteville seemed "as tidy and thrifty" as any manufacturing town in the North. Indeed the whole "busy belt" from Aiken to Augusta was impressive. Here, King pointed out, the visitor "sees manufacturing villages, hears the whir of spindles, and notes on every hand evidences of progressive industry."[98]

Other important industrial activity in the South included the manufacture or processing of flour, tobacco products, glass, salt, phosphate fertilizers, foodstuffs, and various minerals.[99] But industrial development in the region was very uneven. King reported that Memphis and Natchez had little or no significant manufacturing. Industry elsewhere was making only slow gains; for example, in Charleston, West Virginia, and Frankfort, Kentucky, manufacturing was, as a favorite King phrase put it, "creeping" in. King observed realistically that southern industrial progress was "insignificant as compared with the gigantic development in the North." But he believed that the future of industrial development in the South was exceptionally bright. The idea of progress pervaded even the tradition-bound Old Dominion, where "the youth of the new school [were] engaging in commerce, buying and selling mines, talking of opening new railroad routes, and building cotton mills." King predicted, "In twenty years manufacturers will be the aristocrats in Virginia."[100]

The wealth of the South in mineral, agricultural, and forest resources appeared so great to King that substantial economic progress seemed inevitable. Nearly every southern state had mineral resources of significance; he found the mineral wealth of some areas so astonishing that his "wildest ideas" were not exaggerated. He described the mineral stores of Missouri, northern Alabama, West Virginia, and the region around Chattanooga as among the richest in the world, and he predicted that they would last for centuries to come. The South also boasted some of the finest timbered land in the country. King noted that there was considerable activity in lumbering in Missouri and western North Carolina, around Jacksonville and Charleston (West Virginia), and along the Gulf Coast. But he found the bulk of the region's tracts of native forest, rich in a large variety of hard and soft woods, largely untapped.[101]

All the southern states, without exception, possessed extraordinarily rich agricultural resources. Northern Texas, Arkansas, and the Missouri Valley contained some of the "most fertile" farmland in the world, and King noted that one of the major developments in postbellum southern agriculture was the gradual movement of cotton culture from the Atlantic seaboard and the older Gulf states to these "newer and more productive lands" bordering on the Mississippi and west of that stream. The yield of cotton in these areas was surprising, and he observed a "natural tendency . . . towards a rapid and continuous increase" in its production.[102]

Although the lands of some sections of the cotton states were "temporarily

[98] *Ibid.*, 344, 346–47, 334–35. Graniteville, founded by industrialist William Gregg, had been a successful industrial village in the antebellum period.

[99] *Ibid.*, 237–38, 243, 549, 690, 450, 547.   [100] *Ibid.*, 268, 293, 689, 715, 792, 637–38.

[101] *Ibid.*, 240, 239–44, 253, 317, 328–30, 336–38, 381, 488–92, 532–35, 681–91, and sections on natural resources, *passim.*

[102] *Ibid.*, 125, 176, 278–79, 252, 270–71, 51.

exhausted," they held great promise for the future. King described Mississippi's soil as "splendid," and reported that the cotton belt of Alabama was "inexhaustibly rich." The planters of Mississippi, northern Alabama, western Tennessee, western South Carolina, and Georgia were learning a great deal, he believed, and necessity would in time force them to introduce better farming methods, particularly the diversification of crops. The agricultural revolution was already under way in Georgia and Florida. Georgia planters were using fertilizers with the "most remarkable results," and some farmers in the northern sections of the state were beginning to rotate and diversify crops. In Florida northern capital and well-to-do northern immigrants were bringing diversification through the culture of vegetables and fruits, particularly oranges. Here, King predicted, "a great variety of production will henceforth be the rule."[103]

The South possessed other economic advantages in its recreational areas and tourist attractions. The visitor to the region could see some of the "most remarkable lowland scenery in the world" in Florida and Georgia; he could visit the nation's "noblest beach" at Galveston; or he could walk through the "mute, mighty, and passing beautiful" San Jose Mission, the "finest piece of architecture in the United States." The choice of health resorts included San Antonio in the Southwest, Hot Springs, Arkansas, various "watery, sylvan retreats" in Florida, and Greenbrier White Sulphur Springs and other mineral springs resorts in West Virginia and Virginia. In the years to come, King predicted, thousands of tourists would also be attracted yearly to such natural wonders as Mammoth Cave, Lookout Mountain, Mount Mitchell and Whiteside Mountain in North Carolina, and Natural Bridge and the "sublime and haughty" Peaks of Otter in Virginia.[104]

One of the key factors in the development of the South's many resources was the rapid growth of the southern railroad system in the postwar years. Railway development had "metamorphosed the whole cotton trade of New Orleans" and was largely responsible for the fantastic growth of northern Texas. Railroads were bringing greater activity to the mountain region of South Carolina and were of major importance in the remarkable economic recovery of Georgia. Throughout *The Great South,* King points to the direct relationship between railway development and southern economic progress. Railroads brought immigration, destroyed the provincial isolation of the South, and introduced northern and western vigor and enterprise. He thought that railroads alone could solve the problems of such undeveloped areas as western Mississippi and the Arkansas, Missouri, and Texas frontiers. He was confident that the "iron rail," the South's "most effective civilizer," would ultimately bring civilization even to such areas as the wild Texas plains.[105]

In addition to continued progress in industry and railroading, the former slave states greatly needed immigration, education, capital, and a revision of

[103] *Ibid.,* 267–71, 311, 330, 348, 515, 359, 398, 78–81, 403–406. King did not mention specifically the richest of all southern farm land, the Yazoo-Mississippi Delta.

[104] *Ibid.,* 408–13, 358–59, 101–102, 148–54, 285–86, 396–97, 661–77, 699–706, 536–38, 494–514, 561–65.

[105] *Ibid.,* 54, 173–93, 125, 515, 363–67, 311–18, 280, 252–53, 160, 772.

the labor system. King observed that throughout the South the freedmen, who still constituted the main agricultural laboring force, were migrating from their old homes to the cities or to the Southwest. Planters in the lowlands of Arkansas, Mississippi, and Louisiana had "been paricularly troubled" in getting and keeping serviceable plantation labor, and they had begun importing large numbers of black laborers from Alabama. Indeed in the early 1870s, there was a large-scale migration of freedmen from central Alabama and the South Atlantic states to the new cotton lands along the Mississippi. They were fleeing, King wrote, from starvation in the older cotton states. By the spring of 1874, Alabama had already lost "from $700,000 to $1,000,000 in her labor element alone"; in the previous year Georgia had lost twenty thousand black laborers.[106]

With the demise of slavery, "many plans of working large plantations" had come into use, including share cropping, and wage, lease, and squad lease systems. In each of these methods, the planter was usually responsible for providing, on various terms, land, supplies, tools, implements, and work animals. King thought that in the cotton belt the freedmen were generally accorded "very favorable conditions." Cotton planters invariably believed that blacks were irresponsible and needed to be taken care of very much as they had been in antebellum days. But the labor system provided no incentives and no education for black laborers. Hence they worked lazily, if sometimes steadily, were given to "thievish propensities," and remained "densely ignorant." Even when a freedman settled on a tract of his own, he did not care to become a "scientific farmer," and became instead "almost a cumberer of the ground, caring for nothing save to get a living, and raising only a bale of cotton or so wherewith to get 'supplies.' " In view of the Negro's past, King wondered, how could "he suddenly leap forth, a new man, into the changed order of things?"[107]

Throughout the cotton belt, planters were deeply discouraged by the ineffectiveness of the labor system. Black laborers were sinking ever deeper into tenancy, and black emigration made it difficult for planters to employ enough laborers to get their land "worked up to the old standard." Moreover black women and children no longer worked in the fields as commonly as in the past. In Concordia Parish, "once the garden spot of Louisiana," the number of blacks at work was much less than before the war, and cotton production was down fully two-thirds. King reported that the sight of acres of unpicked cotton in January and February was not at all uncommon in some parts of the South. This, he suggested, was the "most effectual proof of the complete disorganization of the labor system."[108]

Southerners overwhelmingly agreed upon the "superiority of free over slave labor," but the labor system was "attended with so many drawbacks and vexations" that many planters desired a complete change. However, their attempts to attract new laborers had not been successful, and most despaired of reorganizing labor upon a more effective basis. King warned, in specific reference to the

[106] *Ibid.*, 740, 275, 299–301, 270–71.   [107] *Ibid.*, 270, 273–77, 306, 310.
[108] *Ibid.*, 301, 305, 274–75, 271, 309.

Lower Mississippi Valley, that "nothing but the education of the negro up to the point of ambition, foresight, and a desire to acquire a competence lawfully and laboriously, will ever thoroughly develop" the cotton belt. Whites, he said, "need to be converted to a sense of the dignity of labor, to learn to treat the laboring man with proper consideration, to create in him an intelligent ambition by giving him education."[109]

Another pressing need of the South was immigration. Internal population shifts were depopulating parts of the region. Since the end of the war, blacks throughout the South had "left the country in swarms and flocked to the towns," and many lower-class whites were being attracted to the large manufacturing centers. The migration of black laborers to the new cotton lands was accompanied by a similar movement among the "poor whites." King described hundreds of refugees leaving the older southern states daily to seek homes on the Texas prairies. Three thousand people of "this great, silent exodus" landed monthly at Galveston. The immensity of the great stream of migration to the Southwest was difficult to appreciate, King suggested, unless one witnessed it "up and down the highways and byways of the South."[110]

Although Virginia and Texas, and to a lesser extent West Virginia, were attracting large numbers of persons from Europe, the North, and other parts of the South, the majority of southern states crucially needed immigration. King observed that population was the "prime need" of Missouri, and Georgia's "only need" was more people. Alabama, Arkansas, and Florida also required large numbers of immigrants. But most of the southern states were finding it impossible to compete with the Northwest. Mississippi's efforts had been largely unsuccessful, and North Carolinians were greatly discouraged that immigrants did not "rush into their State." Politically conservative South Carolinians had encouraged the entrance of "certain Northern classes" but discouraged that of lower-class foreigners; consequently a group of Italian laborers had "haughtily rejected" the meager inducement to settlement offered by the state.[111]

King, noting that white immigrants would not "work and live as the negroes do," warned that an enlightened program must offer good wages and land at cheap rates, as well as promote greater respect for laborers. He was encouraged by the recent improvement of immigration policy in South Carolina, but he was most impressed with the program in Tennessee, where "no stranger is allowed to pass" without hearing the advantages of living in the state. "There is," he concluded, "at least good reason to hope that in a few years immigration will pour into the fertile fields and noble valleys and along the grand streams of the South, assuring a mighty growth."[112]

Self-sufficiency in manufacturing was also necessary for the economic development of the South. The need for manufacturing was particularly crucial in states like Texas, where in nearly every county farmers and merchants were "paying treble and quadruple the prices they . . . [could] afford to pay for

[109] Ibid., 305, 274, 276–77.   [110] Ibid., 740, 774–75, 133, 99, 366.
[111] Ibid., 792, 105, 775, 552–65, 641, 468, 451–52, 316–17, 252, 375, 330, 283, 418, 717. King pointed out that Missouri was also attracting many immigrants but needed more (pp. 219, 252–53).   [112] Ibid., 271, 276, 452, 729, 792.

goods brought thousands of miles." In Georgia, King noted the bitterness with which an unnamed journalist commented on southern economic dependence upon the North: "A Georgia farmer uses a Northern axe-helve and axe to cut up the hickory growing within sight of his door; ploughs his fields with a Northern plough; chops out his cotton with a New England hoe; gins his cotton upon a Boston gin; hoops it with Pennsylvania iron; hauls it to market in a Concord wagon, while the little grain that he raises is cut and prepared for sale with Yankee implements." King suggested that this statement held true for all the cotton states.[113]

Manufacturing and agricultural growth were in turn greatly affected by the availability of capital. "Until her people have recovered from the exhaustion consequent on the war," King wrote, "capital is and will be the crying want of the South." Although southern political difficulties largely checked the investment of northern capital in the South, the North would continue, as it had in the past, to furnish "some portion" of southern capital needs. For example, in the three-state Chattanooga area, foreign and northern capital was "fast finding out the best locations for furnaces and rolling-mills." However, the development of the mineral interests tributary to St. Louis apparently depended primarily upon local capital.[114]

In King's eyes the South's greatest potential lay in its people. "Never were a people more cheery," he wrote of the Texans, and the Virginians particularly impressed him with their courage in the face of the devastation of war. King believed that, in general, Southerners were devoted to building the South anew, and that they largely accepted the main results of the war and the "changing influence of the times." He was convinced that the promise of the region was great. The only exception was South Carolina; the "present condition" of the state, he wrote, "would not seem to justify prophecies of any prosperity within her limits, save in Charleston." But Virginia, Texas, and Missouri were unquestionably destined for great futures, and the other southern states would, under favorable circumstances, ultimately move into the "front rank among the prosperous States."[115]

In short, King foresaw the further development of a New South that differed markedly from the Old. Although strongly influenced by the North, the New South would remain distinctively southern. Perhaps it would not be as intensely materialistic as the North, nor would it embrace all the liberal ideas of that region. But the New South, King concluded, would constitute a departure from tradition: ". . . it will be progressive, more progressive and liberal every year. Its provincialisms will fade gradually away; its educational facilities . . . will increase and flourish. The negro will get justice from the lower classes of

[113] *Ibid.*, 371, 109–10. The journalist may have been Joel Chandler Harris or, more probably, Henry W. Grady. Southerners had used similar arguments for southern self-sufficiency since the 1850s. Grady's description of a funeral in Pickens County, Georgia, is the most famous of such expressions. See Raymond B. Nixon, *Henry W. Grady: Spokesman of the New South* (New York: Alfred A. Knopf, 1943), 10.

[114] King, *Great South*, 793, 535, 244, 730, 335. King noted (p. 403), in Florida "it is mainly Northern capital that is invested in orange culture" throughout the state.

[115] *Ibid.*, 184–85, 801, 339, 342, 793, 437, 419, 126, 255, 644.

whites as soon as those classes are touched by the liberalizing influences of the times."[116]

King and the *Scribner's* sponsors of his southern tour obviously hoped that the "Great South" publications would promote the development of this prosperous, progressive New South. King clearly had established empathy with a region that had suffered so greatly in the "night-mare of civil war" and that in the early 1870s was having to make such difficult social and political adjustments. By stressing the vast, undeveloped resources and the great economic potential of the former slave states, he sought specifically to stimulate the economic growth of the region. As a result *The Great South* definitely belongs to the genre of New South promotional literature.[117]

Indeed King seems to have imbibed deeply of the then current southern attitudes and ideas that underlay the developing "New South Creed." His emphasis on industrialization, agricultural diversification, immigration, and the acquisition of capital as a program of southern regeneration paralleled the promotional efforts of such New South boosters as J. B. D. De Bow, Edwin DeLeon, and Francis W. Dawson. During his tour King may actually have met Dawson, Henry Watterson, Henry W. Grady, and other southern propagandists, or at least may have been influenced by their ideas or writings.[118] In any event his high hopes for the economic and social development of the South (and of the nation) adversely affected his ordinarily keen powers of observation and analysis. As in his treatment of southern urbanization, he tended to overestimate current progress and the prospects for future improvement in the southern economy, in education, and in social justice.

Nevertheless *The Great South* was much more than a purposefully propagandistic and promotional tract, and if King at times exaggerated and overestimated, he rarely led the reader far astray. The substance of his reporting was essentially accurate, even on the subject of economic development. Moreover his account was always honest. Unlike most of the travel narratives of the South published in the 1870s, *The Great South* did *not* omit "the expression of any sentiment which did not tend to soften the Northern attitude toward the South and thus make for better understanding." Nor did King present Radical Reconstruction in a totally negative light or suggest that southern whites understood blacks and should be left alone in the handling of racial matters.[119] In addition, as indicated above, he was sometimes strongly critical of certain aspects of southern society. It is necessary at times, he wrote, "to say some disagreeable things" and "to make severe strictures upon certain people and classes of people." In general King presented the evidence he found

---

[116] *Ibid.*, 792–94.

[117] *Ibid.*, 28; *Scribner's Monthly*, IX (December, 1874), 248–49; Buck, *The Road to Reunion*, 130–33, 151.

[118] For the development of the "New South Creed," see Paul M. Gaston, *The New South Creed: A Study in Southern Mythmaking* (New York: Alfred A. Knopf, 1970.), 17–42; Woodward, *Origins of the New South*, 142–58, 162–74; Buck, *The Road to Reunion*, 130–34, 151–52, 186–95.

[119] Buck, *The Road to Reunion*, 133, 131, 152; and Gaston, *The New South Creed*, 39–40, misrepresent King's treatment of these matters.

candidly and without distortion; as Fletcher Green has noted, he "passed judgments without fear or favor."[120]

Reconstruction and Blacks in THE GREAT SOUTH

Historians have usually looked upon *The Great South* as an unfriendly analysis of Radical Reconstruction and its effects on the South. Unlike the earlier journalistic accounts of the 1860s that had specifically supported Radical Republican policy and had found Southerners generally unrepentant, the King survey reputedly condemned the corruption and misrule of the Radical governments and characterized southern conservative whites as "entirely loyal and trustworthy." According to this view, King argued that "reconstruction had gone too far," that the time had come to end federal interference in the South, and that only when Southerners were allowed to resume full control of the state governments could the social and economic progress of the region be advanced. "Chapter by chapter," Paul H. Buck has written, "the ["Great South"] series piled up an overwhelming mass of evidence pointing to the evil results of Reconstruction."[121]

Although King was more concerned about other aspects of the South, he did devote considerable attention to the course of political reconstruction in each of the former slave states. As suggested above he found a wide diversity in this as in other aspects of the southern scene, and it is extremely difficult to generalize about his views on reconstruction. The interpretation that King was thoroughly critical of Radical Reconstruction and in favor of a hands-off southern policy is a serious oversimplification and distortion that fails to take into consideration his careful observations on and perceptive analysis of a very complex era.

King's view of reconstruction was necessarily influenced by his attitudes about slavery, blacks, and the Civil War. Although available evidence tells little about his early attitudes on slavery, his New England Methodist upbringing may have prompted empathy with the abolitionists. In the early Reconstruction period, he served under abolitionist Samuel Bowles on the Radical paper, the Springfield *Republican,* and he may well have shared the basic social and political views of the *Republican* editorial staff.[122]

In any event King's attitudes surface in *The Great South.* As noted previously he pictured slavery as an oppressive system, a "curse" whose "bitter leaven" had worked to degrade not only blacks but whites as well. Hence it is not surprising that he characterized the work of the antislavery cause as humanitarian, courageous, and noble. For instance, "Bleeding Kansas had indeed bled to some purpose" in contributing to the downfall of slavery and the old regime. And John Brown had "immortalized" Harpers Ferry when in 1859 he "struck the first blow for the freedom of the American slave."[123]

---

[120] King, *Great South,* 138; Green, "The South in Reconstruction," 66–67.
[121] Green, "The South in Reconstruction," 4–5; Buck, *The Road to Reunion,* 131–32; see also Rose, *Rehearsal for Reconstruction,* 378–81.   [122] See p. xxii above.
[123] King, *Great South,* 596–97, 219, 766. King (p. 768) considered John Brown's raid "the first battle of the great war."

Although King never stated explicitly that he considered the war necessary, the conflict and its aftermath had ended the restraints that the old order had placed upon southern progress, had begun the "regeneration" of both blacks and whites, and had substituted a leveling, competitive, open society for a hierarchical and restrictive one. Missourians, King wrote, had shown their "independence and good sense" in refusing to secede. He particularly praised benevolent groups like the American Missionary Association and the American Freedmen's Union Commission for their efforts in the relief and education of black fugitives during the war and the immediate postwar years.[124]

In King's view history had not been kind to the black American. He had been brought in "a low and bestial condition" from the "jungles of Africa" into a "comparatively wild region in America." But it was the slavery experience that had been most degrading. The black man fresh from Africa had "strode defiantly" on American soil, retaining his dignity as a man. Only in the experience of slavery had he acquired that "crouching, abject gait" which he used habitually. In the cotton belt and on South Carolina rice plantations, King observed that the black laborers gave "a shuffling and grimacing assent" to any suggestion from a white person; he was astonished at the "absolute subjection" of the blacks in these areas. The black man, King noted, carried the "crushing burden" of "two centuries of slavery . . . upon his back."[125]

King thought that the former slave could not be "very moral." Under slavery his "moral growth was but lazily helped" and his "lack of moral consciousness" had become more pronounced. "He tries to be a good Christian," King wrote, "and yet is not always satisfied with one wife." It was hard for him "to bear the yoke of the family relation." The freedmen were also prone to stealing. Their best friends would admit, King believed, "that, though very religious, they are also very immoral." The responsibilities of freedom were "almost too much" for some former slaves, who were "almost content to slip back into the old devil-may-care dependence of slavery." King noted that the black man "entered upon a battlefield armed with poor and cumbersome weapons, weighed down with ignorance and 'previous condition.'" He observed that no one felt the difficulty and bitterness of his position more keenly than the freedman himself.[126]

King pointed out that there was a large class of blacks who were "intrinsically mean and gravitating steadily downward toward the worst phases of rascality." Whiskey prompted them to "an indiscriminate use of the revolver and the knife," particularly in the cities, where the freedmen flocked "together idly" and became "more vicious" than in the country. A prominent Mississippi planter expressed the opinion that the "younger generation of negroes was growing up idle and shiftless, fond of whiskey and carousing, and that the race was diminishing in fibre and strength." The ignorance, irresponsibility, and improvidence of black laborers have already been mentioned. Although blacks were generally not "aggressive and insolent" toward whites, King found the

[124] *Ibid.*, 17, 776, 596–603, 256.   [125] *Ibid.*, 780, 22, 303, 430, 276, 596.
[126] *Ibid.*, 277, 453, 427, 780, 309, 272, 33, 779.

"spirit of race" excessively strong in South Carolina, where the black man had let the "African in him run riot."[127]

But King was generally impressed with the progress being made by the freedmen. Even in the South Carolina lowlands, where the race was "really very degraded," blacks were "making gradual progress toward a condition of independence." Although the freedmen might not attend to the details of plantation work with "quite the thoroughness exacted under the rigid discipline of slavery," they generally worked better than they had before emancipation. The testimony of most of the planters throughout the South, he wrote, "is that the free negro works well, and earns his wages, save when he is distracted by politics."[128]

King found encouraging signs throughout the South. In Arkansas the "colored citizens" numbered "many gentlemen of education and refinement"; blacks in Little Rock, most of whom owned their own homes, had done much to demonstrate their capacity for industry and progress. He considered the conduct of black laborers in the cotton belt encouraging, in particular the "tendency to create for themselves homes, and now and then to cultivate the land about them." On large plantations in the cotton country, the grouping of blacks into small villages reduced excessive crowding and encouraged the freedmen to devote greater attention to their homes. Blacks seemed to do particularly well in Texas; throughout the state, King noted, the freedmen constituted "an industrious and prosperous class." But here, and by implication across the South, even those who were making progress were "characterized by the failings of their race, and the crudities consequent on their sudden change of station." Indeed he wondered whether the "slouching and ragged" blacks he encountered on Southern trains could ever become "as useful and trustworthy citizens" as the hardy and ambitious European immigrants.[129]

The answer to this question, King believed, was conditioned primarily by the education that blacks received. The rural blacks of Louisiana, Mississippi, and Alabama were "possessed of no small acuteness" and were "capable of fine development." Whenever there were educational facilities available, the freedmen throughout the South speedily improved their capabilities. Black children in the public schools of Louisiana manifested "an earnestness and aptitude which amply demonstrated their claim to be admitted to them"; and in South Carolina there was a "grand onward movement by the blacks" to begin studies at the state university. Even "severely prejudiced" Southerners conceded that black achievement at such institutions as Hampton, Fisk, Berea, and the University of Atlanta demonstrated the "possibility of the education of the negro masses." Evidence from across the South conclusively proved, King maintained, the fallacy of the popular notion, in both the North and the South, that the "negro would prove susceptible of civilization only to a certain point. . . . the universal testimony of the mass of careful observers is that the negro can go as far in mental processes as the white child. The blacks have wonderful memories and strong imitative propensities; eloquence, passionate and natural;

---

[127] *Ibid.*, 778–79, 274, 297, 430, 452–53.   [128] *Ibid.*, 430, 82, 270, 89.
[129] *Ibid.*, 281–82, 303, 273, 132, 104, 554.

a strange and subtle sense of rhythm and poetry; and it is now pretty well settled that there are no special race limitations."[130]

King recognized the diversity of the black response to freedom. Attempting to generalize, he suggested that about a third of the blacks in the South were in a "very hopeful condition"; another third seemed "to be in a comparatively stationary attitude"; and the remaining third was "absolutely good for nothing" and made "no steady progress in morality, refinement, or education of any kind." But King was essentially optimistic. "[A] . . . mighty uplifting has really been going on since 1865, and," he continued condescendingly, ". . . an influx of good teachers, who shall teach industry, thrift, continence, and self-respect, will in another decade raise the four and a-half million negroes in the South to pretty near the level of Christian manhood and womanhood." He was aware that such progress would not be sudden. "Moral growth is slow," he noted, "and . . . so long as the negro remains in ignorance, and, in a measure, uncertain as to his future condition, he will not develop very rapidly."[131] As it turned out, the black man was not soon afforded that certitude about his status and role which would have been most conducive to his development.

It was from such an attitudinal framework that King viewed reconstruction. He considered it the last phase of the social and political revolution that was sweeping over the former slave states. Radical changes were breaking down the traditional social structure and ushering in a new order, "the prosaic and leveling civilization of the present." Antebellum southern civilization had been unprogressive and unjust; the new was progressive and made greater allowance for human development. Hence, in King's eyes, reconstruction basically was a positive good.[132]

Revolutionary change in itself caused hardship and suffering for many Southerners. Conditions of life and labor became "onerous and disagreeable," the labor system was disorganized, trade was disrupted, capital investment was discouraged, and the traditional means of livelihood were rendered ineffective and obsolete. In parts of the South, it appeared that the social order had been turned upside down, with the bottom rail now on top. One could begin to appreciate the magnitude of the revolution, King wrote, at Hampton and other educational institutions where those who had constituted the bottom rail were beginning the climb toward "a true manhood." In the lowlands of South Carolina, "the revolution [had] penetrated to the quick"; the rice planter returning to the scene of his former domination and prosperity found himself "stripped of everything" and subject to the rule of "ignorant slaves."[133]

But the worst aspect of reconstruction was that an originally humanitarian revolution was turned to "base uses" and "bold and reckless wickedness," particularly in South Carolina and Louisiana. King described reconstruction in South Carolina as a "riot of corruption" and a "total disregard of decency," without "a parallel in the history of revolutions." The whites of South Carolina were "powerless to resist"; they were "trampled completely down."[134] In Loui-

---

[130] *Ibid.*, 606–607, 603–608, 275, 374, 98, 463–64.   [131] *Ibid.*, 779–82.
[132] *Ibid.*, 17, 28–32, 187, 773, 776, 428, 457, 596.   [133] *Ibid.*, 187, 596, 28–31, 34, 453, 426, 428.
[134] *Ibid.*, 455–57. There are interesting similarities between King's treatment of reconstruction in South Carolina and that provided by James S. Pike's 1874 account, *The Prostrate State: South Carolina Under Negro Government,* ed. Robert F. Durden (New York: Harper

siana the Radical Party, led by "reckless and greedy white adventurers, . . .
thrust ruin in a hundred ways upon the unfortunate State." White Louisianians
were pushed to the wall and left in complete despair by "race legislation, retributive tyranny and terrorism."[135] Alabama and Mississippi also "suffered a good
deal from evils incident to reconstruction"; and in North Carolina the unwise
exercise of universal suffrage had produced a "wild carnival of robbery and
maladministration." King observed that reconstruction was a "complete
failure" in Georgia, but he feared that the dominance of a repressive "white
man's government" might prove as "baneful in its results as . . . its degraded
and disreputable opposite."[136]

Although the course of reconstruction "was marked . . . by many political
excitements and troubles" throughout the South, some states did not experience
overwhelming difficulties. In Arkansas and Texas, reconstruction aggravated
frontier-type lawlessness and violence, but in both states this phenomenon appeared to be only temporary. Florida "accepted reconstruction peacefully," and
conservative political opinion was strong enough to prevent the "torrent of
ignorance and vice" that the leaders of the state Republican Party might have
perpetrated. King noted specifically that Virginia and Missouri escaped the
major evils of reconstruction and implied the same of Tennessee. Although
Kentucky was not required to undergo political reconstruction, King observed
that the discussion there of the civil rights bill had been as "furious and illogical" as in any of the former slave states.[137] One of the few generalizations that
one can make from his account of reconstruction is that that process varied
greatly from state to state.

King gave particular attention to the role of blacks in reconstruction. He
observed a great deal of political ignorance, corruption, and vice on the part of
blacks. In Louisiana, he noted, intelligent blacks refrained entirely from politics, and "ignorant and immoral negroes" comprised the rank and file of the
state Republican Party. Similarly in North Carolina, the black voters were
"densely ignorant." Black Louisiana legislators, who commonly propped their
feet on their desks, were "so completely ignorant" that they could not follow the
course of debate; "dusky" speakers in the Alabama house of representatives
were conspicuous in the eccentricity of their gestures and language; and in

and Row, Publishers, 1968). The parallelism between the two authors' comments on such
subjects as the participation of blacks in legislative proceedings, the plan for cumulative
voting, politics in Charleston, immigration, the administration "ring," frauds, the character of
the lowland Negroes, nationalistic sentiment, and the labor question could not have been
produced by chance. Either King used Pike's writings on South Carolina or he and Pike had
common sources of information. The editors lean to the first possibility, partly because of
the striking similarity of some of the phraseology used by King and Pike. King knew of Pike's
book, but oddly referred to it as an "excellent book" on the subject of cumulative voting. One
significant dissimilarity between the accounts is the absence in *The Great South* of the strong
Negrophobia which marked Pike's work. See King, *Great South,* 428–30, 447, 452, 455, 457,
461, 464–65; and Pike, *The Prostrate State,* 18, 19, 21, 43, 52–56, 68, 83, 95, 119, 121, 131, 151,
238–40, 262–63, 268, 273–79.
  [135] King, *Great South,* 91, 34. King doubtless received much of his information on reconstruction in Louisiana from the Louisiana historian Charles Gayarré. King, (pp. 31–34, 53)
carefully presented much of this information as the opinion of a white Louisianian, who, "although by no means unfair or bitterly partisan, perhaps allowed his discouragement to color
all his views."
  [136] *Ibid.,* 311, 468–69, 352, 354, 333.   [137] *Ibid.,* 641–43, 284–85, 129–30, 419, 219, 547, 731.

South Carolina, the parliamentary efforts of black members of the house were extremely ludicrous. King described most of the members of the governing council of a Louisiana parish as "slouching, unkempt, suspicious in their demeanor, and evidently unfit for any public duty."[138]

The blacks who participated in politics were not only ignorant; many were also corrupt, and some were vindictive. For example, in Louisiana only "the rascals and the dubious" got into power, and they practiced "all the vices in the calendar." In Virginia a "disgraceful and lawless rabble" in the Republican convention of 1869 used "violent and offensive measures" to achieve their ends, and consumed an entire day in "brawls, shoutings, and bickerings." South Carolina blacks were "intoxicated with power" and ideas of vengeance and retribution governed their political activity. In contrast some blacks unintentionally became involved in corruption. Georgia blacks were "very easily intimidated" and readily fell into "corrupt practices in election time" because they did not consider the evil effects of such a course. Even in South Carolina, many of the "deluded ignoramuses" in the state legislature were "not aware that they were doing anything especially blameworthy."[139]

Despite these observations, King's comments on politically active blacks were by no means generally derogatory. Many of the black legislators and officeholders were intelligent, able, and honest men. In Mississippi, where they held "a fair share of the offices," black officeholders impressed King "much more powerfully as worthy, intelligent, and likely to progress" than many whom he had seen elsewhere in the South. Some were "very intelligent" and "exceedingly capable"; none of those holding state offices at Jackson was incompetent.[140] The "colored legislators" of Alabama, who were of a "rather higher type" than those in South Carolina and Louisiana, were all "smartly dressed and aggressive in their demeanor." There were a few exceptional black men of "real force and eloquence" in the South Carolina house, and a number of "colored Senators spoke exceedingly well, and with great ease and grace of manner."[141]

King had praise for specific black officeholders, such as David Young, a prominent Louisiana legislator, and the Florida superintendent of education, a "gentleman of considerable culture and capacity." In South Carolina the president of the senate and the speaker of the house, both blacks, "were elegant and accomplished men, highly educated, who would have creditably presided over any commonwealth's legislative assembly." King also reported that blacks participated responsibly in various city and county governments. The black-dominated government of Natchez, he believed, was generally "very satisfactory." At Petersburg, Virginia, blacks were "largely represented in the Common Council," and during the orderly session of the council that he attended, King noted that all the black members "were acting intelligently."[142]

In addition to the intelligence and responsibility displayed by black leaders, King observed other positive aspects of Reconstruction. For instance, in Texas

[138] *Ibid.*, 95–97, 91, 468, 333, 461, 295.   [139] *Ibid.*, 97, 643, 455–58, 426, 461, 355.

[140] *Ibid.*, 314–15. Vernon L. Wharton uses King's comments in support of the contention that the increase in Negro officeholders in Mississippi "did not greatly decrease government efficiency or change its character." Wharton, *The Negro in Mississippi*, 176–77.

[141] King, *Great South*, 332–33, 460–61. For black officeholders in Arkansas, see 281–82.

[142] *Ibid.*, 291–95, 420, 460, 580–81, 113. The superintendents of education or public instruction in Louisiana, Arkansas, and Alabama were also capable and intelligent blacks (pp. 97, 281–85, 316).

the Reconstruction government had passed "wise legislation" which had helped to restore law and order. He reported that "some good laws" had been passed by the Reconstruction legislature of Georgia (1869–71), and he characterized the new constitution of Florida as "on the whole, a good one." In Arkansas the new system of general taxation was liberal compared to that of antebellum days. Unfortunately there was a decided tendency for southern Democratic leaders to undo "all which had been done by . . . [their] Republican predecessors," even when the legislation or constitutional provisions involved were wise and effective.[143]

As historian Harvey Wish has written, King, unlike the later observers of the 1870s, actually "saw many virtues in the Republican regimes" of the southern states.[144] For example, King observed that the administration of Republican Governor Marcellus L. Stearns of Florida had "thus far been satisfactory." But he was particularly impressed by the administration of Governor Adelbert Ames of Mississippi. Ames, who understood "the temper of both whites and blacks . . . very well," was determined to clear the Republican Party in Mississippi of the charge of corruption. His administration followed a policy of "retrenchment and reform" and initiated steps to restore the state's credit and to foster higher education as well as the growth of the public school system. Governor Ames, King concluded, "is firm in his measures, and is not surrounded . . . with men who are inclined to misuse their opportunities." He added: "The motley adventurers in South Carolina might learn a lesson in justice and impartiality from the party in power in Mississippi."[145]

King also praised the work of the Freedmen's Bureau, the Peabody Education Fund, churches, and private charities. The Freedmen's Bureau had "established schools wisely and well," and many other beneficent institutions had been organized and maintained under its auspices. The bureau's chief, General O. O. Howard, had worked effectively, King believed, "to aid the colored man in maintaining his rights." Northern and western philanthropists, church leaders, and teachers had also done much "good work." They had founded and aided churches and schools for the freedmen, giving particular emphasis to schools for the training of black teachers. The efforts in behalf of blacks continued despite intimidation from southern whites. "Wherever one teacher fainted in the ranks," he wrote, "another was quickly found to supply his or her place."[146]

In King's mind the greatest achievement of the revolution that was altering the South was the establishment of permanent public school systems in each of the southern states. "This alone," he argued, "is worth all that the war cost." Before mid-1867 none of the former Confederate states had a "modern school system," but by 1874 each of these states, as well as West Virginia, had established public education by law, and "all but one or two" had "tolerable school systems in operation." King believed that sentiment in favor of public schools was so strong that "no ambitious man of any party, in any Southern state," would dare to oppose public free education.[147]

Progress in education varied widely from state to state. According to the

[143] *Ibid.*, 120–22, 351, 419, 285, 778. [144] Wish, *Reconstruction in the South*, 183–87.
[145] King, *Great South*, 420, 315–16. Vernon L. Wharton agrees substantially with this interpretation. See Wharton, *The Negro in Mississippi*, 176–81.
[146] King, *Great South*, 598–99.
[147] *Ibid.*, 600–601.

testimony of knowledgeable educators like Dr. Barnas Sears, the Conservative-controlled states of West Virginia, Virginia, and Tennessee had the most effective public school programs. Tennessee, which had recently recovered ground it had lost after a good start, and Virginia, which had made "great progress" since 1870, led the South in "good legislation and general activity for schools." Missouri also had an excellent school system, and Baltimore's would "compare favorably with that of any community in the United States."[148] But in North Carolina, the free school system was less than a "thorough success," and public education was inadequately financed in Arkansas, Alabama, Florida, and South Carolina. Efforts on behalf of education were most needed, King thought, in South Carolina, Florida, and Louisiana—the states "under negro rule"—where whites either stood "aloof entirely from many of the public schools," or gave them only "a feeble and reluctant support." Throughout the South educational opportunities in the larger towns and cities were much superior to those in the countryside and small towns.[149]

King believed that southern whites, for the most part, were reconciled to the public education of blacks. Of course, there were exceptions to this generalization. In many parts of Tennessee, "a positive objection" to the education of blacks was freely expressed. But the "better class of Southerners . . . [had] been for some time convinced that they must help the negroes to an education, as a protective measure." Education would provide "incentives to work and to the acquisition of property," thus encouraging blacks to be better laborers and citizens. There was some grumbling by whites at having to pay a highly disproportionate share of the taxes used to support education for the freedmen. Nevertheless southern school laws provided for "buildings and teachers" for blacks, and King noted specifically that in Alabama and North Carolina the same provisions were made for the education of blacks as for whites. King was of the opinion that throughout the South the law guaranteed blacks "exactly equal school facilities, save in a very few instances."[150]

Despite his view that white southerners were generally adjusting well to the changes of the era, King was acutely aware that there was strong resistance to some aspects of reconstruction. In Louisiana, he noted, "there is not much hope that the equality of the races will be at present recognized by the white man." Whites in that state would not admit that the Negro was "at all com-

---

[148] *Ibid.*, 600–601, 547, 575, 228, 765. King's picture of education in Tennessee was somewhat contradictory. In contrast to the comments noted above, King elsewhere (p. 547) pointed out that Tennessee ranked third in illiteracy in the nation and that "thus far no very marked progress has been made" in the support of free schools.

It should also be noted that Virginia's financial difficulties in the late 1870s were severely detrimental to the state's public schools. For an excellent discussion of public education in Virginia in the 1870s, see Jack P. Maddex, Jr., *The Virginia Conservatives, 1867–1879: A Study in Reconstruction Politics* (Chapel Hill: University of North Carolina Press, 1970), 204–17.

[149] King, *Great South*, 470, 601, 463, 281–82, 343, 420, 547, 575, 228, 765.

[150] *Ibid.*, 731, 601–603, 470, 712, 342–43. Henry Allen Bullock, *A History of Negro Education in the South from 1619 to the Present* (Cambridge: Harvard University Press, 1967), 85–86, basically substantiates this last observation: "During the initial stages of the public education movement . . . little difference existed in the financial support given the Negro and white schools. . . . Relatively little racial discrimination had developed in the allocation of school funds as late as 1889. Negro and white schools in the various Southern states were open approximately the same number of days each year, and their teachers received approximately the same monthly salary."

petent to legislate . . . , or to vote . . . on matters of common importance to white and blacks." Indeed they would be very happy to see the "last negro vanish from the soil." Generally southern whites had opposed the elevation of the black man to "political power." In many states the "most barbarous and, in some cases, murderous measures of intimidation were used to prevent the negro . . . from demonstrating his right to be a man." Teachers working with the freedmen were intimidated by "mob violence, Ku-Klux mysteries, and social ostracisms." Whites still objected strongly to sitting on juries with blacks, and there was adamant opposition to any recognition of social equality. Leading politicians intimated that the new state constitutions would ultimately be amended; it was "easy to perceive," King observed, "that the South is not yet reconciled to reconstruction."[151]

In the face of such opposition to one of the principal features of the southern revolution, King was convinced that the federal government and the northern people should continue their active concern for the freedmen. It is true that he spoke out strongly against the "abuses of reconstruction," condemned the activities of the "more odious carpet-baggers," and appealed to the "precious legacy" of Anglo-Saxon blood in suggesting that the current South Carolina government be "[swept] out of existence." But at the same time he denounced the lawlessness and the "atrocious outrages" of the White League and the Ku Klux Klan. In some areas of the South, particularly in Louisiana, Alabama, Georgia, South Carolina, and Kentucky, these organizations had inaugurated "a veritable reign of terror," including whippings, murders, and "midnight massacres." The "Ku Klux," King concluded, had contributed largely to the excesses of reconstruction.[152]

King opposed such violence and argued that it was the responsibility of the federal government to "protect the freedman in the rights given him by the revolution consequent upon the war." Indeed he advocated a greatly expanded role for the federal government in the postbellum South. He believed that Congress "should take earnest measures to foster and protect education in all the Southern states." The reclamation of "the 'poor whites' from . . . barbarism" was "a proper subject for the consideration of the National Government," which "would have done no more than its duty" had it matched the two million dollars given by George Peabody for education in the South. King was particularly critical of the federal government because it did "little but look on" as the southern states and a few individuals and societies did all that was done for the education of the freedmen. He suggested that even more vigor and enterprise by Northerners and Westerners in the promotion of education for blacks was needed in the 1870s than had been the case in the immediate postwar years: "Hundreds of thousands of dollars are needed to supply this people with the barest necessities of their intellectual improvement; a steady charity for ten years to come will be in no wise mistaken. They need, above all, to be taught how to help themselves; and by normal schools and the complete education of

[151] King, *Great South,* 89, 599, 794, 785, 678. Whites particularly objected to any proposal for "an indiscriminate mingling of the races in schools." And only time would tell, King believed, whether southern planters would some day demand compensation for their emancipated slaves or try to establish a labor system relegating the Negro to serfdom (pp. 601–602, 794).

[152] *Ibid.,* 793, 465, 454–57, 722, 88, 333, 351, 515, 715.

the most promising individuals of their race, that will be soonest accomplished."[153]

There were, King argued, numerous other areas of southern life in which the federal government should be actively involved. A federal commission should investigate the "labor question in the South," and the government should make "a final effort to remedy . . . [labor] evils by every proper means." One solution would be the promotion of immigration into such fertile areas as the Mississippi Valley. Another project should be a "grand national work by the General Government" that would prevent the ruinous inundations suffered along the Mississippi; he argued that the federal government should "at once undertake the control and care of the stream and its tributaries." In addition improvements were greatly needed on the Tennessee, the Ohio, and the Cumberland rivers. The federal government was also the only agency which could protect the Indians from the rapacity of the white man. King further urged that the national government establish historic monuments at such sites as the Alamo, Monticello, and Harpers Ferry, and suggested that Hot Springs, Arkansas, be made "a grand sanitary resort free to the people." The federal government, he believed, should be intimately involved in improving the quality of life for all Southerners.[154]

If King could return to the South in the 1970s, a century after his original visits, he would find that the region is much like the New South he foresaw. He was too optimistic about the speed with which progress and social adjustment would come to the South, but progress and change have come. Smokestacks and industrial paraphernalia dot the southern skyline, and a multitude of urban centers pace economic and cultural development.[155] The great majority of white Southerners have a much higher standard of living and greater opportunity for human development than their counterparts of the 1870s; and if there is still vast room for improvement in race relations, whites and blacks have made marked progress in learning to live together. Generally the South has come more and more to participate in the main currents of national life. But the distinctiveness of the southern people and the southern land remains. If King could return, he might still remark upon "the beauty of the fair Southern land" and "the magic of the climate." For instance, he would discover that Virginia's Peaks of Otter, though easier to ascend and visited by thousands of tourists annually, are just as "majestic" as in the bygone days of the 1870s.[156] King would find, in short, that his Great South still lives.

W. Magruder Drake
Robert R. Jones
University of Southwestern Louisiana

[153] Ibid., 608, 277, 94, 602, 608, 277.
[154] Ibid., 277, 263, 329, 339, 530–31, 695–96, 728, 196–203, 163–66, 651–53, 766–78, 286.
[155] King was greatly concerned with the effects of industrialization and the growth of the tourist trade on the southern land. He spoke of the smoke problem in St. Louis and Chattanooga, was indignant at the idea of a proposed construction of a railroad terminus on the site of Fort Marion at St. Augustine, and worried that mobs of tourists would rob the Virginia springs, the North Carolina mountain region, and St. Augustine of their special charm. Ibid., 223, 532, 394, 568, 501, 396–97.
[156] Ibid., 184, 562–65.

THE GREAT SOUTH

ON THE OCLAWAHA FLORIDA.

THE

GREAT SOUTH:

A RECORD OF JOURNEYS

IN

LOUISIANA,   TEXAS,   THE   INDIAN   TERRITORY,   MISSOURI,   ARKANSAS,
MISSISSIPPI,   ALABAMA,   GEORGIA,   FLORIDA,   SOUTH   CAROLINA,
NORTH   CAROLINA,   KENTUCKY,   TENNESSEE,   VIRGINIA,
WEST   VIRGINIA,   AND   MARYLAND.

BY
EDWARD KING.
PROFUSELY ILLUSTRATED FROM ORIGINAL SKETCHES
BY J. WELLS CHAMPNEY.

—— o ——

AMERICAN PUBLISHING COMPANY,
HARTFORD, CONN.
1879.

PREFACE.

THIS book is the record of an extensive tour of observation through the States of the South and South-west during the whole of 1873, and the Spring and Summer of 1874.

The journey was undertaken at the instance of the publishers of *Scribner's Monthly*, who desired to present to the public, through the medium of their popular periodical, an account of the material resources, and the present social and political condition, of the people in the Southern States. The author and the artists associated with him in the preparation of the work, traveled more than twenty-five thousand miles; visited nearly every city and town of importance in the South; talked with men of all classes, parties and colors; carefully investigated manufacturing enterprises and sites; studied the course of politics in each State since the advent of reconstruction; explored rivers, and penetrated into mountain regions heretofore rarely visited by Northern men. They were everywhere kindly and generously received by the Southern people; and they have endeavored, by pen and pencil, to give the reading public a truthful picture of life in a section which has, since the close of a devastating war, been overwhelmed by a variety of misfortunes, but upon which the dawn of a better day is breaking.

The fifteen ex-slave States cover an area of more than 880,000 square miles, and are inhabited by fourteen millions of people. The aim of the author has been to tell the truth as exactly and completely as possible in the time and space allotted him, concerning the characteristics of this region and its inhabitants.

The popular favor accorded in this country and Great Britain to the fifteen illustrated articles descriptive of the South which have appeared in *Scribner's Monthly*, has led to the preparation of the present volume. Much of the material which has appeared in *Scribner* will be found in its pages; the whole has, however, been re-written, re-arranged, and, with numerous additions, is now simultaneously offered to the English-speaking public on both sides of the Atlantic.

To the talent and skill of Mr. J. WELLS CHAMPNEY, the artist who accompanied the author during the greater part of the journey, the public is indebted for more than four hundred of the superb sketches of Southern life, character, and scenery which illustrate this volume. The other artists who have contributed have done their work faithfully and well.

NEW YORK, November, 1874.

DEDICATION.

TO MR. ROSWELL-SMITH,

Scribner & Co., 654 Broadway, New York.

My Dear Sir :—You have been from first to last so inseparably as well as pleasantly connected with "The Great South" enterprise, that I cannot forbear taking this occasion to thank you, not only for originally suggesting the idea of a journey of observation through the Southern States, but also for having generously submitted to the enlargement of the first plan's scope, until the undertaking demanded a really immense outlay.

I am sure that thousands of people will unite with me in testifying to you, and the gentlemen associated with you, their thanks for the lavish expenditure which has procured the beautiful series of engravings illustrating this volume. What I have been able only to hint at, the artists have interpreted with a fidelity to life and nature in the highest degree admirable.

I herewith present you the result of the joint labor of author and artists, "The Great South" volume. Permit me, sir, to dedicate it to you, and by means of this humble tribute to express my admiration for the energy and unsparing zeal with which you have carried to completion the largest enterprise of its kind ever undertaken by a monthly magazine.

Sincerely Yours,

EDWARD KING.

NOVEMBER 1, 1874.

GENERAL MAP OF THE SOUTHERN STATES.

THE GREAT SOUTH.

I.

LOUISIANA PAST AND PRESENT.

Bienville, the Founder of New Orleans.

LOUISIANA to-day is Paradise Lost. In twenty years it may be Paradise Regained. It has unlimited, magnificent possibilities. Upon its bayou-penetrated soil, on its rich uplands and its vast prairies, a gigantic struggle is in progress. It is the battle of race with race, of the picturesque and unjust civilization of the past with the prosaic and leveling civilization of the present. For a century and a-half it was coveted by all nations; sought by those great colonizers of America,—the French, the English, the Spaniards. It has been in turn the plaything of monarchs and the bait of adventurers. Its history and tradition are leagued with all that was romantic in Europe and on the Western continent in the eighteenth century. From its immense limits outsprang the noble sisterhood of South-western States, whose inexhaustible domain affords an ample refuge for the poor of all the world.

A little more than half a century ago the frontier of Louisiana, with the Spanish internal provinces, extended nineteen hundred miles. The territory boasted a sea-coast line of five hundred miles on the Pacific Ocean ; drew a boundary line seventeen hundred miles along the edge of the British-American dominions ; thence followed the Mississippi by a comparative course for fourteen hundred miles ; fronted the Mexican Gulf for seven hundred miles, and embraced within its limits nearly one million five hundred thousand square miles. Texas was a fragment broken from it. California, Kansas, the Indian Territory, Missouri, and Mississippi, were made from it, and still there was an Empire to spare, watered by five of the finest rivers of the world. Indiana, Arkansas, Iowa, Minnesota, and Nebraska were born of it.

From French Bienville to American Claiborne the territorial administrations were dramatic, diplomatic, bathed in the atmosphere of conspiracy. Superstition cast a weird veil of mystery over the great rivers, and Indian legend peopled every nook and cranny of the section with fantastic creations of untutored fancy. The humble roof of the log cabin on the banks of the Mississippi covered all the grace and elegance of French society of Louis the Fourteenth's time. Jesuit and Cavalier carried European thought to the Indians.

Frenchman and Spaniard, Canadian and Yankee, intrigued and planned on Louisiana soil with an energy and fierceness displayed nowhere else in our early history. What wonder, after this cosmopolitan record, that even the fragment of Louisiana which has retained the name—this remnant embracing but a thirtieth of the area of the original province—yet still covering more than forty thousand square miles of prairie, alluvial, and sea marsh—what wonder that it is so richly varied, so charming, so unique ?

Six o'clock, on Saturday evening, in the good old city of New Orleans. From the tower of the Cathedral St. Louis the tremulous harmony of bells drifts lightly on the cool spring breeze, and hovers like a benediction over the antique buildings, the blossoms and hedges in the square, and the broad and swiftly-flowing river. The bells are calling all in the parish to offer masses for the repose of the soul of the Cathedral's founder, Don Andre Almonaster, once upon a time "perpetual regidor" of New Orleans. Every Saturday eve, for

The Cathedral St. Louis—New Orleans.

three-quarters of a century, the solemn music from the Cathedral belfry has brought the good Andre to mind ; and the mellow notes, as we hear them, seem to call up visions of the quaint past.

Don Andre gave the Cathedral its dower in 1789, while the colony was under the domination of Charles the Fourth of Spain. The original edifice is gone now, and in its stead, since 1850, has stood a composite structure which is a monument to bad taste. Venerable and imposing was the old Cathedral, with its melange of rustic, Tuscan, and Roman Doric styles of architecture; with its towers crowned with low spires, and its semicircular arched door, with clustered columns on either side at the front; and many a grand pageant had it seen.

"A blind beggar hears the rustling of her gown, and stretches out his trembling hand for alms."

Under the pavement of the Cathedral lies buried Father Antonio de Sedella, a Spanish priest, who, in his time, was one of the celebrities of New Orleans, and the very recollection of whom calls up memories of the Inquisition, of intrigue and mystery. Father Antonio's name is sacred in the Louisiana capital, nevertheless; for although an enraged Spanish Governor once expelled him for presuming to establish the Inquisition in the colony, he came back, and flourished until 1837, under American rule, dying at the age of ninety, in the odor of sanctity, mourned by the women and worshiped by the children.

Now the sunlight mingles with the breeze bewitchingly; the old square, the gray and red buildings with massive walls and encircling balconies, the great door of the new Cathedral, all are lighted up. See! a black-robed woman, with downcast eyes, passes silently over the holy threshold; a blind beggar, with a parti-colored handkerchief wound about his weather-beaten head, hears the rustling of her gown, and stretches out his trembling hand for alms; a black girl looks wonderingly into the holy-water font; the market-women hush their chatter as they near the portal; a mulatto fruit-seller is lounging in the shade of an ancient arch, beneath the old Spanish Council House. This is not an American scene, and one almost persuades himself that he is in Europe, although ten minutes of rapid walking will bring him to streets and squares as generically American as any in Boston, Chicago, or St. Louis.

The city of New Orleans is fruitful in surprises. In a morning's promenade, which shall not extend over an hundred acres, one may encounter the civilizations of Paris, of Madrid, of Messina; may stumble upon the semi-barbaric life of

"A black girl looks wonderingly into the holy-water font."

the negro and the native Indian; may see the overworked American in his business establishment and in his elegant home; and may find, strangest of all, that each and every foreign type moves in a special current of its own, mingling little with the American, which is dominant: in it, yet not of it—as the Gulf Stream in the ocean.

But the older colonial landmarks in the city, as throughout the State and the Mississippi Valley, are fast disappearing. The imprint of French manners and customs will long remain, however; for it was produced by two periods of domination. The hatred of Napoleon the Great for the English was the motive which led to the cession of Louisiana to the United States: had he not come upon the stage of European politics, the Valley of the Father of Waters might have been French to-day; and both sides of Canal street would have reminded the European of Paris and Bordeaux.

The French Emperor, fearful lest the cannon of the English fleets might thunder at the gates of New Orleans when he was at war with England, at the beginning of this century, sold the "Earthly Paradise" to the United States. "The English," said the man of destiny, "shall not have the Mississippi, which they covet." And they did not get it. Seventy years ago the tide of crude, hasty American progress rushed in upon the lovely lowlands bordering the river and the Gulf; and it is astonishing that even a few landmarks of French and Spanish rule are left high above the flood.

The Archbishop's Palace—New Orleans.

Yonder is the archbishop's palace: enter the street at one side of it, and you seem in a foreign land; in the avenue at the other you catch a glimpse of the rush and hurry of American traffic of to-day along the levée; you see the sharp-featured "river-hand," hear his uncouth parlance, and recognize him for your countryman; you see huge piles of cotton bales; you hear the monotonous whistle of the gigantic white steamers arriving and departing; and the irrepressible negro slouches sullenly by with his hands in his pockets, and his cheeks distended with tobacco.

You must know much of the past of New Orleans and Louisiana to thoroughly understand their present. New England sprang from the Puritan mould; Louisiana from the French and Spanish civilizations of the eighteenth century. The one stands erect, vibrating with life and activity, austere and ambitious, upon its rocky shores; the other lies prone, its rich vitality dormant and passive, luxurious and unambitious, on the glorious shores of the tropic Gulf. The former was Anglo-Saxon and simple even to Spartan plainness at its outset; the latter was Franco-Spanish, subtle in the graces of the elder societies, self-indulgent and romantic at its beginning. And New Orleans was no more and no less the opposite of Boston in 1773 than a century later. It was a hardy rose which dared to blush, in the New England even of Governor Winthrop's time, beīore June had dowered the land with beauty; it was an o'er modest Choctaw rose in the Louisiana of De Soto's epoch which did not shower its petals on the fragrant turf in February.

In Louisiana summer lingers long after the rude winter of the North has done its work of devastation; the sleeping passion of the climate only wakes now and then into the anger of lightning or the terrible tears of the thunder-storm; there are no chronic March horrors of deadly wind or transpiercing cold; the sun is kind; the days are radiant.

Wandering from the ancient Place d'Armes, now dignified with the appellation of "Jackson Square," through the older quarters of the city, one may readily recall the curious, changeful past of the commonwealth and its cosmopolitan capital; for there is a visible reminder at many a corner and on many a wall. It requires but little effort of imagination to restore the city to our view as it was in 1723, five years after Bienville, the second French Governor of Louisiana, had undertaken the dubious project of establishing a capital on the treacherous Mississippi's bank.

Discouraged and faint almost unto death, after the terrible sufferings which he and his fellow-colonists had undergone at Biloxi, a bleak fort in a wilderness, he had dragged his weary limbs to the place on the river where New Orleans stands to-day, and there defiantly unfurled the flag of France, and made his last stand! Bienville was a man of vast courage and supreme daring; he had been drifting along the Mississippi, through the stretches of wilderness, since 1699; had vanquished Indian and beast of the forest; was skilled in the lore of the backwoodsman, as became hardy son of hardier Canadian father.

When he succeeded the alert and courageous Sauvolle as Governor of the colony, which had then become indisputably French, he entered upon a period of harrowing and petty vexations. He had to keep faithful and persistent watch at the entrance of the river from the Gulf, for, during many years England, France, and Spain were at war, and the Spaniards ever kept a jealous eye on French progress in America. The colony languished, and was inhabited by only a few vagabond Canadians, some dubious characters from France, and the Government officers. On the 14th of September, 1712, Louis the Magnificent granted to Anthony Crozat, a merchant prince, the Rothschild of the day, the exclusive privilege, for fifteen years, of trading in all the indefinitely bounded territory claimed by France as Louisiana.

Crozat obtained with his charter the additional privilege of sending a ship once a year for negroes to Africa, and of owning and working all the mines that might be discovered in the colony, provided that one-fourth of their proceeds should be reserved for the king. One ship-load of slaves to every two ship-loads of independent colonists was the proportion established for emigration to Louisiana more than a century and a half ago. Slavery was well begun.

In 1713 Bienville was displaced to make room for Cadillac, sent from France as Governor; a rude, quarrelsome man, who saw no good in the new colony, and hated and feared Bienville. But Cadillac's daughter loved the quondam Governor whom her father's arrival had degraded; and to save her from a wasted life, the proud Cadillac offered her in marriage to Bienville. The latter did not reciprocate the maid's affection, and Cadillac, burning with rage, and anxious to avenge himself for this humiliation, sent Bienville with a small force on a dangerous expedition among the hostile Indians. He went, returning successful and unharmed. Cadillac's temper soon caused his own downfall, and others, equally unsuccessful, succeeded him. Crozat's schemes failed, and he relinquished the colony.

And then? Louisiana the indefinite and unfortunate fell into the clutches of John Law. The regent Duke of Orleans had decided to "foster and preserve the colony," and in 1717 gave it to the "Company of the Indies," a commercial oligarchy into which Law had blown the breath of life. The Royal Bank sprang into existence under Law's enchanted wand; the charter of the Mississippi Company was registered at Paris, and the exclusive privilege of trading with Louisiana, during twenty-five years, was granted to that company.

France was flooded with rumors that Louisiana was the long-sought Eldorado; dupes were made by millions; princes waited in John Law's ante-rooms in Paris. Then came the revulsion, the overturn of Law. Louisiana was no longer represented as the new Atlantis, but as the very mouth of the pit; and it was colonized only by thieves, murderers, beggars, and gypsies, gathered up by force throughout France and expelled from the kingdom.

After the bursting of the Law bubble, Bienville was once more appointed Governor of Louisiana, and his favorite town was selected as the capital of the territory. The seat of government was removed from New Biloxi to New Orleans, as the city was called in honor of the title of the regent of France.

Let us look at the New Orleans of the period between 1723 and 1730. Imagine a low-lying swamp, overgrown with a dense ragged forest, cut up into a thousand miniature islands by ruts and pools filled with stagnant water. Fancy a small cleared space along the superb river channel, a space often inundated, but partially reclaimed from the circumambient swamp, and divided into a host of small correct squares, each exactly like its neighbor, and so ditched within and without as to render wandering after nightfall perilous.

The ditch which ran along the four sides of every square in the city was filled with a composite of black mud and refuse, which, under a burning sun, sent forth a deadly odor. Around the city was a palisade and a gigantic moat; tall grasses grew up to the doors of the houses, and the hoarse chant of myriads of frogs mingled with the vesper songs of the colonists. Away where the waters of the Mississippi and of Lake Pontchartrain had formed a high ridge of land, was the "Leper's Bluff;" and among the reeds from the city thitherward always lurked a host of criminals.

The negro, fresh from the African coast, then strode defiantly along the low shores by the stream; he had not learned the crouching, abject gait which a century of slavery afterwards gave him. He was punished if he rebelled; but he kept his dignity. In the humble dwellings which occupied the squares there were noble manners and graces; all the traditions and each *finesse* of the time had not been forgotten in the voyage from France: and airy gentlemen and stately dames promenaded in this queer, swamp-surrounded, river-endangered fortress, with Parisian grace and ease.

There were few churches, and the colonists gathered about great wooden crosses in the open air for the ceremonials of their religion   There were twice as many negroes as white people in the city.   Domestic animals were so scarce that he who injured or fatally wounded a horse or a cow was punished with death. Ursuline nuns and Jesuit fathers glided about the streets upon their sacred missions.   The principal avenues within the fortified enclosure were named after princes of the royal blood—Maine, Condé, Conti, Toulouse, and Bourbon; Chartres street took its name from that of the son of the regent of Orleans, and an avenue was named in honor of Governor Bienville.

Along the river, for many miles beyond the city, marquises and other noble representatives of aristocratic French families had established plantations, and lived luxurious lives of self-indulgence, without especially contributing to the wealth of the colony.   Jews were banished from the bounds of Louisiana.   Sundays and holidays were strictly observed, and negroes found working on Sunday were confiscated.   No worship save the Catholic was allowed; white subjects were forbidden to marry or to live in concubinage with slaves, and masters were not allowed to force their slaves into any marriage against their will; the children of a negro slave-husband and a negro free-wife were all free; if the mother was a slave and the husband was free, the children shared the condition of the mother.

Slaves were forbidden to gather in crowds, by day or night, under any pretext, and if found assembled, were punished by the whip, or branded with the mark of the flower-de-luce, or executed.   The slaves all wore marks or badges, and were not permitted to sell produce of any kind without the written consent of their masters.   The protection and security of slaves in old age was well provided for; Christian negroes were permitted burial in consecrated ground. The slave who produced a bruise, or the " shedding of blood in the face," on the person of his master, or any of the family to which he appertained, by striking them, was condemned to death; and the runaway slave, when caught, after the first offence, had his ears cut off, and was branded; after the second, was hamstrung and again branded; after the third, was condemned to death.   Slaves who had been set free were still bound to show the profoundest respect to their "former masters, their widows and children," under pain of severe penalties. Slave husbands and wives were not permitted to be seized and sold separately when belonging to the same master; and whenever slaves were appointed tutors to their masters' children, they "were held and regarded as being thereby set free to all intents and purposes."

The Choctaws and Chickasaws, neighbors to the colonists, were waging destructive war against each other; hurricanes regularly destroyed all the engineering works erected by the French Government at the mouths of the Mississippi; and expeditions against the Natchez and the Chickasaws, arrivals of ships from France with loads of troops, provisions, and wives for the colonists, the building of levées along the river front near New Orleans, and the occasional deposition from and re-instatement in office of Bienville, were the chief events in those crude days of the beginning.

I like to stand in these old Louisiana by-ways, and contemplate the progress of French civilization in them, now that it has been displaced by a newer one. I like to remember that New Orleans was named after the regent of France; that the beautiful lake lying between the city and the Gulf was christened after the splendid Pontchartrain, him of the lean and hungry look, and of the "smile of death," him to whom the heart of Louis the Fourteenth was always open; and that the other lake, near the city, was named in memory of Maurepas, the wily adviser of Louis the Sixteenth and unlucky.

I like to remember that Louisiana itself owes its pretentious name to the devotion of its discoverer to the great monarch whom the joyous La Salle could not refrain from calling "the most puissant, most high, most invincible and victorious prince." I like to picture to myself Allouez and Father Dablon, Marquette and Joliet, La Salle, Iberville, and Bienville, following in the footsteps of Garay and Leon, Cordova and Narvaez, De Vaca and Friar Mark; and finally tracing and identifying the current of the wild, mysterious Mississippi, which had been but a tradition for ages, until every nook and cranny, from the Falls of St. Anthony to the Gulf of Mexico, re-echoed to French words of command and prayer, as well as to gayest of French chansons.

Let us take another picture of New Orleans, from 1792 to 1797, thirty years after the King of France had bestowed upon "his cousin of Spain" the splendid gift of Louisiana, ceding it, "without any exception or reservation whatever, from the pure impulse of his generous heart." That a country should, by a simple stroke of the pen, strip herself of possessions extending from the mouth of the Mississippi to the St. Lawrence, is almost incomprehensible.

France had perhaps already learned that her people had not in their breasts that eternal hunger for travel, that feverish unrest, which has made the Anglo-Saxon the most successful of colonists, and has given half the world to him and to his descendants. But the French had nobly done the work of pioneering. Sauvolle, grimly defying death at Biloxi; Bienville, urging the adventurous prow of his ship through the reeds at the Mississippi's mouth, are among the most heroic figures in the early history of the country.

New Orleans from 1792 to 1797? Its civilization has changed; it is fitted into the iron groove of Spanish domination, and has become bigoted, narrow, and hostile to innovation. Along the streets, now lined with low, flat-roofed, balconied houses, out of whose walls peep little hints of Moorish architecture, stalks the lean and haughty Spanish cavalier, with his hand upon his sword; and the quavering voice of the night watchman, equipped with his traditional spear and lantern, is heard through the night hours proclaiming that all is "serene," although at each corner lurks a fugitive from justice, waiting only until the watchman has passed to commit new crime. Six thousand souls now inhabit the city, there are hints in the air of a plague, and the Intendant has written home to the Council of State that "some affirm that the yellow fever is to be feared."

The priests and friars are half-mad with despair because the mixed population pays so very little attention to its salvation from eternal damnation, and
because the roystering officers and soldiers of the regiment of Louisiana admit
that they have not been to mass for three years.   The French hover about
the few taverns and coffee-houses permitted in the city, and mutter rebellion
against the Spaniard, whom they have always disliked.   The Spanish and
French schools are in perpetual collision; so are the manners, customs, diets,
and languages of the respective nations.   The Ursuline convent has refused to
admit Spanish women who desire to become nuns, unless they learn the
French language; and the ruling Governor, Baron Carondelet, has such small
faith in the loyalty of the colonists that he has had the fortifications constructed with a view not only to protecting himself against attacks from without,
but from within.

The city has suddenly taken on a wonderful aspect of barrack-yard and camp.
On the side fronting the Mississippi are two small forts commanding the road and
the river.   On their strong and solid brick-coated parapets, Spanish sentinels
are languidly pacing; and cannon look out ominously over the walls.   Between
these two forts, and so arranged as to cross its fires with them, fronting on the
main street of the town, is a great battery commanding the river.   Then there
are forts at each of the salient angles of the long square forming the city, and a
third a little beyond them—all armed with eight guns each.   From one of these
tiny forts to another, noisy dragoons are always clattering; officers are parading
to and fro; government officials block the way; and the whole town looks like a
Spanish garrison gradually growing, by
some mysterious process of transformation, into a French city.

Yet the Spanish civilization does not
and can not take a strong hold there.
Spain does not give to New Orleans
so many lasting historic souvenirs as
France.   Barracks, petty forts, dragoon
stables, and many other quaint buildings finally disappear, leaving only the
"Principal," next the Cathedral, its
fellow on the other side of the old
church, some aged private dwellings,
rapidly decaying, and a delicate imprint

"Some aged private dwellings, rapidly decaying."

and suggestion of former Spanish rule scattered throughout various quarters
of the city.   But Spanish society still lingers, and in some parts of the old
town the many-balconied, thick-walled houses for the moment mislead the
visitor into the belief that he is in Spain until he hears the French language,
or the curious Creole *patois* everywhere about him.

Let us take another look at the past of New Orleans.   The Spaniard has
gone his ways; Ulloa and O'Reilly, Unzaga, Galvez, and Miro, have held their
governorships under the Spanish King.   Carondelet, Gayoso, Casa-Calvo, and

Salcedo alike have vanished. There have been insurrections on the part of
the French; many longings after the old banner; and at last the government

of France determines once more to possess the grand territory. Spain well
knows that it is useless to oppose this
decision; is not sorry, withal, to be rid
of a colony so difficult to govern, and
so near to the quarrelsome Americans,
who have many times threatened to
take New Orleans by force if any farther commercial regulations are made
by Spaniards at the Mississippi's outlet.
      Napoleon the Great has three things
to gain by the possession of the Territory: the command of the Gulf; the

A brace of old Spanish Governors.—From portraits owned
by Hon. Charles Gayarré, of New Orleans.

supply of the islands owned by France; and a place of settlement for surplus population. So that, at St. Ildefonso, on the morning of October first,
1800, a treaty of cession is signed by Spain, its third article reading as follows: "His Catholic Majesty promises and engages, on his part, to retrocede
to the French Republic, six months after the full and entire execution of the
conditions and stipulations herein relative to His Royal Highness the Duke
of Parma—the colony or province of Louisiana, with the same extent that it now
has in the hands of Spain, and that it had when France possessed it; and such as
it should be after the treaties subsequently entered into between Spain and other
states."

This treaty is kept secret while the French fit out an expedition to sail and
take sudden possession of the reacquired Territory; but the United States has
sharp ears; and Minister Livingston besets the cabinet of the First Consul
at Paris; fights a good battle of diplomacy; is dignified as well as aggressive;
wins his cause; and Napoleon tells his counselors, on Easter Sunday, 1803, his
resolve in the following words: "I know the full value of Louisiana, and I have
been desirous of repairing the fault of the French negotiator who abandoned it
in 1763; a few lines of a treaty have restored it to me, and I have scarcely
recovered it when I must expect to lose it. But if it escapes from me, it shall
one day cost dearer to those who oblige me to strip myself of it than to those to
whom I wish to deliver it." And it is forthwith ceded to the United States, in
1803, on the "tenth day of Floreal, in the eleventh year of the French republic,"
in consideration of the payment by our government of sixty millions of francs.

Half a generation brings the conflicting national elements into something like
harmony, and makes Louisiana a territory containing fifty thousand souls. The
first steamboat ploughs through the waters of the Mississippi, but more stirring
events also take place. In 1812 Congress declares that war exists between
Great Britain and the United States, and early in 1815 General Andrew Jackson
wins a decisive victory over the English arms, on the lowlands near New
Orleans. Fifteen thousand skilled British soldiers are beaten off and sent home

in disorder by the raw troops of the river States, by the stalwart Kentuckians, the hunters of Tennessee, the rough, hard-handed sons of Illinois, the dashing horsemen of Mississippi, and the handsome and athletic Creoles of Louisiana. When the victorious Americans return to New Orleans, a grand parade is held in the square henceforth to commemorate the name of Jackson, and where

"And where to-day stands a fine Equestrian Statue of the great General."

to-day stands a fine equestrian statue of the great general. In front of old Almonaster's cathedral the troops are drawn up in order of review. Under a triumphal arch, from which glittering lines of bayonets stretch to the river, General Jackson, the hero of the Chalmette battle-field, passes, and bows low his laurel-crowned head to receive the apostolic benediction of the venerable Abbé.

II.

THE FRENCH QUARTER OF NEW ORLEANS—THE REVOLUTION AND ITS EFFECTS.

LET me show you some pictures from the New Orleans of to-day. The nightmare of civil war has passed away, leaving the memory of visions which it is not my province—certainly not my wish—to renew. The Crescent City has grown so that Claiborne and Jackson could no longer recognize it. It was gaining immensely in wealth and population until the social and political revolutions following the war came with their terrible, crushing weight, and the work of re-establishing the commerce of the State has gone on under conditions most disheartening and depressing; though trial seems to have brought out a reserve of energy of which its possessors had never suspected themselves capable.

Step off from Canal street, that avenue of compromises which separates the French and the American quarters, some bright February morning, and you will at once find yourself in a foreign atmosphere. A walk into the French section enchants you; the characteristics of an American city vanish; this might be Toulouse, or Bordeaux, or Marseilles! The houses are all of stone or brick, stuccoed or painted; the windows of each story descend to the floors, opening, like doors, upon airy, pretty balconies, protected by iron railings; quaint dormer windows peer from the great roofs; the street doors are massive, and large enough to admit carriages into the stone-paved court-yards, from which stairways communicate with the upper apartments.

Sometimes, through a portal opened by a slender, dark-haired, bright-eyed Creole girl in black, you catch a glimpse of a garden, delicious with daintiest blossoms, purple and red and white gleaming from vines clambering along a gray wall; rose-bushes, with the grass about them strewn with petals; bosquets, green and symmetrical; luxuriant hedges, arbors, and refuges, trimmed by skillful hands; banks of verbenas; bewitching profusion of peach and apple blossoms; the dark green of the magnolia; in a quiet corner, the rich glow of the orange in its nest among the thick leaves of its parent tree; the palmetto, the catalpa;—a mass of bloom which laps the senses in slumbrous delight. Suddenly the door closes, and your paradise is lost, while Eve remains inside the gate!

From the balconies hang, idly flapping in the breeze, little painted tin placards, announcing "Furnished apartments to rent!" Alas! in too many of the old mansions you are ushered by a gray-faced woman clad in deepest black, with little children clinging jealously to her skirts, and you instinctively note by her manners and her speech that she did not rent rooms before the war. You pity her, and think of the multitudes of these gray-faced women; of the numbers of these silent, almost desolate houses.

Now and then, too, a knock at the porter's lodge will bring to your view a bustling Creole dame, fat and fifty, redolent of garlic and new wine, and robust in voice as in person. How cheerily she retails her misfortunes, as if they were blessings! "An invalid husband—*voyez-vous ça!* Auguste a Confederate, of course—and is yet; but the *pauvre garçon* is unable to work, and we are very poor!" All this merrily, and in high key, while the young negress—the housemaid—stands lazily listening to her mistress's French, nervously polishing with her huge lips the handle of the broom she holds in her broad, corded hands.

Business here, as in foreign cities, has usurped only half the domain; the shopkeepers live over their shops, and communicate to their commerce somewhat of the aroma of home. The dainty *salon*, where the ladies' hairdresser holds sway, has its doorway enlivened by the baby; the grocer and his wife, the milliner and his daughter, are behind the counters in their respective shops. Here you pass a little café, with the awning drawn down, and, peering in, can distinguish half-a-dozen bald, rotund old boys drinking their evening absinthe, and playing picquet and vingt-et-un, exactly as in France.

Here, perhaps, is a touch of Americanism: a lazy negro, recumbent in a cart, with his eyes languidly closed, and one dirty foot sprawled on the sidewalk. No! even he responds to your question in French, which he speaks poorly though fluently. French signs abound; there is a warehouse for wines and brandies from the heart of Southern France; here is a funeral notice, printed in deepest black: "The friends of Jean Baptiste," etc., "are respectfully invited to be present at the funeral, which will take place at precisely four o'clock, on the ———." The notice is

"A lazy negro, recumbent in a cart."

on black-edged note-paper, nailed to a post. Here pass a group of French negroes, the buxom girls dressed with a certain grace, and with gayly-colored handkerchiefs wound about an unpardonable luxuriance of wool. Their cavaliers are clothed mainly in antiquated garments rapidly approaching the level of rags; and their *patois* resounds for half-a-dozen blocks.

Turning into a side street leading off from Royal, or Chartres, or Bourgogne, or Dauphin, or Rampart streets, you come upon an odd little shop, where the cobbler sits at his work in the shadow of a grand old Spanish arch; or upon a nest of curly-headed negro babies ensconced on a tailor's bench at the window of a fine ancient mansion; or you look into a narrow room, glass-fronted, and see a long and well-spread table, surrounded by twenty Frenchmen and French-women, all talking at once over their eleven o'clock breakfast.

Or you may enter aristocratic restaurants, where the immaculate floors are only surpassed in cleanliness by the spotless linen of the tables; where a solemn dignity, as befits the refined pleasure of dinner, prevails, and where the waiter gives you the names of the dishes in both languages, and bestows on you a napkin large enough to serve you as a shroud, if this strange melange of French and Southern cookery should give you a fatal indigestion. The French families of position usually dine at four, as the theatre begins promptly at seven, both on Sundays and week days. There is the play-bill, in French, of course; and there are the typical Creole ladies, stopping for a moment to glance at it as they wend their way shopward. For it is the shopping hour; from eleven to two the streets of the old quarter are alive with elegantly, yet soberly attired ladies, always in couples, as French etiquette exacts that the unmarried lady shall never promenade without her maid or her mother.

One sees beautiful faces on the Rue Royale (Royal street), and in the balconies and lodges of the Opera House; sometimes, too, in the cool of the evening, there are fascinating little groups of the daughters of Creoles on the balconies, gayly chatting while the veil of the twilight is torn away, and the glory of the Southern moonlight is showered over the quiet streets.

The Creole ladies are not, as a rule, so highly educated as the gracious daughters of the "American quarter;" but they have an indefinable grace, a *savoir* in dress, and a piquant and alluring charm in person and conversation, which makes them universal favorites in society.

One of the chiefest of their attractions is the staccato and queerly-colored English, really French in idea and accent, which many of them speak. At the Saturday matinées, in the opera or comedy season at the French Theatre, you will see hundreds of the ladies of "the quarter;" and rarely can a finer grouping of lovely brunettes be found; nowhere a more tastefully - dressed and elegantly - mannered assembly.

"The negro nurses stroll on the sidewalks, chattering in quaint French to the little children."

The quiet which has reigned in the old French section since the war ended is, perhaps, abnormal; but it would be difficult to find village streets more tranquil than are the main avenues of this foreign quarter after nine at night. The long, splendid stretches of Rampart and Esplanade streets, with their rows of trees planted in the centre of the driveways,—the whitewashed trunks giving a fine effect of green and white,—are peaceful; the negro nurses stroll on the sidewalks, chattering in quaint French to the little children of their former masters—now their "employers."

There is no attempt on the part of the French or Spanish families to inaugurate style and fashion in the city; quiet home society, match - making and marrying of daughters, games and dinner parties, church, shopping, and calls in simple and unaffected manner, content them.

The majority of the people in the whole quarter seem to have a total disregard of the outside world, and when one hears them discussing the distracted condition of local politics, one can almost fancy them gossiping on matters entirely foreign to them, instead of on those vitally connected with their lives and property. They live very much among themselves. French by nature and training, they get but a faint reflection of the excitements in these United States. It is also astonishing to see how little the ordinary American citizen of New Orleans knows of

"The interior garden, with its curious shrine."

his French neighbors; how ill he appreciates them. It is hard for him to talk five minutes about them without saying, "Well, we have a non-progressive element here; it will not be converted." Having said which, he will perhaps paint in glowing colors the virtues and excellences of his French neighbors, though he cannot forgive them for taking so little interest in public affairs.

Here we are again at the Archbishop's Palace, once the home of the Ursuline nuns, who now have, further down the river, a splendid new convent and school, surrounded by beautiful gardens. This ancient edifice was completed by the French Government in 1733, and is the oldest in Louisiana. Its Tuscan composite architecture, its porter's lodge, and its interior garden with its curious shrine, make it well worth preserving, even when the tide of progress shall have reached this nook on Condé street. The Ursuline nuns occupied this site for nearly a century, and it was abandoned by them only because they were tempted, by the great rise in real estate in that vicinity, to sell. The new convent is richly endowed, and is one of the best seminaries in the South.

Many of the owners of property in the vicinity of the Archbishop s Palace have removed to France, since the war,—doing nothing for the benefit of the metropolis which gave them their fortunes. The rent of these solidly-constructed old houses once brought them a sum which, when translated from dollars into francs, was colossal, and which the Parisian tradesmen tucked away into their strong boxes. Now they get almost nothing; the houses are mainly vacant. With the downfall of slavery, and the advent of reconstruction, came such radical changes in Louisiana politics and society that those belonging to the *ancien régime* who could flee, fled; and a prominent historian and gentleman of most honorable Creole descent told me that, among his immense acquaintance, he did not know a single person who would not leave the State if means were at hand.

The grooves in which society in Louisiana and New Orleans had run before

the late struggle were so broken that even a residence in the State was distasteful to him and the society he represented; since the late war, he said, 500 years seemed to have passed over the common-

The New Ursuline Convent—New Orleans.

wealth. The Italy of Augustus was not more dissimilar to the Italy of to-day than is the Louisiana of to-day to the Louisiana before the war. There was no longer the spirit to maintain the grand, unbounded hospitality once so characteristic of the South. Formerly, the guest would have been presented to planters who would have entertained him for days, in royal style, and who would have sent him forward in their own carriages, commended to the hospitality of their neighbors. Now these same planters were living upon corn and pork. "Most of these people," said the gentleman, "have vanished from their homes; and I actually know ladies of culture and refinement, whose incomes were gigantic before the war, who are 'washing' for their daily bread. The misery, the despair, in hundreds of cases, are beyond belief."

"Many lovely plantations," said he, "are entirely deserted; the negroes will not remain upon them, but flock into the cities, or work on land which they have purchased for themselves." He would not believe that the free negro did as much work for himself as he formerly did for his master. He considered the labor system at the present time terribly onerous for planters. The negroes were only profitable as field hands when they worked on shares, the planters furnishing them land, tools, horses, mules, and advancing them food. He said that he would not himself hire a negro even at small wages; he did not believe it would be profitable. The discouragement of the natives of Louisiana, he believed, arose in large degree from the difficulty of obtaining capital with which to begin anew. He knew instances where only $10,000 or $20,000 were needed for the improvement of water power, or of lands which would net hundreds of thousands. He had himself written repeatedly, urging people at the North to invest, but they would not, and alleged that they should not alter their determination so long as the present political condition prevailed.

He added, with great emphasis, that he did not think the people of the North would believe a statement which should give a faithful transcript of the present condition of affairs in Louisiana. The natives of the State could hardly

realize it themselves; and it was not to be expected that strangers, of differing habits of life and thought, should do it. He did not blame the negro for
his present incapacity, as he considered the black man an inferior being,
peculiarly unfitted by ages of special training for what he was now called
upon to undertake. The negro was, he thought, by nature, kindly, generous, courteous, susceptible of civilization only to a certain degree; devoid
of moral consciousness, and usually, of course, ignorant. Not one out of a
hundred, the whole State through, could write his name; and there had been
fifty-five in one single Legislature who could neither read nor write. There was,
according to him, scarcely a single man of color in the last Legislature who was
competent in any large degree.

The Louisiana white people were in such terror of the negro government that
they would rather accept any other despotism. A military dictator would be
far preferable to them; they would go anywhere to escape the ignominy to
which they were at present subjected. The crisis was demoralizing every one.
Nobody worked with a will; every one was in debt. There was not a single
piece of property in the city of New Orleans in which he would at present
invest, although one could now buy for $5,000 or $10,000 property originally
worth $50,000. He said it would not pay to purchase, the taxes were so
enormous. The majority of the great plantations had been deserted on account
of the excessive taxation. Only those familiar with the real causes of the
despair could imagine how deep it was.

Benefit by immigration, he maintained, was impossible under the present
régime. New-comers mingled in the distracted politics in such a manner as to
neglect the development of the country. Thousands of the citizens were fleeing
to Texas (and I could vouch for the correctness of that assertion). He said
that the mass of immigrants became easily discouraged and broken down,
because they began by working harder than the climate would permit.

In some instances, Germans on coming into the State had been ordered
by organizations both of white and colored native workmen not to labor so
much daily, as they were setting a dangerous example! Still, he believed
that almost any white man would do as much work as three negroes. He
hardly thought that in fifty years there would be any negroes in Louisiana.
The race was rapidly diminishing. Planters who had owned three or four hundred slaves before the war, had kept a record of their movements, and found
that more than half of them had died of want and neglect. The negroes did
not know how to care for themselves. The women now on the same plantations
where they had been owned as slaves gave birth to only one child where they
had previously borne three. They would not bear children as of old; the negro
population was rapidly decreasing. Gardening, he said, had proved an unprofitable experiment, because of the thievish propensities of the negro. All
the potatoes, turnips, and cabbages consumed by the white people of New
Orleans came from the West.

Such was the testimony of one who, although by no means unfair or bitterly
partisan, perhaps allowed his discouragement to color all his views. He frankly

accepted the results of the war, so far as the abolition of slavery and the consequent ruin of his own and thousands of other fortunes were concerned; he has, indeed, borne with all the evils which have arisen out of reconstruction, without murmuring until now, when he and thousands of his fellows are pushed to the wall. He is the representative of a very large class; the discouragement is no dream. It is written on the faces of the citizens; you may read and realize it there.

Ah! these faces, these faces;—expressing deeper pain, profounder discontent than were caused by the iron fate of the few years of the war! One sees them everywhere; on the street, at the theatre, in the *salon*, in the cars; and pauses for a moment, struck with the expression of entire despair—of complete helplessness, which has possessed their features. Sometimes the owners of the faces are one-armed and otherwise crippled; sometimes they bear no wounds or marks of wounds, and are in the prime and fullness of life; but the look is there still. Now and then it is controlled by a noble will, the pain of which it tells having been trampled under the feet of a great energy; but it is always there. The struggle is over, peace has been declared, but a generation has been doomed. The past has given to the future the dower of the present; there seems only a dead level of uninspiring struggle for those going out, and but small hope for those coming in. That is what the faces say; that is the burden of their sadness.

These are not of the loud-mouthed and bitter opponents of everything tending to reconsolidate the Union; these are not they who will tell you that some day the South will be united once more, and will rise in strength and strike a blow for freedom; but they are the payers of the price. The look is on the faces of the men who wore the swords of generals who led in disastrous measures; on the faces of women who have lost husbands, children, lovers, fortunes, homes, and comfort for evermore. The look is on the faces of the strong fighters, thinkers, and controllers of the Southern mind and heart; and here in Louisiana it will not brighten, because the wearers know that the great evils of disorganized labor, impoverished society, scattered families, race legislation, retributive tyranny and terrorism, with the power, like Nemesis of old, to wither and blast, leave no hope for this generation. Heaven have mercy on them! Their fate is too utterly inevitable not to command the strongest sympathy.

Of course, in the French quarter, there are multitudes of negroes who speak both French and English in the quaintest, most outlandish fashion; eliding whole syllables which seem necessary to sense, and breaking into extravagant exclamations on the slightest pretext. The French of the negroes is very much like that of young children; spoken far from plainly, but with a pretty grace which accords poorly with the exteriors of the speakers. The negro women, young and old, wander about the streets bareheaded and barearmed; now tugging their mistresses' children, now carrying huge baskets on their heads, and walking under their heavy burdens with the gravity of queens. Now and then one sees a mulatto girl hardly less fair than the brown maid he saw at Sorrento, or in the vine-covered cottage at the little mountain town near Rome; now a giant matron, black as the tempest, and with features as pronounced in savagery as any of her Congo ancestors.

But the negroes, taken as a whole, seem somewhat shuffling and disorganized; and apart from the statuesque old house and body servants, who appear to have caught some dignity from their masters, they are by no means inviting. They gather in groups at the street corners just at nightfall, and while they chatter like monkeys, even about politics, they gesticulate violently. They live without much work, for their wants are few; and two days' labor in a week, added to the fat roosters and turkeys that *will* walk into their clutches, keeps them in bed and board. They find ample amusement in the "heat o' the sun," the passers-by, and tobacco. There are families of color noticeable for

"And while they chatter like monkeys, even about politics, they gesticulate violently."

intelligence and accomplishments, but, as a rule, the negro of the French quarter is thick-headed, light-hearted, improvident, and not too conscientious.

Perhaps one of the most patent proofs of the poverty now so bitterly felt among the hitherto well-to-do families in New Orleans was apparent in the suspension of the opera in the winter of 1873. Heretofore the Crescent City has rejoiced in brilliant seasons, both the French and Americans uniting in subscriptions sufficient to bring to them artists of unrivaled talent and culture. But opera entailed too heavy an expense, when the people who usually supported it were prostrate under the hands of plunderers, and a comedy company from the Paris theatres took its place upon the lyric stage. The French Opera House is a handsomely arranged building of modern construction, at the corner of Bourbon and Toulouse streets. The interior is elegantly decorated, and now during the season of six months the *salle* is nightly visited by hundreds of the subscribers, who take tickets for the whole season, and by the city's floating population. Between each act of the pieces all the men in the theatre rise, stalk out, puff cigarettes, and sip iced raspberry-water and absinthe in the cafés, returning in a long procession just as the curtain rises again; while the ladies receive the visits of friends in the *loges* or in the private boxes, which they often occupy four evenings in the week. The New Orleans public, both French and American, possesses excellent theatrical taste, and is severely critical, especially in opera. It is difficult to find a Creole family of any pretensions in which music is not cultivated in large degree.

People in the French quarter very generally speak both prevailing languages, while the majority of the American residents do not affect the French. The Gallic children all speak English, and in the street-plays of the boys, as in their conversation, French and English idioms are strangely mingled. American boys call birds, fishes and animals by corrupted French names, handed down through seventy years of perversion, and a dreadful threat on the part of Young America is, that he will "mallerroo" you, which seems to hint that our old French friend *malheureux*, "unhappy," has, with other words, undergone corruption. When an American boy wishes his comrade to make his kite fly higher, he says, *poussez!* just as the French boy does, and so on *ad infinitum.*

Any stranger who remains in the French quarter over Sunday will be amazed at the great number of funeral processions. It would seem, indeed, as if death came uniformly near the end of the week in order that people might be laid away on the Sabbath. The cemeteries, old and new, rich and poor, are scattered throughout the city, and most of them present an extremely beautiful appearance—the white tombs nestling among the dark-green foliage.

It would be difficult to dig a grave of the ordinary depth in the "Louisiana

"The old French and Spanish cemeteries present long streets of cemented walls."

lowlands" without coming to water; and, consequently, burials in sealed tombs above ground are universal. The old French and Spanish cemeteries present long streets of cemented walls, with apertures into which once were thrust the noble and good of the land, as if they were put into ovens to be baked; and one may still read queer inscriptions, dated away back in the middle of the eighteenth century. Great numbers of the monuments both in the old and new cemeteries are very imposing; and, one sees every day, as in all Catholic communities, long processions of mourning relatives carrying flowers to place on the spot where their loved and lost are entombed; or catches a glimpse of some black-robed figure sitting motionless before a tomb. The St. Louis Cemetery is fine, and many dead are even better housed in it than they were in life. The St. Patrick, Cypress Grove, Firemen's, Odd Fellows, and Jewish cemeteries, in the American quarter, are filled with richly-wrought tombs, and traversed by fine, tree-planted avenues.

The St. Louis Hotel is one of the most imposing monuments of the French quarter, as well as one of the finest hotels in the United States. It was originally built to combine a city exchange, hotel, bank, ball-rooms, and private stores. The rotunda, metamorphosed into a dining-hall, is one of the most beautiful in this country, and the great inner circle of the dome is richly frescoed with allegorical scenes and busts of eminent Americans, from the pencils of Canova and Pinoli. The immense ball-room is also superbly decorated. The St. Louis Hotel was very nearly destroyed by fire in 1840, but in less than two years was restored to its original splendor. On the eastern and western sides of Jackson Square are the Pontalba buildings, large and not especially handsome brick structures, erected by the Countess Pontalba, many years ago. Chartres street, and all the avenues contributing to it, are thor-

The St. Louis Hotel — New Orleans.

oughly French in character; cafés, wholesale stores, pharmacies, shops for articles of luxury, all bear evidence of Gallic taste.

Every street in the old city has its legend, either humorous or tragical; and each building which confesses to an hundred years has memories of foreign domination hovering about it. The elder families speak with bated breath and touching pride of their "ancestor who came with Bienville," or with such and such Spanish Governors; and many a name among those of the Creoles has descended untarnished to its present possessors through centuries of valor and adventurous achievement.

III.

THE CARNIVAL—THE FRENCH MARKETS.

CARNIVAL keeps its hold upon the people along the Gulf shore, despite the troubles, vexations, and sacrifices to which they have been forced to submit since the social revolution began. White and black join in its

The Carnival—"White and Black join in its masquerading."

masquerading, and the Crescent City rivals Naples in the beauty and richness of its displays. Galveston has caught the infection, and every year the King of the Carnival adds a city to the domain loyal to him. The saturnalia practiced before the entry into Lent are the least bit practical, because Americans find it impossible to lay aside business utterly even on *Mardi-Gras*. The device of the advertiser pokes its ugly face into the very heart of the masquerade, and brings base reality, whose hideous features, outlined under his domino, put a host of sweet illusions to flight.

The Carnival in New Orleans was organized in 1827, when a number of young Creole gentlemen, who had recently returned from Paris, formed a street-procession of maskers. It did not create a profound sensation—was considered the work of mad wags; and the festival languished until 1837, when there was a fine parade, which was succeeded by another still finer in 1839. From two o'clock in the afternoon until sunset of Shrove Tuesday, drum and fife, valve and trumpet, rang in the streets, and hundreds of maskers cut furious antics, and made day hideous. Thereafter, from 1840 to 1852, Mardi-Gras festival had varying popularity—such of the townspeople as had the money to spend now and then organizing a very fantastic and richly-dressed rout of mummers. At the old Orleans Theatre, balls of princely splendor were given; Europeans even came to join in the New World's Carnival, and wrote home enthusiastic accounts of it. In 1857 the "Mistick Krewe of Comus," a private organization of New Orleans gentlemen, made their *début*, and gave to the festivities a lustre which, thanks to their continued efforts, has never since quitted it. In 1857 the "Krewe" appeared in the guise of supernatural and mythological characters, and flooded the town with gods and demons, winding up the occasion with a grand ball at the Gaiety Theatre; previous to which they appeared in tableaux representing the "Tartarus" of the ancients, and Milton's "Paradise Lost." In 1858 this brilliant coterie of maskers renewed the enchantments of Mardi-Gras, by exhibiting the gods and goddesses of high Olympus and of the fretful sea, and again gave a series of brilliant tableaux. In 1859 they pictured the revels of the four great English holidays, May Day, Midsummer Eve, Christmas and Twelfth Night. In 1860 they illustrated American history in a series of superb groups of living statues mounted on moving pedestals. In 1861 they delighted the public with "Scenes from Life"—Childhood, Youth, Manhood and Old Age; and the ball at the Varieties Theatre was preceded by a series of grandiose tableaux which exceeded all former efforts. Then came the war; maskers threw aside their masks; but, in 1866, after the agony of the long struggle, Comus once more assembled his forces, and the transformations which Milton attributed to the sly spirit himself were the subject of the display. The wondering gazers were shown how Comus,

> " Deep-skilled in all his mother's witcheries,
> By sly enticement gives his baneful cup,
> With many murmurs mixed, whose pleasing poison
> The visage quite transforms of him that drinks,
> And the inglorious likeness of a beast
> Fixes instead."

In 1867 Comus became Epicurean, and blossomed into a walking bill of fare, the maskers representing everything in the various courses and *entrées* of a gourmand's dinner, from oysters and sherry to the *omelette brûlée*, the Kirsch and Curaçoa. A long and stately array of bottles, dishes of meats and vegetables, and desserts, moved through the streets, awakening saturnalian laughter wherever it passed. In 1868 the Krewe presented a procession and tableaux from "Lalla Rookh;" in 1869, the "Five Senses;" and in 1870, the "History of Louisaina;" when old Father Mississippi himself, De Soto and his fellow-discoverers, the soldiers, adventurers, cavaliers, Jesuits, French, Spanish, and American Governors, were all paraded before the amazed populace. In 1871, King Comus and his train presented picturesque groupings from Spenser's "Faery Queene;" in 1872, from Homer's "Tale of Troy;" and in 1873 detailed the "Darwinian Development of the Species" from earliest beginnings to the gorilla, and thence to man. The Krewe of Comus has always paid the expenses of these displays itself, and has issued invitations only to as many people as could be accommodated within the walls of the theatre to witness the tableaux. It is composed of one hundred members, who are severally sworn to conceal their identity from all outsiders, and who have thus far succeeded admirably in accomplishing this object. The designs for their masks are made in New Orleans, and the costumes are manufactured from them in Paris yearly. In 1870 appeared the "Twelfth-Night Revelers"—who yearly celebrate the beautiful anniversary of the visit of the wise men of the East to the manger of the Infant Saviour. In 1870 the pageants of this organization were inaugurated by

"The coming of Rex, most puissant King of Carnival." [Page 41.]

"The Lord of Misrule and his Knights;" in 1871, "Mother Goose's Tea Party" was given; in 1872, a group of creations of artists and poets and visionaries, from lean Don Quixote to fat Falstaff, followed; and in 1873 the birds were represented, in a host of fantastic and varied tableaux.

Another feature has been added to the festivities, one which promises in time to be most attractive of all. It is the coming of Rex, most puissant King of

"The Bœuf-Gras—the fat ox—is led in the procession."   [Page 42.]

Carnival. This amiable dignitary, depicted as a venerable man, with snow-white hair and beard, but still robust and warrior-like, made his first appearance on the Mississippi shores in 1872, and issued his proclamations through newspapers and upon placards, commanding all civil and military authorities to show subservience to him during his stay in "our good city of New Orleans." Therefore, yearly, when the date of the recurrence of Mardi-Gras has been fixed, the mystic King issues his proclamation, and is announced as having arrived at New York, or whatever other port seemeth good. At once thereafter, and daily, the papers teem with reports of his progress through the country, interspersed with anecdotes of his heroic career, which is supposed to have lasted for many centuries. The court report is usually conceived somewhat in the style of the following paragraph, supposed to be an anecdote told at the "palace" by an "old gray-headed sentinel:"

"Another incident, illustrating the King's courageous presence of mind, was related by the veteran. While sojourning at Auch (this was several centuries ago), a wing of the palace took fire, the whole staircase was in flames, and in the highest story was a feeble old woman, apparently cut off from any means of escape. His Majesty offered two thousand francs to any one who would save her from destruction, but no one presented himself. The King did not stop to deliberate; he wrapped his robes closely about him, called for a wet cloth —which he threw aside—then rushed to his carriage, and drove rapidly to the theatre, where he passed the evening listening to the singing of 'If ever I cease to love.'"

This is published seriously in the journals, next to the news and editorial paragraphs; and yearly, at one o'clock on the appointed day, the King, accompanied by Warwick, Earl-Marshal

"When Rex and his train enter the queer old streets, the balconies are crowded with spectators." [Page 43.]

of the Empire, and by the Lord High Admiral, who is always depicted as suffering untold pangs from gout, arrives on Canal street, surrounded by troops of horse and foot, fantastically dressed, and followed by hundreds of maskers. Sometimes he comes up the river in a beautiful barge and lands amid thunderous salutes from the shipping at the wharves. This parade, which is gradually becoming one of the important features of the Carnival, is continued through all the principal streets of the city. The Bœuf-Gras—the fat ox —is led in the procession. The animal is gayly decorated with flowers and garlands. Mounted on pedestals extemporized from cotton-floats are dozens of allegorical groups, and the masks, although not so rich and costly as those of Comus and his crew, are quite as varied and mirth-provoking. The costumes of the King and his suite are gorgeous; and the troops of the United States, disguised as privates of Arabian artillery and as Egyptian spahis, do escort-duty to his Majesty. Rumor hath it, even, that on one occasion, the ladies of New Orleans presented a flag to an officer of the troops of "King Rex" (sic), little suspecting that it was there-after to grace the Federal barracks. Thus the Carnival has its pleasant waggeries and surprises.

Froissart thought the English amused themselves sadly; and indeed, com-paring the Carnival in Louisiana with the Carnival in reckless Italy, one might say that the Americans masquerade grimly. There is but little of that wild luxuriance of fun in the streets of New Orleans which has made Italian cities so famous; people go to their sports with an air of pride, but not of all-pervading enjoyment. In the French quarter, when Rex and his train enter the queer old streets, there are shoutings, chaffings, and dancings, the children chant little couplets on Mardi-Gras; and the balconies are crowded with spec-tators. But the negroes make a somewhat sorry show in the masking: their every-day garb is more picturesque.

Carnival culminates at night, after Rex and the "day procession" have retired.

"The joyous, grotesque maskers appear upon the ball-room floor." [Page 44.]

Thousands of people assemble in dense lines along the streets included in the published route of march; Canal street is brilliant with illumination, and swarms of persons occupy every porch, balcony, house-top, pedestal, carriage and mule-car. Then comes the train of Comus, and torch-bearers, disguised in *outré* masks, light up the way. After the round through the great city is completed, the reflection of the torch-light on the sky dies away, and the Krewe betake themselves to the Varieties Theatre, and present tableaux before the ball opens.

This theatre, during the hour or two preceding the Mardi-Gras ball, offers one of the loveliest sights in Christendom. From floor to ceiling, the parquet, dress-circle and galleries are one mass of dazzling toilets, none but ladies being given seats. White robes, delicate faces, dark, flashing eyes, luxuriant folds of glossy hair, tiny, faultlessly-gloved hands,— such is the vision that one sees through his opera-glass.

Delicious music swells softly on the perfumed air; the tableaux wax and wane like kaleidoscopic effects, when suddenly the curtain rises, and the joyous, grotesque maskers appear upon the ball-room floor. They dance; gradually ladies and their cavaliers leave all parts of the galleries, and come to join them; and then,

"No sleep till morn, when youth and pleasure meet,
To chase the glowing hours with flying feet."

Meantime, the King of the Carnival holds a levée and dancing party at another place; all the theatres and public halls are delivered up to the votaries of Terpsichore; and the fearless, who are willing to usher in Lent with sleepless eyes, stroll home in the glare of the splendid Southern sunrise, yearly vowing that each Mardi-Gras has surpassed its predecessor.

Business in New Orleans is not only entirely suspended on Shrove Tuesday (Mardi-Gras), but the Carnival authorities have absolute control of the city. They direct the police; they arrest the mayor, and he delivers to them the keys, while the chief functionaries of the city government declare their allegiance to "Rex;" addresses are delivered, and the processions move. The theatres are thrown open to the public, and woe betide the unhappy manager who dares refuse the order of the King to this effect. On one occasion a well-known actor arrived in the city during the festivities to fulfill an engagement, but as the managers of the theatre at which he was to act had refused to honor the King's command for free admission to all, the actor was at once arrested, taken to the "den" of the Earl-Marshal, and there kept a close prisoner until a messenger arrived to say that the recalcitrant manager had at last "acknowledged the corn." The violet is the royal flower; the imperial banner is of green and purple, with a white crown in the centre; and the anthem of the mystic monarch is, "If ever I cease to love." The accumulation of costumes and armor, all of which are historically accurate, is about to result in the establishment of a valuable museum.

The artist's pencil has reproduced in these pages one of the many comical incidents which enliven the Carnival tide, and calls his life sketch " Beauty and

the Beast." From the gallery of the Varieties Theatre, many bright eyes are in vain endeavoring to pierce the disguise under which a fashionable member of the Comus Krewe parades before their gaze.

From early morning until nightfall the same quaint, distorted street-cries which one hears in foreign cities ring through the streets of New Orleans; and in the French quarter they are mirth-provoking, under their guise of Creole *patois*. The Sicilian fruit-sellers also make their mellifluous dialect heard loudly; and the streets always resound to the high-pitched voice of some negro who is rehearsing his griefs or joys in the most theatrical manner. Negro-beggars encumber the steps of various banks and public edifices, sitting for hours together with open, outstretched hands, almost too lazy to close them over the few coins the passers-by bestow. A multitude of youthful darkies, who have no visible aim in existence but to sport in the sun, abound in the American quarter, apparently well fed and happy. The mass of the negroes are reck-

"Many bright eyes are in vain endeavoring to pierce the disguise."

"The French market at sunrise on Sunday morning."

lessly improvident, living, as in all
cities, crowded together in ill-built
and badly-ventilated cabins, the
ready victims for almost any fell
disease.

Next to the river traffic, the New
Orleans markets are more picturesque than anything else apper-
taining to the city. They lie near
the levée, and, as markets, are indeed clean, commodious, and always
well stocked. But they have another and an especial charm to the
traveler from the North, or to him
who has never seen their great
counterparts in Europe. The
French market at sunrise on Sunday morning is the perfection of
vivacious traffic. In gazing upon
the scene, one can readily imagine
himself in some city beyond the
seas. From the stone houses, balconied, and fanciful in roof and
window, come hosts of plump and
pretty young negresses, chatting in
their droll *patois* with monsieur the
fish-dealer, before his wooden bench,
or with the rotund and ever-laugh-
ing madame who sells little piles
of potatoes, arranged on a shelf
like cannon balls at an arsenal, or
chaffering with the fruit-merchant,
while passing under long, hanging
rows of odorous bananas and pine-
apples, and beside heaps of oranges,
whose color contrasts prettily with
the swart or tawny faces of the
purchasers.

During the morning hours of
each day, the markets are veritable
bee-hives of industry; ladies and
servants flutter in and out of the
long passages in endless throngs;
but in the afternoon the stalls are
nearly all deserted. One sees deli-

cious types in these markets; he may wander for months in New Orleans without
meeting them elsewhere.   There is the rich savage face in which the struggle of
Congo with French or Spanish blood is still going on; there is the old French
market-woman, with her irrepressible form, her rosy cheeks, and the bandanna

"Passing under long, hanging rows of bananas and pine-apples."   [Page 46.]

wound about her head, just as one may find her to this day at the Halles
Centrales in Paris; there is the negress of the time of D'Artaguette, renewed in
some of her grandchildren; there is the plaintive-looking Sicilian woman, who
has been bullied all the morning by rough negroes and rougher white men as
she sold oranges; and there is her dark, ferocious-looking husband, who handles
his cigarette as if he were strangling an enemy.

In a long passage, between two of the market buildings, where hundreds
of people pass hourly, sits a silent Louisiana Indian woman, with a sack of
gumbo spread out before her, and with eyes downcast, as if expecting harsh
words rather than purchasers.

Entering the clothes market, one finds lively Gallic versions of the Hebrew
female tending shops where all articles are labeled at such extraordinarily low
rates that the person who manufactured them must have given them away; quavering old men, clad in rusty black, who sell shoe-strings and cheap cravats,
but who have hardly vitality enough to keep the flies off from themselves, not
to speak of waiting on customers; villainous French landsharks, who have
eyes as sharp for the earnings of the fresh-water sailor as ever had a Gotham

shanghai merchant for those of a salt-water tar; mouldy old dames, who look
daggers at you if you venture to insist that any article in their stock is not
of finest fabric and quality; and hoarse-voiced, debauched Creole men, who
almost cling to you in the energy of their pleading for purchases. Sometimes, too, a beautiful black-robed girl leans over a counter, displaying her
superbly-moulded arms, as she adjusts her knitting-work. And from each
and every one of the markets the noise rises in such thousand currents of
patois, of French, of English, of good-natured and guttural negro accent,
that one cannot help wondering how it is that buyer and seller ever come
to any understanding at all.

Then there are the flowers! Such marvelous bargains as one can have in
bouquets! Delicate jessamines, modest knots of white roses, glorious orange
blossoms, camelias, red roses, tender pansies, exquisite verbenas, the luscious
and perfect virgin's bower, and the magnolia in its season;—all these are
to be had in the markets for a trivial sum. Sometimes, when a Havana
or a Sicilian vessel is discharging her cargo, fruit boxes are broken open;
and then it is a treat to see swarms of African children hovering about the
tempting piles, from which even the sight of stout cudgels will not frighten
them.

In the winter months the markets are crowded with strangers before six
o'clock every morning. Jaunty maids from New England stroll in the passages,

"One sees delicious types in these markets." [Page 47.]

escorted by pale and querulous invalid fathers, or by spruce young men, who swelter in their thick garments, made to be worn in higher latitudes. While New York or Boston ladies sip coffee in a market-stall, groups of dreamy-eyed negro girls surround them and curiously scan the details of their toilets. Black urchins grin confidingly and solicit alms as the blond Northerner

"In a long passage, between two of the market buildings, sits a silent Louisiana Indian woman." [Page 47.]

saunters by. Perchance the Bostonian may hear a silvery voice, whose owner's face is buried in the depths of a sun-bonnet, exclaim— "There goes a regular Yankee!"

Sailors, too, from the ships anchored in the river, promenade the long passage-ways; the accents of twenty languages are heard; and the childlike, comical French of the negroes rings out above the clamor.

Wagons from the country clatter over the stones; the drivers sing cheerful melodies, interspersed with shouts of caution to pedestrians as they guide their restive horses through the crowds. Stout colored women, with cackling hens dangling from their brawny hands, gravely parade the long aisles; the fish-monger utters an apparently incomprehensible yell, yet brings crowds around him; on his clean block lies the pompano, the prince of Southern waters, which an enthusiastic admirer once described as "a just fish made perfect," or a "translated shad."

Towards noon the clamor ceases, the bustle of traffic is over, and the market-men and women betake themselves to the old cathedral, in whose shadowed aisles they kneel for momentary worship.

"Stout colored women, with cackling hens dangling from their brawny hands."

IV.

THE COTTON TRADE—THE NEW ORLEANS LEVEES.

COTTON furnishes to New Orleans much of its activity and the sinews of its trade. It stamps a town, which would otherwise resemble some decayed but still luxurious European centre, with a commercial aspect. Amer-

"These boats, closely ranged in long rows by the levée."
[Page 52.]

icans and Frenchmen are alike interested in the growth of the crop throughout all the great section drained by the Mississippi and its tributaries. They rush eagerly to the Exchange to read the statements of sales, and rates, and bales on hand; and both are intensely excited when there is a large arrival from some unexpected quarter, or when the telegraph informs them that some packet has sunk, with hundreds of bales on board, while toiling along the currents of the Arkansas or Red rivers.

In the American quarter, during certain hours of the day, cotton is the only subject spoken of; the pavements of all the principal avenues in the vicinity of the Exchange are crowded with smartly-dressed gentlemen, who eagerly discuss crops and values, and who have a perfect mania for preparing and comparing the estimates at the basis of all speculations in the favorite staple; with young Englishmen, whose mouths are filled with the slang of the Liverpool market;

and with the skippers of steamers from all parts of the West and South-west, each worshiping at the shrine of the same god.

From high noon until dark the planter, the factor, the speculator, flit feverishly to and from the portals of the Exchange, and nothing can be heard above the excited hum of their conversation except the sharp voice of the clerk reading the latest telegrams.

New Orleans receives the greater portion of the crop of Louisiana and Mississippi, of North Alabama, of Tennessee, of Arkansas, and Florida. The gross receipts of cotton there amount to about thirty-three and one-third per cent. of the entire production of the country. Despite the abnormal condition of government and society there, the natural tendency is towards a rapid and continuous increase of cotton production in the Gulf States.

But the honor of receiving the Texas crop, doubled, as it soon will be, as the result of increased immigration, favoring climate, and cheap land, will be sharply disputed by Galveston, one of the most ambitious and promising of the Gulf capitals; and the good burghers of New Orleans must look to a speedy completion of their new railways if they wish to cope successfully with the wily and self-reliant Texan.

Judging from the progress of cotton-growing in the past, it will be tremendous in future. In 1824–'25 the cotton crop of the United States was 569,249 bales; in 1830–'31, it ran up to 1,038,000 bales; during '37–'38 it reached as high as 1,800,000 bales; and eleven years later was 2,700,000 bales. In 1859–'60 the country's cotton crop was 4,669,770 bales; in 1860–'61 it dropped to 3,656,000 bales. Then came the war. In the days of slave labor, planters did not make more than a fraction of their present per cent. They themselves attended very little to their crops, leaving nearly everything to the overseers. Cotton raising is now far more popular in the Gulf States than it was before the war, although it has still certain distressing drawbacks, arising from the incomplete organization of labor. The year after the close of the war, 2,193,000 bales were produced, showing that the planters went to work in earnest to retrieve their fallen fortunes. From that time forward labor became better organized, and the production went bravely on. In 1866–'67 it amounted to 1,951,000 bales, of which New Orleans received 780,000; in 1867–'68 to 2,431,000 bales, giving New Orleans 668,000; in 1868–'69 to 2,260,000, 841,000 of which were delivered at New Orleans; in 1869–'70 to 3,114,000, and New Orleans received 1,207,000; in 1870–'71 to 4,347,000, giving the Crescent City 1,548,000; and in 1871–'72 to 2,974,000, more than one-third of which passed through New Orleans. The necessity of a rapid multiplication of railroad and steamboat lines is shown by the fact that more than 150,000 bales of the crop of 1870–'71 remained in the country, at the close of that season, on account of a lack of transportation facilities. From 1866 to 1872, inclusive, the port of New Orleans received 6,114,000 bales, or fully one-third of the entire production of the United States. The receipts from the Red River region alone at New Orleans for 1871–'72, by steamer, were

197,386 bales; for 1870–'71 they amounted to 284,313 bales; and the Ouachita River sent to the metropolis 89,084 bales in 1871–'72, and 151,358 in 1870–'71.

Knowing these statistics, one can hardly wonder at the vast masses of bales on the levée at the landings of the steamers, nor at the numbers of the boats which daily arrive, their sides piled high with cotton. About these boats, closely ranged in long rows by the levée, and seeming like river monsters which have crawled from the ooze to take a little sun, the negroes swarm in crowds, chatting in the broken, colored

"Whenever there is a lull in the work they sink down on the cotton bales."

English characteristic of the river-hand. They are clad in garments which hang in rags from their tawny or coal black limbs. Their huge, naked chests rival in perfection of form the works of Praxiteles and his fellows. Their arms

"Not far from the levée, there is a police court, where they especially delight to lounge."

are almost constantly bent to the task of removing cotton bales, and carrying boxes, barrels, bundles of every conceivable shape and size; but whenever there is a lull in the work they sink down on the cotton bales, clinging to them like lizards to a sunny wall, and croon to themselves, or crack rough and good-natured jokes with one another. Not far from the levée there is a police court, where they especially delight to lounge.

In 1871–'72 (the commercial year extends from September to September) the value of the cotton received at New Orleans was $94,430,000; in 1870–'71 it was $101,000,000; and in 1869–'70 even $120,000,000. The difference in the value of the crops during that period was very great. In 1869–'70 cotton sold for nearly $100 per bale, and in 1870–'71 it had depreciated to an average of $65 per bale. Until the facilities for speedy transportation have been greatly increased, a glut of the market, produced by a successful conduct of the year's labor on the majority of the plantations, will continue to bring prices down.

The whole character of the cotton trade has been gradually changing since the war. Previous to that epoch a large portion of the business was done directly by planters through their merchants; but now that the plantations are mainly worked on shares by the freedmen, the matter has come into the hands of country traders, who give credits to the laborers during the planting seasons, and take their pay in the products of the crop, in harvest time. These speculators then follow to market the cotton which they have thus accumulated in small lots, and look attentively after it until it has been delivered to some responsible purchaser, and they have pocketed the proceeds.

They often pay the planter and his coöperating freedmen a much higher price for cotton than the market quotations seem to warrant; but they always manage to retain a profit, rarely allowing a freedman to find that his season's toil has done more than square his accounts with the acute trader who has meantime supplied him and his family with provisions, clothing, and such articles of luxury as the negro's mind and body crave. Shortly after the war there was trouble between planters and factors; and it is not probable that much, if any, business will hereafter be transacted by the latter directly with the planter, though upon the arrival of the crop in New Orleans the cotton factor becomes the chief authority. Business is largely done between buyer and seller on the basis of a confidence which seems to the casual observer rather reckless, but which custom has made perfectly safe.

The Cotton Exchange of New Orleans sprang into existence in 1870, and merchants and planters were alike surprised that they had not thought its advantages necessary before. It now has three hundred members, and expends thirty thousand dollars annually in procuring the latest commercial intelligence, and maintaining a suite of rooms where the buyer and seller may meet, and which shall be a central bureau of news. The first president of the Exchange was the well-known E. H. Summers, of Hilliard, Summers & Co., of New Orleans; the second and present one is Mr. John Phelps, one of the principal merchants of the city.* The boards of the Exchange are carefully and thoroughly edited, and are always surrounded by a throng of speculators, as well as by the more staid and important of the local merchants. During the busy season, the labor at the Exchange, and in the establishments of all the prominent merchants and factors, is almost incessant.

* The writer takes this occasion to acknowledge his indebtedness to Secretary Hester of the Cotton Exchange of New Orleans, and to Mr. Parker of the *Picayune*, for many interesting details in this connection; to Hon. Charles Gayarré for access to historical portraits; and to Collector Casey and his able deputy, Mr. Champlin, for reference to official statistics.

In the months between January and May, when the season is at its height, clerks and patrons work literally night and day; so that when the most exhausting period of the year arrives, finding themselves thoroughly overworked, they leave the sweltering lowlands, and fly to the North for rest and cool refuge. New Orleans is accused of a lack of energy, but her cotton merchants are more energetic than the mass of Northern traders and speculators, working, as they do, with feverish impulse early and late.   One well-known cotton factor, whose transactions amount to nearly $12,000,000 yearly, gets to his desk, during the season, long before daylight,—and that, in the climate of the Gulf States, comes wonderfully early.

The railroad development of the South since the war has metamorphosed the whole cotton trade of New Orleans.   Cotton which once arrived in market in May now reaches the factor during the preceding December or January.   The Jackson and Mobile roads did much to effect this great change, and when rail communication with Texas is secured, it will bring with it another marked difference in the same direction.

The sugar interest once left the most money in New Orleans; now cotton is the main stay.   It is estimated that each bale which passes through the market leaves about seven dollars and fifty cents.   Most of the business with England is done by cable, and the telegraph bills of many prominent firms are enormous.   The Board of Arbitration and Board of Appeals of the Exchange make all decisions, and have power to expel any unruly member.

The Louisiana capitalists have given some attention to the manufacture of cotton, and the factories which have already been established are clearing from eighteen to twenty-five per cent. per annum.   There are two of these factories in New Orleans, each of which consumes about one thousand bales yearly; a third is located at Beauregard, and a fourth in the penitentiary at Baton Rouge.   The consumption by all the Southern cotton mills, during the three years closing with 1872 amounted to two hundred and ninety-one thousand bales, and is increasing at a rapid rate.   Each new railway connection enlarges the city's claims as a cotton mart.   The Jackson Railroad, during the commercial year 1871–'72, brought into it forty thousand bales, thus adding about four million dollars to the trade.

When the levées are crowded with the busy negroes, unloading cotton from the steamboats, the apparent confusion is enough to turn a stranger's head; yet the order is perfect.   Each of the steamers has its special stall, into which it swings with grace and precision, to the music of a tolling bell and an occasional hoarse scream from the whistle; and the instant the cables are made fast and the gangways swung down, the "roustabouts" are on board, and busily wheeling the variously branded bales to the spaces allotted them on the wharves.

The negroes who man the boats running up and down the Mississippi are not at all concerned in the discharging of cargoes, being relieved from that duty by the regular wharfmen.   There is a rush upon the pile of bales fifty-feet high on the capacious lower deck of a Greenville and Vicksburg, a Red River, or a Ouachita packet, and the monument to the industry of a dozen planters vanishes as if by magic. Myriads of little flags, each ornamented with different devices, flutter from various points along the wharves; and as the blacks wheel the cotton past the "tally-man" standing near the steamer's gangways, he notes the mark on each bale, and in a loud voice calls out to him who is wheeling it the name of the sign on the flag under which it is to rest until sold and removed. While the bales remain on the levées, the cotton thieves now and then steal a pound or two of the precious staple.

"The cotton thieves."

This army of "roustabouts" is an ebony-breasted, tough-fisted, bullet-headed, toiling, awkward mass ; but it does wonders at work. It is generally good-humored, even when it grumbles; is prodigal of rude, cheerful talk and raillery; has no secrets or jealousies; is helpful, sympathetic, and familiar. It leaps to its work with a kind of concentrated effort, and, as soon as the task is done, relapses into its favorite condition of slouch.

Neither the sharp voices of the skippers, nor the harsh orders of the masters of the gangs, nor the cheery and mirth-provoking responses of the help, mingled with the sibilations of escaping steam, the ringing of countless bells, and the moving and rumbling of drays, carts and steam-cars can drown or smother the jocund notes of the negro's song. His arms and limbs and head keep time to the harmony, as he trundles the heavy bale along the planks.

When he pauses from his work, you may see his

"There is the old apple and cake woman." [Page 56.]

dusky wife or daughter, in a long, closely-fitting, trim calico gown, and a
starched gingham sun-bonnet, giving him his dinner from a large tin pail; or
you may find him patronizing one of the grimy old dames, each of whom
looks wicked enough to be a Voudou Queen, who are always seated at quiet
corners with a basket of coarse but well-prepared food.   Small merchants
thrive along the levée.   There is the old apple and cake woman, black and
fifty, blundering about the wharf's edge; there is the antiquated and moss-
grown old man who cowers all day beside a little cart filled with cans of ice-
cream; there is the Sicilian fruit-seller, almost as dark visaged as a negro;
there is the coffee and sausage man, toward whom, many a time daily, black
and toil-worn hands are eagerly outstretched; and bordering on Canal street,

"The Sicilian fruit-seller."

all along the walks leading from
the wharf, are little booths filled
with negroes in the supreme stages
of shabbiness, who feast on chicken
and mysterious compounds of
vegetables, and drink alarming
draughts of "whiskey at five cents
a glass."   The sailor on the Mississippi is much like his white
brother of more stormy seas, who
drinks up his wages, gets penitent,
confesses his poverty, and begs
again for work.

At high water, the juvenile
population of New Orleans perches
on the beams of the wharves, and
enjoys a little quiet fishing.   For
two or three miles down the
river, from the foot of Canal street,
the levées are encumbered with
goods of every conceivable description.   Then the landings cease,
and, almost level with the bank on which you walk, flows the grand, impetuous
stream which has sometimes swept all before it on the lowlands where the
fair Louisiana capital lies, and transformed the whole section between Lake
Pontchartrain and the present channel into an eddying sea.

Up the river, commerce of the heavy and substantial order has monopolized
the space, and you may note in a morning the arrival of a hundred thousand
bushels of grain, on a single one of the capacious tow-boats of the Mississippi
Valley Transportation Company.   Merchants even boast that the port can supply,
to outgoing ships, that quantity daily from the West; and that the lack of
transportation facilities often causes an accumulation of three hundred thousand
bushels in the New Orleans storehouses.   Up and down the levées run the branch
lines of the Jackson, the Louisiana and Texas, and the New Orleans, Mobile and

Texas railways, and teams drive recklessly on the same tracks on which incoming trains are drawn by rapidly moving locomotives. The freight depots, the reception sheds and the warehouses are crammed with jostling, sweating, shouting, black and white humanity; and, in the huge granite Custom-House, even politics

has to give way, from time to time, before the torrents of business. At night a great silence falls on the levée. Only the footsteps of the watchmen, or of the polite, but consequential negro policeman, are heard on the well-worn planks. Now and then an eye of fire, the lamp of an incoming

"At high water, the juvenile population perches on the beams of the wharves, and enjoys a little quiet fishing." [Page 56.]

steamer, peers out of the obscurity shrouding the river, or glides athwart the moonlight, and three hoarse screams announce an arrival. Along the shore, a hundred lights twinkle in the water, and turn the commonest surroundings into

"The polite, but consequential negro policeman."

enchantment. There is little sign of life from any of the steamers at the docks, though here and there a drunken river-hand blunders along the wharves singing some dialect catch; but with early sun-peep comes once more the roar, the rush, the rattle!

The coastwise trade is one of the important elements of the commerce of New Orleans. Of the total tonnage entered and cleared from that port during the fiscal year 1871–'72, fifty-four per cent., or 1,226,000 tons, belonged to this trade, representing something like $125,000,000; while the foreign trade was only $109,000,000 for the same period. During the commercial year ending September 30, 1872, two thousand five hundred and nine steamboats, comprising a tonnage of 3,500,000 tons burthen, arrived at the port. The value of the principal articles brought in by these boats was $160,000,000, the up-river cargoes amounting to about $90,000,000. It is, therefore, fair to estimate the net value of this commerce at nearly $400,000,000 per annum.

Now let us take the actual figures of the commerce of the Gulf for one year: that from September, 1871, to September, 1872.

Coastwise trade	$135,000,000
Galveston trade	25,000,000
Mobile trade	24,000,000
Exports from New Orleans	90,800,000
Imports to New Orleans	18,700,000
Cuban trade	150,000,000
Porto Rico	25,000,000
Mexico	35,000,000

This, exclusive of the Darien and Central American trade, now so rapidly increasing, makes a grand total of more than five hundred millions of dollars.*

* The collection district, of which New Orleans is the chief port, embraces all the shores, inlets, and waters within the State of Louisiana east of the Atchafalaya, not including the waters of the Teche, of the Ohio river, or the several rivers and creeks emptying into it, or of the Mississippi or any of its tributaries except those within the State of Mississippi. The district extends on the coast from the western boundary of Mississippi, on Lake Borgne, to the Atchafalaya; and the ports of delivery, to which merchandise can be shipped under transportation bond, are as follows: Bayou St. John and Lake Port, in Louisiana; Memphis, Nashville, Chattanooga and Knoxville, in Tennessee; Hickman and Louisville, in Kentucky; Tuscumbia, in Alabama; Cincinnati, in Ohio; Madison, New Albany and Evansville, in Indiana; Cairo, Alton, Quincy, Peoria and Galena, in Illinois; Dubuque, Burlington and Keokuk, in Iowa; Hannibal and St. Louis, in Missouri, and Leavenworth, in Kansas. The shipment of merchandise, under transportation bond, has increased steadily from $1,736,981 in 1866 to $5,502,427 in 1872; the value of merchandise imported, from $10,878,365 to $20,006,363; and domestic exports, from $89,002,141 to $95,970,592, in the same period. The total value of the merchandise imported during those years is $102,305,014; the total of domestic exports amounted to $608,871,013, and the whole amount of revenue collected, to $35,140,906.

The receipts from customs at New Orleans for 1872 were very much diminished by the large shipments of goods in bond to the interior cities of Memphis, Nashville, Louisville, Cincinnati, Cairo, St. Louis, Chicago, etc., the duties on which were collected at those ports respectively. From 1866 to 1872 inclusive, the movement of the port included 2,852 foreign vessels, with a tonnage of 1,547,747 tons, and 1,773 American ships, with a tonnage of 1,100,492. The revenue receipts at New Orleans have been largely diminished by the removal of the duties on coffee—the importations of that article during the seven years following 1866 amounting to 155,953,213 pounds, valued at $16,511,602. The magnitude of the trade of the port may also be well illustrated by showing the importations of sugar and railroad iron for the same time. Of the former article there were imported 263,918,978 pounds, worth $14,531,960, and of the latter 480,043 tons, valued at $15,299,642.

It will be seen that the imports are small in quantity as compared with the exports when the cotton is counted in—the imports amounting to only about one-seventh of the exports; but this ratio will be much reduced in time, as New Orleans becomes a more economical port. Five steamship lines now make the city their point of departure. Three of these, the Liverpool Southern, the Mississippi and Dominion, and the State Line Steamship Company, communicate directly with Liverpool, while other lines are projected.

V

THE CANALS AND THE LAKE—THE AMERICAN QUARTER.

NEW ORLEANS is built on land from two to four feet below the level of the Mississippi river at high water mark. It fronts on a great bend in the stream in the form of a semicircle, whence it takes its appellation of the "Crescent City," and stretches back to the borders of Lake Pontchartrain, which lies several feet below the level of the Mississippi, and has an outlet on the Gulf of Mexico. The rain-fall, the sewerage of the city, and the surplus water from the river, are drained into the canals which traverse New Orleans, and are thence carried into the lake. The two principal canals, known as the Old and New Basins, are navigable; steamers of considerable size run through them and the lake to the Gulf, and thence along the Southern Atlantic coast; and schooners and barks, laden with lumber and produce, are towed in and out by mules. The city is divided into drainage districts, in each of which large pumping machines are constantly worked to keep down the encroaching water. Were it not

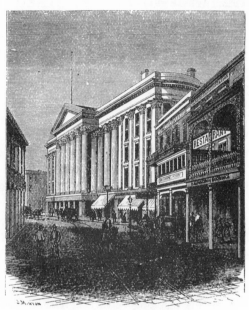

The St. Charles Hotel—New Orleans. [Page 61.]

for the canals, and the drainage system, the low-lying city would, after a heavy rain, be partially submerged. A fine levée extends for four and a-half miles along the front of Lake Pontchartrain, making a grand driveway; and as a complement to this improvement, it is expected that in a few years the cypress swamps will be filled up, and the lake front will be studded with mansions. The building of this levée was an imperative necessity, the action of the lake making the perfecting of the city's present system of drainage impossible otherwise.

On Sundays the shell road leading northward from Canal street past the Metairie and Oakland Parks, by the side of the New Basin, is crowded with teams, and the restaurants, half hidden by foliage, echo to boisterous merriment. But on a week day it is almost deserted. Schooners on the canal glide lazily along; ragged negro boys sit on the banks, sleepily fishing; while the intense green of the leaves is beautifully reflected from the water. Arrived near the lake, you catch a view of dark water in the canal in the foreground, with a gayly-painted sail-boat lying close to the bank; an ornamental gateway just

beyond; a flock of goats browsing at the roadside; and afar off, a white light-house standing lonely on a narrow point of land. You may step into a sail-boat at the lake, and let a brown, barefooted Creole fisherman sail you down to the pier where the railroad from New Orleans terminates; then back again, up the Bayou St. John, until he lands you near the walls of the "old Spanish fort." There you

The New Basin. [Page 59.]

may find a summer-house, an orchard, and a rose-garden. From the balcony you can see a long pier running into the lake; the sun's gold on the rippling water; the oranges in the trees below; the group of sailors tugging at the cable of their schooner; the pretty cluster of cottages near the levée's end; the cannon, old and dismounted, lying half-buried under the grasses; the wealth of peach-blossoms in the bent tree near the parapet; and a bevy of bare-legged children playing about their mother, as she sits on the sward, cutting rose-stems, and twisting blossoms into bouquets.

As evening deepens, you sail home, and, in the dining-room of the restaurant near the canal, look out upon the passing barges and boats gliding noiselessly townward; hear the shouts of festive parties as they wander on the levée, or along the cypress-girt shore; hear the boatmen singing catches; or watch a blood-red moon as it rises slowly, and casts an enchanted light over the burnished surface of the water-way.

A promenade on Canal street is quite as picturesque as any in the French quarter. There is the negro boot-black sitting in the sun, with his own splay-feet on his blacking-block; and there are the bouquet-sellers, black and white, ranged at convenient corners, with baskets filled with breast knots of violets, and a world of rose-buds, camelias, and other rich blossoms. The newsboy cries his wares, vociferous as his brother of Go-tham. The "roust-abouts" from the levée, clad in striped trowsers and flannel shirts, and in coats and hats which they seem to have slept in for a century, hasten homeward to

The old Spanish Fort.

dinner, with their cotton-hooks clenched in their brawny hands. The ropers for gambling-houses—one of the curses of New Orleans—haunt each conspicuous corner, and impudently scan passers-by.

From twelve to two the American ladies monopolize Canal street. Hundreds of lovely brunettes may be seen, in carriages, in cars, in couples with mamma, or accompanied by the tall, dark, thin Southern youth, attired in black broadcloth, slouch hat, and irreproachable morning gloves. The confectioners' shops are crowded with dainty little women, who have the Italian rage for *confetti*, and the sugared cakes of the pastry-cook vanish like morning dew. The *matinées* at the American theatres, as at the French, begin at noon; and at three or half-past three, twice a week, the tide of beauty floods Canal, St. Charles, Carondelet, Rampart, and other streets. At evening, Canal street is very quiet, and hardly seems the main thoroughfare of a great city.

The University of Louisiana — New Orleans. [Page 62.]

The American quarter of New Orleans is superior to the French in width of avenue, in beauty of garden and foliage; but to-day many streets there are grass-grown, and filled with ruts and hollows. In that section, not inaptly designated the "Garden City," there are many spacious houses surrounded by gardens, parks and orchards; orange-trees grow in the yards, and roses clamber in at the windows. The homes of well-to-do Americans, who have been able to keep about them some appearance of comfort since the war, are found mostly on Louisiana and Napoleon avenues and on Prytania, Plaquemine, Chestnut, Camp, Jena, Cadiz, Valence, Bordeaux, and St. Charles streets. Along St. Charles street, near Canal, are the famous St. Charles Hotel; the Academy of Music, and the St. Charles Theatre, both well

The Theatres of New Orleans

appointed theatrical edifices; and the Masonic, City, and Exposition Hails. Opposite the City Hall—one of the noblest public buildings in New Orleans, built of granite and white marble, in Grecian Ionic style—is Lafayette Square. On its south-western side is the First Presbyterian Church; and at

its southern extremity the Odd Fellows' Hall, where the famous McEnery Legislature held its sessions. On Common street, one of the business thoroughfares of the town, is the University of Louisiana. The city is making its most rapid growth in the direction of Carrollton, a pretty suburb, filled with pleasant homes, and within three-quarters of an hour's ride of Canal street.

Canal street is bordered by shops of no mean pretensions, and by many handsome residences; it boasts of Christ Church, the Varieties Theatre, the noted restaurant of Moreau, the statue of Henry Clay, a handsome fountain, and the new Custom-House. The buildings are not crowded together, as in New York and Paris; they are usually two or three stories high, and along the first

Christ Church — New Orleans.

story runs a porch which serves as a balcony to those dwelling above, and as protection from sun and rain to promenaders below. The banks, insurance offices, and wholesale stores fronting on Canal street are elegant and modern, an improvement in the general tone of business architecture having taken place since the war. Under the *régime* of slavery, little or no attention was paid to

fine buildings; exterior decoration, save that which the magnificent foliage of the country gave, was entirely disregarded. Now, however, the citizens begin to take pride in their public edifices.

The bugbear of yellow fever has, for many years, been a drawback to the prosperity of New Orleans. The stories told of its fearful ravages during some of its visitations are startling; but there is hope that the complete and thorough draining of the city will prevent the repetition of such scenes and consequent panics in future. The inhabitants who remain in the city throughout the summer are, in ordinary seasons, as healthy a people as can be found in the United States. Although a lifetime spent in the soft

The Canal street Fountain — New Orleans.

climate of Louisiana may render an organism somewhat more languid and effeminate than that of the Northerner, there are few of the wretched chronic complaints, terminating in lingering illness and painful death, which result from the racking conflict of extremes in the New England climate.

The Charity Hospital— New Orleans.

Many Louisianians disbelieve in the efficacy of quarantine against the yellow fever. They say that, during seventy years, from 1796 to 1870, they had quarantine nineteen times, and in each of those nineteen years the dread fever at least showed its ugly face. The war quarantine, they assert, failed every year of the four that it was in operation. The Charity Hospital has received cases of yellow fever annually for the last fifty years. Only in two cases, however, where the proper quarantine precautions had been taken, had the disease assumed the proportions of a general plague. The general impression is that the fever will certainly carry off unacclimated persons; but physicians in the hospitals assert that there has been no evidence of the transmission of the fever in hospital wards to unacclimated people; and as they have watched cases for weeks after exposure, their testimony should be considered valuable. Previous to the war, no proper attention had been paid to drainage and cleanliness of streets in New Orleans; and it is the opinion of many good authorities that a careful examining of all vessels arriving from foreign ports, and in town a sanitary police of the most rigorous character, will soon make the fever a rare and not a very dangerous visitor.

The Charity Hospital is one of the noblest buildings in the city, and the people of New Orleans have good reason to be proud of it. Dating from the earliest foundation of the city, it has never closed its doors save when acci-

The old Maison de Santé —New Orleans. [Page 64.]

dent has compelled it to do so temporarily.   From the time when the Ursuline
nuns took charge of it under Bienville until now it has been one of the most
beneficent charities in the country.   No question of race, nationality, religion,
sex or character hinders from admission a single applicant for repose and heal-

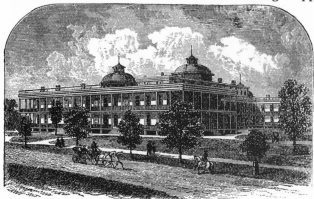

ing within the walls; and
the best medical talent is
placed at the disposition
of the poorest and meanest
of citizens.   The Asylum
of St. Elizabeth, and the
male and female orphan
asylums, are also note-
worthy charities.

The *Maison de Santé*,
long one of the most noted
infirmaries of New Orleans,
is now deserted, and like

The United States Marine Hospital—New Orleans.

the United States Marine Hospital, which has not been used since 1860, is
rapidly falling into decay.   During the war the fine United States Hospital, which once stood at MacDonough's, on the river opposite New Orleans,
was destroyed.

The Protestant churches in the American quarter are good specimens of
modern church architecture.   The oldest of the Episcopal organizations, dating
back to 1806, is Christ Church, on Canal street, founded by Bishop Chase.
This church was the germ of Protestantism in the South-west.   The present
edifice is the third erected by the society.   The fashionable Episcopal churches

Trinity Church—New Orleans.

St. Paul's Church—New Orleans.

are considered to be Trinity and St. Paul's. Annunciation Church is a fine edifice. The McGhee Church, of which Rev. Dr. Tudor is pastor, is the principal of the Methodist Episcopal churches South. The Northern *post-bellum* settlers are mainly Congregational or Methodist, and have gathered at the First Congregational Church, and at the Methodist Episcopal Ames Chapel. The First Presbyterian Church Society long enjoyed the spiritual guidance of the eloquent Dr. Palmer, a divine of national reputation. The principal Baptist society assembles at the Coliseum Place Church. There are great numbers of colored church organizations, many of which are in a flourishing condition, having been largely aided by Northern missions. As there are one hundred and sixteen churches in New Orleans, the visitor can hardly hope to peer into them all; but on Baronne street he may steal for a moment into the shade of the old Jesuit Church, and, entering the dimly-lighted nave, see the black-robed girls at the confessional, and the richly-dressed women making their rounds before the chapels and kneeling, prayer-books in hand, beside the market-woman and the serving girl. The Jesuit Church, St. Augustine's, St. Joseph's, St. Patrick's, and the Mortuary Chapel, are

First Presbyterian Church — New Orleans.

ST. JOSEPH'S   ST. PATRICK'S   JESUIT CHURCH & SCHOOL.

The Catholic Churches of New Orleans.

among the best of the Catholic religious structures. St. Patrick's has a tower 190 feet high, modeled after that of the famous minster at York, England.

The city is not rich in architecture. After the National Capitol, the Custom-House is considered the largest public building in the country. It has a front of 334 feet on Canal street, and nearly the same on the levée. It is built entirely of granite from Massachusetts. Begun in 1848, little has been done since the war to complete it. As the seat of the United States courts, and of the exciting political conventions which have been so intimately

The Custom-House—New Orleans.

connected with the present political condition of Louisiana, the Custom-House attracts an interest which its architecture certainly could never excite. The building still lacks the roof contemplated in the original plan. When General Butler was military commander of New Orleans he proposed to erect a temporary roof, but his recall came before the work was begun.

The Ionic building at the corner of Esplanade and New Levée streets, once used as a United States branch mint, is noted as the place of execution of Mumford, who tore down the flag which the Federal forces had just raised on the roof when in 1862 the city was first occupied by the Northern forces. Mumford was hung, by General Butler's order, from a flag-staff projecting from one of the windows under the front portico of the main building.

The United States Branch Mint—New Orleans.

VI.

ON THE MISSISSIPPI RIVER—THE LEVÉE SYSTEM—RAILROADS.
THE FORT ST. PHILIP CANAL.

THE banks of the Mississippi, within the State of Louisiana, are lovely, the richness of the foliage and the luxuriance of the vegetation redeeming them from the charge of monotony which might otherwise be urged. Here and there a town, as in the case of Plaquemine, has been compelled to recede before the encroachments of the river.

The people of the State have shown rare pertinacity in maintaining the levée system. Like the Dutch in Holland, they doggedly assert their right to the lowlands in which they live, always braving inundation. They have built, and endeavor to maintain in repair, more than 1,500 miles, or 51,000,000 cubic feet of levées within the State limits. Their State engineer corps is always at work along the banks of the Mississippi, above and below Red River, on the Red River itself, on the Lafourche, the Atchafalaya, the Black and Ouachita, and on numerous important bayous.

The work of levée building has been pressed forward even when the Commonwealth has been prostrated by a hundred evils. Detailed surveys are constantly necessary to insure the State against inundation. The cost value of the present system is estimated at about $17,000,000, and it is asserted that the future expenditure of a similar sum will be necessary to complete and perfect it.

Ten years before the war, when Louisiana was in her most prosperous condition, she possessed 1,200 miles of levées, and the police juries of the several parishes compelled a strict maintenance of them by "inspectors of sections." Of course, during the war, millions of cubic feet of levées were destroyed by neglect, and for military purposes; and that the State, in her impoverished condition, should have been able to rebuild the old, and add new levées in so short a time, speaks volumes for her energy and industry,—qualities which find a thorough representative in General Jeff Thompson, the present State Engineer.

The Louisiana people claim that the general government should now take the building of levées along the Mississippi into its own hands, and their reasoning to prove it is ingenious. They say, for instance, that the tonnage of the great river amounts during a given year to 1,694,000 tons. They then claim that the transit of steamboats gives, by causing waves, an annual blow, equal to the whole tonnage of the commerce of the river, against each portion or point of the levées, or the banks on which the levées are erected; and that this blow is delivered at the average rate of about six miles an hour, a force equal to

15,000,000 tons;—a force expended by the commerce of the whole Mississippi basin upon each lineal foot in the 755 miles of Louisiana levées upon the river! On these grounds they object to paying all the expenses of levée building in their own State; and they are supported by able scientists.

"Sometimes the boat stops at a coaling station."

The United States certainly is the only power in America which can ever control the Mississippi, and prevent occasional terrible overflows; and it is its bounden duty to do it.

By day and night, the journey down river in the State of Louisiana is alike beautiful, impressive, exhilarating. But when a moonless night settles down upon the stream, and you float away into an apparent ocean on the back of the white Leviathan whose throbbing sides seem so tireless, the effect is solemnly grand.

Sometimes the boat stops at a coaling station, and tons of coal are laboriously transferred from barges to the steamer. An army of negroes shovel the glistening nuggets into rude hand-barrows, which another army, formed into a procession, carries to the furnaces.

I went down from Vicksburg on one of the larger and finer of the steamers; and the journey was a perpetual succession of novel episodes. At one point, when I supposed we were comfortably holding our way in the channel, a torch-light flared up, and showed us nearing a scraggy bank. The thin, long prow of the boat ran upon the land. Gangways were lowered; planks were run out from the boat's side to the bank; forty negroes sprang from some mysterious recess below, and huddled before the capstan.

The shower of harmless sparks from the torches cast momentary red gleams over the rude but kindly black faces. A sharp-voiced white man, whom I learned afterwards to call the "Wasp," because he always flew nervously about stinging the sprawling negroes into activity, thrust himself among the laborers. Twenty stings from his voice, and the dusky forms plunged into the darkness beyond the gangways. Then other torches were placed upon the bank— lighting up long wood-piles.

The Wasp flitted restlessly from shore to deck, from deck to shore, while the negroes attacked the piles, and, each taking half a dozen sticks, hurried to the deck with them. Presently there was an endless procession of black forms from the landing to the boat and back through the flickering light, to the tune of loud adjurations from the Wasp. Now and then the chain of laborers broke into a rude chant, beginning with a prolonged shout, such as

"Oh! I los' my money dar!"

and followed by a gurgling laugh, as if the singers were amused at the sound of their own voices. When any of the darkies stumbled or lagged, the Wasp, generally kind and well-disposed towards the negroes, despite his rough ways, broke into appeal, threat, and entreaty, crying out raspingly and with, oaths, "You, Reuben!" "You, Black Hawk!" "Come on thar, you Washington! ain't you going to hear me!" Now and then he would run among the negroes, urging them into such activity that a whole pile would vanish as if swallowed by an earthquake. In two hours and a-half sixty cords of wood were transferred from the bank to the boat, and the Wasp, calling the palpitating wood-carriers around him, thus addressed them: "Now, you boys, listen. You, Black Hawk, do you

"The Wasp."

hear? you and these three, first watch! You, Reuben, and these three, second watch!" etc. Then the torches were dipped in the river, and the great white boat once more wheeled around into the channel.

On the shores we could dimly discern huge trees half fallen into the stream, and stumps and roots and vines peeping up from the dark waters. We could hear the tug-boats groaning and sighing as they dragged along heavily laden barges; and once the light of a conflagration miles away cast a strange, dim light over the current. Now and then the boat, whirling around, made for the bank, and the light of our torches disclosed a ragged negro holding a mail-bag.

Up the swinging gangway clambered one of our deck hands; the mails were exchanged; the lights went out once more.

So on, and ever on, a cool breeze blowing from the perfumed banks. Now we could see the lights from some little settlement near a bayou emptying into

"Some tract of hopelessly irreclaimable, grotesque water wilderness."

the stream; now, the eye of some steamer, and hear the songs of the deck-hands as she passed us. Now we moved cautiously, taking soundings, as we entered some inlet or detour of the river; and now paused near some great swamp land—some tract of hopelessly irreclaimable, grotesque water wilderness, where abound all kinds of noisesome reptiles, birds and insects.

One should see such a swamp in October, when the Indian summer haze floats and shimmers lazily above the brownish-gray of the water; when a delicious magic in the atmosphere transforms the masses of trees and the tangled vines and creepers into semblances of ruined walls and tapestries. But at any season you see towering white cypresses, shooting their ghostly trunks far above the surrounding trees; or, half rotten at their bases, fallen into the water; the palmettoes growing in little clumps along the borders of treacherous knolls, where the earth seemed firm, but where you could not hope with safety to rest your feet; the long festoons of dead Spanish moss hanging from the high boughs of the red cypress, which refuses to nourish the pretty parasite; and the great cypress knees, now white, now brown, looming up through the warm haze, and peeping from nooks where the water is transparent, seeming like veins in a quarry riven by lightning strokes.

Vista after vista of cypress-bordered avenues, with long lapses of water filling them, and little islands of mud and slime, thinly coated with a deceptive foliage, stretch before your vision; a yellowish ray, flashing across the surface of the water, shows you where an alligator had shot forward to salute his friend or attack his enemy; and a strange mass hanging from some remotest bough, if narrowly inspected, proves an eagle's nest, fashioned with a proper care for defense.

You see the white crane standing at some tree root, sullenly contemplating the yielding mass of decaying logs and falling vines; and the owl now and then cries from a high perch. The quaint grossbeak, the ugly heron, the dirty-black buzzard, the hideous water-goose, with his featherless body and satiric head, start up from their nooks as you enter; the water moccasin slides warily into the slime; and if you see a sudden movement in the centre of a leaden-colored mass, with a flash or two of white in it, you will do well to beware, for half a dozen alligators may show themselves at home there. You may come upon some monarch-tree, prostrate and decayed within from end to end. Entering it, and tapping carefully as you proceed to frighten away lurking snakes, you will find that you can walk through without stooping, even though you are of generous height.

As far as the eye can reach you will see hundreds of ruined trees, great stretches of water, forbidding avenues which seem to lead to the bottomless pit, vistas as endless as hasheesh visions; and the cries of strange birds, and the bellowings of the alligator, will be the only sounds from life. You will be glad to steal back to the pure sunlight and the open lowland, to the river and the odors of many flowers—to the ripple of the sad-colored current, and the cheery songs of the boatmen.

Some evening, just as sunset is upon the green land and the broad stream, you stand high up in the pilot-house, as you float into a channel between low-lying islands, clad even to the water's edge with delicate shrubs whose forms are minutely reflected in the water. You may almost believe yourself removed out of the sphere of worldly care, and sailing to some haven of profoundest peace.

So restfully will the tender glory of the rose and amethyst of the sunset come to you; so softly will the perfume of the jessamines salute your senses; so gently will avenue after avenue of verdurous banks, laved by tranquil waters and extending beyond the reach of your vision, open before you; so quietly will the wave take from the horizon the benison of the sun's dying fires; so artfully will the perfect purple—the final promise of a future dawn—peep up from the islets' rims ere it disappears, that you will be charmed into the same serene content which nature around you manifests. From some distant village is borne on the breeze the music of an evening bell; from some plantation-grounds, or a grove of lofty trees, comes the burden of a negro hymn, or a jolly song of love and adventure.

Down below, the firemen labor at the seven great furnaces, and throw into them cords on cords of wood, tons on tons of coal; the negroes on the watch scrub the decks, or trundle cotton bales from one side of the boat to the other, or they lie listlessly by the low rails of the prow, blinking and shuffling and laughing with their own rude grace. Above, the magic perfume from the thickets fillled with blossoms is always drifting, and the long lines of green islets bathed by the giant stream, pass by in rapid panorama.

You notice that some little fiend of a black boy, clad in an old woolen cap, a flannel shirt whose long flaps hang over his ragged and time-honored trowsers, and shoes whose heels are so trodden in that when he walks his motion seems to rock the steamer, will, when his comrade is not watching, steal some little article which said comrade can ill afford to lose ; whereupon comrade, in due time discovering the loss, will end by complaining of the suspected boy to the Wasp ; then you see the Wasp come buzzing and stinging and swearing along the broad decks, and calling George Washington to a certain post where he is to face him. Perhaps the Wasp will say: "George Washington, Jack says you stole his belt;" and then will sting and buzz and swear ; whereupon George Washington, mopping his black face with the flap of his red flannel over-garment, will say hastily. in one indignant sibilation: "Deed to God, hope I die, sah—no sah !" Perhaps then the Wasp will make George Washington hold up his hand, and, looking him earnestly in the face, will say, "George Washington, are you going to tell me a lie?" with a buzz and a sting and a swear.

The monument on the Chalmette battle-field.

finally end by rendering up the belt, and retiring to the shade of a cotton bale, followed by the laughter of his comrades.

Whereupon George Washington will again and defiantly sibilate: "If dat nigger say dat, he lied. I do' know nuffin about his belt nohow. Mus' a los' it woodin-up las' night. I did n't tetch it ; " but after various hand-raisings will

You come to a plantation landing where some restive steers are to be taken aboard, and notice the surprising manner in which those playful creatures toss about the negroes who wish to lead them on, until one or two agile fellows, catching the beasts by the tails, and as many more holding their horns, manage to make them walk the narrowest planks.

Or you come to some landing where a smart-looking young negro man comes on board with a quadroon wife ; and you notice a hurried look of surprise on some of the old men's faces as the couple are shown a state-room, or as they promenade unconcernedly.

Or a group of chattering French planters, with ruddy complexions and coal black eyes and hair, arrive, and the village priest, a fat, stalwart old boy in a white choker and a shovel hat, accompanies them; or perhaps a lean, gray-haired man, with a strongly marked dialect and a certain contemptuous way of talking of modern things, tells you that he remembers the first steamboat but three that ever ran upon the Mississippi river, and hints that "times were better then than now. That was a right smart o' years ago."

Descending the river from New Orleans, you go slowly down a muddy-colored but broad and strong current, between low and seemingly unstable banks. You pass the Chalmette battle-field, where Andrew Jackson won his victory over the English, and where Monument Cemetery, the burial place of many thousand soldiers, killed in the late civil war, is located. The monument from which the cemetery takes its name was erected in 1856, to commemorate General Jackson's good fight.

The fears that the levées along the Mississippi would not be able always to resist the great body of water bearing and wearing upon them have several times been realized. Among the most disastrous instances of the "crevasse" is that of May, 1816, when the river broke through, nine miles above New Orleans, destroying numbers of plantations, and inundating the back part of the city. Gov. Claiborne adopted the expedient of sinking a vessel in the breach, and saved the town. In 1844 the river did much damage along the levée at New Orleans; and the inundations of 1868 and 1871 were severe lessons of the necessity of continually strengthening the works.

Within fifty or sixty miles of the river's mouths, the banks become too low for cultivation; you leave the great sugar plantations behind, and the river broadens, until, on reaching the "Head of the Passes," it separates into several streams, one of which in turn divides again a few miles from its separation from the main river. Beginning at the north and east, these passes, as they are called, are named respectively "Pass à l'Outre," "North-east Pass," the "South Pass," and "South-west Pass." Across the mouths of these passes bars of mud are formed, deposited by the river, which there meeting the salt and consequently heavier water of the gulf, runs over the top of it, and, being partially checked, the mud is strained through the salt water, and sinks at once to the bottom.

This separation of the fresh from the salt water is maintained in a remarkable degree. When the river is high, the river water runs far out to sea, and has been seen at fifteen miles from the passes, with as sharply defined a line between them as that between oil and water. This is also true with reference to the upper and lower strata. Sometimes, when a steamer is running through a dense pea-soup colored water on top, the paddle-wheels will displace it sufficiently to enable one to see clear gulf water rushing up to fill the displacement. The flood tide runs up underneath the river water for a long distance, and, at extraordinary high tides, is distinctly visible as far as New Orleans, one hundred and ten miles above.* The bars change their depth constantly.

When the river is high, and consequently brings down most mud, the depth of the deposit increases with great rapidity; while in a low stage of the river the accumulation is slight. The bars are subject to another and great change, believed to be peculiar to the Mississippi; that is, the formation of "mud lumps." These mud lumps are cone-shaped elevations of the bottom, often thrown up in a few hours, so that although the pilot may find ample depth for the largest ship on one day, on the next he may be aground with one of a much lighter draught.

Sometimes the lumps disappear as quickly as formed; at others they spread, show themselves above the water, and gradually grow into islands. It is sup-

* For these and many other interesting details, the writer gratefully acknowledges his obligations to Major C. W. Howell, Captain of United States Engineers, and to Captain Frank Barr, United States Revenue Marine.

posed that this is the manner in which the long, narrow banks on either side of the "passes" have been formed.   These cone-shaped lumps of mud are believed to be started by the action of carburetted hydrogen gas formed by the decay of vegetable matter contained in the river deposits, the substance of the bar being loosened by the action of the gas and forced upward until the lump makes its appearance above the water; when, becoming dry, and being continually fed by the forces from below, it gradually gains consistency, and forms another link in the delta chain, extending into the waters of the Gulf.

The attention of the United States Government to the necessity of improvement at the mouths of the Mississippi was first attracted in earnest in 1837, when an extended and elaborate survey of the passes and mouths was made by Captain Talcot, of the Engineer Corps.   To save the commerce of New Orleans it was necessary to deepen the channel; and the plan of dredging with buckets was carried into effect as far as a slight appropriation permitted.   No farther work was then undertaken until 1852, when $75,000 was set aside for it; and a number of processes for deepening—such as stirring up the river bottom with suitable machinery, and the establishment of parallel jetties, five miles in length, at the mouth of the South-west Pass—were tried.

By 1853 a depth of eighteen feet of water had been obtained in the Southwest Pass by stirring up the river bottom; but in 1856 it was found that no trace of the deepening remained.   In that year the sum of $300,000 was appropriated for opening and keeping open, by contract, ship channels through the bars at the mouths of the South-west Pass.

Contractors began work, but unless they labored incessantly, they could not keep the channels open; and they retired discomfited.   The plan of dragging harrows and scrapers seaward along the bottom of the channel was adopted, thus aiding the river-flood to carry the stirred-up matter to deep water; and a depth of eighteen feet was maintained upon the bar for one year at a cost of $60,000. Other efforts, in 1866 and 1867, were equally costly and of small avail; and in

Light-house — South-west Pass.   [Page 75.]

1868, the "Essayons," a steam dredge-boat, constructed by the Atlantic Works, of Boston, was employed upon the bar at Pass à l'Outre.   The plan of this boat, which had been recommended by General McAllister, was a powerful steamer with a cutting propeller, which could be lowered into the surface of the mud, where its rapid revolutions would effect the necessary "stirring-up."   So far as her draught permits, the "Essayons" has been a complete success; and another steamer, whose cutting propeller can work at greater depth, and which has been named "McAllister," is now engaged upon the work. The main labor with these new boats has been done at the South-west Pass, which has become the principal entrance to the Mississippi, and there the United States Government is erecting a light-house on iron piles, as the marshes offer but an insecure foundation. The improvements at the river's mouth, like those in the Red River, Tone's Bayou, the Tangipahoa River, the harbor of Galveston, and the Mississippi forts, as well as those on the lakes in the rear of New Orleans,

"Pilot Town"—South-west Pass.

are all under the direction of Major C. N. Howell, of the Engineer Department. Pass à l'Outre is generally considered by best authorities the natural channel for eastward-bound and returning ships. With its bar opened, none such would, it is affirmed, ever go to South-west Pass, for the reason that they might save several hours coming in. This pass, properly opened, can accommodate three times the number of ships which now annually enter the Mississippi.

The effect on the commerce of New Orleans of the bar-formations at the river's mouths is depressing. They cause burdensome taxes on the earnings of ships. In 1870 the value of imports at New Orleans amounted to only one-seventh of the exports; but if the port were made as economical as that of New York, by removing all obstacles to free entrance and exit, the imports would soon nearly equal the exports. The Government is at present expending about $650,000 annually on the necessary river and harbor improvements in Louisiana and Texas. Twice that amount might be judiciously invested every year. The work on the channel at the Mississippi's outlet must evidently be perpetual, unless the plan of a canal is adopted.

"The Balize," now a little collection of houses at the North-east Pass, was a famous place in its day—was, indeed, the port of New Orleans; and vessels were often detained there for weeks on the great bar, which had been labored upon to but little advantage before the cession of Louisiana to the United States. The extensive French military and naval establishments at the Balize were utterly destroyed by the great hurricanes of September, 1740. Now-a-days, the venerable port is almost desolate; a few damp and discouraged fishermen linger sadly among the wrecks of departed greatness. "Pilot Town," at the South-west Pass, is interesting and ambitious. The pilots and fishermen are delightful types, and are nearly all worthy seamen and good navigators. At "Pass à l'Outre" and "South-west Pass" the Government maintains a "boarding-station" for protection of the revenue, and an inspector is sent up to the port of New Orleans with each incoming vessel.

Steaming back to the Louisiana capital on one of the inward-bound vessels, leaving behind you the low-lying banks; the queer towns at the mouths of the passes, with their foundations beneath the water; the long lines of pelicans sailing disconsolately about the current; the porpoises disporting above the bars, and the alligators sullenly supine on the sand, you will land into the rush and whir of the great commerce "on the levée." If it be evening, you will hear the hoarse whistles of a dozen steamers, as they back into midstream, the negroes on their decks scrambling among the freight and singing rude songs, while the loud cries of the captains are heard above the noise of escaping steam.

One of the most pressing needs of Louisiana is an increase of railway lines. The New Orleans, Mobile and Texas road has done much for the commerce of the State, and is, undoubtedly, one of the best constructed lines in the country. It drains extensive sections of Mississippi and Alabama toward New Orleans. The extension of this route to Houston in Texas, and the building of a branch from Vermilionville to Shreveport, will do much for the development of the commonwealth. The trade between New Orleans and Shreveport, which is really immense, was much restricted for many years by the difficulty of navigating the Red river, whose tortuous water-ways have latterly been considerably improved. The projected "Louisiana Central" railroad, located along the route of the Red river for about 200 miles, passing through Alexandria and Natchitoches, will make Shreveport within twelve hours of New Orleans. The journey formerly occupied three or four days. Morgan's "Louisiana and Texas" railroad extends from New Orleans to Brashear City on Berwick's Bay, where it communicates with a fleet of first-class iron steamers running to Texas ports. The branch of this road from Brashear City to Vermilionville, graded years ago, might now be completed to advantage.

The New Orleans, Jackson and Great Northern railroad gives a valuable connection with the North, *via* Jackson, in Mississippi. A recent enterprise is the New Orleans and North-eastern road, which is to cross Lake Pontchartrain on a trestle-work, supported on piles, and opening up a delightful location for suburban residences beyond the lake, is to push on into the iron and coal regions of Alabama. The Illinois Central Railroad Company has built a line from Jackson, Tennessee, to the south bank of the Ohio river, opposite Cairo, Illinois, bringing New Orleans as near to Chicago by rail as it is to New York, and creating an important adjunct to the system for transportation from the Northwest to the gulf and the ocean. Railroad routes along the banks of the Mississippi would give new life to such towns as Baton Rouge, the old capital of Louisiana, 129 miles from New Orleans, and Natchez in Mississippi. Baton Rouge now has no communication with New Orleans save by steamer. It is a lovely town, built on gently sloping banks crowned with picturesque houses, the ruined Gothic State Capitol, a substantial Penitentiary, and the Asylum for the Deaf and Dumb. It is one of the healthiest towns in the State, and with proper facilities for speedy communication with other towns, might be the seat of a flourishing trade. Routes parallel with the river would be speedily built if New Orleans had better outlets and more tonnage. Knowing this, the enterprising inhabitants of that city are anxious for the Fort St. Philip canal, which shall render the tedious and risky navigation of the passes at the Mississippi's mouth unnecessary.

The project of the Fort St. Philip canal is not entirely due to the sagacity of this generation. Forty years ago the Legislature of Louisiana, at the suggestion of a distinguished engineer, memorialized Congress on the subject of a canal to connect the Mississippi river with the Gulf, leaving the stream a few miles below Fort St. Philip and entering the Gulf about four miles south of the island "Le Breton." Numerous commercial conventions have endorsed it since that time. It would give, by means of a system of locks, a channel which would never be subject to the evils now disfiguring the passes at the river's mouth, and would communicate directly with deep water. The estimated cost of the work is about eight millions of dollars. It is a national commercial necessity, and should be undertaken by the Government at once. New Orleans would more than quadruple her transportation facilities by means of this canal, not only with regard to Liverpool, Bremen, Hamburg, Rotterdam, Antwerp, Southampton, Havre, and Glasgow, but to New York and Philadelphia. Havana, Lima, and Aspinwall.

'A Nickel for Daddy."

VII.

THE INDUSTRIES OF LOUISIANA—A SUGAR PLANTATION. THE TECHE COUNTRY.

THE main industries of Louisiana at the present time are the growth of cotton, the production of sugar, rice, and wheat,— agriculture in general,— and cattle raising. The culture of the soil certainly offers inducements of the most astonishing character, and the immigrant who purchases a small tract— five to ten acres—of land can, during the first year of possession, make it support himself and his numerous family, and can also raise cotton enough on it to return the purchase money.

Vergennes, in his memoir on *La Louisiane*, printed early in this century, says: "I will again repeat what I have already many times said—that Louisiana is, without doubt, by reason of the softness of her climate and the beauty of her situation, the finest country in the universe. Every European plant, and nearly all those of America, can be successfully cultivated there." This was the verdict of one who had made a careful survey of the great province then known as Louisiana, and especially the tract now comprised in the lowlands. Rice, an important article of food, can be raised on grounds which are too low and moist for any other species of valuable vegetables, and in the Mississippi basin, rice, sugar and corn can be cultivated in close proximity. The fertility of the sugar lands is proverbial; and Louisiana is prodigal of fruit of all kinds. With but little attention orange and fig-trees prosper and bear splendid crops; apples and peaches are produced in abundance; and grape-bearing lands are to be found in all sections of the State. Sugar, cotton, rice and tobacco might all be readily cultivated on the same farm in many sections.

The cultivation of rice, introduced into Louisiana by Bienville, at the time of the founding of New Orleans, may be profitably pursued in all the "parishes," *i. e.*, counties, on the river and Gulf coasts, and on the high pine lands of the northern part of the State. The rice raised on the irrigated lands below New Orleans, and in the immediate proximity of the Gulf, is known as "lowland rice;" that raised elsewhere as "upland."

The quality of the staple is constantly improving by cultivation. In 1860 the rice crop of Louisiana amounted to 6,500,000 pounds. There is no good reason why it should not now be 60,000,000. Barley and buckwheat flourish admirably in the State, and the attention given to the cultivation of wheat since the close of the war has accorded singularly gratifying results. The average yield in the hill portion of the State is fully equal to that of the Northern States, —about twelve bushels to the acre—and in the Red River Valley, where the planters were compelled to devote much of their old cotton land to the production of wheat, for the sake of getting the wherewithal to live, the yield was twenty bushels to the acre.

The wheat yearly gains largely in weight, size and color. It is said that wherever the cavalry of the United States camped in Louisiana during the war, immense grain fields sprang up from the seed scattered where horses were fed. In the swamps of Assumption parish wheat and rye have been known to yield forty bushels to the acre. The wheat may be planted in September, October, or November, and reaped late in April or early in May. Indian corn does not yield well, rarely giving over fifteen bushels to the acre. Marsh, Hungarian herbs, and prairie grasses grow in abundance and make excellent hay. Pasturage is perennial, and in the Attakapas the grazing regions are superb. Cotton may be cultivated throughout the entire arable portion of the State.

The cultivation of the sugar-cane in Louisiana merits especial mention. One of the most remunerative of industries under the slave system, it has been for some time languishing because of the disorganization of labor, and because also of the division of large plantations into small farms. For a whole year before the sugar crop is ready for the market, a constant outlay is required, and the small planters succeed but poorly, while the larger ones have been ruined by the war, and have allowed their sugar-houses to decay, and their splendid machinery to rust in ditches.

In 1751, two ships transporting soldiers to Louisiana, stopped at Hispaniola, and the Jesuits on that island sent some sugar-canes and some negroes, used to their cultivation, to the brothers of their order in the new colony. The Jesuits at New Orleans undertook the culture of the crop, but did not succeed; and it was only in 1795 that the seeds became thoroughly naturalized in Louisiana.

Up to 1816 the cultivation of the cane was confined to the lower parishes, but it is now raised with reasonable success in many other portions of the State. From 1828 to 1833, the sugar production in the commonwealth was about 280,000 hogsheads. The following table will show the amount of the crops of each year from 1834 to 1873 inclusive:

Year.	Production, Hogsheads.	Year.	Production, Hogsheads.	Year.	Production, Hogsheads.	Year.	Production, Hogsheads.
1834	100,000	1844	200,000	1854	346,000	1866	39,000
1835	30,000	1845	186,000	1855	231,000	1867	37,600
1836	70,000	1846	140,000	1856	74,000	1868	84,000
1837	65,000	1847	240,000	1857	279,000	1869	87,000
1838	70,000	1848	220,000	1858	362,000	1870	144,800
1839	115,000	1849	247,000	1859	221,000	1871	128,461
1840	87,000	1850	211,000	1860	228,000	1872	105,000
1841	90,000	1851	236,000	1861	459,000	1873	90,000
1842	140,000	1852	321,000	1864..War,	7,000	......	
1843	100,000	1853	449,000	1865	15,000	......	

The ribbon cane planted in Louisiana was brought from Java, in a ship which touched at Charleston. It was hardy, and was at once adopted in all sections of the State. But it is thought that it has deteriorated very much, and an associa-tion recently sent a gentleman to the islands of the Pacific Ocean and to India to search for a fresh supply. He secured some ten thousand cuttings, which were so long in transit as to be nearly all destroyed, and parties in the sugar interest are now anxious that a government vessel should be sent out to obtain a new supply.

There were, at the time of my visit to Louisiana, 1,224 sugar-houses in operation in the State, 907 of which possessed steam power. The number of large plantations is everywhere decreasing, while small farms take their place.

The coöperative system, as practiced in Martinique and other colonies, has been adopted to some extent in the State. It separates the production of cane from the manufacture of sugar, the small planters taking their cane to the sugar-houses to be worked through on shares. This is much better than the old system, which made the raising of sugar by free labor so expensive as to be almost impossible. The coöperative system will, perhaps, prevail very largely ere long, many extensive planters giving it their sanction. In 1871, there was enough labor and capital expended on the crop to have brought it up to a quarter of a million hogsheads.

The accumulated losses of the last three years have made the trade so dubious that dozens of the largest planters in the State cannot secure a cent of advances. Plantations are deserted; owners are completely discouraged. The present sugar production of this most fertile of cane-growing lands is only two per cent. of the whole production of the world. The consumption of sugars in the United States for the calendar year 1871 was 663,000 tons, of which eighty-five per cent. was foreign. The whole number of acres now devoted to the cultivation of sugar in Louisiana is estimated at 148,840, producing to the acre about 49,000 pounds of cane, or 1,500 pounds of raw sugar. To every thousand pounds of sugar there is also a yield of 666 pounds of molasses.

All the land comprised in the section known as the "Delta proper of the Miss-issippi River," embracing·eighteen parishes and an area of 12,000 square miles, is peculiarly adapted to the cultivation of sugar-cane, as well as of cotton, corn, rice, tobacco, indigo, oranges, lemons and figs. More than half of the population of the State is settled upon this delta; and in 1860, *one hundred and fifty thou-sand* slaves were held in that section, and the total estimate of taxable property there, including the slaves, amounted to $271,017,667, more than half of the State's entire valuation. It is not wonderful that stagnation has fallen upon this once prosperous region, since, reckoning the slaves at the average $1,000 apiece, by their liberation alone $150,000,000 of the above valuation at once vanished into thin air.*

For fifty or sixty miles below New Orleans, the narrow strip which protects the Mississippi channel on either side from the gulf is crowded with plantations. The soil there is all of recent alluvial formation, and is, consequently, extremely

---

* The census of 1870 gives Louisiana 732,731 population, of whom 364,210 were blacks. The population of New Orleans in 1870 was nearly 200,000.

prolific. This section may, without the least exaggeration, be called "of the best land in the world." The rivers and bayous furnish fish and oysters of finest flavor; the earth brings forth fruit and vegetables in tropical abundance; all the conditions of life are easy; and, in addition, there is the profitable culture of sugar and rice.

The negroes themselves are making money rapidly in this section, and show much skill in managing their affairs. In many cases they were aided in purchasing their lands by their old masters, and generally go to them for advice as to speculation and conduct in crop raising. The same negro who will bitterly oppose his old master politically, will implicitly follow his advice in matters of labor and investment in which he is personally concerned.

At every turn, and on every available spot along the shore, as one drifts slowly down the lower Mississippi, one is charmed to note the picturesque grouping of sugar-houses and "quarters," the mansions surrounded by splendid groves, and the rich fields stretching miles away towards a dark belt of timber.

Each plantation has its group of white buildings, gleaming in the sun; each its long vistas of avenues, bordered with orange-trees; for the orange and the sugar-cane are friendly neighbors. When the steamer swings around at the wharf of such a lordly plantation as that of the "Woodlands" of Bradish Johnson, or that of Effingham Lawrence, the negroes come trooping out, men and women dancing, somersaulting, and shouting; and, if perchance there is music on the steamer, no power can restrain the merry antics of the African.

The "Magnolia" plantation of Mr. Lawrence is a fair type of the larger and better class; it lies low down to the river's level, and seems to court inundation. Stepping from the wharf, across a green lawn, the sugar-house first greets the eye, an immense solid building, crammed with costly machinery. Not far from it are the neat, white cottages occupied by the laborers; there is the kitchen where the field-hands come to their meals; there are the sheds where the carts are housed, and the cane is brought to be crushed; and, ranging in front of a cane-field containing many hundreds of acres, is a great orange orchard, the branches of whose odorous trees bear literally golden fruit; for, with but little care, they yield their owner an annual income of $25,000.

The massive oaks and graceful magnolias surrounding the planter's mansion give grateful shade; roses and all the rarer blossoms perfume the air; the river current hums a gentle monotone, which, mingled with the music of the myriad insect life, and vaguely heard on the lawn and in the cool corridors of the house, seems lamenting past grandeur and prophesying of future greatness. For it was a grand and lordly life, that of the owner of a sugar plantation; filled with culture, pleasure, and the refinements of living;—but now!

Afield, in Mr. Lawrence's plantation, and in some others, one may see the steam-plough at work, ripping up the rich soil. Great stationary engines pull it rapidly from end to end of the tracts; and the darkies, mounted on the swiftly-rolling machine, skillfully guide its sharp blades and force them into the furrows. Ere long, doubtless, steam-ploughs will be generally introduced on Louisiana sugar estates. Four of these stationary engines, built at Leeds, England, and supplied with water brought from the river in mule carts, suffice to do the work upon the ample plantation of Mr. Lawrence.

As to the details of plantation work, the negroes, evidently, do not attend to them with quite the thoroughness exacted under the rigid discipline of slavery.

"A cheery Chinaman."

Evidences of neglect, in considerable variety, offer themselves to the critical eye. Entering the sugar-house, the amiable planter will present you to a venerable, mahogany-looking individual in garments stained with saccharine juices, and with a little tone of pride in his voice will tell you that "this is Nelson, overseer of this place, who has been here, man and boy, forty years, and who knows more about the process of sugar-making than any one else on the plantation."

Nelson will, therefore, conduct you into the outer shed, and, while showing you the huge rollers under which the canes, when carted in from the fields in November or December, are crushed, will impress upon you the danger of early winter frosts which may baffle every hope of profit, will explain to you how difficult and how full of risks is the culture of the juicy reed, which must be nursed through twelve or thirteen weary months, and may leave but a meagre result. He will take you across the delightfully-shaded way into one of the fields, passing on the walk a cheery Chinaman wearing a smile which is seven times childlike and bland, and point you to the stalks of the cane left at the last harvest to lie all winter in the furrows and furnish young sprouts for the spring. These shapely and rich-colored stalks have joints every few inches along their whole length, from which spring out the new buds of promise. When the spring ploughing begins, these stalks are laid along the beds of the drills, and each shoot, as it makes its appearance, is carefully watched and cultured that it may produce a new cane, a great portion of the crop being thus reserved, each year, for seed.

The complaisant overseer will give you a profusion of details as to how the cane, if safe from the accidents of the seasons, is cut down at its perfection and brought to the sugar-house; how all hands, black and white, join, for many days, in "hauling" it from the fields, and then keep the mill going for a week night and day; how there is high wassail and good cheer in the intervals of the work, and every nerve is strained to the utmost for the completion of the task. He will show you the great crushers which bring the sweetness out of the fresh canes as they are carried forward upon an endless series of rollers, and will then point out the furnace into which the refuse is thrown to be burned, thus furnishing the motive power for crushing the stalks and for all the minor and subordinate mechanical details in the processes of the manufacture. The *baggasse*, as this refuse is called, usually furnishes steam enough for this purpose, and leaves nothing but a kind of coke in the ash-pit of the furnace; no coal being used except in the refining mill's furnace.

Out from the crushed arteries of the cane wells a thick, impure liquid, which demands immediate attention to preserve it from spoiling; and then the clarifying process is begun and continued, by the aid of hundreds of ingenious mechanisms, whose names even you will not remember when Nelson takes you into the refinery.

You enter a set of huge chambers, the floors of which are sticky with sugar, and watch the juice passing through various processes. There are the great open trays, traversed by copper and iron steam-pipes; there are the filter-pans filled with bone dust, from which the liquid trickles down. Now it wanders through separators, and then through bone dust again, onward toward granulation in the vacuum pans, and then into coolers, where the sugar is kept in a half

Sugar-cane Plantation—"The cane is cut down at its perfection." [Page 82.]

liquid state by means of revolving paddles, until, finally, it comes to the vessels, in which, by rapid whirlings, all the molasses is thrown out; and the molasses, leaving the dry sugar ready for commerce, goes meandering among the pipes under the floors, and round and round again through the whirling machines, until there is no suspicion of sweetness in it, and it is ignominiously discharged.

It seems a pity that such fine machinery should be in use only during one-sixth of the year, as it would be injured far less by being kept constantly running than by remaining idle. The new steam-mills are, in every point of view, so vastly superior to the old horse-mills, that they have been adopted on the greater portion of the sugar plantations, and are desired by every planter; but they are so enormously expensive, that coöperative or joint ownership is, in many cases, essential.

The division of the large plantations into small farms seems, sooner or later, inevitable; as no one owner can, under the new condition of things, make the necessary and continuous outlay. In a few years the cane now crushed at one of these immense sugar-houses in the winter months will belong, in small lots, to a hundred different men, instead of to the one aristocratic and wealthy planter, as under the old *régime*.

There is not a parish in Louisiana which does not offer powerful inducements to immigration; not one which will not most bitterly need it if the present political condition, which is driving the original inhabitants from their homes, is continued. Closely following upon the bloodshed in Grant parish, came a hurried, voluminous emigration of its citizens to Texas. They flocked to the new Eden in the greatest terror, seeming eager to leave their homes forever behind them. Still, these troubles must some day have an end, because, save in the final disruption of the world, there is no end to the fairy beauty and fertility of the bayou lands, or to the luxuriant vegetation of the vast plains.

The parishes bordering on the Red river are especially adapted to the staples—sugar, cotton, wheat, corn, rye and oats—and are always accessible, the river in their vicinity remaining navigable at all seasons of the year. These parishes, six in number, comprise more than 8,500 square miles of rich alluvial land, and some of the largest towns are situated in them. Shreveport, on the west bank of the river, is the second city in the State. It is now the great centre of emigration into Eastern and Northern Texas, and a line of railway is projected to it from Vicksburg, which will give it increased commercial importance.

In the parishes which comprise South-western Louisiana, there are more than 3,000,000 acres of land of almost inexhaustible fertility. The forests are composed of oak, ash, locust, pine, gum, maple, cypress, elm, willow, hickory, pecan, persimmon, dogwood, mulberry, and magnolia trees. The giant cypresses along the lakes and bayous are abundant enough to last for a century. Employment to hundreds of mills and thousands of workmen could readily be furnished, the lumber being easily floated down the innumerable bayous and along the lakes to market.

By the borders of the great desolate sea-marshes of St. Mary and Iberia runs a grand belt of timber from one to two miles wide. A western editor once said that if the Teche lands of Louisiana were in Illinois, they would bring from $300 to $500 per acre. And they could be made worth that sum in their present situation in five years from this writing by the introduction of intelligent and laborious immigrants, and by the amplification of the State's railway system. The "Attakapas" region, as the five parishes or counties of St. Mary, Iberia, Vermilion, St. Martin and Lafayette were originally called, from the name of a tribe of Indians, is certainly seductive enough to tempt the most fastidious.

The cattle-grazing regions are as extensive as remarkable. There are seven great prairies, respectively named Grand Choiseuil, Attakapas, Opelousas, Grand Prairie, Prairie Mamon, Calcasieu, and Aubine, all covered with rich pasturage.

Thousands of cattle roam over these prairies; the population is pastoral and to a certain extent uncultivated. There are Frenchmen and Frenchwomen among them who are as remote from any active participation in the politics of the State or the country at large, as if they lived in France. Cattle and horses subsist even in the marshes, and graze the year round upon a treacherous surface, in which such animals, bred on solider ground, will instantly sink and flounder. I am not willing to vouch for the Louisiana statement that these marsh-bred cattle and horses are web-footed, though such is the affirmation. One informant assured me that a proper system of transportation from the marshes to New Orleans would develop this now almost useless section immensely. Thousands of cattle might be turned in to grow fat and bide the time when their owners should seek them for the New Orleans market. They would not even need a cowherd's care.

All the prairies in Western Louisiana are perennially green; and upon them were once located the largest vacheries in the United States—vacheries whose owners sometimes branded five thousand calves apiece yearly. Sheep by thousands were also raised, but both these important industries seem to have largely fallen off since the war. The French paid great attention to the cattle and sheep husbandry in this section of Louisiana early in the last century, and it has been estimated by a competent authority that, allowing one animal to every five acres, more than 220,000 cattle could be annually reared and transported from the single prairie of Opelousas—a vast expanse of natural meadow. It was not uncommon for a stock raiser to possess from 30,000 to 40,000 head of cattle, and twenty-five years before the war, the stock raisers of one parish in that section owned 100,000 cattle and 30,000 horses.

There is no good reason why Louisiana should not be known in future as an extensive a cattle-raising State as her neighbor, Texas. She has nothing to fear from the dangers incurred by proximity to a foreign frontier, and there are no Indians to manifest their unconquerable longing for " raids."

But if you wish once again to find the lost gate of Eden, if you wish to gain the promised land, if you wish to see in this rude, practical America of ours an "earthly paradise," where life is good, because Nature has invested it with everything that is delicious and fairest; if you wish to see plantations at the height of culture—lawns as fragrant, as clean-shaven, as nobly shaded by graceful trees as any sovereign's—seek the Teche country. It is the pearl of Louisiana; it is the gem of the South. Thither, more than a century ago, when the cruel order of the English dispersed them from their homes, Andry and the exiled Acadians took their mournful way. Thither they went, threading the swamps and wandering up the beautiful Atchafalaya, and her lakes, where

"Water lilies in myriads rocked on the slight undulations
　Made by the passing oars, and, resplendent in beauty the lotus
　Lifted her golden crown above the heads of the boatmen.
　Faint was the air with the odorous breath of magnolia blossoms,
　And with the heat of noon; and numberless sylvan islands,
　Fragrant and thickly embowered with blossoming hedges of roses,
　Near to whose shores they glided along, invited to slumber."

Now, as then, the traveler, pushing his way in a tiny steamer, or in a shallop or pirogue, can hear—

"Far off, indistinct, as of wave or wind in the forest,
    Mixed with the whoop of the crane, and the roar of the grim alligator,"

strange sounds from the dark forests and the lonely lands.

From Berwick's Bay, where the rich fields lie trustingly upon the water, and strange vines and creepers seem to caress the waves, and bid them be tranquil, ascend the Teche bayou, and lose yourself in the tangled network of lake and lakelet, plain and forest, plantation and swamp. By day you shall have the exquisite glory of the sun, which, gleaming on the seigniorial residences, on the great white sugar-houses with their tall chimneys, on the long rows of cabins for the laborers, on the villas peering from orange groves and bosquets of the mespilus, makes all doubly bright and beautiful; and at evening the moon will lend her witchery to swell your surprise and admiration.

You will drift on by superb knots of shrubbery, from which sprightly birds are singing madrigals; past floating bridges and garden bowers; past ruined plantations, the wrecks of the war; past dense cypress swamps, bordered by picturesque groupings of oaks and ash and gum-trees; through that fine region stretching from the entrance of the bayou into the parish of Iberia and the town of New Iberia, where the beautiful water willows and forest trees lean forward from the banks as if to see themselves reflected in the stream; where the wheels of passing steamers rudely brush the arching foliage; where the live oak spreads its ample spray over some cool dell upon whose grassy carpet grow strange bright-hued flowers; and where vistas of forest glade—happy sylvan retreats—open as by enchantment, and moonlight makes delicious checkerwork of gleam and shadow.

Below New Iberia, on Petit Anse Island, there is a salt mine sixty feet beneath the level of the Gulf of Mexico, and you may go down through fifty-eight feet of solid rock-salt, to watch the miners pick out the crystal freight which has proved superior to any other salt found in the Southern market. Or you may penetrate the romantic country near Lake Peigneur, and even hunt the genial comedian—the noble artist who created the rôle of "Rip Van Winkle,"—in his "Orange Island" retreat.

The richness of Louisiana may perhaps be best illustrated by this same island. It is one of many in the lake, rising high above it and the surrounding prairie. It possesses delicious lawns miles in length, sloping gently southward; orange groves, which in 1868, after a neglect of ten years, produced half a million oranges; bold banks and knolls with northward outlook; and delightful sea breezes constantly blowing over the whole length and breadth of its lovely lands. On Grand Cote Island you may wander among wide fields of cotton and of corn, or you may climb steep hill-sides to find a lake of purest water high up among them, its surface covered with water lilies; or you may sit in garden bowers over which the Scuppernong grape-vines run riot, and gaze out upon the towering magnolia, the blooming cotton and the waving cane.

The forests in the parish of St. Martin, in the Teche valley, contain millions of tall, straight cypress-trees; and beyond are stretches of ash, gum, hickory, black walnut, magnolia, live, white and red oaks, linn, pecan, sycamore, and other trees. There are also here some grand estates, notably those of General Declouet, Mr. Lestrapes, and Dr. Wilkins. General Declouet's mansion is a fine type of the old Creole house, with spacious halls and corridors, baronial dining-room, and portrait galleries from which look down the faces of a hundred ancestors. Avenues, bordered with China-trees or with pines, lead up to it; while magnolias, fig-trees, and live oaks are scattered throughout the grounds.

One finds superb forests everywhere in Louisiana. They are among the chief glories of the State. One may purchase, for an insignificant sum, a lovely natural park, with trees in it which an English duke might covet for his estate.

"The beautiful 'City Park'"—New Orleans.

The oaks which stud the beautiful " City Park," and the "race-course" grounds, in New Orleans, are exceedingly fine. City and country alike abound in the most delicious foliage.

St. Mary's parish formerly contained 170 sugar plantations, scattered along the banks of the Teche, the Atchafalaya, and the various bayous and water-ways in that section. In the same parish, 13,000 slaves were owned before the war, and more than 100 vessels plied between Franklin (a pretty, cultured town, twenty miles from Brashear) and various Northern and Southern ports. The fertile lands readily yield a hogshead of sugar to the acre, and

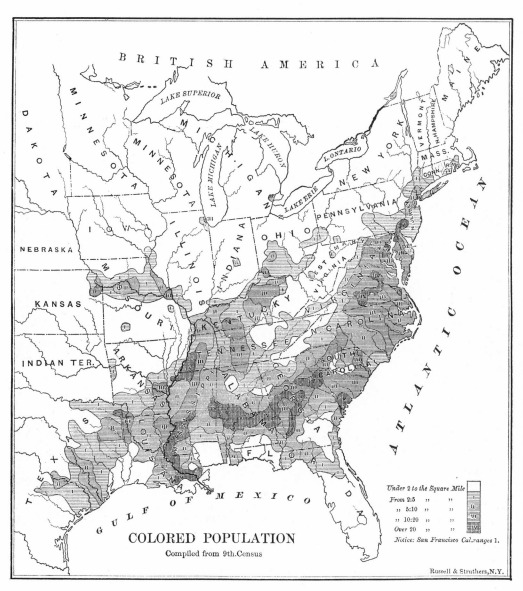

COLORED POPULATION

Compiled from 9th. Census

Under 2 to the Square Mile

From 2:5 ,, ,,

,, 5:10 ,, ,,

,, 10:20 ,, ,,

Over 20 ,, ,,

Notice: San Francisco Cal. ranges 1.

Russell & Struthers, N.Y.

MAP SHOWING THE DISTRIBUTION OF THE COLORED POPULATION OF THE UNITED STATES.

THE GULF STATES AND ARKANSAS.

Physical and Political

By A. Guyot

INDIAN TERRITORY

ARKANSAS

MISSISSIPPI

LOUISIANA

TEXAS

TENNESSEE

ALABAMA

NEW MEXICO

MEXICO

GULF OF MEXICO

LLANO ESTACADO (STAKED PLAIN)

CHEROKEE COUNTRY

CREEK COUNTRY

CHICKASAW

CHOCTAW NATION

APACHES

GYPSUM

APACHE MTS

Rio Grande del Norte

Gulf Stream

PROFILE ON THE LINE A·B.

Elevations increased 50 times

6000 Engl. Feet

Cora Goteville Cameron Pine Hills Caldwell Hempstead Galveston

Mesquite Timber Limestone Hills Gulf of Mexico Llano Estacado

Places near New Orleans.
1 Napoleonville or Assump.
2 Bonfouca (Carrizo). Yum.
3 Lafourche
4 St. Charles
5 St. Carrollton
6 Algiers

Scale
Geographical Miles
English Miles

○ County Towns
Capitals are underlined
Rail Roads .... Canals
☐ General Surface of land below 800 feet Altitude
☐ General Surface of land above 800 feet Altitude

Entered according to Act of Congress in the Year 1878 by Scribner Armstrong & Co. in the Office of the Librarian of Congress at Washington D.C.

the manufacture may begin early in November. Flooded rice-lands produce ten barrels to the acre; unflooded, six. There are orange orchards in this parish producing 3,000,000 of oranges annually. Such facts are eloquent.

Lands in certain of the parishes, not very far from towns and trade centres, can be generally purchased at from $3 to $15 per acre; those more remote are only worth $1 or $1.50 per acre. The general health of South-western Louisiana is good; there is no greater error than the common supposition in the North that the lowland climate is fatal to health. There is not a heartier or healthier population in the Union than that of South-western Louisiana; none more frank, unsuspicious and generous. Of course hostility and even ostracism, at the present time, are the lot of such as take sides for the Kellogg Government; but for him who does not take active part, no matter what his opinions may be, there is never even a harsh word. The recent operations of the "White League" in Northern Louisiana have been prompted by the extremists of the Democratic party, in the vain hope of intimidating negro voters, and driving out "Yankees" who are settled in some of the parishes, and who vote the Republican ticket. The assassinations of which this League has been guilty, and the proscriptive measures which it has adopted, are condemned in the strongest terms by large numbers of native Conservatives in other sections of the State, who realize that no reform is possible on the basis of an exclusive white man's government, and who appreciate the immense harm done the material interests of the commonwealth by a revival of the old Ku-Klux tactics which once disgraced the State.

Louisiana has some few valuable minerals, and the discovery of rock-salt in Vermilion parish, and of crystalline sulphur on the Calcasieu river, has encouraged a search for others. Iron is scattered at various depths below the surface of the State south of Red river, and in some of the parishes it is so abundant as to obstruct the ploughs or the hoes of the farmers. Valuable deposits of organized peat are found in many places near the coast, and the investment of a little capital might soon develop a great industry in the preparation of this important fuel. Coal abounds in certain regions through which railway lines are already projected, and the petroleum wells in Bossier, Bienville, and Natcnitoches parishes, as well as in a broad belt extending nearly to the Gulf in Calcasieu parish, promise a remarkable development. The salt region runs through five islands, ranged along the coast for about twenty miles west of the mouth of the Atchafalaya. One of these islands is 140 feet above the sea-level.

VIII.

THE POLITICAL SITUATION IN LOUISIANA.

THE testimony of most of the planters in Louisiana, as elsewhere throughout the South, is that the free negro works well, and earns his wages, save when he is distracted by politics. Indeed, there are none who are willing to assert that free labor has not been a success; and the majority would prefer it to the most arbitrary days of ownership, if the State were otherwise in a settled condition.

It is, nevertheless, evident that political excitements, gotten up by adventurers with the hope of obtaining power, take the negro's attention altogether too much from his work, and constitute a species of mild intellectual dissipation, which he thinks it vastly fine to indulge in, but which only unfits him for serious efforts at progress, and factitiously elevates him to a position directly opposed to the interests of his fellow-citizens.

Judging from conversations with great numbers of persons, there is not much hope that the equality of races will be at present recognized by the white man in Louisiana. He will not admit that the negro is at all competent to legislate for him, or to vote with him on matters of common importance to white and black.

While he has no desire to see any of the conditions of that kind of society which prevailed before the war re-established, he refuses to recognize or acquiesce in the actual condition. Having been, as he considers, doomed by the revolution, he sits haughtily tranquil, wrapped in reserve, save when he ventures to predict the downfall of the Republic, and to lament the despotism under which he asserts that he is kept. He is fond of gloomy horoscopes, and delights in announcing to the world that the precedent established in Louisiana by the Lynch returning-board and the Durell decision will yet be disastrous to New York and Massachusetts.

He is not more glad to be rid of slavery than he would be to see the last negro vanish from the soil. He is weary of the whole subject of politics; anxious for immigration, yet doubtful of its practical results; willing to guarantee, to the extent allowed by his impaired fortunes, any reasonable enterprise tending toward the commercial development of the State, but discouraged, and oftentimes distracted.

Impulsive, intensely individual, and extremely sensitive, he fancies that he sees fresh humiliations in the thousand changes which are but the inevitable attendants of the revolution. In the parishes, the tyranny of those who use the new political element for base purposes is constantly increasing in boldness and violence—now showing itself in an appetite for public plunder, and now in shielding from richly merited punishment some infamous scoundrel.

Sometimes the negro, annoyed and perplexed, takes the reins into his own hands, and then follow scenes of bloodshed and violence; then comes to the front the question of black *versus* white, and the commonwealth is, as nearly always when the Legislature is in session, convulsed to its centre. Meantime professional politicians and lobbyists constantly arrange new plans for the pacification of parties, for compromises never to be effected, and victories never to be won.

The citizens are willing and anxious to work, but all their energy, all the intense commercial ambition of New Orleans is neutralized by the incubus of a legislature which in no wise properly represents the people. The negro afield, with his sturdy family around him, cultivating the little plot which has at last become his, and the white man, with his own hand to the plough, showing that he no longer thinks labor degrading, are, to be sure, gratifying sights, which present themselves from time to time; but they are by no means so common as they would be if the State were not constantly anguish-stricken, overwhelmed with taxation and myriad debts, and hindered from making the improvements necessary to the securing of new trade and consequent prosperity.

There are in Louisiana men of brilliant and imposing eloquence; men of *entrain* and magnetism, who seem fashioned for leadership; and yet, strange as it may appear, who take but little interest in the affairs of their own State; who either content themselves with deriding their inferiors, or with watching chances for personal elevation by taking advantage of the weakness or insincerity of those in power. They laugh at the discomfiture of their fellows, while the house is being pulled down over their own heads. With anarchy at their doors, they refuse to take the first step toward reconciliation, or a proper understanding between the races now so equally divided as to numbers within the State limits.

In 1864 Michael Hahn was chosen first free State Governor of Louisiana. On the occasion of his inauguration, the celebrated Gilmore, then a band director in the Federal army, gave his first mammoth jubilee. Cannon roared, drums rolled, the earth shook. A constitutional convention was next held, and a constitution prohibiting slavery was a few months later adopted by the Reconstruction party. In 1865 Henry C. Warmoth was elected a delegate from the "territory" of Louisiana to the National Congress. The negroes placed him in office, and supplied him with funds. Under Banks, he had been provost judge of the parish of Orleans, and there had acquired influence over, and the confidence of, the colored voters.

In the fall of 1865 the first general election under the new State constitution was held, and the Democrats were overwhelmingly successful in all sections. They elected J. Madison Wells Governor, and at the first session of their Legislature passed several bills which placed them in direct antagonism with the colored people. Among the measures instrumental in bringing on a conflict of races was a bill for the regulation of labor, which the negroes bitterly opposed.

In 1866 a new constitutional convention was held, the members of the Radical party desiring to check the Democratic successes by remodeling the constitution. Riots occurred, in which white and black men lost their lives. This led to the appointment of a special committee of investigation by Congress, and to the inauguration of the policy of reconstruction.

In the fall of 1867 another convention met, which had been provided for by the Reconstruction Act, and in May of 1868 a thoroughly radical constitution was adopted, Henry C. Warmoth being elected Governor, and a Republican Legislature, of course largely composed of ignorant negroes, coming into power. This legislative session was occupied by petty squabbles, and by the passage of many bills in the interest of corrupt jobs. The Conservatives did not, however, yield their power without some show of resistance, and the Presidential campaign of 1868 was the occasion of much severe fighting in the State. The negroes were very shamefully intimidated, and but few of them succeeded in casting their votes for President.

However, the new party, composed of ignorant and immoral negroes, led on by reckless and greedy white adventurers, held Louisiana completely in its power, and gross frauds were perpetrated. Ignorance, captivated by the glitter of money, and misled by wily sharpers, thrust ruin in a hundred ways upon the unfortunate State. For two or three years the most scandalous plundering was indulged in. The Governor was himself disgusted with such manœuvres, and gradually showed a leaning toward the respectable Conservatives, who now and then gathered around him. But the Conservatives had waited too long before attempting a policy of conciliation. The negroes were thoroughly estranged, and could not be persuaded to listen to anything which they might say. A division took place in the Republican party; the Legislature became hostile to Governor Warmoth, and in the summer of 1871 a new convention was held in New Orleans. Both wings of the now divided Republican party attempted to obtain control of this convention, which was held in the Custom-House. The Federal appointees in New Orleans—Mr. Casey, the collector of the port, Mr. Packard, the United States Marshal, and others—refused the opposite faction admission to the convention, the services of a company of United States infantry being secured to prevent Warmoth's entrance.

Upon this, Warmoth and his party declared war against the Federal appointees, held an opposition convention, and even sent a committee to President Grant asking for the removal of Packard and Casey. The President disregarded this request, and Warmoth and his friends therefore opposed his re-election, Warmoth even braving the anger of the Administration by participating in the Cincinnati " Liberal " convention of 1872.

The division in the Republican ranks grew daily more pronounced, and when the time came to choose a new governor candidates were abundant. The Conservatives finally united upon John McEnery; Warmoth ran on an independent ticket, and the Federal, or "Custom-House" party, brought forward William Pitt Kellogg, the then United States Senator from the State. Mr. Kellogg had been collector of the port of New Orleans under President Johnson, and had acquired some little knowledge of Louisiana politics.   He was, without doubt, beaten in the election for governor, McEnery being unquestionably elected, although it is conceded on all hands that frauds were liberally practiced by both parties.

The Conservatives, who had doubtless learned wisdom from their political experiences since the close of the war, were about to resume power, not a little glad to be freed from the contest of factions which had so long paralyzed the State, when their hopes were dashed by sudden Federal intervention.

The history of the infamy which, in the name of law, was perpetrated in New Orleans, in December of 1872, is well known to all who have taken any interest in general politics.   The non-elected Legislature was placed in power by Federal bayonets, called into requisition by an order issued by a Federal judge named Durell. A returning-board which had not, and did not pretend to have the election returns before it, yet which was the only one recognized by Judge Durell, who was firm in his policy of usurpation, seated the Kellogg government, and struck a direct blow at the will of the majority.   It pushed Louisiana to the very verge of ruin.

The Supreme Court — New Orleans.

In his speech on the Louisiana bill, made before the United States Senate early in 1873, Carl Schurz has briefly summed up the whole matter in the following words. Speaking of the Legislature mentioned above, he says:

"There was, I believe, not a single one of them who was returned by a board that had the official returns of the election in its hands or had ever seen them.   By virtue of what, then, were those men put in the Legislature? Not by virtue of votes, not by virtue of returns, but upon the ground of newspaper reports, of wild guesses, of forged affidavits, of the usurpation of a Federal judge, and of Federal bayonets. That was their whole title to the legislative capacity which they assumed.

"What was their first act ?   They impeached the Governor.   Throwing aside all the forms of impeachment prescribed by law, they impeached and suspended the Governor, if a summary decree can be called impeachment and suspension. They who had not a shadow of right based upon law, upon votes, upon an election, upon legal returns, proceeded to undo one governor and to make another. That second governor was Pinchback.   The National Government recognized him as the Governor of Louisiana.

"Then they proceeded to what they called the canvass of the votes in the Legislature, not canvassing legal returns of voters in any legal form, but a canvass on the ground of newspaper reports, wild guesses, and forged affidavits. What I say here is by no means an exaggerated assertion, for it is distinctly proven by the testimony, and I think it is denied by no one. Then they declared the men of their choice: Kellogg, Governor; Antoine, Lieutenant-Governor, and so on all the State officers of Louisiana.

"Thus the usurpation is consummated—a usurpation without the shadow of a law as an excuse; with nothing but fraud and force to stand upon; a usurpation palpable, gross, shameless, and utterly subversive of all principles of republican government; a usurpation such as this country has never seen, and probably no citizen of the United States has ever dreamed of. The offspring of this Legislature is the Kellogg government."

What has been the result of this usurpation? The State has been broken down by taxation and debt; the negro has been demoralized; the principal cities and towns are impoverished.

Had the usurpation been confined within bounds, the people of Louisiana would doubtless have borne it in silence; but the usurping government was not content with ordinary measures. Possessed of arbitrary power, it proceeded to exercise it in the most odious fashion. Scarcely ninety days after the Durell decision, the judges whom, by large majorities, the people of the parish of Orleans had elected to preside over certain district courts, and who had been commissioned by Warmoth and sworn in, were unseated by force, and the candidates who had been defeated were put in their places.

This was the signal for an uprising. The incipient riot, however, was speedily quelled, and the natives of the State who did not propose to compromise their loyalty by a collision with the United States troops, stationed in New Orleans, were remanded to their condition of a subjugated class.

Resistance to taxation, which began in 1873, was pretty effectually checked by the proclamation of the President, which made such resistance dangerous. People who wish to keep in their hands what little property now remains to them are compelled in one manner or another to pay up.

New Orleans has suffered peculiarly, its taxable property being cumbered with two huge debts, that of the city itself, now estimated at about $22,500,000, and over three-fifths of the State's various liabilities. While the city groans under such enormous taxation, it has been loaded down with grievous licenses on all trades, professions, and occupations, amounting to nearly $1,000,000 annually.

Under these burdens it is not astonishing that real estate in the city has declined from thirty to more than fifty per cent. The double public debt of the city is already more than one-fourth of its property assessment, and many times more than the value of all the available property now owned by

The United States Barracks — New Orleans.

the corporation. The annual expenditures of the city were increased from $3,767,000 in 1862, to $6,961,381 in 1872; and still mount upward. Meantime the streets remain uncared for, and the treasury is empty. Where has the money gone?

The city certificates are sold on the street at enormous discounts; the Legislature's sessions cost the people half a million dollars yearly, instead of $100,000 as in 1860, and this also the city is compelled mainly to pay; whoever, therefore, buys property in the city of New Orleans buys with it a share of a great and discouraging public debt.

There is some hope, however, at present, for the administration of the metropolis. The economy inaugurated in 1873 will be but of small avail for a year or two, for the sums expended around the City Hall in New Orleans' were so enormous that gradual reduction will not relieve the people much. The budget of 1872 provided for the payment of the sum of $229,000 to the various employes about the City Hall, or more than is annually paid to the President, Vice-President, judges of the Supreme Court, and cabinet officers of the United States, and the State officers of Louisiana. There was a veritable army of office-holders and dependents about the municipal head-quarters.

The government of the city is now entirely vested in a mayor, and seven "administrators," respectively charged with the administration of finance, commerce, improvements, assessments, police, public accounts, and water works and public buildings. These eight gentlemen constitute what is known as the City Council, and are elected biennially at the time of the election for members of the General Assembly.

The famous Board of Metropolitan Police, created by Warmoth, is in no manner under the direction of the City Council, the administrator of the police department being merely an ex-officio member of that board. The Metropolitan Police constitute a body directed by a board controlled by the State Executive, and which is paid by taxes levied upon the city.   It is in reality an armed military force which the central State Government maintains in the capital for the enforcement of its measures and the prevention of riots.   Since Warmoth created it, its cost has been enormous, amounting to hundreds of thousands of dollars yearly. The police expenses for the year ending October 1st, 1869, were $930,809.09; for 1870, $725,357.73; and for 1871, about $800,000.   The municipality constantly threatens rebellion against the control of its action by State interference, but, meantime, that control increases in strength and extent.

The speculation in warrants, the creation of certain courts out of elements diametrically opposed to the real interests of the people of the State, are evils which are even worse than they have been represented by the injured, and for which there is no excuse. The Federal Government may and should protect the freedman in the rights given him by the revolution consequent on the war; but it should not permit the use of ignorant masses of negroes as stepping-stones to tyrannical, centralized power; it should not allow interlopers to array the black freedman against the white freeman, under any pretense whatsoever.

To give an account of the condition of the State finances is somewhat difficult. It was stated, in 1872, that the amount of the actual funded and unfunded debt was between $24,000,000 and $25,000,000; that the contingent liabilities amounted to $5,483,602; and that the amount of bonds "authorized" by the Legislature, but not yet issued, was $10,770,000, making a total of actual, contingent, and prospective liability which is far from cheering, especially as from 1860 to 1871 the valuation of property in the State decreased from $435,000,000 to $250,000,000.

With the possibility of a war of races constantly thrusting forward its ugly head, it is easy to perceive how industrial development is hindered and capital frightened away; it is easy to see how passions which should long since have become extinct still smoulder, and are ready at a moment's warning to burst forth into anarchy and chaos.

It is now and then asserted that corruption, consequent upon despair and disgust, has affected the ranks of the native born citizens; and that there have been cases where even they have crowded the lobbies of the hybrid legislature in the interests of corporations. This seems hardly credible, when it is remembered that the masses of the conservative citizens vehemently assert that the returning-board which established that legislature in power had no official statements in its possession on which to base its conclusion, and since they are supported in their assertion by the declaration of a Committee of the United States Senate that the Lynch returning-board's canvass " had no semblance of integrity."

A visit to Mechanics' Institute, the seat of the Kellogg Legislature, during the session, is a curious experience. At the doors stand negro policemen, armed with clubs and revolvers; and crowds of blacks obstruct the passage-ways.

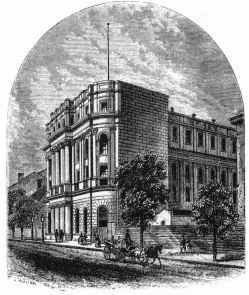

Mechanics' Institute—New Orleans.

Mounting a staircase covered with old, tobacco stained matting, one finds himself in the House of Representatives, where sit the law-makers with their feet upon their desks. Nearly all the honorable members are black; some of them are so completely ignorant that they cannot follow the course of debate. But all are so drilled by the adventurers who control them that their opposition to anything likely to better the present horrible political condition is firm and determined. There are also many blacks in the Senate. When a colored man is in the chair, he is always falling into profound errors with regard to his rulings and decisions. He finds it difficult to follow the course of any bill the moment half-a-dozen members are speaking of it, and constantly submits to corrections and suggestions from some lean white man, dressed in new clothes, who smiles contemptuously, as, from a carpet-bag point of view, he superintends this legislative farce.   And this scene has been enacted for six weary years—the State meantime sinking deeper and deeper into the abyss of crushing taxation.   It is not wonderful that "White Leagues," in opposition to negro government, are springing up throughout Louisiana.

Here are some instances which will show how greatly property has decreased in value under the present crushing taxation and wholesale plundering.

A gentleman in New Orleans was, some time since, offered a loan of $6,000 on the security of certain real estate owned by him.   He did not then need the money; but recently went to the capitalist and said, " I will now accept your kind offer."   Said the capitalist, " I would not now lend you $600 on the property.   It is worth nothing as security.   No property in the city, in the current condition of politics, is worth anything."

A gentleman who purchased, a short time before the war, a finely wooded estate in a rich section of Louisiana, for $100 in gold per acre, informed me that he had tried repeatedly to borrow upon the security of that estate, and that he could not get any one to lend a sum *equivalent to one dollar per acre on it.*

Some three years ago a prominent capitalist was addressed by a citizen of Louisiana, who represented that a great many rich estates could be purchased in various sections of the commonwealth for at least one-third of their original value; and added, as an inducement to speedy decision, that he did not think property would ever be lower in Louisiana.   The capitalist replied that he differed with his much esteemed friend; that in a few years those estates would, by the various derangements consequent on the then predominant legislation, be reduced to almost no value whatever, and that he was therefore determined to wait.

During a visit to New Orleans, in March of 1874, my attention was called to a number of notable instances of the rapid decline of property.   One gentleman pointed out a house which, in 1868, he would have been glad to purchase for $12,000; a little later it was sold for $8,000; then for $6,000, and now no one could be found to take it at $4,000.   Many houses are given rent free to persons who will occupy them, that they may not be allowed to fall into decay.

The sheriff is the prosperous man in New Orleans.   His office has been made worth $60,000 yearly.

The annual session of the Legislature, fortunately limited by the Constitution to sixty days, is a terrible trial.   The state government cannot be depended upon.   Earnest men, on the conservative side, are deterred from conciliatory action by the insincerity of those in power.   At one time the dominant party seemed really desirous of inaugurating reform in the management of certain affairs, and called for a committee of investigation to be composed of the property-holders.   But as, at nearly the same time, it voted away $500,000 worth of State bonds for a doubtful enterprise, the property-holders could not be made to believe that there was, in truth, any desire for " retrenchment " and " reform."

Time and time again the legislature which the Federal Government placed in power in Louisiana has sworn in as members men whom the returning-boards did not even pretend had been elected; and these men have been allowed to sit as representatives of people whom they have never seen.

One of the worst features of the situation in Louisiana is the entire absence of the intelligent and well-to-do negroes from politics there. It is only the rascals and the dubious who get into power; and they are more terrible than the white rogues. They practice all the vices in the calendar; they take the thousands of dollars diverted from their proper channels, and lavish them upon abandoned white women; they enrich themselves and boast of it.

The present condition of the educational system of Louisiana is encouraging, although disfigured by evils which arise from the political disorganization. The State superintendent of education, at the time of my visit, was a mulatto gentleman of evident culture—seeming, indeed, quite up to the measure of his task, if he only had the means to perform it. He could not tell me how many schools were in operation in the State; nor how much the increase had been since the war. There was, he explained, the greatest difficulty in procuring returns from the interior districts, even the annual reports being forwarded tardily, or sometimes not at all. The school-tax has heretofore been two mills on the dollar, but it is to be raised to one-fourth of one per cent. The State is in six divisions, one of which comprises New Orleans, and there is a superintendent for each division.

There are now in Louisiana 291,000 youth between the ages of six and twenty-one; and it is fair to presume that at least one-half of them are children of colored parents, since the population of Louisiana is pretty equally divided into white and black.. The Legislature appropriates half a million dollars yearly for the use of the schools, of which about seven-eighths is annually expended. There are a few mixed schools now in the State, although the mingling of colors has not been insisted upon.

Great numbers of private schools have sprung into existence, especially in New Orleans, where the predominant religion is the Catholic; and the Germans have shown their fear of mixed schools by establishing special schools for their own children. The Catholic clergy in New Orleans have not gone so far as to forbid the attendance of children of Catholic parents in the public schools; but the organ of that clergy announced, some time since, that the poverty, and not the will of the parties, acceded the permission to attend secular schools. Immense progress has certainly been made since the war. In 1868, when the real work of school reform in the State began, there was no supervision whatever exercised over school funds, and millions of dollars were uselessly squandered. There were then less than one hundred public schools in the entire State. But it was estimated at the first educational convention ever held in Louisiana, which met in New Orleans, in 1872, that there were at that time 1,100 schools in operation, with nearly 100,000 pupils. The old system, or lack of system, had had most painful results. There were no means of obtaining proper reports; there was no certainty that the few teachers who were employed did their duty.

The present school-law is well adapted to the condition and wants of the State. There is one ugly fact in the way of progress in the interior of the commonwealth, and that is, as asserted by the superior officials, that the money appropriated to the different parishes for school funds, has, in many cases, never been used for schools; and prosecution of officers supposed to have retained that money is of but small avail. There are ostensibly parish boards of school directors in office in every section of the State; but they do not all perform their duty.

The school-law provides for tne maintenance of a proper normal department; and good teachers are yearly sent out therefrom. New Orleans now has about seventy public schools, and a little more than $700,000 invested in school property. The teachers in those schools exclusively attended by white children are all white; in the few mixed schools there are some colored teachers. The superintendent said that it would not do to insist upon mixed schools in remote districts, as the people would in that case refuse to have any school at all.

The Louisiana State University, temporarily located at Baton Rouge until its new buildings at Alexandria are completed, is a struggling institution, which needs and merits much aid from richer States; and an agricultural college and a system of industrial schools have been projected. The colored children in the public schools manifest an earnestness and aptitude which amply demonstrates their claim to be admitted to them. People in all sections have ceased grumbling at the " school-house taxes," and that in itself is a cheering sign.

IX.

"HO FOR TEXAS!"—GALVESTON.

ONE of the saddest sights in New Orleans or Galveston is the daily arrival of hundreds of refugees from the older Southern States, seeking homes on the Texan prairies. The flood of emigration from South Carolina, Alabama and Georgia is formidable, and turned the tide of politics in Texas, in a single

Going to Texas.

year, from Republican flood to Democratic ebb. Old men and little children, youths and maidens, clad in homespun, crowd the railway cars, looking forward eagerly to the land of promise. The ignorance of these poor people with regard to the geography of the country in general, is dense. "I never traveled so much befo'," is a common phrase; "is Texas a mighty long ways off yet?" The old men, if one enters into conversation with them, will regale him with accounts of life in their homes "befo' the surrender." With them, everything dates from the war, leaving the past irrevocably behind its yawning gulf, while in front there is only poverty—or flight.

The route from New Orleans to Brashear City is, in the delightful months of April and May, one of the most beautiful in the South. The railroad which connects at Brashear City with the Morgan steamers sailing to Galveston, and along which the tide of emigration constantly flows, traverses weird forests and lofty cane-brakes, and passes over bayous, swamps, and long stretches of sugar plantations.

Crossing the Mississippi by the great railroad ferry to Algiers, the traveler soon leaves behind the low, green banks, studded with neat, white houses embowered in a profusion of orange groves; and is borne out of sight of the black lines of smoke left upon the cloudless sky by the funnels of the river steamers. He passes Bayou des Allemands, and a low country filled with deep, black pools; hurries across the reedy and saturated expanse of Trembling Prairie, dotted with fine oaks; rattles by Raceland, and its moist, black fields, to La Fourche Bayou, on which lies the pretty, cultivated town of Thibodeaux.

He next passes Chacahoula swamp, a wilderness of shriveled cypresses and stagnant water; Tigerville, with its Indian mounds; the rich Bœuf country, along the banks of whose lovely bayou lie wonderful sugar lands, once crowded with prosperous planters, but now showing many an idle plantation. He passes immense groves, from the boughs of whose trees thousands of Spanish moss beards are pendent; and through which long and sombre aisles, like those of a cathedral, open to right and left. He wonders at the presence of the bearded moss on all the trees, and his commercial eye perhaps suggests that it be made available in upholstery; but he is told that the quaint parasite already does good service as the scavenger of the air.

At Brashear City he finds a steamer for Texas at the fine docks built by the enterprising proprietor of the " Morgan line," and notes, as he passes out to the blue waters of the Gulf, the richness of the vegetation along the shores of the inlet. An afternoon and a night—and he is in Galveston.

The coast line of Texas, bordering upon the Gulf of Mexico from Sabine Pass to the Rio Grande,—from the Louisiana boundary to the hybrid, picturesque territory where the American and Mexican civilizations meet and conflict, is richly indented and studded with charming bays. Trinity, Galveston, West, Matagorda, Espiritu Santu, Aransas, and Corpus Christi harbors, each and all offer varied possibilities for future commerce. The whole coast, extending several hundred miles, is also bordered by a series of islands and peninsulas, long and narrow in form, which protect the inner low-lying banks from the high seas.

The plains extending back from the coast in the valleys of the Sabine, the San Jacinto and the Colorado, seem in past centuries to have formed a vast delta, whose summit was probably near the Colorado, and whose angles were formed by the Sabine and the Nueces. Great horizons, apparently boundless as the sea, characterize these plains; the wanderer on the Gulf sees only the illimitable expanse of wave and alluvial; the eye is fatigued by the immensity, and gladly seeks rest upon the lines of ancient forest which cover the borders of the Colorado and the Nueces. Beyond these plains comes the zone of the prairies, whose lightly undulating surface extends inland as far as the Red river, while the mountains on the north-west crown the fertile knolls of rolling country.

These mountains are portions of the Sierra Madre, which is itself but a spur from the grand Andean chain. Running to the north-west in the State of Coahuila (once a portion of Texas), the Sierra Madre spur bifurcates to enter the Texas of the present, and continues in a north-westerly direction, under the name of the San Saba, in whose breasts are locked the rich minerals which the Spaniard, during his period of domination, so often and so vainly strove to unearth.

The Texan coast sweeps downward and outward by a wide curve to the Mexican boundary. Approaching it from the sea, the eye encounters only a low-lying level of white sand, with which, however, at all hours, the deep colors of the gulf are admirably contrasted.

The great sea highway to which I have previously alluded, from Brashear City, on Berwick's Bay, on the Louisiana coast, to Galveston, is well known and fascinating to the modern traveler. The enterprise and liberal expenditure of a citizen of New York, Mr. Charles Morgan, has covered the waves of this route with steamships, which, until recently, furnished the only means of communication between Texas and the rest of the United States. The Morgan Line was not merely the outgrowth of an earnest demand; it was the work of an adventurous pioneer; and although its importance, in view of the grand railroad development of Northern Texas, can henceforth be but secondary, its founder will always be remembered for his foresight and daring. The improvements in the channels from Berwick's Bay outward are also the work of the owner of this line. They comprehend the dredging of a great bar which once obstructed the short passage to the Gulf, and when completed will be of infinite importance to the commerce of the whole south-west. Thousands of tons of shells have been dragged out of the dark-blue water to make room for the prows of the Morgan fleet, pointed toward Galveston and Indianola.

And what is Galveston? A thriving city set down upon a brave little island which has fought its way out of the depths of the Gulf, and given to the United States her noblest beach, and to Texas an excellent harbor. Seen from the sea, when approaching under the fervid light of a Southern dawn, or when sailing away from it in the white moonlight, so intensely reflected on the sand, it is indeed a place where

> "Myrtle groves
> Shower down their fragrant wealth upon the waves
> Whose long, long swell mirrors the dark-green glow
> Of cedars and the snow of jasmine cups."

It is a city in the sands; yet orange and myrtle, oleander and delicate rose, and all the rich-hued blossoms of a tropic land, shower their wealth about it. In the morning the air is heavy with the perfume of blossoms; in the evening the light, to Northern eyes, is intense and enchanting.

Thirty-one miles of picturesque beach are constantly laved by the restless waters. It is only a few steps from an oleander grove to the surf, the shell-strewn strand, and the dunes. The approach from the mainland will instinctively remind the traveler of Venice. A great bridge, two miles in length, connects the islet with the continent. Dismantled fortifications near the bridge show one that the war reached even to the Gulf; and the mass of low-lying, white, balconied houses forms a pleasant group.

"It is only a few steps from an oleander grove to the surf."

Much of the island is unkempt and neglected-looking. Cattle wander freely about. There are a few market-gardens, and some meat-packeries in the suburbs of the city. Galveston itself, however, is as trim and elegant as any town in the South. The business quarter looks quaint and odd to strangers' eyes, because of the many long piers and jetties; the mule-carts, unloading schooners anchored lightly in the shallow waves; and the hosts of slouch-ing darkies, shouting and dancing as they move about their tasks.

The "Strand," the main business thoroughfare, has been twice ruined by fire, but has sprung up again into quite a magnificence of shop and warehouse; and Tremont, and other of the commercial avenues, boast of as substantial structures as grace the elder Northern cities. There is a network of wharves and ware-houses, built boldly out into the water, in a manner which recalls Venice even more forcibly than does the approach from the mainland.

The heat is never disagreeably intense in Galveston; a cool breeze blows over the island night and day; and the occasional advent of the yellow-fever,—the dread intruder who mows down hundreds of victims,—is a mystery. It comes, apparently, upon the wings of the very wind which puts health and life into every vein; and many a midsummer is rendered memorable by its ravages.

Yet there could hardly be imagined a more delightful water-side resort than Galveston, during, at least, four months in the year. My first visit to the beach was in February, and the air of Northern June fanned the waves. The winter months could certainly be delightfully spent in Galveston; and the little city has built a splendid hotel as a seductive bait for travelers.

Galveston is memorable in Texan history as the retreat of the dread pirates of the Gulf— the smugglers and outlaws of Barataria. Though discovered in 1686 by La Salle, it remained uninhabited until 1816, when Lafitte and his pirate brethren from the Louisiana coast tested the capacities of the harbor, and shortly after it was occupied by the forces of the "Mexican Republic." Privateers went out from the bay to cruise against Spanish commerce, and the fleets of Spain were swept from the Gulf.

The island also became a depot for the sale of negroes, to be imported into Louisiana, the native African's market value being one dollar per pound. At one time the followers of "Lafitte, the Galveston buccaneer," numbered a thousand refugees from justice. Lafitte was appointed "governor of the island" by the Mexican authorities, who cared little for the character of their public servants, provided they were efficient.

But in due time the prince of pirates was compelled by the Government of the United States to leave Galveston forever, as his followers had so far forgotten themselves as to plunder American shipping. The island again became a waste, and only an occasional superstitious hunter for the spoils of the pirates visited the sandy shores.

As the republic of Texas grew in after years, however, so grew Galveston. It was a promising town before the late war, with perhaps ten thousand population. While the rude interior towns were still in their infancy, Galveston was a port of entry, the station of the navies of the little republic, and the scene of many courtly festivities in honor of foreign ambassadors.

During the war its commerce was, of course, utterly broken, and it was occupied in turn by Union and Confederate soldiers. Latterly it has assumed a commercial importance which promises to make it a large and flourishing city,

"The mule-carts, unloading schooners anchored lightly in the shallow waves." [Page 102.]

although it has many rivals in the field whence it expects to draw its trade. The cotton factors of the city are enthusiastic in their belief that they shall succeed in bringing to their port the majority of the cotton grown in Texas, but they overlook the formidable rivalry of St. Louis. The capitalists of that city intend to control the whole cotton crop of Northern Texas, bringing it into their market over the new Cairo and Fulton line and over the railroads running through Central Northern Texas; and in case the New Orleans, Mobile and Texas railroad should connect Houston with New Orleans, Houston might take the remainder of the cotton crop, diverting it from the Galveston channel, and throwing it into the New Orleans market. Galveston has but one railroad exit, the line leading to Houston, where all the railroads of the grand new system will centre. Although the business men of Galveston are confident that the

"Galveston has many huge cotton presses"

cotton crop will all fall into their hands, those of Houston think differently. Galveston has many huge cotton presses, in whose sheds thousands of bales lie stored.

It is to be hoped that such a large proportion of the twenty millions of acres of cotton-bearing lands in Texas will speedily come under cultivation that all the channels of trade will be filled to repletion. The freed negroes, who are throughout Texas an industrious and prosperous class, although, of course, characterized by the failings of their race, and the crudities consequent on their sudden change of station, are extensively engaged in the culture of cotton. The negro who is fortunate enough to have secured a tract of land, grows all the cotton he can, and if he would take the necessary pains to clean and prepare it, would soon enrich himself in the profitable culture.

The lands at the head of Galveston Bay, and on the adjoining San Jacinto Bay, as well as all the lands in immediate proximity to the Gulf, are well adapted to the culture of sea-island cotton—equal in quality to the best grown upon the islands along the South Carolina and Georgia coasts. It would be difficult to imagine a better paying culture than that of this excellent staple, the yield being from $200 to $300 in gold per acre. The alluvial lands along the Gulf demand the presence of the Chinaman; great fortunes lie hidden in their flats.

The export of sea-island cotton is trivial as yet, but growing daily. In 1870 the exports amounted to $17,719; in 1871, to $44,863, and in 1872, to $84,437. Some of the exports of the ordinary upland cotton from Galveston since the war are shown in the appended table:

Year.	Bales.	Dollars.
1866	16,417	$2,146,224
1867	66,271	6,730,257
1868	87,794	7,687,464
1869	84,485	9,997,661
1870	144,123	14,476,550
1871	233,737	16,060,794
1872	186,073	11,898,870
1873	333,502	32,423,806

The commercial year begins May 1st.

The total amount of dutiable and free imports for each year since the re-establishment of business, May 1st, 1866, in the Galveston Custom-House, until December 31st, 1872, is as follows: 1866, $366,388; in 1867, $766,627; in 1868, $251,052; in 1869, $276,588; in 1870, $774,918; in 1871, $1,586,408; and in 1872, $1,940,292.

The number of entrances of foreign and coastwise vessels in Galveston harbor yearly varies from 700 to 1,400. Steamships loaded with cotton run regularly between Galveston and Liverpool; and, returning, bring out English, Irish, and Scotch emigrants, giving them credit for their passage-money, and binding them by contract to work for a fixed sum for a certain term after their arrival in Texas. This plan has thus far succeeded admirably, and is bringing hundreds of worthy families from the slums of English cities into the inspiring atmosphere of the Texan uplands. The main shipments of cotton are, of course, to Liverpool although London, Bremen, and Hamburg receive some of the crop.

There are now fifteen steamers running to Berwick's Bay; eight to New

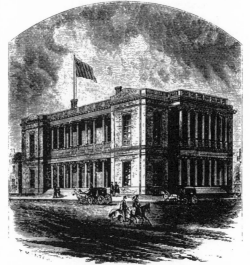

The Custom-House—Galveston.

York; a line to Baltimore; bayou steamers to Houston, and river steamers from the Trinity and the Brazos. The steamship line between New York and Galveston carries about ninety-five per cent. of all the merchandise sent into Texas from New York, Philadelphia, Boston and Baltimore. The foreign trade of the

"Primitive enough is this Texan jail." [Page 107.]

port is increasing with wonderful rapidity; tallow and cotton-seed oil-cake are important exports; and on my second visit to Galveston I saw the famous steamer "Hornet" loading with cattle for Havana. It is proposed to supply the West Indian market hereafter entirely with Texan cattle, the transit requiring only three days; and there are large exports of hides and wool.

The imports are salt, coffee, crockery, iron and tin, and best of all—though non-dutiable—a steady current of sturdy Germans, who tame the wildness of Texas faster than the natives themselves can do it. Galveston is likely to remain the best coffee market in the United States. The importation of lumber from Florida, Louisiana, and Northern ports, employs a large number of vessels yearly, for Galveston stands in a timberless region; there is not an acre of forest land for miles on miles around.

Thus much for the present commerce of Galveston; its future would be perfectly certain were it not for the rivalry forced upon neighboring towns by the marvelously rapid development of transit lines. Very little fear have the Galvestonians, the cheery "sand-crabs," as the people of Houston affectionately call them, of being "left out in the cold." And they go on building superb new avenues, planting their oleanders, and trellising their roses, without any worry for the morrow. The rebound since the war has certainly been surprising. Galveston was almost depopulated at the close of the great struggle, hardly two thousand people remaining there. Let us take a picture or two from the life of the "Island City."

Morning: A bright sunlight on the silver-rippling water, and one catches the inspiring breath of the waves. Yonder is a mass of dense foliage, from whose green peer out faintest red and purest white, the color of the blossoms and the gleam of the house-walls.   Here the oleanders have arched their boughs and made a shaded walk; the magnolia towers above a little balconied cottage, on whose gate a couple of half-naked negro children are swinging; a mocking-bird is imitating the strange whir of the insect-life about him; there is very little din or rattle of carriages or drays; the town seems to have wakened lazily, and to be lolling in the sun-bath, and rejoicing in the hints of the

"Salt and spume o' the sea"

which drift lightly inland.

At the doors of the Custom-House half-a-dozen negroes are lying with their heads upon the broad steps, yawning and joking; at the long, white-painted market-sheds, the market-men and women have done their shouting, and relapsed into a kind of contented rest as they feel the day's heat coming on; under the wooden awnings in the principal avenues of lighter trade a few black-robed, dark-eyed ladies pass quietly to and fro; and from the sea drifts up the chant of dusky watermen loading their mule-carts.

Noon: From this balcony we can overlook the jail, the cathedral, and the town beyond.   Primitive enough is this Texan jail—a common two-story brick structure—surrounded with a high wall, garnished with cruel glass, set in cement. In the jail-yard you may see still life—very still life.   The jailer has just let the prisoners out from their steaming ovens, and they are stretched on the scant grass, a motley crew—an old man, with a hang-dog look, and eyes which seem to fear any one's face as he blinks in the sun's glare; a frowsy, mean negro girl, slouched down upon a water-butt, smoking a corn-cob pipe; and half-a-dozen stout black men, hideous in rágs and dirt.

At the jail's front there is a little tower and a kind of mediæval gate, where the prisoners sometimes huddle to watch a passing circus or to note the advent of a new prisoner.   Invitingly near stands the Court-House, whence now and then issue legal-looking gentlemen, furiously masticating tobacco.

The Catholic Cathedral — Galveston.

Beyond the Cathedral, with its graceful group of roofs, there is a stretch of dusty roadway, and, farther still, a herd of young horses quietly feeding.   Yon dusky horseman means to bring them in.   Ha!   Like the wind they fly—every nerve and sinew strained.   Escaped?   No: The black centaur speeds beyond them like a flash, and the homeward race begins—wild but decisive.   Here and there dead cattle lie scattered.

Here is the very aspect of the San Antonio plains within a mile of the principal seaport of Texas.

Evening: The tide is out, and you may promenade the Gulf shore along a hard, unyielding track left by the receded water, and watch the negro fisherman as he throws his line horizonward, to see it swirl and fall in the retreating surf to come up laden with scaly treasure. The blue of the water, the dark of the seemingly endless strip of beach, the faint crimson, or the purple, or the gold of the sunset sky, form delicious contrasts. A few sails steal seaward like unquiet ghosts; miles away, at a rugged promontory, where the tide is beginning to set about and come in again, the sky seems to have come down to kiss the sea,

"Watch the negro fisherman as he throws his line horizonward."

so exquisitely do colors of heaven and water blend; the long line of carriages hurries cityward; lights seem to spring from the very bosom of the sea, so low and trustingly does the little islet-town lie on the Gulf's surface; the orange-trees and the fig-shrubs send forth a delicate perfume in the cool air of the twilight.

The depth of water on the various bars at the ports along the Texan coast is so shallow that most of them can never receive the largest shipping; but the plan of Captain Howells, the department engineer, for the improvement of the entrance to Galveston Bay, is an excellent one, and contemplates the admission of vessels drawing eighteen feet of water.

The merchants of Galveston will hardly be contented until they have Liverpool ships of largest draught at their very docks. They have built a wharf railroad which enables the loading of vessels directly from the cars, avoiding tedious transfers. They are also planning for a canal to connect the Rio Grande with the Mississippi. This canal would be of immense advantage to South-western Louisiana and South-eastern Texas ; and it is estimated that it would bring into cultivation nearly 4,000,000 acres of land adapted to the raising of sea-island cotton. But this is one of the measures which will probably come with the " moving of the Mexican frontier."

Society in Galveston is good, cultured and refined ; and the standard of education is excellent, judging from the large number of institutions of learning in the city. The Collegiate Institution, the Catholic College, the Convent for Women, the Galveston Female Seminary, the Medical College, and several German schools, all have fine reputations. The new Methodist and Episcopal churches, and the Cathedral are the finest religious edifices in the State.

On Tremont street stands the beautiful Opera House, where is also located the office of *The Galveston News*. This paper, founded by Willard Richardson, is by far the ablest Democratic journal in Texas, and takes high rank in the South-west. Its founder has been conspicuous in aiding by word and work, the upbuilding of Texas, and through a long series of years, has published the " Texas Almanac," a voluminous and faithful record of the great commonwealth's progress.

Galveston also has its Club, " The Gulf City," frequented by many of the prominent citizens of the State. Few cities, with a population of twenty-five or thirty thousand are more spirited ; though manufacturing, as a solid basis is, nevertheless, a supreme need.

X.

A VISIT TO HOUSTON.

THE need of manufactures is, indeed, strongly felt throughout Texas. In nearly every county farmers and merchants are paying treble and quadruple the prices they can afford to pay for goods brought thousands of miles, whereas, local investment in manufacturing establishments would enable them to multiply facilities for agricultural development, and for the comfort and culture of which the interior is now so barren.

Now that transit facilities have come, such an outgrowth of manufactures may be looked for.

The wheat region of Texas comprehends 40,000 square miles. What millions of barrels of flour, if proper mills were at hand, might be placed in the market two months in advance of consignments from the West!

Houston has already begun the manufacture of cotton cloth, and applicants for situations in the mills are so numerous that the employers are embarrassed by them. At Hempstead, New Braunfels, and the State Penitentiary, this manufac-

"The cotton train is already a familiar spectacle on all the great trunk lines."

ture is prosperous; yet I doubt if more than $1,000,000 is thus invested in the whole State. The people of Texas are learning that they have in their very midst all the elements necessary to support life and make it comfortable and even luxurious; and they are making a genuine effort to secure and hold Northern and Western capital.

In a few years cotton and woolen mills will rapidly multiply in Texas; labor will be cheap, because of the cheapness of provisions and the ease with which life is sustained; and Northern capital will find one of its most profitable fields in the very region which, ten years ago, was hardly counted among the cotton and woolen producing sections of the South. The "cotton train" is already a familiar spectacle on all the great trunk lines. It is carefully guarded against danger from fire by vigilant negroes, and when seen at a distance, crawling across the level lands, looks like some huge reptile, from whose nostrils issue smoke and steam.

Houston is one of the most promising of Texan towns. It lies fifty miles inland from Galveston, on Buffalo Bayou, and is now the central point of a complicated and comprehensive railway system. It was christened after the resolute, strong-hearted and valiant man whose genius so aided in creating an independent Texas, and it cherishes his memory tenderly. It is the ambitious rival of Galveston, and because nature has endowed its streets with unusual capacity for muddiness, Galveston calls its inhabitants "mud-turtles." A free exchange of satiric compliments between the two infant cities is of frequent occurrence.

In the days of the Texan republic, when Houston was the capital, it was an important point. Only fifteen miles below the present town limits, on the banks of the picturesque bayou, that republic was born; for the travail of San Jacinto certainly brought it to the light. Audubon, the naturalist, has left a curious memorial of Houston as it was during the republic. The residence of President Houston was a typical Southern log-cabin, two large frame-works, roofed, and with a wide passage-way between. Audubon found the President dressed in a fancy velvet coat, and trowsers trimmed with broad gold lace, and was at once invited to take a drink with him. All the surroundings were uncouth and dirty, in Audubon's eyes; but he did not fail to recognize that the stern men who had planted a liberty pole on that desolate prairie in memory of the battle of San Jacinto would make Texas an autonomy. They did their rough work in their rough way; but it will stand for all time. The old "Capitol," now a hotel, stands on the main street of modern Houston. It is a plain two-story wooden structure, painted white; and contains the "Senate Chamber" which once resounded to the eloquence of the early heroes.

Houston was a little settlement which had sprung up near the town of Harrisburg, the scene of many dramatic events when the republic was struggling with Santa Anna for its life; and the Texan Congress first met there in 1837. There, too, was finally and definitely established the first Texan newspaper, *The Houston Telegraph,* an adventurous sheet which had been forced by Mexican invasion to flee from town to town, until Houston's victory confirmed its right to live. To-day it is one of the institutions of Texas; has been edited by men of rare culture; showed wonderful enterprise in obtaining news during the war of secession, and is a credit to the State.

My first visit to Houston was in winter. It was late at night when, after a long ride from the frontier of the Indian territory, where snow was still on the ground, I

"Dropt into that magic land."

Stepping from the train, I walked beneath skies which seemed Italian. The stillness, the warmth, the delicious dreaminess, the delicate languor were most intoxicating. A faint breeze, with a hint of perfume in it, came through the lattice of my window at the hotel.   The magnolias sent their welcome; the roses, the dense beds of fragrant blossoms, exhaled their greeting.   Roses bloom all winter, and in the early spring and May the gardens are filled with them.

The bayou which leads from Houston to Galveston, and is one of the main commercial highways between the two cities, is overhung by lofty and graceful magnolias; and in the season of their blossoming, one may sail for miles along the channel with the heavy, passionate fragrance of the queen flower drifting about him.

Houston is set down upon prairie land; but there are some notable nooks and bluffs along the bayou, whose channel barely admits the passage of the great white steamer which plies to and from the coast. This bayou Houston hopes one day to widen and dredge all the way to Galveston; but its prettiness and romance will then be gone.

"There are some notable nooks and bluffs along the bayou."

On the morning of my arrival I was inducted into the mysteries of a "Norther," which came raving and tearing over the town, threatening, to my fancy, to demolish even the housetops. Just previous to the outbreak, the air was clear and the sun was shining, although it was cold, and the wind cut sharply.   This "dry Norther" was the revulsion after the calm and sultry atmosphere of the previous day.   A cloud-wave, like a warning herald, rose up in the north, and then the Norther himself

"Upon the wings of mighty winds
Came flying all abroad."

It was glorious, exhilarating, and—icy. Suddenly the cloud vanished; only a thin mist remained, and after his brief reign of a brace of hours, the Norther was over. He is the physician of malarious districts, from time to time purging them thoroughly. Sometimes he blows down houses, trees, and fences, forcing the beasts on the plains to huddle together for safety; rarely, however, in his coldest and most blustering moods, bringing the mercury of the thermometer below twenty-five degrees.

Houston is well laid out, and grows rapidly, prosperous business houses lining its broad Main street. The head-quarters of the Masonic lodges of the State are there; the annual State Fair, which brings together thousands of people from all the counties, every May, is held there; and the Germans, who are very numerous and well-to-do in the city, have their Volks-fests and beer-absorbings, when the city takes on an absolutely Teutonic air.

"The Head-quarters of the Masonic Lodges of the State."

The colored folk are peaceable and usually well-behaved; they have had something to do with the city government during the reconstruction era, and the supervisor of streets, and some members of the city council, at the time of my sojourn there, were negroes. The railroads are hastening Houston's prosperity. The quiet inhabitants who came to the town a quarter of a century ago, and who, frightened by the fancied perils of the Gulf, have never since been back to "the States," hear of the route from "Houston to St. Louis in sixty hours," with

"The railroad depots are everywhere crowded with negroes, immigrants, tourists and speculators." [Page 114.]

superstitious awe. It opens a new country to them. Northern Texas, even, seems to them like a far-off world. They hardly realize that within twenty-four hours' ride a new Texas is springing up, which, in commercial glory and power, will far surpass the old.

The future commercial importance of Houston can readily be seen by examining its location with regard to railway lines. The Houston and Texas

The New Market — Houston.   [Page 115.]

Central connects it by a direct line with Denison in Northern Texas, with the Missouri, Kansas and Texas railway through the Indian Territory and South-western Missouri, and thence by the Missouri Pacific with St. Louis. The Houston and Great Northern route, with which the "International" road has been consolidated (the united lines taking as a new title the "International and Great Northern"), gives a through route from Columbia near the coast to Houston, thence to Palestine and Longview in Northern Texas, and over the "Texas and Pacific," *via* Marshall to Texarkana, on the Arkansas border. There it connects with the new Cairo and Fulton and Iron Mountain route to St. Louis. The Texas and Pacific road also gives it connection with Shreveport and with the road projected from that point across Northern Louisiana to Vicksburg in Mississippi. Houston is connected with Galveston by the Galveston, Houston and Henderson road, now under the control of Thomas W. Pierce of Boston, who is also building the Galveston, Harrisburg and San Antonio road, now completed to within forty miles of San Antonio. The extension of the New Orleans, Mobile and Texas railroad through Louisiana to the Texan border will be of immense advantage to Houston.

At the time of my visit there were about 1,100 miles of completed railroad in Texas; and the projected routes, and surveys, indicated a determination to build at least as many more lines, opening up the whole of Northern Louisiana, Texas and Arkansas. Although the roads have been laid down with surprising rapidity, they are generally good, and bright little towns are springing up at all the junctions and termini. The railroad depots are everywhere crowded with negroes, immigrants, tourists, and speculators. The head-quarters of the Houston and Texas Central,

"The ragged urchin with his saucy face." [Page 115.]

and of the International and Great Northern roads, are at Houston. The former route, of which William E. Dodge, of New York, is president, was chartered in 1848, and had built eighty miles of its line before the war. All the rest has been done since 1861, and it now stretches, 340 miles from Houston to the Red river, 115 miles from Hempstead to Austin, the Texan capital, and 45 miles from Bremond to Waco, one of the most promising towns of the northern section. Galusha A. Grow, the noted Pennsylvania politician, has taken up his abode in Texas, and presides over the destinies of the International and Great Northern railroad.

Thus connected with the outer world, Houston grows daily in commercial importance, and should be made a prominent manufacturing centre. At present, however, there are only the Eureka and Houston City cotton mills, running a few thousand spindles; the various railroad machine and repair shops; a fine new market and opera-house combined; a few brick yards, beef packeries, and foundries. In the vicinity, among the pineries along the bayou, there are numbers

"The negro on his dray, racing good-humoredly with his fellows." [Page 116.]

of steam saw-mills, which furnish lumber to be worked into the "saloons," hotels, and shops of the ambitious new towns in the recently opened northern region.

There is a frankness and cordiality about the society of Houston which is refreshing to one coming from the more precise and cautious East; the manners of the people are simple, courteous, delightful; there are, in the little city, many families of culture and social distinction, whose hospitality renders a sojourn among them memorable. The Texan of the South is, if possible, possessed of more State pride than his brother of Northern Texas: he is never tired of declaiming of the beauties of the climate, and is extremely sensitive to criticism. Above all, do not tell the Texan maiden that her land is not the fairest; for the women of this Southern commonwealth are even more idolatrous of their beautiful homes than are the men. There is a touch of defiance in the loving manner with which they linger over the praise of Texas; they talk best and look prettiest when they are praising "stars which Northern skies have never known." They show the same content with their own section as is found in France, and a leaning toward incredulity if one speaks of landscapes more perfect or of flowers more rare than those of the "Lone Star State!"

The street life is interesting; the negro on his dray, racing good-humoredly with his fellows; the ragged urchin with his saucy face and his bundle of magnolia-blossoms; and the auctioneer's "young man," with mammoth bell and brazen voice, are all interesting types, which, as the reader will observe, the genial and careful artist has faithfully reproduced.

"The auctioneer's young man."

XI

PICTURES FROM PRISON AND FIELD.

ABOUT fifteen miles from Houston, on the banks of the bayou, and upon a dull, uninteresting plain, is the site of the famous battle of San Jacinto. The character of Houston who fought it, annihilating a Mexican force more than twice as large as his own, and capturing the redoubtable Santa Anna, is, and always will be, the subject of much heated discussion in Texas.

Few men have ever left such firm friends and such implacable enemies. There are two versions of every episode of Texan history with which he was connected, his enemies invariably representing him as a man of bad and designing nature, without special ability, while his friends magnify the real excellence of his character into exalted heroism.

"Sam Houston" was a man of extraordinary merit, sternness, strength of will, and was possessed of a foresight quite beyond the ordinary range. He was a Virginian by birth, the hardy son of hardier and noble parents, going in his youth with his widowed mother to Tennessee, then the boundary between the white man and the Cherokee Indian. His education was slight, and, being refused, when at school, the privilege of learning Greek, which he desired after reading a translation of the Iliad, he swore that he would never recite another lesson, and kept his word.

He crossed the Tennessee river and joined the Indians, remaining with them until his manhood. Some time later he distinguished himself in the war against the Creeks, and in 1823 was elected to Congress from

Sam Houston.

Tennessee. An unfortunate marriage seems finally to have decided his career. While governor of Tennessee, in 1829, he suddenly separated from his newly married wife, resigned his high office, and returned to his friends the Cherokees.

After remaining with them for some years he again mingled with white men, and in 1833, entering Texas politics, leaped to the front, became the commander-in-chief of the Texan armies, and, in the face of the determined opposition of an empire of 8,000,000 of people established the independence of the State.

There is but little of interest on the battle-ground of San Jacinto to-day. The ride down the bayou from Houston is delightful ; but, arriving at the plain, one sees only a dreary ex-panse, and the line of rising ground where, on the 21st of April, 1836, the Texans established their camp. On that field, with his little band of war-worn Texans, General Hous-ton made his final stand against the formidable forces of Santa Anna. Suddenly rallying his almost ex-hausted men, he charged upon the

View on the Trinity River.

enemy, smote them hip and thigh, trampled them into the morasses and bayous, and terribly avenged the Alamo, and its kindred massacres.

The Texans engaged in the battle numbered 783, and the Mexicans lost 630 killed ! The next day Santa Anna was found lying prone in the grass near the field of battle,—his disgraced head covered with a blanket,—and was made prisoner. Texas was effectually wrested from the cruel grasp of Mexico.

Houston possessed remarkable eloquence and great magnetic power. His speech had a certain majesty about it which was in itself convincing to the popu-lar ear. A man of many faults, he was full of the pride and joy of life, although at times intemperate and choleric. There are many traditions in Houston of his fondness for gaming, his adventures after drinking freely, and his power of control over others. ·When the late war came he stood a magnificent bulwark against the waves of secession and indecision, and always spoke his mind. Never, in the maddest moments, was he denounced ; his person and his opinions were held sacred, and he died peacefully at Huntsville before the great struggle was ended. In the various portraits extant of him there is as much difference as in the opinions of his friends and enemies. The most authentic gives him a keen, intellectual face, somewhat softened from its original determination by age and repose, but emphatically a manly and powerful one.

The courtesy of President Grow, of the "International and Great Northern" railroad, placed a special train at the disposition of the artist and myself during our stay in Houston, and we visited the banks of that charming stream, the Trinity river, and the fertile lands beside it ; then turning aside to look at the great State Penitentiary, where nearly a thousand convicts are registered, more than half of whom are employed, like galley slaves, as hewers of wood and stone on the railroads and highways.

The sight of the "convict train" is one of the experiences of Texan travel which still clings like a horrid nightmare in my memory. To come upon it suddenly, just at twilight, as I did, at some lonely little station, when the abject, cowering mass of black and white humanity in striped uniform had crouched down upon the platform cars; to see the alert watchmen standing at each end of every car with their hands upon their cocked and pointed rifles; to see the relaxed muscles and despairing faces of the overworked gang, was more than painful.

Once, when we met this train, a gentleman recognized an old servant, and cried out to him, "What, Bill, are you there?" and the only answer was a shrinking of the head, and a dropping of the under jaw in the very paralysis of shame.

"We frequently passed large gangs of the convicts chopping logs in the forest by the roadside." [Page 120.]

The convict labor is contracted for, and is of great value in the building of the railways and the clearing of forests. As a rule, the men are worked from dawn to dark, and then conveyed to some near point, to be locked up in cars or barracks constructed especially for them. They are constantly watched, working or sleeping; and the records of the Penitentiary show many a name against which is written, " Killed while trying to escape."

We frequently passed large gangs of the convicts chopping logs in the forest by the roadside; they were ranged in regular rows, and their axes rose and fell in unison. When they had finished one piece of work, the stern voice of the supervisor called them to another, and they moved silently and sullenly to the indicated task. In the town where the Penitentiary is located, it is not unusual to see convicts moving about the streets, engaged in teaming, carpentry, or mason work; these are commonly negroes, sent to the Penitentiary for trivial offences, and denominated "trusties." Sambo and Cuffee have found the way of the transgressor unduly hard in Texas and most of the Southern States, since the war liberated them. The pettiest larceny now entitles them to the State's consideration, and the unlucky blackamoor who is misty as to the proper owner-ship of a ragged coat, or a twenty-five cent scrip, runs risk of the "convict train" for six months or a year. One good result, however, seems to have followed this unrelenting severity; you may leave your baggage unprotected anywhere on the Texan lines of travel, and no one will disturb it.

A branch line of rail leads from the main trunk of the "International and Great Northern" to the Penitentiary, prettily situated among green fields and pleasant hills. It is vigilantly guarded everywhere by armed men. Inside, the shops are light and cheery, and the men and women, even the "lifers," who have stained their hands with blood, look as contented in the cotton spinning room as the ordinary factory hand does after a few years of eleven hours' toil daily. The prisoners make shoes, clothing, furniture and wagons, weave good cottons and woolens, and it is even proposed to set them at building cars.

The large number of prisoners serving life sentences seemed surprising until, upon looking over the register, we noted the frequency of the crime of murder. The cases of murderous assault—classified under the head of "attempt to kill"—were generally punished by a term of two to five years; never more. At the time of my visit there were seventy persons so sentenced.

Since the passage of the act making the carrying of concealed weapons illegal, these commitments are not so common. Yet the Democratic Legislature last assembled—true to its principle of undoing all which had been done by its Republican predecessors—would gladly have repealed the law.

In a corridor of the Penitentiary I saw a tall, finely-formed man, with bronzed complexion, and long, flowing, brown hair—a man princely in carriage, and on whom even the prison garb seemed elegant. It was Satanta, the chief of the Kiowas, who with his brother chief, Big Tree, is held to account for murder. Being presently introduced to a venerable bigamist who, on account of his smattering of Spanish, was Satanta's interpreter, I was, through this obliging prisoner, presented at court.

Satanta had stepped into the work-room, where he was popularly supposed to labor, although he never performed a stroke of work, and had seated himself on a pile of oakum. His fellow-prisoner explained to Satanta, in Spanish, that I desired to converse with him, whereupon he rose, and suddenly stretching out his hand, gave mine a ponderous grasp, exclaiming as he did so, "How!" He then replied through his interpreter to the few trivial questions I asked, and again sat down, motioning to me to be seated, with as much dignity and grace as though he were a monarch receiving a foreign ambassador. His face was good; but there was a delicate curve of pain at the lips which contrasted oddly with the strong Indian cast of the other features. Although much more than sixty years old, he hardly seemed forty, so erect was he, so elastic and vigorous.

When asked if he ever expected liberation, and what he would do if it should come, he responded, with the most stoical indifference, "*Quien sabe?*" "Big Tree" was meanwhile briskly at work in another apartment plaiting a chair seat, and vigorously chewing tobacco. His face was clear cut and handsome, his coal black hair swept his shoulders, and he paused only to brush it back, give us a swift glance, and then turn briskly to his plaiting as before. The course pursued toward these Indians seems the proper one; it is only by imposing upon them the penalties to which other residents of the State are subject that they can be taught their obligations.*

The Penitentiary in Texas is satisfactorily conducted, being leased from the State by enterprising persons who make it a real industrial school, albeit a severe one. But certain of the jails in the State are a disgrace to civilization, and many intelligent people at Austin spoke with horror of the manner in which criminals were treated in the "black-hole" in that place. All the barbarities of the Middle Ages seemed in force in it.

There is also a certain contempt for the ordinary board or brick county jail, manifested by a class of desperadoes and outlaws, unhappily not yet extinct in

"Satanta had seated himself on a pile of oakum."

the remote sections of the State. During my last visit to Austin, the inhabitants were excited over a daring jail delivery effected in an adjacent county by a band of outlaws. Some of their fellows had been secured, and the outlaws rode to the jail, in broad daylight, attacked it, and rescued the criminals, killing one or two of the defenders, and firing, as a narrator told me, with a touch of enthusiasm in his voice, "about eighty shots in less 'n three minutes." Not long after, tidings were brought us of the descent of an armed body of men upon the jail in Brenham, a large and prosperous town, and the rescue of criminals there.

As a rule, however, such acts of lawless violence are due more to the carelessness of the law officers in securing their prisoners than to any defiance of law. It would be singular if, in a State once so overrun by villains as Texas, there were

* Satanta and Big Tree have since been set at liberty.

no defiant rascals still unhung. Governor Davis, in his last annual message, admitted that in four-fifths of the counties the jails were not secure, and that the constant escape of prisoners was made the excuse for a too free exercise of lynch law upon persons accused of offences. He also added that the jails so constructed as to secure the prisoners confined in them were dens unfit for the habitation of wild beasts.

To the credit of Texas, however, it should be said that political bitterness rarely, if ever, has any part in the scenes of violence enacted in certain counties; the rude character of the people, and the slow return to organized society after the war, being the real causes of the troubles in those regions. Under the reconstruction government, law and order had returned, and it is to be hoped that the now dominant legislators will do nothing to hinder their supremacy in the by-ways as well as the highways of the State. The Democratic Legislature can ill afford to undo the wise legislation which established a State police for the arrest and punishment of outlaws, and which forbade the carrying of concealed weapons.

The little towns along the International and Great Northern railroad are as yet very primitive, and constructed upon the same monotonous, stereotyped plan as those on the Red river. From Houston to Palestine the road runs through a country of great possibilities. On all these new lines the picture is very much the same. Let us take one as it looks in the early dawn.

Morning comes sharply on the great plains, and sends a thrill of joy through all nature. The screaming engine frightens from the track a hundred wild-eyed, long-horned cattle that stand for a moment in the swampy pools by the road-side, jutting out their heads, flourishing their tails angrily, and noisily bellowing, as if resenting the impertinence of the flame-breathing iron monster, and then bound away like deer.

On the slope of a little hill stand a dozen horses, gazing naïvely at the train; a shrill yell from the steam-throttle sends them careering half a mile away, their superb necks extended, their limbs spurning the ground. Behind them gallop a hundred pigs, grimy and fierce, snorting impatiently at being disturbed.

In the distance one can see an adroit horseman lassoing the stupid beef creature which he has marked for slaughter. He drives it a little apart from the herd, and it turns upon him; a quick twirl of his wrist, and he has thrown the deadly noose about its neck; a rapid gallop of a few seconds, and he has tightened the long rope. The horse seems to enjoy the sport, bracing himself as the animal makes a few angry struggles, and then gallops rapidly once more away. The poor beef, now in the tortures of suffocation, falls upon his knees and staggers blindly and heavily forward, bellowing hoarsely and brandishing his horns; again he falls headlong; and once more piteously bellows as much as his choked throat will permit. The disturbed herd walk slowly and mournfully away, huddling together as if for protection. At last the horseman, loosening a little the dreadful noose, forces the subdued creature to follow him submissively, and so takes him to the slaughter.

This wonderful expanse of plain, which melts away so delicately into the bright blue of the cloudless sky, has inspiration in it. The men and women whom one meets at the little stations along the road are alert and vigorous; the glow of health is upon them; the very horses are full of life, and gallop briskly, tossing their heads and distending their nostrils.

Every half hour we reach some small town of board shanties, crowned with ambitious signs. Each of these hamlets is increasing weekly by fifties and hundreds in population. As the train passes, the negroes gather in groups to gaze at it until it disappears in the distance. At one lonely little house on the edge of a superb wheat country a group of Germans, newly come, is patiently

"As the train passes, the negroes gather in groups to gaze at it until it disappears in the distance."

waiting transportation into the interior. The black-gowned, bare-headed women are hushing the babies and pointing out to each other the beauties of the strange new land.

Not far away is the timber line which marks the course of a little creek, whose romantic banks are fringed with loveliest shrubbery. A log cabin's chimney sends up a blue smoke-wreath, and a tall, angular woman is cutting down the brush near the entrance. A little farther on, half-a-dozen small tents glisten in the morning sun; the occupants have just awoke, and are crawling out to bask in the sunshine and cook their coffee over a fire of twigs. The air is filled with joyous sounds of birds and insects, with the tinkling of bells, with the rustling of leaves, with the rippling of rivulets. One longs to leave the railroad, and plunge into the inviting recesses which he imagines must lie within reach.

The Houston and Texas Central railroad route runs through neither a bold nor broken country, but is bordered for at least a hundred miles by exquisite foliage and thickets.   At Hearne, 120 miles from Houston, it meets the International line running to Longview, and furnishing the route to Jefferson, at the head of the chain of lakes extending to Shreveport, in Louisiana.

These lakes were formed by the obstructions created by the Red river raft, and Jefferson has become, by the diversion of the waters of this river from their natural channel, the head of navigation in that section.   An important steamboat commerce with New Orleans, St. Louis, and Cincinnati has sprung up here, and Jefferson now exports nearly 100,000 bales of cotton annually.   Before the Texas Pacific railroad branch from Marshall was completed, 20,000 wagons freighted with cotton yearly entered the town.   Though the war found Jefferson a miserable collection of one-story shanties, it is now a city of 10,000 inhabitants, with elegant brick buildings, and a trade of $20,000,000 annually.   To what it may grow, now that it is connected with the direct route to St. Louis, and that 15,000 square miles of territory in Northern Texas are opened to settlement, no one can tell.   Marshall not only enjoys much the same advantages as Jefferson, but is the head-quarters in Texas of the great Texas and Pacific railway which the famous Scott is stretching across the country to El Paso, and which is already completed beyond Dallas.   The same genius now presides over the destinies of the Transcontinental line, to run through the upper counties from Texarkana to Fort Worth, where the two routes are merged in the main line, which shoots out thence straight to the Mexican frontier.

The International railroad as originally planned was to extend *via* Austin and San Antonio into Mexico; but a Democratic Legislature refused to accord the aid offered by its Republican predecessor.

North-eastern Texas has extensive iron interests, and, throughout the counties in the vicinity of Jefferson, large foundries are grouping villages around them. These beds of iron ore, lying so near the head of steamboat navigation, are destined to an immense development.   All the north of the State is rich in minerals.

In the wild Wichita regions, where exploring parties have braved the Indians, there is an immense copper deposit, continuing thence hundreds of miles, even to the Rio Grande.   The copper ore from some of the hills has been tested, and will yield fifty-five per cent. of metal.   Notwithstanding even the expense of transporting ore 500 miles by wagon, the copper mines of Archer County have proved profitable.   All the requisites for building furnaces and smelting the ores exist in the immediate vicinity of the deposits.   The whole copper region is exquisitely beautiful.   The mountains are bold and romantic; the valleys mysterious and picturesque; the plains covered with flowers—and Indians! But who will let the ignoble savage stand in the way of mineral development?

The Indian troubles in North-western Texas are quite as grave as those in the extreme western part of the State.   Now and then an adventurous frontiersman is swept down by the remorseless savage, who seems to delight in waiting until his victim fancies he has attained security before murdering him and his family.

Government should certainly afford better protection to the settler on the extreme frontier—by some other method if it cannot do it by means of the regular army.

Waco, now a fine town, on a branch of the Texas Central, was once an Indian village, and, long ago, was the scene of a formidable battle between the Wacos and some Cherokee forces. The noble Wacos had acquired, in a surreptitious manner, a good many Cherokee ponies, and, in the pursuit and battle which followed, the Waco village was plundered and burned, and extensive fortifications—traces of which still remain—were heaped with the conquered thieves' dead bodies. Waco, situated on the Brazos river, is to-day a handsome, solidly-built town, possessing many manufacturing establishments. Throughout all the adjacent region stock-raising is fast giving way to agriculture; and great fields of cotton, corn and cane are springing into existence. Every one has heard of Dallas, set down on the banks of the Trinity river, and contributed to by the great feeders of the Texas Central and Texas Pacific. It grows like an enchanted castle in a fairy tale. Dallas is the centre of Northern Texas; has superb water power, and lumber, coffee, iron, lead, and salt fields to draw upon. In the midst of the rich, undulating prairies, and near a plateau covered with noble oaks, elms and cedars, it promises to be beautiful as well as prosperous. It is also one of the centres of the wheat region, some of the finest wheat lands on the continent being in its vicinity. The absolutely best wheat region is said to be in Lamar, Hunt, Kaufman, and Navarro counties.

The eastern corners of the lands now settled in Northern Texas were nearly all held by emigrants from Alabama, Georgia, and Mississippi until the railroad's advent, when the North-westerner joined them in the country, and the Northerner mingled with them in the towns. Slavery flourished there before the war, and the revolution improved neither the negro nor his old master much; so that both are gradually yielding before the new-comers.

In the northern and middle counties, however, slavery never was popular. Some 3,000 families from Indiana and Illinois were introduced into those counties between 1843 and 1854. They owned no slaves and never desired any; and the influence of their example was good even before emancipation came. Hundreds of intelligent and cultured families live there, happy and well-to-do, sowing their wheat and rye in October, and reaping it in June; planting corn in February, to harvest in September; and raising great herds of cattle and horses.

The black, sandy lands are admirably suited for orchards and vineyards; and the "black-waxy,"—a rich alluvial,—for all the cereals. As all the cotton lands of Northern Texas will readily produce a bale to the acre, how many years will pass before the cotton crop of the Lone Star State will be 10,000,000 bales?

The labor question is to be an engrossing one in Texas very soon. The proportion of the colored to the entire population being small, the negroes' share in the labor of cultivation is, of course, not large. The Chinaman is already at St. Louis; the completion of the Texas Pacific railroad will establish him along the whole Texan coast. At present, in great numbers of the counties, there is hardly one negro to fifty white people, so that Cuffee stands no whit in the way of John.

With one single field of coal covering 6,000 square miles; with apparently inexhaustible copper and iron stores; with lead and silver mines; with 20,000,000 of acres of cotton-bearing land, and with agricultural resources equal to those of any State in the Union, Texas can enter upon her new career confidently and joyously. As a refuge for the ruined of our last great revolution, she is beneficent; as an element of greatness in the progress of the United States, she has no superior. She has peculiar advantages over her sister Southern States. While they vainly court emigration, the tide flows freely across her borders, and spreads out over her vast plains. Whatever danger there may be of political disagreements and disturbances within her limits, nothing can permanently impede her progress. Lying below the snow line, she furnishes the best route to the Pacific; fronting on the Gulf, she will some day have a commercial navy, whose sails will whiten every European sea.

Few persons who have not visited the South appreciate the vast extent of territory which the Texas and Pacific route has opened up. Its most beneficent work will be the chasing of the Indian from the vicinity of the "cross-timber" country, which is an excellent location for small farmers. The settlers there are bravely holding on to their lands, keeping up a continual warfare with the redskins, in hopes that they may preserve their lives until the advent of the rail.

The Indian reserves in this section of the State have, according to the testimony of competent authorities, all been failures, whether considered as protection to the white man or as a means of civilization to the Indian. For ten years the savage has been master of all that part of Texas. The new Pacific route will not only send a civilizing current through there, but will also develop a portion of the great "Staked Plain" territory, now one of the unknown and mysterious regions of Northern Texas. The Transcontinental branch is doing good pioneer work in new counties. It also runs through some of the oldest and most cultured sections of the State.

Clarksville, in Red River county, has long been a centre of intelligence and refinement; it was settled early in 1817, and in 1860 had under cultivation nearly 17,000 acres of corn and 8,000 acres of cotton. It is noteworthy that in this county lands which have been steadily cultivated for fifty years show no depreciation in quality. Paris, a handsome town in Lamar county, is also touched by this line. These towns and counties offer a striking contrast to other portions of the northern section which lie within a day's journey of them. They are like oases, but the rest of the apparent desert is being so rapidly reclaimed, that they will soon be noticeable no longer. By all means let him who wishes to cultivate fruit, cotton, or the cereals in Texas visit these elder counties.

XII

AUSTIN, THE TEXAN CAPITAL—POLITICS—SCHOOLS.

M Y various journeys to Austin, the capital of Texas, enabled me to judge of its winter and summer aspects, and I do not hesitate to pronounce them both delightful. The town itself is not so interesting at first sight as either Galveston or Houston; but every day adds to the charm which it throws about the visitor. At Austin the peculiarities of Western and Eastern Texas meet and compromise; one sees the wild hunter of the plains and the shrewd business man of the coast side by side in friendly inter-course. The majority of the public buildings are not architect-urally fine; the Capitol, the Land Office, the Gov-ernor's Mansion, are large and com-modious, but not specially interest-ing. But a touch of the grand old Spanish architect-ure has crept into

The State Capitol—Austin.

the construction of the Insane Asylum, which is built of the soft gray sand-stone so abundant in that region; and the edifice, standing in a great park, whose superb trees seem to have been cultured for centuries, rather than to be mere gifts of nature, is very beautiful.

It is, however, overcrowded with unfortunates, and the State's imperative duty is to build another asylum at once. Under the rich glow of the February sun the white walls of the structure formed a delicious contrast to the foliage of the live oaks near at hand, making it seem more like a temple than like the retreat of clouded reason. In wandering through the wards I came suddenly upon a group of idiot girls, seated on benches in a niche before a sunny window. These poor creatures cowered silently—grimacing now and then—as I stood gazing upon them, when suddenly one or two of them, doubtless excited by the presence of a visitor, rose and began dancing and shrieking.   The suddenness of the transition, and the fearful, mysterious nature of these idiotic saturnalia, appalled me.   I avow that I could hardly drag my limbs to the door, and when once more in the sunlight I felt as if I had come from Dante's Hell.   The

cheery German physician in charge complained of the overcrowded condition of the asylum, adding that as the majority of the cases brought him had already become chronic, it was a hopeless throng with which he had to deal.

In a yard of the asylum, comfortably inclosed, and covered by a picturesque roof upon which a vine had been trained, I saw the sty in which "Queen Elizabeth," a filthy and dreadful old negress, wallowed all day long. Behind green lattices neatly set into the walls of another building, I could hear the furiously insane groaning and shouting.   It is said that there are

The State Insane Asylum—Austin.

more than 1,200 insane in the State, for most of whom an asylum is necessary.

Not far from the Lunatic Asylum, in another beautiful nook, is the institution for the blind, which comprises a school for the industrial training of the patients whose vision is hopelessly lost.   The Colorado river flows to the westward of

Austin, close to the city, issuing from a romantic mountain range, a long gap in which forms what is known as the Colorado Valley; and on the west bank of the river is an efficient and pleasant school and home for the deaf and dumb of the State.

One of the notable sights of Austin, too, is the well-drilled little company of cadets from the "Texas Military Institute," originally located at Bastrop, but now situated on a lovely hill-side near the capital. The school, which is one of general and applied science, is modeled after

The Texas Military Institute—Austin.

West Point and the Virginia Military Institute, and can receive one hundred cadets, whose gray uniformed company is often seen in martial array in the lanes and fields near the town.

Austin is very prettily set down in an amphitheatre of hills, beyond which rises the blue Colorado range.   The little town, which boasts "from 8,000 to

10,000 inhabitants," is very lively during the legislative session. One passenger train daily, each way, connects it with the outer world; beyond are the mesquite-covered plains, and only wagon roads.

The governor, whose term of office lasts four years, has a special mansion, which was the president's house when Austin was the capital of the Texan republic; and the surroundings of his office at the Capitol are of Spartan plainness. In both the Senate and the House of Representatives I noticed a good deal of the freedom of Western and South-western manners, which would be counted strange in the older States. There were no objections, apparently, to the enjoyment of his cigar by any honorable senator on the floor of the Senate, if the session was not actually in progress; senators sat with their feet upon their desks, and the friendly spittoon handy; but these are eccentricities which prevail

in many a State beside Texas. There were men of culture and refinement in the Senate, others who were coarse in manners and dress; the president was amiable and efficient. One or two negroes occupied senatorial chairs, although the Thirteenth Legislature, which I saw, was almost entirely Democratic. The House of Representatives was a sensible, shrewd-looking body of men, with no special Southern type; a Northerner might readily have imagined himself in a New England legislature during the session, save for certain peculiarities of dialect. Here, also, there were negroes, more numer-

The Governor's Mansion —Austin.

ous than in the Senate, and mingling somewhat more freely in the business of the session. The portraits of Austin and Houston looked down benignantly upon the lawgivers.

Texas went through a variety of vexatious trials during the period between the close of the war and the election of what is known as the "Davis party." A. J. Hamilton was appointed provisional governor by President Johnson, but surrendered his power in 1866 into the hands of Governor Throckmorton, the successful "Conservative Union" candidate, who was elected after the adoption of a new State constitution by a majority of more than 36,000 votes over E. M. Pease, the "Radical" candidate. The advent of reconstruction brought Texas into the Fifth Military District with Louisiana, and under the control of General Sheridan. In 1867 Governor Throckmorton, who was considered an "obstacle" to reconstruction, was removed, and the defeated candidate Pease made governor in his stead. During his administration, he had a controversy with General Hancock, who had meantime been appointed commander of the district in place of Sheridan, and was prevented from undertaking several arbitrary measures which the military authorities deemed inexpedient at that time.

The new registration which came into force in Texas, as elsewhere in the South, reduced the number of white voters from 80,000 to a little less than 57,000. A second Constitutional Convention was held in June of 1868, in obedience to an order from the army authorities, then represented by General Rousseau, who succeeded General Hancock in command. This convention was presided over by Edmund J. Davis, an uncompromising loyal man, who had once had a Confederate rope around his neck in war-time. The State was at that time in a very bad condition. Murder and lawlessness were rampant; it was said that there had been nine hundred homicides in the State between 1865 and 1868. The Conservative and Radical wings of the Republican party had much sharp discussion in the convention, which was finally adjourned until the last days of November. Meantime, the differences of opinion between the wings of the party brought forward Mr. Davis as the Radical, and A. J. Hamilton as the Conservative candidate for governor. The constitution was submitted to the people in November, and ratified by more than 67,000 majority. Mr. Davis and his party were at the same time elected to power, and the military force was withdrawn.

Governor Davis certainly succeeded in restoring order and maintaining peace in the State during the four years of his administration, although some of his measures were bitterly opposed. He inaugurated the militia act, which the Democrats of course fought against. It was an act delegating to the governor the power to suspend the laws in disturbed districts, and was perfectly efficient in the only three cases in which it was ever resorted to. During his term, also, the "State Police"—a corps for the maintenance of order throughout the State— was established, and did much to rid Texas of outlaws and murderers.

A tax-payers' convention, held at Austin in September, 1871, united all the elements of opposition against the Davis party. Ex-Governors Throckmorton, Pease and Hamilton participated in it. The Democrats re-organized, and suc- ceeded in securing the Legislature, which is elected annually in Texas. Toward the close of Governor Davis's term, as the tenure of office of some of the State officials was involved in doubt, the Legislature passed an act providing for a general election in December. A new and vehement political contest at once sprang up. The Republicans renominated Governor Davis, and the Democrats, who had been powerfully reinforced by thousands of immigrants from Alabama, Georgia, and other cotton States, put forward Judge Richard Coke as their can- didate. In the election which followed, the Democrats elected Judge Coke as governor by more than 40,000 majority; and the State was completely given over to the Conservative element.

This election caused great excitement among the Republicans. Governor Davis, backed up by the declaration of the Supreme Court of the State that the recent election was unconstitutional, at first refused to yield his power, and called on the President for troops to maintain him in office. But the United States declined to interfere; the Democrats took possession of the Capitol; and Governor Davis finally withdrew his opposition. The Democrats propose in due time to hold another Constitutional Convention, and threaten to undo much of the legislation which, under reconstruction and the *régime* of the Radicals, had proved salutary to the State.

On the steps of the Capitol stands the small and unambitious monument built of stone brought from the Alamo.   It is but a feeble memorial of one of the most tragic events in American history, to which the State would do well to give lasting commemoration by some stately work in bronze or marble on Alamo plaza, in San Antonio.

In the office of the Secretary of State at Austin, one may still see the treaties made with France, England, and other nations, when Texas was a republic, when Louis Phillippe was King of the French, and Victoria was young. Three years after Texas had declared her independence of Mexico, the commissioners appointed under President Lamar's Administration selected the present site on the Colorado as the capital, and, in grateful remembrance of the "father of Texas," called it Austin.   It seems, indeed, strange that it has not grown to the proportions the commissioners then predicted for it; for the best of building stone and lime and stone-coal abound in the vicinity, and it has an immense and fertile back-country to draw upon.

The Alamo Monument—Austin.

These same commissioners also fondly hoped, by building the town, effectually to close the pass by which Indians and outlaws from Mexico had from time immemorial traveled to and from the Rio Grande and Eastern Texas.   In October, 1839, President Lamar's Cabinet occupied Austin,—and, although Indian raids in the neighborhood were frequent, the brave little government remained there.   Those were great days for Texas,—a State with hardly the population of one of her counties to-day, yet holding independent relations with the civilized world.

The European governments had their representatives at the Court of Austin, while hosts of adventurers thronged the Congressional halls.   Gayly-uniformed officers of the Texan army and navy abounded; and the United States daily felt the pulse of the people as to annexation.   Once in a while there was a diplomatic muddle and consequent great excitement, as when,—the owner of some pigs which had been killed for encroaching on the French Minister's premises having abused said minister in rather heated language,—Louis Phillippe felt himself insulted, and very nearly ruined the infant republic by preventing it from obtaining what was then known as the "French Loan."

The Texan government in those early days had always been a great straggler, moving from town to town, and when, in 1842, the Administration proposed to remove the archives to Houston, because a Mexican invasion was feared, the citizens of Austin revolted, and General Houston, the then President, was compelled to leave the records where they were.

In the Secretary of State's office I was shown the original ordinance for the secession of Texas from the Union,—a formidable parchment, graced with a long list of names,—and a collection of the newspapers printed in the State during the war, a perusal of which showed that there are several sides to the history of all our battles, and that in those days the Texans were taught that the Confederates invariably won.

The four presidents of the Texan republic, Burnet, Houston, Lamar and Jones, were all strong men, but of widely different character. Lamar was a brilliant writer and talker, clear-headed and accomplished; Jones was an intellectual man, bitter against the Houston party, and to judge from his own memoirs, jealous and irritable. He died by his own hand.

The population of Texas has increased, since its annexation to the Union in 1845, from 150,000 to more than a million of inhabitants. Its principal growth has, of course, been since the war, for before that time Northern Texas was as much a wilderness as is Presidio county to-day. The greatest needs of the State at the present time are more people, and more improvement along the lines of travel. The coarse cookery, bad beds, and villainous liquor-drinking which one now finds in remote towns will vanish when people and manufactures and inducements to ease and elegance come in.

A favorable sign on the railroads is the occasional entrance of some rough fellow into the Pullman car, and his intense enjoyment of it. I recall now, vividly, the gaunt drover who went to bed before dark in one of the berths of a palace car one evening between Austin and Hempstead. "Never was in one of these tricks befo'," he said; "I reckon I'll get my money's worth. But look yere," he added, to a gentleman near him, confidentially, "if this train should bust up now, where'd the balance of ye go to, d'ye reckon?" He appeared to think the berth a special protective arrangement, and that he was perfectly safe therein.

The negro and the Mexican are both familiar figures in Austin, and the negro seems to do well in his free state, although indulging in all kinds of queer freaks with his money; he saves nothing. Sometimes he undertakes long journeys without the slightest idea where he is going, and finding he has not money enough to return, locates anew. As a rule, he does not acquire much property, expending his money on food and raiment—much of the former, and little of the latter. The commercial travelers in Texas all carry large stocks of confectionery, with which, when they fail to tempt Sambo to expend his little hoard in any other manner, they generally manage to exhaust his means. There is no idea of economy in the Texan negro's head. On the Texas railroads, the candy venders are allowed to roam at large through the trains and practice the old swindle of prize packages, by which they invariably deplete the darkey's purse. They display the tempting wares, and hint at the possibility of gold dollars and greenbacks in the packages; of course, appetite triumphs, and Sambo falls.

The Land Office is one of the important institutions of Texas, and a main feature of Austin. The United States has no government lands in the commonwealth; and the land system, although somewhat complicated, on account of the various colonization laws and old titles acquired under them, is a good one. In the Land Office there is an experienced corps of men, who have the history of each county and its records at their fingers' ends, and who can trace any old title back to its Spanish source. Plans of all the counties, and every homestead on them, are also to be seen. This, in a State where the counties comprise areas of from 900 to 1800 square miles each, is of the utmost importance to persons buying land and wishing to establish a clear title to it; although, as a general rule, the settler who acquires land under the preëmption laws of the State, has no trouble, and runs no risk.

An attempt was once made to sectionize all the State public lands,—now amounting to nearly 90,000,000 of acres,—and to offer them, as the United States does, in open market, but it was thought wiser to continue the original plan. The legislation of Texas favors preëmption, and the new settler had best go with it; but he may also become the legal owner of a portion of the public domain by "locating a land certificate," at from thirty-five to sixty-five cents in gold per acre, and then proving his title to it by forming a perfect chain of deeds from the original grantee down to himself. In doing this the facilities afforded by the Land Office are, of course, invaluable. The State Bureau of immigration, located at Galveston, has commissioners constantly in the Southern and Western States, and in Europe, soliciting immigrants to take up the millions of acres in the Western and Northern parts of the State. Judging from the statistics of 1872–3, I should say that fully three thousand persons

The Land Office of Texas—Austin.

monthly land at Galveston, coming from the older Southern States. How little we at the North have known, in these last few years, of this great, silent exodus, this rooting up from home and kindred, which the South has seen, and the anguish of which so many brave hearts have felt! But your true American is peripatetic and migratory, so that perhaps the struggle is less intense with him than with the Europeans who crowd our shores.

Texas owes but little money—a trifle more than $1,500,000—and her taxable property, which was estimated in 1871 at $220,000,000, and was then thought to be undervalued, must now be nearly $300,000,000. In most respects the outlook of the State is exceedingly good; certainly as favorable for immigration as the majority of the States of the West. The grand middle ground, more than 1,000 miles in extent, between the Atlantic and the Pacific, it must be covered with railroads in every direction; and even the barbarity of the savages can last but little longer.

Journalism has had an astonishing growth in Texas since the war. Out of 140 newspapers now printed in the State, 110 have been started since the close of the great struggle. Most of the small new towns have two or three papers each, and support them handsomely. The proprietor of a weekly journal, in one of the mushroom cities, told me that five columns of his paper paid him $6,000 clear profit yearly.

Everybody—merchant, gambler, railroad contractor, clergyman, desperado—patronizes the newspaper, and pays large prices for advertising. The majority of the papers are Democratic, but in the cities the Republicans usually have influential organs. "Democratic" does not always mean a full support of the party, but a kind of independent journalism, to which the air of Texas is more conducive than even that of the North. The *Age* and *Union* in Houston, the *Civilian, Post,* and *Standard* in Galveston, the *Times* in Jefferson, the *Reporter* in Tyler, and the *State Journal, Gazette,* and *Statesman* in Austin, and the *Red River Journal* in Denison, are among the principal newspapers published either daily or tri-weekly. Almost every county has an excellent weekly, filled with enthusiastic editorials on the development of the State, and appeals to the people to appreciate their advantages. The Germans have also established several influential journals both in Western and Eastern Texas; and all of them are very prosperous. In Galveston, Houston, and all the principal towns there are elegantly-appointed German book-stores, whose counters are freighted weekly with the intellectual novelties of the Old Country.

The school question, so seriously and severely disputed in all the Southern States, has created much discussion in Texas; and, indeed, the people do well to occupy themselves with the subject; for it is estimated that in 1873 there were yet in the State 70,895 white, and 150,617 colored persons over ten years of age who could neither read nor write. This appalling per centage of ignorance is gradually decreasing under the beneficent workings of the new system, which came in with reconstruction, and to which there was, of course, a vast deal of opposition.

Texas has always been reasonably liberal in matters of education; as early as 1829 the laws of Coahuila and Texas made provisions for schools on the Lancastrian plan; the republic inaugurated the idea of a bureau of education, and its Congress took measures for establishing a State university. After annexation, free public schools were established, and supported by taxation on property. In 1868 the reconstruction convention established a school fund amounting to more than $2,000,000; and in April, 1871, the Legislature passed an Act organizing a system of public free schools, and the schools were begun in September of the same year.

The opposition to them took the form of complaint of the taxes, and in most of the leading cities the courts were overrun with petitions asking that collection of the school tax be restrained. In this manner the progress of the system has been very much embarrassed. The Texan of the old *régime* cannot understand how it is right that he should be taxed for the education of his neighbor's children; neither is he willing to contribute to the fund for educating his former bondsmen.

There have been at different times about 127,000 pupils in the public schools of the State, and the average number taught during the year is 80,000, while the whole number of children in the commonwealth is estimated at 228,355. During the first year of the application of the system, over 6,500 teachers were examined and accepted. The number of colored pupils in the public schools cannot be accurately determined, and mixed schools seem to be nowhere insisted upon. In many counties where the opposition to the payment of the tax was persistent, the schools were forced to close altogether.

In the large towns, as in Houston, the Germans have united with the leading American citizens in inaugurating subscription schools in which the sexes are separated, and have introduced into them some of the best German methods. There has been much objection to the compulsory feature of the

"The emigrant wagon is a familiar sight there."   [Page 136.]

free system, parents furiously defending their right to leave their children in ignorance. Texas needs, and intends soon to found, a university and an agricultural college. The latter should be opened at once. There are a good many thriving denominational schools scattered through the counties; the Baptists have universities at Independence and Waco; the Presbyterians at Huntsville; the Lutherans at Columbus; the Methodists at Chappell Hill; and the Odd Fellows have a university at Bryan. Wherever the public school has been established there is a private one which is patronized by all the old settlers, who thus gratify their desire for exclusiveness, and embarrass the growth of the free system.

Between Austin and Hempstead the river Brazos is crossed, and not far from its banks stands the populous and thriving town of Brenham, in Washington county, one of the wealthiest and most thickly settled in the State.   The beauty of the famous La Bahia prairie has not been exaggerated; I saw its fertile lands where the great oaks stood up like mammoth sentinels; where the pecan-tree, the pride of Texas, and one of the noblest monarchs of the sylvan creation, spread his broad boughs; where the cotton-wood, the red cedar, and the ash shot up their noble stems; where the magnolia and the holly swore friendship; where the tangled canebrake usurped the soil, and where upon the live oak the grape-vine hung lovingly encircling it with delicate leaves and daintiest tendrils.   How fair, too, were the carefully cultivated lands, hedged in with the Osage orange and the rose, the vineyards and the pleasant timber lines along the creeks! What beautiful retreats by the Brazos!   One might fancy himself in the heart of the richest farming sections of England.   Tobacco, rye, hops, hemp, indigo, flax, cotton, corn, wheat and barley, as well as richest grapes, can be profitably grown; deer bound through the forests, wild turkeys stalk in the thickets, and grouse and quails hide in the bosquets.   The emigrant wagon is a familiar sight there, and the wanderers from the poorer Southern States find that this rich tract realizes their wildest dreams of Texas.   In this section small farms are rapidly increasing in number, land being rented to new-comers unable to buy.

One's senses are soon dulled by satiety.   When I first traversed Texas, fresh from the white, snow-covered fields of the North, how strange seemed the great cypresses, hung with bearded moss; the tall grasses rustling so uncannily; the swamps, with their rank luxuriance and thousands of querulous frogs; the clumps of live oaks, and the tangled masses of vines!

But a winter in the South had familiarized me with all these things, and on my return I sought in vain the impressions of my earlier trip.   Extraordinary rural charms are like the perfume of the jessamine.   At first it intoxicates the senses, but, as familiarity grows, it ceases to attract attention.   Even absence will not restore its sweetness and subtlety.

XIII.

THE TRUTH ABOUT TEXAS—THE JOURNEY BY STAGE TO SAN ANTONIO.

GALUSHA A. GROW, once speaker of the national House of Representatives, and now the energetic and successful manager of a railroad in the Lone Star State, has changed the once memorable words, "Go to Texas!" from a malediction into a beneficent recommendation. The process was simple: he placed the curt phrase at the head of one of those flaming posters which railway companies affect, and associated it with such ideas of lovely climate and prospective prosperity, that people forthwith began to demand if it were indeed true that they had for the last twenty years been fiercely dismissing their enemies into the very Elysian Fields, instead of hurling them down to Hades.

The world is beginning to learn something of the fair land which the adventurous Frenchmen of the seventeenth century overran, only to have it wrested from them by the cunning and intrigue of the Spaniard; in which the Franciscan friars toiled, proselyting Indians, and building massive garrison missions; which Aaron Burr dreamed of as his empire of the south-west; and into which the "Republican" army of the North marched, giving presage of future American domination.

Austin and his brave fellow-colonists rescued Texas from the suicidal policy of the Mexican Government, and the younger Austin accepted it as his patrimony, elevating it from the degraded and useless condition in which the provincial governors had held it. Under his lead, it spurned from its side its fellow-slave, Coahuila, and broke its own shackles, throwing them in the Mexican tyrant Guerrero's face; its small but noble band of mighty men making the names of San Felipe, of Goliad. of the Alamo, of Washington, of San Jacinto, immortal.

It crushed the might of Santa Anna, the Napoleon of the West; it wrested its freedom from the hard hands of an unforgiving foe, and maintained it, as an isolated republic, commanding the sympathy and respect of the world; it placed the names of Houston, of Travis, of Fannin, of Bowie, of Milam, of Crockett, upon the roll of American heroes and faithful soldiers, and brought to the United States a marriage-gift of two hundred and thirty-seven thousand square miles of fertile land.

The world is beginning to know something of this gigantic south-western commonwealth which can nourish a population of 50,000,000; whose climate is as charming as that of Italy; whose roses bloom and whose birds sing all winter long; whose soil can yield the fruits of all climes, and whose noble coast-line is broken by rivers which have wandered two thousand miles in and out among Texan mountains and over vast Texan plains. It is a region of strange contrasts in peoples and places: you step from the civilization of the railway junction in Denison to the civilization of Mexico of the seventeenth century in certain sections of San Antonio; you find black, sticky land in Northern Texas, incomparably fertile; and sterile plains, which give the cattle but scant living, along the great stretches between the San Antonio and the Rio Grande.

You may ride in one day from odorous, moss-grown forests, where everything is of tropic fullness, into a section where the mesquite and chaparral dot the gaunt prairie here and there; or from the sea-loving populations of Galveston and her thirty-mile beach, to peoples who have never seen a mast or a wave, and whose main idea of water is that it is something difficult to find and agreeable as a beverage.

The State has been much and unduly maligned; has been made a by-word and reproach, whereas it should be a source of pride and congratulation. It has had the imperfections of a frontier community, but has thrown off the majority of them even while the outer world supposed it to be growing worse and worse. Like some unfamiliar fruit supposed to be bitter and nauseous, it has gone on ripening in obscurity until, bursting its covering, it stands disclosed a thing of passing sweetness, almost beyond price.

Much of the criticism to which Texas has been subjected has come from people very little acquainted with its actual condition. Border tales have been magnified and certified to as literally true. The people of the North and of Europe have been told that the native Texan was a walking armament, and that his only argument was a pistol-shot or the thrust of a bowie-knife. The Texan has been paraded on the English and French stages as a maudlin ruffian, sober only in savagery; and the vulgar gossipings of insincere scribes have been allowed to prejudice hundreds of thousands of people.

Now that the State is bound by iron bands to the United States, now that, under good management and with excellent enterprise, it is assuming its proper place, the truth should be told. Of course, it will be necessary to say some disagreeable things; to make severe strictures upon certain people and classes of people; but that is not, by any means, to condemn the State by wholesale or to write of it in a hostile spirit. The first impression to be corrected — a very foolish and inexcusably narrow one, which has, nevertheless, taken strong hold upon the popular mind — is, that travel in Texas, for various indefinite reasons, is everywhere unsafe. Nothing could be more erroneous; there is only one section where the least danger may be apprehended, and that is vaguely known as the "Indian country." Hostile Comanches, Lipans, or predatory Kickapoos might rob you of your cherished scalp if you were to venture into their clutches; but in less than three years they will have vanished before the locomotive — or, possibly before the legions of Uncle Sam, who has a pronounced mania for removing his frontier quite back to the mountains of Mexico.

Indeed, this apprehension with regard to safety for life and property in Texas is all the more inexplicable from the very fact that the great mass of the citizens of the State were and are determined to maintain law and order, and to fight with bitter persistence the outlaws who have found their way into the country.

It is true that during the war, and for two years thereafter, things were in lamentable condition. Outlaws and murderers infested the high-roads, robbed remote hamlets, and enacted jail deliveries. There were a thousand murders per year within the State limits; but at the end of the two years the reconstruction government had got well at work, and annihilated the murderers and robbers.

It is a noteworthy fact, too, that the people then murdered were mainly the fellows of the very ruffians who murdered them—shot down in drunken broils, or stabbed in consequence of some thievish quarrel. Of course, innocent people were occasionally plundered and killed; but then, as now, most of the men who "died with their boots on" were professional scoundrels, of whom the world was well rid.

It may with truth be said that there exists in all of the extreme Southern States a class of so-called gentlemen who employ the revolver rather suddenly when they fancy themselves offended, sometimes killing, now and then only frightening an opponent. These people are not, as yet, treated with sufficient rigor in Texan society. There are even instances of men who have killed a number of persons and are still considered respectable. The courts do not mete out punishment in such cases with proper severity, sometimes readily acquitting men who have wantonly and willfully shot their fellow-creatures on the slightest provocation.

A correct summary of the present condition of Texas may, it seems to me, be stated as follows: A commonwealth of unlimited resources and with unrivaled climate, inhabited by a brave, impulsive, usually courteous people, by no means especially bitter on account of the war, who comprise all grades of society, from the polished and accomplished scholar, ambassador, and man of large means, to the rough, unkempt, semi-barbaric tiller of the soil or herder of cattle, who is content with bitter coffee and coarse pork for his sustenance, and with a low cabin, surrounded with a scraggy rail fence, for his home.

The more ambitious and cultured of the native Texans have cordially joined with the newly-come Northerners and Europeans in making improvements, in toning up society in some places, and toning it down in others; in endeavoring to compass wise legislation with regard to the distribution of lands, and the complete control of even the remote sections of the State by the usual machinery of courts and officials; and in the binding together and consolidation of the interests of the various sections by the rapid increase of railway lines.

It was a charming morning in April that I climbed to the high box-seat by the driver of the San Antonio stage, and sat perched above four sleek and strong horses in front of the Raymond House, at Austin, the Texan capital.

Heavy heat was coming with the growing day; the hard, white roads glistened under the fervid sun, and the patches of live oak stood out in bold relief against a cloudless sky. The shopkeepers were lolling under their awnings, in lazy enjoyment of the restful morning, and a group of Mexicans, lounging by a wall, cast wild glances at us from beneath their broad sombreros and their tangled and matted black hair.   In the distance, Mount Bonnel showed a fragment of its rock-strewn summit, and white stone houses peered from the dark

green of the foliage, while the State House, crowning a high knoll, and flanked on either side by the Land Office and the Governor's Mansion, hid from us the view of the rich plain, extending back to the bases of the hills which form an amphitheatre in whose midst Austin is prettily set down.

Nine inside and three outside.   "Now, then, driver, are you ready? Here is your way-bill; here are half-a-dozen mail bags; ballast up carefully, or you will have your

Sunning themselves. — "A group of Mexicans, lounging by a wall."   coach upset!"   The driver,

a nut-brown man, handsome and alert withal, clad in blue overalls, velvet coat, and black slouch hat, springs lightly into his seat, cracks his long whip-lash, and we plunge away toward the steep banks of the Colorado, bound for an eighty-mile stage ride to the venerable and picturesque city of San Antonio.

Rattle! we are at the bank, and must all dismount to walk down the declivity, and cross the almost waterless river channel on a pontoon bridge.   We toil painfully across a sandy waste, and then up the bank on the other side, turning to look at the town behind us, while the horses pant below.

A cavalcade of hunters passes us, mounted on lithe little horses and grave, sure-footed mules, returning toward Austin.   The men are brown with the sun, and carry rifles poised across their high-peaked Mexican saddles.   Their limbs are cased in undressed skin leggings, and their heads are covered with broad hats, entwined with silver braids.   Each man bows courteously, and all canter briskly down to the stream.

Mounting once more to our perches, beside the driver, artist and writer alike are inspired by the beauty of the long stretch of dark highway, bordered and covered with huge live oaks, or with the wayward mesquite, whose branches are a perpetual danger to the heads of outside passengers.

The driver nervously inspects us; then lights a cigar, and, in a gentle voice, appeals to his horses with: " Git up, ye saddle critturs!"—evidently a mild reproach. The saddle critters dash forward at a rapid gait. Each glossy flank is branded with the name by which the animal is known; and whenever a leader lags or a wheel horse shows a disposition to be skittish, the loud voice says, "You Pete!" or "Oh Mary!" and Pete and Mary alike prick up their pretty ears with new energy. The driver's tones never rise beyond entreaty or derision; and the animals seem to feel each stricture upon their conduct keenly.

So we hasten on, past pretty farm-houses with neat yards, where four-year-old boys are galloping on frisky horses, or driving the cattle or sheep afield; past the suburbs of Austin, and out into the open country, until we have left all houses behind, and only encounter from time to time wagons, drawn by oxen, and loaded with barrels and boxes, with lumber and iron, toiling at the rate of twenty miles a day toward the West. Behind each of the wagons

marches a tough little horse, neatly saddled; and a forlorn dog with a general air of wolfishness about him, and showing his teeth as we dash past, brings up the rear.

Presently the driver turns to us with, "I'm a dreadful good hand to talk, if ye've got any cigars." Then, in another breath, "From New York, hey? Ain't

"We encounter wagons drawn by oxen."

ye afraid to come away out here alone?" (Implying a scorn for the outside impression of Texan travel.) A moment after, in a tone of infinite compassion, as if regarding Gotham as a place to be pitied, driver adds:

"Wal, I s'pose thar are some good souls thar" (confidentially); "I've hauled more 'n two thousand o' them New Yorkers over to San Anton within the last year. Heap o' baggage. We told one young feller on the box here, one day, lots of Injun stories, just as it was gittin dark. Reckon he was n't much afeared. Oh, no!" Suppressed merriment lurking in the handsome brown face. "You Pete! you ain't fit for chasin' Injuns! Git up!"

San Antonio is 2,270 miles from New York by present lines of rail and stage, and is situated in one of the garden spots of South-western Texas. To the newly-arrived Northerner, Galveston certainly seems the ultima-antipode of Gotham; but once across the Brazos and the Colorado, and well into the fertile plains and among the glorious prairies of Western and South-western Texas, the sense of remoteness, of utter contrast, is a thousand-fold more impressive. To think, while clinging to the swaying stage-seat, that one may journey on in this pleasant way for eight hundred miles still within Texan limits, gives, moreover, a grand idea of the great State's extent.

Whirling thus, hour by hour, away from railroads, from houses, taverns, and bridges, and beaver-hatted and silk-bedizened folk, one cannot resist the growing feeling that he is in a foreign land, and as he sees the wild-eyed children staring at him from the fields, or notes the horseman coursing by, with clang and clatter of spur and arms, he has a vague expectation that if addressed it will be in a foreign tongue.

A halt:—at a small stone house, through whose open door one sees a curious blending of country-store, farm-house and post-office. Here the mail for the back-country is delivered. " Morning, Judge," from a lean by-stander, meditatively chewing tobacco, to an outside passenger. " Got them radical judges impeached yet? Driver, won't you bring me a copy of the Texas Almanac next time you come out? Reckon I kin use it." A drove of pigs curiously inspect the open entrance to the store, whereupon two dogs charge them, flank the youngest of the swine, and teach them manners at the expense of their ears.

Lime-flavored water is brought in a tin dipper and passed around; such of the passengers as choose, perfume the vessel with a drop of whiskey. " Wal! sha'n't git ye to San Antonio 'fore this time to-morrow, if ye drink the rivers all dry," is the mild remonstrance. As we move off, the driver vouchsafes:

" Thar was Mose—Judge, you remember Mose; he would n't let no stranger talk to him, he would n't. Crossest man on this line; had a right smart o' swear-words: used 'em mostly to hosses, tho'! Had one horse that was ugly, and always tied his tail to the trace. Outsides mostly always asked him: ' What do you tie that horse's tail to the trace for?' You oughter hear Mose answer. Took him half an hour to get the swear-words out. One day, a feller from New York went over with Mose, and did n't say a word about the horse's tail all the way to the relay; when they got to the unhitching place, Mose offered the New Yorker half a dollar—'Stranger,' he says, 'I reckon you've gin me that worth of peace of mind; you are the first man that never asked me nothing about that 'ar critter's tail.'"

A ford, the sinuous road leading to the edge of a rapidly-rushing streamlet, on whose banks, among the white stones, lie the skeletons of cattle perished by the wayside! Buzzards hovering groundward indicate some more recent demise. Ah! a poor dog, whose feet no longer wearily plod after the wagon train. The collar is gone from his neck, some lonely man having taken it as a remembrance of his faithful companion.

A mocking-bird sings in some hidden nook; a chaparral cock runs tamely before us, fanning the air with his gray plumes, and gazing curiously at the buzzards. An emigrant wagon is lumbering through the shallow, bluish-green water; the children of yonder grim-bearded father are wading behind it: inside, the mother lies ill on a dirty mattress. Two old chairs, with pots and kettles, a Winchester rifle, a sack of flour, and a roll of canvas, are strung at the wagon's back. The horses display their poor old ribs through their hides, and their tongues protrude under the intense heat.

Our steeds splash through the stream. We come upon a Mexican camp, where a group of lazy peons, who have wandered across from Mexico, braving danger and death daily, have at last found a safe haven. The dingy father sleeps under his little cart. His mules crop the dry grass, tethered near a small, filthy tent, wherein reposes an Indian girl, with a cherub-child's head resting upon her exquisite arm. A gipsy-looking hag is munching dried meat before a little fire where coffee is boiling.

Now along a rolling prairie, in a route disfigured by what is known as the "hog-wallow;" then, up to a range of hills: and *O gioja!* the matchless beauty of a wide expanse of vale below filled with masses of dense foliage, and beyond, forest-clad hills peered down upon by a blue, misty range, far away. A comfortable farm-house crowns the hill up which we climb; shepherds are driving flocks of sheep afield; horsemen are mounting and dismounting; bright-eyed maidens flit about the yard, bareheaded and barearmed; half-naked negro

"Here and there we pass a hunter's camp."

children tumble about on the turf, and little white boys on ponies play at Comanche. Majestic waves of sunlight flit across the valley; the campagna to which we are now coming swims in the delicious effulgence of the perfect Texas April noon. Here and there we pass a hunter's camp. We spin forward merrily, having had plenty of relays of fresh horses, and put the Blanco river behind us almost without wetting their hoofs, so low is it; though in times of freshet it holds the whole country round in terror for weeks.

A halt for dinner, which is served in a long, cool kitchen; a swart girl standing at one end and a swart boy at the other. Each agitates a long stick adorned with strips of paper, and thus a breeze is kept up and the flies are driven off. Buttermilk, corn-bread, excellent meat, and the inevitable coffee are the concomitants of the meal.   The landlady stares at the paper-currency offered, as only gold and silver are known in this section.   The farmer comes in from the field for his dinner, and his pleasant, homely talk recalls one to America.   After all, then, this is not a foreign land.   "Stage ready; come, now, if ye want to git anywhar to-night!"

Onward to the San Marcos, another small, but immensely powerful stream, running through rich lands, and passing hard by the prosperous town of San Marcos, the shire of a county whose best products are cotton, corn, and sorghum. The river, which has its source not far from the town, and near the old home-stead of Gen. Burleson, the noted Indian fighter, affords water-power which cannot fail to tempt Northern capital some day.   Wood and building-stone of the best quality are abundant; San Marcos may yet be a second Lawrence or Manchester.   We pass the court-house and the Coronal Institute ; pass the long street lined with pretty dwellings, and ride forward all the hot afternoon towards the Guadalupe.

The fields, in which the corn is already half a foot high, are black; the soil is like fruit-cake.   In obscure corners we find little cabins—erected by the Mexi-cans who abound along the way.   Toward sunset we come upon neat stone houses, with quaint German roofs.   "Everything Dutch now," ejaculates the driver, and indeed we are about to see what German industry and German thrift have done for Western Texas.

The stage rumbles on through the "lane" which extends for miles on either side of New Braunfels, bounded by fertile, well-fenced, well-cultivated fields, such as the eye of even a New England farmer never rested upon.   It is dark as we rattle past the cottages; the German families, mother, father, and the whole gamut of children, from four to fourteen, are coming in from work.

The women have been afield ploughing, with the reins round their necks and the plough handles grasped in their strong hands.   Yet they are not uncouth or ungracious; their faces are ruddy, their hair, blown backward by the evening breeze, falls gracefully about their strong shoulders.   Surely, this is better than the tenement house in the city !

At last we reach the Comal, and crossing its foamy, greenish-blue waters, rattle on to New Braunfels, the cheery town which the German Immigration Company settled in 1845, and which is now an orderly and wealthy community of 4,000 inhabitants, set down in the midst of a county which has probably 10,000 residents.

The Germans were the pioneers in this section, endured many hardships, and had many adventures, many battles with the Indians, before they were allowed to push forward from New Braunfels and create other settlements.   As we enter the long main street of the town, the lights from the cottage doors gleam forth cheerily.   The village maidens are walking two by two with their arms about each others' waists, and crooning little melodies, and the men are smoking long pipes at the gates.   Suddenly we dash up to the hotel, and a pleasant-faced old gentleman, in a square silk cap, hastens to welcome us into a bright room, where little groups of Germans sit ranged about clean tables, drinking their foaming beer from shiniest of glasses. Are we then in Germany? Nay; for supper is spread in yonder hall, and the new driver whom we took up at the last relay is calling upon us, in our English tongue, to make haste.

New Braunfels bears as many evidences of wealth and prosperity as any town in the Middle States. It has always been liberal in sentiment, and for many years boasted of having the only free school in Texas. The shrewd Germans have taken advantage of the admirable water-power of the Comal and Guadalupe, and have established manufactories in the county.

The Comal, one of the most beautiful streams in Texas, gushes out at the foot of a mountain range not far from New Braunfels, from a vast number of springs; and from its sources to its confluence with the Guadalupe, a distance of three miles, has forty feet of fall, and mill-sites enough for a regiment of capitalists. Indeed it is easy to see that the place will, at some future time, become a great manufacturing centre. White labor is easily obtained, and the community is peaceful and law-abiding.

A large cotton factory was established on the Comal some years ago, but was destroyed by an exceptionally disastrous tornado in 1869. There are many water-mills in the county, all engaged in the manufacture of flour for export *via* the port of Indianola, settled by the same immigration company which founded New Braunfels, or *via* Lavaca. The trees along the river and creek bottoms are almost overborne with the mustang grape; the county abounds in fruit, while cotton, corn, and the other cereals are raised in profusion. Irrigation is not difficult.

It is quite dark, and a cool night wind is blowing when we mount once more to the coach-top, and settle ourselves for a ride which will last until two in the morning. The driver cracks his long whip, and we plunge into the darkness. The two great lamps of the coach cast a bright light for twenty feet ahead, and we can see little patches of the landscape, beyond which is the infinite darkness relieved only here and there by the yellow of camp-fires, or by the fitful gleams of the fire-flies. At last we strike across the prairie. The mesquite-trees, which we pass every moment, look white and ghostly in the lamplight, and flit by us like a legion of restless spirits. Then, too, as the horses trot steadily forward, there is the illusion that we are approaching a great city, so like are the innumerable fire-flies to the gaslights of a metropolis. Now we are in a stable-yard, in the midst of a clump of mesquite and oak-trees; the tired horses are unhitched, fresh ones replace them, and away we go again over the prairies. Presently the architecture changes; the little houses, dimly seen at the roadside, from time to time, are low, flat-roofed, and built of white stone; there are long stone walls, over which foliage scrambles in most picturesque fashion, while, sprinkled in here and there, are the shabby Mexican cottages, with thatched roofs and mud floors. There is a hint of moonlight as we approach the hills, and we can see the cattle in relief against the sky, hundreds of them lying comfortably asleep, or starting up as they hear the rattle of the coach, and brandishing their horns or flourishing their tails. Faster, faster flit the mesquite ghosts; faster fly away the oaks and the chaparral; and faster the little streams which we speed across. Now we mount upon a high table-land, from which we can see, faintly defined in the distance, a range of hills, and can catch a glimpse of the beautiful valley at their feet. The hours pass rapidly by; the night breeze is inspiring, and the driver is singing little songs; we dash into a white town; pass a huge "corral," inside

"We pass groups of stone houses."

which stand blue army wagons drawn up in line; pass groups of stone houses, then into a long street, thickly lined with dwellings, set down in the midst of delicious gardens; scent the perfume drifting from the flower-beds; climb a little hill, whirl into a Spanish-looking square, and descend, cramped in limb and sore in bone, at the portal of the Menger House, in the good old city of San Antonio, the pearl of Texas,

XIV.

AMONG THE OLD SPANISH MISSIONS.

THE great State of Texas is usually spoken of by its inhabitants as divided into eight sections—namely, Northern, Eastern, Middle, Western, Extreme South-western, and North-western Texas, the Mineral Region, and the " Pan Handle." This latter section, which embraces more than 20,000 square miles, is at present inhabited almost entirely by Indians. The mineral region proper, believed to be exceedingly rich in iron and copper ores, comprises 50,000

"The vast pile of ruins known as the San José Mission." [Page 154.]

square miles. The vast section between the San Antonio river and the Rio Grande—as well as the stretch of seven hundred miles of territory between San Antonio and El Paso, on the Mexican frontier, is given up to grazing herds of cattle, horses, and sheep, to the hardy stock-raiser, and to the predatory Indian and Mexican. Across the plains runs the famous "old San Antonio road," which, for 150 years, has been the most romantic route upon the western continent. The highway between Texas and Mexico, what expeditions of war, of plunder, of savage revenge, have traversed it! What heroic soldiers of liberty have lost their lives upon it! What mean and brutal massacres have been perpetrated along its dusty stretches! What ghostly processions of friar and arquebusier, of sandaled Mexican soldier and tawny Comanche; of broad-hatted, buckskin-breeched volunteer for Texan liberty; of gaunt emigrant, or fugitive from justice, with pistols at his belt and a Winchester at his saddle; of Confederate gray and Union blue, seem to dance before one's eyes as he rides over it! The romance of the road and of its tributaries is by no means finished; there is every opportunity for the adventurous to throw themselves into the midst of danger even within forty miles of "San Antōn," as the Texans lovingly call the old town; and sometimes in the shape of mounted Indians, the danger comes galloping into the very suburbs of San Antonio itself.

San Antonio is the only town in the United States which has a thoroughly European aspect, and, in its older quarters, is even more like some remote and obscure town in Spain than like any of the bustling villages of France or Germany, with which the "grand tour" traveler is familiar. Once arrived in it, and safely ensconced among the trees and flowerets on Flores street, or on any of the lovely avenues which lead from it into the delicious surrounding country, —there seems a barrier let down to shut out the outer world; the United States is as a strange land.

In San Antonio, too, as in Nantucket, you may hear people speak of "going to the States," "the news from the States," etc., with utmost gravity and good faith. The interests of the section are not so identified with those of the country to which it belongs as to lead to the same intense curiosity about American affairs that one finds manifested in Chicago, St. Louis, and even in Galveston. People talk more about the cattle-trade, the Mexican thievery question, the invasion of Mexico by the French, the prospect of the opening up of silver mines, than of the rise and fall of the political mercury; and the general government comes in for consideration and criticism only when the frontier defenses or the Mexican boundaries are discussed. "What general was that down yer with Gin'ral Sherman?" said a man to me at an out-of-the-way town in Western Texas. "Reckon that was one o' your Northern gin'rals." As he had no interest in following Cabinet changes, he had never heard of Secretary Belknap.

Although everything which is brought to San Antonio from the outer world toils over many miles of stage or wagon transit, the people are well provided with literature; but that does not bring them closer to the United States. Nothing but a railroad ever will; and against the idea of the railroad soon to reach them the majority of the elder population rebels. Steaming and snorting engines to defile the pure air, and disturb the grand serenity of the vast plains! No, indeed; not if the Mexicans could have their way, the older Mexicans, the apparently immortal old men and women who are preserved in Chili pepper, and who, as their American neighbors say, have been taught that they will have but short shrift when the railways do come. "It will bring you all sorts of epidemics, and all kinds of noxious diseases," they have been told by those interested to prevent the road's building. And this the venerable moneyed Mexicans actually consider a valid reason for opposition, since San Antonio now has the reputation of being the healthiest town on the American continent.

The local proverb says, "If you wish to die here, you must go somewhere else;" and, although the logic is a little mixed, it certainly has a *fond de vérité*.

For many years consumptives have been straying into San Antonio, apparently upon their very last legs, only to find renewed life and vigor in the superb climate of Western Texas; and so certain are consumptives and other invalids to be cured in the city and the surrounding region, that retreats and quiet residences for people to enshrine themselves in during recovery are going up in all quarters. A few of the golden mornings—a few of the restful evenings, when the odorous shadows come so gently that one cannot detect their approach —and one learns the charm of this delightful corner of the world.

San Antonio is the cradle of Texan liberty. Its streets and the highways leading to it have been drenched with the blood of brave soldiers. Steal out with me into the fields this rosy morning, friends, and here, at the head of the San Antonio river, on this joyous upland, at the foot of the Guadalupe mountains whence flow a thousand sweet springs, and overlooking the old town, hear a bit about its history and the early struggles of the Texans.

France was a great gainer for a short time by the fortunate accident which in 1684 threw De La Salle's fleet into the bay of San Fernando, on the Gulf of Mexico, during his voyage from La Rochelle to take possession of the mouths of the Mississippi in the name of the king of France. De La Salle virtually opened Texas. After he had discovered his error in reckoning, and that he was on new ground, he established a fort between Velasco and Matagorda; but it was soon after destroyed, and De La Salle's premature death, at the hands of his quarrelsome and cowardly associates, greatly retarded the progress of French discovery. But the expedition, and those which followed it, caused great alarm, and as much indignation as alarm, at the Court of Spain. A century and a-half was yet to elapse ere her feebleness should compel Spain to abandon a conquest whose advantages she had so abused; ere she should see herself driven to give up the immense territory which she had held so long.

Meanwhile De La Salle's expedition caused new activity in Spain; and in 1691, a governor "of the States of Coahuila and Texas" was appointed, and with a handful of soldiers and friars went out to establish missions and military posts. Colonies were planted on the Red river, on the Neches, and along the banks of the Guadalupe; but in a few years they died out. Presently other efforts were made—the Spaniards meantime keeping up a sharp warfare with the Indians, the mission of San Juan Bautista, on the right bank of the Rio Grande, three miles from the river, being created a *presidio* or garrison, and the "old San Antonio road" between Texas and Mexico running directly by it.

Meantime the French were vigorously pushing expeditions forward from the settlements along the Louisiana coast; and so very much in earnest seemed the movements of Crozat, the merchant prince, to whom Louis XIV. had ceded Louisiana, that the Viceroy of Mexico began anew measures for establishing missions and garrisons throughout Texas. And so it happened that in 1715, after a mission had been established among the Adaes Indians, and another, the "Dolores," west of the Sabine river, the fort and mission of San Antonio de Valero was located on the right bank of the San Pedro river, about three-fourths of a mile from the site of the present Catholic Cathedral in San Antonio of to-day.

From this year (1715) may be said to date the decisive occupancy of Texas by Spain, as opposed to France; she drove out the French wherever found, opposed their advances, and finally succeeded in definitely planting fortified missions at the principal important points.   San Antonio was then known as a garrison, and was usually spoken of as the Presidio of Bexar.   Indeed, to this day the elder Mexicans living in the surrounding country speak of going *al presidio* (to the garrison) whenever they contemplate a visit to San Antonio. Texas was then known as the "New Phillippines;" and San Antonio, with its five missions, was one of the four garrisons by which it was protected.

The Marquis of Casa Fuerte had long believed that this post would be a good site for a town, and, having asked the Spanish Government to send emigrants there, "thirteen families and two bachelors" (say the ancient town records) arrived from the Canary Islands, and settled on the east side of the San Antonio river, founding a town which they called San Fernando.   To them came sturdy Tlascalans from Mexico, and the colonists built a stout little hamlet around the great square which to-day is known as the "Plaza of the Constitution," or the main square in San Antonio.   The town was called San Fernando, in honor of Ferdinand, the then king of Spain.   It was rough work to be a colonist in those days, and the Spaniards, friars, soldiers and all, were very glad to get into the great square at night, close the entrance with green hides, set their sentinels on the roofs of the flat houses, and, trembling lest the sound of the war-whoop of the terrible Apaches and Comanches should startle their slumbers, catch a little repose.   These Apaches and Comanches overran in those days the country between San Antonio and Santa Fé, and would swoop down upon the infant settlement from their stronghold in the pass of Bandera.   They swarmed in the Guadalupe mountains, where even now they come in the full of the moon, searching for horses, as their ancestors did.

In due time, there was a town on either side of the San Antonio river, each with its mission and attendant garrison.   Around the mission of the "Alamo" had clustered a little garrison and village.   This mission church, whose history is so romantic, was first founded in 1703, in the Rio Grande valley, by Franciscans from Queretaro, under the invocation of San Francisco de Solano; but, water being scarce, was moved back and forth until 1718, when,

"Borne, like Loretto's chapel, thro' the air,"

it migrated to the west bank of the San Pedro river, and remained in that vicinity until, in 1744, it was removed to the high plateau on the east side of the San Antonio, and the foundations of the Church of the Alamo were laid on the very ground where, ninety years after, Travis and his braves fell as only heroes fall.

The mission was known, until 1783, as San Antonio de Valero, in honor of the Marquis of Valero, the then Viceroy of "New Spain."   The town below the river retained its name of San Antonio de Bexar.

The missions built up around San Antonio were named respectively La Purissima Concepcion de Acuna, San Juan Campitran, San Francisco de Assissis, and San José.   The Franciscans, completely estranged from all the ordinary cares and passions of the world by the vows of their order, gave themselves heartily to their work, and vigorously employed the soldiers allotted them by the Government in catching Indians, whom they undertook to civilize.   The missions were fortified convent-churches, built in massive and enduring form, and surrounded by high walls, so thick and strong that they could resist all Indian attacks. Within these walls the converted Indians and the missionaries and soldiers gathered whenever a sentinel gave the alarm; and the brawny friars joined with the men-at-arms in fiercely defending the stations where the cross had been planted.   The Indians who were induced to settle in the vicinity of the Franciscans, and submit to the religious and industrial training which the friars had prepared for them, were rarely guilty of treachery, and submitted to all the whippings which Mother Church thought good for them.   Barefooted, and clad in coarse woolen robes, with the penitential scourge about their waists, the priests wandered among the Indians at the missions, learned their language, and enforced chastity, temperance and obedience.   Inside the square which the mission buildings formed were the dwellings allotted both the soldiers and the Indians—the savages chafing under this restraint, although they could not doubt the motives of the good fathers in restraining them.   But they toiled well in the fields, went meekly to catechism, and were locked up at night, lest they should be led into temptation.   Whenever the converts rebelled, there were soldiers enough at hand to subdue them; and the commander of the church garrison was a kind of absolute potentate, who made any and every disposition he pleased of a convert's life and property.

In 1729, the right reverend fathers forming the college of Santa Cruz of Queretaro, were authorized to found three missions on the river San Marcos; and, in 1730, a superior order from the Marquis of Casa Fuerte authorized the foundation of these missions upon the river San Antonio, under certain conditions as to their distance from the San Antonio garrison.   The result was that before

1780, four superb mission edifices had been reared, at short distances from each other, and not far from the beautiful San Antonio river.

On the 5th of March, 1731, the foundations of La Purissima Concepcion de Acuna were laid, and, after many vicissitudes and escapes from imminent destruction, it was completed in 1752.   For twenty-one years Indians and friars had toiled upon one of the noblest churches ever erected by Catholics in America.   To-day it is a ruin, de-

The old Concepcion Mission near San Antonio—Texas.

serted save by an humble German family, who exhibit the time-honored walls to visitors, and till the lands in the vicinity. The San josé mission, in all respects the finest, was completed in 1771; that of San Juan in 1746; and the "Espada" in 1780.

As the communities clustered about these missions grew, so grew San Antonio; as they suffered, so it suffered in protecting them. The same Indians who cantered up to the town-gates did not fail to offer some menace to the missions before returning to their mountain fastnesses. In 1758, they went farther, for they assaulted the mission which had been established at San Saba. Pastors and their flocks, as well as the guardian soldiery, were sacrificed. Swarms of the savages surrounded the mission, and the wonderfully rich silver mines which had been developed near it, and not a Spaniard was left alive to bear the news of the dreadful massacre to his trembling comrades at the other missions. Some day the San Saba mines will be re-opened; but their exact location has been long lost to the knowledge of Europeans or Mexicans, and no Indian will point the way to them.

It was sunset, on a beautiful April evening, when I first climbed to the roof of the Concepcion mission. As the day had been heated and dusty in town, I was glad, toward evening, to steal away down the lovely road; past the dense groves and perfumed thickets, along the route which wound among trees and flowers, and fertile fields watered by long canals; past quiet cool yards, in whose shaded seclusion I could catch glimpses of charming cottages and farm-houses, where rosy Germans or lean Americans sat literally under their own "vine and fig-tree."

The carriage rolled suddenly through a ford in the deep, swift stream, came out upon a stretch of open field, and at a distance I saw, peering above some graceful trees, the twin towers of Concepcion—saw them with a thrill of joy at their beauty and grandeur, just as hundreds of weary travelers across the great plains had doubtless seen them a century ago. In those days they were a welcome sight, for they guaranteed comparative security in a land where nothing was absolutely certain, save death. Approaching, I could see that the towers arose from a massive church of grayish stone, once highly ornate and rich in sculpture and carving, but now much dilapidated. The portal was decayed; the carvings and decorations were obscure; a Spanish inscription told of the founding of the mission. A group of awe-struck girls lingered about the door-way as an old man rehearsed some legend of the place.

The edifice bore here and there hints of the Moorish spirit, the tendency to the arch and vault which one sees so much in Spanish architecture. The great dome, sprung lightly over the main hall of the church, was a marvel of precision and beauty. In front, jutting out at the right hand, a long wall now fallen into decay showed the nature of the mission's original defenses. This wall was of enormous thickness, and the half-ruined dwellings in its sides are still visible.

As I wandered about the venerable structure, the gray walls were bathed in the golden light of the fervid Southern sunset; numberless doves hovered in and out of the grand towers; lizards crawled at the walls' base; countless thousands of grasshoppers flashing in the air, nestled on the mission's sides; the stone cross between the twin towers stood up black against the sky. Curious parapets along the roof, contrived at once for ornament and shelter, showed loop-holes for muskets. There were mysterious entrances in the rear, and the stone threw a dark shadow upon the short, sparse, sun-dried grass. I tried to call up the mission fort as it was a century ago, surrounded with smiling fields, cultivated by patient Indians; with soldiers at their posts, diligently guarding the approaches; with the old friars in their coarse robes, building and teaching, and praying and scourging themselves and the Indians. I pictured to myself a cavalcade arriving at sunset from a weary journey; men-at-arms, and gayly-costumed cavaliers entering the gateway; the clatter of swords and the click of musket-locks; the echoes of the evening hymn from the resounding vault of the cathedral;—but the Present, in the shape of a rail-fence and four excitable dogs anxiously peering at me from behind it, would obtrude itself, so I gave meditation the good-by, and asked of the family the way to the roof.

The barefooted German maiden, naïve and bashful, seemed strangely out of place in the shadows of the mission. I wandered through the kitchen, an old nook in the wall, and venturing behind the heels of half a dozen mules stabled in a niche of the sanctuary, mounted a crazy ladder leading to the belfry window.

Getting in at the huge opening, I startled the doves, who flew angrily away, and then clinging to the wall on one side, I climbed still another flight of stone steps, and emerged on the roof. A giant piece of masonry, my masters of to-day! You can certainly do but little better than did the poor friars and Indians a century ago. Being built of the soft stone of the country, the ruin has crumbled in many places; but it looks as if it might still last for a century. For miles around, the country is naked, save for its straggling growth of mesquite, of cactus, of chaparral; the forest has never reasserted itself since the fathers cultivated the fields; and one can very readily trace the ancient limits.

The grant of the mission of Concepcion was about the first by the Spanish Government in Texas of which there is any record. In March of 1731 the captain commanding at San Antonio went to the newly allotted mission grounds, kindly greeted the Indians who had decided to settle there, and caused the chief of the tribe to go about over the ceded lands, to pull up weeds, turn over stones, and go through all the traditional ceremonials of possession. The same formalities were observed in founding all the missions near San Antonio; the transfer of the lands being made to the Indians, because the Franciscans, on account of their vows, could hold no worldly estate.

We Americans of the present should lean rather kindly toward these old Franciscans, for they were largely instrumental in the work of freeing Texas from the yoke of Spanish and Mexican tyranny. As priests, they were too human and sympathetic to enjoy or sympathize with the brutal policy of Spain; and as sensible men, they had Democratic leanings, doubtless enhanced by the Spartan plainness in which they lived.

The various internal troubles undergone by Spain early in this century had only served to make her more arrogant toward her colonies, and a large party in them was anxious to revolt.   At this time there were few Americans in the territory.   Now and then the agents of Wilkinson and Burr ran through it, endeavoring to perfect designs for their new South-western Empire ; but, besides these ambitious schemers, only desperadoes from the United States entered Texas.

In 1813, however, Augustus W. Magee, a lieutenant in the American army, undertook, in conjunction with a Mexican revolutionist, to conquer Texas to the Rio Grande, with a view to annexing it to America or Mexico, as circumstances should dictate.   He resigned his commission and plunged headlong into the invasion, bringing to it many men and much courage, and fighting a good fight at Nacogdoches ; but, finally contemplating a retreat, and unable to carry his men with him in his plans, he is generally believed to have ended his life by his own hands.

A short time thereafter, the invading Americans and the revolting Mexicans arrived before San Antonio, and attacked the city at once.   General Salcedo, the Spaniard commanding, valiantly defended it ; but the Americans and Mexicans won, and as the Indians from the missions had joined in, but few prisoners were taken, more than 1,000 Spaniards being killed and wounded. Salcedo and a number of noted Spanish officials were brutally murdered.

A few days later, the Americans and Mexicans were attacked by other Spanish forces, whom they repulsed with great slaughter.   But a third Spanish force was sent to San Antonio, and 4,000 men gave battle to 850 Americans and twice as many Mexicans, composing the " Republican Army of the North," near the Medina river.   The Spaniards were victorious, and all of the Americans but ninety-three were massacred.   A large number of the Americans were shot on the San Antonio road, their cruel captors seating them by tens on timbers placed over newly-dug graves, and thus despatching them.   This terrible massacre was known as the " battle of the Medina."   Then the brave old town of San Antonio suffered the vengeance of the Spanish authorities.   Seven hundred of its best citizens were imprisoned, and 500 of the wives and daughters of the patriots were thrown into filthy dungeons.

From that time forth the history of San Antonio was one of blood and battle, of siege and slaughter.   The Americans, who, in a reckless manner, had given their blood for Texan freedom, were henceforth to act from the simpler motive of self-defense.

The vast pile of ruins known as the San José Mission stands in the midst of the plain about four miles westward from San Antonio.   Mute, mighty and passing beautiful, it is rapidly decaying.

The Catholic church in Texas, to whom the missions and the mission lands now belong, is too poor to attempt the restoration of this superb edifice which one of the most famous of Parisian architects, in a recent tour through this country, pronounced the finest piece of architecture in the United States.   San José has more claims to consideration than have the other missions, as the king of Spain sent an architect of rare ability to superintend its erection.   This architect, Huizar, finally settled in Texas, where his descendants still live.

It is impossible to paint in words the grand effect of this imposing yellowish-gray structure, with its belfry, its long ranges of walls with vaulted archways, its rich and quaintly carved windows, its winding stairways, its shaded aisles, rearing itself from the parched lands.   As our party entered the rear archways an old, sun-dried Mexican approached, and in a weak voice invited us to enter the church.

The old man and his bronzed wife had placed their household goods in the interior of the edifice; and in the outer porch dried beef was hung over the images of the saints.   An umbrella and candlestick graced the christening font. Lighting a corn-shuck cigarette, the old man lay down on one of the beds with a moan, for he was a confirmed invalid. We climbed to the tower, but speedily came down again, as the great dome fell in last year, and the roof is no longer considered safe.

Returning to the shade, the Mexican woman, clad in a single coarse garment,

An old Window in the San José Mission.

her hair falling not ungracefully about a face which, although she must have been fifty, seemed still young, served us with water in a gourd, and then seated herself on the ground with the hens affectionately picking about her.   Was she born at the mission? we asked.   No, señor; but in San Fernando.   And where had she spent her youth?   In Piedras Negras, señor.   And did she not fear the roof of the old mission might some day fall and crush her?   Who knows, señor, she answered, ambiguously; giving that vague shake of the head by which both Spaniards and Mexicans so accurately express profound unconcern.   In the shade of some of the great walls were little stone cabins, in which lived other Mexican families. Bronzed children were running about in the sun, and bronzed fathers were working lazily in the field.   In the distance, in any direction—chaparral,—mesquite, —cactus,—short, burned grass, and the same prospect all the way to the Rio Grande.

A sun-swept, sun-burnished land; a land of mirages, and long, wearying distances without water; a land of mysterious clumps of foliage, inviting to ambush; where soldiers are always chasing marauding savages whom they rarely catch, and where the Mexican and the Indian together hunt the cattle of

"An umbrella and candlestick graced the christening font."

the "Gringo;" where little towns cluster trustingly around rough fortresses; where the lonely "ranch" is defended by the brave settler with his "Winchester;" where millions of cattle and thousands of horses and sheep roam fancy free from year to year, their owners only now and then riding in among them to secure the increase ;—that is the beyond.

The San Juan mission, a little beyond the San Antonio river, some three or four miles farther down, like the Espada, which stands upon the bend in the river still below, is but a ruin. In its day it was very large, and many families lived within its bounds. Now there is little to be seen, except a small chapel and the ruins of the huge walls. A few families live among the *débris*, and there is even a "San Juan Mission Store."

The scene about the humble abodes of the Mexicans, residing in or near these missions, is very uniform. There is a rude water-cart near the door; a few pigs run about the premises, and a hairless Mexican dog watches them ; two or three men, squatted on their haunches, sit blinking in the sun. No one ever seems to do any work; though the Mexicans about San Antonio have a good reputation as laborers.

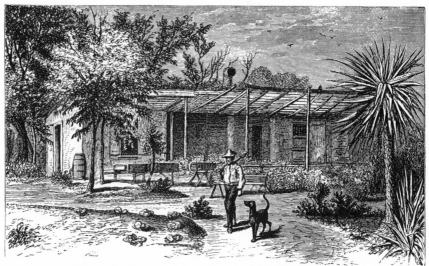

"The comfortable country-house so long occupied by Victor Considerant."

It was at the Concepcion mission that the patriot army of Texas assembled in 1835, after the capture of Goliad; and it was along the river bottom and in the timber by the river, that a battle was fought in which the Mexicans received severe treatment.

On the river road from San Antonio to Concepcion stands the comfortable country-house so long occupied by Victor Considerant, the French free-thinker and socialist. Considerant, after his ineffectual attempt to found a community of the Fourier type in Texas, lived tranquilly with his family near the old mission for many years, going to San Antonio now and then for society, and occupying his leisure with literary work. A strange man, strongly fixed in his beliefs and prejudices, he was not thoroughly understood, though universally respected by the Texans who met him.

XV.

THE PEARL OF THE SOUTH-WEST

SAN Antonio is watered by two beautiful streams, the San Antonio and the San Pedro, the former running directly through the town's centre. Its bluish current flows in a narrow but picturesque channel between bold and rugged banks in some places, and sloping borders in others, and is everywhere overhung with delicate groupings of foliage. It passes under bridges, by arbors and bath-houses; by flights of stone steps leading up into cool, cozy houses, as the stairways lead from Venetian canals; past little lawns, where the San Antonian loafs at his ease at midday; and on through sweet fields, full of a wealth of blossoms. Nowhere, however, is it so supremely beautiful as at its source, on the high plateau at the foot of the Guadalupe range, where it breaks out from a fine spring, and shapes itself at once into a beautiful stream. Around the natural park of several hundred acres which

The San Antonio River—"Its bluish current flows in a narrow but picturesque channel."

lies along the base of the mountains, Mr. Brackenridge, the banker, who purchased the estate, has thrown a protecting wall enclosing a park which an English duke might covet. The stream is a delicious poem written in water on the loveliest of river-beds, from which mosses, ferns, dreamiest green and faintest crimson, rich opalescent and strong golden hues, peep out. Every few rods there is a waterscape in miniature—an apotheosis of color. Noble pecans, grand oaks, lofty ashes, shade the stream, which flows down toward a quarry a little above the town, where it again forms a picture such as only

The Source of the San Antonio River.

the Marne at St. Maur, or the Seine at Marly can rival.   To the people of San Antonio it is a perpetual delight, a constant treasure, of which they speak almost reverently.   The San Pedro is commonly known as a creek, but has many a beautiful nook along its banks; and in one of them, called "San Pedro Springs,"

the Germans have established their beer gardens. There, in the long Sunday afternoons, hundreds of families are gathered, drinking beer, listening to music and singing, playing with the fawns, or gazing into the beer garden and the den of the Mexican panther. There, too, the Turnverein takes its exercise; and in a long hall, dozens of children waltz, under the direction of a gray-haired old professor, while two spectacled masters of the violin make music.   This is the

San Pedro Springs — "The Germans have established their beer gardens."

Sunday rendezvous of great numbers of the citizens of San Antonio, Germans and Americans, and is as merry, as free from vulgarity or quarreling, as any beer garden in Dresden.   The German element has been of incalculable value to Western Texas, and especially to San Antonio.   It has aided much in building

"Every few rods there is a waterscape in miniature."   [Page 157.]

up the material interests of the whole section; has very largely increased the trade of the city; has brought with it conservatism and good sense in manners, so that even a frontier town, eighty miles from any railroad, and not more than thirty miles from Indians, has all the grace and decorum of older societies. The German was a good element, too, when the trying issues of the last war came; and was unwavering in its loyalty. The Germans suffered much, and many were driven out, losing property and money; hundreds were slaughtered in trying to escape to Mexico, or into the North-west; there were shameful massacres; but they were not to be frightened, and they held to their opinions, although often obliged to conceal them.

Texas is a changed place indeed to the people who were afraid to express their views before the war. As a gentleman in San Antonio

"The river passes under bridges, by arbors and bath-houses." [Page 157.]

said to me, "It was like living in an asylum where every one was crazy on one especial subject; you never knew when dangerous paroxysms were about to begin." The Texas of twelve years ago, when it was dangerous for a man to

The Ursuline Convent—San Antonio. [Page 161.]

be seen reading the *New York Tribune*, and critically perilous for him to be civil to a slave, has passed away, and the Texans themselves are glad that they have awakened from their dream of patriarchal aristocracy, which placed such a check upon the development of the State. The Germans have settled several thriving places west of San Antonio, the most noted of which is Fredericksburg. German and Jewish names are over the doors of certainly more than half the business houses in San Antonio; and German or Hebrew talent conducts many vast establishments which have trade with the surrounding country, or with Mexico.

San Antonio has so long been a depot for military supplies for all the forts on the south-western frontier, and for the Mexican States this side of the Sierra Madre, that some of the merchants are not in favor of the advent of railroads, fearing that with them trade will move beyond the venerable city, and forgetting that even in that event there will be ample compensating advantages. The sooner Western Texas has railroads, the sooner will the Indian and Mexican difficulties be settled; the sooner will all the available rich lands be taken up.

St. Mary's Church — San Antonio.   [Page 161.]

Even now the business done by means of the slow wagon trains, which can at best only make twenty miles per day, is enormous, amounting to many millions yearly. What will it be when railroads penetrate to the now untamed frontiers? Many of the appliances of civilization are fast reaching Western Texas for the first time. San Antonio now has four prosperous banks, —she had none before the war,—gas-lights, two daily papers, and a weekly for the Germans; how can she avoid railroads?

Three lines are at present pointed directly at the antique city; the Galveston, Harrisburg and San Antonio railroad, nearly completed; the Gulf, Western Texas and Pacific railroad, which at present extends from Indianola to Victoria, and has been graded to Cuero, thirty miles beyond Victoria; and the International railroad, which contemplates touching both Austin and San Antonio, thus opening a through line to Longview, in Northern Texas, and south-westward to Mazatlan on the Pacific, with a branch to the city of Mexico. There is not much probability that the last line will be finished to San Antonio, at least for many years.

The *plazas*, or public squares of San Antonio, merit special attention. The four principal ones are the Alamo, the Constitution, the Military, and Travis. The latter is a handsome grass-grown common surrounded by pretty residences, some of them fronting upon charming lawns and gardens; a stone church is to be erected there by the Episcopalians. The Ursuline Convent and St. Mary's Church are among the noticeable Catholic edifices of the town.

The old church of San Fernando is now removed from the "Plaza of the Constitution," or rather is enshrined within a new and imposing edifice, built of the white stone of the section. The Constitution plaza is the original garrison square of San Fernando, and streets lead out from it into the open country, the Military plaza, and the main part of the town. The

A Mexican Hovel.   Page 162]

Military plaza is surrounded by storehouses and shops, and is always filled with wagon teams and their picturesque and ragged drivers. From thence it is only a few steps to one of the Mexican quarters of the town, sometimes called "Laredito." There the life of the eighteenth century still prevails, without taint of modernism. Wandering along the unpaved street in the evening, one finds the doors of all the Mexican cottages open, and has only to enter and demand supper to be instantly served; for the Mexican has learned to turn American curiosity about his cookery to account. Entering

The Military Plaza — San Antonio.

one of these hovels, you will find a long, rough table with wooden benches
about it; a single candlestick dimly sending its light into the dark recesses
of the unceiled roof; a hard earth-floor, in which the fowls are busily bestowing
themselves for sleep; a few dishes arranged on the table, and glasses and
coffee-cups beside them.   The fat, tawny Mexican *materfamilias* will place
before you various savory compounds, swimming in fiery pepper, which biteth
like a serpent; and the *tortilla*, a smoking hot cake, thin as a shaving, and
about as eatable, is the substitute for bread.   This meal, with bitterest of coffee
to wash it down, and dulcet Spanish talked by your neighbors at table for dessert,
will be an event in your gastronomic experience.   You will see many Americans
scattered along at the tables in the little houses in Laredito; even where
I went there was a large party of the curious, ciceroned by one of the oldest
and most respected of San Antonio's citizens, "Don Juan" Twohig, the wealthy

"The Mexicans slowly saw and carve the great stones."

Irish banker, who was sixty-five years old that very day, but rolled tortillas as
heartily as when a sturdy youth, and was as gay as when, a gallant revolutionist,
he beguiled the hours of captivity in the Castle of Perote, where the cruel
Mexicans had sent him.

    The residences on Flores street are all completely embowered in shrubbery, and
many of them are intrinsically fine.   There are few wooden structures in the city.
The solid architecture of previous centuries prevails.   Putting up a house is a
work of time; the Mexicans slowly saw and carve the great stones; but the work
is solid when completed, and fire-proof.   Most of the houses and blocks in Commerce and other principal streets are two stories high—sometimes three—and
there are some fine shops—one or two of them being veritable museums of traffic.

    It is from these shops that the assortments are made up which toil across the
plains to the garrisons and to Mexico; and a wagon-train, loaded with a "varied

assortment," contains almost everything known in trade. Through the narrow
streets every day clatter the mule-teams, their tattered and dirty-clothed negro
drivers shouting frantically at them as they drag civilized appliances toward
Mexico. These wagoners lead a wild life of almost constant danger and adventure, but they are fascinated with it, and can rarely be induced to give it up.

The Mexicans monopolize a corner of the town, which has won the *sobriquet*
of "Chihuahua." It is a picturesque collection of hovels, built of logs, stones,

"The elder women wash clothes by the brookside."

and dried mud, and thatched with brush or straw. Little gardens are laid out in
front of the houses, some of which are no larger than a sentry-box, and naked
children play in the primitive streets. Young girls, bold-eyed and beautiful,
gayly dressed, and with shawls thrown lightly over their superb heads, saunter
idly about, gossiping, or staring saucily at strangers; the elder women wash
clothes by the brookside. The men seem to be perpetually waiting for some one
to come and feed them. They wander about in the most purposeless fashion,
and one is tempted to think them on the look-out for a chance to rob or murder;
yet they are, on the contrary, quite inoffensive. "Chihuahua" and "Laredito"
are nooks that one would never suspect could exist on American soil. But
the Mexican is hard-headed, and terribly prejudiced; he cannot be made to
see that his slow, primitive ways, his filth and lack of comfort, are not better
than the frugal decency and careful home management of the Germans and
Americans who surround him.

The Alamo is the shrine to which every pilgrim to this strange corner of
America must do utmost reverence. It is venerable as mission church and fortress, and was so baptized in blood that it is world-famous. The terse inscription
on the Alamo monument, in the porch of the capitol at Austin, "*Thermopylæ had
her messenger of death; the Alamo had none !*" indicates the reverence in
which the ruins are held by Texans. There is now but little left of the original
edifice. The portion still standing is used as a Government storehouse; and
the place where Travis and his immortals fell, which should be the site of a fine
monument, is a station for the mule and ox-teams waiting to receive stores.

It was a noteworthy struggle which led to the massacre at the Alamo, and thence to Texan independence. Moses and Stephen F. Austin, father and son, struggled through a dreary period of colonization from 1821 until 1836. The father died before he had succeeded in availing himself, to any extent, of the hesitating permission he had received from the Spaniards to introduce Americans into Texas; but his son took that permission as his patrimony, and went at the work with a will.

Stephen Austin was obliged to brave a thousand dangers in founding his first colony on the banks of the Brazos; but the colony grew, and acquired a steadiness and prosperity, even while the adjacent Mexican States were undergoing twenty revolutions. The time, however, came, and speedily, when the Government of Mexico perceived that the two races were radically antagonistic, and that American activity would soon conquer the whole territory, unless force were opposed to it. So, with the usual blindness of despotism, Guerrero, the weak and despicable tyrant, began hostilities against the Americans, and detachments of soldiers crept in upon the colonists, occupying various posts, under one pretext or another, until the colonists saw through the ruse, and openly defied the crafty invaders.

Guerrero continued provocative measures; freeing slaves throughout Mexico, and thus violating a treaty made with the American colonists; and at last the Mexican Congress forbade any more Americans to enter Texas.

Then came the thunder-storm! The colonists sent commissioners to complain to the Mexican Government of their ill-treatment. These commissioners were imprisoned and abused, and the colonists flew to arms—took the citadel of Anahuac—took other fortresses and held them—released their commissioners—repudiated Mexico—met in convention at San Felipe, in 1832, and drew up a constitution under which they desired to live. Stephen Austin agreed to present

Mexican types in San Antonio.

it to the parent government in the city of Mexico, but when he reached that place he was thrown into prison.   This and other odious tyrannies of Santa Anna, the new ruler and liberator of Mexico, opened the way to the Alamo, to San Jacinto, and to independence. It was a bloody
path, but bravely trod !
There were giants in those
days, men who gave their
lives cheerfully, men who
held death in contempt.
Such men were Austin,
Houston, Travis, Fannin,
and Milam.

"The remnant of the old fort of the Alamo."

The final struggle be-
tween Santa Anna, dictator
of Mexico, and the Texan-
American army began in
1834. It was a clever pre-
text which brought about the real war.   The Mexican governor of Coahuila, the province allied to Texas, had, in order to meet his expenses, proposed the sale of lands in Texas.

Numerous speculators presented themselves; but they were all Americans, and when this became known, the Mexican Government refused to ratify the governor's action.   The governor insisted; troops were sent into Coahuila to expel the rebel Legislature which had voted the land measure, and the Texan-Americans found themselves, as well as their neighbors, in danger of invasion. They could wait no longer; they raised the standard of revolt on the plains of San Jacinto, August 16, 1835; and as soon as the news of the rebellion came to Mexican ears, General Cos, by Santa Anna's orders, sat down before San Antonio, the rebellious capital, to starve it into submission.   There was fighting everywhere—at Goliad, at Gonzales, in all the towns, and around them.

General Cos took San Antonio; was besieged in it; had to give it up to brave Ben Milam and the "three hundred men who were ready to die;" and, a little time after, the people of Texas, assembled in convention at Washington, on the Brazos river, enthusiastically voted the declaration of the absolute independence of Texas.   So Santa Anna, with three army corps, began the third siege of San Antonio.

As you see the remnant of the old fort of the Alamo now, its battered walls looming up without picturesque effect against the brilliant sky, and the clouds of dust which the muleteers and their teams stir up, half hiding it—perhaps it does not seem to you like a grand historic memorial.   Indeed it is not so grand as in its old days, when, as a church, standing proudly under the shade of the noble cottonwood trees, it was the cynosure of every eye.   It has fallen much into decay, and the Government, which would use Washington's tomb for a storehouse, rather than build a proper one, if Mount Vernon were a military depot, has cumbered it with boxes and barrels.

But you must picture the old fort as it was on Sunday, the 6th of March, 1836, when Texas was a young and war-ridden republic. Santa Anna, with an overwhelming force of infantry, had hemmed in and forced to retreat into the fort a little band of one hundred and forty or fifty men, commanded by Lieutenant-Colonel Travis. In those days the fort extended over two or three acres.

A thousand men would hardly have been sufficient to man the defenses. It was a capacious structure, with chapel, long stone barracks, barrier walls, and intrenchments, fortified with cannon. The barracks were loop-holed, and the doors were barricaded with semicircular parapets, made of double curtains of hides filled with earth. The walls were so tremendously thick and strong that batteries playing upon them night and day produced but little effect.

It was a troublous time for the new republic; the United States had given sympathy, but no aid; the Mexican troops were ten times as numerous as were the patriot armies; terrible struggles against the enemy had been made at Goliad, and at other places, but in vain; all hope of succor was cut off from the soldiers in the Alamo, although Houston's little army was doing its best to rally. Fannin was desperately awaiting the attack upon Goliad. The Alamo and its defenders were left alone, to the mercy of the "Napoleon of the West."

But Lieutenant-Colonel Travis and the little garrison had made up their minds. There was but one idea of duty in the souls of these men. Bowie and Crockett and Bonham, and those noble volunteers who had succeeded in making their way into the fort from the town of Gonzales—one hundred and eighty-eight souls in all, say some chroniclers,—resolved to defend the Alamo to the uttermost. Like Leonidas and his Spartans at Thermopylæ, they pledged themselves to victory or death. Then and there did they consecrate Texas to liberty. The Alamo was stormed by thousands of ferocious Spaniards and Mexicans. The Texans fought like demons, killing hundreds of their assailants, but were finally overpowered, and were all put to death. Two women, their two children, and a negro boy, were the only survivors of this dreadful massacre; and but one, a Mexican woman, is alive to-day. The "Napoleon of the West" gave his name to infamy, and sealed the doom of his own cause by this infamous massacre and the still bloodier one which followed it at Goliad. The heroism of the Alamo was the inspiration of the men who fell upon Santa Anna's army at San Jacinto, destroyed it, and made Texas free. Not even the bones of Travis and his men were preserved. The mutilated bodies were burned a few hours after they fell; and the fierce north winds which now and then sweep over San Antonio, have long ago scattered the ashes which the Texans a year after the massacre had gathered up and reverently buried.

XVI.

THE PLAINS—THE CATTLE TRADE.

THERE are many almost distinctively Mexican types to be seen in the San Antonio streets. Prominent among them are the horsemen from the plains, with their blankets well girt about them, and their swarthy features shaded by broadest of sombreros. Youths mounted on overloaded little mules shout lustily in Spanish. The drivers of the ox-teams swear and swear again as they crack their long whips, and groups of rough, semi-Indian looking men sun themselves at unprotected corners. The candy and fruit merchants lazily wave their fly-brushes, and sit staring open-eyed all day, although the intense sunlight reflected from the hard, white roads is painfully annoying to the stranger. The old beggars, half-blind and wholly ragged, huddle together, howling for alms, and invoking ten thousand saints, or, muttering to themselves, stray aimlessly up and down the avenues.

A residence of a few weeks in San Antonio affords one a good look into the cattle trade of Western Texas, one of the most remarkable industries of the southwest. One might with justice call it an indolent industry—for it accomplishes

J. Tinker, Sc

"The horsemen from the plains."

great results in a lazy, disorderly way, and makes men millionaires before they have had time to arouse themselves for real work.

Cattle-trading is a grand pastime with hundreds of Texans. They like the grandiloquent sound of a "purchase of 60,000 head." There is something at

"The candy and fruit merchants lazily wave their fly-brushes."
[Page 167.]

once princely and patriarchal about it. They enjoy the adventurous life on the great grazing plains, the freedom of the ranch, the possibility of an Indian incursion, the swift coursing on horseback over the great stretches, the romance of the road. Nearly all the immense region from the Colorado to the Rio Grande is given up to stock-raising. The mesquite grass carpets the plains from end to end, and the horses, cattle and sheep luxuriate in it; while the giant pecan throws down stores of oily nuts every year for the wandering hogs to revel over.

The mountainous regions around San Antonio offer superb facilities for sheep husbandry; and the valleys along the streams are fertile enough for the most exacting farmer. There are millions of cattle now scattered over the plains between San Antonio and the Rio Grande, and the number is steadily increasing. It is not uncommon for a single individual to own 200,000 head.

The cattle owners of Western Texas have been much before the public for the last few years, on account of their numerous complaints of thievery on the frontier. While I was in San Antonio a Government commission arrived from a long and tedious journey through the Rio Grande valley and the country between San Antonio and the Mexican boundary, where they had been taking testimony with regard to the Mexican outrages.

Opinion seems somewhat divided as to the extent and nature of the damage done the cattle-raising inter-est by the Mexicans, some Texans even asserting that the Texan claims are grossly exaggerated, and that there has been much stealing on both sides of the Rio Grande. But the commission itself has taken testimony with great care, and, whatever may be the exact nature of the claims against Mexico, they are enough to justify a prompt aggressive policy in case the hybrid neighbor

A Mexican Beggar.

republic does not see fit to take notice of the demands of her more powerful sister. The troubles on the Mexican-Texan frontier have resulted largely from an attack made on the Kickapoo Indians. It appears that these Indians, during our late civil war, left their reservation with the intention of going to Mexico, and while passing through Texas in May of 1864, were mistaken for a hostile force by a Confederate corps of observation, and were attacked. When the mistake was corrected, the Indians were allowed to proceed on their way; but they found the attack a pretext for an offensive policy, and soon after reaching Mexico began a series of distressing frontier depredations. There were only nine hundred and thirty-five of these Kickapoo Indians, originally; and it is now supposed that at least half of them are dead; but those who remain are terrible fellows. The Kickapoo is a kind of perverted Indian; he is unlike the original tribes of Texas, who, like their neighbors in Mexico, were mild-mannered until aroused by ideas of wrong. He was born with the genius of murder and rapine firmly implanted in his breast, and being somewhat civilized, of course he is much worse than if he were a pure savage. He had not been long in Mexico before he began to dominate the native Mexican Indians; and the Comanches joining with them, they soon had things their own way in their new home.

These Bedouins of the West have been a terror to the stock-farmer since 1864. They have acted like fiends; seeming to be far more malignant and savage than their ancestors. Indeed, as the Indian race decreases in Texas, from disease, internal dissensions, and intangible causes, the "type of the decadence" is the most repulsive which the blood has ever produced. It is as if the savage spirit made its last protest against annihilation tenfold more bitter and deadly than its first.

The Kickapoos, in conjunction with Comanches, Apaches, and Mexicans, have carried off immense herds, and committed numberless murders. They have been almost ubiquitous, overrunning that vast section between the Rio Grande and San Antonio rivers, and the road between the towns of San Antonio and Eagle Pass,—a region embracing 30,000 square miles. They were wont to dash into the ranches and stampede all the stock they could frighten, driving it before them to the Rio Grande, and, although well-armed pursuers might be close behind them as they crossed the fords, they would usually escape with their prey, knowing that in Mexico reclamation would be an impossibility.

They came, and still come from time to time, within a few miles of San Antonio, to gather up horses; and if they cannot succeed in escaping with the horses they invariably kill them. At the full of the moon the Indians will usually enter the vicinity of the ranches, on foot, carrying their lassos. They hide carefully until they have discovered where the stock is, and then the gathering up is a speedy matter. An attempt at pursuit is folly, as the pursuer can only travel in the day-time, when he can see the trail, and the only hope of peace seems to be the extermination of the Indians.* The citizens gather at San Antonio, and discuss measures of vengeance; but it is useless.

The Rio Grande valley has always been the paradise of stock-farming. Before the Spaniards had left the Texan country, the whole section between the

* I believe the Kickapoos in question have been removed from Mexico to some reservation, but there are still Indians enough left in Texas to keep stock-stealing up to its old standard.

Rio Grande and the Nueces was covered with stock.   The Indians were in those days employed in herding cattle; imagine one of them engaged in such a gentle, pastoral occupation to-day!   As soon as the influence of the missionaries began to wane, the Indians ceased herding, and returned to their old habits of murder and rapine.

The United States Commissioners to Texas are of opinion that not only have the Indians been aided and abetted by Mexicans in their stealing from the rancheros of Western Texas, but that Mexicans themselves are directly engaged in the stealing.   So great has been the loss from these causes since the war, that the number of cattle now grazing west of San Antonio is between two-thirds and three-fourths less than in 1866.

But the stock-raisers, despite the many dangers and vexations which beset them, are a healthy, happy set.   Their manners have a tinge of Spanish gravity and courtesy; they are sun-browned, stalwart men, unused to the atmosphere of cities, and in love with the freedom of the plains.

"The citizens gather at San Antonio, and discuss measures of vengeance"   [Page 169.]

Their herds of thousands range at will over the unfenced lands, and only once yearly do the stout rancheros drive them up to be examined, branded, and separated.   Ownership is determined by peculiar brands and ear-marks, records of which are kept in the offices of the county clerks, and published in the newspapers.   There is a stock-raisers' association which has decided on rules for mutual protection and aid.

In 1872 there were 450,000 cattle driven overland from Western Texas to Kansas, through the Indian Territory, by Bluff Creek and Caldwell, up the famous "Chisholm trail."   In 1871 as many as 700,000 were driven across. The general value of "Kansas beeves" is $12 to $13 gold; but after deducting all expenses, the average profit on the "drive" is not much more than a fair rate of interest on the money invested.   The cattle interest is rather heavily taxed for transportation, and suffers in consequence.

But few cattle are transported by sea, the outlet for the trade by way of Indianola having never been very successful. The Morgan steamships carry perhaps 40,000 beeves yearly that way. The two great shipping points in 1872–73 were Wichita, on a branch of the Atchison, Topeka and Santa Fé railroad, at the junction of the Arkansas and Little Arkansas rivers, and Ellsworth, on the Kansas Pacific railroad. The whole country, at the time of transit, is covered with vast herds, which begin to arrive in Kansas early in May and await buyers there. A stampede is something which baffles description; you must witness it. It is a tempest of horns and tails, a thunder of hoofs, a lightning of wild eyes; I can describe it no better.

Merely to see a man on foot is sometimes sufficient to set Texan cattle into a frenzy of fear, and a speedy stampede; for the great majority of them have never been approached save by men on horseback. The gathering up of stock is no light task, as a herd of 75,000 cattle will range over an area fifty miles wide by 100 miles long.

A Texan Cattle-Drover.

Large stock-raisers are always increasing their stock by buying herds adjacent to their ranges. Many persons make fortunes by simply gathering up and branding the cattle which the rightful owners have neglected to brand; cattle found unbranded, and a year old, being known as "Mavericks."

The origin of this name is very funny. Colonel Maverick, an old and wealthy citizen of San Antonio, once placed a small herd of cattle on an island in Matagorda Bay, and having too many other things to think of, soon forgot all about them. After a lapse of several years, some fishermen sent the Colonel word that his cattle had increased alarmingly, and that there was not grass enough on the island to maintain them. So he sent men to bring them off. There is probably nothing more sublimely awful in the whole history of cattle-raising than the story of those beasts, from the time they were driven from the island until they had scattered to the four corners of Western Texas. Among these Matagordian cattle which had run wild for years were 800 noble, but ferocious bulls; and wherever they went they found a clear field. It was as if a menagerie of lions had broken loose in a village. Mr. Maverick never succeeded in keeping any of the herd together; they all ran madly whenever a man came in sight; and for many a day thereafter, whenever unbranded and unusually wild cattle were seen about the ranges, they were called "Mavericks." The bulls were long the terror of the land.

The estimated profits of cattle-raising are enormous. Some authenticated instances are worthy especial mention. One man in the vicinity of San Antonio began in 1856 with 150 head of cattle; he now has 60,000, and is considered worth $350,000. Another, who began by taking stock to attend to for one-third of the increase, is worth about the same sum. One ranch, that of Mr. Kennedy, some distance west of Corpus Christi, has an inclosure of 150,000 acres, the fencing for which alone cost $100,000. Many a stock-raiser brands 15,000 head of calves yearly. The profits of horse-raising, making due allowance for losses by Indian raids and American and Mexican horse-thieves, are even greater. The owner of a large horse-ranch near Castroville* told me that he had repeatedly endeavored to get up an issue with the Indians, who often attacked his ranch—hoping to get them indicted and then requisitioned in Mexico; but their tribal arrangements prevent that. The chief alone is responsible for the bad deeds of all his warriors, and any quantity of indictments would never bring him to justice. An attempt to operate under the treaty made by Corwin, in 1862—by which the Government authorized district judges to demand the extradition of criminals,—was equally unsuccessful. The Mexican officers on the frontier recognize no law, no authority except their own.

The head-quarters of such troops of the regular army as are in the Department of Texas, is at San Antonio. A chain of defensive forts extends from Fort Sill in the Indian Territory—in that section occupied by the Kiowas, Arapahoes and Comanches,—south-west and south to the Rio Grande, and along the Mexican frontier. Forts Richardson, Griffin, Concho, McKavett, Clark, Duncan, McIntosh, Ringgold, and Brown, are the most important posts, and each is well garrisoned with several companies of infantry and cavalry. It is at Fort Clark that the gallant Colonel McKenzie has long been stationed. The close proximity

of the fort to the river has somewhat troubled the raiding Indians; but they generally manage to pass between the forts without being observed. Cavalry scouts are constantly engaged along the whole defensive

Military Head-quarters — San Antonio.

line; but the men and horses are but poor matches for the Indians and their ponies. There is no telegraphic communication from fort to fort; therefore the officers at the various posts are never capable of concerted action. The line of forts extending from Concho to Fort Sill is intended to protect against incursions from the "Staked Plains" district, where the Indians still wander at their own

---

* Castroville is one of the most thriving towns in Western Texas. It was founded by Henry Castro, a Frenchman of great culture and executive ability.

sweet will over the grass-carpeted plains, which are seemingly boundless as the ocean. The grandeur, the rugged beauty of these mighty table-lands will for many years yet be enjoyed only by the Indian; he makes a good fight there.

South-west from Fort Concho runs a defensive line, dotted with Forts Stockton, Davis, Hultman, and Bliss, the latter opposite El Paso, at the extreme western limit of Texas, and nearly seven hundred miles from San Antonio, at the entrance of the mountain passes of Chihuahua. Service in this department is no child's play; it is a rough and tumultuous school; and to see the general activity, one wonders that more is not actually accomplished.

Negro Soldiers of the San Antonio Garrison.

Railroads alone can solve the question. As it is, the thirty-five hundred men in the department, whether officered by General Auger, the present department commander, or General Grant, cannot catch and punish the evil-minded Indians. The soldiers are rarely attacked; the alert and logical savage seeks a peaceful prey rather than a fight with men as well armed as himself. Never advertising his coming, as the soldiers too often do, he rarely meets them. He is all eyes and ears; the tiniest cloud of dust on the horizon announces to him the approach of some one; he notes the faintest tremor among the grasses, and knows what it signifies; he detects a little imprint on the turf, and can decide at once whether or not it is that of a soldier's foot, or a white man's horse.

When he mounts a hill, he looks about to see if there is anything stirring on the plain; and if there be, he hides until he knows what it is. It is easy to see that recruits and unpracticed frontiersmen cannot fight such people as these. Very few soldiers are harmed; it is mainly the innocent settlers, who have no

idea of protecting themselves, who suffer.   Since 1866 over 300 unoffending
Texans have been killed by murderous Indians and Mexicans.

Great care is necessary in traversing the plains, even with an escort of soldiers.
A gentleman, returning from Fort Clark, once strayed ahead of the main party
and was found, with arrows sticking in him and minus his scalp, dead.   The
Indians even hovered around the Government commissioners, on their journey
from Eagle Pass to Laredo.   For efficiency's sake, the Texans should be allowed
in some way to take the matter of subduing the Indians and protecting their frontier against the Mexicans into their own hands.

Wonderful land of limitless prairie, of beautiful rivers and strange foliage—
land where there is room to breathe full breaths—land beyond which there
seem no boundary lines—the railroad will yet subdue you !   Then there will be
no more mystery in your plains—your chaparral thickets—your groves of post
oak and pecan—your cypress-bordered streams—your grand ranges—your sun-
burnished stretches.   Stage routes will be forgotten ; the now rapidly decaying
native Indian tribes will stray into some unexplored nook, never to sally forth
again.   The Rio Grande will no longer be a boundary, and the Sierra Madre's
rocky gaps will echo back the sharp accents of the American tongue.   All this
in a few years, unless the tokens fail !

XVII.

DENISON—TEXAN CHARACTERISTICS.

STANDING in the main street of Denison, Texas, the new town near the southern border of the Indian Territory, six hundred and twenty-one miles south-west of St. Louis, it was hard to realize that only four months before my visit its site was almost a wilderness, not a building of any kind having yet been erected there. For all around us was Babel—a wild rush of business, a glory in affairs, an unbounded delight in mere labor, by which I was at once oppressed and appalled.

Scene in a Gambling House—"Playing Keno"—Denison, Texas.

The slightest indication of progress was pointed out as a gigantic foreshadowing of the future preëminence of Denison. "There are from 2,500 to 3,000 people here now," said one gentleman to us; "how's that for four months? That'll make some of the incredulous folks take their frame houses off from the rollers !"—an expression intended to open up a startling prospect for the future of Denison.   But, indeed, all these enthusiastic pioneers of a new civilization were justified in their seemingly wild prophecies of greatness.   Northern Texas, under the beneficent influences of railroad pioneering, is assuming a prominence which had never been imagined for it until within the last five years.

As soon as the Missouri, Kansas and Texas railway had crossed the Red river, a stream of immigration, which the most sanguine had not hoped for, set in.   The North-west seemed to move *en masse*.   The tracts of fertile, black-wax land, which literally needed but to be tickled with the plough to smile a

"Men drunk and sober danced to rude music."   [Page 177.]

harvest, were rapidly taken up, and Denison sprang into existence as the chief town of the newly developed region.   It was organized four months before my visit, and since that time the Denison Town Company had sold $90,000 worth of building lots.   The town stands in a county absolutely free from debt, and is at the outlet of one of the most fertile farming regions of the world.   Two railroads, coming to it from opposite points, and not costing it a cent, laid the foundation for its remarkable advance, an advance more like magic than like the normal growth of a pioneer settlement.

All the lumber for the houses and business establishments was brought hundreds of miles, there being none suitable in the vicinity ; and the car-loads of material were changed into rough but commodious structures in a twinkling. It was exceedingly remarkable, also, that in a community one-half of which was undoubtedly made up of professional ruffians, "terminus" gamblers, and the offscourings of society, and where there was not yet a regularly organized government, there was not more of terrorism.

Every third building in the place was a drinking saloon with gambling appurtenances, filled after nightfall with a depraved, adventurous crowd, whose profanity was appalling, whose aspect was hideous. Men drunk and sober danced to rude music in the poorly-lighted saloons, and did not lack female partners. In vulgar bestiality of language, in the pure delight of parading profanity and indecency, the ruffian there had no equal. The gambling houses were nightly frequented by hundreds. Robberies were, of course, of frequent occurrence in the gambling hells, and perhaps are so still; but in the primitive hotels, where the luckless passengers from the Missouri, Kansas and Texas railway awaited a transfer by stage to Sherman, and where they were packed three or four together in beds in a thinly-boarded room through whose cracks rain might fall and dust blow, they were as safe from robbery or outrage as in any first-class house. Rough men abounded, and would, without doubt, have knocked any one upon the head who should find himself alone, unarmed, and late at night, in their clutches. But the carrying of concealed weapons is so expressly forbidden by the laws of Texas, that cases of shooting rarely occurred, and there was no more danger to the life or limb of the traveler than may be met with on Broadway. I was too late to see the Denison where rascals had held supreme sway. Their _régime_ vanished when the railroad crossed the Red river.

The business men of Denison are a stern, self-reliant, confident company. They have a thorough belief in Northern Texas; intend to tame its wildness, and make it one of the gardens of the world. The Kansas and Missouri and Illinois and Western New York character crops out everywhere in Denison, and is the chief reliance of the town.

The aboriginal Texan looks on, and admires the energy displayed, but he takes good care not to mix in the fray too much himself. There is something sublimely impudent, charmingly provoking, in the manner in which he disappears from work and the street when a cold "Norther" comes on; in the cool, defiant way in which he forces others to work for him, and the utter surprise he manifests when he is accused of droning. He is a child of the sun; he dislikes effort; it gives him no gratification to labor in the rough ways of a new town like Denison.

Yet this same man can leap to the level of a hero when his rights are assailed; can bathe a San Jacinto plain with his best blood; can stand at an Alamo's breastworks until covered with wounds, and can ride at the head of a brigade into the very gates of death without losing one iota of his magnificent equipoise.

But the old population of Northern Texas is rapidly assimilating with the new-comers, and there is no longer any vestige of the intolerance which made a

Texan regard a stranger as an intruder. Neither is it safe in a new town like Denison to judge a man, as we are forced to do in large cities, by his outer garb and manners. The huge hulking fellow with one cheek distended with tobacco, and with his clothes all so disposed that they seem to have been thrown upon him, will answer you with all the courtesy and grace of a high-bred gentleman, and will show a consideration for your opinions and your remarks which you do not always receive from the *habitués* of a city. The roughness is exterior only, and he who contents himself with a passing glance will not penetrate to the sterling qualities which that exterior conceals.

The earnestness of the new town, the almost religious quality of its ambition, were amusing as well as inspiring. Every one talked in exaggerated phrase; land values were fictitious; the estimates of immigration were overdrawn; the "probabilities" were certainly elastic, but there was such hope! Many men who had only been in Texas a year or two had already become rich, enhancing, at the same time, the value of property in the localities in which they had settled. In the little boarded newspaper office there was the same dauntless ambition; in the saloon, again the same. "Sherman ain't nothin' to this yer," said one man to me; "we've got the riffle on her on saloons." He could not even allow a neighbor town a preëminence in vice. "General Sheridan's going to build a supply depot here, 'n' then you'll see!" was the final, annihilating rejoinder administered to a carping Shermanite in our hearing. All the inhabitants were determined to make a magnificent city out of this irregular group of one-story wooden buildings, confusedly located on the high rolling land four miles south of the Red river, and their zeal was both to them and to us "like new wine."

He would, indeed, be a brave man who should, at this writing, prophesy that the great new route to the Gulf will redeem the Indian Territory from its present isolation, and bring it into the Union first as on probation, and finally as a State. Nevertheless, the people of the south-west are firmly convinced that such will be

"Red Hall."

the case, and, for various important reasons, the inhabitants of Northern Texas earnestly desire it. The existence of such an immense frontier, so near to the newly settled districts of Texas, enables rogues of all grades to commit many crimes with impunity, for, once over the border, a murderer or a horse-thief can hide in the hills or in some secluded valley until his pursuers are fatigued, and can then make his way out in another direction.

So frequent had this method of escape become, at the time of the founding of Denison, that the law-abiding citizens were enraged; and the famous deputy-sheriff, "Red Hall," a young man of great courage and unflinching "nerve," determined to attempt the capture of some of the desperadoes. Arming himself with a Winchester rifle, and with his belt garnished with navy revolvers, he kept watch on certain professional criminals. One day, soon after a horse-thief had been heard from in a brilliant dash of grand larceny, he repaired to the banks of the Red river, confident that the thief would attempt to flee.

In due time, the fugitive and two of his friends appeared at the river, all armed to the teeth, and while awaiting the ferry-boat, were visited by Hall, who drew a bead upon them, and ordered them to throw down their arms. They refused, and a deadly encounter was imminent; but he finally awed them into submission, threatening to have the thief's comrades arrested for carrying concealed weapons. They delivered up their revolvers and even their rifles, and fled, and the horse-thief, rather than risk a passage-at-arms with the redoubtable Hall, returned with him to Denison, after giving the valiant young constable some ugly wounds on the head with his fist. The passage of the river having thus been successfully disputed by the law, the rogues became somewhat more wary.

"Red Hall" seemed to bear a charmed life. He moved about tranquilly every day in a community where there were doubtless an hundred men who would have delighted to shed his blood; was often called to interfere in broils at all hours of the night; yet his life went on. He had been ambushed and shot at, and threatened times innumerable, yet had always exhibited a scorn for his enemies, which finally ended in forcing them to admire him. When he visited me on my arrival in Denison, he remarked, " I shall see you in Sherman Monday, as I have some prisoners to take to court there;" but Monday morning, as I was starting for Sherman, he informed me that when he awoke in the morning, he was surrounded by armed men; a pistol was held under his nose ; and he was told that he was arrested at the instance of the United States Marshal, to whom some one had been retailing slanders concerning him. Even as he spoke he was vigilantly guarded by armed men. But in the afternoon he was free again—once more in authority, and awing the ruffians into a proper respect.

The tracks of the great railway connecting Northern Texas with the outer world had but just been completed to Denison when I visited the town, but the huge freight-houses were already filled with merchandise awaiting transportation to the interior. The Overland Transportation Company was closing its books, for the Texas Central railway line was expected in a few weeks to reach the Red river, and the great Gulf route would be complete.

Staging to Sherman, we passed immense wagon-trains of merchandise, creaking forward through the wax-like soil, which clung in such masses to the wheels that the teams stopped from time to time, discouraged. Gangs of stout fellows from Illinois and Missouri were marching along the highways, *en route* for the railroad lines which they were to aid in constructing; mule-teams, drawing loads of lumber, each team driven by a six-foot Texan with a patriarchal beard, passed us; wild-looking men mounted on horses or mules, with rifles slung over shoulders, and saddle-bags stuffed with game, cantered by.

Sometimes we met a discouraged company, painfully forcing its way back toward sunrise, the *paterfamilias* driving a span of sorry mules which dragged a weary wagon-load of grumbling and disheartened family. So, faring forward through forest and brake, over creeks and under hills, beside smiling fields and along mournful wastes, into primitive clearings and out of forsaken nooks, and crannies where civilization had only made the wilderness look worse, we reached Sherman, the forty-year-old shire town of Grayson county.

The Public Square in Sherman, Texas.

Glorious sunlight enlivened the town as we entered it, and intensest activity prevailed, the county court being in session. The town is built around a square, in the centre of which stands a low, unpainted wooden building, known as the Court-House. The "grand jury" was not far from the aforesaid building, as we drew up at the hotel opposite it, and was to outward appearance a collection of rough, sensible farmers, impressed with a full sense of their duty. The horses on which half-a-hundred of the neighboring farmers had ridden in to attend to their marketing and upon the sessions of the court, were hitched at a common hitching frame not far from the court-house; and in the centre of the square a noisy auctioneer, whom the Texans were regarding with admiring eyes, was bawling out his wares. The plank sidewalks were crammed with tall youths, in patched homespun; with negroes, whose clothing was a splendid epitome of color; with

spruce speculators—Northerners and Westerners—dressed in the latest styles;
with dubious-looking characters, who shrank a little apart from the common gaze,
as if afraid of the day-light; with swine, that trotted hither and yon; and with
the hook-nosed and loud-voiced Israelites, who are found in every city and
hamlet throughout the South.

Large numbers of people seemed diligently engaged in doing nothing whatever, or in frankly enjoying the delicious sunlight, which gave new glory and
picturesqueness to everything upon which it rested.   Now and then a soft breeze
came gently from the up-
lands, and softened the effect
of this generous sun.   The
excited gambler came out
to bathe his livid face in
zephyr and sunlight; the

"With swine that trotted hither
and yon."

negro crawled to the sidewalk's edge, and with his
feet in the mud, blinked like
an owl in the fierce glare; the
stage-drivers swore round
but rather jocund oaths at
the rearing and plunging mules drawing the coaches for Denison, McKinney,
and other little towns; and the big negro who guarded the court-house door
twirled the great key majestically, and looked ferocious.

Although it was midwinter, the day was as perfect as one in June at the
North; but the languor which stole over us was purely Southern, as I imagined
myself to be dreaming away the afternoon in lazy abandon and irresolute comfort, spiced only with the charm of studying new types of a common nationality.
Toward evening there was absolute tranquillity all over the place.   Not even
a loud word was spoken.   The dusky figures who sat crouched in the porch of
our hotel, mutely regarding the glories of the setting sun, seemed almost in the
act of worship.

Denison was a yearling when I saw it for the second time, and the most wonderful changes had meanwhile taken place.   The Texas Central railway line was
completed.   Northern and Southern Texas were connected, and Pullman cars
were running through the untamed prairies.   The gamblers and ruffians had fled.
Denison had acquired a city charter; had a government, and the rabble had
departed before law could reach them.   A smart new hotel, near the railroad, was
doing a driving business, hundreds of people thronging its dining-rooms.

Above Denison, at the river, another town had sprung up, a child of the
Texas Central, and ambitiously named "Red River City."   Newsboys called the
daily paper about the streets of Denison; we heard of the opera-house; we saw
the announcement of church services; and the notices of meetings for the discussion and advocacy of new railroad routes were numerous.

I confess to a certain feeling of disappointment in not having found more
marked peculiarities of the people of Texas.   There are, of course, phases and
bits of dialect which distinguish them from the inhabitants of other sections; but
even the rude farmer in the back-country is not as singular as he has been represented.   In extreme Southern and extreme Northern Texas, the visitor from the
North or West sees but little variation from his own types in the cities; and yet
in the remote districts he may find more ignorance and less idea of comfort than
he would have thought possible in America.

There are a good many instances of rude and incult rich men; people who are of the old *régime*, and who, while owning thousands of cattle, sheep, and horses, live in log-houses, eat mean food, and have scarcely more than one suit of clothes in ten years. But these people are quietly disappearing before the new-comers.   At first they are fierce against innovation, and indignant at frame houses, railroad stations, and saloons; but finding that they must yield or retire, they acquiesce.

The general characteristics of an old style Texan farm were unthrift and untidiness; the land was never half tilled, because it produced enough to support life without being highly cultivated.   When a fence fell into decay,—if by some strange chance there was a fence,—the rails or boards lay where they fell; people

Bridge over the Red River—(Missouri, Kansas and Texas Railway).

grew up like weeds, and choked each other's growth.   Those who held slaves counted their wealth in " niggers," and sometimes boasted that they were worth a hundred thousand dollars, while living in meaner and more uncomfortable fashion than the poorest Irishman at the North.

The only amusement of the *paterfamilias* was a hunt, or a ride to the county seat in court time, where, in days when every one carried arms, there was usually some exciting event to disturb the monotony of existence— perhaps to disturb existence itself.   There was no market, no railroad within hundreds of miles, no newspaper, no school, save perhaps some private institution miles from the farm or plantation, and no intellectual life or culture whatever.

The rich slave-owner was a kind of patriarchal savage, proud of his own dirt and ignorance.   The heroic epoch of the struggle for independence being over, thousands of persons settled down to such life as this, and thought it vastly fine. What a magnificent awakening has come to them !

The mass of people in the interior still have a hearty scorn for anything good to eat.   The bitter coffee, and the greasy pork, or "bacon," as it is always called, still adorns the tables of most farmers.   A railroad president, inspecting a route in Northern Texas, stopped at a little house for dinner.   The old lady of the homestead wishing to treat her guest with becoming dignity, inquired in the kindest manner, after having spread the usual food before him, "Won't ye have a little bacon fat to wallop your corn dodgers in now, won't ye ? " This was the acme of hospitality in that region.

Now and then, in these days of immigration, a housewife will venture a timid " Reckon ye don't think much of our home-made fare, do ye? " when the visitor is a stranger; and, indeed, he shows upon his face his wonder that a well-to-do farmer's stout sons and pretty daughters are satisfied with pork and molasses and clammy biscuits, with no vegetables whatever.

The negro is responsible for the introduction of such oceans of grease into Texan cookery; it suited his taste, and the white people for whom he cooked mutely accepted it, just as they insensibly accepted certain peculiarities of his dialect,—notably "dat 'ar" and "dis yer," and "furder" for further; mispronunciation which it makes one stare to hear good-looking white people use, as if they supposed it correct. The Texan has one phrase by which he may easily be recognized abroad : "I reckon *so*," with the accent on the last word, is his common phrase of assent. In the country, when riding on horseback, and inquiring how far it is to a certain place, you will now and then be told that it is "two sights and a look," which you must understand if you can.

There is in Western Texas a more highly-colored, vivid, and dramatic manner of talk than in the rest of the State, doubtless the result of long contact with the Spaniard and Mexican. In parts of Northern Texas, too, among some classes, there is a profanity which exceeds anything I have ever encountered elsewhere. In Western Texas it is fantastic, and, so to speak, playful. I once traveled from Galveston to Houston in the same car with a horse-drover, who will serve as an example. This man was a splendid specimen of the Texan of the plains, robust and perfectly formed. There was a certain chivalrous grace and freedom about all his movements which wonderfully impressed one. His clean-cut face was framed in a dark, shapely beard and moustache, which seemed as if blown backward by the wind. He wore a broad hat with a silver cord around it, and I felt impelled to look for his sword, his doublet, and his spurs, and to fancy that he had just stepped out of some Mexican romance.

His conversation was upon horses, his clear voice ringing high above the noise of the car-wheels, as he laughingly recounted anecdotes of adventures on ranches in the West, nearly every third word being an oath. He caressingly cursed; he playfully damned; he cheerfully invoked all the evil spirits that be; he profaned the sacred name, dwelling on the syllables as if it were a pet transgression, and as if he feared that it would be too brief.

Even in bidding his friend good-by, he cursed as heartily as an English boatswain in a storm, but always with the same cheeriness, and wound up by walking off lightly, laughing and murmuring blasphemous assent to his friend's last proposition.

Some of the small towns in the interior are indeed trials to him who must long stay in them. My severest experience was in a Northern Texan "metropolis,"—its name shall be spared,—where the main hotel was a new board structure, without the suspicion of ceiling or lathing on the premises, and through whose roof one could see the stars. The front office was about the size of a

New England wood-box; and when some twenty persons, variously impregnated with questionable liquids, had gathered therein, the effluvia became shocking.

In the long, creaking supper-room beyond, a dirty cloth was laid on a dirtier table, and pork, fried to a cinder and swimming in grease hot enough to scorch the palate, was placed before the guests. To this was presently added, by the hands of a tall, angular, red-haired woman, a yellow mass of dough supposed to be biscuit, a cup of black, bitter bean-juice named coffee, and as a crowning torture, a mustard-pot, with very watery mustard in it.

This, the regular sustenance, I suppose, of the unfortunate people of that town, was so unusually bad that I forthwith desired to be shown my room; and was ushered into a creaking loft, over a whiskey saloon wherein a mob of drunken railroad laborers were quarreling, and threatening, with the most outrageous profanity, to annihilate each other. To the music of these revels I attempted to lull my wearied body to repose; but did not succeed, and went to the four-in-the-morning train unrefreshed.

Even at the station my troubles were not at an end, for on venturing to expostulate with an *employé* for not checking my baggage, he profanely condemned me, adding that "It's mighty easy to get up a fight in Texas." Had I remained twenty-four hours longer in that town, it is my firm belief that I should have been accommodated with a complete and thorough exposition of all the eccentric features generally accredited to the society of the State.

The people of Texas suffered greatly from the war; thousands were ruined by it. Young and old together went to the fight, returning only to find ruin staring them in the face, and the poverty which was so bitter hangs by them still. The sudden fall from large fortune to day-labor, so general in Louisiana, smote Texas sternly. But never, on the whole, was a people more cheery. It is resolved to rebuild and to accept the advent of

"New men, new faces, other minds."

The beauty of the fair Southern land is but faintly shadowed in these pages. It is too intense to admit of transfer. But no visitor will ever forget the magic of the climate—never guilty of the extremes of heat or cold which we suffer in the North, and yet so varied that the most fastidious may suit themselves within home boundaries; one cannot forget the attractive wildness of the great western plains, nor the tropic luxuriance of the southern shore.

He cannot forget his pilgrimage to rock-strewn Mount Bonnell, Austin's guardian mountain; nor the Colorado running between its steep banks, with the wooded slopes beyond melting softly into the ethereal blue; nor the long, white roads, bordered by graceful live oaks; nor the bayous, along which the whippoor-wills and chuck-will's-widows keep up lively chorus all night long.

Nor will one visitor forget how, just at dawn, he saw a troop of hundreds of Texan cattle fording a shallow stream, and leaving a track of molten silver behind them, as the sun smote the ripples made by their hurrying feet; nor how, by night, as the slowly-moving train stole across the country, millions of fire-flies flashed about the fields; how gaunt and weary emigrants gathered in groups around the camp fires; how, now and then, some weary figure, bent and ragged, stole up behind the train with pack upon its back, plodding its way toward the land of promise; how the darkies at the little stations where the iron horse stopped to refresh himself, sang quaint songs as they threw the wood into the tender; how mahogany-colored old women besieged him with platters, covered with antique "spring chicken" and problematic biscuits; how hale, stalwart old men with patriarchal beards and extraordinary appetites for tobacco, talked with him of the rising glory of Texas, impressing upon him that this is a mighty State, sir; fast rising to the lead, sir; has come out of the war gloriously, sir; and, sir, enough for all the world in her broad acres, sir; yes, sir.

Nor will he forget the motley throng of Mexican prisoners, straggling into the streets of Austin, charged with murder most foul, their great eyes glittering with demoniac hatred under the gray of their sombreros; nor the pretty maidens dismounting from their restive ponies at the "horse-blocks" in front of the shops, and trailing their long overskirts before the merchants' windows; nor the groups of negroes at the corners, chattering like parroquets.

Nor the disguised army detective, slouching about the public places in the clothes of a western ranchero, prospecting for deserters; nor the gaunt teamsters from the borders of the San Marcos, the Guadalupe, or the San Antonio, with their half-melancholy, half-ferocious look; nor the erect military figure of "the governor," with his keen, handsome face and blond Prussian moustache.

Nor the typical land agent, with his bland smile and diffuse conversation about thousand-acre tracts and superb locations; nor the dusty and pallid travelers descending from the El Paso stage, their Winchester rifles in their hands, and their nerves strained with eight hundred miles of adventurous stage travel.

Nor can he forget how, one morning, on the banks of the beautiful Colorado, a ghastly cross-tree affronted the sky, while around a platform a great throng of white, and black, and brown men, American, and negro, and Mexican, gathered to see two men die. He will remember how the criminals came to the gallows and gazed round from the scaffold in search of some sympathetic desperado to help them; how, in his despair at finding none, one of them, in derision, broke into a shuffling dance, and after making a blackguard speech, fainted as the rope was placed about his guilty neck; how the crowd jeered at and mocked the two men until the scene was over, leaving the vacant gallows to stand as a perpetual warning.

Nor will he forget the moonlit evenings in the gardens of the southern coast, where the thick clumps of cedar joined their heavy perfume to that of the magnolia; where the rose and the myrtle vied in fragrance, and the dagger-tree spread its sharp leaves defiantly; where the snow-white of the jessamine peered from the darkness; where the China-tree showered its strange fruit on the turf; the fig put forth its tender shoots; the orange and the oleander, the verbenas and the pansies all looked coquettishly out of their midwinter beds at the Northern new-comer, seeming to smile at his wonder; where the grape trellises were covered with clinging vines; and where strange birds sang songs in consonance with the lapping of the waters on the Gulf shore, and with the intense hum of the unseen insect life, rising and falling like a magnificent harmony.

XVIII

THE NEW ROUTE TO THE GULF.

A JOURNEY from Sedalia, in Missouri, through the Indian Territory to Denison, will enable one to appreciate properly the vastness of the southwest, and the magnitude of the railway projects so constantly carried into execution there.

The ruder aspects of Sedalia, the Missourian terminus of the Missouri, Kansas and Texas railway, have vanished before the march of improvement, and the town has arisen from the low level of a speculative frontier village, where the tenure of life and position in society was very uncertain, to the grade of an important junction, and a city of prominence. It is not very long since the revolver was the supreme arbiter in all disputes in Sedalia,—since, indeed, the streets were cleared of all peaceable men in an instant, whenever there was prospect of a quarrel between the bloodthirsty thieves and ruffians who infested the whole adjacent region.

The drift of iniquity from the impromptu towns along the Union Pacific line came into Missouri, Kansas, and the Indian Territory, as soon as the project of the new route to the Gulf was broached, and brought with it murder and wholesale robbery. The men who had been attracted to Missouri from the States of Illinois and Ohio, and from portions of Kansas, by the excellent chances to enrich themselves in land speculations, were appalled by the conduct of the drunken and ferocious fiends who came to haunt the new towns. The projectors of the new route to the Gulf had to face this criminal element and to submit to its presence in their midst.   Often it was the stronger, and openly defied law, as is now the case in certain sections of the West.   But the pioneers of the route had had their schooling in new lands; the engineers and builders were men of muscle and brain, of coolness and "nerve," and moved quietly but irresistibly forward, amid the harassing outrages of a mean and cowardly banditti, whose chief precept was assassination, and whose trade was rapine.

With dauntless energy, courage, and industry, and by the aid of generously expended capital, these pioneers of the Missouri, Kansas and Texas railway worked steadfastly, and in three and a-half years laid 551 miles of solidly-constructed track, or a little over half a mile for every working day.   When they took up their task, the anguish of the war was hardly ended; the total disorganization of society consequent on the radical changes inaugurated in the lately slaveholding States made many of the conditions of life and labor onerous and disagreeable; but the superb end hoped for always made the difficult means easier to work with.

To-day a tract of country which, two years ago, was comparatively as unknown to the masses of our citizens as Central Africa, is now easily accessible; palace cars convey the traveler over the rich plains of the Indian territory from St. Louis, with its legacy of more than a century's history, to Denison, the young giant of Northern Texas, with its records of a year.

Two New Yorkers, Messrs. George Denison and David Crawford, jr., gave the railway its first financial status, and brought it before the eyes of the world with its respectability thoroughly guaranteed, and its objects all properly explained.   The enterprise, originally known as the Southern branch of the Union Pacific Railway Company, was magnificent in scope, and found ready support from men of large minds and ample means.

The system north of the Red river, when perfected, was intended to comprehend more than 1,000 miles; and the proposed extension south of the Red river would amount to 1,000 more.   The scheme was that of a grand vertebral line through Texas, via Waco and Austin, to Camargo on the west bank of the Rio Grande; thence almost due south, through Monterey, Saltillo, Zacatecas, San Luis Potosi, and Queretaro, to the City of Mexico.

The company, in constructing its railway and branches through Missouri and Kansas, asked but few favors of the States.   It has built the road mainly with its own money, and has shown the true pioneering spirit in boldly pushing its tracks, at an enormous expense, through the Indian Territory, without waiting for the settlement of the question of the distribution of lands there.   The same indomitable pluck and persistent effort will doubtless be shown in the future building of Texas and Mexican extensions.

The Legislature of Texas has accorded the company organization under a special law, and the general law gives to any railway built within the State limits extensive land grants, so that the people will not be subjected to burdensome taxation, and in a few years the outside world will suddenly discover that a journey to Mexico is no more difficult than the present journey to New

Orleans, and that new lands and territories have been opened up to speculation and profit as if by magic. But the plan is not limited merely to this. It is possible that in future the line may extend from where it now joins the Houston and Texas Central railway at Denison, southward, down the valley of the Trinity,

"The Pet Conductor."

—the richest in Eastern Texas,—to Galveston, with a branch to the waters of Sabine Bay, which route to the Gulf, it is claimed, would save from 700 to 1,200 miles of railway transportation upon all the foreign importations and exportations of the West Mississippi States and Territories, over shipments via the Atlantic ports. The value of the Texas business will also be immense; and should the Missouri, Kansas and Texas railway lines touch the Gulf, there will be travel and trade enough for it and for the International and Great Northern and the Houston and Texas Central, even though they double their tracks and rolling stock. Besides this, the branch from Sedalia, extending across the Missouri river at Booneville, to Moberly, Missouri, gives a magnificent direct line from Chicago to Galveston.

As the Indian Territory boasts no towns worthy the name along either of the two lines of rail which penetrate its domain, the railroad company placed at the disposition of our party a superb hotel car, equipped with kitchen, drawing, and sleeping-room. The larder of the traveling-home was well stocked; engineer, fireman, and brakeman took their rifles, prepared for an encounter with deer, or to chase the cautious wild turkey; and a merry party, one frosty morning in January of 1873, rattled out of Sedalia. Both artist and writer were fascinated with this perfection of travel, this journeying so thoroughly at one's own will, with power to stop at every turn, and with no feeling of haste. The presiding genii of the train, "the Pet Conductor" and "Charlie," made the travel through the wilds as comfortable as the journey of an emperor. Wherever it seemed to us good, we dismissed our train to a side track, and wandered off.

"Charlie."

The Missouri towns in this section were passed over with a cursory glance, as being so much alike in general character. Windsor was a sleepy place; Calhoun sleepier and older. The latter village was a cluster of ill-looking buildings, grouped around a muddy square. At the time we saw it, there was also snow enough to make it uncomfortable. "Yer ought to see it Sundays," said an informant at the depot, "when them fellows get full of tangle-foot. They kin just fight!" But the railroad is bringing

Calhoun a better future. A little farther on, we paused before the entrance to a shaft sunk in one of those rich veins of coal which crop out in all this section. An old man, dwarfed and bent, but still vigorous, the very image of a gnome, conducted us into the narrow galleries, a hundred and fifty feet below the surface, where we crawled on our hands and knees along passages scarcely three feet high, examining the superb strata into which the railway company delves for fuel. A railway built over a coal-bed gives its corporation no cause for complaint, although, far as the eye can reach, on either hand, there may be scarcely a stick of timber to be seen.

The men and women in these small Missouri towns had a grave, preoccupied look, doubtless born of the hard ways of the West. The farming population in that section is none too prosper-ous, and rarely has any ready money. The im-mense dispropor-tion between the cost of labor and implements for producing crops, and the prices of the produce it-self, has made sad havoc with many brilliant pros-pects. At that time, throughout that part of the South - west, the tillers of the soil were savagely discon-tent. Many with whom we conversed spoke with great bitterness of the difficulty of obtain-ing proper representation in Congress on the subject of their grievances. In this first day's journeying it was curious to note how the advent of the railway had caused whole towns and villages to change their location, and come tumbling miles across the prairie, to put themselves in direct communication with the outer world. Sometimes, at a little station, we were shown, far off on the horizon, a landmark of the village's former site, and told that the citizens one day set their houses upon wheels, and had them dragged by long trains of oxen to the railway line. For a time everything was in transition; people had to give up church on Sundays until the "meeting-house came over to the new village;" a gambling-hell, and the house of a pious citizen often jogging along for days in friendly company. Sometimes a great wind, turning a whole migratory village

Our Special Train.
[Page 188.]

upside down, would compel the vigorous "bull-whackers" to shout themselves
hoarse in their efforts to right things.

Instances of discouraged towns were abundant on every hand.   Here and
there we came to a long street, bordered by white one-story board structures
and plank walks, and inhabited by a bevy of dejected and annoyed colonists,
forever cursing their lack of judgment in not having selected the site destined
to be the great railway city of the South-west.   Entering the shop of the
humblest tradesman, we were at once the centre of an admiring and awe-
stricken group, every person in it manifesting surprise that commerce in that
especial locality had revived even to the extent of the expenditure of a ten-cent
scrip.   In such towns, the hotel was usually a small, frail, frame structure, kept
by a giant of a man, with a disappointed face and a sour and envious manner

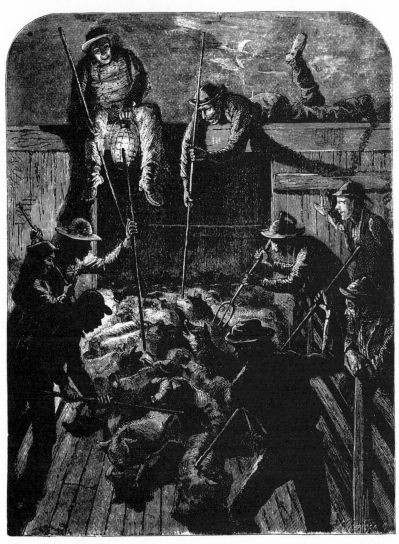

" A stock - train from Sedalia was receiving a squealing and bellowing freight." [Page 191.]

of greeting—a manner grafted upon him by the hard facts of pioneer life, but which it was easy to see belied his real nature. The women were silent, impassive, laborious, seeming to have forsworn folly of every kind, and to be delving at Nature with desperate will, determined to wrench riches from her, even though the golden opportunity had moved on.

"The old Hospital"—Fort Scott. [Page 192.]

After Charles had made all tidy for bed within the palace-car, on the first evening of the journey, we wandered among the drovers and herdsmen at one of the great stock-yards on the railway line. A stock-train from Sedalia was receiving a squealing and bellowing freight as we reached the yards, leading from which to the car door ran an inclined plane. Along the outer side of the fence inclosing this plane stood a dozen stout men, armed with long poles and pitchforks. Presently the figure of a man sprang out of the darkness. "Is your lot ready, Bill?" with an oath. "Yes!" with an oath; and then to the music of other oaths innumerable, a mass of struggling porkers were forced forward to the car door. A rain of curses, yells and sharp pitchfork thrusts fell upon their defenceless backs. They rushed madly over each other along the crowded way into the car, those who lagged behind receiving prods enough to honey-comb an elephant's hide. Now and then, before succumbing to the captivity of the car, some giant porker would throw down one of his human assailants and give him a savage bite—these being none of your luxurious pigs of the civilized sty, but sovereign rooters at large brought forth and reared on the prairie. Many a drover has carried to his grave the ugly scars given him by Texas steers and Missouri swine.

The next day was Sunday, and the one street of the little town of Appleton, where a New York publishing firm has generously built a handsome school-house, was lined with tired-looking women and pretty girls moving churchward. Rough fellows, who had been occupied all the week with hard labor, mounted their ponies and galloped away for a day's hunting. We went on through the towns of Nevada and Deerfield to Schell City, a superb location for a fine town, and one of the especial favorites of the railway corporation. Thousands of acres of rich land are owned there by the company, and many substantial buildings are already in progress. In the afternoon we came to the prosperous little town of Fort Scott, in Kansas, stretched along a range of hills lined with coal.

Situated directly at the junction of the Kansas City, Fort Scott and Gulf railway with the Missouri, Kansas and Texas, and crowded with enterprising and industrious citizens, Fort Scott is destined to a large prosperity. The Government post there was long ago deserted; nothing remains of it but a few barrack buildings, grouped around a weed-grown square, and the old hospital, which decay aids in rendering picturesque. The building of the new Gulf route has had a great influence for good upon Fort Scott and the surrounding country; and although the reclamation of lands of the railway company from people who claim to have acquired a title to them by occupancy has occasioned some trouble, it is expected that a satisfactory arrangement may be reached.

This was a lawless section but a few years ago; now the security of life and property are as great as in any community in the world. The era of crime passed with the building of the new railway, and found no inducement to linger even for a moment. It has been a sweeping change, this metamorphosis

of Kansas, from the condition of a wild territory, whose lands were held and inhabited solely by the Indians driven west of the Mississippi, into a transplanted New England. In 1841 Fort Scott was a post with which to hold the savages in check; now a full-blooded Indian is hardly to be met with in the vicinity. Thirty-five miles below Fort Scott we came to Osage mission, where a good

Bridge over the Marmiton River, near Fort Scott.

Jesuit, Father Schumacher, began his labors among the Indians a quarter of a century ago; and from the mission a rapid run of a few miles brought us to Parsons—a thriving town named in honor of the president of the Missouri, Kansas and Texas railway.

Parsons, of course, owes its existence to this road. From the town the route extends southward to the Indian Territory and to Texas; and north-west, through the thriving towns of Neosho Falls, Burlington, Emporia, and Council Grove, the line stretches to Junction City, where the Kansas Pacific joins it. The *entrepot* for the rich regions between the boundary of the Indian Territory and the plains,—all the wonderfully fertile Neosho Valley,—it is not surprising that the growth of the town has been rapid. Less than a month after Parsons was "started," in 1871, upward of one hundred lots, on which parties were pledged to put up buildings worth at least $1,000, had been sold; and at present the town boasts good hotels, churches, handsome residences, banks, and large stone railway shops. Land has already assumed a marked speculative value in many of these towns; but at Parsons, as indeed throughout the Neosho Valley, the opportunities for investment are still magnificent.

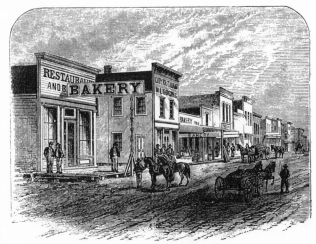

A street in Parsons, Kansas.

The town is one of the great centres for the trade and travel of at least fifty thriving towns and villages, into which the immigration from all parts of the West is rapidly flowing. The valley offers homes to thousands of people, on terms which the poorest man can accept and fulfill. All through this rich country there is abundance of timber—black walnut, ash, maple and oak; and for steam machinery, there is plenty of coal and water; so that the various implements of agriculture, the furniture, the building materials, which are now brought hundreds of miles, from St. Louis and Chicago, may be manufactured near at hand, the moment shrewd men of capital can induce themselves to operate in so promising an enterprise.

The Neosho Valley is a revelation to one who has never before visited the South-west. Miles on miles of wondrously fertile valleys and plains, watered by fine streams, along whose banks is a heavy growth of timber, are now within easy reach by rail. Hundreds of cattle, horses and swine wander at will through the fields, guarded only against straying into the crops by the alert movements of the herdsman, who, well mounted and accompanied by a shepherd dog, spends his whole time in the open air. The houses of the farmers are usually of logs roughly hewn, but carefully put together. Shelter of crops being rarely necessary in such a climate, the granaries are somewhat rudely constructed. A

A Kansas Herdsman.

corn granary is a tower of logs, built like a boy's cobhouse. No one ever thinks of stealing from it. The horses career as they please in the front yard, and look in at the parlor windows; the pigs invade the kitchen, or quarrel with the geese at the very steps of the houses; but whenever the master of the household thinks that discipline has been too seriously infringed, he sends a sprightly dog to regulate matters. Pigs are taken by their ears, geese fly screaming away, and horses scamper into the distance.

As we passed through the reservation of the " Kaw" Indians—the Kansas aborigines—our artist could not refrain from capturing a few types, and has faithfully sketched for us the little grave by the wayside, with the slain horses lying upon it, and the flag floating over it, to mark it as the resting-place of a chieftain ; the stone house which the graceless Kaw has turned into a stable for his pony ; and the warrior galloping across the field in the midst of a pouring rain. The Kaws are dirty, lazy, and frequently dishonest beings,—just as far from civilization as were their ancestors three hundred years ago.

They generally refuse to speak English to strangers, and will only converse by signs. They still sigh for the time when their forefathers were wont to swoop

A Kansas Farm - yard.

down upon the wagon-trains toiling from the Missouri State line to Santa Fé in New Mexico, when the traders were almost at the mercy of the tawny banditti, until the post of Council Grove, now a flourishing town, was established as a general rendezvous, where caravans numbering hundreds of wagons and thousands of mules could form into processions of sufficient strength to protect themselves.

There were at one time nearly 6,000 men, 18,000 oxen, and 6,000 mules engaged in the New Mexico trade, all of whom made Council Grove their headquarters. The villages of the Kaws are remote from the present line of rail, and the Indians rarely patronize the road save when, for the pure delight of begging, they entreat the conductor for a free passage from one village to another. When they are refused the privilege, they break forth into the most violent profanity of which the English language is capable. Their vocabulary of English oaths is more complete than even that of the native American, who, in many parts of the South-west, is charged with violent expletives as a musket is charged with powder.

At Junction City, which stands in a beautiful valley, where the Smoky and Republican rivers join, in a country not so rich as that twenty miles south, yet still wonderfully fertile, we were detained by a sudden snow-fall and a miniature whirlwind, which blockaded tracks and made travel impossible. The beautiful Smoky Valley was, therefore, a forbidden domain to us; and we consoled ourselves with a visit to Fort Riley, an important frontier post, established in 1852, on the left bank of the Kansas river, at the junction of the Smoky Hill and Republican Forks, and three miles from Junction City.

"The little grave, with the slain horses lying upon it." [Page 194.]

General Oakes, in command at the post, welcomed us with true South-western hospitality. He was for many years stationed in Texas, and has had a rich experience of frontier garrison life. This adventurous and isolated existence seems to have a charm for all who have adopted it, and very few of the officers take advantage of their furloughs to visit the Eastern cities. Ladies, too, find rare attractions in a garrison winter, and the forts all along the frontier do not lack good society from November until May. At Fort Riley the soldiers support a good little theatre, much of the talent for which is furnished by members of the cavalry regiment quartered there. Not far from the fort is the "geographical centre of the United States," on a hill-top, where stands a monument erected to the memory of Brevet-Major E. A. Ogden, founder of Fort Riley.

We hastened back toward Parsons, again crossing the great Kaw reservation, and meeting long trains of Indians, mounted on their shaggy ponies. This Neosho Valley line, which we had traversed, was the beginning of the present great trunk route from Sedalia to the Gulf. Work was begun on it, under a contract with the Land Grant Railway and Trust Company, in November, 1868, the line to extend from Junction City to Chetopa, on the frontier of the Indian Territory, a distance of 182 miles; and it was completed in October, 1870.

While this was in construction, the building of the line from Sedalia to Parsons was begun, and the whole route, 160 miles, was completed early in 1871. Meantime work was going forward, at lightning speed, in the Indian Territory. The manager of the line had made a bold stroke in order to be the first to reach the Cherokee country, and obtain permission to run a line through it, as well as

"The stone house which the graceless Kaw has turned into a stable for his pony." [Page 194.]

to get conditional land-grants; and in May of 1870 occurred quite an episode in the history of railway building. On the 24th of that month the line had reached within twenty-four miles of the southern boundary of Kansas. Much of the grading was unfinished; bridges were not up; masonry was not ready. But on the 6th day of June, at noon, the first locomotive which ever entered the Indian Territory uttered its premonitory shriek of progress.

In eleven days twenty-six and a-half miles of completed rail were laid, four miles being put down in a single day. A grant of over 3,000,000 acres of land, subject, under treaty stipulations, to temporary Indian occupancy, has been accorded the Missouri, Kansas and Texas Railway Company, on the line of the

"The warrior galloping across the fields." [Page 194.]

road in the territory between Chetopa and the Red river. The question of the future disposition of the Indian Territory is interesting to the railroad builders, as they have extended their line through the great stretch of country, hoping that the fertile lands now waste may come into market. Until it is opened to white settlement, or until the Indians adopt some new policy with regard to their lands, the Territory is, in many respects, a barrier to the best development of that portion of the South-west. The immense reservation, larger than all New England, extending over 60,000,000 acres, lying between Texas, with her 1,000,000 settlers, Arkansas, with her hardy 500,000, and Missouri and Kansas, with their 2,000,000 of stout frontiersmen, is now completely given over to the Indian, and the white man who wishes to abide within its borders will find his appeal sternly rejected by an Indian Legislature, unless he marries into one of the dusky tribes and relinquishes his allegiance to Uncle Sam.

A little beyond Chetopa lies a long range of low hills. The new Gulf route, cutting through them, carries one out of the United States and into the Cherokee nation. Here the traveler is no longer in the domain of the white man; the Government of the United States can protect him only through the feeble medium of marshals and deputy-marshals, who exercise their own judgment as to whether or not they shall do him justice, the nearest towns lying nestled among the hills, or in the tall timber on the banks of creeks. The railway runs through a seemingly deserted land. Rarely does one see along the route the face of an Indian, unless at some of the little wooden stations, or at a lone water-tank near a stream. The inhabitants have acquiesced sullenly in the opening of their country to railway travel, but they do not build near the line, and rarely patronize it.

Monument erected to the memory of Brevet-Major E. A. Ogden, near Fort Riley, Kansas.

XIX.

THE "INDIAN TERRITORY."

THE Indian Territory is, to its inhabitants and to the Government of the United States, at this present writing, a problem. The area of 52,780,000 acres has as yet scarcely population enough to make a city of tenth rank. The estimated numbers of the tribes scattered over the vast plains and among the mountains are as follows: Cherokees, 17,500; Choctaws, 17,000; Creeks, 13,500;

Chickasaws, 5,500; Seminoles, 2,500; Osages, 3,500; Sacs and Foxes, 468; Shawnees, 670; Cheyennes and Arapahoes, 3,390; Confederate Peories, 170; Eastern Shawnees, 80; Wyandottes, 150; Quawpaws, 236; Senecas, 188. And this little band of 65,000 people is so separated by great distances, unabridged by railways, and by barriers of language and custom, that there is hardly any intercourse between tribes. The land lies waste because there are not hands enough to hold the plough, and the country remains a wilderness because the Indian jealously refuses to allow the white man to make it blossom as the rose.

An Indian Territorial Mansion.

There is something pathetic in the resolution with which the Indian clings to this Territory, the very last of his strongholds. His race and his history are soon to be inextricably mingled with that of the white men, whom he still considers as intruders; and while he recognizes the inevitable fate attending him and his possessions, he fiercely repulses any attempt at a compromise.

He now stands firm by the treaty stipulations; for the treaties made in 1837 by the Government of the United States with the various tribes east of the Mississippi, giving them the "Indian Territory," on condition that they should move into and occupy it, were comprehensive and binding. The Osages had been the virtual owners of these immense tracts of land until the advent of the white man, but to-day have almost entirely disappeared.

To the Cherokees, in 1837, a patent in fee simple was given, while the other tribes held their lands under treaty stipulations. From 1837 to 1845 the task of removing the various tribes from their homes east of the Mississippi went on, and with the unwillingness of the Seminoles to migrate came the Florida war. In the treaties it was provided that the five distinctive tribes, the Cherokees, Choctaws, Chickasaws, Creeks, and Seminoles, should hold the lands of the Territory as homes *forever*. They, in their turn, have allowed smaller tribes to make homes among them. In 1866, the Delawares and Shawnees of Kansas agreed to live thereafter in the Cherokee Nation, and to give up their own nationality, adding the funds resulting from the sale of their Kansas lands to the annuities of the Cherokees.

The annuities of the various nations in the Territory arise from their sales of lands in the past; those of the Cherokees amount to about $350,000 yearly; of the Choctaws, $250,000; the Creeks, $175,000; the Chickasaws, $100,000; and the Seminoles, $10,000. The various treaties were all revised and renewed in 1866—following on the "Treaty of Amity" made at Fort Smith, at the close of the late war.

The Indians of the Territory of to-day are, therefore, just as securely vested with the control of the Territory as against its settlement by white men as they were in 1837, and they manifest no more disposition to yield their claims than they did a quarter of a century ago.

The Cherokees have naturally made the greatest advances in civilization, and are at present the most powerful of all the tribes in the Territory. They have a ruling voice in matters that concern the general polity of the nations, or tribes of the Territory, and their manners and customs are better known to the outside world than are those of any other tribe.

Their general status is not below that of the white frontiersmen. They are industrious and capable agriculturists, and understand the care of stock better than any other people in the South-west. They live remote from each other—on farms which, it is true, they hold in common, yet to which there is an individual and perpetual right of occupancy. All the land is vested in the Nation; a man may sell his improvements and buildings—but not the land.

The Indians throughout the Territory are not, as a rule, farmers in any proper sense, as they raise simply what they need; this, however, is because there is no market for surplus produce. The Government originally supplied them with capital; they do not realize the advantages of gain, they simply desire to "make a living." Throughout the various nations there is an utter neglect of internal improvements. An Indian highway is as difficult as the Vesuvian ascent, and none of the magnificent rivers were bridged before the advent of the Missouri, Kansas and Texas railway.

The "Indian Agents"—who are appointed directly by the President, and who, residing among the different tribes, are properly the interpreters of all the treaties, have charge of the annuities, and make the annual reports—usually have much influence with the Indian chiefs, and, of late years, some few improvements have been introduced at their suggestion. The person of an agent is always respected, and as a rule his word is law.

The government of the Cherokees, as well as that of the other principal nations in the Territory, corresponds in large degree to those of our States. The

Cherokees elect a "principal" and second chief for four years. They also have an upper and lower house of the Legislature, the former continuing in power four, the latter two years. Bills, or acts, are regularly introduced, and passed through the various readings to be engrossed, as in other Legislative assemblies. There

is a supreme court, with three judges, and there are also district judges and sheriffs.

At Tahlequah, the capital, the annual sessions of the legislature are held in the council-house, beginning in November, and lasting thirty days. The legislators are paid out of the annuities of the nation. Tahlequah is an average town of the South-west, with nothing especially denoting its Indian origin. The Choctaws and Creeks have the same general form of government. The Creeks are a fine people; their women are handsome, and their men generally brave and honest. The Seminoles have vested their executive authority in twenty-four band-chiefs, all of whom are controlled and directed by a "principal," who is an absolute autocrat, having an irrefragable veto-power. All the tribes or nations join in a general council, provided for by the treaty of 1866, and it is presided over

A Creek Indian.

by the Superintendent of Indian Affairs for the Southern Superintendency. At this council only such matters are legislated upon as are of comity between the nations—the rendition of criminals, the joint action in regard to land, etc.

This superb country, unquestionably one of the most fertile on the globe, is a constant source of torment to the white men of the border, in whom the spirit of speculation is very strong. The hardy citizen of the South-west bears no ill-will toward the various Indian tribes, but it irritates him to see such vast tracts of land lying idle. He aches to be admitted to the Territory with the same privileges granted Indian citizens, viz.: the right to occupy and possess all the land they may fence in, and to claim all that remains unfenced within a quarter of a mile on either side of their fenced lots. He is crazed with visions of the far-spreading, flower-bespangled prairies, the fertile foot-hills, the rich quarries, mines, and valley-lands. He burns to course at free will over the grazing regions where even the Indians raise such fine stock. And now that the railroad has entered a protest against continued

Bridge across the North Fork of the Canadian River, Indian Territory (M., K. & T. Railway).

exclusiveness on the part of the Indians, he thunders at the northern and southern entrances of the Territory, and will not be quiet.

At the time of the emigration of the Cherokees to the Indian Territory, a powerful feud existed between two influential families in the nation—the Rosses

An Adopted Citizen.

and the Ridges. It grew out of dissatisfaction at a treaty made by the Ridge party. Those hostile to the treaty claimed that the Ridges and others had agreed to sell a portion of the Territory to the United States, contrary to the instructions of the nation.

A vendetta followed, in which Boudinot, Ridge, and all the parties to the treaty were killed, save Stand Weatie, who succeeded in defending himself, single-handed, against a dozen murderous assailants. On the wave of indignation against the Ridges and the other parties to this odious treaty, the Ross party came into power, and has since achieved considerable distinction both by its lead in the affairs of the whole Territory and by its loyalty to the Government during the late war.

At the beginning of the war, the Indians of the various tribes in the Territory were naturally in closer relations with the South than with the North. Their agents had mainly been Southern men, and the annuities, by which they had become rich and independent, had been derived from the South, and paid promptly.

Most of the Indians knew nothing whatever concerning Northern people or politics. They had been residents of a slave-holding section all their lives. Many of the Cherokees had 200 or 300 slaves each, and negroes who had settled among the Indians also held slaves. In May of 1862, when the great struggle was gravely accentuated, the Indians took sides with the South, a regiment being formed among the Cherokees, and placed under the command of General Stand Weatie, a full-blooded Indian.

The principal chief, John Ross, used his utmost endeavors to prevent any of the tribes from further engaging in the struggle. There was presently an engagement between the United States troops and the Cherokee regiment, at Pea Ridge, in Arkansas. A portion of the Cherokees at that time threw down their arms, and returned to their allegiance to the General Government. William P. Ross, the present chief, was among them, and his father, continuing his loyal efforts, went to Washington, and gave a true statement of the situation. He remained loyal until his death, which occurred in Philadelphia, in 1864.

To General Albert Pike was principally due the conversion of most of the Indians in the Territory to Southern sentiment. The Confederates made better treaties with the Indians than ever the United States had made, and even paid them one annuity in Confederate money.

Meantime the fair lands underwent all the ghastly and appalling disasters which follow in the train of war. They were occupied alternately by Northern and Southern armies, and were plundered by both. The Indian adherents of the Southern cause moved their families into Texas, and those who had cast their fortunes with the Government stampeded into Kansas.

The departure of the loyal Indians for the loyal States was the signal for a determined attack upon them, and was the cause of almost unparalleled suffering among the women and children. At one time there were fifteen thousand refugees in Kansas, all supported by the General Government, while hundreds were daily arriving in a starving condition.

The story of Opothlehola, chief of the Creeks, furnishes one of the most striking instances of determined loyalty. The Creeks had long been beset by General Pike, who had finally succeeded in inducing a certain number of them to go South. But the chief Opothlehola, then nearly one hundred years old, and reverenced with almost superstitious awe by the masses of his people, rejected all Pike's advances, and, after a long and stormy council, called on all who wished to seek the Great Father's hand to go northward with him.

He hastily gathered such of his young men and warriors as would join him, with their wives and children, and in midwinter, with but few provisions, and dragging all their household goods, the loyal refugees set forth for Kansas. They were followed by Pike

An Indian Stock-Drover.

and regiments from Texas, and a bloody battle ensued at Honey Springs, in which, as in a succeeding fight, Opothlehola's little band was routed with much slaughter.

But they continued on until January, 1863, when those who remained alive reached Kansas in an almost famished condition. On the dread march more than a thousand men, women and children sickened, died, and were left by the wayside. When the old chieftain reached Kansas, his first act was to enroll his warriors as soldiers of the United States, and every able-bodied man enlisted in the service! Opothlehola died shortly afterward, at Fort Leavenworth, where he was buried with military honors. The various regiments from the territorial tribes on both sides in the war were good soldiers. When they were led well, they fought well. They waged relentless war on one another. The feud is still nourished to some extent, and will be until this generation has gone its way.

Before the war the Indians were rich in stock, and it was not uncommon for a well-to-do stock-raiser to possess 15,000 head of cattle; while it was a very poor and woe-begone Indian, indeed, who had not at least twenty. Then, as now, all the labor necessary was the branding of the beasts, as they grazed at will over the unbounded lands.

But when the war came, the total destruction of this stock ensued! Hundreds of thousands of the beasts were stolen, and taken into the neighboring States: both armies fed from the herds; and so great was the consequent decline of prosperity, and the distress, that the General Government appropriated money

"The ball-players are fine specimens of men."

for the purchase of new stock, and now the tribes have nearly as much as before the war. The only present subject of disagreement among any of the tribes is the land question; the various propositions tending to an opening up of the land to white settlement, which have been made by one party, having all been received with disdainful threats by the other. Death is the speedy fate of any Indian of any tribe who dares to accede to approaches on the part of the white man tending to the sale of lands; and the white man who attempts to ingratiate himself too freely among the Indians runs risk of a sudden and mysterious disappearance.

Religion is creeping into the simple yet logical minds of the various tribes. There are no previous impressions to correct, for these tribes have no mythology, save the gracious and beautiful embodying of some of nature's loveliest forms. After the war, the Cherokees invited the missions and their schools to return to the Territory, and the other tribes followed their example.

There are few, if any, church edifices among the tribes, and the meetings are now held in school-houses. Church expenses are borne by voluntary gifts. Many of the tribes seem to have a dim idea that they are fragments of one of the "lost tribes of Israel," and the Choctaws have a fund of curious legends concerning the wanderings of their forefathers which tend to that belief.

Manners and superstitions are, of course, in many respects still thoroughly Indian. Games in which physical strength and skill are required are popular among all the tribes, and the ball-players are fine specimens of men. Hospitality is unbounded, and as soon as an Indian of wealth and station takes a wife, all her relatives, even the most distant, come to live on his estate, and remain forever, or until they have impoverished him. The tyranny of mothers-in-law in the Territory is something frightful to contemplate. One Indian gave as his reason for not wishing to get rich the torments which his relatives, in case he married, would cause him.

Food is simple among all the "nations." Corn, ground with mortar and pestle, furnishes the material for bread; a few vegetables are grown; and game, pork and beef are abundant.

The hog of the Indian Territory is a singular animal. Having always run wild, he is as distinguished for thinness as are his brethren of civilization for corpulence, and his back well merits the epithet of razor-edge applied to it. Stock feeds itself, winter and summer, and there is rarely a season when it is necessary to put up any hay.   In the winter of 1871 grass along the Arkansas bottom was green until the middle of December.

Marriage is gradually becoming a recognized institution among all the tribes, the efforts of the missionaries tending to encourage it; but heretofore men and women have simply cohabited without formal tie and reared families.   The usual practice has been for a young man who has become enamored of a maiden to ingratiate himself with her brother, or with a near male relative, and for the latter to intercede with the father.   Should the father regard the suitor favorably, he puts him on probation, and at the end of a certain term receives him, and presents him to the daughter as her future husband.   The family relation seems much respected, and is guarded against disorganization by many excellent laws.

A Gentleman from the Arkansas Border.

XX.

RAILROAD PIONEERING—INDIAN TYPES AND CHARACTER.

A FTER leaving Chetopa, a pretty town, with nearly 2,000 inhabitants, and a
point of supply for territorial traders, our special train steamed merrily
along the broad expanse of prairie until Vinita, the junction of the Atlantic and
Pacific line with the Missouri, Kansas and Texas railway, was reached. At
Vinita, the junction has made no growth, because white men are not allowed to
live there, and the Indians content themselves with agriculture and hunting.
We had prepared ourselves for a sojourn of a fortnight between this point and

Limestone Gap—Indian Territory. [Page 212.]

the Red river, and a brief inspection of the
culinary department, over which the ebony Charles
presided, was eminently satisfactory. Telegrams
were received from various gentlemen at each end

of the main line, stating that they would join us at Fort Gibson, and we set out on our journey with delightful anticipations.

The long grasses rustled; the timber by the creeks stood out in bold relief against the Naples-blue of the sky; the distant line of mounds assumed the appearance now of a giant fortification, now of a city, and now of a terraced garden; here and there a gap in the woods lining the horizon, showed a glimpse of some far-reaching valley, on whose bosom still lay a thin snow-veil; and sometimes we saw a symmetrical tree standing midprairie, with a huge white-hooded hawk perched lazily upon a bending bough, and a gaunt wolf crawling away from the base. But nowhere was there any sign of man.

The train halted for water and coal, the engineer and firemen helping themselves at the coal-cars and water-tank, and we moved on. At last, at a little wooden station, we saw half-a-dozen tawny youths, tall and awkward, with high cheek-bones, intensely black hair, and little sparkling eyes, which seemed the very concentration of jealousy. This was a party of young beaux from the

"Coming in the twilight to a region where great mounds reared their whale-backed heights"

nearest Cherokee village. They wore the typical American slouch hats, but had wound ribbons around and fastened feathers in them; their gayly-colored jackets were cut in fantastic fashion, and at their sides they carried formidable revolvers, which they are, however, slower to use than is the native American.

They stared curiously at our party, seated in luxurious chairs on the ample platform of the rear car, and, after having satisfied their curiosity, they mounted their horses and galloped away. So we rattled on, coming in the twilight to a region where great mounds reared their whale-backed heights on either hand. Upon the summit of one of them stands a monument of hewn stone, doubtless to some deity who went his ways long before Columbus uncovered America to European eyes. These mounds seem constructed according to some general plan, and are of immense extent.

We went on in the deepening twilight until we came to Gibson station, the limit of our journey for the day. Only one or two houses were to be seen; a cold wind blew over the prairie, and we betook ourselves to the supper-table, where prairie-chickens, mysteriously purveyed for our surprise by the beneficent Charles, sent up a savory steam.   The stillness of death reigned outside, and we

listened languidly to the conductor's stories of "terminus troubles" a brace of years agone, until we were aroused to welcome delegations brought by the night express trains from each way to join our party, and to prepare for the morrow.

When we were all snugly tucked up in our berths in the gayly-decorated sleeping-saloon, one of the new-comers began dreamily to tell stories of more terminus troubles. "Not much as it was when we were here and at Muskogee in 1870," he said. "Three men were shot about twenty feet from this same car in

A "Terminus" Rough.

one night at Muskogee. Oh! this was a little hell, this was. The roughs took possession here in earnest. The keno and monte players had any quantity of tents all about this section, and life was the most uncertain thing to keep you ever saw.

"One night a man lost all he had at keno; so he went around behind the tent and tried to shoot the keno-dealer in the back; he missed him, but killed another man. The keno man just got a board and put it up behind himself, and the game went on. One day one of the roughs took offence at something the railroad folks said, so he ran our train off the track next morning. There was no law here, and no means of getting any. As fast as the railroad moved on, the roughs pulled up stakes and moved with it.

"We tried to scare them away, but they did n't scare worth a cent. It was next to impossible for a stranger to walk through one of these canvas towns without getting shot at. The graveyards were sometimes better populated than the towns next them. The fellows who ruled these little terminus hells,—where they came from nobody knows—never had any homes—grew up

"We came to the bank of the Grand river, on a hill beyond which was the post of Fort Gibson." [Page 208.]

like prairie grass, only coarser and meaner.   They had all been 'terminuses' ever since they could remember.   Most of them had two, three, and four murders on their hands, and confessed them.   They openly defied the Indian authorities, and scorned Uncle Sam and his marshals.   They knew there was money wherever the end of the road was, and they meant to have it."

"But how long did this condition of affairs continue?"

"It went on steadily until the Secretary of the Interior came down here to see the Territory and to examine the railroads.   He came down in this same car, and was carefully informed of all the lawlessness and flagrant outrages which decent people had been obliged to submit to.   One night the superintendent-in-chief pushed on a little ahead of the train to get a physician, as a gentleman in the special car was taken suddenly ill.   The roughs captured the superintendent and proposed to shoot him, as they fancied that he was a United States marshal.   He explained who he was, however, and begged off.   As they hardly dared to shoot him then, he succeeded in reaching a physician, got back to the train, and next took the Secretary to inspect this specimen of railroad civilization."

"And what did the Secretary see?"

"Oh, all the ruffians flocked to hear what he had to say.   They had killed a man that morning from mere caprice, and he was laid out in a little tent which the party passed while looking around.   One after another of the rough fellows was presented to the party, each one speaking very plainly, and declaring that he had a good right to stay in the 'Nation,' and (with an oath) meant to; and he'd like to hear any one hint that he had better go away.   Then they told stories of their murderous exploits, practiced at marks with their revolvers, and seemed to have no fear of the Secretary."

"What was the result?"

"Well, the Secretary of the Interior took a bee-line for the nearest telegraph station, and sent a dispatch to General Grant, announcing that neither life nor property was safe in the Territory, and that the Indians should be aided in expelling the roughs from their midst.   So, in a short time, the Tenth Cavalry went into active service in the Territory."

"Did the ruffians make any resistance?"

"They got together, at the terminus, armed to the teeth, and blustered a good deal; but the cavalrymen arrested one after another, and examined each man separately.   When one of the terminuses was asked his name, he usually answered that it was Slim Jim, or Wild Bill, or Lone Jack (with an oath), and that he was a gambler, or a 'pounder,' as the case might be, and, furthermore, that he did n't intend to leave the Territory.   Whereupon the officer commanding would say: 'Well, Slim Jim, or Wild Bill, or Lone Jack, I 'll give you twelve hours to leave this town in, and if you are found in the Territory a week from this date, I 'll have you shot!'   And they took the hint."

A moment afterward, the same voice added:

"By the way, at the next station, Muskogee, a man was shot before the town got there, and the graveyard was started before a single street was laid out.   You can see the graveyard now-a-days—eleven men are buried there with their boots on. Good night."

The landscape was snow-besprinkled next day, but our merry party of six climbed into a rickety ambulance, and set out on the seven miles' ride to Fort Gibson. As we rattled along past the dense bosquets, great flocks of prairie-chickens rose in leisurely flight; wild turkeys waddled away; deer fled across the roads after bestowing a scornful gaze upon us; and rabbits jumped painfully in the snow.

The farm-houses which we passed were all built of logs, but were large and solidly constructed ; and the Indian farmers were making preparations for the Spring ploughing. When we came to the bank of the Grand river, on a hill beyond which was the post of Fort Gibson, we found the ferries obstructed by masses of floating ice. Negro cavalrymen from the fort were in midstream, desperately clinging to the guide-rope, and in imminent danger of being carried down river and out into the mighty Arkansas. At last, the dangers over, two lazy half-breeds ferried us across, after infinite shouting and disputing; and we met, on the other bank, "Uncle John" Cunningham, postmaster at Fort Gibson. "I saw you across the stream, and was watching out for you a little carefully," said Uncle John, "for there's a fellow come into town this morning with six gallons of whiskey, and we expect some of the Indians to go circusing around as soon as they get it down."

A Negro Boy at the Ferry.

We climbed the hill to the fort, a well-built post usually garrisoned by three companies either of infantry or cavalry. Fort Gibson is the residence of the present chief of the Cherokee nation, William P. Ross, a cultivated and accomplished gentleman, whom I had previously met in Washington. The fort stands on the Grand river, about two and a-half miles from its confluence with the Arkansas, and is only twenty-one miles from Tahlequah, the capital of the Cherokees. The whole of the adjacent country, except upon the high range of the hills along the Grand, Verdigris and Illinois rivers, is arable and easy to cultivate.

From the verandah of the commanding officer's quarters at the fort, one can overlook a range of hills known as the "Boston mountains," the town, set down in an amphitheatre formed by the slopes, the broad, swift river running between its picturesque banks,—a charming scene.

At Fort Gibson we were in a real Cherokee town, and at every turn saw one of the tall, black-haired, tawny citizens of the Territory. It was evidently a market-day with the farmers for many a mile around. Horses were tied before the porches of the Indian traders and along the bank of the river, and every few moments some stout Indian came rattling into town, his wife mounted behind him on the demure-looking pony, equal to anything, from the fording of a river

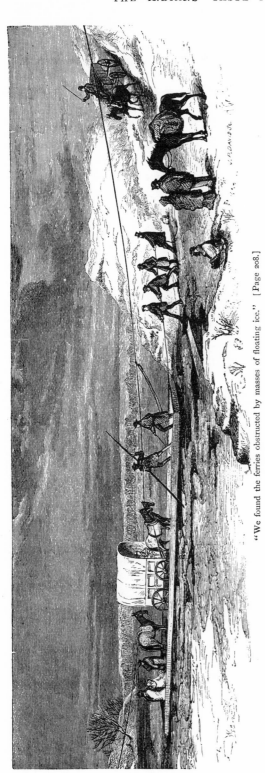

"We found the ferries obstructed by masses of floating ice." [Page 208.]

to the threading of a cañon. Many of the men carried side-arms, but none of them showed any disposition to quarrel, and we saw no one who seemed to have been drinking liquor. Indeed, so severe are the penalties attaching to the sale of ardent spirits in the Indian Territory, that men do not care to take the risk. The United States marshals and the Indian authorities pursue the offenders with great persistence, and a law-breaker rarely escapes.

The Indians—Cherokees, Choctaws, Chickasaws and Seminoles— all have a strange thirst for intoxicating liquor, and often make the most astonishing efforts to secure it. All kinds of patent medicines in which alcohol forms an ingredient find ready sale among the various tribes; and camphor, pain-killer, and similar articles, were for a long time so much in use among the Cherokees as to provoke an examination by the agents, who discovered the braves to be drinking whole bottles at a gulp, in order to feel some effect therefrom. A bottle of whiskey is still one of the most powerful bribes that can be placed before an Indian.

The women were all robust, and not devoid of a certain wild beauty; but they wore a prim, Shakerish costume which defied criticism. A poke-bonnet nearly concealed their features, and a stiff, heavy robe fell down to the ankles, while a shawl was decorously draped about the shoulders. Many of the Indians seemed to have negro wives, and we saw more than one stalwart negress receiving courteous atten-

tion from tall, copper-colored beaux, whose manners would have done no dis-
credit to a *salon* in society.

The men, as a rule, would not respond when addressed in English, and often
turned sullenly away; while younger members of the tribes, both boys and
girls, would chat cheerily, and question us with childish curiosity as to our
reasons for visiting the nation. There were some superb heads among these
Cherokees, with masses of tangled hair peeping in most charming confusion from
under torn hats, slightly shaded faces, with matchless eyes, and features in which
the Indian type of a century agone was yet preserved—all the reserve, all the
immobility, all the silent scorn being still distinctly marked. Yet civilization
was beginning to do its work. The greater number of countenances were losing
their savage traits, and becoming more like those of their fellows in the neighboring States; still there was a certain atmosphere of strangeness about them, born,

"They wore a prim, Shakerish costume." [Page 209.]

doubtless, of their methods
of thought, their traditions,
their almost complete lack of
sympathy with the whites.
Never until the war had they
been called upon to feel that
their territory constituted a
part of a common country;
now they realize it.

From Fort Gibson, where
Lieutenant-Colonel Lawson,
the amiable commanding
officer, and his associates had
made our stay a very pleasant
one, we rode back along the
very rough roadways until we

A Trader among the Indians.

came to Gibson station. The station-agent came to see us, and announced that
some of the "Indians had been having a circus" during our absence. "Came in
here, an old woman did," he said, "with a butcher-knife, and took a piece out
of my chair, and a man with her fired half-a-dozen shots from his revolver
through the roof. But I finally quieted 'em." Liquor, or possibly pain-killer,
was the cause of this sudden outburst.

So we journeyed slowly on through the great Territory, now coming into the
shadows of the prehistoric mounds, and now into delightful valleys, which needed
only human and tasteful occupancy to be transformed into veritable Elysian
Fields. At night the train was switched off at some lonely siding, and the
baggage-car transformed into a kitchen. Then arose the complicated aroma of
broiled venison, savory coffee, and fried potatoes and muffins, or delicate toast,—
the work of the dusky Charles, who could growl fiercely whenever profane eyes
attempted to peer into the arcana of the kitchen. One of the leading citizens of
Parsons, Kansas, presided over the venison; half-a-dozen eager hands conducted
the coffee from the mill in which it was ground into the cup in which it was

poured; and the "pet conductor" watched over the comfort of all, generously forgetting his own.   Late o' nights a thunderous roll and a flash of light would salute our ears and eyes, and sometimes a bundle of letters and home papers, fresh from St. Louis and the East would be handed us out of the darkness by the conductor of the "down express."

Our train was always in motion when we awoke in the morning, reminding us more of life on an ocean steamer than on the "rattling rail-car."   We spent some time at Muskogee, the railway station communicating most directly with Fort Gibson, and a town which owes all its present prosperity to the Missouri, Kansas and Texas railway.   Immense stock-yards have been built there, and the arrival and departure of goods and mails for Ocmulgee, the capital of the Creek nation, forty-five miles to the westward, and We-wo-ka, the capital of the Seminoles, one hundred miles west, gives employment to large numbers of men. Here, too, is a point of debarkation for travel to Armstrong's Academy, the Choctaw seat of government; and to Tishomingo, the principal town in the Chickasaw nation.   Stage routes branch out in all directions from Muskogee, and weekly mails are forwarded thence to the interior.

Between Gibson and Muskogee we had crossed the Arkansas river on one of the immense bridges of the Missouri, Kansas and Texas railway, a grand triumph of engineering skill; and some miles below Muskogee we also crossed the "North Fork" and the "Canadian," both of which run through a singularly wild and beautiful, country.   Near the Canadian we crossed the fields to visit one of the mission schools, of which there are numbers in the Territory.   It is in the Creek domain, and is known as the "Asbury Manual Labor School," being supported by the Methodist Church South. About eighty Indian children of both sexes are boarded, lodged, and taught at this institution, and the school-rooms which we entered were models of order and comfort. The native Creek schools, of which there

"The Asbury Manual Labor School," in the Creek domain.

are twenty or twenty-five, are not very useful; even the examining boards are deficient, and the native teachers are only able to give ordinary elementary instruction. The mission schools throughout the Territory have been of great service. The Presbyterians also support a mission among the Creeks, called the "Tallahassee Manual Labor School," where, as in the Asbury, work afield and in the house is expected from the scholars. The pupils of the Asbury School in one season produced 2,000 bushels of corn from about fifty acres.

In the Cherokee nation much attention is paid to the thirty "neighborhood schools," as they are called, and all the Northern missionaries who, of course, were compelled to retire during the war, were invited to return to their posts, and received cordial welcome, when peace was re-established. The common schools among the Cherokees were established by the Legislature in 1867. There are schools set apart for colored children, but no spirit of exclusion is now manifested; for the Indians, when the war closed and they emancipated all their slaves, frankly placed them on the same basis with themselves. Five orphans are boarded, clothed and instructed in each of the public schools.

Once in two years a superintendent of schools is chosen, and he appoints a board of directors for each school. The district schools are mainly taught by women, and those pupils who desire more than an elementary education are sent to colleges in the South and West. The Choctaws support forty youths and twenty maidens in institutions at Louisville, Kentucky, and other Southern cities. Various influences are gradually doing away with the desire to retain the Indian language in the schools. The Seminoles have thus far established five common schools, and a missionary boarding-school, under the charge of the Presbyterian Church. This little tribe is improving as rapidly in material wealth and in education as any other in the Territory.

On the Canadian river is a town which has at various times possessed the euphonious appellations of "Sandtown" and "Buzzard's Roost." It is now merely a collection of roofless cabins, but was long the rendezvous of all the ruffians infesting the Territory. Perched on a waste near the river's side, it was a convenient location for murder and plunder, and travelers learned to give it a wide berth.

Passing Perryville, an old trading-post of the Choctaws, and now a station of some promise; then along the picturesque and fertile line of Ream's Valley, a magnificent region; dashing through the wonderful coal region near McAllister we came at last to Limestone Gap.

From Limestone Gap to the Red river the country is wonderfully fertile, and in summer beautiful beyond description. Towns of more or less promise are interspersed with solitudes which are very impressive. Stringtown is to be one of the lumber markets of the future; and at Caddo, one of the curious new towns which are plenty in the vicinity of the Texan frontier, the Fort Sill trade debouches, and with the building of a branch railway to Paris, the cotton from that town and other points in Northern Texas will come in.

The railroad runs over trestle-work of the most difficult character between A-to-ka and South Boggy, which latter town was once the capital of the Choctaw nation. Not far from the banks of the Red river, on the Indian side, a small town has grown up, and the Texas Central railroad will soon cause the growth of a hamlet on the opposite side.   The river, at the point where it is crossed by the railroad, on a superb bridge, is not grand, although the banks are high and stony.   There is usually but a small volume of water in the stream, and the sands show on either side.

Not far from the railway bridge we saw a long line of cattle fording the channel; and the answer to our inquiry as to the reason why no bridge had been constructed by the Texas and Indian Governments at those points was that a Chickasaw Indian had long ago secured legislative privilege to charge one dollar for each person crossing the river from either direction, at the very point most available for bridge-building.   The income of this Indian has, for some years, been $100 per day, while the working expenses of the ford are not more than $20 weekly.

As our train lay in the shadow of the hills at Limestone Gap that night, the express from St. Louis went thundering by, and we were awakened to catch a glimpse of cars filled with weary emigrants, their faces eagerly turned toward the South.   Ere I slept again, I followed them in fancy on their journey to the Gulf.

Now they were hurried through sharply-defined hill ranges, and deep, sequestered, fertile valleys, until, the last creek crossed, the last forest of the Territory dominated, the fickle stream that marks the Texan boundary was reached; then, on through new forests, where a gnarled, unprofitable growth rankly asserted itself;

The Toll-Bridge at Limestone Gap, Indian Territory.

and now over uplands, whose black earth needs but a caress to bring forth abundant harvest.

Now through thickets where Spanish moss hung in hundred fantastic forms from the trees it feeds upon; past immense fields, where thousands of cattle were grazing; by banks and braes, in summer-time dotted and spangled with myriads of flowers; along highways where horsemen rode merrily.   Now the train rushed through a still, old town, where negro children were playing about the doors of the dirty, white houses, or a stalwart negress, with a huge bundle on her head, was tramping in the shade of friendly trees; and now along the borders of a marsh in which a million frogs were croaking a dreary burden, their monotonous chorus rising out of little pools from which the flag-lily raised its defiant head.

Or now the train stopped where one could see, in the tremulous air of evening, the reflection of the dying sun in a little lake nestling among the trees, with Spanish graybeards dipping into its clear depths; now where a path wound up a hill-side, and a magnolia tree stood lonely, its green leaves giving promise of future bloom and perfume, and its coarse bark sending forth a subtle odor; now where sombre creeks stole in and out among the crooked trees, as if eager to furnish seductive nooks for the brown, gray and red birds which fluttered and hovered and hopped from a thousand twigs.

Or now where the mesquite quivered in the glare of the generous Texan sun ; where the voices of negroes were heard in loud refrain, singing some bois-terous melody as they loitered home from their half-completed tasks, the urchins somersaulting on the elastic earth ; and now where the shadows in the distance were strangely lighted up by the erratic glow of the moon, which threw a fan-tastic glamour on moss and thicket, on lily, magnolia, and live oak.

XXI.

MISSOURI—ST. LOUIS, PAST AND PRESENT.

MISSOURI is the child of a compromise whose epitaph was written in letters of blood. Her chief city was founded more than a century ago, by a colony of adventurous Frenchmen; and for many years, during whose lapse the title to its soil was savagely disputed by Gaul and Indian, was a fur-trading post.

"Looking down on the St. Louis of to-day, from the high roof of the Insurance temple."   [Page 217.]

When Laclede Liguest and the brave band of men who followed him set out from New Orleans, in 1763, to explore the country whose exclusive trade had been accorded them by charter from the hands of the governor of the province of Louisiana, the lands west of the Mississippi were unexplored and unknown. Beyond the mouth of the Missouri river the bateau of no prying New Orleans trader had ever penetrated.   The song of the *voyageur* was as yet unheard

by the savage; and the inhabitants of the little post of Sainte Genevieve looked with amazement and reverence upon the trappers, hunters and merchants who started from their fort, one autumn morning, to explore the turbid current of the Missouri.

Laclede Liguest and his men did not long remain in the mysterious region adjacent to the junction of the two great rivers, but speedily returned to the site of the present city, and there, early in 1764, a few humble cabins were erected, and the new settlement was christened St. Louis, in honor of the dissolute and feeble Louis XV., of France.   A hardy and fearless youth named Auguste Chouteau was left in command of the few men pro-

"Where now stands the great stone Cathedral." [Page 217.]

tecting the infant town, and at once began negotiating with the Missouri Indians, who came in large bodies to visit the strangers, and to learn their intentions.

The treaty by which all the French territory on the Mississippi's eastern bank, save New Orleans, was ceded to the English, had just been made; scarlet-coated soldiers were daily expected at the forts near St. Louis. Laclede Liguest did not dream that another cession, embracing all lands west of the Mississippi, had been made to the king of Spain, and that his pet town was actually upon Spanish soil; he was happy in the belief that the banner of France would flaunt in the very eyes of the hated English, and was delighted to find that the Indians who surrounded him were resolved to fight the soldiers of Great Britain to the death.

So he merrily extended the limits of his colony; but had been at work hardly a year before he received orders from the governor of Louisiana to surrender to Spain.   The governor himself was so chagrined at the orders he was compelled to communicate, that he died of a broken heart soon after; and Laclede Liguest, mute with rage at the pusillanimous conduct of the Home Government, remained stubbornly at his post, ignoring Spanish claims. The French from all the stations east of the Mississippi took refuge with him, when the English came to their homes, and St. Louis grew more and more Gallic until 1768, when the Spanish came in, and after several unsuccessful attempts to gain the confidence of the early settlers, finally quite disregarded their feelings, and in 1770 pulled down the French flag.

In that year the French had consecrated their little log church, built on the land where now stands the great stone cathedral, and in that humble edifice they assembled to mourn the loss of their nationality, and to listen to the counsels of peace given them by their priests.   The Spanish commanders finally succeeded in fraternizing with the French, and cordially joined them in hating the English.

Laclede Liguest died during a voyage down the Mississippi, and was buried in the wild solitudes at the mouth of the Arkansas river.   His immense properties in St. Louis were sold to strangers.   His valiant lieutenant, Auguste Chouteau, became his administrator, and a few years afterward the Chouteau mansion was built in the field where now there is a continual roar of traffic.

Thenceforward, through the bloody days of the colonial revolution, St. Louis experienced many vicissitudes.   It underwent Indian massacres; suffered from the terrorism of the banditti haunting the Mississippi; began gradually to get acquainted with the gaunt American pioneers who had appeared on the eastern bank of the Father of Waters; and in 1788 had more than 1,000 inhabitants.   In those days it was scoffingly called *"Pain Court"* (short bread), because grain was expensive, and the hunters who came to the "metropolis" to replenish their stock of provisions got but scant allowance of bread for their money.

The Osages were forever hanging upon the outskirts of the settlement, and many an unfortunate hunter was burned at the stake, impaled, or tortured slowly to death by them.   Toward the close of the last century, however, the inhabitants pushed forward into the wilderness, and the fur trade increased rapidly. Numerous neat, one-story cottages, surrounded by pretty gardens, sprang up in St. Louis.   France once more recovered her possessions west of the Mississippi; and in 1804 the settlement which Laclede Liguest had so carefully founded, hoping that it might forever remain French, came under the domination of the United States.

A formal surrender of Upper Louisiana was made to the newly enfranchised American colonies; the stars and stripes floated from the "Government House" of St. Louis; and the Anglo-Saxon came to the front, with one hand extended for a land grant, and the other grasping a rifle, with which to exterminate Indian, Spaniard or demon, if they dared to stand in his way.

Looking down upon the St. Louis of to-day, from the high roof of the superb temple which the Missourians have built to the mercurial god of insurance, one can hardly

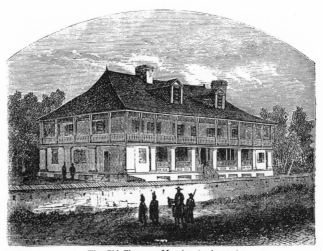

The Old Chouteau Mansion (as it was.)

believe that the vast metropolis spread out before him represents the growth
of only three-quarters of a century. The town seems as old as London.
The smoke from the Illinois coal has tinged the walls a venerable brown, and the
grouping of buildings is as picturesque and varied as that of a continental city.

The St. Louis Life Insurance Company's Building.

From the water-side, on ridge after
ridge, rise acres of solidly-built houses,
vast manufactories, magazines of commerce, long avenues bordered with
splendid residences. A labyrinth of
railways bewilders the eye; and the
clang of machinery and the whirl of a
myriad wagon-wheels rise to the ear.
The levée is thronged with busy and
uncouth laborers; dozens of white
steamers are shrieking their notes of
arrival and departure; the ferries are
choked with traffic; a gigantic and
grotesque scramble for the almost limitless West beyond is spread out
before one's vision.

The town has leaped into a new
life since the war; has doubled its population, its manufactures and its ambition,
and stands so fully abreast of its wonderful neighbor, Chicago, that the traditional acerbity of the reciprocal criticism for which both cities have so long
been famous is latterly much enhanced.

The city which now stretches twelve miles along the ridges branching from
the water-shed between the Missouri, the Meramec and the Mississippi rivers,
flanked by rolling prairies richly studded with groves and vineyards; which has
thirty railroad lines pointed to its central depots, and a mile and a-half of steamboats at its levée, 1,000 miles from the sea; whose population has increased from
8,000, in 1835, to 450,000, in 1874; which has a banking capital of $19,000,000;
which receives hundreds of thousands
of tons of iron ore monthly, has
bridged the Father of Waters, and
talks of controlling the cotton trade
of Arkansas and Texas—is a giant
in comparison with the infant settlement wherein, in a rude cottage,
Colonel Stoddard had his head-quarters when the United States assumed
territorial jurisdiction. In those days
the houses were nearly all built of
hewn logs, set upon end, and covered
with coarsely shingled roofs. The
town then extended along the line of

"In those days the houses were nearly all built of hewn logs."

what are now known as Main and Second streets; a little south of the square called the *Place d'Armes*, Fort St. Charles was held by a small garrison, and in the old stone tower which the Spaniards had built, debtors and criminals were confined together.

French customs and French gayety prevailed; there were two diminutive taverns, whose rafters nightly rang to the tales of hair-breadth escapes told by the boatmen of the Mississippi. The Chouteaus, the Lisas, and the Labbadies were the principal merchants; French and English schools flourished; peltry, lead and whiskey were used for currency, and negroes were to be purchased for them; the semi-Indian garb of the trapper was seen at every street corner; and thousands of furs, stripped from the buffalo and the beaver, were exported to New Orleans. The mineral wealth lying within a hundred miles of St. Louis had hardly been dreamed of; the colonists were too busy in killing Indians and keeping order in the town, to think of iron, lead, coal and zinc.

The compromise which gave the domain of Missouri to slavery checked the growth of the State until after it had passed through the ordeal of the war. How then it sprang up, like a young giant, confident of the plenitude of its strength, all the world knows! St. Louis, under free institutions, has won more prosperity in ten years than under the old *régime* it would have attained in fifty.

It is now a cosmopolitan capital, rich in social life and energy, active in commerce, and acute in the struggle for the supremacy of trade in the South-west. The ante-bellum spirit is rarely manifested now-a-days; progress is the motto even of those men of the old school who prayed that they might die when they first saw that "bleeding Kansas" had indeed bled to some purpose, and that a new era of trade and labor had arrived. The term "conservative" is one of reproach in St. Louis to-day; and the unjust slur of the Chicagoan, to the effect that the Missouri metropolis is "slow," puts new fire into the blood of her every inhabitant.

After the ravages of the war, both State and city found themselves free from the major evils attendant upon reconstruction, and entered unimpeded upon a prosperous career. The 100,000 freedmen have never constituted a troublesome element in the State; no political exigencies have impeded immigration or checked the investment of capital; and the commonwealth, with an area of more than 67,000 square miles of fertile lands, with 2,000,000 of inhabitants, and $1,100,000,000 worth of taxable property; with 1,000 miles of navigable rivers within her territory and upon her boundaries, and with vast numbers of frugal Germans constantly coming to turn her untilled acres into rich farms, can safely carry and in due time throw off the various heavy obligations incurred in the building of the railway lines now traversing it in every direction. The present actual indebtedness of the State is nearly $19,000,000, for more than half of which sum bonds have been issued.

The approaches to St. Louis from the Illinois side of the Mississippi are not fascinating, and give but a poor idea of the extent of the city. Alighting from some one of the many trains which enter East St. Louis from almost every direction, one sees before him a steep bank paved with "murderous stones," and

the broad, deep, resistless current of the great river, bearing on its bosom tree
trunks and branches from far-away forests.

East St. Louis stands upon famous ground; its alluvial acres, which the
capricious stream in past times yearly overflowed, have been the scene of many
fierce contests under the requirements of the so-called code of honor, and its
sobriquet was once "Bloody Island." It is now a prosperous town; hotels,
warehouses and depots stand on the ancient dueling ground; immense grain
elevators and wharves have been erected on soil which the river once claimed as
its own. Huge ferry-boats ply constantly across the river; but the railway
omnibuses and the ferry-boats are soon to be but memories of the past, as the
graceful arches of the new bridge testify.

"The crowd awaiting transportation across the stream has always been of the most cosmopolitan and motley character."

The crowd awaiting transportation across the stream has always been of the
most cosmopolitan and motley character. There may be seen the German emigrant, flat-capped and dressed in coarse black, with his quaintly attired wife and
rosy chilnren clinging to him; the tall and angular Texan drover, with his defiant
glance at the primly dressed cockneys around him; the "poor white" from some

far Southern State, with his rifle grasped in his lean hand, and his astonished stare at the extent of brick and stone walls beyond the river; the excursion party from the East, with its maps and guide-books, and its mountains of baggage; the little groups of English tourists, with their mysterious hampers and packets, bound toward. Denver or Omaha; the tired and ill-uniformed company of troops "on transfer" to some remote frontier fortress; the smart merchant in his carriage, with his elegantly dressed negro driver standing by the restive horses; the hordes of over-clothed young commercial men from the Northern and Western cities, with their mouths distended by Havana cigars, and filled with the slang of half-a-dozen capitals; and the hundreds of negroes, who throng the levées in summer, departing in winter like the swallows, at the slightest hint of snow, or of the fog which from time to time heightens the resemblance of the Missouri capital to London.

Before the bridge was built, the levée on each side of the river was a kind of pandemonium. An unending procession of wagons, loaded with coal, was always forcing its way from the ferry-boats up the bank to the streets of St. Louis, the tatterdemalion drivers urging on the plunging and kicking mules with frantic shouts of "Look at ye!" "You dar!" These wagons, in busy days, were constantly surrounded by the incoming droves of stock, wild Texan cattle, that with great leaps and flourish of horns objected to entering the gangways of the ferry, and now and then tossed their tormentors high in the air; and troops of swine, bespattered with mud, and dabbled with blood drawn from them by the thrusts of the enraged horsemen pursuing them. Added to this indescribable tumult were the lumbering wagon-trains laden with iron or copper, wearily making their way to the boats; the loungers about the curbstones singing rude plantation songs, or scuffling boisterously; the nameless ebb-tide of immigration scattered through a host of low and villainous bar-rooms and saloons, whose very entrances seemed suspicious; and the gangs of roustabouts rolling boxes, barrels, hogsheads, and bales, from wagon to wharf, and from wharf to wagon, from morning to night.

Below the bridge, the river, gradually broadening out, was covered with coal-barges and steam-tugs, and above it, along the banks, one saw, as one still sees, dark masses of homely buildings, elevators, iron foundries, and various manufactories; while along the shore are moored thousands of logs, fastened together in rafts.

XXII.

ST. LOUIS GERMANS AND AMERICANS—SPECULATIVE
PHILOSOPHY—EDUCATION.

THE old French quarter of St. Louis is now entirely given up to business, and but little of the Gallic element is left in the town. Some of the oldest and wealthiest families are of French descent, and retain the language and manners of their ancestors; but there are few exterior traces of French domination. Souvenirs still remain; streets, both English and American in aspect, bear the names of the vanished Gauls. Laclede has a monument in the form of a mammoth hotel; and the principal outlying ward of the city, crowded with vast rolling-mills, and iron and zinc-furnaces, is called Carondelet.

On the Illinois side of the river the village of Cahokia still lingers, a moss-grown relic of a decayed civilization, its venerable church, Notre Dame des Kahokias, being the most ancient building in the West. But not one of the great circular stone towers, erected in early times as defences against the Indians, remain; block-houses and bastions have been replaced by massive residences, in which live the merchant princes of the day.

"The Hill" is traversed in every direction by horse railroads; and a few minutes' ride will take one from the roar of business into a quiet and elegant section, where there are miles of beautiful and costly dwellings. As the ridges rise from the river, so rise the grades of social status. Mingled with the wholesale establishments, and the offices of mining and railway companies in Main and Second streets, parallel with the river, are hundreds of dirty and unhealthy tenement houses; on Fourth, and Fifth, and Sixth streets, and on those running at right angles with them, are the principal hotels, the more elegant of the shops and stores, the fashionable restaurants, and the few places of amusement which the city boasts; beyond, on the upper ridges, stretching back to Grand avenue, which extends along the summit of the hill, are the homes of the wealthy.

The passion for suburban residences is fast taking possession of the citizens of St. Louis, and several beautiful towns have sprung up within a few miles of the

The Court-House—St. Louis.

city, all of which are crowded with charming country houses. Lucas Place is the Fifth avenue of St. Louis, and is very rich in costly homes surrounded by noble gardens. The houses there have not been touched by the almost omnipresent smoke which seems to hover over the lower portion of the town. In

Thomas H. Benton (for thirty years United States Senator from Missouri).

Lucas Place lived the noted Benton, and there he foamed, fretted, planned his duels, nourished his feuds, and matured his magnificent ideas. The avenues which bear the names of Washington, Franklin, Lindell, McPherson, Baker, Laclede and Chouteau all give promise of future magnificence.

St. Louis is not rich in public buildings, although many of the recent structures devoted to business are grand and imposing. The hotels partake of the grandeur which distinguishes their counterparts of other cities; on Fourth and Fifth streets there are many elegant blocks.

The street life is varied and attractive, as in most southern towns; and the auction store is one of the salient features which surprise a stranger. The doors of these establishments are open from sunrise until midnight, and the jargon of the auctioneer can be heard ringing loudly above the rattle of wheels. The genius who presides behind the counter is usually some graduate of the commerce of the far South. Accustomed to dealing with the ignorant and unsuspecting, his eloquence is a curious compound of insolence and pleading. He has a quaint stock of phrases, made up of the slang of the river and the slums of cities, and he begins by placing an extravagant price upon the article which he wishes to sell, and then decreasing its value until he brings it down to the range of his customers.

On Saturday evenings the street life is as animated as that of an European city. In the populous quarters the Irish and Germans throng the sidewalks, marketing and amusing themselves until midnight; and in the fashionable sections the ladies, seated in the porches and on the front door-steps of their mansions, receive the visits of their friends.

A drive through dozens of streets in the upper portion of the city discloses hundreds of groups of ladies and gentlemen thus seated in the open air, whither they have transferred the etiquette of the parlor. A far more delightful and agreeable social freedom prevails in the city than in any Eastern community. The stranger is heartily welcome, and the fact that most of the ladies have been educated both in the East and the West, acquiring the culture of the former and the frankness and cordiality of the latter, adds a charm both to their conversation and their beauty.

At the more aristocratic and elegant of the German beer gardens, such as "Uhrig's" and "Schneider's," the representatives of many prominent American families may be seen on the concert evenings, drinking the amber fluid, and listening to the music of Strauss, of Gungl, or Meyerbeer. Groups of elegantly dressed ladies and gentlemen resort to the gardens in the same manner as do the denizens of Dresden and Berlin, and no longer regard the custom as a dangerous German innovation.

The German element in St. Louis is powerful, and has for the last thirty years been merging in the American, giving to it many of the hearty features and graces of European life, which have been emphatically rejected by the native population of the more austere Eastern States. In like manner the German has borrowed many traits from his American fellow-citizens, and in another generation the fusion of races will be pretty thoroughly accomplished.

There are more than fifty thousand native Germans now in St. Louis, and the whole Teutonic population, including the children born in the city of German parents, probably exceeds one hundred and fifty thousand. The original emigration from Germany to Missouri was largely from the thinking classes—professional men, politicians condemned to exile, writers, musicians, and philosophers, and these have aided immensely in the development of the State.

The emigration began in 1830, but after a few hundreds had come out it fell off again, and was not revived until 1848, when the revolution sent us a new crop of patriots and statesmen, whose mother country was afraid of them. Always a loyal and industrious element, believing in the whole country, and in the principles of freedom, they kept Missouri, in the troublous times preceding and during the war, from many excesses.

The working people are a treasure to the State. Arriving, as a rule, with little or nothing, they hoard every penny until they have enough with which to purchase an acre or two of land, and in a few years become well-to-do citizens, orderly and contented. The whole country for miles around St. Louis is dotted with German settlements; the market gardens are mainly controlled by them; and their farms are models of thorough cultivation.

In commerce they have mingled liberally with the Americans; names of both nationalities are allied in banking and in all the great wholesale businesses; and the older German residents speak their adopted as well as their native tongue. At the time of my visit, a German was president of the city council, and bank presidents, directors of companies, and men highly distinguished in business and society, who boast German descent, are counted by hundreds.

German journalism in St. Louis is noteworthy. Carl Schurz and his life-long friend and present partner, Mr. Pretorius, are known throughout the country as distinguished journalists, and have even, as we have seen in these later days, played no small role upon the stage of national politics.

The failure of the Liberal Republican movement rather astonished the masses of the Germans in Missouri, who had the most unwavering confidence in the ability of Schurz to accomplish whatever he chose; and has left them somewhat undecided as to what course to pursue in future.   There are four daily German newspapers in St. Louis, one of which has been recently planted there by the Catholics, who have also started a clever weekly, in the hope of aiding in the fight against the new principles put in force by the Prussian Government—principles, of course, largely reflected among the Germans in America.   The sturdy intellectual life of the Teuton is well set forth in these papers, which are of great ability.

The uselessness of the attempt to maintain a separate national feeling was shown in the case of the famous "Germania" Club, which, in starting, had for its cardinal principle the non-admission of Americans; but at the present time there are 200 American names upon its list of membership.   The assimilation goes on even more rapidly than the Germans themselves suppose; it is apparent in the manners of the children, and in the speech of the elders.

German social and home life has, of course, kept much of its original flavor. There are whole sections of the city where the Teuton predominates, and takes his ease at evening in the beer garden and the arbor in his own yard.   At the summer opera one sees him in his glory.

Entering a modest door-way on Fourth street, one is ushered through a long room, in which ladies, with their children, and groups of elegantly dressed men are chatting and drinking beer, into the opera-house, a cheery little hall, where very fashionable audiences assemble to hear the new and old operas throughout a long season.   The singing is usually exceedingly good, and the *mise en scène* quite satisfactory.   Between the acts the audience refreshes itself with beer and soda-water, and the hum of conversation lasts until the first notes of the orchestra announce the resumption of the opera.   On Sunday evenings the opera-house is crowded, and at the long windows of the hall, which descend to the ground, one can see the German population of half-a-dozen adjacent blocks, tiptoe with delight at the whiff of stolen harmony.

The "breweries" scattered through the city are gigantic establishments, for the making of beer ranks third in the productive industries of St. Louis.   Iron and flour precede it, but a capital of nearly $4,000,000 is invested in the manufacture, and the annual productive yield from the twenty-five breweries is about the same amount.   Attached to many of these breweries are concert gardens, every way scrupulously respectable, and weekly frequented by thousands.

The Germania and Harmony Clubs, and a hundred musical and literary organizations use up the time of the city Germans who are well-to-do, while their poorer brethren delve at market gardens, and are one of the chief elements in the commerce of the immense and picturesque St. James Market, whither St. Louis goes to be fed.   The Irishman is also prominent in St. Louis, having crept into the hotel service, and driven the negro to another field.

The operation of the German upon the American mind has been admirably exemplified in St. Louis by the growth of a real and noteworthy school of speculative philosophy in the new and thoroughly commercial capital, at whose head, and by virtue of his distinguished preëminence as a thinker, stands William T. Harris, the present superintendent of the city public schools.   Mr. Harris, during his stay at Yale, in 1856, met the venerable Alcott, of Concord, and was much stimulated by various conversations with him. At that time he had studied Kant a little, and was beginning to think upon Goethe.

The hints given him by Mr. Alcott were valuable, and some time afterward, when he settled in St. Louis, and came into contact with Germans of culture and originality, his desire for philosophical study was greatly increased and strengthened. In 1858 he became engaged in teaching, for eight years conducting one of the city graded schools.

The first year of his stay in St. Louis he studied Kant's "Critique of Pure Reason," without, as he says, understanding it at all. He had been solicited and encouraged to these studies by Henry C. Brockmeyer, a remarkable and brilliant German, and so enthusiastic for Kantian study that he awoke a genuine fervor in Mr. Harris. They arranged a Kant class, which Mr. Alcott on one occasion visited, and in a short time the love for philosophical study became almost fanaticism. A number of highly cultured Germans and Americans composed the circle, whose members had a supreme contempt for the needs of the flesh, and who, after long days of laborious and exhaustive teaching, would spend the night hours in threading the mysteries of Kant. In 1858 Mr. Harris claims that they mastered Kant, and between that period and 1863 they analyzed, or, as he phrases it, obtained the keys to Leibnitz and Spinoza. The result of this long study is written out in what Mr. Harris calls his "Introduction to Philosophy," in which he deals with "speculative insights." Every one, he claims, will

William T. Harris, editor of the St. Louis "Journal of Speculative Philosophy."

have the same insight into Kant, Leibnitz and Spinoza as he did, by reading his "Introduction." He already has a large number of followers, many of whom, according to his confession, apply his theories better than he does himself: and his *Journal of Speculative Philosophy*, started boldly in the face of many obstacles, has won a permanent establishment and gratifying success.

Among the most prominent members of the Philosophical Society, definitely organized in 1864, were Mr. Brockmeyer, J. G. Werner, now a probate judge, Mr. Kroeger (a stern, unrelenting philosopher, enamored of Fichte, translator of the "Science of Knowledge," and author of a "History of the Minnesingers"), George H. Howison, now in the Boston Institute of Technology, and Mr. Thomas Davidson, one of the most profound students of Aristotle in this country. Mr. Brockmeyer is the accomplished translator of Hegel's "Logic."

The *Journal of Speculative Philosophy* was prompted in this wise: Mr. Harris wrote a "Critique upon Herbert Spencer's First Principles," which was offered to *The North American Review,* but the editors failed to discover anything in it save that it was very audacious, and returned it to the author. Mr. Harris thereupon boldly started his own journal in April of 1867. The publication is gaining ground in this country, and has won a very wide and hearty recognition in Germany and among thinking men throughout Europe.

Mr. Harris has been an indefatigable worker, as well as a deep thinker, for a score of years. The impetus given by him and his confreres to the growth of a deep and pure literature in the West and South is as yet too little appreciated. A brilliant talker, a man of great originality, and of positive genius for analysis, he is fitted to shine in the brightest of the world's capitals, but loves his Southwestern home, and will doubtless remain in it. The teachers grouped around him in his work of directing the schools of the new metropolis are brilliant men and women, thoroughly in love with their work, and animated by his inspiring presence with the proper spirit.

The Germans have, as a rule, frankly joined hands with the Americans in the public schools, and have imparted to them many excellent features. The composite system differs largely from that in vogue in other cities. There is, of course, a very large Catholic population in St. Louis, but it is pretty evenly balanced by German skepticism.

The city public schools are utterly secular in their teaching, but, notwithstanding that fact, the priesthood makes constant and successful efforts to keep Catholic children from them; and wherever a new public school building is erected, Holy Church speedily buys ground and sets up an institution of her own. The Catholic laity of St. Louis, however, are, perhaps, if they spoke their real sentiments, in favor of the public schools; and there has been a vast advance toward liberalism on their part within the last few years. The Catholics have eight or nine out of the twenty-four members of the school board, and of course have much to say.

It is wonderful that in a capital where the population is so little gregarious, and where, up to last year, it has been so comparatively indifferent to lecture courses, such an earnest interest should be taken in the schools by all classes. All the powers relating to the management of the schools are vested in a corporate body called " the Board of President and Directors of the St. Louis Public Schools," the members of the board to be elected for terms of three years. The school revenue is derived from rents of property originally donated by the General Government, by the State school fund, and from taxes of four mills on the dollar on city property, the yearly income from these sources averaging perhaps $700,000. The school board has authority to tax to any amount.

Between the district and the high schools there is a period of seven years, during which the pupil acquires a symmetrical development admirably fitting him for the solid instruction which the finishing school can offer. But out of forty thousand children enrolled upon the public school list, only about two and a-half per cent. enter the high school. The feature of German-English instruction has become exceedingly popular, and the number of pupils belonging to the classes increased from 450 in 1864–65, to 10,246 in 1871–72. The phonetic system of learning to read was introduced in the primary schools in 1866, and has been attended with the most gratifying results.

The city acted wisely in introducing the study of German, as otherwise the Teutonic citizen would doubtless have been tempted to send his child to a private school during his early years. Now native American children take up German reading and oral lessons at the same time as their little German fellow-scholars; and in the high school special stress is laid upon German instruction in the higher grades, that the pupils may be fitted for a thorough examination of German science and literature.

The growth of St. Louis is so rapid that the school board has been compelled to build several large new school buildings annually, each capable of containing from seven to eight hundred pupils.   The introduction of natural science into the

The High School—St. Louis.

district schools is indicative of liberal progress.   Normal schools in St. Louis and at Kirksville and Warrensburg are annually equipping splendid corps of teachers.   The public school system throughout the State is exceedingly popular, judging from the fact that a quarter of a million of children attend the schools during the sessions.

The State fund appropriated to school purposes is usually large, and although there have been objections to local taxation for school support in some of the counties, the taxes have generally been promptly paid.   The largest and finest edifices in such flourishing cities as St. Joseph, Kansas City, Sedalia, Clinton, Springfield, Mexico, Louisiana, and Booneville are usually the "school-houses;" and in Kansas City, which was without railroad communication in 1865, the school buildings are now as complete, elegant, and large as any in Boston or Chicago.   The School of Design in St. Louis, conducted by Mr. Conrad Diehl, is rapidly growing, and has already won enviable praise in the most cultured art circles of the East.

The Catholic population within the archdiocese of St. Louis is certainly very large, probably numbering two hundred thousand persons; and from this population at least twenty-five thousand children are furnished to the one hundred parish schools attached to the various churches in the diocese.   None of these schools receive any aid from the common school fund, and the pupils are in every way removed from the influences of secular education, and made a class by themselves.

It is estimated that the Catholics now own more than four million dollars' worth of church and school property in Missouri; and in their various colleges, convents, seminaries, and academies in St. Louis and the other large cities of the State they have at least fifteen hundred students. They have kept well abreast of the tide of secular education, and bid it open defiance on all occasions, while the skeptical and easy-going German laughs at their zealotry, and the American shuts his eyes to their growing power.

Vast as is the growth of colleges and schools of various other denominations, such as the Baptist, the Methodist, and the Methodist Episcopal Church South, the Catholics keep even with them all. Ever since old Gribault, the first pastor in St. Louis, led his little flock of five hundred Frenchmen to the altar, Mother Church has been bold, dominant, defiant in the young capital of the West.

In St. Louis I was especially interested in "Washington University,"

Washington University — St. Louis.

conducted by Rev. Dr. Eliot, so long pastor of the First Unitarian Church in that city. The institution has had a superb growth since its founding in 1853–54, despite the unfortunate intervention of the war, and now has more than eight hundred students in its various branches. Nourished by generous gifts from the East, it has made great progress in its departments of civil and mechanical engineering, mining and metallurgy, and architecture, and its law department is ably supported.

To that section of the University devoted to the special education of women, known as " Mary Institute," the flower of Missourian girlhood annually repairs. The University seems to have had an almost mushroom growth; yet its culture is solid and substantial. The State University is located at Columbia, and has also been characterized by a remarkable growth since the war. During the struggle its buildings were occupied by United States troops, and its sessions were entirely broken up ; the library was dispersed, the warrants of the institution were afloat at a discount, and various prejudices had nearly ruined it.

At last Rev. Dr. Daniel Read took the presidency ; and the reorganized University comprises a normal college, an agricultural and mechanical college, opened in 1870, law and medical schools, and a department of chemistry, and now has attached to it a "school of mines and metallurgy," established at Rolla, in South-eastern Missouri. Into this mining school students flock from all directions, turning their attention toward a scientific development of the mineral resources of the State. Women have finally been admitted to the University, and, at the commencement of 1872, a young lady was advanced to the baccalaureate grade in science.

XXIII.

COMMERCE OF ST. LOUIS—THE NEW BRIDGE OVER THE MISSISSIPPI.

THE midsummer heats, during which I visited the Exchange of St. Louis, seem to make but little difference with the ardor and energy of its members. The typical July day in the Missourian capital is the acme of oppressive heat; before business hours have begun, the sun pours down bewildering beams on the current of the great river, on the toiling masses at the levée, and along the airless streets rising from the water-side.

The ladies have done their shopping at an early hour, and gone their ways; *paterfamilias* seeks his Avernus of an office, clad only in thinnest of linen, and with a palm-leaf fan in his hand; a misty aroma of the ices of Hellery or Gregory floats before him as he seats himself at his desk, and turns over the voluminous correspondence from far Texas, from the vexed Indian Territory, from the great North-west, from Arkansas, or from the hosts of river towns with which the metropolis does business.

At eleven the sun has become withering to the unaccustomed Easterners, but the St. Louis *paterfamilias* dons his broad straw hat, and, proceeding to the

The new Post-Office and Custom-House in construction at St. Louis.

"Merchants' Exchange," a large circular room into which the thirteen hundred members vainly try each day to cram themselves, he makes his way to the corner allotted to his branch of trade, and patiently swelters there until nearly one o'clock. In this single room every species of business is transacted; one corner is devoted to flour, a second to grain, a third to provisions, a fourth to cotton, etc.

A whirlwind of fans astonishes the stranger spectator; people mop their foreheads and swing their palm-leaves hysterically as they conclude bargains; and, as they saunter away together to lunch, still vigorously fan and mop. The tumult and shouting is not so great as in other large cities, but the activity is the same; the participants from time to time refreshing themselves at great cans filled with sulphur water. But in a few years the magnificent new Exchange building, which will be, in many respects, the finest on the continent, will be completed, and trade will not only be classified, but will have far greater facilities for public transactions than at present.

St. Louis has determined to become a leading cotton market, and, in view of the new railroad development ministering directly to her, it seems probable that she will take position among the cotton marts of the world. The opening of Northern Texas, and of the whole of Arkansas, to immediate connection by rail with the Missourian capital, and the probability—alas, for the faithlessness of nations!—of white settlement and increase of cotton culture in the Indian Territory, will give a back-country capable of producing millions of bales annually for St. Louis to draw upon. She will eventually become a competitor with Houston, Galveston, and New Orleans for the distribution of the crop of the South-west, and has already, as she believes, received sufficient encouragement to justify the building of large storehouses along the line of the Iron Mountain railroad.

A good deal of the cotton once handled in New Orleans has lately been going to New York by rail, and the St. Louis merchants and factors are now using a "compress," by means of which 23,000 pounds of cotton can be placed in a single freight car. The city is receiving only 40,000 to 60,000 bales annually, but confidently counts on several hundred thousand as soon as it has perfected arrangements for transportation. It will, without doubt, control the cotton in certain sections of Arkansas, and the southern portions of Missouri, and can make very seductive bids for the crops of many sections of Texas.

To draw the attention of cotton-growers toward the St. Louis market, the Agricultural Association recently offered premiums of $10,000 for the best specimens of various grades of cotton. The Atlantic and Pacific, the Missouri, Kansas and Texas, the St. Louis and South-eastern, the Mobile and Ohio, and the Iron Mountain roads will probably bring large quantities of cotton to St. Louis in the future. The testimony of many of the planters of Northern Texas is that their shipments to St. Louis have been far more satisfactory than those to Galveston.

St. Louis is emphatically the railroad centre of the Mississippi valley, being the actual terminus of no less than fourteen important railroads, while at least thirty are pointed toward her. By all the railroads and by river routes she received, in 1872, nearly 4,000,000 tons of freight, being a vast increase over her receipts of 1871, and shipped 2,009,941 tons. In 1872 the railroads alone brought her nearly 800,000 tons of coal. In 1872 she expended $7,000,000 in new buildings, and in 1873 about $8,000,000.

Through her vast elevators, four of which are located along the banks of the Mississippi, and one of which has a capacity of 2,000,000 bushels, passed more than 28,000,000 bushels of grain in 1872; and in 1873 the receipts and exports were largely increased over this figure. She contributed $2,500,000 in duties from her custom-house in 1872; manufactured in 1873, 1,384,180 barrels of flour, and received nearly that number by various rail and river routes; received 279,678 cattle, and shipped 188,306; imported and exported more than 1,000,000 swine; took nearly 30,000 bales of hemp into market; handled hundreds of millions of feet of lumber, shingles and laths drifted down from the Upper Mississippi, the Black and the Wisconsin rivers; and consummated vast bargains in wool, hides and tobacco.

The river trade has many peculiar features, and is subject to a thousand fluctuations and adversities which make it, at all times, hazardous. For many years past the steamboat men have had unprofitable seasons to bewail. Their especial enemies have been low water and railroad competition. The railways may in future gradually absorb the carrying trade of the Mississippi valley; but such is not at present the case. The rivers have thus far remained the principal arteries of commerce; and the moment that low water is reached, or ice closes navigation, the greatest depression is visible in St. Louis; trade is at an absolute stand-still.

The Mississippi is the main outlet possessed by the city for her supplies for southern consumers. In view of this fact, it is of the greatest importance that the river should receive the improvements so much needed between the mouths of the Missouri and the Ohio. A formidable system of dykes and dams, it is confidently believed, would make open navigation feasible throughout the year.

It is impossible to give an adequate idea of the picturesqueness and vivacity of the river trade; it must be seen. One appreciates the real volume of the current of the "Father of Waters" only after he learns something of the multitude of boats, barges and rafts on its ample breast. Every conceivable variety of river-boat grates its keel against the St. Louis levée: the floating palace, the "Great Republic;" the "Natchez," or the "Robert E. Lee;" the strong, flat-bottomed Red river packet; the cruisers of the Upper Mississippi and of the turbid Missouri; the barges, in long procession, laden with coal and iron and lead and copper ore; the huge arks of the Transportation Company, each capable of receiving 100,000 bushels of grain within its capacious bosom; while rafts of every size and shape are scattered along the giant stream like chips and straws on a mountain brook.

Nearly 3,000 steamboat arrivals are annually registered at the port of St. Louis. Drifting down on the logs come a rude and hardy class of men, who chafe under city restraint, requiring, now and then, stern management. Sometimes one of these figures, suddenly arriving from the ancient forests on the rivers above, creates a sensation by striding through a fashionable street, his long hair falling about his wrinkled and weather-beaten face, and his trusty rifle slung at his shoulder.

The steamboat men on these upper waters of the Mississippi suffer when the "ice gorges" come. Faces become dark with anxiety or black with fear at the news of each fresh disaster. Even the dreaded "low water," with all the dangers of "snags" and sunken wrecks, is not so much to be feared as one of the great ice sweeps which, with its glittering teeth, will in a few moments grind to atoms hundreds of thousands of dollars' worth of property.

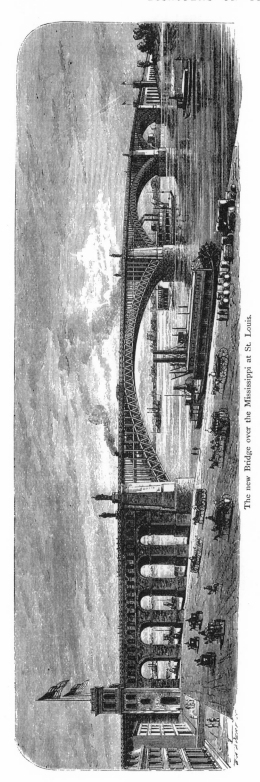

The new Bridge over the Mississippi at St. Louis.

In December the Mississippi, at St. Louis, is sometimes closed by ice, and before the great bridge was built, hundreds of teams crossed upon the natural bridge to and from the Illinois shore. The breaking up is sudden — dozens of boats and cargoes being swept away and annihilated. Then come the stories of romantic and hair-breadth escapes; the population along the banks becoming wild with excitement over the pending fate of some unfortunate family swept out into the ice-filled current. Steamboat owners even hardly dare look in a newspaper.

In 1872 there were over five hundred and fifty disasters on the Mississippi river and her tributaries — by few of which, however, was there any loss of life, although the annual destruction of property is enormous, occurring in almost every conceivable manner. But the record of these disasters is not without its grim humor. One can hardly repress a smile at the announcement, in the terse, expressive language of the river, that "Phil. Sheridan broke loose at St. Louis," or that "Hyena broke her engine," "Lake Erie ran through herself," "Mud Hen blew up at Bellevue," "Enterprise broke a wrist at Cairo," "Andy Johnson blew out a joint near Alton," "Wild Cat sunk a barge at Rising Sun," "Humming Bird smashed a shaft," "St. Francis broke her doctor," "Daniel Boone was crowded on shore by ice," or "John Kilgour, trying to land at Evansville, broke nine arms." The river-men have not been satisfied to confer upon their beloved craft the names of heroes and saints. They rake up all fantastic cognomens which the romance of the centuries or the slang of the period can afford, bestowing them upon clumsy and beautiful crafts alike, while they pay but little regard to incongruities of gender or class: the "Naiad" may be a coal-barge, or the "Dry Docks" a palace steamer. The ice makes short work of even the largest cargoes; the river will swallow up several hundred thousand bushels of coal or grain as if it were the merest bagatelle, while the gorges gape for more.

Great numbers of barges ply between St. Louis and Pittsburg, via the Ohio, engaged in the transportation of iron ore. It is a long and wild journey, moving slowly upon the treacherous currents of the two great streams, the men on the barges sometimes contenting themselves for a month without going on shore, living on rude fare, and cuddling with their families in little cabins in the boats'

View of the Caisson of the East Abutment of the St. Louis Bridge, as it appeared during construction.

sides, like the Belgian canal-men. Dozens of these barges are always moored at Carondelet, waiting the freights which pour into them from the mines in the south-east of the State. When navigation throughout the Mississippi valley shall have been properly improved, the river trade of St. Louis will be quadrupled.

The triumph in engineering, won by Captain Eads in the successful completion of the great bridge, is a magnificent one. This was not, however, the first important work accomplished by him. He built the vessels "Benton," "Baron de Kalb," "Cincinnati," and others, used with such effect by Admiral Porter during the war. He afterward constructed fourteen iron clads for the United

States, and he invented various improvements in military and naval defences. He was the first man in America or Europe to devise successful means for operating heavy ordnance by steam. He knows the Mississippi as well as any one can know that most capricious and uncertain of streams, and was, of all men, best qualified for the work of bridging the current.

It was evident from the first that the Father of Waters would not consent to be bridged without a struggle. The main obstacles to the construction were, of course, the width, the depth, and the shifting sands of the river. It was necessary to take into account the certainty of an enormous increase of transportation, and to obstruct navigation as little as possible. The foundations must be planted on the rock-bed below the fickle and dangerous sands.

Two companies for building the bridge were at first organized, one chartered by the Missouri Legislature, the other by that of Illinois. The company chartered in Missouri was naturally somewhat jealous of the other, fearing lest Chicago might play some game against the interests of St. Louis, and quite a contest ensued until, in the spring of 1868, a consolidation was effected, and the

The building of the East Pier of the St. Louis Bridge.

work was placed under the direction of Captain Eads as chief engineer. The new corporation, which has been ably officered, assumed the title of the Illinois and St. Louis Bridge Company. The original estimate of the cost of the structure was $5,000,000; but the whole cost will probably reach $10,000,000, two-thirds of which sum have been supplied by J. T. Morgan & Co., American bankers in London.

The greatest difficulties in the work were encountered in the sinking of the piers. Captain Eads decided to construct them of solid masonry, and to sink them by means of pneumatic caissons, many of the features of which had been designed by him expressly to meet the exigencies of the case. The caisson for the first pier was made of heavy wrought iron, weighed 500,000 pounds, and was 82 feet long, 60 feet wide, and 18 feet high. It had seven air-chambers, with thirteen girders, and nearly 200 workmen were employed on it for four months in reaching to the rock-bed in the stream. This was effected at a depth of 93 feet and four inches below the surface of the water, in March, 1870. In November of 1870, the launch of the caisson to be used in laying the eastern abutment pier was made the occasion of quite a public celebration. That pier now rests on the rock at a depth of 130 feet below high water mark. The work in the air-chambers during the building of these piers was difficult and dangerous, and from time to time the river, as if angry at the intrusion, required a sacrifice of human life. Sometimes in winter the work was interrupted by the vast masses of ice hurled against the bridge-works; now and then the sand outside the caissons was scoured away, causing the sand inside (put there to equalize the pressure) to burst the walls; and at the banks great trouble was experienced in setting the coffer dams.

But all obstacles were finally overcome, and in June of 1874, trains began crossing the Mississippi on the new bridge. It now stretches from the foot of Washington avenue in St. Louis to a corresponding point on the Illinois shore, at an elevation of fifty feet above high water.

Its extraordinary breadth of span and depth of foundation are its chief merits. In the western abutment there are 2,500 tons of stone, and in the eastern abutment pier 45,000. The bridge has three spans, each formed with four ribbed arches made of cast-steel. The centre span is 520 feet, and the side ones are each 500 feet in the clear. The four arches forming each of these spans consist each of an upper and lower curved rib, extending from pier to pier, and between these ribs there is a horizontal system of bracing for the purpose of securing the arches in their relative distances from each other. Two centre arches of each span are thirteen feet nine and a-half inches apart from centre to centre, and the upper member of one arch is secured to the lower one of the other by a system of diagonal bracing. The roadways are formed by transverse iron beams twelve inches in depth, suitably separated.

The bridge accommodates two double steam railway tracks, and one for street railways, besides footwalks and a carriage-way. It is estimated that the annual saving to St. Louis by the facilities for transportation accorded by the bridge will amount to a million of dollars.

In the mere item of coal, which is carried to St. Louis from the Illinois side, hundreds of thousands of dollars will be saved yearly. A fine union depot will soon be erected at the end of the tunnel through which trains will enter and leave St. Louis via the bridge.

XXIV.

THE MINERAL WEALTH OF MISSOURI.

L ET us peer into that busy suburban ward of St. Louis which still clings so
fondly to its old French name of "Carondelet." The drive thither from
the city carries you past the arsenal, where Government now and then has a
few troops, and past many a pretty mansion, into the dusty street of a prosaic
manufacturing town, near the bank of the Mississippi.

Descending toward the water-side from the street you find every available
space crowded with mammoth iron and zinc-furnaces, in whose immense structures of iron, wood, and glass, half-naked men, their bodies smeared with
perspiration and coal dust, are wheeling about blazing masses of metal, or guid-

In the "Cut" at Iron Mountain, Missouri. [Page 241.]

ing the pliant iron bars through rollers and moulds, or cooling their heated faces
and arms in buckets of water brought up fresh from the stream. Here, in a zinc-
furnace, half-a-dozen Irishmen wrestle with the long puddling rods which they

thrust into the seventy-times-seven heated furnaces; the green and yellowish flames from the metal are reflected on their pale and withered features, and give them an almost unearthly expression.

Farther on, the masons are toiling at the brick-work of a new blast-furnace, which already rears its tall towers a hundred feet above the Mississippi shore; not far thence you may see the flaming chimney of the quaint old Carondelet furnace—the first built in all that section; or may linger for hours in such immense establishments as the South St. Louis or Vulcan iron works, fancying them the growth of half a century of patient upbuilding, until you are told that nearly every establishment has been created since the war.

At the Vulcan Iron Works — Carondelet.

The Vulcan Iron Works, which now employs twelve hundred men in its blast-furnaces and rolling-mills, overspreads seventeen acres, boasts $600,000 worth of machinery, and has two furnaces smelting 25,000 tons of ore annually, while its rolling-mill can turn out 45,000 tons of rail in a year, was not in existence in 1870; indeed, there was not a brick laid on the premises. There is nothing else so wonderful as this in the South or South-west; Kansas City, in the north-western part of the State, is the only other place in Missouri which can show similar material progress.

The little *Rivière des Pères*, where the holy Catholic fathers once had a mission among the Osage Indians, empties into the Mississippi, close beside the Vulcan iron works; its banks are piled high with coal and refuse. The fathers would know it no more. They would stare aghast at the thousand horse-power pump; at the myriads of fiery snakes crawling about on the floors of the rolling-mill; at the troops of Irish laborers, the cautious groups about the doors of the sputtering blast-furnace, and the molten streams pouring into the sand-beds to form into "pigs" of iron; and could hardly credit the statement that Carondelet furnaces alone can manufacture 140,000 tons of iron yearly.

This sudden and marked progress at Carondelet is significant. Such amazing growth is indicative of a splendid future. The elder England is fading out; her iron-fields are exhausted; and her producers growl because American iron-masters can at last undersell those of England. The heart of the republic, the great commonwealth of Missouri, is to be the England of to-morrow.

Her mineral stores are inexhaustible. There are a thousand railroads locked up in the great coffers of the Iron Mountain. A thousand iron ships lie dormant in the ore-pockets scattered along the line of the Atlantic and Pacific railway, and a million fortunes await the men who shall come and take them. Missouri is one of the future great foundries of the world; the coal-fields of Indiana and Illinois are near at hand; the earth is stored with hematites; the hills are seamed with speculars. The work has already begun in earnest.

Enough good iron can be produced from Missouri ores and Illinois coal to supply the wants of the United States henceforth; and at the rate at which furnaces are at present multiplying throughout the State, this consummation will be reached. All the conditions for a favorable competition with England have at last been arrived at, for the cost of labor in Missouri furnaces to-day is but a trifle more than it is in the cheapest furnaces in Wales. The four or five millions which St. Louis now has invested in the manufacture of pig-iron will, in a few years, become forty or fifty; and the furnaces in South-eastern Missouri, aided by those in Pennsylvania supplied with ore from the same source, will girdle the world with their products. The aggregate production of pig-iron in Missouri in 1870 was 54,000 tons; in 1880 it will be ten times that amount, for the capacity of Carondelet alone in 1873 was nearly three times as much as that of the whole State three years ago.* If St. Louis, unaided by any special interest, could increase the value of her manufactured products from $27,000,000 in 1860 to more than $100,000,000 in 1870, what may she not be expected to accomplish, with the Iron Mountain at her back, in the decade at whose very beginning she has demonstrated such wonderful capacity for progress?

How long, before, with proper investment of capital, St. Louis may be the centre of a region producing as many millions of tons of pig-iron annually as are now produced in England? Continuing as she has begun, less than twenty years will place her at that pinnacle of commercial glory.

I will not follow the ingenious individuals who have lightened the *ennui* of their leisure by computing, upon a highly speculative basis, the exact number of tons of ore contained in the famous Iron Mountain. But there is no doubt that the term inexhaustible can with justice be applied to its stores.

Certain acute English witnesses have recently, after a careful survey, declared that the coal and iron deposits of Alabama are now the most deeply interesting material facts on the American continent. Whether or not this statement is at all influenced by the knowledge that numerous investments in Alabama's iron-fields have been made by Englishmen, or by ignorance of the quantity and

---

* The coal used at Carondelet comes from the Illinois side of the Mississippi, and a new bridge across the stream at that point is contemplated, that the high prices charged during the icy season may be avoided.

quality of the ore in Missouri, I do not know; but the latter State may certainly claim an equal share in the interest which her sister of the South has
awakened, so far as the value of her deposits is concerned.   If it can be said that
the hematites of Alabama, which yield fifty-six per cent. of pure iron, will
compare favorably with the best ores of Cumberland and the North of Spain,
what shall we say of the ores of Missouri, which in many cases boast a proven
yield of sixty-six per cent.?

The main iron region of Missouri is situated in the south-east and southern
portions of the State, and the greater portion of it is adjacent and directly tributary to St. Louis.   The hundreds of thousands of tons of ore annually sent out of
the State to be smelted all pass through or near the great city.

My visit to the Iron Mountain had been resolved upon before I entered Missouri; but my wildest ideas of its importance were none too exaggerated for the
reality.   The "mountain" is situated eighty-one miles south-west of St. Louis,
on the Arkansas branch of the Iron Mountain railroad.   The route thither in
summer-time is charming.   The railroad runs so near to the banks of the Mississippi (there high and rugged), that nervous people, not fascinated by the grand
outlook over the current, may confess to a tremor now and then.

But the exquisite shapes of the foliage on the one bank, and the great
expanse of the "bottoms" on the other, made a pleasing picture, to which the
dazzling sheen of the broad sheet of smoothly-flowing water, bearing lightly
forward the white steamers and the dark, flat barges, lent a strange charm.
From Bismarck, a pretty little station among pleasant fields, it was but a brief
ride to Iron Mountain station, the town which has grown up out of the mining
interests managed and owned in these latter years by Chouteau, Harrison, and
Vallé.   Three of the wealthiest families in Missouri are represented in the ownership of this and the adjacent region, and each has been much interested in the
material development of the State.

The "mountain," which rises rather abruptly from a beautiful valley, land-
locked and filled with delicious fields, was originally rather more than 200 feet
high, and its base covers an area of 500 acres.   All the country round about is
still crowded with reminiscences of Spanish domination.   The names of some of
the counties and towns are French and Spanish souvenirs; and the "King's
Highway," running through St. François county, is still often called by its
original name.

The people in the vicinity are quiet and usually well-to-do farmer folk, and
look upon the mountain as the most wonderful of natural phenomena.   The
French and Spaniards seem never to have suspected the rich nature of the
queerly-shaped elevation and its surroundings; for the original possessor, Joseph
Pratte, who obtained it by a grant from Zenon Trudeau, the Spanish governor,
in September of 1797, mentions in his petition for a grant that the land is sterile,
and only fit for grazing.

Pratte's grant composed some 20,000 arpents, or 17,000 English acres, and
from his hands it became the property of Van Doren, Pease & Co., who, in 1837,
were recognized as the Iron Mountain Company.   Congress had meantime con-

firmed the Spanish grants. In 1843 the American Iron Mountain Company took the place of the above-mentioned firm. August Belmont, of New York, was among the subscribers to the capital stock, which was $273,000; and James Harrison, of St. Louis, one of the most energetic iron workers of the West, was its first president.

For many years the investments of the original companies did not pay, and the investors were sneered at as guilty of an act of folly.

In those days the Iron Mountain railroad was not, and all the ore dug out was hauled painfully forty-five miles in carts to the ancient town of St. Gene-vieve. But when pig-iron became worth $85 per ton, there was no lack of energy in examining the real resources of the mountain, and since 1862 the company has taken millions of tons of ore from the surface and from the deep incisions made in the hill-sides.

The ores there, as throughout the section, are mainly rich specular oxides, and were originally pronounced too rich to work. Even to this day the surface specimens are plenteous, and one could readily pick up a cart-load of lumps all ready for the furnace. In the deep cuts and along the mountain sides more than 1,000 men were at work at the time of my visit, Irishmen, Swedes and Germans predominating.

The Furnace—Iron Mountain, Missouri. [Page 242.]

The mountain is composed almost exclusively of iron in its purest form, and the regiment of laborers mine ore enough to load 125 cars, carrying 10 tons each, daily, besides supplying two furnaces of large capacity, established at the base of the mountain. A century of hammering at the hill's sides will not bring it level with the valley. The surface ore is so intermingled even with the earth, that I found a number of stout Swedes washing it very much as gold is washed for, and extracting tons which, in more careless days, had been thrown away.

Iron Mountain is a typical Missouri mining town.   It was mainly built up by Hon. John G. Scott, of St. Louis, an ex-Congressman, and largely identified with all the iron interests of that section.   Mr. Edwin Harrison, the present president, and one of the principal owners, is an accomplished metallurgist, one of the most active business men in the South-west, and interested in a dozen large and successful enterprises connected with the development of metal.   Both at Iron Mountain and at Irondale, as well as at other mining towns which I visited, the workmen have built handsome cottages, and liquor and the other debasing influences sometimes found at mines are beyond their reach.

There was a subtle charm about the roar and ominous hum of the great furnaces after dark, when the clink of the hammers and the noise of the blasting on the mountain had ceased, and darkness had shrouded the little valley.   The chimneys of the " blasts" glowed like dragons' eyes; the semi-nude figures flitting in the huge open sheds, before the doors of the furnaces, looked like demons.

When the masses of broken and carefully-selected ore, together with the requisite charcoal and limestone, had been transfused in the fearful heat, and the blast was ready to be drawn off, the workmen gathered half timorously about the aperture whence the molten iron was to flow, and gave it vent.   Then first sprang out a white current—the slag—looking like gypsum, and hardening as it touched the sand.   Finally came the deep fiery glow of the iron itself, as it flowed resistlessly down the channels cut in the sand to receive it, hissing fiercely from time to time, and lighting up the great stone vault of the furnace with an unearthly glare, then "dying into sullen darkness," and forming the cold, hard, homely bars which are one day rolled into the rails by means of which we annihilate distance, and build cities like St. Louis.

The whole region round about is rich in mines and minerals.   A few miles below Iron Mountain rises Pilot Knob, a stately peak towering far above the lovely Ozark range which surrounds it in every direction; and from the porphyry there and on Shepherd Mountain great quantities of ore are extracted. It is the boast of the people of the section that Iron county, in which lie Shepherd, Arcadia and Bogy mountains and the Knob, contains more iron than any other equal area known on the globe.

From this valley more than 100,000 tons of iron have been shipped since the formation of the Pilot Knob Iron Company.   The works there and elsewhere in this section were much injured, and some of them were burned, during the war, by Price's raiders.   The silicious and magnetic and specular oxides found in the Pilot Knob and Shepherd Mountain region are abundant and pure.   The specular oxides abound in Dent, Crawford, Phillips and Pulaski counties.   The beds of bog ore extend for miles among the swamps and cypresses in Southeastern Missouri; and hematite ores are found in almost every county in the south of the State.   Throughout the coal-measures of the commonwealth there are vast beds of spathic ore, which will serve when the more available deposits have been exhausted.

And this is not all.   For miles and miles along the Missouri river, iron crops out from the bold and picturesque bluffs, and it is estimated that it can be easily mined and placed in barges for less than a dollar per ton.   On the line of the Atlantic and Pacific railroad also, vast deposits of the blue specular variety are gradually being un-

earthed.   At Scotia, at Sullivan, at Jamestown, at Salem, the treasures of iron are astonishing.

Missouri should take care to keep the furnaces for smelting these ores within her borders, for pig-iron and Bessemer steel can to-day be made cheaper there, at the present prices of labor and coal, than in Pennsylvania.   If America desires or intends one day to supply Europe with

The Summit of Pilot Knob—Iron County, Missouri. [Page 242.]

the ore which she is beginning to clamor for, the policy of transporting the ores from these fresh fields to the furnaces in the Quaker State seems neither wise nor economical.   The stores of coal match those of iron; it was long ago estimated that Missouri had an area of 26,000 square miles of coal-beds between the mouth of the Des Moines river and the Indian Territory; and along all the railroads in Northern Missouri, and beside the Missouri Pacific, coal-veins have proved very extensive.

The development of the lead mines of Missouri is full of romance.   De Soto, disdaining any thing save gold, carelessly passed them by.   One hundred and fifty years ago Renault and La Motte hunted in the Ozark hills for the precious metal, but only found lead, and to-day La Motte's mine is still called by his name.   As early as 1819 the annual yield of the lead mines in the State was 3,000,000 of pounds; in 1870 the annual production amounted to nearly 14,000,000; and in 1872 it had risen to over 20,000,000.

The revival of the lead mining interest, in 1872, created almost as much excitement in certain sections as if gold had been in question.   The largest investments were made in South-western and Central Missouri; old mines were reopened, new machinery was hurried in, and in Jasper county, a wild section on the borders of Kansas and the Indian Territory, a new town sprang up as by magic in the midst of a section where lead lay near the surface.   There was genuine California enthusiasm; furnaces, stores, shops, hotels and churches arose on Joplin creek, and the town of "Joplin" was born.   An impulse was given to the lead production of Missouri, which will not decline until the imports of lead from Europe to this country have been vastly reduced.

The area of the lead region comprises nearly 7,000 square miles. In the neighborhood of Jasper and Newton counties are large stores of zinc ores, supposed to extend into the Indian Territory. In the counties of St. François and Madison there is a fine vein of lead, of great length, "running at large" through limestone strata. Upon this vein are the splendid properties of the Mine La Motte Company. Most of the lead in that vicinity, and in Franklin, Washington, Jefferson, Crawford, Phelps, Dent, and other counties, carries cobalt and nickel in abundance, and not far away, brown hematite iron ores are found in profusion. The extension of the Iron Mountain and the Atlantic and Pacific railroads through the mineral regions has done more for the future development of the State than all other efforts put together.

In a few years both roads will be lined with furnaces and mines of all descriptions, and will extend branches in every direction. Several varieties of copper are found in the State, and the mines in Shannon, Madison, and Franklin counties have been worked successfully. New discoveries of zinc ore are daily made in all sections; cobalt, nickel, manganese, tin, and marble are also found. The Ozark marbles of Missouri are already famous; they aid in the adornment of the national capital. Excellent building limestones, coarse, reddish granite and various shades of sandstones, are to be found in all quarters.

But the iron and coal interests tributary to St. Louis dominate all others, and give the finest promise. It is evident that Missouri is about to enter as a formidable competitor upon one of the greatest industrial fields in the world. She has cheap food in a strong new country, rapidly receiving immigration. She has ores of surpassing richness lying close to the surface. She has coal in vast areas, easily mined—coal, too, which does not require coking before it aids in the smelting of iron ore. She has an economical system of inter-communication by river and rail, backed, we may hope and predict, by plenty of money in the strong boxes of the fathers of St. Louis. The time is coming when that capital, which has so long lain dormant, will be awakened, and turned into the service of the industry that in less than a generation is to make St. Louis a city with a million inhabitants.

The "Tracks"— Pilot Knob, Missouri. [Page 242.]

Here we are again at Carondelet —passing the long ore-trains hourly arriving from the Iron Mountain. What crowding, what noise and clang of machinery, what smoke and stench of coal! The workmen, with thick leather aprons about their waists, and gloves on their hands, are bringing the bars of pig-iron from the blast-furnaces, and cording them up by hundreds. Here is a crowd of perturbed Irish laborers, shrieking and dancing around a prostrate man, whose limbs have been scarred and seared by a sudden spurt of hot iron from the furnace. His comrades are bending over him, eagerly cutting away his garments with their knives, while the iron burns its way into his flesh.

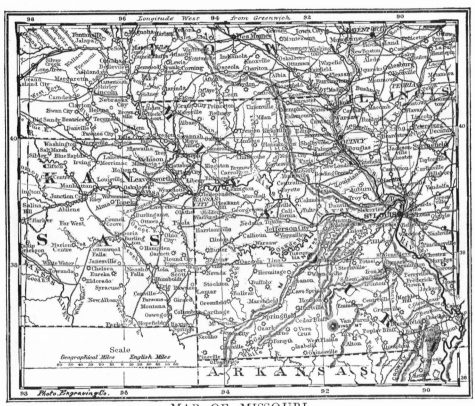

MAP OF MISSOURI.

XXV.

TRADE IN ST. LOUIS—THE PRESS—KANSAS CITY—ALONG THE MISSISSIPPI—THE CAPITAL.

Fᴿᴼᴹ Carondelet we may return cityward by another route, climbing the hill which leads to Grand avenue, and wandering up a country road to a vineyard, and a "garden-close" among beautiful shrubbery. The hills around are covered with vineyards, or rich fields of corn and other cereals. Returning to Grand avenue, you may drive through the new "Tower Grove" park, with its

View in Shaw's Garden—St. Louis.

pretty arbors, rustic houses, and clumps of trees; past Lafayette park, much like one of the great squares in the West End of London, and, rattling through street after street, lined with elegant houses, descend at last toward the banks of the river and the business section of the town.

Although the suburbs of St. Louis are not remarkable, there are many attractive parks and parklets near at hand. The superb botanical garden known as "Shaw's," adjoining the "Tower Grove" park, is the especial pride of Missouri. The Forest park, containing fourteen hundred acres, clothed in delicious foliage, dotted with elms, oak, ash and sycamores, festooned with grape-vines, and watered by the capricious little *Rivière des Pères*, is not as yet improved, but will doubtless be the principal recreation ground of the city in time. Lindell, Belmont, and the Park of Fruits, are all beautiful; and the park upon which the famous St. Louis fair is annually held has many lovely winding walks, garden-spots, and knots of shrubbery.

To this fair-ground every October many thousands of visitors flock from the whole Mississippi valley; and the vast amphitheatre, which will seat twenty-five thousand people, is daily crowded by a constantly changing audience. St. Louis worships annually one day at the shrine of this fair, which is mechanical as well as agricultural in its scope. All business is suspended; schools are closed, and a species of high carnival is inaugurated. Inside the amphitheatre there is a huge procession of horses, cattle, sheep, and swine, at which the good burghers look on something after the fashion of ancient Romans at the Coliseum.

The stranger will do well to wander the whole city over—dine at Porcher's, and loiter in the pleasant parlors of the "University Club;" to attend the concerts at Uhrig's, and the mass in the old cathedral; inspect the plafonds and other gorgeous splendors of the palace in which the St. Louis Life Insurance Company transacts its business; see Benton on his pedestal in Lafayette park; and visit the burial grounds of beautiful Bellefontaine. He may dive into the great vaults of the Imperial Wine Company, where a million bottles of native champagne lie always cooling; or do reverence to the Water Works, where two powerful engines each force the Mississippi river to contribute seventeen million gallons daily to supply the wants of the city; or have a peep at the prisons of the "Four Courts," and even be a looker-on at the matinee, locally known as "The Terrible Court," where a police judge dispenses justice, sends vagrants to the workhouse for a thousand days, and suspicious charac-ters across the river in twenty minutes. Or he may explore the score of mam-moth foundries, where iron is manu-factured in every form, from gas-piping to architectural work for houses; or

Statue to Thomas H. Benton, in Lafayette Park.

gaze at the dome of the imposing Court-House,—a kind of miniature "St. Paul's,"—or climb the hill at the city's back, on which the ungainly Lunatic Asylum stands. Or he may visit the First Presbyterian and Christ churches; or inspect the Gratiot street prison, where many sympathizers with the cause of the South were confined during the late war. But after all this, he may look about and be surprised to find that a city of four hundred and fifty thousand inhabitants cannot boast a first-class theatre,* and is compelled to

The "Four Courts" Building—St. Louis. [Page 247.]

have its opera season in a second-rate variety hall.

If one insists on being amused, however, he can read the editorial columns of the leading newspapers, and note the playful animosity which evidently guides the editorial pens, getting a lesson or two, meanwhile, in journalism; for St. Louis is as rich in journals as it is poor in theatres,— *The Democrat, The Republican, The Globe,* and *The Times* all showing admirably equipped establishments. The *Republican* building is one of the most elegant and complete newspaper offices in the world; there is but one in the country which equals it, and that is in New York. *The Democrat* is a Republican journal, and *The Republican* is Democratic.

The first number of *The Republican* was issued in 1808, as *The Gazette,* printed on a rude press of Western manufacture. It has twice arisen, an untiring phœnix, from the ruins of great fires. Mr. Knapp, its editor, was always an opponent of secession, although strictly his paper might now be classed as an opposition sheet. *The Democrat* was an early advocate of free soil principles, and a stout defender of the new Republican party in the troublesome times following the election of Buchanan. It is now ably managed by George W. Fishback, one of the leading journalists of the West. *The Globe* grew out of a division of interests in *The Democrat;*

The Gratiot Street Prison—St. Louis. [Page 247.]

both it and *The Times* have grown up handsomely. *The Dispatch* and *The Journal* are evening papers, respectively Democratic and Republican. The

---

* There are several theatrical buildings, but there is no regularly organized theatre.

religious and literary press of the city numbers several able periodicals, among which is *The Southern Review*, a quarterly of national reputation.

The higher intellectual life in St. Louis is not apparently so vigorous as that of many of the Eastern cities. The nature of its population prevents a large and symmetrical growth at present in that direction. A great portion of that population is either foreign born, or in the transition from the old to the new nationality; and the material growth of the city and the neighboring country is so "fierce and vast"* that people have little time for abstractions, or for the graces and culture which come with literature and art. There are one or two promising artists, and Mr. Diehl and Mr. Pattison have done some good work.

It has been said that no course of lectures has ever paid in St. Louis; this seems astonishing, if, indeed, it be the fact. The libraries are numerous and good. The Mercantile is the largest, and its spacious rooms are adorned with statues by Miss Hosmer, and other sculptors of note.

Of course the city boasts many splendid interiors and almost princely establishments. It could hardly fail to produce them, with a dry-goods trade which, in 1872, aggregated fifty millions of dollars, and is steadily increasing at the rate of thirty per cent. yearly. Before the war the dry-goods business engaged but from ten to twelve millions. The retail trade of one dry-goods establishment in St. Louis now amounts to more than six million dollars annually, and there are two which boast a million, and four half-a-million each. The trade in groceries spreads over an

First Presbyterian Church—St. Louis. [Page 247.]

immense section, there being in this business three firms whose transactions amount to two millions each annually, and no less than seven which claim a million each.

The sales of sugar by one of the principal sugar refinery companies amounted to 32,000,000 pounds in 1872, and yielded the Government nearly $1,000,000 of revenue. The wholesale trade in hardware counts up several millions, and in 1871 seven wholesale firms reported sales varying from $600,000 to $150,000. More than one hundred million feet of lumber are usually on hand in the St. Louis markets. From five to seven million dollars are invested in leather manufactures, and the annual sales exceed fifteen millions. Three-fourths of all the sheetings sold in St. Louis are now manufactured in cotton mills in the Mississippi valley, and St. Louis herself has considerable capital invested in the manufacture of textile fabrics for her own market.

* See General Walker's preface to last Census Report.

The gain which the city has made since the war is shown by the statement that in 1860 the capital invested in manufactures there was about $13,000,000, while it is now more than $60,000,000. Fine churches, hospitals, and many worthy charities show that much of the profit from these immense businesses is properly employed.* In the local and municipal politics there are but few excitements. The Germans are not so readily welcomed in official positions as they once were, because a pretty liberal exercise of power had revived their feeling of nationality rather too strongly, and they were making German blood an overweening qualification for office.

Christ Church—St. Louis.   [Page 247.]

The true valuation of the property within the limits of St. Louis city is $475,000,000. The bonded debt of the metropolis is a little over $14,000,000; the floating debt is $543,669; the amount of cash and assets now in the sinking fund, $805,744. It is impossible in the limits of a work of this description to give an exact statement of the amount of trade, and increase in wealth and manufactures. I have endeavored merely to show how vigorous and substantial that increase has been. New industries are constantly locating at St. Louis, or in its immediate vicinity; and a persistence is shown in their establishment which augurs grand results. The history of glass manufacture there has been one of disaster for many years; it is said that a million dollars has been sunk in unsuccessful efforts to establish it, but at last St. Louis has the credit of an establishment which can produce plate-glass, said to be equal to the best of European manufacture.

St. Louis is, I believe, the only city in the United States which ever adopted the Continental method of licensing the social evil, and there has been a great battle recently fought over it, in which church, society, and the Legislature took active part. Mayor Brown, progressive and liberal in municipal matters, sided with the license system, maintaining that it was the only means to the much desired end—reform and control of the fallen. The money received from license fees was devoted purely to the furthering of reformatory measures. The Legislature was induced to consider the matter seriously, and St. Louis was finally compelled to relinquish a system which has been so much debated. Missouri maintains a State lottery, and that too has been somewhat discussed. It is honestly administered, but seems poor business for a State to lend its sanction to.

---

* These figures only serve to show the condition of trade in St. Louis in 1873–74; the growth and increase is so rapid that it is almost impossible to collect statistics one month which will be correct the next.

The Missouri river, flowing from west to east through the commonwealth, divides the State into northern and southern portions, the rich agricultural lands of which Missourians are so proud lying mainly north of the muddy, lazy stream. Where the river first touches the Kansas line there is, as has been already intimated, another instance of marvelous growth, still more wonderful, perhaps, than the progress of St. Louis.

Kansas City, the young colossus bestriding the bold and irregular bluffs on the southern bank of the Missouri just below the mouth of the Kansas, was, in 1850, a shabby town, vainly struggling upon the flats by the river side. It had once been a station for the wild "bull-whackers," who came to load their "prairie schooners" from the Missouri river boats; and even several years afterward it was graceless enough to be thus touchingly characterized by one of the rude men of the frontier: "There's no railroad west of Junction City, no law west of Kansas City, and no God west of Hays' City." During the war the forlorn and remote town suffered all kinds of evils; but in 1865 the Missouri Pacific railroad reached it. Then it sprang up! It is now the terminus of nine splendid railroads, which stretch out their long arms over Kansas, Missouri, across the great desert to Colorado, give direct connection with Omaha, Chicago and the North, and tap Texas and her newly developed fields.

The city seems to have sprung out of the ground by magic. Upon its scraggy bluffs, pierced in all directions by railroad tracks, more than 40,000 people have settled, and built miles of elegant streets, lined with fine warehouses, school and church edifices. They have bridged the Missouri, erected massive depots and stock-yards, fine hotels and many princely residences, and have two of the best newspapers in the North-west. They control the market from the Missouri river to the Rocky Mountains, have a valuation of $42,000,000, instead of the $1,000,000 which they boasted twelve years ago. The jobbing trade of the city alone amounts to $17,000,000. The aggregate deposits in the banking institutions in 1872 reached $72,000,000. Eighty railway trains arrive and depart from the crowded depots daily. During the last seven months of 1871, 200,000 cattle were received in its stock-yards. More beef is packed there than in any other city in the United States.

In the lower town, which lies down close to the Kansas line (a portion of it, indeed, being in Kansas), one sees throngs of drovers and cattle-dealers; clouds of dust arise in the wake of the bellowing and plunging herds in transit; there is a lively stock-market, where hundreds of persons are buzzing about from sunrise until sunset; and the railway lines through the streets are so numerous that a stranger's life is constantly in danger. Four great packing-houses have facilities for dressing 2,000 cattle daily; the spectacle within their vast interiors, where hundreds of grimy and bloody butchers dexterously rend the vitals of the animals, and convert their flesh into carefully cured and packed provisions, being as imposing as it is disagreeable. In 1872 more than 20,000 cattle and 120,000 swine passed through the hands of Kansas City butchers.

As the eastern terminus of the great Texan cattle roads of the West alone, Kansas City can become one of the largest cities in the West. It is a busy, bustling town, in whose streets the elegantly dressed business man jostles the slouching, unkempt farmer from the back-country; where the hearty currents of frontier rudeness meet and mingle with the smoothly-flowing and resistless streams of business civilization. Energy is necessary—for, when a new street is to be laid out, a bluff has to be leveled; the town has only been fastened to its place by sheer audacity and tremendous pluck. Thousands of Germans and Jews have settled in all the region round about.

The hard riding, hard drinking, blustering Missourian, who carries bowie-knife and revolver—the type of those adventurous knights who used to amuse themselves by crusading into Kansas, and committing "border-ruffian" outrages, is rarely to be seen; and when one of them finds himself by accident in the roaring, trafficking town, he feels so uncomfortably out of place that he immediately turns his horse's head toward the open country again. Where in 1860 there was nothing but a desolate moor, now stands a depot through which 1,000,000 people annually pass. In twenty years Kansas City will become one of the great manufacturing centres of the country.

The influence and mark of Southern manners have vanished from the north-western sections of Missouri. A new type has arisen, and swept out of sight those who prevailed "befo' the waw." The same remark may be made of St. Louis. Once a thoroughly Southern city in all its attributes, it is now cosmopolitan. In the northern and north-western portions of the State there are large numbers of New England people; the tone of society and manners is a curious mixture of Colorado and Maine. In some of the counties there is wild life, and the enforcement of law is rather difficult; but such counties are the exceptions. The Missouri farmers can never allow a court to try a horse-thief; they always give him short shrift. Popular justice is very healthful in many instances, and keeps down future rascality.

Population is the prime need of Missouri. The agricultural resources of the State are immense. The river-bottoms along the Missouri are as rich as the valley of the Nile. In journeying beside them on the Missouri Pacific railroad one sees immense spaces but recently cleared of forests, dotted with log-cabins, and barns and their omnipresent appendages, the hog-yards filled with dozens of swine; yellow corn-fields, acres on acres, extending as far as the eye can reach among the girdled trees; men and women cantering to market on bareback horses, and grimy children staring from the zig-zag fences.

The life is like the products of the soil, dusty and coarse; there is a flavor of corn and pork about it, but it is full of vigor. The country north of the Missouri river is rich, undulating prairie, watered by abundant streams. The Platte country is famous for hemp, grain, and superb stock; and, indeed, there is no section of Missouri which is not well adapted to stock-raising. The climate is so mild that there is rarely any necessity of shelter for stock in the winter. The State is covered with a network of small streams; the grasses everywhere are rich, and grain crops are unfailing. Countless swine, sheep and cattle now roam over the vast swelling prairies; the swine, I am sorry to say, roaming with equal freedom in the streets of most of the towns. Immense tracts of good land south of the Osage river—a grand section for vineyards, sheep-farms, and fruit—can be had for from fifty cents to five dollars per acre. The bottom lands along the Mississippi river are very rich, and are all capable of cultivation. The staple products of the State—Indian corn, wheat, rye, oats, barley, buckwheat, potatoes, tobacco, hay, grapes, wool and hemp*—grow luxuriantly and yield largely.†

The foliage of the Missouri forests is exquisitely beautiful. The timber-lines along the creeks, and the great woods, covering hundreds of acres, are alike charming. Even in sections where there has been no cultivation, one finds delicious lawns shaded by trees, as graceful and luxuriant as if the product of the care of centuries.

The sycamores and oaks are of marvelous height, sometimes measuring 130 or 140 feet, and on all the forest monarchs hang graceful festoons of wild grape-vines, the trumpet-flower, and many pretty winding parasites. In the south-east of the State are enormous groves of yellow pine, in whose aisles wild animals still stalk fearlessly. But the woodman's axe is rapidly annihilating all these beautiful sylvan retreats.

In journeying across the State along the line of the Kansas City and North-ern railroad, I found many little towns of the same unsubstantial outward appearance as those I had seen in South-western Missouri during our journey Texas-ward. The little villages seemed like those toy ones we play with in childhood, and were all of one general plan. "Saloon—Wines and Liquors" is always a conspicuous sign; and the hum and bustle of the town centres about the depot.

Such places are the outgrowth of the railway; but the older towns are more substantial and interesting. Lexington, Moberly and Mexico are flourishing communities in the midst of fertile regions. St. Joseph is perhaps the most attractive, as it is the largest, in North-western Missouri. In aspect it is a New England town, and is built on hills along the Missouri river—hills which slope gently away until they reach rich prairies extending over thousands of acres. The sum total of its wholesale and retail trade averages $25,000,000 annually. It has costly hotels, theatres, churches, residences, a mammoth bridge across the great river,—and 25,000 inhabitants. From St. Joseph a railroad stretches across the State to Hannibal, another thriving city.

But this is digression. These cities properly belong to the North-west, whose spirit they manifest, and whose manners and energy they represent. St. Louis and the country tributary to it, however, are Southern in interest, and must so remain. St. Louis will become one of the greatest clearing-houses of the South. Its interests are allied with those of Texas, Arkansas, the Indian Territory, and the Mississippi valley. Its rolling-mills must make rails with which to lay Southern railroads, and its capital must build mills in which to manufacture Southern cotton.

* In 1870 Missouri produced nearly 4,000,000 pounds of wool; more than 1,000,000 pounds of honey; sorghum to the amount of 1,731,000 gallons, and 1,000,000 gallons of wine.

† There are at present more than 150,000 farms in Missouri, and there is ample room for five times as many more.

Along the Atlantic and Pacific railway line must come a trade which will build St. Louis marvelously fast. Pierce City, Joplin, and dozens of other small towns, will become wealthy and important. Springfield, now pioneering in cotton manufacture, will be a great spindle centre, like Lowell or Lawrence.

St. Charles, the little town nestled at the junction of the Missouri and Mississippi rivers, looks charmingly picturesque seen from the high bridge over the Missouri. The houses are nearly all German in architecture, and their low, broad, sloping roofs are huddled into artistic groups. A few steamers lie at the levée, others drift lazily along the broad, sheeny tide, between the rich green banks. The pretty town is really older than St. Louis, for as *"Village des Cotes"* it was settled two years before Laclede visited the site of St. Louis, and was once the seat of the State government, before the legislators betook themselves to the rather prosaic Jefferson City.

Sainte Genevieve is another romantic old town, and a few venerable Frenchmen, lingering on the edge of these moving times, give many stories of the good old days when the trappers and *voyageurs* made it a rendezvous, and the people of St. Louis came there to buy provisions. They cannot comprehend the grand movement which has made St. Louis a metropolis, and left their village to its primitive quiet. They see hundreds of steamers and barges slip down the broad current, and it seems to them all a dream.

There are many pretty, and some prosperous towns along the Mississippi, on the Missouri shore, between St. Louis and the section opposite the Ohio's mouth. St. Mary's, Wittenberg, Cape Girardeau, are thriving settlements, indicating a vigorous growth in the back-country, whence come rough farmers, mounted on tough horses, to see the boats come in, to get the mails, and, mayhap, a little whiskey.

The Missouri Capitol, at Jefferson City.

Southward of Cape Girardeau begins the " Great Swamp,"—a magnificent wilderness, extending to the mouth of the St. Francis river, a region picturesque enough in its wildness and desolation as I saw it, when the giant stream had overflowed all the lowlands, and left nothing visible but a half-submerged forest. Cape Girardeau lies on a solid bed of marble, and is called the Marble City. New Madrid, a small and unimposing town in the south-eastern portion of the State, and on the river, was the scene of the colossal earthquake in 1811, when the whole land was moved and swayed like the ocean, and the tallest oaks bent like reeds.

There are but four States in the Union which out-rank Missouri in the amount of manufacturing done within their limits.   Those States are New York, Pennsylvania, Massachusetts, and Ohio.   It is true that Missouri and Illinois are so closely abreast that the supremacy is keenly disputed.   The rate per cent. of increase in Missouri has, however, been 394 since the war, while that in Illinois has been but 257.

There is an earnestness in the manner in which the Missourian declares his determination to place his State at the head of all others, which almost convinces one that he will do it.   The cash value of the farm lands in the State is fully four hundred million dollars, and is steadily increasing.   In 1872 the State produced almost one hundred million bushels of corn, nearly eight million bushels of wheat, and seventeen million bushels of oats.   So uniting agriculture and the rapid development of manufactures, Missouri has a wonderful future before her.

"The Cheery Minstrel." [Page 256.]

St. Louis certainly has considerably more than four hundred thousand inhabitants ; the citizens claim 450,000, and, indeed, it is not improbable, judging from the rapidity with which the currents of immigration pour into it and through it.   The people of Missouri have wisely left their capital in a small town, never entrusting it to the influences of a large metropolis, and at Jefferson City a legislature assembles, which is usually, though not always, up to the level of the State's progress.   Jefferson City itself is a prosperous town of seven thousand inhabitants, situated on the south bank of the Missouri river, 125 miles west of St. Louis.   It has been the capital since 1828, the seat of government having previously been rather peripatetic, making visits to St. Louis, St. Charles, and Marion.

The State-House occupies a bluff overhanging the river; the handsome residence of the governor, a crowded penitentiary, the Lincoln Institute, and the Court-House are the other public buildings. There is abundant and admirable limestone in the vicinity, and this alone, so well adapted to the construction of serviceable public buildings, may induce the Missourians to locate the capital permanently at "Jefferson." The Democrats have been for some time in power, and have distinguished themselves rather by a lack of progressive legislation than by any tendency to undo the advance already made.

The State withheld itself from the cause of secession, and the memorable phrase of Governor Stewart, in his valedictory in 1861, shows the independence and good sense of the masses in the commonwealth: "Missouri will hold to the Union so long as it is worth the effort to preserve it. She cannot be frightened by the past unfriendly legislation of the North, nor dragooned into secession by the restrictive legislation of the extreme South." To-day the best spirit prevails; old enemies work in the upbuilding side by side, and the animosities of the past are buried under the impressive and fascinating opportunities of the present.

The cheery minstrel, whose portrait our artist has given, makes music on the cars between St. Louis and the State capital. He is one of the celebrities of Missouri, known to thousands of the traveling public, and when the Legislature is in session, and the tide of travel is strong, coins many an honest penny, the fruit of much manipulation of harmonicon and triangle.

XXVI.

DOWN THE MISSISSIPPI FROM ST. LOUIS.

"O, starboard side!"
"Oo-le-oo-le-oo!"
"Nudder one down dar!"

THE roustabouts were loading sacks of corn from one of the immense elevators at East St. Louis into the recesses of that mammoth steamboat, the "Great Republic," and singing at their toil. Very lustily had they worked, these grimy and uncouth men and boys, clad in soiled and ragged garments, from early morning, and it was full midnight as we stood listening to their song. In their voices, and in the characteristic wail with which each refrain ended, there was a kind of grim passion, not unmixed with religious fervor. The singers' tones seemed to sink into a lament, as if in despair at faulty expres-

The Steamer "Great Republic," a Mississippi River Boat.

sion. But the music kept them steadily at their work,—tugging at the coarse, heavy sacks, while the rain poured down in torrents. The "torch-baskets" sent forth their cheery light and crackle, and the heat-lightning, so terrible in Missouri, now and then disclosed to those of us still awake the slumbering city, with its myriad lights, and its sloping hills packed with dark, smoke-discolored houses, beyond the river.

Toward morning, the great steamer turned swiftly round, the very spray from the boiling water seeming crowded with oaths, as the officers drove the negroes to their several tasks; and the "Great Republic" glided slowly, and with scarcely a perceptible motion, down the stream. The blinking lights of the ferries behind us faded into distance. We passed tug-boats fuming and growling like monsters, drawing after them mysterious trains of barges; and finally entered upon the solitude which one finds so impressive upon the Mississippi.

A journey of 1,200 miles by water was before us. We were sailing from the treacherous, transition weather of Missourian March to meet loveliest summer robed in

"Down the steep banks would come kaleidoscopic processions of negroes and flour barrels." [Page 259.]

green, and garlanded with fairest blooms. The thought was inspiring. Eight days of this restful sailing on the gently-throbbing current, and we should see the lowlands, the Cherokee rose, the jessamine, the orange-tree. Wakeful and pacing the deck, across which blew a chill breeze, with my Ulster close about me, I pondered upon my journey and the journey's end.

The "Great Republic" is the largest steamer on the Mississippi river,—literally a floating palace. The luxuriantly furnished cabin is almost as long and quite as ample as the promenade hall in the Hombourg Kursaal, and has accommodations for 200 guests. Standing on the upper deck or in the pilot-house, one fancies the graceful structure to be at rest, even when going at full speed. This is the very luxury of travel. An army of servants come and go. As in an ocean voyage, breakfast, dinner and tea succeed each other so quickly that one regrets the rapid flight of the hours. In the evening there is the blaze of the chandeliers, the opened piano, a colored band grouped around it and playing tasteful music while the youths and maidens dance. If the weather is warm, there are trips about the moonlit wilderness of decks—and flirtations.

The two-score negro "roustabouts" on the boat were sources of infinite amusement to the passengers.   At the small landings the "Great Republic" would lower her gang-planks, and down the steep banks would come kaleidoscopic processions of negroes and flour barrels.   The pilots, perched in their cosy cage, twisted the wheel, and told us strange stories.   Romantic enough were their accounts of the adventures of steamers in war time,—how they ran the gauntlet here, and were seized there; and how, now and then, Confederate shells came crashing uncomfortably near the pilots themselves.   The pilots on the Western rivers have an association, with head-quarters at St. Louis, and branches at Louisville, Pittsburg, and Cincinnati.   Each of the seventy-four members, on his trip, makes a report of changes in the channel, or obstructions, which is forwarded from point to point to all the others.   They are men of great energy, of quaint, dry humor, and fond of spinning yarns.   The genial "Mark Twain" served his apprenticeship as pilot, and one of his old companions and tutors, now on the "Great Republic," gave us reminiscences of the humorist. One sees, on a journey down the Mississippi, where Mark found many of his queerest and seemingly impossible types.

Our first night on the river was so extremely dark that the captain made fast to a shelving bank, and the "Great Republic" laid by till early dawn.   Then

The Levée at Cairo, Illinois.

we sailed down past the fertile bottom lands of Missouri and Illinois, past Grand Tower, with its furnaces and crowded villages, past the great cypress swamps and the wooded lands, until we came to Cairo, in Illinois, at the junction of the Ohio and Mississippi.   One broad lake spread a placid sheet above the flat country at the Ohio's mouth. The "Great Eastern" might have swung round in front of the Illinois Central tracks at Cairo. Stopping but to load more bags of corn and hogsheads of bacon, with hundreds of clamorous fowls, we turned, and once more entered the giant river, which was then beginning to show a determination to overflow all proper bounds, and invade the lands upon its banks.

An Inundated Town on the Mississippi's Bank.

When the rains have swollen its tributary rivers to more than their ordinary volume, the Mississippi is grand, terrible, treacherous. Always subtle and serpent-like in its mode of stealing upon its prey, it swallows up acres at one fell swoop; on one side sweeping them away from their frail hold on the main land, while, on the other, it covers plantations with slime, and broken tree trunks and boughs, forcing the frightened inhabitants into the second story of their cabins, and driving the cattle and swine upon high knolls to starve, or perhaps finally to drown. It pierces the puny levées which have cost the States bordering upon it such immense sums, and goes bubbling and roaring through the crevasses, distracting the planters, and sending dismay to millions of people in a single night. It promises a fall on one day; on another it rises so suddenly that the adventurous woodmen along the border have scarcely time to flee. It makes a lake of the fertile country between the two great rivers; it carries off hundreds of woodpiles, which lonely and patient labor has heaped, in the hope that a passing steamer will buy them up, and thus reward a season's work. Out of each small town on its western bank set too carelessly by the water's edge, it makes a pigmy Venice, or floats it off altogether. As the huge steamer glided along on the mighty current, we could see families perched in the second stories of their houses, gazing grimly out upon the approaching ruin. At one point a man was sculling from house to barn-yard with food for his stock. The log barn was a dreary pile in the midst of the flood. The swine and cows stood shivering on a pine knoll, disconsolately burrowing and browsing. Hailed by some flustered *pater-familias* or plantation master bound to the nearest town for supplies, we took him to his destination. As we got below the Arkansas and White rivers, the gigantic volume of water had so far overrun its natural boundaries that we seemed at sea, instead of upon an inland river. The cottonwoods and cypresses stood up amid the water wilderness like ghosts.   Gazing into the long avenues of the sombre forests, we could see only the same level, all-enveloping flood.   In the open country the cabins seemed ready to sail away, though their masters were usually smoking with much equanimity, and awaiting a "fall."

While we are gossiping of the river, let us consider its peculiarities and the danger of its inundations more fully.   Below the mouth of the Missouri, the great river takes a wholly different appearance and character from those of the lovely stream which stretches from Lake Pepin down; and some of the old pilots say that section of it below St. Louis should have been called the "Missouri" rather than the Mississippi.   The Missouri, they claim, gives to the Father of Waters most of the characteristics which dominate it until it has been reinforced

The Pilot-House of the "Great Republic."   [Page 259.]

by the Ohio, the Arkansas, the White and the Red.   The river is forever making land on one side, and tearing it away on the other, the bends in its course not permitting the current to wash both banks with equal force.   The farmer on the alluvial bottoms sees with dismay his corn-field diminish year by year, acres slipping into the dark current; yet the ease with which corn, cotton and sugar are raised in their respective localities along its banks is such that they willingly run the risk.   The pilots complain bitterly of the constant changes in the channel, which it requires the eyes of Argus almost to detect.   They say that the current might be made to bear more upon the rocky shores, thus avoiding disastrous losses of land and many "crevasses," as the gaps made in the levées by the encroaching water are called. The stream is so crooked that a twenty miles sail by water is sometimes necessary where the distance across the promontory, round which the steamer must go, is not more than a mile. Sometimes the current, tired of the detour, itself brushes away the promontory, and the astonished pilots see a totally new course opened before them.

The occasional inundations of the alluvial lands are so little understood, and the general course of the Mississippi is comprehended by so few, that a little idea of its progress downward to the Delta country may prove interesting.

At the junction of the Mississippi and Missouri rivers properly begins what is known as the Lower Mississippi, although the name is not usually applied to the stream until it has crossed the grand " rocky chain" or bed extending across its channel between St. Louis and Cairo. All below this "chain," in the Mississippi valley, is alluvium, through which the river meanders from one bluff to another —the bluffs being from forty to one hundred miles apart. Touching these bluffs at Commerce, Missouri, on the west bank, it courses across the valley, passing the vast prairies of Lower Illinois, known as "Egypt," on the east, meets the Ohio at Cairo, then strikes the bluffs again at Columbus, on the eastern or Kentucky shore. It skirts these bluffs as far as Memphis, having on its west the broad earthquake lands of Missouri and Arkansas. It then once more crosses its valley to meet the waters of the White and Arkansas rivers, and skirts the bluffs at Helena in Arkansas, flanking and hemming in the St. Francis with her swamps and "sunk lands." Reinforced by the White and Arkansas, it again crosses its valley to meet the Yazoo near Vicksburg, creating the immense Yazoo reservoir on the east bank, extending from the vicinity of Memphis to Vicksburg, and the valleys and swamps of the Macon and Tensas, on the west side. These latter have no terminus save the Gulf of Mexico, as the river does not approach the western bluffs after leaving Helena. From Vicksburg to Baton Rouge the river hugs the eastern bluffs, and from Baton Rouge to the mouth is

A Crevasse in the Mississippi River's Banks.

the pure "delta country," for a distance of more than 200 miles.

All of this valley below the rocky chain crossing the river channel lies lower than the high water line of this powerful current, and the efforts of men to stay an inundation seem very puerile. The valley is divided into several natural districts, one embracing the lands from the chain to the vicinity of Helena, where the St. Francis debouches; another from Helena nearly to Vicksburg on the east bank, for the Yazoo valley; a third comprises the country from the Arkansas to the Red river, known as the Macon and Tensas valley; a fourth runs from the Red river to the Gulf, on the west side; and a fifth from Baton Rouge to the Gulf on the east side.

Some of these districts have been imperfectly levéed; others have never been protected at all, and the general opinion is that when high water does come the fact that there are a few levées increases the danger of a complete inundation, as the stream, finding itself restrained, breaks the barriers which attempt to control its current. Under the slave system, the planters on the lowlands were able to guard against ruin by water by elaborate preparation and vigilance, which they cannot summon now; and it is believed that nothing but the execution of a grand national work by the General Government will ever secure to the delta that immunity from ruin so desirable for people already savagely stripped by war and political knavery.

Yet the inundations do not come with alarming frequency. In 1867 the lowlands were overflowed and distress ensued; and in this year, 1874, the confusion, distress, and trepidation have been terrible to witness. Starvation has stood at thousands of doors, and only the hands of the Government and charity have saved hundreds from miserable deaths. Below Memphis, and in a wide belt of country round about, along the bottom lands in the State of Mississippi, and throughout the Louisiana lowlands, there has been immense damage. In an hour the planter is doomed to see a thousand acres, which have been carefully prepared for planting cotton, covered with water two or three feet deep. The country round about becomes a swamp—the roads are rivers, the lakes are seas.

As the Mississippi valley, south and north, will in future be one of the most populous sections of the American Union, and as the great network of rivers which penetrate to the Rocky Mountains, and the mighty cañons of the *Mauvaises Terres* are so well adapted for commercial highways; as a score of States and Territories border on the Mississippi alone, why should not the National Government at once undertake the control and care of the stream and its tributaries?

XXVII.

MEMPHIS, THE CHIEF CITY OF TENNESSEE—ITS TRADE AND CHARACTER.

PASSING Columbus and Hickman,—two thriving towns on the Kentucky shore,—and the ruins of the fortifications on "Island Number Ten," an island rapidly sinking in Mississippi's insidious embrace, past Fort Pillow, now rounding bends which took us miles out of our way, and now venturing through "cut-offs," made by the sudden action of the resistless flood, we skirted along the vast desolate Arkansas shore, reached the third Chickasaw bluff on the Tennessee side, and saw before us the city of Memphis.

Memphis is the chief city of Western Tennessee, and, indeed, of the whole State. It has been well and widely known ever since the five thousand acre

View in the City Park at Memphis, Tennessee.

tract on the fourth Chickasaw bluff, on which the town now stands, came into the possession of Judge Overton, Major Winchester, and General Andrew Jackson, the original proprietors. From the river, Memphis presents quite an imposing appearance, stately piles of buildings running along the bluff, at whose foot stretches a levée, similar to those of all the other river towns. Opposite to it, on the west bank of the Mississippi, is the level line of the Arkansas bottom, whose lowlands are often submerged; and from a ferry station at Hopefield a railroad leads to Little Rock, the Arkansas capital. The streets of Memphis are broad, regular, and lined with handsome buildings; there is but one drawback to their perfection, and that is a wooden pavement, so badly put down, and so poorly cared for, that a ride over it in an omnibus

is almost unendurable. In the centre of the town is an exquisite little park, filled with delicate foliage, where a bust of Andrew Jackson frowns upon the tame squirrels frisking around it, or climbing on the visitor's shoulders and exploring his pockets for chestnuts. Since the terrible visitation of yellow fever in 1873, the City Government has made most extraordinary efforts to secure perfect drainage and cleanliness in the streets; and Memphis certainly compares favorably in this respect with any of its riparian sisters, Northern or Southern. On the avenues leading from the river toward the open country there are many lovely residences surrounded by cool and inviting lawns; the churches and school buildings are handsome and numerous, and there is an air of activity and thrift which I was not prepared to find manifested after the severe experiences through which the city has passed. Several good newspapers—the *Avalanche*, the *Appeal*, the *Ledger*, and the *Register*, do much to enliven Memphis and the highly prosperous county of Shelby, in which it stands; and the carnival in winter, and the cotton trade until midsummer, make excitement the rule. Those who fancied Memphis "dead" after the yellow fever's ghastly visitation are wrong; the number of business houses in the city has increased ten per cent. since that terrible event, the number of physicians, curious to note, decreasing in exactly the same proportion. The wholesale trade has been growing enormously, and the influx of population has been so very considerable, that Memphis claims to-day about 65,000 inhabitants. Great injustice has been done the city in former times by the false statement extensively published that, after Valparaiso and Prague, Memphis had the highest death-rate in the world. The cemetery on the Chickasaw bluff, besides receiving the dead of the city itself, serves as the burial place for the dead of all the migratory multitudes who toil up and down the currents of the half-dozen giant streams which bring trade and people to Memphis. It is quite probable, whatever appearances may indicate, that the death-rate of Memphis is no higher than that of any city in the central valley of the Mississippi. The city itself occupies a tract of three square miles. Opposite it is the centre of a district, one hundred miles square, east of the White and St. Francis rivers and west of the Mississippi, which has been for ages enriched by the alluvial deposits brought down by the mighty river. It is said that in this area there are 5,000,000 acres, each one of which is capable of producing annually a bale of cotton. This plain, says a local writer, "was the rich granary of the city of the mound-builders, once occupying, as suggested by the great mounds on the city's southern confines, the heights on which Memphis stands." North of the city lies the famous Big Creek section, the home of many opulent cotton-planters before the war, but now but little cultivated, and with many of its fine lands deserted.

Memphis is very near the centre of the cotton belt, and has an enormous supply trade with Arkansas, Mississippi, Western Tennessee, and Northern Alabama. The export trade of inland ports like Memphis, Macon, and Augusta has become so great that the railroads have accorded them very low rates. Much of the cotton once sent to New Orleans is now shipped directly across the country to Norfolk. The railroad system of Memphis is already very important—as follows: The Memphis and Charleston road extends to Stevenson in North Alabama, and connects with routes to Norfolk and the sea, as well as with those

running northward. It is at present under a lease to the Southern Railway Security Company, but it is expected that the control of the line will in time return to
the stockholders. Next in importance is the Louisville and Nashville and Great
Southern railroad, sometimes called the Memphis and Ohio. This line extends
to Paris, Tennessee, connecting thence to Louisville, Kentucky, and with the
Memphis and Clarkville and Louisville and Nashville roads. The Mississippi
and Tennessee road extends from Memphis to Grenada, a smart town in the
former State, and runs through an excellent cotton-raising, although thinly
settled country, for one hundred miles, connecting by the Mississippi Central
with New Orleans. The road to Little Rock gives connection with the network
in which Texas is tangled; and the Memphis and Paducah, only partially
completed, will give almost an air-line to Chicago. The Memphis and Selma
road is also begun. But the project considered of most importance by the
citizens of Memphis is the contemplated road from Kansas City to Memphis,
which would render the latter independent of and in direct competition with
St. Louis.

The cotton trade of Memphis represents from $35,000,000 to $40,000,000,
annually. Its growth has been extraordinary. In 1860–61 Memphis received
nearly 400,000 bales. She then had also an extensive tobacco trade, which the
war took from her, and which has never been returned. After the war, production was so crippled that there was but a gradual return to the old figures in the
cotton trade, as shown by the appended table:

Year.	Bales.	Year.	Bales.
1867–68	254,240	1871–72	380,934
1868–69	247,698	1872–73	414,955
1869–70	247,654	1873–74 up to April	398,637
1870–71	511,432		

The cotton received at Memphis comes mainly from Western Tennessee,
Northern and Central Alabama, the same sections of Mississippi, and Arkansas, as
far south as Chicot. The south-eastern portion of Missouri also furnishes some
cotton to Memphis. The market is made up of buyers from New England
and the Northern spinning element generally, and from Liverpool, Manchester,
and the continental ports. Nearly one-third of the receipts, it is said, are now
taken by foreign shippers. Of course most of those purchases go to Europe
via Norfolk, New York, or Boston, but one German buyer this season shipped
forty thousand bales via New Orleans and the Gulf. The character of the cotton
is such as to make it specially sought after by all classes of spinners. As a cotton-
port Memphis is independent of New Orleans, and this independence has been
recently achieved. Of the entire crop brought into Memphis in 1860–61 there
were 184,366 bales sent to the Louisiana metropolis: whereas in 1872–73 scarcely
25,000 bales were sent there for market. The prices are so nearly up to those
of New Orleans as not to leave a margin. The Louisville and Nashville road
takes a great deal of cotton northward, and the various packet lines to St. Louis, to
Cairo, to Cincinnati, Evansville, and Cannelton, carry many hundreds of bales.

There are so many lines that Memphis is never blockaded. As a single item of commerce, that of cotton is enormous, amounting, at an average estimate, to something like $28,000,000. It is calculated that the whole commerce of Memphis foots up $62,000,000 yearly. Thousands on thousands of barrels of flour, pork, bales of hay, sacks of oats, barrels of corn-meal, are brought in on the Mississippi river and thence dispersed. Besides handling one-eighth of the entire cotton crop of the United States, Memphis has thus far kept in food as well as in courage a very large portion of the half-discouraged planters of the South; her merchants having made great efforts to accommodate themselves to the new order of things. So changed are all the conditions under which planters labor, and so evident is it that the character of planting or farming must change a good deal, that the merchants themselves are beginning to doubt the real beneficence of the supply system.

Memphis now has a prosperous Cotton Exchange, and has had an excellent Chamber of Commerce for many years. Shelby county is rich. Its people were wont to grumble about taxes, but have at last become wiser, and it was even expected, at the date of my visit, that the Mayor, a Republican, would succeed in collecting $700,000 of " back taxes." Party lines are not especially regarded in city politics, there being a general happy determination to take the best man. The negroes have great numbers of societies, masonic, benevolent, and strictly religious; and one often sees in a dusky procession, neatly clad, the " Sons " or " Daughters of Zion," or the " Independent Pole Bearers," or the " Sons of Ham," or the " Social Benevolent Society."

Memphis has a banking capital of $2,000,000, which for six months of the year is ample, but during the cotton season is by no means enough. Her schools are excellent, both for white and black, and there is a State Female College in the neighborhood. There are numerous excellent Catholic schools, to which, as elsewhere in the South, those Protestant parents who do not yet look with favor on the free system send their children. For about a year the number of pupils in the public schools has been increasing at the rate of two hundred monthly. One-fourth of the children in the free schools are colored, and one of the school-houses for the blacks contains seven hundred pupils.

In the busy season, there are seven steamers a week from St. Louis to Memphis, and there are three which extend their trips to Vicksburg—a voyage of nine hundred miles. The Memphis and St. Louis Packet Company brings down about one hundred and fifty thousand tons of freight yearly, and carries up stream perhaps forty thousand bales of cotton in the same period. The gigantic elevator at Memphis, built on the sloping bluff so that next the water it is of the height of an ordinary three-story house, showed only its top floor, so high ran the Mississippi, at the time of my visit. From Memphis, steamboats run up the Arkansas and the White rivers, threading their way to the interior of Arkansas. There is a line to Napoleon, Arkansas, two hundred miles below; one to the plantations on the St. Francis river, and one direct to Cincinnati. The lack of confidence between merchant and planter sometimes causes a diminution

in amount of supplies forwarded; but the dull seasons are brief.* The manufactures of Memphis are not numerous; there are some oil-mills, a few
foundries, and steam saw-mills for cutting up the superb cypresses from the
brakes in the western district of Arkansas.

The yellow fever came to Memphis in 1855 and again in 1867, each time
having been brought by steamer from below. In 1867 it was quite severe in its
ravages, but was confined to the section of the city where it first appeared. In
August of 1873 it came again, and nothing stayed its course. Two boats arrived
during the month of August, the "George C. Wolf," from Shreveport, and the
tow-boat "Bee," from New Orleans, each with a sick man on board. These men

The Carnival at Memphis, Tennessee — "The gorgeous pageants of the mysterious Memphi." [Page 269.]

were put off at the upper levée, where there is a coal-fleet, and in front of what is
known as "Happy Hollow," not far from the remains of the Government navy-
yard which Memphis once boasted. It is a low, marshy place, which the genius
of Dickens would have delighted to picture, filled with shanties and flat-boats,
with old hulks drifted up during high water and then adopted by wretched 'long

* The writer desires to express his obligations to Mr. J. S. Toof, Secretary Memphis Cotton
Exchange, and to Messrs. Brower and Thompson of the *Avalanche*, for many interesting facts
concerning the city's growth.

shoremen as their habitations. One of the two men died before he could be taken to hospital; the other shortly after reaching it, and the physicians hinted that they thought the disease the yellow fever. For three weeks it was kept in "Happy Hollow," then it moved northward through the navy-yard, and suddenly several deaths on Promenade street, one of the principal avenues, were announced.

The authorities then went at their work, but it was too late, except to cleanse and disinfect the city. The deaths grew daily more numerous; funerals blocked the way; the stampede began. Tens of thousands of people fled; other thousands, not daring to sleep in the plague-smitten town, left Memphis nightly, to return in the day. From September until November hardly ten thousand people slept in town over night. The streets were almost deserted save by the funeral trains. Heroism of the noblest kind was freely shown. Catholic and Protestant clergymen and physicians ran untold risks, and men and women freely laid down their lives in charitable service. Twenty-five hundred persons died in the period between August and November. The thriving city had become a charnel house. But one day there came a frost, and though suffering too severely to be wild in their rejoicings, the people knew that the plague itself was doomed. They assembled and adopted an effective sanitary code, appointed a fine board of health, and cleansed the town. Memphis to-day is in far less danger of a repetition of the dreadful scenes of last year than are Vicksburg or New Orleans or half-a-dozen other Southern cities. Half-a-million dollars contributed by other States were expended in the burial of the dead and the needed medical attendance during the reign of the plague.

This terrible visitation did not, however, prevent Memphis from holding her annual carnival, and repeating, in the streets so lately filled with funerals, the gorgeous pageants of the mysterious Memphi—such as the Egyptians gazed on two thousand years before Christ was born,—the pretty theatres being filled with glitter of costumes and the echoes of delicious music. The carnival is now so firmly rooted in the affections of the citizens of Memphis that nothing can unsettle it.

XXVIII.

THE "SUPPLY" SYSTEM IN THE COTTON COUNTRY, AND ITS
RESULTS — NEGRO LABOR — PRESENT PLANS OF WORKING
COTTON PLANTATIONS — THE BLACK MAN IN THE MISSIS-
SIPPI VALLEY.

A T Memphis I heard much concerning the miseries and revelations of both
capitalists and laborers in the cotton country. It is easy to see that the
old planters are in trouble under the new order of things. They are not
willing to become farmers. "These people will never," said to me a gentleman
familiar with the whole cotton-planting interest, "grow their own supplies until
they are compelled to." They choose to depend upon the West for the
coarse food supplied to negro laborers, and seem totally unconscious of the fact
that they can never secure white immigration, so much desired, until they raise
the status of the laboring man. White labor has proved a failure in a great
many sections of the South, because the laborers who come to make trial are
not properly met. They are offered strong inducements—can purchase good
lands on almost unlimited credit, and are kindly received—but they find all
the conditions of labor so repulsive that they become disheartened; and give
up the experiment. The negro along the Mississippi works better than ever
before since freedom came to him, because he is obliged to toil or starve, and
because, being the main stay of the planters, they accord to him very favorable
conditions. Self-interest is teaching the planters a good deal, and in the
cotton-growing regions of Northern Alabama and Mississippi, as well as generally throughout the older cotton States, a diversity of crops will in time force
itself upon them as a measure of protection.

It is noticed that cotton culture is gradually moving from the Atlantic sea-
board to newer and more productive lands. The States west of the Mississippi,
and bordering on that stream, are receiving immense colonies of negroes fleeing
from the temporarily exhausted sections of Alabama, and the lands which they
have left will soon come under the influence of fertilizers, and corn and rice and
wheat will be raised. In consequence of the gradual change in the location of
the planting interest, buyers from the North in such markets as Memphis hear
from time to time that less cotton is planted than heretofore, and are led to figure
on higher prices; but they find that new lands are constantly opened up, and that
the yield on them is surprising. It is the belief of many acute observers living at
important points along the Mississippi river that the ultimate home of the black
man is to be west of that stream, on the rich bottom lands where the white man
has never been known to labor, and where it would be perilous to his health

to settle. In the fall and winter of each year the migration to Arkansas and Louisiana is alarming to the white planters left behind. In Western Tennessee the exodus has not been severely felt as yet, but it will doubtless come. The two hundred thousand negroes in that rich and flourishing region are reasonably content. They do not, in the various counties, enter so much into politics as they did immediately after the war. They show there, as, indeed, almost everywhere in the Mississippi valley, a tendency to get into communities by themselves, and seem to have no desire to force their way into the company of the white man.

There must, and will be, a radical change in the conduct of the rising generation of planters. The younger men are, I think, convinced that it is a mistake to depend on Western and Northern markets for the articles of daily consumption, and for nearly everything which goes to make life tolerable. But the elders, grounded by a lifetime of habit in the methods which served them well under a slave *régime*, but which are ruinous now-a-days, will never change their course. They will continue to bewail the unfortunate fate to which they think themselves condemned—or will rest in the assurance that they can do very well in the present chaotic condition of things, provided Providence does not allow their crops to fail. They cannot be brought to see that their only safety lies in making cotton their surplus crop; that they must absolutely dig their sustenance, as well as their riches, out of the ground.

Before the war, a planter who owned a plantation of two thousand acres, and two hundred negroes upon it, would, when he came to make his January settlement with his merchant in town, invest whatever there was to his credit in more land and more negroes. Now the more land he buys the worse he is off, because he finds it very hard to get it worked up to the old standard, and unless he does, he can ill afford to buy supplies from the outer world at the heavy prices charged for them—or if he can do that, he can accomplish little else. As most of his capital was taken from him by the series of events which liberated his slaves, he has been compelled, since the war, to undertake his planting operations on borrowed capital, or, in other words, has relied on a merchant or middle-man to furnish food and clothing for his laborers, and all the means necessary to get his crop, baled and weighed, to the market. The failure of his crop would, of course, cover him with liabilities; but such has been his fatal persistence in this false system that he has been able to struggle through, as in Alabama, three successive crop failures.

The merchant, somewhat reconciled to the anomalous condition of affairs by the large profits he can make on coarse goods brought long distances, has himself pushed endurance and courage to an extreme point, and when he dare give credit no longer, hosts of planters are often placed in the most painful and embarrassing positions. So they gather up the wrecks of their fortunes, pack their Lares and Penates in an emigrant wagon or car, and doggedly work their way to Texas.

The appalling failure of crops in certain sections has not, however, lessened the cotton production of the region supplied from Memphis. In the aggregate it is greater than ever before, and I was informed that its increase would be even more than it is if so many planters did not "overcrop"—that is, plant more than they can cultivate. Those who plant a little land, and care for it thoroughly, usually make some money, even although they depend upon far-off markets for their sustenance, and are completely at the mercy of the merchants. It is believed that the crop failures will induce planters, in the sections which have suffered, to make an effort to grow their own supplies, and until that effort has been successful, there can be no real prosperity among them. Even when fortune smiles, and they make a good crop, but little is left after a settlement with the merchant. Life is somewhat barren and unattractive to the man who, after a laborious season spent in cultivating one staple, finds that, after all, he has only made a living out of it. He has done nothing to make his surroundings agreeable and comfortable; his buildings are unsightly and rickety, and there are very few stores in his cellar, if indeed he has any cellar at all.

The region which finds its market and gets its supplies in Memphis, Vicksburg, and Natchez, is probably as fair a sample of the cotton-producing portion of the South as any other, and I found in it all the ills and all the advantages complained of or claimed elsewhere. Imagine a farming country which depends absolutely for its food on the West and North-west; where every barrel of flour which the farmer buys, the bacon which he seems to prefer to the beef and mutton which he might raise on his own lands, the clothes on his back, the shoes on his feet, the very vegetables which the poorest laborer in the Northern agricultural regions grows in his door-yard—everything, in fact,—has been brought hundreds of miles by steamer or by rail, and has passed through the hands of the shipper, the carrier, the wharfmen, the reshipper (if the planter live in a remote section), and the local merchant!

Imagine a people possessed of superior facilities, who might live, as the vulgar saying has it, on the fat of the land, who are yet so dependent that a worm crawling over a few cotton leaves, or the rise of one or two streams, may reduce them to misery and indebtedness from which it will take years to recover! Men who consider themselves poorly paid and badly treated in Northern farming and manufacturing regions live better and have more than do the overseers of huge plantations in this cotton country. If you enter into conversation with people who fare thus poorly, they will tell you that, if they raise vegetables, the "niggers" will steal them; that if times were not so hard, and seasons were not so disastrous, the supply system would work very well; that they cannot organize their labor so as to secure a basis on which to calculate safely; and will finally end by declaring that the South is ruined forever.

These are the opinions of the elders mainly. Younger men, who see the necessity of change and new organization, believe that they must in future cultivate other crops besides cotton; that they must do away with supply-merchants, and try at least to raise what is needed for sustenance. There are, of course, sections where the planter finds it cheapest to obtain his corn and flour from St. Louis; but these are small items. There are a hundred things which he requires, and which are grown as well South as North. Until the South has got capital enough together to localize manufactures, the same thing must be said of all manufactured articles; but why should a needless expenditure be encouraged by the very people whom it injures and endangers?

There are many plans of working large plantations now in vogue, and sometimes the various systems are all in operation on the same tract. The plan of " shares " prevails extensively, the planter taking out the expenses of the crop, and, when it is sold, dividing the net proceeds with the negroes who have produced it. In some cases in the vicinity of Natchez, land is leased to the freedmen on condition that they shall pay so many bales of cotton for the use of so many acres, furnishing their own supplies. Other planters lease the land in the same way, and agree to furnish the supplies also. Still others depend entirely upon the wages system, but of course have to furnish supplies at the outset, deducting the cost from the wages paid hands after the crop is raised. Sometimes the plantation is leased to " squads," as they are called, and the " squad leader " negotiates the advances, giving " liens " on the squad's share of the crop and on the mules and horses they may own. This plan has worked very well and is looked upon favorably.

Under the slave *régime*, the negroes working a large plantation were all quartered at night in a kind of central group of huts, known as the " quarters;" but it has been found an excellent idea to divide up the hundred or five hundred laborers among a number of these little villages, each located on the section of the plantation which they have leased. By this process, commonly known as "segregation of quarters," many desirable results have been accomplished; the negro has been encouraged to devote some attention to his home, and been hindered from the vices engendered by excessive crowding. On some plantations one may find a dozen squads, each working on a different plan, the planters, or land owners, hoping in this way to find out which system will be most advantageous to themselves and most binding on the negro.

Clairmont, a plantation of three thousand acres, of which one thousand are now cultivated, on the Louisiana side of the Mississippi river, opposite to Natchez, is cut up into lots of one hundred acres each, and on each division are ten laborers who have leased the land in various ways. It was amusing, by the way, to note the calculation that one negro made when negotiating for one of these tracts. He was to be allowed one-half, but was vociferous for one-tenth. As ten is more than two, he supposed a tenth to be more than a half. On this Clairmont, in 1860, the owner raised 1,000 bales of cotton and 8,000 bushels of corn; now he raises about 500 bales, and hardly any corn.

Still, the conduct of the laborers is encouraging. The little villages springing up here and there on the broad acres have a tendency to localize the negroes, who have heretofore been very much inclined to rove about, and each man is allowed to have half an acre of ground for his garden. The supplies spoken of as furnished the negroes are of the rudest description—pork, meal and molasses—all brought hundreds, nay, thousands of miles, when every one of the laborers could, with a little care, grow enough to feed himself and his family.

But the negro throughout the cotton belt takes little thought for the morrow. He works lazily, although, in some places, pretty steadily. In others he takes a day here and there out of the week in such a manner as to render him almost useless. The planter always feels that the negro is irresponsible and must be taken care of. If he settles on a small tract of land of his own, as so many thousand do now-a-days, he becomes almost a cumberer of the ground, caring for nothing save to get a living, and raising only a bale of cotton or so wherewith to get "supplies." For the rest he can fish and hunt. He does n't care to become a scientific farmer. Thrift has no charms for him. He has never been educated to care for himself; how should he suddenly leap forth, a new man, into the changed order of things?

Nevertheless, some of the planters along the river near Natchez said, " Give the negro his due. The merchant will ordinarily stand a better chance of collecting all his advance from fifty small black planters than from fifty whites of the same class, when the crop is successful." But if the negro's crop fails, he feels very loth to pay up, although he may have the means. He seems to think the debt has become outlawed. In success he is generally certain to pay his "store account," which is varied, and comprehends a history of his progress during the year.

The shrewd Hebrew, who has entered into the commerce of the South in such a manner as almost to preclude Gentile competition, understands the freedman very well, and manages him in trade. The negro likes to be treated with consideration when he visits the " store," and he finds something refreshing and friendly in the profuse European manner and enthusiastic lingo of Messrs. Moses and Abraham. The Hebrew merchants have large establishments in all the planting districts. In Mississippi and in some other sections they have made more than 100 per cent. retail profit, and excuse themselves for it by saying that as they do not always get their money, they must make up for bad debts. They are obliged to watch both white and black planters who procure advances from them, to make sure that they produce a crop. If the merchant sees that there is likely to be but half a crop, he sometimes notifies the planters that they must thereafter draw only half the amount agreed upon at the outset. In short, in some sections the Hebrew is the taskmaster, arbiter and guardian of the planters' destinies.

Some of the elder planters are liberal in their ideas, and would welcome a complete change in the labor system, but they do not believe one possible. One of the best known and influential in the valley told me that he and his neighbors in the magnificent Yazoo country, where the superb fertility of the soil gives encouragement even to the rudest labors, had tried every expedient to bring new labor into their section, but could not succeed. His laborers were now practically his tenants; but he had to supply them and to watch over them, very much as he did before the war. He was willing to admit that the negro was better adapted to the work than any white man who might come there; but thought the younger generation of negroes was growing up idle and shiftless, fond of whiskey and carousing, and that the race was diminishing in fibre and strength. Those who had been slaves were industrious, and conducted themselves as well as they knew how; but the others, both men and women, seemed to think that liberty meant license, and acted accordingly. They were wasteful, and there was but little chance of making them a frugal and foresighted farming people. Whenever they could secure a little money the ground in front of their cabins would be strewn with sardine boxes and whiskey bottles.

The planters in the lowlands of Arkansas, Mississippi, and Louisiana have been particularly troubled to get and keep serviceable plantation labor; and are now importing large numbers from Alabama. In truth, the hundreds who flock in from the older cotton States were starving at home. On a plantation in Concordia parish, in Louisiana, opposite Natchez, there are many of these Alabama negroes. One planter went into the interior of that State, and engaged a hundred and twenty-five to follow him. They did not succeed in leaving without meeting with remonstrances from the colored politicians, but were glad to flee from an empty cupboard.

Densely ignorant as these negroes are, they are yet capable of fine development. They have sound sense, and some idea of manners, seem well-inclined toward their employers, and appear to appreciate their own defects. On many of these plantations on the lowlands the negroes do not vote; on some they are even hired with the distinct understanding that they shall *not*, unless they wish to be discharged. But sooner or later the politicians reach them, and they become political victims.

I took a ride one morning in this same Concordia parish for the purpose of conversing with the planters, and getting testimony as to the actual condition of the laborers. Concordia was once the garden spot of Louisiana; its aspect was European; the fine roads were bordered with delicious hedges of Cherokee rose; grand trees, moss-hung and fantastic in foliage, grew along the green banks of a lovely lake; every few miles a picturesque grouping of coarsely thatched roofs marked negro "quarters," and near by gleamed the roof of some planter's mansion. In this parish there was no law and but little order—save such as the inhabitants chose to maintain. The negroes whom I met on the road were nearly all armed, most of them carrying a rifle over their shoulders, or balanced on the backs of the mules they were riding. Affrays among the negroes are very common throughout that region; but, unless the provocation has been very great, they rarely kill a white man.

In a trip of perhaps ten miles I passed through several once prosperous plantations, and made special inquiries as to their present condition. Upon one where six hundred bales of cotton were annually produced under slave culture, the average annual yield is now but two hundred and fifty; on another the yearly average had fallen from one thousand to three hundred bales; and on two others which together gave the market fifteen hundred bales every year, now barely six hundred are raised. The planters in this section thought that cotton production had fallen off fully two-thirds. The number of negroes at work on each of these plantations was generally much less than before the war. Then a bale to the acre was realized, now about one bale to three acres is the average.

Much of this land is "leased" to the negro at the rate of a bale of cotton weighing four hundred and thirty pounds for each six acres.

The planters there raise a little corn, but are mainly supplied from the West. The inundation was upon them at the epoch of my visit, and they were in momentary expectation of seeing all their year's hopes destroyed. The infamous robberies, also, to which they had been subjected by the Legislature, and the overwhelming taxation, had left them bitterly discouraged. One plantation which I visited, having sixteen hundred acres of cleared land in it, and standing in one of the most fertile sections of the State, was originally valued at one hundred dollars per acre; now it could not be sold for ten dollars. In Madison parish recently a plantation of six hundred improved acres, which originally cost thirty thousand dollars, was offered to a neighboring planter for *seven hundred dollars.*

The "wages" accorded the negro, when he works on the wages system, amount to fifteen or sixteen dollars monthly. But few ever save any money; and this remark will, I think, apply to the majority of the negroes engaged in agriculture throughout the cotton region of the Mississippi valley. Still there are praiseworthy exceptions to this general rule. Enormous prices are placed upon everything, because of the cost of transportation. The grangers have accomplished some good in the cotton States by buying for cash and selling for cash, the object being to keep supplies as near the wholesale price as possible, and have already become a formidable organization there, having scores of societies, small and large, in Alabama, Georgia, Tennessee, and Mississippi.

While there is no doubt that an active, moneyed, and earnest immigration would do much toward building up the southern portion of the Mississippi valley, it is evident that so long as the negro remains in his present ignorance, and both he and the planter rely on other States for their sustenance, and on Providence never to send them rainy days, inundations, or caterpillars, the development of the section will be subject to too serious drawbacks to allow of any considerable progress. All the expedients, the tenant systems, and years of accidental success will not take the place of thorough and diversified culture, and intelligent, contented labor resulting from fair wages for fair work. Nothing but the education of the negro up to the point of ambition, foresight, and a desire to acquire a competence lawfully and laboriously, will ever thoroughly develop the Lower Mississippi valley. As the negro is certainly to inhabit it for many years at least, if not forever, how shall he learn the much-needed lesson?

On the other hand, the whites need to be converted to a sense of the dignity of labor, to learn to treat the laboring man with proper consideration, to create in him an intelligent ambition by giving him education. Something besides an introduction to political liberties and responsibilities is needed to make the negro a moral and worthy citizen. He is struggling slowly and not very surely out of a lax and barbarously immoral condition. The weight of nearly two centuries of slavery is upon his back. He needs more help and counsel. An old master will tell you that he can discover who of his employés has been a slave, "for the slave," he says, "cannot look you in the eye without flinching."

Neither can the ex-slave be very moral, if indeed moral at all. It is hard for him to bear the yoke of the family relation. Although conscious that he is a freeman, and can leave his employer in the lurch if he chooses, he is, here and there, almost content to slip back into the old devil-may-care dependence of slavery. The responsibilities of freedom are almost too much for him. He has entered upon a battle-field armed with poor and cumbersome weapons, weighed down with ignorance and "previous condition;" and I venture to say that no one feels the difficulty and bitterness of his position more keenly than he does himself.

Unable as he is to aid in his own upbuilding, it is to be considered whether there is not really more room now for educational enterprises, and for a general diffusion of intelligence among his race, by Northern and Western men and women, than there was immediately after the war. Might it not be wise to appoint commissioners to investigate thoroughly the labor question in the South, and to make a final effort to remedy its evils by every proper means? Events have shown that the National Government must undertake the improvement and the control of the Mississippi river; why ought it not to devote some little attention to the removal of the obstacles to immigration into the most fertile sections of the Mississippi valley?

A Steamboat Torch-Basket.

XXIX

ARKANSAS—ITS RESOURCES—ITS PEOPLE—ITS POLITICS.
TAXATION—THE HOT SPRINGS.

NEARLY two hundred miles below Memphis, at the mouth of the Arkansas river, and on lowlands which, when I saw them, were drowned and buried under the combined flood of the two great rivers, stands Napoleon, once a flourishing town, but now gradually slipping away into the stream. The only other towns on the Arkansas bank of the river, of importance, are Sterling, which lies at the mouth of the St. Francis river, and Helena, a rather thriving and vigorous community of five thousand inhabitants. The White river, which was the scene of much fighting during the war, comes down from the wilds a little above Napoleon, and pours its floods into the Arkansas. Napoleon did not have a good reputation in past days. Various anecdotes, not entirely devoid of grim humor, were told of it, as illustrating the manners of the town. It was at Napoleon that the man showed a casual passer-by on a steamboat a pocket full of ears, and, with a grin, announced that he was among the boys while they were having a frolic last night. Murder, daily, was the rule, and not the exception. Brawls always ended in burials. Even now-a-days there are occasional scenes, which end in furious free fights. A pilot on one of the up-river steamers one day went into a saloon where a group were playing cards. The bystanders laughed at the loser, and the pilot laughed too. Being a stranger, his laughter was resented by the loser, who pulled a bowie-knife from his boot, and made a desperate lunge at him. The pilot returned to his boat. But the river is yearly more and more closely embracing the doomed town, and the roughs, like the rats, will leave before the final engulfing comes. In war time, Napoleon was an important rendezvous for gunboats and other warlike craft; the United States Marine Hospital there had been seized by the Confederates when Arkansas seceded, but was recovered as soon as the Mississippi was partially opened.

These wild and weird forests and swamps bordering the junction of the Arkansas and Mississippi were threaded by the French as early as 1671, and the State now known as Arkansas was a part of Louisiana until the purchase made by the United States in 1812. It had a varying fortune for some time thereafter; was made a territory in 1819, then became part of Missouri territory, but was finally admitted into the Union as a separate State in 1836. Arkansas is in area one-sixth larger than the State of New York, comprising more than fifty-two thousand square miles. It is separated by Nature into two important divisions—the one comprehending some of the richest agricultural bottom lands in the world, the other containing vast deposits of valuable minerals. The mountain ranges, beginning in the south-western part of the State, develop into the Masserne range, and toward the north and east become broad, elevated tracts until they reach the Ozark mountains, which run from the vicinity of Little Rock, north and west, into Missouri. The often-repeated remark that "Arkansas is all swamp and backwoods" is an error inexcusable in one who travels so much as does the average American. There are tracts along the Mississippi which certainly are swamps, and will remain such until reclaimed by some general system of drainage; but they comprehend but a small portion

View on the Arkansas River at Little Rock.

even of the lowlands. Drainage is necessary both to render the land productive, and to guard against the spread of pernicious climatic diseases.* The lands which extend from Napoleon to Memphis on the Arkansas side form the nucleus of a mighty lowland empire. Drained, settled, and carefully cultured, they would produce almost incalculable wealth. The negro is the man for this work. He is adapted to the climate, and if he had but the ambition, could speedily enrich himself.

The Arkansas river journeys two thousand miles to meet the Mississippi coming eastward from the mountains of Colorado; and the entrance from it into the White river, near its mouth, is easy. The White river drains, with its tributaries, a large expanse in the north-western, middle, and south-eastern parts of the State, and renders the transportation of products easy and inexpensive. The Arkansas forms a superb water-way directly across the State, and into the recesses of the Indian Territory. It is navigable for several months in the year, and with needed improvements might be always serviceable. The Ouachita and its contributing streams drain that part of the State lying south of the Arkansas river, and the Red river gives drainage to the south-west. It would be difficult to find another State of which it can be said that of its seventy-three counties fifty-one are watered by navigable streams. The climate varies with the location, but none could be healthier than that of the romantic mountain region; more invigorating than that of the thick pine forests in the lower counties; or more malarial than are the undrained and uncleared bottom lands.

* "Resources of Arkansas," by James P. Henry.

Time was when a journey up the Arkansas river was not devoid of thrilling adventure; when the passengers stopping at Little Rock laid their bowie-knives and pistols beside their knives and forks, on the hotel table, at supper; and when along the river-bank could be heard the pistol-shot from time to time. Great numbers of outlaws from the older States came to Arkansas when it was first opened up, and, fascinated with the grandeur and beauty of the more elevated portions of the State, they remained there,—some to become honest and hard-working citizens, others to pursue their old callings of robbery and murder, and finally to die at the muzzle of a rifle. Wild life and careless culture of the soil, disregard of humanizing influences, and a general spirit of indifference, character-ized large numbers of the people; while others were as orderly, enterprising and industrious as those to be found in any of the older States. But the common-wealth has thus far been completely *terra incognita* to the people of the North and East. No railroads, up to a very recent date, have penetrated its fertile lands; river navigation has been tedious and unattractive; and the stories, more or less exaggerated, told of the sanguinary propensities of some classes of the inhabitants, were such a grotesque mixture of fun and horror, that civilized peo-ple had no more desire to go there than to Central Africa.

But now the most effective civilizer, the iron rail, has been laid across the State. The St. Louis, Southern, and Iron Mountain railroad has stretched an arm from the Missouri border down the Black and White River valleys to Little Rock, the pretty and flourishing capital of the commonwealth; thence through Arkadelphia, along the Ouachita valley, and across the Little Missouri and the Red River valley to the Texas boundary, where it connects with the Inter-national and Great Northern and the Trans-Continental. In other words, it has placed Arkansas on the direct high road to Texas, and opened up to settlement, on terms which the poorest immigrant can accept, good lands for raising corn and the smaller grains; uplands wooded with pine, and bottoms all through the Red River valley timbered with walnut, oak and ash, noble cotton lands, and a fine country for fruit and grapes. The wild grape grows abundantly in the forests, and to large size. Along the line of this railroad also are scattered iron, coal, kaolin, and clay in large deposits. That portion of the road extending from the Missouri border down was built as the Cairo and Fulton railroad, giving a through line from Cairo, on the Mississippi, to Fulton, on the Texas line; but it is now consolidated with the St. Louis and Iron Mountain road, which has recently completed its line from St. Louis to Little Rock, running through the range of mineral mountains in South-eastern Missouri, and uniting with the Cairo and Fulton route at Newport. In the White River valley there are some of the loveliest river bottom lands on the continent, where cotton yields a bale or a bale and a-half, corn seventy-five bushels, and wheat twenty-five bushels to the acre. This section of Arkansas is also admirably suited for the culture of tobacco and hemp, besides being an excellent fruit and stock country. Along this mammoth line of rail, nearly two million of acres, confirmed to the company by act of Congress, are now in market, and immigrants are rapidly settling at distances of five and ten miles from the railroad.

The Arkansas river at Little Rock is broad and noble, and here and there the bluffs are imposing. The town is said to take its name from a small rock on the west side of the stream,—the first one encountered on that side from the mouth of the Mississippi to that point,—so level is the alluvial. Some distance up stream, on the east bank of the Arkansas, stands Big Rock, a bluff of a little prominence. The river is handsomely bridged for the railroad's convenience, and Little Rock, since the iron horse first snorted in its streets, has had a wonderful growth. It is a handsome, well laid out town, containing 20,000 inhabitants; and one can see, from any eminence, hundreds of small, neat houses—the best testimonials to individual thrift in a community. The handsome but somewhat dilapidated State Capitol, the picturesque Penitentiary, perched on a rocky hill, the Deaf and Dumb State Asylum, the Asylum for the Blind, the land offices of

The Arkansas State Capitol—Little Rock.

the railroad companies, St. John's College, and St. Mary's Academy, are among its best public buildings. Many of its streets are beautifully shaded, and the peach-trees were in bloom on the March days when I visited it. The main part of the city lies on a high, rolling plateau overlooking the river; back at some distance from the stream is the arsenal and post where United States troops are still stationed, and near by is a national cemetery. Little Rock was for many years the home of General Albert Pike, the noted Confederate general and poet, and his mansion is pointed out with pride by the people of the State. There, too, lived for many years the original of the "Arkansas Traveler," whose story has penetrated to the uttermost ends of the earth; and there the negro has done much to increase one's faith in his capacity for industry and progress.

The colored citizens of Little Rock and of Arkansas in general, number many gentlemen of education and refinement. The Superintendent of the Penitentiary, the Commissioner of State Lands, the Superintendent of Public Instruction, some of the State senators, police judges, and many preachers of excellent ability, are colored men. Among these gentlemen are graduates of Harvard University and of Oberlin, and of many of the best Western schools. A large proportion of the colored people at Little Rock own their own homes, which are mainly in the third ward, whence two aldermen,—black men and slaves up to the war, but now worth from $5,000 to $10,000 each,—are sent up to the Council. At Helena and Little Rock there have been many noteworthy instances of progress among the negroes. This is not so common in the back-country, although some of the counties have colored sheriffs and clerks. One of the most intelligent of his race in the State told me that the negroes had, as a rule, a horror of clearing up new land, and that they had been a good deal hindered from undertaking cotton-farming by the lack of means to begin with,—this requiring quite an outlay. The large landholders, too, have generally been averse to selling land in small parcels. For these reasons the country negroes are mainly " hired laborers, working on shares, or tenants by ·rental, payable in produce." In either case the landlord often furnishes the supplies of food, seed and stock, and at the, annual settlement has the lion's share of the proceeds, the laborers making little more than their living for the· year. A very reliable colored man told me that if the freedmen of Arkansas had made less progress since the war than those of the elder States since emancipation, he believed it to be because the white population of Arkansas was also, in many respects, behind that of the other States, being more sparsely settled and isolated, without large towns, railroads, and other improving agencies. The educational societies of the North had comparatively neglected the State. Political commotions had been the rule ever since reconstruction, and the State was already bankrupt at the outbreak of the war. The Republican party, which came in with reconstruction, inaugurated vast schemes for " internal improvements," and to obtain means to carry on said improvements, funded the old ante-bellum bonds of the State as a pledge of good faith. This process, he thought, had resulted in a large increase of the State debt, the debt in onerous taxation, and the taxation in a high rental. The State bonds outstanding March 14, 1874, are classified as follows :

Railroad aid bonds.................................. $5,350,000
Funded bond, July 1, 1869.......................... 2,000,000
Funded bond, January 1, 1870...................... 2,350,000
Levée bonds.. 2,208,500
Outstanding insurance certificates.................. 1,600,000

Some manufacturing has been introduced at Little Rock, and the wholesale trade of the town is very large, although as no organized chamber of commerce yet exists, I could not discover its amount. At the close of the war it was only a small village, with little or no railroad outlet, and with a minor trade. Planters had been in the habit of bringing almost literally everything which they needed from Memphis; the idea of keeping supplies in the State had never occurred to them. Now the through route to Texas, the Memphis and Little Rock, and the

Little Rock and Fort Smith railroads give plenty of outlets, and are bringing the town considerable new population. The latter route, in which a good many Eastern men are interested, is not yet completed, and is in wretched financial and material condition, but it runs through a fine country, and, if ever finished, will develop the most interesting portion of Arkansas. The noble country along the borders of the Indian Territory needs developing : it is rich in minerals and in grand mountain scenery, but is now in semi-barbaric hands, and it will take a persistent effort to improve the tone of society there. Fort Smith is on the Arkansas river and the border of the Territory, has a population of 3,000, is a military post whence offenders from the Indian Territory are taken to be tried, and once had a very extensive Western trade, which has been taken away by the passage of the Missouri, Kansas and Texas line of rail within sixty-five miles of the town. Society throughout this section is said to be improving. My own opinion is that it will never improve much in the face of ignorance, whiskey, and weapons. Most of the deadly broils occur between drunken ruffians, whose only sentiment is revenge by pistol-shot, and whose chief amusement is coarse and bestial intoxication. The " Fort Smith road " runs through the counties of Pulaski, Vincennes, Faulkner, Conway, Pope, Johnson, Franklin, Crawford, and Sebastian. Conway, Lewisburgh, and Russelville promise to be important towns along the line, although the local business is thus far slight.

Over the 33,000,000 of acres in Arkansas are scattered barely 500,000 people, and the nature of their employment forbids the building of many large towns. The grade of intelligence in the interior districts, where they have never had schools, is much the same as in Eastern Tennessee. There are fewer churches than school-houses in the " up-country." The masses of the whites are ambitionless ; and even the most enthusiastic that I met seemed dubious about the State's prospects. The north-eastern current of immigration is wanted, and would do much toward reforming the State. Something beyond a rough prosperity in cotton-raising and whiskey seems to be demanded ; and the cultured people living in the larger towns are making special efforts to redeem the commonwealth from the bad name it has received. Certainly Little Rock's handsome development should do much to make one believe in the State's possibilities ; it has a flourishing library, a dozen good churches, several well-ordered banks, and fine streets ; society and schools are as good as in Eastern towns of the same size. But in the back-country !—there the prospect is very different. Little Rock, with its streets and gardens filled with azaleas, japonicas, China and peach-trees, the queenly magnolia, and the lovely box-elders and elms, is a striking contrast to some of the rude lowland towns near the river, or the log-built, unkempt settlements in the interior, where morals are bad, manners worse, and there are no comforts or graces. The Presbyterian Church South is the prevailing denomination at Little Rock, and Northern people worship in it, politics being eschewed. The schools are, of course, classified for black and white ; mixed schools having been nowhere attempted, or, indeed, demanded. The Industrial University at Fayetteville is to be a powerful institution, and the Judsonian University, located at Judsonia, in White county, is one of the hopes of the future.   Schools have been organized and maintained for a number of years in Fort Smith, Pine Bluffs, Helena, Arkadelphia, Dardanelle and Camden, and have been well attended by both white and black children.   The State Superintendent could not inform me how many schools were in operation in the community; inasmuch as he had to operate with only the semi-annual apportionment of $55,000 in State scrip, worth forty cents on the dollar, he could not make much new effort.   He admitted that but little progress in education had as yet been made in the remote parts of Arkansas; the thinly settled character of the region preventing neighborhood schools.

The vexed condition of politics in the State since the war has greatly hindered its development.   People complained a good deal of the manner in which the Arkansas Central (narrow gauge) railroad scheme was conducted.   This road is now in operation from Helena to Clarendon, and is eventually to be completed to Little Rock.   It traverses one of the best cotton-producing regions in the South. Its completion is hindered by the anomalous condition of affairs in the State, and by the various accusations brought against its builders as to the manner in which they obtained the money to build it with.   The Little Rock, Pine Bluff and New Orleans road now runs from Chicot to Pine Bluff, and will this year reach Little Rock.   The Mississippi, Ouachita and Red River road is intended to run across the State from Chicot, on the Mississippi, to Texarcana, on the Red river.   The Ouachita Valley road extends from Arkadelphia to Camden, and thence will connect with Monroe in Louisiana.   Camden is one of the largest towns in Southern Arkansas, in the heart of a fine cotton-growing section.   It will be seen that as soon as these projected lines are completed, Arkansas will be very thoroughly traversed by roads, and, with her splendid river highways, will find no difficulty in annually sending an early crop to Memphis and New Orleans.   Steamers can reach Camden from New Orleans coming up the Red and Ouachita rivers, and thousands of bales of cotton annually go to New Orleans that way.   But these facilities for communication cannot enrich the State so long as an appeal to arms by a discontented faction may at any time overthrow law, destroy order, and turn towns into camps.   There seems to have been, since the close of the war, the most bitter struggle between the different factions, sometimes resulting in bloodshed, and always in a paralysis of the State's vitality for some time after the combat.   The partisans in a State where the use of arms is so common as it is in Arkansas are, of course, violent and vindictive, and a good many lives are wasted in useless struggling to prevent those sudden changes in party sentiment which are inevitable..   When Governor Clayton was elected to the United States Senatorship, he was seemingly unwilling to allow his successor to take his office, for fear that he might change the course of the party.   So, recently, the Republican Governor now in office, having inaugurated his course by promising something like an honest administration, and by uniting around him the more reputable of the old Conservatives—in other words, by bringing politics, to a certain extent, back to their normal condition, and not controlling the intelligent property-owners by ignorant and incompetent office-holders—was temporarily ousted by the beaten candidate, who brought a formidable army at his back, expelled the rightful Governor, Mr. Baxter, and opened the way to a series of arrests and counter-arrests, which would have been laughable had they not been so disgusting to any one possessing a high ideal of republican government. It required the interference of the Federal Government to secure the reinstatement of Governor Baxter, and the would-be usurper, who had mustered at his back a Falstaffian army of idle and worthless fellows, retired only when the proclamation of the President warned him to do so. The re-establishment of law and order was followed by a popular vote on the question of holding a new constitutional convention. The election occurred in July, and the people of the State affirmed, by more than seventy thousand majority, their desire for a convention. Several important amendments to the constitution will, doubtless, be made; some of the elder Democrats have already manifested a disposition to return to the illiberal ante-bellum policy with regard to general taxation.

Taxes in the State now are nearly six per cent. The vicious system of issuing State warrants is pursued in Arkansas as in Louisiana, and with the same disastrous results. A stern reign of law and order for four years would fill Arkansas with immigrants; but a *coup d'etat* every four years will not be very reassuring. The Legislature should enact a law forbidding the bearing of arms, and should enforce it if possible. Murder is considered altogether too trivial an offense in Arkansas. I walked through the Penitentiary at Little Rock, and saw a large number of white and black criminals who were serving life, or long term sentences for homicide. A brace of negroes working at the prison forge were murderers; an old man, peacefully toiling at a carpenter's bench, was a murderer; a young negro, hewing a log, was a murderer; and in a dark cell, a murderer, stretched on his iron bedstead, was sleeping off the terrors which had partially subsided with the reprieve just sent him. The Governor had fifteen proclamations, offering rewards for murderers, flying about the State at the date of my visit. The day before I left Little Rock, however, a desperado was hung in the neighboring town of Clarksville, and it was thought that the execution would have a salutary effect on the lawless element.

The resources of Arkansas are, like those of all the other Southern and Southwestern States, as yet but little drawn upon by the resident population; and they are immense. Arkansas contains twelve thousand square miles of coal,* and a valuable coal-basin is situated along both sides of the Arkansas river. In Sebastian county there are veins from three to six feet thick. A lead belt extends diagonally across the State; the lead and silver mines in Sevier county promise much clay. Kaolin, gypsum, copper, and zinc are found in profusion, manganese, ochre, and paint-earths are to be had in many counties; and there are vast quarries of slate, whetstone, limestone, and marble. Iron ore has been discovered at various points; but the coal-stores are the great treasure, and must some time enrich the State.

The St. Louis, Iron Mountain, and Southern railroad has brought the Hot Springs, that famous Bethesda of the rheumatic and scrofulous unfortunate, within convenient distance of a Pullman palace-car. The staging is now eighteen

* Testimony of the State Geologist.

instead of eighty-five miles to this Bad-Gastein of America, which lies in a wild, mountainous region near the line of the St. Louis, Southern and Iron Mountain road. The hot springs issue from the western slope of a spur of the Ozark range, about fourteen hundred feet above the sea-level. There are now nearly sixty of these springs, new ones appearing annually. Their temperature varies from ninety-five to one hundred and fifty degrees Fahrenheit, and they discharge something like three hundred gallons per minute. Thousands of discouraged pilgrims flock to Hot Springs yearly, and return much recovered; while those who do not achieve a cure experience great relief. The town lies in a valley which follows the Hot Spring creek, and is very well supplied with

The Hot Springs, Arkansas.

hotels and neat but inexpensive residences. I did not penetrate to the Springs, but heard very powerful testimony in their behalf. It is expected, and, I think, desired, that the United States, which has a disputed claim to the " Hot Springs reservation," should succeed in getting possession, and making the valley a grand sanitary resort free to the people.

The forests of Arkansas offer the most stupendous chances for the development of State wealth. The yellow pine and cypress, the cedar, the cottonwood, the mulberry, the oaks, hickories, pecans, and ash, can be borne easily to market on the bosoms of the great currents near which they grow. There are still eight millions of acres of land belonging to the United States subject to homestead entry, and these are among the best in Arkansas. A decent State government, and the progress of education among the masses, would enable the State to leap into as wonderful a growth as that achieved by Texas and Missouri. But there is a great deal to do before that prosperity can be achieved.

XXX.

VICKSBURG AND NATCHEZ, MISSISSIPPI—SOCIETY AND POLITICS.
A LOUISIANA PARISH JURY.

THE journey along the Mississippi river from Napoleon, on the Arkansas
shore, to Vicksburg, the largest town in the State of Mississippi, discloses
naught save vast and gloomy stretches of forest and flat, of swamp and inlet, of
broad current and green island, until Columbia, a pretty town on the Arkansas
side, is passed. Below Columbia the banks of the river are lined with cotton
plantations for more than 150 miles.

Vicksburg, the tried and troubled hill-city, her crumbling bluffs still filled
with historic memorials of one of the most desperate sieges and defences of
modern times, rises in quite imposing fashion from the Mississippi's banks in a

Vicksburg, Mississippi.

loop in the river, made by a long delta, which at high water is nearly submerged.
The bluffs run back some distance to an elevated plateau. In the upper streets
are many handsome residences. The Court-House has climbed to the summit
of a fine series of terraces; here and there a pretty church serves as a land-mark;
and the remains of the old fort from which " Whistling Dick," a famous Confed-

erate gun, was wont to sing defiance to the Federals, are still visible on a lofty eminence. From the grass-grown ramparts one can see "Grant's Cut-off" in the distance; overlook the principal avenue—Washington street, well-lined with spacious shops and stores, and unhappily filled at all hours with lounging negroes; can see the broad current sweeping round the tongue of land on which the towns of De Soto and Delta stand, and the ferries plying to the landings of the railroad which cuts across North Louisiana to Shreveport; can see the almost perpendicular streets scaling the bluff from the water-side, and, down by the river, masses of elevators and warehouses, whence the white, stately packets come and go. There is evidence of growth; neat houses are scattered on hill and in valley in every direction; yet the visitor will find that money is scarce, credit is poor, and that every tradesman is badly discouraged.

The river is so intricate in its turnings that one is at first puzzled on seeing a steamboat passing, to know whether it is ascending or descending; at the end of the "loop," near the mouth of the Yazoo river, and at the point where Sherman made his entrance from the "Valley of Death," is the largest national cemetery

The National Cemetery at Vicksburg, Mississippi.

in the country, in whose grassy plats repose the mortal remains of sixteen thousand soldiers. The view from the slopes of the cemetery, reached by many a detour through dusty cuts in the hills, is too flat to be grandiose, but ample enough to be inspiring. The wooded point; the cross-current setting around it; the wide sweep away toward the bend, are all charming. The old Scotch gardener and sexton told me that twelve thousand of the graves were marked "unknown." The original design contemplated the planting of the cemetery with tree-bordered avenues intended to resemble the aisles and nave of a cathedral. This was impracticable; but oaks have been planted throughout the ground, and the graves were covered with lovely blossoms. The section of Vicksburg between the cemetery and the town is not unlike the park of the Buttes Chaumont in Paris. Grapes grow wild in the adjacent valleys, and might readily be cultivated on the hill-sides. A simple marble shaft in the cemetery is destined to commemorate the spot where Grant held his famous interview with Pemberton.

Vicksburg has acquired a not altogether enviable notoriety as a town where shooting at sight is a popular method of vengeance, and, shortly before my second visit there, three murders were committed by men who deemed it manly to take the law into their own hands. There is still rather too much of this barbarism remaining in Mississippi, and it has not always the excuse of intoxication to palliate it. The Vicksburg method seems not to be the duel, but cold-blooded murder. The laws of the duello are pretty thoroughly expunged in Mississippi, although I was not a little amused to learn from Governor Ames that the ultra-Democratic people in those counties of the State bordering on Louisiana refused in any manner to aid the authorities in securing duelists who steal out from New Orleans to fight on Mississippi soil, on the ground that the " d——d Yankees want to do away with dueling so as to make their own heads safe." Mississippi is a sparsely settled State, and in some of the counties life is yet as rough as on the South-western frontier. But that open and

The Gamblers' Graves—Vicksburg, Mississippi.

deliberate murder should be encouraged in a city of fifteen thousand inhabitants, where there is good society, and where church and school flourish, is monstrous!

Vicksburg was once the scene of a terrible popular vengeance. A number of gamblers persisted in remaining in the town against the wishes of the citizens, and having shown fight and killed one or two townsmen, they were themselves lynched, and buried among the bluffs. The town gets its name from one of the oldest and most highly respected families in Mississippi,—the Vicks,—whose family mansion stands on a handsome eminence in the town of to-day. Colonel Vick, the present representative of the family, is a specimen of the noble-looking men grown in the Mississippi valley,—six feet four in stature, erect and stately, with the charming courtesy of the old school. The picture which our artist has given of him does justice only to the fine, manly face; it cannot reproduce the form and the manner. Mississippi raises noble men, and they were wonderful soldiers, showing pluck, persistence, and grip. Nineteen lines of

Colonel Vick, of Vicksburg, Mississippi, Planter.

steam-packets ply between New Orleans and Vicksburg, and from Vicksburg up the Yazoo river. The scene in the elevators at the river-side, as in Memphis, is in the highest degree animated. Thousands of bales and barrels roll and tumble down the gangways which communicate with the boats, and the shouting is terrific. The railroad from Vicksburg to Jackson, the Mississippian capital, runs through the scene of some of the heaviest fighting of the war, crossing the Big Black river, and passing Edwards and other flourishing towns, set down between charming forests and rich cotton-fields.

Sailing on through the submerged country from Vicksburg was sorrowful work; every one was depressed with imminent disaster. We passed into the great bend, or lake, where, on Hurricane Island, lie the plantations formerly owned by the Davis Brothers,—famous for their wealth. The broad acres once known as the property of Jefferson Davis are now in the hands of his ex-slave, who, by the way, is said to be a miracle of thrift and intelligence.

Negroes were toiling in the mud at some of the landings, building ineffectual dams, around which the current of the great river, sooner or later, remorselessly ran. The white men, splashing along the overflowed roads on horseback, looked grimly courageous, and gave their orders in a cool, collected manner. The whole land seemed one treacherous morass; the outlook was very discouraging.

We passed several rude villages on the eastern bank, which had been built by colonies of negroes, who had fled as the floods came upon them. These blacks gain a precarious livelihood by cutting wood and growing chickens for passing steamers; they depend on the captains of the boats for their supplies of corn-meal, molasses, pork and whiskey, and are sometimes reduced almost to starvation when their natural recklessness and improvidence have resulted in empty larders.

At one of these primitive settlements, known as "Waterproof" (it was by no means proof against the water, however), there were once two negro preachers who were extravagantly fond of whiskey. As each desired to maintain in the eyes of the other a reputation for strictest temperance, some secrecy in procuring the supplies of the coveted article was necessary, and each made the clerk of the "Great Republic" his confidant. Whenever the boat stopped at "Waterproof," the preachers were promptly on hand, each one obtaining of the clerk a private interview, and imploring him to bring, on the return trip, a good keg of whiskey, carefully enveloped, so that "dat udder nigger" should not know what it was. When the clerk complied, he received at the hands of the grateful preachers thank-offerings of chickens and fat ducklings, and whenever he mischievously threatened to expose the reverend sinners, he would hear the frightened words:

"'Fo' de Lord, you's gwine to ruin me!'"

When the river destroys the land upon which the negroes have built a town, and tumbles their cabins and their little church into the current, they retire to the higher lands, a few miles back, or seek a new water-side location. They cultivate but little corn, and give much of their time to merry-makings, "meetings," mule races, and long journeys from one settlement to another. As we passed a little village where there were, perhaps, a hundred negroes, comfortably installed in weather-proof cabins, a passenger on the "Great Republic," who was a planter of the old *régime*, indulged in the following monologue:

"Thar's what they call free niggers. Thar's a change from a few years ago, sir. Them poor things thar are just idlin' away their time, I reckon; and you notice, they're mighty ragged and destitute lookin.' Thar's a d——d nigger a-ridin' a mule, as comfortable like as ye please. Not much like the old times, when they were all working quiet-like in the fields. Sundays yo'd seen 'em in their clean white clothes, singin' and shoutin' or may be doin' a bit of fishin', and at night, when the plantation bell rung, agoin' peaceful as lambs to quarters. Now it's all frolic. I reckon they'll starve. What kin they do alone, sir?"

Natchez-under-the-Hill, Mississippi.

"I hain't nothin' agin a free nigger," said a tall native of Mississippi bound for Texas, "but I don't want him to say a word to me. The world's big enough for us both, I reckon. We ain't made to live together under this new style o' things. Free niggers and me could n't agree." And the two spat sympathetically.

The negroes in the valley cheered the "Great Republic" as she passed; the swart mothers, fondling their babes, looked up and waved their hands, and some of the men doffed their hats, unconsciously retaining the respectful manner which they had been forced to observe under the stern domination of slavery.

The western bank of the river below Vicksburg, even to the Gulf of Mexico, is within the bounds of Louisiana. The eastern bank, to a point nearly opposite the Red river, is in Mississippi. The characteristics of the river-side populations in both States are much the same. The negroes in many of the counties are largely in the majority, and hold responsible offices. One of the prominent citizens of Natchez, who was in former days a man of large wealth,

owning several hundred negroes, was sitting on his verandah one day, when a negro with a book under his arm approached, and with the dignity befitting a state official, said to the Caucasian:

" I 's de century-man, sah ! "

He was the officer appointed to take the census for the county. He could not read well, and his chirography was painful, but he showed diligence and determination.

Grand Gulf, in Mississippi, is a pretty town, lying on romantic hills,

View in Brown's Garden—Natchez, Mississippi. [Page 293.]

whose bases are bathed by the great stream. A railway extends from Grand Gulf to Port Gibson, eight miles distant, and a thriving trade is done with the interior. The hills overhanging the river were advantageous positions for the Confederates in war time, and the Federal fleet of gun-boats shelled the town and its battery-crowned heights in 1862. Below Grand Gulf there are no towns of importance on either side of the river until Natchez, one of the loveliest of Southern towns, and without exception the most beautiful in Mississippi, is reached.

Natchez, like Vicksburg, lies on a line of bluffs which rear their bold heads from the water in an imposing manner. He who sees only Natchez-under-the-Hill from a steamboat's deck gets an impression of a few prosaic houses huddled together not far from a wharf-boat, a road leading up a steep and high hill, and here and there masses of foliage. Let him wander ashore, and scale the cliff, and he will find himself in a quiet, unostentatious, beautifully shaded town, from which, so oppressive at first is the calm, he almost fancies

" Life and thought are gone away ; "

but he finds cheeriest of people,—cheery, too, under heavy misfortunes,—and homes rich in refinement and half buried under the lustrous and voluptuous blossoms which the wonderful climate favors. Natchez has an impressive cathedral, a fine court-house, a handsome Masonic temple, and hosts of pretty houses. You walk beneath the shade of the China-tree and the water oak, the cedar and the laurimunda. Nowhere is there glare of sun on the pavement ; nothing more clamorous than the galloping of a horse stirs the blood of the nine thousand inhabitants.

There were, before the war, great numbers of planters' residences in the suburbs,—beautiful houses, with colonnades and verandahs, with rich drawing and dining-rooms, furnished in heavy antique style, and gardens modeled after the

finest in Europe.   Many of these homes have been destroyed.   We visited one or
two whose owners have been fortunate enough to keep them.   The lawns and
gardens are luxurious.   The Mississippian wealth of roses is inconceivable to
him who has not visited such gardens as Brown's, in Natchez-under-the-Hill, and
that of Mr. Shields, in the suburbs of the upper town.   I remember no palace
garden in Europe which impressed me so powerfully with the sense of richness
and exquisite profusion of costly and delicate blooms as Brown's, at Natchez,
which a wealthy Scotchman cultivated for a quarter of a century, and handed
down to his family, with injunctions to maintain its splendor.

From the bluff above this indescribably charming spot one can overlook the
plain of Concordia, in Louisiana, on the west side the broad, tranquil river, and
catch the gleam of the lake among the mammoth trees.

There are still many wealthy families in Natchez, independent of the war and
its abasements.   Here and there a French name and tradition remind one that
the town is of French origin, that D'Iberville founded it in 1700, and that
Bienville once had a trading-post there among the Natchez Indians.   There
that tribe, fire-worshipers and noble savages, passed an innocent and Arcadian
existence, keeping ever alight on their altars a fire in honor of the sun.   But the
white man came; the fire on the altars went out; the Indian was swept away.
Gayarre, who has written well concerning these Southern Indian tribes, says the
Natchez were the Athenians of Louisiana, as the Choctaws were the Bœotians.   A
hundred years after the Natchez had first seen the French, Fort Rosalie, on
the bluff,—its site is still pointed out to the stranger,—was evacuated by the
Spaniards, that the flag of the United States might be raised over it, and
since 1803 Natchez has been an incorporated American city.   It has no manufactures now; its trade depends entirely on cotton.   No railroad reaches it,
but a narrow-gauge, called the Natchez, Jackson, and Columbus road, has been
begun.   The adjoining counties furnish from five to twenty thousand bales of
cotton annually, which are shipped to New Orleans for sale.

Natchez was out of debt when it was given over to the Republican party, but
has acquired quite a heavy indebtedness since.   The negroes came into power
there in 1867.   The present Sheriff, the County Treasurer and Assessor, the
majority of the magistrates, and all
the officers managing county affairs,
except one, are negroes.   The Board
of Aldermen has three negroes in it.
There is the usual complaint among
the Conservatives that money has been
dishonestly and foolishly expended;
but the government of the city
seemed, on the whole, very satisfactory.   About a thousand children are
at school in the public schools, and
four hundred of them,—the colored
pupils,—have a handsome new school-

Avenue in Brown's Garden—Natchez, Mississippi.

house, called the "Union," built expressly for them.   Natchez had an excellent system of public schools before the war, and the "Natchez Institute," the original free-school, is still kept up.   The Catholic institutions are numerous and thriving.   A good many of the negroes, as in Louisiana, are Catholics.

One-half of the population of Natchez is black, and seems to live on terms of amity with the white half.   White and black children play together in the streets, and one sometimes feels like asking "Why, if that be so, should

A Mississippi River Steamer arriving at Natchez in the Night.

they not go to school together?"   But the people of Mississippi, like the people throughout the South, will not hear of mixed schools.   The negroes are vociferously prominent as hackmen, wharfmen, and public servants generally; but they do not like to leave the town and settle down to hard work on the worn-out hills at the back of the city.

On the bluffs, some three miles from the town, is a national cemetery, beautifully planned and decorated, and between it and Natchez stands the dilapidated United States Marine Hospital, and the grass-grown ramparts of Fort McPherson mark the site of a beautiful mansion which was razed for military purposes.   When its owner, a rich Frenchman, was offered compensation by the army officer superintending the work, he gruffly refused it, saying that he had enough still left to buy the United States Government.

The taxes in Natchez and vicinity are very oppressive, amounting to nearly six per cent. The State and county tax touches four per cent., and is based on full two-thirds the valuation. The railroad movement has, however, done something to increase these burdens.

Many of the Natchez planters own plantations on the Louisiana side of the river, but, of course, have no political influence there, and are dependent on the negroes for the local legislation necessary to secure them in their rights, and for measures to prevent inundation. I attended a session of a parish jury in Vidalia, opposite Natchez, and was surprised to find it almost entirely composed of blacks. The white planters with whom I conversed grumbled bitterly over their hard fate, and recounted thrilling stories of the exploits of carpet-baggers in their vicinity. From the tone of their conversation, it was easy to see that they believed these carpet-baggers had misled the negroes, who would otherwise have been well enough disposed.

The jury, whose office corresponds, so far as I could learn, very much to that of our county commissioners in the Northern States, comprised men of various grades of intelligence. One or two of the negroes were well dressed, and quiet and gentlemanly in their manners; the others were slouching, unkempt, suspicious in their demeanor, and evidently unfit for any public duty. The planters addressed them familiarly, stating their needs, and making hearty appeals to the common sense of the most intelligent of the number. As the inundation was rapidly invading all the neighboring lands, the negroes recognized the necessity of action.

At Vidalia I also met one of the prominent negro members of the Louisiana Legislature, Mr. David Young, a coal black man. When I first saw him he was addressing a row of his fellow-citizens, who were seated upon a fence in that nerveless, unexpectant attitude so characteristic of the lowland negro. As an election was about to occur in Vidalia, he was endeavoring to impress on the colored voters the necessity of electing reform officers, and indulged in some general remarks on the importance of a purification of Louisiana politics. Brandishing his ballots, he warned the listeners to vote for honest representatives; whereupon one ragged negro said sullenly:

"I's done gwine to vote to suit myself. Dave Young nor no udder man ain't gwine to tell me nothin' 'bout my vote."

Mr. Young then proceeded to explain to them that Northern sentiment was beginning to rebel against the misrule at the South, and that the colored voters throughout the State must be "wise in time." The listeners shook their heads suspiciously, although evidently impressed with what they had heard. As we drew near, and entered into conversation, Mr. Young turned his attention to us, and expressed himself desirous of a fair government in the State for both whites and blacks. While he gave his views, in plain but well chosen language, I noticed that the other negroes listened intently, making whispered comments on his remarks. They were far from friendly toward Young, as he was a candidate for re-election to the Legislature against a white man who had a notoriously evil reputation as a carpet-bagger, yet who had obtained the firm support of a majority of the negroes in the parish.

"We do not object," said one planter to me, as we left Vidalia, "to the presence of the negro in the parish jury, we complain because nine out of ten who sit upon the jury are ignorant and have no property at all, and yet are permitted to judge of what is best for the interests of property-holders.   We are often compelled to submit questions of vital importance to the judgment of irresponsible and suspicious fellows, who, because they are opposed to us politically, seem to think it their bounden duty to do nothing for our material well-being. But such men as Dave Young do some good.   They are teaching the negroes a little prudence and moderation.   I would rather have a nigger like David, than a white man like ——— " (mentioning the wicked carpet-bagger).

"Sah?"

XXXI.

LIFE ON COTTON PLANTATIONS.

DURING my stay in Natchez, one of the many gentlemen interested in cotton-planting on the west or Louisiana side of the river, invited me to accompany him on a tour of inspection. The rapidly-rising river threatened to inundate the lands on which hundreds of negroes had been expending weeks of patient care, and the planter felt it his duty to take a horseback ride over the trio of plantations under his charge; so we crossed the Mississippi, and rode twelve miles into the interior of Louisiana.

On the road, which led along the lovely banks of Lake Concordia, the planter chatted of some of the vexations by which he is daily beset, and spoke rather hopelessly of the labor problem. The condition of society, too, he thought very bad, and that it was an actual hindrance to the development of the section.

"Are the negroes," I asked him, "aggressive and insolent toward the white people?"

But as the planter was about to answer this question, we approached a ferry-boat, or barge, in which we were to cross an arm of the lake to the island on which my friend's plantations were situated. An old negro man, much the worse for liquor, was preparing to monopolize the boat with his mule-team, but held back the mules, and touched his hat with drunken courtesy as we came up.

"Stand aside, uncle," said the planter firmly, but very politely; "we wish to cross at once, and there is not room for us all."

"Yas, sah; yas, Colonel," said the old man. "I's willin' to wait on you gemmen, 'cause you is gemmen; but ef yer was no count folks, I'd go for yer. Ride in, Colonel."

When we were some distance from shore, the planter said:

"That old man made way for us simply out of deference to our social position. The negroes are courteous enough to us; it has been their habit so long that they cannot forget it. But they will kill our deer and steal our poultry and bacon, and we have no redress."

After an hour or two of journeying over rough roads, we came to one of the plantations. A host of negroes were busily filling a breach in a dyke which the treacherous water might sweep away if rains came to swell the already ominous floods of the Mississippi. A pack of hounds came yelping to meet the planter; and the black women in the cabin courtesied obsequiously.

We crossed the field, bordered by noble cypresses and oaks, stopping now and then to watch the negroes as they carefully prepared the ground which an inundation might, in less than a day, reduce to a hopeless wilderness of mud. Entering the house of the overseer, we found that functionary smoking his pipe and reposing after a long ride over the plantation. He was a rough, hearty, good-natured man, accustomed to living alone and faring rudely. I asked him what he thought of the negro as a free laborer.

"He works well, mostly, sir. These yer Alabama niggers that's workin' on our plantations now do well on wages. They make some little improvements around their cabins, but mighty little, sir. Ef politics would only let 'em alone, they'd get along well enough, I reckon."

"Do the negroes on this plantation vote?"

"I reckon not (laughing). I don't want my niggers to have anything to do with politics. They can't vote as long as they stay with us, and these Alabama boys don't take no interest in the elections here."

"What do they receive as monthly wages?"

"From ten to sixteen dollars. It costs us about fifteen dollars per head to bring 'em from Alabama. These niggers likes wages better than shares. We keep a store here, and, Saturday nights, most of the money they have earned comes back to us in trade. They're fond o' whiskey and good things to eat."

"What is the routine of your work on a large plantation like this, and those adjoining it, throughout the year?"

"Wal, sir, I reckon that's a long story. We don't have much spare time, and mighty little amusement. Wal, sir, the first thing we do, sir, we begin early in January, a few weeks after the old crop is all gathered in, to repair fences and clean out all the ditches, sir. Then we pull down the old stalks, and start the ploughs to throw quadruple furrows in the fields. Then we throw out the 'middles.'"

"What are they?"

"Wal, sir, we throw out soil at the sides so as to leave a slope bed of fresh ground to plant on, and loose earth to cover it with. If the spring freshet breaks on to this yer prepared earth, we've got to begin over again, and that makes the season very late.

"Planting begins about the last of March, or very early in April. Piles of cotton seed are laid along some ways apart on the field, and then the niggers sow it along the beds, a ton of seed to eight acres. Then it is 'barred off'— covered up, that means.

"Ez soon as the cotton stalks begin to peep up, 'scraping' begins. The hands weed every row carefully, and don't leave any weakly plants. That, and looking after the caterpillars, keeps 'em busy till July. Caterpillars ain't the only danger we have to fight against. Thar's a hundred others. Cotton's a ticklish plant to raise. You've got to watch it mighty close, and then the worms and the weather will sometimes ruin the crop.

"Between July and September we keep the hands busy, getting out baskets, and setting things in order; then we pile in new help, and for the rest of the season, employ three times as many hands as thar's in the fields now. Up to Christmas it's picking and ginning, and it's right lively, you can be sure."

From the overseer's conversation I learned that cotton-picking is done quite as thoroughly under the system of free labor as in the days when slave-driving was permissible; but that the "niggers" require constant watching. On many plantations where the yield is abundant, it is difficult to concentrate labor enough at the proper time to get the cotton into the gin-house the same year that it is planted. I have seen cotton-fields still white with their creamy fleeces late in December, because the negroes were either too lazy or too busily engaged in their annual merry-makings to gather the harvest. But on the large lowland plantations along the Mississippi, the crop is usually gathered early, and the picking is very thorough. I could not discover that there was any system of "forced labor" now in use, and I thought the overseer's statement, that a "good field-hand now-a-days would pick 250 pounds of cotton daily," was excellent testimony in favor of free labor. He added, however, that on many plantations the average hands would not pick more than 100 pounds per day.

The laborers were coming in from the field in a long picturesque procession. As it was spring-time many of them had been ploughing, and were mounted upon the backs of the stout mules which had been their companions all day. Some of the men were singing rude songs, others were shouting boisterously and scuffling as they went their way along the broad pathway bordered by giant cypresses and noble oaks. The boys tumbling and wriggling in the grass perpetually exploded into guffaws of contagious laughter. Many of the men were tall and finely formed. They had an intelligent look, and were evidently not so degraded as those born on the Louisiana lowlands. The overseer sat on the veranda of his house, now and then calling out a sharp command or a caution, the negroes looking up obsequiously and touching their hats as they heard his voice. When the mules were stabled the men came lounging back to the cabins, where the women were preparing their homely supper, and an hour afterward we heard the tinkle of banjos, the pattering of feet and uproarious laughter. The interiors of the negro cabins were of the rudest description. The wretched huts in which the workmen live seem to them quite comfortable, however. I saw no one who appeared discontented with his surroundings. Few of these laborers could read at all. Even those who had some knowledge of the alphabet did not seem to be improving it.

Late in the evening, as the planter, with his heavy cloak thrown about his shoulders, was reposing from the fatigues of a wearisome ride over the broad acres, a delegation of field-hands came to see him, all to ask favors of "de Cunnel,"—to get him to write a few letters, or to bring some tiny parcel from the town on his next visit to the plantation. The men came huddling in, bowing awkwardly, and stood with their caps in their hands as near the door as possible, as if ready to run on the slightest provocation. If I looked at them steadily they burst into uneasy laughter and moved away, while the black women in the door-way and on the porch re-echoed the merriment. Meantime the planter listened to one after another of the delegation. Charles, a black boy, six feet tall, and with sinews strong as steel, stepped forward to the flickering light given by the candles and the burning logs in the fire-place.

"Cunnel, I wish you read me dat letter, please, sah."

The "Cunnel" read it, Charles meantime standing erect, with his great arms folded across his mighty chest and the massive column of his throat throbbing with scornful emotion. There was a strange, baffled expression in his face; a look of contempt for his own helplessness which was painful.

The letter was common-place enough, reproaching Charles for having left Alabama before liquidating the pressing claims of certain swarthy creditors. Having, after some trouble, deciphered the letter's meaning, the Colonel said, gently but coldly:

"Stand aside, Charles. Andy, who is the likeliest negro from Alabama now on the plantation?"

No answer for a minute. Andy stepped forward into the light, looking first into the fire-place, then at the deer's horns over the mantel, then at the shining revolver on the rough wooden table, while his immense lips worked nervously, as if endeavoring to draw in inspiration from the air.

"Did you hear me, Andy?"

"Cunnel, I's a studyin', sah."

After having studied some time, Andy darted out without a word, and presently returned with three hulking black giants, who huddled together in the same helpless way that the first arrivals did. They held their shapeless felt hats in their enormous hands, glancing from them into the faces of the white men; then exchanging significant looks with each other, burst into the regulation laugh.

"Did the colored politicians try to keep you from leaving Alabama to come here with me, boys?" inquired the Colonel.

Intense surprise on the part of the negroes.

"No, sah; reckon not, sah."

"Did you vote in Alabama?"

"Yas, Cunnel; yas, sah, always voted, sah."

"Can you do better here than in Alabama?"

After mature reflection, the trio responded in the affirmative.

"Would you care to vote here?"

Hesitatingly, "No, sah;" whereupon the three negroes were dismissed into the darkness.

The Alabama papers at the beginning of the current year reported that the colored laborers were leaving that State in troops of thousands. They were nearly all *en route* for the cotton plantations of Mississippi, and on the Louisiana bank of the Father of Waters. Central Alabama appeared at that time to be undergoing rapid depopulation for the benefit of the richer lands along the Mississippi bottom. It was estimated in the spring of 1874 that Alabama had already lost from $700,000 to $1,000,000 in her labor element alone. How long the influx of the freedmen into Mississippi and Louisiana from the South Atlantic States and from Alabama will continue is uncertain. In 1873 Georgia lost fully 20,000 of her able-bodied colored laborers, and gained but little in white immigration to balance it.

The women and children on the cotton plantations near the Mississippi river do not work in the fields as much as they used. Rude as are their surroundings in the little cabins which they now call their own, they are beginning to take an interest in their homes, and the children spend some time each year at school. The laborers on the plantations in Louisiana have sometimes been paid as high as thirty dollars per month, and furnished with a cabin, food, and a plot of ground for a garden; but this is exceptional.

While supper was being prepared the master of the plantation apologized for what he modestly called the homely fare which, he said, was all that he could set before us.

"We are so far from town here," he said, "that we can offer you only plantation fare—rough meat and eggs, with bacon, a loaf of baker's bread, and some bottles of claret which I brought from Vidalia."

I ventured to suggest that on the plantation he had every facility for a superb garden, and to wonder that the overseers did not employ some of the negroes to cultivate a plot of ground that its fruits might appear on the table.

"Oh, oh," laughed the overseer. "Make a garden here; reckon it would have to have a mighty high wall; the niggers would steal everything in it as fast as it was ripe."

But I suggested that if each of the negroes had a small garden, which he seemed to have ample time after hours to cultivate, he would not desire to steal.

The Colonel smiled gravely, and the overseer shook his head incredulously, adding:

"These is good niggers, but stealing is as natural as eating to them;" and, with this remark, we were ushered into the supper-room, where two black servant girls ran nimbly about, bringing in plain but substantial fare, which our hard riding made thoroughly palatable.

There was no white lady on the plantation. The overseer and his two assistants were busy from dawn till dark, and when night threw its shadows over the great cypress-bordered aisles of the forest and the wide expanse of the fields, they dismissed the negroes about the store and the stables and retired to rest. But on the occasion of our visit we saw unusual activity. A violent storm arose while we were at supper, and the overseers mounted their horses and rode off in different directions to inspect the levées. Troops of negroes were dispatched in skiffs along the lake with hundreds of sacks, which they were instructed to fill with sand and place at weak points on the levées. All night they fought the slowly but steadily-rising waters, while my companion and I slept on a mattress on the floor of the overseer's room, undisturbed by anything save the sighing of the winds through the noble trees surrounding the house, and the clatter of rain upon the shingles.

With early morning back came the Colonel, pale and worn with a night of battle with the steadily-rising water, and, as he laid aside his heavy cloak, placed his revolver on the table, and sat down with a weary sigh, he said it was hardly worth while to try to be a successful cotton-planter now-a-days; things human and things divine seemed to conspire to make it impossible to succeed. I thought of his sigh and of his helpless look a day or two afterward, when I was told that one thousand acres of his plantation had been flooded and badly injured by the offensive policy of a neighbor planter, who had cut the Colonel's levées to save his own.

With daylight also, although the rain was steadily falling, the plantation blossomed into activity. The overseers had arisen long before the dim streaks of the dawn were seen on the lowland horizon; had galloped over many a broad acre, but returned gloomily, announcing that the land was too wet to work that day. The negroes slouchingly disposed themselves about the store and the overseer's "mansion," keeping at a respectful distance from the kitchen, where sat the overseer himself, surrounded by his dogs. Nothing more dispiriting could be imagined than the atmosphere of this lowland plantation over which imminent disaster seemed breaking. From right and left came stories of trouble and affliction. Here and there a planter had made a good crop and had laid

A Cotton Wagon-Train.

aside a little money, but the evidences of material prosperity were painfully few. The overseers, while doggedly persistent in working the plantations up to their full capacity, still seemed to have a grim sense of a fate which over-hung the whole locality, and which would not permit consecutive years of pros-perity and plenty.

There is still much on one of these remote and isolated plantations to recall the romance which surrounded them during the days of slavery. The tall and stalwart women, with their luxuriant wool carefully wrapped in gayly-colored handkerchiefs; the picturesque and tattered children, who have not the slightest particle of education, and who have not been reached even since the era of re-construction, by the influences of schools and teachers; the groups of venerable darkeys, with their gray slouch hats and impossible garments, who chatter for hours together on the sunny side of some out-buildings, and the merry-makings at night, all recall a period which, the planter will tell you, with a mournful look, comprised the halcyon days of Louisiana.

The thing which struck me as most astonishing here, in the cotton-lands, as on the rice plantations of South Carolina, was the absolute subjection of the negro. Those with whom I talked would not directly express any idea. They gave a shuffling and grimacing assent to whatever was suggested ; or, if they dissented, would beg to be excused from differing verbally, and seemed to be much distressed at being required to express their opinions openly. Of course, having the most absolute political liberty, because in that section they were so largely in the majority, numerically, that no intimidation could have been practiced, it seemed astonishing that they should be willing to forego the right to vote, and to willingly isolate themselves from their fellows. I could not discover that any of the negroes were making a definite progress, either manifested by a subscription to some newspaper or by a tendency to discussion ; and, while the planter gave me the fullest and freest account of the social status of the negroes employed by him, he failed to mention any sign of a definite and intellectual growth. The only really encouraging sign in their social life was the tendency to create for themselves homes, and now and then to cultivate the land about them.

The rain continued to fall in torrents as we rode across the island along the muddy roads, under the great arches of the cypress-trees, on our return to Natchez. Here and there a few negroes were desperately striving afield, endeavoring to effect something in spite of the storm ; but the planter shook his head gravely, and said that all agricultural operations must now be two months later than usual. The lack of concerted operations among the planters against the inroads of the floods, and the disastrous consequences of an incompetent labor system, were, to his thinking, effectual drawbacks to much material progress for a long time. In a previous chapter I have shown how the production of Concordia parish has fallen off since slavery was abolished ; and he could not give any encouragement to my hope that this wretched state of affairs would soon be changed.

At last we reached the arm of the lake where we expected to find our sable ferry-man, but the rain had washed the waters into quite a fury, and we could see neither ferry-man nor barge. Half-an-hour's hallooing at last brought the old man from his cabin on the opposite side, and another half hour brought him, dripping wet, with the gray wool of his beard glistening with rain-drops, to the shore on which we stood. He complained bitterly of his poverty, yet I was surprised to learn that each time the Colonel visited his plantation he paid this venerable boatman a dollar for his ride across the lake. Although I diligently endeavored to enter into conversation with the aged black man, he steadily avoided any reference to political topics, and assumed a look of blank amazement when I appealed to him for a direct opinion. But he was always civil, courteous to a degree not discoverable among people in his rank of life in the North. His character swayed and bent before any aggression, but did not break ; it was as stubborn as elastic.

In the forest through which ran the road leading to the Colonel's plantation, we met a brown man mounted on a stout horse, and loaded down with a small armory of fire-arms, in addition to which he carried a long knife and a hatchet, evidently intended for dissecting some deer.

"Ha!" said the Colonel pleasantly, yet with a touch of annoyance in his voice, "so you are going poaching on my land again? There will soon be no deer left."

"Yas, Cunnel," said the fellow, impudently shifting his long rifle from his right to his left shoulder. "I reckon ef I see any deer I's gwine to go for 'em, sho;" then, putting spurs to his steed, he galloped off.

There was no redress, and the Colonel was compelled to submit anew to the plundering of his preserves.

Driving homeward with my artist companion, the Colonel having left us to return to his fight with the levées, we were struck with the picturesque clusters of negro cabins by the wayside. Nowhere else in the agricultural regions of the South had we perceived such a tendency to an artistic grouping of buildings. Along the road, which was now so covered with water that we could hardly pick our way, a few uproarious negroes, with whiskey bottles protruding from their pockets, were picking their dubious way. As we approached they saluted us, touching their hats with sudden dignity. Everywhere in this lowland region we found the negro courteous more from habit than from desire. Even when he fell into the sullen silence which marks his supremest dissent, he was deferential and polite to a degree which made that silence all the more exasperating. I have never in my life seen a more gracious and civil personage than the weather-stained and tattered old negro who stood on a shelving bank by the lake-side, and carefully pointed out to us the best spots in the submerged road, as we drove through the little village of which he was an inhabitant.

A Cotton-Steamer.

The local river packets, which depend mainly upon the commerce of the cotton plantations between Vicksburg and New Orleans, are the only means which the planters possess of communication with the outer world. The arrivals of the "Robert E. Lee," or of the "Natchez," at the plantation landings, always furnish picturesque and interesting scenes. We had occasion to journey from Natchez to Vicksburg, departing from the former town late at night. The negro hackman who was to transport us from the upper town to Natchez-under-the-Hill for the moderate sum of three dollars, bade us remain quietly in our rooms until "de Lee whistled." So, toward midnight, hearing the three hoarse yells from the colossal steam-pipes of the Robert E. Lee, we were hurried down to the great wharf-boat, where we found a motley crowd of negro men and women, of sickly, ague-stricken, poor whites, and smartly-dressed planters, whose immaculate linen and rich garments betrayed but little of the poverty and anxiety now afflicting the whole section.

Presently, out of the gloom which shrouded the great river, a giant shape seemed slowly approaching, and while we were endeavoring to discover what it might be, flaring pine torches sent forth an intense light which disclosed the great packet, with her forward deck crowded with negro roustabouts, whose faces shone as the flame was reflected upon them. The tall pipes sent out sparks and smoke, and the river-monster, which seemed stealthily drawing near to us to devour us, winked its fiery eyes and sleepily drew up at the wharf, where, with infinite trouble, it was made fast with many stout ropes, while the mates screamed and cursed as only Mississippi boatmen can.

The cabin of one of these steamers presents quite a different aspect from those of the Northern packets which come from St. Louis and Cincinnati. The bar is a conspicuous object as one enters, and around it cluster eager groups busily discussing the latest phase of the Kellogg usurpation, or, in such times of depression and disaster as during my visit, lamenting their fate with a philosophic air doubtless somewhat enhanced by the soothing nature of the liquids imbibed.

As the traveler goes to register his name and purchase his ticket, the obliging clerk hands him the latest file of the New Orleans papers, of which hundreds of copies are given away at all the ports where the packets stop. No planter along the line thinks of buying a newspaper, but depends on the clerk of the steamer, who willingly furnishes him the news of the day.

About the card-tables men are busily absorbed in the intricacies of " poker" and " seven-up," and the talk is of cotton and of corn, of the rise and fall of the river, and reminiscences of adventures in forest and on stream during the " waw." On the " Robert E. Lee " I found a number of prominent young cotton-planters, all of whom were complaining of the effects of the inundation. Many of these planters were educated gentlemen, familiar with life at the North, and with the best society. None of them. were especially bitter or partisan in their views; their material interests seemed to command their immediate attention, and they, as others throughout the cotton country of the South, complained of the seeming impossibility of reorganizing labor upon a fair and proper basis. All were unanimous in their testimony as to the superiority of free over slave labor, but all asserted that it was attended with so many drawbacks and vexations that they feared it would end in the promotion of much distress, and in the ruin of hundreds of planters. They, however, were by no means confronted with the worst aspects of the labor question, since labor was flowing to them, and not receding from them, as from the planters in Central Alabama, and in certain portions of Mississippi.

Mr. Robert Somers, in his excellent observations on the labor question, as viewed in Alabama, made during a journey throughout the Southern States in 1870–71, hits upon some truths with regard to the relations of the planter and freedman, in the following manner:

"What the planters are disposed to complain of is, that while they have lost their slaves, they have not got free laborers in any sense common either in the Northern States or in Europe.   One cannot but think that the New England manufacturer and the Old England farmer must be equally astonished at a recital of the relations of land, capital and labor, as they exist on the cotton plantations of the Southern States.   The wages of the negroes, if such a term can be applied to a mode of remuneration so unusual and anomalous, consist, as I have often indicated, of one-half the crop of corn and cotton, the only crops in reality produced.

"The negro on the semi-communistic basis thus established finds his own rations; but, as these are supplied to him by the planter or the planter's notes of credit on the merchants, and as much more sometimes as he thinks he needs by the merchants on his own credit, from the 1st of January onward throughout the year, in anticipation of crops which are not marketable until the end of December, he can lose nothing by the failures or deficient out-come of the crops, and is always sure of his subsistence.   As a permanent economic relation, this would be startling anywhere betwixt any classes of men brought together in the business of life.   Applied to agriculture, in any other part of the world, it would be deemed outrageously absurd, but this is only a part of the 'privileges' (a much more accurate term than 'wages') of the negro field-hand.   In addition to half the crops, he has a free cottage of the kind he seems to like, and the windows of which he or his wife persistently nail up; he has abundance of wood from the planter's estate for fuel, and for building his corn-cribs and other out-houses, with teams to draw it from the forest.   He is allowed to keep hogs and milch cows and young cattle, which roam and feed with the same right of pasture as the hogs and cattle of the planter, free of all charge.   Though entitled to one-half the crops, he is not required to contribute any portion of the seed, nor is he called upon to pay any part of the taxes on the plantation.   The only direct tax on the negroes is a poll tax."   Mr. Somers declares that he found this tax "everywhere in arrear, and, in some places, in a helpless chaos of non-payment.   Yet," he adds, "while thus freed from the burden of taxation, the negro has, up to this period of reconstruction, enjoyed the monopoly of representation, and has had all legislative and executive power moulded to his will by Governors, Senators and Deputies, who have been either his tools, or of whom he himself has been the dupe.   For five years," he con-cludes, "the negroes have been kings, lords and commoners, and something more, in the Southern States."

"But to come back," continues Mr. Somers, "to the economic condition of the plantations, the negro field-hand, with his right of half-crop and privileges as described, who works with ordinary diligence, looking only to his own pocket, and gets his crops forward and gathered in due time, is at liberty to go to other plantations and pick cotton, in doing which he may make from two to two and a-half dollars a day.   For every piece of work outside the crop that he does even on his own plantation, he must be paid a dollar a day.   While the land owner is busy keeping account betwixt himself and his negro hands, ginning their cotton for them, doing all the marketing of produce and supplies, of which they have the lion's share, and has hardly a day he can call his own, the hands may be earning a dollar a day from him for work which is quite as much theirs as his. Yet the negroes, with all their superabounding privilege on the cotton-field, make little of it. A ploughman or a herd in the Old World would not exchange his lot for theirs, as it stands and as it appears in all external circumstances."

I have quoted these excellent remarks, as they afford a glimpse into some of the causes of the discouragement which prevails among large numbers of cotton-planters.

Nothing can be more beautiful than the appearance of a cotton-field, extending over many hundreds of acres, when the snowy globes of wool are ready for

Scene on a Cotton Plantation.

picking, and the swart laborers, with sacks suspended from their shoulders, wander between the rows of plants, culling the fleeces. The cotton-plant is beautiful from the moment when the minute leaflets appear above the moist earth until the time when it is gathered in. In June, when it is in bloom and when the blossoms change their color day by day, a cotton plantation looks like an immense flower garden. In the morning the blooms of upland cotton are often of a pale straw color; at noon of a pure white; in the afternoon perhaps faint pink, and the next morning perfect pink. It is noticed, however, that the blossom of the sea-island cotton always remains a pale yellow. When the flowers fall away, and the young bolls begin to grow, the careful negroes watch for the insidious approach of the cotton-worms, terrible enemies to plantation prosperity. There are many kinds of these worms; they multiply with astonishing rapidity, and sometimes cut off the entire crop of whole districts. Their presence cannot be accounted for, although elaborate investigations into the cause of their appearance have been undertaken ever since 1800, when they first appeared in the South. There is a popular belief that they come at intervals of three years in the same districts, and that their greatest ravages occur after intervals of twenty-one years. Their appetites are exclusively confined to cotton, of which they devour both the long and the short staples greedily.

The planters build fires in the fields when they perceive that the insects are about to visit their crops, hoping to attract and destroy the moths which are the parents of the worms; but in many cases this proves insufficient. When the cotton-worm appears early in the season there are usually three broods. If the fires are built exactly at the time of the appearance of the first moths, then their speedy destruction, preventing the appearance of the second and third broods, aids in limiting the ravages; but the remedies are rarely undertaken in time. The ally of this vicious destroyer of the planter's fondest hopes is the boll-worm moth, a tawny creature who in the summer and autumn evenings hovers over the cotton-blooms and deposits a single egg in each flower. In three or four days this egg is hatched, and out of it comes a worm who voraciously eats his way into the centre of the boll, and then, ere it falls to the ground, seeks another, in which he in like manner buries himself. In Central Alabama, in 1873, we were told that plantations were so devastated by worms that they seemed as if lightning had passed over them and scathed them. The bolls were, in many cases, cut down for entire acres as completely as if the reaper's sickle had been thrust into them.

During picking season in the States of North and South Carolina, Georgia, Northern Florida, Louisiana, Alabama, and Mississippi, the southern half of Arkansas and the eastern half of Texas, plantation life is busy and merry. If the planter has made a good crop, he calls in multitudes of negroes from the surrounding country to help him pick. These laborers sometimes wander from plantation to plantation, like the hop-pickers in the West; but where labor is not scarce, an extra force for a few days is all that is required.

By the middle of October the season is at its height. Each person is expected to pick two or three hundred pounds of cotton daily, and as fast as the fleeces are picked they are carried either in wagons or in baskets, on the heads of negroes, to the gin-house. There, if the cotton is damp, it is dried in the sun, and then the fibre is separated from the seed, to which it is quite firmly attached.

Nothing can be simpler or more effective than the machinery of the ordinary Whitney cotton-gin. Its main cylinder, upon which is set a series of circular saws, is brought into contact with a mass of cotton separated from the cylinder by steel bars or gratings. The teeth of the saws, playing between these bars, catch the cotton and draw it through, leaving the seeds behind. Underneath the saws a set of stiff brushes, revolving on another cylinder moving in an opposite direction, brushes off from the saw-teeth the lint which was taken from the seed, and a revolving fan, producing a rapid current of air, throws the light lint to a convenient distance from the gin. The ginning of sea-island cotton is practiced in South Carolina and Georgia, and requires the use of two fluted rollers, commonly made of wood, but sometimes of vulcanized rubber or steel, placed parallel in a frame which keeps them almost in contact. These rollers revolve in opposite directions, and draw the cotton between them, while the seeds, owing to the lack of space, do not pass through.

Horse power is ordinarily used on small plantations in ginning cotton, while the great planters employ steam. But now a host of enterprising individuals have set up gin-houses in neighborhoods central to many plantations, and to them flock the many whites and blacks who cultivate one or two acres in cotton. The gins in these houses are usually run by steam, and many a man has made a small fortune in two or three years since the war by preparing the cotton brought to him from the country round about. Fires are frequent in these gin-houses,

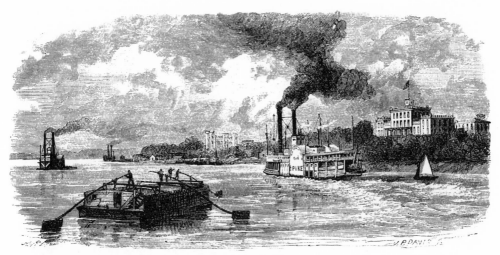

Baton Rouge, Louisiana.

and sometimes the freedmen revenge themselves upon their ex-masters by sending their expensive machinery heavenward in a blaze. Such malice as this, however, is not common, although there are some instances of planters who have lost many thousands of dollars by the torch of the incendiary.

After the cotton leaves the gin it passes to the press, where it is packed into bales. On small plantations these presses are worked by hand or by horse power, while on the great and finer ones hydraulic presses are common. On well-ordered lands the picking is, of course, over before Christmas, and the planters and laborers alike give themselves up to the jollity of holidays; but, as I have already mentioned, the sight of acres of unpicked cotton in January and February in some parts of the South is not at all uncommon. It is the most effectual proof of the complete disorganization of the labor system.

One of the peculiar vexations which the planter suffers is the constant stealing of cotton by the negroes during picking time. They manage to abstract it in petty quantities; and after having accumulated a little stock, they take it, if they live in the vicinity of a city, to what is known as a "dead fall house," where a clever "fence," or receiver of stolen goods, buys unquestioningly whatever they bring. If they live in some remote section, they boldly carry the cotton to the local merchant, who receives it in barter, very likely before the eyes of the planter from whom it was stolen, and who knows that he has no practical redress. Most of the negroes on the plantations have not the strong sense of honor which should lead them to consider their employers' interests as their own, and many of the merchants encourage them in their thievish propensities.

Sixty-five miles below Natchez the Red river empties into the Mississippi. The recent improvements made by the General Government upon this river,

The Red River Raft as it Was.

under the direction of the Board of Engineers, in the removal of the raft of drift-wood, have given it new commercial possibilities. The raft, which was thirty miles long, had, for many years, rendered navigation north of Shreveport impossible. The sketch, which the kindness of one of the engineers who had been employed in the removal of obstructions placed at the disposal of our artist, will serve to show what the Red river raft was. The river runs through one of the finest cotton regions in the country, and, in its ample and fertile valley, immense quantities of cotton and sugar, grain and tobacco will, in future, be produced. Not only Louisiana, but Arkansas and Texas, have been directly benefited by the improvement of the stream.

XXXII

MISSISSIPPI and Alabama together form a mighty domain; many an empire has been founded upon a less extent of territory than either contains. Both States have suffered a good deal from evils incident to reconstruction; both, I believe, are destined to a recuperation soon to come, and to a wealth and position such as neither, in the palmy days of slavery, dreamed of. Alabama, with her million of inhabitants, and Mississippi, with her nine hundred thousand, seem, to an European or Northern visitor, almost uninhabited. In each State there is still an immense tract of native forest. The railway lines, almost as numerous in Mississippi as in Alabama, run for scores of miles through woods and uncleared or unreclaimed lands. The slave-holders naturally sought out the best land to mass their negroes upon, and now the freedmen are settled there, rudely trying to work out the problem of self-government, a problem extremely difficult for the wisest community to solve, and, of course, utterly beyond the scope of a horde of newly emancipated negroes. There has been a marvelous widening and heightening of sentiment in each State, and something of national feeling is now manifested in both. A little money and consequent independence would enable the capable people to do a great deal, despite the encumbrance of the incapables. Mississippi has no minerals from which to predict a future growth; but her splendid soil grows cotton superbly, and Indian corn, tobacco, hemp, flax, silk, as well as all kinds of grains and grasses. At one end of the State the apple flourishes; at the other, one may luxuriate in orange groves and under the shade of the fig-tree. The sixty counties in Mississippi contain farms and plantations whose cash value, in 1870, was nearly $100,000,000. The rivers run south-west, to pay tribute to the mighty stream from which the State takes its name—save a few in the eastern section, which flow into the Alabama rivers, and thence reach the Gulf of Mexico. Property has fallen ruinously in both Alabama and Mississippi; the former boasted, in 1860, a valuation in real estate and personal property, of nearly $450,000,000; in 1870, $155,000,000. Mississippi, at the outbreak of the war, had a valuation of $509,472,912; and in 1870, $154,535,527. The cotton production of Mississippi fell from 1,202,507 bales in 1860, to 564,938 bales in 1870; and the wealthy planter vanished before the storm of revolution.

Corinth, in Mississippi, with its memories of terrible battles, is at the junction of the Memphis and Charleston railroad with the Mobile and Ohio. There Beauregard once sat haughtily entrenched until Halleck's persistence in assault

COTTON.

Compiled from 9th. Census.

Russell & Struthers, N.Y.

MAP SHOWING THE COTTON REGION OF THE UNITED STATES.

SOUTH CAROLINA, GEORGIA, FLORIDA AND ALABAMA.

Physical and Political.

By A. Guyot.

drove him away; and there occurred that ghastly encounter between Rosecrans and Van Dorn, which looms up, like a hideous vision, through the battle-smoke of our recent history.   The land was as thoroughly camped upon as any in Virginia, and to-day the tracks of the contending armies are still visible, in the devastated timber and waste lands.   There is good soil thereabouts.   Located on so important a line as the Memphis and Charleston, Corinth is gradually gaining, and a few thousand bales of cotton annually go to market from its vicinity.   A cotton and woolen manufacturing company, an extensive enterprise, with large capital, has been started near by.   Pushing down the Mobile and Ohio railroad to Meridian, past renaissant Okalona, which received such a terrible shattering during the war; past tiny towns and villages where cotton bales, small wooden houses, and the depot, are the principal features; along the rich prairie lands, world-famous; over the pine slopes—one comes upon the rich woodlands which fringe the country in which Meridian stands.   From Okalona a branch line runs off to the new and thriving town of Aberdeen; from both towns and their neighborhood large quantities of cotton are annually sent to market.

Meridian, Mississippi, a new town in the woods, yet pretty withal, is the southern terminus of the Alabama and Chattanooga railroad, which runs through Birmingham, in Alabama, to Chattanooga, in Eastern Tennessee.   At the time of my journey along the line from Birmingham northward, the road was in the anomalous condition into which Southern railways sometimes get; a condition in which no one knows, or scarcely considers it worth while to inquire, who owns it, so hopeless is the embarrassment.   No tickets were to be had at the depot; I was informed that it was uncertain whether there would be any train that night.   "Reckoned the conductor ('captain,' my informant called him) was running the train, and making what he could of it."   But the line is a remarkably fine one, and as soon as population comes in to support it, will be one of the great routes of the South.   It passes, on its way northward, through Eutaw, Alabama, pretty in its bowers of shade trees; along the fertile prairies, with their underlayers of limestone; and crosses the Tombigbee river at a point where the whitish limestone bluffs are ranged in rows, forming high banks, as picturesque and imposing as the walls of an ancient temple. Here once was great wealth, and here toiled thousands of slaves.   Now they have vanished; so has the wealth, and the planter is left behind to worry along as best he can.   Tuscaloosa, named after a valiant Indian chief of Alabama's early history, was for many years the capital of the State, and is the site of the State Lunatic Asylum, a United States land office, and many flourishing schools. The State University, already alluded to, has a group of handsome buildings on a commanding eminence not far from the banks of the Black Warrior river. Few students frequent it now, though there is some hope that it may be revivified as Alabama grows prosperous once more.   Situated on the borders of both the agricultural and mineral region of the State, Tuscaloosa has always been interested in the mining of both the iron and the coal abundant near by, and the Kennedale cotton-mill, near the town, has been in prosperous operation since 1868. The Black Warrior* is a fine stream, and serves as a high-way for the transportation of coal and iron to Demopolis, and thence via the Tombigbee toward the Gulf. Demopolis was settled in 1818 by a colony of French imperialists whose devotion to Napoleon the First had compelled them to fly from France. Among them were many noted soldiers and ladies of the fallen Emperor's court. Many afterward returned to France, and but few of their descendants at present remain in Alabama.

Scattered over the fifty-five thousand square miles which make up the State of Mississippi, there are but half-a-dozen towns of considerable size. It can readily support on its thirty-five millions of acres a dozen millions of people. Vicksburg, Natchez, Jackson, and Columbus are the principal towns; the rest are villages, into which the trade created by the surrounding country has crowded.

The Mississippi State Capitol at Jackson.

All the good lands are very accessible; railroads run in every direction through the State. The Vicksburg and Meridian route runs from Meridian through Jackson to the Mississippi river; the New Orleans, Jackson and Great Northern gives the capital easy communication with New Orleans and via the Mississippi Central, which runs from Jackson to Grenada, and from Grenada through Holly Springs and Oxford to the Tennessee line, sends a current of Northern trade and travel through the State. Columbus, Mississippi, is an enterprising town on the Tombigbee river, in the centre of a rich planting region, and depends mainly for its support upon the shipment of cotton to Mobile. Vicksburg and Natchez have already been described in their relations to the Mississippi river and the

* Tusca-loosee—meaning Black Warrior—was the Choctaw term for the river, and the town took its name from it.

country which contributes to their trade ; it remains, therefore, to give some idea of Jackson, the capital of Mississippi.

First of all, Jackson is very pretty—a quiet, unambitious village of five or six thousand inhabitants, on the banks of the Pearl river, a charming stream, which makes its erratic way through lovely forests and thickets, and whose current is strewn with the drift-wood torn from them. At Jackson one begins to feel the ripeness and perfection of the far South; he is only twelve hours from New Orleans, and sees in the gardens the same lustrous magnificence of blossom which so charmed his eye in the Louisiana metropolis. The evenings are wonderfully beautiful, silent, impressive. Reaching Jackson from Vicksburg at dark, I strolled along the half-mile of street between the hotel and the business centre of the town ; there was no stir—no sound; one might as well have been in a wood. At last, encountering a mule-car, whose only occupant was the negro driver, I returned in it to the hotel, where I found that every one but the watchful clerk had retired.

The State Capitol, a solid and not unhandsome building, the Penitentiary, the Insane Asylum, the Land Office, a fine Governor's residence, and the Asylum for the Deaf and Dumb and Blind, compose Jackson's public buildings, all well built and commodious. At the proper seasons, one sees in the long main street of the town, lines of emigrant wagons, filled with hard-featured men and women bound for Texas or "Arkansaw." These Ishmaels are not looked upon with any especial love by the inhabitants who intend to remain in their native State, and are often the subjects of much satire, which they bear good-humoredly. Hebrew names appeared to predominate on the signs; the Jews monopolize most of the trade; negroes lounge everywhere, and there are large numbers of smartly

"At the proper seasons, one sees in the long main street of the town, lines of emigrant wagons."

dressed mulattoes, or sometimes full blacks, who flit here and there with that conscious air which distinguishes the freedman. I wish here to avow, however, that those of the negroes in office, with whom I came in contact in Mississippi, impressed me much more powerfully as worthy, intelligent, and likely to progress, than many whom I saw elsewhere in the South. There are some who are exceedingly capable, and none of those immediately attached to the Government at Jackson are incapable. In the Legislature there are now and then negroes who are ignorant; but of late both branches have been freer from this curse than have those of Louisiana or South Carolina.

A visit to the Capitol showed me that the negroes, who form considerably more than half the population of Mississippi, had certainly secured a fair share of the offices. Colored men act as officials or assistants in the offices of the Auditor, the Secretary of State, the Public Library, the Commissioner of Emigration, and the Superintendent of Public Instruction. The Secretary of State, who has some negro blood in his veins, is the natural son of a well-known Mississippian of the old *régime*, formerly engaged in the politics of his State; and the Speaker of the House of Representatives at the last session was a black man. The blacks who went and came from the Governor's office seemed very intelligent, and some of them entered into general conversation in an interesting manner.

The present Governor, ex-United States Senator Adelbert Ames, was four years Military Governor of Mississippi, and knows the temper of both whites and blacks in the State very well. To his military *régime* succeeded the Government of Mr. Alcorn, now United States Senator from Mississippi, and when Mr. Alcorn was sent to the Senate, Lieutenant-Governor Powers took his place. Alcorn, returning from the Senate last year, contested the Governor's chair with Ames, but, not succeeding in a re-election, returned to Washington. At the outset of Governor Ames' civil administration, which began recently, he affirmed his determination to redeem the Republican party in that section from the charge of corruption, and the Legislature has taken measures to second his laudable resolve.

Mississippi's State debt is but little—some three millions;. she was fortunate enough not to have any credit in the markets of the world when reconstruction began, and therefore escaped a good many financial dangers. Her repudiation of her honest indebtedness, years ago, did her infinite harm, and it would be wise to take up that debt, and pay it in future. Part of the money at present owed by the State is due the schools. The State tax is not large; it is the city and county taxation which is oppressive, but that is mainly because of the straitened circumstances of the people.

The vicious system of issuing State warrants has been for some time pursued, but a bill was passed at the last legislative session, funding all these warrants; which had the effect of bringing them up at once from sixty to eighty cents. A new law also requires that all taxes be paid in greenbacks. The State paper has, at times since reconstruction, been sold on the street in Jackson at forty per cent. below par. The return to a cash basis will, it is estimated, save twenty-five per cent. in the cost of government alone. A general movement in favor of "retrenchment and reform" on the part of the dominant party is manifest, the natural result of which will be the restoration of the State's credit. Governor Ames is firm in his measures, and is not surrounded, to judge from a brief look at them, with men who are inclined to misuse their opportunities.

The State Superintendent of Education informed me that there are about 75,000 children now in attendance upon the State schools, fully 50,000 of whom are colored. He believed that there was at the time of my visit $1,000,000 worth of school property owned in the State, which proved a great advance since the war. In counties mainly Democratic in sentiment, there is formidable opposition to anything like a public school system, but in those where Republican or negro officials dominate, schools are readily kept open and fully attended. The Superintendent said that he had in only one case endeavored to insist upon mixed schools, and that was in a county where the white teachers had refused to teach negro scholars. He had found it necessary to inform those teachers that, in that case, they must not attempt to keep the black children from the white schools, since he was determined that they should receive instruction.

The school fund is quite large; there are normal schools at Holly Springs and Tougaloo; and the blacks have founded a university named after Ex-Governor and Senator Alcorn. It occupies the site of the old Oakland College near Rodney, on the Mississippi river, and receives an annual appropriation of $50,000.

A successful university has also been in operation in Tougaloo for several years. First-class teachers for the public schools are very much needed. Large numbers of very good private schools are maintained in the State by those citizens who still disbelieve in free public tuition.

The University of Mississippi,* at Oxford, an old and well managed institution, exclusively patronized by whites, receives, as does Alcorn University, an annual subsidy of $50,000 from the State, and its average attendance is fully equal to that before the war. It has been properly fostered and nourished by the Republican Government, and the motley adventurers in South Carolina might learn a lesson in justice and impartiality from the party in power in Mississippi.

As soon as the funds devoted by the State to educational purposes are paid in greenbacks, or, in other words, when the evil system of "warrants" is thoroughly extinct, Mississippi will make sterling progress in education, and, in proportion, will grow in thrift, wealth and importance.

Jackson has two flourishing newspapers, *The Pilot* being the Republican, and *The Clarion* the Democratic organ. Socially, the town has always been one of high rank in the South, although some of the rougher Mississippian element has at times been manifest in that section. The residence once occupied by Mr. Yerger, who killed the military Mayor of Jackson, shortly after the close of the war, because that Mayor had insisted upon the collection of certain taxes, is still pointed out to visitors. There are many charming drives in the town; a little beyond it, the roads are rough and the country is wild. A garrison is maintained at Jackson, and now and then the intervention of United States authority is necessary to quell disturbances in interior districts.

The State has made efforts to secure immigration, but, like many other Southern commonwealths, finds it impossible to compete with the North-west,

* Both this and Alcorn University have agricultural departments.

and becomes discouraged in presence of the objections made by white laborers to settling within its boundaries. The south-western portion presents really fine inducements for the cultivation of cotton, corn, tobacco, sugar-cane, peaches, pears, apples, and grapes. In several of these south-western counties the yield of sugar has been one thousand pounds to the acre. The average yield of cotton is a bale to the acre. Fruit culture could be made a paying specialty throughout that part of the State.

The rich stores of pine, pecan, hickory, oak, walnut, elm, ash, and cypress timber form also an element of future wealth. Those lands fronting upon the Gulf of Mexico offer, in orange orchards and the miraculous oyster-beds along the shores, rare prizes for the emigrants who will go and take them. The counties a little remote from the coast are rich in a luxuriant growth of pine, and there too, the culture of sugar and the grape has already been successful.

The stock-grazier, also, can find his paradise there; and there the ample water power of the Pearl, the Wolf, the Pascagoula, the Escalaufa, the Leaf and the Chickasawha rivers can turn the largest mills. The average price of lands in the State, accepting the testimony of the Government immigration agent, is five dollars per acre.

Life and property are probably as safe at present as in any other State in the South. The reputation of Southern Mississippi has not heretofore been of the best in respect to law and order; but the State seems to be now entering upon an epoch of peace and confirmed decency. Mississippi has, undoubtedly, suffered immensely, in a material point of view, since the close of the war, but is now on the road to an upbuilding, and would spring into astonishing growth if the vexed labor question could only be settled in some manner.

An immigration to the Mississippi sea-board, where there is so much magnificent timber, would be peculiarly advantageous to young men possessed of small capital. Pascagoula river and its tributaries give a water line thirteen hundred miles in extent through a dense timber region. Millions of feet of good lumber are now shipped from this section. The improvement of the harbor and the deepening of the channel at Pascagoula, and the elevation of that place and of Bay St. Louis into ports of entry, would greatly increase the trade of Mississippi in that direction.

The people of the State have also long desired the connection of the Gulf coast with the central interior, by a railway line, and will demand it soon. Until it is accomplished Mississippi will, perforce, pour streams of commerce into Mobile and New Orleans, while her own grand harbors remain unimproved and empty. Meantime, the completion of the network gradually covering the State goes on; and the Memphis and Selma, the Mobile and North-western, the Vicksburg and Memphis, the Vicksburg and Nashville, the Prentice and Bogue Phalia, and the Natchez, Jackson and Columbus roads are projected, and, in some cases, the routes have been partially graded.

The Vicksburg and Nashville road has no very powerful reason for existence, as its projected line is intersected at equidistant intervals by three rich and

powerful lines in successful operation ; and there has been a good deal of opposition to the surrendering to that road of the trust funds known as the three per
cents., and the agricultural land scrip, amounting in all to some $320,000.

Along the line of rail from Jackson to New Orleans there is much growth of
substantial character.   Mr. H. E. McComb, of Wilmington, Delaware, has built up
a flourishing town not far from the Louisiana line, and named it McComb City.
But the country is still mainly in a wild state, and one cannot help feeling, while

borne along in the palace-car through
forests and tangled thickets, that he is
gradually leaving the civilized world
behind.   He imagining each village
which he sees, like an island in the
ocean of foliage, to be the last, and
experiences a profound astonishment
when he comes upon the cultivated
and European surroundings of New
Orleans.   Northward, along the railway lines, it is much the same.

All one day we traversed the line
from Jackson to Memphis, coming to
but two towns of any mentionable size
in the whole distance.   The others
were merely groupings of a few unpainted houses built against the hill-
sides, among the trees, and on the
open plains.

Plantation life is much the same
in all sections of the State, although
the methods of culture and the amount
of results may differ.   The white man
and the negro are alike indifferent to

"The negroes migrate to Louisiana and Texas in search
of paying labor."

a safe and steady provision for the future by growing their own supplies.

The planters are nearly all poor, and very much in need of ready money,
for which they have to pay exorbitant rates of interest.   At the end of a year
of pretty hard work,—for the cotton planter by no means rests upon a bed of
roses,—both whites and blacks find themselves little better off than when they
began, and feel sore and discouraged.   The negroes migrate to Louisiana and
Texas in search of paying labor, while the planters complain very generally
of the scarcity of help.

XXXIII.

MOBILE, THE CHIEF CITY OF ALABAMA.

THERE was a delicious after-glow over sky and land and water as I left New Orleans for Mobile one warm evening in March, the month which, in the South, is so radiant of sunshine and prodigal of flowers.

Nothing in lowland scenery could be more picturesque than that afforded by the ride from New Orleans to Mobile, over the Mobile and Texas railroad, which stretches along the Gulf line of Louisiana, Mississippi and Alabama. It runs through savannahs and brakes, skirts the borders of grand forests, offers here a glimpse of a lake and there a peep at the blue waters of the noble Gulf; now clambers over miles of trestle-work, as at Bay St. Louis, Biloxi (the old fortress of Bienville's time) and Pascagoula; and now plunges into the very heart of pine woods, where the foresters are busily building little towns and felling giant trees, and where the revivifying aroma of the forest is mingled with the fresh breezes from the sea.

The wonderful charm of the after-glow grew and strengthened as the train was whirled rapidly forward. We came to a point from which I saw the broad expanse of water beneath the draw-bridge over the Rigolets, and the white sails

On the Bay Road, near Mobile, Alabama. [Page 321.]

hovering far away, like monster sea-gulls, on either side the railroad. The illusion was almost perfect; I seemed at sea. Along the channel I could see the schooners, and now and then a steamer, coming from the deep canals that run from New Orleans to Lake Pontchartrain, and communicate with Lake Borgne. At a little pine-built village, completely shrouded in foliage, and seemingly lulled to sleep by the murmurous song of the birds and drowsy hum of the insects, a party of roystering negro men and women, carrying banjos and guitars on their shoulders, left the forward car. Suddenly my next neighbor said:

"Did you see that white man thar, 'mong the niggers, with a beaver on, 'long o' that big black wench?"

"Do you really think he was a white man?"

"Yes, d——n him; p'r'aps his heart's black, though. Looks like that big nigger was his wife."

Then the voice grumbled itself away into silence.

This somewhat deadened the romance with which I was beginning to invest the journey—for the mystical twilight creeping on, the strange panorama of vegetation flitting before my eyes, the sudden transition from forest to Gulf shore, and the sombre calm of the horizon where blue wave seemed mutely kissing bluer sky, all combined to throw one into delightful musings. I retired to the platform of the Pullman car, and was once more giving way to the spell of the sunset, when a sharp voice behind me said:

"Mobile bay lay spread out before me." [Page 321.]

"Cap'n, can't you set inside, 'n let us shet the do'? The mosquitoes is gitting so they bite powerful sharp."

Then darkness came treacherously and suddenly, as it does in that strange Southern land; and we rolled rapidly through the edge of Mississippi; past the pretty Gulfside towns, whither beauty and fashion fly in spring and summer; past inlet, across river, and turned landward to Mobile.

The lovely bay on which the chief city of Alabama is located extends thirty miles inland to the mouth of the Alabama river. One of the most charming promenades near Mobile lies on the bay shore. Bowling merrily over the shell road one superb March day, I was impressed with the tranquil beauty of the spot. There was a light haze; Mobile bay lay spread out before me, a dimly seen vision, the foreground dotted with masses of drift-wood brought in by the tide, and with the long piers running out to pretty bathing-houses.

There was a strange and sleepy air of quiet about the place; a tropical luxu-riance of sunlight and blossom, so curiously at variance with one's preconceived notions of March, that it was a perpetual puzzle! A gentle breeze blew steadily inland; it seemed perfume-laden. The tide was com-ing in. Here and there we had glimpses of long beaches as fine in their rounded sweep as Castella-mare, and massive magnolias, sixty or seventy feet high, threw noble shadows over the sheeny water, from which the haze gradually lifted. Vines, water oaks, and pines tall enough for the masts of Vikings' ships, bordered the way. Neat residences peered from rose-smothered gardens; a negro woman fished silently in a little pool made by the tide, never catching any fish, and seemingly content to regard the reflections of her own ebony face in the water; a swart farmer lazily followed the

"A negro woman fished silently in a little pool."

mule-drawn plough afield; urchins tumbled among the snags and drift-wood hauled up to dry; and goats and kids lingered and skipped distrustfully on the knolls by the roadside.

Here was a garden filled with arbors and benches in cozy nooks; in its centre, a latticed café, whose proprietor was opening soda bottles, and, barearmed, dis-pensing cooling drinks to customers sprawling on seats, with their faces raised to catch the inspiring breath of the sea. There was no whir of gilded equipages; the long avenue seemed all my own; I could almost fancy that the coast was mine, the islands and the light-houses were mine, and that the two negro hunters, loitering by with guns on their shoulders, were my gamekeepers, come to attend me to the chase. The delicate hint of infinity on the mingled wave and haze-horizon; the memories of siege and battle awakened by the sight of the dim line of Blakely coast; the penetrating perfume wafted from magnolias and pines; the soul-clarifying radiance of the sunshine, which industriously drove away the light mist, all conspired to surround me with an enchantment not dis-pelled until I had once more gained the streets of the town.

We are indebted to Bienville, that prince of colonial guardians, for Mobile, as well as for New Orleans. He it was who, in 1711, built the defense called Fort

Condé, on the present site of the town, and who gave the name of Mobile to the bay, because the Indians inhabiting that section called themselves Mobilians. On the west side of the bay he at one time erected a fort called "St. Louis de la Mobile." For half a century the present city was only a frontier military post, carrying on a small trade with the Indians. It was French in character and sentiment, and although but few of the Gallic characteristics are now perceptible in the manners of any of its inhabitants, there are hints of the departed French in the architecture and arrangement of the town. It fell into British hands in 1763, by the treaty of Paris between Great Britain and France, and was too remote from the other colonies to succeed in doing anything against British rule during the American Revolution.

After the British came the Spaniards, who drove out the former, and partially burned Mobile during the siege. In due time, as tract after tract was wrested from the Indians, the territory of Mississippi was formed, with Winthrop Sargent of Massachusetts as Governor, and to this Government Mobile and its tributary country were accountable, after the departure of the Spaniards, until the thorough subjugation of the savage, and his expulsion from the Tennessee valley, and from his hunting grounds on the Chattahoochee, had opened the whole domain to the white man, and a portion of Mississippi territory was organized in March of 1817, under the name of "Alabama." By 1819, white settlers had flocked into the country in such numbers that Alabama was admitted to the Union.

Mobile is to-day a pretty town of 35,000 inhabitants, tranquil and free from commercial bustle, for it has not been as prosperous as many of its southern sea-port sisters. Government street, its principal residence avenue, has many fine

The Custom-House—Mobile, Alabama.

mansions situated upon it; the gardens are luxuriant, and give evidence of a highly cultivated taste. Superb oak-trees shade that noble street, as well as the public square between Dauphin and St. Francis streets. The streets and shops are large, and many are elegant; but there is no activity; the town is as still as one of those ancient fishing villages on the Massachusetts coast when the fishermen are away. Yet there is a large movement of cotton through Mobile yearly. A cotton exchange has grown up there within the last two years, and when I visited it, already had 100 members. Mobile annually receives and dispatches from 325,000 to 350,000 bales of cotton, most of which comes from Mississippi, much of whose carrying trade she controls. Some of the cotton brought to Mobile goes eastward, but the mass of it goes to the foreign shipping in the "lower bay." The port needs many improvements, and the Government has for some time been engaged in a kind of desultory dredging out there, but has not yet succeeded in affording a sufficient depth of water to allow large vessels to come directly to the wharves; and the lines of artificial obstruction, built across the channel of the bay during the war, to impede the passage of vessels, have not yet been removed.

In due time, with a revival of commerce and the development of the immense resources in cotton, coal and iron in the State, the channel through the bay will be properly deepened, and Mobile will have a wharf line along its whole front. At present, however, it seems that foreign captains rather prefer to have their ships loaded from small crafts which come twenty or twenty-five miles down the bay with the cotton, as they thus avoid port dues and the danger of desertion of sailors. It costs but twenty cents per bale to convey the cotton down the

harbor, and the captains, anxious to get their lading and depart, have none of the customary port delays and exactions to complain of. In 1867–68, Mobile exported 358,745 bales; in 1868–69, but 247,348; in 1869–70, sent away 298,523; in 1870–71, the number rose to 417,508; but in 1871–72, fell again to 295,629; and in 1872–73 was over 300,000. Of this cotton the greater portion was sent directly to Liverpool, the amount going northward yearly varying from 80,000 to 160,000 bales. Down the Alabama river, from the rich but lately unfortunate country around Montgomery and Selma, come thousands of bales on the light-draft

Bank of Mobile and Odd Fellows' Hall—Mobile, Alabama.

steamers; and the river banks form one continuous line of cotton plantations. Nearly 400 vessels, employing 7,500 sailors, and having a tonnage of 275,000 tons, are annually employed in direct commerce with the port. This cotton movement does not, however, make Mobile either especially rich or active as a town, inasmuch as, aside from a few manufactories of minor importance, it constitutes the sole business.

The railroad connections of the city are excellent, and her citizens are anxious to improve them still farther. The New Orleans, Mobile and Texas line gives direct communication with New Orleans and Brashear City, the point of departure of the Morgan steamships for Texas; the Mobile and Ohio road connects Mobile with Columbus in Mississippi; the Mobile and Montgomery gives it a highway to the State capital, and thence via the South and North Alabama road through the wonderful mineral region, to Decatur and Nashville. It is intended to create a road from Mobile to Tallahassee in Florida, in due time, and the city already has connection with Pensacola, the most important of the northern Florida ports. All that section of the "land of flowers" contiguous to Alabama will doubtless be annexed sooner or later; there is a growing sentiment in both

The Marine and City Hospitals—Mobile, Alabama.

States in favor of annexation. The present route to Pensacola from Mobile is roundabout; one has to make a triangular detour from Mobile to Pollard, on the Montgomery road, and thence return coastward on the Pensacola and Louisville route. At present the only connection which Pensacola has with Eastern Florida is via steamers to St. Mark's, and thence by rail across the peninsula to Jacksonville. Pensacola has one of the most remarkable harbors in the world; it is thirty miles long, from six to eight wide, and nearly thirty-five feet deep. The average depth on the bar at the harbor entrance is twenty-four feet. Any ship, however heavily loaded, can readily approach Pensacola at any season of the year, and can reach the open sea in a couple of hours. The harbor is safe—differing in that respect from many of the Florida ports, and is amply defended by three forts in good condition. A naval station, and boasting a marine hospital and a custom-house, Pensacola, with its four thousand inhabitants, already talks grandly of its great future. The immense quantities of fine timber which grow in lower Alabama and upper Florida furnish the city with an extensive lumber trade. The completion of the North and South railroad gives it also almost an air line to Nashville and Louisville, and promises to make it in future one of the outlets, like Brunswick on the South Atlantic coast, for the trade of the West.*

Trinity Church—Mobile, Alabama.

The Mobile and Montgomery road has done much for Mobile, placing the town upon one of the main lines of travel across the country. Two excellent bridges span the Mobile and Tensaw rivers; the old and tedious transfer

---

* In 1872, eight hundred foreign ships entered Pensacola harbor, and probably a thousand come there yearly. Few come save in ballast, their object being to procure outward freights of cotton and lumber.

by boats is done away; and to-day a stream of freight and travel passes through the city from North to South, bringing with it visitors and investors. The projected "Grand Trunk" railroad has not yet made much progress. It is intended to give an additional route from Mobile to the mineral regions, and its completion would develop a large section of valuable country. It will stretch four hundred miles into the interior, making new trade for Mobile, but it is not likely to be built at once. It has been completed to Jackson, fifty-nine miles from Mobile.

In the City Park, Mobile— "Ebony nurse-maids flirt with their lovers."

Mobile does not rank as high, as a commercial city, as in the palmy days gone by; but the peculiar advantages of her location, and the vast resources of the State whose chief seaport she is, can but bring her a good future. At present her banking capital is small, hardly aggregating a million and three-quarters, and outside rates for money are ruinously high. There is a large and increasing capital concentrated in fire and life insurance companies; the manufactories are all of minor importance, except the Creole and the Mobile cotton-seed oil works. Alabama produces nearly three hundred thousand tons of cotton-seed annually, of which fully one-half can be spared for sale. There is a similar prosperous factory at Selma. This industry may attain large proportions. Mobile has made active efforts to become one of the principal coffee markets of the Union, and claims that direct importation from Rio to Mobile is easier, less expensive, and more direct than to New Orleans. The retail trade of the city has been greatly injured by the establishment throughout the State of a vast number of new stores, where the freedmen on the adjacent plantations now purchase the supplies which they once bought in bulk in Mobile. There is some hope that the city may become the coaling station for the steam navigation of the Gulf. The Cedar Keys and Florida railroad is the medium of shipping much cotton and other produce directly to New York from Mobile, which would have been diverted elsewhere were it not for this advantageous route.

The construction of the proposed ship canal across Florida would be very beneficial to Mobile, in affording her a cheap water-way, while the South Atlantic ports must necessarily be restricted in growth by expensive railroad transportation.

My visit to Mobile was in spring-time, when the whole land was covered with blossoms. The City park is filled with noble trees, in whose shade ebony nurse-maids flirt with their lovers and squirrels frolic with the children. The drive along the quiet and secluded by-way to "Spring Hill" reminded one of the rich bloom and greenness of England, save that here and there were semi-

In the City Park, Mobile—"Squirrels frolic with the children."

tropical blossoms. Climbing to the roof of the Jesuit college on Spring Hill, I looked out over a lovely plain, once studded with beautiful homes, many of which have now fallen sadly into decay. A dense growth of forest still shrouds much of the surrounding country; in the distance the faint line of the Gulf seemed a silver thread. Along the hills, over which I wandered, flourished all the trees peculiar to the far South, and the Scuppernong grape grew magnificently in the college vine-yards.   The fresh and aromatic atmosphere of the woods, mingled with the delicate breath from the sea, made it difficult for one to fancy that pestilence could ever spread its wings above Mobile. Yet there, as elsewhere, from time to time the death angel inaugurates his terrible campaign, and the citizens are compelled to flee to the mountains.

Mobile bay is replete with historic interest. One may perhaps think, in look-ing out over its placid waters, of Iberville's colonists coming, in 1799, a motley and sea-stained gang, to land on Dauphin's Island, and finding there so many human bones, that they called it Massacre Island; but one cannot forget the mighty naval battle when grim old Commander Farragut forced his way past the fire of Fort Morgan and Fort Gaines, whose Confederate guns were at all hazards to be silenced. One cannot remember, without a thrill, how one day the squadron, which had hung steadfastly at the mouth of the bay during three long years of war, transformed itself into a fiery antago-nist—a war-fleet, breathing forth fire and destruction; nor how, after the admiral had fought his way with his fleet past the forts into the harbor, the giant ram, the "Tennessee," the pride

Barton Academy—Mobile, Alabama.

and glory of the Alabamians who built her, stood out to meet her formidable foes, although she had seen the decks of all her other Confederate consorts transformed into slaughter-pens.   One cannot forget how, even after the harbor was taken, and closed against the blockade-runners, the little city held valiantly out another twelve months, until the attack by Canby on the defenses along the eastern shore was crowned with victory, until the Spanish Fort and Blakely, Batteries Hager and Tracy were invested, besieged and taken.

Mobile is the home of some Southern celebrities; among them are Admiral Semmes, who lives peaceably and handsomely, following the profession of law; Madame Octavia Walton Le Vert, Augusta J. Evans, authoress of "Beulah" and one or two other ultra-scholastic novels, and General John Forsyth, ex-diplomat, and one of the ablest jour-nalists in the country.   The *Register*, which General Forsyth edits, is some-times a little bitter in partisan politics, but altogether highly creditable to Mobile.   The city is also famous for having inaugurated the masked secret societies, which have lately become such a feature of the Southern carnival, and which for several years held the field with the "Cowbellions" and the "Strikers," whose representations were always looked forward to with pleas-ure by the citizens of the Gulf coast. The Cowbellions, the Strikers, and the " T. D. A's," are New Year's Eve societies ; and among the Mardi-Gras companies are the " Order of Myths,"

Christ Church—Mobile, Alabama.

and the " H. S. S." Not even the war and the depression of commerce have been able to deaden the jollity of the genial maskers.

The home of many lovely women, Mobile has a thoroughly good society, cultivated and frank, and the assemblages of its citizens are as brilliant gatherings as are to be found in the country.   There are no public buildings of special beauty ; the Custom-House, the Odd Fellows' and Temperance Halls, the Catholic Cathedral, the First Presbyterian and Christ Churches, Mobile College, the Academy, the Bank of Mobile, are all pleasing structures, but devoid of any remarkable features.   Both Catholics and Protestants have well-conducted orphan asylums ; in the numerous public schools the white and black children are pretty well provided for, education making progress as grati-fying in the city as it is meagre and discouraging in the country.   Immigration and manufactures would make of Mobile one of the most attractive of Southern towns; it needs but a little aid to establish itself firmly and handsomely.   The cemetery is somewhat dilapidated, yet filled with pretty monuments and those sweetest memorials of the dead—a profusion of delicious flowers.

XXXIV.

THE RESOURCES OF ALABAMA—VISITS TO MONTGOMERY AND SELMA.

THAT which chiefly astonishes the stranger in visiting Alabama is that the superb material resources of the State should have remained undeveloped so long. He is told that, in a little less than a century, Alabama expended two hundred millions of dollars in the purchase of slaves; had she spent it in developing her elements of wealth, she would have been to-day one of the richest commonwealths in the world. The extraordinary extent and nature of her mineral stores, the fertility of her fields for cotton, the cereals and fruits, the grandeur of her forests, the length of her streams, and her lovely climate, will render her, after the dreary transition period is past, one of the most opulent of the Southern States.

The expedition of De Soto through Alabama, three centuries and a-half ago, was among the most remarkable of his time. This brave Spaniard, with his little band, while pushing across the new and hostile country to the harbor at Pensacola, where ships with supplies from Havana awaited him, was attacked by swarms of warriors under the chief Tuscaloosa, at an Indian town, said to have been near the present site of Selma, and there fought one of the bloodiest battles of early American history. Turning his face northward and westward once more, he fought his way, step by step, to the Mississippi river, leaving the savages some ghastly memorials of Spanish pluck and valor, but having done nothing toward the colonization of the great territory later known as Alabama.

One hundred and sixty-two years thereafter, another European expedition appeared at Pensacola, but finding the Spaniards in possession there, cast anchor at Ship Island, and finally at Biloxi. Iberville, who had been commissioned by France to found settlements on the Mississippi, planted the seed of the colonies, which Bienville brought to such abundant harvest. Slaves were introduced into Alabama, then a part of Louisiana, under the *régime* of John Law's great Mississippi Company, and rice and tobacco and indigo were successfully cultivated. A little more than a century after the first French occupation, Alabama had nearly 200,000 whites, and 117,000 blacks within her borders, and seemed springing more rapidly into development than most of the other States of the Union.

The area of Alabama is 50,722 square miles, of which the cotton and timber regions comprise about 10,000, and the mineral section 15,000 square miles. The cotton-fields have been the basis of the State's wealth, and will continue one of her chief supports; but to her minerals and manufactures must she look for that development of large manufacturing towns and wonderful increase of population which has marked the growth of other States, uniting, as she does, a superabundance of agricultural and mineral resources. It is supposed that not more than half the available cotton lands are at present under cultivation. From the rich Tennessee valley to the fertile Gulf coast there is such a combination of natural treasures as no country in Europe can boast. Alabama can produce all the grains and esculents of the Northern States, yet to-day whole sections of the State are dependent on the North-west for bread, because the foolish "all cotton" policy is continued from slave times.

Lying at the foot of the Alleghany mountains, which, in the north-western portion of the State, bow their giant heads stupidly, and lean lazily toward the level earth, she possesses grand mineral beds, similar to those which crop out at intervals along the range through Pennsylvania, Virginia and Tennessee. Her river system is one of the noblest on the continent. It comprehends the Tennessee, which courses through eight northern counties, and affords a fertile, although somewhat exhausted, cotton valley; the Alabama and her tributaries; and the Tombigbee, the Black Warrior and the Coosa. These are all navigable. The Chattahoochee river is the boundary line between Georgia and Alabama; and in the lower part of the State several of the rivers flowing through Florida to the Gulf furnish navigation to the border counties.

The improvement of the Coosa and the Cahawba rivers, so that they shall be navigable all the way from the mineral fields to their junction with the Alabama, is considered of the utmost importance. Some of the richest iron mines and coal-fields in the State are on the Upper Coosa, beyond its navigable portion. Surveys have been provided for under the reconstruction governments, but as yet little has been accomplished. The upper portion of the Black Warrior river drains the Warrior coal-field, and could be made of vast service in future.

The opening of the Coosa river would give to the markets of Montgomery and Mobile the produce of a section of Alabama which now finds its outlet in Georgia, and it would furnish the cotton belt of the State with cheap grain—a most important consideration; while, at the same time, it will afford fine water power for manufactures. Mobile is anxious to become a grain depot, like New Orleans, for the corn trade of the West with Europe. The improvement of the Coosa river and of Mobile harbor would accomplish this.

The needed opening of the Tennessee river, which I have alluded to elsewhere, would be of the greatest value to Northern Alabama; and a canal from the Tennessee to the Coosa, cut through at a point where the streams are not more than forty miles apart, would give a continuous water line from the northwest to Mobile bay.* This would become one of the most popular and economical of national highways, and would be lined, throughout Alabama, with manufacturing towns.

The timber region of Alabama comprises a belt extending entirely across the lower portion of the State, bordering on Florida and the Gulf. It is rich in

* "Alabama Manuals."

forests of long-leaved pine, and on the river lowlands grow white, black and Spanish oaks, and the black cypress. Cotton can be produced in the light, sandy soil of this section, but the gathering of naval stores is a more productive industry in these border counties. Between Mobile and Pascagoula bays many settlements are springing up, and enterprising young men from the North and West are sending millions of feet of lumber to the New Orleans market. The lands can be purchased for a trifle; and there are many small bays and estuaries where vessels for any port in the world might load directly at the saw-mill.

In the cotton belt, which also extends across Alabama, from the Mississippi to the Georgia line, there are many large towns which would, in happier times, be flourishing, and whose appearance testifies to a long reign of wealth, elegance, and culture within their limits. Montgomery, Selma, Demopolis, Livingston, Eutaw, Greensboro, Marion, are all inhabited or surrounded by planters who are, or have once been wealthy, and who have gathered about them fine private schools, libraries and churches.

South-eastward through the cotton country, from the capital, runs the Montgomery, Eufaula and Brunswick railroad, intended as part of a gigantic line some day to be completed from Brunswick, Georgia, on the Atlantic coast, to Vicksburg, on the Mississippi; and other lines are here and there projected. It often occurs to one that Alabama is indulging in an "overcrop" of railways, considering the abundance of her superb water-courses.

The soil of the Alabama cotton belt is inexhaustibly rich. This is the testimony of all observers, native and foreign. That it has in some sections been forced, so as to be, for a time, less productive than usual, there can be no doubt; but with anything like decent care it will grow cotton as long as will the soil of Egypt. But there has been a terrible fall in prices, and hundreds, perhaps thousands, of planters have been utterly ruined. Good lands there once commanded $50 per acre; those same lands now command possibly $10, in some instances $5. The enormous fertility of this section is shown by the fact that in 1860, just before the slave system was broken up, it produced 997,978, almost 1,000,000 bales of cotton, or one-fifth of the whole crop of the United States for that year. The planters there, as elsewhere, would prefer the free labor which they now employ, rather than slaves, if the free labor could be relied on to work with a view to getting as good results for his employer as the slave did for his owner.

There are, of course, great multitudes of negroes on these cotton lands, who, as a rule, labored well, in spite of the savage reverses experienced by the whole planting interest of Alabama for some years, until the continuous disaster discouraged them, and they took refuge either in emigration or a precarious dependence upon the charity of others but little richer than themselves. But whatever may be the condition of large planters, or of the freedmen, who are, of course, more or less ignorant and irresponsible, there is no doubt that industrious and capable immigrants, settling in the cotton belt, and carefully cultivating from forty to fifty acres of land, with ten in cotton and an equal number in grain and provisions, could become wealthy. The main suffering, which has been great in Alabama, has occurred because the people raised but little food. Relying entirely upon cotton, when that failed they found themselves penniless and starving. This suffering does not come, however, save when the crops are absolutely destroyed by caterpillars or by rains. If the Alabama planters could succeed for a few years, they might have money to invest in the much needed local manufactures, but at present they have none, and foreign capital does not flow to them.

Going from Opelika, by rail, to Montgomery, I found in the cars the usual number of rough but honest folk bound for Texas; a sprinkling of commercial Hebrews, who bitterly bewailed the misfortunes attendant on the failure of the cotton crop during two successive years; and some very intelligent colored men journeying to the Legislature, then in session.

People generally complained of a desperate condition of affairs, consequent upon the crop failures, and spoke with bitterness of the poverty which had overtaken both whites and blacks. The lands around Montgomery were, every one admitted, wonderfully rich, but the caterpillar had devastated the fields as fast as the planter had planted them; and the consequence was that many persons were not only overwhelmed with debt, but hardly knew where they were to get anything to eat. My visit to Montgomery fully demonstrated to me that these statements were in no wise exaggerated.

Montgomery county, in which the capital of the State is situated, once comprehended a large portion of Central Alabama, but now includes only eight hundred square miles. There are nearly three times as many blacks as whites within its limits. It has usually been considered first on the list of the agricultural counties of the State, and in the first rank in wealth. No section of the South, not even the wonderfully rich Mississippi delta, offers better soil for the growing of cotton and corn. The undulating prairie and the fertile alluvial afford every chance for the amassing of riches. Five great railways run through the town and the county, and the river navigation is excellent.

It was difficult to conceive how this marvelous section had fallen into such decay that the market-place of Montgomery was filled with auctioneers presiding over sheriffs' sales, and that there was a general complaint of poverty, much destitution, and, in some cases, despair. The citizens explained that the failure of the "crops" (the crops meaning cotton) during two years, and the arrival of the panic, had completely worsted them. The negroes employed by planters were discharged by hundreds when the panic came, and having, as a mass, no means, constituted a "bread or blood" populace, whose presence in the country was in the highest degree embarrassing. The Mayor of the city gave these unfortunate people charity out of his own purse for a long time, until other cities and towns rallied and sent in help. Stealing was, of course, frequently resorted to by the freedmen as soon as they were idle, and the whole country round was pillaged. Owing to the ravages of the caterpillar, Montgomery's tributary crop, which usually amounts to 60,000 or 70,000 bales, had fallen to one-third that amount.

Montgomery has a double historic interest as a capital, for it was there that the Confederacy first established its seat of government; there that its "provisional congress" assembled for two months; and the house occupied at that time by Jefferson Davis is still pointed out.   The town is prettily situated on the Alabama river, and used to export 100,000 bales of cotton, much of which was floated down the current of the great stream.   As a manufacturing centre, it would be very advantageous, but, although Alabama has exempted manufactures from taxation, no effort has, as yet, been made there to establish them.   Montgomery, therefore, a town of fourteen thousand inhabitants, with fair transportation facilities, many elegant business blocks, fine churches, a good theatre, an elegant court-house, and a mammoth hotel, has a valuation of only $6,500,000, and its streets are filled with black and white idlers.

If the negroes could be persuaded to show the same industry in manufacturing that they do in attending mortgage sales, the section would not lack capable workers.   I was told in the market square that some of the negroes had come sixty miles—many from the mountains of Coosa county—to attend upon the sales, and on these expeditions were accustomed to be absent from their farms for days together.   The plantations in all the adjacent belt were expected to go

off at sheriffs' sales at the time of my visit.   How many of them the original owners managed to retain in their possession, I know not, but I think the number must have been small.

The Capitol building, crowning a fine eminence, from which one could get a view of the town spread out over the undulating country, was surrounded with the usual number of negroes, old and young, who seemed to have no thought whatever for the morrow.   A few gray-headed Africans were seated on the gateway steps as I went in,

The Alabama State Capitol at Montgomery.

and moved lazily and grumblingly aside to let me pass.   The colored legislators lounging about the lobbies, waiting for the session to begin, were of a rather higher type than those in South Carolina and Louisiana.   There were a good many among them who were lightly tinctured with Caucasian blood, and all were smartly dressed and aggressive in their demeanor.

When the "House" assembled, I went in, and found the honorable representatives engaged in a stirring battle over some measures which the Conservatives desired to pass before, and the Radicals to hinder, until the close of the session.   The speaker, the Honorable Lewis E. Parsons, was the first provisional Governor under reconstruction, and remained in office until, under the new constitution, provision had been made for the election of a Governor and General Assembly in 1865.   He is a good Republican and an honest man, and has done much in staying the tide of ignorance and oppression from overwhelming the State.

Alabama, even after she was supposed to be reconstructed, flatly refused to recognize the Fourteenth Amendment, and was consequently remanded to her provisional condition as a conquered province, and Robert M. Patton, the successor of Governor Parsons, found himself under the supervision of the Brigadier-General commanding the district, of which Alabama formed a part. A new constitutional convention was held ; blacks carried over whites the adoption of a constitution in complete harmony with the requirements of Congress, and in the summer of 1868, William H. Smith became the Republican Governor of the State. Under his administration began the era of domination of the hybrid legislature, and it is not surprising that the State was shaken to its centre by the ensuing legislation. The Legislature was besieged by persons interested in railway schemes, and the State's credit was pledged in the most prodigal fashion. At the same time immigration to the State was hindered by the operations of the Ku-Klux and by the exaggerated bitterness of the white Alabamians, who did not seem willing to forgive the North for having forced negro suffrage upon them ; and in the counties where the negroes were in the majority there was the mismanagement, turmoil, and tyranny which prevailed in other States of the South. In 1870, Robert B. Lindsay was elected Governor, but Governor Smith refused to vacate his office, on the ground that Lindsay had been fraudulently elected, and surrounded himself with Federal soldiers. Lindsay was, however, declared elected, and the State had two Governors and two Legislatures, until Governor Smith was ousted by a writ from the Circuit Court. Governor Lindsay was succeeded, in 1872, by David P. Lewis, who was in power at the time of my visit. The various railroad complications have somewhat impaired the State's credit, and Alabama has latterly found it very difficult to meet the interest upon bonds which she had endorsed for some of the new railroad enterprises. The Alabama and Chattanooga road, the Montgomery and Eufaula, the Selma and Gulf roads have all aided in the embarrassment in which Alabama is plunged to-day by the lamentable condition of her State indebtedness.

In the House of Representatives the colored members appeared to have voluntarily taken seats on one side of the house, and the Conservatives, who were in like manner assembled on the other, were overwhelmed by a deafening chorus of " Mr. Speaker ! " from the colored side, whenever they proposed any measure. Sometimes the colored opponents would show that they misapprehended the attitude of their white friends, and then long and wearisome explanations and discussions were entered upon, enlivened only by an occasional outburst of a dusky member, who fiercely disputed the floor with his ex-master, and whose gestures were only equaled in eccentricity by his language. The Senate was a more dignified body ; in it there were some gentlemen of distinguished presence and considerable eloquence.

But at Montgomery, as elsewhere throughout the reconstructed States, it was easy to see that ignorance and corruption had done much to injure the *morale* of the State. The worst feature observable was a kind of political stagnation in the minds of the white people—a mute consent to almost any misfortune which might happen. This was more dreadful and depressing than the negro igno-

rance. I do not mean to have it inferred that the whites in Alabama are all
educated. The ignorance of the poorer white classes in the country is as dense
as that of the blacks; and there is evidence of rough and reckless manners
of living. Nothing but education and a thorough culture of the soil—a genuine

The Market-place at Montgomery, Alabama.

farming—will ever build up the broken fortunes of this once wealthy section of Alabama. Coming down from the Capitol, one sunlit autumn morning, I was fairly amazed at the great congregation of idle negroes in the market
square. They were squatted at corners; they leaned against walls, and cowered
under the canvas of the huge country wagons; they chattered like magpies at the
shop doors, and swarmed like flies around the cheap and villainous grog-shops
which abounded. No one was at work; none had any thought for the morrow.
Those with whom I stopped to converse " cursed their dull fate " in the mild,
deprecatory manner peculiar to the African. Their descriptions of the caterpillar,
who feeds upon the leaves of the cotton plant, and of its able assistant, the boll-
worm, who buries himself inside the cotton-boll, and feeds on it until it is entirely
gone, were graphic and amusing, but it would require almost countless pages
to translate them here.

   The strip of country extending between the cotton and mineral regions, and
running from the north-east to the middle and eastern part of the State, is
admirably adapted both to agriculture and manufactures. Opelika, Wetumpka,
Centerville, Tuscaloosa, Scottsville, Prattsville, Tallassee, Autaugaville, and other
flourishing towns, are located in it. It is traversed by the Selma and Rome,
the Montgomery and West Point, the South and North, and the Alabama and
Chattanooga railroads.

   Lying directly on the high road between New York and New Orleans, and
traversed by rivers flowing from the mountains over many rocky barriers toward
the lowlands,—thus forming innumerable falls suitable for maufacturing power,—
it has already attracted much attention, and many factories are established
within its limits. A number of prosperous factories were destroyed during the
war; but the extensive cotton-mills at Tallassee, on the Tallapoosa river, the

Granite factory in Coosa county, the mills in Prattsville, and the Bell factory near Huntsville, all demonstrate the success which might attend similar new enterprises.

It is observed that, in spite of the cheapness of labor in England, Alabama manufacturers will soon be able to take cotton from adjacent plantations, spin it into yarn, and sell it in England at a greater profit than the English manufacturer, who buys American cotton in Liverpool and makes it into yarn in England, can ever obtain.* The advantage of the water power in such States as Alabama over the steam power necessarily employed in Great Britain is very large.

The crying need of the State is capital ; she is like so many of her neighbors, completely broken by the revolution, and unable to take the initiative in measures essential to her full development. With capital operating beneficently, Alabama could so bring her cheap cotton, cheap coal, cheap iron, and cheap living, to bear, as to seize and firmly retain a leading position among manufacturing States.

North of the manufacturing region, and extending 160 miles from north-east to south-west, is the mineral region of the State. Railroads traverse it in all directions ; the South and North binds it to Montgomery, and gives it an outlet toward Nashville and Louisville, via Decatur ; the Alabama and Chattanooga gives it easy access to the rolling-mills of Chattanooga ; the Selma, Rome and Dalton cuts through it to connect with the Kennesaw route to New York. It is as yet in many respects a wild country, sparsely populated, and rough in appearance. In one day's journey along the line of the North and South railroad, I saw hardly any town of considerable size ; in the forest clearings there were assemblages of rough board houses, and brawny men and scrawny women looked from the doors ; now and then we passed a coal-shoot, and now long piles of iron ore. There was little of interest save the material fact of the abundant riches of this favored section. The mountains were nowhere imposing ; they were humpbacked and overgrown ; but they held, it was easy to see, mighty secrets.

There are three distinct coal-fields in the carboniferous formation, which, with the silurian, shares all but the south-east corner of this mineral region.

The most extensive is the Warrior field, which has an area of three thousand square miles of a bituminous soft coal, lying in horizontal beds from one to four feet thick. It covers that portion of the State drained by the Black Warrior river and its tributaries, and extends quite into the north-eastern corner, between Lookout mountain and the Tennessee river. The field along the Cahawba river has beds from one to eight feet thick, extending over an area of 700 square miles. The Tennessee field, north of the Tennessee river, has large stores of bituminous coal, and the three together cover 4,000 square miles. Close beside them, from

---

* There are now a dozen prosperous cotton factories in Alabama, in its middle and northern portions. The Tallassee mills have 18,000 spindles ; two at Prattsville have 4,000 each ; and others, averaging about the same, at Huntsville, Florence, Tuscaloosa, Autaugaville, and in Pickens county, are prosperous. These mills regularly pay large dividends ; it is not uncommon for cotton-mills in the South to pay twenty per cent., and twelve to fifteen is the average. White labor exclusively is employed.

north-east to south-west, run beds of red and brown hematite, and limestone and sandstone are near at hand. The South and North railroad runs through the Warrior coal-field for more than fifty miles. It is surprising that, with such superb facilities for transportation, more has not been done toward the development of this section. Grand highways run in all the principal directions across iron-beds; a few branch tracks only being needed to cover every square mile with a network of communication.

I made a journey to Birmingham, the four-year-old child of the mineral development, and was surprised to note how solidly it had grown up. The route, from Montgomery to within a few miles of Calera, where the Selma, Rome and Dalton road crosses the South and North, lay through forests of yellow pine. We saw few farms and but little cleared land. A little above Calera, we came into the Coosa river section. That stream runs to the eastward of the railroad, and for many miles offers excellent sites for the establishment of manufactures. Lime-kilns are to be seen scattered all through the country; one hundred and fifty thousand barrels of lime being annually made, it is said, at and near Calera. The blue limestone of the silurian formation, so abundant there, is especially valuable. The road also traverses the zone of the deposits of fibrous brown hematite, extending north-easterly from Tuscaloosa, where it is said to be a hundred feet thick. On this ore belt several prosperous furnaces—the Roup's Valley, the Briarfield, the Shelby, and the Oxford—are located. An able engineer, Mr. Hiram Haines, of Alabama, says that the cost of the reduction of this iron at these furnaces is about twenty dollars per ton.

Crossing the Cahawba coal-field, and Red mountain, which forms the western boundary, I came into the valley of Shades creek, which presents a very advantageous position for the location of iron works. Here are the Red Mountain and Irondale Iron Works, whose furnaces can produce forty tons daily. The vast bed of fossiliferous ore which extends along the northern ridge of Red mountain runs from a point a score of miles east of Tuscaloosa to the north-eastern limit of the State. Where the railway crosses it, it is thirty feet in thickness. Like its famous compeer in Missouri, the "mountain" hardly merits its name, being simply an elevated ridge. The ore is everywhere easily accessible; I noted from point to point very successful excavations close to the railroad. The "mountain" is said to be one hundred miles in length, and it is estimated that it bears fifteen million tons of iron ore to the mile.

The Pennsylvania iron-masters have not allowed this ore to go unnoticed, and the English have made it an especial study. A little beyond the gap which allows the railroad to leave the coal-field, the projected route of the Mobile Grand Trunk road crosses the South and North; and, a short distance farther on, at the intersection of the Alabama and Chattanooga with the South and North, the town of Birmingham has sprung into a praiseworthy activity. In eighteen months from the date of building the first house there was a permanent population of four thousand people. The town was handsomely laid out in streets lined with imposing brick blocks, and the two finely built railways running through it brought to it crowds of daily visitors. If the development of the

South justifies the building of the proposed route from Atlanta, Georgia, through Birmingham to connect with the Southern Trans-Continental; of the connecting link from Opelika north-westerly through Birmingham to the Tennessee at Pittsburg Landing; of the Grand Trunk road, and the Ashley branch of the Selma, Rome and Dalton road, giving a short line from the coal and iron country to the Gulf—the new mineral capital will be indeed fortunate!

Birmingham is very centrally located in the mineral region, which comprises most of Shelby, Jefferson, Bibb, Walker, Tuscaloosa, Blount, St. Clair, Calhoun, Talladega, Randolph, and Cherokee counties. Red mountain seems to have been pushed above the unattractive soil in these rude fields as a beacon, and a temptation to explorers. It looms up in Jones's valley, the site of Birmingham, as the creator and guardian of the little city's destinies, and offers its treasures freely to the miner, the iron being covered with but a thin coating of soil. The Red mountain ores have a usual yield of fifty to fifty-eight per cent; and this mountain stretches, a narrow strip, for miles and miles, between two of the most wonderful coal-beds on the continent!

On my arrival at Birmingham, one afternoon, I found the good Mayor of the little city in bed, he, with other citizens, having been engaged all the previous night in quelling a negro riot, caused by the discontent and pressing necessities of the inhabitants of the back-country. An armed band of blacks had ridden into the town, and some fires had been started in a low quarter, evidently with the design of diverting attention to the conflagration while the provision stores were robbed. But the citzens succeeded in capturing the would-be robbers, and providing them with food and lodging in jail. This incident served to show the really hazardous position in which the negro is placed in some portions of the State. Untoward circumstances and outside financial pressure leave him absolutely without anything to eat; for he depends almost entirely on the outer world for his supplies.

Birmingham lies in the centre of a charming valley about ten miles wide, and about eighty miles in length. It is, perhaps, six hundred feet above the sea-level, and the valley is supposed to be the result of a vast upheaval of the silurian rocks, which upheaval or convulsion was evidently instrumental in dividing what was one huge coal-field into several. Another result of the rupture is a range of hills running down the centre of the valley, and containing deposits of brown hematite. Along the slope of the Red mountain there is a notable outcrop of variegated marble and sulphate of barytes, and lead ores are scattered throughout the neighborhood. The hematites on the northeastern slope of the Red mountain are exposed for a thickness of from fifteen to twenty-five feet; and many believe that a complete examination will show deposits one hundred feet thick. Here is a supply of iron for centuries to come; but Birmingham does not depend on the Red mountain alone. To the west, the north-west, and the north, there are fine deposits of ore, situated close to coal unsurpassed in quality for the manufacture of iron. The Elyton Land Company, which owned extensive tracts in Jones's valley, took the initiative in building Birmingham, and succeeded so well that the little town is expected to have a cotton factory and extensive car shops, as well as to be girdled by a ring of iron-furnaces. In the vicinity there are already numerous furnaces. Pennsylvania iron-masters are developing Irondale; the Red Mountain Iron Works are undergoing revival, after a long sleep since the war; and the largest Southern and English firms interested in iron manufacture are investigating the resources of Alabama iron tracts. The coal interests are receiving equal attention, and shafts have been sunk in the Warrior and Cahawba fields. The Irondale and Ironton furnaces are undoubtedly the most extensive on Red mountain, the two together producing about forty tons of pig-iron daily, while the Alabama Iron Company, located seventeen miles above Birmingham, is yearly sending North great quantities of ore. All the way from Jefferson county, through St. Clair, until it loses itself in the Lookout range, the Red mountain carries abundant stores. In Cherokee, Calhoun and Talladega counties, within easy reach of the Selma, Rome and Dalton railroad, there are furnaces in operation. At the Shelby Iron Works, in Shelby county, there is an extensive foundry for working up the famous "brown ore." The Briarfield Iron Works, in Bibb county, are also famous, and in Clay county it is believed that there are sufficient indications of magnetic ore to justify the establishment of furnaces. It is evident that a large town is to arise at some point in this region, and Birmingham seems to have secured the precedence.

The stores of copper and marl in Alabama are quite remarkable. In Randolph, Clay and Coosa counties, copper has been mined successfully, and lead has been found in Baker county. Gold has been mined from time to time since 1843, in Eastern Alabama, being found in small quantities. Silver shafts are said to have been sunk there by De Soto. The marble, granite and slate quarries of the State are rich, and will furnish cheap material for future cities, when the iron interest shall begin to build them. Of tin, plumbago, fire-clay, and kaolin and lime, there are abundant stores. The marls of Alabama are expected, in due time, to furnish a very important branch of industry. They contain properties of the highest fertilizing character when applied to worn-out lands, and offer the sections of the State which have been overworked under the old planting system a chance of renewal.

It is certain that large manufacturing communities are to spring up within the next few years, in the mineral region of Northern and North-eastern Alabama. The facility with which iron, coal and limestone can be reached, mined, and sent to furnaces or to market; the cheapness of labor and land, and the facilities for intercommunication, both by rail and water, are great recommendations. The iron ores are so rich, and such fine steel can be readily made from them, that they are certain to tempt capitalists to unearth them. The manufactured iron can be produced at about the same price as that of the cheapest regions in England.

The Alabama and Chattanooga railroad, consolidated from several lines, and purchased by a number of Boston capitalists, runs through the beautiful Wills' valley, near Chattanooga, and will, doubtless, draw much of the mineral interest of the Alabama district toward that city.

XXXV

NORTHERN ALABAMA—THE TENNESSEE VALLEY—TRAITS OF CHARACTER—EDUCATION.

THERE is much of quiet beauty in Northern Alabama, much also that is bold, rugged, even grand. The Tennessee valley seems to combine the loveliest characteristics of a Northern, with all the fragrant luxuriance and voluptuousness of a Southern climate. Here and there arise grand mountains; one encounters rapids and noisy waterfalls; vast stretches of forest; huge areas covered by ill-kept and almost ruined plantations, where the victims of the revolution are struggling with the mysteries of the labor question, and the changing influences of the times. The Memphis and Charleston railway, which runs through this valley from Chattanooga, and which is the connecting link in the great through route from the Mississippi to the Atlantic ocean, has done much in developing the country, but does not seem to have increased population to any large degree. There are some handsome and thriving towns along its line; pretty Huntsville, Decatur, Tuscumbia with its miraculous spring, and Florence, Tuscumbia's near neighbor, at the present head of navigation on the Tennessee, with its cotton factory, are all indications of the beauty and vivacity which this section will boast when new people come in. At Stevenson, whither the Nashville and Chattanooga railroad comes in its search for a passage through the apparently impassable mountains, the beauty of the great ranges is indescribable. The red loam of the valley will produce the best of cotton and corn, rye and barley, and small farmers, in this favorable climate, and with some little capital to start upon, could once more give this section its old name of "the garden of the South." The large plantations are much neglected, in many cases ruined; the planters are discouraged, and the negroes perplexed and somewhat demoralized by the great changes of the past few years. There has undoubtedly been a large falling off in the amount of cotton production in this section of Alabama, since the close of the war; and as the trail of the armies through it was marked with blood and fire, it is, perhaps, not very astonishing that the delay in restoration has been so great. If any portion of the South needs a total renewal of its population, it is this one; and an influx of Northern or foreign farmers would build it up in a short time.

Inasmuch as the Tennessee river passes through the entire breadth of North Alabama from east to west, the State is as much interested as Tennessee in the opening of navigation at Muscle Shoals, feeling convinced that the manufacturing interests at Florence would be revivified, that the valley would thus secure a cheap transportation route to market, and that the carrying of minerals, especially coal, would be made one of the great businesses of the section.

Huntsville has the honor of being the county seat of the richest agricultural county in the Tennessee valley, and is noted as the location of the convention that formed the State constitution, as the seat of the first Legislature of the commonwealth, and the place at which the first Alabama newspaper was issued. The city, which has some five thousand inhabitants, sits upon a low hill, from whose base gushes out a limestone spring, ample enough to supply the population with water. Through this country the weight of war was felt heavily; the people of Huntsville suffered much, and the devastation in the country, caused by both armies, was very great. Huntsville has some fine schools for young ladies; the Greene Academy, a resort of great numbers of the young men of Tennessee, was destroyed during the war by the Union troops.

Decatur was nearly submerged when I saw it, so that I can hardly attempt a description. Rain poured heavily down; the Tennessee, on whose south bank the town lies, was rampant, and the railroad seemed running through a lake. From Decatur toward Nashville, Tennessee, the railway route leads through a wild, hilly country, where the land is not especially good. Tuscumbia also suffered greatly in war time. It is noted for a spring, like Huntsville, but that of Tuscumbia is of pure freestone water, and springing from the plain in which the town is built, discharges 17,000 cubic feet of water every minute. Florence is connected with Tuscumbia by a branch of the Memphis and Charleston road, and was once a formidable commercial rival to Nashville. It was hindered by the war from completing the fine manufacturing enterprises which it was inaugurating, but is now making new efforts to centralize cotton spinning there. The Wesleyan University and the Synodical Institute, flourishing institutions, are located at Florence.

Farmers, and real farming,—not a loose planting and dependence on cotton,—are the principal needs of this section of the Tennessee valley.

The people of Alabama are as varied as is the topography of their lovely State, but most of them distinguished for frankness and generosity of character. It is a land of beautiful women; one even now and then sees among the degraded poor whites, who "dip snuff" and talk the most outrageous dialect, some lovely creature, who looks as poetic as a heathen goddess, until one hears her speak, or she pulls from her pocket a pine stick, with an old rag saturated in snuff wrapped around it, and inserts it between her dainty lips.

Here and there, in my journeys up and down the State, I saw the tall, long-haired, slender men who were so common a sight in the Alabama regiments during the war, and whose extraordinary height sometimes puzzled even the giants from Maine and Minnesota. The countrymen in the interior districts were much like those all through the cotton districts, bounded, prejudiced and ignorant of most things outside the limits of their State; difficult to drive into any conclusion, but easy to lead; generally conciliatory in their demeanor toward Northerners, but possessed of some little distrust of their alert and earnest ways. The gentlemen of means and culture whom I met were charming companions, and usually accomplished. They had the flavor of the country gentleman, and much of his repose, with the breeding and training of city life.

Of course I encountered many bitter people—men who were not at all friendly toward the North, and who declared that they were dissatisfied with the present condition of affairs; who cursed the negro, their own fate and the Federal Administration; but these were certainly the exceptions. The citizens of Alabama, as a mass, are as loyal to the idea of the Union to-day as are the citizens of New York, and have at times gone very far to welcome such reconstruction measures as are not instruments of oppression. In the sections where the lands are exhausted for the time being, or where crops have failed persistently, and the wolf of poverty is at the door, people have ceased to take any interest in State affairs, and are settling up their business and hastening to Texas. Now and then one sees a few tired and soiled men and women on the trains, and on inquiring their destination, finds they are on the return from Texas, which has not treated them as kindly as they anticipated; but, as a rule, those who go remain.

Here and there ostracism shows itself. There is some bitterness in Mobile, but I doubt if ordinarily a Northern Republican, voting there conscientiously for the best men,—not installing ignorance and vice in power under the Republican colors,—would be criticised on account of his sentiments. In the back-country he would meet with more intolerance. The negro has such absolute freedom in Alabama that the whites have long ago given up any endeavor, save at election times, to check his extravagances. There is a law which prevents challenge at the polls, and gives the right to the challenged party to sue for damages. When a native Southerner turns and joins the Republicans, he is usually pretty thoroughly ostracised; and this was the case with the gentleman who was Mayor of Mobile when I visited that city. As soon as he had joined the dominant party, he was "cut" in all the social relations; his wife and children were badly treated, and no name was thought too harsh to apply to him, although he had once been considered a citizen of distinction.

In some of the towns, as in Montgomery, and smaller communities in the region where the most distress prevails, the negroes seem to be absolutely dependent upon the charity of the white folks. Their lives are grossly immoral, and the women especially have but little conception of the true dignity of womanhood. One sees men and women, like Italian and Spanish beggars, slouching all day, from sun to shade, from shade to sun, living on garbage and the results of begging and predatory expeditions—a prey to any disease that comes along, and festering in ignorance. Some of them have been trying agriculture, and have given it up in disgust, because they do not understand farming, and there is no one to teach them. They have flocked into the towns, and there remain, seemingly nourishing a vague idea that something will turn up. It often struck me that the thousands of idle negroes I saw were in the attitude of waiting. Their expectant air was almost pathetic to witness. It was the same thing which we so often remark in animals—that quaint and curious, yet despairing look in the eyes and poise of the body, which seemed to say : " I would like to read the riddle of my relation to the universe, but I cannot." So they occupy themselves lazily in lounging about the sheriff's sales of mortgaged property,—always a prominent sight in the South now-a-days, alas !—or in begging of citizens and strangers with the greatest persistency.   On the plantations they are the same as every-where else in the cotton States : not always honest when they work for other people, and reckless and improvident when they work for themselves.

That there is plenty of enterprise in the State, there can be no doubt—no more doubt than that there is no money to assist it.   Indeed, it is safe to predict for Alabama a sudden upspringing sometime into a marvelous growth, something like that of Texas, because the railroad communication is already so perfect, and the resources are so immense.   As soon as a little money is accumulated, or foreign capital has gained courage to go in, we shall see an awakening in the beautiful commonwealth.   It is rich in grand mountains, noble rivers, swelling prairies, mighty forests, lovely sea-coast, and everywhere there is a wealth of Southern blossom and perfume.   The Northerner from America or Europe can readily accommodate himself to its climate, and can find any combination of resources that he may desire to develop.

Something should be done to arrest the drainage toward Texas ; it is dwarf-ing the development of the Alabamian towns, and leaving them in an unpleasant predicament.   There is a very large discouraged class in the State—people who were willing enough at the close of the war to accept its main results, and to devote themselves to a rebuilding, but who have been so embarrassed and hin-dered by the anomalous condition of labor and politics, and are so destitute of means with which to carry on new enterprises, that they prefer to fly to newer States.

The spirit of nationality among the people in those sections of Alabama which have suffered most, has been somewhat broken, yet, according to the statement made to me by one of the most distinguished of Alabama's citizens, these same people need but the return of a little prosperity to make them con-tented.

The commonwealth labors under a dreadful burden of ignorance ; the illit-eracy in some sections is appalling.   With a population of a little over 1,000,000, Alabama has more than 380,000 persons who can neither read nor write ; and of these nearly 100,000 are whites.   There are also large classes who can both read and write, but whose education goes no farther.   Among the 175,000 voters in the State, there is a newspaper circulation of 40,000 only. The negro does not seem to care for the papers.   A good public school system was inaugurated in Alabama in 1854, and three years later nearly 90,000 children were attending school in the State ; but the advent of the war annulled the progress already made, and since reconstruction educational matters have been somewhat embroiled.   The conduct of the schools is now in the hands of what is known as the State Board of Education, composed of the State Superintendent and two members from each Congressional district.   This Board has full Legisla-tive powers, the Legislature being only revisory of its acts.   The school fund receives from $500,000 to $600,000 annually from the State, one-third of it being interest on the fund bestowed by the General Government, and the remainder being made up of one-fifth of the commonwealth's general revenue—all the poll tax, the licenses, and the tax on insurance companies.   This fund is nominally apportioned impartially to the whites and blacks in each county, and the trustees in each township are informed what their share is. Under this system, the average attendance at the various schools opened throughout the State, has been 150,000; but in 1873 the schools were all closed (save those in the large cities) on account of the inability of the State to pay teachers ! This cessation has been productive of much harm and disorganization. Efforts have, however, been made to resuscitate the State University at Tuscaloosa, which is not in a flourishing condition, and a normal college, for teachers of both sexes, has been started at Florence, in the northern part of the State. In Western Alabama, a colored university and normal college has been established at Marion, and a colored normal school is opened at Huntsville. The American Missionary Society also maintains a college for colored people at Talladega.

The Cotton-Plant.

XXXVI.

THE SAND-HILL REGION—AIKEN—AUGUSTA.

AFTER many weeks of journeying in the South, through regions where hardly a house is to be seen, where the villages, looming up between patches of forest or canebrake, seem deserted and worm-eaten, and the people reckless and idle, the traveler is struck with astonishment and delight when he emerges into the busy belt extending from Aiken, in South Carolina, to Augusta, in Georgia. There he sees manufacturing villages, hears the whir of spindles, notes on every hand evidences of progressive industry, and wonders why it was

A Street Scene in Augusta, Georgia.

not so years before. Alas! who can compute the sum of the lost opportunities of the Southern States?

This "sand-hill region," extending from the north-eastern border of South Carolina to the south-eastern border of Georgia, has many noteworthy aspects. Its climate has wonderful life-renewing properties for the invalid worn down with the incessant fatigues and changes of severer latitudes, and its resources for the establishment of manufactures, and for the growth of some of the most remarkable and valuable fruits, are unrivaled.

The upper limit of the sand-hills in South Carolina is very clearly defined. They are usually found close to the rivers, and are supposed to be ancient sand-banks once not far from the sea-shore. They pass through the State, half-way between the ocean and the Blue Ridge, and are most thoroughly developed near Aiken, Columbia, Camden, and Cheraw. They are usually clothed in aromatic pine forests.

Down the slopes, in Georgia and South Carolina, run rivers, which in winter and spring are turbid with the washings from the red clay hills to the northward; and in the flat valleys scattered along these streams cotton and corn grow with remarkable luxuriance. In Georgia the hills run from the falls of the Savannah river at Augusta, south-west and north-east, as far as the Ogeechee river. The highest point in this curious range, at the United States Arsenal at Summerville, near Augusta, is hardly more than six hundred feet above the sea-level. The sand-hills are the home of the yellow and the "short-leaved" pine, the Spanish and water oak, the red maple, the sweet gum, the haw, the persimmon, the wild orange, and the China-tree; the lovely *Kalmia Latifolia* clothes the acclivities each spring in garments of pink and white; the flaming azalea, the honey-suckle, the white locust, the China burr and other evergreens, the iris, the phlox, the silk grass, flourish there.

In the open air, in the gardens, japonicas grow ten feet high and blossom late in winter; and the "fringe-tree" and the *Lagerstremia Indica* dot the lawns with a dense array of blossoms. Although the unstimulated surface soil of all this section will not produce cotton and the cereals more than two years in succession, yet it is prolific of the peach, the apricot, the pomegranate, the fig, the pear, all kinds of berries, and the grape, which grows there with surprising luxuriance; and all vegetables practicable in a northern climate ripen there in the months of April and May.

A pleasant land, one is forced to declare. But this productiveness is the least of its advantages. The kindly climate is the chief glory of the sand-hill country. Aiken has achieved a great reputation as a winter residence for pulmonary invalids. The mild and equable temperature, and the dryness of the air, which allows the patient to pass most of his winter under the open sky, inhaling the fragrance of the pine woods, have, year after year, drawn hundreds of exhausted Northerners thither. Before the war, the planter of the lowlands, and the merchants of New York and Boston alike, went to Aiken to recuperate; the planter occupying a pleasant cottage during the summer, and the Northerner arriving with the first hint of winter. But now the planter comes no more with the splendor and spendthrift profusion of old, and the Northerner has the little town very much to himself.

The accommodations have, for several years since the war, been insufficient; but as the inhabitants creep back toward their old prosperity, they are giving Aiken the bright appearance of a Northern town, and the ill-looking, unpainted, rickety houses of the past are disappearing. Originally laid out by a railroad company, in 1833, as a future station of commercial importance, Aiken prospered until fire swallowed it up a few years later. When the war came, great numbers

of refugees rushed into it, and the misery and distress there were great. The
tide of battle never swept through the town, Kilpatrick contenting himself with
a partially successful raid in that direction when Sherman was on the road to
Columbia; and as soon as peace was declared the invalids flocked back again
to haunt the springs and the pleasant woody paths, over which the jessamine
day and night showers its delicious fragrance.

Aiken is situated seventeen miles from the Savannah river and from Augusta,
on the South Carolina railroad, which extends southward to Charleston. The
inhabitants of the hill-country, a little remote from the towns, are decidedly
primitive in their habits, and the sobriquet of "sand-hiller" is applied by South
Carolinians to specimens of poor white trash, which nothing but a system of
slave-aristocracy could ever have produced. The lean and scrawny women,
without animation, their faces discolored by illness, and the lank and hungry
men, have their counterparts nowhere among native Americans at the North;
it is incapable of producing such a peasantry.'

The houses of the better class of this folk,—the prosperous farmers, as distinguished from the lazy and dissolute plebeians,—to whom the word "sand-
hiller" is perhaps too indiscriminately given, are loosely built, as the climate
demands little more than shelter. At night, immense logs burn in the fireplace,
while the house door remains open. The diet is barbarous as elsewhere
among the agricultural classes in the South—corn-bread, pork and "chick'n;"
farmers rarely killing a cow for beef, or a sheep for mutton. Hot and bitter
coffee smokes morning and night on the tables where purest spring water,
or best of Scuppernong wine, might be daily placed—the latter with almost as
little expense as the former.

But the invalid visiting this region in search of health, and frequenting a
town of reasonable size, encounters none of these miseries. At Augusta and
at Aiken he can secure the comforts to which he is accustomed in the North,
to which will be added a climate in which existence is a veritable joy. In
the vicinity of Aiken many hundreds of acres are now planted with the grape;
and 2,500 gallons of wine to the acre have been guaranteed in some cases,
although the average production must, of course, fall very much below that.

The development of the resources for manufacturing in the region extending
between and including Aiken and Augusta merits especial mention, and shows
what may be done by judicious enterprise in the South. The extensive cotton
manufactories at Augusta and Graniteville employ many hundreds of hands.
Scarcely a quarter of a century ago the Augusta cotton manufacturing enterprise
was inaugurated with but a small capital. It was the outgrowth of a demand
for labor for the surplus white population—labor whose results should accrue at
once to the benefit of the State, and of that population. In due time the canal at
Augusta was constructed.

The Augusta cotton factory, which was not at first prosperous, now has a
capital stock of $600,000, upon which a quarterly dividend of five per cent. is
paid. Thousands of spindles and hundreds of looms are now busy along the
banks of the noble canal, where, also, have sprung up fine flour-mills and

tobacco factories. The cotton-mill is filled with the newest and finest machinery, and has received the high compliment, from Senator Sprague, of Rhode Island, of being "the best arranged one in the United States."

At Graniteville, in South Carolina, two or three miles beyond the Savannah river, extensive mills have also been erected, and eight million yards of cotton are annually made there. The manufacturing village is as tidy and thrifty as any in the North, and there is none in the South which excels it in a general aspect of comfort, unless it be that of the Eagle and Phœnix Company at Columbus, Georgia. Six miles from Augusta there is an extensive kaolin factory.

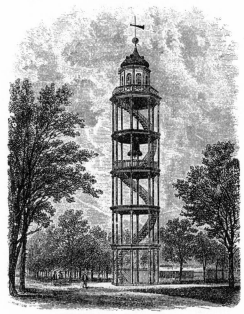

Early on a bright summer morning, while the inhabitants were still asleep, I entered Augusta, and walked through the broad, beautifully shaded avenues of this lovely Southern city. The birds gossiped languidly in the dense foliage, through which the sun was just peering; here and there the sand of the streets was mottled with delicate light and shade; the omnipresent negro was fawning and yawning on door-steps, abandoning himself to his favorite attitude of slouch.

I wandered to the banks of the Savannah, which sweeps, in a broad and sluggish current, between high

A Bell-Tower in Augusta, Georgia.

banks, bordered at intervals with enormous mulberry trees. Clambering down among the giant boles of these sylvan monarchs, and stumbling from time to time over a somnolent negro fisherman, I could see the broad and fertile Carolina fields opposite, and scent the perfume which the slight breeze sent from the dense masses of trees in the town above me.

Returning, an hour later, I found the place had awakened to a life and energy worthy of the brightest of Northern cities of its size. The superb Greene street, with its grand double rows of shade trees, whose broad boughs almost interlocked above, was filled with active pedestrians; the noise of wagons and drays was beginning; the cheery markets were thronged with gossiping negro women; and around the Cotton Exchange groups were already gathered busily discussing the previous day's receipts.

Augusta's excellent railroad facilities, and her advantageous situation, have made her an extensive cotton market. The Georgia railroad is largely tributary to the town, although Savannah is of late years receiving much of the cotton which properly belongs to Augusta. The new railway stretching from Port Royal, in South Carolina, to Augusta, furnishes a convenient outlet, and the South Carolina and Central roads give communication with Charleston and Savannah.

The Cotton Exchange was founded in 1872. For the cotton years of 1872–73, Augusta received 180,789 bales. The cotton factories in the city consume 200 bales daily, and the Langley and the Hickman factories in South Carolina, and the Richmond mills in Georgia, are also supplied from this point. Cotton culture throughout all this section has greatly increased since the war. I was told that one man in Jackson county now grows a larger number of bales than the whole county produced previous to 1860.

The use of fertilizers, once so utterly discarded, is now producing the most remarkable results. But the planters in all the surrounding country give but little attention to a rotation or diversity of crops, so that any year's failure of the cotton brings them to financial distress, as they depend entirely upon the outer world for their supplies; although, in some of the northern sections of the State they show an inclination to vary their course in this respect. Conversation with representative men from various parts of the State, who naturally flock into Augusta to inspect the market, showed, however, that there was a steady and genuine improvement in agriculture throughout Georgia. Lands which heretofore have been considered of superior quality for cotton-growing have, under the new *régime*, with careful fertilizing and culture, produced twice as much as during the epoch of slavery.

According to universal testimony, the negro on these cotton-lands usually works well, "and when he does not," said a planter to me, "it is because he is poorly paid." Small farms seem to be increasing in Middle Georgia, and much of the cotton brought into Augusta is raised exclusively by white labor. The small farmers, who were before the war unable to produce a crop in competition with those who possessed a larger number of slaves, now find no difficulty in placing their crop in market, and securing good prices for it.

Augusta, like Savannah, is a town built in the midst of a beautiful wood. The public buildings are embowered in foliage; the pretty City Hall, the Medical College, the Masonic and Odd Fellows' Halls peering out from knots of trees.

A Confederate Soldier's Grave at Augusta, Georgia. [Page 349.]

Broad street, the main thoroughfare, is well lined with commodious stores and residences, and the streets leading from it are well kept and shaded. In front of the City Hall stands a simple but massive monument, erected to the memory of the Georgian signers of the Declaration of American Independence.

Tall men, as well as tall and graceful trees, abound in the streets, for the Georgian is dowered with a generous height. The policemen are clad in an amicable mingling of gray and blue. On the road to Summerville, the pretty suburb on one of the sand-hills three miles away, one sees the powder-mill, now disused, which supplied the Confederates with ammunition for many a day; and in a lovely location, at the hill's top, is the extensive United States Arsenal, around which are grouped many workshops, built and occupied by the Confederates during the war.

Nothing can exceed in quiet and reverent beauty the floral decoration of the principal cemetery of Augusta. Loving hands have lingered long over the Confederate soldiers' graves, and the white headstones, neatly surrounded with box-wood hedges, nearly all bear inscriptions like the following, which show that even as in the North, the young were the first to go, and first to fall:

"JOE E. R——,
Co. E., 4 Tenn. Cav.
Died Feb. 17, 1863,
Aged 19."

Here and there tall posts have decorative mottoes worked in evergreen upon them, such as

"The Sacred Trust of Heroes."
"Our Boys in Grey."

Augusta escaped the scourge of Invasion, but did not escape the ghost of Bereavement, who has claimed such a large space among the pleasant shadows for his own particular ground.

The old town had a stormy revolutionary history. Named after one of the royal princesses of England by Oglethorpe, it was an Indian outpost after 1735, and in constant danger from the savages, until taken and retaken by Briton and American during the revolution. The churches and the institutions of learning in Augusta are numerous, and the extensive fair-ground of the Cotton States' Mechanical and Agricultural Association occupies many pleasant acres just outside the eastern limits of the city.

XXXVII.

ATLANTA—GEORGIA POLITICS—THE FAILURE OF RECONSTRUCTION.

FROM the ashes of the great penitential conflagration in which the exigencies of war enveloped Atlanta, from the ruins of the thousand dwellings, factories, workshops, and railroad establishments totally destroyed in the blaze of 1864, has sprung up a new, vigorous, awkwardly alert city, very similar in character to the mammoth groupings of brick and stone in the North-west. There is but little that is distinctively Southern in Atlanta; it is the antithesis of Savannah. There is nothing that reminds one of the North in the deliciously embowered chief city of Georgia, surrounded with its romantic moss-hung oaks, its rich lowlands, and its luxuriant gardens, where the magnolia, the bay, and the palmetto vie with one another in the exquisite inexplicable charm of their voluptuous beauty. Atlanta has an unfinished air; its business and residence streets are scattered along a range of pretty hills; but it is eminently modern and unromantic. The Western and Atlantic railway unites it with Chattanooga,

Sunset over Atlanta, Georgia.

running through a country which was scourged in bitterest fashion by the war; the Georgia railroad connects it with Augusta; the Macon and Western with handsome and thriving Macon; the Atlanta and West Point road to the town of West Point, Alabama, gives a continuous line to Montgomery; and the new

Piedmont Air Line, which has opened up the whole of Northern Georgia, gives it new and speedy communication with the North via Charlotte, in North Carolina. Great numbers of Northern people have flocked to Atlanta to live since the time when General Pope's will was law, and when the Bullock administration was just arising out of the chaos of the constitutional convention. The removal of the State capital from Milledgeville to Atlanta also gave the renaissant city a good start, and the wonderful manner in which it drew trade and capital to it from all sides made it the envy of its sister Georgian cities.

A brief review of the progress of politics in the State since Atlanta became its capital will aid in arriving at an understanding of the present social and political condition of the commonwealth.

When the reconstruction policy of the General Government began, a large number of the citizens of Georgia declared for it, and among them was Mr. Bullock, subsequently Governor of the State. In the political campaign which ensued, the opposite faction, which totally repudiated the reconstruction acts, condescended to much proscription and denunciation, and numbers of Union men were driven from the State. It was out of this campaign that the Ku-Klux conspiracy, as manifested in Georgia, is supposed to have grown. Prominent Republicans received lugubrious letters containing pictures of coffins, and acts of violence were not wanting. Native Georgians, who were leading Republican officials, were hunted down and assassinated; Republican meetings were dispersed, not without slaughter; and it was manifest from the outset that there was to be a decided upsetting of the attempt to enforce the policy inaugurated by the war. But the Republican party was organized, and its Legislature, in which there were many negroes, went into session.

The first trouble that occurred was due to a discussion of the question whether or not men who had held office previous to the war, and then had taken part in the rebellion, were eligible for the Legislature. The debate upon this matter was heated and angry, and the final decision was in favor of extreme liberality toward all who had fought on the Confederate side. Many of these were admitted to the State councils, and after a time, getting control of the middle-men, they had the Legislature in their hands. Their first act was to oust all the colored members—some thirty-six—and to proceed on the basis that a white man's government was the only one for Georgia. The expulsion of the negroes was corrected by act of Congress; and in 1869 the colored element was readmitted to the Legislature. After this, Bullock, who was the first Governor chosen under the operation of the reconstruction laws, had full sway for about two years. Some good laws were passed during that time, but the railroad legislation was the occasion of veritable disaster to the progress of reconstruction in Georgia. Bullock was in due time compelled to depart from the State, to save himself from imprisonment; and the Democratic party, completely triumphant, now and then announces its convictions through the medium of Robert Toombs, who has been its leader, and, in some measure, its exponent for many years. It is not long since this gentleman, in a speech made at Atlanta in favor of a convention to revise the constitution of the State, made use of the following language : " Why, look at that miserable thing you call a constitution ! It commits you to all the lies of the revolution against you. It says your allegiance is first due to the Federal Government before it is due to your own State ? Do you believe that ? When you can wrench that from the constitution, do it ! ''

Under the administration of Governor Bullock, a system of internal improvement was inaugurated, theoretically granting State aid to naissant railroads in the proportion in which the companies building those roads aided themselves. But bonds were over-issued, and were negotiated by prominent bankers in New York city. The Brunswick and Albany railroad was the principal project. About $6,000,000 worth of bonds were actually issued during the two years, all of which went to the Brunswick and Albany railroad, with the exception of $600,000 granted to the Cartersville and Van West road. The party now in power has repudiated all the railroad bonds issued under Bullock's *régime*. The New York bankers have not suffered very much by this, but the repudiation will give the credit of the State a severe blow.

The Governor, during these two years in which the reconstruction policy of Congress was upheld, seems to have had an agitated and miserable existence. He spent a great deal of time and money in Washington before he succeeded in procuring the legislation which restored the negroes to their places in the Legislature in 1869. It is alleged that when he took the reins of government in Georgia he was worth no money, but that, a little time after he had assumed the office, he paid his debts, and became reasonably prosperous. But he was surrounded by an atmosphere of corruption, and it is difficult to say that he was individually dishonest. In his defense, which gives a very clear idea of the immense obstacles which wily and subtle men placed in his path, it is evident that he required the shrewdness of an archangel to march without stumbling. It was for the interest of the Democratic party in the State to make reconstruction unsuccessful, and toward that end they unceasingly toiled.

The material on which one was compelled to work, to maintain the power of the reconstruction government in those days, was unreliable. One never knew when he was to be betrayed by the weak-kneed or ignorant legislators who were his own friends. Prominent State officials were applied to to contribute money for " election purposes,"—*i. e.*, for the purchase of votes. I was told by those who did not fear sincere contradiction, that as much as two thousand dollars was sometimes paid at that epoch for a single vote. Often in danger of losing his life, and always in danger of betrayal, the head of the newly organized party was haunted by horrors.

The career of H. I. Kimball in Atlanta, and in various enterprises in the commonwealth, has not a little to do with the present condition of politics in Georgia. In 1865, Mr. Kimball made his appearance in the State, and began by perfecting arrangements for placing sleeping-cars on all the roads in the South. Atlanta was even then peering from beneath the ashes under which she had been buried, and was vaguely whispering prophecies of her future commercial greatness. The capital was likely to be removed from Milledgeville to that city as soon as a regular State government should be resumed, and Kimball, doubtless, saw that as readily as did any of the Atlantians. The Kimball-Ramsey-Pullman Sleeping-Car Company was the name of the organization with which he started ; and he intended, it is said, to get rich out of it by means of $300,000 franchise stock, which he was to have. This venture was not successful, and many people who furnished the money to buy the necessary cars were sufferers. His next venture was the "Atlanta Opera House." The original

company which had contemplated erecting a mammoth block for an opera house, and for stores and public offices, had failed; the unfinished building was considered worth $115,000, but Mr. Kimball obtained possession of it for $33,000. This purchase gave him the means of raising money; he finished the Opera House, furnishing it as a legislative edifice. At that time the Legislature was in session in the City Hall in Atlanta. The city rented Kimball's new building, as soon as it was completed, for a State-House. Kimball had fitted it up with $55,000, advanced to him, it is said, by Governor Bullock from the State

The State-House—Atlanta, Georgia.

funds. The Legislature entered the new Capitol, and no sooner had they assembled than Mr. Kimball besought them to buy it. They at first refused, but subsequently purchased it for $300,000. As soon as this was decided on, the $55,000 loaned by the Governor to Kimball were returned, thus presumably securing Governor Bullock from impeachment.

Having prospered so well in the Opera House project, the ingenious Kimball conceived the scheme of the Kimball House, at present the largest hotel in Atlanta, and one of the largest in the Southern States. A bill was passed by the Legislature allowing an advance to the Brunswick and Albany railroad— that is to say, two acts allowed Kimball, who was the contractor, to build the road, to draw respectively $12,000 and $15,000 per mile, before building each section of twenty miles. By this issue he obtained the funds with which to build the Kimball House. He constructed the first twenty miles of the Brunswick and Albany railroad in good faith, then gradually encroached, until there was no longer any semblance of adherence to the letter of the act, which naturally required him to build the road as fast as the money was advanced. Meantime the Democrats were vigorously attacking Governor Bullock, charging him with every kind of theft, and he was in a precarious situation, when he suddenly found that he had not a majority that he could count on in the Legislature. Then ensued a severe struggle on his part against the ousting which was threatened. Kimball continued to unfold superb schemes, and turn them to his private account. In the fall of 1871, Governor Bullock paid a visit to California, whence he was hurried home by the announcement that the Legislature was to meet in December. He returned; surveyed the political field; found that he was in imminent danger of being complicated and possibly impeached, and went North and resigned.   Shortly after, Kimball disappeared from Atlanta and from his Southern field of operations, and the bubble burst.

The State railroad, running from Atlanta northward to Chattanooga, had been leased under Bullock's administration.   The Democrats, who now came into power, charged that the Governor was guilty of gross official misconduct in leasing the road, although it was done in obedience to an act of the Legislature, and they proceeded to prosecute every one who had been connected with the management of it under the Bullock *régime*.   They based their charge against the Governor upon the theory that he was personally and pecuniarily interested in the road, as Kimball was one of the lessees, and the Governor was alleged to be Kimball's partner.   This, however, the Governor expressly denies, showing that the road, which, for the twenty years from its building up to 1868, had been an expense to the State, and a fruitful source of political corruption, was made profitable under the lease system.   The prosecutions by the Democratic party were characterized by a great deal of acerbity, and in one case the Supreme Court decided that much injustice was inflicted upon a prosecuted party.   The Democratic Legislative Committee appointed to investigate the official conduct of the late Governor was in session seven months, and confined its final report mainly to denunciations of the Governor's course, on the supposition that he was Kimball's partner.   They took complete control of the State Government, gloried in the repudiation of the various bonds issued from 1869 to 1871, and maintained that the reconstruction acts of Congress were "unconstitutional, revolutionary, null, and void."

Certainly reconstruction is null and void in Georgia.   It has been a complete failure there.   That there have been instances of glaring injustice practiced on both sides no fair-minded man can for an instant doubt.   The Republican administration lasted scarcely three years; and the legitimate results of the war were not maintained so long as that after 1868.   Out of the 90,000 colored voters in the State, scarcely 30,000 vote to-day; free schools are almost unknown outside the large cities and towns; and there has not been a Republican inspector of election since the Democrats assumed power.   To judge from the testimony of native Georgians who are Republicans, and who have never been suspected of any dishonesty or untruth, the negroes are very grossly intimidated; and the Ku-Klux faction still exists as a kind of invisible empire.   This is naturally to be expected after the occurrences in Louisiana, South Carolina, and Alabama; it is the revulsion from tyrannical ignorance and carpet-baggery; and may prove as baneful in its results as has its degraded and disreputable opposite.   The Democrat of Georgia talks with all the more emphasis of a white man's government in his commonwealth, because he feels that there is a black man's government in a neighboring State; if he has ever had any exaggerated fears as to a too free assumption of civil rights by his ex-slave, those fears are accented ten-fold since he has seen the real injustice practiced by negroes where they have attained supreme, unrestricted power.

Both the whites and blacks in the State have large and effective military organizations, and drill constantly, as if dumbly preparing for some possible future strife. The battalions of the white race still cling to the Confederate gray, in some cases; the negro militiaman blossoms into a variety of gorgeous uniforms. I saw a company of blacks assembling in Atlanta; they were good-looking, stalwart men, and went about their work with the utmost nonchalance, while here and there a white muttered between his teeth something unmistakably like " d——n niggers." There is a very large negro population in Atlanta and the surrounding country.

But few traces of the war are now left in Atlanta. The residence streets have a smart, new air; many fine houses have been recently built, and their Northern architecture and trim gardens afford a pleasant surprise after the tumble-down, unpainted towns of which one sees so many in the South. The banks, the theatres, the public business blocks, the immense Kimball House, all have the same canny air—seem to be boasting of their tidy looks and prosperity to the countrymen who come into town to market. I strolled into the Capitol (the quondam Opera House, which Kimball sold the Legislature). In the office of the State Treasurer I encountered some gentlemen who seemed inclined to believe that the State would not suffer if all debts contracted under the Bullock *régime* were repudiated. One said that he could not inform me how much the State debt, as construed by the reconstructionists, was; he reckoned no one knew; the scoundrels who had contracted the debt had run away; if they could lay hands on Bullock they would put him in the penitentiary. I found, everywhere I went in the Capitol, a spirit of extreme bitterness prevailing against the departed carpet-baggers; and all complained that the State affairs had been left in a wretched condition.

The attempt to establish free common schools throughout Georgia has thus far resulted in failure. Prior to the war there was but little effort made for the education of the masses. A small sum was appropriated as the "indigent school fund," but the majority of the poorer classes in the back-country remained in dense ignorance. In the present State School Commissioner's office I was informed that there had been no common school open outside the large cities for some time. It was alleged that the school fund had been diverted to unlawful purposes during the "previous administration," and that the State had been much embarrassed by a debt of $300,000, incurred in prematurely putting schools into operation. There seems no doubt of a sincere desire on the part of the Georgia Conservatives to maintain free schools; and it is, by the way, noteworthy that three of the Southern States that are Conservative in politics are leading all the others in education. Local taxation is the principal bugbear. The farmer dislikes to be taxed for schools; he still has various absurd prejudices; thinks the common school a pauper institution, and gets angry if there is any talk of compulsory education. The school population of the State is about 370,000, and the annual school revenue, derived from interest on bonds, from the poll tax, from taxes on shows, and from dividends on railroad stock, amounts to $280,000. This is, of course, ridiculously small, and, now that Georgia has arrived once more at some degree of material prosperity, will, doubtless, be increased, and amends will be made for the shameful negligence which allowed the whole school machinery to stop and rust for a year. A praiseworthy but fruitless effort has recently been made in the Legislature to follow in the steps of Tennessee, by favoring local taxation, a limit to the amount of which is to be fixed, to guard against the creation of excessive taxes by negro votes; and the Peabody fund is employed in aiding the proselyters who preach the cause of common school education in the back counties. The illiteracy in Georgia previous to 1860 was alarming; the most moderate estimates showed that eighteen per cent. of the adult native white population could not even read; and, in 1860, when the State had a scholastic population of 236,454, only 94,687 attended school. Prejudice is strong, but the free school will establish itself in Georgia, as everywhere South, in due time. I think that the mass of Georgians respect an educated negro, but are determined to make him do the work of educating himself. The negro needs a good general education, mainly because it will strengthen his character, and make him more independent. He is at present very easily intimidated with regard to his voting, and readily falls into corrupt practices in election time, because he does not consider the evil effects of such a course.

The manufactures of Atlanta are not extensive; there are some large rolling-mills, and a good deal of iron is brought down from the country to the north-ward, and worked over there. Of course there is a large cotton movement through the town; and, in the late autumn, a journey along the railroad to Chattanooga discloses hundreds of teams toiling over the rough roads, bringing goodly stores of cotton bales to the stations. Journalism in Atlanta is vivacious and enterprising, and the *New Era* and the *Herald* are newspapers of metropolitan dimensions. The Governor's residence is a pretty building, on an ambitious avenue, where stand many handsome mansions; the City Hall is quite imposing. Atlanta is the home of General John B. Gordon, one of the present United States senators, and a noted Confederate general. On the road from Atlanta to Augusta, and but fifteen miles from the capital, is the remarkable " Stone Mountain," a peak of solitary rock, 3,000 feet in height, and several miles in circumference. Near its top are the remains of an ancient fortification; and along the sides there are little patches of soil, but from a distance the great pyramid stands out seemingly naked before the sky, its dark gray looming up angrily against the crystal vault.

Northward, twenty miles from Atlanta, at the base of the Kenesaw mountain, lies the pretty little town of Marietta, once the location of a flourishing military academy, and now a summer resort for the well-to-do of Atlanta's 30,000 residents. The country between Atlanta and Chattanooga seems as peaceful as if never a soldier had set his foot upon it; yet it needs no stretch of memory to recall those wild days when the giant strategists, Sherman and Johnston, bitterly fought and fortified, and marched and countermarched during long months, from Dalton to the Chattahoochee river, whence Sherman pushed on against Hood and the desperate Confederate armies, whose command Hood had taken after the

Richmond Government's fatal error,—the removal of Johnston,—until the great granary and storehouse of the Confederacy, with Atlanta for its centre, was conquered by the Union arms.   The "State," or Western and Atlantic road, once the object of so many hostile cavalry raids, does a thriving trade.   At all the stations, in harvest time, are groups of jovial and contented agriculturists, white and black, their garments flecked with cotton.   Near Marietta, at Roswell, there are flourishing cotton factories.   Allatoona and Resaca, memorable for the scenes of 1864, lie in a broken, picturesque and fertile country; the lands along the creeks are especially rich.   Dalton, the junction of the "State," the branch of the East Tennessee, Virginia and Georgia, and the Selma, Rome and Dalton railroads, is a flourishing grain depot for Atlanta; here and there on the adjacent mountains may be seen fast-crumbling remnants of Johnston's fortifications, erected a decade ago.   At Cartersville, fifty miles from Atlanta, fine crops of wheat and cotton are raised; large quarries of slate and marble have been opened and worked successfully; and in the vicinity manganese has been found.

An Up-Country Cotton-Press.

XXXVIII

SAVANNAH, THE FOREST CITY—THE RAILWAY SYSTEM OF
GEORGIA—MATERIAL PROGRESS OF THE STATE.

THE transition from the brisk air and reddish uplands of Northern Georgia
to the sluggish atmosphere and sombre voluptuousness of the lowlands of
the coast, is startling.   One seems to have come upon another country, to have
passed beyond seas, so great is the difference.   The Savannah river, up which
you sail, returning from Florida some radiant morning, seems to you to have no
affinity with the Savannah which, far among the Northern mountains, you saw
born of the frolicsome or riotous streamlets forever leaping and roaring in the
passes or over mighty falls.   Here it is broad, and deep, and strong, and, near
the bluff on which the city stands, it is freighted with ships from European ports

View on the Savannah River near Savannah, Georgia.

and from the Northern cities of our own coast.   The moss-hung oaks, the magnolias, the orange-trees, the bays, the palmettoes, the olives, the stately shrubs
of arbor vitæ, the Cape myrtles, the oleanders, the pomegranates, the lovely
japonicas, astonish the eyes which have learned to consider a more Northern
foliage as Georgian.   Very grand in their way were the forests of pine, with

their sombre aisles, and the mournful whispers of the breeze stealing through them; but here is the charm of the odorous tropical South, which no one can explain. Yet it is not here that one must look for the greatest wealth of the State; for Middle Georgia is, perhaps, the richest agricultural region in the commonwealth, and the hundreds of farms along the western boundary are notable instances of thorough and profitable culture.

But here at Savannah began the existence of Georgia; here it was that Oglethorpe planted his tiny colony hardly a century and a-half ago; here, on the pine-crowned bluff, where an Indian tribe dwelt in a village called Yamacraw, he disembarked the adventurers who had come with him from England, under the sanction of the charter accorded by George the Second, and in due time established a group of tents defended by a battery of cannon. From this humble begin-

General Oglethorpe, the Founder of Savannah.

ning Savannah soon grew to the proportions of a town, and was laid out into squares. As the colonists had first landed on the shore of South Carolina, and been very kindly received by the Carolinians, they named the streets of the new settlement after their benefactors,—Bull, Drayton, Whitaker, St. Julian and Bryan,—and some of them still bear those names. Savannah, in 1734, was a little assemblage of squares in a clearing in the pine forest. The inhabitants locked themselves into their cabins at night, because the alligators strolled through the town, seeking whom they might devour; and the Indians, who now and then threatened to "dig up the hatchet" when the colonists encroached, kept all in constant alarm. Two years later, the distinguished founder of Methodism, John Wesley, preached his first sermon in America in Savannah.

An English gentleman who visited the colony in this same year tells us that " the houses are built at a pretty large distance from one another, for fear of fire; the streets are very wide, and there are great squares left at proper spaces for markets and other conveniences." To this fortunate early arrangement the town owes its beauty to-day. No other American city has such wealth of foliage, such charming seclusion, such sylvan perfection, so united with all the convenience and compactness of a large commercial centre. The trustees of the colony, appointed under the royal charter, made a strict agrarian law, which divided the original town into two hundred and forty "freeholds;" the town land covered twenty-four square miles, every forty houses (each house being located on tracts of land of exactly the same size) making a ward; each ward had a constable, and under him were four tithing-men. Every ten houses made a tithing; and to each tithing there was a mile square, "divided into twelve lots, besides roads." Every freeholder of the tithing had a lot or farm of forty-five acres there, and two lots were reserved by the trustees. Great efforts were used to make Georgia, as the new colony was called, after the English king who had granted the charter, "a silk and wine-growing country;" but after protracted trials the colonists gave up their dreams of speedily realizing immense fortune, and set to work at more practical schemes.

Savannah, escaping, as by miracle, from Indian malice and the tyranny of the "trustees," who were of small benefit to the rest of the settlers, grew and flourished until John Reynolds came out from England as Governor in 1754, the trustees having resigned. The colonists welcomed him joyously at first, but afterward regretted it, for he was not specially interested in them. He allowed the town to fall into decay, and, notwithstanding the ·fact that the General Assembly of Georgia had met at Savannah in 1750, even considered the question of the removal of the capital. This was not effected; a new Governor was sent over, but the people were rapidly becoming independent, and the "Stamp Act" put the same fever into their blood that stirred the pulses of their cousins in Massachusetts. It is curious to note, in view of later events, that Savannah sent to the Old Bay State much of the powder used in the defense of Bunker Hill.

Among the early excitements of Savannah was the trouble with the Spaniards in Florida, which finally culminated in open war. Spain, with her wonted arrogance, had firmly bidden the Georgians quit their newly established homes; but Spanish bravado did not frighten them. Anglo-Georgian and Hispano-Floridian fortified one against the other; the same Spanish intrigue, which was at work among the thousands of negroes in South Carolina, was active among the Indians in Georgia. When at last England and Spain went to war, Oglethorpe and his colonists played an important part in 1740, and penetrated to the very walls of St. Augustine in Florida, though they did not succeed in taking it.

The Pulaski Monument in Savannah, Georgia. [Page 361.]

Although last settled of the old thirteen States of the Union, neither Georgia nor her chief city was backward in accepting the issues of the revolution. A Georgia schooner was the first commissioned American vessel, and made the first capture of the war—sixteen thousand pounds of powder. Savannah revolted against its royal Governor early in 1776, and imprisoned him; and the next year the convention, which formed the State constitution, met in the city.   Toward the close of 1778, the British, after a savagely disputed battle, captured the city; a brutal soldiery shot and bayoneted many citizens in the streets, and imprisoned others on board the English ships.   British rule, with all the rigor of

military law, was enforced until an evacuation was rendered expedient by the success of American arms elsewhere.

There is one history-picture which the memory of Savannah's trials during the revolution should ever bring to mind, a picture which has in it the sparkle of French color, and which may serve as a noble remembrancer of French gallantry and generosity. In the dull and dreadful days of 1779, when English rule had become all but intolerable, a superb fleet anchored off Tybee one day in September, and the amazed English saw the French colors displayed above twenty ships of the line and eleven frigates, commanded by Count D'Estaing, sent by the King of France to aid the struggling Americans.   Five thousand of the best

A Spanish Dagger-Tree — Savannah.

soldiers of the French army, united with such as the American Government could muster, laid vigorous siege to the town; troops were landed, and lively attacks were made upon the British positions by the combined forces; a strong bombardment was kept up for some time; but the besiegers were finally compelled to withdraw, leaving the unfortunate town to the mercies of the enraged English.

In this long and brave assault, which lasted nearly two months, the chivalrous Pulaski, who had devoted himself to the cause of American liberty, lost his life; and there, fighting to save the beloved flag which he had grown to cherish more than life, perished Sergeant Jasper, who had already immortalized himself by keeping the American colors, at imminent risk of death, still waving over the battlements of Fort Moultrie in Charleston harbor, in the thick of a terrific bombardment.

Savannah was, in her early history, one of the most patriotic of American towns.   She not only produced men renowned for bravery and true chivalric qualities, but she took every occasion to demonstrate her faith in the Union. She received the new President, Washington, with joyous enthusiasm, gave Lafayette an overwhelming welcome, and during his visit laid the corner-stones of two handsome monuments, which are to-day counted among the city's treasures—those to Pulaski and General Greene.

"The Forest City," as the Georgians affectionately call it, is situated on a sandy plain, only fifty feet above sea-level, and eighteen miles from the mouth of the Savannah river.   From the northern bank stretch away the vast lowland rice-fields of South Carolina, once under perfect cultivation, but now only here and there cultured, and serving mainly as the homes of a mass of ignorant and dissolute negroes.   The city to-day is simply the amplification of the old plan of Oglethorpe and the trustees.   It is divided by many wide streets and lanes which intersect at right angles, and there are many large squares at regular distances.   There is little noise of wheels or clatter of hoofs in the upper town; the streets are filled with a heavy black sand over which dray and carriage alike go noiselessly; one wanders in a kind of a dream through the pretty squares, so gay in their dress of flowering shrubs and tall and graceful trees; it is a city through which he moves, yet as tranquil and beautiful as a village.   The winter climate is delicious; the cold weather lasts hardly six weeks; many flowers bloom in the open air from November to April; in February the jessamine and the peach-tree are radiant with blossoms; and a wholesome sea-breeze continually sweeps inland.   In summer, that is, from April to November, there is a mild malaria in the atmosphere, but it has been much reduced during the last quarter century, and the visitations of yellow fever have been rare.   Savannah certainly possesses the advantage of an equable temperature, for during ten months of

"Looking down from the bluff"—Savannah.

the year, the range is from 70 to 92 degrees.   The mean temperature is the same as that of Gibraltar, Bermuda, Palermo, Shanghai, or Sydney.   The Northern invalids who have been helped by a winter or two in Savannah number hundreds; and many persons traveling to Florida in search of restored health, have become so fascinated with the Forest City as to prefer stopping there.

The levée of Savannah is as picturesque, though not as extensive, as that of New Orleans.   Looking down from the bluff, along whose summit "the Bay," the principal commercial avenue, runs, one sees a forest of masts; a mass of warehouses, not unhandsomely grouped; cotton-presses, surrounded by active, chattering toilers; long processions of mule-teams, crowds of sailors talking in every known language, rice-mills, high mysterious stairways, with wondrous effects of light and shade on their broad steps, winding walls, and railroad wharves. Along the water-front the business blocks are so constructed that they rise above the bluff, and are connected with Bay street by means of platforms and balconies from which one can look down, as from house-tops, on the busy life of the port. The few buildings which the great fire of 1820 spared give an air of quaintness and age to the whole.

As we walked, day by day, through the Savannah streets, late in autumn, we were amazed at the masses of cotton bales piled everywhere. They lined the commercial avenues for hundreds and hundreds of rods; down by the water-side they were heaped in mammoth piles, and the processions of drays seemed endless. The huge black ships swallowed bale after bale; the clank of the hoisting-crane was heard from morning till night. At the great stone Custom-House the talk was of cotton; at the quaint old "Exchange," in front of which Sherman reviewed his army in 1865, cotton was the theme; and in all the offices from end to end of long and level Bay street, we encountered none save busy buyers and factors, worshiping the creamy staple, and gossiping rapturously of "middlings" low, and profits possible.

"The huge black ships swallowed bale after bale."

Savannah's progress since the war has not been less remarkable than that of the whole State. The recuperation of its railroad system has been astonishing. Sherman's army, in its march to the sea, destroyed one hundred and ten miles of the Georgia Central railroad track between Savannah and Macon, and thirty-nine miles between Savannah and Augusta. The military authorities returned the road to the control of its directors, June 22, 1865, and early in 1866 it was reconstructed so as to answer the public demand. This immense corporation at present operates in its interest, with its tributaries, 1,545 miles of railway. It extends from Savannah to Macon, thence by the South-western and Muscogee road to the thriving cotton-spinning town of Columbus, thence by the Columbus and Opelika route to Opelika, a brisk manufacturing town in Alabama, thence to Montgomery, and through Selma gets an unbroken rail communication with the Mississippi river at Vicksburg. This, it is expected, will be the connecting point of the Southern Pacific route with the roads leading to the Atlantic coast.   The Central's connections also give Savannah direct communication with New York and Memphis via the Atlanta and Chattanooga route, and connection at Augusta with the South Carolina road.   From Macon it sends out another arm to grasp Atlanta,—the Macon and Western road,—and there, also, connects

An old Stairway on the Levée at Savannah.

with the Georgia railroad to Eufaula, Alabama, whence, by steamers on the Chattahoochee river, it secures an outlet to the Gulf of Mexico.   It is interested in a host of small local lines, and has, indeed, spread an almost perfect network over the State, contributing in the highest degree to the prosperity of Georgia, by the superb facilities which it has afforded for transportation of products.   On its trunk lines, during harvest, immense cotton-trains run night and day, bringing to Savannah the fleeces plucked from the fields of Georgia, Alabama, and Tennessee.   The Central has long been a banking as well as a railroad company, and has always paid large dividends.   The railroad interest in Georgia is secondary to none other but agriculture.   The various companies, great and small, are managed with much ability, and new projects for local and through routes are rarely received with disfavor.   Savannah is somewhat excited over the possibilities of the completion of the Southern Pacific route to San Diego, in California, as the surveys have shown her to be the nearest Eastern port on an air line from the Pacific terminus.*

The Atlantic and Gulf railroad is another important feeder to Savannah.   It is the main thoroughfare connecting Savannah with Florida, Southern and Southwestern Georgia, and Eastern Alabama, and extends to Bainbridge on Flint river, 237 miles from Savannah.   From Lawton to Live Oak runs a branch road connecting the Florida system with that of Georgia—at present the only Northern outlet for the dwellers in the flowery peninsula.   A road from Macon crosses the Atlantic and Gulf route fifty-six miles from Savannah, and gives Brunswick, which was at one time expected to be a great city, an important outlet by land. The Savannah and Charleston railroad, completely destroyed during the war, has

* Savannah would be, by shortest distance from San Diego, 2,070 miles; Charleston, 2,184; Norfolk, 2,331.   The completion of a Southern Pacific railway will certainly add immensely to the commercial importance of Savannah.

been rebuilt, but is so poorly stocked that it is a penance to ride over it, although the lowland scenery through which it runs is among the most exquisite in the Atlantic States.   The grand canebrakes, unsubdued and seemingly impenetrable, extending on either side the track for miles; the stretch of lovely field,

with the fawn and rabbit bounding across it; the odorous forest, with its stately avenues of pine; the little villages of the gatherers of naval stores; the mossy boughs and tangled vines; the muddy-colored rivers, and the marshes filled with wildest masses of decaying vegetation—all add to the charm.

The numerous steamship lines from Savannah to Liverpool, New York, Philadelphia, and Boston, carry away enormous quantities of cotton, and if the needed improvements at the mouth of the river were made, the commerce of the port would be very

The Custom-House at Savannah.

much increased.   The entrance is considered one of the easiest on the Southern coast, the bar having a depth of nineteen feet of water upon it at

View in Bonaventure Cemetery—Savannah. [Page 368.]

mean low tide, and a rise of seven feet on the flood; but it is now necessary that the obstructions placed in the stream in war time be removed, and that extensive dredging be accomplished.

The total amount of upland cotton exported from Savannah in American vessels, from July 1, 1865, to June 30, 1872, was 704,373 bales, or 323,202,812 pounds, valued at $59,537,460; total amount of sea-island cotton exported in American vessels, 12,437 bales, valued at $2,062,576.   In foreign vessels during the same period, 1,292,979 bales of upland cotton, valued at $124,562,590,

and 21,899 bales of sea-island cotton, valued at $4,057,708, were exported. The coastwise trade was also very large, amounting to 1,539,560 bales of upland and 40,574 bales of sea-island cotton.

The value of both exports and imports since 1866 has been as follows:

1867	$41,225,488	1870	$58,850,198
1868	50,226,209	1871	64,893,892
1869	49,152,639	1872	68,100,164

and in 1873 they did not fall short of the amount in 1872. Savannah and Charleston are rivals in the cotton trade, and the newspapers of the two cities fight at every opportunity with an eager fierceness. Savannah is now receiving more than 700,000 bales of cotton yearly. The crop of Georgia alone, I should say, is rather more than that in successful years; and, at the rate at which the production in the regions tributary to the Forest City is increasing, she will soon rank with New Orleans. There is an enormous disparity between the amount of exports and imports; most of the vessels which enter the port of

The Independent Presbyterian Church — Savannah.
[Page 369.]

Savannah are compelled to go there in ballast. If cotton were taken away from the town, there would be little vivacity left. The aim of the port is to control the cotton of South Carolina, Georgia, Alabama and Florida, and it is entered in the lists as a formidable competitor with Charleston for supremacy. A flourishing cotton exchange, earnest merchants and manufacturers, and certain advantages of location, are doing much to place Savannah first among the Southern Atlantic cities.

There is a constant drain of emigration from the poorer districts of Georgia, as from Alabama, and, indeed, from most of the cotton States. Hundreds of poor Georgians, unable to make a living from the worn-out soil, under the new order of things, fly to Texas. Yet Georgia certainly does not grow weaker. Her material progress is in the highest degree encouraging.

Her valuation, in 1858, counting the slaves as capital, was over $600,000,000; the revolution decreased it to $148,122,525, on a gold basis, in 1866. The commonwealth had been racked literally to pieces by the invasion and support of a merciless army. She was weighted down so heavily that recovery seemed impossible. Yet she grew in strength and prosperity year by year thenceforward. In 1872 she returned a valuation in gold of $213,160,808, a substantial increase in six years of nearly $75,000,000 in currency. In other words she increased her wealth by about the total gold value of all her lands—some 30,000,000 acres.

This liberal increase was accomplished despite a decrease in the number of laborers, for although the aggregate population had increased since the war, there were only 114,999 laborers reported in 1871, while in 1866 there were 139,988. In 1872 the number had still further decreased, and it is estimated that in six years near-ly 30,000 laborers have been lost to the State.* But the im-proved methods of culture, and the use of powerful fertilizers, as well as the influence of an energetic spirit which perhaps distin-guishes the Georgian above his neighbors of the other States, have enabled the lessened number of workers to do what few dared to predict as possible. It is estimated that in six years and a-half the increase in the total

View in Forsyth Park—Savannah. [Page 369.]

value of the property of the State has been forty-four per cent. It is to be regretted that the legislators of a commonwealth which has shown itself capable of such an elastic rebound from ruin and misfortune should embarrass their future prospects by ominously talking of repudiation. Now that the majority of the plantations are in good condition; now that the farming implements destroyed in the war have been replaced; now that the quantity of live stock in all sections has been nearly doubled since 1867; and that the planters look confidently forward to the time when Georgia shall produce a million bales yearly,—in spite of all the drawbacks and failures of an imperfect and vexa-tious labor system,—it is hardly wise to threaten the State's credit with destruction, because of the irregularities which the government inaugurated by reconstruction brought into existence. With caution in future, and with some check upon the multitude of railway schemes constantly proposed, Georgia can easily carry all the debt she has contracted, until she finds herself able to discharge it honorably. Railroad building and speculation have always been passions dear to the Georgian heart; and, within thirty years, more than $40,000,000 were invested in lines built in the State.

So feverish has become the railroad mania that there is a class who are in favor of an inhibition of State aid to works of internal improvement, and who

* The population of Georgia, in 1860, was 1,057,286, divided into 591,550 whites, 2500 free and 462,198 slave blacks. In 1870, the population was 1,200,609; number of blacks, 545,132.

would be glad to see a clause to that effect inserted in the Constitution.   It is expected that in due time a convention will be called for the purpose of altering the Constitution in many ways, as the Georgia Conservative press and politicians are clamorous for one to take the place of "the instrument dignified with that name and forced upon the people by Federal intervention."

Autumn-time in Georgia, when harvest is nearly over, is brisk and redolent of inspiring gayety.   In the last days of November the towns and cities are filled with the planters from hundreds of miles round about; money flows plentifully; at Savannah there are agricultural fairs, races, reviews of the fine military organizations which the city boasts, balls, and wassail.   The halls of the Screven and the Pulaski, Savannah's two prime hotels, echo to the cheery laugh of the tall and handsome planter, as well as to the cough of the Northern invalid.   On a bright day in December, when a stiff breeze is blowing through the odorous foliage, Savannah presents an aspect of gayety and vivacity hardly Southern in character.   Elegant equipages dash along the hard white roads leading to the pretty river-side resort known as "Thunderbolt," or the sombre, mystical aisles of the "Bonaventure" cemetery.   Where the Tatnall family once lived in regal splendor, Savannah now buries its dead.   There are many fine monuments in the Forest Cemetery, but no marble can vie in beauty and grandeur with the mighty yet graceful live oaks which spread their arched boughs and superb foliage.

"Forsyth park contains a massive fountain." [Page 369.]

From Bonaventure one may look out across the lowlands traversed by estuaries, along which steamers crawl on the inland route to Florida; or may stray into cool pineries; and, returning, find himself beneath such lofty domes, or such broad and majestic aisles, with pavements of tesselated sun and shade, that he will start with surprise to discover, upon awaking from his day-dream, that he is not wandering in some giant cathedral.   The inhabitants of Savannah have the delights of sea-bathing and sea air within a few miles of town at such pretty resorts as the "Thunderbolt," the Isle of Hope, Beaulieu, Montgomery, and White Bluff.

From the steeple of the venerable Exchange one can get, here and there, glimpses of Savannah's especial curiosities. On Bull street he can see the Masonic Hall, where the ordinance of secession was passed in 1861 ; and, piercing the foliage, the tall spire of the Independent Presbyterian Church, or St. John's, or the Ionic proportions of Christ Church, in the parish over which John Wesley was once rector ; and may look down into parks where flashing fountains scatter their spray-jets upon lovely beds of flowers. Forsyth park contains a massive fountain, around which, as in continental cities, troops of children and their nurses are always straying. In Monument square rises a handsome shaft to the memory of Greene and Pulaski. Monument square is one of the principal centres in Savannah, and around it are grouped the hotels and the State Bank edifice; the Bank itself exists no longer. The Pulaski monument, a beautiful marble shaft, surrounded by a figure of the Goddess of Liberty, ornaments still another square. Wandering up Bull, or Drayton, or along Broad streets, one sees shop, theatre, public hall, market, luxurious private dwellings, many-balconied and cool, and fountain and monument; yet feels around him the tranquillity and beauty of the Southern forest. Each one of the 30,000 inhabitants of Savannah should carry a benediction in his heart for the founders of the colony, who gave Savannah such scope for gardens and parks, for fountains and shaded avenues.

A Savannah Sergeant of Police.

The municipal control of the town thus pleasantly situated is very nearly perfect. The police corps is a military organization, clothed in Confederate gray, subject to strict discipline, armed with rifles, revolvers and sabres, and occupying a handsome garrison barracks in a central location. It is one of the prides of the city, and General Anderson, an ex-United States and Confederate officer, keeps it in perfect discipline. Only now and then, in the troublesome days of reconstruction, did it come into collision with the factions at election time. One policeman wanders over each ward every night. There is but little violation of law, save in the brawls incidental to a seaport, and the larcenies arising from the undeveloped moral consciousness of the freedman. The negroes no longer have any voice whatever in political matters, and are not represented in the City Government. The registration law in the city, which was in force at the outset of reconstruction, has been abolished. There are only 400 negro voters registered in the city. The banking capital of Savannah was decreased from $12,000,000 to $3,000,000 by the war, but the city owes comparatively little money, has a valuation of $16,000,000, and manages to do much business on small capital.

Education in the city, and in the thickly settled county of Chatham surrounding it, is making far better progress than in the back-country. In 1866 the Board of Education in Savannah was made a corporate body, and a most excellent system of schools for white children was inaugurated, to which have now been added several schools for the colored children. The Peabody Fund does its good work there, as elsewhere. Twenty-five hundred white children attend the sessions, but only 400 or 500 out of the 3,000 negro children in Savannah have been accorded facilities.   There is a good deal of absurd prejudice in Savannah against the colored man yet, and, although the Board seems inclined to do its duty, the citizens do not urge any effective effort to raise Sambo out of his ignorance. Savannah is quite rich in private, educational, charitable and literary institutions,

General Sherman's Head-quarters — Savannah.

prominent among which are the Union Society and the Female Asylum for Orphans, the former on the site of the Orphan House which Whitfield established in 1740.   The Georgia Historical and Medical Societies are flourishing, and of excellent reputation.   The house occupied by General Sherman as his head-quarters, after the capture of Savannah during the late war, is still pointed out to visitors.

XXXIX.

GEORGIAN AGRICULTURE—"CRACKERS"—COLUMBUS—MACON.
SOCIETY—ATHENS—THE COAST.

IT is not without some little bitterness that a Georgia journalist recently
wrote: "A Georgia farmer uses a Northern axe-helve and axe to cut
up the hickory growing within sight of his door; ploughs his fields with a
Northern plough; chops out his cotton with a New England hoe; gins his
cotton upon a Boston gin; hoops it with Pennsylvania iron; hauls it to market in a Concord wagon, while the little grain that he raises is cut and prepared
for sale with Yankee implements. We find the Georgia housewife cooking
with an Albany stove; and even the food, especially the luxuries, are imported
from the North. Georgia's fair daughters are clothed in Yankee muslins and
decked in Massachusetts ribbons and Rhode Island jewelry."

Yea, verily! Throughout the cotton States this statement holds true.
In the interior cotton districts of Georgia there is often a great deal of
pecuniary distress, because the condition of the market or the failure of the
crop presses sorely on those who have given no care to raise anything for
self-support, and who have staked their all on cotton. Diversified industry
would make of Georgia, in twenty years, a second New York; for even in
her present ill-organized condition she actually makes great progress. · The
creation of manufacturing centres like Columbus, Macon, Albany, Thomaston,
Augusta, Atlanta, Marietta, Athens, and Dalton is encouraging, but much
remains to be done. Only about five millions of dollars are invested in the
manufacture of cotton and woolen goods in the State as yet, and the grand
water power of the Chattahoochee still remains but little employed. Agriculture must, therefore, be the main stay of the commonwealth, and the prospect is, on the whole, encouraging.

The present cash value of the farms in Georgia is considerably more than
one hundred million dollars, and might be doubled by something like systematic and thorough cultivation. The number of small farms is steadily increasing,
and the negroes have acquired a good deal of land which, in the cotton sections, they recklessly devote entirely to the staple, with an improvidence and
carelessness of the future which is bewildering to the foresighted observer.
They are fond of the same pleasures which their late masters give themselves
so freely—hunting, fishing, and lounging; pastimes which the superb forests,
the noble streams, the charming climate minister to very strongly. In the
lower part of the State, in the piney woods and swamps, the inhabitants are
indolent, uneducated, complaining and shiftless. They are all of the same

stamp as the old woman who explained to a hungry and thirsty traveler that they could n't give him any milk, "because the dog was dead!" Applying his perceptive powers to this singular remark, he discovered that the defunct dog had been wont to drive up the cows to be milked at eventide, and that

since his death it had not occurred to any of the family to go themselves in search of the kine. People who have plenty of cattle, and might raise the finest beef and mutton, rarely see milk or butter, and wear out their systems with indigestible pork and poor whiskey. Their indolence, ignorance, and remoteness from any well-ordered farming regions are the excuses. These are the sallow and lean people who always feel "tollable," but who never feel well; a people of dry fibre and coarse existence, yet not devoid of wit and good sense.

The Georgia "cracker" is eminently shiftless; he seems to fancy that he

A Pair of Georgia "Crackers."

was born with his hands in his pockets, his back curved, and his slouch hat crowded over his eyes, and does his best to maintain this attitude forever. Quarrels, as among the lower classes generally throughout the South, grow into feuds, cherished for years, until some day, at the cross-roads, or the country tavern, a pistol or a knife puts a bloody and often a fatal end to the difficulty. There is, in all the sparsely settled agricultural portion of Georgia, too much popular vengeance, too much taking the law into one's own hands; but there is a gradual growth of opinion against this, and even now it is by no means so pronounced as in Kentucky and some other more northward States. The "d——n nigger" is usually careful to be unobtrusive in quarrels with white men, as the rural Caucasian has a kind of subdued thirst for negro gore, which, when once really awakened, is not readily appeased. Yet, on the whole, considering the character which the revolution has assumed in Georgia since the fall of the reconstruction government there, it is astonishing that the two races get on so well together as they do.

Columbus, on the border of Alabama, separated from that State by the Chattahoochee river, which gives it an outlet to the Gulf, through Florida, is a lively, thriving town, which must one day rival Lowell or Manchester, because its water power is exceptionally fine. The river, some distance above the city, flows through a rugged and beautiful ravine, where the best building stone is to be had. It is said by competent authorities that along the stream, within two miles of the city, there are sixty sites, each large enough for the establishment of a capacious factory. Columbus impressed me more favorably than any other manufacturing town I had seen in the far South. It lies right at the centre of the cotton belt, is pierced by six important railways, receives about 130,000 cotton bales yearly, and in the mills of the Columbus Manufacturing, and Eagle and Phœnix Companies, employs hundreds of women and children. The streets are wide and cheery; the shops and stores quite fine; the residences pretty; the little town of Girard across the river, built by the mill proprietors as a home for their operatives, is charming; there is an aspect of life, and energy, and content in the place strongly contrasted with the dead and stagnant towns, of which I had seen so many. True, there were hosts of idle negroes roosting in shady places about the squares, and under the porticoes, but they are found everywhere in the South. The managers of the cotton-mills will not employ them in their establishments. When I asked one of the superintendents why not, he smiled quaintly, and said: "Put a negro in one of those rooms with a hundred looms, and the noise would put him to sleep." To which, never having seen the "man and brother" under the specified circumstances, I could, of course, make no answer.

Columbus has direct water communication with Texas, the great wool market of the future, and could supply woolen-mills very readily and cheaply. The Columbus manufacturers claim that a bale of cotton can be manufactured twenty-two dollars cheaper there than in or near Boston, and that their labor is thirty per cent. cheaper, while they are never subject to obstructions from ice.* The operatives in the mills were evidently saving money, and their houses and gardens were models of neatness and

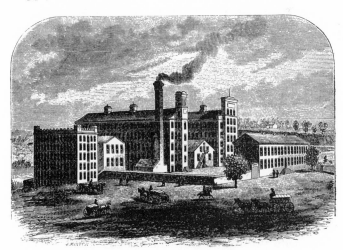

The Eagle and Phœnix Cotton-Mills—Columbus, Georgia.

comfort. After riding all day through regions where the log-cabin was oftener seen than the frame-house, and where the forests still hold possession of nine-

* The first cotton factory established at Macon has sometimes divided twenty-one per cent. yearly, and is gradually accumulating a very large surplus fund.

tenths of the land, it was refreshing to come upon a town of such energy, activity and prospects as Columbus.

The journey from Savannah to Macon carries one well out of the lowlands into a high, rolling country, admirably suited to cotton-raising. Macon is the site of the annual Georgia fair, which, late in autumn, all the planters attend. The smaller towns around about it on the various lines of rail are not very promising in appearance. The unpainted houses seem deserted until one sees half-a-dozen negro children pop their heads above the window-sills, and the "judge," and the "colonel," and the "doctor" come lazily to the train to get the mail and the newspaper. In most of the towns the train-conductor is looked upon with awe, and is invariably addressed as "captain." The railroads are well managed in everything save speed, and the natives traveling are always civil and communicative. Macon is picturesquely perched on a hill, around which a densely wooded country stretches away in all directions. The Ocmulgee river winds between broken and romantic banks not far from the town; and near it are many Indian mounds and the site of a venerable fort, used during the wars with the Cherokees. The cotton factories, large iron foundries and the railway activity of Macon, give it even a more sprightly appearance than Columbus; but the latter has 15,000 population, while Macon has but 10,000. The Wesleyan Female College and the Southern Botanic-Medical Institute, as well as the State Academy for the Blind, are located at Macon. From the pretty Rose Hill cemetery the outlook over the Ocmulgee is very fine.

Society is good and cultured in Savannah and in most of the large towns through the State. There is still bitterness and ostracism for him who votes the Republican ticket, whether he comes with the odor of carpet-baggery about him or not. Savannah is more courteous and liberal in her sentiments than a few years since, but keeps up a latent bitter feeling, ready to be flashed out on good occasions. These remarks do not apply with so much force to the gentlemen as to the ladies, for the average Southern man is altogether too American and too frank to show resentment toward individuals because they represent the best element of a party whose worst elements are obnoxious to him. There is a tendency among large numbers of the men to sink politics, and to attend with all their energies to business. But all seem determined to make Georgia's government one "for white men;" and whenever there is any need for concerted action, every one is alert. Still it is morally certain that before a continued prosperity all political troubles will finally disappear. The labor question is the important one for Georgia, and all the other cotton States, to settle. The negro, after he discovers what he loses by allowing himself to be intimidated or talked out of his vote, will learn to respect it, and use it intelligently. The negroes of the State are possessed of no small acuteness and power of development, and, wherever there are educational facilities for it, they speedily improve them. The especial need of the race is good teachers, raised from its own ranks, and the creation of the university at Atlanta for the colored population was one of the most beneficent works of the American Missionary Society.

The Georgia University at Athens, frequented, of course, exclusively by whites, is an excellent institution. It was endowed by the Legislature in 1788, but did not begin its sessions until 1801, since which time it has been noted among Southern literary institutions. Milledgeville, the quondam capital of Georgia, is a quaint and pretty little town on the Oconee river, not far from Macon. The State asylum for the insane is located there, and the legislators now and then ominously mutter that they would like to remove all the governmental machinery from Atlanta back to the old governmental seat; but the Atlanta influence is powerful against such a movement.

The deft and graceful pen of that sprightly and distinguished Georgian poet, Mr. Paul H. Hayne, is fitter than mine to paint aright the charms of the Georgia lowland scenery. To a poet's verse belong the inexpressible charms of the dark green and sombre foliage, the hurry of waters on the white, low beaches, the sighing of the wind through the long and dainty moss-beards, and the magical effects of sunrise and moonrise on the broad and placid current of the Savannah. To verse belong the many stories and legends of the chain of fertile islands strung along the Georgian coast, from Tybee to Cumberland. These island plantations have been fast falling into decay since the close of the war, and the culture of sea-island cotton on them has experienced many sad reverses. The war left its scars on these islands. The Union troops seized Tybee, near the mouth of the Savannah, as early as 1862, and from it bombarded that superb fortification, Fort Pulaski, on Cockspur Island. The massive walls of Pulaski, on which the United States had lavished money and skill, only to

The old Fort on Tybee Island, Georgia.

find it turned against them, yielded to the terrible summons hurled at them from the mouths of rifled cannon and mortars; and the battered stones loom up to-day, a sad memorial to the passer-by on the river of the havoc wrought by civil war.

Journeying along the coast, one passes Warsaw Sound, where the plucky little monitors captured the iron-clad "Atlanta" in 1863; and a sail up the Ogeechee river will bring one to the scene of the brave defense of Fort McAllister, whose little garrison, stirred by a sense of duty, held grimly on, long after Sherman was at the gates of Savannah with a victorious army, and the Union fleet kept the coast blockaded—long after they had been cut off from all hope of relief; held on until captured and literally crushed down by overwhelming numbers. The many lagoons which penetrate the low and fertile lands are easily accessible, and on the islands there will in future be delightful homes, when a fresh and numerous population shall have come to a State whose only need is more people. The Atlantic coast of Georgia, seen from the deck of an ocean steamer, seems low and uninteresting,—only a few, sand-hillocks now and then looming above the level of the waves,—but a nearer approach shows luxuriant vegetation and enviable richness of soil. From Fernandina, in North-western Florida, one can easily reach Cumberland Island, the old home of General Henry Lee of revolutionary fame, and the scene of sharp fighting between British and Americans in 1815. On this, as on the neighboring islands, the orange grows luxuriantly, and, with a return to careful and thorough culture, the cotton crop there could be made of immense value.

Fernandina is a fine old seaport, with a land-locked harbor in which more than 300 square-rigged vessels were anchored at one time during the war of 1812. The largest ships can unload without difficulty at its excellent wharves, and vessels from all climes come there to load with the lumber which is the main article of export. The sugar and cotton plantations, and the orange groves in the vicinity were highly prosperous before the war. The beach, eighteen miles long, affords delightful drives, and many Northern visitors remain in the venerable town throughout the winter months. Fernandina is the seat of the Episcopal bishopric of Florida, and the bishop there has charge of a flourishing academy for young ládies.

Happiness.

XL

THE JOURNEY TO FLORIDA—THE PENINSULA'S HISTORY. JACKSONVILLE.

I ENTERED Florida on a frosty morning. Thin flakes of ice had formed in the little pools along the railway's sides, and the Northern visitors in the Pullman car shrouded themselves in their traveling-blankets and grumbled bitterly. Here and there, in the forests' gaps, the negroes had kindled huge

Moonlight over Jacksonville, Florida.

fires, and were grouped about them, toasting their heads and freezing their backs. Now and then we caught glimpses of beautiful thickets; we passed long stretches of field carpeted with thick growths of palmetto; with intervening pine-barrens, and freight platforms of logs.

It is 263 miles by the present rail route from Savannah to Jacksonville, the chief city of Florida, and the rendezvous for all travelers who intend to penetrate to the interior of the beautiful peninsula. The train traverses the distance at the comfortable speed of twelve miles an hour; from time to time, half an hour is consumed in wooding up,—an operation performed in the most leisurely manner

by the negroes,—and one arrives in Jacksonville after a night's travel.   The currents of Northern comers pour in by three great streams—the Atlantic and
Gulf rail route from Savannah, the outside steamers from Charleston, which
ascend the St. John's river as far as Palatka, and the inland route from Savannah,
which conducts the traveler along a series of estuaries and lagoons between the
fertile sea islands and the main-land.

By the first of these routes, one passes but few towns of importance.
Neither at Live Oak, the junction where one reaches the Jacksonville, Pensacola
and Mobile railroad, nor at Wellborn, nor at Lake City, is there anything to
answer to one's ideas of the typical Florida town.   The rail route passes Olustee,
the site of a fierce engagement in February, 1864, between Federals and Confederates, in which the former were defeated.   At Baldwin one comes to the
Florida railroad, grappled to Fernandina, northward, on the Atlantic, and
stretching away through Duval, Bradford, Alachua, and Leroy counties to Cedar
Keys, on the Gulf coast.

When we reached Jacksonville the frost had vanished, and two days thereafter the genial December sun bade the thermometer testify to 80 degrees in the
shade.   Here and there we saw a tall banana, whose leaves had been yellowed
by the frost's breath; but the oranges were unscathed, and the Floridians
content.

Pause with me at the gateway of the great peninsula, and reflect for a moment
upon its history.   Fact and fancy wander here hand in hand; the airy chronicles
of the ancient fathers hover upon the confines of the impossible.   The austere
Northerner and the cynical European have been heard to murmur incredulously
at the tales of the modern writers who grow enthusiastic upon the charms of our
new winter paradise.   Yet, what of fiction could exceed in romantic interest the
history of this venerable State ?   What poet's imagination, seven times heated,
could paint foliage whose splendors should surpass that of the virgin forests of
the Oclawaha and Indian rivers ?   What "fountain of youth" could be imagined
more redolent of enchantment than the " Silver Spring," now annually visited by
50,000 tourists ?   The subtle moonlight, the perfect glory of the dying sun as he
sinks below a horizon fringed with fantastic trees, the perfume faintly borne from
the orange grove, the murmurous music of the waves along the inlets, and the
mangrove-covered banks, are beyond words.

> " Canst thou copy in verse one chime
>   Of the woodbell's peal and cry ?
> Write in a book the morning's prime,
>   Or match with words that tender sky ?"

Our American Italy has not a mountain within its boundaries.   Extending
from 25 degrees to 31 degrees north latitude, it has an area of 60,000 square
miles.   Nearly 400 miles in length, it has the latitude of Northern Mexico, the
desert of Sahara, Central Arabia, Southern China, and Northern Hindostan; but
its heats are tempered by the Gulf of Mexico on the one hand, and the Gulf
Stream, which flows along the eastern coast for 300 miles, on the other.   Over

the level breadth of ninety miles between these two waters constantly blow odorous and health-giving ocean winds, and under their influence and that of the genial sun springs up an almost miraculous sub-tropical vegetation.   It is the home of the palmetto and the cabbage palm, the live oak and the cypress, the mistletoe with its bright green leaves and red berries, the Spanish moss, the ambitious mangrove, the stately magnolia, the *smilax china*, the orange, the myrtle, the water-lily, the jessamine, the cork-tree, the sisal-hemp, the grape, and the cocoanut.   There the Northerner, wont to boast of the brilliant sunsets of his own clime, finds all his past experiences outdone.   In the winter months, soft breezes come caressingly; the whole peninsula is carpeted with blossoms, and the birds sing sweetly in the untrodden thickets.   It has the charm of wildness, of mystery; it is untamed; civilization has not stained it.   No wonder the Indian fought ferociously ere he suffered himself to be banished from this charming land.

The beautiful peninsula has been the ambition of many nationalities.   First came the hardy Venetian, Cabot, to whose father Henry the Seventh accorded the right to navigate all seas under the English flag.   In 1497, groping blindly, doubtless, like his father before him, for the passage to Cathay, Cabot touched at Florida.   Early in the sixteenth century came Ponce de Leon, the chimerical old Governor of Porto Rico, who vainly sought in the recesses of the peninsula for the fabled " Fountain of Youth," and perished in a broil with the savages.   To him our gratitude is due for the name which the fair land has kept through all the changes of domination which have fallen to its lot.   During his second search after the treasure, landing on Palm Sunday,* amid groves of towering palm-trees, and noting the profusion of flowers everywhere, the pious knight christened the country " Florida."   After him came other Spaniards, bent on proselyting Indians by kidnapping and enslaving them; but speedy vengeance fell on these ignoble fellows; the Indians massacred them by scores.   Then Narvaez, and the Spaniards in his train, waded through the dangerous lagoons and dreary swamps, fought the Indians from behind breastworks made of rotten trees, and finally perished in storms along the treacherous coast.   Nothing daunted, and fresh from triumphs in other lands, De Soto followed, overrunning with his army the vast extent of territory which the Spaniards claimed under the name of Florida, and which extended from the Chesapeake to the Tortugas.

The definite settlement of Florida by Europeans was consecrated by a massacre, by which the fanatical Spaniard added fresh infamy to his already tarnished name.   When Coligny had received from Charles the Ninth of France permission to found a colony upon the peninsula, and Ribault's expedition had erected a monument near the mouth of the St. John's river, ere sailing to found the settlement at Port Royal, the Spaniards were enraged; and as soon as, in 1564, Laudonniere's expedition had founded Fort Caroline on a little eminence a few miles from the mouth of the St. John's (then called the river May), active hostilities were begun by Spain.   The counter expedition of Menendez de Avila resulted in the massacre of all the Huguenots at Fort Caroline; and the grim Spaniards placed an inscription on the spot stating that " the murdered ones had

* In Spanish, *Pascua Florida.*

been slain, not as Frenchmen, but as heretics." Two years later came Nemesis, in the person of the brave Protestant Chevalier, Dominique de Gourgues of France, who relentlessly slew the Spaniards settled on the site of the old Fort Caroline, and hanged many of them, averring by an inscription above them that it was not done "as to Spaniards, but to traitors, robbers, and murderers."

The town which Menendez established on the site of the Indian village of Seloo, and which he named St. Augustine, was the first permanent European settlement in North America. In the eighteenth century the British gained possession of Florida. The American colonists had already unsuccessfully tried to gain St. Augustine; but were destined to wait a century longer. In 1781 the English lost their hold, and the territory reverted to Spain, only to be purchased by the United States in 1819, after Fernandina and Pensacola had been taken by American arms. Ceded and re-ceded, sacked and pillaged, languishing undeveloped through a colonial existence of 200 years, shocked to its centre by terrible Indian wars, and plunged into a war of secession at the moment when it was hoping for rest and stability, the lovely land seems indeed to have been the prey of a stern yet capricious fate.

It is not wonderful, in view of the perturbed condition of the peninsula, since its discovery, that to-day it has hardly more than a quarter of a million of inhabitants, and that its rich lands remain untilled. The weight of the slave system kept it down, after the Government of the United States had guaranteed it against the wonted invasions and internal wars; the remoteness from social centres enforced by the plantation life made its populations careless of the enterprise and thrift which characterize a country filled with rich and thriving towns; and the few acres which were tilled were forced to exhaustion by the yearly production of the same staple. Now, with more than 33,000,000 of acres within its limits, it has barely 3,000,000 partially improved, and on its 10,000 farms much is still woodland. Large farms and plantations have, throughout the State, decreased, and small ones have multiplied, but the total yearly value of farm products now rises hardly above $11,000,000 or $12,000,000, while the value of its home manufactures is but a couple of hundred thousand dollars. With 1,100 miles of practicable coast line, studded with excellent bays, and with such noble navigable rivers as the St. John's, the St. Mary's, the Appalachicola, and the Suwanee, it is strange that a larger commerce has not sprung up within the State limits.

We will not be too statistical. Imagine yourself transferred from the trying climate of the North or North-west into the gentle atmosphere of the Floridian peninsula, seated just at sunset in an arm-chair, on some of the verandas which overlook the pretty square in Jacksonville. Your face is fanned by the warm December breeze, and the chippering of the birds mingles with the music which the negro band is playing in yonder portico. The lazy, ne'er-do-well negro boys playing in the sand so abundant in all the roads, have the unconscious pose and careless grace of Neapolitan beggars. Here and there among the dusky race is a face beautiful as was ever that of olive-brown maid in Messina. This is the South, slumbrous, voluptuous, round and graceful. Here beauty peeps

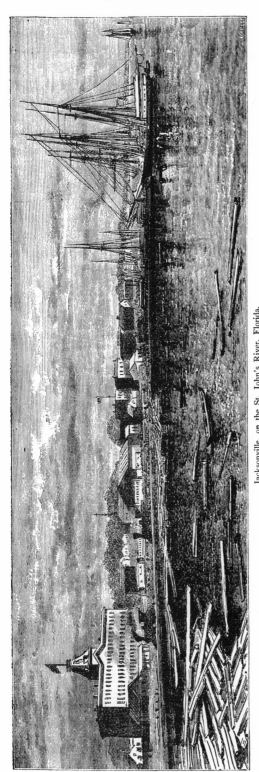

Jacksonville, on the St. John's River, Florida.

from every door-yard. Mere existence is pleasure; exertion is a bore. Through orange-trees and grand oaks thickly bordering the broad avenues gleams the wide current of the St. John's river. Parallel with it runs Bay street, Northern in appearance, with brick blocks on either side, with crowds of smartly dressed tourists hurrying through it, with a huge "National Hotel," with banks, with elegant shops. Fine shell roads run out beyond the town limits, in either direction. Riding toward the river's mouth, which is twenty-five miles below the town, one comes to marshes and broad expanses of luscious green thicket. Passing the long rows of steam saw-mills,—Jacksonville is a flourishing lumber port,—one comes to the point of debarcation for millions of feet of pine lumber, shingles and staves, and great quantities of naval stores. The fleet of sailing vessels used in this trade find at the new city as fine a port as the country can boast.

The St. John's, at Jacksonville, makes a crescent bend, not unlike that of the Mississippi at New Orleans. Nearly two miles broad directly in front of the wharves, it widens to an expanse of six miles a little way above, offering superb opportunities for commerce. The bar at its mouth is nearly always practicable for large ocean steamers, and they run with ease to Palatka, sixty miles above Jacksonville. The journey is charming from the river's mouth, past Baton island, the residence of the hardy river pilots, and the site of two excellent light-houses; past the mounds of oyster-shells, through which tangled shrubbery has pierced a difficult way; past the intensely white dunes, glistening under the sun, and ghastly and weird under the moonlight; past the little eminence known as St. John's Bluff, the location of old Fort Caroline, where Menendez massacred the unfortunate Huguenots; and past Yellow Bluff, with its ancient Spanish ramparts. Along the river-side, on elevated ground beyond the commercial part of the town, many New York and Boston gentlemen have erected elegant residences, and the climate has already seduced them from even a summer allegiance to their Northern birthplaces. The view from " Riverside " is charming.

It is not a score of years since there was a corn-field on the site of Bay street, now the chief avenue of a city of twelve thousand inhabitants. Jacksonville was once known as "Cow Ford." There the "King's Road," in the old days, crossed the river, and connected the northern settlements with St. Augustine. During the war it ran to decay; it was strongly fortified, and was clung to desperately by the Confederates. The Union troops occupied it then several times, and on the third assault a fire sprang out, which did much damage. At the close of the great struggle, the grass stood waist-high in the streets, and the cattle had taken refuge from the sun in the deserted houses. But the North has swept on in such a resistless current that, so far as its artificial features are concerned, the city has grown up according to the New England pattern, though foliage, climate, sun— all these are the antipodes of those of the North !

A good many people fancy that, in going to Florida, they are about to absent themselves from all the accessories of civilization,—that they must undergo considerable privation. Nothing could better correct this impression than a stay of a few days in Jacksonville. Such good hotels as the St. James and the National, such well-ordered streets, such charming suburbs as " Brooklyn " and " Riverside " and " La Villa " and " Wyoming," where the invalid can find the coveted repose and enjoy the delicious climate; such an abundance of newspapers and books, of carriages and saddle-horses, and such convenient access to all other desirable points along the great river, are sufficient to satisfy even the most querulous. Jacksonville is filled with pleasant houses where lodgings are let; and from December until April its population is doubled; society is active; excursions, parties, and receptions occur almost daily; gayety rules the hour. For it is not invalids alone who crowd Florida now-a-days, but the wealthy and the well. One-fourth of the annual visitors are in pursuit of health; the others are crusading to find the phantom Pleasure. Fully one-half of the resident population of Jacksonville is Northern, and has settled there since the war. The town boasts excellent public schools for white and black children; the Catholics have established educational institutions there, and there are several fine churches. The winter evenings are delightful. In the early days of December, on my first visit, the mercury during the day ranged from 79 to 80 degrees, but at nightfall sank to 70 degrees, and the cool breeze from the river produced a most delicious temperature.

XLI.

UP THE ST. JOHN'S RIVER—TOCOI—ST. AUGUSTINE.

THE St. John's river is a capricious stream, and the Indians characterized it for its waywardness as "Il-la-ka,"—meaning that "it had its own way, which was contrary to every other." Its actual source no man knows, though it seems to be formed by a myriad of small streams pouring out of the unexplored region along the Indian river. It is four hundred miles in length, and here and there broadens into lakes from six to twelve miles wide. The banks are low and flat, but bordered with a wealth of exquisite foliage to be seen nowhere else upon this continent. One passes for hundreds of miles through a grand forest of cypresses robed in moss and mistletoe; of palms towering gracefully far above the surrounding trees, of palmettoes whose rich trunks gleam in the sun; of swamp,

white and black ash, of magnolia, of water oak, of poplar, and of plane-tree; and, where hummocks rise a few feet above the water-level, the sweet bay, the olive, the cotton-tree, the juniper, the red cedar, the sweet gum, the live oak, shoot up their splendid stems; while among the shrubbery and inferior growths one may note the azalea, the sumach, the sensitive-plant, the agave, the poppy, the mallow and the nettle. The vines run not in these thickets, but over them. The fox grape clambers along the branches, and the woodbine and bignonia escalade the haughtiest forest monarchs. When the steamer nears the shore, one can see far through the tangled thickets the gleaming water out of which rise thousands of "cypress-knees," looking exactly like so many champagne bottles set into the

Residence of Mrs. Harriet Beecher Stowe, at Mandarin, Florida. [Page 386.]

current to cool. The heron and the crane saucily watch the shadow which the approaching boat throws near their retreat. The wary monster-turtle gazes for an instant, with his black head cocked knowingly on one side, then disappears with a gentle slide and a splash. An alligator grins familiarly as a dozen revolvers are pointed at him over the boat's side, suddenly "winks with his tail," and vanishes! as the bullet meant for his tough hide skims harmlessly over the ripples left above him.

The noble stream appears of a dark blue, as one sails along it, but, taken up in a glass, the water is of a light coffee color, a thin scum sometimes rising to its surface. Its slightly brackish taste is accounted for by the fact that the ocean tides are often perceptible as far up as Lake George. Many insist that there must be springs along the channel of the river, as they cannot otherwise account for its great volume. For its whole length of four hundred miles, it affords glimpses of perfect beauty. One ceases to regret hills and mountains, and can hardly

Green Cove Springs, on the St. John's River, Florida. [Page 386.]

imagine ever having thought them necessary, so much do these visions surpass them. It is not grandeur which one finds on the banks of the great stream, it is nature run riot. The very irregularity is delightful, the decay is charming, the solitude is picturesque. The bitter-sweet orange grows in wild profusion along the St. John's and its tributary streams; thousands of orange-trees demand but transplanting and careful culture to become prolific fruit-bearers.

The local steamers which ascend the river from Jacksonville regularly leave the wharves at eleven in the morning, though advertised for nine, as it has been a tradition, time out of mind, that they shall be two hours late. This brace of hours will be well spent by the traveler, however, if he seats himself on the deck and watches the proceedings on the wharf. A multitude of drays, driven by

ragged negroes, come and go incessantly, bringing every conceivable kind of merchandise and household goods; the deck hands carry piles of lumber, baskets of
eggs, crates of crockery, hoist in kicking and biting mules, toss aboard half-a-
hundred chickens tied by the legs; stow away two or three portable houses destined for the far interior, where some lone lumbermen are felling the massive
cypresses; and finally fill in the interstices with coal, chains, fertilizers, salt pork,
garden seeds, mail-bags, and an unimaginable hodge-podge.   Meantime, if the
boat you have taken be her favorite, "Aunt Rose," the venerable river steward-
ess,—one of the characters along the Jacksonville wharves,—has danced up and
down the gang-planks a hundred times with various letters and packages.   Even
though the day be hot, you find that a cool breeze comes from the dense thickets
and forests bordering the current, for you go up the stream at a rapid pace when
at last the little craft moves off.

It used to be said, a few years since, that the St. John's banks, from its
mouth to its source, were strewn with the wrecks of orange groves.   After the
war, hundreds of Northerners who knew little of Florida rushed in, dug up the
wild orange-trees from the swamps, and transplanted them along the river banks;
leaving them with the firm belief that they would care for themselves, and that,
in a few years, golden fortunes would hang on every tree.   But these careless
cultivators were doomed to bitter disappointment; hardly any of them succeeded.
In their train, however, came Northerners who made a study of the culture, and
now there are dozens of noble groves scattered up and down the river, and a
score of years hence the perfume of the orange leaf will be encountered at every
point along the stream.

When the war closed there was not a wharf left on the river.   Federal and
Confederate had warred and wasted, and to-day for memento there lies in the
stream, some distance above Jacksonville, a sunken gun-boat, its engine gear just
showing above the waves.   Inquiring of a venerable Floridian how it happened
to be there, I was informed that "the durned Yankees' shot was too hot for
her."

The journey from Jacksonville to Tocoi is delightful, though one's first experience of the great river has a zest which no subsequent one can rival.   Stemming
the current, which, under the brilliant noonday sunshine, seems a sheet of
molten silver, the steamer passes little tugs, drawing in their train immense rafts
of cypress and pine logs; or salutes, with three loud shrieks, the ponderous "City
Point" or "Dictator," from Charleston.   The cattle, knee-deep in water, are feeding on the fresh herbage springing from the sand-bars; hundreds of little fish are
leaping out of the current and falling back again, their shining bodies coquettishly
bent as if they were making mock of the sun.   Sometimes the boat enters a
pleasant inlet, where the pines on the shores have cut across the "hummock"
and stand quaintly draped in Spanish moss, as if they had come to be baptized.
Fifteen miles from Jacksonville, on the eastern shore, is the pretty town of Mandarin, so called from the culture there of that variety of the orange.   Through
the trees gleam white cottages.   Orange groves, with the golden fruit glistening
among the dark leaves, come to the very water's edge.   There, in winter, lives

Mrs. Harriet Beecher Stowe, besieged by hundreds of visitors, who do not seem to understand that she is not on exhibition.   Mandarin was once the scene of a dreadful Indian massacre; a generation ago, the Seminoles fell upon it and massacred all within its limits.

"Hibernia," on its island, with a lovely promenade under the sheltering branches of live oaks, and "Magnolia," where a large establishment was erected

On the Road to St. Augustine, Florida.

especially for invalids many years ago, and is now very successfully conducted, are on the right, as you ascend, and are much frequented by Northerners.   Oak forests border the water, and pines and palmettoes form a striking background. Throughout the winter months these health-resorts have the climate of Indian summer, and at Green Cove Spring, just above Magnolia, where there are sulphur waters of peculiar healing virtues in rheumatism and dyspepsia, a goodly company usually assembles with the first advent of "the season."   Crossing the river to Picolata, a wharf with a prospective town, the steamer follows the eastern bank until it arrives at Tocoi, whence an extempore horse-railway conducts the traveler to St. Augustine.   The traveler was formerly condemned to journey from Picolata to St. Augustine, over a terrible road, through cypress clumps and masses of briars, and palmettoes, in a species of volante, in which his bones were so racked that he rarely recovered before it was time to make the journey again.

It is expected that a railroad will one day penetrate the country between Jacksonville and St. Augustine, and following the coast as far as Cape Sable, be conducted over trestles to Key West, thus placing Cuba within three or four hours' sail. The road could be built for a comparatively small sum, as it would run through an absolutely level country.

But that road would rob good old St. Augustine of its romance. I object to it on that account; and so, I am sure, will many hundred others. What! must we lose the pleasure of arriving at nightfall at the Sebastian river, and hearing the cheery horn sounded as we dash through the quaint streets, and alight at the hostelry? *A bas* the railroad! rather let us have the diligence, the mules with tinkling silver bells, the broad-hatted, velvet-jacketed drivers of primitive Spain.

Useless—vain—these protestations; as I stand on the wharf, at Tocoi, I can see that modernism is already here. A horse-car! Ye guardians of the venerable!

Out through a seemingly interminable forest leads a straight road, bordered here by pines, and there by the palmettoes which spring in dense beds from the rolling ground. There is a little group of houses at Tocoi, and along the river bank, under the shade of the beautiful moss-hung oaks, several Northerners have established charming homes. A few miles back from the river, on either side, are good sugar-lands, and the negroes about the station are munching stalks of cane. An old mill near by is half-buried under a wilderness of tropical vegetation. At intervals in the forest, palm-trees shoot up their slender, graceful trunks.

A Street in St. Augustine, Florida. [Page 388.]

It is eighteen miles from Tocoi to St. Augustine. The journey is made partly on iron, partly on wooden rails; but is comfortable, and affords one an excellent chance to see a veritable Florida back-country. There is not a house along the route; hardly a sign of life. Sometimes the roll of the wheels startles an alligator who has been napping on the track; and once, the conductor says, they found two little brown bears asleep in the run directly in their path. It is night ere you approach the suburbs of the old city. The vegetation takes on a ghostly aspect; the black swamp canal over which the vehicle passes sends up a fetid odor of decay; the palm thickets under the moonlight in the distance set one to tropical imaginings. Arrived at the Sebastian river, an arm of the sea flowing in among long stretches of salt-marsh clad in a kind of yellowish grass, and inhabited by innumerable wild fowl that make the air ring with their cries, the horse-car stops, you are transferred to an omnibus, brown-skinned Minorcans and French touters for hotels surround you; the horn sounds ta-ra! ta-ra-ta-ra! and you rattle through the streets to the hotel.

St. Augustine, Florida—"An ancient gateway."

There is no noise in the town; evening has brought with it profound quiet. As for me, alighting at the "Magnolia," in a street as narrow as any in Valencia or Genoa, I stroll, after supper, into the dark and mysterious lanes. This moonless night is kindly; it lends the proper weirdness—the charm which should be thrown about St. Augustine. Walking in the middle of the street, which is overhung by wide projecting balconies, I detect a murmur, as of far-off music—a soft and gentle monotone. Now that I hear it clearly, surely it is the rhythm of the sea, and the warm breeze which blew across my face had a smell of the ocean. There is plainly the sound of water lapping on the shore. Ah! here is a half-ruined cottage built of coquina, with a splendid palmetto overshadowing its remains, and some strange vines which I cannot identify in the darkness, creeping about the decaying windows! A little farther on, an open plain—and here an ancient gateway, with a fragment of a high wall adjoining it; to the right—looming up through the shadows at a little distance—the massive walls and mauresque towers of an antique fortress. Yonder is the beach, and, as I draw near to it, I see two or three stalwart figures pulling in a boat.

I turn again, and wander through other streets, Hypolita, Bay, Treasury Lane. Some of the little alleys are barely eight feet wide. Where is the bravo with his dagger? Not here. St. Augustine is most peaceable of towns. No moss-grown corner of Europe, asleep these two hundred years, shall boast a steadier population than this—our oldest town in the United States.

Here is a sea-wall wide enough to walk upon. Against it the waves are gently beating. The fort yonder seems now but a great blot on the sky. I come to the Plaza, a little park in the city's midst. A few fishermen, a soldier or two, and some visitors are lazily reclining on the benches opposite the venerable Cathedral. A tall white monument stands in the park's centre. I light a match, and climb the pedestal.

PLAZA DE LA CONSTITUCION.

Monument to one of the short-lived forms of government in Spain. Nothing but a plain shaft.

Now every one has left the square. There are no lights, no voices. So I go home to bed.

Morning, in mid-December, brings warmth and sunlight; noon, slumbrous heat. Still roaming in the quiet streets, I see few signs of activity. Hammers are ringing on the walls of the new wooden hotel in which Northern tourists are to be lodged, a splendid coquina wall, which might have stood for another century, having been torn down to make room for this ephemeral box. The old arch, which marked the site of the Treasury, is crumbling, and will soon vanish. The quondam residence of the Spanish Governors, on the west side of the Plaza, has been rebuilt and altered until there is nothing antique in its appearance. It is now a prosaic court-house and post-office, and around its doors daily gather swarms of Northern tourists awaiting their mail. The balconies of the huge St. Augustine Hotel are crowded at evening when the band of the crack artillery regiment plays.

XLII.

ST. AUGUSTINE, FLORIDA—FORT MARION.

ST. AUGUSTINE, which a proud Spanish monarch once called the "Siempre fiel Ciudad," is situated on the eastern coast of Florida. The town is built on a small peninsula between the St. Sebastian river and the harbor. Menendez drew the attention of the Spanish nation to the spot by landing there in 1565; by his joyous return to the little garrison there, and his reception by the priesthood, who glorified him for the zeal he had displayed, after the massacre of the Huguenots at Fort Caroline; and by the subsequent bloody deeds among the dunes of Anastasia Island, at Matanzas Inlet. Menendez, finding that Ribault's Huguenots had been wrecked near this inlet, went to them with seeming protestations of friendship. He heard their pitiable story; how they had lost four galleons in the mighty storm, and that other vessels were missing; how they desired boats with which to traverse the inlet, and to pass through St. Augustine on their way to a fort "which they had twenty leagues from there." Menendez was too thorough a scoundrel and too little of a gentleman to declare open war against them, but he announced boldly that he had massacred the garrison and destroyed the fort. Then they desired that he should enable them to return to France, since "the kings of Spain and of France were brothers and friends." But Menendez told them that, as they were of the new sect, he held them for enemies, and if they would throw themselves upon his mercy he would *do with them what God should of His mercy direct.* Thus, having shifted the responsibility of his crime from himself to his Maker, he enticed the unfortunate Frenchmen into his clutches, and, after tying their hands, his soldiers massacred every one of them. As the two hundred and eight prisoners came, one by one, into a lonely place among the sand-hills, they were poignarded and stricken down by the swords of their treacherous and murderous assailants. It is not strange that the Floridian should to this day speak of the "bloody Matanzas river."

But this was not all. On the very next day after the massacre, the Spaniards, who had returned to St. Augustine, learned that large numbers of Frenchmen had been seen "at the same part of the river as the others had been." This was Ribault himself, with the remains of his shipwrecked company. The Adelantado, Menendez the infamous, at once pushed forward to meet them. A conference was had; the Frenchmen were shown the dead bodies of their comrades, and grimly directed to surrender to the clemency of the noble hidalgos. Terrified and shocked, starving and without any means of escape, Ribault surrendered himself and 150 of the men-at-arms with him, as well as the royal standards, into the hands of Menendez. Two hundred of Ribault's men, well knowing the fate in store for them, had braved the horrors of the wilderness during the night, preferring them to Spanish "clemency." Ribault and the others who surrendered, save sixteen persons, were ruthlessly slaughtered.

In the world's history there is recorded no more infamous massacre than this. The two hundred who fled the night before the final massacre built a fort at some distance from St. Augustine, but were finally attacked by the Spaniards, and great numbers were made prisoners. Menendez did not kill them, perhaps fearing that a fourth slaughter would arouse even the tardy fury of the King of France, but pressed them into his service.

That was three hundred years ago. The remains of a citadel are still visible at Matanzas Inlet, and a Government revenue officer keeps as regular watch there as ever did Menendez, but not exactly with the same intent. The first fort built at St. Augustine is de-

The Remains of a Citadel at Matanzas Inlet.

scribed by the ancient chroniclers as built of logs, and it is said to have been the council-house of the Indian village, on which site the town is founded. The ruins at Matanzas are undoubtedly more ancient than any building in St. Augustine.

Menendez went to his reward in 1574, and for two centuries thereafter the records of the settlement were eventful. Sir Francis Drake attacked and burned it in 1586; the buccaneers now and then landed and plundered the helpless inhabitants, and Indians massacred the missionaries. At the end of the seventeenth century the Spanish Government saw that the sea threatened to wash away the town, and for half a century thereafter the inhabitants toiled at the erection of a massive sea-wall, the remains of which may now be seen in the middle of Bay street, and which has been superseded by the fine breakwater built by the United States Government between 1837 and 1843.

At the beginning of the eighteenth century, the South Carolinians came in hostile array against St. Augustine by land and sea. The siege by land was successful, the attack by sea was a fiasco, and the invasion failed after having cost South Carolina £6,000, for which she issued promises to pay. A quarter of a century later the Carolinians raided again upon the old town, but went no farther than the gates. In 1740 Governor Oglethorpe, of Georgia, led a movement of Georgians, Carolinians and English against it; but retired, after an unsuccessful siege and bombardment. Shortly thereafter, the garrison of St. Augustine retaliated, and attacked the English settlements in Georgia with a formidable force; it was profitless. Back came Oglethorpe in 1743, carrying fire and death to the very walls of the old fort.

At the time of Oglethorpe's siege, St. Augustine was stoutly walled about and intrenched, with salient angles and redoubts. On the principal fort, fifty pieces of brass cannon were mounted, and growled defiance across a moat two score feet wide to any enemy prowling beneath the walls. There were twenty-

View of Fort Marion, St. Augustine, Florida. [Page 394.]

five hundred inhabitants—of which nearly one-half were Spanish soldiers. Out-posts were maintained on the St. John's river, and scouts quickly brought intelligence of any hostile movement.

England obtained the province of Florida by treaty in 1763, and when the red-coats came to St. Augustine, the Spanish inhabitants nearly all left. Many of them or their descendants, however, returned when the English had decided to get rid of the troublesome colony, and recession to Spain occurred in 1783, in exchange for the Bahama islands. In 1821, the standard of Spain, which had been raised by Menendez and his men, 256 years before, over St. Augustine, was hauled down, and the stars and stripes were raised in its place.

Since then, the old town has had its share of vicissitudes. It changed hands three times during our civil war.

A century ago, St. Augustine was, in general plan, very much as it is now. The "Governor's official residence," the present court-house, has lost the beau-tiful garden which surrounded it ; a Franciscan convent stood on the site of the artillery barracks of to-day. An Indian village was still standing upon the little peninsula in those days, and to the town's fortifications had been added a ditch, along whose sides were planted thick rows of the Spanish bayonet, forming an almost impenetrable *chevaux de frise.*" The outer lines of defense can still be traced. The gardens surrounding the solidly built two-story flat-roofed houses were still filled with fruit-trees, as the Spaniards had left them ; the fig, pomegranate, lemon, lime, orange, guava and the bergamot, flourished then as now ; and over the lattices great vines trailed, bending under loads of luscious grapes.

The romance of the place is now gradually departing.   The merry processions of the carnival, with mask, violin and guitar, are no longer kept up with the old taste; the rotund figure of the *padre*, the delicate form of the Spanish lady, clad in mantilla and basquina, and the tall, erect, brilliantly uniformed cavaliers, are gone; the "posy dance," with its arbors and garlands, is forgotten; and the romantic suburbs are undergoing a complete transformation.

The wealth of Northern cities is erecting fine pleasure houses, surrounded with noble orchards and gardens, and in a few years there will be as many villas as at Newport within a half hour's drive from the centre of St. Augustine.   A brilliant society already gathers there every winter, and departs reluctantly when the long summer heats begin.   Although the majority of those who visit the venerable town are not in search of health so much as of an agreeable climate, and an escape from the annoyances of winter, still, the preservation of health has been found so certain in the genial air of Florida, that hundreds of families have determined to make it henceforth their winter home.

Those invalids who cannot endure a sea-air would do well to avoid St. Augustine, and seek some of the interior towns; but the overworked and careworn, the sufferers from nervous disease, can find speedy relief in the permeating influence of the genial sunshine, which continues almost uninter-

Light-house on Anastasia Island, near St. Augustine, Florida.

ruptedly throughout the winter months.   In December, the days are ordinarily bright and sunny, a salt sea-wind blowing across the peninsula; from ten until four o'clock, one can sit out of doors, bathed in floods of delicious light.   During my stay at St. Augustine, in December, there were two days in which I gave myself completely up to the mere pleasure of existence.   I seemed incapable

of any effort; the strange fascination of the antiquated and remote fortress-
town was upon me.   The sunshine penetrated to every corner of my room.
There was no broad and unpleasant glare—no impertinent staring on the sun's
part, but a gladsome light which I have never seen elsewhere.   I walked out
at noonday; the town seemed transfigured: the shadows thereon from the
balconies, from the date-trees, from the thickets of roses, were mystical; I sat
down on the grass-grown rampart near old Fort Marion, and (forgetting the
gnats) let the gentle sea-breeze caress my temples, and memories of by-gone
centuries take complete possession of me.   At that moment, the rest of the
world seemed as remote as Paradise, vague as Ilium, foreign as the Zendavesta.

Falling, at last, to contemplation of the ancient fort, I could not repress my
indignation as I remembered that when there was talk of building a railroad to
St. Augustine, some enterprising company wished to buy and demolish the quaint

View of the Entrance to Fort Marion, St. Augustine, Florida.

landmark, that they might establish a railway terminus there.   Such vandalism
would be a disgrace to us.   The fort should be tenderly clung to.   The
more moss-grown it becomes, the more we should love it.   It is a grand monument.   For more than a century hundreds of men toiled in the quarries on
Anastasia Island and along the bay shore, wresting out the material now in the
massive walls.

Coquina, of which the fort is built, is a kind of concretion of shell-fragments,
often very beautiful.   This formation extends along the Floridian coast for more
than a hundred miles.   It crumbles when exposed for a very long time to the
air, but rarely falls to pieces.   Coquina resists a bombardment better than ordinary stone, as it is elastic and will bend before the fiery messengers; so that it is
quite possible that Fort Marion, decaying and aged though it seem, would stand
the broadsides of a foreign man-of-war better than the forts which have been
built but a few years.

This fort is built after Vauban's principles, in the form of a trapezium, with
walls twenty-one feet high and enormously thick, and with bastions at each

corner, originally named after St. Paul, St. Pierre, etc. The Castle of San Marco was its former title. On it the Appalachean Indians labored for sixty years. The garrison was also compelled to contribute to the work, and convicts were brought from far Mexico to labor in the quarries. Thousands of hands must have been employed for half a century in transporting the giant blocks across the bay, and raising them to position in the thick walls. As one traverses the draw-bridge, coming down the town, he sees over the main entrance the arms of Spain, with the globe and cross above them, and an inscription showing that in 1756 Field-Marshal Don Alonzo Fernando Herrera, then "Governor and Captain of the City of San Augustin de la Florida," finished the castle, "Don Fernando Sixth being then King of Spain."

"San Marco," now Fort Marion, has never been taken by a besieging enemy. It is a noble fortification, requiring one hundred cannon and a thousand men as complement and garrison; and it has been so strengthened by the water-battery added to it since the United States came into possession that it is a very formidable defense. The old sergeant in charge exhibits the interior to visitors. You penetrate the cell which was suddenly discovered some years ago by a break in

a wall, and which the Spaniards had concealed before ceding the fort to our Government. In this cell were found cages in which men had been confined. Torch in hand, the sergeant leads you through the chapel in the casemate, to the cell whence a Seminole chief once made his escape during the war with his countrymen, and mounts with you to the breezy promenade overlooking the water-battery, flanked at either end by the little Moorish sentry-boxes whence the men-at-arms were wont to watch the forest and the sea for the approach of the enemies who came so frequently. The moss-grown and discolored walls, the worn coquina slits, the gloomy corridors, the mysterious recesses, the grand old moat, with the gigantic walls above it, are too perfect reminders of the past to be allowed to perish. The vandal who shall destroy Fort Marion will deserve banishment.

"The old sergeant in charge."

The cathedral is in real Spanish style, and although it is neither large nor imposing, there is a subtle charm about its gray walls, its time-eaten doorway, its belfry from which bell-notes are always clanging. On Sunday evenings, crowds assemble in the Plaza, and listen to the sweet-voiced choir at vespers, while from the Episcopal Church across the way, one can now and then hear the murmur of Protestant song. I shall not soon forget the startling contrast which I observed one Sabbath evening in the Plaza.   The cathedral bells tolled

solemnly. I could see, in the open belfry, three bright-faced lads striking the notes on the bells; while out from under the gray portal came a funeral procession,—the young aco- lytes in their long robes of black and white, then the priests and the mourners, strange, dark- bearded men, and dark-skinned women, facing in sombre fash- ion toward the little cemetery. It was like a bit out of the seventeenth century. Turning, I saw, on the Plaza's other side, the congregation leaving the Episcopal Church—hosts of richly dressed ladies chatting gayly together; the row of

The Cathedral—St. Augustine, Florida.

young gentlemen ranged outside to criticise the belles admiringly; an army officer passing, and touching his cap with lofty courtesy; and half-a-dozen Northerners eagerly discussing the latest news from the stock market;—this was the nineteenth century come to St. Augustine.

The brown maidens, the olive-colored women that you see in the streets, are the descendants of that colony from the Minorcan Islands, which one Dr. Turn- bull induced to settle on the coast, at a place called New Smyrna, more than a hundred years ago.   Fourteen hundred persons were brought out, and engaged in the culture of indigo, which then commanded an enormous price.   Turnbull succeeded in obtaining absolute control over the defenseless colonists, cut them off from all communication with other settlements, and was rapidly reducing them to a condition of actual slavery, when they revolted, but in vain ; and it was not until the English attorney-general of the province interfered in their behalf, that they were emancipated from Turnbull's tyranny, and allowed to remove to St. Augustine, where they and their descendants have now been a part of the population for nearly a century.   Their old habits and customs, brought from the islands, are rapidly dying out; and the dialect songs which Mr. Bryant heard during his visit, in 1843, have almost entirely disappeared. Many of the women are extremely beautiful in their youth, but they fade early. The men are bold, hardy fishermen, Greek and Italian in type and robustness— while the women have much of the delicacy of form and feature of their American sisters.

Much as one may fear that the influx of Northern fashion may rob the old town of its chief charm, it is easy to see that a delightful watering-place is to be created.

The people of New England, who seem to have taken Florida under their especial tutelage, there meet and mingle freely with those from other sections; even the English and French are beginning to find attractions at St. Augustine, and my lord doffs his shooting suit to spend a few days in the pleasant society gathered in the shade of the orange-trees and the pines. The Florida *Press*, which Mr. Charles Whitney, of New York, has established at St. Augustine, represents Northern sentiment, and in its pleasant editorial parlors gentlemen from all the Northern and Western States gather every morning to exchange opinions. Meantime the ladies are shopping in the tiny box-like shops in the toy streets. They buy rich stores of brilliant wings of flamingoes, or pink curlews (all the hues of the rainbow are found on the feathers of the Floridian birds); or they fill their pockets with alligators' teeth, curiously carved, or send home coquina vases, or box a young alligator a foot long, in Spanish moss, and express him North to a timid friend. Or they visit such superb orange groves as that of Dr. Anderson, where eight hundred noble trees hang loaded with yellow fruit; or visit the cemetery where repose Dade and the brave soldiers who lost their lives in the Seminole war, under the tomahawks of Osceola and his men; or peer into the two convents; or at evening, when the sky near the horizon is filled with Daubigny-tints, wander on the beach, the warm, moist wind blowing across their faces, and the shells and brittle sea-weeds crackling beneath their feet.

The war did not greatly impair St. Augustine. A few fine homes were destroyed, and much suffering and privation were caused by the removal to the Nassau river of such families as refused to take the oath of loyalty. The Federal Government obtained possession in 1862, and kept it. Of course many fortunes were completely broken, and scores of people in the town, as throughout Florida, are living in straitened circumstances doubly painful because they have never before known self-dependence. The town now has good educational facilities for white and black, although before the war it had none. The natives of St. Augustine rejoice as much as do the Northerners at the progress of the free and public schools. But in the back-country, so far as l could learn, there are neither school-houses, schools, nor sentiment in favor of either.

XLIII.

THE climate of Florida is undoubtedly its chief charm. Its beauties and virtues have for a hundred years filled the homes of St. Augustine with people striving to recover from the effects of severer surroundings; and it will always be a refuge. The equable temperature is one of the great excellences of the climate. The thermometer rarely falls below 30 degrees, or rises above 95 degrees. The mean temperature of the winter months at St. Augustine, for 100 years, according to the old Spanish records, averaged a little over 60 degrees. The climate of the State is of course varied, as it extends through six degrees of latitude. The greatest heats in summer are never equal to those experienced in New York and Boston. One writer, who is considered good authority, says that during his eighteen years of residence in Florida, the greatest heat was 96 degrees in the shade. The climate of the whole State from October to June has been characterized as "one continuous spring." Periods of cold or frost never last but a few hours, and rarely come, save in January, once or twice. The nights, whatever the character of the days preceding them, are always cool. Both the winter and summer weather in East Florida is delightful. The winters in that section are so mild that "the most delicate vegetables and plants of the Caribbean Islands," says one writer, "experience there not the least injury from the season;" and the orange, the plantain, the banana, the guava, and the pine-apple attain a luxuriant growth. The medical statistics of the army show that the climate of the State as a whole ranks preëminent in point of salubrity. Solon Robinson, formerly the agricultural editor of the *Tribune*, who now resides at Jacksonville, tells me that he considers the climate of East Florida undoubtedly the best in the country. A general impression prevails in the North that on account of the large bodies of swamp land in the State, any one going there to reside, even temporarily, will incur danger of malarial disease. It is, however, established beyond controversy that there is never any danger from malaria in the winter months; and that it is, to quote Mr. Robinson once more, "certainly no worse for immigrants from any of the Northern States than central New York was in its early settlement for those who went into the forests from New England." Despite the fact that there are malarial diseases which attack the careless and unacclimated who remain in the State through all the seasons, it is still true that even with the moribund from half-a-dozen harsh climates sent to her to care for, Florida can show cleaner bills of health than any other State in the Union.

Frost reaches all parts of the State on rare occasions, but has seldom been known to go below latitude 27 degrees. It has sometimes visited Jacksonville and other points along the St. John's river when the mercury stood at 40 degrees. In Eastern Florida it rarely does damage to the sweet oranges, or the banana. In West Florida there is, say the authorities, " a constant struggle between the north-west wind and the trade-wind, and fruit growing incurs dangers." The seasons are the wet and the dry; the rains, which come with astonishing regularity at certain hours during the summer days, fall in heavy showers, and leave a cloudless sky behind them. There is rarely any rain during the winter months. Surgeon-General Lawson in one of his reports announces that while in the middle division of the United States the proportion is one death to thirty-six cases of remittent fever; in the northern division, one to fifty-two; in the southern division, one to fifty-four; in Texas, one to seventy-eight; and in California, one to one hundred and forty-eight,—in Florida it is only one to two hundred and eighty-seven.

If a perfectly equable climate, where a soothing warmth and moisture combined prevail, be desirable for consumptives, it can be found nowhere in the Southern States, save in South-eastern Florida. The number of persons whom I saw during my journey, who had migrated to the eastern or southern sections of the State many years before,— " more than half-dead with consumption," and who are now robust and vigorous,—was sufficient to convince me of the great benefits derived from a residence there. Physicians all agree that the conditions necessary to insure life to the consumptive are admirably provided in the climatic resources of the peninsula. That great numbers of invalids find the localities along the St. John's river, and even on the coast, distressing to them, is said, by some physicians, to be due to˙ the fact that those invalids go there after disease has become too deeply-seated. The European medical men are beginning to send many patients to Florida, cautioning them where to go. It would seem impossible for the most delicate invalid to be injured by a residence anywhere on the eastern or south-eastern coast from St. Augustine down. For those who, from various causes, find that each successive Northern winter,—with its constantly shifting temperature and its trying winds, which even the healthy characterize as " deadly,"—saps their vitality more and more, Florida may be safely recommended as a home, winter and summer. For the healthy, and those seeking pleasure, it will become a winter paradise; for the ailing it is a refuge and strength; for the severely invalided its results depend entirely upon choice of location and the progress which the disease has already made. The perfection of the Floridian winter climate is said to be obtained at Miami, near Key Biscayne bay, on the Miami river. There, among the cocoanuts and the mangroves, invalids may certainly count on laying a new hold upon life.

Returning from St. Augustine to the St. John's river, I continued my journey southward from Tocoi, the terminus of the horse-railroad before mentioned. Over this road, by the way, thousands of Northern people journey yearly; and the wharf, during the winter months, is crowded at the arrival and departure of the boats with fashionably dressed tourists, who seem strangely out of place in the semi-tropical forests. The "Florence," a sprightly steamer, brought me to Palatka early in the afternoon, affording all the way a delightful view of the wide stream, on whose sun-transfigured breast the wild ducks were flushing their eager wings; and over which, now and then, flew the heron and the water-goose uttering strange cries. Dr. Westcott, at Tocoi (a gentleman who spent thirty-three years of his life in the Floridian forests, and who has once been Surveyor-General of the State), told me that the Spaniards called the river at that point Lake Valdes. One finds it wide and narrow alternately until Palatka is reached. There the stream has formed a broad lake, from which there seems no outlet whatever. Palatka is a very pretty town of fifteen hundred inhabitants, on the west bank. It is at the head of navigation for ocean steamers, and is characterized by a richness of vegetation, and a mildness of climate which is not found at Jacksonville. It has become a favorite resort for the Northerners, and I found the Vermonters there in force. Colonel Hart, who went to Florida to die, some

The Banana—"At Palatka we first found the banana in profusion."

years ago, now owns fine properties near and in Palatka, and has drawn around him the sterling New England thrift and management, of which he is such an admirable example. Steamers arrive daily from North and South, and the facilities for travel are quite as numerous and as good as upon the Hudson. The consumptives from the North return yearly to this vivifying and delicious climate, in which they find an arrest of Death's decree against them.

At Palatka we first found the banana and the orange in their richest profusion, and noted what culture would do for them both. The town is backed by an interminable pine forest, through which run but few roads; but the ample space along the river front abounds in grand groves of oak, draped with the cool mosses, hung in most ravishingly artistic forms; and the wild orange grows in the streets. This town has a cheery, neat, New England look; the white painted houses, with their porches nestling in vines and shrubbery, invite to repose. The two old-fashioned, roomy hotels (to one of which an immense wooden addition has been made) are cool and comfortable.

The mornings in December, January, February and March, the four absolutely perfect months of Eastern Florida, are wonderfully soft and balmy; the sun shines generously, but there is no suspicion of annoying heat. The breeze gently rustles the enormous leaves of the banana, or playfully tumbles a golden orange to the ground, that a plump goose or duckling may at once thrust its bill into the tender fruit. The giant cactus in a neighboring garden peers out from among the fruit-trees like some scaly monster. The cart of the "cracker" (the native farmer's appellation), laden with game and vegetables, plies from door to door, and wild turkeys and dappled deer are purchased for dinner. Little parties lazily bestow themselves along the river bank, with books or sketching materials, and alternately work, doze, or gossip, until the whistles of the ascending or descending steamers are heard, when everybody flocks to the wharves. At evening a splendid white moonlight transfigures all the leaves and trees and flowers; the banjo and guitar, accompanying negro melodies, are heard in the streets; a heavy tropical repose falls over the little town, its wharves and rivers.

This was not always so. After the war was over, a few adventurous Yankees betook themselves to Palatka, but were not heartily received by the rude back-woodsmen and dubious "cracker" element which still lingered about there. In war time, 15,000 Union troops had been quartered at Palatka, and previous to that the town had on one occasion been bombarded. The Floridians had suffered a good deal, and there was severe enmity toward the "Yankees." The first attempt to open a hotel by a Northern man was severely resented. Parties of rough horsemen used to ride in and attempt to provoke a fight by sticking their bowie-knives in the hotel door. Shooting affrays were common. I was shown a spot where the sheriff himself tore up the turf during a fight of an hour or two with his own brothers-in-law, who were determined to kill him because he supported the "Yankees," then gradually creeping in. Now and then a negro was massacred.

The river's banks were sometimes the scene of terribly bloody affrays. Of course it was only the rougher classes who had a hand in this—people who rather objected to the march of civilization. It made them uncomfortable. Now the town is as peaceable as the mountain resorts in New Hampshire and Vermont. Property is good there, and has taken on prices which show a real demand for it. Three thousand dollars are asked for a little house and lot which would hardly bring any more in the North. But all the region adjacent to Palatka, and especially on the opposite side of the river, is getting settled up and cultivated.

XLIV.

ORANGE CULTURE IN FLORIDA—FERTILITY OF THE PENINSULA.

JUST across the river from Palatka lies the beautiful orange grove owned by Colonel Hart, in which seven hundred trees, some forty years old, annually bear an enormous crop of the golden fruit, and yield their owner an income of $12,000 or $15,000. The trees bear from twelve to twenty-five hundred oranges each; some have been known to bear four or five thousand. The orchard

"Just across the river from Palatka lies the beautiful orange grove owned by Colonel Hart."

requires the care of only three men, an overseer and two negroes. The myriads of fish to be caught at any time in the river furnish material for compost heaps, with which the land is annually enriched. At the gateway of this superb orchard stand several grand bananas; entering the cool shade— some resplendent December day—one finds the negroes gathering the fruit into bags strapped at their sides, and bearing it away to storehouses where it is carefully packed for the steamers which are to bear it North. On the sand from which the hardy trunks of the orange spring there is a splendid checker-work of light and shade, and one catches through the interstices occasional glimpses of the broad river current. In an adjacent nursery, a hundred thousand young orange-trees await transplanting and "budding."

This culture of oranges will certainly become one of the prime industries of Florida. The natives of the poorer class, who might make fortunes by turning their attention to it, are too idle to develop the country. They prefer to hunt and fish, and, as a rule, cannot be prevailed upon to undertake serious work. The mass of Northern men who undertook orange-raising directly after the war, failed because they did not employ skilled labor. The eastern bank of the river is considered safer than the western for the culture, as frosts rarely reach the former. But for many miles up and down the stream, the culture has proved reasonably successful on both sides. The property is becoming exceedingly good, yearly rising in value. Colonel Hart thinks his grove is worth at least $75,000. In a few years such establishments as those of Mr. Stockwell of Maine, with four hundred bearing-trees; Mr. Burr of Morristown, N. J.; the estate of Masters (two hundred trees); Mr. Brown, a New Yorker (two thousand young trees); Dr. Parsons, the Long Island nurseryman, and others adjacent to Colonel Hart's property, will yield fortunes to their owners. Connected with most of the orchards are many fine lemon and lime-trees. Colonel Dancey, six miles below Palatka, has a lemon grove of two hundred trees. Among the other noticeable groves below Palatka, are those of Dr. Cowgill, the State Comptroller; Colonel Cole of Orange Mills, who has some two thousand trees well started; Doctor Mays, at Orange Mills; a number of New York gentlemen at Federal Point; that of Captain J. W. Stark, nearly opposite Orange Mills, and the fine estate of Captain Rossignol.

Above Palatka, on the eastern banks, where the bluffs are quite high for Florida, and where the magnolia and water oak alternate charmingly with the cypress, the swamp-ash and the palm, there are also many successful orange groves scattered along from Rawlestown (where a hundred years ago an unsuccessful attempt was made to found an industrial retreat for the unfortunate women of London) to San Matteo, Murphy's Island, Buffalo Bluff, Welaka, and Beecher. There are many young groves on the Oclawaha river, and more than a million trees are already budded there. Before the war, acres of land covered with the wild orange were ruthlessly cleared to make room for cotton and cane. It is mainly Northern capital that is invested in orange culture throughout the State at present. In the Indian river region, the woods along the banks are, according to one account, "great gardens of the sour, wild orange, and we often," says the traveler, "had to clear the ground of vast quantities of the fruit before we could pitch our tents." These wild trees can be set out in new lands, and at a proper time budded with the sweet orange. Any time during the winter months is proper for transplanting. The "buds," or grafts, grow enormously the first year; and, in five years at most, if one hundred transplanted trees have been set out on an acre, that acre will yield 10,000 oranges; next year the yield will be doubled, and in ten years from the date of transplanting, with anything like reasonable success, one is sure of an income for life. For the orange is a hardy tree, gives a sure crop, has few insect enemies, and lives for more than a hundred years.   A good tree will bear from one thousand to three thousand oranges yearly. Some of the trees in an orchard at Mandarin have produced as many as 5,500, many of the oranges weighing nearly a pound each.   One single grove on the

Entrance to Colonel Hart's Orange Grove, opposite Palatka.

Indian river, with 1,350 trees, produced in a season 700,000 oranges. Only a small capital is needed for the starting of a grove, and the rewards of a successful one are very great.   Oranges sell at from $25 to $68 per thousand in Jacksonville, and are readily salable in any of the Atlantic seaports.   When the necessary dredging and building of canals has been accomplished, so that the Indian river may have an outlet via St. John, the North will be supplied with oranges of more delicate texture than any it has yet seen; and the number of groves along the river will be legion.

The fitness of Florida for the growth of tropical and semi-tropical fruits is astonishing.   Not only do the orange, the lemon, the lime, and the citron flourish there, but the peach, the grape, the fig, the pomegranate, the plum, all varieties of berries, the olive, the banana, and the pine-apple grow luxuriantly.   Black Hamburg and white Muscat grapes fruit finely in the open air; the Concord and the Scuppernong are grown in vast quantities.   The guava, the tamarind, the wonderful alligator-pear, the plantain, the cocoanut, and the date, the almond and the pecan luxuriate in Southern Florida.   We have within our boundaries a tropic land, rich and strange, which will one day be inhabited by thousands of fruit-growers, and where beautiful towns, and perhaps cities, will yet spring up.

Nothing can be more beautiful than one of the Floridian cottages, surrounded with a flourishing grove of orange-trees.   That of Dr. Moragné, at Palatka, is one of the best examples.   Down at the river front the good doctor has a long row of flourishing bananas, beyond which the great river is spread out—a gentle lake—before him.   From his porch he looks upon several acres of noble trees, with thousands of oranges nestling among the dark green leaves.   They come without care; one man picks them and prepares them for market, and they leave a golden, or, at least, a paper harvest annually behind them.   Some of the 200 trees within the doctor's inclosure yearly produce 3,000 to 4,000 oranges, and will go on their round of blossom and fruit for half a century.*

---

* The Union officer in command at Palatka during the war was ordered to destroy all the trees around the town for military purposes.   He could not find it in his heart to ruin Dr. Moragné's beautiful grove; so he picketed his cavalry there, and evaded the order.

Palatka was an Indian trading post in 1835. The Government built a road thence to Tampa, and kept a guard upon it, in the days when the Seminoles were still vigorous in their warfare. There are now but few Indians left in the State, and they, though peacefully inclined, remain buried in the Everglades, or among the forests of Indian river. Great numbers of them were ignominiously hunted down at various periods after the wars, and rewards were set upon their heads as if they had been criminals. Soldiers wers employed, or induced, by the hope of money, to follow them into their remotest fastnesses, and to disperse them. Now an occasional warrior, scantily clad, and dejected in appearance, is at rare intervals seen in some of the towns.

At Palatka one may gain a good idea of what culture and the advent of ambitious Northerners can do for Florida. There are so many superior inducements offered by the peninsula to those in search of new abiding-places, that I must content myself with a brief summing up of each. I suppose that the average observer, unfamiliar with the character of a sub-tropical country, would traverse the peninsula constantly remarking that he had never before seen so much good-for-nothing land. The eternal pine woods in many sections would prepossess him unfavorably; he would not even appreciate the exceeding richness of the hummocks until he had been instructed in their qualities. The lands of the State are usually classified into hummocks, pine, and swamp. Through the first-rate pine lands, where forests of pitch and yellow pine grow rankly, runs a dark vegetable mould, under which lies a chocolate-colored sandy loam, mixed with limestone pebbles, and resting on a substratum of marl. Lands of this class are so fertile that they have yielded 400 pounds of long staple cotton to the acre for fourteen successive years without any fertilizing. The second-rate pine lands offer excellent pasturage, and, when re-enforced, will yield 3,000 pounds of sugar to the acre. Upon them also can be grown oranges, lemons, and Cuba tobacco. Even the poorest pine lands have been found admirably adapted to the growth of hemp, and also give a good income from the naval stores which the trees yield.

Throughout these pine lands, at intervals of a few miles, there are hummocks of every size, varying from an acre or two to tracts of 20,000 or 30,000. These are wonderfully rich, and persons wishing to cultivate them can choose their residences on the higher pine lands, where there will be no danger of malarial fevers, and only spend their days among the hummocks. The low hummocks are very fertile, and before the war were the seats of many fine sugar plantations. The high hummocks are considered among the best lands in Florida; their fertility is really extraordinary, and the only preparation which they need for the production of luxuriant crops is clearing and ploughing, while, in addition, the low hummocks require draining.

The swamp lands of the peninsula are still, as it were, in process of formation, and are thought to be of even more durable fertility than the hummocks. They are of alluvial formation, occupying basins into which immense deposits of decaying vegetable matter have been washed from higher lands. Some astonishing results in sugar-planting have been obtained in those swamps. Four hogsheads to the acre were produced near New Smyrna, in East Florida, a production which completely overtops that of Louisiana. While Texas and Louisiana cane-planters are obliged to cut their cane in October, because of early frost, in Florida it may stand unharmed until late in December. Vast bodies of these swamp lands are now lying untilled in Florida, and may be had at two dollars per acre. In Leroy county alone there are said to be 100,000 acres of the best kind of sugar-land.*

While the tracts along the St. John's river are not considered extraordinary in point of fertility, still, within a mile of the banks, there are thousands of acres of fine hummock land which might be tilled with great profit. The counties of Middle Florida offer abundant high hummock lands ; so do many counties in the eastern section. As soon as production begins in earnest the producer will learn to appreciate the advantageous situation of Florida. Lying directly across one of the great highways of traffic, and within a day and a-half of New Orleans, three days of New York, and one of Cuba, by steamer; with such harbors as Tampa, Fernandina, Pensacola, Cedar Keys and Charlotte, and with reasonably good means of internal communication by road, and superb ones by river, the State has no reason to complain. Cotton was, of course, the principal staple before the war; but a great variety of production will henceforth be the rule. Indian corn will grow throughout the State, and has been liberally raised, although not yet in sufficient quantities to supply the home demand. Fruit and vegetable culture along the lines of the rivers, with reference to the Northern markets, is becoming one of the principal industries. The culture of cotton at present does not pay in the State; and the production, which in 1860 amounted to 63,000 bales of ginned cotton, is gradually decreasing. Sugar-cane is one of the great hopes of the commonwealth. It is confidently asserted that the yield of this staple in Florida is twice that of Louisiana. Solon Robinson says that "small farmers can grow cane upon any good pine land, and can make sugar as easily as Yankee farmers make cider." He evidently does not believe that the successful culture of the cane is inseparable from the old plantation system. Rice, indigo, silk, coffee, tea, and the ramie plant are likely to be among the other agricultural interests of Florida. The palmetto, scattered so luxuriantly through Florida, is now extensively used in the manufacture of paper, and forms the basis of a great industry. On the entire coast are excellent locations for salt works, and at the commencement of the war, large works had been established on Key West Island for the manufacture of salt by solar evaporation. Along the coast, too, there is such a multitude of oysters, fish, and game, that enter-prises for supplying the market from that section should be very successful. The turtle and the fish are celebrated everywhere; and the Indian river oyster deserves a ballad to his charms by some noted gastronomer.

The natural resources for fertilizers are abundant in the State. From the swamp lands may always be had a muck which serves admirably, and the clay itself, which lies next to the sandy soil in a large part of the State, is a fine fertilizer when mixed directly. There are also immense accumulations of shells,

* See Adams on Florida.

of the periwinkle and conch, which are well calculated to strengthen land, and deposits of green marl are easily accessible.

The expense of building is very slight in Florida, for the houses need none of the plastering and weather-tightening so necessary in Northern climates. Simple houses, cellarless, and raised some two feet from the ground on posts, with large, airy rooms, battened instead of plastered, and surrounded by verandas, are best adapted to the climate. In the towns, as a rule, rents are rather high, owing to the lack of building during the past perturbed years.

The Guardian Angel.

XLV.

THE Oclawaha is a small stream running through swamps and still lakes in Putnam and Marion counties. It empties into the St. John's about twenty-five miles south of Palatka, and opposite the settlement called We-la-ka. The river took its name from that of one of the seven clans of Seminoles who once wandered through the swamps which border it, and hunted in the beautiful lakes above it. It is but a few years since the stream was rendered navigable, and to-day its mouth is so embowered in foliage—such great curtains of vines and water plants overhanging it—that the passer-by on the St. John's would hardly notice it. Boats leave Jacksonville and Palatka every Thursday for Lake Griffin, and, traversing the whole forest range through which the Oclawaha runs, furnish the traveler with an admirable opportunity to see some of the most remarkable lowland scenery in the world.

The invalid from the North, anxious to escape not only from the trying climate which has increased his malady, but also the memories of the busy world to which he has been accustomed, could not do better than to drift up and down this remote and secluded stream, whose sylvan peace and perfect beauty will bring him the needed repose. Some years since, an enterprising Yankee, familiar with the charms of the little river, conceived the project of a floating hotel to constantly make trips between Palatka, on the St. John's, and the Silver Spring, one of the most beautiful resorts on the Oclawaha, but until this mammoth project is put into execution the traveler must content himself with the wheezy little steamboats which lazily mount the current, or must come in his own yacht.

Yachting on the Oclawaha and St. John's rivers would certainly be prime amusement in the winter season. There are some curious characters along the little stream,—hunters and trappers, who have spent many years in the woods and swamps, and who could teach the amateur sportsman how to hunt the alligator in his lair, to snare the turtle, and now and then to shoot a noble wild turkey. If neither the floating hotel nor the new line of steamers is placed on this charming water-way, it is to be hoped that large caravansaries for fashionable visitors may be erected at such lovely resorts as Silver Spring and Ocala. The hotel accommodations in the interior of Florida are generally far from excellent, but the tide of travel which is beginning to penetrate even to the remotest corners of the peninsula will soon cause the establishment of hotels which will be thoroughly satisfactory to Northern and foreign visitors. The whole Oclawaha region had not been properly explored until toward

1867, although many travelers who had penetrated as far as the then supposed
head of navigation, had told strange and seemingly exaggerated stories of its
wonderful beauty.   The tales of floating islands, of the grandeur and almost
frightful calm of the mighty swamps—of the curious colonies of birds and

A Peep into a Forest on the Oclawaha.

animals—the superb lakes, and the lucent waters, had thrilled many a brain; but
only a few had penetrated these watery, sylvan retreats until the prying Northern
element demanded to be shown all.   Now a journey up the Oclawaha is as
fashionable as a promenade on the Rhine, and really more interesting and
amusing.

Our party embarked at Palatka on the little steamer " Marion," one cool
evening, just after the arrival of the boat from Charleston; and while the officers
of her huge sister were still shouting themselves hoarse with commands to the
slouching negroes about them, our tiny bark slipped out into the broad current,
and set slowly off midstream at the rate of four miles an hour, for a journey to
Silver Spring.   Although cool, it was not uncomfortable, and one was from time
to time startled, as on the Mediterranean, by a warm breath across his face, perfumed with the scent of oranges and the rich forest growth.   The lights of
cottages along the banks blinked cheerily; occasionally a descending steamer
yelled her warning, and we blundered leisurely forward, still in the great stream
when midnight came, and sleepily sought the tiny cabins allotted us.

It must have been two o'clock in the morning when I was awakened by a
violent brushing and scraping noise, as if the boat were held fast amid the boughs

of trees. Lazily gazing out of the cabin I saw, with surprise, the bough of a stout shrub entering the window, then vanishing with a shriek and a whisk, as if it had merely looked in to frighten me.

The whole thicket was lighted up as by some supernatural agency. I saw giant cypresses, their dirty white trunks seeming about to topple down upon me; saw acres of glimmering water, in which the mysterious light cast a thousand fantastic gleams, which shifted uneasily every moment; saw the cypress-knees dotting the thicket in every direction; saw lovely green vines, literally spangled with white and blue flowers, and arrayed in such dense and symmetrical masses that I could not persuade myself they grew wild in the thicket; saw a heron sitting, low-perched, on a shrub; and saw the flash of wings, as from time to time our advancing boat's monotonous refrain of sighs from its two steam-pipes startled the birds reposing in the tree-tops.

The red-bay, the holly, the ash, the maple, the cypress, *toujours* the cypress, floated before my half-closed eyes; then vines again, then more birds,—wondered if I should see an alligator—what they would have for breakfast—another tree coming in at my window—"Look out thar, Bill, for them torches!" and at that point, I think, I fell asleep again.

In the morning it was all explained. I had awakened just after we had entered the Oclawaha, and had seen the glare of the torches by which we groped our way in the narrow channel filled with spring-water. Had we entered in the

"We would brush past the trees and vines." [Page 411.]

day-time, I should have seen immense floating islets of lilies and barnets, gently swayed by the tremulous currents, and hundreds of light-footed birds poising airily upon them; the haughty kingfisher diving for his prey; the wild turkey uttering his startled cry; the crane making himself as invisible as possible, by shrinking until he seemed merely a feather-ball; and the rose-colored curlew rising into the air like a flash of light from a ruby. Then, too, I should have noted the rafts of cypress-trees, girded together with bark and palmetto strings, and as we approached the shores, might have caught sight of the wrinkle-throated alligator wagging his huge tail cheerily in the sunshine.

All day we wound in and out of the recesses of this delicious forest. The banks of the stream were scarcely thirty feet apart, as a rule, although sometimes the current broadened to twice that width. We were perpetually coming to a point in the forest from which there seemed no possible egress, when, rounding a sharp corner, the negro boatmen pushing with their long poles, we would brush past the trees and vines, and once more plod on by cypress, water oak, ash, and orange-tree.

The richly variegated colors of the far-extending thickets were mirrored so completely in the water, that we seemed suspended or floating over an enchanted forest. The clumps of saplings garnished with vines; the stately bosquets of palms, now growing a score together on a little hillock, and now standing apart, like sentinels; the occasional magnolias; the long swamp-ways out of which barges, rowed by negroes, would come to receive the mail, and into which they vanished again, the oarsmen hardly exchanging a word with our captain; the fierce-faced, bearded men, armed with rifles and revolvers, who sometimes hailed us from a point of land, to know if we "wanted any meat," and showed us deer and turkeys, and perhaps the skin of a gray wolf or a black bear,—all these novelties of the tropics and the backwoods kept us in perplexed wonder. When evening came slowly on again, a round moon silvered the water, and enabled us to see even the ducks that floated half submerged, and curiously eyed our little boat. By day, one sees hundreds of turtles, as on the St. John's, sunning themselves. The birds are legion. They chatter in the tree-tops; they offer themselves freely as marks for revolver-bullets; they scold at night as the torchlight awakes them; and they accompany the echo of each unsuccessful shot with loud derisive singing.

The torches of pine-knots placed securely on the boat's roof, and watched there by a habile negro boy, aid the reflection in the water to a new beauty. The cypresses seem more ghostly; the vines more luxuriant; the long-necked white birds more comical; the palms more majestic than by day. Now and then a beacon disclosed some lonely cabin, thatched with palmetto, beside which stood a solitary figure with gun strapped over his back. "Got any terbacker, Cap'n?" or some such question, and we left the figure behind. Penetrating Eureka creek, we wormed our way through a little streamlet only twenty feet wide. At Fort Brooke, large quantities of the rich crops of Alachua county were formerly shipped, but the railroad now transports them.

A little above Fort Brooke one comes to Orange creek, the outlet of a charming lake, in Masson and Alachua counties, with lovely orange groves upon its banks and sulphur springs near by. In conversation with people who came and went at the wayside stations in the swamps, I found that they had all been well-to-do "before" the war, and that they were healthy and happy in their tropic wilderness home. The needs of Florida in the lines of canals and convenient short-cuts were well exemplified in the case of a planter from the St. John's river, who, with some friends, was going on a hunting excursion near Silver Spring. From his home on the St. John's by land across to Silver Spring, it was only at best forty miles; but by the only practicable route he was compelled to travel 175 miles, and spend three entire days on the road.

Silver Spring is certainly one of the wonders of the world. The tradition that it is the "Fountain of Youth," of which the aborigines spoke so enthusiastically to Ponce de Leon, seems firmly founded. The river or spring rises suddenly

The "Marion" at Silver Spring.

from the ground, and after running nine miles through foliage-shrouded banks, more luxuriantly beautiful than poet's wildest dream, empties into the Oclawaha. Transparent to the very bottom, the waters show one, at the depth of thirty or forty feet, the bottom of this wonderful basin, with bubbles here and there denoting one of the sources; and the refraction of the rays of light produces most brilliant effects.

We rowed about on the bosom of this fairy spring, quite overcome with the strangeness of the scene. There is nothing like it elsewhere either in Europe or America; the foliage is even more gorgeously tropical than along the Oclawaha, and its arrangement is more dainty and poetic. We spent hours rocking in little skiffs among the oases of lily pods which extend along the borders of the spring; or in threading the forests which set boldly out into the tranquil stream, not without occasional misgivings as to the quantity and temper of the alligators that might be lurking there.

Nothing befell us, save headaches from the too zealous sun. The thermometer confessed to 90 degrees, and the little boat seemed to bake as she lay at the wharf receiving cotton bales and bags of cotton-seed from Ocala, Marion county's principal town, and from its surroundings. The planters and the negroes from the neighborhood, each superintending the loading of his own cotton, formed a lively group under the wharf-shed at Silver Spring. The tiny steamer was by no means equal to the task demanded of it, and left great quantities of freight awaiting its return. Half concealed among the tall, rustling flags, we sat in our boat watching the grimy negroes as they tussled with the cotton; the young Floridians practicing at the curlews and the herons with their revolvers; and the wonderful dreamy green of the foliage, through which peered hundreds of strange plants and flowers.

Silver Spring was once considered the head of navigation in this direction, but steamers now run far beyond it on the Oclawaha, through lakes Griffin, Eustis, Harris, and Dora, to Okahumkee, a little settlement in the wilderness, where sportsmen delight to spend much of their time while in the peninsula. All the lands near the lakes are specially valuable for cane-growing, and for cotton, corn and fruit. In the vicinity of Lake Harris, frost is seldom known; and sugar-cane matures so as to tassel, which the early frost never permits it to do in Louisiana and Texas.

Colonel Hart, of Palatka, was the explorer of this region, and when his adventurous steamer pushed up through the encumbered channel, the crew had to combat sunken logs, fallen trees, and labyrinths of overhanging limbs. Then "floating islands" were encountered, formed of water-flags securely rooted in a soil under which the current had made its way. These islands are sometimes borne down into the larger streams by the winds and the rising of the waters; and those which had become stationary in the river channel were so tough that a saw was required to cut them in pieces.

This whole lake region seems gradually becoming a marsh, and much labor and expense is required to keep the channel open as far as Okahumkee. A project for cutting a canal through to the Gulf by this route, taking advantage of the lakes and their outlets, has been conceived, and would be of great commercial importance to Florida. The country around Lake Apopka, the source of the Oclawaha river, is considered one of the most remarkable in Florida, and cannot fail when communication is more thoroughly established, to attract large numbers of immigrants. At Okahumkee the waters divide, running into the Gulf by way of Lake Pansoffkee and the Withlacoochee rivers—the route of the contemplated ship canal across the State. The Oclawaha is navigable for about 250 miles, and a semi-weekly line of small steam-packets gives the up-country connection with the outer world. A charter has been obtained for the " Great Southern " railroad to run from Augusta, Georgia, via Millen and Jessup in that State, to Jacksonville in Florida—thence to Palatka, and soon to Key Biscayne Bay and Key West. A large land grant from the State has been accorded the

projectors, and the work of laying down the track from Jessup to Jacksonville
has been contracted.

Our captain, the cheery and active skipper of the "Marion," had navigated
the Oclawaha river for nearly a quarter of the century, and his pilot, formerly
his slave, still stands at the helm, a post requiring no small skill in view of the
sharp turns which the "Marion" is compelled to make to avoid being ignominiously stuck fast in the swamp thickets. The captain expressed himself better
satisfied, on the whole, with free than slave labor; thought that it released

Shooting at Alligators. [Page 415.]

employers like himself from a great many obligations. But he said that the
sudden advent of emancipation had greatly hindered the development of hundreds of plantations along the Oclawaha, chiefly because the planters did not
wish to encourage more negroes to come into the country, as they were already
so formidable a political element. Planters cannot work their broad acres without
the very immigration which they dread, and so they suffer them to lie idle. But
industrial progress had been very marked in many things since the war. A few
manufactories scattered through some of the rich counties traversed by these
steamers would, he thought, add greatly to the wealth of those sections. People
suffered a great deal from the large prices which they were obliged to pay for

manufactured articles brought many hundreds of miles, in a toilsome manner, from the outer world.

Sailing back, we were treated to the sight of an alligator fifteen feet long, sunning himself on a hummock of yellow grass. The wrinkle underneath his lower jaw gave him a good-humored look, and he seemed actually to smile as the bullets hissed around him. The alligator is by no means a trifling enemy; and the Floridian tells strange stories of the creature's strength, fleetness, and strategy. An alligator hunter in Jacksonville gave me an idea of these characteristics, somewhat after the following fashion:

"The 'gaiter, sir, is ez quick as lightning, and ez nasty. He kin outswim a deer, and he *hez* dun it, too; he swims more 'n two-thirds out o' water, and when he ketches you, sir, he jest wabbles you right over 'n over, a hundred times, or mo', sir, ez quick ez the wind; and you 're dead in no time, sir. When a dog sees one he always begins to yelp, sir, for a 'gaiter is mighty fond of a dog and a nigger, sir. Nobody can't tell how old them old fellows is, sir; I reckon nigh on to a hundred years, them biggest ones. Thar 's some old devils in them lagoons you see off the St. John; they lie thar very quiet, but it would be a good tussle if one of you was out thar in a small boat, sir. They won't always fight; sometimes they run away very meek; the best way to kill 'em is to put a ball in the eye, sir; thar 's no use in wasting shot in a 'gaiter's hide. When the boys wants sport, sir, they get a long green pole, and sharpen it; 'n then they find a 'gaiter's hole in the marsh, and put the pole down it; then the 'gaiter he snaps at it, 'n hangs on to it, 'n the boys get together, 'n pull him out, 'n put a rope aroun' his neck and set him to fightin' with another 'gaiter. O Lord! reckon t' would make yo' har curl to see the tails fly."

XLVI.

THE UPPER ST. JOHN'S—INDIAN RIVER—KEY WEST—POLITICS. THE NEW CONSTITUTION.

SOUTHWARD and up the St. John's river from Palatka, the vegetation becomes more tropical, the river narrowing so that one can comfortably inspect the thickets, and widening out only to be merged in grand Lake George, twelve miles wide, Dexter's Lake, and Lake Monroe, at Enterprise. The steamers make the run from Palatka to Enterprise in about twelve hours. In March, when the flowers on the banks are at their perfection, if the moonlight be brilliant, do not

View on the Upper St. John's River, Florida.

neglect the journey by night. The glamour of the Southern moon throws an enchantment over all the splendid foliage which makes it doubly bewitching; the lilies and barnets on the water, and the palms and cypresses on shore, form perfect pictures which none can forget. Welaka, opposite the mouth of the Oclawaha, was well supplied with accommodations for visitors before the war destroyed them. There is a grand hotel there now, near some excellent sulphur springs; and Dunn's Lake, abounding in game, and with many rich plantations on its shores is but eight miles distant. At the southern end of Lake George lies Drayton's Island, where it is said there are some remarkable Indian mounds. A barren rib of land divides the St. John's and the lake from the Oclawaha. The steamers dexterously skim over the dangerous bar at the southern extremity of Lake George, and passing Volusia and Fort Butler, a noted relic of the Indian wars, enter Dexter's Lake, surrounded by its wild and seemingly limitless marshes and hummocks. Beyond this lake, the river flows through a very narrow channel, whose banks are clothed with the omnipresent palm, the maiden cane, and the tall sedge in the meadows. At Lake Monroe, one lands at Enterprise, where a Maine man keeps a hotel, of which, and one or two other houses, the town consists. This is a famous rendezvous for sportsmen who are about to visit the Indian river. On the opposite shore is Mellonville, a promising settlement. All along this lake there is superb hunting and fishing; and the invalid who comes pale and racked with a harrowing cough, is, after a few weeks, seen tramping about in the cool of the morning with gun and fishing rod, a very Nimrod and Walton combined.

The source of the St. John is higher up, in some unknown marsh, and after one has penetrated to Lake Harney and Salt Lake, there is little left to see on the noble stream which, at a distance of nearly three hundred miles from its mouth, flows within seven miles of the ocean into which it empties.

Indian river is difficult of access, but swarms of travelers are now finding their way there. One of the favorite means of reaching it is to row from Enterprise to Lake Harney, and to take a portage across to Sand Point. The entrance from the coast is decidedly less easy than from the St. John's; the deepest of the outlets, Fort Pierce channel, having rarely more than seven feet of water at high tide. The so-called river is really an arm of the sea; its waters are salt; its westward shore was once very highly cultivated by the Spaniards, and it could, with a little renewed attention, be made one of the richest garden spots in America. The westward side presents a sad panorama of ruined sugar plantations and houses, of superb machinery lying idle—and of acres of wild orange-trees, which only need transplanting and budding to produce fruit equal to the best which we receive from Havana. The sportsman who pitches his tent for a few days on the splendid camping ground of this same shore, will see the pelican, the cormorant, the sea-gull, and gigantic turtles, many of them weighing five hundred pounds; may see the bears exploring the nests for turtles' eggs; may "fire-hunt" the deer in the forests; chase the alligator to his lair; shoot at the "raft-duck," and fish from the salt-ponds all finny monsters that be. Hardly a thousand miles from New York, one may find the most delicate and delightful tropical scenery, and may dwell in a climate which neither Hawaii nor Southern Italy can excel. Settlements throughout this section are few and far between. The mail is carried down the great silent coast by a foot-messenger— for there is a stretch of nearly one hundred miles along which there is not a drop of fresh water for a horse to drink.

The islands extending along the south coast, from Cape Florida to the "Dry Tortugas," lie close to the Gulf Stream, and between the mainland and the dangerous reefs on which so many vessels are annually wrecked. They are only a few feet above tide-water, and are wooded with the mangrove, the bay, the palmetto, the oak, the cocoa and the pine-apple tree, all of which thrive in the rocky soil of these keys.   A large trade is here carried on in the gathering of sponges and turtles.   The traveler in search of health will find a pleasant recreation in sailing about Biscayne Bay, and penetrating thence into the vast shallow lakes of the "Everglades," where a thousand islands are covered with a wealth of live oaks and cocoas, and with masses of trailing vines, on which, in the season, hang gigantic clusters of grapes.   There one may see miles of flower-beds, where every conceivable hue greets the eye; and will find some of the richest lands in the world lying idle, and to be purchased for a trifle.   North of Biscayne Bay, on the coast, tobacco, bananas, plantains, oranges, coffee, dates, pine-apples, rice, indigo, sugar and cassava will flourish admirably.   The production of sea-island cotton on the Florida coast requires but about one-half the labor necessary in South Carolina, and it is contended that a sugar plantation there can be made for one-fifth of the money required in Louisiana.   Biscayne Bay is within four' days' easy sail of New York, and there is no reason why vegetables and the great variety of tropical fruits which can be grown there should not find a ready market in the metropolis.

Of course, the labor question in Florida, as elsewhere in the Southern States, is perplexing and startling.   The only means by which the State can secure the full development of its extraordinary riches is by inducing immigration on the part of people who live in similar latitudes, and who will find it agreeable and easy to develop the resources of the vast sub-tropical peninsula.   While it is evident that Northern and Western people will develop the region bordering on the St. John's, and possibly the northern part of the commonwealth, those who do the work on the vast sugar plantations of the future, and who develop the whole south-eastern coast, must be native to the South.   The Floridians have already given some attention to the subject of immigration, and a bureau to take charge of that matter was appointed under the new Constitution.   The "Agricultural and Immigration Association of Florida" was organized in 1868, and is composed of the officers of the county associations of the same nature, and of those of the various boards of trade.

Key West, only a short distance from Cuba, is an important Government naval station, and is connected with the world by semi-monthly steamship to Baltimore, Havana, and New Orleans; semi-weekly to Galveston and New York, and by the United States dispatch boats to Fort Jefferson, Tampa, Cedar Keys, St. Mark's, Appalachicola, Pensacola, and Iobile.   One may stand on a cracker-box and look over the whole island, which is formed of a species of coralline limestone.   Key West town is prettily situated amid "groves of cocoa and of palm;" has five thousand inhabitants; becomes quite lovely in aspect when the fleet rendezvous is fixed there; is famous for the beauty of its ladies, the matchless flavor of its green-turtle, the dexterity of its wreckers, the extent of its salt works and cigar manufactories, its naval hospital and its formidable Fort Taylor, with two hundred heavy guns pointing seaward.   All winter long at Key West*

* The name Key West is a corruption of the Spanish *Cayo Hueso*, "Bone Key."

the south winds blow; the air is loaded with warmth and perfume; the moonlight is brilliant, and the "northers" considerately come only two or three times a year. From this port steamers run occasionally to the Dry Tortugas, where a thousand prisoners were confined during the war, and where the "conspirators" found a forced seclusion.

Florida accepted reconstruction peacefully, and the new Constitution is, on the whole, a good one. It makes proper provision for schools, and the management of the courts and the provisions with regard to the distribution of lands are wise.

Sunrise at Enterprise, St. John's River, Florida.

The Republican party of the State has suffered a good deal at the hands of some of the men who have been intrusted with its interest, so that many citizens of the State who, on national questions, always vote with Republicans, array themselves so far as regards their local interests with the Conservative faction. The balance of power in the State is at present held by the blacks, led by a few white men; but the Conservative element is rapidly gaining strength, and it is noted as somewhat remarkable that Northerners who settle there gradually find themselves leaning to Conservatism, as they are compelled to do to protect themselves against a torrent of ignorance and vice. Congressman Cox, of New York, was one day at a Republican meeting at Jacksonville, and was invited to address it. He professed great surprise, and inquired how it was "that a Democrat was asked to make an address in a Republican caucus?" He was thereupon informed that it was not a party meeting, but that it was an effort to secure the best men and the best ideas for the service of the State, even if they were found outside party limits. There has been a great deal of fraud and plundering on the part of county officers who, dazzled by the possession of newly acquired power, have not hesitated to put both hands into 'he public purse. Many have been detected, but some have been so adroit as to completely cloak their iniquities. A firm and thoroughly honest administration of State affairs would bring Florida into front rank among the prosperous States in a short time.

Taxation is about $2.38 on every hundred, but the property owner is allowed to fix his own valuation. This includes a school and county tax amounting to one cent on a dollar. The various railroad enterprises into which the State has been urged have done considerable to embarrass it. The present State debt is nearly $1,350,000, exclusive of a contingent liability of $4,000,000 of bonds, issued by the State to those insincere adventurers who pretended that they desired to complete the Jacksonville, Pensacola and Mobile railroad. This important route is now finished to the town of Chattahoochee, in Florida, the location of the State Penitentiary. The road would be of great advantage to the State, if it were possible to get it freed from the endless litigation surrounding it, and to put even the section which is already completed into decent running order.

It was an enterprise of too much magnitude for the capital or the management of the clever adventurer who got it into his possession, and who obtained everything that he desired from the reconstruction legislature. He having sunk beneath its weight, without having made the tremendous progress anticipated, the project languishes. An act of the last Legislature but one has prohibited the further issuing of bonds for any purpose whatever. The Administration of Governor Stearns has thus far been satisfactory.

At the period of my visit to Florida, the State Superintendent of Education was a negro, and a gentleman of considerable culture and capacity. But neither he nor his predecessors had succeeded in doing much for common schools. The same prejudice which existed against them elsewhere in the South was felt in Florida up to a very recent date; and possibly exists in some degree now, because of the lurking fear of the whites that some day mixed schools may be insisted upon by the black masters of the situation. In such counties as Duval, where the influence of a large and flourishing town has been felt, there are many schools, well supplied and well taught; but as a rule, throughout the back-country, there are no schools, and there is no immediate prospect of any. The scrip which came to Florida, as her share of the national gift for the founding of an agricultural college, was swallowed up by some financial sharks in New York; it amounted to more than $80,000. The establishment of such a college would have been of great value to the State, giving an impetus to effort in exactly the necessary direction.

The educational affairs of each county are managed by a " board of public instruction,'' consisting of five men recommended by the representatives of the Legislature, and appointed by the State Superintendent. There are about 700,000 acres of " school-lands " in the State, and there are some funds which are used in aiding counties to start schools. There are about 63,000 pupil-children in the State, not more than one-fourth of whom are supplied with good facilities for instruction. The amount annually expended for free education by the State, including donations from the Peabody fund, is $100,000. It was claimed that in 1873, 18,000 children attended the schools. At Gainesville, Key West, Tallahassee, Pensacola, and Madison, there are successful schools for both colored and white children, and at Ocala, Quincy, and Appalachicola, there are colored free schools, liberally aided by the Peabody bequest.

In the backwoods there is an alarming amount of ignorance among the adults; there are hundreds of men and women who have not the simplest rudiments of education, and many amusing stories are told of the simplicity and boorishness of the "crackers." They are a soft-voiced, easy-going, childlike kind of folk, quick to anger, vindictive when their rage is protracted and becomes a feud; and generous and noble in their rough hospitality.   But they live the most undesirable of lives, and, surrounded by every facility for a luxurious existence, subsist on "hog and hominy," and drink the meanest whiskey.

The Florida Constitution, adopted under reconstruction, contains some novel features.   One clause provides that the Legislature shall enact laws requiring educational qualifications for electors after the year 1880, but that no such law shall be made applicable to any elector who may have registered and voted at any election previous to that time.   The Governor is elected for four years.   The blacks predominate in the tiny Senate and Assembly, composed of twenty-four and fifty-three members, respectively; and during the sessions, Tallahassee, the capital, situated in a rolling country, in the midst of a beautiful spring region, is the scene of tyro legislation such as at present distinguishes the capitals of Louisiana and South Carolina.

Quincy, St. Mark's, and Monticello, all offer attractions to the traveler; the latter is the site of a sanguinary fight between the forces under General Jackson and the Miccosakie Indians, and there, too, De Soto is said to have encamped on his way to the northward.

A Country Cart.

XLVII

SOUTH CAROLINA—PORT ROYAL—THE SEA ISLANDS.
THE REVOLUTION.

PORT ROYAL, in South Carolina, was once first cousin to Plymouth Rock, in Massachusetts. The rugged New England headland was the refuge and the fortress of the English Puritan; the fertile plain at the mouth of the broad and noble Carolinian river was the resort of the French Huguenot, who preferred exile and danger to the sacrifice of his faith. Jean Ribault and his hardy men-at-arms, sailing northward from the blooming banks of Florida, in 1562, anchored their ships during a great storm at the mouth of a "fair and large harbor," and named it, and the river emptying into it, Port Royal.

The good Frenchmen who had been sent by brave old Admiral Coligny to found an asylum for the oppressed in the New World, wandered delightedly along the shores of the stream, under moss-grown oaks and lofty pines, beneath the cedars and the palmettoes, and shaped visions of future glory. They pictured to themselves the time when the waters of the vast harbor should be covered with noble fleets; when spacious gardens should dot the luxuriant shores; and, after a few days of repose, they raised a stately pillar of stone, with the arms of France graven on it, and in honor of Charles IX., built a fort on an island in the river. A little garrison was placed in charge, and Ribault returned to France, to recount with enthusiasm the wonders of that part of the then province of Florida, destined in future to be named, as the Frenchman called his fort, Carolina.

To-day, more than three centuries after Ribault's adventurous voyage, the site of the old fort and pillar is not even definitely known. Port Royal is an infant town just springing into commercial activity, under the influence of slowly reviving commerce; and the negro slouchingly tills the soil and lounges in the sun on the shores from which the tide of revolution has swept his late master.

In the sixteenth century, the country claimed in America by the Spaniards as Florida, and by the French as "New France," was supposed to extend from the Chesapeake to the "Tortugas," along the coast, and inland as far as the exploring foreigners might choose to penetrate. During many perilous years the States now known as Florida and South Carolina had a common history. The Huguenots continued their explorations until the treachery and murderous fury of the Spaniards had exterminated all of them who ventured into the Florida lands; and had Menendez of Avila, the blackest villain whose life-record blots the annals of American discovery, died in his cradle, South Carolina would, perhaps, at this day have been peopled by Protestant Gauls.

The little settlement at Port Royal suffered many ills. The soldiers left by Ribault, borne down by misfortune and sickness, determined to return home. The Indians aided the soldiers to construct a brigantine, with which the miserable men tried to make their way to France; but they were reduced to starvation on the voyage, and it was only after they had begun to eat each other, that the survivors were rescued by an English vessel.

The settlement founded by Ribault was thus abandoned; and two years elapsed before another Huguenot expedition, led by Laudonniere, founded a settlement near the mouth of the river May, as the St. John's, prince of the streams of Florida, was then called. Had Laudonniere prospered, the Port Royal fort might have been rebuilt; but the Spaniards from St. Augustine, who fell upon both Laudonniere and the re-enforcements which Ribault had brought him, rendered the second of Coligny's attempts disastrous. Even the colossal vengeance which that *preux chevalier*, Dominique de Gourgues, took upon the Spaniards in Florida, two years afterward, did not establish French influence there; and no Huguenot came again to our Southern shores until one hundred and thirty years later, when the revocation of the edict of Nantes in France sent hundreds of the descendants of Coligny's followers to South Carolina. Their illustrious names are still borne by many worthy families in Charleston.

Under the "Palatinate" the development of the province now known as South Carolina was begun. Under a charter from the crown, after the Restoration, all the lands lying between the 31st and the 36th degrees of north latitude were granted to a proprietary government.

The utmost religious liberty prevailed in the newly-organized province. The Constitution, under which the noble dukes and earls who had received the charter proposed that their colonists should live, was framed by the philosopher, John Locke. The eldest of the "lords proprietors" was Palatine, the seven other chief officers were Admiral, Chamberlain, Chancellor, Constable, Chief Justice, High Steward and Treasurer. The province was subdivided into counties, signories, baronies, precincts and colonies. Each signory, barony and colony consisted of 12,000 acres, and it was provided that after a certain term of years the "proprietors" should not have power to alienate or make over their proprietorship, but that "it should descend unto their heirs male." Here was a good foundation for a landed aristocracy. Every freeman of Carolina was authorized to "have absolute power and authority over his negro slaves;" and no person could hold or claim any land in the province except from and under the "lords proprietors."

The first attempt of the English experimenters to settle the country was at Port Royal, in 1670. William Sayle was appointed Governor of the colony, and great inducements were offered to English immigrants. The first site of "Charlestown" was on the western bank of the Ashley river, and the estate where that site was is still known as "Old Town." Subsequently the settlement was removed to the confluence of the Ashley and Cooper rivers.

It was not until 1783 that the town was incorporated.   The original expedition of the proprietary government cost £12,000, and in the years between 1670 and 1682, 100 houses were built at "Charlestown," and an ancient chronicler adds that many who went there as servants had become worth several hundreds of pounds, with their estates still increasing.

The Constitution which Locke had framed, after the pattern of Plato's model Republic, was sufficient for the Carolinians only until 1693, and in 1719 Carolina put itself under the protection of King George.

As a colony, a rapid development and a large prosperity were experienced at once, and the people began to turn their attention to their superb material resources with a vigor never before manifested.

One century after the granting of the charter by Charles the Second to the proprietors, Carolina had arisen to considerable commercial eminence. "Charlestown," Beaufort, Purysburg, Jacksonborough, Dorchester, Camden and Georgetown were the principal settlements, but no one, save the first, consisted of more than thirty or forty dwellings.   The negroes already outnumbered the whites. In Charleston they were as eight to five ; and while the white population of the colony did not exceed 40,000, the negroes numbered 80,000 or 90,000.

At that time it was said of the whites that, "in the progress of society they had not advanced beyond that period in which men were distinguished more by their external than internal accomplishments."   They were chiefly known in England "by the number of their slaves, the value of their annual produce, or the extent of their landed estates."   They were lively and gay ; "all novelties in fashion, ornament and dress were quickly introduced, and even the spirit of luxury and extravagance, too common in England," was beginning to creep among them.   It was said that "there were more people possessed of five and ten thousand pounds sterling in the province" than were to be found anywhere else among the same number of persons.   "Their rural life and their constant use of arms" kept up a martial spirit among them.   The Indians hated the negroes, and there was, consequently, no danger of their conspiring together. The Carolina merchant was an honest, industrious, and generous man.

The province readily obtained all the credit it demanded ; the staples which it produced were very valuable, and agriculture and trade were constantly enlarged in their scope by the importations of ship-loads of negroes.   A little before the time of the American revolution, the exports from "Carolina" in a single year amounted to £756,000 sterling ; but the imports were so extensive that the colony remained indebted to the mother country.

Still the old English critics thought the Carolinians rather slovenly husbandmen, and were astonished at the manner in which they managed their estates. Freeholds of land were easily obtained by patent or purchase, and were also alienable at will; so that the system of husbandry was not carried on according to any established principles or plans.   The planter ordinarily cleared a wooded tract, planted it with rice or indigo until it was exhausted, and then neglected it for a fresh location.   Nowhere was the soil improved, nowhere were grass seeds sown for enriching the pastures, and the only study was the putting of the largest crop into market. Safe and prosperous, guaranteed royal protection, possessing unlimited credit and indulgence, and owning the labor necessary to produce wealth, the Carolinian of one hundred years ago seemed a most fortunate mortal, and his carelessness was accounted a princely quality.

Port Royal Island and its chief town, Beaufort, are monuments to the disastrous effects of the revolution which has swept over South Carolina within the last generation. Everywhere on the chain of beautiful sea islands along the low coast one finds the marks of the overturn. But Port Royal, situated on the river terminating in what is perhaps the grandest harbor on the American coast, has hopes, and may bring new life to decaying Beaufort.

A railroad has penetrated the low lands, creeping across marshes and estuaries upon formidable trestles, and now drains the rich cotton-fields around Augusta, in Georgia, toward the Broad river. The town is laid out into lots, and the numbers of the avenues run ambitiously high already; an English steamship line has sent its pioneer vessel to the port; and the Home Government talks of establishing a navy-yard upon the stream.

With commercial facilities which neither New Orleans, Savannah, nor Norfolk can boast, Port Royal deserves a great future. The harbor which Ribault 300 years ago enthusiastically described as so large that "all the argosies of Venice might safely ride therein," is certainly ample for the accommodation of the largest fleets known, and is easy and safe of access.

The lowland scenery of South Carolina is as varied as tropical. From the sea the marshes, or savannahs, stretching seventy miles back from the coast, seem perfectly level; but there are in many places bluffs and eminences crowned with delicate foliage. A vast panorama of fat meadows, watered by creeks; of salt and fresh marshes; of swamp lands of inexhaustible fertility, from which spring the sugar-cane and cypress; of the rich, firm soil, where the oak and the hickory stand in solid columns, and of barrens studded with thousands of young pines—salutes the eye.

The innumerable branches which penetrate the low-lying lands from the sea have formed a kind of checker-work of island and estuary. The forests along the banks of the streams, and scattered on the hedges between the marshes, are beautiful. The laurel, the bay, the palmetto, the beech, the dog-wood, the cherry, are overgrown with wanton, luxuriant vines, which straggle across the aisles where the deer and the fox still wander.

In the spring the jessamine and the cherry fill the air with the perfume of their blossoms; in winter the noble oaks, in their garments of moss, and the serried pines, preserve the verdure which the other trees have lost, and give to the landscape an aspect of warmth and life. When the rice plantations are submerged, and the green plants are just showing their heads above the water, and nodding and swaying beneath the slight breeze passing over the hundreds of acres, the effect is indescribably novel and beautiful.

Beaufort, in a soft, delicious climate, where the orange flourishes, is beautifully located, and was once the abode of hundreds of proud and wealthy planters. One reaches it by rail from Yemassee, a little junction in the midst of a pine forest, where the trains from Charleston, Savannah, Augusta, and Port Royal all meet at midday, and indulge in delays which in the North would be thought disastrous, but which seem quite natural in the slumbrous climate of the lowlands.

The journey from Yemassee is through rich woods, and along high ridges; past newly cleared lands, where the freedmen are grubbing for existence; past old and worn-out plantations, now deserted, with no smoke curling upward from the chimneys of the long rows of negro cabins, and no signs of life about the huge, white mansion in the clump of oaks, or in the centre of a once lovely garden. At the little station one sees smartly dressed men mounting fine horses, and galloping down the long, straight avenues in the forests, to the plantations which they own many miles away. One also sees colored people everywhere, of every shade and variety, lounging, riding, talking in high-pitched voices, and with an accent which renders their speech unintelligible to the stranger.

Sometimes a startled doe, followed by her fawns, bounds across the track. There are but few houses to be seen, and they are miles away. You catch a glimpse of some mighty lagoon, lonely and grand; now you are whirled into the lonely forests—along a river bank—across a wide arm of the sea; now through swamps in which innumerable cypress-knees and rotting boughs seem like snakes and monsters in the stagnant water, and now where you note the gleam of the sun on the white walls of some deserted Beaufort mansion.

The long street by the water-side, in Beaufort, was as still when I entered it as if the town were asleep. The only sign of life was a negro policeman, dressed in a shiny blue uniform, pacing languidly up and down. But there was not even a dog to arrest. On the pretty pier in front of the Sea Island Hotel two or three buzzards were ensconced asleep; half way across the stream a dredge-boat was hauling up phosphates from the channel-bed.

I wandered through the town. It was evidently once very beautiful, and even now there are many remains of the ancient beauty. But a silence as of the grave reigned everywhere. Many of the mansions were closed and fallen into decay. The old Episcopal church, surrounded by a high moss-grown wall, seemed indignantly to have shut itself in from the encroachments of the revolution. The whole aspect of the place was that which I afterward found pervading other South Carolinian towns—that of complete prostration, dejection, stagnation.

Here the revolution penetrated to the quick. The planter, when he returned from his enforced exile during the war, found that the negro had installed himself upon his lands, and would not give them up. A practical confiscation had been operated. There was no redress; the government was in the hands of the negroes. It is true that they were the majority, as they had been for many years before they received their civil rights. The victory of the Union armies meant land to these negroes. They had some idea of vengeance; they did not care to respect property, and hundreds of white families were left homeless, moneyless, and driven into cities where they were friendless. The great plantations of sea-island cotton were left untilled; the negro was too busy with politics to work; and the General Government was in no mood for listening to individual complaints. The "acts of forfeiture," passed in 1862, swept all the lands in St. Helena parish and thousands of acres on Port Royal Island into the hands of the United States Government, by whose authority they were in turn sold on long time to the negroes, and liens taken as security. The original owners who dared to return, protested,* but it was of no avail. The lands have been taken from them, and the negro rules over both them and their lands. He and his fellows dispose not only of the revenues of Beaufort, but of the State. The idle and vicious of his race huddle together in gorgeous parlors, once decorated with elegant furniture, purchased by the planters with the proceeds of slave labor.

The City Hall is controlled by the blacks, and the magistrates, the police, and the representatives in the Legislature, are nearly all Africans. In Beaufort township there are ten negroes to one white person; and in all towns in the adjacent country it is a similar story. At Hilton Head there are about 3,000 colored persons and hardly 100 whites. On St. Helena's Island, still in the same county, there are 6,000 negroes and about 70 whites; in Yemassee, nearly 3,000 blacks and barely 200 whites. In the adjoining counties, Colleton and Charleston, the proportions in the towns are about the same, except in Charleston city. On Edisto Island there are nearly 3,000 negroes, and hardly any white persons.

The blacks have formed communities by themselves. They have left the country and gone to town. The result is that in the chief centres of every township they are immensely in the majority. They monopolize everything. Naturally enough, they are in possession of a great deal which they cannot use. They seem, especially on Port Royal Island, contented with a small tract of land on which to raise cotton, and over which their hogs may wander. Some are very industrious; others never do any work; the masses are satisfied with getting a living. They know little about markets, surplus crops, and the accumulation of riches, and care less. They love hunting and fishing; they revel in the idleness which they never knew until after the war. But they are cumberers of the soil; their ignorance impedes, their obstinacy throttles. They are tools in the hands of the corrupt. They lack moral sense, as might have been expected, after a few generations of slavery. They are immoral and irresponsible; emotional and unreliable; not at all unfriendly in spirit toward the whites, their old masters, yet by their attitude in reality doing them deadly harm.

* The act of 1862 provided that if a property owner should fail to pay, within sixty days, the amount assessed by the Land Commissioners for South Carolina, appointed by the General Government, "the title to his land should thereupon become forfeited to the United States;" and that after such forfeiture a sale should follow, by which the title should be vested in the purchaser or in the United States. This act was, of course, based upon the assumption that the States in which it was operative were out of the Union. Inasmuch as the Land Commissioners for South Carolina did not enter upon their duties until one year after the establishment at Beaufort of the military and civil authority of the Federal Government, a large number of those Carolinians who have suffered by confiscation claim that the whole sale of the lands is illegal, and that the titles of the present owners are equivocal and false.

The undoing of the old relations between the two races, and the conferring of political privileges upon him who was formerly the inferior, have been the ruin of certain sections of these fertile lowlands. Neither race seems likely to resume operations on anything like the old scale of grandeur. The sea-island cotton crop, once a source of such wealth, is small now, yet the negroes, with industry, might raise immense crops. In 1870, Beaufort county, with 150,000 acres of improved land, sent to market but a little over 7,000 bales; it has done somewhat better of late. The culture has met with some disasters; caterpillars and foul weather have interfered. The negroes usually plant a little sea-island cotton, no matter how small may be their farms.

The Northern capitalists who have undertaken this difficult but once very profitable culture, have, as a rule, sunk the better portion of their invested capital; and the native planters have gradually taken to planting a less number of acres yearly. During the three years preceding the war, South Carolina sent to market 54,904 bales of sea-island cotton; but in the three years ending September 1st, 1873, only 23,307 bales were sent out. The control of prices abroad has also been lost to the sea-island planter in South Carolina, as, in the days of slavery, he carelessly sold the finer seeds to any one from other countries who wished to buy, and now encounters formidable foreign rivalry in Egypt, the Sandwich Islands, and in South America, as well as in our own Gulf States.

If a planter of the days when the royal colony of South Carolina was in the height of its glory could return now, and wander through the streets of moss-grown Beaufort, he would be amazed, but no more so than would the planter of 1850 or 1860, if he too might return.

For it would be found that in a decade and a-half one of the most remarkable revolutions ever recorded in history has occurred. A wealthy and highly prosperous community has been reduced to beggary; its vassals have become its lords, and dispose of the present and pledge the future resources of the State. In ten years the total valuation of the commonwealth has been reduced from nearly $500,000,000 to barely $150,000,000 at the present time; the banking capital of Charleston from $13,000,000 to $3,000,000; the insurance capital is entirely destroyed. The taxes have been increased from $392,000 in 1860, to $2,000,000 in 1870; slaves valued at $174,000,000 have been freed, and set to learn the arts of self-government and civilization. More than 400,000 blacks now inhabit the State, and their number is constantly increasing. Thousands of planters have been so utterly ruined that they can never hope even to attain comfortable circumstances again.

Opposite an elegant mansion, on one of the main streets of Beaufort, is a small, unambitious structure, in which the former occupant of the grand mansion is selling goods at retail. He returned after the capture of the town to find himself stripped of everything, and has been living in view of his former splendor ever since. His fields are held by strangers; his house is converted into offices. In a day, as it were, he and thousands of others were reduced to complete dependence, and compelled to live under the government of the ignorant slaves whose labor they had grown rich upon.

XLVIII.

ON A RICE PLANTATION IN SOUTH CAROLINA.

THE lowlands of South Carolina are the most interesting portion of the State, in a commercial and picturesque point of view, and there the political outlook is also most depressing. The masses of the freedmen and women on the sea islands and in the sea-board counties are very ignorant, and vastly inferior, in natural intelligence and ability, to the negro of the upper and middle sections of the same State, or the type met with throughout Virginia, Maryland, Tennessee, and Kentucky.

The lowland negro of South Carolina has a barbaric dialect, which no external influences have as yet impressed in the slightest degree; the English words seem to tumble all at once from his mouth, and to get sadly mixed whenever he endeavors to speak. The phraseology is usually so odd, too, that even after the

View of a Rice-field in South Carolina. [Page 434.]

stranger has become a little accustomed to the thick tones of the voice and the awkward enunciation, he cannot readily understand. Certainly a Virginian negro from the town could not comprehend these low-country people at all, until his ear had become habituated to the apparent mumbling.

The children of the planters, brought up on the plantations, and allowed to run in the woods with the little negroes, acquired the same dialect; and to-day many a gentleman's son regrets that it is apparent in his speech. These negroes also have their peculiar religious superstitions and ceremonies. I repeatedly asked planters in Beaufort and Colleton counties if the negroes there had changed much in manners and habits since their slave days, and the invariable answer was, "No!" They have learned to understand that the vote gives power; they find work in large bands together on the rice plantations distasteful to them, and they are perfectly happy when they succeed in obtaining an acre or two of land, and in erecting a cabin. To own a mule is the acme of bliss.

The men and women still maintain their old-time servility toward their former masters. When they meet them on the roads the men always touch their hats, and the women, no matter how huge the basket they may happen to be carrying upon their heads, courtesy profoundly. The word "mas'r" is still used, being so intimately associated in the negro's mind with certain individuals, that he has no inclination to drop it.

Friendliest exterior relations are maintained between ex-master and ex-slave, as a rule; and the white Conservatives sometimes bitterly regret that they did not come boldly forward, at the outset of reconstruction, and themselves guide the negro votes. There would, at one time, have been a fair chance for such a fusion; but the races soon drifted into a separate political current, and the negro appeared in his present rôle of corrupt and ignorant legislator. At present, the whites cannot get a fair hearing, and are subject to many tyrannies at the hands of negro justices and constables.

There are honorable exceptions to all the general criticisms which may be made upon the character of the lowland negro; but, as a mass, the race is really very degraded. It is making gradual progress toward a condition of independence; yet ignorance and irresponsibility are still the rule. The marriage relation is almost unknown in many of the lowland counties; men and women live together as long as they can agree, and are called husband and wife.

Passing through a rice-field one morning, in which there were, perhaps, four hundred black men and women at work, I requested the owner of the plantation, whom I accompanied, to ask four men, who were sitting by a rice stack awaiting a barge, some leading question calculated to throw light on their morality. Each of the four had had two "wives," as they termed it; one of the oldest had had four. The causes of separation were various—infidelity, abuse, a hasty word, or laziness. The children who were the fruit of these careless unions were kept by either father or mother, as the couple might agree.

Jealousy is a terrible passion among these people, and sometimes leads to capital crime. All, without exception, are religious; they find a temporary relief and an excitement in the "meetings," and will go to one, no matter how distant it may be. Most of the men are armed; they manage to secure a pistol or a gun, and are as fond of hunting as their white employers. The situation of those gentlemen who had been slave-holders and large planters before the war, was dreadful for a year or two after the fall of the Confederacy. The freedmen were difficult to manage, could not be got to work, and were jealous of anything which seemed like an attempt to get them back to their old places. The intervention of soldiery was constantly necessary to keep the peace.

The low-country planter lived in a luxurious but careless way. Although some few were ignorant, and cherished the belief that there was nothing else in the country so fine as their forests and swamps, most of them were court-eous, unaffected, and devoid of pretension. They resided with their families at their country-seats on the plantations, during the winter months, and in the summer removed to pleasant mansions along the Ashley river or on Sullivan's Island, near Charleston. The Heywards, the Manigaults, the Lowndes, the Mid-dletons, the Hugers, the Barnwells, the Elliotts, the Rhetts, went annually to Charleston, where there was choice and polished society.

To-day, the majority of those engaged in planting at the outbreak of the war, are pitiably poor; and just at the close of the war, the spectacle of men who had owned two hundred or five hundred slaves, reduced to driving a cart or tending a grocery, was quite common. The enforced poverty of many is even bitterer

Negro Cabins on a Rice Plantation.

now than it was then, for they are compelled to see, day by day, the poor State, which has already been so impoverished, plundered anew and embar-rassed further by the action of the ignorant and vicious legislators.

Many of the lowland negroes were firmly impressed, when first called to use the ballot, that they were to gain property by it, and great numbers of them still have an idea that they have been defrauded of what they were entitled to. They have also been told by so many legislators of their own race, that all the property once their masters' now properly belongs to them, that they literally believe it, in many cases, while, in others, they consider the whole thing a muddle entirely beyond their comprehension.

This assertion that the negroes ought to take the planters' lands has been often made by white politicians who gained control of the negro at the time that the white natives refused to take active part in the elections, or the reörganization of the State.   The whole theory of taxation in the commonwealth, as evolved by Nash and the few other colored men of talent in the Legislature, is summed up in these words, from the present Governor's last message : "The taxes fall chiefly where they belong—upon real estate.   The owner cannot afford to keep thousands of acres idle and unproductive, merely to gratify his personal vanity, and because he inherited them from his father.   Stern necessity, therefore, will compel him to cut up his ancestral possessions into small farms, and sell them to those who can and will make them productive ; and thus the masses of the people will become property holders."

Swart Demos in the legislative chair, with artful rogues around him, remembers only that the tax was not raised from land, but upon the slaves, previous to 1860 ; and when he thinks of it, very likely his blood is hot, and he willingly applies a slashing tax to the land owners.   "In the old days," he says, "your cotton acres, worth hundreds of dollars, were only taxed four cents an acre, but on 400,000 wretches, such as I, you placed a tax of sixty cents per head, and made us work it out, thus getting nearly half a million of revenue.   Now we will make you work out your tax, and we will wrest your lands away from you." And so bitterness is needlessly provoked on both sides, and oppression flourishes.   It is not taxation, nor even an increase of taxation, that the white

people of South Carolina object to ; but it is *taxation without representation,* and *unjust, tyrannical, arbitrary, overwhelming taxation,* producing revenues which never get any further than the already bursting pockets of knaves and dupes !

Rice culture has been the prominent industry of South Carolina since the time of the Landgrave Thomas Smith, under the proprietary government.   With the determination of the planters to make it the chief object of their care, came the necessity for importing great numbers of slaves, and the sacrifice of many hundreds of lives, in the arduous labors of clearing the ground and preparing the soil. The cypress forests gave place to

"The women were dressed in gay colors."   [Page 435.]

"With forty or fifty pounds of rice stalks on their heads." [Page 435.]

the fields of waving green, and the rivers were diverted from their channels to flood the vast expanse in which the negroes had set the seeds.

In 1724, 439 African slaves were imported to South Carolina, together with a vast amount of other commodities, in exchange for which the citizens gave 18,000 barrels of rice and 52,000 barrels of naval stores. Year by year the importations of negroes increased in numbers; year by year the planter became "more eager in the pursuit of large possessions of land," and "strenuously vied with his neighbor," says a chronicler, "for a superiority of fortune."

The Carolinians were compelled to keep up fortifications on the borders of the Spanish domains, to prevent the negroes from escaping into foreign territory; but they had few other external cares. Their trade grew constantly with New England, New York and Pennsylvania; and in 1738, when there were fully 40,000 negroes in South Carolina, Spanish policy provoked a formidable insurrection on the part of the blacks. This brought on open hostilities between Spaniards and Carolinians, and the latter made an unsuccessful expedition against St. Augustine.

It should be borne in mind that the following statistics, showing how rapidly the exportation of rice increased in quantity, also shows how swiftly the slave population of the province grew. From 1720 to 1729, the export was 44,081 tons; from 1730 to 1740, it was 99,905 tons; and in the single year of 1740, 90,000 barrels were sent away, the gain upon which was estimated at £220,000. In 1771, the exports of the State amounted to £756,000 sterling. Shipping crowded the harbors; money was plenty; the planters commanded the best of everything from Great Britain and the West India Islands. There were at that period no taxes whatever upon real or personal estate; but the revenues were raised by duties on "spirituous liquors, sugar, molasses, flour, biscuit, negro slaves," etc., and amounted to several thousand pounds per annum.

And so, for many generations, the rice culture and the slave system went hand in hand upon the fertile Carolina lowlands. Good authorities have assured me that they believe there were 1,000,000 acres of rice-lands in cultivation in South Carolina at the outbreak of the civil war. At the present time there is hardly one-fourth of that area cultivated, but there is a steady increase.

The blows struck by immediate emancipation upon this once gigantic industry were crushing. Under the slave *régime*, the planters successfully competed with other producers in all the markets of the world. From 1850 to 1860, they exported 705,317,600 pounds of rice, valued at $24,619,009. The total production of rice in the United States in 1850 was 215,313,497 pounds; even in 1860, it was 187,162,032. Such figures are eloquent. The rice-producing States suffered severely at an early period of the war; the fields were abandoned; and in South Carolina the production has decreased from 119,100,524 pounds, in 1860, to 32,304,825, in 1870. The annual product in Georgia, Louisiana and the Carolinas, from 1865 to 1871, will show that the industry is gradually struggling to its feet once more:

Year.	Pounds.	Year.	Pounds.
1866	12,002,080	1869	48,837,920
1867	19,368,060	1870	54,117,320
1868	27,566,740	1871	59,000,000

Some of the rice plantations cover thousands of acres even now; and the employment of from five to eight hundred men, women and children by a single person, is not at all uncommon. I visited the celebrated plantation at Green Pond, in Colleton county, the property of Mr. Bissell, who has 3,500 acres under his control. He, in common with others, was broken by the war, and is struggling with the hundred ills which beset the planter in the changed condition of affairs.

A Pair of Mule-Boots.
[Page 435.]

Mr. Bissell's broad fields lie seven miles from the Charleston and Savannah railroad, at the rear of extensive pine forests, in which, now that the white man is so poorly represented in the Legislature, the poacher wanders un- reproved. The plantation extends across the Combahee river into Beaufort county, and at various points rice- pounding mills and little villages, in which the workers live, are established. A morning ride in the soft, Italian-like autumn across this or similar planta- tions, is a delicious experience. Mounted on a stout mule or on a Kentucky horse, you gallop through the perfumed avenues of the forests until you reach the wide expanse of fields, cut into squares by long trenches, through which water from the river in the background is admitted to every part of the land.

The breeze rustles musically in the tall cane along the banks, in whose sedgy recesses the alligator and the serpent hide. In the distance an antlered deer may break from his cover, and after one defiant glance, stamp his foot, and be gone! A white sail glides on the horizon's rim, as the little schooner from Charleston works her way around to the mill, where long processions of black boys and girls, with baskets on their heads, and their mouths filled with horrible jargon, are waiting to load the rice.

The injury done to all the plantations in these low- land counties, by the neglect consequent on the war, is incalculable. Most of these plantations have been re- claimed from the waters; have been diked, ditched, furnished with "trunks," by means of which the planter can inundate or drain his land at will.* A rice plantation is, in fact, a huge hydraulic machine, maintained by con- stant warring against the rivers. The utmost attention and vigilance is necessary, and the labor must be ready at a moment's notice for the most exhaustive efforts. Alter- nate flooding and draining must take place several times during the season, and one part of the crop must be flooded, while the other adjacent to it is dry.

Fields are divided into sections, and trunks or canals convey water from the river to each separately. "The whole apparatus of levels, flood-gates, trunks, canals, banks, ditches," says a prominent planter, "is of the most extensive kind, requiring skill and unity of purpose." The slightest leak in the banks or dikes may end in the ruin of the whole plantation. Freshets, too, commit frightful havoc from time to time. At one fell swoop the produce of a

A "Trunk-Minder."
[Page 435.]

* Speech of Hon. F. A. Sawyer, of South Carolina, in the U. S. Senate, in 1872.

thousand acres on Mr. Bissell's plantation was swept away in 1872. The cost of reclaiming rice-lands, and fitting them for culture, was about $100 per acre before the war, and so greatly had they been damaged by long neglect that more than half that sum has been expended in their rehabilitation. Once well prepared, the annual cost of cultivation is now about thirty dollars, as compared with ten dollars in former days; but it is steadily decreasing.

We wandered over perhaps 700 acres, in Colleton and Beaufort counties. The men and women at work in the different sections were under the control of field-masters. The spectacle was lively. The women were dressed in gay colors, with handkerchiefs uniting all the colors of the rainbow, around their temples. Their feet were bare, and their stout limbs encased in uncouth flannel wrappings. Most of them, while staggering out through the marshes with forty or fifty pounds of rice stalks on their heads, kept up an incessant jargon with one another, and indulged in a running fire of invective against the field-master.

Unloading the Rice-Barges.

The "trunk-minders," the watchmen on whose vigilance the plantation's safety depends, promenaded briskly; the flat-boats, on which the field hands deposited their huge bundles of rice stalks, were poled up to the mill, where the grain was threshed and separated from the straw, winnowed, and carried in baskets to the schooners which transported it to Charleston, and the "pounding-mills." During harvest-time 800 hands are employed on this plantation.

Harvest is hardly completed by March, when the sowing begins again. The trunks are opened in each section the day it is planted, and the fields are flooded. The mules, that annually drag the ploughs through the marshes, are booted with leather contrivances, to prevent them from sinking into the treacherous ooze. To the negroes is given the rice that grows along the margins, and considerable profit is obtained from its sale. The fields in autumn are yellowish in hue, tinged here and there lightly with green, where young rice is upspringing from the shoots recently cut down.   The rice lies in ricks, but is ill protected, swarms of birds carrying away great quantities.

While we were strolling afield, one stout negro came up and asked " Mas'r Ben" to buy him a mule with $100 which he had saved.   " Mas'r Ben" agreed to do it, and informed me that such a purchase was a sign of a negro's assured prosperity.   The wages paid the rice-field hands ranged from twenty-five cents to one dollar and seventy-five cents daily, but the manager on this, as on many other plantations, found great difficulty in keeping the labor organized and available.   The men found that by two or three days' work they could procure money enough to support them in idleness the next week, and sometimes the overseers were at a loss what to do for help.

Beautiful were the broad and carefully cultivated acres, stretching miles away on either side of the placid, deep, and noble Combahee ; picturesque were the granaries, almost bursting with the accumulated stores of the precious grain; and novel and inspiring the vistas of the long sedge-bordered canals, through which the morning breezes lightly whistled.   The sea-myrtle was neighbor to the cane, and the tall grasses twined lovingly around them both.

At the "store," about whose entrance were grouped packs of hounds, leaping and fawning about their masters, who were mounting their horses, we saw crowds of negresses, barefooted and barelimbed, bringing poultry or eggs to exchange for corn, or chattering frantically, or bursting into boisterous laughter which echoed over many a broad acre.

One could not help thinking that in due time a vast amount of labor-saving machinery must come to take the place of this rude and careless negro element upon the rice plantation.   At present, the planters admit, there is an enormous waste, and the climate's character renders it impossible to introduce white labor and intelligence into the section.   The negro men and women whom I saw were certainly of a low and degraded type, distinctively,—as a Frenchman, with his quick instincts, said on seeing a group of these same lowland people,—"a broken down race !"

At the threshing-mill, at the winnowing-machine, among the great rice stacks where they were packing and sorting and unloading from barges, the women were coarse, brutish, and densely ignorant; the men, in the main, the same.   There were types of face in which the savage still stood out in splendor.   Many women of sixty or seventy years of age were at work in various places about the field.   They had evidently been untouched by the spirit of the war.   I doubt if they realized the change in their condition.   Their conversation with me was confined to inquiries as to how much tobacco I would give them, and an appeal to me to tell Mas'r Ben that they "bin want" a new handkerchief, and hoped he would not forget them.   The men as a rule were civil, but a little suspicious in

"At the winnowing-machine."

demeanor, as if they did not intend to allow any advantage to be taken of them.   If looked at sharply, they would wince, and finally, wreathing their lips with broad grins, would bow and shuffle away.

The planters throughout this section, where the Middletons and the Heywards once tilled so many acres, and whence they drew great incomes, admit that the labor question is the most serious one with them.   The profits of rice-planting are enormous, but the system of large plantations will, perhaps, have to be adhered to, and African or Chinese labor can alone sustain the trials of the summer climate.   The production of the State, and the adjacent lowlands in other States, will doubtless again reach the figure attained before the war, although the present condition of South Carolina would not seem to justify prophecies of any prosperity within her limits, save in Charleston.

"Aunt Bransom."—A venerable ex-slave on a South Carolina Rice Plantation.

XLIX.

CHARLESTON, SOUTH CAROLINA.

AND why prosperity in Charleston? Mainly because the venerable city has established in addition to her important cotton trade, a large number of manufacturing enterprises, for which her location is particularly advantageous; and because her business men have an elastic spirit and a remarkable courage, which reflect the highest credit upon them. A veritable phœnix, always springing triumphantly from the ashes of terrible conflagrations, as well as from the ruins caused by hurricanes and bombardments, the South Carolinian metropolis is, in itself, a standing reproof to the too oft-repeated assertion that the ancient commonwealth lacks enterprise.

When the war closed there was not a completed railroad ending in Charleston. Those now known as the North-eastern, giving connection with the

View from Fort Sumter, in Charleston Harbor. [Page 440.]

route to Wilmington; the South Carolina, running north-westward to Columbia, Aiken, and Augusta; and the Savannah and Charleston, penetrating the lowlands and reaching to the Georgian seaport, were worn down and almost completely wrecked. Costly bridges and trestles had been destroyed, depots burned, tracks torn up, and the amount of rolling-stock was absurdly inadequate to immediate wants. The rebuilding and equipment were begun in 1866. All the old rail connections are now resuscitated, and Charleston is reaching out for a wider range of commerce than, before the war, she would have deemed possible. The South Carolina railroad and its feeders, the Greenville and Columbia, and the Macon and Augusta, in Georgia, send vast quantities of freight, which heretofore went northward, to the Carolinian metropolis. The North-eastern, and the Savannah and Charleston, are important links in the shortest route from New York to Florida, and with the sea-board line, from New York to New Orleans. Many steamship companies were compelled to suspend communication with the city during the war; now there are two steamer lines between New York and Charleston, comprising eight fine steamers, capable of carrying away 30,000 bales of cotton monthly. On the Baltimore line there are three steamers, on the Philadelphia two, on the Boston two, with a carrying capacity altogether of about 14,000 bales monthly. The splendid line to Florida has been reopened, and the connections with Savannah, Beaufort, Georgetown, Edisto, and the Peedee river are also resumed, and are very prosperous.

The increase in steamship freights from Charleston since 1860 has been 300 per cent., but the sail tonnage is not larger than it was in 1862, as much of its trade has been transferred to steamers. The following receipts of cotton at Charleston for eight years since the war also indicate a marked prosperity :

Years.*	Bales of Cotton.	Years.	Bales of Cotton.
1865–66	111,714	1869–70	250,761
1866–67	165,316	1870–71	356,544
1867–68	246,018	1871–72	282,686
1868–69	200,764	1872–73	385,000

A large proportion of this cotton was sent to Charleston for sale, not merely to pass through. The exports of rice from Charleston, from September, 1865, to September, 1873, amount to about 250,000 tierces. The increase in the number of naval stores reported has also been remarkable, as shown by the following table :

Years.	Barrels.	Years.	Barrels.
1865–66	32,136	1869–70	79,156
1866–67	54,026	1870–71	90,297
1867–68	62,852	1871–72	151,553
1868–69	72,279	1872–73	225,683

The lumber exports since the war have also been large, footing up at least 140,000,000 of feet. The rich pine forests of the State are annually of increasing importance. Charleston, Beaufort and Georgetown are all daily receiving great stores of lumber from the forests, which still stretch over thousands of acres. The swamps furnish the best of material for ship-building, and Charleston has built many fine lumber-mills in which to prepare the pine and other useful trees for shipping. The city sadly needs the addition of several millions to its banking capital to enable it to carry out its schemes. The three National and four State banks now have hardly $3,000,000 of paid up capital. There are four savings banks, with a little more than $1,000,000, much of which represents the savings of the freedmen, on deposit. Private bankers are also doing a good deal for the city's interests.

Very lovely is the old city, lying confidingly on the waters, at the confluence of the broad Ashley and Cooper rivers, and fronting on the spacious harbor, over whose entrance the scarred and ever memorable Sumter keeps watch and ward.

* The commercial year begins September 1.

Nature has lavished a wealth of delicious foliage upon all the surroundings of the city, and the palmetto, the live and water oaks, the royal magnolias, the tall pines, the flourishing hedges, and the gardens filled with rich, tropical blooms, profoundly impress the stranger. The winter climate is superb, and the sunshine seems omnipresent, creeping into even the narrowest lanes and by-ways.

In 1680, the people who had been encouraged to remove from the badly chosen site of a settlement which they had selected on the banks of the Ashley river in 1671, laid the foundations at Charleston, and the town at once sprang into activity. It began its commerce in dangerous times, for pirates hovered about the mouth of the Ashley, and many a good ship, laden with the produce of the plantations, and bound for Great Britain, was plundered, and its crew set on shore, or murdered, if resistance was offered. A hurricane also swept over the infant town, half ruining it; and then began a series of destructive fires, which, from 1680 to 1862, have, at fearfully short intervals, carried havoc and destruction into the homes of the wealthiest.

In later years, too, the fleets of hostile Spaniards or Frenchmen sometimes brought panic even to Charleston bar; and the beacon fires on Sullivan's Island, in the harbor, warned the citizens to be on their guard. In 1728, a hurricane created an inundation, which overflowed the town and lowlands, forced the inhabitants to take refuge on the roofs of their dwellings, drove twenty-three fine ships ashore, and leveled many thousands of trees. In the same year came the yellow fever, sweeping off multitudes of whites and blacks. After the surrender, by the proprietary government, of its control of the province, into the hands of the sovereign of Great Britain, on the payment of a round sum of purchase money, Charleston became more prosperous than ever before. In 1765 it was described as "one of the first cities in British America, yearly advancing in size, riches and population."

The old Charleston Post-office. [Page 441.]

The approaches to Charleston from the sea are unique, and the stranger yields readily to the illusion that the city springs directly from the bosom of the waves. The bar at the harbor's mouth will allow ships drawing seventeen feet of water to pass over it. The entrance from the sea is commanded on either side by Morris and Sullivan's Islands, the former the scene of terrific slaughter during the dreadful days of 1863, and subsequently one of the points from which the Union forces bombarded Charleston; and the latter at present a fashionable summer resort, crowded with fine mansions. On the harbor side of Sullivan's Island, Fort Moultrie, a solid and well-constructed fortification, frowns over the hurrying waters. Passing Sumter, which lies isolated and in semi-ruin, looking, at a distance, like some coral island pushed up from the depths, one sails by pleasant shores lined with palmettoes and grand moss-hung oaks, and by Castle Pinckney, and anchors at the substantial wharves of the proud little city.

Many ships from many climes are anchored at these wharves, and the town seems the seaport of some thriving commercial State, so little does it represent the actual condition of South Carolina. The graceful Corinthian portico and columns of the new Custom-House, built of pure white marble, rise up near the water-side. There is a jolly refrain of the clinking of hammers, the rattling of drays, and the clanking of chains, which indicates much activity. Here some foreign vessel, which has come for phosphates, is unloading her ballast; here a rice-schooner is unloading near a pounding-mill. On one hand are lumber-yards; on another, cotton-sheds, filled with bales. Hundreds of negroes, scream-

Houses on the Battery—Charleston.

ing and pounding their mules, clatter along the piers and roadways; a great Florida steamer is swinging round, and starting on her ocean trip to the Penin-sula, with her decks crowded with Northern visitors. Along "East Bay" the houses are, in many places, solid and antique. The whole aspect of the harbor quarter is unlike that of any of our new and smartly painted Northern towns. In Charleston the houses and streets have an air of dignified repose and solidity. At the foot of Broad street, a spacious avenue lined with banks and offices of professional men, stands the old "Post-office," a building of the colonial type, much injured during the late war, but since renovated at considerable expense. Most of the original material for the construction of the edifice was brought from England in 1761. Within its walls the voices of Rutledge, Pinckney, Gadsden, Lowndes and Laurens were raised to vehemently denounce the Government against whose tyranny the "Thirteen original States" rebelled; from the old steps Washington addressed the Charlestonians in 1791; and for many years during this century it was an Exchange for the merchants of Charleston and vicinity.   When the British occupied Charleston, the building was the scene of

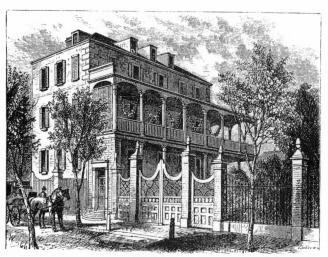
A Charleston Mansion.

many exciting episodes. The basement was taken for a prison, and all who were devoted to the cause of American liberty were confined therein.   From that prison the martyr, Isaac Hayne, was led to execution; and in the cellar one hundred thousand pounds of powder lay safely hidden from the British during the whole time of their occupation.   On the site of this building stood the old council-chamber

and watch-house used in the days of the "proprietary government."

The original plan of Charleston comprised a great number of streets running at right angles, north and south, east and west, between the two rivers.   But many of these streets were very narrow, being, in fact, nothing more than lanes; and they have remained unchanged until the present day.   The darkness and narrowness of the old lanes, the elder colonists thought, would keep away the glare of the bright sun; but the modern Charlestonians do not seem of their opinion, for they open wide avenues, and court the sun freely in their spacious and elegant mansions on the "Battery."   Some of the Charleston avenues present a novel appearance, bordered as they are on either side by tall, weather-stained mansions, whose gable-ends front upon the sidewalks, and which boast verandas attached to each story, screened from the sun and from observation by ample wooden lattices, and by trellised vines and creepers.   The high walls, which one sees so often in France and England, surround the majority of the gardens, and it is only through the gate, as in New Orleans, that one can catch a glimpse of the loveliness within.   In some of the streets remote from the harbor front, the stillness of death or desertion reigns; many of the better class of mansions are vacant, and here and there the residence of some former aristocrat is now serving as an abode for a dozen negro families.

On King street one sees the most activity in the lighter branches of trade; there the ladies indulge in shopping, evening, morning, and afternoon; there is located the principal theatre, the tasty, little "Academy of Music," and there also, are some elegant homes.   Along that section of King street, near the crossing of Broad, however, are numerous little shops frequented by negroes, in which one sees the most extravagant array of gaudy but inexpensive articles of apparel; and of eatables which the negro palate cannot resist. The residence streets of the "Palmetto City," on the side next the Ashley river, are picturesque and lovely. They are usually bordered by many beautiful gardens. A labyrinth of long wooden piers and wharves runs out on the lagoons and inlets near the Ashley, and the boasted resemblance of Charleston to Venice is doubtless founded on the perfect illusion produced by a view of that section from a distance. The magnificent and the mean jostle each other very closely in all quarters.

The Spire of St. Philip's Church—Charleston.

The stranger visiting Charleston is surprised to find that little has been done toward rebuilding that portion of the city swept away by fire in 1861. There are still gaps left in the heart of the populous sections; one suddenly comes upon the scarred and scorched walls of a huge church, or the foundations of some immense block, in a location which it seems folly to leave unimproved. But the Charlestonians explain that they do not need to rebuild as yet, for though the population is gradually increasing (it is now more than fifty thousand) the altered circumstances of some classes in society have compelled them to retire and make room for others.

L.

THE VENICE OF AMERICA—CHARLESTON'S POLITICS.
A LOVELY LOWLAND CITY—IMMIGRATION.

I F we climb into the tower of the stately building known as the "Orphan House," some pleasant evening, when the sunset is beginning to throw the dark walls and picturesque groupings of the sea-girdled city into strong relief, we can get a panoramic glimpse of all the chief features of Charleston's

The Orphan House—Charleston.

exterior. We shall, perhaps, be too far from the Battery and its adjacent parks to note fully the effect of the gay group promenading the stone parapet against which the tides break gently, or to catch the perfect beauty of the palm-girt shores so distinctly visible beyond the Ashley's current, now that the sunset has given them a blood-red background. The Battery is not crowded with carriages, as in those merry days when the State was still prosperous, or on that famous day when yonder black mass in the harbor was aflame, and when the flag of the nation which floated over it was hauled down. But it is one of the airiest and most elegant promenades possessed by any Southern city, and the streets leading to it are quaint and beautiful. The church spires here and there are noticeable, and that one glistening in the distance was a white mark for many a day for the Federal batteries; yet few shells struck the stately steeple of St. Michael's, the old-fashioned, staid Episcopal house of prayer.

Beyond this church one sees a mass of buildings, whose queer roofs and strangely shapen chimneys remind him of Antwerp or of Amsterdam. These date from colonial times; it is the Charleston of pre-revolutionary days which one sees clustered around St. Michael's. The bells were removed during the siege of Charleston to Columbia; were captured and accidentally cracked; were recovered, sent to England, and recast in the foundry in Whitechapel, from whence they were originally obtained. After the war they were put back in their place in the steeple with great rejoicing amongst the old Charlestonians. Yonder, nearer the harbor, out of Church street, arises another spire, the counterpart of St. Martin's in the Fields in London. It is the tower of St. Philip's, also an Episcopal church, and in the old graveyard opposite is a simple tomb in which repose the bones of John C. Calhoun. The statesman rests in an antiquated, yet beautiful corner of the town. The venerable cemetery is embowered in trees, and hemmed round about by old buildings with tiled roofs. The remains were removed when the Union forces seemed likely to capture Charleston, but were replaced in 1871. The formidable ruin, which the sunset-glow throws so sharply upon your vision, is the old cathedral of St. John and St. Finbar, destroyed in the last great fire. On its site, when the Charlestonians were compelled to surrender to the British, occurred a tremendous explosion, occasioned by the rage of the conquered.

The Battery—Charleston.

They were compelled to deposit their arms at the arsenal, which was also a powder magazine, and all coming at once, and hurling down upon the ground hundreds of fire-arms, an explosion took place, igniting twenty thousand pounds of powder and blowing to atoms the adjacent Lunatic Asylum, Poor-House, Guard-

House, and Barracks, as well as conquerors and conquered.   The city has many
other interesting churches, among them the Huguenot, which has on its walls
numerous interesting ancient inscriptions.   Grace Church (Episcopal) is the
resort of the fashionable worshipers.

There is nothing remarkable in the secular architecture of Charleston; yet
this old Orphan House, from whose tower we survey the others, with its lovely

The Grave of John C. Calhoun—Charleston.   [Page 445.]

garden hedged in from the street, with its statue of William Pitt, which the grateful citizens erected when the "stamp act" was repealed, is imposing.   It was
founded in 1790, is bountifully endowed, and thousands of orphan boys and girls
have been well cared for within its walls.   John C. Fremont and the Carolinian
Memminger were educated there.   There is an institution of the same class
for the colored people.   Neither the hotels nor the banks are distinguished for
architectural excellence.   The Charleston Hotel has an immense stone-pillared
piazza fronting on Meeting street, but the Mills House and the Pavilion are
simply solid blocks.

The Charleston Club-House is an elegant structure, and the building of the
South Carolina Hall is fine in interior arrangement.   The Club-House has become
the seat of the Federal courts, and white and black men sit together in juries
there.   The Court-House and the City Hall are substantial edifices, fronting each
other on corners of Broad and Meeting streets.   Around them are always lounging crowds of negro men and women, as if they delighted to linger in the atmosphere of government and law, to the powers and responsibilities of which they
have lately been introduced.   At the Guard-House one may note white and
black policemen on terms of amity.

Charleston prospers despite the anomalous condition of politics and society in
the State.   What might she not become if the commonwealth were developed to
its utmost?   The citizens suffer many trying ills, the most aggravated of which
is the small rôle that the present leaders of the majority permit them to play in
State politics.   The Legislature has out-Napoleoned Napoleon III in measures for
the corruption of suffrage, and has enacted an infamous law, which allows Governors of the State to control the ballot-box completely through commissioners

appointed virtually by himself. Its vote is swallowed up in the vote of Charleston county, and consequently it is represented only at second-hand in the State Assembly, getting but a meagre and partial hearing through a score of ignorant negroes, sent from the plantations and small towns in the vicinity.

The first election in Charleston after reconstruction was held in 1868, and the Republican candidate for Mayor, Pillsbury, was elected by a majority of twenty-three in a poll of 10,000. He remained in office until the summer of 1871, when the Conservatives attempted a fusion, and ran a ticket composed of white and black candidates, against the Republicans, with John A. Wagener, a German, for Mayor, and elected him by 777 majority. This administration had continued to the date of my visit, in 1873, when a new election took place, and exhibited in the most glaring light some of the atrocities of the present system. The Conservatives alleged, and it was, indeed, clearly proven, that four hundred negroes were imported from Edisto Island at one time, to create a majority in Charleston for the so-called "Republicans." None but Radical supervisors of the elections were appointed, and the right of challenge at every poll-precinct was denied. The law required every person voting to swear that he was a citizen of Charleston, but the imported voters were provided with the printed forms of the oath, from which the clause concerning the place of residence was omitted.

With no power of interference, and no chance to dispute at the polls or in the counting of the votes, this city of 50,000 inhabitants, possessing $30,000,000 worth of taxable property, was delivered over, bound hand and foot, to the tender

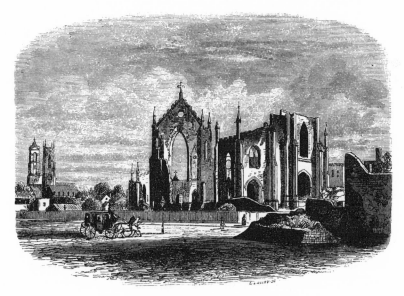

The Ruins of St. Finbar Cathedral—Charleston. [Page 445.]

mercies of the ignorant and the vicious. The party then in power admitted the abnormal condition of affairs. Governor Moses told an editor in Charleston that every citizen of South Carolina could vote in that city, if he chose, without hindrance; the Charlestonians could not help themselves.

The result of this latter election, in which the negro party was, of course, victorious, was a ferment, culminating in mass-meetings, investigations, and finally in a series of arguments. It was charged and shown that the commissioners for the elections did not designate all the polling-places so that the general public would know where they were, but that they stealthily opened them during the election, and there " rushed through" the illegal voters. It was also affirmed by the supporters of the corrupt State Government that a "residence in the city without limit as to time," in the county, sixty days, and in the State, one year, were qualifications sufficient for a voter under the act of 1873. The board of managers consisted, at the city election in 1873, almost entirely of negroes. Several hundred special deputy sheriffs were appointed to " maintain order " if the Conservatives made any attempt to challenge voters at the polls; and the managers refused to give the reporters of the city press any information concerning the changes made in the polling-places the night before the election. The Republican or Radical ticket was elected, and the protest of the citizens of Charleston having been entered, the " board of commissioners," appointed by the Legislature, then published a formal announcement that the election was " legal and valid," and that the " protest was overruled."

The Conservatives were bitterly grieved at this, as they had made a very firm stand, and it showed them how completely they were at the mercy of their present masters. They were not especially dissatisfied with the choice for Mayor, as the successful candidate, Mr. Cunningham, is an honest man; but the other municipal officers elected they regarded quite differently. The present police force of the city is about equally divided into black and white, and there are nine colored aldermen in the new board. It is not because of the presence of the negro in these offices of trust and honor that the Charlestonians are angry and grieved, but because he refuses them their proper share in the government. As they are now situated, the intelligence and property of the city are as completely shut out from political representation as if they were imprisoned within walls of adamant.

Charleston's city tax, in 1872, amounted to two per cent., but in 1873 was somewhat reduced. The combined city, county, and State tax, however, now amounts to three and a-half per cent. The assessments are always fully up to, and usually over, the actual value of property. The property holder, in the first instance, makes his returns. If the county auditor is not satisfied with the estimates, he changes them to suit himself; and the citizen then has the refuge of appeal to a " board of equalization." The Constitution requires that all property be taxed at its value.

The present city debt is nearly $5,000,000, some of which was incurred by subscriptions to railroads before the war. The city, before the war, invested $1,000,000 in the Blue Ridge railroad, and the State about $1,300,000. In 1868 or '69, the State stock, a majority, was sold for $13,000, to a ring. Shortly before this the State had guaranteed $4,000,000 of bonds of the road; these were hypothecated by the company. The ring secured the passage of a law authorizing the State Treasurer to issue $1,800,000 of revenue bond scrip upon the surrender to him of the $4,000,000 guaranteed bonds, said scrip receivable for taxes. Exchange was made, and bonds have been canceled, but the State Supreme Court has decided that the act authorizing the issue of the scrip is unconstitutional and void. The "licenses" which business and professions are already compelled to submit to are grievous burdens, and the people consider them such an odious form of municipal taxation that when the Legislature passed a law for collecting State licenses also, it was resisted, and finally its repeal was deemed expedient. The astute legislators even imposed a license-tax upon the railroads, which were, of course, already licensed by charter.

"The highways leading out of the city are all richly embowered in loveliest foliage." [Page 451.]

Thus cut off, politically, Charleston, with grim patience, awaits a turn in the tide of affairs, and catches a little inspiration from the development of the scheme for a new railway route from Chicago to Charleston. This superb air line, when built, will pass by Columbia and Spartanburg, in South Carolina, northward to Asheville, in the North Carolina mountains—thence through Cumberland Gap into Lexington, in Kentucky, and so onward to Chicago, giving an outlet on the sea 100 miles nearer the North-west than New York now is by any existing line. The towns mentioned above are situated directly on the route originally projected for the connection between the North-west and the Atlantic, and pronounced by all who have surveyed it as one of the most economical and practical ways across the Blue Ridge and the Alleghanies "to be found from the head-waters of the Susquehanna to the southern termination of those ranges."

The extensive marl-beds of the South Carolina lowlands, all comparatively near Charleston, have long been known; but they were first especially noticed by Edmund Ruffin, of Virginia, a noted agriculturist, who had been very successful in renovating worn-out lands in his own State with marl. He examined the South Carolina marls, and found them much richer in carbonate of lime than those of Virginia, but the carbonate was so combined with and mineralized by silex, oxide of iron, phosphate of lime, and other substances, as to necessitate a chemical change by burning before it could be applied to agricultural purposes.

Among these marl deposits, which abound in the immediate vicinity of Charleston, are found hard nodular bodies of all sizes, varying from that of a pin's head to masses weighing hundreds of pounds. These nodules are now known as phosphate rock, and have been described as "incalculable heaps of animal remains thrown or washed together." Beautiful specimens of ribs, vertebræ, and teeth of land and sea monsters of the early tertiary period are found in profusion at a little distance below the surface, and are readily dug up with pick and shovel. The negroes are said even to dive for them to the river-beds, and to bring up large quantities.

The people have at last awakened to the immense value of these deposits, and a number of establishments devoted to their conversion into phosphate-manures have sprung up since the war. In these manufactories the nodules are baked thoroughly dry, then ground to a powder, which is finally mixed with sulphuric acid and charged with ammonia. The Wando Company, which first

Magnolia Cemetery — Charleston. [Page 451.]

undertook the production of these fertilizers, made thirty per cent. profit, and there are now two dozen companies in the State organized for the purposes either of mining or manufacturing these phosphates. One company is organized with a capital of $2,000,000 to mine in all the navigable rivers in the State; and there are several manufacturing corporations which have each a million dollars capital. The Etiwan Company claims to have the largest acid-chamber in the United States; and in the Wando, Etiwan, Pacific, Guano, Atlantic, Stono and Wappoo mills, four or five millions of dollars have been invested since 1868.

Important as is this industry, there are a variety of others already developed in Charleston which promise great future success. In the manufacture of doors, blinds, sashes, and machinery, and in ship-building, a large capital is invested. The enterprising citizens are even constructing ready-made houses and churches, which can be shipped in sections to new States and territories. A cotton-mill and several tanneries are projected. The "truck farms" vie with those of Norfolk, and are supplying the Northern markets with early vegetables. The city's jobbing trade amounted to about $6,000,000 in 1872, and steadily increases at the rate of twenty-five per cent.

The highways leading out of the city are all richly embowered in loveliest foliage ; the oak, the magnolia, the myrtle, the jessamine, vie with each other in tropical splendor. Splendid shell roads have been projected, but are not yet completed. The visitor hardly knows which most to admire—the cultivated bloom and glory of the gardens, the tangled thickets where the luxuriant cane rises thirty and forty feet, the shimmering sheets of water on the marshes, or the long sandy pathways, over which stretch the long arms of moss-hung oaks. A palmetto, standing lonely under the rich glow of the splendid Southern moon, will fill even the prosaic with poetic enthusiasm ; a cabin, overgrown with vines and tendrils, and half concealed in a green and odorous thicket, behind which one catches the gleam of the river current, will make one enamored of the sweet silence and restful perfection of the lowland capital's suburbs. The mansion with closed doors, and decaying verandas, from which

" Life and thought have gone away,"

will recall the late revolution's worst phase to him who had almost forgotten it in the city's commercial bustle.

Along the Ashley, the old manorial houses and estates, like Drayton Hall and the Middleton homestead, stand like sorrowful ghosts lamenting the past; on James's Island one may wander among rich cotton plantations, now overspreading the maze of fortifications which sprang up during the war ; there is no more silence and absolute calm, as there is no more of beauty and luxuriance, in Magnolia cemetery, than in the vast parks surrounding these ruined and desolate homes. The monuments in the cemetery to Simons, and Legare, and Colonel Washington, and Vanderhorst, are beautiful and tasteful ; so are the battered and broken monuments to a dead civilization and a broken-down system which one finds upon the old plantations.

There is a wide belt of forsaken plantations near the Cooper river, along the famous Goose creek, upon whose banks stands the venerable St. James's Church, built in 1711. Around this ancient building the ambitious forest is fast weaving a network difficult to penetrate; and the very graves are hidden under festoons of wild vines and flowers. Along the harbor there are also deserted and bankrupt towns, like pretty Mount Pleasant, filled with moss-grown and rotting houses, whose owners have fled, unless too poor to get away.

The climate of South Carolina being as mild and genial as that of the most favored portion of southern Europe, it is not strange that the lower classes of Italy and other countries should feel inclined to emigrate to the Palmetto State. But the people have been slow to show a proper intelligence

on the subject of immigration. The legislators have taken care to encourage certain Northern classes to come—since they are sure that they will not; and have
discouraged foreigners from attempting to settle in the State, since they fear that
might lead to a new deal in politics. The Italians who went into the commonwealth some time since were offered $100 per year, and a little meal and
bacon weekly; but they haughtily rejected any such terms. The white laborer
who enters South Carolina must be offered good wages and given land at cheap
rates; and the sooner the natives learn that he is not to be expected to work
and live as the negroes do, the better it will be for their interest.

Recently the whites have become thoroughly aroused to the importance of
this subject, and there is a great change in the temper with which immigrants
are now received. The determination seems to be to make much of them as

Garden in Mount Pleasant, opposite Charleston. [Page 451.]

a sure, if slow, means of working out the political regeneration of the State,
and securing its material prosperity. A State Commissioner of Immigration
was appointed by the late Taxpayers' Convention, and the counties are appoint-
ing local Commissioners. An effort is now making at Charleston to establish
a direct steamship line to Liverpool, which, it is hoped, will not only give a
stimulus to immigration, but to inward freights as well.

The negro is not especially anxious to see immigration come in. The
spirit of race is strong within him. He is desirous of seeing the lands in the
commonwealth in the hands of his own people before the rest of the world's
poor are invited to partake. He is impressed with the idea that South Carolina should be in some measure a black man's government, and is jealous of

white intervention. This is not the sentiment, certainly, of the intelligent and refined colored people, but the mass are ignorant, and think that they are right in taking that stand. The black man lets the African in him run riot for the time being. He even dislikes to see the mulatto progress; and when he criticises him, it is as he were necessarily an inferior.

So, too, the negro secretly dislikes the white adventurer, or " carpet-bagger," as our Southern friends call him. Black rogue has quickly learned from white rogue all he wishes to know, and now proposes to go alone. The idea of Nemesis, added to the negro's lack of moral consciousness, which has become so pronounced in the two centuries of servitude, makes the negro believe that he is right in stealing and oppressing. He has found, now that he has obtained power, a strange fascination in the use of political machinery for purposes of oppression and spoliation. He thinks too, grimly, in the words of the Carolinian black's savage song :

"De bottom rail 's on de top,
An' we 's gwine to keep it dar."

Peeping Through.

LI

THE SPOLIATION OF SOUTH CAROLINA.

THE political troubles between the white and the black natives in South Carolina began directly after the close of the war. The mass of undisfranchised whites, embittered by and disgusted with the revolution, refused to have anything whatever to do with the new edifice which the negroes were trying to upbuild. Had they frankly accepted the situation, they might have had a share in the framing of the new Constitution. The negroes, left alone, were soon interested in the advent of white strangers, who agreed to teach them the political rôle they were called upon to play. Some of these new-comers were honest men; others were thieves. The convention for the making of a new Constitution was at once a ludicrous and an impressive gathering. The Constitution was ratified at a general election, held on the 14th, 15th, and 16th days of April, 1868. South Carolina then entered upon her first experience of negro government.

Governor Orr left the State executive chair on July 6, 1868. The commonwealth then had a bonded debt of about $5,500,000, and a floating indebtedness amounting to perhaps $1,500,000 more. While the condition of the finances was not hopeful, it was still far from desperate. People hoped that a new railroad development would open up fresh trade, that money would flow in. The abominable and atrocious outrages of the Ku-Klux, however, were an effective obstacle to Northern immigration.

The Klan was imported into South Carolina in 1868, before the present State Government was organized; and the white population of the ruder and remote counties tried to inaugurate a reign of terror among the negroes. The chairman of the Republican State Central Committee was brutally murdered in the fall of 1868. Hundreds of men were taken from their homes at night and whipped; some were murdered. The result was the interference of the Federal Government, the arrest and imprisonment of members of the organization, and the breaking up of its secret operations.

But while society was completely unsettled, while the whites were smarting under the humiliation of being crowded out of the representation to which they were entitled, while the negro was master, and was beginning to be insolent and aggressive, the Legislature met. The first session after reconstruction was held in August of 1868. At a later session, Governor Scott, formerly an agent of the Freedmen's Bureau, sent in his first message, in which he reviewed the financial condition of the State, and the Ku-Klux outrages, then at their height, and counseled moderation and firmness.

The negroes nearly filled both Senate and House; there were but few white members during the first session, when the ignorant blacks were learning parliamentary forms, for which, by the way, they have an extraordinary aptitude. Jobs began to appear, and the first drawing of blood may be said to have been in connection with the job for the redemption of the bills of the bank of the State. The strong influenced the weak; the negro, dazzled and enlivened by the prospect of the reception of sums which seemed to him colossal fortunes, soon became an apt scholar, and needed but little prompting from his white teachers. Measures for authorizing the Governor to borrow on the credit of the State were at once inaugurated; and then began a series of acts whose results are without a parallel in the history of revolutions:

During the four years from 1868 to 1872 inclusive, the bonded debt was increased from five and a-half to sixteen millions, and the floating debt, which could be only vaguely ascertained, amounted to several millions more. The following tabular statement of the debt is compiled from the books of the State Treasurer:

Legal bonded debt	$9,886,627.35
Illegal bonded debt	5,965,000.00
Legal floating debt	2,429,272.95
Illegal floating debt	2,692,102.94
Contingent liabilities	4,797,608.20
Total	$25,770,611.44

If the actual and contingent liabilities, bonded and floating debt, legal and illegal, are to be taken into account, then the actual debt is the whole amount stated above; and less in proportion as any of the constituent items are excluded.

Honest Republicans had raised their voices loudly against the infamies which were the cause of this terrible increase; had endeavored to oust the thieves, and failing, had left the party in disgust. The negroes were intoxicated with power, and would hear of nothing which seemed likely to better the condition of their old masters.

In 1870, the Conservatives, as the white natives style themselves, alarmed at the riot of corruption and the total disregard of decency manifested by the governing powers, rallied and made a decided effort to get the State into their own hands. They nominated R. B. Carpenter, a Republican Circuit Judge, for Governor, on the simple yet broad platform of retrenchment and reform. On their tickets a few negroes were represented, and for the first time in the history of the State, negroes and Conservative whites spoke upon the same political stump. But the leaders of the negroes refused to believe in the sincerity of the ex-Confederates, and Governor Scott was re-elected over Carpenter. The Ring which was soiling its guilty fingers with plunder was jubilant; honest Republicans hung their heads with shame and gave up all hope of the State; the native white Carolinians, angered and distressed, and fearing that the negroes might undertake some measures to which resistance would be necessary, formed themselves into a "council of safety." This is said really to have been simply an organization to enable planters to protect themselves against strikes, at most a purely defensive organization, and not an attempt at a revival of Ku-Kluxism, as it has sometimes been called. It had no hold in the lower part of the State, but in the upper counties seems to have been perverted into Ku-Kluxism.

The offer of amity which it had cost the pride of the Conservatives such an abasement to make is not likely to be repeated at once. The struggle was great, the result unsatisfactory. People now grimly submit to be robbed without attempting resistance save at election-time. But the hostility which they naturally feel toward the acts of the present State Administration is constantly increased; and in the biting criticisms evoked from the press of Charleston so much truth has been told that the outside world has begun to believe in the statement that the revolution has been made an instrument of fraud and oppression.

Although it would seem an infamy simply to deliberately increase the debt of a State which had been so terribly impoverished as had South Carolina by the war (her total valuation having decreased in ten years from $489,319,128 to $164,409,941), this was but the beginning of the outrage. Not only was the debt increased, but the revenues of the State were diverted from their proper channels into the pockets of the thieves; and it has been incontrovertibly proven that millions have been added to the State debt without the authority of the Legislature. By the official statement of the Treasurer of the Commonwealth, the public debt at the close of the fiscal year ending October 31, 1871, amounted to $15,851,327.35. This showed an actual increase since the advent of the reconstruction legislature of $10,500,000, of which amount only $4,389,400 had ever been in any manner authorized by the legal representatives of the State. And it is considered certain that in 1872 there were already afloat upon the market, very possibly in the hands of innocent holders, without any authority in their original issue, some $6,000,000 in conversion bonds; and it was found necessary to introduce an act, in 1872, to ratify and confirm this illegal issue, for which the "Financial Board," composed of the Governor, the State Treasurer, and the Attorney-General, were responsible.*

Immense sums of money were collected during the four years from 1868 to the beginning of 1872. The people of the State contributed $3,780,000 in taxes, and the financial agents at New York sold bonds to the amount of $2,282,000. Add to this $1,000,000 of taxes collected up to the close of 1872, and it will be seen that more than $7,000,000 went into the Treasury during two administrations.

This revenue, which, in view of the impoverishment caused by the war, was very encouraging, has been stolen from the State in a variety of ways. The officers have never been governed by the Appropriation acts; have never been limited by them. The money appropriated for one purpose has been unblushingly expended for another. No honest debts were paid with all the money collected from the white people who are denied the right of representation in this

---

*At the last session, 1873–'74, an act was passed declaring that these bonds, known as Conversion Bonds, amounting to $5,965,000 were put upon the market "without any authority of law," and were "absolutely null and void." A joint resolution was passed for the prosecution of the ex-State Treasurer, but this joint resolution is "lost" from the records.

black Legislature,—not a debt during the year 1873. The bondholders have not received the interest upon their bonds.

The frauds to which the Legislature lent itself and which private individuals perpetrated, were contemptible. A land commission was established. It was ostensibly beneficent. Its apparent purpose was to buy up lands, and distribute them among the freedmen. An appropriation of $700,000 was granted for that purpose. The State was at once robbed. Worthless land was purchased and sold at fabulous sums to the Government. The commissioners were generally accused of extensive corruption. When at last an honest commissioner came in it was found that a quarter of a million dollars had been stolen. The "Sinking Fund Commission," is another "oubliette" into which money raised from the State sinks mysteriously. The commissioners of this fraud were authorized to take and sell real and personal property belonging to the State, and to report annually to the Legislature the sums received. Public property has rapidly disappeared, but no report has ever been made.* The pockets of an unknown few contain the proceeds of much valuable State property.

This is mighty theft; colossal impudence like this was never surpassed. Never was a revolution, originally intended as humane, turned to such base uses. Never were thieves permitted to go unpunished after such bold and reckless wickedness. Never before were a people, crushed to earth, kept down and throttled so long. The manliness which we received as a precious legacy with our Anglo-Saxon blood demands that we should cry out, "Hold off your hands! Fair play!"

The complete centralization which has been the result of the long continuance in power of an ignorant Legislature, controlled by designing men, is shown in the history of the elections since reconstruction. The Governor has the power to appoint commissioners, who in their turn appoint managers of elections in the several counties. In this manner the Governor has absolute control of the elections, for the managers are allowed to keep and count the votes, and are not compelled to report for some days.

The chances thus given for fraud are limitless. For the last four years men who have been elected by overwhelming majorities have been coolly counted out, because they were distasteful to the powers that be. The negroes intimidate their fellows who desire to vote reform tickets, very much as the Ku-Klux once intimidated them. "The villainy you teach me I will execute."

People will say that this is a black picture. It is; there is no light upon it. There seems small hope for a change. The election this year will oust some plunderers, but will not be likely to check corruption. The white people of the State are powerless to resist; they are trampled completely down.

It is impossible to here review in detail all the transactions of the Legislature since 1868. Besides the schemes for corruption above mentioned, there

---

*An investigating committee of the State Senate on the sinking fund reported, in February 1874, that the proceedings of the Sinking Fund Commission have resulted in nothing but loss to the State; that a large amount of property had been sold, and not a dollar of the public debt had been extinguished.

have been very many others. Nothing has been safe from the taint. Bribery
has been necessary to secure the passage of almost every bill. Railroad legislation has been a stench in honest men's nostrils. The pay certificates of the
Legislature have even been abused. The Speaker of the House has issued these
certificates to the amount of *more than a million dollars*, while the legitimate
demand for them has not amounted to $150,000. They have been spread broad-
cast. The refurnishing of the new State-House cost hardly $50,000, but a bill
for $95,000 was presented. Members of the Legislature, both black and white,
publicly threatened that unless they received sums which they named they would
vote against certain bills. A Governor stands charged by men of his own party
with spending nearly $400,000 of the public money to get himself re-chosen. A
bill to establish a militia became a gigantic "job." The whole course of legislation in the State tended to absolute tyranny, which is all the more dreadful
because the deluded ignoramuses who make up the body of the assemblies are
not aware that they are doing anything especially blameworthy. They look
upon it as the result of a normal condition of things, and intend to keep it up as
long as there is any vestige of State credit left.

Columbia has been the capital of South Carolina since 1790. It occupies a
high and commanding position in the centre of the State, and is but 130 miles
from Charleston. It borders upon the Congaree river, near the mouth of the
Saluda, in the heart of a rich cotton region. The water power which might be
made available in its immediate vicinity is much superior to that of most of the
New England manufacturing towns. The canal near by was purchased from
the State several years ago by Governor Sprague, of Rhode Island; but no cotton factories have as yet arisen along the banks. The town is one of the most
beautiful in the South; its climate rivals that of Italy; and the broad, richly
shaded avenues; the gardens filled with jessamines and japonicas, laurels and haw-
thorns and hollys, and the perfect groves in which the live oaks, the pines, the
magnolias, and the wild oranges vie with each other in charm, give it an especial
fascination. Columbia arose with sorrowful but reliant air out of the ashes
in which it was laid by the war; and if its people had not been weighted down
by the incubus of an ignorant and dishonest government, they would have done
more even than they already have toward rebuilding. The little city, which now
has about 12,000 inhabitants, is on the through route from Charlotte in North
Carolina, to Augusta in Georgia, and also sends its commercial influence into the
north-western counties, along the line of the Greenville and Columbia railroad,
on which Newberry and other thriving towns are located. It has also an excellent connection with Wilmington on the North Carolina coast via Sumter, a busy
town, a short distance to the westward of Columbia.

The counties of Richland, Sumter, Orangeburg, Lexington, and Clarendon, in
the neighborhood of the capital, are exempt from the malaria of the lowlands, and
cotton, corn, and other cereals, grow superbly. The great conflagration at the
time of the evacuation of the city by the Confederates, swept away the Government armory, the old State-House, some manufactories, all the railway stations,
a fine legislative library, St. Mary's College, with many valuable collections of

paintings ; the retreating Confederates destroyed the bridges over the river, and ruin reigned everywhere.

The exterior aspects of Columbia are to-day fair indeed. The venerable University (from which all the white professors and scholars retreated when the first black student was received) nestles charmingly in the midst of a grand tree-dotted park ; the State Lunatic Asylum, a noble building, is likewise embowered in a splendid shade ; the city buildings and hotels are large, and in excellent taste; a fine United States court-house is springing out of blocks of native gran-ite ; and the numerous private institutions of learning give the casual visitor the impression that he is visiting a "grove of Academe," rather than a perturbed and harassed capital. Many Northern families have purchased fine estates in the neighborhood; at evening the avenues are crowded with splendid teams, whose owners drive to the parade ground, and loiter, while six companies of United States troops go stiffly through the prescribed drill, and the band thunders the hackneyed music.

A Future Politician.

LII

THE NEGROES IN ABSOLUTE POWER.

BUT it is at the State-House in Columbia that one arrives at the truth. The mammoth building, which yet lacks the stately cupola to be given it in a few years, is furnished with a richness and elegance which not even the legislative halls of States a hundred times as rich can equal. In the poorly constructed and badly lighted corridors below are the offices of the State Government—that of the Governor, the Treasurer, the Secretary of State, and

the Superintendent of State Schools—each and all of them usually filled with colored people, discussing the issues of the hour. The Secretary of State is a mulatto, who has entered the law school at the University, and carries on his double duties very creditably.

In the House and Senate the negro element stands out conspicuous. On the occasion of my first visit I was shown into the

The State-House at Columbia, South Carolina.

room of the House Committee on the Judiciary for a few moments. While awaiting the assembling of the honorable members a colored gentleman, in a gray slouch hat, and a pair of spectacles, engaged me in conversation, and, as I inquired what was the present question which was exciting the patriotism and sacrifice of the virtuous members, he rolled up his eyes, and with a tragic air, said:

"Dar's a heap o' bizness behin' de carpet heah, sah."

It was true, in more senses than one.

The House, when I visited it, was composed of eighty-three colored members, all of whom were Republicans, and forty-one whites; the Senate consisted of fifteen colored men, ten white Republicans, and eight white Democrats. The President of the Senate and the Speaker of the House, both colored, were elegant and accomplished men, highly educated, who would have creditably presided over any commonwealth's legislative assembly. In the House the negroes were of a much lower grade, and more obviously ignorant, than in the Senate. They were perpetually preventing the transaction of necessary business by " questions of privilege," and " points of order," of which, sometimes, as many as a hundred are raised in a single day. It being an extra session, they were endeavoring to make it last until the time for the assembling of the regular one ; and their efforts were extremely ludicrous. The little knot of white Democrats, massed together in one section of the hall, sat glum and scornful amid the mass of black speakers, a member only rising now and then to correct an error of " his friend" the colored man, who had the floor.

But some of the sable brethren were trying to the visitor's patience, even, and after I had heard one young man talk for a half hour upon the important subject of what his constituents would say if he allowed himself to be brow-beaten into an immediate adjournment, it was with difficulty that I could suppress a yawn. This youth persisted in repetitions ; his voice occasionally would be heard rising above the general hum, precisely reiterating the words he had uttered five minutes before.

The negro does not allow himself to be abashed by hostile criticism. When he gets a sentence tangled, or cannot follow the thread of his own thought in words, he will gravely open a book—the statutes, or some other ponderous volume lying before him—and, after seeming to consult it for some minutes, will resume. He has been gaining time for a new start.

There are men of real force and eloquence among the negroes chosen to the House, but they are the exception. In the Senate I noticed decorum and ability among the members. Several of the colored Senators spoke exceedingly well, and with great ease and grace of manner ; others were awkward and coarse. The white members, native and imported, appeared men of talent at least. The black pages ran to and fro, carrying letters and documents to the honorable Senators ; and a fine-looking quadroon, or possibly octoroon woman, and the ebony gentleman escorting her, were admitted to the floor of the Senate, and sat for some time listening to the debates.

To the careless observer it seems encouraging to see the negroes, so lately freed from a semi-barbaric condition, doing so well, because their conduct is really better than one would suppose them capable of, after having seen the constituency from which they were elevated. One cannot, of course, prevent reflections upon vengeance and retribution drifting into his mind,—it was, doubtless, to be expected that some day the negro would lord it over his master, as the law of compensation is immutable,—but there is danger in the protraction of this vengeance. We must really see fair play. Ignorance must not be allowed to run riot. If we saw it consummating, as a Commune assembled in Paris, one thousandth part of the infamy which it effects as a Legislature in South Carolina, we should cry out angrily for interference.

But this is an epoch of transition. When the negro is a little older as a politician, he will be less clannish. The masses of the blacks will divide more fully into parties. Then there will be some chance for the setting aside of the dreadful question of race against race. At present the blacks in the State move solidly together.   Their eyes are fixed on the spoils which the white men have taught them to gather.   They have not yet begun to understand that in stripping the State, compromising her credit and blackening her reputation, they injure themselves much more than they harm their old masters.   They will learn in time that they have committed a grave error in allowing the whites to be virtually excluded from representation, and that both races will be forced to labor together, honestly and faithfully, to save the State, and to insure their own future prosperity.

I visited the University a day or two after the revolution caused there by the entrance of the first colored student, the Secretary of State himself.   In the library, where the busts of Calhoun and Hayne seemed to look down from their

Sketches of South Carolina State Officers and Legislators, under the Moses Administration.

niches with astonishment upon the changed order of things, I saw the book from whose lists the white students had indignantly erased their names when they saw the Secretary's round, fair script beneath their own.   The departure of the old professors and scholars was the signal for a grand onward movement by the blacks, and a great number entered the preparatory and the law schools.   They have summoned good teachers from the North, and are studying earnestly. The University attained its present title in 1866. It was founded as a college at the beginning of the century, but now consists of ten distinct schools, and is rich in libraries and apparatus for scientific studies. While I was in the library, a coal black senator arrived, with two members of the House, whom he presented to the head of the faculty as desirous of entering the law class. I was informed that dozens of members were occupied every spare moment outside of the sessions in faithful study; but this has been the case for a short time only.

Except in the large towns, however, the educational prospects throughout the State are not very good. In 1873, the schools were much cramped for resources. Not a cent of an appropriation of these $300,000 for educational purposes, made in that year, reached the schools, and great numbers of them were closed. The difficulty of obtaining good teachers has also been very great. Charleston has had a fine school system for many years. Another High School there, an excellent institution, has been established since 1839. The local school tax for 1873 was nearly $45,000. There are about 2,500 white children in the public schools, and about the same number of colored pupils, for whom separate accommodations are provided. One single edifice for the black has room for 1,000 scholars.

Four colored schools are supported in Charleston by Northern funds: The Shaw Memorial, a large and efficient institution, assisted by the New England Freedmen's Aid Society; the Wallingford Academy, by the Presbyterian Church North; the Avery Institute, by the American Missionary School Association; and the Franklin Street High School, by the Episcopal Church North. All the city free schools are considered exceedingly good. The Normal School in Charleston has a fine edifice, and is sending out some excellent teachers. The Peabody fund has given aid here and there throughout the State to great advantage.

There are, at least, two hundred thousand children in the commonwealth; and it is safe to assert that not more than seventy-five thousand have been afforded school facilities. Charleston county shows an attendance of nearly 8,000; in the other coast counties there has latterly been a large decrease in attendance. On the sea-islands there are still some schools. An educational effort was first made there in 1862, and the school originally established in St. Helena is yet in existence, supported by Philadelphia societies. At one time there were twenty schools on St. Helena Island alone, supported by Northern funds. But now that this aid has been generally withdrawn, education there languishes. The school tax of three mills on the dollar would serve very well, if the State's affairs were not so wretchedly confused, and the pay of the teachers so uncertain. The corruption in the legislative halls demoralizes even the free school system, which the negro once so longed for, as the lever which was to lift him up to happiness. Columbia, Beaufort, the mountain towns of consequence, and the shire towns of the upland counties, take much interest in the free school system, and encourage it as their means will permit.

The private institutions of learning in Charleston and the State are remarkably excellent. Few cities can boast of better medical colleges than that in

Charleston. It was first incorporated half a century ago, and had a brilliant career until the late war, during which it was nearly ruined. The Roper Hospital, which adjoins it, is a fine institution. Charleston is divided into health districts, over each of which a physician is appointed, with orders to give daily attendance upon the poor. This was a much needed charity, since the mortality among the negroes who came flocking into the city after the war was fearful, and the blacks neglect themselves, unless looked after, until it is too late to heal them.

The burden of charity is by no means small. The alms-house has more than sixteen hundred regular " outdoor pensioners," that is, poor residents who receive " rations or half-rations," regularly. The city and main hospitals are filled with colored patients, who are cheerfully cared for at the city's expense. Charleston is jealous of her sanitary reputation, and each successive year that passes without bringing the yellow fever only makes her more vigilant in the matters of her tidal drainage, her well-ordered markets, her cleanly docks, and her careful supervision of the personal health of her citizens.

Two of the noted institutions of Charleston are a little fallen into decay, but are still interesting. The Military Academy, a quaint, mauresque building, has become the head-quarters for the United States troops quartered in the city; and its splendid school is broken up. The Charleston College is still in operation. It was chartered in 1795, and has graduated many distinguished men. The establishment of the museum of natural history at the college was first suggested by Agassiz in 1850, and it is to-day, although a portion of the collection was burned in war-time, one of the finest in the country. The libraries of the private institutions are good, but Charleston greatly needs a public one, such as all the Eastern cities possess.

The development of South Carolina presents an interesting problem for solution. It seems, now, as if the system of large plantations were the only one under which rice culture can be successfully pursued. Yet the freedmen yearly manifest stronger disinclination for work in gangs on other people's land, and desire to acquire small farms, and to live independently, however rudely. It is singular that some of them have not developed the business capacity requisite to establish large plantations of their own, and to influence their fellows to work well with them on a coöperative basis.* The wealth in the great pine forests cannot be made available until some one besides the negro goes to work in them. The sea-island cotton-lands are certainly very unlikely to get the needed recuperation by much effort on the part of the negro. A new element of immigration must be had ; but it will not go to the State in its present political condition.

Will, then, the State extricate herself from that position ? There seems but little hope of any thorough immediate change, perhaps not for four years. Cumulative voting has been advocated in the State for some time, and in 1870 the Attorney-General and Governor Scott professed to be strongly in favor of the adoption of that principle. If this plan, as suggested by Mr. Pike in his

---

* There is, I am told, one highly prosperous colored settlement on the communal plan in Marlborough county.

excellent book on the subject, or some other method of gaining protection for the rights of the minority, could be successfully adopted; and if Charleston could receive her just dues politically, the course of events would, in due time, be changed. Her phosphates, her railway connections, her cotton receipts, her manufactories cannot fail to make her rich; but that will not benefit the State, as she is at present situated. Very little reliance is to be placed on any hopes of immigration, save of families who are well-to-do, toward centres like Aiken and Columbia.

The farmers in the upland regions are forcing their lands too harshly in their desperate effort to make a great deal of cotton, and are neglecting the needed diversity of crops, so that they will, perhaps, be in distress by and by. There are hundreds of superb chances for investment in the State which will never for a moment be considered by capitalists so long as a State Government so unjust, tyrannical and centralized as the present one maintains itself in office. It is a frightful incubus which drags down every earnest man who desires to make an effort at a rebound after the collapse caused by the war; it is a disgrace to our system; it is a stumbling-block to the negro; an embodied corruption which public opinion ought to sweep out of existence; a usurpation for which there is no excuse save the complete ignorance of one race, and the utter helplessness of the other.

Iron Palmetto in the State-House Yard at Columbia.

LIII.

THE LOWLANDS OF NORTH CAROLINA.

NORTH CAROLINA comprises an area of a little more than 50,000 square miles, or 34,000,000 of acres. From the Atlantic ocean it stretches 500 miles, back to the Tennessee line, and is from 100 to 150 miles wide, between Virginia and Georgia. It embraces within its limits almost every variety of soil and climate. It is very plainly separated into three natural divisions. The first is the "flat country of swamps and marshes and sluggish streams, supposed by geologists to have been upheaved by the sea."[*] This extends 100 miles inland from the coast. This is the country of the long-leaved pine, the sandy bottoms, and the turpentine forests, inhabited by a low and almost worthless population. There, too, however, are flourishing towns and prosperous people.

The second region is that of wheat, corn, tobacco, and cotton. The soil is undulating, fertile, and the rivers afford fine facilities for transportation. The third division is that of the mountains.

There is a marked difference between the upland and lowland people of North Carolina. The mountaineers seem, in some measure, a race by themselves, and have sometimes made strong efforts to secure a division of the State. To-day there are a few enthusiastic advocates of the creation of a new commonwealth out of the mountain regions of North Carolina and Tennessee. The mountains have certainly supplied North Carolina with many of her famous politicians, with fine instances of prosperity, and with the example of loyalty when she sadly needed it. But the residents of the two sections know little of each other. The railroads through the mountains will open to the lowlanders a Paradise which has been at their very doors, yet little known by them.

The North Carolina coast, as seen from the ocean, is flat and uninteresting. There is an aspect of wild desolation about the swamps and marshes which one may at first find picturesque, but which finally wearies and annoys the eye. But the coast is cut up into a network of navigable sounds, rivers and creeks, where the best of fish abound, and where trade may some day flow in. The shad and herring fisheries in these inlets are already sources of much profit. The future export of pine and cypress timber, taken from the mighty forests, will yield an immense revenue. The swampy or dry tracts along the coast are all capable of producing a bale of cotton to the acre. They give the most astonishing returns for the culture of the sweet potato, the classic peanut, or

---

[*]From a published letter from Rev. Dr. Mason, rector of Christ's Church, Raleigh, North Carolina.

"guber," the grape, and many kinds of vegetables. Malarial fevers will, of course, seize on the inhabitant of this region who does not pay proper attention to the drainage all about him. It is believed that along this coast great numbers of vineyards will in time be established, for there are unrivaled advantages for wine-growing.

The extreme eastern limit of the State is a narrow strip of land, separating the ocean from the interior waters. It is called the Banks, and is here and there broken by inlets, the most important of which are Hatteras, Ocracoke, Beaufort, and the mouth of the Cape Fear river. On this narrow strip, which the ocean has with great unwillingness conceded the State, lives a singular race, "half-horse, half-alligator," subsisting by fishing and pilotage. The central point of this projecting and protecting arm of land is the far and ill-famed Hatteras, the terror of the voyager along the stormy coast.

"Currituck Sound," one of the notable features of the lowlands of North Carolina, separates the "Banks" from the main land just south of the Virginia line. It is a fresh-water strait, varying in width from three to fifteen miles, and in winter is a sportsman's heaven. Myriads of wild ducks, geese and swans resort there during the cold months, and amateurs from every climate under heaven visit the marshes and slaughter the fowls for months together. Albemarle and Croatan sounds are also notable fishing resorts ; through Croatan one enters into Pamlico, and thence penetrates to Beaufort Inlet, on which the town of Beaufort stands.

Beaufort possesses one of the best harbors on the Atlantic coast. Vessels can come directly from the deep sea to the wharves of the Atlantic and North Carolina Railway Company at Morehead City, opposite Beaufort. The town has relapsed into comparative obscurity since its brilliant war history, when it was the rendezvous of many navies, and the point of departure for many hostile expeditions. Fort Macon, at the entrance of its harbor, and its surroundings, are interesting, and there are throngs of summer visitors along the ample beach. The railroad, connecting Beaufort with the interior of the State, runs northwestward through Newbern to Goldsboro. The former is an old and pleasant town of five or six thousand inhabitants, at the confluence of the Neuse and Trent rivers, and the latter is a newer and smarter place, owing its growth mainly to the increase of railroad facilities. Newbern boasts a line of steamers to New York, and once had many elegant mansions and gardens, most of which have latterly fallen into decay.

North Carolina is very well supplied with railways in her lowland and middle districts. The North Carolina road extends from Goldsboro to Charlotte; the Raleigh and Gaston road, from Raleigh to Weldon, thence giving an outlet through Virginia ; the Western road from Fayetteville, on the Cape Fear river mountainward (probably before many years to be completed) ; the Wilmington and Weldon road runs directly north and south through the State; and the Chatham railroad penetrates from Raleigh to the coal and iron-beds in Chatham county. The Air Line road from Atlanta gives a direct route from Charlotte in North Carolina, to Danville in Virginia, and thence north and east.

The lower regions of the State abound in beautiful though quiet rural scenery. There are no towns of considerable size. Raleigh is a sleepy, delightful, shaded old place. Wilmington, although busy, is not large; Charlotte is small but lively. Salisbury and Greensboro are in the centre of a rich mining region, where copper, iron, coal, and gold are to be found; the former is the centre of a lively tobacco trade, and the latter is the point whence one takes the railroad to States-ville and Morganton, the charming towns at the outer line of the mountain region. Salisbury was the seat of a famous Confederate prison in which many a Union soldier languished and died, or starved through weary months.

The North Carolinians are accustomed now-a-days to wonder why immi-grants do not rush into their State, and settle upon the lands which can be had so cheaply; and finding that but few come, and that the State is in a general condition of discouragement and decay, financially, they have relapsed into an indolent attitude, and let progress drift by them. In some of the small towns I found the people more inclined to bitterness and less reconciled to the results of the war than anywhere else in the South. Many towns, too, had a deserted and neglected look which was painful.

The State, of course, suffered greatly by the war. It was one of the fore-most of pro-slavery communities; held nearly 350,000 slaves when the war broke out; and had a firmly-seated and exclusive aristocracy, which has natu-rally been very much broken up by recent events. The present population is 1,071,361, of whom 678,470 are blacks, of by no means the highest type. The revolution decreased the value of real and personal estate in North Carolina from $292,297,602, in 1860 to $132,046,391 in 1870, and the decrease within the last four years has been very rapid.

The evils of universal suffrage have been very great in this State. The great mass of densely ignorant and ambitious blacks suddenly hurled upon the field created the wildest confusion, and crushed the commonwealth under irredeema-ble debt. The villainy and robbery to which the white population of the State was compelled to submit, at the hands of the plunderers maintained in power by the negro, did much to destroy all possibility of a speedy reconciliation between the two races. Still, the citizens are loyal to the Union, and are anxious to be on friendly terms with the North; yet continue to regard Northerners as in some way the authors of the evils which have befallen them. They do not, however, reproach the North with having sent them a carpet-bagger; as the man who did them most harm, and whose conduct has been most sharply criticised, was a citizen of their own State.

The reconstruction convention in 1868 was a singular gathering. Its pro-ceedings bordered on the ridiculous. It finally secured a Constitution which has since been much amended. The judges and other officers placed in power were notoriously incompetent; and Mr. Holden, who was appointed first pro-visional Governor of the State under reconstruction, was the author of so much questionable work that he was successfully impeached and removed. There was, at one time, imminent danger of civil war in the State; several counties were in insurrection; the Ku-Klux flourished and committed all kinds of infamous outrages.   Holden was an original secessionist, and his newspaper, the *Standard*, printed at Raleigh, was the mouth-piece of the Democracy until 1860, when this unblushing "scallawag," as the Southerners call political renegades, threw his Democratic sentiments out at window, and went in for the Union cause.   Of course he did this with an eye to future plunder.   Mr. Holden was, in 1873, Postmaster at the State Capitol, and seemed but little affected by his forcible removal from the executive chair.

At the close of the wild carnival of robbery and maladministration which marked the career of the first reconstruction government, North Carolina found that her debts were between $36,000,000 and $40,000,000.   This was an appalling exhibit, for the mere payment of the interest was enough to stagger the impoverished and struggling agriculturists.   The money had gone, alas! none save the thieves knew where.   The plundered people only knew that out of $16,000,000 voted by the Legislatures for "public works of improvements," but $500,000 had ever been devoted to that purpose; and the ignorant negro himself was puzzled to discover what had become of the resources which, at the outset of his political career, he had imagined to be unfailing.

The main villainies had been consummated at a time when the mass of the white natives who took part in the war were excluded from office, and when the negro vote was overwhelming.   As soon as Governor Holden was impeached, the white population succeeded in gaining a fair share of influence again, and when he was removed they came into power, Governor Caldwell, Holden's successor, working pretty harmoniously with them.   The political troubles may now be considered as nearly over, and if the industrial opportunities of the State are improved, there will be a return to some degree of prosperity.   Many of the most influential citizens believe that an attitude of perfect frankness on the part of North Carolina toward its creditors will be the only thing that can save the State.   They are anxious to see a compromise effected as speedily as possible, that both white and black may know just how they are situated, and may set their shoulders to the wheel in earnest.*

The State-House at Raleigh is delightfully situated in the midst of lovely foliage, and its massive granite columns and superb dome, modeled after the Parthenon, are very imposing.   Raleigh once boasted an exquisite statue of Washington, from the master hand of Canova; but it was destroyed with the first State-House in the disastrous fire in 1831.   The town, which was named for Sir Walter Raleigh, and was established as the seat of government in 1788, is built around a ten-acre lot called Union square, in the centre of which the State-House stands.   It would not be an excess of generous remembrance on the part of the North Carolinians to erect in their capital a statue of the illustrious Essex, who did so much three hundred years ago to further the colonization of the region now within the State's limits.   At Raleigh there is a large and well-filled Penitentiary, and the Deaf and Dumb and Lunatic Asylums are situated in the outskirts.   The town has only 8,000 inhabitants, half of whom are negroes.

* This chapter was written in the summer of 1874.

Northward from Raleigh, toward Charlotte, lie many fertile counties, filled with the remnants of once famous plantations, and with small farms, even now prosperous. At Chapel Hill the State University, now much fallen into decay, is located; and at Hillsborough, one of the oldest towns in the State, the visitor is still shown the house once occupied by Lord Cornwallis, and is reminded that Governor Tryon had his home there; that there the provincial Congress and the Legislature of North Carolina first assembled, and there, too, many unhappy "Regulators" were executed.

The State certainly needs to make progress in education, for the illiteracy at present within its borders is shocking. One of the United States Senators gave it me his belief that there were as many as 350,000 persons in North Carolina who could neither read nor write. The State Superintendent of Instruction said that, late in 1873, there were only 150,000 out of the 350,000 pupil-children actually at school. The free school system, he thought, up to that date, could by no means be called a thorough success; coming, as it did, directly after the war, when people were striving to save money with which to replace their lost stock and farming implements, the dollar tax demanded for the schools was odious to the masses. Still, from $250,000 to $400,000 is annually collected for school purposes; while before the war there was no system worthy the name. The same provision is made for whites and blacks; there is not much desire on the part of ex-Confederates there to deprive the negro of the advantages of an education, as they now realize that it helps him to become a better laborer. There are 40,000 colored children now in the free schools of the State; 530 black teachers passed the Board of Examiners in 1873, and these teachers were paid $46,000 per year. There are several small colleges, each having five or six score students. Prominent among them are Trinity, at Hyde Point (Methodist), Davidson, at old Mecklenburg, where the State first publicly renounced her allegiance to the British crown (Presbyterian), and the Wake Forest (Baptist) College, near Raleigh.

The school law of the State requires that public free schools shall be maintained "four months every year in every school district in each county of the State in which the qualified voters shall vote to levy the additional school-tax for that purpose." This, of course, gives people an opportunity to reject the system entirely, but there are few counties so rude as to refuse all educational facilities, although nearly all the people in the back-country have a most unaccountable aversion to paying "school-taxes." If the Legislature would inaugurate a system which would bring the people up to its level, as was done in Virginia, a reform might be readily effected. Wilmington has at last made the free schools which have long existed in its midst city institutions, and it is hoped that this good example will be followed by a like movement in all the large towns. Raleigh, strange to say, is hindered from taxing itself to support a system of graded schools by the State law, which is very crotchety, and needs amendment. The Peabody fund distributes $12,000 to $13,000 annually in the State, supporting some two score thriving schools. At Newbern and Washington the citizens have shown considerable spirit in establishing free schools.

The capital receives 35,000 or 40,000 bales of cotton yearly, but the great bulk of the State's crop goes by rail to Wilmington.   Edgecombe, Caswell, Rockingham, Stokes, and Warner are the great cotton counties, the former growing 18,361 bales in 1872.   The cotton production of the State varies from 100,000 to 150,000 bales annually.

The range of climate covered by the State may be taught by the statement that buckwheat can be grown on the mountains in Ashe county, and oranges flourish in the soft, sweet air of Wilmington.   There is a tropical luxuriance of flowers and trees in Wilmington, which is almost astonishing, for one sees all plants possible at Charleston or Savannah flourishing in the gardens of this more northern town.   Wilmington lies on the banks of the Cape Fear river, and on the hills which extend backward from those banks.   It is but twenty-eight miles from the mouth of the river, and was one of the havens most sought after by blockade-runners during our civil war.   At the mouth of the river stand Forts Fisher and Caswell, the former one of the strongest forts on the Atlantic coast, as it proved itself in the terrible days of 1865, when Porter and Terry knocked at its doors and finally burst them open.

Wilmington has important railway connections, notably the Wilmington, Rutherford, and Charlotte road, which will give the port direct communication with Tennessee, Kentucky, Ohio, and Illinois, and will immensely increase her trade.   All the counties through which the road, when completed, will pass, are rich in mineral and agricultural resources.   The other routes leading to Charleston and Richmond also command a considerable trade.

The Cape Fear river, at Wilmington, is a wide and noble stream, and the scene along its banks, in the brilliant sunshine of the autumn morning when I saw it, was inspiring.   Cheerful gangs of negroes were rowing huge scows from side to side of the stream, standing upright and steering by means of long poles or sweeps; one might have fancied them a species of African gondoliers.   Swedish ships were loading with naval stores; huge piles of lumber, and heaps and long rows of barrels of turpentine, and pitch and rosin, were ranged on the wharves. There were great numbers of negroes who looked idle, although many were employed.   Some were fishing, others slept in corners; one or two groups seemed discussing politics, and in the centre of a crowd of jet black men I heard the following question and answer, isolated fragments of a deep religious discussion :

"Wha's de reason dar's so many degrees (sects) o' Baptis' now, when dar wa'n't on'y one John de Baptis', hey?"

"Lor, nigger, we ain't 'sponsible fur dat; dat a'nt got nuffin to do wid godliness!"

Front street is a fine avenue, lined with many elegant blocks devoted to business.   Market street is a broad, central promenade, crowded with the omnipresent negroes, who chatter and "discuss" all day long.   The blacks seem to fancy that labor is incompatible with the enjoyment of a city life.

In that portion of the town devoted to the residences, churches, and public buildings, perfect tranquillity prevails.   Nowhere is there hum of wheels, clatter of teams, or braying of whistles. On Third and Fifth streets there are many elegant mansions, and gardens filled with rarest tropical and costly plants. The City and Thalian halls, the jail, and one or two of the churches are quite imposing, but the city is not rich in architecture. The cemeteries are pretty sylvan retreats, and the sleepy moss-grown suburb of "Hilton" is a favorite resort for excursions.

Commercially, Wilmington has every reason to hope for great development. The principal articles of export are spirits of turpentine in barrels, crude turpentine, rosin, tar, pitch, cotton, peanuts, and lumber in all shapes.* The foreign trade is mainly with Liverpool, Queenstown, Antwerp, Belfast, London, Cardenas, Rotterdam, Havana, Bristol, Hamburg, Cape Haytien, Demerara, Jamaica, Nassau and Hayti. The steamship lines running to Philadelphia, Baltimore and New York, have an aggregate tonnage of 40,000 tons monthly. In 1872, 22,000,000 feet of lumber were shipped from the port. After the war, the exports of spirits of turpentine and rosin were encouraging until 1870; since then their development has not been so great, but the constant growth of the cotton trade makes amends for their failure. The fine regions extending along the road to Weldon, and on both sides of the Wilmington, Columbia and Augusta railroad, as well as on the new Rutherford route, are very rich in turpentine and timber. The section traversed by the two Cape Fears and the

* Comparative statement of exports, coastwise and foreign, from Wilmington, North Carolina, from January 1, 1860, to December 31, 1870:

ARTICLES.	COASTWISE.		FOREIGN.	
	1860.	1870.	1860.	1870.
Spirits Turpentine, bbls..	127,562	68,966	20,400	32,889
Crude Turpentine, bbls..	52,175	12,929	23,548	3,258
Rosin, bbls.............	440,132	483,546	57,425	26,127
Tar, bbls.............	43,056	54,090	6,120	6,107
Pitch, bbls	5,489	4,624	784	190
Cotton, bales	22,851	51,617	....	20
Cotton Yarn, bales	1,561	72	....	....
Cotton Sheeting, bales...	1,750	547	....	....
Peanuts, bushels........	99,743	124,296	....	....
Lumber, P. P., feet	9,126,176	11,515,123	9,882,078	8,378,861
Timber, P. P., feet......	22,600	290,789	20,000	85,400
Shingles	730,880	4,804,890	2,887,870	2,339,334
Staves, Cypress.........	....	482,253	....	....
Staves, Oak	94,723	....	10,000	....

It will be seen by the above that the export of naval stores, both coastwise and foreign, except in one instance, has fallen off greatly during the past decade, while, on the contrary, there has been a heavy increase, say about 120 per cent., in the shipments of cotton. This is due, mainly, to the fact that latterly, and in the country supplying the city, every interest was made subservient to the culture of cotton. Even the production of turpentine was of secondary importance compared with the zeal with which cotton was planted, so that Wilmington, the greatest naval store depot in the world, only exported coastwise one and one-third barrels of spirits turpentine to the bale of cotton; that is to say, the number of bales of cotton exported was seventy-five per cent. of the number of barrels of spirits turpentine.

South and Black rivers are, perhaps, richer in turpentine stores than any other in the world.   A new railway line on the lowlands of the coast, and terminating at Wilmington, is contemplated.

The little city has a valuation of only $7,000,000, a debt of $600,000, an excellent city government, and many enterprising merchants.   There is still some bitterness among those of the aristocrats who were ruined by the war, but it is rapidly mellowing into a regret which has but little of unkindly feeling toward the North mingled in it.   A determination on their part to make Wilmington all that it has opportunities to be, would soon increase its population from 14,000 to many times that number.

Fayetteville and Charlotte are the sites of prosperous cotton factories.   The water power of the former place has never been utilized; and it is astonishing that it is not taken advantage of.   Fayetteville is connected by rail with the mining region in Chatham and Moore counties, and is on the line of one of the important routes to the South, *via* Columbia and Augusta.   Charlotte bids fair to become a prominent centre for manufacturing interests, on account of its railroad facilities and fine water power.   Its historic importance, as the place where the first American Declaration of Independence was made in 1775, by the patriots of Mecklenburg county, assembled in convention, cannot be denied. The British troops occupied Charlotte in 1780; and there it was that General Greene took command of the Southern army, after the departure of Cornwallis. The United States Government has an assay office at Charlotte, and gold mining is from time to time carried on in the adjacent counties.   The town also boasts a military institute, and a prosperous seminary for young ladies.

A Wayside Sketch.

LIV.

AMONG THE SOUTHERN MOUNTAINS—JOURNEY FROM EASTERN TENNESSEE TO WESTERN NORTH CAROLINA.

"YOU ain't a show, be ye?" said the small boy.

The question was pardonable; the travelers alighting, that rainy June evening, from their weary and mud-bespattered horses at the door of a little tavern in a Tennessee mountain town, and proceeding to unload their baggage-wagon, certainly presented a singular spectacle. Such mysterious array of traps the small boy's round, wondering eyes had never seen before. He controlled his

"The Small Boy."

curiosity until a tin case containing artists' materials was produced, when he gave a prolonged whistle, and forthwith proceeded to inquire our qualities. Visions of magic lanterns and traveling mountebanks danced before his eyes; his heated imagination hinted at even the possibility of play-actors.

Two days of swift railway travel had brought me from St. Louis to join a merry party of excursionists through the noblest mountain ranges of the South. We had come from Morristown, in Eastern Tennessee, and at the end of our first day's journey on horseback, crawled, drenched and fatigued, into a hamlet for shelter. Let me show you the party as it then appeared.

First alighted the Colonel, coming down with a solid thump in the sticky mud, and unbuckling from his saddle capacious bags and rolls of blankets; then taking from the wagon certain mysterious packages, he propounded the inquiry which is of such thrilling interest to mountain travelers after nightfall :

"Can we get to stay here to-night?"

"Reckon we can accommodate ye."

Next descended the Judge, his long, gray beard and Arabian mustache streaming with rain, his garments bedraggled, and his eyes dim with the sky-spray. He, likewise going to the wagon, took from it seductive valises, boxes which gave forth a cheering rattle of apparatus, and cans of various patterns, and hastened to shelter. A new accession of small boys silently viewed these proceedings with awe.

But ah! the next figure which galloped lustily to the door, mounted on a prancing, delicate Kentucky mare! How did the juvenile by-standers gape at that short, alert youth, with spectacles on nose, and riding-whip swung cavalierly in hand; with white Marseilles trowsers mottled and drenched with mud and water; with jaunty gray hat, flabby and drooping; with overcoat tied about his neck, and a collection of minerals knotted in his handkerchief at his saddle-bow. He was no common traveler. It must—it must be a show!

Or he with camp stool and dripping umbrella slung on his shoulders, with broad slouch hat crushed down over his eyes, and a variegated panorama of the road along which he had passed painted by the weather upon his back—the artist, whose hands were filled with the mystic tin box; behold him! the envied cynosure of boyish eyes.

Then the writer,—clambering down from his horse's smoking sides, and hastening to join the others before the crackling and leaping flame in an old-fashioned fire-place, overhearing as he entered, however, a new come boy's wild guess:

"If 't ain't a show, it 's 'rock-hunters,' *I* reckon."

What mattered rain and mud, the ferrying of swollen streams, the breaking down of wagons, and the weary climbing of hills? The prospect before us was none the less inspiring. We were about to enter upon that vast elevated region which forms the southern division of the Appalachian mountain system, and constitutes the culminating point in the Atlantic barrier of the American continent. We stood at the gate of the lands through which runs the chain of the Iron, Smoky, and Unaka mountains, separating North Carolina from Eastern Tennessee.

Beyond the blue line of hills faintly discerned in the rainy twilight from the windows of our little room lay the grand table-land, 2,000 feet above the heated air of cities and the contagion of civilization; and there a score of mountain peaks reached up 6,000 feet into the crystal atmosphere; torrents ran impetuously down their steep sides into noble valleys; there was the solitude of the cañon, the charm of the dizzy climb along the precipice-brink, the shade of the forests where no woodman's axe had yet profaned the thickets. It was a region compared to which the White mountains seemed dwarfed and insignificant, for through an extent of more than 150 miles, height after height towered in solemn magnificence, and the very valleys were higher up than the gaps in the White mountain range! Through the thick rain-veil, during our first day's wandering, we had seen the noble outlines of English mountain, and the distant and rugged sides of the Smoky; had passed over hill-sides covered with corn, where the white tree-trunks in the "deadenings" stood like spectres protesting against sacrilege; along banks of streams overhung with dense and richly-colored foliage, and past log farm-houses, where tall, gaunt farmers, clad in homespun, were patiently waiting for the rain to cease—until we came to the "Mouth of

Chucky," as the ford just above the junction of the Nolichucky and French Broad rivers is called.

Time was when all the country bordering the rivers at their junction was romantic ground. The "great Indian war trail," upon which so many scenes of violence and murder were enacted, ran not far from the banks of the Nolichucky, and the war-ford "upon the French Broad" was but a short distance from Clifton, where we had halted for the night. From the time of the settlement along the banks of the two rivers, one hundred years ago, until early in the present century, the settler took his life in his hands daily, and the war-cry of the Indian was a familiar sound to his ears.

The Nolichucky, at the ford, ran rapidly between great mountain banks, whose sides were so steep as to be inaccessible on foot, and just below gave itself to the racing and roaring rapids of the "French Broad," which seemed angry at being pent up among the cliffs. A long halloo brought the ferryman with his flat-boat from the opposite bank; the clumsy ark drifting us safely over to the stretch of winding road which finally led us through a still old town, hidden and moldering at the base of a hill, whence we followed along picturesque paths until we reached the placid Pigeon river, with the mountains near it mirrored in its bosom, and, crossing it, dismounted at Clifton, to be confronted by the small boy with the abnormal appetite for "shows."

The rain ceased when we were safely housed; and having placed our drenched garments by the fire to dry, we waited for the supper of bacon and

"The Judge." [Page 473.]

biscuits, flanked by molasses-syrup and the blackest of coffee, meanwhile catching a glimpse of the prosperous little town set down in a nook in the mountains, with a single railroad line, running directly through the main street, giving it a hold on the outer world. The river was fringed with trees and overhanging vines and creepers; in every direction was the blue stretch of far-away hills, or the shadow of luxuriant woods. Our lullaby that night was the murmur of the river and the cry of the whip-poor-will. Before dawn we were astir, and while the dwellers in cities were still asleep our little cavalcade was vigorously *en route* for the North Carolina line.

Ahead, caracoling merrily from side to side of the highway on his coquettishly-pacing mare "Cricket," whose very motions were poetry, rode Jonas of the blond locks, our German companion, in his saddle graceful as a Centaur, in his motions alert as a cat, for he had ridden to many a battle in the cavalry of Prussian William's victorious army. There was a dash of the trooper in him still—the erect military port, the joyous outburst into song, now roystering, now tender; the enviable familiarity with all the secrets of road and woodland life, and a calm, æsthetic sense, never disturbed by weather or the rude inconvenience of travel.

Our route that morning lay through the forest, along unused road-ways; and, constantly ascending, we caught from time to time exquisite views of the summits of English, the Smoky, and other mountains. Great mists were moving lightly away; now and then some monarch of the ranges had his lofty brow wrapped in the delicate embrace of white clouds, which spread into fantastic shapes of smoke-wreaths and castles and towers, sometimes even seeming to take the contour of the mountains themselves.

Now we came to a log-house, with sloping roof, set on some shelf of a hill-side, whence one could look down into deep valleys, and around whose doors sheep and goats were huddled, lying in the shelter of the fences until the sun came out. A shepherd dog would bark at us; a tall maiden, clad in the blue or greenish homespun of the region, would tell us which road to take, and how to turn and "foller the creek," and so we wandered on. Sometimes the hill-sides were so steep that we preferred to dismount and lead our horses rather than take the risk of being pitched over their heads. Rapid little streams here and there foamed across the roadways, and hid themselves in the forests.

Beneath a great oak, or wide-spreading willow, we found a cool spring with a gourd upon a board above it, and travelers halting for shade and rest, with whom our party would exchange courtesies and interrogatories. Still we went on climbing up and up—nearer to some of the peaks, and within view of the clearings upon their sides, and the bald patches where the rocks stood out in the light.

By and by, at a lonely log-house, on a beautiful mountain side, whence one could see the hills craning their long necks in every direction, we halted for dinner; but before we had hitched our horses there came a sudden blinding storm of wind and rain, in the midst of which we hurriedly gave the animals over to our impervious mulatto wagon-driver, and with the lunch baskets beat a retreat for the cabin porch.

The typical Tennessee woman of the mountains, tall and thin, but kind and graceful, the mother of ten children, who stood ranged around her in inquiring attitude, welcomed us, and a loaf of hot corn-bread soon smoked upon the table. Very humble and simple were the appointments of this cabin home. The bare floor, however, was extremely clean; the spinning-wheel, with the flax hanging to it, stood in a corner of the porch; in the great kitchen in the rear of the cabin was a fire-place, in the ashes of which another corn-cake was baking, and the good woman offered us wild honey, buttermilk, and the berries of the mountains.

"No man-folks nigh home now," she said. "Air you rock-huntin'?"

Assuring her that we were not looking for minerals, she questioned us no farther, and seemed to be puzzled when the Colonel hinted that we were in "search of information."

Once more the rain-cloud lifted and the skies were clear. Andy hitched up, singing a cheerful melody, and we rode on; now through gaps in the chain of hills where level fields were in cultivation, and where the women were at work side by side with the men hoeing corn; now by the banks of some creek which rippled merrily over a pebbly bottom, and was overhung by short, densely-set willows; until, at last, we came into a valley where there were a few scattered frame houses and a little mill, around which were gathered some twenty mountaineers. Here our over-loaded wagon suddenly broke down, directly opposite a cabin, in which, through the interstices, we could see anvil, bellows, and other appurtenances of the blacksmith's trade.

The afternoon was waning, and the punctual Judge had planned that we should spend that night in North Carolina. But before us lay a tremendous height, whose rugged sides seemed interminable. Riding on in haste to find the blacksmith, we were suddenly surrounded by a threatening mob of half-drunken mountain men clad in rude garb, some mounted, some on foot, but not one of them with a friendly look. Our inquiry for help, as Jonas and the writer backed their horses rapidly, was met with an oath, and a peremptory demand why we were "racketing about the country."

This not being answered in the most satisfactory manner, demonstrations of violence were made, and it dawned upon the advance guard of the wagon that perhaps a retreat would be prudent. There were bad and drunken faces among the rough men; two or three hands were clutching stones plucked from the wet roads, while the circle gradually narrowed in toward us. So galloping back, we reported "breakers ahead." Patching up the wagon we all moved forward together; but upon our approach to the mill the threatening attitude of the mountaineers was resumed, the motley crowd falling in behind when we had passed, and seeming to await some signal. Presently the Colonel and the Judge were assailed with questions like this from the pursuing group: "Reckon ye don't want to steal nothin', do ye?" This being succeeded by more pointed remarks.

At last hostilities became so imminent that we were forced to stop and explain. Gathering around the wagon, we answered the inquiries, "Whar be ye from?" "What do ye want yer?" "What mout your name be?" etc., and by much parleying demonstrated that we meant no harm. Finally man by man dropped off, but, much to our discomfort, two or three of the more drunk and uproarious followed us toward the ford at the base of the mountain in a manner which plainly indicated attack.

We were now entering upon a wild and lonely by-road, and even the heretofore incredulous of our party had suspicions of mischief afoot. The ascent, wooded and sombre, was before us.

At this juncture another man approached, and said he would walk with us to the mountain top. He was sober, and, producing from his pocket a flask of "moonshine" whiskey, invited us to drink. The secret was out. We had evidently been mistaken for a party of revenue officers, on a mission to seize some of the concealed stills in the gorges and caves of this wild region.

We drank of the blistering fluid, and presently, to our great relief, the drunken horsemen behind reluctantly retired. After consulting vaguely together for a little time in the road, they disappeared, our companion assuring us that they would do us no harm. "But ye can't always tell," he added. "A man wants to keep his eye out in these regions when the boys 've ben drinkin'."

The ascent of the Chestnut mountain now became tedious and painful. The road ran zigzag along the edges of banks and rocks, and over our heads hung mammoth embankments, which might have crushed a caravan. But how delicious the sunlight on the tree-stems, through the forest glades; how delicate the green mosses clothing the trunks of fallen monarchs; how crystal and sweet the water which we drank from the foamy brooks!

For miles we clambered along this lofty road until night was at hand. Our companion, who paused from time to time to treat himself from the bottle, and to importune us to drink, finally left us at a cross-road, advising us to stay at Parson Caton's. We could get to stay with the parson—he kept folks; would we have some more "moonshine?" No? Good luck to us. So we hurried on to Parson Caton's.

A by-road, leading into a thicket where wild vines grew luxuriantly; steep descents and lofty knolls, crowned with strong tree-stems; a woodland path; then a clearing, and we were at the humble cabin of the parson.

The Judge shows the Artist's Sketch-Book.

LV.

ACROSS THE "SMOKY" TO WAYNESVILLE—THE MASTER CHAIN OF THE ALLEGHANIES.

ON our way up the mountain we had passed "the church." It was a rude structure of boards and logs, which we should have mistaken for some deserted shanty, had not our friend of the "moonshine" whiskey pointed it out.

The parson's cabin stood in an enclosure, guarded by a rough fence, and, as we approached, a stalwart young fellow opened the little gate, and some hounds followed him out, making the woods ring with their yelping. A tall matron and two of "the girls"—young women, at least five and a-half feet high, dressed in straight, homespun gowns—peered out at us, and we were presently invited to remain at the cabin all night, as "the parson never refuses nobody."

The pigs and the geese had just come home together from their day's ramble in the woods, and were quarreling over the trough which ran along the fence. The cows wandered about the clearing, watched by the hounds; and the "boys" busied themselves in hewing logs of wood into sticks for the fire. Behind the cabin rose a rib of the mountain, on which was a corn-field, and near this ran a brook.

The whole cabin did not seem large enough to house a family of four; yet Parson Caton's stalwart brood of ten children lived there happily with himself and wife, and found the shelter ample. There were but two rooms on the lower floor, each lighted by the doors only; above was a loft, in which were laid truckle-beds. Supper was speedily cooking on the coals in the fire-place; the scent of bacon was omnipresent. In the smaller of the two rooms there were four large beds, covered with gay quilts, and shoved closely together. Around the room hung collections of herbs and several rifles; for furniture there were a few rude chairs, and a small table, on which were some antiquated books.

As we returned from a wash at the brook the parson came home, and was greeted with a cheery welcome from the hounds. Every inch of his face was filled with rugged lines, which told of strong character. He stood leaning on his staff and looking us over intently for some moments before he said, "Good evening, men." Then he greeted us heartily, and our invalid wagon was forthwith dispatched to the rustic forge near the cabin for repairs. There Andy held a pine knot, while the parson's son, a stout smith, worked.

This old man, in his mountain home, was as simple and courteous in his demeanor as any citizen. After the frugal supper was over, he asked us many questions of the outer world, which he had never visited; New York and Louisville seemed to him like dreams. By and by the family came crowding in to evening prayers. It was quite dark, and the forest around us was still.

The parson took down a well-worn Bible, and opening it at the Psalms, read, in a loud voice, and with occasional quaint expoundings, one or two selections; after which, taking up a hymn-book, he read a hymn, and the family sang line by line as he gave them out. They sung in quavering, high-pitched voices, to the same tunes which were heard in the Tennessee mountains when Nolichucky was an infant settlement, and the banks of the French Broad were crimsoned with the blood of white settlers, shed by the Indians.

The echoes of the hymn died away into the depths of the forest, and were succeeded by a prayer of earnestness and fervor, marked here and there by strong phrases of dialect, but one which made our little company bow their heads, for the parson prayed for us and for our journey, and brought the prayer home

"The family sang line by line."

to us. Another hymn was lined, during which the hounds now and then joined in with their musical howls, and at last the family withdrew, leaving us in the spare-room. Presently, however, the parson reappeared, and announced that he and his wife would share the room with us, which they did; and we were wakened to the six o'clock breakfast by the good woman, who joined with her husband in reproving us for continuing our journey on the Sabbath day.

As we started once more, the wagon, carefully mended overnight, broke down again! So then the parson stripped a hickory bough with his own hands, and bound together the pieces. A mile farther on, coming to another forge, we halted until a second smith tried his hand at a permanent mending, although he said he "mout get fined by the authorities for working on a Sunday." The

Judge amused the smith's children with the artist's sketch-book, while the hammer rang on the anvil.

The country here and henceforward was of the wildest and most romantic character. The mountaineers, scattered sparsely along the ridges, cultivated the

A Mountain Farmer.

land in corn, of which there were huge fields visible in the clearings, but sent nothing to market in winter, and, while the crops were growing, were idle. The houses were almost invariably of logs. Often, as in Switzerland, looking down a high bank, we could see the tree-tops in a long valley below us, and the cabin of some farmer, with his cob-house granary and little cattle-pen nestling by a creek. Here, by the hard, firm roadways, the mountain laurel, the ginseng and the gentian abounded, and pines and spruces, poplars, hickories, walnuts, oaks, and ash grew in the valleys and along the banks.

We were now climbing over the hills of the Great Smoky range, making our way toward the elevated gap, through which we were to enter North Carolina. Every turn in the angular highway brought a new vista of mountains, blue and infinite, behind us; now in serrated ranks, receding into distance; now seeming to close up near at hand, and shut out the world from us. The rare atmosphere of these high regions gave new zest to the journey, and we hardly knew that evening was at hand when we reached the State line and began to descend into the valley to "Hopkins's," the first station in North Carolina.

In this remote and mountain-guarded dell,—this cup hollowed out of the Great Smoky range, visited only by the post-rider once a week, and the few farmers who go to the far towns of Eastern Tennessee to market,—we found the mountaineer in his native purity. No contact with even the people of the lowlands of his own State had given him familiarity with the world.

The people whom we passed as we rode on to Hopkins's, traveling along the roads out of Tennessee into North Carolina, were tall and robust; their language was peculiar, and their manners, although courteous, were awkward and rough. The gaunt, yellow-haired women were smoking, and trudged along contentedly beside the men, saying but little. They were neatly dressed in home-made clothes, and their hair was combed straight down over their cheeks and knotted into "pugs" behind. There were none of the modern conventionalities of dress visible about them. The men were cavalier enough; their jean trowsers were thrust into their boots, and their slouch hats cocked on their heads with bravado air. The hills rose high up around the humble log-dwelling of Hopkins, and a little road ran beside a roaring torrent which came down from the mountain through a delicious valley, making charming nooks and niches among the round polished stones.

Once a prosperous farmer, the war had left the venerable mountaineer only the wrecks of his home. Both parties had guerrillaed through the gorges and gaps; one "army" burned Hopkins's cabin, and the other stole his produce. High on the hill-sides grew the native grape; a little cultivation would have turned the whole valley-cup into a fruitful vineyard; but Hopkins said it was too late for him to try. It was, too, an excellent sheep-grazing country; the wolves sometimes made cruel havoc, but shepherd-dogs could easily keep them off. Along the slopes of the Smoky beyond his home grew the finest of building timber, and water power was abundant; yet there were no frame houses for miles around.

"Wal, you uns don't understand, I reckon," said Hopkins. "I hain't had a mighty sight o' git up since the war."

Supper was served in the kitchen by one of the tall females we had observed upon the road, who was Hopkins's housekeeper, and who laid aside her pipe to come to the table and wait upon the strangers, whom, she said, she did not understand, "for you uns don't talk like we uns;" adding that she "reckoned we found this a mighty fine country."

Half a day's journey from this nook in the mountains brought us to the gap near Mount Starling, where we crossed through the Smoky range, and began to descend on the other side into Haywood county, a division of North Carolina, extending over 750 square miles, and annually producing more than 200,000 bushels of corn. The chain of the Smoky mountain which we had traversed extends for about sixty-five miles, from the deep gorge through which the French Broad river flows at "Paint Rock" to the outlet of the Little Tennessee; and Professor Guyot, who is authority upon the Appalachian system, calls it the master chain of the whole Alleghany region.

The dominant peaks in this line of mountains north of Road Gap are Mount Guyot, 6,636 feet high; Mounts Alexander, Henry, South, and Laurel Peaks, the True Brother, Thunder, Thermometer, Raven's, and Tricolor Knobs, and the Pillar Head of the straight fork of the Oconaluftee river. South of Road Gap rise the peaks known as "Clingman's Dome," 6,660 feet high; Mounts Buckley, Love, Collins, and a dozen others, more than 5,000 feet high.

Each of these rises to 6,000 feet elevation above mean-tide water, and many of them overtop Mount Washington, the monarch of the East, by several hundred feet. Seen from a distance, these mount-

"We caught a glimpse of the symmetrical Catalouche mountain." [Page 484.]

ains seem always bathed in a mellow haze, like that distinguishing the atmosphere of Indian summer. The gap through which we passed was at an elevation of at least 5,000 feet; beneath us were vast cañons, from which came up the roar of the creeks.

We looked down upon the tops of mighty forests, and now and then, descending, caught a glimpse of the symmetrical Catalouche mountain, fading away into distant blue. There are no gaps in the Smoky range which fall below the level of 5,000 feet, until Forney Ridge is passed; and there is a surprising number of peaks and domes rising higher than 6,000 feet.

The Cañon of the Catalouche as seen from "Bennett's." [Page 485.]

Once having traversed the barriers created by this vast upheaval, one enters the mountainous region comprised between the Blue Ridge and the chain of the Iron, Smoky, and Unaka peaks. This region properly begins at the bifurcation of the two chains in Virginia, and extends across North Carolina and into Georgia for 108 miles. The chain of the Blue Ridge to the eastward is fragmentary, and the gaps are only from 2,000 to 3,000 feet high.   All the interior region between the Blue Ridge and the Smoky is filled with spurs and chains, of which, perhaps, the most noticeable is the great Balsam, whose highest point, called the Richland Balsam, or Caney Creek Balsam Divide, reaches the height of 6,425 feet. Into this cluster of highlands, extending to the extreme western boundary of North Carolina, we now daily made our way.

This day's journey was but a succession of grand panoramic views of gorge and height. Descending, we rode for several miles along a path cut out of the mountain's steep side; and hundreds of feet below us saw the tops of tall pines and spruces. Not a human habitation was to be seen; there was no sign of life save when a ruffled grouse or a rabbit sprang across the track.

Now we came into a valley, through which a wide creek flowed rapidly, finding its outlet between two hills towering thousands of feet above us, and there, at a rude cabin, stopped to feed our weary horses, and to partake of the milk, the honey, and the corn-bread set before us; to lie on the turf beside the cool stream, and to drink in at every pore the delicious inspiration of the pure mountain air. Remounting, we climbed along the side of shaggy "Catalouche," until, late in the afternoon, we came to "Bennett's."

Imagine a little frame house set on a shelf on the road, so that its inmates can look for miles down a deep straight valley, through which flows a river between banks fringed with dense foliage, and by rocks over which pines lean and straggle in wildest confusion. At the far end of this river valley looms up a tall mountain peak, so beautiful that one's soul is lifted at very sight of it. As our little company drew rein at the edge of the steep bank leading to the cañon, there was a universal cry of delight. Bennett's folks called to us at that moment, "Won't you 'light,' strangers, 'n come in?" We sat long in the little porch, gazing at Oconoluftee's height, and the Balsam mountains, dimly shadowed beyond the point where the valley was lost in the breast of the hills. The grandeur of the sentinel mountain, standing alone at the end of the chasm; the reflections of high rocks and mighty tree-trunks in the far-away stream; the dizzy precipices which overhung the rarely frequented valley, lent a charm which carried its terror with it.

The road grew narrower and rockier as we clambered along Catalouche; but the air was cooler, purer, the laurels more abundant, the vistas more charming; until just at sunset we came to the "Cove Creek Gap." In front lay a narrow valley, over which the mountain known as Jonathan's Bald threw his shadow; but beyond!—

High on the horizon lay a wavy line of hills, sharply outlined in the strong glare of the sunset, their delicate blue colors springing so suddenly upon our vision against the purple and crimson of the evening tints that we were surprised and delighted. As far as eye could reach, to right, to left, in front, stood the long line of uplifted crags, from which there seemed no outlet! Turning our horses on the crest of the mountain, and looking Tennesseeward, we saw our old friends of the Great Smoky, scattered for miles in friendly groups among the dark forests; westward and eastward deep ravines, and, beyond them, uncounted peaks, which the very sky seemed tenderly to bend over and kiss.

It was fast growing dark as we rode on to the winding road in the valley of Jonathan's creek. As we were rattling by a log farm-house in a deadening, a loud voice cried:

"Strangers, wait a minnit till I ketch my ole mule, or he 'll foller you uns clean down to Boyd's, I reckon."

The owner of the voice, carrying a log on his shoulder, came up through the fields as he said this, and, throwing down his burden, secured the restive mule, who was looking over the low fence; after which he turned to each one of the party, and asked:

"What mout be your name?"

Having satisfied his curiosity thus, he gave us good evening civilly enough, and struggled with his log again.

Farther on a young farmer crossing the creek came to us as we inquired the distance, and, before giving us the desired information, said, "What mout be your names?" "Whar are ye from?" After which he added carelessly, "Mile 'n half; good evenin'."

Mount Pisgah, Western North Carolina. [Page 487.]

Troops of children played about the doors of all the cabins along these roads. Families of ten and twelve are by no means uncommon. Girls and boys work afield with their parents in the summer, and pass the winter with but limited chances for culture.

Passing around the base of "Jonathan's Creek Bald," we came into a more open and fertile country, where the farm-houses were neatly built and painted, and the wheat-fields were wide and well stocked. The creeks were numerous, and everywhere bordered by fascinating foliage; at each turn in the road there was a picture; one was constantly reminded of the rich views in the Loire country in France, or of the fat fields of Alsatia.

On the plain of Waynesville, 2,756 feet above the level of tide-water, and in the shadow of the great Balsam range, stands Waynesville town. The approaches to it are lovely, but the view from the town itself is lovelier still. On all sides rise the mountains; the village nestles between the forks of the Pigeon river, nowhere more beautiful than within a few miles of this nook.

To the westward lie the Balsam peaks, seven of which, Amos Plott's, the "Great Divide," Brother Plott, Rocky Face, Rockstand Knob, and the two Junaleskas, tower more than 6,000 feet high. They are clad, upon their summits, in the sombre garb of the balsam, the sad and haughty monarch of the heights, whose odorous boughs brush against the clouds, and whose deep thickets, into which the sun himself can hardly penetrate, afford a refuge for the wolf and the bear. The balsam is emphatically an aristocratic tree; it is never found in the humble valleys, and rarely lower than an elevation of 4,000 feet; it consorts with the proud rhododendron, whose scarlet bloom was the object of the Indian's most passionate adoration, and its grand stem springs from among the decaying and moss-grown rocks.

On these Balsams, as on the great Black mountains, the moss offers an elastic carpet sometimes a foot thick, and is tough and hard as the hides of the bears who delight to disport upon it. Here and there on the sides of the Plott peaks there is a long furrow which marks the path cut by some adventurous woodsman. The peaks are not romantically named; the unimaginative early settlers called them after the men who owned or lived near them; and many of the most imposing heights are still nameless.

The Bald mountains,—so called because their summits are destitute of forest, and because the sun makes the rocks on their tops glisten like a bald man's shining poll,—are numerous in the vicinity of Waynesville. North and north-east of the town lie the "Crab Tree" and "Sandy Mush" Balds, and beyond them in the same direction rises "Bear Wallow" mountain. On the south and south-east are "Mount Pisgah," the "High Tower," and Cold mountain, which rises 6,063 feet out of the "Big Pigeon" valley; and away to the south and south-east stretches the chain of the "Richland Balsam."

The dry and pure air of Waynesville gives new value to life; the healthy man feels a strange glow and inspiration while in the shadow of these giant peaks. The town is composed of one long street of wooden houses, wandering from mountain base to mountain base. It has a trio of country stores; a cozy and delightful little hotel, nestling under the shade of a huge tree; an old wooden church perched on a hill, with a cemetery filled with ancient tombs, where the early settlers lie at rest, and an academy.

The Carpenter—A Study from Waynesville Life.

There is no whir of wheels. The only manufacturing establishments are flour-mills located on the various creeks and rivers, or a stray saw-mill; while here and there a wealthy land owner is building an elegant home with all the modern improvements. By nine o'clock at night there is hardly a light in the village; a few belated horsemen steal noiselessly through the street, or the faint tinkle of a banjo and the patter of a negro's feet testify to an innocent merry-making. The Court-House of Haywood county, and the Jail, both modest two-story brick structures, are the public buildings, the Jail having only now and then an inmate, for the county is as orderly as a community of Quakers. The Marshal, as in most of these small Western North Carolina towns, is the power which maintains and enforces the law. No liquor is sold within a mile of the town's boundary; some lonely and disreputable shanty, with the words "BAR-ROOM" inscribed upon it, on a clearing along the highway, being the only resort for those who drink "spirits." The sheriff, the local clergyman, the county surveyor, and the village doctor, ride about the country on their nags, gossiping and dreamily enjoying the glorious air; nowhere is there bustle or noise of trade. The county court's session is the event of the year; the mail, brought forty-five miles over the mountain roads from the nearest railroad, is light, and the stage-coaches bring few passengers from the outer world.

But what a perfect summer retreat; what chances for complete rest; what grandeur of mountains; what quiet rippling of gentle rivers; what noble sunsets; what wealth of color and dreaminess of twilight; what breezy morn-

View on Pigeon River, near Waynesville.

ings, when the mists fly away from the deep ravines in the mountain chains, and shadow and sun play hide and seek on the dense masses of the Balsam tops!

The great counties of Haywood, Jackson, Macon, Cherokee, Buncombe, Henderson, Madison and Yancey, contain the principal portion of the mountain scenery of western North Carolina. The mighty transverse chains of the Nantahela, Cowee, Balsam and Black mountains, run across these counties from the Smoky range to the Blue Ridge, and the traveler wandering from county seat to county seat must constantly climb lofty heights, pass through rugged gaps, and descend into deep valleys.

Western North Carolina is not only exceedingly fertile, but abounds in the richer minerals, and needs but the magic wand of the capitalist waved over it to become one of the richest sections of this Union. Occupying one-third of the entire area of the State, and possessing more than a quarter of a million of inhabitants, its present prospects are by no means disagreeable; but its prominent citizens, of all walks in life, are anxious for immigration and development of the rich stores of gold, iron, copper, mica, and other minerals now buried in the hills.

Let no one fancy that this mountain region is undesirable as an agricultural country; there are few richer, or better adapted to European immigration. The staple productions of Haywood county are corn, wheat, rye, oats and hay; all vegetables grow abundantly, and the whole county is admirably fitted for grazing. The level bottom-lands on Pigeon river and its numerous tributaries are under fine cultivation; the uplands and the slopes produce rich wheat; the ash, the sugar maple, the hickory, and the oak, are abundant; and white pine is rafted down the Pigeon river in large quantities yearly.

But the exceptional fertility of most of the ranges throughout all the counties mentioned is the great pride of the section. The sides and tops of the mountains are, in many cases, covered with a thick, vegetable mould,* in which grow flourishing trees and rank grasses. Five thousand feet above the sea-level one finds grasses and weeds that remind him of the lower region swamps. Cattle are kept in excellent condition all winter on the "evergreen" growing along the sides of the higher chains. Winter and summer, before the ravages of the war thinned out their stocks, the farmers kept hundreds of cattle on the mountains, feeding entirely on the grasses. In the spring the herds instinctively seek the young grasses springing up on the slopes, but with the coming of winter they return to the tops to find the evergreen. The balsam-tree can easily be banished, for, after being felled for a few months, it will burn easily, and in its stead will spring up thick coats of evergreen. On some of the mountain farms corn yields one hundred bushels to the acre, and wheat, oats, rye and barley, flourish proportionately. In the "deadenings," where the large timber has been girdled and left to die, and the undergrowth has been carefully cleared, timothy and orchard grass will grow as high as wheat.

The native grape, too, flourishes on all the hill-sides, within certain thermal lines established by observation of the elder mountaineers; and varieties of grapes can be selected, and so planted as to ripen at different periods of the autumn. The negro population is not numerous in Western North Carolina. Wherever the black man is found, however, he is industrious, faithful, and usually quite prosperous. In some of the small tows, as at Waynesville, we found a gentleman's valet of other days officiating as village tailor, barber, errand boy, coachman and "factotum."

* Testimony of Professor Richard Owen, of the Indiana State University.

LVI

THE "SUGAR FORK" AND DRY FALLS—WHITESIDE MOUNTAIN.

IT is sometimes said that Western North Carolina is shaped like a bow, of which the Blue Ridge would form the arc, and the Smoky mountains the string. Within this semicircle our little party, now and then increased by the advent of citizens of the various counties, who came to journey with us from point to point, traveled about 600 miles on horse-back, now sleeping at night in the lowly cabins, and sharing the rough fare of the mountaineers, now entering the towns and finding the mansions of the wealthier classes freely opened to us. Up at dawn, and away over hill and dale; now clambering miles among the forests to look at some new mine; now spurring our horses to reach shelter long after night had shrouded the roadways, we met with un-varying courtesy and unbounded welcome.

The Dry Fall of the Sugar Fork, Blue Ridge, North Carolina. [Page 497.]

As a rule, the younger men with whom we talked were hopeful, very much in earnest, generally free from the mountain rustic dialect; took in one or two newspapers, and were in-terested in the outer world and general legislation; but their fathers, the farmers of the "befo' the waw" epoch, were discouraged and somewhat discontented at the new order of things; looked upon mineral hunters and railroad route surveyors with coldness or contempt; and were wont to complain of their own lot and of all the results of the war. The young and prominent men in most of the counties were good companions and enthusiastic friends; they had none of the artificial manners of the town, none of its guile.

Wherever we went we found the "rock-hunters" had been ahead of us, and a halt by the wayside at noon would generally bring to us some denizen of the neighborhood, who would say, "Good mornin', gentlemen. After rocks?"—and would then produce from his pockets some specimens which he was "mighty certain he did n't know the name of." Many a farmer had caught the then prevalent mica fever, and some had really found deposits of the valuable mineral which were worth thousands of dollars.

There is little danger of overestimating the mineral wealth of this mountain country; it is really very great. There are stores of gold, silver, iron, copper, zinc, corundum, coal, alum, copperas, barytes, and marl, which seem limitless. There are fine marble and limestone quarries whose value was unsuspected until the railroad pioneer disclosed it. The limestone belt of Cherokee county, a wild and romantic region still largely inhabited by Cherokee Indians, contains stores of marble, iron and gold; Jackson county possesses a vast copper belt; and the iron-beds of the Yellow mountains are attracting much notice. The two most remarkable gold regions are in Cherokee and Jackson counties.

The Valley river sands have been made, in former times, to yield handsomely, and now and then good washings have been found along its tributaries. The gold is found in veins and superficial deposits in the same body of slates which carries limestone and iron. Before the war liberal arrangements had been made for mining in Cherokee, but since the struggle the works remain incomplete. It is supposed that the gold belt continues south-westward across the country, as other mines are found in the edge of Georgia.

The gold of Jackson county is obtained from washings along the southern slopes of the Blue Ridge, near the mountains known as "Hogback" and "Chimney Top;" and Georgetown creek, one of the head streams of the Toxaway, yielded several hundred thousand dollars a few years ago. In this wild country, where the passes of the Blue Ridge rise precipitously 800 and 1,000 feet, there lie great stores of gold.

Overman, the metallurgist, unhesitatingly declares that he believes a second California is hidden in these rocky walls. The monarch mountain "Whiteside" is said to be rich in gold.

It is possible that the iron ore of these mountains will not be speedily developed, as capital is now so powerfully attracted to Missouri, and other States, where remarkable deposits exist; but there is no denying the richness of Cherokee, Mitchell, Buncombe, Haywood, Jackson, and Macon counties in that mineral. In Cherokee the hematite ores outcrop in immense quantities along the Hiawassee and Valley rivers, and, when wrought in the commonest county bloomeries, have yielded an astonishing per cent. Rivers flow directly through the iron regions in this section, furnishing every needed facility for transportation; and limestone and forest fuel abound. Magnetic ores are found in Madison, Haywood and Macon counties; and there are large outcroppings of hematite in Buncombe.

Our expedition grew rapidly after we left Waynesville, and our group of horsemen, followed by "the baggage train," toiling along the mountain roads, caused a genuine excitement at the farms by the way. One of our most memorable trips was that from Waynesville to Whiteside and the return.

Upon the beautiful country through which we were now wandering the Indian lavished that wealth of affection which he always feels for nature, but never for man. He gave to the hills and streams the soft poetic names of his expansive language—names which the white man has in many cases cast away, substituting the barbarous commonplaces of the rude days of early settlement.

The Cherokee names of Cowee and Cullowhee, of Watauga, of Tuckaseege, and Nantahela, have been retained; and some of the elder settlers still pronounce them with the charming Indian accent and inflection. The Cowee mountain

View near Webster, North Carolina.

range runs between Jackson and Macon counties, and the valley of Tuckaseege, walled in four crooked, immense stretches, includes all of Jackson county which lies north of the Blue Ridge.

The river itself, one of the most picturesque in the South, "heads" in the Blue Ridge, and swelling into volume from a hundred springs of coldest, purest, most transparent water, which send little torrents down all the deep ravines, it goes foaming and dashing over myriads of rocks, sometimes leaping from dizzy heights into narrow cañons, until it comes to, and is lost in, the Tennessee. Where the Tuckaseege forces its way through the Cullowhee mountains there is a stupendous cataract.

The little inn at Webster, the seat of justice of Jackson county, was none too large to accommodate our merry cavalcade. We came to it through the Balsam mountains from Waynesville, along a pretty road bordered with farms and giant mulberry-trees. In the valleys we saw the laurel and the dwarf rosebay, the passion flower and the Turk's-cap lily, and on the mountain sides the poplar or tulip-tree, the hickory, ash, black and white walnut, the holly, the chincapin, the alder, and the chestnut, each in profusion.

Webster is a little street of wooden houses, which seem mutely protesting against being pushed off into a ravine. For miles around the country is grand and imposing. A short time before our arrival the residents of the county had been edified by the execution of the only highwayman who has appeared in Western North Carolina for many years. The hanging occurred in front of the jail in the village street, and thousands flocked to see it from all the section round about.

Sunset came with a great seal of glory. Before the dawn we were once more in the saddle, *en route* for the Cowee range. Just below Webster we crossed the Tuckaseege river at a point where once there was a famous Indian battle, and wound up the zigzag paths to the very top of Cowee, now and then getting a glimpse of the noble Balsam left behind. Now we could look up at one of the "old balds," as the bare peaks' tops are called. (The Indian thought the bare spots were where the feet of the Evil One had pressed as he strode from mountain to mountain.) Now we stopped under a sycamore, while a barefooted girl brought a pitcher of buttermilk from the neighboring house ; now a group of negro children, seeing a band of eight horsemen approaching, made all speed for the house, evidently thinking us Ku-Klux or " Red Strings " resuscitated ; and now a smart shower would beat about our heads, and die away in tearful whisperings among the broad leaves. The mile-stones by the roadside were notched to indicate the distance ; and from hour to hour, in the mountain passes, stops were made to whoop up the laggards.

In the rich coves in Jackson county the black mould is more than two feet in depth, and the most precipitous mountain sides are grazing pastures, from which thousands of fat cattle are annually driven down to the seaboard markets. In the ranges, too, where the winter grass grows luxuriantly from November until May, great numbers of horses and mules are raised. Fruit grows with Eden-like luxuriance ; the apple is superb, and on the thermal belt in all this section the fruit crop never fails.

Near Franklin, close to the site of an old Indian fortification, we crossed the " Little Tennessee," a stately river, along whose banks are noble quarries of marble, never yet worked. The chief town of Macon county was fair to look upon, seated amidst well-cultivated fields, and in the immediate vicinity of a grand grazing country ; but we pushed on into the mountains once more, anxious to pass the Blue Ridge and climb the ribs of " Whiteside." Three hundred thousand acres still remain unimproved in Macon, and at least one-third of these are rich in minerals.

We were now approaching the extreme western border of the State. A little beyond lay Cherokee and Clay counties, a territory taken from the Indians by treaty no later than 1835-36. They lie in the valley of the Hiawassee, which is famous as the place where the first successful treaty was made. We pushed on until dark, and our little party was dispersed at the various farm-houses on the road, with instructions to gallop up and meet in the morning before reaching the foot of the Blue Ridge.

The stream along whose banks we were now ascending the mountain is known as the "Sugartown" or "Sugar Fork" of the Tennessee river, and comes foaming down the wild slopes of the Blue Ridge through some of the most romantic scenery in America. Beautiful as the Rhone in the Alps, majestic in its tremendous waterfalls, and the wild grandeur of the passes through which it flows, it is strange that few travelers from other States have ever penetrated to its upper waters.

It was not without difficulty that our party reassembled the next morning. The Colonel and the sprightly Jonas came galloping from a town ten miles away, where they had been compelled to remain overnight, and the others came straggling to the rendezvous. The village physician from Webster, who knew every foot of the way for forty miles around, the cheery landlord from Waynesville, and the writer climbed the steep hill-side slowly under a broiling sun; the artist, hungry for sketches, browsed lightly on the delicate vistas afforded by every turn in the road; and the Judge, who had enlisted in our service that genial and venerable mountaineer, Silas McDowell, was actively hunting for the obscure pathway leading to the lower falls; while the colored servant guided an overloaded buggy along the rocky road.

As we reached the crest of the hill a sound like the sweep of the wind through the forest in autumn, or the distant echo of the rush of a railway train, drifted to our ears. Now it was swept away, now came back again powerfully. It was the voice of the fall in the cañon below, and old Mr. McDowell, reining in his horse and placing his hand to his ear, listened intently a minute, then announced that the pathway to the falls was not far, between Lamb and Skittles mountains, from that spot. So we began to search for it, some one meantime volunteering the information that the ravines abounded with rattlesnakes, and that one must tread carefully.

"What do you think of that?" said one, turning to the gray-haired guide. "Had we better go down this way?"

"Sir," said he, fiercely, "I have a contempt for snakes, sir. I kick them out of my way, sir. I kill them before they have a chance to bite me, sir."

Cold comfort, but no alternative; and, Indian-file, we moved toward the descent. After a walk of 200 yards through a pleasant grass-grown space, we came to the hill's abrupt sides, broken by ledges and clothed with tangled vines and underbrush. A slight and scarcely perceptible trail led along the dizzy height, but was now and then lost entirely as one came to a rock, over which he was compelled to crawl and drop cautiously into black-looking caves and dens, out of which the only sortie was another still more difficult scramble.

Bears are often seen in these mountains now-a-days, and "hard times" will bring them into the vicinity of the farmers' cabins. The bear of this region is black, grows somewhat larger than in the swamps of the eastern part of the State, and has a glossy fur-like coat of hair. One sometimes comes upon the wallows in the moss where Bruin has been taking his siesta.

Half-way down the mountain we could hear the roar of the fall, and sometimes, through an opening in the trees, catch a glimpse of the white foam as it
poured over the rocks. Guided by the Judge's cheery halloo, and the occasional crack of a revolver, we reached the valley, swinging down by branches
of trees, and tearing our hands against the rough rocks. The Colonel suddenly
disappeared.

Many a halloo failed to bring him, and I waded through the cold pool at the
foot of a great ledge, staggered out of the knee-deep, chilly water on to a

Lower Sugar Fork Fall, Blue Ridge, North Carolina.

shelving platform, clambered over a half-rotten tree-trunk, and reached a pinnacle midstream, from whose jagged summit I could see the top of the falls and
the twin pine-trees leaning over the huge chasm as if it awed at the spectacle.
Around this pinnacle ran a whirlpool, which made a fierce eddy at the very base
of the projection on which I stood. Forcing myself up among the extending
boughs of another pine-tree, with my boots in one hand and my staff in my

mouth, I was just reaching the top when a limb gave way, and I slid rapidly down twenty feet directly toward the pool. A desperate wrench at a knot on the tree stopped me, however, and I finally reached my perch in safety.

To the right was a ledge, a hundred feet high, down which trailed moss and vines, and along which grew tiny white blossoms in dense masses. Far below this ledge on a rock, which he had reached by a dexterous drop, sat the artist, sketching. In the distance was Jonas, clambering on all fours up a wet stone directly under the shadow of the fall, and now and then turning to whoop at the others. No Judge, no Colonel visible! but now and then a faint halloo showed them still struggling in the glens.

A gap in the mountains, high up, was pierced by a rapidly flowing stream, which boiled into whitest foam as it sprang down the sides of a great rock from a shelf jutting out of the mass. At the right grew tall trees and infinite small foliage, clothing the walls, which descended hundreds of feet, with living green, and with blue, white, and red blossoms; on the left the ledge ran up into a peak in front, then receded toward the crest of the hill which we had left. Eighty or ninety feet below the shelf from which the foam leaped it met some obstacle, and, springing to the right in blinding clouds of spray, which at times filled the cañon for some distance, it formed a second fall extending thirty feet down to the lower channel.

On the left, across the face of the lower part of the cliff, ran minor torrents, bubbling and seething, and everywhere the current was swift, strong, and musical. Landing as I did midstream, and facing the fall, there seemed no exit from the valley save by balloon. On every side the walls appeared to rise perpendicularly, and, indeed, the trail was found only after vexatious scrambling among the rocks. When I reached the top, the others had departed, and I overtook them at a log-cabin, where they had halted for dinner. The Colonel smilingly presented himself.

"I got a fall from a high rock," said he, in apology, "and lost the antidote for rattlesnake bites, which I carried for you others, out of my pocket. It took me a good hour to find it again. Besides, I have seen the falls once before."

The cabin where we rested stood on a very steep hill-side, and was composed of two solidly-constructed square log buildings, connected by a porch. The furniture was of the simplest character. There was a fire-place, a rough board-table, with benches around it, a spinning-wheel, and a quilting-frame, at which three tall girls were busily working. The rude walls and the plank floor were bare.

In the other room stood one or two high bedsteads, of simple pattern; a mirror, a few inches square, hung near them; a little stand with a Bible on it, and a rustic bureau pushed against the wall. The venerable matron of the household, with her gray hair combed smoothly back under her sun-bonnet, which she kept on, stood guard over the table with a fly-brush, and while she gossiped with the Doctor, served buttermilk from an earthen jar.

"Jeems—Jeems is my youngest son's name, Doctor. He'll be eighteen this year; 'n he's a right smart boy."

Although sixty, at least, the matron was strong and hearty; had reared a large family, and never felt the need of anything more than she possessed. "Reckoned them folks that was huntin' for rocks better tend to ther corn, *she* did."

A little higher up the mountain, in the mica-lands, our artist was confronted by the belle of that region. She was pretty. She had evidently been informed as to our coming by the cunning mischief of the urbane Colonel, and approaching the man of pencils remarked, with a delightful bashfulness:

"I want you to take my picture."

Imagine him trying to explain.

"Well, they said anyway that you 'd take all our pictures, 'n my sister 's waitin' up t' our house's, 'n law! how fur'd you uns come this mornin'? Jim Lawson! ef you don't keep thet horse's heels away from me!" to a North Carolina cavalier, anxious to show us his horsemanship by plunging down a steep bank.

Straightway she led the gentle artist captive,—the pretty mountain girl with her hair combed smoothly down over her cheeks, and with her comely form robed in green.

By and by, in the afternoon, the reunited party, as it crept skyward, plunged, Indian-file, into the forest, and took its way to the " Dry Falls." A silence, not of gloom but of reverence, seemed to fall upon all as we entered the aisles of the grand wood, and climbed the knolls which rose like whales' backs every few hundred yards. We were already well upon the Blue Ridge, and crossing toward its southern side, in which the monarch rocks "Whiteside," "Black Rock," "Stooly," and "Fodder Stack," are rooted. Here and there the "Surveyor," who had joined us, stopped to look for his mark on a tree, and his sturdy little horse seemed by instinct to find his way athwart the furze.

After two miles of climbing, sometimes where the hills were so steep that in descending a misstep of the horse would have cost one a broken limb, we came to a long line of laurel thicket. Here, taking our oil capes, we scrambled into the bushes, and, stooping, worked our way to a cliff, down which rugged steps were cut, and stood where we could overlook the cañon into which the upper fall of the Sugar Fork sent its leaping water.

The Hibernianism by which this glorious cascade gets its designation of the "Dry Falls," was suggested by the possibility of passing beneath the giant shelf, over which it pours, without severe wetting, although the spray is at times blinding. The river, coming to a dizzy height, leaps out with such force, that the water is projected far from the rock, and the beholder seems to see a lace veil, at least sixty feet long, dependent from the hoary walls of the cañon. Passing under it, along the slippery rocks, one comes out upon another stone under beetling precipices, from which little streams run down, and around which the mist and spray rise, and can note the changing gleams of the sunshine as they play on the immense mass of foam suspended between earth and sky.

Below, the stream passionately clutches at the rocks, and now and then throws them down into the chasm; there are hollows in the stones, which have been worn to a considerable depth by the pattering of the spray upon them for hundreds of years. Here a mass of wall rises dozens of feet from the chaos of rocks which is huddled at the fall's bottom. Many of the rude figures seem to have human resemblances, and one might imagine them giants rising from the cañon's depths to tear away the veil which has been drawn across the entrance to their cavern.

A hundred and fifty feet below the summit of the falls, the stream runs on in whirlpools and eddies, now forming into inlets in which reeds, ferns and blossoms flourish, and now making a deep, steady current, cold and crystal clear. The pines and spruces seventy feet high seem but toys by the sides of these immense walls; the light, too, in the gap through the mountain, is strange and fantastic, and seems to cast a glamour over every minute object. Even the pebbles, and the ferns and tiny grass-sprouts in the soil beneath the shelf over which the fall pours, are purple.

Then the voice—the voice of the fall! Heard from the laurel thicket, it seems to come from the very ground under your feet; heard from the cavern into which you pass, it is sombre and complaining, like the winter wind about the house chimneys; and its echoes from the foot of the rapids, to which you may descend if you have firm nerves and a quick step, are like those from some unseen choir in a cathedral gallery,—some chant of priests at High Mass, monotonous, grand, inspiring; "the height, the glow, the gloom, the glory," all blended, shock and awe the soul.

Here is a fall upon whose virgin rocks no quack has painted his shameless sign; whose precipices have not been invaded by the mob of the grand tour; whose solitary magnificence thrills and impresses you as if in some barren land you came upon the dazzling lustre of a priceless diamond. But to this, and its brother a few miles below, the feet of thousands of the curious will hereafter wander.

The shadows were creeping over the mighty hills as we hastened back across the wooded slopes, and leaving the main road a little farther on, entered a narrow trail, obstructed by swampy holes and gnarled tree-roots. Three miles brought us to "Wright's"—the little farm-house in a deadening from which we obtained a view of "Short-Off,"—and the forest which hid the approaches to "Whiteside." For some time we had felt the exhilarating effects of the keen, rarefied air, and had noticed the exquisite atmospheric effects peculiar to these regions. The figure of the distant mountain stood out with startling clearness against the heavens; it seemed near at hand, whereas it was in reality miles away. The land is of wonderful fertility; even the imperfect cultivation which it has received in the clearings gives surprising results; and the timber is magnificent. All the land is suitable for small grains and roots, gives fine pasturage, and there are numerous quartz veins running through the hills, indicating the presence of gold in large quantities. The Indians once mined successfully for silver along the slopes of the Blue Ridge, near "Whiteside;" but, although they left the region only thirty years ago, and search has often been made for their riches, no traces of them have yet been found.

The Spaniards once prospected for minerals, and with evident success, in all these regions; and in Cherokee county immense excavations, supposed to be the work of De Soto and his army, have been discovered. Some years ago copper crucibles, with traces of white metal still remaining in them, were unearthed at a place where a vein of lead, silver and gold may be noted.

The summit of Whiteside is perhaps 5,000 feet high, but its peculiar location enables one to gain from it the most striking prospect in North Carolina. It overlooks a country of peaks and projections, of frightful precipices, often of naked rock, but generally fringed with delicate foliage; a country dotted with fertile clearings set down in the midst of forests; of valleys inaccessible save by

The Devil's Court-House, Whiteside Mountain.

narrow passes; of curious caves and tangled trails; of buttes and knobs, reached only by dangerous passes, where one finds the bluff's base thousands of feet down in some nook, and as he looks up sees the wall towering far above him.

At dawn of next day we plunged into the woods beyond "Wright's," and wound through a trail whose trace we of the cities should soon have lost, but in which our companions of the neighborhood easily kept until we reached a wooded hill-side, whence we could see the "Devil's Court-House," and catch a glimpse of "Whiteside's" top.

The former is a grand, rocky bluff, with its foot planted among the thickets, and its brow crowned with a rugged castle-like formation. The ragged sides are here and there stained like the walls of an old building, and it is not difficult to imagine that one is beholding the ruined walls of some giant castle. The "Surveyor" urged us forward, and our stout horses soon brought us to the clearing, where we were compelled to leave them, and climb the remaining distance on foot.

Here, more than 4,000 feet above the ocean-level, the sun beat down with extreme fierceness, and was reflected back from the hard white of the rocks with painful intensity. The horses tethered, the Judge sprang up the narrow pathway, and regardless of rattlesnakes, we clambered on all fours, clinging sometimes to roots, sometimes to frail and yielding bunches of grass and ferns; now trod breathlessly a path in the black dirt on the edge of a rock sixty feet high; now hung, poised by our hands, from one ledge while we swung to another; and now dug out footholds in the stone when we ascended an almost perpendicular wall.

Finally we came to a plateau covered with a kind of gorse, and with laurel bushes scattered here and there; pushing through this, we wound, by a gradual ascent, to the summit of Whiteside, and the edge of the precipice. There we were face to face with the demon of the abyss.

Let me tell you how the Surveyor saw him.

"One day," said the Surveyor, seating himself with admirable carelessness on the dreadful slope of a rock overhanging the awful depths, "I was taking some levels below, and at last thought I would climb Whiteside. While I was coming up a storm passed over the mountains, and when I reached the top everything was hidden in such a dense mist, fog, or cloud, that one could hardly see his hand before his face. I strolled on until I reached a spot which I thought I recognized, and sat down, stretching my feet carelessly.

"Luckily enough, I did n't move; I was mighty still, for I was tired, and the fog was solemn-like; but pretty soon it blew away right smart, and dog my skin if I was n't perched on the very outer edge of this line of rock, and about two inches between me and twelve hundred feet of sheer fall.

"I saw the trees in Casher's valley, and the clearings, and then the sky, for I did n't look twice at the fall below me; but I flattened myself against the rock, and turned over; and I never want to come up here in a fog again."

Imagine a waterfall 2,000 feet high suddenly turned to stone, and you have the general effect of the Whiteside precipice as seen in the single, terrified, reluctant glance which you give from the top. There is the curve and the grand, dizzy bend downward; were it not for occasional clumps of foliage down the sides, the resemblance would be absolute.

The mountain itself lies rooted in the western slope of the Blue Ridge. The veteran McDowell has compared it to the carcass of some great monster, upon whose head you climb, and along whose mammoth spine you wander, giddy with terror each time you gaze over the skeleton sides.

The main rock stands on a hill 1,600 feet high, and its upper crest is 2,400 feet above the branch of the Chattooga river, which runs near the hill's base.

From top to tail of the mammoth skeleton the distance is 800 feet. Viewed at a proper distance, in the valley below, from its south-east front, it is one of the sublimest natural monuments in the United States. The sunshine plays upon walls which are at times of dazzling whiteness, and the sheer fall seems to continue to the very level of the valley, although it is here and there broken by landings.

But the outlook! It was the culmination—the finishing stroke of all our rich and varied mountain surprises! When  we were seated on the white crag, over which a fresh breeze perpetually blew, the "wrinkled" world beneath us literally "crawled." Everything seemed dwarfed and insignificant below. Even the brother crags — to the south-west, Fodderstack and Black Rock, and Stooly, to the north-west—although in reality rising nearly to the elevation of Whiteside, seemed like small hills.

To the north-east, as far as the eye could reach, rose a multitude of sharply defined blue and purple peaks, the valleys between them, vast and filled with frightful ravines, seeming the merest gullies on the earth's surface. Farther off than this line of peaks rose the dim outlines of the Balsam and Smoky ranges. In the distant south-west, looking across into Georgia, we

Jonas sees the Abyss.

could descry " Mount Yonah," lonely and superb, with a cloud-wreath about his brow ; sixty miles away, in South Carolina, a flash of sunlight revealed the roofs of the little German settlement of " Walhalla ; " and on the south-east, beyond the precipices and ragged projections, towered up " Chimney Top" mountain, while the "Hog Back" bent its ugly form against the sky, and " Cold " mountain rose on the left. Turning to the north, we beheld "Yellow" mountain, with its square sides, and " Short-Off." Beyond and beyond, peaks and peaks, and ravines and ravines ! It was like looking down on the world from a balloon.

The wealthy citizens of South Carolina have long known of the charms of this section, and many of them annually visit it. In a few years its wildness will be tamed; a summer hotel will doubtless stand on the site of "Wright's" farm-house, and the lovely forests will be penetrated by carriage roads ; steps will be cut along the ribs of Whiteside ; and a shelter will be erected on the very summit. A storm on the vast rock, with the lightning playing hide and seek in the crevices of the precipice, is an experience which gives one an enlarged idea of the powers of Heaven.

There is one pass on Whiteside which, though eminently dangerous, is now and then essayed, and Jonas and one of the woodmen of our party resolved to try it. While we commoner mortals drank in the wonderful view, and hob-nobbed with the clouds, these adventurers climbed down the precipice's sides, and coming to a point not far from the Devil's Court-House, where the pass begins, launched themselves boldly forward. To gain a cave which is supposed in former times to have been the abode of an Indian sorcerer or medicine man, they were compelled to step out upon a narrow ledge running along the very side of the cliff, turning a corner with no support above or below. The ledge or path is, at its beginning, two feet wide, and as it nears the cavern, not more than eighteen inches in width. A single misstep or a failing of the nerves would have precipitated them a thousand feet into the valley, and above them the com-fortless rock rose 300 feet. Hugging the wall, and fairly flattening themselves against it, they calmly went forward and reached the cavern in safety. Return-ing, with their eyes blinded by the shadows of the rocky crevice, the demon of the abyss seized upon Jonas, and prompted him to look down. One glance, and the awful depths seemed to claim him. He shrank toward the wall, dug his finger-nails into the crevices, uttered a faint cry, looked up, and was saved. His com-panion, following imperturbably behind, did not trouble himself about the depths, and striding coolly forward, with his hand filled with mineral specimens, came out upon the plateau unmoved, while Jonas seemed to have seen spectres.

From time to time "Indian ladders,"—huge trunks of trees with the boughs so chopped off as to form steps,—have been found on Whiteside, indi-cating that the savages frequently visited the mountain, and the tradition that it was the scene of some of their superstitious rites seems well authenticated. Now-a-days a few young men wander about its hills and ravines, inspecting their bear-traps, and sometimes are fortunate enough to encounter a shaggy bruin, wallowing in moss or ensconced near a tree.

At evening, as we reposed at Wright's, the thunder broke along the sky, and the lightning struck among the rocks on the adjacent hills. The storm was mighty and beautiful; a strange, rushing wind came with it, bending the forest growths like willows, and then the clouds covered the mountain top, and a fine mist fell. The sky was luminous, the lightning seeming to rend it in twain, and we were mute and frightened before the terrific grandeur of the battling elements.

"Whiteside" stands near the extreme south-eastern border of Macon county. We descended from it down the Tuckaseege valley into Jackson. Through both these counties runs an extensive copper belt; the ore in Jackson county being mainly bisulphuret or green carbonate of copper. In this region the advan-tages for the location of grazing-farms are superb, because the high mountains arrest the passing clouds, and condense them into rain so often that the lands are never parched or dry. Snow rarely lingers long there, and even in a hard winter the mountain herbage and ferns are readily made into hay.

LVII.

ASHEVILLE—THE FRENCH BROAD VALLEY—THE ASCENT OF MOUNT MITCHELL.

ON a bright Sunday we descended toward the course of the Tuckaseege, and a violent storm delayed us at a lowly cabin, near the path by which a visitor now and then penetrates to Tuckaseege cataract. According to the custom of the country, we carried our saddles into the porch and sat down on them to talk with the residents. The tall, lean, sickly farmer, clad in a home-spun pair of trowsers and a flax shirt, with the omnipresent gray slouched hat, minus rim, drawn down over his forehead, courteously greeted us, and volun-teered to direct us to the falls, though he " was powerful afeard of snakes."

Buttermilk and biscuit were served; we conversed with the farmer on his condition. He cultivated a small farm, like most of the neighbors in moderate circumstances; only grew corn enough for his own support; " did n't reckon he should stay thar long; war n't no schools, and he reckoned his children needed larnin'; schools never was handy; too many miles away." There was very little money in all the region round about; farmers rarely saw fifty dollars in cash from year to year; the few things which they needed from the outside world they got by barter. The children were, as a rule, mainly occupied in minding the innu-merous pigs about the cabin, and caring for the stock. The farmer thought sheep-raising would be "powerful peart," if folks had a little more capital to begin on; thought a man might get well-to-do in a year or two by such invest-ment.

He welcomed the mineral movement gladly; reckoned may be we could send him some one to buy his farm, and let him get to a more thickly settled region; but seemed more cheerful when we suggested that emigrants might come in and settle up the country, bringing a demand for schools with them. " He reckoned there war n't no Ku-Klux these days; never knew nothin' on 'em. Heerd nothin' furder from 'em sence the break-up."

The housewife was smoking her corn-cob pipe, and sitting rather disconso-lately before the fire-place, warming her thin hands by the few coals remaining in the ashes. The rain dripped in through the roof, and the children were hud-dled mutely together where it could not reach them. The furnishings were, as everywhere among the poorer classes in the mountains, of the plainest character. But the log barns were amply provisioned; stock looked well, and a few sheep and goats were amicably grouped under the shed.

The rain had so submerged the country that we gave up a visit to the cataract, said to be superior to the two other falls we had seen; and, as we rode

on, there came a pause in the shower.   Presently we overtook a party of mountaineers going to church.   The women, perched on the horses behind the men,
peered curiously at us from beneath their large sun-bonnets, and the men talked
cheerily.   The church, which we passed, was ruder than Parson Caton's in Tennessee.   It was merely a log-cabin, inside which benches were placed.   The
congregation was singing a quaint hymn as we rode by, and a few men, for whom
there was no room inside, lounged near the saplings where their horses were
hitched, listening intently.

The copper region of Jackson county is fascinatingly beautiful.   While there
is the same tropical richness of foliage which distinguishes the other counties,
there is a greater wealth of stream-side loveliness; there are dozens of foamy
creeks and by-ways, overhung with vines.

The hills are admirably fertile in the vicinity of the Way-ye-hutta and Cullowhee copper mines, and many of the vineyards are exquisitely cultivated.
The Cullowhee mountain is charming; no region in the South can furnish
stronger attractions for emigrants.   "Look at that valley," said an English
resident to me, "a few farmers from England, with their system of small farms
and careful cultivation, would make this an Eden."   And he did not exaggerate.

Asheville, North Carolina, from "Beaucatcher Knob."

Give all that section immigration, and railroads cannot be kept out of it, even
by the rascality of such gigantic swindles as have been forced upon North
Carolina.   The copper mines in Jackson were worked extensively before the
war, and Northern capital and shrewd English mining experience are once more
developing them.

The ore is "hauled," as the North Carolinians say, more than forty miles
over a wagon road.   The Blue Ridge tracts and the lands in Jackson county
demand the attention of such men as Joseph Arch and other English agitators of
the agricultural revolution in Great Britain.   Vast tracts of the lands in Western
North Carolina can be sold to colonists or capitalists at from one to two dollars
per acre.

Some days later, the Judge enthusiastically pointed out to us the beauties
of Asheville, the Mecca of the North Carolina mountaineer.   We had journeyed
thither down the valley of the Pigeon river,—a tranquil stream, with flour-mills

here and there perched in cozy nooks along its banks. A thirty mile wagon ride from Waynesville landed us at the great white "Eagle Hotel," from whose doors the Asheville stages ply over all the roads west of the Blue Ridge. In the valley where Asheville lies the capricious "French Broad" receives into its noble channel the beautiful Swannanoa, pearl of North Carolinian rivers.

Around the little city, which now boasts a population of 2,500 people, are grouped many noticeable hills; out of the valley of "Hommony" creek sombre Mount Pisgah rises like a frowning giant, and from the town the distant summits of the Balsam range may be faintly discerned. From "Beaucatcher Knob," the site of a Confederate fort, overhanging Asheville, the looker toward the south-west will see half-a-hundred peaks shooting skyward; while in the foreground lies the oddly-shaped town, with the rich green fields along the French Broad beyond it. Asheville Court-House stands nearly 2,250 feet above the level of the sea; and the climate of all the adjacent region is mild, dry, and full of salvation for consumptives. The hotels, and many of the cheery and comfortable farm-houses are in summer crowded with visitors from the East and West; and the local society is charmingly cordial and agreeable.

Buncombe county, of which Asheville is the central and chief town, was named after Colonel Edward Buncombe, a good revolutionary soldier and patriot; and its name has become familiar to us in the quaint saying so often used in the political world, "He's only talking for Buncombe," when a legislator is especially fervent in aid of some local project. At Asheville, we were once more in a region of wooden and brick houses, banks, hotels and streets; and although still some distance from any railroad, felt as if we had a hold upon the outer world.

Asheville has heretofore been comparatively unknown. Enthusiastic inva-lids, who there regained their health, have from time to time sung its charms, but the little town, situated 250 miles from the State capital, has only a fleeting fame. The war brought it now and then into notice; General Stoneman, with his command, fought his way through the passes to Waynesville, and at a short distance from Asheville the last Confederate battle east of the Mississippi occurred.

The town has grown steadily and remarkably since the war, and now has banks, good churches, well-furnished stores, three newspapers, and ample hotels; while in the vicinity the tobacco which grows so abundantly in Buncombe is prepared for the market, and great quantities of cheese are annually manufac-tured. Beautiful natural parks surround it; superb oaks cast their shadows on greenest of lawns, and noble maples, ash and walnuts border the romantic road-way. A few miles from the town's centre are excellent white sulphur springs, from which a variety of exquisite views are to be had, and only nine miles north of the town are the so-called "Million Springs," beautifully situated in a cave between two ranges of mountains, where sulphur and chalybeate waters may be had in profusion.

The town of Asheville will in future be the railroad centre of Western North Carolina, and must grow to be a large and flourishing city. The present pov-

erty of the section as to railroad communication is largely due to the discouragement consequent on the manner in which the confidence of those subscribing
to the principal enterprise has been betrayed. The unfinished embankments,
the half-built culverts and arches of the Western North Carolina railroad, which
are to be seen in many of the western counties, are monuments to the rapacity
and meanness of a few men in whom those counties placed confidence.

The plan of this railroad is a fine one, and would soon develop the noble
mountain country into a very wealthy section. It proposed to supply a route
from Salisbury, North Carolina, to Asheville, and thence by two lines to give
advantageous outlets. One of these was to run down the valley of the French
Broad river to "Paint Rock," on the Tennessee line, connecting with the Cincinnati, Cumberland Gap, and Charleston railroad, leading to Morristown, Tennessee, which would have connections with the through route from New York
to New Orleans, at Morristown, and would complete the great air line from
Charleston, in South Carolina, to Cincinnati in Ohio, by connecting at Lexington

View near Warm Springs, on the French Broad River. [Page 507.]

or Paris, in Kentucky, with the Kentucky Central road. The other outlet was to
be by the main line passing due west from Asheville through the western counties
to Ducktown, in Cherokee county, and thence on to Cleveland in Tennessee,
whence it is but a short distance to Chattanooga. Thus the gates of this now
almost unknown region would be unlocked, and the best sections penetrated by
rail routes. But the work lies incomplete under the very eyes of the hard-working mountaineers who have been swindled. The money which they subscribed
has been spirited away, and still the eastern division of the road has only reached
Old Fort, twenty-five miles from Asheville.

The other routes are few and insufficient. The "Central North Carolina,"
formerly the Wilmington, Charlotte, and Rutherford railroad, is to run from Wilmington on the coast via Wadesboro', Charlotte, and Lincolnton to Cherryville,
and is intended to reach Asheville, but has eighty-five miles yet to build from
Cherryville.

The Union and Spartanburg railroad, leading from Alston, in South Carolina, to the Greenville and Columbia route, twenty-five miles north of Columbia, is to be extended to Asheville, a distance of seventy-four miles, crossing the Blue Ridge at Butt Mountain Gap; and the Laurens and Asheville Railroad Company intends to build a road from Laurensville via Greenville, in South Carolina, to Asheville, which will furnish a means of connection with the Atlanta and Richmond Air Line.

The importance of the extension, which would give a through direct line from Cincinnati to Charleston, can hardly be overestimated. The links still to be built would develop not only a rich, but a wildly romantic and picturesque country. The valley of the French Broad river conforms with perfect accuracy to the general direction of an air line between the two cities.

And what a valley it is! The forty-four miles from Asheville to Wolf creek form one of the most delightful of mountain journeys. The rugged wagon road runs close to the river's banks all the way to Warm Springs, a charming watering-place a short distance from the Tennessee line. As you penetrate the valley the river grows more and more turbulent; its broad current now dashes into breakers and foam-flakes, as it beats against the myriads of rocks set in the channel-bed; now twirls and eddies around the masses of drift-wood washed down from the sides of the gigantic mountains which rise almost perpendicularly from the tiny stretches of sand at the water's edge; now, deep and black, or in stormy weather yellow and muddy, it flows in a strong, steady current beside banks where the trees are grouped in beautiful forms, creating foregrounds over which the artist's eye lovingly lingers.

The Indians named the French Broad "the racing river;" and, as it hurls its wavelets around the corner of some islet or promontory, one sees how faithfully the name describes the stream. Each separate drop of water seems to be racing with every other. A party of American hunters named the stream after their captain, French, during the days of early settlement, and from "French's Broad" the name finally assumed its present form.

One can hear the voice of the river always crying among the cliffs, and moaning and sighing as it laps the low banks in the narrow gorge. It was the rare good fortune of our party to journey beside the stream during a terrific storm. As we reached the little town of Marshall,—a few white buildings grouped beneath immense cliffs,—a wild tempest of wind and rain, which snapped the locusts like paper twine, blew down oaks, made "land slides," and prostrated the crops, came through the valley; and then the roar of the river was sublime.

Straggling along in the storm, we gave ourselves completely up to the grandeur of the occasion. The creeks which came down from the rocks were so swollen that they would have carried the stoutest horse out into the wild chaos of the dashing and leaping stream, and drowned him in the mysterious eddies.

Night came, and we slept in a little farm-house, with the river singing its delicious songs of unrest and impatience at its mountain bounds in our ears. Skillful fording in the morning enabled us to pursue our journey along the washed-out road, where beetling crags almost shut the light; where there was not room for two carriages abreast, and some stone monarch of the glen leaned toward the stream's edge as if just about to topple downward.   For miles the rocks towered up loftily, and miniature torrents ran down their sides, rippling across the road into the river, upon whose farther bank there was no refuge what-

Lover's Leap, French Broad River, Western North Carolina.

ever; only the sheer rock with its coating of foliage; the tangled thickets on the height; the gleam of the streamlet piercing its way athwart the stones 1,500 feet in air!

The traveler who is not strongly moved by his first gaze upon this valley must be indeed *blasé*.   The approaches to Warm Springs exceed in grandeur any other portion of the gorge.   Pyramidal hills rise on either hand; the soft breeze of the south brings perfume from the borders of little river lakes, where the current has set backward, and is held in place by banks covered with delicate flowers.

Mountain Island," two miles from the Springs, is a hilly islet in the impetuous stream; its shores and its slopes are rich in beauty, carpeted with evergreens, and all the colors of the rich North Carolinian flora.   Below it the river becomes smooth, and moves majestically, only to break up anew into sparkling and fantastic cascades.   Suddenly leaving the looming mountains, with the famous rock "Lover's Leap" on the right, one finds that the south-west bank of the river recedes, and gives place to a level plain, in whose centre is a beautiful grove.   From this clump of trees peer out the white pillars of the Warm Springs Hotel.   It is not far from the banks of the French Broad, which there is more than 400 feet wide, and traversed by a high bridge.

The Warm Springs were discovered late in the last century by some adventurous scouts, who had penetrated farther than was prudent into the then Indian country.   The springs boil up from the margins of the river, and of "Spring Creek," and have a temperature of 105 degrees.   Thither the rheumatic, and those afflicted with kindred diseases, repair yearly in large numbers, and find speedy relief.   From a spacious lawn one can look up-river at massive cliffs and mountains clad in rich foliage; and for miles and miles around there is a succession of quaint and oddly shaped rocks.   Nine miles beyond the Springs the railroad from Wolf creek gives prompt connection with the through line to New York.

Five miles below, on the Tennessee line, is the "Paint Rock," 200 feet high, a titanic mass of stone whose face is marked as with red paint, and which seems

to have been pounded by some terrible Thor-hammer into multitudinous fragments, some of which overhang the highway. Not far from this point one comes
also to the "Chimneys,"—the unpoetic name given to jagged stone monuments
rising 400 feet into the air, serene, awful, gigantic, while the "racing river" cries
and caracoles at their bases. Hundreds, nay, thousands of fragments, shaped like
diamonds, or squares, of round flint and sandstone, and almost every other kind
of stone, lie scattered below, as though hurled down by a thunderbolt; and
swarms of turkey-buzzards hover in and out among the crags.

Buncombe county is very fertile; the tobacco raised there has frequently
taken the first and second premiums at the Virginia State fair. Fruit culture
prospers; iron ores crop out here and there. Stock-raising is one of the chief
occupations of the wealthier residents. Beaufort harbor will be Asheville's
nearest port, and a very convenient one, if ever the Western North Carolina railroad is completed. Manufacturing is needed, and would find superior advan-

View on the Swannanoa River, near Asheville, Western North Carolina.

tages, in all the region round about Asheville. In the valley of the French
Broad there are many admirable mill sites, the river at Asheville being quite as
large as the Merrimac at Lowell, in Massachusetts. The water power is generally
superb, because most of the mountain streams, before they flow out into Tennessee, have a fall of 1,000 feet. Timber is abundant, and when the railroad comes,
it will run through finely-timbered regions.

Our journey along the Swannanoa was a revelation. We missed the noisy
grandeur of the French Broad valley, but we found ample compensation in the
quiet loveliness of the stream which the reverent Indian named "beautiful."
Four miles from Asheville, going north-eastward, toward the Black mountains,
we reached the river, and followed its placid current through a beautifully-culti-
vated valley. A rich carpet of green covered its banks, and there was the same
charming effect produced by the trailing of the vines over the trees which we
had noticed in the mountains.

The river was sometimes deeply dark in color; now and then faintly blue or purple, as the sunshine played upon it through the thickets; here and there we came to a place where it had formed a little lake, across which a rustic bridge was thrown, and where one of the long, slender canoes of the country was

First Peep at Patton's.

moored to a sapling; now, where some rich farmer's mansion stood on a lawn, dotted with oaks and hickories; now, where we caught a glimpse of the distant Potato Top mountain; now, where an old mill was half hidden under clusters of azaleas and the low-laurels.

The summit of the Black mountains is the highest point in the United States east of the Mississippi river, and the rugged range, clad in its garments of balsam and moss, glorious with its vistas of apparently endless hills and fancifully-shaped valleys, is the chief pride of the North Carolinian mountaineer. Our party left Asheville late one bright morning, sped along the Swannanoa to "Alexander's," a good halting-point, seven or eight miles from the mountain's foot, and then pushed on to Patton's, the collection of humble cabins nestled at the very base of the chain of peaks. Our German companion sang his merriest songs that afternoon, and the Judge's cheery halloo was heard at every mile, for the loveliest phases of nature gave us their inspiration.

As we approached Patton's, the long ridges of "Craggy" loomed up like ramparts to the eastward, and the sun tinged the sky above them crimson and purple. The music from the ripples of the fork of the Swannanoa, which we were now ascending, drifted on the evening air; the kalmias, the azaleas, and the honeysuckles, sent forth their perfumes; the wood-choppers, their feet well protected against the snakes by stout boots, were strolling supperward, and gave us hearty good evenings; the cow-bells tinkled musically, and in a corner of Patton's yard a mountain smith was clanging his hammer against his anvil, seemingly keeping time with the refrain to which all nature was moved. The evening was still and warm, even in that elevated region. While some of us remained in the cabin below and listened to tales of Black Mountain adventure, the aspiring Jonas, with a companion, pushed on a few miles beyond, that he might see sunrise from the heights, even though he had to sleep in a crazy and decaying house on the edge of a dizzy cliff, with the floor for his bed and his saddle for a pillow.

It is twelve miles from Patton's to the summit of Mitchell's Peak, and the ascent, which is very arduous, is usually broken by stop at the "Mountain House," four miles from the foot, and another at the point where the Government once maintained an observatory, on a rock 6,578 feet high, and three miles

from the topmost height, which rises suddenly from the range, a mass of ragged
projections, covered with deadened tree-trunks.

At early dawn we were on our road to the Mountain House, at first through
thickets, then along a creek-bed, where the cautious mountain-horses walked with
the greatest difficulty; now fording a creek twenty times in half an hour, now
bending as we came to tree-trunks half-fallen across the trail. A slip upon a
smooth stone frightened one of the horses so that he stood still and trembled
for a moment, so well did he realize the result of a fall or roll backward; sometimes the animals would stand and listen, with their ears ominously cocked as
if watching for snakes; often they paused as if in mute despair at the task
before them.

But after an hour and a-half of this laborious climbing, during which we
had ascended at least 1,500 feet, we heard the halloo of Jonas and his companions, and scrambling up the track of a little water-course, came out upon the
plateau on whose edge stands the Mountain House.

The "house" is a small Swiss cottage, once solidly built of stout beams, but
now fast decaying. It was built by William Patton, a wealthy citizen of Charleston, and before the war was often the resort of gay parties, who dined merrily on
the cliff's verge, and saluted the sunset with champagne. It stands but a few
yards from the edge of the Balsam growth, where the vegetation changes and the
atmosphere is rarer than below. It is 5,460 feet above the sea-level at the
point in front of the
Mountain House, where one
looks down into the valley,
and sees the forest-clad
ridges creeping below him
for miles; notes the twin
peaks of Craggy and their
naked tops; then turns
in wonder to the wood
above him, and searches
in vain for the peaks be-
yond. While at the win-
dows of the Mountain
House we seemed to be
gazing from mid-air down
upon the Blue Ridge.
The illusion was perfect.
Below us the mists were
rising solemnly and slowly;
peak after peak was unveil-
ed; vast horizons dawned
upon us; we seemed to

The "Mountain House," on the way to Mount Mitchell's Summit.

have risen above the world. We turned from this view of the valleys and
entered the balsam thickets, pushing eagerly forward to Mount Mitchell.

And now we came into the region of the pink and scarlet rhododendrons. Whenever there was an opening in the trees the hill-side was aflame with them. Masses of their stout bushes hung along our path, and showered the fragile red blossoms upon us. The white mountain laurel, too, was omnipresent, but the scarlet banner usurped the greatest space.

When we came to a narrow trail, where slippery rocks confronted us, and ragged balsam-trunks compelled us to clamber over dangerous crags, we found the way strewn with a crimson carpet after our horses had struggled through. Here, too, were masses of evergreen, and red-pointed mosses, and the azaleas again along the border of streamlets, and purple rosebay and the tall grasses in the clearings, in whose midst nestled timorously tiny white blossoms and ground berries.

View of Mount Mitchell.

To climb Vesuvius is no more difficult than to scale the Black mountain, for although one can reach the very top of the latter on horseback, he is in constant danger of breaking his limbs and those of his horse on the rough pathway. By the time we had reached "Mount Mitchell" and seated ourselves upon its rocks, our horses were as thoroughly enthusiastic as we were, and peered out over the crags with genuine curiosity.

From Mount Mitchell we saw that we were upon a centre from whence radiated several mountain chains. To the south we could see even as far as the Cumberland line, and could readily discern the "Bald" mountain and our old friend the Smoky; while nearer in the same direction, we noted the Balsam range. Sweeping inward from the north-east coast were the long ridges of the Alleghanies; on the north the chain of the Black culminated in a fantastic rock pile; while on the south the ridges of Craggy once more stood revealed.

To the east we could overlook the plains of North and South Carolina; on the north-east we saw Table Rock and the "Hawk Bill," twin mountains, piercing the clouds; while beyond them rose the abrupt "Grandfather" mountain, and the bluff of the Roan. On the south were the high peaks of the Alleghanies, the Pinnacles, Rocky Knob, Gray Beard, Bear Wallow, and Sugar Loaf.

Another hour and a-half of climbing; then, dashing through a clearing, we suddenly saw above us a crag 200 feet high, with a stone-strewn path leading up it. Our horses sprang to their risky task; they rushed up the ascent,—slipped, caught against the edges of the stones, snorted with fear, then laid back their ears and gave a final leap, and we were on Mitchell's high peak, utterly above Alleghanies, Blue Ridge, or Mount Washington. Our horses' ears brushed the clouds. In a few moments we were at Mitchell's grave.

Here we were above the rhododendrons, and only a gnarled and stunted growth sprang up. The trees were nearly all dead; those still alive seemed lonely and miserable. The rude grave of the explorer, with the four rough slabs placed around it, recalled the history of the man, and the origin of the peak's name.

The Rev. Dr. Elisha Mitchell, a native of Connecticut, graduate of Yale and an eminent professor in the University of North Carolina, established the

The Judge climbing Mitchell's High Peak.

fact by measurements, made from 1835 to 1844, that the Black was the highest range east of the Rocky mountains in the United States. He grew very much to love the work of studying these heights, and spent weeks in wandering alone among them. The rough mountaineers learned to revere him, and he became as skillful a woodsman as any of them.

In June of 1857, after accomplishing some difficult surveys, and, as it is supposed, having ascended the pinnacle which now bears his name, he was descending into Yancey county, when, overtaken by night and a blinding storm, he strayed over a precipice on "Sugar Camp" creek, and was discovered some days afterward, dead, at the bottom of a waterfall, his body perfectly preserved in the limpid pool. His friends the mountaineers, who mourned his loss bitterly, buried him in Asheville; but a year later his remains were carried to the mountain top and there placed in a grave among the rocks he had loved so well.

Near the grave the Government has established a signal-house, where two brave fellows dare the storms which occur almost daily. The anger of the heavens, as witnessed from this stony perch in mid-air, is frightful to contemplate, and many a day the lonely men have expected to see their only shelter hurled down into the ravines below.

The view from the topmost peak is similar, in most respects, to that from lower Mount Mitchell; but the effect is more grand and imposing, and the mountains to the south and east seem to stand out in bolder relief. A tremu-

Signal-Station and "Mitchell's Grave," Summit of the Black Mountains.

lous mist from time to time hung about us; the clouds now and then shut the lower world from our vision, and we seemed standing on a narrow precipice, toward whose edges we dared not venture.

As we descended, that afternoon, the pheasant strutted across our path; the cross-bill turned his head archly to look at us; the mountain boomer nervously skipped from tree to tree; the rocks seemed ablaze as we approached the rhododendron thickets; the brooks rippled never so musically, and the azalea's perfume was sweeter than ever before.

Each member of the party, dropping bridle-rein on his weary horse's neck, as we came once more into the open space where stands the "Mountain House," and looked down thousands of feet into the yawning valley; as the peace and silence, and eternal grandeur of the scene ripened in his soul, involuntarily bared his head in reverence. Goethe was right:

"On every height there lies repose."

LVIII.

THE SOUTH CAROLINA MOUNTAINS—THE CASCADES AND PEAKS OF NORTHERN GEORGIA.

THE new link in the New York and New Orleans Air Line, connecting Charlotte in North Carolina with Augusta in Georgia, had been finished but a few days when I passed over it. This road, which gives the most direct route from Atlanta to Richmond, opens up a large portion of North-eastern Georgia, and traverses a rich mineral region for 600 miles.

The country between Charlotte and Greenville in South Carolina is interesting, though still in the rough. The better class of people all through this section, and especially in North Carolina, possess and manifest that boldness and independence of spirit which made the colony the first of the original thirteen to claim independence, and prompted the settlers on the Cape Fear river to refuse a landing to the stamps brought from England in one of King George's sloops-of-war. There is a good deal of ignorance and prejudice among the low class of whites; they are hardly the stuff out of which the old heroes were made.

The mountain region of South Carolina, lying between North Carolina and Georgia, contains some of the most exquisite scenery in the United States. Entering it from Charlotte, one passes Spartanburg and near the site of the famous battle of King's Mountain, and following the Air Line may pause at the busy town of Greenville.

I found there more activity and less embarrassment on account of the distressing political situation than anywhere else in South Carolina south of Columbia, the State capital. The negroes were far less ignorant than their fellows of the coast and the central counties, and were disposed to be more reasonable in their political views. It is true that, after the war the Ku-Klux organization committed abominable outrages throughout York, Union, Spartanburg, Laurens and Chester counties. It was shown, at the time of the exposure consequent on the military arrests, that 2,000 male citizens of a single county belonged to the Ku-Klux, and actively participated in the coercive measures which it had foolishly adopted.

But the mountaineers have learned the folly of such attempts, and there are no longer any reports of whippings and midnight massacres. The railroad and the advent of Northern men here and there, as well as the impetus which the universal use of the new fertilizers has given to the production of cotton upon lands where, before the war, it would not have been deemed wise to plant it—all have aided in building up new feeling, and in banishing most of the old bitterness. Had it not been for the supreme rascality of the hybrid State Government, the citizens of this upland region might have possessed even more railroad facilities than they at present enjoy. The "Blue Ridge" route was intended as a railroad into Kentucky and Tennessee, running across the southern end of the Blue Ridge, in South Carolina, which latter State and the city of Charleston owned nearly all the stock in the road up to 1871.

After about $3,000,000 had been expended in the construction of a portion of the road, and the State had guaranteed $4,000,000 of bonds, in support of fur-

The Lookers-on at the Greenville Fair. [Page 517.]

ther construction, upon certain conditions intended to protect its own interests, a gigantic fraud was consummated. The "sinking fund commission," composed of the State officers, self-appointed, passed the railroad into the hands of a corporation, robbing the State of its interest in the work, and then secured a legislative enactment annulling the conditions on which depended the issue of the four millions in bonds.

In addition to this, the Legislature authorized a further issue of "Blue Ridge" scrip to the amount of $1,800,000, and made it available by declaring it receivable for taxes. This afforded "operators" the chance they desired for plundering the State treasury; and meantime the Blue Ridge railroad remains unfinished.

It was late in the autumn when I reached Greenville, but the weather was warm and delightful. The small planters from all the country round were crowding the roads with their mule-carts, laden with one, two, or three bales of cotton. The agents for the sale of fertilizers were busy in the town looking after their interests, for many a planter had given them a lien upon his crop, and they wished to claim their money when the crop was brought to market.

There was a variety of testimony as to the profit made by the cotton-raisers who only planted two or three acres each; some insisted that they made handsome profits, others that, after they had paid for their fertilizers, and their own support during the year, they usually had nothing left. The "lien" which the seller of phosphate takes, when he delivers a ton of the coveted stimulating substance to the farmer, is a formidable document. It engages not only the growing crop, but in many cases the household goods, if the crop fails, and sometimes the unlucky wight who has a poor crop on his few acres finds himself in danger of a practical eviction.

But a good crop puts money and prosperity into this section, where the people are altogether better off than in the lowlands. They have every facility for enriching themselves, as soon as they can and will diversify the culture of their farms; and I noticed with pleasure the introduction of the "Agricultural fair" as a means of creating ambition in the direction of thorough farm culture. Greenville held its first fair of the kind during my stay there.

All along the highways leading into Greenville cotton whitened the fields; although it was late in November, there were immense fields yet to pick; and I was told that the whole crop is often not all picked before the advent of the spring months. The bareheaded negroes were lazily pulling at the white fleeces, wherever we passed, but seemed animated by no desire for results; it was easy to see why the crop was not all gathered before spring. Emigrants from other States would find every chance for enriching themselves in these charming uplands, where the climate is so delicious; where the streams and the hills are so beautiful, and where the soil is so fertile.

Greenville lies at the base of the Saluda, near the Paris mountain, and is delightfully situated on a range of breezy hills. Summer visitors from the lowlands crowd its hotels and private mansions; it has, like its neighbor, Spartanburg, a number of excellent schools and colleges, and a university. It is near the source of the Reedy river, and the approaches to it from Columbia are along the banks of that lovely stream, the Saluda. To the eastward, daintily enshrined in a nook in the Blue Ridge, near the North Carolina frontier, lies Walhalla, a German settlement, where the vine is cultivated with rare success; the county of Pickens is rich in mountain outlooks and noble waterfalls; and not more than twenty miles from Greenville, that superb monarch of the glens, Table mountain, with its ledges, each a thousand feet high, rises in rocky grandeur to the height of 4,300 feet above sea-level.

From the Greenville post-office, the stage-coach will speedily convey one into the heart of the Swannanoa and French Broad valleys in North Carolina. The road to Asheville leads through Saluda Gap, and past the beautiful summer resort, once the refuge of so many wealthy lowlanders, "Flat Rock." This was a species of Saratoga for the South Carolinians, and in the sweet valley there are still some noble mansions, like those of the Draytons and Memmingers, surrounded by gardens filled with rarest and costliest of shrubbery and flowers. Another route from Greenville leads to "Cæsar's Head," a lofty mountain like the "Whiteside," and a trysting place for hundreds of merry pilgrims during summer months.

Along the road, between Greenville and Asheville, and the rugged yet delightful routes which lead from Asheville to Charlotte, lies one of the great

Table Mountain — South Carolina.

pleasure regions of the future. The falls of Slicking, at the base of the Table mountain, the banks of that prince among mountain streams, the wonderful Keowee, the sweet vale of Jocasse, and the adjacent Whitewater cataracts, vie with Mount Yonah, Tallulah, Toccoa, and Nacoochee, their Georgian neighbors, in variety and surprising beauty.

From Charlotte to Centreville the scenery is sublimely beautiful. By this route one passes through the Hickory Nut Gap, a grand gorge in the Blue Ridge, through which a creek flows until its waters are merged in those of the rocky Broad river. Where the latter stream forces its passage through a spur of the Blue Ridge, its bed is encumbered with myriads of rocks, rooted deeply in the almost unyielding soil; mountain bluffs hem it in; the scene is one of fearful solitude and grandeur. The Gap is hardly anywhere more than half a mile wide, and, seen from a little distance, it seems but a narrow path cut between gigantic buttresses of stone, which rise 2,500 feet.

Midway up the front of the highest bluff, on the south side of the Gap, stands an isolated rock resembling some antique and weather-beaten castle turret. The rains of thousands of years have washed the granite cliffs smooth, and one may fancy them the walls of some huge fortification. Shooting out over the cliff, and falling into some as yet undiscovered pool, a spray-stream comes pouring; and near the base of the awful precipice are three violent and capricious cascades, which, by centuries of persistence, have worn wells from forty to fifty feet deep in the hard stone beneath them. When one approaches the Gap, he sees before him nothing but the limitless ocean of peaks, pointed sharply, like the apexes of waves, against the crystal vault of the sky. Everywhere Nature seems to have thrown out barriers, and to have determined to prevent one from entering her favorite retreat.

Then suddenly one comes upon the narrow defile of the "Hickory Nut Gap."

Beyond it, penetrating to Rutherfordton, one sees the sublime sentinels of the Blue Ridge range jealously guarding the approaches, and at last reaches a point whence the panorama of the Pinnacle, and Sugar Loaf, and Chimney Rock, and Tryon mountains all burst at once upon the vision. The road thither winds along a ravine-side; steep rocks overhang it, and beneath it a rushing torrent screams its warning. An opening in the forest shows anew the vast expanse of peaks, and in their midst the Monarch, the Cloud-piercer, the sombre controller of the whole magic realm, Mitchell's high peak!

Miles away, to the westward, one can dimly discern a silver line on a faintly defined mountain: it is a torrent leaping down the almost perpendicular sides of its parent height.

Southward from Greenville toward Atlanta, the Air Line road runs through the forests of Northern Georgia. I found many small towns, built of rough planks, growing briskly in the forest clearings. The railway station and a long platform, a store, a few plain houses, with fat hogs rooting among the stumps in their immediate neighborhood, a carpenter's shop, and, possibly, some small and primitive manufactory, made up each of these "towns." The hotels were two-story wooden buildings, through whose thin walls came the keen autumn winds, and whose slender partitions allowed one to hear every movement and tone of voice of all his adjacent fellow-sleepers.

The fifteen counties of North-eastern Georgia cover a territory of 7,000 square miles, traversed here and there by the Appalachian chain, which, leaving North Carolina on its western boundary, pushes into hundreds of spurs and outliers which shape the romantic scenery of Rabun, Habersham, Towne, Union, White, Fannin, Gilmer, and Lumpkin counties. There, in valleys elevated nearly 2,000 feet above the sea-level, are rivers and rivulets upon whose courses some of the most majestic cascades on the continent are found. Attracted by the fame of those noble waterfalls, Toccoa and Tallulah, I left the line of rail, and with a friendly company, wandered in and out among the peaks and ravines for several days.

Rabun Gap is the passage from Western North Carolina, through the Blue Ridge, into the Georgia gold and iron field. Rabun county itself is one succession of dark blue giant ridges, over which, descending gradually, one reaches the little town of Clayton. The populations in the mountains along the border devote some attention to illicit distilling, and are, consequently, a little suspicious of strangers who penetrate to their fastnesses. A worthy clergyman from the lower counties was journeying peacefully on a religious errand to the neighboring

State, through the passes of Rabun, shortly before our visit, when he suddenly, one day, saw thirteen guns pointed at him by as many men, and had to dismount and prove, at the rifles' muzzles, that he was not a revenue officer.

From "Whiteside," in North Carolina, to Rabun Gap, it is only forty-five or fifty miles on an air line, but the detours through the ravines make it farther to the traveler. When one arrives at Clayton he feels much as if he had left the world behind him. The quaint hamlet lies in a valley encircled with mountains. As you enter, you have that feeling of being imprisoned and of desire to escape, so common to the wanderer among the Alleghanies and on the Blue Ridge. There seems no possible outlet; the town appears to have been conveyed there by enchantment; yet a little careful observation will show you the

"Let us address de Almighty wid pra'r." [Page 521.]

roads piercing the passes in the valleys. Not far from Clayton are the falls of the Estatoia, or, as the mountaineers call them, "Rabun Falls," where a succession of brilliant cascades plunge down the chasm in a mountain-side. Clambering to the top of this natural stairway in the rocks, one may obtain an outlook over the valley of the Tennessee, miles beyond Clayton, and may note the mountain billows rolling away, apparently innumerable, until the eye tires of the immensity!

I have had occasion to describe the mountain "hack" to you—a red wagon mounted on super-fragile springs, and graced with seats, which, at every start made by the horses, bid fair to leave the vehicle. In such a conveyance, behind two splendid horses, did we depart from one of the forest towns on the Air Line railway one morning in mid-October, and climb the red hills of Northern Georgia. Mile after mile we journeyed through lands which might be made very valuable by a year or two of careful culture, by plantations or farms whose owners had deserted them, or tracts which the old settlers, having adopted the

Mount Yonah, as seen from Clarksville, Georgia. [Page 522.]

new labor system, were putting into most wonderful order ; now dashed over firm roads, through stretches of dreary forest, where battalions of black-jacks guarded the solemn way ; and now along mountain-sides, where paths were narrow and ravines were on either hand.

A few miles from the little hill-town of Clarksville, whither we were journey-ing, we came upon a large assembly of negroes in a high, open field, backed by a noble uplift of mountains in the distance. It was Sunday afternoon, and the dusky citizens were returning to their devotions, the scene of which was a log-cabin, inhabited by a negro, whom we judged to be the neighborhood blacksmith, as a shop near by was encumbered with wheels and old iron.

As we approached the " bars " leading into the meadow, the mass of the negroes had gathered inside and outside the cabin, and were singing a wild hymn, marked with that peculiar monotonous refrain which distinguishes all their music. Nothing could have been more picturesque than this grouping of swart and gayly-costumed peasantry, disposed around the humble cabin, with the afternoon sun glistening on their upturned faces. The noble peaks in the far background, mysterious in their garments of subtle blue, and inspiring in their majesty, added deliciously to the effect of the whole.

As the singers became excited, their bodies moved rhythmically, and cling-ing to each other's hands, they seemed about breaking into the passionate warmth of some barbaric ceremony. But our momentary fears of barbarism were checked when we heard the cracked voice of the venerable pastor, and saw the assembly kneel, and bow their heads at the words—

"Let us address de Almighty wid pra'r."

While the minister was praying, the young negroes who, during the sing-ing, had been disporting near a neighboring brook, left off their pranks, and hastened to join the kneeling throng about the cabin. As we drove away we could hear the solemn pleading of the ebony Jacob as he wrestled with the angel of prayer, and the nervous responses of the brethren and sisters when their souls took fire from the inspiration of the moment.

The "Grand Chasm," Tugaloo River, Northern Georgia.
[Page 524.]

From Clarksville, pleasant summer resort of the citizens of Savannah and other land towns, we caught a new glimpse of Mount Yonah, that lonely monarch of the northern counties. The village is small and quiet; there are few farm-houses in the immediate vicinity; there is no bustle of trade, no railroad, and no prospect of one. Seven miles away the new Air Line gives communication with the outer world. Habersham county, of which Clarksville is the county seat, was laid out by the famous "lottery act" of 1818, and has in it many valuable lands adapted to the raising of wheat and corn.

A ride from Clarksville to the valley of Nacoochee, which comprises within its limits a series of the most exquisite landscapes in the world, is one of the charming specimens of this mountain journey. There a gentleman who has forsaken the lowlands has built a grand mansion with conservatories, lawns, and parterres; there he and his visitors strike terror into the hearts of the mountain trout, and wander over the peaks and down the valleys at their will. Mount Yonah's summit affords beautiful glimpses of a wide expanse, covered with rich farms—for the Nacoochee valley is fertile, and its vicinity is thickly settled.

The other visitors at Clarksville considered us aristocrats because we maintained the dignity of a red wagon on our journey to Tallulah Falls. They had usually accomplished the route in the somewhat fatiguing but cautious ox-cart. The famous falls, unquestionably among the grandest objects of natural scenery in America, are thirteen miles from Clarksville, and a portion of the journey lies over a new road through the forest, which I may safely condemn as execrable.

On the border of a vast rent in the hills stands a little hotel built of pine boards. From its verandas you look up at ravine-sides of solid brown stone; down into leaping and foaming rapids, which seem singing war songs; over the tops of swaying pines, which, in the rich moonlight of a delicious autumn evening, stand out, black and frightful, like spectres; and along paths cut in the steep descents, leading to rocky projections and treacherous knolls.

These falls were named by the Cherokees, who called them Tarrurah or Tallulah—"the terrible." The stream in which they are formed is the western branch of the Tugaloo river, and the rapids are, perhaps, ten miles from its junction with the Chattooga. For more than a mile the impetuous stream passes through a ridge of mountains, with awful parapets of stone piled upon either side, and finally rattles away through the "Grand Chasm."

The rocky banks are in some places five hundred, in others not more than two hundred feet high; their bases are worn into fantastic and grotesque forms by the action of the dashing waters; and the stream, at no point very wide, breaks into four cataracts, which vary from fifty to eighty feet in height, and into many others from twenty to thirty. From the highest points on the cliffs to the bottom of the river-bed, at one or two localities, the depth is nearly 1,000 feet; and the spectator, dizzy and awe-struck, can but do as we did—look once, and turn his frightened and bewildered eyes away!

The "Lodore," the "Tempestia," the "Oceana," and the "Serpentine," are the names given to the four principal falls. The third fall, sometimes called the "Hurricane," is the most remarkable and interesting. Climbing to a rock directly overhanging it, and beneath which the waters are breaking across irregular shelving masses of stone, and foaming and dancing in passion in a whirlpool eighty feet below, one may gaze down stream to the sortie from the cañon.

There the whole valley seems to pitch violently forward, as if it were the entrance to Avernus; its rocky sides are mottled with lichens and the beautiful colt's-foot; and on the crests of the cliffs flourish pines, hemlocks, masses of ferns, and a profusion of grays and browns which no painter's brush can reproduce. Many trees lean as if looking shudderingly, and drawn involuntarily, toward the abyss. Beyond is a sheer precipice draped in hemlocks only, and still beyond, a projection which, when I saw it, was ablaze with the strong autumn colors of the leaves, red, and scarlet, and yellow, above which runs up a hundred and fifty feet of naked, glittering rock, towering tremendously above the tallest trees, and standing in giant relief against the sky.

Coming back to the banks near the "Hurricane" fall, we noticed that the ledges bent downward in three or four immense layers of dark flint, and that grasses grew over them, like strange beards upon monsters' faces. Here and there an old white tree-trunk hung tottering on the ravine's edges. The descent to this fall is down a gully almost perpendicular in steepness: one is also compelled to pass through the "Needle's Eye," a low passage beneath rocks, and the "Post-office," where it was once the custom for the hundreds of visitors to write their names upon the smooth walls of a cave.

The cascades themselves are not so remarkable as the scenery around them. The rocks and the precipices are so gigantic that the stream seems but a silvery thread among them. Seen from the dizzy height known as "The Devil's Pulpit," or "The Lover's Leap," the cascades are like tiny lace veils, spread in the valley, or like frostbeds, such as one sees on meadows in the morning.

Toccoa Falls, Northern Georgia.   [Page 525.]

The effect of a sojourn among the rocks at Lover's Leap at night, when the moonlight is brilliant, is magical. Far below you the valley seems sheathed in molten silver; the song of the cascades is borne, now fiercely, now gently, to your ears by the varying breezes; while you grovel among the slippery pine and hemlock sprays and twigs, clinging to a rock, which is your only protection against a fall of a thousand feet down to the jagged peaks below.

At the "Grand Chasm," which is properly the end of the ravine, where the stream, free from its barriers, becomes tranquil,—after it has fought its way around the base of a mountain of dark granite,—the formation of rock changes. There are no more of the slanting shelves, of the Avernus gates; but instead, there are rounded battlements, which, sloping and yielding, end in a ragged hill-side, strewn with bowlders, with blackened hemlocks, and with tree-trunks prone, as if waiting for some landslide to hurl them into the stream.

On the right looms up another cliff, with a slope like that of walls rising from a castle-moat; this is thatched with foliage; hemlocks straggle along its summit; and in the recesses of the thickets which stretch in all directions from it, the holly spreads its thorny leaves, and the laurel its pendants.

Finally the stream is lost to view and flows under rocks, through a symmetrical gap half a mile away,—beyond which one can see a succession of peaks, whose heads are wrapped in cloud.

After "Tallulah," the falls of Toccoa, a single spray jet, falling one hundred and eighty-five feet, over a shelving rock, is a relief. Seated in a quiet and forest-enshrouded valley, through which Toccoa creek runs, one can look up to the pouring waters with a sense of admiration, but without the awe inspired by the chasms and cascades of "The Terrible." Toccoa is situated near Toccoa City, an ambitious fledgling town on the Air Line railroad, and thousands of visitors yearly watch its tremendous leap from the crag, around which a steep road winds along the ascents that conduct to "Tallulah."

The copper region of Northern Georgia is a continuation of the remarkable one in Eastern Tennessee. A vein of copper seventeen feet thick has been found in one of the counties. In Fannin county there are large bodies of marble, and there is an iron-field on the southern slopes of the Iron mountain range. A great deal has been said about the gold mines in the northern counties. There are, no doubt, extensive deposits there. The mines in the Nacoochee valley, when first worked, on a very small scale, and with rude machinery, yielded from $2,000 to $3,000 to each workman yearly; and several millions of dollars have been obtained from the deposits since 1828. The Loud, Sprague, and Lewis mines, in the vicinity of Nacoochee, are believed to be exceptionally rich. In Rabun, Habersham, Carroll, and White counties there are known to be extensive deposits. In the Nacoochee valley immense works for carrying out the California hydraulic process were erected before the war; but have since that time been only feebly worked.

In the section between the Tray and Yonah mountains some few diamonds have from time to time been found. Not far from this point are the head-waters of the Tennessee, which, passing through Rabun Gap, plunge downward through the Appalachian, the Smoky, the Chilhowee, and Cumberland ranges, until, merged in a broad and noble stream, they enter the fertile fields of Tennessee and Alabama. There, too, the Savannah rises; there the waters of the rain-storm divide, and flow in separate directions in the channels of the two mighty rivers. It is said that several good gold mines in Hall county have been opened, and worked as low as the water-level, and that they pay a small but steady profit. In Hall county is also situated the "Harris Lode," a notable silver mine; and in the neighboring divisions of Lumpkin, Forsyth and Clarke, topaz,

amethysts, beryl, gold, plumbago, iron, granite, and gneiss have been found.*
In Clarke county, where the Georgia University is located, there is remarkable
water power, and some cotton and woolen factories have been erected.

This mountain region, so rich in resource, has been as yet but little developed.
With the completion of the railroad system, which is very comprehensive, and
puts almost every county within easy reach of markets, the more enterprising of
the present residents think that new population and new methods of agriculture
will come in.

The valley lands now readily yield twenty to thirty bushels of corn and fifteen
of wheat to the acre, without manures, and with no culture of consequence; deep
ploughing and rotation of crops would treble these amounts. The local farmers
need the example of Northern agriculture before their eyes. With lands which
will produce infinitely finer and larger crops of clover and timothy than
those of Massachusetts, they still send to the Bay State for their hay. But living
is cheaper than in the Western States, game is plentiful, and good land,
"improved" in the Georgia sense, is to be had at reasonable prices.

*At Dahlonega, in Lumpkin county, a pretty town commanding fine mountain views, the
United States has a branch mint, and gold mines are quite extensively worked in the vicinity.

A Mail-Carrier.

LIX.

CHATTANOOGA, THE GATEWAY OF THE SOUTH

AT a little distance from the locality known as Bird's Mill, not far from
the boundary line between Tennessee and Georgia, and within the limits
of the former State, there stands, among tangled underbrush, a massive yet
simple monument. Around it the envious brier has crept, and the humbler
headstones which here and there dot the thicket are also hedged about with

Mission Ridge, near Chattanooga, Tennessee. [Page 528.]

weeds and creepers. Neglect and oblivion seem, to the hasty observer, to have
so effectually covered the spot with their wings, that even the dwellers in the
neighborhood hardly know whom or what the marble and the stone represent.

Yet these obscure memorials call to mind some of the most touching and
remarkable episodes in our history as a nation. They point backward, through
the miraculous years of the last half century, to the time when the Cherokees held
all the country about them; to the time of the mission-schools, and the heroic
efforts of the "American Board" to establish them. A weather-beaten inscription
on the marble monument discloses the fact that beneath it is the resting-place of
the good Dr. Worcester, first Secretary of the Board, and an enthusiastic laborer
among the Cherokees. A hundred rods away stands one of the old mission-
houses, now a decaying ruin, inhabited by a horde of negroes. Cherokee and
missionary have gone their ways together; there is not one to be encountered in

any nook of the forest; the current of Fate has swept the Indian to the West, and the priests who labored for him into almost forgotten graves.

At the beginning of the present century the Indian still held the territory of North-western Georgia secure against the intrusion of the white man's laws, and also roamed over extensive tracts in Alabama, Tennessee and North Carolina. In the deep coves between the parallel ranges of the Cumberland, along the vast palisades by the winding Tennessee, and through the furrowed and ridgy lands extending toward Virginia and Kentucky, he wandered unrestrained. But the pale-race was on his track, anxious first to gain his good-will, and then to reason him into a cession of his beautiful lands. It was with the bitterness of despair in his heart that one of the chieftains said he had "learned to fear the white man's friendship more than his anger."

But the Cherokees did not seem to dread or detest the missionaries of the American Board. They knew them for men without guile or desire for personal gain, and they learned to love them. When good Cyrus Kingsbury founded the mission of Brainard, in 1817, on the banks of that Chickamauga whose waters, a few years since, ran red with the blood of civil war, it was with the cordial consent of all the principal chiefs. Schools and churches were founded; log mission-houses erected; even the President of the United States allowed the use of the public funds for the building of a school-house for girls. Kingsbury, Cornelius, Evarts and Worcester became eloquent champions of the Indians when their rights were assailed, and each missionary successively risked his liberty and life for the much wronged aborigines. At last a crisis arrived. The State of Georgia began to extend her criminal jurisdiction over the lands claimed by the Cherokees, and with scorn disregarded all efforts of the Indians to protect themselves by an appeal to the Supreme Court of the United States. Angered because the missionaries sided with the Cherokees in the exciting question, the officers of the Georgia Government imprisoned the noble Worcester and one of his fellow-laborers in the penitentiary, for "illegal residence among the Indians," and "because they gave advice on political matters." This last charge the missionaries solemnly denied, but refused of their own will to quit their posts, and the pardon which had been offered them was withdrawn. While they spent weary months in prison, the Cherokees were occupied with internal dissension, and with ineffectual resistance to the encroaching Georgians. At last the treaties which virtually banished the Indians from their homes were signed, and in 1838 the troops gathered up into one long and sorrowful procession thousands of men, women and children, and hurried them from the State. Depleted and worn down by every imaginable privation, more than 4,000 of the unfortunates died on their long march of 600 miles to their new homes west of the Mississippi,— forming a ghastly sacrifice to commemorate the white man's greed.

Leaving the brier-invaded grave-yard and the tumbling mission-houses, and climbing to the summit of Mission Ridge, a vision of perfect beauty is before one. To the east is Chickamauga valley, following the course of the historic creek, and dotted with pleasant farms and noble groves; westward one looks down upon a rich and broad interval, bounded by high bluffs with rocky faces, along whose bases the noble stream of the Tennessee flows with many an eccentric turn, until, as if amazed and startled at the grandeur of Lookout mountain, which rises just within the vale to 2,400 feet above the sea-level, it turns inland once more in a western course, becoming rapid and turbulent as it descends through gorges and forests, to Northern Alabama. "Lookout" is an outlier of the Cumberland table-land, and extends across the Tennessee line into Georgia. One may travel for more than forty miles along its breezy height without finding anywhere a really advantageous point at which to descend. Between Mission Ridge and Lookout mountain lies Chattanooga valley, the "Crow's Nest," as the Indians called it, and as its name signifies. It is, indeed, not unlike a nest or cup securely set down among huge mountain barriers, through which one can discern no pass,

Lookout Mountain, near Chattanooga, Tennessee.

and which only the birds can afford to despise. Everywhere ridges, sharply-projecting spurs from the Cumberland, caves, forests, rocks, bluffs! How can traffic find its way through such a country?

Far below, as you stand on Mission Ridge, with "Lookout's" shadow thrown across the brilliant sunlight, falling on the slopes up which Grant sent his men on that day of blood in 1863, you may see the city of Chattanooga, "the gateway of the South." On the present site of the town, the south bank of the Tennessee river, there stood, in 1835, a Cherokee trading post. In 1837 a good many white families from Virginia and the Carolinas had moved there, and a post-office called Ross's Landing was established. The original lots into which the town was partitioned were disposed of by lottery, after the expulsion of the Indians, and the vast commerce that to-day uses the Tennessee's current as the chief transporting medium soon created quite a trading post. From upper Eastern Tennessee came iron and ironware, corn, wheat and whiskey, and Virginia sent down great quantities of salt. In 1838 a new town was started and christened Chattanooga.* Ten years later, railroad communication, via Atlanta, with Charleston and Savannah, gave the little town 40,000 bales of cotton as its annual shipment; and when Robert Cravens began to manufacture charcoal iron there, at a cost of $10 to $14 per ton, shipping it to New Orleans, St. Louis and Cincinnati, for from $30 to $40 per ton, the settlers multiplied very rapidly. The cotton trade was lost to Chattanooga by the building of the Memphis and Charleston railroad, which did away with the painful navigation of the Tennessee up from Alabama, and the portage around " Muscle Shoals;" but the grain and stock trade steadily increased, and in 1861 the town boasted 3,500 population. Then the war came to it.

Planted at the very mouth of the narrow passes, through which trade and travel pick their difficult way, Chattanooga has sprung, since the war's close, from a village into a prosperous city of 12,000 inhabitants. Its aspect to-day is that of a North-western settlement, Northern and Western men having flocked to it in large numbers. The men who campaigned among the mountains around it, and who fought so desperately to get to it, year after year, noted its wonderful advantages as a railway centre in one of the richest mineral regions in the world, and when they were mustered out settled there. The march of progress began. It was a revelation to the people of the surrounding country—that steady and rapid improvement at Chattanooga. They had always known that there were coal, iron and oil in the vicinity in such quantities that, in the words of a public speaker who once upbraided them for their lack of enterprise, "within sight of the city might be found Pittsburg ploughs that had been worn out upon the iron ore lying loosely on the hill-sides; " yet they had not dreamed that with cheap iron and cheap coal at their doors they had the elements of empire in their hands. To-day Chattanooga is connected with the outer world by five trunk lines of rail, and the surveys for the sixth, and in some respects the most remarkable, have been completed. The Western and Atlantic connects the city with Atlanta and the South; the Nashville and Chattanooga line pierces the Cumberland, and gives a route to Louisville and the Ohio; the East Tennessee, Virginia, and Georgia road reaches to Bristol, giving direct connection with Lynchburg, Washington and New York; the Alabama and Chattanooga runs through marvelous coal and iron fields to Meridian, in Mississippi, whence there is a direct line to the "Father of Waters," and the Memphis and Charleston opens up a vast fertile section in Northern Alabama and a corner of Mississippi, a section unhappily strewn at present with wrecks of once prosperous plantations. The track of the war is visible through all the beautiful Tennessee valley, and for miles one sees nothing but ruins and neglected lands. The "Cincinnati Southern" railroad is intended to run from the Ohio metropolis to Chattanooga, and

* This was done at the suggestion of Mr. John P. Long, one of the prominent citizens of Chattanooga, who is very familiar with the Indian language and legends.

will operate as an outlet from the Ohio valley to the south-eastern seaboard, while it will also furnish a desirable connection with the Gulf system of roads. It will penetrate some of the richest regions of Kentucky, will cross the Cumberland river at Point Burnside, and run through the Sequatchie valley, along an almost unbroken coal-field.

With so many important and really finely - built lines of travel stretching from it in all directions, one would naturally suspect Chattanooga of an inclination to

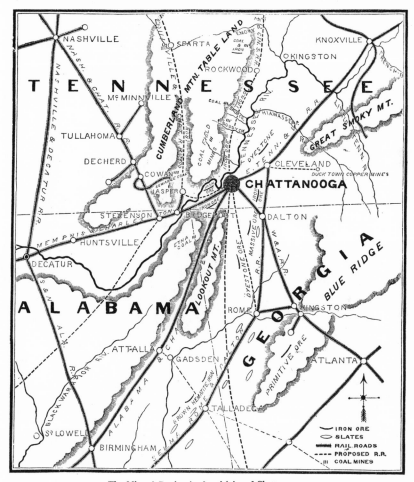

The Mineral Region in the vicinity of Chattanooga.

disregard her river traffic, yet she is by no means unmindful of it. Operating as the distributing point for the whole river-valley, and indeed for the far South, the city crowds her storehouses yearly with corn, wheat, and bacon, brought hundreds of miles in flat-boats and small steamers along the winding river from Kentucky, Virginia and North Carolina. At high water season the stream is crowded with rustic crafts of all kinds, and the jolly raftsmen who have been for months in the forests, and have drifted down stream on broad platforms of pine logs, make merry in highways and by-ways. Transportation of coal

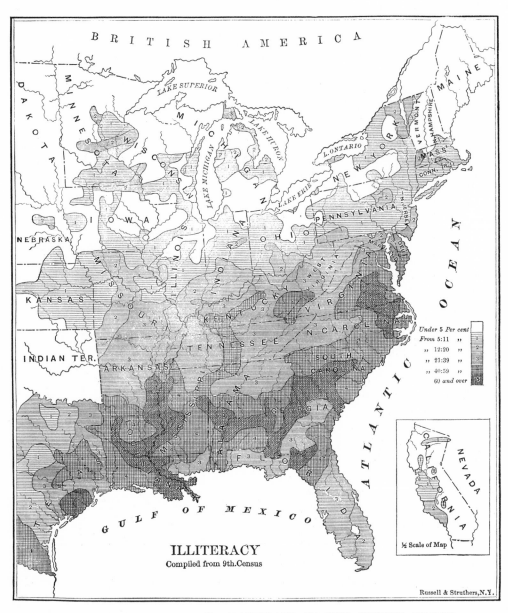

ILLITERACY
Compiled from 9th. Census

Under 5 Per cent
From 5:11 „
„ 12:20 „
„ 21:39 „
„ 40:59 „
60 and over

½ Scale of Map

Russell & Struthers, N.Y.

MAP SHOWING GRADES OF ILLITERACY IN THE UNITED STATES.

MIDDLE ATLANTIC STATES, SOUTHERN SECTION, AND NORTH CAROLINA. By A. Guyot.

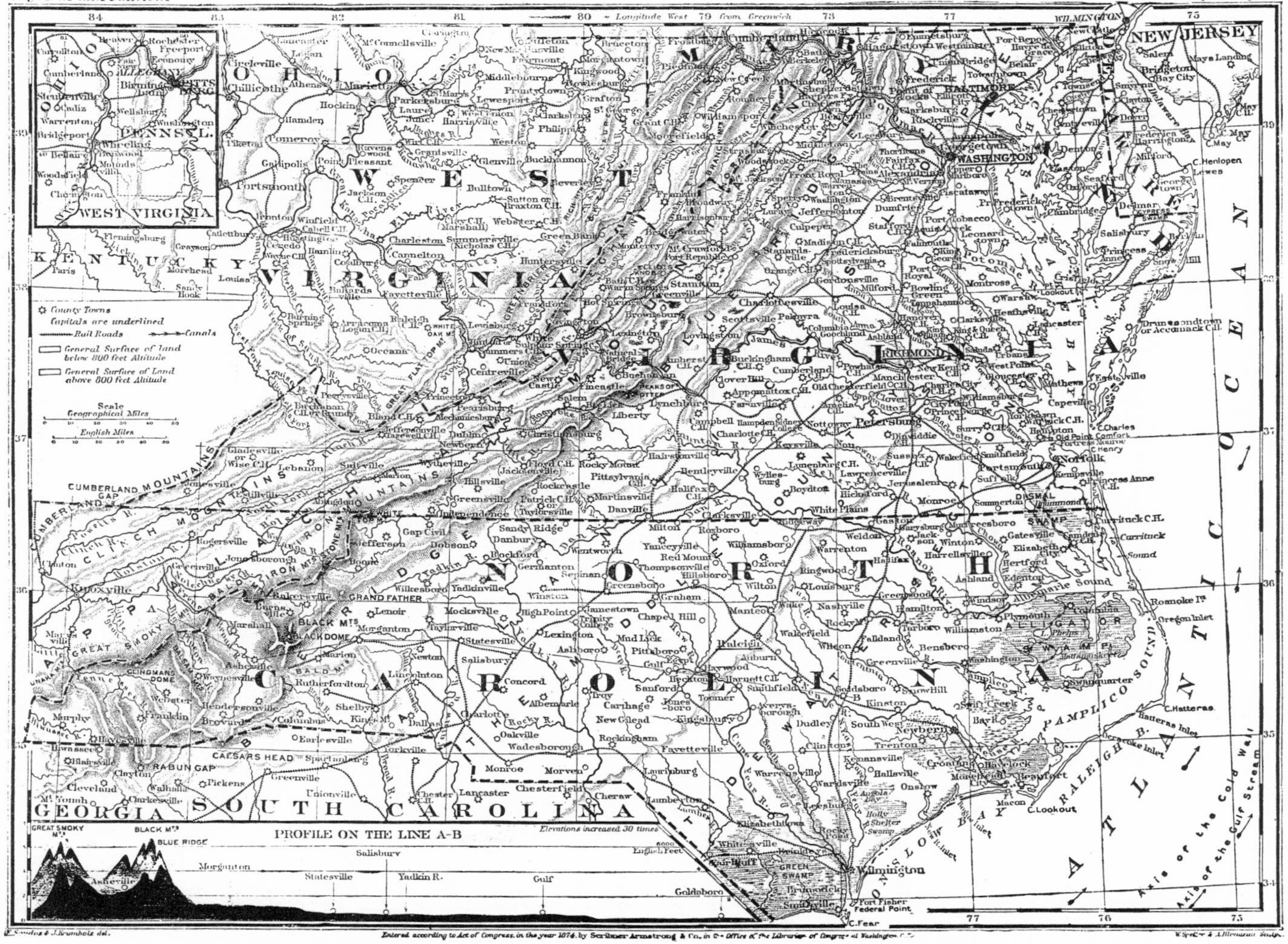

Physical and Political

PROFILE ON THE LINE A—B

Entered according to Act of Congress in the year 1874 by Scribner, Armstrong & Co., in the Office of the Librarian of Congress at Washington.

and iron by river would not cost more than one-fourth the sum demanded by the railways.

The surroundings of Chattanooga are of the wildest and most romantic beauty, and in gazing down from " Lookout," or from the humbler Mission Ridge, upon the lovely valley, with its majestic river and lordly ledges, one cannot repress a fear that some day all these natural beauties will be hidden by the smoke from the five hundred chimneys which will be erected in honor of the god Iron.   For it is to be a town of rolling-mills and furnaces, giant in its traffic, like Pittsburg and St. Louis, and inhabited by thousands of hard-handed, brawny-armed artisans.   There is hardly a county in Eastern Tennessee where the resources destined to make Chattanooga one of the commercial centres of the country do not abound.   Along the Great Unaka chain, in those counties bordering upon the Smoky, over which we passed on our way to the North Carolina mountains, lie some of the richest sections of the "eastern iron belt"—which extends northward into Virginia and southward into Georgia.   In the " Valley," that rich and populous quarter of Tennessee, on whose ridges and in whose nooks are raised some of the noblest physical specimens of the American man, the mineral development seems incredible.   In what is known as the "Dyestone Belt" the immense layers of red hematite run without a break for 150 miles, swelling sometimes to eight or ten feet in thickness, but never sinking below five. One hundred pounds of this stratified red-iron rock, soft and easily crushed, will yield seventy pounds of pure iron.   It is the same ore which, outcropping in Virginia, has for years supplied the splendid furnaces of Eastern Pennsylvania, and extending through North-eastern Georgia into Alabama, is known as the " Red Mountain " ore of the latter State.   And this grand belt lies at the very base of the coal-measures !

The East Tennessee valley extends north-east and south-west about 280 miles from Chattanooga to the Virginia line.   North-west of it is the Cumberland table-land, which Andrew Jackson was wont to declare would one day be the garden of the United States; and one of the outlines of this plateau, extending from the vicinity of Chattanooga to Cumberland Gap, is known as "Walden's Ridge." This is the south-eastern limit of the great Appalachian coal-field, which covers 6,000 square miles—considerably more than the entire coal area of Great Britain.   All the ridges in the " Valley " contain minerals; they are ribbed with iron ore of every variety.   In some cases the veins of red fossiliferous ore extend under the coal-fields.

The numerous rivers heading in the North Carolina and Western Virginia mountains drain north-west toward the Tennessee, and form natural highways upon which to bear the ore to the beds of coal.   The stores of red and brown hematites in the Alleghany chain and the Cumberland range are absolutely inexhaustible.   This grand mineral-field is blessed with a delicious climate, which the high mountain walls render temperate in winter and cool and entirely free from malaria in summer.

Before 1860 numbers of furnaces were worked in the " Dyestone Belt," and excellent ore was produced ; but an especial impetus has been given to the production of that section since the war. General John T. Wilder, of Ohio, while campaigning under Rosecrans against Chattanooga, in 1863, at the head of a brigade of mounted infantry, became interested in the hills, from which might be blasted thousands of tons of ore in a day, in the great veins of hematites, sometimes covering hundreds of acres, and in that mighty stretch of 200 miles along the now famous ridge, where coal and iron lie only half a mile apart, with massive limestone between them. When he laid by his sword, he continued the study of these mineral deposits, and after purchasing the site on which· the village and furnaces of Rockwood now stand, associated with himself a company of capitalists, and in 1867 organized the Roane Iron

The Rockwood Iron-Furnaces—Eastern Tennessee.

Company, with a capital of $1,000,000. This company purchased the rail-mill at Chattanooga, which had been built by the Federal Government; tunneled the Cumberland mountain for coal; and in 1868 began to manufacture pig-iron cheaper than it has been made elsewhere in the country, and to supply it to the rolling-mills, sending it down the Tennessee river in steamers and barges.* Rockwood is now a brisk village of 2,000 inhabitants, of whom about one-half are workmen in the furnaces and the coal mines. It is situ-

---

* According to the census of 1870, there were then in Tennessee fourteen establishments manufacturing pig-iron, with twenty-three blast-furnaces and $1,103,750 capital, producing 28,688 tons, worth $1,147,707. There were eighteen rolling-mills with a capital of $253,750, producing rolled iron worth $369,222, and thirty-three manufactories of cast-iron, with a capital of $331,392, the products of which annually amounted to about $500,000. The number of establishments has much increased since that time.

ated seventy miles north-east of Chattanooga, in the heart of a rugged mountain region.*

The energetic Western men who have it in charge are confident that in a few years the city of Chattanooga will rival Pittsburg in growth, for they

The "John Ross House," near Chattanooga. Residence of one of the old Cherokee Landholders.

claim that they can manufacture iron at least ten or twelve dollars per ton cheaper than it can be made anywhere else in the United States. It would certainly be remarkable if a mineral region so vast and well stocked as that of Northern Georgia, Northern Alabama, and Eastern Tennessee,—in the midst of which Chattanooga stands,—should not produce at least one city of a hundred thousand inhabitants within a few years. The new aspirant for the honors of rapid growth has made sterling progress. Cotton-mills and car works are springing up beside the rolling-mills and foundries; many fine mansions already grace the principal residence streets, and hundreds of mechanics are building neat cottages along the slopes on both sides of the Tennessee. Swiss capital is engaged in the manufacture of cotton, and English investors are carefully studying the iron and coal fields with a view

* Twenty-five thousand tons of ore are mined at Rockwood yearly, and about 12,000 tons of pig-iron are sent thence to Chattanooga, Atlanta, St. Louis, and Louisville. The rolling-mill at Chattanooga produces about 15,000 tons of rails annually. The impetus given to the growth of Chattanooga by the establishment of this mill and the Vulcan Iron Works has been tremendous. The price paid the Government for the rolling-mill and 145 acres of land at Chattanooga by the Roane Iron Company, was $225,000. The patent puddling apparatus of an Englishman named Danks—an apparatus which is expected to revolutionize iron manufacture by an immense saving in cost—has been introduced into the works. The cost of ore at the Rockwood furnaces is about $2 per ton; that of coal, $1.40 per ton; limestone, eighty cents. It is not astonishing, in view of these prices, that the company hope eventually to manufacture rails and deliver them in Pittsburg cheaper than they can be made there.

to finally erecting large rolling-mills in the city; banks, good hotels, well-planned streets, and excellent schools and churches have arisen like magic within seven years; and the constant stream of produce transferred from the river to the rail-roads gives an activity and feverishness to the aspect of the streets, at certain seasons, which is quite inspiring. Even within the town limits iron ore is to be found. It lies in the north-west slopes of "Cameron Hill," a high bluff from which one can overlook the Tennessee and the busy town stretched along its banks, even to the base of "Lookout." In the Eastern, Dyestone, and Western iron belts of Tennessee there were more small furnaces before the war than at present; but it is doubtful if so much iron was manufactured then as now. Capital is fast finding out the best locations for furnaces and rolling-mills in each of the three States whose commercial centre Chattanooga properly is, and hundreds of thou-sands of acres have recently been purchased by companies, who will probably develop them within the next five years.

Catching a "Tarpin."

LX.

LOOKOUT MOUNTAIN—THE BATTLES AROUND CHATTANOOGA. KNOXVILLE—EASTERN TENNESSEE.

MOST persons in this country or in Europe who have heard of Lookout mountain since "the war" have also been told of the "battle above the clouds." It was my fortune to scale the remarkable palisade at a time when the broad plateau which runs along its summit was literally enshrouded in formidable mists. The rain was falling in torrents as, with two companions, I galloped through the little town at the foot of the mountain; but ere we had scaled the winding road, the shower was over, and a brisk wind began to stir the

View from Lookout Mountain, near Chattanooga.

mists. We could see little but the ledges along whose sides the route ran, but as we arrived nearly at the summit, the mist-curtain was lifted for an instant, and revealed to us a delicious expanse of valley, with sunlight's smiles here and there chasing away the rain's tears. Then we were shrouded in again; and our horses, apparently inspired by the gloomy grandeur of the occasion, rattled furiously along the hard roads, over which the boughs hung uncomfortably near our heads. The red sandy clay nourishes enormous pines, whose roots have here and there been disturbed by the sandstone bowlders, and stretched out their fibres in a desperate grasp; beside the pathways great blocks of stone, carved by the storms and polished by the winds, are scattered. We galloped nearly to the massive perpendicular wall which arises directly out of the valley, and disdainfully frowns down upon the Tennessee, spurned from its base fourteen hundred feet below; and tethering our horses, approached to the very edge. There we seemed shut off from all the world. Now and then a hum from the valley—the growl of a locomotive or the rolling of wheels—came faintly up; we heard the cow-bells and the bleating of the sheep on the hill-sides behind us; and just as we were trying to imagine how "the battle" must have been, the wind came sweeping away the mist-curtain, and—we beheld the whole!

Umbrella Rock, on Lookout Mountain.

From "Umbrella Rock" we saw "the Moccasin," that curious point of land made by the Tennessee's abrupt turn. The streets and houses of Chattanooga seemed like toys, or little blocks of wood. Mission Ridge was an insignificant blue line. The Tennessee seems to turn in deference to Chattanooga, for it might readily inundate it, and has once compelled the citizens to navigate their streets in boats. Beyond it, northward and westward, the eye encounters forests and ridges where the mountains seem to have been split asunder by some convulsion of nature—until at last, on the east, the Cumberland range springs up, and forbids you to choose any other horizon. Southward, beyond broad and quiet vales, richly cultured, are the mountains of Georgia, and westward the tree-crested ridges in Alabama.

We clambered down a flight of wooden steps to a secure point of the crags, and looked over the valley out of which Hooker hurried his troops on to the summit when he broke the left of Bragg's formidable army. It was a wild struggle, a running and leaping fight among rocks and behind trees, when men carried their lives in their hands, and their swords in their teeth, as they wormed their way through the fastnesses, and then made their charge upon the foe so strongly intrenched above the very clouds, upon "Point Lookout."

The old Government hospital still stands on its picturesque bluff, deserted now save by curious visitors; here and there along the broad plateau are scattered comfortable houses, and log-cabins; good roads lead into the northern counties of Georgia. Near "Rock City,"—a gigantic series of galleries in disrupted stone pinnacles which rise amid the ragged brush and saplings,—is another enormous uplift of limestone, from which one may see the whole of Chattanooga valley, the Raccoon and Lookout ranges, and the battle-field of Chickamauga. Descending five or six miles from the point where the turnpike from the city reaches the summit, into the valley of Walker county, in Northern Georgia, one comes to a region of precipices and waterfalls, of tarns and caves, of landslides and bluffs.

Near "Lake Seclusion," an apparently bottomless well, sunk a hundred feet below the surrounding rocks, the scenery is exquisite. In autumn the foliage on the cliffs bordering the stream which flows through this lake, and plunges farther on down a ravine in a blinding spray-cloud, which the Indians named "Lulah Falls," is so rich in color that the whole country seems aflame. From one or two of the highest points the ragged ends of the Lookout plateau, and the pleasant expanse of valley beyond, may be seen.

Riding day by day along the broad tables of the Cumberland, in the nooks on the banks of the Tennessee, and up and over the ridges near the scene of Chickamauga, it was pleasant to hear anew the story of the great fight around Chattanooga from the lips of those who had been participants. But it was all unreal, dreamlike. When we stood with our feet in half-filled rifle-pits, or

Looking from "Lookout Cave."

among the shattered and cannon-scorched tree-trunks on the field of combat, it was still remote, indefinite. I fancy even the natives of the country round about only remember the whole struggle vaguely now and then; although a Chattanooga man once said to a newcomer from the West that when he wanted some paper which the invading army had burned up for him, or remembered the losses of property he had suffered, he "hated the whole Yankee nation for a minute or two;" but he added, "it's only for a minute or two, and those minutes don't come as often as they did."

Chattanooga's possession by the Union army cost many thousands of lives; but it opened the way to Atlanta and the sea. The line which stretched from Lookout's northern crag to Mission Ridge, on the night of November 24th, 1863, might have been quadrupled in strength if the dead warriors from Murfreesboro and Chickamauga could have been marshaled into it. There was an especial bitterness in the struggle for this rocky gateway. After the staggering blows which both armies had received in the terrible fight by Stone river, Bragg and Rosecrans were both willing enough to rest for a little; but when Bragg had withdrawn, and it was evident that his formidable campaign, which had carried terror even to the gates of Louisville and Cincinnati, was at an end, the Union standards led the way to Chattanooga. There, strongly intrenched, Bragg defied his old antagonist. On the morning of August 21st, 1863, General

Wilder, commanding the advance of Rosecrans' army, began shelling the city which he now makes his home, from the hills at the north side of the river.

Meantime day by day the Federal forces were investing Chattanooga, having crossed the Tennessee at Bridgeport, at Battle Creek, and at Shell Mound. On the 4th of September Burnside occupied Knoxville. Bragg moved the Confederate forces away toward Dalton, and Rosecrans entered the town, and followed the enemy, who turned fiercely, and stood at bay on Chickamauga. Longstreet's Virginians and Bragg's hardy army fought with the energy of desperation; and if, on that memorable 19th of September, when the combatants waded in blood, Longstreet had had another than Thomas to encounter, he might have carried the Federal left which he so furiously attacked. Thomas drove Longstreet back a mile or two, but, as the centre failed to keep pace with his advance, he was compelled to halt.

Then Bragg fell upon the forces under command of McCook and Crittenden, and the waves of battle flowed to and fro until night, when the Federal army still held its own ground. Early in the morning Thomas had the enemy once more hurled at him, but repulsed him as before. The Union right and centre were driven back; McCook was confused and demoralized; Thomas alone stood like a rock, and kept the enemy at arm's length until night, when he fell back to Rossville, to be attacked again, and to once more repulse his foes the next day. Fifteen thousand men had been lost to the Union army, in killed, wounded and missing, in these two days; and the Confederates had lost 18,000. The field of Chickamauga was piled with the dead, and the rivulets literally ran blood.

The flushed and defiant enemy now stood ready to again fall upon Chattanooga. They had struck some terrible blows. Rosecrans, McCook, and Crittenden, were removed from command. The Confederate forces occupied Lookout mountain and controlled the valley, cutting off rail and river communication. Provisions were hauled over the rough hill-roads and through the narrow passes on the north side

"Rock City," Lookout Mountain. [Page 537.]

of the river, for seventy miles, by animals worn to skeletons, and by men who were half starved; and so, on mountain and in forest, along the valleys and the rivers, the vigilant combatants stood, patiently awaiting the next move, when there came upon the scene a man named Grant.

As soon as General Grant had taken command of the military division of the Mississippi, communication, both by river and rail, was gradually re-established, and Chattanooga was unlocked. Sherman reinforced the army there in mid-November. Grant's next move was to allow Longstreet to do what he had several times unsuccessfully tried, pass the Federal army to the east of Chattanooga and march against Burnside and the army of the Ohio. Longstreet had 20,000 splendid soldiers, and Burnside far less; it might fare hardly with the latter, but it was one of the moves on Grant's chessboard, and there was nothing to be said. It resulted in checkmating Bragg at Mission Ridge.

Twenty thousand men having been taken from the line which the Confederates had stretched along the Lookout plateau,—eastwardly across Chattanooga valley to Mission Ridge, at or near Rossville Gap, and thence northwardly

View from Wood's Redoubt, Chattanooga.

on the Ridge toward Chickamauga creek,—by the departure of Longstreet, that line was attacked. The plan was to assault the wings, to cause Bragg to throw large forces to their protection, and then to break the centre.

Hooker and Sherman began working in earnest. The 24th of November saw the left of the enemy driven from Lookout, and the right forced out of its position. Next day the wave of war swept up Mission Ridge, over the charming slopes where now the great National cemetery is situated, up to the summit; and at sunset General Grant moved his head-quarters from Wood's Redoubt to the Ridge, which in the morning had been guarded by sentinels in gray. The enemy was next day driven from his base of supplies.

The siege was over. The pathway to the sea lay before Sherman.

Wood's Redoubt is still one of the most striking objects in the valley of Chattanooga. Standing on the grass-grown ramparts one has an exquisite view of Lookout, the Tennessee's abrupt recoil at its base, and the sharp peak of Eagle Point, and can note the two turns of the river, with the Moccasin Point between, around whose southern bend, on a November midnight in 1863, Sherman moved 3,000 soldiers in pontoons. Northward, and opposite the redoubts, overhanging the Tennessee, is Cameron Hill, from whose wind-swept height one can look down upon Chattanooga's busy streets as from a balloon. On the slopes adjacent to Cameron Hill there are many handsome residences, and Wood's

Redoubt itself will in a few years be lost sight of under the foundations of some charming villa. On many of the hills a faint outline of the old fortifications may be traced; but they will soon have vanished forever.

It would be difficult to imagine more romantic approaches than those through which the Nashville and Chattanooga railroad finds its way to the latter city. For seventy-five or eighty miles it runs through a bold, mountainous country; but about twenty-five miles before reaching Chattanooga it bends downward into the mighty passes among the Cumberlands in Northern Alabama, and crawling under rocks and on the brinks of chasms, now running on the edges of valleys clothed in perfect forests, and now shooting into long tunnels, works its way to the valley. As one approaches Lookout by this route, the effect is extremely imposing; a new and striking view is presented at each instant; the cliffs seem to present no outlet; the train is apparently about to be cast down some yawning ravine, when one sees the continuation of the route.

Sixty-two miles from Chattanooga, on a spur of the Cumberland, at Sewanee, in Tennessee, is situated the " University of the South." This remarkable institution owes its origin to the late Bishop Leonidas Polk, of Louisiana. He desired to concentrate the interests of the several Southern dioceses of the Episcopal Church upon one school where religious education might be given in a thorough manner; and in 1836 he issued an address to the bishops of the various States of the South, proposing to establish a Christian University. The result was a large assembly of bishops and lay delegates at a meeting on Lookout Mountain's summit, in 1837, at which the general principles of union were discussed; and the city of Sewanee was chosen some time thereafter. The Tennessee Legislature granted a liberal charter, and a domain of ten thousand acres of land had been secured, five hundred thousand dollars obtained toward an endowment, and the corner-stone of the central building laid, when the war began. In 1866 very little remained save the domain; but in 1868, after some aid from England, the University was definitely established, and the more important of the schools are now well organized, with able professors at their head. The institution is under the perpetual control of a board of trustees composed of the bishops of the various Southern States, the senior bishop being, *ex officio,* Chancellor of the University.

The location is charming. The University was started in the midst of an almost unbroken forest, but has now grouped around it a pleasant and refined community. It is about nine miles from the Nashville and Chattanooga railroad, and the great tunnel on that road passes under its lands. From Cowan, on the line, to Sewanee, the local coal mining company has built a good railroad. The Sewanee plateau is 2000 feet above the sea-level, in a richly-varied country, abounding in cascades, ravines, groves, and uplands.

There is an abundance of building material in the quarries of gray, blue, dove-colored and brown limestone, which lie beside the Sewanee Company's railroad, and as soon as the present insufficient endowment is enlarged, the erection of permanent buildings will be begun. There are chalybeate springs in the vicinity, and the slopes of the Cumberland here are admirably adapted for grape

culture.   Nearly 300 students are gathered into the various schools.   Bishop
Quintard, of Tennessee, has done the University great service in collecting
money in England for its establishment, and he and others are now anxiously
trying to secure $500,000 as an enlargement fund.

Riding through the wooded country on the Tennessee's banks, not far from
Chattanooga, one autumn day, we dismounted, a large and hungry party, before
the door of a log-cabin, built on a hill-side, and hailed the inmates.   A fat negro
woman appeared at the corner of the rude veranda, and four plump negro babies
regarded us through the crevices between the logs with round-eyed fear.
" Reckoned she could n't give us no dinner—no way;" finally was very positive,
and said "she had nothing in the house."   But persistence was rewarded by

On the Tennessee River, near Chattanooga.

permission to return in an hour, and she would see what could be improvised.
At the hour's end we found in the cabin a rough table spread with bacon, and
corn-bread just baked in the ashes; a few sweet potatoes were presently proffered,
and some tea was made.   By the fireside, rocking a black cherub, was another
woman, younger and more comely than our host.   These two cultivated a little
field; their " husbands," or the men of the house,—for marriage is not always
considered necessary among the negroes,—were away at work in another
county; and the children rolled in the dirt, and had no thoughts of school.   It
was the very rudest and most incult life imaginable; the cabin was cleanly,
but primitive in all its furnishings; the round of these people's lives seemed
to be sleeping and waking, with a struggle between morning and evening to

get enough to put into their mouths; they had no thought of thrift or progress. Now and then they went to a religious gathering, and, perhaps, had
"experiences," and were converted; then they gradually relapsed into their
dull condition.

The mountain roads in all the section bordering on the Tennessee are
beautiful. There are many bold bluffs, one and two hundred feet high, which

The "Suck," on the Tennessee River.

overlook the stream.; and one comes upon stretches of fertile fields. The
inhabitants, white or black, are invariably civil and courteous. The farmers,
clad in homespun, mounted on raw-boned horses, are willing and eager to
compare notes with strangers. They have caught a touch of the inspiration
Chattanooga diffuses around itself, and carefully explore their lands in the
hope of finding minerals.

The Tennessee is receiving some improvement here and there. At the point
called the "Suck," where the waters rush through a gorge in the mountains, over
a rocky bed and in a shallow channel, we saw dredge-boats at work. The river
has ordinarily more water than the Ohio, and a permanent bed, with little
or no sand or gravel, so that there is no danger of the formation of those bars
which obstruct the navigation of so many Western rivers.

The attention of the Government has been directed toward the needed
improvements ever since 1828, and the ruins of the Muscle Shoals canal, which
originally cost $700,000, testify to the thoroughness of the plans then made. If
that canal were put in condition again, and the obstructions between Muscle
Shoals and Knoxville were removed, America would be the richer by one grand
water highway.

Knoxville, once the capital of Tennessee, and one of the most illustrious
and venerable of its communities, is situated on the Holston river about 100
miles above Chattanooga. It is to-day as actively engaged in developing the
mighty resources of Eastern Tennessee as is its sister of the valley, and a
generous rivalry exists between the two towns, represented in the newspapers
by good-humored raillery, in which the editors of both cities seem admirable
proficients. Five miles east of Knoxville the lovely French Broad river empties
its dancing and frothing current, released from the passes of the North Carolina
mountains, into the Tennessee. Knoxville was named for that worthy Knox

who was Secretary of War under the presidency of Washington. The town dates from 1794, when Colonel White, proprietor of the lands, laid it out into lots. Three years before, on the 5th of December, 1791, in the midst of Indian massacres and battles, the first Tennessee newspaper was issued by George Roulstone. Although it was printed at Rogersville, it was called *The Knoxville Gazette*, and was identified with the interests of the then territorial seat of government.

The section of which Knoxville thus became the chief town has a most romantic history. In 1760 there was not a single civilized inhabitant in Tennessee. A few daring woodsmen pushed into the wilderness a few years later, and founded settlements on the Watauga and the Holston, to which flocked settlers from North

A Negro Cabin on the bank of the Tennessee. [Page 542.]

Carolina and Virginia. North Carolina, in those days a province, was disquieted by taxation which she considered illegal; and thousands who had been compelled to fly from their homes, because they had actively resisted the oppression of Governor Tryon, took refuge with the adventurers at Watauga. In a few years the surrounding country re-echoed to the blows of the woodsmen's axes, and the Indians began to regard their encroachments with alarm and resentment. But shortly before the outbreak of the Revolution, and the downfall of royal government in North Carolina, the members of the Watauga Association had a peaceable meeting with the Cherokees and their chiefs, and purchased from them, for £2,000, all the lands on which they had settled. The Elizabethton of to-day, a little mountain hamlet, occupies the site of the old Watauga. Shortly after the purchase, the Cherokees began open hostilities, and the Tennessean had then, as for many a long year thereafter, to risk his life daily. Battles ensued; the Indians organized expeditions to cut off and annihilate the infant colonies; war raged through all the North Carolina mountains and along the Unaka range. The result was an invasion of the Cherokee towns by the militia of North Carolina and the settlements. Eighteen hundred men, armed with rifles, tomahawks, and butcher knives,—thus saith the ancient chronicle,—marched across the Holston and the French Broad, and drove the Indians everywhere before them. A pious chaplain accompanied this little army of invasion, and was the first Christian minister that ever preached in Tennessee. Immigration flowed after the army, and the Indians were dismayed. The Watauga settlement, triumphant, petitioned for annexation to North Carolina, and its prayer was granted. The Legislature of that State, in 1777, founded Washington county, which occupied the whole district now included within the present boundaries of Tennessee. Two years later explorers had planted a field with corn on the spot where the present city of Nashville stands.

The recital of the border wars, and of dashing expeditions down the Tennessee river, would require volumes. Men sprang up, rude, hardy, brave—the outgrowth of their time; their brains were filled with visions of empire; they fought by day and planned by night. After the independence of the United States had been acknowledged by Great Britain, each State endeavored to relieve the indebtedness of the country, by cessions to Congress, of their unappropriated lands; and, accordingly, North Carolina ceded her new acquisition, now known as Tennessee. This made political orphans of our brave Watauga settlers and their followers, so they forthwith created an independent State called Franklin, which was ruled over by an energetic and daring man named Sevier, and maintained a stormy existence from 1784 to 1788, during much of which time it was considered by the Government of North Carolina as practically in revolt. Sevier was engaged in many a daring battle and mountain skirmish; was once carried off by his friends at the moment a court in North Carolina was trying him for his offenses; and was, after Franklin became United States territory, sent to Congress. His associates in the Government of Franklin,—Cocke, White, the founder of Knoxville, Ramsey, Doak, Center, Reese, Houston, Newell, Weir and Conway,—were, subsequently, leading spirits in the affairs of Tennessee. Greenville, the present home of ex-President Andrew Johnson, and a pretty village set down graciously among exquisite mountains, was founded in the days of Franklin, and was the original seat of government. In 1785 the third Franklin convention was held there, in a court-house built of unhewn logs, and there the State Constitution was finally adopted.

White's Fort, the location of Knoxville, was, at the time of the fall of Franklin, a stockaded settlement, to which settlers were rapidly flocking. On the high plateau which, extending southward, terminated in a bold bluff on the Holston river, they saw excellent chances for defense; and thus the site of the city was determined. In 1794, Governor Blount, controlling the territory for the United

States, had his cabin at Knoxville, and was kept busy day and night devising measures for the defense of the young settlement against the thoroughly maddened Cherokees. At one time, when the fighting force of Knoxville was forty men, more than fifteen hundred Indians marched against the town, but were turned aside by some trivial circumstance, and the colony was saved.

As Knoxville had been the seat of the Territorial Government, so in 1796 it became the State capital, and there the convention met, and the first Constitution was adopted. There, too, the "Washington College, in honor of the illustrious

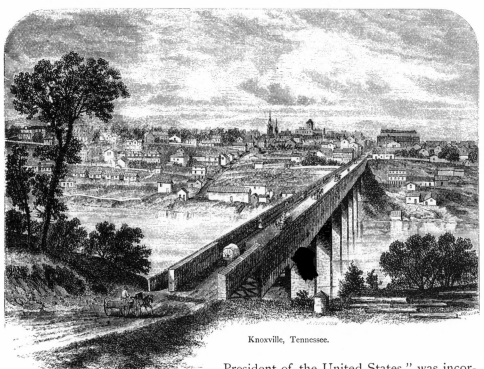

Knoxville, Tennessee.

President of the United States," was incorporated; and there General Jackson, in the convention, suggested that the new State adopt the beautiful Indian name of Tennessee. Knoxville shared the honors of the government seat with Kingston, Murfreesboro, and Nashville alternately, but in 1817 it became the capital for the last time. The centre of population moved beyond the Cumberland mountains, and the State officials went with it. To Knoxville were left the souvenirs of the bloody times in which it sprang into being, of councils with Cherokee chieftains, and struggles against their warriors, before the current of immigration came.

Knoxville is to-day a flourishing town with nearly 15,000 population. It has more capital than Chattanooga, but not the same wonderful transportation facilities. More actual business is, however, probably done there; the town has a large wholesale trade, and is a kind of supply depot for the mountains. On the line of the road from New York to New Orleans, it has hopes of other communication shortly. The subject of narrow-gauge railroads has very much interested the people of Eastern Tennessee, and they will, in a few years, traverse the valleys in all directions. A direct line from Knoxville to Macon in Georgia has been projected; and the completion of the Knoxville and Kentucky roads would be a great aid to the local commerce. The General Government is erecting a fine custom-house and post-office in the city. Thirty miles to the northward are large coal-fields, close to veins of iron; in Carter and Greene counties there are iron mines which supply the rolling-mills and car-wheel establishments at Knoxville. There is an extensive manufacture of glass in that section; the lumber interests are large, and considerable shipments are made to New England. Five miles east of Knoxville is a fine marble quarry, operated by capitalists from St. Louis. At Coal creek and Caryville, some thirty-five miles north of the town, there are extensive coal mining interests. The whole of Eastern Tennessee offers the best of inducements for the practical farmer, the wool-grower, and the investor in mines and minerals.

The social condition of the people varies with the location. In previous chapters I have described the dwellers in the mountains bordering on North Carolina; those living in other remote counties are very similar in habits and intelligence. The political sentiment is yet, as it was during the war, difficult to classify. There were then hosts of uncompromising Union men in Eastern Tennessee; but there were, also, many committed to the interests of the Confederacy, and both classes were much broken in fortune, and possibly discouraged, by the marching and counter-marching of the troops. Their farms were plundered by both armies; and they often came near starvation themselves. In Knoxville the majorities are usually Republican, although the struggle is sometimes very close. In Chattanooga Republican municipal rule is also purchased at the expense of a careful fight. In the mountain counties people are not very much engrossed with general politics; their local affairs alone occupy their attention. At the period of my visit the school law allowed each county to decide for itself as to taxation for the support of free schools, and thus far no very marked progress has been made in the State. Tennessee admits the disagreeable fact that she ranks third in illiteracy in the Union, but her population does not seem as yet to feel the situation very keenly. Knoxville has good schools, with about 1,400 scholars as an average attendance; it also supports four colored schools. Chattanooga's regular attendance is about 1,000, and it also has two large colored schools. On the whole, Eastern Tennessee seems to make as much progress in education as other sections of the State in proportion to its population. Some of its counties have totally refused to have any public schools; while others have levied small taxes for supporting winter sessions. The Peabody fund has been very active in East Tennessee, and it is largely due to its influential distribution that a feeling in favor of schools is gradually taking root among the masses. The founding of two or three Normal schools in the State is a prime necessity. In a commonwealth which has thus far succeeded in getting only one-fifth of its 400,000 pupil-children into schools, the education of capable teachers is certainly of first importance.

Knoxville is the seat of the East Tennessee University, and the State Asylum for deaf and dumb persons. The University has latterly received a large share of the $200,000 appropriated as the "Agricultural Fund" of the State, and will serve as the Agricultural College. It now has some 300 students. The Methodist Episcopal Church contemplates founding a college at Knoxville; and there, or at Chattanooga, the people of one of the grandest mineral regions on this continent should not fail to establish a school of mines.

The peaks of the Cumberland, the Clinch and the Smoky, furnish Knoxville with many beautiful mountain views; and the eye dwells with delight on the

The East Tennessee University—Knoxville.

route from Chattanooga even to Greenville, upon the fields so beautifully cultivated, on the noble orchards, and the forests of mammoth corn stalks. The soil in this elevated valley is generally rich, second only to that of the Western prairies; the summers are long, but never excessively hot; there is only a light snow-fall in winter; in the valleys the water is limestone; on the hills freestone and chalybeate. On the table-lands grow rye, oats, and all vegetables; in the valleys wheat and corn attain extraordinary size. Apples, pears, peaches and wild grapes are cultivated in profusion, and the grazing-lands are no whit poorer than those of the North Carolina mountain region, which are so perfect and inexpensive. Land ranges in value from $5 to $35 per acre.

Through this fruitful country, and almost on the line of the railroad of to-day, ran the " great Indian war-path " eighty years ago. When one reflects upon the vast territory cleared, settled, and dominated within three generations, by the Tennessean, he cannot refrain from admiration, nor will he refuse to believe in the greatest possibilities in the future.

The Ducktown copper region in Eastern Tennessee, near the North Carolina line, is worth a visit from all interested in the State's development. It is the only locality in the commonwealth yielding copper ore in any considerable quantity. Although traces of the metal are to be met with in the Unaka mountains, they do not indicate veins of any importance. Ducktown is a mountain basin that belongs physically to Georgia and North Carolina. In the vicinity of the mines, 2,000 feet above sea-level, deep ravines alternate with sharp ridges, at whose base the Ocoee river worms its way toward the main Unaka range—when it becomes a torrent, roaring over huge rocks in its passage through the narrows. As early as 1836, the attention of geologists was drawn to the mineral deposits near the junction of the Ocoee and the Hiawassee rivers, and indications of copper were finally discovered by men who were searching for gold.

One of these men, while washing in the Hiawassee for gold, found great numbers of crystals of red copper ore. Soon after, the black oxide, which has thus far been the most important ore of the mines, was found; but it was not until 1850 that mining was begun in earnest. The gentlemen who opened the mines found themselves surrounded by a rough population, who took no interest whatever in any improvements; and on one occasion, when they had called a meeting of the township, and explained to the assembled citizens that civilization and wealth would follow upon the opening of the mines, one of the assembly arose and said that most of those present had come to the mountains to get away from civilization, and if it followed them too closely, they would migrate again!

This was discouraging; but the owners of the mines opened day and Sabbath schools, and built roads over the hitherto almost impassable mountains; meantime sinking shafts and employing the few whom they could prevail upon to undertake regular labor. Between 1851 and the close of 1855 a number of mines were opened and worked successfully in this region, and during that time eight of them produced and shipped 14,291 tons, worth more than a million of dollars. A few years later a consolidated company, called "The Union," was formed from a number of the most prosperous organizations, and its works now extend over 2,500 acres. Refineries were constructed, and although the company was prevented from working much of the time during the war, it has been very prosperous. The refining works have yielded nearly 1,500,000 pounds of refined copper since the war. In most of the Ducktown mines the operations have been confined to the zones of black and red copper ore, below which lie zones of iron and copper pyrites. The smelting works of the Union Consolidated Company are very extensive.

Lead and zinc are pretty liberally scattered through Eastern Tennessee, and in Bradley and Monroe counties lead mines have been opened. At Mossy Creek, in Jefferson county, and in the mountains beyond, there are numerous irregular veins of zinc ore. The gold found in the eastern portion of the State has been insignificant in quantity, although, in 1831, there was a genuine gold fever concerning the discoveries along the Hiawassee.

The most important coal mining establishments in the State are the Ætna mines, in Marion county, and the Sewanee Company's mines, which extend several miles underground, not far from the location of the "University of the South." Some of the veins at these latter mines are seven feet thick.

At the Ætna Coal Mines.

The coal in these mountains can be mined for three cents per bushel, and the freights for coal on all the roads south of Nashville are low. All the Tennessee coals are bituminous; but as such they present numerous varieties.

One of the sources of future wealth for Eastern Tennessee consists in its immense stores of variegated marble, the veins of which run through ten or twelve counties in that section. Besides the finer marbles, there are, in the extreme eastern counties, black or dark-blue limestones, which, when polished, would make elegant marble slabs. There is marble enough in this section to build all the public buildings of the United States for the next five centuries.

The siege of Knoxville, in 1863, is called to memory, but faintly, by the earthworks scattered about the town, and now nearly obliterated; but it was one of the most desperate struggles of the whole war. Longstreet and his men, fresh from their triumphs at Chickamauga, fell upon Burnside's little force in the mountain city with savage eagerness, but were hurled back into the jaws of death. They charged toward the ditches only to be pitched headlong over the wires strung to trip them, and to be massacred. But the living charged over the dead who filled the ditches, and twice had planted their flag or leaped upon the fortifications before they were finally swept away. Pools of blood six inches deep were found in the bottom of the trenches when the assault was made on the morning after the repulse of November 29th, and hundreds of corpses were hastily buried in heaps. On the 5th of December following, the little army of the Ohio, which was literally at the point of starvation, was at liberty once more. The siege was raised.

The magnitude of the mineral resources in this section perhaps affords the strongest argument in favor of the immediate removal of the obstructions in the Tennessee river; but the arguments are really legion. This noble stream, sixth in magnitude in the United States, intersecting ten rich commonwealths—in connection with the Ohio, draining the gigantic coal-areas of Tennessee and Alabama—never bearing upon its current, from its sources to its mouth, winter or summer, a particle of ice, and having half-a-dozen tributaries which could be rendered navigable by slack-water improvement, should be made one of the main commercial arteries of the South. With the necessary improvements, navigation could be rendered practicable for thirteen hundred miles above Muscle Shoals in Alabama. Only steamers of the lightest draught now succeed in running to Knoxville and beyond during six or nine months of each year.

The soil of the great Tennessee plateau, the Cumberland table-land, is no less remarkable than the climate of that favored region. For the production of fruit, and for the raising of sheep and cattle, the immigrant will find it most admirably suited. Extending across the State from north to south, the plateau is at least forty miles wide from east to west, and can furnish homes for thousands of farmers, who need but little capital.

"Down in a Coal Mine."

LXI.

A VISIT TO LYNCHBURG IN VIRGINIA.

"TIME to get up, boss!"

I hastily adjusted my garments, and hurried from the sleeping-car of the Richmond train on to the Gordonsville platform, where I was speedily

The old Market at Lynchburg. [Page 554.]

lost in a whirlpool of English and Scotch immigrants, surrounded by their numerous wives and children; of negro touters, shouting, "Dis way, boss,—

don' ye trust dat ar nigger, he don tole ye wrong 'bout de hotel,—take yer bag, *sar ?* "—of stout colored damsels, hastening to and fro with platters of cold and antiquated provisions, and blue-looking eggs; of farmers coming from markets, and of through passengers shivering in the cool night air.

"Now, boss, dar 's de Orange train!"

You must know that in the South the African is wont to designate strangers to whom he is indifferent by the euphonious title of "boss." It is, perhaps, a kind of compromise with his inclination to still cling to the old word "mas'r," and, at the same time, embodies as much respect as he cares to bestow on the "casual" whom he is called to serve. When familiar with your face, he will call

The James River, at Lynchburg, Virginia.

you "captain," if you are young; "major," if you are middle-aged, and "general" or "judge," if you are advanced in years. He has even been known to heap these titles upon strangers under the genial influence of the respect-provoking twenty-five cents. But at one o'clock in the morning, in hurrying you from one sleeping-car to another, it would take the potent influence of a brand-new dollar bill to wring from him any salutation save the accustomed "boss."

The train from Washington came crawling along the Orange road, and received me, while the one I had just left rushed forward into the mountains, and by the side of the deep ravines of Western Virginia, toward the Ohio river.

Among the immigrants there were many Englishmen of education and refinement, country gentlemen's sons who had made up their minds to try farming in the new country, or to purchase coal or iron tracts for speculation. Even the least cultured and rudest of these people wore the look of health and prosperity. Their advent was an encouraging symptom.

But in the car where the colored people were seated there were a good many discouraging signs. Was it possible to mould these slouching and ragged fellows, who talked so rudely, whose gestures were so uncouth, and on whose features had been stamped the seal of ignorance, into as useful and trustworthy citizens as these newly-arrived Britons, with their hardy cleanliness and bluff ambition, were likely to become? And if not, what would be the future condition of the lately liberated slave? Was he prospering, and hastening forward to the consummation of the independent manhood promised him? These questions, idly drifting in my sleepy mind without expecting answers, served to amuse and keep awake a tired body until the train trembled to a stand-still at the foot of the steep hill along whose sides Lynchburg lies.

At midday I strolled out to survey the town. The September sun poured terrible heat upon the broad James river, which, opposite the network of tracks at the depot, flowed placidly at the base of an immense cliff, from whose stony sides quarrymen were blasting and chiseling blocks for building purposes. A few rafts and flat-boats, steered by barearmed and bareheaded negroes, drifted lazily on the stream. A long covered bridge spanned the water, and a glance through its little windows showed quaint mills and houses upon the banks ; high bluffs, crowned with humble cabins, were rendered accessible by precipitous paths and flights of stone steps ; and, in the distance, were blue outlines of mountains, with little cloud-wreaths around them.

Returning from the bridge toward the town I came to a wide street, stretching straight up the hill. On either side were stone pavements, crowded with negroes; colored children gamboled on the flags ; colored mammas smoked pipes in the doorways of shops, where colored fathers sold apples, beer, and whiskey ; colored damsels, with baskets of clean linen in their stout arms, joked with colored boatmen from the canal ; colored draymen cursed and pounded their mules ; and colored laborers on the streets enveloped one in a cloud of suffocating dust as he hastened by. Toward the water sloped other streets lined with roomy tobacco warehouses ; half-way up the hill a broad and well-built business avenue crossed at right angles, and there, at last, one saw white people, and the ordinary sights of a city.

Finally I came into an open air market, picturesque as any in Italy or Spain. On the curbing of the sidewalk, and even on the stones in the middle of the square, dozens of negro women were seated before baskets containing vegetables, or various goods of trivial description. One venerable matron, weighing perhaps 200 pounds, had her profuse chignon overtopped by a dilapidated beaver, and was smoking a clay pipe. Many young women were cleanly and nicely dressed, and had folded back the huge flaps of their starched sun-bonnets, so that they seemed to imitate the head-dresses of the Italian maidens at Sorrento. Hosts of colored buyers, market-baskets in hand, hovered from one seller to another, talking in high-pitched voices, and in a dialect which Northern ears found difficult to understand. Leaving the market, and yet ascending, I came to another broad street lined with comfortable dwellings, and looking up saw, still far above me, the " Court-House" perched on the topmost point.

Lynchburg lies among the mountains, on the south bank of the James river, nearly in the centre of the Piedmont district of Virginia, and not far from the base of the Blue Ridge. The Virginians of all sections speak affectionately of it as "Old Lynchburg." It was once the wealthiest city in the United States, in proportion to its population, and one of the most remarkable tobacco marts in the world. Colossal fortunes were amassed and enjoyed there, in the days when internal revenue was not, and slave labor tilled the fields. Then the products of the Virginia and North Carolina plantations filled its warehouses and manufac-

A Side Street in Lynchburg, Virginia.

tories to bursting, and all Europe came to buy. An Irish emigrant gave his name, in 1786, to the town; and the famous term " Lynch law," now so universal, sprang from the summary manner in which this hot-headed Hibernian— a colonel in the Revolutionary army—treated such tories as were caught by him. During the late war the town did not fall into Federal hands. The tide of war flowed all around it, but never mounted to the reddish hills where it had safely perched.

Lynchburg's great natural advantages of situation will, in a few years, increase it from a city of 12,000 population to a huge overcrowded railway centre. It possesses superb and abundant water power. Coal is to be had in the immediate neighborhood cheaper than in most of the other cities in the Atlantic States.

Two important railway lines intersect at Lynchburg, the Atlantic, Mississippi and Ohio, now connecting Norfolk on the Atlantic with Memphis on the Mississippi, and destined also to connect Norfolk with Louisville on the Ohio; and the Washington City, Virginia Midland and Great Southern road which connects from Alexandria, in North-eastern Virginia, with Danville in the southern part of the State, and forms a link in the great Air Line between the cities on the Gulf and New York. The latter road opens to Lynchburg the whole Piedmont district, so rich in grains, grasses, fruits, tobacco, minerals and timber. The James river and Kanawha canal now extends from tide-water at Richmond, about 200 miles through the centre of the State, to a point near the base of the Alleghanies, but if carried to the Ohio, by means of liberal improvements in the Kanawha river, would revolutionize American internal commerce. This canal winds in pleasant curves between green banks through the mountains and at the base of the Lynchburg hills; and the horn of the boatmen is heard, making cheery melody at sunset. It was a grand mistake to locate the canal on the river-level. People have grown somewhat wiser since 1841, when the route was opened to navigation, and now regret that they did not place it high enough to secure the water power. The Chesapeake and Ohio rail route runs a little to the north of Lynchburg.

Finding the old town standing so "amid the fertile lands," with such excellent chances for growth, the new-comer feels, at first, like reproaching its inhabitants, despite the shock which they received in the war, for want of enterprise. But a careful examination shows that Lynchburg boasts a considerable activity. It has thirty-five tobacco factories, employing great numbers of negroes, men, women, and children. These negroes earn good wages, work faithfully, and turn out vast quantities of the black, ugly compound known as "plug," which has enslaved so many thousands, and promoted such a sublime disregard for the proprieties in the matter of expectoration. The appended note will give an idea of the trade of the tobacco district of which Lynchburg is the centre.* In the manufactories the negro is the same cheery, capricious being that one finds him in the cotton or sugar-cane fields; he sings quaintly over his toil, and seems entirely devoid of the sullen ambition which many of our Northern factory laborers exhibit. The men and women working around the tables in the basements of the Lynchburg tobacco establishments croon eccentric hymns in concert all day long; and their little children, laboring before they

*A comparative statement of the tax paid on manufactured tobacco shipped from the Fifth District of Virginia, in the fiscal years of 1871–72 and 1872–73, show that during the first period the amount manufactured was 5,351,894 pounds, on which was paid a tax of $1,501,526; and for the latter period 10,774,611 pounds, on which the taxation amounted to $2,154,922.20. The total weight of tobacco, in hogsheads, in boxes, and "loose," inspected at Lynchburg from October 1, 1870, to October 1, 1871, was 17,425,439 pounds, of which 11,629,239 pounds were brought in loose or unpacked; and for the same period in 1871–72 the total weight was 14,323,708 pounds, more than 10,000,000 pounds of which quantity was brought in unpacked. Campbell, Bedford, Pittsylvania, Halifax, Charlotte, Appomattox, Amherst, Nelson, Rockbridge, Botetourt, Roanoke, Franklin, Montgomery, Giles, Washington, Floyd, and Mercer counties furnish most of the tobacco received at Lynchburg.

are hardly large enough to go alone, join in the refrains. Tobacco is the main article of Lynchburg trade. Buyers from all parts of the Union crowd the streets; the warehouses are daily visited by throngs. Other manufactures are slowly creeping in, and the venerable town will probably yet do its share in developing the iron so profusely scattered through South-western Virginia. Lynchburg stands in the centre of a region richly supplied with educational institutions. Within a radius of sixty miles Roanoke and Hampden-Sidney Colleges, the Virginia Military Institute, the University of Virginia, and the Washington - Lee University, are all situated. Its own public and private schools are numerous and of excellent character. *The Virginian* and the other Lynchburg newspapers hold high rank among the journals of the State.

Scene in a Lynchburg Tobacco Factory.

The annual fairs of the Agricultural and Mechanical Society bring together hundreds of farmers from all parts of the commonwealth.

Down the steep hills every day come the country wagons (often with a bull, a mule, and an old mare harnessed together as the team), loaded with the dark sheaves of tobacco; and the groups of men standing about the parks and public places are almost certain to be discussing the favorite staple.

Something of the old Scotch and English manners are still perceptible among the people in this part of Virginia; and there are bits of dialect and phrase which show how little the communities have been affected during the last century· by the influences which have so transformed the populations of other sections of America. While England has gone on from change to change, and has even been capable of complete revolution in certain matters, Virginia has altered but little. Until now immigration has had no inducements to come and unlock the treasure-house of the grand mountains of the South-west, and so the people have lived under pretty much the same laws and customs that prevailed in England two centuries ago.   Yet the absence of the rushing, turbulent current of immigration has had its compensating advantages in allowing the growth of families in which the hereditary love of culture and refinement, and the strictest attention to those graces and courtesies which always distinguish a pure and dignified society, are preëminently conspicuous.

"Down the steep hills every day come the country wagons."   [Page 557.]

South-western Virginia is a region which will in time be overrun by tourists and land speculators.   The massive ramparts of the Alleghanies are pierced here and there by cuts through which crawls the line of the Atlantic, Mississippi and Ohio railroad; and towns are springing up with almost Western rapidity.   Stores of coal and iron are daily brought to light; and the farmer of the old *régime* stares with wonder, not wholly unmixed with jealousy, at the smart new-comers who are agitating the subject of branch railroads, and searching into the very entrails of the hills.

The sea-board link of the Atlantic, Mississippi and Ohio railroad was originally known as the Norfolk and Petersburg road, and was completed in 1858, under the direction of William Mahone, an engineer of decided talent.   At the close of the war this line, as well as the Southside, running from Petersburg to Lynchburg, and the Virginia and Tennessee road, extending from Lynchburg to Bristol, were in a lamentable condition, having been completely worn down by the heavy traffic and constant wear and tear during the great civil struggle. A measure for the consolidation of these roads, and their rebuilding and thorough equipment as a grand inter-State highway, was brought before the Virginia Legislature, and became the subject of much discussion.   The engineer, Mahone, had been for many years prominent in the railway affairs of the commonwealth, and was now the foremost advocate of the unification measure. He had also been a brilliant fighter on the Confederate side, had gone through the struggle to the bitter end, standing by Lee at Appomattox, and, as in the battle years he had been impetuous, persistent, and unsparing of self, so now, in the pursuit of this great scheme for a route from Norfolk to the Ohio and the Mississippi rivers, he was characterized by the same qualities.

Ever since George Washington plainly pointed out the advantages of a route between the Atlantic coast and the Ohio river, the attention of Virginian statesmanship has been directed to the subject; but it remained for General Mahone, with his clear logic and irresistible array of facts, to exercise the influence which finally brought about the needed legislation, and on the 12th of November, 1870, resulted in the organization of the present line, merging together the Norfolk and Petersburg, the "Southside," the Virginia and Tennessee, and the Virginia and Kentucky railroads.

By this there were placed under one management five hundred miles of railroad lying upon the best and shortest location afforded by the continent between the centres of Western trade and the finest harbors on the Atlantic sea-board. This continuous line, running east and west between the extreme western border of the State and the sea-board, will bestow its trade within, and confer its benefits upon, towns and cities in the limits of Virginia; and by building up large centres, will gradually reduce the rate of taxation levied upon the agricultural population. In its completed form it will be, in the words of a distinguished Virginian, "a line which spans one-half the continent at its narrowest breadth, which begins at that point of the very sea-board nearest the western trade centre, and reaches out not only to the proper west in its middle, but also to the north-west and the south-west "—a line, in fact, which will make the Atlantic via Norfolk 351 miles nearer Louisville, 260 miles nearer Cincinnati, and 400 miles nearer Cairo, than via New York city. Traversing the most prosperous and fertile portion of Virginia, it diverges at Bristol, to penetrate, by means of its present and future connections, the entire South and South-west, and via Cumberland Gap, the State of Kentucky and the huge North-west. The three railroads now composing this main line were placed under the management of General Mahone as early as 1869 (he having been successively chosen president of each one), but they continued for some time afterward to act under their separate charters.*

* In 1866–67, before the three lines above-mentioned were placed under one general management, the number of tons transported upon them was 145,000. During the year ending September 30, 1872, the amount transported by the consolidated line was 205,000 tons. In 1866–67, the average charge per ton per mile was five and a-quarter cents; in 1871–72 it was two and three-fourth cents. This great reduction of rate was followed by an increase of revenue from $1,000,000, in 1866–67, to $1,969,000 in 1871–72, and for 1872–73, to over $2,000,000. The Norfolk and Petersburg road was in active operation as an independent road in 1860. Its entire revenue for that fiscal year was $96,621.74. That same division of the consolidated road earned for the year ending September 30, 1872, $376,531. The cotton transported over this route all goes to Norfolk, except that taken by the Petersburg and Richmond mills, which yearly increases in amount. The number of bales carried in 1871–72 was 130,000; in 1872–73, 177,000, coming mainly from Memphis, Selma, Nashville, Huntsville and Dalton. Some of the other, and no less important, fruits of the consolidation measure are seen in the following statistics: In 1866–67 the quantity of minerals transported was but 13,000 tons; in 1871–72 it was 31,000 tons. In 1866–67, the weight of live stock moved was 3,000 tons; in 1871–72 it was 15,000. The contrast in the amount of wheat is still more striking: it has increased from 17,000 bushels in 1866–67, to 263,000 bushels in 1871–72. In this same latter year there were delivered to Virginia cities 88,000 tons of agricultural and mineral products, and 47,000 tons were sent North.

The traveler who hastens through Lynchburg, repelled by the uncouth and prosaic surroundings of the railway station, will lose real pleasure. A residence of a few days in the old town will show him much that is novel and interesting. He may wander along the beautiful banks of the James below Lynchburg; by the canal whereon the gayly-painted boats slip merrily to their destination; or he may climb the steep hills behind the town, and get a glimpse of the winding stream which looks like a silver thread among the blue mountains. At noontide he may hear the mellow notes of the horn by which buyers are summoned to a tobacco sale; and at sunset he may watch the curious groups of negroes returning from their labors singing and chattering, or noisily disputing some momentous political issue.

Summoning Buyers to a Tobacco Sale.

LXII.

IN SOUTH-WESTERN VIRGINIA—THE PEAKS OF OTTER. THE MINERAL SPRINGS.

IT was in the brilliant early autumn that I visited South-western Virginia. Leaving Lynchburg, just at sunset, for the mountains beyond, I was impressed with the beauty of the soft light which gently rested upon the lovely stream, and was gradually losing itself in the mysterious twilight. The foliage was at its completest still; the gay loungers at the pretty little fashion-resorts scattered through the mountains were giving their sprightliest balls before retiring to the solitude and routine of their plantations. The tobacco-fields were yet resplendent with green. The farmers were fallowing the lands on the rich hill-sides for winter wheat. Every day the sun shone with inspiring splendor on the blue lines of monarch mountains, which, clothed in their beautiful forests,

reared their crests against the unclouded sky. I did not wander along the winding canal, in the recesses of the hills, as far as the famous "Natural Bridge," but he who wishes to inspect that massive arch, spanning the chasm in which flows the little stream called Cedar creek, can reach it by a night's journey along the canal, from Lynchburg to the mouth of Cedar creek, within two miles of the bridge. The route, on a moonlit evening, is delightful, as the banks of the canal afford a constant succession of beautiful mountain pictures. But we leave the description of the approach to the bridge, and the great monumental wonder's special characteristics, to the pen of a native Virginian:

Evening on the James River—"The soft light which gently rested upon the lovely stream."

"The first view of the bridge is obtained half a mile from it, at a turn on the stage-road. It is revealed with the suddenness of an apparition. Raised a hundred feet above the highest trees of the forest, and revealed against the purple side of a distant mountain, a whitish-gray arch is seen, in the effect of distance as perfect and clean-cut an arch as its Egyptian inventor could have defined. The tops of trees are waving in the interval, the upper half of which we only see, and the stupendous arch that spans the upper air is relieved from the first impression that it is man's masonry, the work of art, by the fifteen or twenty feet of soil that it supports, in which trees and shrubbery are firmly imbedded —the verdant crown and testimony of Nature's great work. And here we are divested of an imagination which we believe is popular, that the bridge is merely a huge slab of rock thrown across a chasm, or some such hasty and violent arrangement. It is no such thing. The arch and whole interval are contained in one solid rock; the average width of that which makes the bridge is eighty feet, and beyond this the rock extends for a hundred feet or so in mural precipices, divided by only a single fissure, that makes a natural pier

In the Gap of the Peaks of Otter, Virginia.

on the upper side of the bridge, and up which climb the hardy firs, ascending step by step on the noble rock-work till they overshadow you.

"This mighty rock, sunk in the earth's side, of which even what appears is stupendous, is of limestone, covered to the depth of from four to six feet with alluvial and clayey earth. The span of the arch runs from forty-five to sixty feet wide, and its height to the under line is one hundred and ninety-six feet, and to the head two hundred and fifteen feet. The form of the arch approaches the elliptical; the stage-road which passes over the bridge runs from north to south, with an acclivity of 35 degrees, and the arch is carried over on a diagonal line, the very line of all others most difficult for the architect to realize, and that best calculated for picturesque effect."

Promising myself a visit to the Natural Bridge in the future, I made all speed to the other wonder of the neighborhood—the keen, sublime and haughty "Peaks of Otter."

Tenderly outlined against the exquisite pearl gray of the morning sky was the Blue Ridge, as I looked at it from the windows of the little inn of Liberty, the shire town of Bedford county, the point of departure for the Peaks of Otter. I noticed but little life or activity in the long street on Liberty hill; some negroes were at work in one or two tobacco warehouses; farmers were bustling in on the red country roads leading toward the purplish hill-background; and miles away two sharp, yet symmetrical peaks, connected by a gap, perched high up on the Blue Ridge chain, sprang into view.

There were the mighty twins! Two splendid guardians of the sweet valley spread out at their bases, they rose in indescribable grandeur. Where they take root in the gradually ascending earth, a capricious creek, the Otter, from which they get their name, eddies and bubbles and ripples in poetic confusion through rich fields, and by humble farm-dwellings, and granaries fashioned from the mountain trees. The northern and highest peak is rarely visited; it rises 5,307 feet above the level of the sea. The other, more symmetrical in shape,—something like an enormous pyramid, and capped by a chaotic mass of rock reaching seemingly into the clouds,—we determined to scale.

The negro livery-man had promised us a "hack," and consequently arrived with a red spring-wagon, perched high upon four clumsy wheels, and drawn by two unambitious horses. The road, for a mile or two after leaving Liberty, was good; then we fell upon the ordinary back-country route in Virginia, which is simply abominable. Square brick mansions with an air of solid respectability, standing in the middle of green and well-kept lawns, occupied the environs of the town; but we gradually left them, and passing through stretches of forest, along the beds of dissolute creeks which seemed determined not to go in the narrow way accorded them by nature, and by fields rich in culture, and abounding in delicious foliage, we began to climb around the mountain base.

We followed a vagrant road skulking apparently away from the sun. Now the road huddled under oaks, and now scurried up a thinly-wooded slope; now toiled over masses of loose stones; now coursed majestically along a plateau whence one could see the valley spread out like a map; now catching a glimpse of the overhanging peak toward which we toiled, and then, as if frightened at it, entered the wood forthwith. The cabins by the way were rude; rail-fences, chin high, through which white-headed children peered suspiciously, ran by the front doors; near which the cow-yards were conspicuous. Log barns were partially filled with hay, while tobacco hung from the rafters. Glancing upward, we could frequently see the pinnacle apparently suspended in mid-air. It seemed remote from, and disconnected with, the hill up to which we toiled, frowning upon us like a giant spectre.

At last, reaching the gap, more than three thousand feet above sea-level, we saw before us a pyramid of rough soil thickly sown with trees, and dotted with cabins in a few clearings. On the right, the northern peak showed its wooded sides, where the bear still wanders undisturbed; and a little in front of us stood the primitive hotel surrounded by flourishing orchards. The vine grows with surprising luxuriance along these mountains, the dry air and genial warmth giving every encouragement for the largest experimenting in vine-yards.

We now began gradually to master the ascent, and after half an hour of painful climbing over rudest roads, and a long scramble up an almost perpendicular hill-side, we came to a point in the forest where a high rock seemed to offer an impassable barrier; but around which led a path on a narrow ledge. We stumbled forward, and dizzy with the effort, stood on the summit.

Jagged and irregular masses of rock projected over a tremendous abyss, into which we hardly dared to look. A strong wind blew steadily across the height. We could not help fancying that some of the masses of stone, apparently so tightly suspended, might fall and crush us. Under the great dome of the translucent sky we stood trembling, shut off from the lower world, and poised on a narrow pinnacle, from which we might at any moment, by an unwary step, be hurled down. An old stone cabin, which had once served as the lodging for such adventurous persons as desired to see sunrise from the peak, but which had been partially destroyed during the war, was perched on one of the corners of the mighty crag; from it a slender board was laid to a sharp corner in the uppermost cliff, and up that we scrambled. Then, making our way on to the topmost stone, we gazed down on the valley

The Summit of the Peak of Otter, Virginia.

of Virginia. In front of us, looking over fertile Bedford county, it seemed a garden; from point to point gleamed the spires and roofs of villages; mountains of every imaginable shape rose on all sides; and the forests at the edges of the gaps in the Blue Ridge seemed delicatest fringes of purple. We could trace the massive and curving ranges of the Alleghanies, and the rudely-gullied sides of the nearest peaks. Their reddish soil, showing up strongly under the bright sun, produced a magical effect. Nowhere were the adjacent peaks, however, so near as to lessen the sublime illusion of seeming suspension in mid-air, produced by our climb to the highest rock of the peak. The cabins along the roads below looked like black dots; the men at work in the fields like ants. From the rocky throne one seemed to have the whole map of Virginia spread out before him; 'and the backbone of the Alleghanies appeared but as a toy which one might stride over, or displace at will.

Talks with the farmers and business men along the roads were full of information encouraging to would-be immigrants. Titles to land are usually good, because the estates rarely changed owners before the war, but descended from father to son, and one can more readily trace the title in Virginia on that account than in most of the other Southern States. The prices of farms in the south-western section of the State, although somewhat influenced by local causes, and, therefore, a little perplexing to the stranger, are reasonably low. Land of the best quality can be had at from $40 to $80 per acre, and the ridges of the mountains for almost nothing. The present prices there are, on the whole, an advance on the old ones.

In Rockbridge, Botetourt, and Roanoke counties, all surprisingly rich in resources, lands have declined in value so that they may be purchased at excellent bargains. In the Upper Piedmont counties prices are variable, but under the impetus given them by a steady English immigration show a tendency to rise. In Bedford, Amherst, Nelson, Campbell, and Appomattox counties, there are thousands of acres of good grazing and fruit-lands to be bought for from $2 to $5 per acre; while farms of the best quality, easily accessible to market, are sold at from $10 to $30. In the James River valley great numbers of slaves were held before the war. Emancipation ruined hundreds of planters and farmers, and caused a decline in the price of the lands. Many a fine old colonial estate is in the market at a small sum. The bottom lands in this attractive valley have been cultivated for two centuries, but are still fertile and unexhausted. The staples in the hill-country in the vicinity of Lynchburg are mainly wheat, Indian corn, oats, hay, and tobacco. The fruits are unrivaled, and along the eastern slopes of the Blue Ridge mountains the grape flourishes luxuriantly, and needs no protection from the cold. The farmers in the James River valley say that the bottom lands there will yield from sixty to one hundred bushels of corn to the acre.

The taxes are not heavy. On real estate in the counties they amount to one per cent., and the property is usually rated at only two-thirds of its cash value. Negro farm labor can be engaged for from $8 to $12 per month, with board; but "board" means only rations of bacon, molasses and corn, which the negro is supposed to cook for himself. In the forests of the hill-country black-walnut, cherry, and maple abound, and the oak, locust, chestnut, hickory, and pine are spread over one-half of the counties of the Piedmont section. Here and there one notices rank growths of pines, poplars and locusts, which have sprung up on the neglected land, whose owners have no longer capital to employ in cultivation. There is a statutory provision allowing each head of a family to hold, exempt from any process of execution or levy, real and personal property to the amount of $2,000. One-fifth of the tax money is devoted to the uses of free schools; but I am inclined to believe that in back sections of most of the

counties these schools do not flourish to any extent—not so much because of
any hostility toward them as because of the general apathy of the native farming population on the subject of education.

At every town throughout this region there are lovely mountain views.   One
has lost sight of the twin peaks of Otter ere he arrives at Blue Ridge Springs,
a charming resort ensconced in a nook between two huge ridges, situated upon
the railroad, and connected with the outer world by telegraph and numerous
daily trains, the waters being noted for their efficacy in special cases.   The route
continues through a rich farming country, and passes hill-sides covered with flourishing vineyards.   The farmers on the ridges are quiet and well-disposed folk.
Corn-fields grow up to the very doors of their humble houses.   The negroes

Blue Ridge Springs, South-western Virginia.

have little patches of land here and there, and seem industrious in their cultivation.   Chalybeate and sulphur springs are the attractions around which revolves,
all summer long, a pleasant *coterie* from the extreme South.   The whole spring
region of this section of Virginia is crowded from July until the last of October
with Southern visitors.

The mountain-passes about Blue Ridge Springs, the delightful roads running
out from thence to Coyner's and Bonsack's, the lovely stretches of the Roanoke
valley, the mystic recesses of the hills about "Alleghany," the sweet tranquillity
of the "Montgomery White Sulphur," and the half-dozen other retreats in the
vicinity, are all sought by the overworked and climate-worn who have come thou-

sands of miles for a sniff of fresh air.   The railroad, seeking a way through the most practicable passes of the Alleghanies and the Blue Ridge, has established stations convenient to all these springs.   For fifty miles the Atlantic, Mississippi and Ohio route runs through a wild and romantic section, abounding in richest mineral springs, as well as in minerals of value.   The most noticeable of the fashionable resorts are the "Alleghany" and the "Montgomery White."   Both have long been famous among Southerners; and hundreds of Northern pleasure-seekers now yearly find their way there.

Alleghany Springs, in Montgomery county, are near the Roanoke river, at the eastern foot of the Alleghany mountains.   The hotel, surrounded by a chain of picturesque and comfortable cottages, is only three miles from the railroad, and in all directions there are ravines and recesses containing some of the great wonders which Nature has so lavishly scattered through the State.   The saline waters which are abundant at Alleghany draw around them hosts of invalids, and the more robust visitors find health and pleasure in the exploration of such rocky cañons as Puncheon Run Falls, where, through the rent side of the hills a foamy series of cascades leap down 2,000 feet into abysses, shrouded in leaves and vines, where the black mosses cling to the blacker rocks; where the laurel sways rhythmically to the music of the spray and the sombre refrain of the fall.   He who would see billowy mountains, rolling miles and miles away, should climb to "Fisher's View," at a short distance from Alleghany. Along the by-ways of this region he will meet the rustic, clad in homespun, with an ancient rifle slung at his shoulder, and will be surprised at his uncouth speech and quaint suspicions of the traveler.   The mountaineer looks scornfully upon the crowds of city butterflies who flit back and forth through his country retreats in summer, and stands, dumb with amazement, before the doors of the hotel ball-room, through which he sees the gleam of rich costumes and the sparkle of jewels.

The routine at all the springs is much the same.   The hotel is usually a roomy building, surrounded by porches or verandas, and stands in the middle of a green lawn, dotted with the white oak or some other of the superb trees abounding in the Virginian mountains.   In the hotel are grouped the ball and dining-rooms and the general reception parlors; while in the small, neatly-painted, one-story cottages, ranged in rows, equidistant from the hotel, the visitors are. lodged.   There is a host of attentive and polite colored serving-men and women, ex-valets and ex-nurses of the "before-the-war" epoch, and they will tell you, with pardonable pride, "I used to belong to ole Mars' ——," mentioning some name famous in the annals of slave proprietorship.   Here one can establish the charm and seclusion of a home, and combine with it the benefits accruing from a sojourn at a watering-place.   Society, usually very good, crystallizes in the parlors of the hotels and in the ball-rooms, where bands of colored musicians discourse the latest themes of Strauss and Gungl. When one tires of dancing and of the promenades to the "springs," there are the mountains, and the strolls along ridges thousands of feet above the level of the sea, where the air is always pure and inspiring.   There is no gaming, save an innocent whist party by some sleepy old boys who lurk in the porches, keeping out of the strong morning sun; there is no Saratogian route of carriage and drag; no crowded street, with ultra style predominant in every costume; nothing but simplicity, sensible enjoyment, and excellent taste.   In the sunny mornings the ladies and their cavaliers wander about the mountain pathways; dress does not exact homage until dinner-time, and the children join with their parents in the strolls and promenades, followed by the venerable "aunties," black and fat, who seem indispensable appendages to every Southern family having young children.

Montgomery White Sulphur Springs lie even nearer to the main route of travel than those of Alleghany.   A pleasant ride of a mile and a-half from the Atlantic, Mississippi and Ohio line, on a horse-railroad brings one to a lawn, planted round about with fine trees, and watered by a rippling brook.   The hotel and cottage buildings are comfortable and elegant; the sulphur and chalybeate springs are daily visited by hundreds in the season; and the ragged spur of the Alleghanies which backs the lawn is traversed by smooth, well-kept roads, over which visitors trot on the brisk mountain horses.   At the season's height Southern statesmen, lawyers, planters, journalists, ex-warriors, poets and speculators make the Montgomery White their rendezvous; and illuminations, balls, tournaments and meetings follow one upon the other. Four miles south-west are the "Yellow Sulphur Springs," loftily situated near the head-waters of the Roanoke, and reached from the railway via Christiansburg.   These springs, whose waters are celebrated for the cure of children's diseases, and are said to impart a rare purity to the complexion of women, are noted as a quiet resort for families.

This spring region, abounding in all the resources for the restoration of health and energy, and so rich in natural beauty, is as yet comparatively unknown to the mass of Northern and Western people.   For cheapness of price and for convenience of access it has in America hardly an equal; and in Europe but few watering-places can claim any superior advantages of that nature.   When the great commonwealth is thoroughly developed, these beautiful summer resorts will gradually become large towns, and the charm of the restful stillness, the possibility of intimate communion with some of nature's grandest phases which they now afford, will be gone.   The mob of the summer grand tour will rob them of their chief charm.

LXIII.

AMONG THE MOUNTAINS—FROM BRISTOL TO LYNCHBURG.

A JOURNEY from the Tennessee line, northward toward Lynchburg, gave me enlarged ideas of the possibilities of South-western Virginia. Bristol bestrides the line between Virginia and Tennessee, and consequently has a double municipal existence. Two Mayors and two sets of minor municipal officers have jurisdiction within its limits. It is a pretty collection of neat houses and busy shops, ranged along lightly-sloping hills; and beyond the Tennessee boundary, the blue range of the Iron mountains stands out sharply against the clear sky.

The streets are usually crowded with wagon-trains, immense canvas-covered vehicles, drawn by sober mules, and driven by brawny, long-bearded backwoods-

Bristol, South-western Virginia.

men, or by tattered and slouching negroes. These trains ply back and forth along the difficult routes not yet reached by any railways, and at night the men and mules camp together under the open sky. Stout farmers, splashed with the reddish mud of the highways, rattle up and down the main avenues on alert little horses. At evening the through train from New Orleans, bound for New York, shrieks the note of warning as it rolls into the overcrowded depot, and the passengers pour out to the roomy, old-fashioned brick hotel, and, seated on wooden stools around a long table, absorb the smoking fragments of hot chicken and corn-bread set before them. Here and there the noise of factory wheels is heard, and the hills are crowned with neat edifices containing flourishing schools. On the Tennessee side stands King's College, supported by the Presbyterian Church South, and there are also one or two excellent seminaries for women.

The 1,800 people settled at Bristol seem prosperous and contented, as they may well be, in view of the chances for future growth which the rapid multiplication of railway lines with important connections is to give the town. The extension of the Atlantic, Mississippi and Ohio railroad from Bristol to Cumberland Gap will develop a rich country; and when Bristol is receiving the great currents of traffic directly from Memphis and Louisville, it will fully merit the

White Top Mountain, seen from Glade Springs.

title now and then given it, of "the most active town in Virginia." The "Natural Tunnel," forty-two miles from Bristol, near the ford of the Clinch river, is a passage, about 800 feet in length, through battlements of solid stone. The vaults of the tunnel rise to the height of eighty feet; and, where the arch finally terminates in the mountain slope, there is a sheer precipice 500 feet high. In a few years, it is confidently expected, a railroad will find its way through this wonderful tunnel, and the locomotive's scream will be heard on the path over which Daniel Boone painfully toiled, more than a century ago, on his pioneering pilgrimage to the Kentucky wilds. Straight across Powell's mountain and Powell's valley to the rock-ribbed Cumberland range runs the projected route of the railway which is to forge one more link in the great chain binding the West to the East. The whole region adjacent to the main road leading to Cumberland Gap is rich in tradition and natural wonders. Not far from the Natural Tunnel is a massive cave, in whose chambers hang thousands of stalactites; and near the little town of Estillville, in Scott county, are the "Holston Springs," where chalybeate, thermal and white sulphur waters rise from sources within a few hand-breadths of each other. Around Estillville the lands are rich in minerals; iron and copper abound; and the lead deposits along the Clinch river have long been considered remarkable.

The journey backward toward Lynchburg took me through Abingdon, a flourishing trade centre in Washington county, and to Glade Springs, whence one gets a peep at White Top mountain's lofty brow. From Glade Springs I turned aside to Saltville, a busy town connected with the outer world by a branch rail-road running in among the queer hill-knobs filled with plaster, and through the valleys where salt-wells are sunk. The country round about, until one reaches the Alleghany ridge, is not unlike that portion of England lying near Eastbourne, with its chalk hills sparsely covered with grass. Saltville is a neat manufact-uring village, nestling in a valley near a defile in Walker's mountain. The basin of salt-water there yields nearly eighty per cent., and, ever since a Scotchman named King opened a well in 1780, the salines have been extensively worked. During the last war the Confederacy depended almost entirely upon these works for salt, and the tremendous draft of ten thousand bushels per day was promptly met by the wells. About two thousand men were constantly employed; the town was thoroughly fortified; each Southern State had its private establish-ment, and the various furnaces are to-day known by the names of the States which originally established them. There was some savage fighting along the mountain-sides, and in the defiles, when General Stoneman tried to force his way into Saltville and destroy the precious stores; but, after a severe repulse, he succeeded in gaining possession and burning everything. The stock company now owning and working the wells, manufacture but three thousand bushels of salt daily, sending it mainly to the Southern markets.

Making Salt, at Saltville, Virginia.

The stout negroes working over the boiling salt were both delighted and amazed when their pictures appeared in the artist's sketch-book; they had never seen "no such writin' befo'." Great stores of gypsum are annually mined and prepared for fertilizers in this valley, where also there are some superb model farms, well stocked and separated one from another by beautiful hedges. Not far from Saltville is Clinch mountain, over which the traveler to Tazewell county, a wonderfully beautiful mountain region, must climb. The fighting around Saltville was severest at the time that Burbridge came from Kentucky, intending to break up the Confederate works there. It was, I believe, the first fight in which colored troops entered as an important element, and the slaughter of them, as they came struggling up the difficult hill-sides, is said by eye-witnesses to have been dreadful. About six thousand troops were engaged on each side.

In Tazewell county, twenty-five miles from the line of the Atlantic, Mississippi and Ohio road, coal crops out literally everywhere. It furnishes a rich field for investment. The mountain population is rude, but, as a rule, law-abiding, and sensible. Along the valley of the Clinch river, in this county, are many stretches of fertile fields, contrasting strangely with the rocky cliffs rising around them. "Wolf Creek Knob," clad in laurel and ivy, and "Dial Rock," near Jeffersonville, are worthy many visits. Railroads, schools and mines will give this country great riches, and a much needed increase of education in a few years. The dialect of the people is strange and hard; their hospitality is unbounded, and their love for the peaks, among which they raise their droves of cattle, horses, and hogs, amounts to devotion. Their homes are cleanly, although simple almost beyond belief; their manners are frank, and their instincts usually noble.

At Marion Court-House—a pleasant village near the Brush mountain, and a fair type of the average Virginian county seat,—we arrived at a time when the Conservative candidate for Governor of the State, General Kemper, was addressing the citizens of the county. Marion consists mainly of one long street, on one side of which is the Court-House, with a lawn in front, and a stout jail in the rear. It was court-day as well as a political occasion; and the farmers had assembled from many miles around.

The negroes are very numerous in the vicinage; but, constituting a party by themselves, did not flock about the Court-House, although two of the better class of them lingered near, as if appointed as reporters. The court-room in which the political meeting was held, after the session of the court had been adjourned over for a day in deference to the discussion of pending issues, was small and destitute of seats. The farmers and town residents dropped in at intervals during the lucid and fluent speech made by General Kemper, and listened for some little time with respectful attention, although they did not seem to take that thrilling interest in the irrepressible conflict which I had been led to expect.

The speeches of the candidate (since elected Governor) and his friends were somewhat condemnatory of the Administration's course with regard to certain Southern States. It was evident that the hearers present, with the exception of the negroes, were all of one mind, and would vote the Conservative ticket without fail. But as soon as the farmers had seen the candidate of their party for Governor, and heard him make a few remarks, many of them strolled back upon the lawn, and began discussing crops and comparing notes on horses. They

Wayside Types—A Sketch from the Artist's Virginia Sketch-Book.

regarded the election of the Conservative ticket in the State as a foregone conclusion, and were apparently tired of all political talk, preferring to attend to
their home matters, and the bettering of their agricultural prospects, rather than
to a revival of past memories. By noon many of them had completed their
errands, and were riding out of town on their smart horses, as grimly and
silently as they had entered.

The negroes seemed to consider the Conservative triumph as certain ; and
those who were intelligent were basing all hope of an improvement in their condition on the influences of time rather than on anything else. They hope to
make education general among their race ; and, during the four years that the
Conservatives will remain in power, they think that a more intelligent ground-
work of politics may be formed. In the back counties it will be found difficult

Wytheville, Virginia.

to establish the free common school on a good and reliable basis ; but, certainly,
both whites and blacks enjoy excellent school facilities in most of the larger
towns. A careful canvass of the counties in South-western Virginia, and the
Piedmont district, in 1872, shows that, while there was still some marked opposition to the free public school, the sentiment of the mass was gradually becoming favorable to it.

There has never been, since the war, any inclination on the part of the whites
to hinder the negro from getting as much education as he can himself pay for ;
and, although some resistance to the collection of taxes for school purposes was
anticipated at the time the system went into operation, in 1870, there never has
been any worthy of the name. The negroes in many of the counties manifest
more eagerness to enter school than do the whites, but they are not always willing

to pay something to support the school.   On the whole, great progress has been made; the Peabody fund has done, and still does good work in Bristol, Abingdon, Marion, Salem, Wytheville and Lynchburg; the number of school edifices is increasing, and good teachers are more readily procured than at the outset.   The mass of the people throughout that region, as in other parts of Virginia, would, I think, prefer that the Legislature should take the responsibility of raising the funds

Max Meadows, Virginia.

to support the schools.   At present the supervisors and judges in each county have the power to regulate the local school taxes, and the result of this is that the school trustees, who are required by law to provide good school edifices for the pupils, have not the money with which to build them.   But experience and improved sentiment are gradually regulating all these matters.

Near Marion, and in the mountains back of the town, the deposits of iron ores promise to be very rich, and furnaces will soon be established there.   Barytes has long been mined in the vicinity.   In the adjoining county, at Wytheville, a pretty town lying on the western slope of a spur of the Alleghanies, 2,000 feet above tide-water, we saw fine specimens of coal, iron, lead and zinc ore, mined in the vicinity.   The Austinville lead mines, near by, have been worked for more than a century.   All the zinc is at present transported to the Eastern States before being smelted.

A little more than six miles from Wytheville several extensive coal veins have been opened, and ample stores of limestone are found near these veins, so that furnaces and rolling-mills would get their material ready to hand, if erected at such an excellent point on the Atlantic, Mississippi and Ohio line as Wytheville.   The water power in the vicinity is magnificent.   Beyond lie Kent's Mill and Max Meadows, the latter a lovely pastoral landscape dotted with fine stock.   To Max Meadows zinc and pig-iron are brought in large quantities from the country between the station and the North Carolina mountain frontier.   In that section there are also extensive lead and shot works, and silver enough is scattered in the zinc-beds to pay the men mining the latter for their work.   At

Dublin, a little village in the midst of fertile fields, there are large iron interests. This is a depot whence many shipments of the celebrated short-horn beef cattle are made. As soon as the railway now prompting the growth of these interests can shoot out its feeders on either side, the number of tons of minerals annually exported from Virginia will be quadrupled. Not far from this point the owners of the Radford Iron Works of Philadelphia are shipping pig-iron from a newly-erected furnace.

The banks of New river are so lovely in the autumn time, that we determined not to hasten by them in the express train; so we mounted upon a hand-car, which the strong arms of two stout negroes sent down grade at thirty, and up the toilsome ascents at five, miles an hour. The river, a few miles beyond Dublin, is broad and wonderfully clear, mirroring in its placid breast the verdure-bordered banks, and the rich foliage of the forests along the cliffs, to whose sides the railway confidingly clings.

The Roanoke Valley, Virginia. [Page 577.]

Traversing the stream, and mounting a little hill, we caught a view of "Bald Knob." The bare poll of the venerable mountain was touched by the afternoon sunlight as we looked, and the great height formed an admirable background to the richly broken landscape along the riverside. One may make a pleasant voyage on the New river from this point to Eggleston's Springs, twenty-five miles further down the current, taking one of the many bateaux which ply constantly on the stream, and simply drifting on the lazy wave until the destination is reached. Within easy distance of these springs one comes upon the greatest natural wonder of the Virginian mountains,—a pond or lake, having no visible source of supply, sunk in a kind of earth cup, on a height 4,500 feet above the level of the sea. It has been forming and enlarging for more than sixty years, and is now about three-quarters of a mile long by a third of a mile wide. Submerged trees can be seen beneath its pellucid surface; and a line hundreds of feet long, if let down its middle waters, will not touch bottom.　Higher up, in the same range, is the " Bald Knob," the view from whose summit is considered quite as grand as that from the Peak of Otter.

A little beyond New river we stopped at a primitive coal station, where great heaps of the black diamonds, newly brought from "Brush" mountain, were lying. As I inquired the name of the mine from which they came, a by-stander answered, "The mountain is all coal, and every farmer is his own miner."

At Christiansburg, which is in the spring region, we were not far from the site of the new State Agricultural and Mechanical College at Blacksburg.　The "farm" attached to the college comprises two hundred and fifty acres, lying in the fertile " Valley of Virginia," and with veins of coal of superior quality, and large bodies of timber within easy reach.　Climbing over the huge grades which dominate the Alleghanies at this point, and passing through the deep cuts in the rock-ribbed hills near the stations giving access to Montgomery White Sulphur and Alleghany Springs, we came suddenly upon the delicious expanse of the Roanoke valley, bathed in the splendid shimmer of an afternoon autumn sun, and fading into delicatest colored shadows where the mountains rose gently, as if loth to leave the lowly retreat.　The vale was filled with wheat and corn fields, and with perfect meadows, through which ran little brooks gleaming in the sun.

After crossing the Roanoke river we came into a region covered with fine fields of tobacco, which extended far up the hill-sides.　Just below is the pleasant station of "Big Spring," to which we had been gradually descending for some

View near Salem, Virginia.

time on the high cliffs along the side of the Roanoke valley.　At Big Spring a profusion of iron and copper ore has been found.　Salem, the site of Roanoke College, is surrounded by charming hills, and stands in one of the richest agricultural regions in the United States.　Near Salem are some lovely streams, bordered by rich foliage.　Throughout the adjacent sections the farmers are very well-to-do, many owning from 1,200 to 1,300 acres of land, worth $80 to $90 per acre. Tobacco and the cereals are grown there in large quantities. Salem and "Big Lick," just beyond, export immense quantities of cereals. Salem stands at the head of navigation on the Roanoke, and communicates with Weldon, in North Carolina. Here, too, it is hoped that a road, opening up the Shenandoah valley, will connect with the Atlantic, Mississippi and Ohio line.

The wealth of this region is by no means developed yet. South-western Virginia proper, which remained so long unexplored after the valley and the Potomac shores had been carefully studied, has a grand future. As a field for immigrants who have capital and intelligence, for the better class of large farmers, and for workers in metal, it cannot be surpassed. An empire in itself, with every resource conceivable, it is not wonderful that that rare soldier, General Lee, boasted that he " could carry on the war for twenty years from those western mountains."

View on the James River below Lynchburg.

LXIV.

PETERSBURG—A NEGRO REVIVAL MEETING.

THE journey from Lynchburg to Petersburg calls up many memories. Eight years ago the mad rush of desperate and final battle swept across it. From the log and earth parapets of Five Forks, where Pickett's forces met their doom at the hands of Sheridan; from the Appomattox and from Hatcher's Run; from Fort Gregg, where the splendid Mississippians held on against hope and fate until nearly all of them had perished; from the intrenchments of deserted Petersburg; from Burkesville; from the road to Jetersville, over which Sheridan and the "Fifth" went clattering; from Amelia Court-House and from Sailor's Creek; from the High Bridge, and from Cumberland Church near Farmville, where Mahone made his heroic stand, and would not be driven; from all the bloody and memorable fields which stretch, sunlit and peaceful now, from the

Appomattox Court-House—"It lies silently half-hidden in its groves and gardens." [Page 580.]

hills around Petersburg to the village of Appomattox Court-House, come echoes which recall to us some faint impressions of the splendor and the grandeur of that last resistance of the broken army of Northern Virginia.

Along the line of rail where now currents of trade flow stronger and more steadily than in the most prosperous days of the old *régime*, raged a gigantic struggle, the very traces of which seem to have passed away. Now and then the eye catches the outline of a grass-grown intrenchment, in the midst of some well-cultivated field; but there are notably few marks of that wild series of battles by day and flights and pursuits by night which ended when Gordon, with the advance guard of Lee's exhausted army, had charged successfully against the cavalry ranged in front of him, only to find that behind that cavalry were the blue infantry lines which foretold the necessity of surrender.

There is nothing especially interesting in Appomattox Court-House. The little village lies at a short distance from the railway station, around which idle negroes are always lounging.   It lies silently half-hidden in its groves and gardens, as if frightened at the notoriety it has achieved.   The house where Lee and Grant arranged the terms of surrender is pointed out to the Northern visitor; but aside from its associations, it has nothing to recommend it to attention.   The surrounding country, however, is quite beautiful.   Farmville, so memorable for the battles in .its vicinity, seems alert and full of energy; it has the stamp of a New England town in the vivacity of its streets, as I saw them.   It has long been an important tobacco market, and the people are prosperous and progressive.   Hampden-Sidney College is not many miles away; and a short distance below the town is the famous " High Bridge," simply a railway viaduct, where General Mahone had proposed, in those terrible days of April, 1865, to make one of his stubborn fights, but whence he was forced to fall back to his position at " the church." The fields on which one looks down from this great bridge—a triumph of engineering—are beautifully cultivated in tobacco and corn.   The valley was delicious in color, as I passed through it in an autumn sunlight.

Below Burkesville the cotton-fields were numerous; acres were white with the pretty shrub's blossoms, and the intrenchments of eight years ago were here and there covered with them.   Seen from a distance, Petersburg presents the appearance of a lovely forest, pierced by church spires and towers.   On entering it, one sees many signs of commercial prosperity.   Along the railroad line in the suburbs are large cotton-mills, and the much beleaguered town now echoes to the whirr of spindles, and the ring of hammers on tobacco-hogsheads.

The negroes were slightly in the majority in Petersburg at the time of my visit.   As at Lynchburg, the Northerner is at first amazed by the mass of black and yellow faces.   The hackmen who shriek in your ear as you arrive at the depot, the brakeman on the train, the waiter in the hotel, all are African.   In the tobacco factories hundreds of dusky forms are toiling, and an equal number are slouching in the sunshine.   On the day of my visit a colored Masonic excursion had arrived from Richmond, and the streets were filled with stout negro men, decently clothed, and their wives and sweethearts, attired in even louder colors than those affected by Northern servant girls.   Each was talking vociferously; officials, in flaunting regalia and sweating at every pore, rushed to and fro; bands thundered and urchins screamed.   The Virginia negro has almost the French passion for *fête*-days; he is continually planning some excursion or " reunion," and will readily consent to live in a cellar and submit to poor fare for the sake of saving money to expend in frolic.

At Petersburg the negroes are from time to time largely represented in the Common Council, and sometimes have a controlling voice in municipal affairs. The white citizens have readily adapted themselves to circumstances, and the session of the Council which I attended was as orderly and, in the main, as well conducted as that of any Eastern city.   There was, it is true, an informality in the speech of some of the colored members which was ludicrous, but it was evident that all were acting intelligently, and had come to some appreciation of their responsibilities. Most of the colored members were full types of the African. In some matters they readily admit the superiority of the white man in legislation, and in Petersburg willingly gave the management of the city finances into the hands of the elder Conservative members of the Council. The Commissioner of Streets and the Engineer of the Board of Waterworks were both negroes. The mayoralty and the other city offices remained, at the epoch of my visit, in the hands of white Radicals, and the negroes had made no special struggle to secure them, although they are to the whites in the city as eleven to

"The hackmen who shriek in your ear as you arrive at the depot." [Page 580.]

nine. The Conservatives allege that they are unable to compete with the negroes in tricks at election-time. They say, among other things, that they have never been able to secure burial records of the negro population, since it is their custom to make a dead voter renew his life in the person of one of his friends.

The Petersburg schools are noteworthy examples of Virginian progress since the war, and merit the warmest encomiums. No attempt has been made by black or white to insist upon the education of the races together, it being tacitly allowed on both sides that it would not be wise. Petersburg's general free system of public schools was founded in 1868, when $2,000 of the " Peabody

Fund" was contributed, on condition that the city should raise $20,000, and with it establish schools for all classes and colors. By the second year nearly 3,000 pupils were enrolled, and both whites and blacks are now given all facilities for a thorough education. The colored young men have not, as a mass,

"The 'Crater,' the chasm created by the explosion of the mine which the Pennsylvanians sprung underneath Lee's fortifications."

made any special demand for instruction in the higher branches; their main desire is for a knowledge of reading, writing, arithmetic, and such general study as will enable them to speak in public or to preach; but the girls in many of the negro schools are capable of mastering Cæsar, and can write correct French exercises.

About 5,000 negroes are at work in the tobacco warehouses; in the cotton-mills white labor exclusively is employed. Eight of these mills are established in and near the city, viz.: the Mattoaca, Ettricks, Battersea, Davis, Roper & Co's, Swift Creek, Kevan, and Lynch. Two thousand operatives are employed in manufacturing cotton. Numbers of Scotchmen have settled in the vicinity, and some of them are largely interested in the mills. Petersburg's annual receipts of cotton and tobacco are very large. During the last year 42,500 bales of cotton and 14,000 hogsheads of tobacco were received. The flouring-mills of the city have a capacity of 1,000 barrels daily. This thriving community of 18,000 persons has shrewdly thrust itself between Richmond and the northern counties of North Carolina, and has thus secured a large portion of the trade which the capital considered its own. Petersburg supplies the planters and farmers of the adjacent State with bacon and corn, and in return takes tobacco and cotton. The Atlantic, Mississippi and Ohio railroad opens up to it long stretches of fertile country.

The town contains many charming avenues, bordered with elegant mansions embowered in foliage; some of the business streets are quaint and almost foreign in aspect. The Appomattox makes here and there a picturesque waterfall; the hill on which the old cemetery and ruined, ivy-mantled Blandford Church stand commands a lovely view of the city, around which, in every direction, miles on miles, stretch the decaying intrenchments, batteries, and forts of the great siege. The lines along the eastern and southern suburbs are still pretty clearly defined; but the traces of the battles have nearly all vanished. The " Crater," the chasm created by the explosion of the mine which the Pennsylvanians sprung underneath Lee's fortifications, on that dread day of the unsuccessful assault in July, 1864, is overgrown with shrubbery; and the farmer, who points out the old lines of the two armies, says that he himself can hardly realize that his farm was once a mighty fortified camp. Along what was known as the "new intrenched line," constructed after the explosion and the consequent battle,—and around the worn earthworks of Forts "Hell" and "Damnation,"*—some marks of strife are yet noticeable. The National cemetery, with its 3,000 graves, near the "Poplar Spring Church," and the lot on Cemetery Hill, devoted to "Our Soldiers," where sleep the Confederate dead; the little church which a regiment of New York engineers erected during the weary months of the siege, and (when they left for Five Forks) presented to their enemies; the "Signal Tower," built by the same hands; and, scattered in the vales and along the slopes, some vaguely-defined ruins of rifle-pit and subterranean passage, of bomb-proof and sharpshooter's lurking-hole, are all that remain as memorials of the fierce and deadly struggle which lasted ten months, and cost many thousands of lives.

During our stay in this section a "revival meeting" was announced by the colored brethren of the surrounding country, to be held at a little station half-way between Richmond and Petersburg, and we determined to be present. On a beautiful Sunday morning we drove out through the fields, in which, the oak timber having been cut away, a rank growth of pine had sprung up; and stopping a massive coal black man, dressed in white duck, with a flaming red necktie at his throat, we inquired "the way."

"Ef yo' want to go to Zion's Hill, dat yer 's de way; but ef yo' want to go whar de good preachin' is, dis yer road 'll take yo' to it."

Presently we arrived at a large frame building, much like a country school-house, save that

"The old cemetery, and ruined, ivy-mantled Blandford Church." [Page 582.]

it was neither ceiled nor plastered, and therein the revivalists were gathered. A powerful spiritual wave had swept over the colored population, and dozens of carts, loaded with dusky searchers for truth, came rolling along the rough

* Sobriquets given Forts Sedgwick and Mahone.

roads, and stopped before the primitive door.   Entering, we found represented
every shade of color, from the coal black full-blood to the elegantly dressed
and well-mannered octoroon.   The congregation was not large.   Owing to
the excitement which had prevailed for several previous Sabbaths, many had
retired, worn out, from the spiritual feast.   The women sat on the left side, the
men on the right of a broad aisle, running to a plain wooden pulpit, in which
were three moon-faced negroes, two of them preachers, and the third a State
Senator.

In front of the pulpit, behind a little table, stood an olive-colored elderly
man, neatly dressed, and with a wildness in his eyes, and an intensity written
upon his lips which reminded me of what I had read of the " Convulsionists of
St. Médard."   The audience was breathless with attention as the preacher, a
strolling missionary, supported by Quakers in Louisiana, took up the great Bible,
and, poising it on his lean, nervous hand, poured forth such an impassioned
appeal that I fairly trembled.   I was not prepared for such vehemence.   Never,
in the history of New England revivalism, was there such a scene.   The preacher
stood with many of his hearers well around him; one of the deacons and
exhorters, a black giant in spectacles, was his *point d'appui*, and to him he
appealed from time to time, shaking him roughly by the shoulder, and hissing
his words in his ear with fiery vehemence.   The proposition with which he
started was somewhat incomprehensible to us, viz.: " Christ is the creating power
of God;" but the proposition was of no consequence, because every few moments
he would burst into paroxysms of exhortation, before which the emotional
audience rocked and trembled like reeds in a wind.   He had a peculiar way of
addressing himself suddenly and in a startling manner to some individual in the
congregation, dancing, and pounding the table furiously with both hands, in the
agony of his exhortation to that person.

From time to time he would draw in his breath with great force, as if repress-
ing a sob, and, when speaking of love and salvation, he inevitably fell into a
chant, or· monotone, which was very effective.   Under the hurricanes of his
appeal, the fury of his shouting, the magnetic influence of his song, one of the
old deacons went into a spasm of religious fervor, and now and then yelled vociferously.   A milder brother ventured to remonstrate, whereupon the Quaker
preacher turned upon him, saying loudly:

" Let dat brudder shout, an' 'tend to dine own business !"

Then he began preaching against hypocrisy.   He seemed especially to chide
the women for becoming converted with too great ease.   " Woe !" he cried, "woe
unto dat woman what goes down into the water befo' she ready; woe *unto* her !"
with a long, singing descent on the last words; and then he added, *sotto voce*,
" Dat what make so many women come up stranglin' an' vomitin' an' pukin' outen
de water; de debbil dat still in 'em git hole on 'em, an' shake 'em an' choke 'em
under de water!   Let no woman shout for Jesus what don't know 'bout Jesus!
It's one thing to git to Heaven, but it's anudder to git in !   Don' ye know what
Heaven is ?   Heaven's God !   We must know what we is preachin' about, an' ef
we don't we ought to SET DOWN !"   (This with terrific emphasis.)

In describing the creation, he said: "Breddren, it's now 12,877 years sence de good Lord made de world, an' de morning stars sung togedder. *Dat wa'n't yesterday!* Ha! read de Book o' Job, 'n see for yerself! *Dat wa'n't a month ago! I was n't dar den!*" (thus illustrating with sublime scorn the littleness of man), "but by de grace of God, I 'll git dar by 'n' by!" (here his voice was faint and suggestive of tearful joy) "to join de mornin' stars, an' we 'll all sing togedder!

"Oh, yes! oh, yes! Heaven's God made de world an' de fullness darof, an' hung it up on de high hooks of heaven. Dar wa'n't no nails dar; no hammer dar; no nothin' but de word of God." In hinting at the terrors of death to the unconverted, he sang wild word-pictures which had a certain rude force even for us, and then shrieked out these sentences: "Ef de brudders don't want to die in de dark, dey must git Christ to hole de candle. God's grace shall be de candle in de good brudder's heart. Devils may howl, lions may roar, but nothin' shall daunt dat brudder's heart. Angels shall come down with lighted candles in deir hands to congratulate de brudder." Then, once more screaming and dancing and weep-

"Seen from a distance, Petersburg presents the appearance of a lovely forest pierced here and there by church spires and towers." [Page 580.]

ing, he uttered these words: "Die right, brudder, 'n' yo' shall not die in de night; yo' shall die in eternal day. Ef Christ don't bring light enough, den God will come wid his candle; an' ef dat ain't enough, den de Holy Ghost 'll come wid his candle, too, an' dar can't be no more night wid dat brudder's soul."

At another period in the sermon, he said: "Ef we can't preach God, we can exhort Him; ef we can't exhort Him, we can live Him; an' ef we can't live Him, we can die Him. I 've served under Him forty-two long year—longer dan Moses led Israel in de wilderness; an' ef I don' know what God is, den I 'd better *shut up* an' go home!!! Jesus snatched my soul from hell forty-two year ago in Fredericksburg, in old Vaginny! Praise Him! O praise Him! Let no brudder shout for Jesus who don' know Jesus."

After the more furious passages of exhortation were over, he gave his ideas upon prayer, something in this wise: "Dar was ole Fadder Jupiter (a colored preacher). Now Jupiter he used to git a Bible in one han' an' a pra'r-book in anudder, an' a hymn-book under his arm; an' den he 'd start out to see de widders 'n' de fadderless; 'n' one day I met old Fadder Jupiter, 'n' I say to him: 'Fadder Jupiter, how many pounds of meat have yo' prayed? How many pounds of sugar have yo' exhorted? How many cups of coffee have yo' sung to dem pore widders 'n' fadderless?' 'N' he says: 'Not one.' 'N' den I say: ''Pears like, Fadder Jupiter, yo 'll sing here, and pray dar, 'n' yo 'll pray every widder to death 'n' sing every fadderless child to de grave; 'n' call in help to bury 'em.' 'N' den I told him dat when he sung he must call a bar'l o' flour long metre, 'n' fur short metre he must take a keg of lard, 'n' dat 's short enough, anyhow; and fur particler metre nice ham 'n' some coffee; 'n' den he mus' take de Quaker pra'r-book, a two-wheeled cart, 'n' fill up de ole pra'r-book with coal; 'n' when de col' wedder come he must drive de ole pra'r-book down to some widder sister's, 'n' say: 'Sister, I 've come to pray six bushels of coal with yo', 'n' den open de cellar door, dump de ole pra'r-book, 'n' pray de cellar full o' coal.'"

The sermon was interspersed with impassioned recitations from Watts and Wesley. There was no logic, and no clear idea of anything except the love of God and charity. Now and then, with pompous air, the speaker would say: "An' now, breddren, we will proceed to consider de third (or fourth or fifth) point," and after a moment of solemn cogitation, would plunge into exhortation, appeal, and sarcasm, and yell until the rafters rang. His face was convulsed, and sobs shook his whole frame when he sat down. A strange wild hymn was sung, the singers waving their bodies to and fro to the measure of the music.

One of the ministers then arose, and bade those who desired the prayers of the church to come forward and lay their sins upon the altar. An indescribable rush of some twenty persons ensued. Old men and young girls hastened together to the pulpit, and knelt with their faces bowed upon their hands, and a low tremulous prayer to "O my Heavenly Fadder," was heard, as one of the old deacons poured forth his soul in supplication. During the prayer an exhorter passed around among the congregation, singling out the impenitent, and personally addressing them: "Yo' better go now!" "How 'll yo' feel when it 's too late, 'n' dar ain't no gittin dar?" In a short time the church resounded to groans and prayers, high over all of which was heard the clear voice of the colored Quaker chanting:

> "For everywhar I went to pray
> I met all hell right on my way,"

"but Heaven's God, 'n' we 'll get dar by 'n' by. O praise Him! O bless Him, 'n' sing 'wid de mornin' stars!"

Some of the colored preachers, although they make extravagant pretensions, are by no means so moral as our "Fadder Quaker," and, exercising absolute spiritual control over their ignorant flocks, prompt them to unworthy deeds, and fill their minds with wrong ideas. There is also a multitude of quacks and false prophets who seek to make money out of a revival of the barbaric superstitions still prevalent among certain classes of negroes.

On one occasion a huge negro created quite a clamor among the blacks in Petersburg, by announcing that he could cure any one afflicted with disease. He practically revived many of the features of Voudouism, and was rapidly fleecing his victims, when a pitying white man interposed and tried to expose the swindler.

But it was of no avail. The quack boldly challenged the would-be exposer to witness a cure of a long standing case of dropsy. At the house of the sick man the incredulous Caucasian found a large crowd of faithful believers assembled in front of a circle of bones, old rags, and other trash, over which the quack was muttering some gibberish. Finally the announcement was made that there was something in the sick man's bed which had made him ill; and, after a little search, a mysterious packet was found beneath the mattress.

While the horror-stricken crowd were bewailing this evidence of witchcraft, the white man insisted on opening the packet, found it filled with harmless herbs and minerals, and endeavored to convince the negroes that the doctor's confederate had undoubtedly concealed it there. But they would not believe him, and insisted on considering the doctor great at divination, although their confidence was a little shaken when the man stricken with dropsy died, despite the discovery and removal of the hurtful charm.

A Queer Cavalier.

LXV.

THE DISMAL SWAMP—NORFOLK—THE COAST.

CITY POINT, the historic peninsula upon the winding James river, is connected with Petersburg by a branch of the Atlantic, Mississippi and Ohio railroad, and steamers come up from the coast to carry away coal and iron. The route from Petersburg to Norfolk lies through Prince George, Sussex, Southampton, Isle of Wight, Nansemond and Norfolk counties. General Mahone's splendidly-constructed railway runs in a perfect air line for at least seventy-five of the eighty-one miles between the two cities, and is in all respects a model highway to so important a port as Norfolk. It takes the traveler

City Point, Virginia.

through fine cotton-fields; then along stretches of plain covered with thin swaying pines; now through clearings where rows of cabins are erected, and stalwart negroes are hewing wood and digging drains; now into thickets through which rough roads lead to some remote plantation; now through smart little villages, until at last he reaches Suffolk, the pretty shire town of Nansemond county. Suffolk is energetic, and well supplied with railways and river navigation; manufactories are springing up; the Sea-board and Roanoke railway touches there; the county has about 11,000 inhabitants, most of whom are prosperous. The climate in that section is usually delightful; the thermometer ranges from 22 degrees in winter to 94 degrees in summer, with seasons long enough for the maturity of all crops; and, indeed, the same land often produces two crops in one season. Cotton and all the cereals yield immensely. Many Northern people and a large number of English families have settled in the vicinity.

In Norfolk county we entered the edge of the Great Dismal Swamp, which extends far downward over some of the northern portions of North Carolina, and is intersected by canals, on which there is quite an extensive transportation business. The "swamp" is a succession of wild and, apparently, irreclaimable marshes, through which run black currents of water, and in the midst of which spring up thousands of dead tree-trunks. Many of these trunks are charred or blackened by the progress of some recent fire. Some are fantastically shaped, and have been imagined to bear resemblance to well-known statues. The passer-by has his attention invited to the "Column Vendome."

For miles the eye encounters nothing save the bewildering stretch of swamp and dead trees, or the dreary country covered with rank growth of pines and underbrush. The only signs of life are occasional groups of negroes about some saw-mill, on a "hummock," or a glimpse of dusky forms on a barge floating along one of the Stygian canals, as the train glides

A Peep into the Great Dismal Swamp.

smoothly and swiftly by. Drummond's Lake, penetrated by a feeder from the "Dismal Swamp" canal, is about thirty miles long.

Norfolk has a real English aspect. It is like some of the venerable towns along the southern coast of England, and the illusion to which the traveler readily yields is heightened by the appearance of many English names on the street corners, over the doors of some business houses, and at almost every turn. The grand current of the Elizabeth (opposite Fort Norfolk) is so broad and deep that the largest ship that floats can swing around there. Midstream, there is much clatter and activity; ships and steamers arrive and depart, and the hoarse shout of the sailor is heard all day long, vying in strength with the scream of the steamboat whistle. In the streets remote from the water-side, not so much activity is apparent, but there are long rows of staid, comfortable-looking houses, embowered in trees, many fine churches, and an ambitious custom-house. The trains of the Atlantic, Mississippi and Ohio railroad discharge their freights of cotton and grain directly upon wharves at the steamers' sides, and the unusual facilities are yearly increased and improved.

The people of Norfolk are beginning to understand the consolidation policy in railroad matters now-a-days. Time was when they could hardly perceive the advantages of a road laid through the treacherous "hummocks" of the Dismal Swamp, and they called the iron bridge over the Elizabeth "Mahone's Folly" when it was first built, thinking that it would cripple the line. But now that they have grappled hold of the commerce of the West, and have begun to compare their advantages with those of New York, they cannot enough praise the sagacity of those who labored until the great through line was an accomplished fact.

The importance of Norfolk as a port of the future is certainly indisputable; and it is not at all improbable that within a few years it will have direct communication with European ports, by means of ocean steamers, owned and controlled in this country. The Norfolk people have made an effort to turn the European emigration, bound to Texas, through their town, forwarding it over the lines penetrating South-western Virginia and Tennessee. But, thus far, only a fortnightly steamer of the Allan Line has touched at Norfolk, bringing, usually, many English families for the lands around Charlottesville and Gordonsville. The Elizabeth river is not so lively now as when, at the beginning of this century, the river could not be seen, so thick was the shipping between the Norfolk and Portsmouth shores. In the financial crash which came at that time, sixty Norfolk firms interested in maritime commerce failed; the modern town does not boast as many.

Norfolk* lies within thirty-two miles of the Atlantic. Northward stretch the Chesapeake and its tributaries, navigable nearly a thousand miles; westward is the James, giving communication with Richmond, and five hundred miles of water-way; southward run the canals to Currituck, Albemarle and Pamlico, communicating with two thousand miles of river-channel. She affords

---

* The eastern and southern branches of the Elizabeth river are superior in depth to the Thames at London, or the Mersey at Liverpool. The depth of water in the harbor at Norfolk is twenty-eight feet, or nearly twice that regularly maintained at New Orleans; and the harbor is spacious enough to admit the commercial marine of the whole country. It has been estimated that thirty miles of excellent water-front for wharfage can readily be afforded.

Eastern North Carolina is the natural ally of Norfolk in commerce. Behind the barrier of sand-hills, extending along the Carolina coast, lies one of the most fertile regions on the continent, which can find no more convenient outlet than Norfolk. The Sea-board and Roanoke railroad penetrates North Carolina, a little above the point at which the trade becomes tributary to its canals, and connects with the Raleigh and Gaston, and Wilmington and Weldon railroads, at Weldon. The Norfolk and Great Western road is a projected route to run through the southern counties of Virginia, touching at Danville and terminating at Bristol. The natural seaport of the Chesapeake and Ohio railroad, which, coming from the Ohio river, penetrates the mountains of Western Virginia, is, of course, Norfolk. The Albemarle and Chesapeake canal, through which, during eleven years from the 30th of September, 1860, more than thirty-five thousand vessels of all classes passed, penetrates a country rich in cereals, woods, and naval stores, all of which it brings directly to Norfolk. The river lines of steamers, running to Yorktown, Hampton, and Old Point, Elizabeth City, and Washington, N. C., Roanoke Island, and other places, are rapidly re-establishing the local trade of the Chesapeake and its tributaries, interrupted by the war. The receipts of cotton at Norfolk in 1858 were 6,174 bales; we have seen that in 1872 they were more than 400,000.

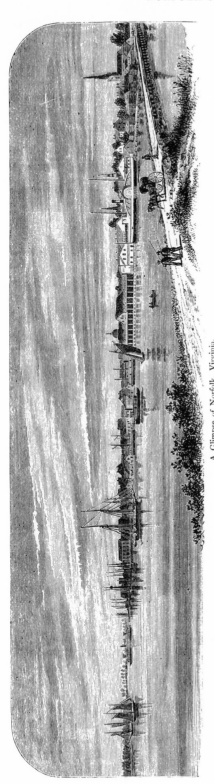

A Glimpse of Norfolk, Virginia.

naturally the best seaport for most of North Carolina and Tennessee, besides large sections of Northern Georgia, Alabama, Mississippi, and the Southwest. A thorough system of internal improvements in Virginia, giving lines leading from tide-water in that State to the North-west, would enable Norfolk almost to usurp the commercial preeminence of New York. Pittsburg, and Wheeling, and Toledo are geographically nearer the Capes of Virginia than to Sandy Hook; and it is almost certain that in the future many of the highways to the sea from the West will run through Virginia, and the ports furnishing outlets to the Western cities will be along the beautiful and capacious Chesapeake bay. Ingenious minds have already mapped an ocean route from Norfolk to the Holland coast—one possessing great advantages—and it is to be hoped that a company may be formed to place steamers upon it.

There are good steamship lines between Norfolk and New York, Boston, Baltimore, and Philadelphia. The Boston steamers carry a great deal of cotton to the New England factories. Norfolk received in 1873 *four hundred and six thousand* bales of cotton, an enormous increase over her receipts in 1872. The amount brought by the Atlantic, Mississippi and Ohio railroad alone in 1873 was 158,000 bales. The produce business of the port is very great; during the active season a daily steamer is sent to New York, Boston, and Baltimore, and three weekly to Philadelphia. The "truck farms"—*i. e.*, the market gardens in the vicinity,—give the shippers business at a time when "all cotton" towns are afflicted with dullness. The receipts of truck for 1872 amounted to $3,500,000; and the value of all the receipts was

$21,000,000.* The duties on imports into the district of Norfolk and Portsmouth, from 1866 to 1871 inclusive, amounted to more than $800,000.

There is a large negro population in Norfolk, and the white citizens make great struggles at each election to keep the municipal power in their own hands. They have long had excellent free schools, on which they are now expending $10,000 yearly; their city affairs are in good condition. The estimated real value of assessable property in the city is $17,000,000, and the .greater part of the tax thereon is readily collected; the citizens have built fine water-works at a large expense; the shops are excellent; society is exceedingly frank, cordial and refined.

This goodly ancient town, with its 20,000 inhabitants, was laid out more than a century and a-half ago, but the British burned it in the Revolution, and it had to grow again. It has seen troublous times since then. The yellow fever has made one or two ghastly visitations, and war has disturbed the even tenor of its way. There came a day, too, when Portsmouth, the pleasant town just across the Elizabeth from Norfolk, and where one of the principal naval depots of the United States is situated, seemed enveloped in flame, and when the new-made Confederate on one side of the stream watched with mingled regret and exultation the burning of the vast ship-houses and the ships-of-war which the United States were unwilling to allow him to capture.

A promenade along the Elizabeth, in company with an ex-Confederate officer, was fruitful of souvenirs. It was toward sunset of a September day when we clambered upon the parapet of old Fort Norfolk, and gazed out over the broad expanse of sparkling water toward the horizon, delicately bordered with foliage, which masked the embouchure of the James, and the black spots further down, indicating Crany Island and the entrance to Hampton Roads, where those two sea-devils, the "Merrimac" and the "Monitor," had their fierce battle. Fort Norfolk is now, as it was when the Confederates seized it, a magazine. The powder captured there at the beginning of the war long defended many a Southern town.

From the quaint walls of the venerable fort we saw pretty villages and villas, and the noble United States Marine Hospital, on the opposite shore; could watch the schooners coming in with the tide, as the sunset deepened from blood-red until it mingled its last gleam with the strange neutral twilight; the sudden advent of a Baltimore steamer looming up like a spectre, with its dark sides and black wheels half-shrouded in smoke; could see the rows of mansions extending

---

* Some idea of the produce business may be had from the following enumeration of the articles which passed through Norfolk, bound mainly to Northern cities, in 1872, and the various articles received at the port. The receipts of corn were 1,628,940 bushels; of peanuts, 544,025 bushels; of dried fruit, 346,542; oats, 329,110; peas, 152,420; wheat, 75,210; flour, 100,640 barrels; rosin, 129,586 barrels; turpentine, 14,940 barrels; pitch, 3,240 barrels; tobacco, 3,525 hogsheads, 2,520 tierces, 34,270 cases, and 38,920 boxes. In the same time, 1,000,000 dozens of eggs; 14,280,170 pounds of rags; $175,000 worth of shad; 6,000,000 bushels of oysters, amounting to nearly $4,000,000; 37,775 barrels of salt fish; 8,381,860 staves, 53,392,221 shingles, and 57,496,290 feet of lumber were also received. The Sea-board and Roanoke railroad annually brings in more than 180,000 bales of cotton.

out to the very water's edge, and the piers jutting from their front doors, with
rustic arbors and awnings, where one might sit and woo the fresh sea-breeze;
could see the gracefully tapering masts, and the massive walls of the warehouses,
and could hear the rattling of the chains, and singing of sailors.

Strolling back, we noted the barelegged negro boys sculling in the skiffs
which they had half-filled with oysters, and passed through streets entirely devoted
to the establishments where the bivalve, torn from his shell, was packed in cans
and stored to await his journey to the far West.   Driving on the hard shell road,
later in the evening, we passed long trains of fish-carts, in each of which lay a

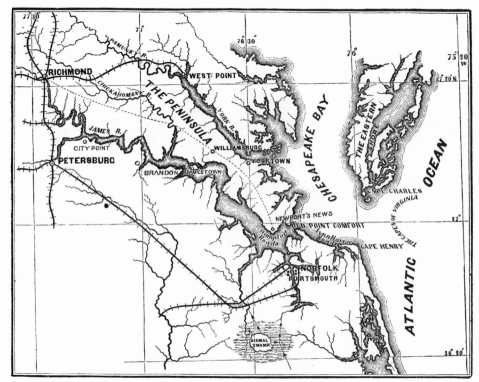

Map of the Virginia Peninsula.

sleepy negro, growling if we asked one-half of the road; saw the fields where,
during the civil war, the Confederates had prepared to defend Norfolk from approach of the blue-coated soldiery by land—fields occupied by carefully-tilled
farms, near which were the cabin and garden patch of the freedman; saw evidences
on every hand of growth and progress, and found it hard, indeed, to convince
ourselves that half a century had not passed since the " war for the Union "
closed.

The map given above shows the configuration of the Virginia peninsula, and
the location of Hampton Roads, one of the most superb expanses of land-locked
water in the world.   This grand refuge, in which all the navies of the world
might at one time find shelter from storm, is but fifteen miles from Norfolk.
Entering from the Atlantic, between the two capes of Virginia, Charles and

Henry, the ships of Newport, Smith, and Gosnold, the daring English explorers and colonists, penetrated more than two and a-half centuries ago to Hampton Roads and anchored opposite the point now known as Newport News.   Northward from Old Point Comfort, stretches the mighty Chesapeake bay, along whose richly-indented shores are some of the finest harbors on the American coast.

Hampton Roads.

Hampton Roads and Lynnhorn bay, lying between the capes, and under their shelter, are sometimes called the "Spit Head" and the "Downs" of the United States.   The York, the Potomac, the Rappahannock and the James rivers empty their ample currents into the Chesapeake bay, which the Virginians claim as "Virginia water," because it passes through her borders to the sea, and flows to it between the capes.

The "northern neck" of Virginia is that portion of her territory situated between the Rappahannock and the James rivers, and extending from the Chesapeake bay to the Blue Ridge mountains.   The four counties in this section, Lancaster, Northumberland, Richmond and Westmoreland, contain four hundred and sixty-six thousand acres, on which only 26,000 people are settled.   Along the rivers and the bay there are beautiful plains, which run back some two miles to a ridge two hundred feet higher than the shores.   This ridge extends throughout the length of the neck, and is intersected every few miles by streams of soft, fresh water.   Many of these streams are navigable, and producers settled along their banks can have easy water communication with the principal Northern ports.   The prodigal abundance of food to be had with very little effort, has thus far been an effectual hindrance to the proper development of this favored region; the negroes, who constitute a good part of the population, spend a few hours of each day in securing the fish, oysters, and wild fowl with which the inlets abound, but do not possess sufficient ambition to become either fruit-raisers, market gardeners or oystermen.   If they would work they might be prosperous; but they prefer a life of idleness.

The soil of the Neck along the rivers is mainly composed of alluvial deposits. It was for years cultivated recklessly, and very seriously exhausted, under the *régime* of the slave-holder; yet to-day, without thorough culture, produces paying crops.   The climate is delightful; the winters are very short and by no means severe.   Almost all varieties of fruit, save those peculiar to the tropics, can be cultivated to perfection there.   Labor is cheap; the negro is, of course, the only workman, and does as well as his limited knowledge and indolent dis-position will allow.   He needs the example of ambitious immigrants to encourage him to a right development of the excellent resources so lavishly scattered around him.   The white inhabitants eagerly welcome skilled workers, and offer them lands on favorable terms.

The tide-water region of Virginia extends from the coast to an imaginary line drawn across the State, and touching at Fredericksburg, Richmond, and Petersburg.   It includes the northern neck just described, and consists of a series of peninsulas whose sides are washed by the Chesapeake bay, and the great tidal rivers emptying into it.   Throughout this section the principal item of land culture is market gardening; good farms are to be had for small prices.   The lands are well drained; reasonably free from marsh, with a soil of clay, marl and sand, and an overgrowth of pine and oak.   It is estimated that 30,000,000 bushels of oysters are annually drawn from the waters in this region; a State tax is collected yearly on 20,000,000 bushels.   Malarial fevers are the draw-back, and historical memorials are the boast of the section.   Fevers prevail only during the autumn months, and will doubtless disappear entirely as the country becomes more densely populated, and sufficient attention is given to drainage.   They are at present the curse of the river-side populations, and nothing is more common than to meet a lean, discolored individual who explains his woe-begone look by announcing that he has just had a " right smart shake."

LXVI

THE EDUCATION OF NEGROES—THE AMERICAN MISSIONARY
ASSOCIATION—THE PEABODY FUND—THE CIVIL RIGHTS BILL.

A T Hampton one begins to appreciate the magnitude of the revolution
which has overtaken the South. There it was that, more than two
hundred and fifty years ago, the first cargo of slaves was landed on American
soil. There the curse began, and there its bitter leaven worked until the time of
deliverance arrived, and it was ordained that, on the very ground where the negro
had first been enslaved by the white man in Virginia, efforts for his elevation to
a true manhood should be undertaken.

Everywhere that the Union armies went in the South, they found the negro
anxious for knowledge. The wretched slave was like a blind man who heard
around him tumult and struggle, and who constantly cried aloud for light, for
the power of vision. He was weighted down with the crushing burden of his
past life; he saw the great chance slipping away from him, and in his intense
desire to become intelligent and independent, he fairly laid hold upon the soldiery
for help. But the officers and men of the army knew not what to do with the
negroes who took refuge in the Union camps. Sometimes they sent them back
to their masters; at others they protected and fed them, while at the same time
denying any intention of interfering with the institution of slavery.

But the day came when General Butler pronounced the freedmen who, by
thousands, had flocked into the country around Fortress Monroe, "contraband of
war." Hungry, homeless, and filled with nameless dread, these rude exiles from
the plantations of their late masters turned toward the National Government,
and held out their hands for protection. They knew not what to do. The
future lay dark before them. The cannon still thundered throughout Virginia.
The negroes stood on the threshold of liberty, still fearing that they might be
dragged away to their old condition of servitude. The country came to their
aid. The National Government found the key-note of the situation in Butler's
sharp, coarse proclamation, and held the negro refugees under its protection.
Then the American Missionary Association came to the front.

This noble Association, for so many years before the war an earnest worker
in the antislavery cause, was ready and anxious to send material relief to the
negroes. It was willing to aid in feeding their bodies as well as their souls. It
had had its missionaries in all parts of the South, undergoing persecution and
abuse for the sake of preaching the gospel and telling the truth. Its envoys had
been driven out of some of the States; others, as the outbreak of the war
approached, were arrested and imprisoned. But the work went on !

In August of 1861, Lewis Tappan, Esq., then Treasurer of the American Missionary Association, wrote to General Butler, at Fortress Monroe, asking what could be done to aid the negroes.   The General answered, showing the unhappy condition of the freedmen and women, and welcoming any assistance. Letters came from soldiers and officers in the army to the charitable throughout New York and the East, asking help for the negroes.   Rev. L. C. Lockwood was sent out to investigate the condition of the great mass of refugees in Virginia, and in September he opened a Sabbath school in the deserted mansion of ex-President Tyler.   On the 17th day of the same month, he started the first day school for the freedmen.   It was held in an humble house not far from Fortress Monroe, and was taught by Mary A. Peake, an excellent woman, whose father was an Englishman of rank and culture, but whose mother was a free colored woman.   She, the representative of both the oppressing and oppressed races, began her work of regeneration of the blacks on the very coast where the degradation began, and near a proud seminary where the daughters of Southern aristocrats had received the education paid for by the unrequited labor of slaves.

As the war progressed, the work of teaching grew and strengthened among the freedmen.   The Union forces made their way on to the sea-islands along the South Carolina coast in November of 1861, and the usual swarms of ignorant and half-starved negroes flocked around them.   The envoys sent from the North to examine into the condition of these wretched people gave such thrilling accounts of their needs, that public meetings to devise measures for relief were held in Boston, New York, and Philadelphia.   Societies for the establishment of schools and forwarding of supplies were speedily formed; the " Boston Education Society," the "Freedmen's Relief Association" of New York, and others, sprang into existence early in 1862.   Men and women were at once sent out as teachers. They began by first relieving the physical wants of the distressed, and then tried to teach them the dignity of labor.   The " Port Royal Society" of Philadelphia sent funds, provisions, and teachers.   Cincinnati, Chicago, Cleveland and Pittsburg sent workers and money.   Societies multiplied so rapidly that it was finally deemed advisable to consolidate them; and it was accordingly done in 1866, the combined bodies taking the title of the "American Freedmen's Union Commission."   This colossal organization worked in perfect harmony with the American Missionary Association for a short time, then gradually withdrew some of its branches from the work as reconstruction progressed, and ceased to be a really national body.

From the date of the founding of the school near Fortress Monroe, the American Missionary Association pushed its work with exemplary vigor.   The opening of 1863 brought with it the proclamation of emancipation, and settled forever the question of the condition of negro fugitives who escaped to the Union lines.   Then the North put forth its strength.   Hundreds of refined and delicate ladies voluntarily engaged in the work of teaching the blacks—living amid cheerless surroundings, on poor fare, and meeting with contempt and vulgar ostracism, which many a one who was guilty of it then would to-day be ashamed of.   At Hampton, Norfolk, and Portsmouth, day and Sabbath schools for the negroes were held in the colored churches; evening schools for adults were established, and men and women flocked to them after the fatigues of the day. On the estate of ex-Governor Wise, of Virginia, near Norfolk, the Missionary Association established schools, and the Governor's mansion became a school and a home for colored teachers.

Wherever the freed negroes gathered, as at Newbern in North Carolina, at Nashville in Tennessee, on Roanoke Island, in the Port Royal Islands, at Vicksburg, at Columbus, at Memphis, at President Island, at Camps Fisk and Shiloh, teachers were furnished, charities were bestowed, and the good work went nobly on. In 1864 the Association's workers in the field of the South numbered 250, mainly employed in Virginia and along the line of the Mississippi. In Louisiana General Banks had introduced an efficient system of public instruction, supported by a military tax, and there, too, the Association sent its teachers. The colored troops enlisted in the Union armies were instructed, and while the negroes rested from drill, they pored over the Readers and text-books which had been distributed among them.

The bodily needs of the freedmen were always as great and extreme as their spiritual necessities. Thousands died of neglect and starvation. The hand of Northern charity could not reach one-third of the sufferers. Many died under the despair and unrest occasioned by their change of condition. They became wanderers, and set out upon long journeys hither and yon, blindly straying toward some dimly-defined goal. Their darkened minds were impressed with the belief that somewhere a great material heritage awaited them. They were in an attitude of intense suspense when the war ended. Virtually the wards of the National Government, which had been compelled to undertake their support wherever they claimed aid, they relied implicitly upon the promises given them. Unable to help themselves, or to understand the dignity of the future to which they had suddenly been introduced, they could but hope and wait.

Behind the army of Sherman, and the forces which entered Richmond, marched resolute teachers. Schools were established in the slave-marts of Savannah, and were in due time placed under the control of the American Missionary Association. In Augusta, in Charleston, in Wilmington, and Richmond, teachers did all they could to shape the minds of the negroes to a sense of the responsibilities of manhood and the dignity of womanhood. Early in March of 1865 the Freedmen's Bureau was formed, and placed under the direction of General O. O. Howard, who, as its chief commissioner, did much to aid the colored man in maintaining his rights. The Bureau established schools wisely and well; and under its fostering care many now prosperous institutions were started and maintained, until they showed their beneficent character, and received large support from private charities.

As the Missionary Association had been from the first frankly unsectarian, it from time to time received the cordial coöperation of the different churches. The Wesleyan Methodists went into its work with the fervor which characterizes all their movements. The Free-Will Baptists supported many of its teachers. The National Council of Congregational Churches, which assembled in Boston in June of 1865, recommended the raising of a quarter of a million of dollars, to be placed in the hands of the Missionary Association, for carrying on the work among the freedmen. This generous gift came into play in 1866, and orphan asylums and normal schools were founded. The first asylum was located at Wilmington in North Carolina; the second, founded by a donation from Hon. I. Washburn of Worcester, Massachusetts, at Atlanta, Georgia.

Aid from abroad meantime came generously in. Great Britain sent more than $1,000,000 in money and clothing to the freedmen. The envoys of the Missionary Association were gladly and hospitably received in England, Scotland and Wales.

With the advent of reconstruction came a change in the aspect of the educational situation. The Southern people were not satisfied to see the black men elevated to political power; and in many States the most barbarous and, in some cases, murderous measures of intimidation were used to prevent the negro from gaining instruction, and from demonstrating his right to be a man. Mob violence, Ku-Klux mysteries, and social ostracisms were tried as agencies to deter Northern teachers from doing their good work. But the labor was continued as zealously as before. Churches were founded, the normal schools were liberally aided and encouraged in their work of equipping colored teachers, and wherever one teacher fainted in the ranks, another was quickly found to supply his or her place.

The operation of the Peabody fund, and the constant beneficence of the wealthy in the North and West, are still doing much to second the efforts which the Southern people are now themselves making in the cause of free public education. The negroes have as yet done but little to help themselves; they are not property holders to any extent, nor do they seem likely to become such, until they have been educated for at least a generation. Instances of thrift and thorough independence among them are not wanting, it is true; but the mass of negro males in the Southern States aid comparatively little in paying for the school privileges which they receive, under the operation of school laws in most of the reconstructed commonwealths.

The North has done much; yet it is by no means a proper time for it to relax its efforts. There never was a period when the money, the intelligence and the energy of Northern people were so much needed in the cause of education in the South as now. There was never a time when so much real missionary work could be done among the negroes. Now that they are beginning to take active part as citizens in the affairs of their sections they need the best instruction and the wisest advice. Their ignorance has already been made the means of infamous tyranny; their accession to political power has been marked by much injustice and wrong, of which they have been unwittingly the instruments; and the North owes it to them and to herself to aid in rescuing them from the adventurers into whose clutches they have fallen.

The seven chartered normal schools which have grown up under the American Missionary Association in the South are annually equipping fine corps of teachers for colored schools. Hampton, in Virginia; Berea College, on the border line between the blue grass and the mountain regions of Kentucky; Fisk University, at Nashville, Tennessee; Atlanta University, in Atlanta, Georgia; Talladega College, in Alabama; Tougaloo University, in Mississippi; and Straight University, in New Orleans, are but the precursors of other similar institutions to be placed in each Southern State. The Association will not rest contented with its labors until it has established normal schools in each of the ex-slave States west of the Mississippi river. In addition to these normal institutes, the American Missionary Association now has graded and normal schools combined in Wilmington, North Carolina; in Charleston, where the Avery Institute has more than four hundred pupils, and owns twenty thousand dollars' worth of property; in Greenwood, South Carolina; in Andersonville, Atlanta, Macon, and Savannah, Georgia; in Athens, Marion, Mobile, Montgomery, and Selma, in Alabama; in Chattanooga and Memphis, Tennessee; in Lexington and Louisville, Kentucky; in Columbus, Mississippi; in Galveston, Texas; and in Jefferson City, Missouri. It has under its charge, mainly in the Southern field, although some few of the institutions are on the Pacific coast, forty-seven churches, with a membership of 2,898; the seven normal and nineteen graded and normal schools mentioned above; forty-seven common schools; three hundred and twenty-three ministers, missionaries and teachers; and more than fourteen thousand pupils. As the work of thirteen years, in the face of the most remarkable obstacles and with a degraded population born in slavery to operate upon, this merits the world's applause.

The efforts of this brave Association and kindred societies have not been in vain. The Southern States at last have school systems of their own, and seem likely to maintain them. This alone is worth all that the war cost.

When Dr. Sears, the able and generous agent of the Peabody fund, went South in July of 1867, there was, strictly speaking, no modern school system in any of the twelve States in which the fund now operates. Tennessee inaugurated one, however, in that same year, under General Eaton. To-day all of those twelve States have by law, and all but one or two have in fact, tolerable school systems. West Virginia, Virginia and Tennessee, now have the most effective plans. Tennessee, after originally taking the lead, nearly abolished its schools on changing its politics three or four years ago. It adopted the miserable county system, with no State Superintendent. But for the last year or two, it has not only recovered what it had lost, but is now surpassed in good legislation and general activity for schools by no Southern State unless it be Virginia. At this time it is, in some respects, the most zealous and active State in the South concerning educational matters, and the prospects for public schools for years to come, at least in the large towns, are most encouraging.

West Virginia, which adopted a pretty good system early after the war, did not suffer much by a change from Republican to Democratic politics. The Convention for revising the Constitution made no change in that portion relating to schools. The latest legislation, leaving it optional with the counties to supplement the inadequate State taxation, was supposed to be disastrous; but the people have fortunately shown a disposition to vote a liberal tax.

It is the testimony of Dr. Sears and other intelligent men, who have carefully studied the subject, that three of the Conservative States are now leading all the others of the South in education. The feeling in favor of schools of some kind is so strong that no ambitious man of any party, in any Southern State, dares to oppose public free education. This is certainly a radical change in seven years !

Arkansas has a good school system, inadequately supported; Mississippi has good schools in the cities, but very few in the country. Alabama's progress is marred by unwise legislation, which gives the Legislature the power to veto the laws that only a Board of Education can pass.

The American Missionary Association, and all Northern enterprises in the cause of education, cannot do better for the next decade than to put all their money and talent into the States which are now, and are likely from time to time to be, under negro rule. In South Carolina, Florida, and Louisiana, the white people either stand aloof entirely from many of the public schools, or give them but a feeble and reluctant support. Normal schools and thorough teaching are needed bitterly in those States, and will be required for ten years to come.

At the commencement of the educational work in the South, there were three grand hindrances to the establishment of public schools.

The first was prejudice against them as a Northern institution, not adapted to the condition of the Southern people. This is now so far overcome as to cause no anxiety.

The second was the burden of taxation; but men are now beginning, all through the South, to see the necessity and economy of free schools. The opposition is mainly, to-day, among the ignorant, against whom the enlightened are gradually prevailing.

The third and most potent, still existing, is the dread of mixed schools. This should not be understood, as it so often is at the North, as arising from a desire on the part of the Southerner to deprive the negro of his chances for an education. The objection to mixed schools is a graver one, and may be considered sufficient. Until the masses of the black population in the South have acquired a higher moral tone than at present characterizes them, it will not be well to admit them freely into that communion which an education in the same rooms and under the same teachers as white children would give.

It is noteworthy that where the negroes have full and unrestrained political power, as in South Carolina and Louisiana, they have not even demanded mixed schools to any extent. They know that it would be useless; and it would be quite as repulsive to most of the blacks as to the whites to have an indiscriminate mingling of the races in schools. The negro in the Conservative States gains many more educational advantages by a separate school system than he could by mixed schools. Although he rarely pays more than one-sixth as much in taxes as his white fellow-citizen, the school law guarantees him exactly equal school facilities, save in a very few instances, and supplies him with buildings and teachers. It would be as absurd on the part of Congress to pass a bill a section of which should require the co-education of the sexes in the South, as to enact the mixed school section of the proposed "civil rights" bill. The good sense of the negroes rejects the section, as it enables them to see that a law odious to the whites would have for its natural result a cessation of effort in behalf of the blacks. The mixing of the races is not a matter for national legislation. Both races now have the vote; each has an equal chance with the other to acquire property and enjoy it; each can have all the education that it is willing to buy, besides what is freely given it. The course of a Congress which seriously discusses the passage of a bill which would block the whole educational system of the South, and at the same time never thinks of voting any appropriation to aid in carrying on the work of education there, is certainly open to criticism. The practical tendency of the attempt at enforcement of the mixed school clause would be the turning out of doors of the million and a-half of white and black children now in the public schools of the fifteen ex-slave States.

Taking the statistics of the Southern public schools, as given in 1871 and 1872, it will be seen that seven years after the close of the war the impoverished Southern States had managed to bring under the operation of a school system proportionally four-sevenths as many children as are at school in the North, and to keep them at school three-fourths as long.* In view of the fact that great numbers of the Southern people (*i. e.*, the negroes) own little or no property, it may be asserted that the Southern property holder is paying a much heavier school tax than is his Northern brother.

Congress, instead of threatening the South with the destruction of her school system, should take earnest measures to foster and protect education in all the Southern States. The ignorance prevalent in that section is the cause of many phases of its unhappy condition. It is believed that the registered adult illiterates in the South constitute more than one-half the adult population. There is indisputable evidence to show that the percentage of illiteracy has increased among the whites in the South since the outbreak of the war. The reclaiming of the "poor whites" from the barbarism in which they have been plunged for so many years is certainly a proper subject for the consideration of the National Government. If that Government had carefully and wisely supplemented, by an equal sum, such a generous donation as the $2,000,000 given by George Peabody for education in the South, it would have done no more than its duty. The negroes have been called *the wards of the nation;* yet we find the Southern States and a few individuals and societies doing all that is done for them. The nation does little but look on.

* Vide Report of General Ruffner, Virginia Superintendent of Education, for 1873.

LXVII

THE HAMPTON NORMAL INSTITUTE—GENERAL ARMSTRONG'S
WORK—FISK UNIVERSITY—BEREA AND OTHER COLLEGES.

THE better class of Southerners have been for some time convinced that
they must help the negroes to an education, as a protective measure.
They have discovered that the free laborer must possess a certain amount of
intelligence, and that he must have the incentives to work and to the acquisition
of property which knowledge gives. But the great difficulty has been to procure
a sufficient number of capable colored instructors for work throughout the back-
country. In the cities white teachers have been readily procured; but in the
interior those of their own race were needed for the negroes. To insure the
elevation of the blacks, they must have before them the daily example of one of
their own people who has been instructed, and who is anxious to instruct them.

The establishment of the normal schools mentioned in the previous chapter
proved the solution of this difficulty. The Northern people, who had been the
closest observers of the freedmen, readily recognized that the first need was the
spread of rudimentary education. After the new generation had been taught to
read and write, had been shown the dignity of labor, and had received the much-
needed lessons in morality, it would be time enough to found a college with a
classical course for the freedmen, or to insist on the privilege for them of entrance
into the colleges now occupied by the whites. So the sensible Northerners went
at the work of educating negro teachers.

"What the negro needs at once," wrote General Samuel C. Armstrong, in his
report on the system and condition of the Hampton Normal Institute, made to
the Virginia Superintendent of Education in 1872, "is elementary and industrial
education. The race will succeed or fail as it shall devote itself with energy to
agriculture and the mechanic arts, or avoid these pursuits, and its teachers must
be inspired with the spirit of hard work, and acquainted with the ways that lead
to material success. An imitation of Northern models will not do. Right
methods of work at the South must be created, not copied, although the under-
lying principle is everywhere the same." This is the truth, and those of the
negroes who have been taught under such men as General Armstrong are telling
it to their fellows.

General Armstrong, who had been Colonel of the Eighth Regiment of United
States colored troops during the war, was the chief official of the Freedmen's
Bureau at Hampton when the thousands of blacks were helplessly gathered there.
As early as 1867, he had set forth, in an able article, the need of normal schools
for the colored people. The son of a missionary who was for sixteen years the
Minister of Public Instruction in the Hawaiian kingdom, General Armstrong thor-

oughly understood the establishment of schools upon a "manual labor" basis, as they had been established in the Sandwich Islands. A man of quick sympathies, tremendous will and iron courage, he determined to see what the manual labor school would do for the freedmen and freedwomen. With the coöperation of the American Missionary Association, he began his work and, in April of 1868, inaugurated the labors of the institution which was chartered in 1867 by the Virginia Legislature as the Hampton Normal and Agricultural Institute, with a board of eminent Northern gentlemen as trustees. General Howard, as head of the Freedmen's Bureau, helped the work generously; money was given, a large farm was purchased, and in 1872 the school received its first aid from Virginia, in land-scrip to the amount of $95,000, bestowed on the institution in its character of agricultural college. Thus encouraged, the school prospered, and colored pupils flocked to it from nearly all the States of the South. The division of labor and study partaken by both male and female pupils has been satisfactory to both teachers and scholars, and the pecuniary results have been better than were anticipated. Each male student has, each week, from a day and a-half to two days' labor on the farm, for which he is credited a fair sum. The young women are provided with an industrial department, where they are taught to use sewing-machines, and are familiarized with all the ordinary duties of housekeeping. There is a printing-office attached to the school, and a monthly paper is issued by the labor of the scholars. One of the fundamental principles of the school is that nothing shall be given which can be earned by the pupil, and this has the desired effect of encouraging a spirit of independence. Since the founding of the institution, it has sent out nearly one hundred well-trained teachers, earnest, honest Christian men and women, who propose to devote their lives to the elevation of their race. At the closing exercises of the term of 1874, when a large class graduated, Virginians and New Englanders united in pronouncing the school a thorough success, and one of the most effective agents for the elevation of the negro.

The normal work has had great and encouraging growth in Tennessee. The people of Nashville had the problem of the care of freedmen presented to them early in 1862, and in 1867 the Freedmen's Bureau and the American Missionary Association together had succeeded in securing the charter of Fisk University in that city. Early in 1867 the State Superintendent of Public Instruction and other Tennesseans announced that "the best way to permanently establish and perpetuate schools among the colored people is to establish good normal training schools for the education of teachers." The University was developed from the Fisk school, opened in 1866, and named for General Clinton B. Fisk, who was for a time in charge of the work of the Freedmen's Bureau at Nashville. The attendance at this school had averaged over a thousand pupils, until Nashville herself adopted a public school system. The Missionary Association then placed a suitable location for buildings at the disposition of the trustees of the new University, and a little band of the students, young men and women, went out into the North to sing the "heart-songs" in which the slaves used to find such consolation, and by means of concerts to secure the money with which to erect new University buildings. The success of that campaign, in this country and in

England, is now a matter of history. The "Jubilee Singers" have found the means to build Jubilee Hall, an edifice which would be an ornament to any university, and around which will in time be grouped many others.

This University began with the alphabet in 1867. It teaches it still, but it offers in addition a college classical course of four years, with a preparatory course of three years, and two normal courses of two years each. The following paragraph from a report of a recent commencement will show what progress the ex-slaves have already made:

"On Thursday the freshman class in college was examined in Virgil's Æneid, Geometry, and Botany, the latter with the sophomores. The sophomore class was examined in the De Amicitia and De Senectute of Cicero, and Livy, in Latin; in Homer's Iliad, in Greek, and Botany, in all of which the members of this class acquitted themselves with marked ability, showing conclusively that the people of the colored race are capable of acquiring and mastering the most difficult studies, and attaining the highest culture given by our best colleges. The promptness and beauty of their translations, together with their accuracy, showing a knowledge of the structure of the language as well as the thought of the classics they translated, was most gratifying to the friends of education, as well as to their instructors. So, too, in Botany, pursued but a single term, the examination was most satisfactory in the knowledge of the terminology of the science, the principles of classification, and the ability to analyze plants, explain their structure, and determine their order and species in the vegetable world."

The normal instruction of Fisk University is constantly supplying the colored race with efficient and pious teachers. The privations which the negro will inflict upon himself for the sake of maintaining himself in the University (for it is not, like Hampton, a manual labor school) are almost incredible. The University stands upon the site of Fort Gillam, in a beautiful section of Nashville, and the town negroes never pass it without a lingering look at the doors of the building, as if they all would enter if they could.

At Berea College, near the old estates of Cassius M. Clay, the famous abolitionist, in Madison county, Kentucky, the spectacle of both races studying in the same institution in completest harmony may be seen. A prosperous school was started at Berea several years before the war by a missionary who had been successful in founding antislavery churches in the South; but when the John Brown raid occurred, the slaveholders broke up Berea. At the close of the war the teachers returned, and found their homes and buildings uninjured. They at once opened a school into which both races were received upon equal footing. This was a source of great astonishment to the white Kentuckians for a time; but they finally began to send their children, and now the regular proportion of white students is about two-fifths, many of whom are young ladies. The annual commencement exercises bring together audiences of a thousand or fifteen hundred persons, black and white, ex-Confederate and Unionist, who look approvingly upon the progress of students of both colors. Rev. E. H. Fairchild, brother of the President of Oberlin, presides over the faculty. Donations from the North are rapidly building up this institution, one of the few in the ex-slave States where blacks and whites study harmoniously together.

The University at Atlanta met with much opposition; the Georgians seemed disinclined to believe in the sincerity of those who had come to teach the negroes.

After the institution, which was incorporated in 1867, had been in operation two years, it was visited by a committee of prominent Southern gentlemen, many of whom were severely prejudiced against negro schools, but who were forced to admit, in their report made to the Governor of the State, that "the system of intellectual and moral training adopted in the school" was eminently practical. It was evident, also, from other sentences in their report, that they began to believe in the possibility of the education of the negro masses, as they added that the satisfactory answers of the pupils "to questions tended to define the character of their moral training, their polite behavior, general modesty of demeanor, and evident economy and neatness of dress, are indicative of a conviction on the part of the pupils that they are being educated for usefulness, and not for mere ostentation or to gratify a selfish ambition." They found that the African could stand very rigid tests in algebra and geometry, and "fully comprehend the construction of difficult passages in the classics." Atlanta University has two hundred and fifty students, has received aid from the Legislature, and annually sends out well-educated colored teachers from its normal department.

The college at Talladega, Alabama, was chartered in 1869, and has already sent out many faithful workers. A paragraph from the pen of Rev. George Whipple, of New York, concerning a recent examination of the classes at Talladega, contains some important testimony:

"Those who know anything of the educational work among the colored people need not be told that they are seldom at fault in studies exercising mainly the memory; but many, if not most, have doubted their ability in studies requiring the exercise of the reasoning faculty. There was here, however, no failure. On the contrary, that which made the most marked impression on those who were familiar with schools in the North twenty and twenty-five years ago, was the well-sustained examination in English Grammar and Algebra, showing a power of analysis, under the circumstances, really surprising."

In the theological department of this University, young colored men are prepared for the ministry, and are given an impulse in the direction of real missionary work, so much needed among the reckless emotional negroes in the interior districts of the South.

The Straight University at New Orleans has nearly 250 pupils, and among the dusky attendants there are diligent students in Greek, Latin, and Algebra. The importance of this institution to the negroes of the South-west cannot be overestimated. In no other State does the negro, when left to himself, touch so closely upon barbarism as in the remote portions of Louisiana; and the training of colored teachers who can reach the untaught masses is a work of the highest beneficence. The programme of the University is certainly ample; how necessary its existence to the good of the State is may be understood from the statement of what it proposes to do:

"To train the half-heathen preachers of this State into a useful Christian ministry; to give its colored legislators so much knowledge of history and law as to make their votes intelligent, and to awaken as much self-respect as shall lift them above temptation to take a bribe; to furnish teachers to our crudely-organized public schools; to gather into the fold of the Church this vast Roman Catholic population; to win them to us by showing them that Straight University is, in its instructors, buildings, libraries, apparatus, discipline, Christian courtesies, scholarship, and general management, wholly superior to, and broader than, their parochial and conventual schools; to make it safe for the republic that the newly-created citizens of Louisiana should retain their franchise, and to prevent Louisiana from being Mexicanized by frequent revolutions; in brief, to infuse a wholesome Christian life into the mingled mass of negro and Latin blood,—is a work which must be done for its own sake, for the sake of the nation, and for Christ's sake."

There is but one chartered normal school for the tens of thousands of freedmen in Mississippi, the one heretofore mentioned as at Tougaloo. It has nearly 300 students; the manual labor system has been introduced to some extent; the normal school is successful; but half-a-dozen such institutions, amply endowed, are necessary to give proper facilities for education to the swarming masses of blacks.

It has been the fashion in both North and South to believe that the negro would prove susceptible of cultivation only to a certain point. But the universal testimony of the mass of careful observers is that the negro can go as far in mental processes as the white child. The blacks have wonderful memories and strong imitative propensities; eloquence, passionate and natural; a strange and subtle sense of rhythm and poetry; and it is now pretty well settled that there are no special race limitations. Why, then, should they not go forward to a good future? Is it not the duty of that section which gave them political power before they were fit to use it, to give them every opportunity to fit themselves for its exercise? It will be long before they can, of their own effort, supply the funds needed for their education; until they can, the North should not fail to foster all the schools which, like the normal institutions whose history has been reviewed in this chapter, sow the good seed.

The schools are doing much to lift up the negro's idea of the dignity of religion. Emphatically Christian institutions, they strive to inculcate that morality and self-denial which it seems so difficult for the blacks to exercise. Although there are many exemplary Christians among the freedmen and freedwomen, it may safely be said that the majority do not allow their religion to interfere with their desires. They believe in the spasmodic shouting, stamping, and groaning which characterize their meetings as essentials of true worship; they are excited to the most exalted state by the rude and picturesque harangues of their preachers, and obey them implicitly, so far as they understand them. But they often make their camp-meetings and revival assemblies the scenes of indecent orgies, and in some States where great numbers of ignorant negroes are gathered together, they turn the church into a den of roystering drunkards. The preachers are sometimes very immoral, and now and then, after exhorting for an hour or two in such a violent manner that one might imagine them possessed by the spirit, they will join in the worst carousals of their parishioners. But wherever education goes, this conduct ceases. The missionaries from the normal schools strive against the besetting sins of the African, and are gradually helping him. The school-house and the church together, with intelligent and earnest advisers in each, will transform the character of the freedman in another generation.

The negroes have a profusion of churches, organized by themselves, in all the large cities of the South and South-west; in Memphis, in New Orleans, in Richmond, and in Charleston the churches are very well sustained, and are attended by immense congregations. The preaching is sometimes absolutely fine; there are colored men of great culture and natural talent in the ministry; but, as a rule, the ministers are rude in their language, forcible in their illustrations, and possessed of an enthusiasm which, whether or not the proof of a rare spirituality, is certainly inspiring to any one who witnesses it. The emotional part of the black man's worship is, of course, that which develops the greatest number of peculiarities. It will always, even when the race is educated, remain a striking feature in his churches; but will be chastened and subdued. The rapturous shoutings, the contortions of the body, the desire to dance and to yell, the mysterious trances, now-a-days seen, as they were before the war, in assemblages of blacks overcome with religious excitement, will be greatly modified, but will never be lost sight of. Under powerful mental excitement of any kind, the American negro finds it difficult to "keep still." The exuberance of his animal spirits gets relief only in dancing, in gambols high in air, in grotesque gestures; and this is all the more noticeable from the fact that in repose his favorite attitude is slouching and inactive.

The theological department in the excellent Howard University at Washington, and the classes in theology in the other universities, are kept well recruited, and the graduates go out to teach the negroes a "different kind of religion from mere shouting and confusion." In the back-country, log churches are built; in the towns, houses are rented, or neat brick edifices are erected. The ministers who go into the interior districts make efforts to have the negroes from several contiguous plantations unite in building a church, and are generally successful. In many sections negroes have been converted from practices resembling barbarism to sincere Christian worship. But for the millions of freedmen and women in the South the work which has already been done is only as a drop in the bucket. Hundreds of thousands of dollars are needed to supply this people with the barest necessities of their intellectual improvement; a steady charity for ten years to come will be in no wise mistaken. They need, above all, to be taught how to help themselves; and by the normal schools and the complete education of the most promising individuals of their race, that will be soonest accomplished.

LXVIII.

NEGRO SONGS AND SINGERS.

THE negro would deserve well of this country if he had given it nothing but the melodies by which he will be remembered long after the carping critics who refuse to admit that he is capable of intellectual progress are forgotten. His songs of a religious nature are indisputable proofs of the latent power for an artistic development which his friends have always claimed for him. They are echoes from the house of bondage, cries in the night, indistinct murmurs from an abyss. They take directly hold upon the Infinite. They are sublimest and most touching when they partake of the nature of wails and appeals. They have strange hints and gleams of nature in them, mingled with intense spiritual fervor. In this song, which the toilers in the tobacco factories of Virginia used to sing, there is a wild faith, and a groping after the proper poetry in which to express it, which touch the heart :

> " May de Lord — He *will* be glad of me,
>   In de heaven He 'll rejoice ;
>   In de heaven once, in de heaven twice,
>   In de heaven He 'll rejoice.
>   Bright sparkles in de churchyard,
>   Give light unto de tomb ;
>   Bright summer, spring 's ober,
>   Sweet flowers in de'r bloom."

This is the incoherence of ignorance ; but when sung, no one can doubt the yearning, the intense longing which prompted it. The movement of the melodies is strong and sometimes almost resistless ; the rhythm is perfect ; the measure is steady and correct.

But little idea of the beauty and inspiration of the " slave music " can be conveyed by the mere words. The quaintness of the wild gestures which accompany all the songs cannot be described. At camp-meetings and revival-gatherings the slaves give themselves up to contortions, to stampings of feet, clappings of hands, and paroxysms affecting the whole body, when singing. The simplest hymns are sung with almost extravagant intensity.

The songs are mainly improvisations. But few were ever written ; they sprang suddenly into use. They arose out of the ecstasy occasioned by the rude and violent dances on the plantation ; they were the outgrowth of great and unavoidable sorrows, which forced the heart to voice its cry ; or they bubbled up from the springs of religious excitement. Sometimes they were simply the expression of the joy found in vigorous, healthy existence ; but of such there are few. The majority of the negro songs have a plaintive undertone. They are filled with such passionate outbursts as the following:

"Nobody knows de trouble I see, Lord,
  Nobody knows de trouble I see;
Nobody knows de trouble I see, Lord,
  Nobody knows like Jesus!
Brudders, will you pray for me,
  And help me to drive old Satan away?"

The improvisations are in some cases remarkable. A student at the Hampton Normal School has given to the public a long rhapsody on the judgment day, improvised by an old slave who was densely ignorant, but who embodied his dreams in song, as follows:

"I'm a gwine to tell yo' bout de comin' of de Savior,
        Far' you well, Far' you well;
Dar's a better day a comin',
        Far' you well, Far' you well;
When my Lord speaks to his Fader,
        Far' you well, Far' you well;
Says Fader, I 'm tired of bearin',
        Far' you well, Far' you well;
Tired o' bearin' for pore sinners,
        Far' you well, Far' you well;
Oh! preachers, fold your Bibles,
        Far' you well, Far' you well;
Prayer makers, pray no more,
        Far' you well, Far' you well;
For de last soul's converted,
        Far' you well, Far' you well;
In dat great gittin'-up mornin',
        Far' you well, Far' you well."

The terrors of the judgment day are portrayed with a vivid and startling eloquence, and these verses are usually sung with a rude dramatic force which is really fine:

"Gabriel, blow your trumpet!
Lord, how loud shall I blow it?
Loud as seven peals of thunder,
Wake de sleeping nations;
Den yo' see pore sinners risin',
See de dry bones a creepin',
        Far' you well, Far' you well.

"Den yo' see de world on fire,
Yo' see de moon a bleedin',
See de stars a fallin',
See de elements meltin',
See de forked lightnin',
Hear de rumblin' thunder;
Earth shall reel and totter,
Hell shall be uncapped,
De dragon shall be loosened,
Far' you well, pore sinner,
        Far' you well, Far' you well."

Nothing can exceed in beauty and fervor this little hymn, sprung out of great sorrow and affliction. It lays hold upon Heaven, and will not be thrust aside:

> " O Lord, O my Lord,
> O my good Lord,
>   Keep me from sinkin' down!
> O my Lord, O my good Lord,
>   Keep me from sinkin' down!
> I tell you what I mean to do,
>   Keep me from sinkin' down;
> I mean to go to Heaven too,
>   Keep me from sinkin' down!"

One of the most notable of the songs refers to a "great camp-meeting in the promised land," and is said to have been first sung by a company of slaves, who were not allowed to sing or pray where the master could hear them; but when he died their mistress granted them the privilege of singing and praying in their cabins at night, and they often joyfully sang this hymn:

> Dere's a better day comin', don't you get weary,
> Better day a comin', don't you get, &c., *(bis)*
> Dere's a great camp-meetin' in de Promised Land,
> Oh slap your hands childron, don't, &c.,
> Slap your hands childron, don't, &c., *(bis)*
> Dere's a great camp-meetin' in de Promised Land.
> Oh pat your foot children, don't you get weary,
> Pat your foot childron, don't, &c., *(bis)*
> Dere's a great camp-meetin' in de Promised Land.
> CHO.—Gwine to live wid God forever,
>   Live wid God forever, *(bis)*
>   Dere's a great camp-meetin' in de Promised Land.

> Oh, feel de Spirit a movin', don't you, &c.,
> Feel de Spirit movin', don't, &c., *(bis)*
> Dere's a great camp-meetin' in de, &c.
> Oh now I'm gettin' happy, don't you get weary,
> Now I'm gettin' happy, don't, &c., *(bis)*
> Dere's a great camp-meetin' in de, &c.
> I feel so happy, don't you get weary,
> Feel so happy, don't you get weary, *(bis)*
> Dere's a great camp-meetin' in de, &c.
> CHO.—Oh, fly an' nebber tire,
>   Fly an' nebber tire, *(bis)*
>   Dere's a great camp-meetin' in de Promised Land.

Throughout the South, wherever the negroes have gathered into large communities by themselves, one will generally find a very good brass band; yet probably not one of its members can read music. They play by rote with remarkable accuracy, and they learn a song by hearing it once. The rhythm mastered, they readily catch the tune, and never forget it. Every one sings; man, woman and child croon over their toil, but never with that joyous abandon so characteristic of other races. In the churches the hymns are often "lined

out "—that is, each line is read by the deacon or preacher, and then sung by the
congregation; but this is quite unnecessary, as all are usually familiar with the
words.   In hymns and songs which are purely enthusiastic, the lines are never
read; the worshipers will sometimes spontaneously break into a rolling chorus,
which almost shakes the rafters of the church.   Then their enthusiasm will die
away to a tearful calm, broken only now and again by sobs and "Amens!"
The appended hymns, sung in seasons of great enthusiasm by the negroes in
and around Chattanooga, Tennessee, will serve to indicate the character of all
of that class:

> "Oh, yonder come my Jesus,
>   Hallelujah! Hallelujah!
> Oh, how do you know it's Jesus?
>   Hallelujah! Hallelujah!
> I know Him by his garments,
> I know him by his garments.
> His ship is heav-i-ly loaded,
> His ship is heav-i-ly loaded,
>   Hallelujah! Hallelujah!
> It's loaded wid bright angels,
> It's loaded wid bright angels,
>   Hallelujah! Hallelujah!
> Oh, how do yo' know dey are angels?
>   Hallelujah! Hallelujah!
> I know dem by deir shining,
> I know dem by deir shining,
>   Hallelujah! Hallelujah!
> *   *   *   *
>
> "O, John! my Jesus' comin',
> He is comin' in de mornin';
> Jesus' comin'; He's comin' by de lightning,
> Jesus' comin'; He's comin' in de rainbow.
> Don't you want to go to Heaven?
> Jesus' comin."
> *   *   *   *   ¢
>
> "Oh, rock away chariot,
> Rock all my crosses away;
> Rock me into de Heavens.
> I wish't I was in Heaven—
> I wish't I was at home.
> I wish't I was in Heaven—
> Lord, I wish't I was at home!"

The pilgrimages of the " Jubilee " and Hampton singers through this country and England, and the brilliant success which attended their concerts, is a
notable event in the history of the American negro.   When the Jubilee Singers
first went North to earn money for the University which was giving them their
education, they met with some slights—were now and then called "niggers"
and "negro minstrels," and were variously scoffed at.   Here and there in the
North and West they were refused admission to hotels on account of their
color; their success was at first a matter of doubt; but their mission pleaded its
way into the hearts of men when the sweet melodies and wild burdens of their

songs were heard. In all the great cities of the North their concerts were attended by large audiences; Henry Ward Beecher welcomed them in Brooklyn, introducing them to his congregation at a Sunday evening prayer-meeting, when they sang some of their most effective songs; and straightway thereafter they were the rage in the Metropolis as well as in Brooklyn. Their tour through the Eastern States was productive of much profit, and the little band of singers carried home twenty thousand dollars to place in the treasury of Fisk University, as the result of their first campaign in the North.

Encouraged by this success, Prof. George L. White, who originally conceived the idea of teaching these emancipated slaves to sing the plantation hymns of the old times, and to give a series of concerts embodying them, took the singers to England. All the world knows how enthusiastically they were received in Great Britain. The Queen, the nobility, and the great middle class heard them sing, gave them kind words and money, and praised them highly; and in March of 1874 this little band of blacks had collected ten thousand pounds, to be used to pay for the building of Jubilee Hall, at the University at Nashville. Of the eleven singers, eight are emancipated slaves.

The Hampton Student Singers at first numbered seventeen. They made their first appearance in 1872, under the direction of Mr. Thomas P. Fenner, of Providence, Rhode Island, who was of peculiar service in aiding them to a faithful musical rendering of the original slave songs. The singers were all regular students of the Hampton Normal Institute, and, even while journeying on their concert tour, carried their school-books with them. Their songs were heard with delight throughout the Middle, Eastern, and Western States, and their concerts have been attended with financial success.

The spirituality, the pathos, the subtle plaintiveness of the fresh, pure voices of these bands of black singers, invest the commonest words with a beauty and poetry which cannot be understood until one hears the songs. Once while listening to the singing of " Dust an' Ashes," one of the sweetest and sublimest chorals ever improvised, I tried in vain to analyze its mysterious fascination. The words were few and often repeated; the melody was from time to time almost monotonous. I could not fix the charm; yet the tears stood in my eyes when the wild chant was over,—and I was not the only one of the large audience gathered to hear the singing who wept. I give some of the words; but they will hardly serve to convey to the reader's mind any idea of the beauty of the choral:

> " Dust, dust an' ashes
>   Fly over on my grave.
>   Dust, dust an' ashes
>   Fly over on my grave, *(bis)*
>   An' de Lord shall bear my spirit home. *(bis)*
>   Dey crucified my Savior
>   And nailed him to de cross, *(bis)*
>   An' de Lord shall bear my spirit home.
>   He rose, he rose,
>   He rose from de dead, *(repeat)*
>   An' de Lord shall bear my spirit home."

One of the most effective of the spiritual songs is "Babylon's Fallin'," which is often used at Hampton Institute as a marching song. The words are as follows:

"Pure city,
  Babylon's fallin' to rise no mo'.
Pure city,
  Babylon's fallin' to rise no mo'.
Oh, Babylon's fallin', fallin', fallin',
  Babylon's fallin' to rise no mo'.
Oh, Jesus tell you once befo'
  Babylon's fallin' to rise no mo';
To go in peace and sin no mo'—
  Babylon's fallin' to rise no mo'."

Another note of aspiration is sounded in the hymn "Swing Low, Sweet Chariot," the music of which is full of earnest prayer:

"Oh, swing low, sweet chariot;
    Swing low, sweet chariot, (bis)
  I don't want to leave me behind.
Oh de good ole chariot swing so low,
    Good old chariot swing so low,
  I don't want to leave me behind."

Even the religious hymns and songs are not devoid of that humor with which the negro is so freely endowed, and some of the words to hymns intended to be of the most serious character are highly ludicrous, as when we are informed, concerning a "pore sinner," that

"Vindictive vengeance on him fell,
  Enough to sqush a world to hell;"

or when we hear a hundred negroes loudly singing—

"Jesus ride a milk-white hoss,
  Ride him up and down de cross—
    Sing Hallelujah!"

It is difficult to repress a smile when listening to the story of the deluge and Noah's voyage, as detailed in the popular choral hymn entitled, "De Ole Ark a-Moverin' Along." The last verse will give the reader a taste of its quality:

"Forty days an' forty nights, de rain it kep' a fallin',
    De ole ark a-moverin', a-moverin' along;
  De wicked clumb de trees, an' for help dey kep' a callin',
    De ole ark a-moverin', &c.,
  Dat awful rain, she stopped at last, de waters dey subsided,
    De old ark a-moverin', &c.,
  An' dat old ark wid all on board on Ararat she rided,
    De old ark a-moverin', &c.
CHORUS—Oh, de ole ark a-moverin'," &c.

A hymn called the "Danville Chariot," which is very popular with the negroes in Virginia, has this verse:

"Oh shout, shout, de deb'l is about;
Oh shut yo' do' an' keep him out;
    I don' want to stay here no longer.
For he is so much-a like-a snaky in de grass,
Ef you don' mind he will get you at las',
    I don' want to stay here no longer.
CHORUS—Oh, swing low, sweet chariot," &c.

The quaintness of the following often induces laughter, although it is always sung with the utmost enthusiasm:

"Gwine to sit down in de kingdom, I raly do believe
        Whar Sabbaths have no end.
Gwine to walk about in Zion, I raly do believe,
        Whar Sabbaths have no end.
Whar ye ben, young convert, whar ye ben so long?
Ben down low in de valley for to pray,
And I ain't done prayin' yit."

"Go, Chain de Lion Down," is the somewhat obscure title of a hymn in which this verse occurs:

"Do you see dat good ole sister,
    Come a-waggin' up de hill so slow?
She wants to get to Heaven in due time,
    Before de heaven doors clo'.
        Go chain de lion down,
        Go chain de lion down,
Befo' de heaven doors clo'."

Many years before the period of bondage was over, and when it seemed likely to endure so long as the masters pleased, the negroes hinted in their hymns at their coming deliverance. They often compared themselves to the Israelites, and many of their most touching songs have some allusion to King Pharaoh and the hardness of his heart. A few of the more noted of the songs, which were the outgrowth of the negro's prophetic instinct that some day he should be free, are still sung in the churches and schools. This is a favorite among the blacks:

"Did n't my Lord deliber Daniel,
Did n't my Lord deliber Daniel,
    And why not ebery man?
He delibered Daniel from de lion's den,
And Jonah from de belly of de whale,
An' de Hebrew children from de fiery furnace,
    And why not ebery man?"

"Go Down, Moses," was another warning of the "wrath to come," which those in power did not soon enough accept. It was sung at many a midnight meeting, when the masters did not listen; and the oppressed took comfort as they joined in its chorus.   The free children of parents who were born in slavery will look upon this song with a tearful interest:

"When Israel was in Egypt's land,
    Let my people go;
Oppressed so hard dey could not stand,
    Let my people go.
Go down, Moses,
    Way down in Egypt land,
Tell ole Pha-roh,
    Let my people go.

"Thus saith de Lord, bold Moses said,
    Let my people go;
If not I'll smite your first-born dead,
    Let my people go.
        Go down, Moses," &c.

"No more shall dey in bondage toil,
    Let my people go;
Let dem come out wid Egypt's spoil,
    Let my people go.
        Go down, Moses," &c.

The "first-born" have indeed, been smitten, and Israel has come up out of Egypt.

Mr. Theodore F. Seward, of Orange, New Jersey, in his interesting preface to the collection of songs sung by the Jubilee Singers of Fisk University, makes the following remarks, which may help to a proper comprehension of the negro's heart-music:

"A technical analysis of these melodies shows some interesting facts.   The first peculiarity that strikes the attention is in the rhythm.   This is often complicated, and sometimes strikingly original.   But although so new and strange, it is most remarkable that these effects are so extremely satisfactory.   We see few cases of what theorists call *mis-form*, although the student of musical composition is likely to fall into that error long after he has mastered the leading principles of the art.

"Another noticeable feature of the songs is the entire absence of triple time, or three-part measure, among them.   The reason for this is doubtless to be found in the beating of the foot and the swaying of the body which are such frequent accompaniments of the singing.   These motions are in even measure, and in perfect time; and so it will be found that, however broken and seemingly irregular the movement of the music, it is always capable of the most exact measurement.   In other words, its irregularities invariably conform to the 'higher law' of the perfect rhythmic flow.

"It is a coincidence worthy of note that more than half the melodies in this collection are in the same scale as that in which Scottish music is written; that is, with the fourth and seventh tones omitted.   The fact that the music of the ancient Greeks is also said to have been written in this scale suggests an interesting inquiry as to whether it may not be a peculiar language of nature, or a simpler alphabet than the ordinary diatonic scale, in which the uncultivated mind finds its easiest expression."

The teachers attached to the educational mission of the Port Royal Islands carefully studied the music of the half-barbarous negroes among whom they were stationed, and the result was an excellent collection of slave songs, which, without their efforts, would have been entirely lost.

The old planters sometimes say, with a shake of the head and a frown, that the negroes no longer sing "as they used to when they were happy." It is true that the freedmen do not sing as of yore; that they sing as much, however, there is little doubt. We have seen that the better class of their songs is filled with a vein of reproachful melancholy, that it everywhere has the nature of an appeal for help, a striving for something spiritual, dimly seen, and but half understood. These were the songs which the slaves sung at their work, but since their emancipation they are no longer compelled to voice their talents in such sombre music. The Port Royal teachers took down from the lips of the colored people hundreds of songs whose crude dialect and cruder melancholy rendered the task very difficult.

According to the testimony of the teachers the negroes always keep exquisite time in singing, and readily sacrifice a word and the sense attached to it if it stands in the way of the rhythm. The voices have a delicate and mellow tone peculiar to the colored race. There is rarely part singing, as it is not generally understood, and yet the Port Royal teachers say that when a number of blacks are singing together no two appear to sing the same thing. The leaders start the words of each verse, improvising many tunes, and the others, who "base" him, as they call it, will strike in with the version, or when they know the words, will join in the solo. They always succeed in producing perfect melody, out of whose network the transcribers have found great difficulty in extracting sounds that can be properly represented by the gamut.

The teachers testify that "the chief part of the negro music is civilized in its character, partly composed under the influence of association with the whites, and partly actually imitated from other music; but," they add, "in the main it appears to be original in the best sense of the word." Passages in some of the songs are essentially barbaric in character, and the teachers believe that most of the secular songs in use among the negroes contain faint echoes from the rude music of the African savages. A gentleman visiting at Port Royal is said to have been much struck with the resemblance of some of the tunes sung by the watermen there to boatmen's songs he had heard on the Nile. Colonel Higginson, who spent some time among the negroes on the South Carolina islands, gives a curious description of the way in which negro songs were originated. One day, as he was crossing in a small boat from one island to another, one of the oarsmen, who was asked for his theory of the origin of the spirituals, as the negroes call their songs, said, "Dey start jess out o' curiosity. I ben a raise a song mysel' once," and then described to Colonel Higginson that on one occasion when a slave he began to sing, "O, de old nigger-driver."

Then another said, "Fust ting my mammy tole me was, notin' so bad as nigger-drivers." This was the refrain, and in a short time all the slaves in the field had made a song which was grafted into their unwritten literature. Another negro, in telling Mr. J. Miller McKim, one of the teachers on the island, how they made the songs, said, "Dey work it in, work it in, you know, till dey get it right, and das de way."

The "shout," one of the most peculiar and interesting of the religious customs of the slaves, still kept up to some extent among the negroes on the coast, is discountenanced by many of the colored preachers now-a-days. It is what may be called a prayer-meeting, interspersed with spasmodic enthusiasm. The population of a plantation gathers together in some cabin at evening, and, after vociferous prayer by some of the brethren, and the singing of hymns in melancholy cadence by the whole congregation, all the seats are cleared away, and the congregation begins the genuine "walk-around" to the music of the "spiritual."

The following description of the dance, which is a main feature of these shouts, appeared in the New York *Nation*, in 1867:

"The foot is hardly taken from the floor, and the progression is mainly due to a jerking, pitching motion, which agitates the entire shouters, and soon brings out streams of perspiration. Sometimes they dance slowly; sometimes, as they shuffle, they sing the chorus of the spiritual, and sometimes the song itself is also sung; but more frequently a band composed of some of the best singers and of tired shouters stands at the side of the room to "base" the others singing the body of the song, and clapping their hands together or on their knees. Singing and dance are alike extremely energetic, and often when the shout lasts into the middle of the night, the monotonous thud of the feet prevents sleep within half a mile of the 'Praise-House.'"

I append three or four of the most beautiful of the songs sung by the negroes of the lowland coast of South Carolina. That entitled "Lord Remember Me" attracted universal attention when it first appeared, shortly after the war, at the North. It was set to weird music, and had the genuine ballad flavor:

I HEAR FROM HEAVEN TO-DAY.

Hurry on, my weary soul,
And I yearde from heaven to-day,
My sin is forgiven, and my soul set free,
And I yearde, etc.
A baby born in Bethlehem,
De trumpet sound in de oder bright land;
My name is called and I must go,
De bell is a-ringin' in de oder bright world.

LORD REMEMBER ME.

Oh Deat' he is a little man,
And he goes from do' to do';
He kill some souls and he wounded some,
And he lef' some souls to pray.

Oh, Lord, remember me,
Do, Lord, remember me;
Remember me as de year roll round,
Lord, remember me.

NOT WEARY YET.

O me not weary yet, *(repeat)*
I have a witness in' my heart;
O me no weary yet, Brudder Tony,
Since I ben in de field to fight.
O me, etc.
I have a heaven to maintain,
De bond of faith are on my soul;
Ole Satan toss a ball at me,
Him tink de ball would hit my soul;
De ball for hell and I for heaven.

HUNTING FOR THE LORD.

Hunt till you find him,
   Hallelujah!
And a-huntin' for de Lord,
Till you find him,
   Hallelujah!
And a-huntin' for de Lord.

I SAW THE BEAM IN MY SISTER'S EYE.

I saw de beam in my sister's eye,
Can't saw de beam in mine;
You'd better lef' your sister's door,
Go keep your own door clean.

And I had a mighty battle, like-a Jacob and de angel,
Jacob, time of old;
I did n't 'tend to lef' 'em go,
Till Jesus bless my soul.

RELIGION SO SWEET.

O walk Jordan long road,
And religion so sweet;
O religion is good for anything,
And religion so sweet.
Religion make you happy,
Religion gib me patience;
O 'member, get religion.
I long time ben a huntin',
I seekin' for my fortune;
O I gwine to meet my Savior,
Gwine to tell him bout my trials.
Dey call me boastin' member,
Dey call me turnback Christian;
Dey call me 'struction maker,

But I don't care what dey call me.
Lord, trial 'longs to a Christian,
O tell me 'bout religion;
I weep for Mary and Marta,
I seek my Lord and I find him.

MICHAEL, ROW THE BOAT ASHORE.

Michael, row de boat ashore,
            Hallelujah!
Michael boat a gospel boat,
            Hallelujah!
I wonder where my mudder deh,
See my mudder on de rock gwine home,
On de rock gwine home in Jesus' name;
Michael boat a music boat,
Gabriel blow de trumpet horn,
O you mind your boastin' talk;
Boastin' talk will sink your soul.
Brudder, lend a helpin' hand;
Sister, help for trim dat boat.
Jordan's stream is wide and deep;
Jesus stand on t' oder side.
I wonder if my massa deh;
My fader gone to unknown land,
O de Lord he plant his garden deh.

I WISH I BEN DERE.

My mudder, you follow Jesus,
My sister, you follow Jesus,
My brudder, you follow Jesus,
To fight until I die.

I wish I ben dere,
To climb Jacob's ladder;
I wish I ben dere,
To wear de starry crown.

JESUS ON THE WATER-SIDE.

Heaven bell a-ring, I know de road,
Heaven bell a-ring, I know de road;
Jesus sittin' on de water-side,
Do come along, do let us go,
Jesus sittin' on de water-side.

LXIX.

A PEEP AT THE PAST OF VIRGINIA—JAMESTOWN.
WILLIAMSBURG—YORKTOWN.

A T Jamestown, on the river James, one comes suddenly upon memorials of a vanished past. The Virginia whose life once centred around the village on the placid stream has passed away. Jamestown, the first prominent Anglo-Saxon settlement on this continent, is to-day a melancholy nook where historic memories play at hide-and-seek among moss-grown ruins. The remains of the venerable church there are surrounded with a graveyard filled with mouldy tombstones, whose inscriptions are scarce-ly legible. Tall trees tangle their roots in the brickwork of the decaying tower. Silence and desolation brood over this ancient edifice, destroyed nearly a century and a-half ago. It is supposed to have been built a little after Bacon's rebellion in 1676, and is known to have been in use as late as 1733, for in that year a silver baptismal font was presented to it. Some of the pieces of silver plate that belonged to the church may still be seen in the library of the Theological Seminary near Alexandria.

The Ruins of the old Church at Jamestown, Virginia.

After Captain John Smith and his brave knights, as well as all the swaggering, starveling gallants and tavern-haunting vagabonds who first colonized Jamestown, had crumbled into dust and made way for the more enterprising and industrious native Virginians, the town was deserted. The transfer of the seat of the Colonial Government to Williamsburg in the beginning of the eighteenth century ruined the prospects of Jamestown, and the swiftly-moving years have now swept everything away save this one tower of the old church, the reflection of whose image upon the river's gleaming surface seems like a ghost from the past, peering out of the depths into which the present has banished it.

Williamsburg and Yorktown, on the peninsula between the York and James rivers, contain some of the most interesting souvenirs of early civilization in America. Williamsburg, half-way between the two streams, is the oldest incorporated town in the State, was the seat of the Colonial Government before the

Revolution, and the capital of the Dominion until 1779.   On the lawn in front of William and Mary College, the oldest of American educational institutions except Harvard, stands the statue of Lord Botetourt, who ruled over the Virginians some years previous to the troubles between the mother country and the colonies, and who died two years before the advent of the great Revolution.

Statue of Lord Botetourt at Williamsburg, Virginia.

The tide of war has from time to time swept round the College buildings, but has always respected the old statue.   The Virginians of revolutionary days did not bring the good Lord down from his pedestal, for he had been a faithful Governor, zealous and never forgetful of their interests.   The marble image, however, once lost its head, a college student, who afterward became Governor of Virginia, having taken a fancy to knock it off; but it was carefully replaced.   William and Mary College has had the rare honor of educating several Presidents of the United States. During the late civil war it suffered much, and to-day stands in serious need of financial aid.

A century ago a noble avenue, known as Gloucester street, extended from the venerable college for a mile in a straight line to the then Capitol of Virginia.   Along its sides were ranged the palace of the Governor, of which only one wing remains to-day, the rest having long since been destroyed by fire; the " Court-House of James City County;" the old Raleigh Tavern; the octagonal powder magazine which served as the colonial arsenal of Virginia, and from which on the night of April 20, 1775, the royal Governor stole away all the powder; and the old church of Bruton parish.   The, powder magazine to-day serves as the stable for the principal inn of Williamsburg.   The College chapel, designed by Sir Christopher Wren, has vanished from the western extremity of the great avenue, which it once adorned.   Old Bruton Church, standing midway between the College and the site of the ancient Capitol, was erected shortly after the noted James Blair, commissary to the Bishop of London, and President of William and Mary College, became minister, when Spotswood was Governor in 1710.   Whitfield often preached in the church, and the parish became noted as the ground on which, more than sixty years before the outbreak of the American Revolution, the battle of the rights of the people against privilege and irresponsible authority was fought.   The Rev. Mr. Blair had a hearty quarrel with Spotswood, the Governor insisting upon the right of choosing parish clergymen, while Blair contended for the right of the vestries to make that choice.   By their firm attitude the vestries at last compelled the Governor to yield his point.

Spotswood, although hard-headed and obstinate, was one of the ablest and purest of Virginia's chief magistrates in her colonial days. He it was who built the first iron-furnaces in the colonies, and who first rode across the great Blue Ridge, the barrier in his day between civilized Virginia and the wilderness beyond. When he and his goodly company returned to Williamsburg from their long and adventurous journey across the mountains, the Governor caused a golden horseshoe, set with precious stones, to be given to each of his fellow cavaliers as a badge of knighthood, bearing the motto, *"Sic juvat transcendere montes."* This was the origin of the order of the Knights of the Golden Horse-shoe.

Yorktown and Williamsburg are both destined to be important termini of the Chesapeake and Ohio railroad. Yorktown, which lies within a few miles of the colonial capital, still possesses some of the picturesque and semi-decayed mansions of the old Nelsons and Pages, and other noble families of Virginia. The traveler is yet shown the precise spot at Yorktown where, on the 19th of October, 1781, the surrender of Lord Cornwallis to the combined American and French forces took place, the remains of the intrenchments cast up by the British, on the south and east sides of the town, being still visible. An excavation in the bluff on which the village stands is called Cornwallis's Cave, and is reputed to have been made and used by Lord Cornwallis as a council-chamber during the siege. Round about both Williamsburg and Yorktown there are many newer and fresher memorials of war than those half-forgotten ones of the Revolution.

A journey up the York river from Yorktown takes one past the site of the Indian settlement which John Smith described as "Werowocomoco," and where he was rescued from death by the fair Pocahontas. Not far from the site of this romantic rescue stands "Rose-well," formerly the estate of Governor Page, a princely edifice, whose materials were all brought over from England in colonial days, and which now stands lonely on a barren hill. On the Pamunkey river is "White House," said to be the scene of Washington's marriage with Martha Custis in 1759. During the late war, White House was an important depot of supplies, and the fine mansion there and all the supplies were burned in the course of military operations.

The old Colonial Powder Magazine at Williamsburg, Virginia.

In 1584, Queen Elizabeth licensed Sir Walter Raleigh to search for remote heathen lands "not inhabited by Christian people," and granted to him in fee simple "all the soil within two hundred leagues of the places where his people should, within six years, make their dwellings or abidings," reserving only, to herself and her successors, his allegiance and one-fifth of all the gold and silver he should obtain.   Sir Walter at once sent out two ships, which visited Wococan Island, in North Carolina, and the next year he dispatched seven ships, with 107 men, who settled on Roanoke Island.   The Indians there soon acknowledged

The old Church of Bruton Parish—Williamsburg, Virginia. [Page 622.]

themselves the homagers of the brave Sir Walter, and in 1586 and 1587 he sent a Governor, with twelve assistants and a charter of incorporation, instructing them to settle on Chesapeake Bay.   They landed, however, at "Hattorask," now known as Hatteras. In 1588, when a fleet was ready to sail with a new supply of colonists and supplies, it was detained in English ports by Queen Elizabeth to assist against the Spanish Armada; and Sir Walter, who had expended £40,000 in these enterprises, was obliged to get others to adventure their money.   In 1589, he therefore deeded to other colonists the liberty of trade to his new country free from all taxes for seven years, excepting the fifth part of the gold and silver ore due the Queen.   At different times thereafter, however, he sent off fresh expeditions to the American coast, but the fate of the last colonists sent hither was never known, and Sir Walter died on the scaffold without seeing the realization of his bright dreams of a new empire on the American Continent.

Cornwallis's Cave, near Yorktown, Virginia. [Page 623.]

Those who supposed that Raleigh's grant was forfeited by his alleged treason petitioned King James, the successor of Elizabeth, for a new grant of Virginia to them.   It was executed to Sir Thomas Gates and others, and in 1607 a settlement was effected at Jamestown, on the river James.   This grant "was superseded by letters patent of the same King in 1609 to the Earl of Salisbury and others, incorporating them by the name of 'The Treasurer and Company of Adventurers and Planters of the City of London for the First Colony of Virginia;' granting to them and their successors all the lands in Virginia from Point Comfort along the sea-coast to the northward two hundred miles, and from the same point along the sea-coast to the southward two hundred miles, and all the space from this precinct on the sea-coast up into the land, west and north-west, from sea to sea, together with the islands within 100 miles of it." This grant was added to in 1612.

In 1621 this Company established two Supreme Councils in Virginia, one called "The Council of State," the other "The General Assembly," to be convened by the Governor once yearly or oftener, the latter body to consist of the Council of State and two burgesses out of every town, hundred, or plantation, to be chosen by the inhabitants. In due time King James and "The Company of Adventurers" quarreled, and the latter's powers were superseded by a proclamation in 1624. As Charles I. then took the government of England, the colonists of Virginia passed under his control, and in this they heartily accorded, loving and admiring the cavalier King.

But presently the northern parts of their colony were granted away to Lords Baltimore and Fairfax, the first of whom also obtained the rights of separate jurisdiction and government. After the deposition of Charles I., the English Parliament, standing in the deposed King's stead, began to tyrannize over the colony and to impose grievous restrictions upon it. But the Virginian colonists had, from the first, maintained a vigorous opposition to Cromwell and the Parliament, and did not lay down their arms until, as they fancied, they had secured their rights by a solemn covenant with the deputies from Parliament. These rights, which, with arms in their hands, they sternly insisted upon, were that Virginia's ancient limits should be restored to her; that the colony should be freed from all taxes and impositions; that the colonists should have all the rights of free-born Britons; that the Assembly should convene as formerly, and that trade should be free. Every one of these rights, so strongly insisted upon, was subsequently violated by English kings and parliaments. "The General Assembly was split into two houses; appeals from their Supreme Court, which had been fixed by law in that Assembly, were arbitrarily revoked to England, to be there heard before the King and Council."* The colony saw its sea-coast reduced in thirty years from 400 to 100 miles; its foreign trade was suppressed; and the gradual restriction and oppression practised by England, under the long line of royal governors, and the intolerable grants of land made to the detriment of the colonists after the Restoration, finally resulted in the Virginia phase of the revolution which became so general throughout America. England lost a proud domain when the Virginians were alienated from her. The State which produced Marshall, Madison, Monroe, Mason, Nicholas, Henry, Randolph, Lee, Pendleton, Washington, Wythe, and other members of the Convention which assembled in Richmond in June, 1788, to ratify the Federal Constitution, deserved deference and generous treatment rather than oppression and abuse. Time was when England, Scotland, Ireland, and Virginia had their arms quartered on the same shield.

* Jefferson's "Notes on Virginia."

LXX.

RICHMOND—ITS TRADE AND CHARACTER.

THE view of the Virginian capital as one approaches it on the James river, is singularly fine. One gains the impression that Richmond is an immense metropolis, the hills seem so packed with streets lined on either side with solid blocks of stone and brick. From the ample foliage peep church-spires and towers, and the roofs of spacious mansions are seen on Cary, Main, Franklin, Grace, Marshall, Clay and Leigh streets, and in the pretty suburbs of " Chim-

View of Richmond, Virginia, from the Manchester side of the James River.

borazo" and Union, Church and Navy, Gamble's and Libby's Hills. The splendid steamers of the Old Dominion Company, which controls the line between New York and Richmond, ply slowly along the stream through the level plains bordered with forests, and give one ample time to study the city which was so lately the Confederate capital. Its grouping of houses and streets, seen at a distance, is picturesque; as one approaches it the ordinary aspects of an American city appear in their customary prosaic form.

One is not sorry to see hills again, after the lowlands of the serpentine James, and he climbs with gusto the steep streets leading to the Capitol, whence he can get a look over the broad plains beyond the stream. A few years ago the dwellers in Richmond watched those plains with keenest anxiety, when cannon thundered and battles were fought in the forests and along the roads. The traveler remembers that he saw many church-spires in the vicinity of the Capitol as he looked at the city from the river; from Capitol Square he can hardly distinguish them, they are so concealed, save their very tops, by the ample foliage. From the front porch he can look down upon the James, flowing hurriedly through the city over a rocky bed which makes Richmond the head of navigation; and can note the barges clustered about the flour-mills, and the groups of negroes at the doors of the tobacco warehouses.   The State Penitentiary's white-washed walls, on a neighboring hill, form a group as picturesque as an Italian monastery.   On the Richmond bank of the river the immense array of shops, known as the Tredegar Iron Works, lies half-concealed beneath clouds of smoke, and beyond them are the "Old Dominion Nail Works," on the famous "Belle Isle," where Federal prisoners were confined during the war.   Manchester, on the opposite side of the stream, is a thriving village, with two fine cotton-mills

Libby Prison—Richmond, Virginia.

employing three hundred workers, and with many neat houses, which testify to the prosperity of the villagers.   Farther down the James, one can see the unsightly group of buildings around the low, dirty-looking, ancient edifice, known as "Libby Prison."   Not far away, on the opposite side of the street, is the famous "Castle Thunder."   These once noted prisons, whose walls are covered with the names of the hapless Union officers who sweltered and starved in them during the civil war, have been relegated to their previous condition of tobacco warehouses.

At the foot of the hill occupied by Capitol Square stands the pretty Custom-House, built in the Italian style from the granite of which inexhaustible beds lie all around Richmond.   From the Square, avenues running down toward the river open into Main street, a broad business thoroughfare, extending along the hills and into the valleys, and lined with the principal shops, banks and offices of the town.   Below Main, on all the streets by the river-side, are located the wholesale establishments, the manufactories, and the warehouses.   A vacant spot here and there, blackened by fire, is the only reminder of the great conflagration which ran riot for a mile through the business section of the city on the night when the Confederates were forced to evacuate the capital which they had defended so long and so well.   Richmond lost a thousand buildings in that fire; but now builds half as many every year.   In 1873, the city expended a million and a-half dollars in the erection of new edifices.

"Shockoe Hill," on which the Capitol stands, is a goodly eminence.   Its picturesque height was so attractive to the eyes of old Colonel Byrd, of West-over, in 1733, that he decided to lay the "foundation of a large city there."   He had found a promising site for another metropolis at the falls of the Appomattox river, where Petersburg stands, and recorded in his diary that Richmond and

Petersburg, being the uppermost landings of James and Appomattox rivers, "were naturally intended for marts where the traffic of the outer inhabitants must centre." The good Colonel's judgment has been proved accurate. "Shockoe's" height was once furrowed by deep ravines on either side, and weeds flourished where now dainty flower-beds and trim lawns delight the eye. The modest three-story wooden house in which Henry and Jefferson, when Governors of Virginia, lived, has been succeeded by a handsome "Executive Mansion." The Capitol itself, modeled, according to Thomas Jefferson's suggestion, after the celebrated Maison Carré at Nismes, in France, has an imposing front, but is insecure and insufficient for the uses of a great commonwealth. A horrible accident occurred in the building in April of 1870, by which over fifty

Capitol Square, with a view of the Washington Monument—Richmond, Virginia.

people were killed and hundreds were wounded. The flooring of the room situated directly above the Hall of the House of Delegates, and used as the Court of Appeals, gave way, and precipitated a large audience, gathered to hear the decision of an important case, into the legislative chamber.

The Capitol contains the celebrated statue of Washington, by Houdon, made in 1788, and erected in the same year by the grateful State, which would not wait until its hero was dead before it deigned to honor his deeds. In the square "hall of entrance," where this statue stands, there are also a marble bust of Lafayette, and an antique English stove, used to warm the House of Burgesses at Williamsburg in colonial days. The stove is three stories high, and when sent to the Colonies its founder, Buzaglo, wrote concerning it: "The elegance of the workmanship does honor to Great Britain. It excels in grandeur anything ever seen of the kind, and is a masterpiece not to be equaled in all Europe." It was given to the House of Burgesses by the Duke of Beaufort, and is the most interesting of colonial memorials, except the chair in which the Speaker of the House of Burgesses once sat, and which is now in the Capitol. A fine portrait of General Lee, by Elder, graces the Hall of Delegates. The only bronze statue which Richmond possesses is the most remarkable in the United States. It is the equestrian statue of Washington, upon which Crawford lavished so much labor, and in which his splendid genius shines more conspicuously than in any other of his works. The statue, completed by Randolph Rogers, stands on the esplanade leading from the Governor's house to the west gate of the Capitol Square. Around the colossal Washington, mounted on a finely modeled horse, which seems vaulting airily from a massive pedestal of granite, stand bronze figures of Patrick Henry; Thomas Jefferson; John Marshall, one of the bravest fighters in the Revolution, as well as a most illustrious Chief-Justice of the United States; Andrew Lewis, one of the giants who supported Washington in the earliest struggles against Great Britain; George Mason, author of the Virginia "Bill of Rights;" and Thomas Nelson, a Governor of the old commonwealth during the Revolution and a brilliant soldier. Around the lower pediments military and civic decorations are emblazoned in bronze. The Capitol Square also contains a marble statue of Henry Clay. Northward from the square is the City Hall, and not far from it the stately mansion which Jefferson Davis chose for his residence when Richmond was the Confederate capital. Near at hand is St. Paul's Church, in which Davis was seated at worship when the messenger brought him the fatal news of the final disaster to Lee's army, and the necessity of flight from Richmond.

St. John's Church—Richmond, Virginia.

There are three churches in the Virginian capital which possess especial interest for the traveler. One of them, St. John's, dates from before the Revolution, and is celebrated as the edifice in which Patrick Henry uttered his immortal words—"Give me liberty

or give me death!" Modern improvements are crowding thickly around this
venerable structure, which was also filled, long after the Revolution had been
successful, by the delegates that Virginia sent up to Richmond to ratify the
Federal Constitution.   The second church is a long, low building on steep Broad

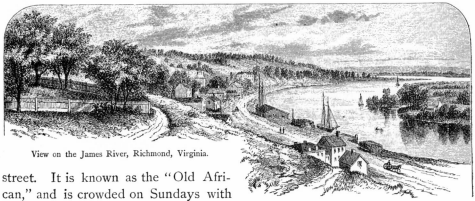

View on the James River, Richmond, Virginia.

street. It is known as the "Old African," and is crowded on Sundays with
the dusky population of the negro
quarters.   During the late war, and the troublous times following it, this humble
but spacious building was the scene of many tumultuous political gatherings.
Now-a-days the white visitor, unobtrusively seating himself in one of the rear
pews, can look over a vast congregation of blacks listening with tearful and
rapt attention to the emotional discourse of their preacher, or singing wild
hymns, as they are read out, line by line, by the deacon.   The singing is one of
the most remarkable features in all the African churches in Richmond; every one
joins in it, and it is not uncommon to see the churches so crowded that the
doors are blockaded, the worshipers obstructing even the sidewalks, as they
unite with enthusiasm in the simple yet really beautiful service.

   The third noticeable church is the Monumental, built on the spot on Broad
street where, in 1811, the Richmond Theatre took fire during an evening per-
formance, and a great number of the most beautiful women and eminent men
in the State, including the Governor and other personages of distinction, were
burned and crushed to death.

   Richmond's principal cemetery, Hollywood, has long been noted as one of
the most lovely in the South.   It occupies a wide tract in the western limits
of the city, picturesquely broken into hill and dale, and decorated with prettiest
of shrubs and flowers.   From a slope in the cemetery one gets a fine outlook
over the winding James river and Kanawha Valley canal; on the fretted current of the James river itself, with its waterfalls and clusters of green islets; and
on the northern and eastern hills of the city, covered with masses of well-
grouped buildings and remnants of fortifications.   In the southern section of
the cemetery stands the tomb of President Monroe, whose remains were
escorted to Richmond from New York by the Seventh Regiment several years
before that noted organization had any idea that it would ever make a hostile
incursion into the "Old Dominion."   From the hill one can see the ruins of

the old State Armory near the canal. The Confederates used it during the war, and when the evacuation of Richmond was ordered, the Armory was swept away in the conflagration kindled by the retreating army.

Monument to the Confederate Dead—Richmond, Virginia.

In the soldiers' section are the graves of hundreds of Confederate dead, and from the centre of this tract springs a rough stone pyramid, which the clinging ivy is gradually clothing in green. Soldiers from all the Southern States are buried under the shadow of this pyramid, and late in the month of May, a few days before the North observes the ceremonies of Decoration, the gray-coated veterans and the militia regiments parade in solemn procession to the cemetery, and thousands of ladies dressed in black wander silently and tearfully among the graves. There are rarely any speeches; there is no display of flags and emblems of the lost cause; the grief is too deep for words, too sacred to be associated with the vulgar details of politics.

Richmond is chief among Virginia cities, no less because of its proud position as the capital than because of its enterprise and its rapid growth. It now has nearly fifty-five thousand inhabitants, and its population is steadily increasing. The total assessed value of its real estate and personal property amounts to $37,000,000. Its exports amounted in the year 1873 to $3,026,492, an increase in one year of $1,026,123; its trade with other countries, to which it sends wheat, flour, leaf and manufactured tobacco, resin, lard, stoves, and furniture, is steadily increasing. The aggregate product of the manufactories in the city in 1872 was $16,199,870. The most important and oldest industries of the town are the manufacture of chewing tobacco and the milling of flour.

The Gallego Flouring-Mill—Richmond, Virginia.

The Gallego flour-mill, which produces fifteen hundred barrels daily, has a monopoly of the Rio de Janeiro and Australian trade, where the Richmond flour is preferred to all others, because it suffers no injury from transportation through the hot latitudes near the equator. From "Rockitt's," the "port" of Richmond, on the James, thousands of barrels of flour are weekly carried away in small sailing vessels, which ply constantly between Brazil and Virginia, bringing coffee on their trips to America. Richmond was, up to 1860, the third coffee mart in the United States, and will perhaps be the first when her Western connections have been so perfected that wheat enough to supply the hoppers of the flour-mills can be obtained, and the commerce with South America

Scene on a Tobacco Plantation— Burning a Plant Patch.

assumes the mammoth proportions it promises some day to take. The city suffered the loss of one of its largest flour-mills by fire a year since; but the citizens propose speedily to replace it by another and ampler one. The present Gallego mill has twice arisen from the ruins caused by conflagrations. This mill was owned successively by Mr. Gallego and Mr. Chevallie, both accomplished Frenchmen, the latter being especially distinguished for his literary culture and his courtly manners.

The tobacco trade of Richmond has long been of great importance to the city, and is one of the mainstays of its commerce. The trade is by no means as large as it was before the war, when slave labor made a mammoth production more certain than now, and when there was no revenue officer with vigilant eyes in every town.   There are at present in Richmond about forty-five tobacco fac-

Tobacco Culture—Stringing the Primings.

tories in operation, each employing from fifty to two hundred hands, and each producing from fifteen hundred to twenty thousand pounds of manufactured tobacco daily.   The revenue which this article pays to the General Government is enormous.   The collections of internal revenue for the year 1872 in the Richmond district of Virginia averaged a quarter of a million dollars monthly; and during the year amounted to more than three million dollars.   While the reve-

nue collected from the tax on ardent spirits in the Richmond district in 1873 was but $34,476, that on tobacco was $3,064,293, many hundred times more than the amounts collected there by the General Government from all other sources.   The collections in that district from the various taxable articles since May 1, 1869, amount to $12,251,537.

When the tobacco comes from the plantations throughout Virginia and North Carolina to the Richmond market,

A Tobacco Barn in Virginia.

it is first taken to some of the great warehouses on the border of the James, where it remains until the commission merchants to whom it is consigned desire to dispose of it. It is then "sampled" by a sworn State Inspector, who is responsible for the quality of each package from which he takes a sample. The "samples" are carried to the "Tobacco Exchange," where they are exposed for sale, either to private parties or at public auction. There are annually inspected in the Richmond warehouses from 40,000 to 45,000 hogsheads, or more than three-fourths of the entire crop of the State. The finest grades of tobacco come from Halifax and Charlotte counties in Virginia, and from Granville and Caswell counties in North Carolina. The tobacco leaf is the most troublesome as well as the most remunerative staple which the Virginian planter can raise. The old ex-slaveholders are wont to moan bitterly over the

The Old Method of Getting Tobacco to Market.

oss of the good old days when there were from six hundred to a thousand slaves upon a tobacco plantation, and when the lands were taxed almost beyond the limits of their strength that the greatest possible results might be secured. But now-a-days the work that previous to 1860 was done on one plantation is divided between a hundred "landed proprietors." *

The Richmond dealers cluster daily around the Tobacco Exchange, where they find an epitome of the whole tobacco production of the State neatly arranged in samples. Hundreds of negroes toil in the warehouses, as in Lynchburg and Petersburg, opening the hogsheads for the inspectors, and arranging the

---

* In 1873 there were inspected in Richmond 42,054 hogsheads, 8,201 tierces, and 1,218 boxes, besides 2,834,100 pounds of loose tobacco. The latter is mainly grown within a radius of forty miles from Richmond, and is brought to market in wagons. The Tobacco Exchange, started as a private speculation in 1857 by William Y. Sheppard, Esq., has now passed into the hands of the tobacco trade.

lots. Half a century ago the tobacco warehouses in Richmond were mere wooden sheds; the cask containing the weed was rolled to these warehouses on its own periphery. The rough farmers who had spent a whole season in cultivating a crop packed it tightly into a cask, then drove a long wooden spike into the centre of each end of the compressed mass. This served as an axletree; a split sapling was transformed into a pair of shafts, rude tires were placed around each end of the cask, and a stout horse and a steer trundled this extempore wagon to the capital, where its contents were inspected, and then sold. Near each warehouse stood a furnace, into which all tobacco unfit for exportation was thrown to be burned.

The water power of Richmond is not quite so limitless as an enthusiastic Virginian once declared it, viz.: "Sufficient to run all the machinery in the New England States;" but the best authorities have pronounced the available power very large, certainly much ampler than the entire mill privileges combined of Lowell and Lawrence in Massachusetts. There is enough for three or four times as many manufactories as are now established along the James at Richmond and Manchester, and within a short distance of this power ships drawing thirteen feet of water can come at all seasons of the year. The prominent citizens of Richmond are anxious for the establishment of more cotton-mills on the James; and it is possible that in future the Virginia capital will become the rival of Fall River and Lowell. The present ratio of increase in the value of products manufactured in the city is certainly as rapid as could be

Getting a Tobacco Hogshead Ready for Market.

expected after the trials undergone by Virginia during the last decade. The tobacco factories, the iron works, and the flour-mills showed a product amounting to twelve million dollars in 1873; and the manufacturers of agricultural implements, of fertilizers, the preparers of sumac, the makers of clothing, paper, and a hundred miscellaneous articles, are all prosperous and active. The receipts of corn, of wheat, of coal and iron are increasing immensely from year to year as the Western railroad connections are perfected and the

mineral deposits in the mountains are unearthed. * The Tredegar Iron Works now employs a million dollars capital and two thousand workmen; its buildings cover fifteen acres, and it annually works up tens of thousands of tons of crude iron.

There seems but little doubt that Richmond will become one of the most important Southern centres of iron manufacture. Now that the Virginian has learned to aspire to something besides "land and negroes," and that new railroads enable him to utilize the immense coal and iron deposits of the common-

Scene on a Tobacco Plantation—Finding Tobacco-Worms.

wealth, it is reasonable to believe that he will improve his opportunities, and will make of the pretty capital on the James one of the most prosperous of manufacturing towns. The Richmond, Piedmont, Dan River, and New River coal-fields will add their stores to those of the mighty Kanawha valley; and the iron region

* Leading articles brought into Richmond during three fiscal years, ending September 30th of each year:

	1871.	1872.	1873.
Coal, tons	31,220	59,188	64,916
Corn, bushels	107,456	133,696	209,225
Fish, barrels	7,824	8,153	5,819
Guano, tons	1,901	5,507	13,179
Hay, bales	1,744	3,815	12,248
Ice, tons	7,817	8,994	9,101
Iron, tons	......	36,225	21,519
Lime, barrels	28,834	18,389	17,523
Lumber, feet	5,005,000	6,771,000	6,474,419
Plaster, tons	4,916	1,903	1,208
Salt, sacks	64,798	66,773	52,230
Shingles	1,272,000	2,252,000	2,353,000
Wheat, bushels	239,213	185,383	174,355

The Tredegar Iron Works—Richmond, Virginia.

which Richmond can draw upon is very extensive. Louisa, Spottsylvania, Albemarle, Nelson, Amherst, Fluvanna, Powhatan, Cumberland, Buckingham, Campbell and Appomattox counties possess fine deposits of iron ores; and as furnaces spring up in those sections, the capital will give added attention to the manufacture of iron. As the mineral development of South-eastern Missouri has aided in building up St. Louis, so will the unearthing of the treasures in that part of Virginia tributary to Richmond give that city added strength and size. The resources of the hematite beds of Augusta, Rockbridge, Bath and Alleghany counties, can be readily united at Richmond with those of the Kanawha coal-seams. It is safe to predict that in a generation the whole character of the city will be changed; that it will have become a sprightly centre, devoted to manufactures, and filled with huge establishments for turning raw cotton, crude tobacco, and pig-iron into serviceable articles. In twenty years manufacturers will be the aristocrats in Virginia. What planter of the Old Dominion twenty years ago would have believed such a thing possible?

The rapid growth of Richmond doubtless carries sadness to the heart of the Virginian of the old school. For in the steady progress of the capital toward prominence as a manufacturing centre he sees the symbol of the decay of the society which produced him and his. He hates large cities, with their democratic tendencies, their corruption, and their ambitious populations. He looks upon the rich manufacturer as a *parvenu ;* the lordly agriculturist is still, in his mind, the only fitting type of the real aristocrat. He shudders when he sees the youth of the new school engaging in commerce, buying and selling mines, talking of opening new railroad routes, and building cotton-mills. He flies to the farthest corner of the lands that have been spared to him out of the wrecks caused by the war, and strives to forget the present, and to live as he did "before the surrender," like a country squire in England two hundred years ago.

Richmond, in the conduct of her schools, does not belie the reputation for advanced progress in education which Virginia has gained. In April of 1869 her citizens of all parties petitioned the City Council for a system of public schools, and in due time a school ordinance was adopted, and a Board of Education was appointed. To the insufficient appropriation made by the city authorities, generous donations from the Peabody fund, the Freedmen's Bureau fund, and Northern educational societies, were added, and fifty-two schools, with a pupil membership of twenty-four hundred, were opened. At the close of this first session the citizens voluntarily agreed to continue the schools, and the city took control of those for black and white alike. In the season of 1870–71, the attendance had increased to 3,300, and the schools of the city were finally made a part of the State system. The School Board turned the Davis Mansion, once the "White House" of the Confederacy, into a school building.

The Richmond schools for both white and colored pupils rank among the best in the country. The schools are grouped in houses holding six hundred pupils each, and are divided into six grades of primary and four of grammar, with an advanced high school grade. No Virginian living in Richmond is able to say that his children cannot receive as good an education in the public as they can obtain in private schools. In 1873 Richmond had fifty-five schools for white and thirty-two for colored children, and expended about seventy thousand dollars in supporting them. The instruction is the same in each, and competent white teachers are employed when good black ones are lacking for the colored schools. No one thinks of refusing to aid the negro in obtaining his education, although he contributes little or nothing toward the school tax.

The white and colored normal schools of Richmond have done noble work in sending out well-equipped teachers to encourage the growing sentiment in the State in favor of universal education and free schools. The colored normal school was incorporated by special act of the Virginia Legislature, and opened in 1867. It is supported by the Freedmen's Bureau and the Peabody fund. It receives pupils mainly from the city public schools, and gives them a careful three years' course. The Richmond Institute, for the training of colored preachers and teachers, is a protegé of the American Baptist Home Mission Society. The Baptist and the Virginia Medical Colleges, located in Richmond, are flourishing institutions ; and there are more than a score of well-conducted private schools, seminaries, "institutes," and academies, in which several hundred pupils are annually received.

LXXI.

THE PARTITION OF VIRGINIA—RECONSTRUCTION AND POLITICS IN WEST AND EAST VIRGINIA.

AT the time of the secession of the Cotton States, Virginia was apparently attached to the Union. Shortly after that secession, at an extra meeting of the Legislature, a State Convention was called, the members of which were to be elected on the 4th of February, 1861. On the 23d of January of the same year, a bill was passed appropriating a million dollars for the defense of the State, and Virginia began to show signs of adhesion to the cause of the South. The Governor sent messages to the Legislature, in which hostility to the North and Northern institutions was exhibited. Ten Virginia members of Congress published an address denouncing the Republican party, and declaring that it was vain to expect reconciliation. Many of the delegates elected to the State Convention were conditional Union men; some few were unconditional in their support; but the majority avowed the doctrine of State Rights, condemned interference with slavery, asserted the right of secession, and defined the circumstances under which Virginia would be justified in exercising that right. These circumstances were the failure to procure such guarantees from the Northern States as Virginia demanded, the adoption of a war policy by the General Government, or the attempt to exact payment of duty, or to reinforce or capture forts.

On the 17th of April, 1861, after the call of the President for troops, the ordinance of secession was passed by 88 to 55 votes. War measures were begun, and on the 25th of April the Convention passed an act for the adoption of the Constitution of the Provisional Government of the Confederate States, and Virginia was fairly out of the Union.

In the western section of Virginia, a public meeting was held in Clarksburg, in Harrison county, on the 28th of April, 1861, to decide what measures should be taken in view of the recent action of the State. Delegates from twenty-five counties met at Wheeling, condemned secession, and provided for a convention to represent all the counties in the State favorable to a division thereof, in case the people of Virginia ratified the ordinance of secession, against the vote of the western section. The popular vote, ratifying the secession ordinance, is said to have given 94,000 majority for secession, Eastern Virginia voting solidly for and Western Virginia against it.

On the 11th of June, at Wheeling, the Convention of West Virginia, representing forty counties, passed a declaration of independence from the action of the State Convention, and took measures for establishing a provisional government. Later, the representatives of Western Virginia met as a State Legislature, and elected Senators to the United States Congress, passed a stay law, and appropriated $200,000 for carrying on the war, and the same amount to support the new Government. The proposition for a division of the State was voted down, but subsequently the Convention, at an adjourned session, passed an ordinance organizing the western counties into a new State to be called "Kanawha." Thirty-nine counties, with a population of nearly 300,000 people, thus gave in their adhesion to the Union.

On the 24th of October the Provisional Legislature, in session at Wheeling, sanctioned the setting off of the new State, and in October the act was approved by the people of thirty-nine counties by an almost unanimous vote. Western Virginia, as it was finally decided to call the new division, applied for admission to the Union at the first regular session of the 37th Congress, and on April 20th, 1863, after the Provisional Legislature had ratified an amendment to the Constitution, permitting free negroes to enter the State, and inserting certain provisions relative to freeing the slaves, Western Virginia was admitted to the Union, and the new State was inaugurated at Wheeling, June 20th, 1863, with imposing ceremonies.

Old Virginia thus lost one of the fairest portions of her domain, an immense amount of material resources, a mineral region almost unequaled upon the continent, and a large population.

The people of Western Virginia unanimously adopted their new Constitution in a Convention comprising 66 Democrats and 12 Republicans, on the 9th of April, 1872. The Constitution guarantees West Virginia a continued separate existence, secures free schools, and is, withal, quite liberal, although some members of the Convention tried to have the negroes deprived of their newly-acquired right to vote. It also recognizes the obligation of West Virginia for whatever she may justly owe the parent State as her share in the latter's debt of $44,000,-000, and declares her willingness to pay it when it is properly ascertained. The new Constitution was ratified August 22d, 1872, by a small majority. It fixes the term of the office of Governor and other important State officers at four years, and that of the Judges of the Supreme Court of Appeals at twelve years. The Democrats, in 1872, nominated Johnson M. Camden, of Wood county, as Governor, but John J. Jacob, the then incumbent, was re-elected by a small majority.

There have been at times, serious disagreements between the Governor and the Legislature of the State; the former interpreting the Constitution as giving him appointive power with regard to almost all officers, and in 1873 these disagreements became the cause of quite serious disturbances in the new commonwealth. The estimated expenditures of the State, under the new Constitution, are somewhat more than a quarter of a million of dollars yearly, to which may be added the "State fund," distributed for free schools in 1873, amounting to about the same sum. The number of pupil-children enrolled in that year was 170,031, of which about one-half attended school. The University of Western Virginia, under the exclusive control of the State, has a permanent endowment of $100,000. The "Normal Schools" at Fairmont, West Liberty, Shepherdstown, and Marshall College are flourishing. The indebtedness of the State is very slight; taxes are not burdensome; the State institutions are well maintained, and the present population, constantly increased by immigration of excellent character, mainly from the middle classes of England, is now nearly 500,000.

After the division of territory, the progress of reconstruction in Virginia proper was marked, as in all the other States, by many political excitements and troubles. President Johnson's order, issued May 9, 1865, recognized Francis H. Pierpont, who was originally elected Governor in West Virginia, and who had subsequently moved his Government seat to Alexandria, and exercised jurisdiction over a few counties adjacent to Washington during the war. His Legislature consisted of members from ten counties, and was known to loyal men in war time as the "Legislature of Virginia." Governor Pierpont went to Richmond shortly after the surrender at Appomattox Court-House, and called a special session of the Legislature.

In October, 1865, the restriction in the Constitution prescribing the oath relative to freedom from sympathy with the late Confederacy was removed. The Legislature met at Richmond on the 4th day of December, 1865.

During this year the Conservatives attempted to inaugurate a practical serfdom of the freedmen, by means of vagrant laws; and other evidences of a determination to revert to the old system were given. But the State Government, which had been established by merely a handful of votes in the northern counties, was nevertheless honestly and creditably sustained, and Governor Pierpont suddenly found himself in full jurisdiction over Virginia.

In May of 1866, a "Republican State Convention" met at Alexandria, and a Special Committee reported a resolution declaring the so-called Legislature illegal and unconstitutional, and sent a memorial to Congress demanding the revocation of Governor Pierpont's powers, and asking for a "policy of reconstruction." How far this policy had been rendered necessary by the action of the Conservatives with regard to the negroes, it is not necessary here to inquire. As soon as the Reconstruction Act of Congress had become a law, General Schofield was placed in command of the First Military District, which comprised the territory of Virginia. The Conservatives, who had intended to hold a convention at Richmond in May of that year, and to so amend the Constitution as to make it coincide with the reconstruction policy of Congress, were too late to escape military rule. Governor Pierpont issued orders commanding all State officers to continue the exercise of their duties until a new election could be held under reconstruction. A Board of Army Officers selected the officials to superintend a new registration, which was at once begun. On the 2d of April, 1867, an order appeared, superseding all elections under the "Provisional Government," until the registration should be completed. The Commanding-General at that time made all appointments. The Conservatives were opposed to this action, and the local press was violently critical.

On the 17th of April, 1867, at the call of the "Union party of Virginia," a convention assembled in the African Church in Richmond, of which, out of two hundred and ten delegates, only fifty were white. Other political meetings were elsewhere held about the same time by freedmen and the whites allied with them. Many negroes sided with the Conservatives. General Schofield found it necessary to disband all armed organizations in the State. On the 3d of June orders for reconstruction were issued, and 116,982 white, and 104,772 colored voters were registered. In Amelia, Brunswick, Charlotte, Dinwiddie, Elizabeth, Halifax, Powhatan, and York counties the negroes were overpoweringly in the majority.

Meantime, the Conservative wing of the Union party, so called, decided to hold a convention at Charlottesville on the 4th of July, 1867, but it was finally determined to call a " convention of all the unconditional Union men of Virginia," to meet in the African Church in Richmond on the 1st of August, to secure the coalition of the two wings of the Republican party of the State. This convention was packed with ignorant negroes, and but little good was effected.

A number of ex-officers and soldiers of the Union held a convention at Richmond on the 25th of September. Vacancies in offices were filled by temporary appointees. Military commissions continued to try offenders, because the strong caste prejudice prevalent in the State endangered the lives and property of persons who sat upon mixed juries.

On the 22d of October a Constitutional Convention was decided upon by a popular vote and a majority of 45,455. Of the 105 delegates chosen to this Convention the mass were white people. The Convention, which met on the 3d day of December, proposed to provide in the organic law of the State that negroes should be allowed equal privileges with whites in horse-cars, public places, &c. Meantime the Convention of the Conservatives of the State assembled at Richmond on the 12th of December. It disclaimed all hostility to the blacks, but hotly condemned reconstruction *in toto*. The Republican Constitutional Convention finally adopted an article making every male citizen 21 years old, who had been or might be a resident of the State for twelve months, and of a county, city, or town three months, a voter, excepting only those who had been engaged in insurrection. The test oath was brought in, and the Conservatives at once rebelled against this, as did also the commander of the military district, General Schofield. The operation of the test oath, inasmuch as all the native white Virginians had been engaged in the work of secession, would not have left voters enough to carry on the Government intelligently; but the odious provision was not modified, and the new Constitution, with the test oath in it, was adopted by the Convention April 17, 1868. It had then to go before the people for ratification. Virginia remained, however, under military law.

On the 4th of April of the same year, Governor Pierpont's term of office expired. Henry H. Wells was appointed, by military authority, Governor of the State. Hon. Joseph Mayo, who had been Mayor of Richmond for fifteen years, was removed, and George Chahoon was appointed his successor. General Schofield was shortly afterward made Secretary of War, and Major-General Stoneman took his place as Military Governor of Virginia. Things went on quietly thereafter until 1869. The Constitution which the Republican Convention had adopted had not yet been presented for ratification. It was evident that under its provisions the more intelligent and capable citizens of the commonwealth were to be excluded from office. President Grant, being authorized to submit the Constitution to the voters of the State and to allow them to vote separately on the separate provisions, appointed the 6th of July as the time for ratification. Wells was meantime removed from the Governorship. General Stoneman was superseded by Major-General Canby, and the political parties continued an active canvass of the State.

Shortly afterward the Republican delegates assembled in convention at Petersburg and renominated Mr. Wells for Governor. It was my rare fortune to assist at the session of this Convention, which was held in a negro church. Never in the history of Republicanism was there a more disgraceful and lawless rabble assembled together. Gratifying as it was to see those who had lately been slaves learning something of Government affairs, it was utterly discouraging to note the violent and offensive measures which they took to obtain their ends. Brawls, shoutings, and bickerings consumed an entire day, and the police were called upon four times to clear the building before a temporary president was chosen.

Another wing of the Republican party of the State, which had always acted with the National party, but which took no part in the Petersburg Convention, nominated Gilbert C. Walker of Norfolk, an accomplished and amiable gentleman of Northern parentage, as its candidate for Governor. On the 28th of April, 1869, the Conservatives, highly pleased with this nomination, met at Richmond, and favored the election of Mr. Walker, but decided to use all their efforts to vote down the odious Constitution which the Republicans had prepared. The Constitution was accepted, however, on the 6th of July, at a general election, by a majority of 197,044 votes, but the "disfranchising clause," which had been the cause of much of the ill feeling toward the reconstruction policy in the South, was voted down squarely by a majority of 39,957 votes, and the test oath clause was also lost by a majority of 40,992 votes. Mr. Walker was elected Governor, with the coöperation of the Conservatives, by a majority of 18,317 votes. In the Legislature which then assembled there were 95 Conservatives and 42 Republicans, with 18 negroes in the House and 6 in the Senate. The Conservatives at once assumed an attitude of conciliation, and, forgetting the old issues and prejudices of the past, ratified the 14th and 15th amendments to the Constitution of the United States. The Republicans were discontented, attributing their failure to the separate votes on the clauses of the State Constitution.

Virginia was readmitted to the Union on the 26th of January, 1870. On the following day, General Canby retired from his authority; Governor Walker assumed his office, and for four years thereafter governed the State well and fairly. Had all the other Southern States been as fortunate as Virginia in escaping the major evils of reconstruction, the South would have been far more prosperous than she can now hope to be for many years.

It is noteworthy with regard to Virginia politics, that whenever the Conservative politicians make a campaign up and down the State, sometimes flying the old Confederate colors a little, they do not awaken any intense enthusiasm among the working population. The farmers of Virginia are too much occupied with their own immediate concerns to give great attention to State politics. They feel determined to keep the negro from attaining such power as he has gained in South Carolina and Louisiana ; but they are apathetic, and any attempt to organize them into a party of extremists would be an inevitable failure.

The present government of the State is in good hands. The officers of the State Government are allied to the Conservative party, but seem determined to do equal and exact justice to all classes of citizens. Governor Kemper, elected over Mr. Hughes, the Republican candidate, in 1873, was a Confederate General, and is an old-school Virginian, but has a sufficient appreciation of the necessities of the time to avoid the narrow and mean-spirited policy which has latterly characterized some of the other Southern States. He has thus far done everything that he could to develop good-will and confidence between the races. When the Legislature of the State proposed, shortly after General Kemper's election, to invade the liberties of the city of Petersburg and to take from it its self-government because the majority of the voters there were negroes, the Governor stood up boldly against this movement and vetoed the bill. In his veto message, he said :

"In view of the fundamental conditions on which Virginia stands as a member of the Federal Union ; in view of our own solemn and sworn recognition of the political equality before the law of all men, irrespective of race, color, or previous condition, the proposed measure, if enacted, could not fail to subject us to disastrous misconstruction at home and abroad. It would renew and intensify the race agitations of the past, which are being happily settled ; it would present Virginia to the world as being torn by intestine feuds of an apparently interminable character ; it would discourage and postpone, if not repel, the approach of the immigration and capital to which our most ardent hopes are directed ; and, more to be deplored than all, it would sound a provocation to Federal interference in our domestic affairs."

In these words of Governor Kemper one may find expressed the attitude of the better class of Virginian Conservatives. The determination to avoid everything which might be construed as ungenerous toward the negro ; to build up his character by education, and to urge him to accumulate property ; the gradual change and softening of public sentiment among the elder aristocrats with regard to the introduction of manufactures and the dignity of labor,—all point to a change in the character of the Old Dominion, which will result in making her one day as rich and mighty as Pennsylvania or Missouri.

The aggregate of assessed values of taxable property of all kinds in Virginia, in 1873, was not quite $337,000,000. In 1860 the assessed value of the real and personal property actually subjected to taxation in the State was $585,099,-382, and the official reports show that property of the value of $163,556,100 was then exempted from taxation, thus making the actual aggregate resources of the State in that year about $748,000,000. The aggregate value of real and personal property within the 38,348 square miles in the present limits of Virginia proper, in 1860, was $632,000,000. It will be seen from these figures that the decline in taxable values has been very great and rapid. The losses in production have in some cases been startling, as instanced in that of tobacco, the crop of which in 1860 amounted to 123,968,312 pounds, but in 1870 to only 37,086,364. The decrease in production is largely due to the fact that the slave population, which constituted the most valuable producing class before the war, numbering more than half a million persons, now produces little but a bare living for itself. Until the Virginian negroes learn to be enterprising and industrious, and to produce surplus crops, the cultivation of the great staples in the State will languish.

Of the 1,125,163 inhabitants of Virginia, more than 512,000 are blacks. It would seem that both whites and colored people spend even the small amount of ready money which they have upon things which do not profit their souls; for General Ruffner, the able State Superintendent of Public Instruction, asserts that the consumption of liquors in Virginia amounts to something like $19,000,000 annually. During the fiscal year 1872, the revenue officers of the United States collected from liquor dealers in Virginia $71,000 in licenses. General Ruffner is probably very nearly right when he puts the cost of the liquor yearly drank *as a beverage* in the State at $12,000,000, and he shows the folly and criminality of the general indulgence in whiskey, by stating that the gross annual product of seven of the best counties in the State is not sufficient to pay for the liquor consumed by the people of the commonwealth ; that the gross production of nearly half the small counties would not compensate for annual loss by drink ; that the Virginians drink up the value of their wheat crop every year ; and that the legislative cost and the expenses of courts and civil officers and State institutions and the public free schools, and the interest on the enormous public debt, only amount to a little more than one-quarter of the sum which the people of Virginia yearly spend upon liquor. Colonel Burwell, of Richmond, estimates the annual consumption of liquor in Virginia at 2,500,000 gallons, and he latterly introduced a bill into the Legislature, imposing a tax of 30 cents per gallon upon this liquor, which would, if collected, yield the State a revenue of $750,000. But this bill has not yet become a law.

The State is now seriously considering the sources from which it may derive increased revenue, but doubts the expediency of increasing the taxation upon lands, as it would result in a virtual confiscation of private property. The State credit is severely prostrated; for, while the debt is enormous, considering the present condition of the commonwealth, the interest is largely in arrears. The act known as the Funding act pledged the State to the regular and punctual payment of interest on the debt, which it provided to be newly funded in the name of Virginia; but the State was unable to fulfill these obligations, and both debtors and creditors were but poorly satisfied with the results. The sum then funded, the interest upon which is largely overdue, was $30,478,741.48, excluding the amount assigned for settlement with West Virginia. The revenues of the State, as compared with her available resources, are quite large; yet they are usually less than enough to support the Government and to pay full interest on the debt. The Conservatives will take care to do nothing tending

to impair the public credit.   No partial or total repudiation will ever be considered, and the impolicy of taxing capital heavily is thoroughly understood.
Virginia will not fail to treat liberally all capital invested in the establishment of
new manufactures within her boundaries.

The favorable advance in public sentiment regarding general free education
in Virginia grows more noticeable yearly.   It is largely due to the energetic
campaign upon which General Ruffner, the State Superintendent of Education,
entered under the Administration of Governor Walker.   By able reports, lectures, figures, and liberal as well as daring policy, he has revolutionized opinion
in many parts of the State.   The organization of the graded schools is rapidly
becoming general in thickly-populated localities, and 160,859 pupils were in
1873 enrolled upon the books of the public schools.   The total cost to the
public fund for education was $707,835, and the total cost to all sources nearly
$800,000, of which the Peabody fund contributed $31,450.   There were 2,070
students in the various universities and colleges of the State, 1,207 of whom
were native Virginians.

A Water-melon Wagon.

LXXII.

FROM RICHMOND TO CHARLOTTESVILLE.

RICHMOND is well supplied with railroads. The Richmond, Fredericksburg and Virginia road extends northward to Alexandria, the Potomac, and Washington; the Richmond and Petersburg road southward to Petersburg; south-eastward runs the rail route connecting the capital with Yorktown; south-westward the road to Danville, and thence to Greensboro' in North Carolina, and westward the Chesapeake and Ohio. By the York River railway route one may reach the battle-fields of Seven Pines and Fair Oaks, only four miles away.

A Marl-Bed on the Line of the Chesapeake and Ohio Railroad.

The Chesapeake and Ohio railroad at present extends from Richmond through the Piedmont country, the Blue Ridge, and the Alleghanies, to Huntington on the Ohio river. It was formed by a consolidation of the roads, properties and franchises of the Virginia Central and the Covington and Ohio railroad companies. Its charter privileges cover the line from tide-water on the James to the Ohio river, at or near the mouth of the Big Sandy, where the borders of the States of West Virginia, Kentucky and Ohio touch each other. This is a distance of 427 miles. Several important branches and extensions are contemplated. One is a line from Richmond down the peninsula, between the York and James rivers, to a point on the deep waters of the Chesapeake bay, near the Capes. They further propose to give Richmond its long de-sired direct communication with the West by the completion of the Elizabeth-town, Lexington and Big Sandy railroad in Kentucky to Huntington. At Lexington this will connect with Louisville, Cincinnati and Lexington, one of the oldest roads in Kentucky, and there will then be a direct all-rail line 640 miles in length between Richmond and Louisville. The road from Richmond to the Ohio river was opened for traffic on the 1st of April, 1873. This great central highway crosses both the Blue Ridge and the Alleghany mountains by easy grades, the highest elevation attained being about two thousand feet. It offers special advantages for the transportation of the surplus productions of the

Earthworks on the Chickahominy, near Richmond, Virginia.

West directly to the largest, deepest, and most secure harbor on the eastern Atlantic coast of the United States. Along the greater portion of the route the best coals abound, in thick seams, close to and above the level of its track; and this coal can be supplied to its locomotives at the bare cost of handling. As it lies near the 38th parallel of latitude, it is never liable to obstruction from deep snows, nor interruption from severe frosts.

The journey from Richmond to the Piedmont country along this line of rail takes the traveler through little that is noteworthy. The Chickahominy river, which the railroad crosses five miles from the capital, is, at the point where the right wing of McClellan's army rested in June and July of 1862, an unimpressive stream. Various dilapidated and grass-grown earthworks are still to be seen, and are amicably pointed out and discussed by ex-Confederate and ex-Federal as the train passes. A few miles beyond are extensive marl-beds, whence Virginia draws much of her fertilizing material; although her planters also rely largely on the guano brought from the Chincha Islands for the renewal of their fields.

A little farther on is Hanover Court-House, where Henry Clay was born, and where Patrick Henry first gave evidence of his wonderful oratorical powers, by his famous plea against "the parsons," who had brought an action for the recovery of certain amounts due them by the people.

Here and there along the route are corn-sheds, unpretending buildings in which the farmers store their grain until the railway officials are ready to transport it to Richmond.

Bending northward and westward, through the rich Hanover and Louisa counties, and crossing at right angles the belt of iron and gold deposits extending through the State, Gordonsville, seventy-six miles from Richmond, is reached. This is an important junction. The line of road from Lynchburg to Washington there unites with the Chesapeake and Ohio, and the trains of the two roads

run thence to Charlottesville on the same track.   Gordonsville straggles along
a rocky road running through a beautiful country, upon which a range of mountains looks down.   There are many fine farms in the vicinity, and the English
immigrants have done much to give the section the air of peace and homely
thrift so marked in some British agricultural regions.   The negroes, who swarm
day and night like bees about the trains, look with amazement upon the brisk rosy
young men and women who throng the cars, and who daily appear in increased
numbers on all the fine farming tracts in the neighborhood.

The three counties of Henrico, Hanover and Louisa, through which the
Chesapeake and Ohio railroad passes between Richmond and Gordonsville, con-
stitute a fine specimen section of the tract in Virginia known as the "Middle
Country," which has an area of twelve thousand square miles, and is sixty miles

Scene at a Virginia "Corn-Shed."   [Page 648.]

wide.   At Gordonsville, at the South-west mountain, the surface of the country is
about five hundred feet above sea-level.   The light brown soil of the ridges and
the rich dark brown of the bottom lands are each very productive; and even
the sides and summits of the mountain are arable.   Tobacco, wheat, corn, flax,
oats and sweet potatoes grow in this section abundantly and well.   In the three
counties nearly a million and a-half pounds of tobacco were produced in 1870;
and in 1860, the average production of tobacco there was 246 pounds to each
inhabitant.   The mud-beds, sometimes fifteen feet deep, furnish inexhaustible
supplies of fertilizers; the counties contain good grazing-lands, and large herds
of cattle and flocks of sheep roam in the valleys.

At Gordonsville one is at the door of the Piedmont region, which extends
from the head of tide-water to the Blue Ridge mountains.   The lower part of
this fertile section is gently undulating; the upper is quite hilly, but nowhere so

broken as not to admit of cultivation. The tier of counties included in this region comprises an area of six thousand square miles. At the outbreak of the war, nearly half the land in these counties had been put under culture, and the population of two hundred thousand persons scattered through the district raised annually about twenty-five million pounds of tobacco.* The lands are among the very finest in America; the red, crumbling loam is easily worked, and from it spring noble grass, excellent grain, and delicious orchard fruits.

The approaches to Charlottesville, the principal town of Albemarle county, afford a glimpse of the beauties of the Piedmont section. The mountains show

Gordonsville, Virginia—"The negroes, who swarm day and night like bees about the trains." [Page 649.]

their blue outlines; the slopes are dotted with rich farms; the landscape is radiant with peace and plenty. Before the war this county was a region of large plantations, principally devoted to tobacco, of which hundreds of slaves raised five millions of pounds annually. Now the production amounts to but little more than a million and a-half pounds yearly; but it will in due time regain the old number; for no section of Virginia is more rapidly recovering from the disorganization of labor, and the discouragements which followed upon the war, than Albemarle and her fertile sister counties at the foot of the Blue Ridge.

* The whole amount of tobacco raised in Virginia in 1870 was 37,086,364 pounds.

English immigrants are bringing money and accurate knowledge of scientific farming into the country, and are prompting to a new vigor the natives who had begun to yield under the pressure of the adverse fortunes of the past few years.

Charlottesville is one of the loveliest of Virginia towns. It has an air of dignified quiet which befits so ancient and distinguished a seat of learning as the University of Virginia, and the neighbor of such historic ground as Monticello, the home of Thomas Jefferson. The town stands on a moderate elevation, shut in on the south-west by hills beyond which rise the ridges known as the "Ragged" mountains. To the north-west one sees in the distance the symmetrical outlines of the Blue Ridge. On the east is the Rivanna, a pretty stream, although its waters are discolored by the reddish loam through which it flows around the base of Monticello. The railroad is an ungracious intruder, as locomotives saucily shriek at the very doors of sleepy taverns, and trains rattle through streets where everything seems to resent the outbursts of steam and the clang of wheels. The negro is omnipresent, the blacks appearing at first vastly to outnumber the white folks. Many pleasant mansions are surrounded with gardens embowered in shrubbery.

A storm was muttering overhead as I climbed, one midsummer day, the steep road which leads from Charlottesville to Monticello. Here and there a turn in the route gave me exquisite glimpses of the valley below; the old town with its many dingy brown houses, asleep on the plateau; the dome of the University peeping above the foliage, and the delicate blue of the far-away mountains. Just as I was beginning to suspect that I had lost my way, I came to an ill-kept road branching away from the main one. Ascending this, while rain-drops clat-

tering on my face warned me to seek shelter, I came suddenly upon the tomb of the author of the "Declaration of Independence."

I rattled at the rusty iron gate set in the shabby brick wall; but, observing an enormous padlock, I turned away and continued the ascent toward the hill-top, when I noticed an ancient negro man in the pathway, vainly endeavoring to force an unruly yoke of oxen to obey him. The snows of eighty or ninety winters had frosted his wool; the labors of many years of servitude had bent him double. He did not at first hear my salutation, but continued his husky appeals to the oxen. "Debbil in dem critturs, sho;" then spying me, he took off his greasy hat with an explosive "Sah!" A sprightly negro urchin ran

The Tomb of Thomas Jefferson, at Monticello, near Charlottesville, Virginia.

out to aid the venerable blackamoor, but seeing me, grinned good-day, and led the way to the house. On the right, as we approached, stood a row of negro cabins, from one of which a black woman came out, courtesying, and as it was at last raining rapidly, I entered her door. The cabin or hovel was wretched in the extreme; a small window lighted a poor room, in which there was scarcely any furniture. On an uneven hearth a weak fire struggled with the

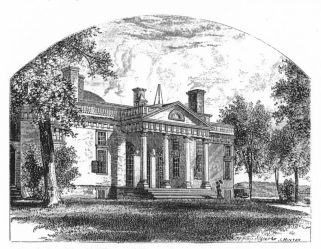

Monticello—The Old Home of Thomas Jefferson, author of the Declaration of American Independence.

dampness. On the lawn near the path which led, by a gentle ascent, to the mansion, was the body of an old infantry baggage-wagon, marked "U. S." Evidently the "late unpleasantness" had penetrated even to Monticello.

The house, surrounded by beautiful aspen trees, and with its chances for an outlook over an ocean of foliage on one side, and a lovely valley hemmed in by lofty mountain ranges on the other, must have been a pleasant retreat in the last century. I could almost fancy that the long-vanished master of the estate would throw open the great door at which I knocked, under the lofty portico, and usher me into the dining-room, where I should find the Marquis de Lafayette gayly chatting with some country squire, or mayhap reading the memoranda for the "Notes on Virginia" which Mr. Jefferson prepared mainly for the instruction of his French friends. While I stood at the door, a sharp voice inside commanded various colored servants to look "yere" and there after the key, and I was presently ushered in, not by the ghost of the great patriot, but by a sour-looking man, who collected a small fee before I could set foot upon the sacred threshold. He then proceeded to inform me that the estate was in litigation, and that it had "run down" very much, which indeed was quite easy to see. The interior of the mansion, although stripped of nearly everything placed there by Jefferson, has yet a few reminders left. A curious old clock stands in a corner of the entrance hall, and a marble bust of Jefferson himself occupies a dusty niche. The little dining-room with polished inlaid floor, and gilt Parisian mirrors, where the great man was wont to hob-nob over dinner with Lafayette, or distinguished chance visitors, is still in good order; the dumb waiter yet creaks solemnly in its grooves, and from the old-fashioned windows one can look out upon a charming lawn, and on leafy hill-sides. The house is a fair specimen of the commodious and not inelegant structures erected in Virginia in colonial times, and when filled with Jefferson's superb collections of sculpture, paintings, medallions, engravings and books, must have been an oasis of peace to gentlemen of culture who traveled slowly on horseback through the Virginia woods a hundred years ago. The library building, separated from the house, but communicating with it by means of a covered passage-way, still stands. The whole is fast decaying, however, and if the State will not, the country should, see that the home of Jefferson is, like that of Washington, preserved as an historic shrine to which the lovers of liberty may repair for many generations to come.

The little negro boy, carrying an immense key, bounded before me to the tomb, whither I went once more, despite the rain, which now came heavily. Entering, I found that the enclosure was a family burying-ground. Over the grave of the great statesman stands a simple, almost rude granite obelisk, eight feet high, on which is the epitaph which he himself desired to have inscribed on his tomb:

" Here Lies Buried
THOMAS JEFFERSON,
Author of the Declaration of Independence
Of the Statute of Virginia for Religious Freedom
And Father of the University of Virginia."

The University at Charlottesville is Jefferson's noblest monument. So long as it endures, the admirers of the great Virginian can afford to forego lamentation over the ingratitude of republics, and refrain from criticising the Government which is too niggardly to place a marble shaft over his grave. Jefferson founded the University in 1819, and watched with tender care its early growth and im-

The University of Virginia, at Charlottesville.

mediate success. Always an ardent admirer of the school system prevalent in New England in his time, he urged Virginia to adopt it, even while she was struggling in the Revolution. His zeal was so great that, after persistent labor for many years, he succeeded in influencing the State Legislature to adopt a free-school system; but its practical operation was prevented by a proviso which some

Conservative legislators managed to attach to the bill, giving the county courts, whose officials were unfriendly to Mr. Jefferson's plan, the privilege of declaring when the schools should be established in each county.

He was not discouraged, although he saw that the commonwealth gave more attention to internal improvements than to the education of her people; and he never forgot, even when seemingly absorbed in national politics, his schemes for making universal free education popular in Virginia. When, after retiring from the Presidency in 1809, he again took up his residence in the State, he returned to the work with new energy. A "literary fund" was founded by an act of the State Legislature in 1810; the proceeds of this fund were designed to be used exclusively for the purposes of common school education. The principal had at one time grown to two millions of dollars; but since the war it has yielded nothing. Its original nucleus* consisted of fines, forfeitures, and escheats. Mr. Jefferson succeeded, in 1818, in obtaining another legislative enactment, which allowed an appropriation of $15,000 yearly to endow and support a university. A report recommending the establishment of this university, various colleges, and a scheme for general public education, had been made to the Legislature in 1816, doubtless at the instance of Mr. Jefferson, and in 1821 the institution whose noble rotunda to-day rises in graceful relief against the blue mountains near Charlottesville began to receive State aid, which continued without interruption until toward the close of the late war.

Jefferson planned the University, and it still retains the characteristics which he gave it. In the departments of languages, literature, science, law, medicine, agriculture, and engineering, it has to-day eighteen distinct schools. For more than half a century it has been preëminent among the higher institutions of learning in the country, and Northern colleges and universities have borrowed from it the feature of an elective system of study. It has latterly established excellent agricultural and scientific schools, has a fine laboratory, with an extensive collection of raw and manufactured materials, and an experimental farm inferior to none in the country. Its government is vested in a rector, and two visitors from each grand division of the State, except Piedmont, which, because it is the location of the University, is entitled to three. The institution bestows no honorary degrees, and makes the attainment of its "Master of Arts" so difficult that it will serve as a certificate of scholarship anywhere. Nearly one hundred and fifty of the graduates of the several schools are now professors in other colleges. The University is by no means aristocratic in its tendencies; a large proportion of the students pay their expenses with money earned by themselves, and, since the war, there have been many "State students" who are provided with gratuitous instruction. The alumni form an army fourteen thousand strong.

The buildings of the University are not architecturally fine, although the main edifice has a rotunda modeled in part after the Pantheon at Rome. The country around the elevation a mile west of Charlottesville on which they stand, is exquisitely lovely. The great porticoes, whence one can look out upon lawns,

* Report of Dr. Ruffner, State Superintendent of Education in Virginia.

on the trim houses where the professors live, and on the dormitories for the students, are beautiful. In the well-arranged and amply-stocked library hangs a fine portrait of General Lee, by Elder. Among the academic groves, Long, and Key, and Silvester, whose names are eminent both in England and America, and Courtenay, Rogers, Emmett and Bonnycastle, famous instructors, once had their homes.

A Water-melon Feast.

LXXIII.

FROM CHARLOTTESVILLE TO STAUNTON, VA.—THE SHENAN-
DOAH VALLEY—LEXINGTON—THE GRAVES OF GENERAL
LEE AND "STONEWALL" JACKSON—FROM GOSHEN TO
"WHITE SULPHUR SPRINGS."

THE route from Charlottesville to Staunton, through Albemarle and Augusta
counties, passes some of the finest farming-land in the Piedmont section.
In summer, one sees fields clad in the green of the tobacco leaf, or in the luxuriant clover, timothy, blue, orchard, and herds' grasses. The fruits flourish in
perfection; the pippin, the pear and the grape attain unusual size, and yet have

Piedmont, from the Blue Ridge.

delicate flavor. Looking out from the train as it begins to scale the base of the
Blue Ridge, one gazes down into fertile valleys, with little streams flowing
through them; upon expanses of meadow; and on lusty vineyards clothing
the hills.

The Chesapeake and Ohio railroad traverses the Blue Ridge at a point no
less rich in mountain scenery than that section near the Peaks of Otter through
which the Atlantic, Mississippi and Ohio road runs; but it slips under the great
ridges, instead of winding among them. The Blue Ridge tunnel, seven-eighths
of a mile long, was built by Virginia, under the supervision of her State Engineer, Colonel Claude Crozet, an old soldier of Napoleon the Great. This
persevering engineer worked seven years at the tunnel before he saw light
through it.

Coming out from the "great bore," the traveler descries the Shenandoah valley, the pride of Virginia, outspread in its loveliness before him. As far as he can
see, his gaze rests upon highly-cultivated farms and noble woodlands.

"This valley," to quote the words of Major Hotchkiss, of Staunton, author
of the "Resources of Virginia," "forms the north-eastern third of the great val-

ley that extends for nearly three hundred and sixty miles diagonally across the State." This latter valley in turn "forms about one-tenth of the Appalachian valley, that, under the various local designations of Champlain, Hudson, Goshen, Kittatinny, Lebanon, Cumberland, Shenandoah, James, Roanoke, New River, Holston, East Tennessee, and Warrior, extends from the St. Lawrence to the Alabama river," a distance of fifteen hundred miles. It is walled on the east

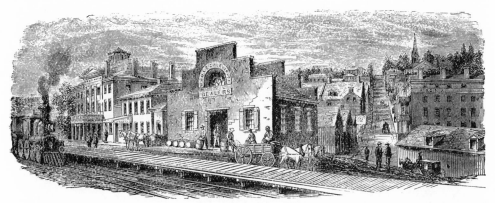

View of Staunton, Virginia.

throughout its whole extent by the Blue Ridge, on the west by the ranges locally known as the Catskill, Shawangunk, Blue, North and Cumberland, and is a limestone tract "embracing thirty thousand square miles of the best farming and grazing-land on the continent, margined on each side by inexhaustible deposits of richest hematite iron ores.

The "Shanando'," as the negroes call it, includes about five million acres of land, of which nearly two-thirds are either under cultivation or enclosed in farms; the remainder is open to immigrants. The valley is especially noted for its grain and grass-growing capacity. In 1866 its wheat product was three and a-quarter million bushels; it produced three million pounds of tobacco, and five and a-half million bushels of corn. At the outbreak of the war, it was one of the finest stocked farming countries in the world. In Augusta county, at the head of the valley, English settlers have purchased many estates. That county is well underlaid with mineral treasure. Jefferson, in his "Notes on Virginia," mentions that, in his time, iron mines were worked in Augusta county. Great impetus has been given to the mineral development there by the extension of the railroad through the Kanawha valley, which is stocked with cheap and abundant fuel, to the furnaces along the Ohio river for which the Virginia ores are always eagerly demanded. Lands which contain veins of hematite ore are easily obtainable; good agricultural tracts may be purchased from $25 to $30 per acre.

Twelve miles from the base of the mountain through which the tunnel is pierced lies the pretty hill-town of Staunton, where two of the principal State charities, the Western District Asylum for the Insane, and the Institution for the Deaf, Dumb and Blind, are located. As Staunton is also a very central point,

and one of the healthiest places in Virginia, it is the seat of several seminaries for young ladies. A walk along its steep streets induces the stranger
to believe that the town has more beautiful girls than are to be found anywhere else in the South; but the presence of so many lovely creatures is
explained by the fact that six hundred lady pupils are gathered there from
the Middle, Southern and Western States, and that they represent the best
society of the whole country. The town is also the residence of Dr. Sears, the
dispenser of the educational fund donated to the Southern States by George
Peabody. Staunton has a large trade in tobacco and whiskey; many wealthy
people have fine mansions on the hills which rise in the rear of the business
section; and in summer the hotels are crowded with tourists on their way to the
mineral springs of Virginia, and to the natural wonders in the vicinity of the
town. One of the most remarkable of these wonders is Weyer's Cave, a "vast
subterranean labyrinth of glittering grottoes and galleries," where stalactites
sparkle in the light of the torches carried by the guides, and "hang from the
fretted roof like the foliated pendants of a Gothic cathedral." The cave was

Winchester, Virginia. [Page 659.]

discovered in 1804, by Bernard Weyer, a hunter of the neighborhood. The
direct course through it is sixteen hundred feet long; the main path usually
taken by visitors to the principal apartments and galleries is six hundred and
fifty feet long. Washington's Hall, the chief curiosity of the cave, takes its
name from a calcareous formation six or seven feet high, which bears a close
resemblance to a statue in classic drapery. "Madison's Cave," not far from
Weyer's, is on the north side of the Blue Ridge, near the intersection of the line
of Rockingham and Augusta counties with the south fork of the southern Shenandoah river. In Jefferson's "Notes" it is thus described: "It is in a hill of
about 200 feet perpendicular height, the ascent of which on one side is so steep
that you may pitch a biscuit from its summit into the river which washes its
base. The entrance of the cave is in this side, about two-thirds of the way up.
It extends into the earth 300 feet, branching into subordinate caverns, sometimes
ascending a little, but more generally descending, and at length terminates in
two different places at basins of water of unknown extent. The vault of this
cave is of solid limestone, from 20 to 40 or 50 feet high, through which water

is continually percolating. This, trickling down the sides of the cave, has incrusted them over in the form of elegant drapery, and, dripping from the top of the vault, generates on that, and on the base below, stalactites of a conical form, some of which have met and formed massive columns."

Northwest of Staunton, in Augusta county, are the Cyclopean Towers, formed of limestone. They rise to the height of seventy feet, and resemble the battlements of a feudal castle.

Staunton is certainly one of the pleasantest summer retreats in Virginia. The road-bed of the Chesapeake and Ohio railroad there is 1,386 feet above tidewater. The atmosphere is dry and cool. Sheltered on the east by the barrier of the Blue Ridge, and on the west by a loftier range, from which Ellsworth's Knob rises to the height of 4,448 feet above the sea-level, the piercing blasts which sweep down from the Alleghanies in winter are broken. The Valley of the Shenandoah is often free from snow when the less protected regions adjacent are covered with the white veil of winter.

The Valley railroad now runs from Staunton through Harrisonburg, Strasburg, and Winchester, to Harper's Ferry, at the confluence of the Potomac and Shenandoah rivers. I made the journey from Staunton to Harrisonburg, twenty-five miles, in a stage, before the railway was completed. The route stretches through a rich, farming country, studded with fine square, antique mansions surrounded with tall trees. The roads are excellent; the fields are divided by walls of the limestone which abounds thereabout, and are well cultivated. Harrisonburg is an old-fashioned Virginian town which has awakened into activity since the railroad reached it; the citizens are anxious to join in the efforts to make a "New Virginia" out of the "Old Dominion." The Shenandoah valley felt the shock of war as keenly as any section of the South. It was overrun by the contending armies; exhausted by the repeated foraging expeditions of Confederates and Federals; and at the close of the contest its inhabitants were pretty thoroughly discouraged.

Half-way between Staunton and the Potomac river two ranges of mountains run parallel for twenty-five miles, finally uniting in Massanutten

Buffalo Gap and the Iron-Furnace. [Page 660.]

mountain, which separates the branches of the Shenandoah river, and ends abruptly to the southward in Rockingham county. These parallel ranges hold

between them "Luray," a charming valley which was the theatre of many of
the exploits of Stonewall Jackson early in the war, and through which Sheridan
campaigned later, leaving devastation in his train.   Through the gaps the Confederates kept up communication with the forces on the lower lands of Northern
Virginia, along the Rapidan and the
Rappahannock.

Elizabeth Iron-Furnace, Virginia.   [Page 661.]

At Strasburg, one of the prettiest
towns in the valley, one gets a fine
view of the Massanutten range, whose
steep wooded sides seem inaccessible.
The Virginians still point with pride
to the pass through which Stonewall
Jackson withdrew his army when
closely pressed by McDowell and
Fremont in 1862.   The wily General
saw that the Federals were determined,
if possible, to capture him, so he led
his hosts through the upper valley,
and speedily placed the Massanutten
ridge between his army and the
enemy, his guides finding paths along
the precipices where none but natives
of the region could possibly have
discovered them.

Winchester is one of the oldest
towns in the valley, and has, since
the earliest settlements there, been an
important trade centre.   It is the
chief town of a region rich in historic souvenirs and beautiful scenery.   Washington made it his head-quarters when commanding the army of operations
against the French and Indians in 1756.   Lord Fairfax and General Morgan
were both buried there.   Not far from Winchester, on the lower Opequan,
is Traveler's Rest, whither General Horatio Gates retired after his disgrace at
the battle of Camden.   Leetown, still nearer Winchester, was long the home
of another fallen General, Charles Lee, who conducted himself so badly at the
battle of Monmouth that he received a stinging reproof from the lips of
Washington.   Lee and Gates were fond of each other's company, but rarely
visited any of their neighbors.   The former lived and died a sceptic.   The
skirmishes and battles around Winchester in which Jackson, Banks, Ewell and
Sheridan, played important roles, are still talked of.

Returning to Staunton, and continuing along the line of the Chesapeake and
Ohio railroad, the traveler will pass through a remarkable cleft in the mountains
known as Buffalo Gap.   It is a passage between tall cliffs which seem to have been
rent asunder by earthquake or lightning stroke, and through it the buffaloes once
passed in their annual migrations.   Here some Baltimore capitalists have erected

an iron furnace, and six miles distant, at the ore bank of Elizabeth Furnace, rich seams of brown hematite may be seen. A little beyond this is the highest point

reached by the railroad between the Chesapeake and Ohio rivers, 2,073 feet above the tide. To the west are the numerous Pasture rivers, variously known as the Cow Pasture, the Bull Pasture, the Big Calf Pasture, and the Little Calf Pasture, and Jackson's river, which are the principal sources of the James. Goshen,

The Alum Spring—Rockbridge Alum Springs, Virginia.

on the "Big Calf Pasture" river, is the point of departure for the town of Lexington, for the Natural Bridge, for the Cold Sulphur and Rockbridge Alum Springs, and for the Rockbridge Baths.

Rockbridge Alum Springs, one of the most celebrated of Virginian wateringplaces, is in the northern portion of Rockbridge county, seventeen miles from Lexington, and is now easily reached by an eight-mile ride in a stage-coach southward from Goshen. The springs lie in a shallow basin between pretty

The Military Institute—Lexington, Virginia. [Page 662.]

mountain ridges. From beneath slate-stone arches issue five fountains, whose waters have proven efficacious in a variety of chronic ailments. A pretty hotel stands at the base of a high mountain; the lawns are girdled with neat cottages, secluded among the trees. The waters contain, in common with the alum which gives the Springs their name, protoxide of iron, sodium, potash, lime, magnesia and ammonia, and sulphuric, carbonic, chloric, and silicic acids. The invalid who is tired of the glare and bustle of the crowded Northern spring resorts can find at the " Rock-bridge Alum" absolute tranquillity and the charms of a virgin forest within a mile from his hotel. The Rockbridge Baths, near the North river, are richly impregnated with iron, and are so buoyant with carbonic acid gas that the bather floats without effort in the refreshing waters.

Lexington, twenty miles from the Rockbridge Alum Springs, is filled with solemn memorials for Virginians. From the Military Institute* there, the "West Point" of the Old Dominion, went out some of the best talent engaged in the service of the Confederacy; three of its professors and one hundred and twenty-five of its alumni were killed, and three hundred and fifty of the graduates of the institution were maimed in the war. The grave of "Stonewall" Jackson, who left the peaceful retreat of his college home to fight for his State against the Union, is in the Presbyterian burying-ground. Above the simple mound a board

Washington and Lee College—Lexington, Virginia.

headstone, painted in imitation of marble, is now the only memorial of the brave General's resting-place; but latterly an effort has been made to secure funds for the erection of a memorial chapel, at the Institute where he was for fourteen years a professor, to perpetuate his memory. The Institute was destroyed in 1864 by the Federal troops, but has succeeded in securing new buildings and re-establishing itself completely without demanding the aid of a dollar from the State treasury. In a commonwealth where military discipline and training are considered as indispensable parts of a general education, the Institute is a great power, and will, doubtless, in future, be fostered and encouraged by the State. Since the war it has extended the benefits of its course to pupils from all the States of the Union.

* The Virginia Military Institute was organized in 1839 as a State military and scientific school, on the basis of the U. S. Military Academy at West Point.

"Washington," or, as it is now called, "Washington and Lee College," also located at Lexington, is one of the oldest literary institutions in the South. It was established as an academy in 1776, by the Hanover Presbytery, which then embraced the whole of the Presbyterian Church in Virginia, and was christened Liberty Hall. In 1796 it obtained its first regular endowment at the hands of Washington. The Father of his Country had received from the Legislature, as a testimony of gratitude for his services, some shares in what was then known as the "James River Improvement." He was unwilling to accept them for his private gain, and therefore presented them to "Liberty Hall." This generous act induced the trustees to change the name of the academy

Portrait of General Thomas J. Jackson, known as "Stonewall Jackson.
[From an engraving owned by M. Knoedler & Co., N.Y.]

to "Washington," and it kept it when it became a college. Rockbridge county gave birth to McCormick, the noted inventor of the reaping-machine. He has furnished the money to build an astronomical observatory at Washington and Lee College, and the Peabody Fund has also given the institution a generous sum.

After the fall of the Confederacy, General Robert E. Lee took the presidency of the college, which before the war had rarely gathered more than a hundred students at a time within its walls. The fame of the soldier-president, and the affection of the Southern people for him, brought the number up to five, and sometimes seven hundred.   General Lee held the presidency of the college until his death, on the 11th of October, 1870.   The name of the institution was then changed to Washington Lee, and George Washington Custis Lee, a son of the deceased General, is now president of the institution.

The University Chapel, in the basement of which are the tombs of General Lee and his wife, is a plain brick building, with an auditorium capable of holding from eight hundred to a thousand persons.   The basement is built of gray Virginia limestone blocks, large and rough.   The building was planned and its

General Robert Edward Lee, born January 19, 1801; died October 11, 1870.

erection superintended by General Lee himself.   It is unfinished, from lack of funds.   At the time of General Lee's death the basement was used as a library, and near it was the General's private office, which remains exactly as he left it when he went out of it for the last time.   After his death the trustees and faculty of the University appropriated the basement as a place of sepulture for the Lee family. A vault or pit was dug, and walled and cemented in the middle of the large room formerly used as a library. The burial case containing the

The Great Natural Arch—Clifton Forge, Jackson's River. [Page 668.]

General's remains was placed in this vault, and over it were laid two strata of marble slabs, on the upper of which is the following simple inscription:

GEN. ROBERT EDWARD LEE,
Born
Jan. 19, 1801;
Died
Oct. 11, 1870.

The wife and daughter of the great Confederate chieftain, who speedily followed him to rest, repose beside him. Around the graves of General and Mrs. Lee there is a railing of black walnut, and some dark cloth hangings extend

Beaver Dam Falls. [Page 668.]

from the tops of the corner-posts to the ceilings above. The present surroundings will remain only until the monument, or sarcophagus, now in preparation by the sculptor Valentine, of Richmond, is finished. When that is completed, the whole basement will be modeled into a "Memorial Room," where as now, one of the students of the University will each day stand guard as a "watcher at the tomb." The monument will cost fifteen thousand dollars.

The railroad route from Goshen to White Sulphur Springs, the famous watering-place in the West Virginia mountains, is lined on either hand with exquisite scenery. It extends through Rockbridge, Bath, and Alleghany counties, entering, in the latter, the mountain or Appalachian belt of country, which has a width of from twenty to fifty miles, and is very equally divided between the States of Virginia and West Virginia. In the twenty counties—ten on each side of the State line—included in this region, there was, in 1870, a population of only 148,509 persons, or twenty to the square mile. Hundreds of thousands of acres of dense forest still clothe the mountain-sides; hickory, all varieties of the oak, wild cherry, spruce, pine, black walnut, ash, chestnut, all abound; finely-timbered land being held at from $10 to $25 per

Falling Springs Falls, Virginia. [Page 667.]

acre. All the slopes and hill-sides and the table-lands are covered with a rich and mellow soil that gives a fine yield, when properly cultivated, of wheat, corn, oats, potatoes, and all root crops. Mr. Howell Fisher, a Pennsylvania iron-master, who has carefully studied this Appalachian belt, says that cattle and sheep "fatten and flourish on the herbage and undergrowth without other food, and with literally no care." The opening of a railroad through this region has made it one of the most desirable in the two Virginias. On the extensive plateaus between the depressions formed by the washing of the streams there are fine grazing and orchard-lands, and millions of acres, now held as wild lands, are available for field culture, vineyards, or sheep pasturing, and can be purchased for trifling sums.

A little beyond Goshen the rail penetrates the rocky pass of Panther Gap, so called because the early settlers found to their sorrow that panthers loved to disport therein. From North mountain to the Alleghanies the scenery is wildly beautiful. Ravines, hill-sides, with ragged forests, log cabins beside rushing streams, vistas of perfect valleys, the high peak of Griffith's Knob, blue outlines of massive mountains, charm the eye. The "Cow Pasture" river flows beside the tracks for some distance, then disappears among the hills. From

Griffith's Knob, and Cow Pasture River.

Millboro' one may take stage for the "Warm Springs," fifteen miles away, in a lovely valley in Bath county. At the lower end of this valley is the famous "Cataract of the Falling Springs," where a stream flowing down from the "Warm Spring" mountain falls over a rock two hundred feet high, jeweling with its many cascades the bright grasses and ferns below. The view from Warm Spring mountain is accounted one of the most beautiful in Virginia, and not far from it, on the banks of the Cow Pasture river, is the "Blowing Cave," from which such a current of air constantly comes that the weeds for twenty feet in front of the cavern are prostrated. The Hot and Healing Springs are but a few miles from the Warm Springs valley.

At Millboro' for many years the trains of the Virginia Central railway crossed a yawning ravine by means of a temporary track, running down one slope and up the other at a grade of hundreds of feet to the mile. But when the Consolidated railroad line was completed, this ravine was filled up, and the occupation of "Mac," the old engine driver, whose locomotive, "Mountain Climber," used to push the trains up the hill, was gone. The artist has rescued him from oblivion.

At Clifton Forge, where Jackson's river rushes through a gorge, to unite with the many bright streams flowing down to form the James, a mighty arch of a half-mile chord, and a thousand feet to the keystone, is visible on the mountain-side. In this defile the clink of hammers on the anvils of numerous forges was once heard; but only the walls of the buildings, overgrown with vines, remain. The James River and Kana-wha canal is one day to have a channel here, and the wild loneliness and romance of the place will then be gone.

Clay Cut, Chesapeake and Ohio Railroad.

Covington, a sprightly town on Jackson's river, is a favorite point of departure from the railroad for the Hot and Healing Springs. On the road leading from it to the Sweet Springs, the clear waters of a little creek come rushing from a rocky cleft at Beaver Dam with a noise and patter far exceeding Lodore, which Mr. Southey made so many rhymes about; and with picturesqueness of dark green in the foliage, and brilliant refractions and reflections of broken sunlight in the descending drops.

At Covington one is confronted by the Alleghanies. Here, more than two hundred miles from Richmond, a city was once laid out, but it has never grown beyond the dimensions of a village. Covington was to have been the western terminus of the Virginia Central railroad, and the canal was to have been extended to this point. A road was to have been built from it to the Ohio by the State of Virginia, and the products of the mines and fields of the West were to be reshipped at Covington. This was a part of the internal improvement system which the Old Dominion was inaugurating when the war came. The great fight over, Virginia found that she had no funds with which to carry on the important enterprise, and offered all that had been done in improvements from Rich-

"Mac, the Pusher." [Page 667.]

mond to the Ohio river to any company that would complete the task.   Both
Virginia and West Virginia readily agreed upon a harmonious policy with regard
to the line, and the Chesapeake and Ohio Company finished the road on the
terms offered by the two commonwealths.

Jerry's Run.

At Jerry's Run a mighty ravine has been carved and cut away, to allow the
road a passage among the mountains.   For miles the roadway is carried over a
succession of artificial embankments and through long cuttings in the crags.
The train traverses the ravine so high above the stream that the water looks like
a silver thread stretched through the valley.   Then, at an elevation of more than
two thousand feet above the level of the sea, the road passes under the mountains by the "Alleghany Tunnel," and gradually descends toward the "Greenbrier White Sulphur," the most noted of Southern watering-places.

LXXIV.

GREENBRIER WHITE SULPHUR SPRINGS—FROM THE "WHITE SULPHUR" TO KANAWHA VALLEY—THE MINERAL SPRINGS REGION.

THE White Sulphur Springs are situated on Howard's creek, in Greenbrier county, West Virginia, and on the western slope of the Appalachian mountain chain, which separates the waters that flow into Chesapeake bay from those

Scene on the Greenbrier River in Western Virginia.

that empty into the Mississippi. On the south is Kates' mountain; on the west the Greenbrier range, and northward and eastward, at a distance of five miles from the springs, the Alleghanies tower in lovely confusion. The valley in which the springs lie is one of the most beautiful in the mountain region of the South. It is planted with great numbers of noble and finely-grown trees, and in early autumn the leaves of the maple, the hickory, the oak, the chestnut, the sweet gum, and the pine, vie in color with the gay toilets in which the Southern belles clothe themselves for the final hops and "Germans" of the season. The lawn around which the cottages are grouped is rich in foliage; in the hottest days of summer, when the lifeless atmosphere of Richmond seems like a curse suspended over the heads of the citizens, the air is cool and delightful at the "White Sulphur."

The Hotel and Lawn at Greenbrier White Sulphur Springs, West Virginia.

All the region round about was once a hunting ground of the Shawnee Indians, who knew the Greenbrier valley as one of the most frequented "licks" of the deer and the elk. The valley takes its name from the river, which was christened by old Colonel John Lewis, an early explorer, who once became entangled in a brier-thicket on the banks while exploring, and vowed that he would ever after call the stream Greenbrier. Toward the close of the last century, the Indians often brought those of their number afflicted with difficult diseases to the valley, where the unfortunates were speedily cured by drinking the water and bathing in it.

But in those days there were no roads; the Indians were far from friendly, and our revolutionary fathers had neither the time nor the money to spend in improving the beautiful resort. The Virginia planters learned of its charms, and as early as 1818 the tract was somewhat improved; but it was not until 1837 that the White Sulphur Spring Company was formed by a number of Virginians, who made the place what it is to-day. They erected a mammoth hotel covering an acre of ground; surrounded it at a convenient distance with neat cottages, built upon terraces, on the hill-sides and on the borders of the lawns; laid out serpentine walks, and gave the hitherto crude valley the aspect of a fashionable watering-place. The springs had been frequented, up to the date of these changes, almost exclusively by Southern people. The planters from the lowlands came in their carriages, attended by troops of servants, scattering plenty in their path; money flowed like water during the two or three months of the season; and when the merry company departed a wail of anguish went up from the mountaineers, who saw their golden harvest checked for a twelvemonth. During the war the place was alternately a Federal and a Confederate head-quarters. The cavalry of both armies clattered over the mountain roads, leaving destruction behind them. But the growth of railway enterprise in Virginia, during the last dozen years, has given the watering-place a railroad; and the lawns, the springs, and the mountain roads of the White Sulphur are rapidly gaining a national reputation.

The Eastern Portal of Second Creek Tunnel, Chesapeake and Ohio Railroad.

It must have been a tedious journey to the valley in the days of stage-coaches and private carriages, for the springs lie in a difficult mountain region. The Chesapeake and Ohio Railroad Company had to build some of its highest trestles, and dig some of its longest tunnels, within a few miles of "White Sulphur." At one point between Staunton and the springs, the tunnels, within a few minutes' ride of each other, aggregate more than two miles in length. One of them, called the "Big Bend," is 6,400 feet long.

Now-a-days, however, the traveler may ensconce himself in his berth in a luxurious sleeping-car at Richmond in the evening, and awaken at White Sulphur in the morning, just as the first breakfast bell is warning the sleepy ladies to prepare for their conquests of the forenoon. The journey from Washington to White Sulphur occupies but fifteen hours.

From July until September the season is at its height. The trains bring hundreds of passengers every evening; the cottages and hotels, as well as the few surrounding farm-houses, are crowded. The lawns are dotted with sprightly

parties, representing the society of every Southern, and latterly of most of the
Northern and Western States. The "hotel" is a remarkable structure, resembling the "Kursaal" at the German baths rather than the vast palaces in
which the habitués of Saratoga dance, flirt, eat, and sleep in the season. It is
amply provided with long and solid verandas, with a huge ball-room and a
colossal reception parlor. Between ball-room and parlor is a dining-room three
hundred feet long, in which twelve hundred guests may at once be seated. There
are but few rooms for lodgers in the hotel. From the cottages on Alabama,
Louisiana, Paradise, Baltimore, Virginia, Georgia, Wolf, and Bachelor rows, or on
Broadway, or in the "Colonnade," or on "Virginia Lawn," or at the "Spring,"
the belles come skipping across the green sward to dinner, attired in full evening
dress. There are never a dozen carriages at the White Sulphur during the
season. There is no whirl and glitter
of ambitious equipages, the whole life
and charm of the society being concentrated in the mammoth building called
the hotel. At early morning the par-

A Mountain Ride in a Stage-Coach. [Page 675.]

lor is filled with ladies who make their engagements for the day, and with the
customary rows of invalids who chat cheerily, or listen to the music of the pianos
or the band upon the lawn. After breakfast there are sometimes from five
hundred to a thousand persons gathered in the parlor, promenading for an hour,
after which the crowd separates into small parties, who linger on the verandas,
or under the oaks, or along the shaded paths in that famous resort known as
the "Lovers' Walk," where hundreds of hearts have been broken.

As the hour for the evening meal, dinner or tea, according to the visitors'
taste, approaches, the parlor is once more crowded. At dinner an army of four
hundred waiters skillfully supplies the guests with food. The scene is novel and
dazzling. Hundreds of beautiful girls from every part of the South, clad in ball-
room costume, are seated at the round tables in the long hall. The dark-haired,
languishing Creole of Louisiana is contrasted with the robust and bewitching
Kentucky belle; the delicate blonde of Richmond chats amicably with the

stately Mississippian; the lovely Baltimore ladies twirl their fans and frown defiance at Northern beaux; the sparkling belles of Charleston and the pretty mountain maids from the West Virginian capital may be seen side by side. The West and the East, the South and the North seem to have forgotten their sectional bickerings, and to have come together in friendliest mood. Ex-Generals of the Confederate army—Beauregard, Johnston, the Lees—chat amicably with United States Senators from the North and West; men who would gladly have flown at each other's throats a few years ago now reviewing the war with utmost calm. The South sends its best representatives to the White Sulphur Springs every year, and the result is a delightful, unostentatious, cultured society. The "hops" and the Germans given by the fashionable Philadelphia and New York ladies are the only dissipations; neither regattas, nor horse-races, nor tumultuous tumbling in surf distract one. Every morning the groups gather in the pavilion, under which the sulphur water bubbles up from the spring; the young ladies make the wonted wry faces over the unsavory beverage; while the venerable planters from the lowlands, with many a thought upon their damaged livers and yellow faces, swallow the fluid as if it were nectar.

"Greenbrier White Sulphur," as the Southerners call it, is a pleasure resort. Not one-tenth of the throng which crowds cottages and hotel in the season comes to regain its health. It comes rather to rejoice in a superabundance of life and vigor. But the waters are singularly efficacious in many obstinate diseases.* As an alterative they have no superior. The effect of a free use of the

---

* The White Sulphur Water was analyzed in 1842, by Professor Hayes, of Boston, with the following results:

"Fifty thousand grains (about seven pints) of the water contain, in solution, 3.633 water-grain measures of gaseous matter, or about 1.14 of its volume, consisting of—

Nitrogen gas	1.013
Oxygen gas	.108
Carbonic acid	2.444
Hydro-sulphuric acid	.068
	3.633

"One gallon, or 237 cubic inches, of the water, contains 16.739-1000 cubic inches of gas, having the proportion of—

Nitrogen gas	4.680
Oxygen gas	.498
Carbonic acid	11.290
Hydro-sulphuric acid	.271
	16.739

"Fifty thousand grains of this water contain 115.735-1000 grains of saline matter consisting of—

Sulphate of lime	67.168
Sulphate of magnesia	30.364
Chloride of magnesium	.859
Carbonate of lime	6.060
Organic matter (dried at 212° F.)	3.740
Carbonic acid	4.584
Silicates (silica 1.34, potash .18, soda .66, and a trace of oxide of iron)	2.960
	115.735"

waters much resembles that produced by mercury, without any of the disagreeable contingencies attendant on the employment of that medicine. The
sulphur baths, which constitute one of the attractions of the place even for well

Anvil Rock, Greenbrier River.

people, are admirably kept. A visit
to the spring, a bath, and a horseback
ride among the mountains, or a walk
along "Dry Creek" before breakfast, will certainly fit one for the
fatigues of the merry "evening," even
if there be a "German" which lasts
until daybreak.

Within a radius of forty miles from
the Greenbrier White Sulphur lies the
most interesting portion of the Virginia Springs region. Northward are
those already mentioned, the Hot, the
Warm, the Healing, and the Alum

Springs. Seventeen miles eastward from the White Sulphur are the Sweet
Springs; twenty-four miles to the south the Salt Sulphur; forty-one miles to the
south the Red Sulphur; and twenty-two miles to the west the Blue Sulphur. At
all these springs fine hotels have been built, and as the season wanes at one it
waxes at another, so that one may make a jolly round for three or four months.

At some of these resorts the furnishings of the cottages are primitive, and
one sadly misses the elegance of city
life; but the natural beauties and the
delicious atmosphere amply compen-
sate for all other deficiencies. Although most of the Springs are now
either directly accessible by rail, or
within easy distance of the railroads,
it is the fashion to make the tour in
such a stage as our artist has given a
picture of, although the passes in the
mountains are rarely as rough as they
are depicted in the engraving. Many
parties adjourn to the Old Sweet
Springs after the season at the Greenbrier is over, stopping on the way for
picnics. The "Old Sweet" always has
a company of distinguished guests.
It is located in a charming valley in
the eastern part of Monroe county,

A West Virginia "Countryman."

with the high Sweet Spring mountain on the south, and the Alleghanies only
a mile away. The buildings are elegant and commodious; the lawns as beauti-

ful and richly studded with trees as those in the Greenbrier valley. The baths are frequented from dawn until dusk by crowds who represent the best talent of the West and South. The predominance of carbonic acid in the waters of these springs induces physicians to recommend invalids who have been drinking the White Sulphur water for some time to try those of the "Old Sweet" for perfecting and fixing the cure already reasonably well established.

The Red Sweet Spring, situated but one mile from the Old Sweet, is one of the prettiest retreats in the mountains. The chalybeate and tonic waters annu-

A Freighters' Camp, West Virginia. [Page 679.]

ally draw hundreds of visitors to them. The Salt Sulphur, shut in among the mountains near the town of Union, has three springs, one of which is called the "Iodine," and is strongly recommended for chronic affections of the brain, and for nervous diseases. The Red Sulphur, in the southern portion of Monroe county, is romantically situated on Indian creek, in a deep ravine to which the traveler descends along the side of a picturesque mountain. The waters of this spring have been found a powerful adjunct in the management of difficult cases of phthisis and consumption. At the "Blue Sulphur" a spacious hotel, a beautiful lawn, and a fine establishment of medicated baths are the attractions grouped about the spring, which is covered by an imposing temple.*

The Northerner is especially welcome at all these watering-places. There is none of the bitterness and occasional small spite manifested toward him which he might perhaps encounter in some of the Southern capitals. The courtesy and hospitality of the Virginians are proverbial; their frankness and kindliness toward strangers are shown in their best light at the "Springs." The subject of politics is pretty thoroughly eschewed at White Sulphur during the season, except when the President goes there to hear what the Southern politicians have to say, or when some injudicious relict of the late war utters something fiery at a reunion or a convention. The whole company of distinguished Southerners at White

"The rude cabin built beneath the shadow of a huge rock." [Page 679.]

Sulphur, in 1873, condemned the bitter and hostile speech made by Jefferson Davis at a meeting of the Southern Historical Society at the "Montgomery White" that season. The Northern or Western man at these springs is never likely to hear disagreeable sentiments unless he provokes them by illiberality on his own part. He will find the Southern people assembled there amply able to take a fair and dispassionate view of our national politics. Gentlemen of culture and refinement will show him how possible it was for the South to believe that it was right in the war. But all will convince him that they are much more interested in the material development of the Southern States than in quarreling over

* See appendix for complete table of routes in and about the Virginia Springs region.

old issues. Leading politicians will now and then intimate that some day the Southern State Constitutions will be amended; and from this it will be easy to perceive that the South is not yet reconciled to reconstruction.

The Springs region of Virginia seems likely to become a favorite meeting-ground for Northern and Southern people. As soon as the Chesapeake and Ohio railroad was opened to the Ohio river, Cincinnati sent a large quota of visitors to the "Greenbrier White Sulphur," and the Virginians have found, much to their surprise, that there is a fair share of culture and manners at the West. The free and friendly intercourse between citizens of the different sections, which has been the result of yearly visits to the charming resorts in the mountains of Virginia and West Virginia, cannot fail to have an influence for good in their future political relations. The wild life of the mountaineers, and the

"The rustic mill built of logs." [Page 679.]

strange humors and habits of the negroes scattered through the Springs region, offer an interesting study to the visitor from the North and West. The country

in the vicinity of the White Sulphur Springs has many prosperous farms; fine cattle are to be seen in the fields; the grazing is excellent the year round.

West Virginia does not bear the aspect of a slave State; its farms have the same thoroughly cultured and well-kept appearance as those at the North. But few slaves were owned in the mountain region; the wealthy families had some house-servants' who, as a rule, still remain with them. The negroes who come to these mountain regions from the lowlands seem to thrive. They proved themselves one of the most useful laboring forces that could be employed in the building of the new railroad. They were en-

The Junction of Greenbrier and New Rivers.

dowed with vigorous health, were easily managed, sober, and quick to learn. The beautiful Greenbrier river flows downward from Greenbrier mountain through Pocahontas, Greenbrier, and Monroe counties, to unite with the New river, which rises in North Carolina, and courses through some of the most romantic mountain scenery in West Virginia, until it meets and joins with the Great Kanawha river at the entrance of the famous Kanawha valley. Along the Greenbrier and New rivers adventurous boatmen ply in "batteaux," carrying merchandise or travelers who wish to explore the wonders of the New River cañon. The lofty and thickly-wooded hills; the vales carpeted with flowers and overhung by giant trees; the camps of the "freighters" who transport goods over the rough roads along or near the banks; the rustic mill built of logs, and insecurely set beside some treacherous hill-side stream; the rude cabin beneath the shade of a huge rock; and the types of "countryman," inquisitive and sus-

picious—all are strangely interesting, and amply repay the traveler for the fatigues of the journey.

Our artists, who made the tour of the New river cañon in a batteau, found it an exciting experience. At the junction of the Greenbrier and New rivers they engaged one of the boats used in running the rapids. This boat was sixty feet long

Descending the New River Rapids.

by six wide, and was managed by three negroes,—the "steersman," who guided the boat with a long and powerful oar; the headsman, who stood on the bow to direct the steersman by waving his arms; and an extra hand, who assisted with an oar in the eddies and smooth parts of the river. The merry artists not only found time for exciting scrambles along the rocky banks, in search of pictures, but even when descending the New River rapids managed to obtain the necessary notes from which to give the world a faithful representation of the event.

The country near the junction of the Greenbrier with the New river literally stands on end. The people live on hill-slopes so steep that the horses can hardly keep their footing when they plough; and it is sometimes said that the farmers in the cañon stand on one bank and shoot their seed corn into the field on the other from a rifle.

The New River cañon is one of the most remarkable natural wonders of the eastern portion of the United States. It is a deep crack in the earth, a hundred miles long, a mile wide at the summit, from eight to fifteen hundred feet deep, and traversed at its bottom by a turbulent stream. The railroad builders found this cañon practicable for the passage of their route. They blasted out fragments of rock until they had made a shelf along the perpendicular rocky side of the cañon. Entering this strange gorge by train, one scarcely realizes that he is hundreds of feet below the level of the surrounding country. The scenery is grand. The journey along the rocky shelf, whence one can look upon the enormous masses of stone hurled down to make room for the track, or look up to the streams of water flowing from the sides of the cliffs, is an experience never to be forgotten.

But there is one remarkable characteristic of the cañon which the traveler through it by rail or in batteau will notice with care. He will observe that the stratification of the rocks is very singular; that they lie evidently as they were deposited; that there has been no upheaval, no disorganization. The earth has simply been cracked asunder, and the traveler is able to enter, without difficulty, a coal-shaft which is open to the sunlight, and through which a railroad runs.

A coal-shaft? Yes; out of the high bank a coal-seam crops. In some places many seams are visible. The railroad has here and there cut through veins of the best cannel coal, and the miner has only to dig into the mountain. The mine drains itself, and the precious mineral is dumped directly into cars which carry it to Richmond. In 1871 it was impossible to ride through this cañon on horseback. Now it is as easily accessible as any manufacturing town in the North. The coal and limestone in this New River valley lie within a hundred miles of some of the richest and most important deposits of iron ore in the United States.

A hard road for artists to travel.

LXXV

THE KANAWHA VALLEY—MINERAL WEALTH OF WESTERN VIRGINIA.

EMERGING from the New River cañon, one reaches the Great Falls of the Kanawha, a stream formed by the junction of the New and Gauley rivers. The country surrounding was the scene during the late war of much strife between the Federal Rosecrans and Wise and other Confederate officers. A few miles from Kanawha Falls, in the direction of Greenbrier White Sulphur, the "Hawk's Nest," an imposing bluff rising a thousand feet above the bed of the New river, frowns upon the railroad. From this height, to which a winding path leads, one may look down over perfect valleys, unsurpassed by those of Rhine or Moselle. The scene at Miller's Ferry, where the stream winds through deep recesses in the hills, is one of the most sublime in the South. The "Richmond" and "Big Dowdy" Falls on the New river, and "Whitcomb's Boulder," in this vicinity, are worthy of the traveler's attention.

The "Hawk's Nest," from Boulder Point.

The Kanawha and Ohio valley, or trans-Appalachian region, which lies along the western foot slopes of the Alleghany range, has an area of seventeen thousand five hundred square miles in West Virginia. Most of this area is seamed with wonderful strata of bituminous, splint, and cannel coal. Its agricultural advantages also are con-

siderable, tobacco, corn, and root crops paying well. As a live-stock country, this valley resembles the "blue-grass" lands of Kentucky, which join it on the west. The farmers are industrious, intelligent, and reasonably prosperous.

Great Kanawha Falls. [Page 681.]

But the mineral wealth of the Kanawha valley now usurps all the attention directed to that quarter. The coal-measures there actually cover sixteen thousand square miles. They make their appearance at the surface, in the New River and Kanawha valleys, to the number of fourteen distinct strata, "with an aggregate thickness in some

Miller's Ferry, seen from the Hawk's Nest.

places of one hundred feet, more than half of which is in workable seams from three to eight feet thick." The coal crops out on the hill-sides, high above the water and railroad levels, allowing easy and inexpensive excavation. The testimony of Mr. Howell Fisher upon this point is as follows :

"In respect to conditions most essential to cheap and profitable working, this region stands unrivaled. The chasm of the river renders it most peculiar service in its relation to the coal. Cutting all the coal strata for nearly its whole length entirely through, and getting down among the shales under the coal, the river has caused the numerous streams which pierce the whole coal region to cut down through most of the coal-bearing strata on their courses, leaving the coal entirely above water-level, accessible at hundreds

of points by simply scraping off the surface soil, so that, as far as the mere getting of coal is concerned, two thousand dollars will open a mine ready to ship
one thousand tons per week. There is no region in the world where less
physical labor will prepare a mine for the delivery of coal at the drift's mouth.

"This will be made clearer by a comparison of the position of coal here and
in Great Britain in this respect. In Great Britain, and in fact in almost all of the
European coal-fields, the coal is deep below the water-level. To reach the
seams requires the expenditure of years of labor and vast sums of money in
sinking shafts or pits, and in erecting pumping and hoisting machinery, to be
maintained and renewed at heavy annual expense. It is authoritatively stated
that the cost of sinking shafts in the Newcastle region of England to the depth
of one thousand feet, has been, in many instances, one thousand dollars per
yard. In the great Northern coal-field of Great Britain, producing twenty million tons per annum, there are two hundred pits or shafts, costing, in first outlay,

Richmond Falls, New River. [Page 681.]

for sinking and machinery, fifty millions of dollars, to which must be added the
necessary expense of constructing and maintaining proper air-courses, and their
accessories requisite to the safety of the employés.

"Now in this great Kanawha coal-field nature has already sunk all the necessary pits and shafts, which need neither repair, renewal, nor labor to work them.
The laws of gravity have provided the most perfect, permanent, and costless
pumping machinery; and the ventilation of the mine and safety of the employés,
instead of requiring scientific knowledge and anxious thought, is simply a matter
of the most ordinary care, the freedom from noxious gases being the natural
result of the position of the coal strata."

There is coal enough along the line of the railroads and rivers in this favored
section to supply the American market for several centuries. Professor Ansted,
of England, explored this region nearly a quarter of a century ago, and gave
his testimony at a meeting of the Society of Arts in London, two or three years
since, that "there was no coal-field more important than that of Virginia;

none where the coal-seams were more accessible or of a better quality.   The coal-fields in the Appalachian range were nearly all horizontal, intersected by convenient valleys, could be worked from numerous points at the same time with ease, and might be looked upon as inexhaustible."

Big Dowdy Falls, near New River. [Page 681.]

Professor Hotchkiss, of Staunton, Virginia, in a paper on the Resources of the State, speaks as follows of the Kanawha coal-field :

"On the eastern border the seams of the lower coal-measures are found, having an exposed aggregate thickness of some fifty feet in the gorge of New river—the line of the Chesapeake and Ohio railway—a cañon from 1,200 to 1,500 feet below the general level of the country.   One of these seams is over six feet thick, furnishing a good coking coal; another seam of block coal is four and a-half feet thick.   There are several other seams three and four feet in thickness, furnishing bituminous coals of good quality.   These seams have only a moderate inclination to the north-west, and are all above the river and railroad-level.   These lower measures descend more rapidly than the rivers, and so pass beneath the water-level some fifty miles from their eastern outcrop. The strata of the upper coals come to the horizon as the mouth of New river is approached, and not far below the junction of that river with the Gauley to form the Great Kanawha. At Armstrong's creek, a section in the 600 feet of bluff above the level of the Kanawha shows thirteen seams of coal varying in thickness from two and a-half to nine feet, with an aggregate of sixty-one feet. Below this place, at Cannelton, on the other side of the Kanawha, there are five seams of coal open, in the 1,300 feet of the face of the bluff, aggregating twenty-nine feet. More than 100 feet of stratified coal has been proved here. The seams vary from eight to fourteen feet in thickness, and embrace gas, shop, splint, and cannel varieties. The seam producing the cannel is double, giving four feet of cannel and two and a-half of splint coal. This cannel will yield sixty gallons of oil to the ton of 2,000 lbs. A section on Cabin creek and

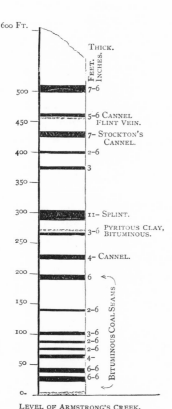

SECTION OF KANAWHA COAL-SEAMS.

Whitcomb's Boulder. [Page 681.]

vicinity, ten miles below Cannelton, by Prof. Ansted, gives sixty-eight feet of coal, in some thirteen seams, varying from two and a-half to eleven feet; twenty-two feet of these seams are cannel and from seven to eleven splint coal. At Campbell's creek, still lower down the river, in the 400 feet of bluff, are six seams, from four and a-half to six feet thick, that furnish twenty-nine feet of coal. This coal is peculiar in its formation. Near Clay Court-House, on Elk river, the coal strata are from four and a-half to eleven feet thick, making forty-one feet of coal in the 500 feet of bluff; nineteen feet of the coal being splint and six cannel. At the mouth of Coal river a stratum of coal, from four to eight feet thick, is found at a depth of 300 feet; of course the other seams are found there also, but at greater depths. These may be considered fair samples of the sections throughout this great coal-field, ample enough to satisfy the wants of untold generations, and so accessible as to require no special skill in mining; nor expenditure for drainage and ventilation.   The Baltimore and Ohio railway, with its Parkersburg and Wheeling arms and numerous branches, now crosses the northern part of this field and opens it to markets. The Chesapeake and Ohio railway has just crossed it in the south, where the Great Miner has ' torn asunder the mountains,' and well and wisely cut an open gangway, more than a thousand feet deep, across the rich strata, exposed them to daylight, and at the same time made way for the railroad, at very low grades, to carry this ' bottled sunshine' to the great markets.   The coals found here are used in making iron without coking, and the choice for any special purpose is very great, the quality being unexceptionally good."

Cannelton, mentioned by Professor Hotchkiss, was established by a Rhode Island company, who built works there for the milling of coal into oil.   Just as the work was progressing fairly, the oil region of Pennsylvania was dis-

The Inclined Plane at Cannelton.

covered, and the proprietors of Cannelton, unable to compete with the flowing wells of Titusville, closed their works, for without transportation facilities their coal was worthless.   But with the advent of the railroad came a fortune into their hands, and to-day they let coal down an inclined plane 1,100 feet long from the almost perpendicular side of the mountain, directly into cars waiting on side tracks to receive it.

In previous chapters I have given some idea of the extent of the stores of iron in South-western Virginia and the Piedmont country.   The deposits of iron ore are no less remarkable along the line of the Chesapeake and Ohio road.   In that part of Piedmont penetrated by this line, there are hematite and magnetic ores of the best quality.   In the spurs of the Blue Ridge, near Fisherville, a seam of hematite ores exists, and rich lodes of hematite and specular ores are found running along the foot of the Blue Ridge; at intervals, in the whole breadth of the Shenandoah valley; "and in continuous seams of great thickness along the north and parallel mountains beyond."

"The mineral wealth of the Blue Ridge," says Professor Hotchkiss, "is great, and destined to be quite important, from its nearness to the sea-board.   In the ranges of foot-hills lying along the western base of these mountains, the whole three hundred or more miles of their length, are found very extensive deposits of brown hematite iron ores of the best character, giving from sixty to seventy-five per cent. of metallic iron in the yield of the furnace.   It is not correct to say that these deposits are continuous, and yet they have been so regularly found, when sought after, as almost to justify the use of that term.   In some places they are deeply buried in the *debris* of the mountain; at others they show themselves as interstratified masses, conforming for long distances to the formations of the district, as near where New river leaves the Ridge, at Radford Furnace, where the stratum is over thirty feet in thickness, while at other places the ore, in a soft state, forms hill-like masses, as at the Shenandoah Iron Works, in Rockingham. At one place in Rockbridge, where the stratification is nearly vertical, striking with the mountain, this one appears as a hard central stratum, forming the crest of a spur more than 600 feet above its base. The western flank of the table-land in the south-west is known as the Iron mountain, from the quantity of this ore there exposed. There are numerous furnaces now in blast, and others are being built along the line of these deposits, making charcoal iron of a high character, such as now readily commands sixty dollars a ton in the United States. One of these had a yield of sixty-five per cent. of iron from the ore put into the furnace in the run of a season. Between these hematites and the main ridge is found a deposit of specular iron-stone."

Fern Spring Branch, a West Virginia Mountain Stream.

In the slopes of the North mountain there are numerous lodes or pockets of ore inter-stratified with limestone. The ore-beds in the western portion of Augusta county, and in one or two adjacent counties in Virginia proper, are very extensive. Their astonishing bulk and their convenient position near the surface have prompted trustworthy experts to declare them among the most remarkable on the continent. From Gordonsville in the Piedmont district, to Huntington on the Ohio river, a distance of three hundred and twenty-five miles by the railway line, there is a constant succession of minerals. All the elements of successful and profitable coal mining and manufacture are there found closely associated. The iron ores are rich and of great variety; the carboniferous limestone is excellent for fluxing purposes, and there are inexhaustible stores of coal. In Greenbrier valley the limestone is bordered by deposits of ore on one side, by coal-measures on the other.*

* See appendix for article on the Iron of the Virginias.

Charleston, the capital of West Virginia, is pleasantly situated near the confluence of the Elk and Kanawha rivers, in a bold mountain country.   A

Charleston, the West Virginia Capital.

steamboat plies between the city and the railroad depot on the steep side of a rocky ledge.   The deck hands may any day be seen shoveling coal from a vein in the riverbank into the coal-bunkers of the steamer, and in the hills which overhang the stream veins crop out at points where they can be very easily mined.   At the close of the war Charleston was a small village, but its selection as the State capital, and the completion of the Chesapeake and Ohio railroad, gave it a new start. It now has three or four thousand population ; a cultured society ; one of the best hotels in the South, the Hale House ; an elegant State capitol ; an opera house ; fine structures for schools and churches, and many handsome private mansions. For forty years before the war the people of Charleston were wealthy and cultured.   The saltmills and furnaces along the Kanawha, and the cultivation

The Hale House—Charleston.

of the fertile bottom lands, brought plenty and prosperity. But no farmer or land-owner ever thought of opening coal mines—of developing the riches which they daily trampled under their feet. Even to-day the old-school farmers seem hardly to appreciate the value of their mineral lands, and show a decided disin- clination to develop them. When they can get what they consider a good price, they will gladly sell; but they cannot be induced to risk much of their own capital in mining. Charleston is the central point and the most convenient outlet for five great sections of Western Virginia, all of which in a few years will doubt- less be provided with railroads. There is no city within one hundred miles of it which can become a rival in the lumber, coal, salt, and manufacturing interests

Rafts of Saw-Logs on a West Virginia River.

of the Kanawha, Elk, and Coal River valleys. The lumber trade along the Elk river is very important; hundreds of rafts are floated down that stream to the mouth of the Kanawha, and thence into the Ohio. A single company sends twelve hundred thousand bushels of coal down the Coal river annually. The Elk River railroad will soon connect Charleston with Pittsburg and the East, and the Parkersburg, Ripley and Charleston road is an important route recently projected. Manufactures are creeping into the West Virginia capital. It begins to assume the thrifty and active appearance of a New England city. On the banks of the Kanawha there are many pleasant towns, rapidly increasing in population. Prominent among them are Point Pleasant, Buffalo, Raymond City, Winfield, St. Albans, Brownstown, Coalburg and Cannelton.

The completion of the James River and Kanawha canal would undoubtedly aid immensely in the development of the resources of the Kanawha valley. The canal is now completed from Richmond to Buchanan, 197 miles, leaving a gap of 303

The Snow Hill Salt Works, on the Kanawha River.

miles yet to be built between that point and the mouth of the Kanawha. The importance to Virginia and the Western States of a line of cheap water transportation from the Ohio river to the Chesapeake bay can hardly be overestimated.

Indian Mound, near St. Albans   [Page 691.]

The salt region tributary to Charleston extends from that place fifteen miles on either side up the Kanawha river. The annual product from the wells in the region is about two million bushels. It might readily be increased to twenty. The Snow Hill furnace, owned by Dr. Hale, of Charleston, is one of the largest in the world, and in 1870 produced more than four hundred thousand bushels of excellent salt.* This important interest and

* At the Snow Hill works the brine is drawn from nine wells, each from eight hundred to one thousand feet deep. They are bored through about three hundred feet of sandstone, below which the brine is found. From forty-five to fifty gallons make a bushel of salt. Attached to the salt works is a bromine factory, where a hundred pounds of this odorous drug are daily made. The coal used for fuel for all this work is taken from a five-foot seam on the adjacent hills.

View of Huntington and the Ohio River.

the lumber trade will in a few years make Charleston a large city. The Kanawha river and its tributaries drain one of the finest bodies of timbered land in the United States. The white oak, the white and yellow poplar, the black walnut, the shell bark and "white heart hickory," grow to enormous heights; the white ash, the locust, the linden, the birch, the sycamore, and the iron-wood exhibit a development rarely seen in the Northern forests.

The agricultural advantages of the country surrounding Charleston are numerous. Not only are the river bottom lands fertile, but the mountain-sides may be profitably cultivated. Corn, wheat, rye, oats, and barley are profitable; the culture of tobacco, the grape, and orchard fruits, has proved very successful. There is nowhere a better country for sheep-raising, and the English settlers have given much attention to this specialty.

On the road from Charleston to the Ohio river, one passes through a rich and extensive timber country. Between Charleston and St. Albans there are some singular conical-shaped hills, supposed to be the work of that lost race known as the "Mound Builders." Crossing the Coal, the Scary, the Hurricane, the Mud, and the Guyandotte rivers, the Chesapeake and Ohio railroad reaches the Ohio river at Huntington, a new and pretty town, ambitiously laid out as a "future great city." It stands at the head of what is known as reliable navigation on the Ohio; steamers of light draught can reach it at all seasons, and there is never danger of any interruption of transportation.   Huntington is an important supply point for the inhabitants of the lower Ohio valley, who, before the building of the route from Richmond through the mountains, often suffered a coal famine because the upper Ohio was obstructed.   From Huntington the supply will be constant and regular.   South of the town lie deposits of splint and cannel coal, and the neighboring counties in Kentucky are rich in both coal and iron.   The State Normal School of West Virginia, formerly Marshall College, one of the elder collegiate schools of the Old Dominion, stands within the " city limits."   The Chesapeake and Ohio Company have also established their construction shops, in which an army of operatives work, at Huntington.

Guyandotte is prettily situated on the river of the same name, at its confluence with the Ohio.   It was once a trading place of much importance, and still has a commerce of its own with the back-country.   The farmers and lumbermen from the mountain districts come down the river in barges, which they propel with long poles; and one of the most curious sights in the Southern highlands is a group of these rustic watermen storing their boats with provisions purchased from the merchants at Guyandotte.

The result of climbing a sapling — An Artist in a Fix.

LXXVI.

DOWN THE OHIO RIVER—LOUISVILLE.

THE French explorers called the Ohio *La Belle Rivière;* and certainly, when its banks are full, and a profusion of flowers dot the cliffs here and there overhanging the stream, or are reflected from the lowlands in the shining water, one readily recognizes the appropriateness of the term. But the Ohio river, on a foggy morning, late in autumn, when sycamores are stripped and flowers are gone, hardly recalls the affectionate name which the Frenchmen bestowed upon it.

The traveler, journeying from Huntington to Louisville on the Ohio, finds but little in natural scenery that is impressive; much, however, that is very beau-

The Levée at Louisville, Kentucky.

tiful. In summer, when the shores are clothed in green and the vineyards are resplendent with foliage, there are many landscapes which charm the eye. Inasmuch as the channel in midsummer contains little more than a "light dew," as the Western captains call it, navigation is attended with peculiar difficulties, and steamboats of lightest draught are often detained for days on a treacherous bank suddenly laid bare.

No river is more subject to extreme elevations and depressions. The average range between high and low water is said to be more than thirty feet. The highest stage is in March, and the lowest in August. In times of flood the variations are so rapid that the river at Cincinnati has been known to rise at the rate of one foot per hour during half a day.   It requires no little skill and sea-manship to navigate this peculiar stream.   Obstructions were originally very numerous, and the passages between the exquisite islands and the sand-banks require the tact and courage of ocean sailors.   The days of keel-boat, of Ken-tucky float, of pirogue, of gondola, skiff, and dug-out, are past.   Lines of rail have superseded the noble packets which sailed from Louisville to New Orleans, and much of the romance of the river has departed.   Yet there is a certain fascination in the journey by night along the great current which slips, although rapidly, apparently with a certain laziness, past the low shores sprinkled with log cabins.

From Huntington, the terminus of the Chesapeake and Ohio railroad, in West Virginia, to Cincinnati, the voyage is exceedingly interesting.   The towns on the Kentucky shore, while few of them are large or bustling, have a solid and substantial air.   Around the various taverns in each of them is grouped the regulation number of tall, gaunt men, with hands in pockets, and slouched hats drawn over their eyes.   A vagrant pig roots here and there in the customary sewer.   A few cavaliers lightly mount the rough roads leading into the unimposing hills; a few negroes slouch sullenly on a log at the foot of the levée, and on a wharf-boat half a hundred white and black urchins stare, open-mouthed, as if they had never seen steamboats or strangers before.

On the Ohio side of the river there are large manufacturing towns, evidences of thrift, industry and investment; iron-furnaces smoke; and the clatter of ham-mers and the roll of wheels are heard.

The distance from Pittsburg, in Pennsylvania, to Cairo, in Illinois, where the Ohio pours its muddy flood into the muddier waters of the Mississippi, is 967 miles.   The tourist who takes a packet from Wheeling, in West Virginia, to Parkersburg, will see some noble scenery; for the upper Ohio, when navigation is practicable there, far surpasses in beauty the lower portion of the stream. Descending from Parkersburg he will pass Pomeroy, Gallipolis, Catlettsburg, Ironton, Portsmouth, Maysville, Ripley, and Cincinnati, and will note on the banks many salt, nail, and iron manufactories.   From Cincinnati he can have his choice of two or three steamers daily for Louisville, and from the Ken-tucky metropolis can drift on to Evansville, in Indiana, and thence to Cairo. At Maysville, in Kentucky, between Huntington and Cincinnati, there are two extensive cotton factories and several iron foundries.   The town contains many handsome streets, and is the entry port for the north-eastern section of the State. It is also the most extensive hemp market in the whole country.

Between Cincinnati and Louisville there are but few towns of importance on the Kentucky shore of the Ohio.   At Big Bone Lick, in Boone county, great numbers of bones of the mastodon and the Arctic elephant were once found. At Warsaw, a few miles below, there are many tobacco factories.   Carroll-ton, formerly called Fort William, stands at the junction of that beautiful stream, the Kentucky, with the Ohio.

The scenery along the Kentucky river justly ranks among the wildest and most picturesque in the United States.   For more than 200 miles, as the stream flows north-west to empty into the Ohio, it passes through massive limestone ledges, arranged upon either side of its narrow channel in great cliffs, forming irregular cañons, or pours over rapids, or glides between precipices 500 feet high, whose tops almost touch, like roofs in the streets of an old Italian town.

The river flows through Middle Kentucky for the greater portion of its course. The confluence of the small streams which make it is at the spot known as the "Three Forks," in Lee county, the very heart of the coal and iron region which stretches away for miles in every direction. During the winter and spring coal and pig-iron are floated down the river in barges.

A familiar scene in a Louisville Street.

The improvement of the Ohio river and its tributaries is highly necessary. It is demanded by more than one-fifth of the States, and one-third of the whole population of the country, and inasmuch as that population has hitherto paid thirty-five per cent. of the internal taxation of the Union, and as it raises forty per cent. of the farm products of the land, owns forty per cent. of the farm-lands and of the live stock, and thirty-six per cent of the capital in farming implements and machinery, it would seem that it has a right to ask of the Government this boon. The sum demanded for the work will depend largely upon the plan adopted for its accomplishment. The estimates of engineers have varied from seventeen to sixty millions. No definite decision as to the wisest plan has yet been reached. Those most directly interested are still in doubt whether to decide upon supplying the required volume of water by aid of reservoirs, or maintaining the proper navigation by low dams with open chutes, or slack-watering the entire stream.

The commerce of the river is immense. The amount of coal transported from Pittsburg down the Ohio increased from fifty million bushels in 1869 to ninety millions in 1872, or more than twenty-six per cent. per annum. The tonnage of the port of Pittsburg in 1869 was estimated at eight hundred thousand tons; in 1872 it was one million six hundred and sixty-nine thousand tons. The commerce along the stream amounts to nearly nine hundred millions of dollars yearly. The Ohio drains an area of 214,000 square miles, and could furnish cheap transportation for the commerce of fifty millions of people.

Louisville, the chief city of the goodly commonwealth of Kentucky, lies on the southern bank of the Ohio river, at a point where the navigation of the stream was originally obstructed by rapids. For six miles above the site of the city, the stream stretches out into a smooth sheet of water, a mile wide, and embraces within its limits the mouth of Bear Grass creek, which affords a safe harbor for the myriad barges and flat-boats which drift on the bosom of the great stream. Situated centrally between the cotton-fields of the South and the grain-

A Waiter at the Galt House, Louisville, Kentucky.

fields of the West, amply supplied with railways piercing both West and South in all directions, and with ten miles of river-front from twenty to twenty-five feet above highest flood mark, the city has a promising commercial future. Its levées, while they are not so picturesque, and the life along them is not so vivacious as that which one sees at New Orleans, Savannah, and Charleston, are yet quite as fine as those of any Southern or Western city. What Louisville has lost in river trade, since railroads came in, she has gained in railway commerce. The days of tedious steaming from Louisville to the Louisiana lowlands, in roundabout ways and along treacherous currents, are gone, and have pulled down with them into oblivion many noble fortunes; but the city grows and prospers despite the misfortunes that have overtaken the commerce once its mainstay. Opposite Louisville, on the Indiana shore, are the towns of Jeffersonville and New Albany; the former pretty and dull, the latter a kind of Western Brooklyn, having ready communication with Louisville by means of the great railroad bridge, a triumph of mechanical engineering, which has long spanned the stream.

West and south of the city the lots are lovely, and admit of unlimited extension; and on the broad and shapely streets which are one of its peculiar features stand many handsome mansions, each one of which is set down in a capacious yard, well kept, and now and then embellished with terraces. The streets which run parallel with the river, and not far from the levée, are long, and flanked with solid business blocks, very uniform in architecture, and as devoid of pretense and show as is the character of the men who built them. Main, Market, Jefferson and Green streets are all filled with large and handsome shops and warehouses, and many of those which cross them at right angles, extending indefinitely into the vast plains, are devoted to residences.

Scene in the Louisville Exposition.

Louisville is famous for several excellent institutions, noteworthy among which are the "Galt House," a massive stone structure in the English style, long celebrated by foreign travelers as the best hotel in the United States; the Louisville *Courier-Journal*, the successor to the old *Journal*, on which Prentice expended his wit, and upon which those who were wounded by his shafts vented their spleen; and the "Public Library," the outgrowth of an ingenious lottery scheme conducted by an ex-Governor of the State, and now a thriving institution with museums and lecture-rooms attached. The *Courier-Journal*, edited to-day by the sprightly Watterson, whose courageous attitude in reproving many of the prime faults in Kentucky politics and civilization, and whose trenchant style in his editorials, have rendered him famous, has long had a sensible influence on the political and social life of the State.

The *Commercial*, a Republican newspaper, has grown and prospered, as its party grows in Louisville, steadily and surely.

The City of Louisville was surveyed as early as 1770, when parties came from Fort Pitt, now known as Pittsburg, and examined the land adjacent to the Falls of the Ohio, with a view to parceling it as "bounty territory." In 1773, Captain Thomas Bullitt, the deputy of a special commission from William and Mary College in Virginia, moored his bark in Grass harbor, and with his little band of hunters made numerous surveys. Death, however, interrupted his labors, which were largely instrumental in the definite settlement of Kentucky. In 1778, Colonel George Rogers Clarke, who had for some time fought the British along the Ohio, took possession of and fortified Corn Island, opposite the spot now occupied by Louisville. In 1779, Louisville was permanently established; cabins, block-houses and stockades were erected. Clarke and his hunters lived in constant danger, and battled with the Indians for many a long day. In succeeding years, Louisville grew up a scraggy, rude town, whose streets were here and there intersected with ponds of stagnant water;* and so unhealthy was the location considered that it was known as the "grave-yard of the Ohio." If the denizens of the Louisville of the past could visit the thriving and healthy Louisville of to-day, with its miles of elegant streets, its smooth pavements, its fine hospitals and churches, its mammoth hotels and pretty theatres, its bustling "Exposition," and its brilliant society, they would hardly believe the evidence of their senses.

Life in this pleasant metropolis of 130,000 inhabitants is socially very attractive. Nowhere in the country is frankness and freedom of manner so thoroughly commingled with so much of high-bred courtesy. The people of Kentucky really, as Tuckerman says, illustrate one of the highest phases of Western character. They spring from a hardy race of hunters and self-reliant men, accustomed to the chase and to long and perilous exertion. The men of Kentucky, while they are not afflicted with any peculiar idiosyncrasies, are intensely individual. There is something inspiring in the figure of a grand old patriarch like Christopher Graham, now in his ninety-second year, erect, vigorous, and alert as an Englishman at sixty. Born in the wild woods of Kentucky five years before it became a State, he has lived to see a mighty change pass over the commonwealth where he cast his fortunes; and he delights to tell of the days when men went, rifle in hand, about their daily work, and when the State was constantly troubled with Indian incursions. Mr. Graham was long noted as the best marksman, with a rifle, in America, and has had, in his eventful life, a hundred adventures with Indian, guerilla, and bandit. The product of a rough, and, in some respects, barbarous time, when shooting, swimming, leaping, wrestling, and killing Indians were the only exercises considered manly, he is to-day a gentle old man, busied with works of charity, and with the upbuilding of a fine museum of mineralogy in Louisville.

* See "Casseday's History of Louisville."

LXXVII.

A VISIT TO THE MAMMOTH CAVE.

THE country along the line of rail from Nashville, in Tennessee, to Cave City, in Kentucky, whence travelers depart in rickety stages over the rough routes for the Mammoth Cave, is especially rich in fine farms. In autumn, when golden sunlight lingers lovingly over the great arched trees, and makes

Mammoth Cave, Kentucky—The Boat Ride on Echo River.

checker-work upon the reddish soil, a ride through this highly-cultivated country is thoroughly charming. The people one meets are mainly rough country farmers, plodding sturdily to court on fine horses, or journeying from farm to farm.

At Glasgow Junction and Cave City, on the Louisville and Nashville railroad, primitive hotels receive the visitor, and rival stage-drivers fill his ear with alarming rumors of each other's incapacity. At Cave City a sleepy waiter drowsily gives inexact information, and negroes, with persistent demand for *backshish*, follow the unfortunate Northerner and clutch his carpet-bag, despite his efforts to retain it.

Edmondson county, in which the Mammoth Cave is situated, is rich in natural curiosities. On Dismal creek, a perpendicular rock, 163 feet high, towers like a black spectre against the crystal vault of the sky, and the inhabitants invest it with many strange and highly apocryphal legends. Near the town of Brownsville is a large cave containing a petrified tree, and on Indian Hill are the remains of a fortification, with mounds and burial-places scattered over the acres in the vicinity.

The Entrance to Mammoth Cave (Looking Out).

The visit to the Mammoth Cave, which we made with a merry party, was in autumn, when the sunlight, tempered by fresh breezes, seemed to permeate every nook and cranny of the forests through which the road wound over hill and across plain. The vehicle in which we embarked at Glasgow was rickety and venerable, as also was the horse which drew it; and the driver beguiled the way with stories not calculated to impress us favorably with the hotel near the cave. Indeed, so great was his animosity toward the proprietors of that hotel, that he refused to set us down within the high fence which inclosed the building, and indulged in a lively passage-at-words, calculated to awaken quarrelsome feelings with the host when he came up to welcome us.

The hotel is a huge, rambling structure, built in Southern style, with long porches and surrounded by a pleasant lawn dotted with noble trees. Passing the primitive counter, on which lay the "Mammoth Cave Register," and paying the fees exacted from every visitor, we donned overalls, blouses, and flannel caps, and found ourselves face to face with an amiable darkey, who, taking up two swinging lamps, led the way down a rocky descent toward a black opening from which came a rush of cold air. Over the yawning mouth of the cave a stream of water was pouring, and around the sharp rocks on the brow of the hill were graceful fringes of mosses and leaves, and festoons of ferns. Shadows fell gloomily against the sunlight as we hastened down the declivity, and a wandering bat, giving a faint scream, flew directly in my face, and then darted back into the darkness.

A tree, apparently growing out of the solid rock, stretches its trunk over the chasm. This trunk is moss-grown, and both the moss and the leaves upon it have a pale yellowish tinge. Descending a few steps, and suddenly losing the genial warmth of the sun, we were forced to stoop, and to plunge forward, almost upon all fours, into the stony recesses.

Our dusky guide now supplied us each with a swinging lamp, by whose dim light we soon became accustomed to the narrow pathway, everywhere singularly free from obstacles. The cool air was so exhilarating, that after a march of several miles, clambering over stones, filing carefully along the edge of abysses, and escalading innumerable cliffs, we scarcely felt fatigue.

Unlocking a rude iron gate, the guide ushered us into a second narrow corridor, from the roof of which, as the light penetrated the gloom, hundreds of bats flitted down and circled about our heads, screaming, as if resentful of the intrusion. On the return journey the bats usually make the promenade through this gallery quite exciting, and many a timid lady remembers with horror the gauntlet she there ran.

We wandered on for several hours, the cheery guide singing psalms in a round musical voice, and turning from time to time to caution us against venturing into unexplored by-ways where pitfalls were numerous. Now we plodded through a mighty gallery, whose walls and ceilings seemed frescoed by the hands of man rather than incrusted with stalactite formations; now climbed miniature mountains; now looked down hundreds of feet into deep wells. Each of the galleries and recesses has been christened, but the visitor sometimes finds it difficult to detect in the fantastic forms of rock the resemblance suggested by the names. We visited the Rotunda, a vast chamber which seemed like the council-room of some ancient castle. Then, after exploring many antechambers and halls, we entered Audubon avenue. After wandering in that mighty gallery, whose roof is sixty feet above its smooth floor, we returned to the passage through which we had entered, passing into the main cave, and visiting, in rapid succession, the "Church," the ruins of some old saltpetre works, the Kentucky Cliffs, the Gothic Gallery, the Gothic Arcade and Chapel, the Register Hall, the Altar, Vulcan's Forge, and, finally, the Devil's Arm-Chair, a huge stalactite, beautiful in color, in which we enthroned one of the ladies accompanying the party. The Gothic Chapel, through which we wandered half-convinced that we were dreaming, is rich in noble ornaments, its columns rivaling in the nicety of their proportions those of the finest cathedrals. The

Gothic avenue, reached by a detour from the main cave and an ascent of some thirty feet, is two miles in length, and a promenade along it discloses an uninterrupted panorama of natural wonders which seem the work of giant architects rather than the result of one of nature's convulsions. All the stalactites

Mammoth Cave –In "the Devil's Arm-Chair."

and stalagmites in the cave are extremely rich in color, and look as if they had been carefully polished. The ceiling of the "Gothic Avenue" is as smooth as that of any mansion. Passing the "Devil's Arm-Chair," and stopping for a moment to inspect the "Elephant's Trunk" and the "Pillars of Hercules," we came at last to the "Lover's Leap," a large pointed rock more than ninety feet above the roadway, and projecting into an immense rotunda.

The "Ball-Room" is a mighty chamber, admirably fitted for the dance, with a rocky gallery even, in which from time to time an orchestra has been placed when gay parties from Louisville and other neighboring cities have engaged in festivities, with music and torches. A short distance beyond looms up a huge mass of rock, known as the Giant's Coffin. Passing the deserted chamber, the "Wooden Bowl Cave," where oxide of iron and lime are sprinkled on the floor, and crossing the "Bridge of Sighs," we came to the "Star Chamber," where our guide had prepared for us a genuine surprise. Mysteriously commanding us to be seated in a dark corner, and saying that he would return to find us on the morrow, he suddenly seized the lights and withdrew. We heard his sonorous voice echoing along the galleries as he hurried back over the pathway, and while we were yet wondering what was the object of this sudden manœuvre, we saw above us twinkling stars, and seemed to catch a glimpse of the blue sky from which we had thought ourselves shut out by the solid rock. Indeed, so strange was the illusion, that we fancied we could feel the fresh air blowing upon us, and, for a few moments, imagined that the guide had conveyed us by some roundabout way to the mouth of the cave, and then had hastily left us, that he might enjoy our surprise. But presently we heard his voice, confessing the cheat. The dark ceiling of the Star Chamber is covered with a myriad incrustations, sparkling like stars; and the artful guide, by a careful arrangement of his lamps and the use of Bengal lights, had produced a magical effect. The ceiling, which was not more than forty feet from our heads, had seemed remote as the heavens. It was like the very early dawn, when the stars are gradually fading and seem no longer to belong in the sky. The guide, in the distance, imitated to perfection the crowing of the morning cock, and then burst into loud laughter as, removing the lamps, he exposed the trick, and returned to us.

From the Star Chamber we descended to "Wright's Rotunda," which has a ceiling of four hundred feet span without a single pillar to uphold it, and wandered on through the Black Chambers, where masses of shelving stone reminded us of old baronial castle walls and towers ; and ascending thence into an upper room, in which we caught the whispers of a far-away waterfall, translated, upon our crossing the room, into the roar of a cataract falling sullenly down deep and hidden recesses. Next, crawling upon our hands and knees under a low arch, we entered the Fairy Grotto, whence we retraced our steps to the entrance of the cave. The bats gave us a lively reception as we passed through the gate around which they flitted as sentinels, and it was not until after we had climbed the hill, and stood in the hotel garden for some time, that we missed the sun, so accustomed had we become to the darkness during our long sojourn in the cave.

Early next morning we were once more treading the corridors, and by nightfall had made a journey of eighteen miles. The experiences of this second day were far more novel and interesting than those of the first.

The various passages of the cave have a total of more than two hundred miles in length, and many of those not often seen are said to surpass in beauty those commonly visited. To my thinking, nothing, however, in subterranean scenery can be finer than the mighty and ragged pass of El Ghor, whose jagged peaks, frightful ravines, and long recesses, filled with incrusted rocks, on which the swinging lamps threw a changeful shimmer, extend for long distances. On this day we also made the acquaintance of the "Fat Man's Misery," which the artist has faithfully depicted, and through which some of our party found no little difficulty in pressing.

The Mammoth Cave—"The Fat Man's Misery."

Crossing the black and deep river Styx by a natural bridge, and safely ferrying over Lake Lethe, we passed through a level and lofty hall called the " Great Walk," and soon arrived at "Echo River," on whose moist and muddy shore a rude barge was drawn up. The stream seemed shut in by a huge overreaching wall of solid stone, and we turned in amazement to the ebony guide, who motioned us to take seats in the boat, jumping in when we had obeyed, and rowing boldly forward into the blackness. From time to time the wall seemed to press down upon us, and we were obliged to bend close to the seats. The guide sang loudly as we floated through the darkness, our little lights making but tiny specks in the gloom. The sense of isolation from the world was here complete. We seemed at last to have had a glimpse of the infernal regions, and imagined our-

selves departed souls, doomed to a reluctant ride in Charon's bark. A deep silence fell upon all the visitors; but the guide still sang loudly his pious psalms, only ceasing them to burst into laughter when the ladies cowered as we rounded some rocky corner, and seemed about to be crushed against a lowering wall.

After half an hour of this mysterious journeying we approached another shore, and left behind us the archway. Before us lay a vast region of black and desolate pathways over high rocks and under huge boulders, along avenues brilliant with stalactites and resplendent with sparkling ceilings. Here we were recalled to a knowledge of the outer world by encountering a return party, escorted by Stephen, one of the first guides who ever penetrated the cave, and concerning whom a curious story is told.

Stephen had for many years urged a white man living near the cave to build a boat with which to explore the Echo river. When at last it was built, and a voyage under the arches was decided upon, he (Stephen) was afraid to undertake it, but was compelled at the pistol's mouth to enter the boat and proceed. Neither he nor the white man entered upon

Mammoth Cave—"The Subterranean Album."

this daring feat without fear and trembling, for no one could have predicted that the stream would find its outlet beyond the cave, in Green river. Echo river is certainly one of the most remarkable streams in the world. It is here and there wide and deep enough to float a steamer of the largest class. A few fish are now and then caught in it. They have no eyes, and certainly need none.

The journey from this stream through the pass of El Ghor, Silliman's Avenue, and Wellington's Gallery, all the latter leading up to St. Mary's Vineyard and the Hill of the Holy Sepulchre, was fatiguing; and when we returned at nightfall we found that the day's journey had quite demolished our stout walking shoes.

The burning of blue lights in various places where the ceilings are covered with sulphate of iron produces marvelous effects. No palaces, no castles, ancient or modern, rival in beauty or in grandeur the corridors and passages of the Mammoth Cave. In one of the long avenues we saw the Veiled Statue, a perpendicular rock which, from a distance, as one turns around the angle of the way, looks exactly like the figure of some ancient goddess clad in draperies. Many of the incrustations or "formations," as our guide called them, are in the form of *rosaces*, some rivaling the most beautiful bits of Gothic architectural decoration. The shading is bold and beautiful, and the lines and curves delicious. The pillars seem to flit away like ghosts as one comes suddenly upon them in the dim light given by the lamps. Occasionally one reaches a place where the cave seems to afford no outlet into passages beyond; but the guide turns suddenly to right or left through narrow archways, or down little steps to new wonders. The journey is a succession of surprises. One of the most curious experiences is a look into the "Bottomless Pit," which is reached from the "Deserted Chambers;" and a glance at the Dead Sea, into which one may shudderingly peer from a precipice eighty feet high, is not without its fascination. A young telegraph operator from Michigan once descended into a hitherto unexplored pit in the cave, and found bottom 198 feet down. He narrowly escaped death, however, for the rope with which he was lowered was cut nearly in two by the sharp rocks in which it caught. The best features of the cave are the Dome, the Bottomless Pit, and the Pass of El Ghor. Their grandeur and beauty amply repay the journey of thousands of miles which European and American tourists make to see them.

Vandalism has made its way into the Mammoth Cave. The lamps given visitors are sometimes attached to a rod, by means of which industrious snobs smoke the letters of their names upon the sides and roofs of some of the corridors. Thousands of people have thus testified their thirst for notoriety, and many a shock is given the impressible traveler by finding the name and date of some obscure mortal recorded on a rock which he had fancied heretofore unseen by men.

The cave is said to have been first discovered in 1802 by a hunter, who strayed into it in pursuit of an animal that had taken refuge there. It now belongs to nine heirs, who each receive about $1,000 yearly income from it. Were the facilities for reaching it better, the heirs might readily receive $50,000 annually for an indefinite period.

The cave has repeatedly been offered for sale for half a million dollars, and Louisville capitalists have talked from time to time of forming a company for its purchase, and erecting a new and splendid hotel in its immediate vicinity.

Gathered about the great fire-place of the hotel office in the evening, the conversation drifted to Kentucky politics, and one of the Englishmen who had been exploring the cave with us inquired curiously about the Ku-Klux. The Kentuckian in charge of the hotel answered that the Ku-Klux in that section were called Regulators, and they never troubled any except bad people. "They are composed," he said, "of the gentlemen in the neighborhood, and when those gentlemen are annoyed by vicious neighbors they warn them to move away. If they will not move, they move them, and if they resist they force them." This he asserted was only done in cases when great provocation had been received, and he insisted that politics had little to do with the operations of the Klan. Carelessly dropping his reserve, the Kentuckian added: "We don't do anything wrong; we simply correct those who don't behave right," thus unconsciously intimating that he himself was one of the Knights of the "Invisible Empire."

A Country Blacksmith Shop.

LXXVIII.

THE TRADE OF LOUISVILLE.

THE trade of Louisville, long dwarfed by the oppressive slave system to which Kentucky was utterly devoted, and which prevented the growth of large manufacturing towns, is gradually springing into vigorous life. Louisville has long been one of the most important tobacco markets in the United States. Situated near the centre of the largest tobacco-growing district of the country, with an admirable system of railroad connections North and South, and a noble water outlet, she has superior facilities for this branch of trade. The

The Court-House — Louisville.

bulk of the staple raised in Kentucky, the chief tobacco-growing State of the Union, is sold in the Louisville market. The Kentucky crop for 1871 amounted to 66,000 hogsheads, of which nearly 50,000 were sold in Louisville. Buyers for American and foreign markets reside permanently in the city, and those European Governments which have found it wise to enjoy a monopoly of their home tobacco trade are represented by local agents who make their purchase from the planters. Thousands of whites and blacks are employed in the huge warehouses, and nineteen factories, with a capital of 850,000 dollars, are engaged in the manufacture of chewing tobacco. The city also produces twelve millions of cigars annually. In the whiskey trade a large capital is invested. From the distilleries in the Blue Grass region thousands of barrels, filled with the fluid which prompts so large a proportion of the homicides in the State, are brought to Louisville, and it is said that the transactions amount to five millions annually. Pork-packers also make the city their head-quarters, and in the sixty days of each year between November and January a million swine pass through their hands.

As a live-stock market, Louisville has been rapidly growing in importance for many years. The stock-yards there now cover twenty acres, and the value of the stock received annually is between twenty and thirty millions. The flour-mills yearly yield a product worth four millions. The trade in provisions aggregates from eleven to fifteen millions; the annual product of iron foots up five millions, and more than 1,500 hands are employed in the manufacture of iron work, while in the foundries 500 hands are employed. In brief, the amount of capital invested in manufacturing enterprises in the city is about twenty millions, the annual product fifty-five millions, the number of hands employed 16,000, and the amount of wages paid eight millions.

The Cathedral—Louisville.

Louisville would be an admirable point for the establishment of cotton-mills, and as its capitalists have had their attention favorably directed to the large dividends which Southern mills are yearly paying, it is hoped that the city may speedily secure several mills. The building of steamboats for the Western waters has long been one of the leading industries of Louisville and the villages clustered about the Falls of the Ohio. The water power of the Ohio Falls is very remarkable, and ought to place Louisville among the first manufacturing cities of the country. It has thus far been but little utilized. The same negligent and reckless spirit which pervaded others of the slave States in regard to the improvement of natural advantages controlled the Kentuckian mind, and was even more pronounced in Louisville and its vicinity than in many places further south. The law of Kentucky, which allowed only six per cent. interest, was an effectual barrier to the investment of foreign capital in Louisville, and drove away much local capital which might have been invested. The enlargement of the present Louisville and Portland canal, which was completed in 1828 at a cost of $750,000, would render transportation to and from Louisville more feasible; and the building of a new canal through Portland town would furnish a superb location,

The Post-Office—Louisville.

with enormous water power for miles of factories and mills. The Louisville and Nashville railroad gives a grand trunk line from Louisville to Montgomery,

Alabama, a distance of 490 miles, and connection with the railroad system of the Southern States, which are Kentucky's chief market. Louisville is also connected by the Great Bridge spanning the Ohio, with all the railroads north of that river, and is directly on the through route from the north and west to the extreme south. The main trunk of the Louisville and Nashville railroad extends through Jefferson, Bullett, Nelson, Hardin, Larue, Hart, Edmondson, Barren, Warren, and Simpson counties. Branch railroads, connecting with Memphis and South-eastern Kentucky, have served largely to develop the regions through which they run. The so-called Richmond branch runs to within a short distance of the richest iron region of the State. The Elizabethtown and Paducah railroad extends from Elizabethtown, on the Louisville and Nashville railroad, forty-two miles from Louisville, to Paducah, a thriving city on the Ohio, fifty miles from its junction with the Mississippi. Paducah is the commercial market of Western Kentucky. The Owensboro, Russelville

and Nashville, the Evansville, Henderson and Nashville, the Paducah and Memphis, and the Nashville and Ohio roads also traverse Western Kentucky. The last-named route gives an important connection with the city of Mobile.

Louisville has connection with the eastern section of the State and Cincinnati, by the Louisville, Frankfort and Lexington, and the Short Line, railroads. The former runs through Frankfort, the charming capital of Kentucky, to the staid and solid old city of Lexington, which is the western terminus of the Big Sandy railroad. This road passes through some of the finest agricultural districts of the State, pierces the very heart of the mineral region of

The City Hall — Louisville.

Kentucky, and is designed to furnish connection with the Atlantic ports via the Chesapeake and Ohio Railroad through Western Virginia.

At Lagrange, twenty-eight miles from Louisville, the Short Line railroad to Covington, opposite Cincinnati, on the Ohio river, crosses the Louisville, Frankfort and Lexington road. The Kentucky Central railroad runs through Middle Kentucky, and from Paris, in the Blue Grass region, the Maysville and Lexington road branches out.

Many new railroads are chartered in Kentucky, and of those most likely soon to be built, the Cincinnati Southern, intended to furnish a line from Covington, on the Ohio, to Chattanooga, Tennessee, and to pursue a central route through Middle Kentucky, is the most prominent. The Ohio and Cumberland railroad,

as projected, will run from Covington to Nashville, in Tennessee, and the Louisville, Memphis, and New Orleans road is intended to pierce from Louisville
through rich agricultural and mineral districts, and intersecting important lines
of rail, to Union City, where it will
connect with routes tributary to Memphis.   The railroads that are already
completed in Kentucky penetrate sixty-
one counties, and the majority of them
contribute directly to the prosperity of
Louisville.   In addition to these, as a
means of distributing its manufactured
wares, that city has the advantage of
navigable streams, embracing an extent
of 16,000 miles.

George D. Prentice—(From a Painting in the Louisville
Public Library).

The capital stock at present invested
in banks and banking houses in Louisville is about ten millions, and the
deposit capital amounts to more than
eight millions.   In addition to these
amounts, Louisville has many private
capitalists.   The law of Kentucky now
allows ten per cent. interest upon loans,
and it is probable that capital from all sections of the Union will flow to
Louisville within the next few years.   The bonded debt of the city was
$6,153,509 in 1872, and the taxable property of the city is estimated at

$80,000,000.   The credit of the city is
excellent; the taxation is not burdensome; the municipal government is
good.   There are few better lighted,
better paved, or better policed towns
than Louisville.   For a community
where three-fourths of the male citizens habitually bear arms, shooting
is reasonably rare, although not
properly punished when, under the
influence of liquor or passion, it does
occur.   The city spreads over thirteen
square miles, a space amply sufficient
to furnish dwellings for a population
of half a million.   Building is cheap,
tenement houses are rare, and although
a motley gang of rough men from the

The Colored Normal School—Louisville.

rivers is gathered in some quarters of the city, but little lawlessness prevails.
The public buildings of Louisville are not architecturally fine.   The City Hall
is the most ambitious structure, and the council-room in which the municipal

fathers discuss popular measures is palatial. The Court-House on Jefferson street, the Louisville University Medical College, the Blind Asylum, the male and female High Schools, the Custom-House and Post-Office and Masonic Temple are solid and substantial edifices. In autumn and in winter, fogs hover over the city, and the coal smoke, joined to the mists, colors the walls of houses with the same brown so noticeable in London and St. Louis. The Cathedral on Walnut street, St. Paul's Episcopal Church, and the First Presbyterian, opposite it, are fine houses of worship. Louisville boasts accommodation for 50,000 worshipers, and amongst its noteworthy divines is the Rev. Dr. Stuart Robinson, whose Confederate predilections during the war were strongly marked, and whose

Louisville, Kentucky, on the Ohio River, from the New Albany Heights.

ability is unquestionable. The new Public Library at present occupies a small and commodious building, soon to be replaced, when the drawings of the Lottery are completed, by a finer structure. This library, although at present no larger than those in many New England cities one-third the size of Louisville, is admirably selected, finely officered, and contains, among other curiosities, a painting of George D. Prentice, as he appeared in middle-life. The celebrated journalist, poet and politician, lies beside his son, who was killed while in the ranks of the Confederates, in Cave Hill cemetery, near the city.

The schools of Louisville merit great praise. The public school system is taking a firm hold there, and even the "Steel Blue" tendencies of the majority

of the population, and their refusal to believe in the ultimate elevation of the
222,000 blacks in the State, have not hindered them from supplying the colored
population with excellent facilities for education. Louisville has two high schools,
which are, in every respect, first-class seminaries, twenty-three ward schools, and
a host of private institutions for English and classical training. The school buildings will seat 12,000 pupils. Nearly three-quarters of a million is invested in
school buildings and lots, and $150,000 is annually paid in salaries. The German
language is taught as one of the regular branches in the public schools, a measure
rendered necessary, as in St. Louis, by the influx of the Teutonic population. The
Colored Normal School building, dedicated in Louisville last year, is probably the
finest public school edifice designed for the instruction of negroes in the country.
The School Board has established training departments in connection with some
of the ward schools, and these are rapidly equipping teachers.

Although there is no impressive scenery in the vicinity of Louisville, the
green lowlands, the wide river, and the vast expanse of wooded plain are very
imposing. From the hills back of New Albany, on the Indiana shore, one can
look down on the huge extent of Louisville half-hidden beneath the foliage which
surrounds so many of its houses; can note the steamers slowly winding about
the bends in the Ohio, or carefully working their way up to the broad levées;
can see the trains crawling like serpents over the high suspended bridge, and the
church spires and towers gleaming under the mellow sunlight. In a few years,
if the improvements now in progress are continued, Louisville will be one of the
most delightful of American cities.

Chimney Rock, Kentucky.

LXXIX.

FRANKFORT—THE BLUE GRASS REGION—ALEXANDER'S FARM. LEXINGTON.

OWHERE is the Kentucky river more beautiful than where it flows past the pretty and cultured town of Frankfort, the capital of Kentucky, sixty miles above its entrance into the Ohio. For many miles in every direction superb landscapes are spread out before the traveler's vision. He will have found the ride of sixty-five miles from Louisville a constant panorama of fine fields, well-

Frankfort, on the Kentucky River.

kept farms, stone-fenced and thoroughly cultivated. Their solid building and general air of thrift offers a sharp contrast to the scraggy sheds and unpainted mansions of Southern plantations. In the train the traveler will find the typical Kentuckian, tall, smooth-faced, with clear complexion, and bright eyes, his manners deferential, and his conversation enjoyable. In the manners of the better class of Kentuckians there is no familiarity, no grossness or coarseness, but a frankness only slightly tinged with formality.

We arrived at Frankfort at nightfall, and were ushered by an attentive negro into a great stone caravansary known as the Capitol Hotel, which, during the sessions of the Legislature, is crowded, but for the remainder of the year is almost empty. In the morning, while a delicious haze, through which the sun was

The Ascent to Frankfort Cemetery, Kentucky.

striving to peep, overhung the hills, we walked through the still streets bordered with pretty mansions, and stole along the steep and picturesque banks of the Kentucky to the cemetery, perched on a high bluff, where stands the monument above the grave of Daniel Boone. Clambering up to this lovely spot by a flight of ancient stone steps, and passing the crags known as Umbrella and Boone rocks, we paused from time to time, fascinated with the beauty of the tranquil stream hundreds of feet below us, its banks fringed with loveliest foliage and trees. On the river lay moored great rafts of logs which had been drifted down from the mountain torrents above.

Frankfort lies in a deep valley surrounded by sharply-defined hills, the river there flowing between high limestone banks, from which is quarried the admirable building stone of which the town is partially constructed. From the cemetery bluff the town looks as picturesque as an Italian city. Clustered together on the river-bank the wide buildings form a group which has none of the unpleasant angles so common in America. The village of South Frankfort is connected with the main town by a covered bridge over the stream, and in all directions smooth, wide, macadamized roads stretch out over the hills and through the ravines. Near the city there are many fine estates, on which the noted horses and cattle of the Blue Grass regions are raised. The State Arsenal is an unimposing building on a pretty eminence. The ruins of the old State Capitol occupy a conspicuous elevation, and the new State-House, now in process of completion, stands on a handsome lawn. The Penitentiary—where, at the time of our visit, 700 convicts, equally divided among whites and blacks, were engaged in manufacturing hemp into matting—is an unpicturesque structure, whose high walls have not prevented the occasional escape of prisoners. Each convict is compelled to weave 150 yards of matting daily, and, after his task is completed, is allowed to repose until nightfall, when he is locked up in his cell. We saw several of the blacks improving their time by reading, but most of the prisoners who had finished their daily toil were sullenly chewing tobacco, and contemplating the gloomy walls of the dark rooms in which they had been working. The keepers of the Penitentiary regaled us with stories of adventurous people who in the old days had been confined for negro stealing. In the Hospital we saw a fine athletic man crouching over a table with his head held wearily behind his hands. This was the forger Atwood, whose reckless folly brought him from the centre of a brilliant society to a term of twenty years in jail.

Manufacturing is creeping into the capital, although prominent society neither seeks nor cares for it. Farming, the distilling of pure whiskeys from the golden grain which grows so abundantly in the vicinity, the breeding and care of race-horses, and visiting and junketing in all the country side, content the Kentuckians. Aside from the stir created by the assemblage of politicians there is but little thus far to trouble the dreamy repose and enviable tranquillity by which Frankfort is characterized. It is the home of many of the loveliest women in the country, and its society is largely represented in all the cities of the world. Its belles, and those of Lexington, lead the fashion at the Southern "Springs."

While we were at Frankfort the Ku-Klux were engaged in active operations in the neighboring counties, and the residents of Frankfort denounced them as a band of ruffians whose main object was revenge. One gentleman asserted that he would at any time help with his own hands to lynch a certain member of the gang, if he could be caught. In Owen and Henry counties these midnight marauders had inaugurated a veritable reign of terror. They took "niggers" from their houses and whipped them on most trivial provocation. They waylaid those who had dared to testify against them in court, and "fixed" them from behind bushes. Clad in fantastic disguises, they hovered about the confines of large towns, carrying dread into the hearts of superstitious blacks. The colored people living in the outskirts of Frankfort had deserted their homes and flocked into the town, giving as their reason that they were afraid of the Ku-Klux. It is hardly fair to presume that political bitterness has

The Monument to Daniel Boone in the Cemetery at Frankfort, Kentucky.

been so much concerned in prompting the actions of these prowlers as have ignorance and the general lawlessness—all too prevalent in the back-country of Kentucky.

Between Louisville and Frankfort, at La Grange, a branch road diverges to Shelbyville. This pretty town stands in the midst of a luxuriantly fertile country, has many manufactories, a fine court-house, numerous churches, three flourishing seminaries, and is the seat of Shelby College, founded in 1836. Thirty miles below Frankfort, on an eminence near the far-famed Salt river, so well known in political jargon, is Harrodsburg, the oldest settlement in the State, where Captain James Harrod, in 1774, erected a cabin in the wilderness. Harrodsburg has been visited by thousands from East and West, and it is to-day the most famous summer resort in the State, its mineral springs being a prime attraction. It is also the seat of old Bacon College and a good military academy. In 1819 Christopher Graham went to Harrodsburg with a few dollars in his pocket, and for thirty-two years thereafter was the patron of the springs, bringing into the State more than $4,000,000, the expenditure of visitors from all parts of the world. The Presbyterian Female College and the Christian Baptist College

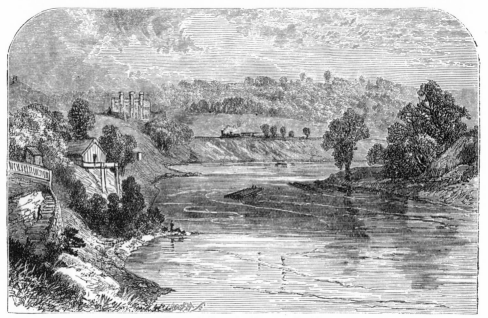

View on the Kentucky River, near Frankfort.

at Harrodsburg owe their existence to Doctor Graham. He also created and paved, at his own expense, the first street in the town. In three decades, and by his own exertions, he so beautified this lovely spot that when Generals Scott and Wool were delegated by Congress to prepare an asylum in the West for invalid soldiers, they bought a site at Harrodsburg for $100,000, and built on it a fine edifice, which was long ago burned.

Nine miles from Frankfort, on the road to Lexington, stands one of the finest and richest farms in Kentucky—that owned by Mr. Alexander. On this superb stock-farm we saw 300 blooded horses, ranging in rank from old "Lexington," the monarch of the turf, to the kittenish and frisky yearling. Here also Mr. Alexander has collected $100,000 worth of cattle, comprising some of the finest stock in the world. Peeping into the inclosure where the costly cattle were kept, we saw one diminutive heifer worth $27,000, and a variety of foreign creatures

whose value seemed almost fabulous.   On this farm are bred the great majority
of the fine trotting and running horses which appear in our parks during the
racing season.   Mr. Alexander's estate, which is admirably stocked with fine
farm-houses, barns and stables, and is more like a ducal manor than the
ordinary American farm, extends over 3,200 acres.   Near by is old John
Harper's modest farm of 2,000 acres.   The roads, the stone walls, and the fine
lawns covered with massive shade-trees, make a series of delightful pictures.

Asteroid Kicks Up.

The annual sale of horses on the Alexander farm occurs in June.   Only yearling
colts are sold.   Hundreds of people from all the country around, and from
every State in the Union, flock to this sale.   An immense barbecue is held, and
high wassail marks the conclusion of the occasion.

   We paid a respectful visit to old "Lexington," the mighty sire of a mightier
equine family.   He is now quite blind, a veteran of twenty-two, afflicted with
goitre, and stood gazing in the direction from which our voices came, a melancholy wreck of his former greatness.   The princes of the race-course of the
present galloped by, neighing and pawing the ground, as if annoyed at our
presence.   One of them, named "Asteroid," so far forgot his princely dignity as
to charge incontinently upon the fence where we were seated, and the artist has
depicted the result in a spirited sketch.   The negro men who manage these
erratic brutes undergo all sorts of perilous adventures, but they seem to possess
as many lives as a cat, and, like that animal, always land on their feet, no matter
how far the plunging and rearing horses may throw them.

   Except the negligence of her people with regard to their own interests, and
the prejudices which still, in many quarters, survive the death of the slavery
régime, there is no reason why Kentucky should not already have received a
mighty current of immigration.   Rich in all the elements of material greatness,
abounding in mineral and agricultural lands, noble rivers, and superb forests, it is

astonishing that great wealth is not more general among the people of the State. Lying between 39° and 36° 30′ north latitude, her climate is delightful, and her situation, between the two greatest water-sheds of the continent, affords her easy communication with twelve of the largest and wealthiest of her sister States.

The Green, the Kentucky, and the Barren rivers are all navigable, and run through regions which can readily furnish them an immense commerce. The area of the State is 37,700 square miles, the larger part of which is more than eight hundred feet above the level of the sea. The farming region, in Middle Kentucky, which includes the territory between the mountains of the east and the lower lands lying west of the Louisville and Nashville railroad, and extending from the northern to the southern boundary, is superb. Within this tract of ten thousand square miles all the cereals, hemp, flax, and every kind of vegetable and fruit flourish magnificently. In Middle Kentucky lies the famous "Blue Grass Region," of which I have already spoken, which has long been noted for its beautiful women, its Bourbon whiskey and Bourbon Democrats, its Lexingtons and Asteroids, its Alexanders, and its "Old John Harper." Fayette, Bourbon, Scott, Woodford, Clark, Jessamine, and portions of other counties in this region, owe much to the beds of blue shell limestone and marble which underlie them, the upper soil, which is a dark loam with a red clay subsoil, being astonishingly fertile. These fair lands are carpeted throughout the year with a brilliant blue grass. Even in midwinter a deep green clothes the soil, and, when summer comes, the grass sends up slender shafts to the height of several feet, crowned with feathery tufts of a bright blue color. The effect of a landscape clad in this noble herbage, and dotted here and there with fine oaks and well-kept farm-houses, is exceedingly fine. Throughout Fayette, Woodford, Scott, and Bourbon counties, lands are worth from $80 to $140 per acre, and highly-cultivated farms of from 250 to 300 acres are abundant. There hemp yields from eight to fourteen hundred pounds per acre, and tobacco flourishes even on the second-rate lands. Montgomery county is interspersed with fields and meadows, studded with stately forests in which the blue grass grows as luxuriantly as in the cleared lands. In the forest pastures are bred the magnificent cattle and horses for which Kentucky is so famous. The chief advantage which the Blue Grass region possesses over any other in the State is in its unequaled pasturage, and in the richness of its timber-lands. From it are annually exported thousands of noble horses and cattle, and immense droves of sheep, mules and hogs are sent to the cotton-fields of the South.

Lexington, one of the most wealthy and beautiful of Kentucky cities, is charmingly situated on the lower fork of the Elkhorn river. The early pioneers and adventurers, who established the town in the midst of a wilderness, found there the remains of a great fortress and a mighty people whose history has not been written. The present city is built above the ruins of mounds and fortifications, totally different from those erected by the Indians, and evidently of great extent and magnificence. A few years before the first prominent white settlement was made there, the entrance to an ancient catacomb was discovered by some hunters, and embalmed bodies were found in it. For three-quarters of a century the entrance to this subterranean cemetery has been hidden, and the Kentuckians of to-day even doubt its existence.   Lexington was the starting-point of Kentucky and the centre from which radiated all the movements that finally ended in the conquering of the savage and the domination by the whites in the West.   In 1775, the hunters from Harrodsburg took possession of the north side of the Kentucky river, and the place where they first halted was near Lexington.   A spring from which they drank is still pointed out.   The town was named after Lexington in Massachusetts by the hunters, into whose forest retreat

A Souvenir of Kentucky.

the news had crept that King George's troops, on the 19th of April, had shot down the American rebels in Massachusetts colony at Lexington.   Kentucky was then a wild territory, belonging to the royal province of Virginia, and it is not a little strange that there, in the midst of an unbroken forest, was raised the first monument to the first dead of the American Revolution.

The founder of Lexington was Colonel Robert Patterson, the compeer of Boone, Kenton, and other forest pioneers whose names are famous.   For half a century after its foundation, Lexington had a brilliant history. To-day it is a quiet town, the home of many wealthy families and the Mecca of thousands of pilgrims, as it contains the old residence and the grave of Henry Clay. A monument to the illustrious statesman stands in the beautiful cemetery of Lexington, on an eminence near the centre of the grounds, and is a landmark for miles around. It was completed in 1860, at a cost of $50,000.

"Ashland," the old Clay homestead, is situated a mile and a-half from the city, in the midst of beautiful parks, closely resembling the manors of England. During Mr. Clay's lifetime the estate was ornamented with loveliest shade-trees and orchards in profusion, and the road which leads to the mansion, now the residence of Regent Bowman, of the Kentucky University, is lined with locusts, cypresses, and cedars, through which peep the rose, the jessamine, and the ivy. The old mansion, replaced in 1857 by a beautiful modern residence, was a plain, unpretending structure, in which Mr. Clay at various times had entertained a host of distinguished Americans and foreigners. Lexington is also the location of the Kentucky University and the State Lunatic Asylum; the former institution, founded on the ruins of Transylvania University, has an endowment of $500,000, a fine library, and its law and medical schools have long been renowned. The present University was incorporated in 1858, its original endowment having been obtained by the efforts of the present Regent, John B. Bowman, a native of Kentucky, who was also instrumental in the consolidation of the Universities of Harrodsburg, Transylvania, and the Agricultural College at Lexington. The first session of the Kentucky University was in 1865, and the grounds of the Agricultural and Mechanical College, which now comprise "Ashland," and the adjoining estate of "Woodlands" were purchased in 1866.

A little Adventure by the Wayside.

LXXX.

POLITICAL questions in Kentucky have lately been more agitated than for many years since the war. The discussion of the Civil Rights bill has been as furious and illogical there as in any other of the ex-slave States. The freedmen do not constitute a troublesome element in the commonwealth. There are 222,000 of them, while the whole population of the State is 1,331,000 souls. Some of the oldest and stiffest Bourbon Democrats have of late shown gratifying tendencies toward liberality in educational matters, and, indeed, it may with reason be hoped that Kentucky will soon be ranked among the progressive States which desire immigration, education, and manufactures,—the three things which alone can build up States once consecrated to slavery.

A brief sketch of the progress of Kentucky politics may not be uninteresting. Kentucky was a Whig State, faithful to Henry Clay as long as he lived, and a worshiper of his theories after he died. The Whig feeling is still very strong among some of the older voters. A prominent editor in the State told me that he could remember when it was not good *ton* to be a Democrat, just as since the war it has not been fashionable to be a Republican. When the Whig party died, after Scott's defeat, the masses of the Whigs went into the Know-Nothing movement, and the Democrats opposed it, although, during the battle, a good many Whigs and Democrats changed sides. In the Fillmore and Buchanan canvass, the State sided with Buchanan, and the Know-Nothing party died.

Then the Whigs, still unwilling to coincide with the Democrats, formed what was called the Opposition Party, and, in 1859, ran Bell for Governor against McGoffin, who was a Douglas Squatter-Sovereignty Democrat; but Bell, for the purpose of making political capital, took extreme views with regard to the rights of the South in the territories, and compelled McGoffin to come on to his ground. This, it is considered, was very unfortunate in its effect on the temper of the State.

When the Secession movement came up, eighteen months afterward, it had a good deal to do with creating the neutrality position taken by the leading men of the State, in the winter of 1860, as a measure of necessity for holding the masses of the people steady for a time against the wave of Secession excitement. The division of the Democrats between Breckenridge and Douglas, in 1860, gave the State to Bell and Everett. The Douglas men were nearly all Unionists. When the Southern States began the Secession movement, after the election of Mr. Lincoln, the Kentucky Legislature, which had been elected in 1859 during the excitement raised by the Bell-McGoffin canvass for the Governorship, was found to be nearly divided between Union men and Southern sympathizers.

In the election of 1861, for "Peace Commissioners," Congressmen, and Legislators, the Union men were successful by large majorities, and they retained control of the State until 1866, although it is said that the Emancipation Proclamation, and the course of injudicious military commanders in the State, greatly weakened the Union party, which was gradually divided into unconditional Union men and "Union Democrats." The straight-out Democrats, mostly Secessionists, tried to hold a convention at Frankfort in 1862, but were prevented by the Post Commander. They sent delegates, however, to the Chicago Convention in 1864. Those delegates were received, and divided seats with the Union Democrats. The unconditional Union men, who voted for Mr. Lincoln in 1864 in Kentucky, formed the basis of the present Republican party in the State, but did not call themselves Republicans until the convention of May, 1867.

The Union Legislature, during the war, passed an act expatriating all citizens who had left the State for the purpose of aiding the Confederacy. The last Union Legislature, in 1865 and '66 repealed this act, and welcomed the return of the Confederates to their allegiance. The Democratic party was organized in 1866, and gained possession of the county offices. The unconditional Union men coöperated with the Union Democrats in this canvass. The next year the Union men took their stand with the Republican party, and nominated a candidate for Governor. The Union Democrats also nominated a candidate. They were called before the election the "third party," and after it, from their small show of strength, the "one-third party." The Democrats, embracing the Secession element, and the dissatisfied Union men, also made a nomination.

The "third party" embraced nearly all the old Union leaders, but few of the rank and file, and cast but 13,000 votes. A Democratic Governor was elected, and Secession Democrats have filled the Governor's chair ever since.

By the adoption of the fifteenth amendment about 45,000 additional voters were placed upon the lists, but not more than 35,000 of them have ever voted at an election. The Republicans have been slowly but steadily gaining ground in the Legislature for some years. They are still in a small minority. Their policy has been to win back the old Union men from the Democracy, with whom their associations have not always been pleasant. It is from that source mainly that the Republicans have gained their strength. The Democrats are divided up by lines which cross one another in a variety of ways, into the "Stay-at-home sympathizers," the Confederate soldiers, the Bourbons, and the "Progressives." The Stay-at-homes have repeatedly concluded that the Confederates were too grasping, and the Bourbons have shriekingly accused the Progressives of infidelity to party. The balance of power has swayed in every direction; but the Bourbons and Confederates now control the State. The feeling that the Democratic party of Kentucky was in many respects an "unreconciled" party, and that it sanctioned the lawlessness of the Ku-Klux, has led the Republicans to adhere to the national organization of their party, without paying much attention to the questions which have caused dissension among Northern Republicans. They still regard the predominance of the Republican party in national affairs as more important to them than the justification of party measures. If the negro question were out of the politics of the State, there would be no trouble on account of the old Union and Secession differences. The feeling in relation to it had been toned down to a manageable point, when the discussion of the Civil Rights bill revived it in all its old bitterness and intensity.

The Progressives in the Democratic party have among them individuals who take strong ground in favor of general education, but the opposition to common schools among the wealthier classes is very powerful. The first law for the establishment of a general system of common schools in Kentucky was enacted in 1838, but the continued war made upon it disgusted the friends of the movement, and they did but little for many years thereafter. In 1867 a series of liberal reforms in the then prostrate school system was planned, and a bill inaugurating the reform finally passed the Legislature in 1869–70. The result of the operation of the new law was the doubling of the number of children in the common schools, and a general advance in education throughout the State. The Board of Education is composed of the Attorney-General, the Secretary of State, and the Superintendent of Public Instruction.

While it may be said that there are free schools in most of the districts in Kentucky, it is evident that many of them are but poorly sustained for a few months in the year, and are not patronized enough by the influential classes to give them vitality and value. All the populous and flourishing towns have high schools and private academies, and the many colleges, either sectarian or established by private enterprise, receive the youth who, in other States, are educated in public schools. Outside of the cities, although some provision is made for the education of the colored children, the whites feel but little interest in it, and Berea College, in the mountain district, is probably the only mixed college in the State. An address recently made by Colonel Stodart Johnson, of Kentucky, containing a strong plea for educational progress, excited considerable unfriendly criticism.

The public debt of Kentucky is but a trifling sum, and the "powers that be" are very scrupulous with regard to incurring liabilities,—so much so that they begrudge the money which might be expended in furthering the State's interest. The total State tax, at present, is forty-five cents on one hundred dollars, and real estate is rarely assessed at more than half its value.

Eastern Kentucky may be said to be one immense bed of coal and iron. The territory of the State extends over much of the area of two of the largest and richest coal-fields on the continent. The great Appalachian coal-field extends through its eastern section, and extensive coal-measures are found, and have been worked, in a score of the eastern counties. This coal-field embraces nearly all the mountain counties drained by the Big Sandy river, the Kentucky above its forks, and the Cumberland above its shoals. The upper coal-measures of this eastern coal-field embrace very rich beds, containing from sixty to sixty-three per cent. of fixed carbon. The yield of the entire region is rich, averaging from fifty-eight to sixty-three per cent. Coal crops out along the banks of the Big Sandy river, and is easily worked and readily transportable to market. On the Kentucky and Cumberland fine workable beds of coal are also found. The iron ore is always closely associated with coal. Iron-furnaces might be established with profit throughout the entire group of mountain counties, from the Big Sandy to the level lands of Middle Kentucky, and from the Ohio river to the Tennessee line.

In many counties red and brown hematites and the Black Band ores, resembling those from which iron is chiefly made in Europe, are abundant. The minerals of Eastern Kentucky are its main resource, for the only lands of medium fertility are to be found along the streams. The hill-sides, from which the inhabitants dig with difficulty a scanty sustenance, are poor in quality. Mineral springs are scattered throughout the eastern section, and the fine climate and the lovely scenery of the Kentucky mountains will doubtless give them in due time the reputation won by those of Western and South-western Virginia.

In Estill county, on the Red river, a small tributary of the Kentucky, is an iron district which has attained a world-wide reputation. The Red River Iron Works, located near the mouth of the stream, began operations in 1808. Rude furnaces were built there in that year, and the soft ores of the district were roughly converted into pig-iron. In succeeding years better furnaces were erected, and since the war the property has passed into the hands of a wealthy stock company, which now owns 60,000 acres of mineral and timber lands, and is much in need of railroad facilities. Another corporation, known as the Cottage Iron Company, also owns 13,000 acres of fine mineral land in the vicinity. These companies together employ a thousand workmen, and annually expend half a million dollars in the manufacture of metals used exclusively for car-wheels. When these furnaces are put in connection with the markets, by an already projected railway, the number of tons of pig-iron manufactured in the State, which in 1870 was 37,548, will be vastly increased.

The coal-field of Western Kentucky is seventy-five miles in length and fifty-five miles in width at the widest part, having an average width of perhaps forty miles. The Elizabethtown and Paducah railroad runs through its entire length, and it is traversed by several other railroads. The coal and iron ores have as yet been but little developed, but will evidently repay an active mining. Through the southern portion of Western Kentucky there are large veins of lead ore said to contain considerable silver, but the operations in mining these ores have been very imperfect. Twelve of the western counties overlie coal-measures, and in Union, Henderson, and Davis counties there are many workable beds of coal with an average thickness of four feet. According to the testimony of General Basil Duke, the richest coals of the Western Kentucky fields, possessing an average of more than fifty per cent. of fixed carbon, are found in the lower coal-measures, which in a depth of 900 feet contain ten workable beds having a united thickness of more than thirty feet.

The above-mentioned counties are also exceedingly rich in agricultural resources. Alluvial deposits in the bottoms along the Ohio river, and the loam of the uplands, furnish a superb soil on which fine crops of tobacco are raised and the Indian corn is as large as that of the best blue grass land. All these counties lying along the Ohio are very fertile, and their lands command high prices. The counties near the confluence of the Ohio and Mississippi rivers, composed of the sediment of both streams, produce fine crops of tobacco, wheat, corn, and grasses. Labor and immigrants are everywhere in demand in this part of the State. Western Kentucky produces the great bulk of the tobacco crop of the State, although this staple is cultivated in many other counties. The farms in some portions of this section are now too large to be managed under the present labor system, and proprietors will occasionally sell acres which before the war brought $90, for $35 or $40. In the counties lying adjacent to Middle Kentucky small improved farms of reasonably good soil can be had at trivial prices.

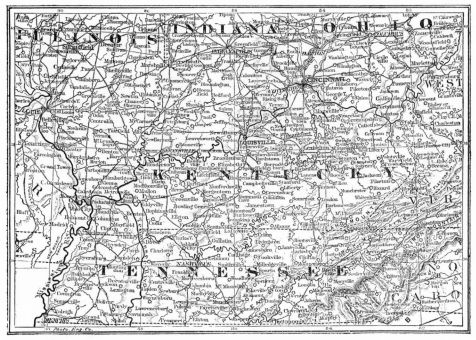

TENNESSEE, KENTUCKY, and the REGION DRAINED BY THE OHIO RIVER.

LXXXI.

NASHVILLE AND MIDDLE TENNESSEE.

WHEN I first saw Nashville, the capital of Tennessee, its streets were almost deserted. The only signs of activity were at the railway stations, where thousands of people were crowding the trains which were to bear them beyond the reach of cholera. The city received a dreadful visitation of this destroyer in 1873, and the dispatches which brought from Memphis the accounts of the horrors of the yellow fever were the only news which I found in the papers of Nashville. But visiting the pleasant town a few months afterward, when the cholera had passed away, and the inhabitants had regained their courage, I saw plenty of life, activity, and industry. During my stay the city was visited by a furious and protracted rain-storm which flooded the lower part of the town, and raised the Cumberland river, which at Nashville flows between high banks, so that a disastrous inundation was feared. Houses were set afloat, negroes were driven from their cabins to the streets, and poverty and distress were great.

The Tennessee State Capitol, at Nashville.

Nashville was once one of the most famous towns in the United States. Its men and women were noted for their wit and beauty,—qualities which are conspicuous to-day, but which have not been so prominent in the society of the National Capital as previous to 1835. The town is situated on the left bank of the Cumberland river, a little north of the centre of the State. It is founded almost literally upon a rock, the river-bluffs rising nearly eighty feet above low water mark. The city stretches along irregular and gradual slopes, and is picturesquely grouped around Capitol Hill, on which stands the State-House, one of the most elegant public buildings in the country. From its beautiful porticoes one may look over the wide expanse of plain dotted with groups of houses; over the high trestle-works on which run the railways leading toward Memphis; or may gaze upon the winding Cumberland, along whose banks the high business blocks are not ungracefully packed; or out to the hill on which stand the ruins of Fort Negley, a remnant of the fierce siege during the war.

The Capitol is built of laminated limestone, which softens by exposure to the air, and some of the stones are already beginning to show signs of exfoliation. On the streets near the Capitol I saw gangs of negro convicts from the State Penitentiary, which is situated in the city, working at street and wall making, while guards with cocked rifles kept constant watch over them.

Nashville now has about 40,000 population, and is rapidly growing in wealth and commercial importance. Its receipts of cotton annually amount to nearly 100,000 bales; it has a large trade in leaf tobacco, which comes from the adjacent counties; its provision trade is with the far South, and is very extensive. Its sales of dry goods annually amount to about four million dollars. It also deals very extensively in liquor. The flouring-mills in the city and vicinity manufacture 450,000 barrels of flour and 1,200,000 barrels of meal annually. The Southerner has a marked fondness for Tennessee whiskey, and Nashville sends the favorite beverage into every Southern State. During the year 1873 the sales amounted to more than one hundred thousand barrels. Nashville is also a

View from the State Capitol, Nashville, Tennessee.

central point for drovers, and thousands of cattle, sheep, and swine are yearly sent down from the great Blue Grass region to be marketed at the capital. The whole trade of the town amounts to more than fifty millions yearly, and this will probably soon be doubled by the rapid increase of the coal trade and manufacturing and mechanical interests.

Three coal-fields are easily accessible from the town. One lies along the Nashville and Chattanooga railroad, the second is drained by the upper Cumberland river, and the third, that of Western Kentucky, is penetrated by the St. Louis and South-eastern railroad. Six important railways centre in Nashville. The Louisville and Nashville, and Nashville and Decatur roads, consolidated, give a route from the Ohio river through the Tennessee capital to the junction with the road leading, by the Memphis and Charleston line, to Memphis. The Nashville and Chattanooga road runs through the loveliest mountain scenery in the South to Chattanooga. The Tennessee and Pacific road extends to Lebanon in Tennessee, and the St. Louis and South-eastern line gives a direct route via Henderson, Kentucky, and Evansville, Indiana, to St. Louis.   Other roads are now under contract, and are opening up the entire country of Middle Tennessee.

The Cumberland river, upon whose banks are many flourishing towns, is navigable for nine months in the year, and large quantities of coal and lumber are floated down to Nashville during high water.   The value of the exports and imports along this river exceeds ten million dollars yearly, and if the improvements could be effected which are needed to render it thoroughly navigable, even at an expense of four or five million dollars, the trade would doubtless be quadrupled.   Little has been done since Andrew Jackson's time to construct the necessary dams and deepen the channel of the stream.

In North Nashville stands one of the largest cotton factories in the country. Although it has been established but a short time, the annual dividends of the company amount to twelve per cent.   Factory-hands receive but little more than five dollars weekly, and the cheapness of cotton and labor enabled the proprietors last year not only to issue bonds which are at par in financial circles, but to declare a net profit of more than forty thousand dollars.   Nashville is making an effort to secure the establishment of other cotton factories within her limits.

At Edgefield, across the Cumberland, there are many prosperous manufactories ; and many Nashville people, finding that the neighboring town has thus far enjoyed complete immunity from cholera, have built handsome residences there.

Tomb of Ex-President Polk—Nashville, Tennessee.

The Nashville people, during the visitation of their town by the plague, accepted the suggestion that Edgefield escaped the scourge because its inhabitants drank only cistern water; but this cannot be the case, as the water procured for Nashville by her fine system of water-works can hardly be inferior to that used in Edgefield.

Davidson county, in which the capital is situated, is highly prosperous. Manufacturing establishments are springing up in many towns; food can be produced cheaply, and great quantities of coal and iron lie within convenient distances of each other.   The public schools in Nashville are exceedingly good. More than 2,500 children regularly attend them, and the course of study, which requires ten years, and embraces primary, intermediate, grammar and high school departments, is admirably comprehensive.   Nashville is likely to become a prominent educational centre in the South.   The Vanderbilt University, the outgrowth of the magnificent donation of half a million of dollars to the Methodist Episcopal Church South, by Commodore Vanderbilt, of New York, is in process of erection. The Fisk University, for the colored people, and several excellent seminaries for young ladies, have an enviable reputation. The University of Nashville, whose buildings were used as a hospital during the civil war, has been revived, and its literary and medical departments are now successfully conducted.

The Hermitage—General Andrew Jackson's old homestead, near Nashville, Tennessee.

From the suspension bridge spanning the Cumberland one gets a view of the pretty stream, with rafts of logs moored along its banks; of busy and prosperous Edgefield; of old Fort Negley's wind-swept height, and the many elegant streets along the hills, with cozy mansions and fine churches embowered in foliage. The market square is large, but there is not much of the picturesque activity which one finds in the markets further South; so, also, there is less of the lounging and laziness which a more genial sun prompts in the Gulf States. The town is quiet, but not sleepy. The numerous daily newspapers, and the elegant book stores, than which there are no finer south of Baltimore, as well as a good public library, and the collection of volumes at the Capitol, testify to a literary taste. The society is exceedingly cordial, and hospitality is of the genuine Southern kind, diffuse and deferential.

A few miles from the town, on the line of the Louisville and Nashville railroad, is a large national cemetery, an effective testimonial to the sharpness of the fighting around Nashville in 1864, when General Thomas sallied out to meet Hood, and in a two days' battle drove the Confederates from their intrenchments, following them until they escaped across the Tennessee river.

No State is making more earnest endeavors to secure immigration than Tennessee. In the cars, on the steamboats, on the rivers, in the hotels, at the Capitol, in all public places, one hears the resources of the State earnestly discussed, and no stranger is allowed to pass without giving him thorough information as to its splendid mineral wealth and remarkable agricultural facilities.

The population of the State is at present 1,258,526, of whom 322,000 are colored. Over seventy-two per cent. of the people are engaged in agriculture. The area of improved land in the State is but small, when one considers that there are twenty-five millions of acres within the State limits.

The tendency is to small farms. The entire value of the farms is more than $218,000,000. The total valuation of the taxable property in 1873 was $308,000,000, while the true valuation was probably two-fifths more. From these few statistics it will be seen that Tennessee has an industrious and capable population, although in some parts of the State one cannot but look with displeasure upon the rough-riding, hard-drinking, quarrelsome folk who grumble at the new order of things, and spend their nights at corner-groceries, inveighing against "free niggers" and free schools.

The astonishing cheapness of land is accounted for by the want of home markets, of good roads, and cheap means of transportation in many sections in the State. The war also ruined many farmers who held slaves, and instances have been known of the sale of estates worth $100,000 for one-fifth of that sum. Among the other drawbacks to farming are the want of active capital and of good labor. Great inducements are offered immigrants who are willing to work, and who have a small capital to invest; for good lands, partially improved, may be had in the eastern, middle, or western divisions of the State for from eight to thirty dollars an acre.

Many Northern immigrants who have entered Tennessee have been disappointed because they expected to find labor less necessary than in the country

Young Tennesseans.

whence they came. The winters are short and the products are abundant; but a farmer must labor in Tennessee as in New York or Ohio. The Secretary of the State Board of Agriculture, Mr. J. B. Killebrew, who has written an excellent book on the resources of the State, urges immigrants to go to Tennessee in colonies, as they can generally, by buying land together, secure it at much cheaper rates, and can have a society of their own, whereas a single individual settling in the back-country of Tennessee, among populations somewhat ignorant, and generally prejudiced against innovations, would find his habits constantly clashing with those of the people around him, and would end by leaving in disgust. The impression that the better class in Tennessee does not respect laboring men is incorrect. It is becoming yearly more and more disgraceful to be an idler, and the influential people heartily welcome all who go to the State for the purpose of establishing manufactures or engaging in agriculture. Outrages against persons and property are, on the whole, rare. In the rougher mountain regions, and some of the sections bordering on the Mississippi, strangers are looked upon with suspicion, and Northern men are considered as natural enemies; but this by no means represents the feeling of the mass of the people of the State.

Tennessee is gradually reducing her debt, which, in April of 1874, was $23,995,337. In 1875, nearly every railroad within her boundaries will be liable to taxation, and, judging from the present aspects, many millions of dollars will be invested in the manufacture of cotton and woolen goods, and the development of the coal and iron-fields so prodigally scattered over the State. The Tennessee, the Cumberland, and numerous other rivers, serve as important avenues of transportation, and the unflagging zeal manifested by the State authorities in demanding the improvement of these streams will soon result in some action by the General Government. Western Tennessee has already more than seven hundred miles of rail, and had it not been for the financial crisis of '73, the mileage would have been largely increased.

Tennessee Log Cabins.

The public school system is not yet very efficient, although much labor has been expended in its enforcement by native Tennesseans. There is a positive objection freely expressed in many parts of Tennessee to the education of the negro, but the colored element in the Republican party seems quite competent to assert its own interests and to provide for them. The blacks are clamorous for many of the privileges which would be secured to them by the Civil Rights bill, and Congressman Maynard, their present candidate for Governor (October, 1874), is helping them in their crusade. The permanent school fund for the State is more than two and one-half millions, and an additional annual income is derived from numerous sources. The school districts are authorized to levy taxes for the support of schools and the erection of buildings. As the matter of taxation is left to their option, the more illiberal of the districts are, of course, unprovided with schools. It is asserted that but thirty-five counties in the State have really levied a tax for school purposes. The fact that the whites are positively determined to provide completely separate schools for the colored people, and that the latter are not rich enough to supply themselves with schools, renders the subject a difficult and disagreeable one, especially at the present time. The scholastic population of the State was, in 1873, one hundred and seventy-three thousand. The number of teachers is insufficient, and their qualifications are not always of a high order.

The Cumberland University at Lebanon has a good legal department, and the Presbyterians propose shortly to establish a fine University, with an endowment of half a million, which shall rival the famous institution founded by Vanderbilt at Nashville.

Middle Tennessee, in which Nashville stands, is at present the most valuable division of the State. It contains more than half a million people, and several hundred prosperous towns and villages. It is one of the healthiest sections of America. The Cumberland, Duck, and Elk rivers flow down through deep gorges in the mountains, and the hundreds of small streams in the recesses among the hills furnish abundant water power. The variety of crops is almost astonishing; wheat and fruits, tobacco, corn, cotton, and everything that grows above the thirty-fifth parallel of latitude,—even the fig and the magnolia,— can be cultivated without injury from the climate. In what is called the Central Basin of Middle Tennessee, as in Kentucky, much of the fine stock used in the Cotton States is bred. The fleet horses and the slow and laborious mules, the fine short-horned and Ayrshire cattle, are sought by buyers from all the States as the most perfect types of these animals. As a wool-growing region the basin has few equals and no superiors.

Tomb of Andrew Jackson, at the "Hermitage," near Nashville.

LXXXII.

A GLANCE AT MARYLAND'S HISTORY—HER EXTENT AND RESOURCES.

WHEN the first Lord Baltimore, George Calvert, found that his efforts to establish a colony in Newfoundland were unavailing, he visited Virginia, in 1628. While there, he undertook the examination of the Chesapeake, which John Smith had explored many years before. Journeying along the mighty

View from Federal Hill, Baltimore, Maryland, looking across the Basin.

stretch of water 200 miles from the ocean, and, noting its numerous tributary rivers, he doubtless saw the wonderful advantages which these offered for colonization, and as soon as he returned to England he procured from Charles I. the promise of a grant of territory on the Chesapeake. The Virginians were not pleased with the prospects of the establishment of Lord Baltimore's colony, and took occasion to voice their discontent in the hearing of the English officials. Lord Baltimore died early in 1632, before the promised charter had been accorded; but when it was issued it passed to his son, the second Lord Baltimore, and "all that part of the peninsula lying in the parts of America between the ocean on the east and the Bay of Chesapeake on the west" was erected into a province and called Maryland. This was England's first province, and it was intended to call it Crescentia; but Charles I., when the charter was presented for his signature, struck out Crescentia and substituted Maryland, in honor of his queen, Henrietta Maria, of France. Lord Baltimore was made absolute lord and proprietary of the province, giving only two Indian arrows annually, and one-fifth of all the gold and silver ore found within the limits of Maryland, as a pledge of his allegiance to the crown. The proprietary was accorded power to enact laws, with the advice and assent of the freemen of the province and their delegates. He had arbitrary power to impose taxes, and to deprive citizens even of life and liberty.

The boundaries of Maryland were the occasion of much dispute in later days, the present limits being much less than those originally accorded the province. Delaware was formerly part of the territory of Maryland. The boundary between Maryland and Pennsylvania was disputed until Mason and Dixon drew their famous line between the two States in 1763 — since recognized as the dividing line between Northern and Southern territory and sentiment. Virginia also revived her old quarrel with regard to the boundaries, and it may be said to have existed in a modified form up to the present day.

In 1633, on the 22d of November, about two hundred colonists, many of whom were Roman Catholics, set sail from the Isle of Wight, arriving off Point Comfort in Virginia early in 1634. On the 25th of March they celebrated mass on the banks of the Potomac and took formal possession of the country. They then occupied an Indian town which the natives had ceded to them, named St. Mary's, and for more than half a century this town was the capital of the province. The capital thus established was almost at the southern extremity of the province, and for many years thereafter the extension of settlements into the interior was hindered by internal commotion and wars with the Indians. The proprietary government during the first century of its existence twice met with serious interruptions: once when it was usurped by Cromwell's Commissioners during the rule of the English Commonwealth, and once when it was displaced by the rule of William and Mary. At a time when religious toleration was unknown elsewhere in America, or at all in Europe, it was inaugurated under the proprietary government. Maryland soon became a refuge for all who suffered from religious persecution. Quakers and Puritans and members of the Church of England fled thither from New England and Virginia, and Protestants from France, Portugal, and the Netherlands, took refuge in Lord Baltimore's colony from Catholic rage. The population of the province enjoyed religious equality until 1692, when the royal government which had usurped the powers of the proprietary, made, for the first time, ecclesiastical establishment in Maryland.

In 1659 Baltimore county was created. At that time the territory was almost a wilderness occupied by the Indians, but the colonists gradually extended the limits of civilization.

In 1662 the first land within the limits of the present Baltimore city was patented by Thomas Gorsuch, a member of the Society of Friends. This was a tract of fifty acres on Whetstone Point, where to-day the gigantic grain trade of the West is centring. The first actual settler on the site of the city is believed to have been a Mr. David Jones, who gave his name to the erratic little stream known as Jones's Falls, which has often overflowed its banks and caused serious damage.

In 1723 ships began to enter the Patapsco from London, and in 1729 an Act of Assembly was passed for erecting a town on the north side of the Patapsco, in Baltimore county. In 1730 the town was laid out into lots, and called Baltimore in compliment to the proprietary. It was evidently not the expectation of the early settlers that the town would grow to its present size, or they would not have established it in a location surrounded by hills, water-courses and marshes ; but they found abundance of stone, lime, iron and timber, and excellent sites for water-works near the harbor. The expense to which the modern Baltimoreans have been subjected for extending and grading streets along the numerous hills, and for covering marshes and small streams, is enormous.

In 1752 Baltimore had but twenty-five houses. St. Paul's Church, which was begun by the members of the Church of England in 1731 and completed in 1744, was a quaint building occupying the site of the present church, at the corner of Charles and Saratoga streets. Although the population of the county at that time was more than seventeen thousand, that of the town was but two hundred. The sloop " Baltimore " and the brig " Philip and Charles " were the only sea-going vessels owned in the town. The warehouse near the

harbor, for tobacco inspection, was one of the principal centres of trade. The growth of the city was promoted during the war between the English and the French by the necessity which the inhabitants felt of flocking together for protection, rather than penetrating into the country.

In 1755 the Indians came within eighty miles of Baltimore, and made numerous destructive raids. Palisades were constructed, and the women and children were placed by the colonists upon vessels in the harbor. In 1756 numerous Acadians, refugees from the harsh policy of the English in Nova Scotia, settled in Baltimore. The town began to grow in com-

The Oldest House in Baltimore.

merce ; ship-yards were established at Fells Point, and many merchants had their residences there. In 1761 the population of the province was 164,007, of which 49,675 were negroes.   The good people of Maryland were greatly annoyed at this time by the number of convicts imported from England, estimated at not less than twenty thousand.   These convicts were brought over under contract by private shippers, and sold into servitude for the entire term of transportation.   In due time many of them were transformed into useful citizens, and some of them attained considerable distinction.

In 1761 the Maryland exports of tobacco to England amounted to 140,000 pounds.   Wheat, lumber, corn, flour, iron, skins, and furs were also exported, and Maryland would have grown with astonishing rapidity from that date if England's policy of stifling manufacturing industry in the colonies, that she might send her own productions to them, had not been vigorously carried out. The iron and shipping business was greatly restricted, but, although commercially dependent upon England, the province managed to develop her natural resources to a considerable extent.   Although Maryland acquiesced in the restrictions made by England upon her commerce, she heartily joined with the colonies in asserting the right to regulate her own internal government and to impose her own taxes.   The freemen of the province were exceedingly jealous of the privileges accorded to them by the charter, and when England began to take the matter of taxation into her own hands by establishing the stamp tax, Maryland promptly expelled the stamp distributor from the province upon his arrival, and forbade the landing of the stamped paper which had been brought in the same ship with him.   The attempted tax upon tea, which was the occasion of the sudden rebellion in Boston, was also the occasion of an outbreak at Annapolis, the then capital of Maryland.   The colonists had refused from the very first to allow the tea sent from England to be unloaded, and in 1774 a vessel with eighteen packages of tea on board was burned at Annapolis.

At the time of the declaration of independence by the Continental Congress in Philadelphia, the proprietary government of Maryland was held by an illegitimate son of Lord Baltimore, who died in 1771.   The people of Maryland had always entertained a strong loyalty toward the Baltimores, but this bastard ruler was promptly objected to.   His government was overthrown, and a convention was called to frame a Constitution for the new State of Maryland.

The convention assembled at Annapolis on the 14th of August, 1776, and Maryland entered into the Revolutionary war with an earnestness and gallantry which made the name of the "Maryland line" conspicuous in Revolutionary annals.   At the battle of Brooklyn Heights in 1776 a part of a battalion of Maryland troops repeatedly charged with bayonets a whole brigade of British regulars.   They were the first American troops to use that weapon, and used it to such advantage that on many occasions thereafter they both charged and repulsed the enemy with unloaded muskets.   Maryland also maintained a marine service during the Revolution, to protect her shores from the English cruisers.

After the establishment of the independence of the colonies there was for some time an almost complete paralysis of commerce in Maryland.   The low price of tobacco and flour, the principal articles of export from the State, added to the distress. But a period of marked commercial activity soon followed. The tobacco trade revived, English merchants who had sought to re-establish the agencies which they had maintained before the Revolution at Annapolis, Bladensburg, Upper Marlborough and Elk Ridge Landing, being superseded by Baltimore capitalists, who began to make shipments in their own vessels and for their own account. The trade of the city was greatly improved; canal companies along the Susquehanna and the Potomac were formed; streets were extended and paved; and the population, which in 1782 was nearly 8,000, became energetic and progressive. Sugar refineries, glass-works and flour-mills were established, and the Baltimore clippers carrying their products to foreign ports became famous everywhere. As the West began to develop, Baltimore laid hold from time to time upon its trade, and became the first, as it is to-day the natural, market for the productions of that section.

Baltimore bore an important part in the war between England and America in 1814, and was one of the chief sufferers by it. The British fleet blockaded the Chesapeake bay, and commerce was seriously affected. Many privateers were fitted out at Baltimore and did good service. After the burning of Washington by the British, a force of 5,000 English was landed at the mouth of the Patapsco river, a sharp battle taking place there between this force and the Maryland and Pennsylvania militia. On the 13th of September, 1814, the British made a vigorous attack upon Fort McHenry, an important fortification which had been established on Whetstone Point in 1794. The little fort, with its finely planned batteries, completely repulsed the attacking fleet, and compelled the retreat of the invading forces. During the night of the bombardment, upon which the English admiral relied so much that he had sworn to take the fort in two hours, Francis S. Key, a noted Marylander and a prisoner in the British fleet, wrote the celebrated national song called "The Star-Spangled Banner."

This song, which has justly been accorded the honors of the "national hymn," was suggested by the hopes and fears which filled the poet's heart during the long and terrible night, and the anxiety with which he looked at the walls of the fort in the morning to see if the flag was still there:—

"Oh, say can you see by the dawn's early light
What so proudly we hailed at the twilight's last gleaming;
Whose broad stripes and bright stars, through the perilous fight
O'er the ramparts we watched, were so gallantly streaming?
The rockets' red glare, bombs bursting in air,
Gave proof through the night that our flag was still there.
Oh, say does that star-spangled banner still wave
O'er the land of the free and the home of the brave?"

While the bombs of the English ships were bursting in hundreds about the parapets of Fort McHenry, an adventurous rooster mounted the walls and crowed heartily and repeatedly. One of the defenders of the fort then declared that if he ever lived to see Baltimore the rooster should be fed with pound cake; and the day after the bombardment, although the man was so worn down with fatigue as to be unable to leave the fort, he sent to the city, procured the cake, and treated the patriotic fowl.

Maryland has an area of about 9,500 square miles of land, and the Chesapeake bay covers 4,000 more. It may be said with truth that the land beneath the waters is quite as productive as that above, for the oyster-beds, the abundance of excellent fish, the flocks of wild ducks and the multitudes of terrapins and crabs afford an immense commerce. The thousands of acres along the shores of this beautiful bay are crowded with market gardens, which supply Baltimore, Philadelphia, Washington, and New York with all the most delicate fruits and vegetables.

The estuaries and navigable arms of the Chesapeake are so numerous that there are many counties bordering on the water, no point in which is many miles from a good landing. Although the actual sea-coast of Maryland is but little more than thirty miles, the tide-water margin, including that along the islands, is over 500 miles. The largest vessels can ascend the bay, pass St. Mary's, Calvert and Anne Arundel counties to Annapolis, and, entering the Potomac river, can

Fort McHenry — Baltimore Harbor. [Page 737.]

pass up by St. Mary's, Charles, and Prince George's counties to Washington. The Chesapeake, the Nanticoke and the Patuxent, as well as nearly fifty other streams, are navigable for many miles. Maryland is divided into three sections, two of which, separated by the Chesapeake, are very similar in formation. In the tide-water district, which embraces nearly one-half of the territory of the State, and which is supposed to have formed the bed of an ancient ocean, lie rich deposits of marl and shell lime. The surface is but slightly elevated above the sea, and the forest-growths are mainly oak, hickory, chestnut, walnut, gum, cedar, pine and beech. Emery, bog iron ore, kaolin, or porcelain clay, and gray, red and blue clays are found in profusion. In this section there is an excellent opportunity for the establishment of glass manufactories, as the pure sand is admirably adapted for that purpose. Wheat, Indian corn, tobacco, and cotton in the southern sections, are the grains mainly cultivated.

On the "eastern shore," which embraces the counties of Worcester, Somerset, Dorchester, Talbot, Caroline, Queen Anne's and Cecil, the soils were originally among the most fertile in the State. Reckless management in slave-holding times injured their productive value, but careful culture is gradually restoring them. The sections remote from tide-water produce wheat and corn mainly, while in the southern portion flax and cotton are raised. In Worcester county there are immense cypress swamps, but the soil, in many portions, where it has been drained and reclaimed, is of unsurpassed fertility. Wild ducks and oysters abound along the Atlantic coast of this county.

The grape grows in great perfection along the eastern shore, and in some counties excellent wines are manufactured. Along the western shore dwell many hardy fishermen, the shad and herring fisheries of the Potomac being as extensive as those of any other portion of the United States. As many as four hundred thousand barrels of herring have been taken from the Potomac, within a hundred miles of Washington, in a single year, and sent to the Baltimore market. On this, as on the eastern shore, the lands suffered for a century from an exhaustive system of planting, and being deserted by their owners, as their fertility gradually lessened, the section had a smaller white population in 1860 than just before the Revolution; but the means of reclaiming all the lands exists in the great beds of shell marl which abound throughout many of the counties. In the southern part of the district tobacco is one of the principal crops, Prince George's county alone having produced as much as ten million pounds in a year. The clay-beds which extend through the district from the Potomac to the Susquehanna, and which here and there attain an elevation of two hundred feet above tide-water, are very valuable. The iron which the clay contains gives the pottery made from it a red shade, which renders it unfit for the choice wares; but for the manufacture of brick, these clay-beds are the best in the world. Prince George's county, whence in the latter part of the seventeenth century a hundred sail of ships annually carried tobacco to England and the West Indies, possesses the State Agricultural College, which is located near Bladensburg. On the southern border of Montgomery county are the great falls of the Potomac, one of the finest water powers in the United States. In this county many of the wealthy citizens of Washington have built handsome residences. The section suffered greatly from raids during the war, but is rapidly regaining its original prosperity. On the Patapsco river, in Howard county, there are numerous excellent granite quarries, and in Baltimore county there are fine-grained white and blue-gray marbles.

The mountain district of the State, which includes Carroll, Frederick, Washington, and Alleghany counties, is fertile and interspersed with beautiful valleys. It is admirably adapted to the raising of stock, and large crops of wheat and thousands of pounds of maple sugar are annually manufactured there.

At Wedverton, in Frederick county, a noble water power has been made available by a dam across the Potomac, and here in due time an extensive manufacturing town will doubtless spring up. In the rugged and broken Alleghany county there are extensive glades or meadows whose grasses are famed for their luxuriance, and over which, before the late war, thousands of cattle from Virginia roamed while fattening for the stall. The iron ores of Cumberland and the coal mines have already been alluded to. The capital invested in mines in Alleghany county is nearly seven million dollars.

Eighty-five thousand slaves were emancipated as the result of the war, and these persons constituted the main agricultural laboring population of the State. As elsewhere throughout the South, they have left the country in swarms and flocked to the towns, and the owners of large plantations, finding that their ex-slaves have deserted them, are anxious to divide up the broad tracts which have now become a burden to them into small vendible portions. Nowhere is there a better opportunity for the purchase of cheap and good lands, or for the practice of the highest scientific farming.

Jones's Falls — Baltimore.

LXXXIII.

THE BALTIMORE AND OHIO RAILROAD—GROWTH OF TRADE.

BALTIMORE, the Maryland metropolis, not only enjoys the honor of having received the first telegraphic message in the United States, but it was also the first to inaugurate a railroad. To that road, which has become one of the most gigantic powers in the land, it owes much of its present astonishingly rapid growth. The last surviving signer of the Declaration of Independence, the illustrious Charles Carroll, of Carrollton, laid the corner-stone of the Baltimore and Ohio railroad, on the 4th of July, 1828. Within half a century since the road was projected, Baltimore's population has increased from 62,000 to 350,000, and her trade has grown so enormously that the stranger who visited the town in 1860 would hardly recognize it now.

When the first rails were laid down, there were very few who contemplated the completion of the road even to the Alleghanies, and none believed that it would touch the Great Lakes and make Chicago and Pittsburg its tributaries. The material obstacles which beset its construction were by no means so great as the financial difficulties. From 1828 until

Exchange Place, Baltimore, Maryland.

January in 1853, when the completion of the Wheeling and Ohio railroad was celebrated, the company was engaged in perpetual struggles to maintain its existence. As soon as the first rails were laid in the city, in 1828, a car which resembled a country market wagon, and which was drawn by a single horse, was placed upon them, and the leading citizens of Baltimore made trips backward and forward in it. No one had then dreamed of employing steam to draw the cars; but as soon as steam was introduced · in England, Mr. Peter Cooper, of New York, who had invented a locomotive with a boiler about the size of those used in hotel kitchens, forthwith solicited the privilege of trying his new and wondrous invention upon the Baltimore and Ohio railroad. His was the first locomotive for railroad purposes ever built in America, and Mr. Cooper successfully drove his own engine, to which was attached a car filled with the Directors and prominent citizens, a distance of thirteen miles on the new road in fifty-seven minutes.   But as ill-luck would

have it, on the return trip, his engine was beaten by a smart trotting-horse, whose owner, from the highway parallel with the road, saw the daring experimenters at work, and mischievously resolved to test horse-flesh against steam.   The veteran philanthropist, Cooper, must look back upon those days of primitive experiments with a smile when he remembers that from New York to St. Louis is hardly a journey of forty-eight hours to-day.

From such humble beginnings the road rapidly grew, and, as it reached the Alleghanies, began to draw toward Baltimore a traffic in coal which has since been developed into colossal proportions.   Millions of tons, in cars

The Masonic Temple—Baltimore, Maryland.

expressly constructed for the purpose, annually pass over the road; and the traveler who, seated in the hotel-station at Harper's Ferry, looks down the

line of rail which runs along the ravine, sees immense trains, drawn by enormous engines of a peculiar build, whizzing over the tracks within ten minutes of each other all day long.

In 1831 the then President of the railroad, in a report made to the Governor of Maryland, boasted that the State had within her limits the longest continuous railway in the world.   This was the road from Baltimore to Frederick, sixty-one miles in length.   In the same report he foreshadowed the future effort to draw the trade of the West to Baltimore, when he referred to the fact that the State was so situated as to afford the surest and most convenient route of communication between the navigable Western waters and the

The Shot-Tower—Baltimore, Maryland.

ocean.   Baltimore, with her splendid advantages of precedent, however, required many severe lessons before she could be made to improve her opportunities.

One by one her rivals laid hold of the treasures of the West, while the Directors of the Baltimore and Ohio railroad were battling with the great canal company, which had so long monopolized the trade between the Chesapeake and the Ohio; and while the legislation of Baltimore itself so restricted the road that it could not obtain proper development.   In 1842 the line was opened to Cumberland, now a fine commercial town, beautifully located in the mountains; and on the completion of the road to Wheeling in 1854 the commerce of Baltimore began to increase with tremendous rapidity.   The freight to the State in 1832 had amounted to scarcely 30,000 tons; in 1852 it had reached 252,000 tons; in 1854 it amounted to 661,000 tons.   All the old methods of transportation were thenceforth unavailing.   The products of the West were no longer floated down the Ohio and Mississippi to New Orleans, there loaded into schooners, and thence carried by sea to the Chesapeake, and so to Baltimore.

Just as the people of the State were beginning to despair, and to fancy that New York and Philadelphia had completely distanced them, their best commercial development began.   Had the road been completed to the Ohio river twenty years sooner, the river system of the West would not to-day have converged toward Lake Erie.   The wisdom of the commercial men of the North who had hastened to construct the Erie and New York Central road, which, with the Erie canal, seemed to secure to New York the great body of the Western trade, had been so often demonstrated to the Baltimoreans that they had quite despaired of longer endeavoring to make Baltimore a rival of New York, and were contenting themselves with the supply trade of the South.   But the vigorous policy of the railroad men who pushed the Baltimore

Scene on the Chesapeake and Ohio Canal.

and Ohio road into the West, and courageously combated New York, has worked a complete revolution.   Now that grain seeks quick transportation by rail, and that the Baltimore and Ohio road, whose connections extend through the length of the South and West, has reached out an arm to Chicago, Baltimore seems likely to be a most important tide-water terminus of the West.

The war interrupted the many projects which President Garret, to whose past and present vigorous management the railroad owes much of its prosperity, had been maturing, and after four years of civil strife the work was begun anew. In 1865 the company commenced to lease Western railroads, and to elaborate its terminal facilities at Baltimore.   As the result, it has to-day under its management a continuous direct road of 512 miles in length, furnishing for West Virginia and much of Ohio, Indiana, Illinois, Missouri and Kansas, the surest and cheapest path to the sea. It has thoroughly attached itself to the trade of the valley of the Ohio, Pittsburg, Wheeling, Marietta, Parkersburg, Portsmouth, Cincinnati, Louisville, and other centres, which have branches extending to them from the main stem. The road to Chicago completes the system, and the Baltimoreans

The House of Refuge—Baltimore.

claim that it relegates New York to the commercial inferiority which her inactive policy of late has been bringing upon her. Within the past few years, also, the metropolitan branch of the Baltimore and Ohio railroad, shortening the line between Washington and the West nearly fifty miles, has been completed; and a new branch is in construction downward through the Valley of Virginia, and will doubtless drain that wonderful agricultural region into the Baltimore basin, opening up, by its connection with the Chesapeake and Ohio railroad at Staunton, the coal, salt and iron industries of Western Virginia. The road has also seized on the Orange, Alexandria and Manassas line from Washington to Lynchburg, and given to it and its extensions the new name of the Washington City, Virginia Midland, and Great Southern.

The contest with the Chesapeake and Ohio Canal Company for the right of way along the Potomac, when the Baltimore and Ohio railroad was in its infancy, brought into play the abilities of some of the finest leaders of the bar. In the trials of the Court of Appeals, where the struggle for the choice of route was a prolonged one, and where the decision was finally given in favor of the railroads, the clear-headed Taney, the commanding Webster, the majestic and elegant Wirt, the philanthropic Mercer, the accurate Gwynn, and the then young and aspiring Reverdy Johnson, made brilliant speeches. Among the men who planned and executed the through route were some of the most noted citizens of Maryland; the names of Robert Oliver, of Alexander Brown, of William Lorman, of Isaac McKim, of William Patterson, Talbot Jones, George Hoffman, John B. Morris, William Stewart, and Philip E. Thomas, are inseparably connected with the projection of this great work. They were, in a measure, the pioneers of the railway system of this country, and to them and the thousands who have emulated their example in every State of the Union we owe our material prosperity as a nation.

The men who determined to make Baltimore the chief of American ports did not overlook the necessity for proper terminal facilities. This subject engaged the attention of the company from the moment of its organization; but during its early years, the main terminus was a small depot, which has since expanded into the great Mount Clare Station, where to-day there are acres of repair shops and locomotive houses. When the company had once resolved to provide a tide-water terminus, it lost no time in selecting and purchasing the grounds at Locust Point, a narrow strip of land at the entrance of Baltimore harbor, admirably adapted for the construction of wharves. The misguided stranger who fancies that Baltimore is a torpid town, where business enterprise is rarely hinted at, would do well to visit Locust Point, and correct his previous impressions.

The whole peninsula, of which Locust Point is the terminus, has always been considered most advantageous for shipments. Early in the Revolution an English corporation obtained possession of it; but the plans of the company were overthrown by an act of confiscation, under which the Point was taken by the State and sold. In later years, the peninsula was selected as the site for Fort McHenry, the principal defense of the harbor. The peninsula has about five miles of water-frontage, along every portion of which there is a depth of from seventeen to twenty-one feet, easily increased to twenty-five. Locust Point proper comprises a water-front of about 3,600 lineal feet, and an area of eighty acres, seamed with railway tracks, covered with gigantic sheds and warehouses, and dotted with immense wharves, on which stand two mammoth elevators, one of which has a capacity of 600,000, and the other 1,500,000

bushels. These elevators, through which the grain, poured into Baltimore by thousands of cars from the great West, passes directly into the holds of Norwegian, Danish, and English vessels, are superior to any buildings of the kind on the Atlantic coast. Their foundations rest upon thousands of piles, driven deep into the harbor-bed, and covered with oak cappings, upon which the massive granite is laid. The elevator last built stands upon no less than twelve thousand piles. Both are surrounded by water upon three sides, and the vessels flocking about them seem like swallows nestling on the sides of some huge barn. To the great steamship piers, which are covered with iron sheds and into which double track

The Blind Asylum — Baltimore, Maryland.

lines of railway run, come weekly steamships from Bremen, and thousands of emigrants annually pass westward through Baltimore.

The present piers are already inadequate to the business which is poured on to them, and new ones will soon be erected. A huge ferry, upon which cars coming from the West with freight for Eastern cities are transferred to the opposite side of the harbor, where connection is made with the Philadelphia, Wilmington and Baltimore railroad, is another of the noted sights at Locust Point. When trade is busiest more than two hundred and fifty cars a day are thus transferred, and the company intends hereafter to obviate the necessity of

The Eastern High School—Baltimore, Maryland.

hauling passenger trains, by horse power, through the city, by running them to Locust Point across the harbor in barges of the ferry. A huge coffee warehouse has been erected near the elevator.

The activity at this point is simply wonderful. A walk along the piers shows an immense panorama of stores of railroad iron, iron ore, bonded warehouses crammed with imported merchandise; great double piers along which hover coastwise steamers; the huge bulk of a Liverpool steam-liner discharging its freight; the graceful outlines of a " North German Lloyd,"

with its flat-capped and clumsy-looking sailors peering over the sides; while thousands of cars rattle forward and backward into and out of mysterious sheds, and floods of grain pour down from spouts into quaint little barks, whose captains tranquilly smoke their pipes as the process of loading goes on. When one understands that a thousand coal-cars can be daily unloaded at Locust Point, and that all the coal for the huge fleet of ocean steamers plying between New York and Europe is shipped from Baltimore, he begins to comprehend the reasons for the constant arrival of trains filled with their sooty freight.

For the month ending June 30, 1874, 13,861 coal-cars, 2,072 grain-cars, and 3,512 cars loaded with miscellaneous freight were received and emptied at Locust Point. The elevators are monuments to the astonishing increase of the grain trade of Baltimore. In 1871, the exports of bulk grain from the city were hardly 2,000,000 bushels. As soon as the first elevator was opened, they increased to 4,000,000 bushels annually, and in 1873, they amounted to 7,250,000 bushels. The citizens of Baltimore, who once fancied that the improvements in terminal facilities would only enrich the company and not aid the city, have been shown conclusively that all kinds of property in Baltimore increases in ratio with the increase of export trade. The exports for the six months ending July 1, 1874, amounted to more than $15,250,000, or $6,000,000 more than the corresponding six months of 1873, and exceeding by $3,000,000 the entire exports of 1870. Now that the elevators are in direct connection with railway tracks penetrating the West, the grain receipts for the first six months of 1874 amounted to but 600,000 bushels less than those of the entire year of 1873, and the close of 1874 will witness the completion of elevators at Locust Point and at Canton whose united capacity will increase the grain trade at Baltimore to 10,000,000 bushels for the last half of the current year. Certainly, it is not without some reason that the enthusiastic Baltimore merchants predict that they may claim $50,000,000 in exports annually in a few years.

The improvement of the harbor of Baltimore was for many years talked of as desirable, but did not become an imperative necessity until the action of the railroad company had made the town one of the most important of American ports. It was evident that if Baltimore was to have a large European trade, her ship-channel, leading from the Patapsco river into the Chesapeake, must be deepened. Large appropriations were made by Congress and the city of Baltimore, in equal portions. The new channels will permit the approach to the city at low water of vessels drawing from twenty-two and a-half to twenty-three feet; and at high water, of those drawing twenty-four to twenty-five feet. The only improvements now necessary are such as will allow vessels of the largest draft to load directly at the wharves, and this work, which is being rapidly effected by the River and Harbor Commission, comprehends the deepening of the channel to the wharves from Fort McHenry.

View of a Lake in Druid Hill Park, Baltimore.

LXXXIV.

THE TRADE OF BALTIMORE—ITS RAPID AND ASTONISHING GROWTH.

THE view of Baltimore harbor, as one enters it from the Chesapeake on one of the noble steamers of the Norfolk and Baltimore line, is highly picturesque. At the narrow mouth of the long and irregularly-shaped basin, which is thronged on either side with groups of imposing buildings, stands Fort McHenry.

On the eastward shore, and nearly opposite Locust Point, is Canton, which was laid out by a company organized in 1828, and has sprung into a wonderfully active life during the past few years. In addition to its wharf property, the Canton Company to-day owns twenty-eight hundred acres of land, and a water-front of twenty thousand feet. Many of the most important manufacturing interests of Baltimore are located in this active suburb. Oyster and fruit packing-houses, sugar refineries, brick-yards, foundries, steam saw-mills, iron and copper smelting fur-naces, coal oil refineries, breweries and distilleries, ship-yards and bat-ting factories are densely crowded together along the streets arising from the water, and five to six thousand operatives are employed in the various works.

Maryland Institute — Baltimore.

The Canton Company has shown itself capable of the largest enterprise in increasing the terminal facilities of Baltimore, and is constantly adding to its wharfage forests of piles, their scraggy heads, which appear above the dark water, testifying to the rapidity with which new wharves can be built as soon as they are needed. The railroads centring at Canton drain a vast extent of rich country, and the elevators to be erected there will make it, in time, as important a terminus as its busy neighbor, Locust Point. The Union railroad, projected mainly under the auspices of the Canton Company, was a gigantic undertaking, adding immensely to the commercial advantages of Baltimore,—its double tracks connecting the Baltimore and Potomac, the Western Maryland, the Northern Central, and the Philadelphia, Wilmington and Baltimore railroads. Much of it was constructed at great outlay through tunnels under the city and over treacherous soil; but the two million dollars which it cost are a mere bagatelle when compared with the increase of trade which it will give the city, as it affords another long-needed outlet to tide-water. It is, indeed, precisely the kind of road so much needed to-day in Boston and New York, and which neither of those great cities has yet shown sufficient sagacity to provide. All the railroads passing through Baltimore are entitled to its use at a fixed rate per mile.

When the Canton elevators are completed, Baltimore harbor will be richer in facilities for immediate and convenient shipment to Europe of Western produce than any other city on the continent. The grain trade now centring at Canton is enormous, but the elevators there are totally insufficient to meet the demand.

Woodberry, near Druid Hill Park.

The sugar refinery at Canton has large piers, and the chemical and oil works, and the distilleries, together covering many acres, require extensive wharf accommodation. Large coal oil manufactories are shortly to be established along the water-front at Baltimore, and will add much to the business of the new Union railroad.

The completion of the Baltimore and Potomac railroad, in 1873, forming a new connection between Baltimore and Washington, opened up five of the most fertile lower counties on the western shore of the State—counties which heretofore have had no ready means of communication with the metropolis except by water. The railroad included the construction of large tunnels both at Baltimore and Washington, and forms a very important link in the great Southern line of the Pennsylvania Central railroad. It has had a marked influence upon the character of the population of the western shore.

The residents of that section before the war were large slave-holders, and contented themselves with an unambitious life, devoted mainly to the raising of large crops of tobacco and cereals, and with the ordinary enjoyments of the country gentlemen of Maryland. Among them, however, there were many who, before the slavery *régime* had passed away, saw the necessity of a means of speedy transit to and from the sea-board, and at the close of the war they were prominent in aiding in the building and equipment of the road.   This great work, which is one of the most solidly constructed in the United States, cost nearly six and a-half millions of dollars, one hundred thousand cubic yards of rock having been blasted through during the construction of the tunnel in Baltimore. It has already given an important impetus to forming a trade along its whole line.   The Western Maryland railroad, which extends from Williamsport on the Potomac river to tide-water at Baltimore, was completed in December of 1873.   It is a work which called for the best engineering talent, built as it is across the very summit of the Blue Ridge. From this summit a fine view is obtained of the vast valley of the Cumberland, which, backed with its rugged mountain slopes, and filled with flourishing farms and villages, presents a constant panorama of charming

The New City Hall— Baltimore, Maryland.

scenery.   The road's main service to Baltimore will consist in the current of coal which it can pour from Williamsport on to the wharves at Canton.

The Northern Central railway, formerly known as the Baltimore and Susquehanna, was one of the first routes to import locomotives from Liverpool in the early history of rail-road travel; and by its connection to-day with the great Pennsylvania road, and, through that route, with the Lakes, the West, the North-west, and the South, is a valuable feeder to Baltimore commerce.   The Northern Central Railroad Company has invested very largely in lands at Canton, and proposes the erection of spacious piers, wharves, and elevators, for the reception of the grain from the West.   It runs through a line of busy suburban villages, filled, like the manufacturing towns in the most prosperous sections of New Eng-

Lafayette Square, Baltimore, Maryland.

land, with small manufacturing establishments; passes Timonium, where the old Maryland families were wont to attend the annual State races; passes

Cockeysville, near which marble, granite, and lime quarries, and important iron works are located; and crosses the Gunpowder river, a small tributary of the Chesapeake, which winds picturesquely among overhanging rocks. Over this route to Harrisburg, and thence by Altoona across the Alleghanies, goes a great share of the through travel from South and East to West.

The coal trade of Baltimore has been very largely increased by the rapid railroad development of the past two years. The Maryland coal regions, which stretch away through the George's Creek valley from Piedmont to Frostburg, furnish millions of tons yearly. In this Cumberland region, situated about two hundred miles from Baltimore, the stores of coal are almost inexhaustible. The city can certainly count upon supplies from them for many centuries. It is but a few years since seventeen hundred tons were considered a heavy shipment yearly from the Cumberland mines, but in 1872 1,915,000 tons were shipped thence to Baltimore, while in the same year the city received 600,000 tons of gas and anthracite coal from Western Virginia and Pennsylvania. Baltimore can to-day supply coal freights for five thousand vessels. Her coastwise trade in coal is enormous, and within the past two years her foreign trade has sprung into proportions which bid fair to rival those of any port in the world. The demand in the Baltimore market has at all times latterly been difficult to meet, and vast as are the resources of the Baltimore and Ohio railroad and the Chesapeake and Ohio canal, they are quite insufficient. It is proposed to extend the Western Maryland line until it taps the Pennsylvania railroad, thus giving a shorter route than any present one to Pittsburg, by means of which the trade will be still further increased.

In 1873 the Baltimore and Ohio railroad brought 2,752,178 tons of coal to Baltimore.

The comparative receipts of grain for four years are as follows:

	1873.	1872.	1871.	1870.
Wheat,	2,810,917	2,456,100	4,076,017	3,039,357
Corn,	8,330,449	9,045,465	5,735,921	3,831,676
Oats,	1,255,072	1,959,161	1,833,409	1,243,720
Rye,	100,519	90,938	88,956	77,778
Peas,	10,000	10,000	10,000	10,000
Beans,	30,000	30,000	30,000	30,000
Total,	12,536,967	13,571,664	11,774,303	8,232,531

The coffee and flour trades of Baltimore are very extensive. In the importation of coffee Baltimore stands second among the ports of the United States, the receipts there being more than twice the aggregate entries at the chief ports of Boston, Philadelphia and New Orleans. It has indeed become a port of entry for New York coffee merchants because of the facilities offered for economical handling. The imports for 1873 amounted to 384,808 bags. The receipts of flour for the same year from the West footed up 1,054,033 barrels, and the product of the city mills during that time was 258,579 barrels. The trade in flour has steadily increased for the past seven years, and the exports of that article from the city for 1873 amounted to 359,566 barrels, many of which went to Brazil and the West Indies.

The sugar trade of Baltimore is also very extensive, and the Baltimore, Maryland, Calvert and Chesapeake refineries work up more than 100,000,000 pounds of the crude material annually. In 1871 these refineries produced 91,000,000 pounds of refined sugar, and the total supply for 1873 was 96,387 tons. In 1873 the sugar refineries of Baltimore took 75,000 tons of sugar and 30,000 hogsheads of molasses. The six refineries which work up pure sugar and molasses produced in that same year 75,000 tons of refined sugars and syrups. Baltimore ranks now only second to New York as a sugar market. The tobacco trade has long been of great importance to the city. In colonial days it was the chief dependence of its commerce, and the old inspection laws, which were very judicious, still remain in force. The city has now six large tobacco warehouses. During 1873, 65,067 hogsheads were inspected, and more than 50,000 were exported to Bremen, Rotterdam, Amsterdam, England, France, Spain, Trieste, Italy and Antwerp. Most of the tobacco sold at Baltimore comes from the interior of Maryland, from Ohio, and from Kentucky, and is principally used in Germany and France. Baltimore has many large factories for the manufacture of tobacco, and millions of cigars are made there every year.

The City Jail—Baltimore, Maryland.

In lumber, iron, cotton, and petroleum the trade of this active commercial centre is also rapidly increasing. The export of lumber to Germany now forms a very lucrative branch of trade. The receipts of oil from Western Virginia and Pennsylvania wells in 1873 were 399,360 barrels, and there are numerous oil refineries which prepare the crude petroleum for export. The total exports of oil in 1873 were 3,470,995 gallons; and 66,415 bags of oil-cake were also sent abroad.

Not so much progress has been made latterly in the iron trade as in other branches. In 1872 there were in the State twenty blast furnaces, producing upward of 54,000 tons, but the production in 1873 did not probably reach 50,000 tons. The importations of English and Scotch iron to Baltimore are yearly decreasing. There are a number of bar and plate iron works in the city which do a very heavy business. One company alone controls four plate-mills which yield an annual product of a million dollars in value. The rolling-mills of the great railroad corporations are vast. A journey through the shops of the Baltimore and Ohio railroad at Mount Clare is the work of a day. Two regiments of laborers are employed. It is not generally known that Maryland, particularly in the vicinity of Baltimore, produces some of the best charcoal pig-iron in the country, and in such quantities that this city may be considered the principal market for that staple.   Orders are constantly received, even from St. Louis, for "charcoal pig."   There are eleven charcoal furnaces in the State, which produced during 1873 nearly 25,000 tons.   The oldest now in operation is the Catoctin furnace, quite recently built.   Pig-iron was exported from Maryland to England as early as 1717, but in 1737 the colonists were graciously permitted to make bar iron,—the act, however, providing that they should build no rolling-mills which should interfere with the manufactories of Great Britain.   Along the lines of the Philadelphia, Wilmington and Baltimore railroad, and the Washington branch of the Baltimore and Ohio, for a distance of fifty miles, there is a bed of ore six to eight miles wide, and in many places fifty feet deep.

The Peabody Institute—Baltimore, Maryland.

This is a carbonate of iron peculiar to Maryland, imbedded in clay, and yielding from 32 to 40 per cent. at the furnaces.   In Maryland it is known as chocolate ore.

The copper smelting works at Canton are the largest on the Atlantic coast, producing from 8,000,000 to 10,000,000 pounds of refined copper per annum.

The annual cotton receipts usually amount to from 100,000 to 120,000 bales, fully one-third of which is exported to Liverpool and German ports.

Millions of swine, slaughtered at the various packing points throughout the West, and thousands of beef cattle, are annually received in Baltimore markets, whence they are dispersed through the South and the East.

More than a thousand vessels arrive at Baltimore yearly.   The total value of the imports in 1873 was $32,116,721 ; the exports, $23,387,812.   The receipts of customs at Baltimore for the same period, notwithstanding the free entry of coffee and the reduction of duties on many other articles, amounted to nearly $7,000,000.   The manufacture of boots and shoes in Baltimore gives employ-ment to four thousand persons, and the total value of the trade in 1873 was more than $23,000,000.   The jobbing and provision trade makes steady and rapid progress.   More than two hundred houses are engaged in the liquor trade in Baltimore.   The capital invested in whiskey is $3,000,000 ; the receipts from sales average $6,000,000.

The gentle oyster furnishes the means of livelihood to more than twenty thousand men, women, and children, in this liveliest of Southern cities.   The resources of the Chesapeake bay and its tributaries are so vast that no competition with Baltimore in this trade is possible. More than thirty years ago, an enterprising individual established a house on Federal Hill for the canning of cooked oysters. He had discovered the secret of hermetically sealing the cans, and fancied that he was to become a millionaire, but a hundred ambitious rivals sprang up, and whole streets in Baltimore are to-day lined with the oyster packeries. Eight hundred small schooners and three thousand little boats are engaged from the middle of September until early in the spring in lifting the oysters from their tranquil beds with dredges, tongs and rakes, and in bringing them to the packing establishments, where they are ruthlessly torn from their shells, packed, raw or cooked, in cans from which air is carefully excluded, and shipped for inland consumption as a much-coveted luxury. In

First Presbyterian Church — Baltimore.

one single house fifty thousand cans of raw oysters are daily packed, while another establishment prepares thirty thousand cans of cooked bivalves in the same time. The manufacture of cans in which oysters and prepared fruits are transported is not a small item in the trade of Baltimore, nearly thirty million cans being annually manufactured for that market. Half-a-dozen large printing houses are occupied in preparing labels for the cans, and long lines of lime-kilns, with a capacity of one thousand to twelve hundred bushels each, dispose of the millions of oyster shells which otherwise would block the streets. One firm alone makes more than 600,000 bushels of pure white lime in a year. Farmers are paid to carry away the shells used in the construction of roads, or in the improvement of lands near the city.

When spring comes, and the great army of employés who have been occupied with the oyster during the winter would otherwise be idle, the fleet of schooners and boats penetrates all the streams flowing into the Chesapeake, and their crews purchase from the orchards and market gardens along those streams thousands of tons of fruit and vegetables. The oyster packeries are transformed into manufactories of savory conserves. Peaches, pears, apples, berries, tomatoes — pickles of every imaginable kind — are so prepared that they can be exported to any part of the world. Large kegs are annually sent to Hindostan, to China, to Japan, and throughout middle and western Europe. The oyster-beds of Maryland extend, from a point in Kent county opposite Baltimore, southward down to and up the Potomac forty miles, a total of one hundred and twenty-five miles, and east and west across the Chesapeake bay and Tangier sound, and up all their tributaries as far as salt water reaches. Maryland maintains a State oyster police force, employs a cruiser to protect her interests, has an elaborate oyster law, and in the shape of licenses, fines, &c., draws an annual revenue from the trade of between $50,000 and $60,000.

From this slight review of the commercial interests of Baltimore, it is easy to see that this city has become the most formidable commercial rival of New York on the Atlantic sea-board. It has the shortest inland lines to the Western granaries; its terminal facilities are superb; its rates for transportation are reasonable; imports pass with readiness and dispatch through the Custom-House, and importers are free from the many vexatious delays that have made New York a disagreeable port of entry. It requires seventy-two hours longer for a steamer of 3,000 tons to bring her cargo to Baltimore, but this extra charge is offset by the $2,000 which its owner may save by buying its coal in Baltimore instead of New York, while the difference between the terminal and berth charges of Baltimore and New York is great.

The recovery of the prestige of Baltimore has greatly encouraged her leading merchants and business men, and has done away to some extent with that provincial spirit so long characteristic of the place. In 1798, when Baltimore was a struggling village, it ranked as the third commercial port in the United States, had more than 30,000 tons of registered shipping, and exports amounting to about $12,000,000 annually. Twenty years later, the fleetest vessels that floated on the high seas under any flag were the Baltimore clippers, those renowned specimens of marine architecture whose praises were sung in every clime, and of whose captains there are yet few equals and no superiors. These clippers were schooner-rigged, and so built as to sail within four or four and a-half points of the wind. This enabled them to elude the pursuit of any vessels belonging to blockading squadrons in the stormy days between 1790 and 1807, and they did the chief part of the American and West Indian trade for this country, besides a large carrying trade for European nations. But as the clippers vanished from the seas, and Baltimore seemed over-whelmed by that disastrous lack of energy which was the natural consequence of the system of slavery, her commerce slipped away, and it was only by the projection and completion of that mighty work, the Baltimore and Ohio railroad, which spanned the Alleghanies and laid hold upon the fertile fields of the West, that she succeeded in regaining her proud position. For the first five months of 1874, the aggregate shipments of wheat and corn have been 5,277,000 bushels. The Liverpool Steamship Line has been sending extra steamers for the shipment of grain, and everything indicates a massive and tremendous increase of trade in the old city from month to month and from year to year for many decades to come.

From Federal Hill, the lofty bank south-west of the inner basin of Baltimore harbor, a fine view may be had of the city and the blue waters of the bay. Federal Hill is an historic eminence. It was christened by the Federalists of 1787, who on the adoption of the Constitution of the United States testified their joy by having a grand procession, and rigging and equipping a model ship called the "Federalist," which, after being paraded through the streets of the town, was burned on the hill. Four thousand persons there sat down to a grand dinner at which speeches were made in favor of the new Constitution.   The little ship of State was afterward launched and navigated down Chesapeake bay to the mouth of the Potomac and thence to Mount Vernon, where it was presented to General Washington.   It was on Federal Hill also that a disturbance occurred in the early days of Secession, when an attempt was made to display the flag of the South, and to fire one hundred guns in honor of South Carolina. There, too, General Butler posted his troops when he took possession of the city; and there are seen to-day the earthworks thrown up by the soldiers from Massachusetts and New York.   Opposite Federal Hill, beyond the basin, the steep streets rise to lofty heights, along which are built the fashionable residences, many of the public buildings, the monuments, the churches, the theatres and the banks.   At the foot of the hill, and grouped about the unsavory basin, which emits odors similar to those of the Amsterdam and Rotterdam canals, are long and by no means cleanly streets, lined with petty shops and crowded with piles of wood and lumber, with bustling stevedores and roustabouts, negro wood-sawyers and wholesale shipping merchants.

Looking out over this solid commercial town, and meditating on its trade's enormous growth, one is almost inclined to forget that it has any love for art. Yet it has two of the finest private picture galleries in the country.   The collections of Mr. William T. Walters and Colonel J. Stricker Jenkins are world-famous.   Mr. Walters' gallery is enriched with the paintings of Delaroche, Meissonier, Gérome, Edouard Frère, Corot, Plassan, Troyon, Achenbach, and dozens of other celebrated artists.   The best efforts of the French pencil, and some of the finest works of American artists, grace the halls of Colonel Jenkins. Rinehart, the sculptor, who died recently in Italy, has left to Baltimore much good statuary.

The "Maryland," "Allston," and "Baltimore" Clubs are remembered with pleasure by all visitors to the metropolis.   Their graceful hospitality and the memories of the luxurious terrapin which they recall can never fade away.   The theatrical edifices are very good, and when the new "Academy of Music" is completed, the town will have a charming opera house.

LXXXV.

BALTIMORE AND ITS INSTITUTIONS.

BALTIMORE well deserves the name of the "Monumental City," many years ago bestowed upon it. The stately column which rises from a hill in the fashionable quarter of the city, and known as the Washington Monument, is 180 feet high. It is surmounted by a colossal statue of the Father of his Country, and on the great pedestal, from each side of which radiate pretty parks and fine avenues, are the following inscriptions:

To
GEORGE WASHINGTON,
by the
State of Maryland.

———

Born February 22, 1732.

———

Commander-in-Chief of the American Army, June 15, 1775.
Trenton, December 25, 1776.
Yorktown, October 19, 1781.
Commission Resigned at Annapolis, December 23, 1783.

———

President of the United States, March 4, 1782,
Retired to Mount Vernon, March 4, 1797.
Died December 14, 1799.

The square in which the monument stands is called Mount Vernon, after the home of General Washington. On the south side of the square is the Peabody Institute, founded by the famous banker, George Peabody, who never forgot, in his liberal series of donations, his adopted home and the scene of his early business success. On the 12th of February, 1857, Mr. Peabody donated $300,000 to the city for the establishment of an Institute, and appointed a number of prominent citizens as trustees of the fund. It is devoted to the selection of a fine library and the creation of an academy of music, and is intended to foster the elevation of the middle class. Every citizen of Baltimore can avail himself of the advantages of the Institute, which has already done much for the encouragement of public taste and knowledge in special branches of art.

A little to the west of the Peabody Institute stands Grace Church, and north of it the First Presbyterian Church, one of the most beautiful religious edifices in the country. A little south of the monument is the old cathedral. This noble building, which was begun in 1806, is in the form of a Roman cross, and is a massive and imposing structure. It was finally completed only in 1865. The interior is decorated with many paintings, some of which are of rare merit.

The Battle Monument, which stands in Monument Square, was erected in

Mount Vernon Square, with a view of the Washington Monument, Baltimore, Maryland.

memory of the citizens who fell in defense of Baltimore at the battle of North Point, at the bombardment of Fort McHenry in 1814. The shaft of the monument is a fasces, symbolical of the Union, and the rods are bound together by a fillet on which are inscribed the names of those who were killed. On the north and south fronts of the base of the fasces are two excellent bas-reliefs, one representing the death of General Ross at the battle of North Point, and the other the bombardment of the fort. The column is surmounted by a statue of Baltimore, and at the feet of the statue stands an eagle. The monument is enclosed with an iron railing, outside of which are chains fastened to marble cannon. Around Monument Square are grouped the City Hall, formerly the residence of Reverdy Johnson; Barnum's Hotel, which Charles Dickens praised as one of the best hotels in the country; and the famous Guy's Restaurant, where the terrapin and soft-shelled crab are served in all the glory and perfection of Baltimore cookery.

Wildey Monument, on Broadway, above Baltimore street, is an imposing column designed to perpetuate the memory of Past Grand Sire Thomas Wildey, the founder of the Odd-Fellows in America. In the Green Mount cemetery stands the McDonough statue, erected to the memory of a philanthropic merchant, who was a son of Baltimore, and a prominent citizen of New Orleans; and in Ashland Square a plain but massive column commemorates the two youths who slew General Ross, the Commander of the British forces, in the battle in 1812.

Prominent among the public buildings of Baltimore is the new City Hall, which is an imposing structure of composite architecture, in which the Renaissance predominates. It fills the entire square enclosed by Holliday, Lexington, North, and Fayette streets. The dome, which adds but little in beauty to the building, is 222 feet above the level of the ground. The City Hall is situated in the business portion of the town; and, if it were not walled in by numerous inferior buildings, would be a fine ornament. The Exchange, in Gay street, is a noticeable building, with fine Ionic columns on its east and west sides, and is also surmounted by a huge dome, something like an inverted butter-bowl. The Custom-House and Post-Office are in this building, the former fronting on Lombard street, a busy and substantial avenue. On Baltimore street, the main commercial avenue of the town, is the Maryland Institute for promoting the mechanic arts. It is a handsome and commodious structure, the ground floor of which is occupied by the Centre market. The main hall of this building is one of the largest in the country, and during the annual Mechanics' Fair thousands of visitors from all parts of the State flock into it. It was in this hall that Breckenridge was nominated by the Southern politicians in 1860, and that

the great Union Sanitary Fair in 1863, and the Southern Relief Fair in 1866, were held. The schools of design connected with the Institute are in admirable condition, and the library is large and constantly increasing in size. The Court-House, at the corner of Monument Square and Lexington street, is a highly ornamented marble and brick building, surrounded by streets filled with the offices of the legal fraternity. The new United States Court-House, at the corner of North and Fayette streets, is a massive building. On Madison street stand the City Prison and the State Penitentiary.

Baltimore is very rich in charitable institutions. The Maryland Hospital for the Insane, a fine building on East Monument street in the eastern part of the city; the Mount Hope Hospital, conducted by the Sisters of Charity; the Baltimore Infirmary, controlled by the regents of the University; the Washington

The Battle Monument, seen from Barnum's Hotel—Baltimore.

Medical College, the Washington Infirmary, many "Homes" for aged people, the Maryland Institution for the Instruction of the Blind; the Church Home, conducted by the Protestant Episcopal Church of the city; the orphan asylums of St. Anthony and St. Vincent de Paul (Bay View Asylum, or the Work-house, which stands on the Philadelphia road, a short distance from the eastern limits of the city, can accommodate twelve hundred persons, and cost a million of dollars), the Maryland State Insane Asylum, on the Frederick road, six miles from the city, and the Sheppard Asylum for the Insane, are all testimonials to the liberality and beneficence of the wealthy. The will of Mr. McDonough, by which very large sums were left to Baltimore and New Orleans to be devoted to the education of poor children, gave the former $800,000, which the trustees have expended in purchasing a large farm ten miles from the city, and where they propose to erect a fine institution in which hundreds of pupils will receive constant instruction in English studies, music, and agriculture.

The Battle Monument—Baltimore, Maryland.   [Page 758.]

Beggars are rarities in Baltimore. The "Association for the Improvement of the Condition of the Poor" has the most prominent of the citizens enrolled upon its books, and all who are worthy objects of charity receive prompt assistance. A host of minor charitable institutions, under the charge of the Catholic and Protestant Churches, aid the above-mentioned useful society; and, as the system of tenement houses is almost entirely unknown in the city, but little of the misery and wretchedness so peculiar to large towns is noticeable. The munificent donation of $600,000, left Baltimore some years ago by Moses Sheppard for the establishment of a hospital for the insane, has, by judicious investments, increased to nearly a million dollars, and a beautiful Elizabethan structure, which is to be surrounded by one of the most exquisite landscape gardens in the United States, is now arising a few miles from Baltimore. The establishment is mainly designed as a curative hospital, while Mount Hope, in the north-western centre of the city, is devoted to the treatment of the incurably insane. The Deaf and Dumb Asylum, which has been established by the State in Frederick City, has also received liberal donations from the people of Baltimore. The venerable Thomas Kelso, for eighty-two years a citizen of the Monumental City, some time since endowed a Methodist Episcopal Orphan Asylum with $100,000, and a wealthy lumber dealer has left nearly half a million for the establish-

The Cathedral—Baltimore, Maryland.

ment of an asylum for female orphans. The House of Refuge for vagrant and vicious children, opened in 1855, is a noble range of buildings situated

a short distance beyond the western limits of the city, and within its walls nearly 2,000 boys and girls have been taught trades and received a plain but comprehensive education since the inauguration of the city. The Baltimore Orphan Asylum, founded in 1801, the Children's Aid Society, the Baltimore Manual Labor School, the Male Free School for Baltimore, and the Maryland Industrial School for Girls, have all been amply .and generously supported since their foundation.

Mr. Johns Hopkins, one of the merchant princes of Baltimore, and identified with its history for more than half a century, left the bulk of his immense fortune to the city. The whole of his donations amount to

The Wildey Monument—Baltimore, Maryland.

nearly seven millions of dollars, two millions of which he devoted to the establishment of one of the finest hospitals in the world, for the treatment of sur

Entrance to Druid Hill Park—Baltimore, Maryland.

gical cases and general disease. The site of the old Maryland Hospital was purchased by Mr. Hopkins, and the new edifice will arise thereon. Under the supervision of the trustees of this hospital is also an asylum for the education and maintenance of several hundreds of colored orphan children. The remainder of the donation is devoted to the establishment of a university at Clifton, the beautiful country residence of Mr. Hopkins. This university will have law, medical, classical, and agricultural schools, and its endowment of $4,000,000 with 400 acres of land should make it one of the most famous sites of learning in the country. Mr. Hopkins died in December, 1873. He was connected with almost all the great

enterprises that have entered into the history of Baltimore; and from 1847 until the day of his death was a Director in the Baltimore and Ohio Railway

Company. When the Company was fighting through the embarrassments which constantly crippled it until 1857, he often voluntarily endorsed its notes. By the liberal manner in which he sustained the credit of the corporation the completion and success of the great road were insured. Mr. Hopkins' interest in the Company was only exceeded in value by that held by the State of Maryland and the city of Baltimore. He owned at one time shares of the stock whose actual market worth was $3,000,000. He was almost the controller of the various banks of Baltimore, and a large stockholder in them all, as well as in many of the Virginia banks. In 1873, when the news of the great panic in New York swept down through the business quarter of Baltimore, and the alarm which had been so disastrous in other cities was about to strike terror in the Maryland metropolis, Mr. Hopkins announced his determination to avert the calamity from his native town. He held at that time $2,000,000 worth of commercial paper, and had some investments which were affected by the sudden

Scene on the Canal, near Harper's Ferry.

crisis; but he put his shoulder to the wheel, loaned his money until it was exhausted, then loaned his name, which was as good as money, charging nothing for it in many cases, and, thanks to his generous efforts, Baltimore was uninjured by the financial crisis.

Prominent among the more beautiful churches of Baltimore is the superb Gothic structure near the Washington Monument, known as the Mount Vernon Place Methodist Episcopal Church, completed in 1872. The First Presbyterian Church, on Madison and Park streets, built of New Brunswick freestone in the pointed Gothic style; the Independent Methodist Church, and the Eutaw Place Baptist and St. Paul's Churches, are all imposing religious edifices. The Masonic Temple on Charles street, and the noble building which the Young Men's Christian Association of Baltimore is now erecting at the corner of Charles and Saratoga streets, the former of white marble, are substantial buildings of the modern type. It is astonishing that Baltimore is not built entirely of this marble, as there are inexhaustible supplies of the rich material within easy access of the city.

The parks and suburbs of the "Liverpool of America" are on the same magnificent scale as the charitable institutions and terminal facilities. Druid Hill park was purchased in 1860 for half a million dollars. It is within half a mile of the present city limits, and the Park Commissioners found the five hundred acres which comprise it already laid out; for the Rogers family, whose estate it once was, fashioned the superb grounds a century ago into the style of the English parks of the period. Situated on the highest point of land near the city, there are many noble views of the great town and the blue bay beyond; downward, toward Kent Island and Annapolis, and eastward and westward, fertile valleys and sweet landscapes salute the eye. The Rogers family owned the present

The Bridge at Harper's Ferry.

park for one hundred and fifty years, and carefully shielded many noble sylvan monarchs from the profanation of the woodman's axe. Great bouquets and masses of superb trees dot the lawns; antique woodlands skirt the roadways; and in autumn the rich orange and crimson of the sassafras and dogwood leaves contrast charmingly with the deep browns and purples of the oaks and the gold of the hickory.*

From the terrace in front of the mansion in the centre of Druid Hill park, there are many pretty glimpses of the city, the river, the bay; and all the country may be seen through lovely frame-works of foliage. Druid Hill was once known as the largest pear orchard either in America or Europe, and on its western and south-western slopes were forty thousand pear-trees, with six hundred varieties of that fruit upon them. A tract of country has been set apart for the establishment of a botanical garden. From the noble gateway on Madison avenue lead long walks and roads, adorned with ornamental summer-houses, marble statues, vases and urns; water-ways dotted with swans and ducklings; lawns across which deer bound undisturbed, and a lake whose icy surface in winter is gay with thousands of skaters. On fine days streams of handsome equipages wend their way in procession to the centre of the park, where beauty and fashion pass in grand review. The distance to the central entrance-gate at Druid Hill from Charles and Baltimore streets, which are at present the most thickly-populated portions of the city, is two and a-half miles. Within the bounds of the park lies Druid lake, a mighty stone-wall reservoir which has a storage capacity of 493,000 gallons. This reservoir is only supplemental, however, to the ample system of city water-works which draw their supplies from Lake Roland, six miles from the city, on the Northern Central

*See Weishampel's "Stranger in Baltimore."

railway. From this lake, which is seven miles in circumference, run conduits to Hampden and Mount Royal reservoirs. The city has recently purchased, at the cost of $350,000, the water rights of the Great Gunpowder river, and has already provided a supply of pure water for a population of a million inhabitants. The drives along Charles Street avenue, which leads from the city six miles out into a lovely wooded country sprinkled with fine villas and cottages to Lake Roland, to the Sheppard Asylum for the Insane, and to numerous other institutions, are all crowded in summer with lines of carriages and pedestrians. In Green Mount cemetery, at the junction of Belvidere street and North avenue, there are many beautiful monuments, and the grounds of Loudon park, Mount Olivet, Mount Carmel, and the "Western," all within short distances of the city, are beautifully laid out and planted with fine trees.

Patterson park, in the eastern section of the city, is but small as compared with its gigantic neighbor of the west, but has been very handsomely adorned, and from it superb views of the harbor and of the mighty Chesapeake are to be had.

The proposed enlargement of the city, which now covers but 10,000 acres, will embrace within Baltimore limits Clifton park, the site of the projected Hopkins University, and many pretty suburban villages into which manufacturing enterprise has already begun to penetrate. In addition to its parks, Baltimore has many beautiful public squares scattered throughout the different sections. In the western portion are Union, Franklin, and Harlem Squares, all surrounded by choice and commodious mansions. In the north-west is Lafayette Square; in the centre stands the noble Monument Square; in the north-east and the east Madison and Jackson Squares give shady refuges to the inhabitants, and the population in the southern portion flies from the summer heats to the cool breezes in Battery Square.

View of the Railroad and River, from the Mountains at Harper's Ferry.

The extension of the city limits is imperatively demanded by most of the citizens. The inhabitants are anxious to see the straggling villages, located within one or two miles of Baltimore's boundaries, compelled to contribute to the support of the metropolis from which they derive so many benefits. Their ambition, also, to rank Baltimore as the fourth city in the United States makes them anxious for increase of population, and many favor the annexation of the whole of Baltimore county, thus giving the city a chance for indefinite expansion. The old boundaries established by legislative enactment in 1816 are ridiculously within the proper limits of the present metropolis. Waverley, a lively village north of Baltimore, and the former seat of wealthy Maryland families; Woodberry, under the shadow of Druid Hill, an extensive cotton and machine manufacturing point; Mount Washington, perched on picturesque hills within a few minutes' ride of Baltimore by the Northern Central railway; Brooklyn, south-east of the city, possessing a land-locked harbor and a water-front nearly two miles in length; Towsontown, Govanstown, and Picksville, the last noted as the location of one of the earliest built arsenals of the General Government, are all destined to come under the control of Baltimore.

The school system of Baltimore is admirable, and will compare favorably with that of any community in the United States. The schools are under the control of a board of twenty commissioners, presided over by one chosen from their number and by the Superintendent of Schools and his assistants. The youth who passes through the primary and grammar schools and the City College of Baltimore, receives a liberal education. The total number of pupils enrolled in the public schools of the city in 1873 was 40,185; and the expenditures for white and colored schools, of which latter there are at present fifteen, amounted to nearly $500,000. The sexes are educated separately. The female high schools are the most admirable institutions of their kind in the South, and there are few in the North which equal them. The Baltimore City College, which has been granted $150,000 for the erection of a new building, has a high scholastic standard, and is eminently prosperous; and the normal school for the education of teachers yearly sends forth many competent graduates.

The press of Baltimore is enterprising in aiding to develop the commercial greatness of the city. The *American*, the *Gazette*, and the *Sun*, all have large and finely-equipped establishments. The *American* was founded in 1773 as the *Maryland Journal and Baltimore Advertiser;* the *Sun* and *Gazette* are younger. The *Bulletin* is a literary journal of much excellence. In Baltimore is also the office of the *Southern Magazine*, the only monthly periodical of any importance issued in the South.

Leaving Baltimore by the Baltimore and Ohio railroad, and crossing over Gwynn's Falls, on the superb Carrollton viaduct, the traveler will find at almost every turn a profusion of bold and romantic scenery. At Washington Junction, formerly known as the Relay House, a fine hotel has been erected by the railway company; and in summer hundreds of youths and maidens, from Washington and Baltimore, angle for trout and for each other's hearts beside the little stream which comes down from the mountains.

From the Thomas viaduct, the noble granite structure which spans the stream sixty-six feet above its bed, one can see the pretty village of Elkridge Landing. Time was when vessels of small tonnage from London used to come up the stream, which now would scarcely float a skiff, and anchor at Elkridge Landing to be loaded with tobacco.

At Ellicott's Mills, a charming old town, the Patapsco river runs through a bold and rocky passage, and from the railroad one may see the huge mass of granite known as the Tarpeian Rock. At Mount Airy and at Frederick Junction there are many fine out-looks over the fertile valleys and broken hills. At Frederick Junction, or as it is better known, Monocacy, one may visit the battle-ground where General Lew. Wallace made his gallant stand at the Monocacy bridge, on the 9th of July, 1864, and prevented the enemy from making a victorious advance upon Washington.

From Frederick Junction a branch line of rail communicates with Frederick City, a well built town with broad, straight streets, bordered with stone mansions, and possessing many handsome churches and flourishing educational institutions. From Monocacy the Baltimore and Ohio railroad traverses the beautiful valley lying between the Monocacy river and the Catoctin mountains. At Point of Rocks, a bold promontory formed by the profile of the Catoctin mountain, whose base is washed by the Potomac on the Maryland side, the railroad passes through a tunnel drilled fifteen hundred feet into the solid rock. It traverses the battle-field at South Mountain, running at the foot of a precipice for three or four miles, and, passing Hagerstown Junction, enters the great gorge at Harper's Ferry.

Thomas Jefferson immortalized Harper's Ferry by his words as John Brown did by his deeds. The rock on which Jefferson is said to have sat when he wrote his "Notes on Virginia" commands a fine view of the junction of the Potomac and the Shenandoah rivers, in the great gorge which forms one of the most picturesque bits of mountain scenery in the South. On either side of the eminence known as Cemetery Hill, on which Jefferson's Rock stands, rise up majestic mountains, rugged and difficult of access—the Maryland and Loudon Heights. The Maryland hills rise to 2,000 feet above the level of the sea, and the others are still clad in primitive forests, where the foot of man seldom treads. The Potomac, which rises in Western Virginia, and rushes

Jefferson's Rock, Harper's Ferry.

impetuously, like some mountain sprite, down through the Alleghanies, traverses the northern extremity of the valleys of West Virginia, and forms the boundary between that State and Maryland.

On the rugged cliffs are various fancied shapes and faces, and travelers are invited to discover, in a rock on the Maryland side, a fanciful and certainly feeble resemblance to George Washington.

The village of Harper's Ferry, before the war, contained 3,000 population, and was the site of a national armory, for which the immense water power rendered it valuable. When the late war broke out many of the old inhabitants cast their lot with the Confederacy, but great numbers also sided with the Government of the Union. The population has been materially changed, and to-day is composed of 1,600 whites and 700 blacks. The Baltimore and Ohio railroad has pushed its tracks across the Potomac at this point on a magnificent bridge, and the Winchester and Potomac railway has its northern terminus at Harper's

Cumberland Narrows and Mountains.

Ferry. The scenery along the Chesapeake and Ohio canal, whose banks the line of railway follows for many miles between Harper's Ferry and Washington, and by the rugged edges of the great cliffs westward from the little mountain town, is exceedingly fine. In summer a ride on the banks of this canal affords a constant succession of delicious landscapes, still-life pictures, and sweet vistas of romantic woodlands.

Harper's Ferry was named after Mr. Robert Harper, a native of Oxford in England, who established the first ferry over the Potomac in the mountains, and who was shrewd enough to join the American colonists when they made their strike for freedom. The Ferry is said to have been chosen as the site of a national armory, in 1794, by General Washington himself. The establishments there were very extensive, and their ruins—for the buildings were burned during the war—extend for a long distance beside the tracks of the Baltimore and Ohio railroad.

In the little engine-house, still pointed out from the platform of the depot of the railway station, John Brown made his defense against the excited inhabitants and the Virginian militia when he was inaugurating his raid for the purpose of liberating the slaves of Virginia. The engine-house is a small brick building near the old armory gate, and the Government would do well to see that it is preserved as an historical memorial, for around it and from it was fought the first battle of the great war which finally raged for four years throughout the South.

Not far from Harper's Ferry, on the Winchester and Potomac railroad, is the little hamlet of Charlestown, where John Brown was executed under the laws of the State of Virginia in 1859. Early in 1861 the armory buildings were burned, together with fifteen thousand stand of arms stored in them, to prevent the Confederates from profiting by their capture, and the Southern forces soon took possession of Harper's Ferry. Throughout the war it was occupied and re-occupied by the Union forces; the heights around glistened with bayonets; and the town has not yet fairly recovered from the demoralization consequent on its unfortunate condition during the civil struggle. Harper's Ferry was long the base of supplies for the armies of Banks and Fremont when they were operating against Stonewall Jackson in the Valley. In September of 1862 there was a grand artillery duel between the opposing forces stationed on the heights, when Jackson and Hill attacked Harper's Ferry with their army corps. On that occasion the Maryland heights were abandoned by a Federal officer, who was cashiered for his misconduct, but killed by a shell shortly after he had given the order for the surrender of Harper's Ferry to the Confederates.

Cumberland Viaduct, Maryland.

The scene on the whole peninsula formed by the Potomac and Shenandoah, at the time that McClellan's army was concentrated about Harper's Ferry, has been described as exceedingly fine. All the heights were aglow with thousands of watch-fires, and from Camp Hill, a ridge dividing the villages of Harper's Ferry and Bolivar, one could hear the hum of voices, like the murmur of the ocean, rising up from the valleys and drifting down from the mountains.

The village clusters picturesquely among the sides of the steep hills; no hum of spindles or plying of hammers disturbs its primitive quiet. An ancient flight of stone steps leads up to a quaint church on the hill-side, and beyond the path conducts the visitor to Jefferson's Rock.	Hardly a quarter of a mile from the engine-house where John Brown struck the first blow for the freedom of the American slave, rise the walls of Storer College, an institution endowed by private munificence for the education of freedmen, and sending out every year, competent teachers of both sexes, who labor to educate the colored race.

A short distance to the west, beyond Harper's Ferry, the Baltimore and Ohio railroad passes through a projecting rock in a tunnel eighty feet long, whence a magnificent view of the pass through the mountains to the confluence of the Potomac and Shenandoah is presented.	The road also passes through Kearneys-ville in West Virginia, the scene of many sharp cavalry fights between Generals Pleasanton, Averill, Custer, and Merritt with the Confederates under Fitz Lee and Stewart, and within seven miles of Sharpsburg, whence the tourist can reach the celebrated battle-field of Antietam.

Harper's Ferry, Maryland.

Sharpsburg bears many marks of the great fight of 1862, and near the battle-field is a monument to the slaughter of those dread September days, in the shape of a fine national cemetery.

Martinsburg, in West Virginia, on the line of the Baltimore and Ohio railroad, was the scene of many Confederate raids, but is now a prosperous town, whose chief reliance is upon the extensive iron works established there by the railroad company.	At St. John's Run travelers leave the rail for Berkley Springs, a favorite summer resort at the eastern base of the Warm Spring Ridge in West Virginia.	At Cumberland one enters into the mountain region of the narrow western part of Maryland, and into the magnificent valley from which Baltimore draws its enormous coal trade.	Cumberland is a handsome town with many fine churches and banks.	It lies in a noble amphitheatre of mountains, and all around it and beyond it the scenery is very picturesque.

At Piedmont, twenty-eight miles beyond Cumberland, the foot of the Alleghanies is reached, and the road, climbing the mountains, passes Altamont on the extreme summit of the Alleghany ridge, where the streams divide, flowing in one direction toward the Gulf of Mexico, and the other toward the Atlantic; then passes by pretty Oakland, a famous resort for summer tourists, and descends rapidly along high and precipitous embankments to the banks of the Cheat river, a turbulent mountain stream, whose waters are of sombre hue.

For many miles beyond the Cheat river the road winds down the steep sides of the mountains, and, entering the great Western coal-fields, passes through the Ringwood tunnel, 4,100 feet long, and completed at the end of five years' labor at a cost of a million dollars. From the tunnel at Newburg, in Western Virginia, the railway line descends a steep hill-side, and thence finds its way through a country rich in coal and petroleum, but only sprinkled here and there by small and uninteresting villages, to Pittsburg, on the Ohio river.

The old town of Annapolis, on the Severn, near Chesapeake, still the capital of Maryland, is the seat of the United States Naval Academy, established there in 1845. It was founded in 1649, and in 1708, in honor of Queen Anne, its name was changed from Anne Arundel Town to the present one. It was at Annapolis that General Washington resigned his commission at the close of the Revolution. The State-House, and St. John's College, founded in 1784, are the only important public buildings.

The present debt of the State, over and above its assets, is $6,219,172; but when the indebtedness of the Chesapeake and Ohio Canal Company to the commonwealth, which amounts to more than twenty million dollars, is transferred from the schedule of unproductive assets to that of interest-paying securities, a fund will be furnished by which the entire State debt can be taken up. The last Legislature appropriated $50,000 for the establishment of schools for colored children, and a colored normal school is in excellent condition.

Old John Cupid, a Negro Herb Doctor.

LXXXVI.

SOUTHERN CHARACTERISTICS—STATE PRIDE—THE INFLUENCE OF RAILROADS—POOR WHITES—THEIR HABITS.

WHILE I cannot agree with the amiable gentleman in Savannah who one day assured me that the people of the North and South were two distinct nations, and that the time would come when they would separate, I still recognize essential differences between the inhabitants of the Northern and Southern States. These differences are not merely climatic; they were inbred by the system and tendencies which have been so lately done away with. Between the citizen of Massachusetts and the dweller in South Carolina a broad and deep gulf so long existed, that it is not strange that the habits, the customs, and the language of the people should differ in many particulars.

The first thing, however, which strikes the stranger as peculiar in visiting the Southern States is that the inhabitants of each State have remarkably distinguishing characteristics. Because one knows the Virginian character he cannot safely draw inferences as to that of the South Carolinian; because he has studied the types in the bayou regions of Louisiana he cannot presume to a knowledge of the Mississippian of the Gulf coast. In short, the variety of origin and ancestry in the Southern States has left indelible marks upon the populations.

People in all the States, however, take what seems to Northern men, and also to the European, overweening pride in their State, their county, and even the immediate neighborhood

Southern Types—Come to Market.

in which they were born. Nothing is more common than to hear a Southerner announce himself, on being introduced, as from a certain county, and he will very likely add that it is a section famed for certain excellences and for the valor of its inhabitants. This is not said from any motives of self-conceit, because the same man who vaunts the virtues of his neighbors will willingly compare himself unfavorably with them; but it is due to a genuine love and a deep-seated affection for the soil. The Southerners have been so long emphatically an agricultural people, and have conquered at such expense and with such difficulty a great portion of the land which belongs to them, that they love it with an intensity and devotion equaled in the world only by the attachment of the Swiss peasant to his peaks and the Frenchman to his vineyard.

The railroads which now penetrate the South in every direction, and the prosaic yet cosmopolitan "through routes" which, to Southern eyes, dash with such irreverent lack of compunction across State boundaries, and annihilate so recklessly all local sentiment, are doubtless doing much to annul the devotion to State rights. Curious travelers in the South have remarked that, as fast as a railroad penetrates a section, sentiment with regard to matters in the outside world becomes liberalized along the line. The current of through travel pouring over the great roadways from New York to New Orleans, and from the West and St. Louis to the Atlantic coast, has done much to shake that isolated independence once so conspicuous in the Southerner of the country regions, and to render him more like his bustling and active fellow-citizen of the North and West.

However much the hundred railroads covering the South with an iron network may do to destroy the old and too earnest attachment of each individual

Southern Types—A Southern Plough Team.

to his particular State and neighborhood, that attachment will still remain for many years one of the salient points of Southern character. Two gentlemen meeting upon a railway train often introduce themselves something after this fashion:

" Are you from this State, sir ?"

" No, sir, I am from Kentucky, sir," or " Tennessee, sir," as the case may be; whereupon the first interlocutor immediately defines his nativity, and the two enter into an amicable discussion of political and social issues. It is not unusual for strangers thus meeting to inquire of each other the counties and even the towns in which they were respectively born, and from the gravity and dignity of their conversation, and the evident pride which each takes in detailing the advantages and peculiar blessings of his neighborhood, one might fancy them a couple of foreigners from distant lands who had accidentally met. As a rule, two Southerners traveling in a State remote from that in which they were born find an instant bond of communion in the fact that they are from the same commonwealth.

Sometimes one sees on the cars or on the steamers a tall, lank Southerner anxiously inquiring if there be among the passengers any one from his native State; and if he finds such a one, he goes to him with effusive friendship and adopts him as his comrade. A friend has told me a curious incident of this kind which he saw in a rough part of the South-west. While traveling on an obscure railroad in some forest, the car door opened; and a lank individual thrust his countenance through the aperture, crying out in an appealing manner: "Is there any one heah from Tennessee?" No response being made, his voice was presently heard repeating the same inquiry in the neighboring car.

There are, of course, several important facts to bear in mind when one is judging of the peculiarities of the Southern people. It should be remembered

Southern Types — Negro Boys Shelling Peas.

that there were but two classes in the South under the old system, the high up and the low down, Dives in his hall and Lazarus among the dogs at the gate,— the gentleman planter and the ruffian, brawling, ill-educated, and generally miserable poor white. The negro did not count; he was a commodity, an article of barter, classed familiarly as "nigger;" had no identity; was supposed to possess little consciousness, moral or otherwise; and while practically·he was every now and then treated with great kindness and forbearance by those who were his absolute masters, still he did nothing either to build up or solidify society. Now-a-days a middle class is gradually springing into existence, bridging the once impassable gulf between the "high up" and the "low down," and some of the more intelligent and respectable negroes are taking rank in this class. The low down element has perhaps received more benefit from the results of the war than has the negro or his master.

The introduction of manufactures here and there in the South has drawn into large towns some of the white population which was once utterly useless and degraded. A noteworthy instance which I have already mentioned is that of the hundreds of cleanly and handsome girls in the cotton-mills of Georgia. Many of them have been transformed from slouching, unkempt, and gawky country girls into tidy and thrifty operatives, with some little money in bank, and prospects of a social position far higher than they could ever have hoped to gain under the old system.

The poor white still clings to many of his eccentricities. One finds an excellent chance to observe the peculiar habits of this class by traveling with the great current of emigration from Alabama, Georgia, and Mississippi south-westward to Arkansas and Texas. Now and then, in our long journeys from one end of the South to the other, we fell in with, and traveled for days in the company of, representatives of what was formerly the low down class. We chatted in the friendliest and freest manner with the pretty, soft-voiced girls from Alabama, as we rode across the great plains of Texas, and were no whit deterred from conversation by the fact that they dipped long pine sticks in yellow snuff, and chewed the sticks while they talked with us. Sometimes, however, we felt like remonstrating with the mothers who gave their children sticks from the family snuff-bottle, and taught them the disgusting habit.

The men were almost without exception clad in homespun garments of a blue or butternut color, always neatly made. A slouch hat was their invariable head-gear—a hat, too, which seemed to have undergone more than the ordinary vicissitudes, which one could never imagine to have had band or buckle or definite color—a hat much battered by the elements, and occasionally perforated with buckshot. Out of ten thousand people of this class, not one had in his face a particle of color; all had the same dead, pallid complexion. The women whom we saw, and who were doubtless fair specimens of their class, were, when young, quite pretty; gracious, but exceedingly timid. On the whole, when the snuff-stick was laid by, and their lustrous brown eyes were playing at hide-and-seek with thought, they seemed charming as Italian peasant girls, or maids of Marseilles; but when from their sweet lips came the flat and harsh accents of their native mountains and plains, the illusion was dispelled.

My observation justifies me in the conclusion that the poor white always has a numerous family. It was not at all uncommon to see lean fathers and lank and scrawny mothers entering the cars, followed by a brood of ten or, more children of all sizes. There was something touching, too, in the rough sympathy and helpfulness of the members of these families one for another, during their long and weary journeys. The little girls, whose thin but pretty faces were hidden beneath sun-bonnets, and the rough boys, with fists like sledge-hammers, and faces drawn down with wrinkles of fever and ague, each carried some bundle of household gear; the mother usually bore a basket containing a ham, some coarse corn-bread, and, mayhap, a package of fruit, as well as the snuff-bottle; and the father bore the family rifle, its long barrels weather-stained and rusty.

The ignorance and timidity of these poor people, during their journeys to new homes, was painful as well as ludicrous to witness. Sometimes a family on entering a car would stand utterly bewildered, not seeming to know whether to sit or slink into a corner, until the conductor, or the "captain," as he is called in the South, marshaled them to seats. On one occasion, being startled by the pressure of a brawny hand on my shoulder, I turned to confront the father of an interesting family of eleven, who, pointing to his wife, said in a hoarse whisper:

"Stranger, the captain did n't give her no yaller ticket; I reckon he done forgot."

Then showing me the yellow check which the conductor had given him in return for his ticket, he earnestly inquired the meaning of the lettering upon it. Surprised that a man whose appearance indicated intelligence of no mean order could not read, I ventured to ask him if such was the case, and if his family was unable to read or write. I found that no member of the party had the slightest acquaintance with anything educational, and that in the whole course of half a century of toil, the old man had rarely been more than ten miles from home. Now he was about to try the far-away plains of Texas, and he looked forward to it as a mighty change. The future seemed a great gulf before him, and he informed me, with the ghost of a sigh, as he shifted his tobacco from one cheek to the other, that he never would have believed "befo' the surrendah" that he could have undertaken a wholesale emigration.

Southern Types—A "Likely Girl" with her Baby.

Few people who have not wandered up and down the highways and byways of the South can appreciate the immensity of the emigration from the old cotton States to the extreme South-west. That Texas will speedily have a vast population, drawn from these cotton States, and bitterly necessitous in matters of education and elevation, there is no doubt. The destiny of these poor whites, who have fled before the changed order of things in their homes, is somewhat uncertain. If they could but acquire habits of solid industry, and learn to accumulate in their rough way some little surplus means, they might easily be redeemed from their present degraded condition; but Texas is vast, the means of living easily to be had there, and so it is to be feared that the mass of the poor white race will be improved in little except its material condition. Those who remain at home are certainly, as I have said, improving as a whole; yet the Sand-hillers of South Carolina, the Crackers of Georgia and Florida, the wretched masses along the lowlands of the Atlantic coast, and the mountaineers in some portions of Virginia, Eastern Tennessee, and

Western North Carolina, present many discouraging signs. In some cases, they do not advance as rapidly as does the negro; but the latter, immediately after the war, had a great incentive to a rapid growth, and it was to be expected that

Southern Types—Catching his Breakfast.

he would improve his newly-acquired opportunity. I do not think the mass of poor whites really appreciated the immense difference which the war effected in their social position, nor will they thoroughly understand it for many years to come—not until the progress of events under the new *régime* has wiped out the old aristocracy, and brought its genuine leveling influence wholly to bear. Should immigration make as great progress in the other States of the South as it is now making in Virginia, there will, of course, be a radical change in the character of the poor white population. We may expect in a few years, as the country fills up, and the persistent idlers are crowded to the wall, to see the Southern poor white transformed into an industrious and valuable member of society. The pride of State, heretofore alluded to, has doubtless made it much harder for the native Southerner to emigrate than it would have been for citizens of other sections. I shall not readily forget the intense delight with which a Mississippian, returning from a disastrous colonization experiment in Brazil, hailed the bluffs and the rose-embowered gardens of beautiful Natchez as we drew near to them one spring evening.

"Thar," he said, "is ez good a country ez the sun shines on, and if all them cussed fools as went to the Brazils was hyar now, they would say so too. Give me old Mississippi in mine."

The affection for the State as distinguished from the section was shown all through the late war. When we were called upon to listen to the recital of battles, in which, by the way, it was noteworthy that the Confederates always won, we remarked the pride and dignity with which the superior excellences of any special State in question were asserted. In fact, we learned to believe that the Southerner often thinks, as the Englishman said of all Americans, that "he is as good as any one else, and better too."

LXXXVII.

THE CARRYING OF WEAPONS—MORAL·CHARACTER OF THE NEGROES.

SOME people are inclined to place a good deal of stress upon the supposed fact that the mass of Southern males carry weapons, and that their sense of honor is so highly wrought that their conversation is guarded. While it must be admitted that great numbers of Southerners habitually go armed, and that in some States they are prone to fight on small provocation, my experience has been that the most cultured and refined gentlemen rarely bear a weapon, and scoff at the idea of the necessity of carrying one.

In our journeys, we traveled not unfrequently in regions remote from the railroads, or along rivers, where the people were somewhat rough, but never on any occasion did we see pistol or knife drawn or displayed during our  fourteen months' stay in the South. While, however, we never saw weapons displayed, we heard plenty of stories to confirm the impression that large classes carried them and used them freely.

There is no doubt that a great proportion of the Southern people believe that they must avenge any fancied slight upon their honor by personal punishment of the individual who has offered it, and so they have recourse to the revolver and the knife, where the Northern man would carry the case into the courts. The worst phase of the Southern character is illustrated in the unwillingness to adopt legal methods in the settlement of dis-

Southern Types—Negro Shoeblacks.

putes. Under the *régime* of reconstruction the juries of the Federal Courts are detested, appeals to them being considered a greater ignominy than those to the State Courts. The higher class of gentlemen rarely settle disputes by shooting or stabbing, but it is probable that the only thing which will restrain the rougher whites from a practice unworthy of our civilization, and from ideas of personal satisfaction which are alike murderous and contemptible, will be the progress of education.

It is, perhaps, too true that the recent accession of the Democrats to power in Texas and Arkansas has increased the number of misdeeds there. That the Democratic party in the South is the party of law and order is by no means strictly true; the leaders of the Democratic party are unfortunately people of inflammable methods of speech, and often, in the excitement of political harangues, give advice which their rude followers interpret to suit themselves, and which sometimes results in bloodshed. The public, however, should be extremely careful not to judge of the Southern character by the greatly exaggerated accounts of outrages with which many political newspapers are filled during the progress of a campaign. The fact that in a journey of 25,000 miles, nearly a thousand of which I traveled on horseback, through mountain regions, I saw no weapons drawn, and not a single instance of assault, lynching, or even drunken brawls, ought to be considered as good testimony in favor of the Southerners. The Northern people in their judgment are too apt to confuse the classes, and it is undoubtedly true that in some parts of the North prejudiced persons still fancy the South a barbarous region infested with ruffians of the old border type.

The negroes certainly rejoice in the possession of weapons to a large extent. Since the war every black man has felt himself called upon to own a shot-gun, but to his credit be it said that very rarely in his history as a freedman has he been guilty of the murder of white people for purposes of vengeance. He is deterred in a large measure from the greater crimes to which his ignorant condition and lack of moral training may impel him by the certainty of punishment, just as he is deterred in some of the States, where he has not political power, from petty and grand larceny. When traveling through sparsely settled regions in many of the Southern States one may generally leave his personal property unprotected by lock or key. The negro will not steal it. In some of the States petty larceny by negroes is punished with undue severity, in imitation of the barbarous English sentences which send a man to jail for eighteen months for taking a loaf of bread. Rape and similar crimes, of which in all the States negroes are occasionally guilty, are invariably punished with death; and the rape, justly considered a capital offence by all nations, is almost always avenged at the hands of Judge Lynch.

The negro is far from being a savage, even in his most degraded condition. Whiskey, however, operates as badly upon him as upon the whites; it prompts him to an indiscriminate use of the revolver and the knife, when, if he were in his sober senses, he would be contented with a solid bout at fisticuffs. The negro, however, rarely cherishes a feud for many years, as the low whites do. His vengeance is prompt, or his careless nature leads him, if he delays, to forget it. No Southern man, even when surrounded by a hundred negroes politically hostile to him on any remote plantation, fears for his life. A kind of tacit confession of his superiority pervades his dusky dependents, and he might kill half-a-dozen of them without incurring any danger of Lynch law. In the cities where the negroes flock together idly and become more vicious than in the country, occasional cutting and shooting among themselves are not uncommon; and now and then when a white man kills one of their number, they resent the slaughter by riot, but they rarely bring the offender to justice. It would, I think, be perfectly fair to say that not half-a-dozen white men have been hung in the South since the war, for the murder of negroes. I believe conviction for such a crime would be quite impossible in the present state of opinion in some Southern States.

That there is a large class of negroes who are intrinsically mean and gravitating steadily downward toward the worst phases of rascality, there is no

Southern Types—A Little Unpleasantness.

doubt. About one-third of the negroes in the South is in a very hopeful condition; another third seems to be in a comparatively stationary attitude; another third is absolutely good for nothing, prefers theft to honest labor, and makes no steady progress in morality, refinement, or education of any kind. The religion of the negroes in many parts of the South appears pretty completely divorced from morality.

It is difficult to persuade one's self that the blacks as yet deserve recognition as a moral race. Their best friends will admit that, though very religious, they are also very immoral. Adultery, which is a mortal sin among the Northern and Southern white religionists, is simply venial to the black man. His conver-

sion to the religion of the Lord does not seem to build up the negro's conscience.
The tough moral fibre of the Anglo-Saxon, which came only by slow growth, is
not perceptible in the negro; neither could it be expected, considering that he
was brought from the jungles of Africa into a comparatively wild region in
America, and that, under the dominion of slavery, his moral growth was but
lazily helped.   That the negro has made progress no one will be inclined to
dispute, but he started from such a low and bestial condition that he has as yet
reached only the confines of real Christianity.   He tries to be a good Christian,
and yet is not always satisfied with one wife.   He is not restrained by the
fear of what people will say of him, as the whites universally are.   The moral

Southern Types—"Going to Church."

tone of all his fellows is so low, the temptations to occasional lapses from virtue
on the part of his spiritual advisers of his own color are often so great, that it is
not astonishing that his backslidings are frequent.   His idea is that salvation is
attained by shouting.   The Anglo-Saxon believes that salvation can only be
attained by self-denial, faith, and hard work.   In some parts of the South the
negro, while under conviction, goes into spasms, and is unfit for his daily duties.
If he is a cook he spoils the dinner, and if he is a field-hand his master finds
occasion to complain of him.   In Virginia, and doubtless in many other States,
the negro alludes to this spiritual condition as being "in the wilderness."

He has found no peace, he cannot profess to be converted until he sees a great light, hears a voice from Heaven, and has a visitation from an angel of God. Then his spirit is filled at once with brightness and light, and in the public revival-meetings he often jumps six feet into the air, embraces with effusion all the deacons and ministers, and in some of the States he is not considered as converted unless he can say this formula:

" The Lord has taken my feet out of the miry clay and set them on the rock of ages, where the very gates of hell shall not prevail against them."

If the brother or sister under conviction cannot say this phrase exactly, the preachers and deacons will tell them that they are not yet out of the wilderness, and will refuse to admit them to religious communion.

All the negro meetings which I attended were marked by intense convulsions of the muscles on the part of all the people present. Even the best educated colored ministers seemed to rely upon theatrical contortions of face, and mighty. stampings of feet and waving of arms, for effect on the congregations. Listening outside the open windows of a negro church in Florida one evening, I heard the preacher furiously pounding the Bible which lay on the sacred desk. His words were incoherent, his logic was sadly at fault; some of his appeals seemed ludicrous, but every thump on the holy volume brought a tempest of shoutings, sighs, and moans from the dusky hearers. On the plantations the camp-meetings and revivals sometimes totally unfit the negroes for labor during the whole week. Men and women foam at the mouth, wander about the fields and forests half distracted, a spasm of spiritual insanity having taken possession of them. In such moments of rare enthusiasm they sometimes descend to orgies; whiskey and licentiousness do their work, and the whole meeting will be transformed into an assembly of blackamoor maenads and satyrs. A clever Northerner, who has for many years dwelt in the South, once told me that

Southern Types— A Negro Constable.

he considered the Christianity of the negro as Fetichism with a Christian cloak on.

This may seem a hard and unfriendly judgment of negro character, but the careful observer who studies the characteristics of the whole black population will yet not fail to see signs of encouragement. He will discover that a mighty uplifting has really been going on since 1865, and that an influx of good teachers, who shall teach industry, thrift, continence, and self-respect, will in another decade raise the four and a-half million negroes in the South to pretty near the level of Christian manhood and womanhood.   Such discouraging views of the negroes in the Gulf States as are taken by many of the native whites, are the result of a mistaken judgment.   Even Caucasian ministers of the gospel, whose hearts are supposed to be filled with charity for and faith in all men, refuse to see any tendency on the part of poor Sambo to improve his advantages.   They do not seem to understand that moral growth is slow, and that so long as the negro remains in ignorance, and, in a measure, uncertain as to his future condition, he will not develop very rapidly.

Traveling one day from Jackson to Grenada in Mississippi, I observed a bright, intelligent-looking negro woman seated near me in the smoking-car which I had entered for a moment.   By her side was her little girl, three or four years of age.   At one of the wayside stations a smart mulatto man entered the car, and, being acquainted with the young woman, speedily addressed her thus:

" Why, Sister Smith, how is you ?"

" Why, Brudder Brown, tol'able, thank you; how is yourself ?"

" I 's tol'able; always tol'able, thank you."

" Is you quite sho' you is tol'able ?"

" Oh, yas; I 's tol'able, very tol'able, thank you."

" Whar is you gwine, Brudder Brown ?"

" Oh, I 's gwine up hyar to 'tend a meeting; is dat your little gal, Sister Smith ?"

" Yas, dat 's my little gal."

" How is your little gal, Sister Smith ?"

" Oh, she is tol'able, thank you, very tol'able; is your children tol'able ?"

" Yas, yas thank you."

" Is you married, Sister Smith ?"

" No, Lor! I is n't married; what would I be married for ?"

" Whar did you get dat little gal, Sister Smith ?"

" Dat 's one I done foun', Brudder Brown ;" whereupon the two indulged in a sympathetic giggle.

But the teachers of the various Freedmen's Aid and Missionary Associations, as well as Southern people of high character, such as the daughters of Christian ex-Confederate soldiers, who do not count it a shame to teach the ignorant negro, are gradually shaping opinion favorable to marriage among the blacks; and while great numbers of ex-slaves still prefer the old fashion of living together so long as they can agree, without having any sacred compact between them, they feel that they still have a duty toward their offspring, and illegitimate birth is slowly becoming among the blacks, as among the whites, a cause for reproach.

In many of the States until very recently, the railroad stations had rooms over the doors of which were signs marked, " For colored people only."   But this odious distinction against race is, I believe, gradually dying out.   I do not remember to have noticed it often.   In some sections of Georgia it may perhaps still be seen, but I would not affirm that it is general even in that State. Negroes and whites, however, do not ride together in the same railway cars, in those States where the blacks are absolutely masters of the political situation, nor do I believe that the whites would tolerate the admission of the black race to an equal share in the first-class accommodations of travel. The blacks usually buy second-class tickets, and as the Southern railroads are very poor in rolling stock, black men and black women are crowded together into smoking-cars of trains where the white men who enter to smoke, pay as little attention to the etiquette of travel as if no members of the female sex were present. There is an occasional outburst on the part of the whites when an aggressive negro attempts to assert his right to a berth in a sleeping-car or to enter a first-class carriage.

In South-western Virginia I once entered the smoking-car of a through train, and was suddenly accosted in a fierce manner by an intelligent looking mulatto who inquired if I was born in the South, and if I ever owned slaves. Responding in the negative, he began a violent harangue against the railroad authorities, saying that it made his blood boil to be refused a first-class ticket; that he was from Tennessee, and as good as any white man, and added very bitterly that he was "damned if he appreciated it." He was well dressed, cleanly, and appeared decently educated. In a New York horse-car, room would have been made for him even on a crowded seat, but the Southern people dislike to establish a precedent for the admission of the colored race to the same facilities of travel enjoyed by the whites.

In Louisiana and South Carolina the negroes do from time to time monopolize the trains, and create disturbance when their presence is objected to; but if they insisted upon it as a general thing the whites would arm themselves and speedily check any such aggression. The negroes as a mass have not, however, even where their civil rights are practically gained, been difficult to manage in this delicate matter. They avoid a collision with white prejudices as much as possible; as great numbers of them are ragged and engaged in menial occupations, their presence in a car where elegantly-dressed ladies and gentlemen are seated would certainly be far from agreeable, and they recognize this fact quite as readily as they could be expected to do. Until they have gained much more property than they at present possess as a class, they will not be likely to secure the recognition of their equality, which they certainly desire, however little they may assert it.

LXXXVIII.

DIALECT—FORMS OF EXPRESSION—DIET.

THE noticeable differences in dialect and mode of expression between the North and South have been noted, caricatured, and exemplified hundreds of times. The lower class of Southern whites have undoubtedly caught some methods of speech, and certain fatal defects of pronunciation, from the negro.

Southern Types—The Wolf and the Lamb in Politics.

Sometimes, as we have seen in South Carolina, the rude and coarse dialect of the plantation hand, who never in his long life had an instant's education, is reflected in the speech of the haughty and high-bred gentleman's son. But this will no longer be so. The intimate communion which was possible in the days of slavery between the white and the black is now, for a dozen obvious reasons, impossible. The intermixture of dialects is as sure to be stopped as the commingling of bloods. Competent observers say that miscegenation was nearly ended by the war and the emancipation of the slave; that the social equality which certain of the whites in the South now seem to fear has been rendered impossible by the very event which established the independence of the negro. The two races are steadily drifting apart, so far as all intimate association is concerned.

No one can doubt that the negro who was born a slave still retains the profoundest respect for, and in general also a kind of admiration with regard to, his late master; but, except on remote plantations where, thus far, but small change in the habits and customs of the natives has resulted from the war, the white and black children do not associate in the friendly comity of old; a kind of barrier seems to have been erected between them, and it is but right it should be so. There seems no reason for believing that the negro cherishes any insane desire to promote miscegenation. There is a tendency in some sections of the South among the full-blacks to marry, as the whites phrase it, "above their color," or, as the negro himself would express it, "into America, and not back into Africa." A jet black man often shows a marked preference for a mulatto woman, and a full-black girl will not hesitate long in expressing her preference for a smart yellow boy of the modified and subdued African type over the thick-lipped, long-heeled negro who may also be enamored of her charms. A pupil in one of the Virginia schools for the colored people told a teacher that of her two suitors she liked the character of the one who was jet black the best, but that, altogether, she preferred the mulatto who also wooed her, because of his color and his refinement. But the full-blacks are gradually beginning to assert themselves, and certainly in South Carolina, and in many other sections, they have as much pride of race as has the haughty Caucasian.

Just how much influence the incapacity of the negro to pronounce many of our English words has had upon the speech of the Southern people it would be difficult to say. It is not probable that the masses in the lower class at the South would feel flattered if told that their speech much resembles that of the Africans. It may be said without exaggeration that all classes of Southerners find it impossible to pronounce the letter "r." They seem to have the same difficulty that the Parisian has in giving it its full roundness and completeness. Such words as "door" and "floor," and "before," are transformed into "do'" "flo'" and "befo'" by the lower class, while some educated and refined people pronounce them "doah," "floah," and almost invariably allude to our late unpleasantness as the "waw." The use of "I reckon," for "I guess," or "I think," is, of course, universal. Now and then the Southerner says "I calculate," or "I allow," but rarely "I guess," or "I think," unless in delicate deference to his Northern visitor.

The highly educated people of the South speak an elegant and chaste English, in which, by the way, they take an especial pride. The planter, the city merchant, the factor, the professional man of eminence, the lawyers and physicians, the doctors, and even the country squires, judges, and militia colonels, all are distinguished for an exactness and nicety in the use of language which is very agreeable. There is a refinement and courtesy in the manners of the country gentlemen, and an absence of anything like a relapse into the slang of the day, or familiar forms of expression, which are perhaps more noticeable in the North and West than in the South.

The joking and chaffing so common among acquaintances, and even strangers, in many parts of the North, is not understood at the South, and a Southerner will often fancy his dignity seriously offended by some sally which would pass unnoticed among other people. There is also an occasional undue assumption of dignity on the part of employés in public offices.

On one occasion, remonstrating with a clerk in the office of a Texas stage company because he demanded the moderate sum of four dollars and a-half in gold for transporting my trunk eighty miles, he flew into a towering passion and inquired if "I meant to tell him that he lied." Nothing would have been easier than to quarrel with him, yet a moment afterward he was convinced that my inquiry was justifiable.

A Northern gentleman, venturing to question the price of a telegram in the office of the telegraph company in a Mississippi town, was haughtily reminded by the chief clerk that he did n't allow his statements to be questioned. This excess of individualism, however, is perhaps a mark of provincial manners quite as much as of Southern breeding, and does not in any sense apply to the educated and refined Southerner.

To note the characteristics of the South properly, one would be compelled to classify them by States, as the citizen of Maryland would be loth to admit the justness of a judgment which would be reasonable with regard to Texas, and the Virginian would repel with indignation the assumption that he has a few traits which might very properly be ascribed to the people of Louisiana.

Recurring to the matter of speech and its peculiarities in the Southern States, it may be said that it is among the poor whites that eccentricities are mainly found.

The Union soldiers brought home with them an inexhaustible fund of stories illustrating the dialect of these people, and relate with gusto the anecdote of the venerable Georgia cracker dame, who, when a company of Kentucky Confederate cavalry passed her house, inquired:

"Be you-uns kim all the way from Kintuck, critter back, to fight for we-uns?"

The use of "we-uns" and "you-uns" is very noticeable in North Carolina and Eastern Tennessee, both in the mountains and valleys. The same thickness of pronunciation in certain words which is remarkable in the West, but never in the East, as in the words "there" and "where," and "here," which become, "thar," "whar" and "hyar," are observable among the lower classes in the South.

There are also certain shibboleths by which the traveler from south of Mason and Dixon's line is always marked in the North and in Europe. These are the before-mentioned inability to give the letter "r" its due, and the transformation of such words as "car" into "cyah."

Some waggish Northern critic has asserted that the mass of ex-slave-holders find great difficulty in pronouncing the word "negro," from their long habit of alluding to the black man only as a "nigger," and that they now-a-days call him a "niggro." But I suspect that there is a spice of malice in this hyper-critical statement.

The use of "I don't reckon" sometimes strikes one unpleasantly, coming, as it often does, at the end of a sentence. "Right smart" is used in a variety of ways never employed at the North. The Southerner says, "We shall have a right smart crop this season," or, "There was a right smart of people at the last meeting," or, "I shall have a right smart chance of business." "Right" is used pretty generally throughout the South in the sense in which Northerners use "very." Of a lady they say that she is right pretty, of a fruit that it is right good, of scenery that it is right magnificent.

Southern Types — Two Veterans Discussing the Political Situation.

With regard to distance, there seems in the back-country a charming disre-gard of actual measurement. The negro is especially vague in his statements as to the number of miles between any two towns. He will either tell you that it is a "right smart distance," or may state that it is "two good looks and a dog bark," or that it is "a hop, skip, and a go-so." This would hardly be credited unless one heard it. The negro was, up to the date of the war, intensely local in feeling. The boundary of his little neighborhood was to him the horizon where the world stopped, and, traveling but little, he got but slight idea of distances. In some portions of the Southern mountains we found the whites were very familiar with distances in their own State and counties, but not outside of those limits. The chief difficulty in obtaining accurate information from the negroes seemed to be their disinclination to assertion. A visitor to the Virginia springs noted as curious that the negroes there would not, as a rule, dissent from remarks by white people. If asked, " Does this stream run up hill?" the negro would be apt to say: "Yas, sah, reckon it do, sah;" but if the question were put in a leading form, as: "This stream runs down hill, of course, does it not?" he would say: "Sartinly, sah."

The use of the word "stranger," as applied to an individual whose name one is not familiar with, so common in the extreme West, we found to prevail among the mountain populations of the South, but so far as my observation went, nowhere else. Sometimes the natives whom we encountered would say, " Mistah," and pause, as if expecting you to supply your name. If you did not do so they would inquire, "What did you say your name was," or more frequently, "What mout your name be?" A curious form of assent, which must be heard to be appreciated, and which Dickens caricatured mercilessly when he first visited this country, prevails in the mountains of Eastern Tennessee and Western North Carolina. The following will serve as an example:

While discussing the outer world with old Parson Caton, in a remote mountain district of Tennessee, he inquired if New York was not a right smart place, and being assured that it was, he said with a rising inflection, "Yes, sir?" Whereupon I responded, "Yes, sir." "As likely a place as Louisville, I reckon," he added; to which I answered, "Yes, sir," he chiming in interrogatively, "Yes, sir?"

These mountain peculiarities of speech demand more study than we were able to give them. They strike the visitor at first very strangely, but he gradually becomes accustomed to them. They differ considerably from the barbarous nasal Yankee slang spoken in certain sections of New England, but they have, nevertheless, many points of resemblance to it. There is nowhere in the South any such conspicuous difference from Northern habits of speech as is found between the dialects of the French peasants living in two towns near each other. Some of the mountaineers speak of "hit," instead of "it," and emphasize the word as in this case: "I meant to have brought my gun, but I forgot *hit*."

Words of endearment between husband and wife in the South often show an unconscious borrowing from the negroes. Where the Northern husband habitually calls his wife "dear" or "darling," the Southern man says "honey," alike to his spouse and to his offspring.

The negro in South Carolina, and in other adjacent States, shows a tendency to render the English language more musical than it is when spoken by Anglo-Saxons. He gives an extra syllable to words which end abruptly, and puts a kind of rhythm into all that he says. The Virginia negro, especially when he shows the influence of mixed blood, copies the speech of the whites as nearly as possible, making some ludicrous errors when he attempts to catch the sonorous refrain of long words. He still speaks of people who impress him favorably as "quality folk," and now and then, when disdainfully describing some unimpressive people, will denominate them "white trash," or even admit that they are "worse than niggers." Entering Barnum's Hotel, in Baltimore, one evening, I found the colored bell-boys gathered round an old negro servant, who was reading from the evening paper some instance of unparalleled meanness which a white man had been guilty of. After he had finished the anecdote he said: "Boys, dat's— dat's real niggerism," thus expressing his contempt for the conduct of the white man in question.

In Natchez, on the Mississippi, I noticed that some of the white children, even those who attended private schools and were evidently kept from street communion with the negroes as much as possible, copied the defects of the colored man's speech. Our landlord's son, for instance, pointing to our carriage which had arrived at the door, said: "Da he," which was plantation slang for "There it is." Since the negroes gained their freedom, those among them who had been servants of wealthy gentlemen, and who had consequently been thrown into the company of white people, speak very good English, except when they endeavor to use long words, when they sometimes mix their meanings.

In San Antonio I saw an officer of the garrison handing some invitations for a reception to the old darkey who was to distribute them through the town.

"Now, Uncle," he said, "mind you do this promptly." "Yes, sah," said the old man, "I will regenerate dem," meaning that he would distribute them.

Here and there the polite black servants in the first class hotels hinted that "renumeration," instead of "remuneration," would be agreeable. The negro is almost as quick of wit of a certain kind as the Irish peasant. He is disposed, as European servants are, to presume upon the good-natured familiarity of his superiors in position, and serves one best when a dignified and distant demeanor is maintained toward him.

At Lynchburg we noticed that "Charles," one of the colored waiters, black as the traditional ace of spades, and very clumsy withal, made extravagant professions of his willingness to serve us, but managed to make his fellow-servant, "Harry," do all the work. I therefore ventured a remark something in this wise :

"It appears to me, Charles, that Harry does all the waiting and you do all the talking."

"Yas, sah," he answered, civilly but quickly, "I does de talkin', and de smokin' too, when de gemmen gives me cigars."

After that we considered Charles incorrigible.

The negro valet, taught by years of experience under the slave system, is probably the best in the world. He is always civil, attentive, deferential, and adheres to his master's fortunes, good or ill, with remarkable tenacity. It is not from him that you will hear complaints of his old position. Indeed he looks backward half regretfully to the days of the slave-holders' domination, and often gazes with proud scorn upon the struggling blacks who are playing fantastic tricks in the political world.

The teachers on the Port Royal islands, in South Carolina, in the book called "Slave Songs of the United States," give many interesting instances of what is probably the most remarkable negro dialect in the South. They say that, "With these people the process of 'phonetic decay' appears to have gone as far, perhaps, as is possible, and with it an extreme simplification of etymology and syntax. There is, of course, the usual softening of *th* and *v*, or *f*, into *d* and *b* ; likewise a frequent interchange of *v* and *w*, as *veeds* and *vell*, for *weeds* and *well; woices* and *pumkin wine*, for *voices* and *pumpkin vine*. ' De wile' *(vilest)* sinner may return.' This last example illustrates also their constant habit of clipping words and syllables, as *lee' bro'*, for *little brother ; plant'shun*, for plantation. The lengthening of short vowels is illustrated in both these (*a*, for instance, rarely has its short English sound) ' Een (in) dat mornin' all day.'

"Strange words are less numerous in their *patois* than one would suppose, and, few as they are, many of them may be readily derived from English words. Besides the familiar *buckra*, and a few proper names, as Cuffy, Quash, and perhaps Cudjo, I only know of *churray* (spill) which may be 'throw' way;' *ouna* or *ona*, 'you' (both singular and plural, and used only for friends), as ' Ona build a house in Paradise ;' and *aw*, a kind of expletive, equivalent to ' to be sure,' as, ' Dat clot' cheap.' 'Cheap aw.' ' Dat Monday one lazy boy.' ' Lazy aw — I 'bleege to lick 'em.' "

These interesting quotations illustrate the linguistic peculiarities of the South Carolina negro. It is supposed that the fashion which the negroes in all parts of the South have of speaking of their elders as uncles and aunts, or as daddy and mammy, arose originally from a feeling of respect, and as they were not allowed to call each other Mr. or Mrs. they adopted this.

Almost universally on the sea-islands they call their equals also cousin. Their speech has but little inflection or power of expressing grammatical relation in any way. Even to-day they make little distinction of tense, gender, case, number, or person. " He " is most common as a possessive pronoun. Thus the teachers say that "him" might mean a girl as well as a boy. I quote the following specimens of negro talk from the volume published by the teachers mentioned above, as it gives, better than any one else has been able to show, the peculiarities of this remarkable dialect.

" A scene at the opening of a school:

" ' Charles, why did n't you come to school earlier ? ' ' A-could n't come *soon* to-day, sir ; de boss he sheer out clo' dis mornin'.' ' What did he say to you ? ' ' Me, sir ? I ain't *git;* de boss he de baddest buckra ebber a-see. De morest part ob de mens dey git heaps o' clo'— more 'n nuff; 'n I ain't git nuffin.' ' Were any other children there ? ' ' Plenty chil'n, sir. All de chil'n dah fo' sun-up.' ' January, you have n't brought your book.' ' It *is*, sir ; sh'um here, sir ? ' ' Where is Jim ? ' ' I ain't know where he gone, sir.' ' Where is Sam ? ' ' He did n't been here.' ' Where is the little boy, John ? ' ' He pick up he foot and run.' A new scholar is brought: ' Good mornin', maussa; I bring dis same chile to school, sir ; *do* don't let 'em stay arter school done. Here you, gal, stan' up an' say howdy to de genlm'n. De maussa

lash 'em well ef he don't larn de lesson.' 'Where's your book, Tom?'
'Dunno, sir. Somebody mus' a tief 'em.' 'Where's your brother?' 'Sh'im
dar? wid bof he han' in he pocket?' 'Billy, have you done your sum?' 'Yes,
sir, I out 'em.' 'Where's Polly?' 'Polly de-de.' Taffy comes up. 'Please,
sir, make me sensible of dat word—I want to ketch 'em werry bad, sir, werry
bad.'"

Probably, no Northern traveler ever went South without returning to complain with great bitterness of the poor food which he finds even in prosperous
regions. Horace Greeley told the people of Texas that their prime need was a
thousand good cooks; and, doubtless, a few regiments of Frenchmen, well
dispersed throughout the South, would succeed in giving the Southern people
some much needed instruction in this respect. Yet criticism of the Southern
cuisine cannot be general. Nowhere in the world is there better cookery or a
richer bill of fare than that offered in Baltimore, in Charleston, in Savannah, and
in New Orleans; yet within a few miles of any of those cities one comes into a
region where coarse bread, coarser pork, and a few stunted vegetables are the
only articles of diet upon the farmers' tables. In regions where the best of
mutton and beef can be raised at trivial expense, where with slight cultivation the
land will produce a profusion of vegetables, and where good wines can be
raised from vines of two or three years' growth, the farmers are a lean,
ill-fed race. Nowhere was this more apparent to us than in the mountains,
where, save at the hotels and in the comfortable mansions of well-to-do agriculturists, we were usually invited to partake of hot and indigestible corn bread, fried
and greasy ham, or bacon, as it is universally called in the South; and whenever
by rare chance a beefsteak found its way to the table, it had been remorselessly
fried until not a particle of juice remained in its substance.

People who subsist upon such food as this must of necessity use some stimu-
lant, and they make up in corn whiskey and leaf tobacco what they lack in
nourishing meats, good soups, and a general variety of vegetables. Wherever
culture and refinement prevail, however, there one finds the best of cookery,
an educated taste in wines, and a thorough appreciation of good things.

LXXXIX.

IMMIGRATION—THE NEED OF CAPITAL—DIVISION OF THE NEGRO VOTE—THE SOUTHERN LADIES.

THERE is much that is discouraging in the present condition of the South, but no one is more loth than the Southerner to admit the impossibility of its thorough redemption. The growth of manufactures in the Southern States, while insignificant as compared with the gigantic development in the North and West, is still highly encouraging; and it is actually true that manufactured articles formerly sent South from the North are now made in the South to be shipped to Northern buyers.

There is at least good reason to hope that in a few years immigration will pour into the fertile fields and noble valleys and along the grand streams of the South, assuring a mighty growth. The Southern people, however, will have to make more vigorous efforts in soliciting immigration than they have thus far shown themselves capable of, if they intend to compete with the robust assurance of Western agents in Europe. Texas and Virginia do not need to exert themselves, for currents of immigrants are now flowing steadily to them; and, as has been seen in the North-west, one immigrant always brings, sooner or later, ten in his wake. But the cotton States need able and efficient agents in Europe to explain thoroughly the nature and extent of their resources, and to counteract the effect of the political misrepresentation which is so conspicuous during every heated campaign, and which never fails to do those States incalculable harm. The mischief which the grinding of the outrage mill by cheap politicians, in the vain hope that it might serve their petty ends, at the elections of 1874, did such noble commonwealths as Alabama, Georgia, and Mississippi, can hardly be estimated.

The Italians have been favorably looked upon by the Southerners as possible immigrants, and many planters in some of the States have offered them liberal inducements to settle on the lands which now lie wholly uncultivated; but it will probably be some years before any considerable body of Italian settlers take up those lands. Many foreign immigrants show an indisposition to settle among the negroes, and an especial unwillingness to accept the wages offered them by the old school of planters—namely, a trivial sum yearly, and the rations of meal, pork, and molasses, with which the negro is easily contented. The immigration question can only be settled by time ; but an exposé of the material resources of the South is an important aid to such settlement, and I have endeavored, in the foregoing pages, to give some adequate idea of those resources, and the possibility of their development. The attentive reader of this book will not fail to discover that the mineral wealth ascertained since the war to exist in some of the States of the South is likely to be of far more importance to their future than all the broad cotton-fields, once their sole dependence.

Until her people have recovered from the exhaustion consequent on the war, capital is and will be the crying want of the South. The North will continue to furnish some portion of that capital, but will be largely checked in its investments in that direction, as it has been heretofore, by its lack of confidence in the possibility of a solution of the political difficulties.

If we may rely upon the figures given in the last census, the black race is increasing in numbers. Many travelers through the South, however, have expressed a contrary opinion, some enthusiastic correspondents asserting that the negroes, by flocking into the large cities, and there living in idleness and vice, are contracting the seeds of disease, which will eventually sweep the race away. But in spite of the fact that on many of the plantations fœticide, which in the days of slavery was of course almost unknown among the negroes, has become quite common, there seems no good reason to doubt that their numbers have increased nearly half a million within ten years. The black population will long be migratory, and will show the same tendency which has been so noticeable since the war to seek the attractive life of the town.

Still, as white families are, as a rule, much larger in the South than in the North, and as the increase of the native Caucasian population there is, on the whole, greater than in any other section of the country, there is not much danger of the Africanization of any of the States of the South. The whites and blacks will have to learn to live and vote amicably together, and in time they will do so.

As soon as the negro vote in the South is divided, and the black man learns to respect the merits of a candidate in spite of his political complexion, there will be but little of the trouble now-a-days so conspicuous in Louisiana, Alabama, and some of the other States. Within the last few months the South Carolina Conservatives have frankly allied themselves with those of the negroes who have shown a disposition to encourage honest government in the State, and this is a movement which will be general throughout the South as the abuses of reconstruction are corrected, and some of the more odious carpet-baggers, who have arrayed the negro wrongfully against the principal property-holders, are summarily dismissed from the arena of politics.

The South can never be cast in the same mould as the North. Its origin was too different; it will not be thoroughly emancipated from the influence of the old system for several generations. It will still cherish some prejudices against that utter freedom of speech, that devotion to "isms," and possibly that intense desire for immediate material development that distinguish the North; but it will be progressive, more progressive and liberal every year. Its provincialisms will fade gradually away; its educational facilities, despite the occasional hindrances imposed by such unwise manœuvres as the projected passage of the Civil Rights bill, will increase and flourish. The negro will get justice from the lower classes of whites as soon as those classes are touched by the liberalizing influences of the times. There is, of course, still much objection to sitting with him on juries, or otherwise acknowledging his equality.

It is not the province of this volume to indulge in theories as to the grave dangers which many politicians fancy still environ the Southern question, nor is it important to speculate upon the possible determination on the part of the planters to demand compensation some day for their emancipated slaves, or to hint that they may try to establish a labor system which shall relegate the negro to serfdom. Time alone can disclose the rôle which the Southern Conservative will play when he returns to power.

The Southern ladies during the trying years since the war have developed many noble qualities. It is hardly necessary to eulogize their beauty, their wit, their vivacity, or even to hint that they still cherish a few of the animosities which their husbands, brothers, and lovers have long ago laid aside. It is but natural that they should yet feel some of the bitterness of the war, for latterly its burdens have fallen quite as heavily upon them as upon the survivors of the Confederate ranks. They have toiled unceasingly and uncomplainingly.

The frankness and earnestness with which these ladies accepted a changed order of things, the smile with which they have cheered the humble homes for which many of them have been compelled to leave noble mansions, and the charity and kindliness that they have shown toward their ex-slaves, entitle them to the highest honor. They have not been ashamed to teach negro schools now and then; they have contentedly worn calico instead of satin when rude poverty made it necessary, and they have graced with the nameless charm of their manner circumstances which have made many men harsh and sour for life. It is but natural that, as they stray among the graves of the loved and lost, or amid the ruins of their homes and hopes, they should sometimes recall with strange affection the memory of a lost and mistaken cause, to which they gave themselves with a passionate devotion which has few parallels in the history of the world.

XC.

RAMBLES IN VIRGINIA—FREDERICKSBURG—ALEXANDRIA.
MOUNT VERNON—ARLINGTON.

THE journey from Richmond to Washington, via the battle-scarred town of Fredericksburg, takes one through Henry, Hanover, Caroline, Spottsylvania, Stafford, Prince William and Fairfax counties. This route is now a favorite one from Wilmington in North Carolina, and other large cities in the Southern Atlantic States, to the North, and sleeping-cars daily cross the Rappahannock, which a few years ago was red with the blood of Northern soldiers. In the vicinity of Ashland, the site of a flourishing Methodist college, fifteen miles from Richmond, there are thousands of uncultivated acres which might readily be turned into profitable farms. The birthplace of Henry Clay is not far from Ashland. Fredericksburg is a venerable town, pleasantly situated on the south shore of the Rappahannock, seventy miles from Washington. The "Falls," a mile above the place, afford an extensive water power. Falmouth, on the north side of the river a little above Fredericksburg, is a small village of the ordinary Virginian type.

Fredericksburg is, historically, one of the most interesting places in Virginia. The birthplace of George Washington is near the town, half a mile from the junction of Pope's creek with the Potomac, in Westmoreland county, on the "Wakefield" estate. The old farm-house, a rude building with enormous stone chimneys at each end, in which Washington was born, was destroyed some time before the Revolution. The only memorial on the spot to-day is a freestone slab, erected by George Washington Park Custis in 1815, and bearing these words:

"Here, the 11th of February (O. S.),
1732, George Washington
was born."

Near Fredericksburg, too, repose the remains of the mother of Washington, who lived for many years in the town. Some time before her death, she selected the spot, and often retired to it for meditation and prayer. In 1833 the corner-stone of a fine monument was laid above the grave by Andrew Jackson, then President of the United States; but the monument is still unfinished. The house in which the last memorable interview between the mother and her distinguished son occurred still stands in Fredericksburg. The old Masonic Hall, in which Washington was initiated into the Masonic Order, is also yet standing.

But the reverence which the mass of Americans a generation since felt for these important memorials has been dulled by the newer and sadder souvenirs which fill the minds of all visitors to the Fredericksburg of to-day. The

heights on either side of the little river have been the scene of one of the greatest battles in our history; the old town has echoed to the noise of fratricidal
strife, has been riddled by shot and shell, and some portions of it have been
burned.   It is wonderful that it was not entirely torn to pieces by Burnside's
guns in 1862.   Many a European village, far more solidly built, was crushed
into ruins under the shock of battle between the contending hosts in the last
struggle in France, while Fredericksburg yet shows a smiling front.   The old
steeples, around which raged tempests of bombs and bullets, still point serenely
heavenward; and the rows of houses by the river, past which went the torrent
which poured up Marye's Hill to attack the Confederate position, seem but
little damaged.   The stranger can readily convince himself, however, that the
tide of battle has swept over Fredericksburg, if he will but climb the hills
which lie beyond the plain at the rear of the town—those eminences along
which Lee posted his army of defense, from Hamilton's Crossing to Marye's
Hill.   There he will find, charmingly laid out in terraces like some vast garden,
a huge national cemetery, where many thousand soldiers sleep the sleep that
knows no waking upon earth.

At the foot of Marye's Hill may still be seen the stone wall behind which
the Confederate infantry were posted on that dread day in 1862 when the
Northern troops, time and time again repulsed, were finally compelled, by the
artillery fire from the hill, to retire across the Rappahannock.   That stone wall is
a monument to the bravery of the Irish troops who there fought for the Union.
If mortal men could have taken it, it would have been theirs; but it was an
impregnable position.   Blackened with smoke, and scarred with bullets, it is a
ghastly reminder of the days when Northern Virginia was a battle-ground where
two giant antagonists had declared war against each other to the death.   Lee's
Hill, where General Lee stood during the fight in December of 1862, and
Chatham, on the north side of the river, where General Burnside had his head-
quarters, are interesting points, both offering a good view of the surrounding
country.

A journey into the battle-grounds of the " Wilderness"—that vast tract
stretching southward from the Rapidan, and westward from Mine Run, may
be readily made on horseback or in private conveyance from Fredericksburg.
The Wilderness, which has been described as a "darkling wood" covered with
"a dense undergrowth of low-limbed and scraggy pines, stiff and bristling
chincapins, scrub oaks, and hazel," is not looked upon with much affection by
Virginians, as the lands in that section are not valuable.   On the road to
Chancellorsville one passes Salem Church; and not far from that point is the
"Mountain Way" estate, where General Sedgwick had his head-quarters when
he was fighting his way to Chancellorsville in 1863.   The view of Fredericksburg, the Rappahannock, and the distant summits of the Blue Ridge from this
place, is delightful.   In the vicinity of Chancellorsville one may still see the
outlines of the Federal works, the tree under which Stonewall Jackson lay for
a time after he received his fatal wound, the old Wilderness Tavern, and the
Wilderness Church.

Hanover, Caroline, and Spottsylvania counties produce excellent crops of tobacco, winter wheat, rye and Indian corn; the farmers are intelligent and capable, and saw enough of Northern men during the war to wear away a good deal of their old-time prejudice against the "Yankees." There are still large tracts of unimproved land in these counties; industrious and frugal immigrants can readily turn them into paying farms.

The old town of Alexandria, seated on the Potomac shore, seven miles from Washington, is now accessible by rail from Richmond. Before the completion of the Richmond, Fredericksburg and Potomac railroad, trains from the Virginian capital stopped at Acquia creek, on the river, whence passengers were conveyed in boats to Alexandria and Washington. The Orange, Alexandria, and Manassas railroad procures for Alexandria trade with many of the counties along the line, and, by the "Washington and Ohio," lays hold upon fertile Halifax and Loudon counties. The town has a cotton-mill, a brewery, some private iron workers and machinists, a few repair shops for railroad works, and it makes extensive transfers of coal. It occupies a position admirably fitted for large industrial activity. Its frontage on the Potomac is better than that of any other town on the river, and yet it languishes. Its inhabitants seem to lack the vigor and the enterprise needed to seize upon and improve their fine advantages. They are in the attitude of waiting for something to turn up, yet do not even display the impracticable enthusiasm of Micawber when an opportunity presents itself. The streets were not paved until a Northern officer, during the occupation in war times, insisted upon having a pavement of cobble stones laid down, and met the expense by fines levied upon whiskey-selling. Few repairs have been made, and the avenues are filled with ruts and hollows. The inhabitants seem to feel, with regard to the changed order of things upon which they have fallen, very much as did the old negro whom I met there in 1869.

"'Pears like, boss," said the venerable darkey, as he looked up the river toward the dome of the National Capitol, the Mecca of his dreams, and then glanced over his broken down chest and withered limbs, "'pears like I 's come too late for de good times."

One sees nerveless unthrift in many small Virginian towns. It seems graven in the nature of whites and blacks. An occasional conversation with the negroes led me to believe that they offer as many hindrances to the advent of capital as their ex-masters do. Both seem suspicious that some improper and undue advantage is to be taken of them. The negro appears oftentimes suspicious of those who are making strenuous endeavors to elevate him out of his shiftless and helpless condition into something like manly independence.

Alexandria was once a part of the District of Columbia, but was retroceded to Virginia in 1846, when the Old Dominion regained all the territory which had before been national ground. The town was founded in 1748; Washington was a frequent visitor there, and the pew in which he used to sit, in Christ Church, is still pointed out. The hourly steamboat line which plies between Washington and Alexandria affords communication with the Washington City and Potomac line of steamers, with Norfolk, Philadelphia, New York and Boston.

A new commercial exchange, and a fine Government custom-house and post-office have recently been erected in the town.

In summer and autumn the journey down the Potomac from Washington is usually interesting. There is a certain picturesqueness in the great stream and the quaint towns and fortifications along its banks; Forts Foote and Washington, on the Maryland side, being especially noticeable. On the little steamer which plies regularly to and from Mount Vernon, the old home of the Father of his Country, may sometimes be found a few Virginians clad in rusty black, who confidentially discuss with the stranger the painful issues of the present.

Mount Vernon is fifteen miles from the Capitol, and the traveler will not fail to observe, while sailing down the river, that the fields on the Virginia side have not yet recovered from the devastation of war. The whole country has the trampled aspect which the passage of the myriads of men and horses, and the location of the thousand camps, naturally gave it. Fort Washington, on the Maryland side, was blown up in 1814 when the British occupied Washington, but is now thoroughly restored. On a fertile slope on the Virginia shore, in the midst of noble groves and on a pretty lawn, overlooking the wide and winding river, one may see here and there a few substantial mansions, once the homes of prosperous planters. The woods near Mount Vernon, like many bits of forest along the Potomac, are untamed, but a pretty road leads up the hill-side to the tomb, and thence wanders to the lawn, where stands the Washington mansion with its little cupola, its quaint roof and its veranda with eight stately pillars.

Nothing can be simpler than the tomb in which the first President of the United States reposes. It is of quadrangular form, built on a sloping hill-side, painted red and white, a high iron gate guarding the entrance. Above the gate is the inscription, "Within this enclosure rest the remains of General George Washington." There is no attempt at decoration. One sees nothing but two marble coffins lying on the brick floor; the one on the right has upon its lid a spread eagle, a flag and a shield, and beneath these emblems the single word, "Washington." The coffin on the left is plain, and contains the remains of Mrs. Washington. Above the door which opens into another vault are the following words:

"I am the resurrection and the life; he that believeth in me, though he were dead, yet shall he live."

Near the tomb are several other family monuments, much more showy and pretentious than that which covers the mortal remains of our chief patriot. The old tomb, in which the body of Washington remained for thirty years, was situated between the present vault and the house.

The mansion commands a fine view of the river, and, were it not for its low ceilings and its lack of all the comforts of modern residences, would be a desirable country residence for a century to come; for, although it is now more than one hundred and twenty-five years old, it is still solid and enduring. The wood of which the house is built is cut in blocks in imitation of stone; on the sloping sides of the roof there are dormer windows, and the portico, which covers the whole front of the building, is quite imposing.

The gardens and the lawn in the rear of the house, with the walks extending to what were formerly the negro quarters, are extensive and pleasant, and one or two colored families supply the visitor with luncheon, and nosegays from the garden. Mrs. Cunningham, the present guardian of that portion of the estate purchased by the patriotic ladies of the country some years ago and preserved as a National treasure, lives at Mount Vernon some portion of the year. The farms round about are owned by Northern men, and the old lordly life of the planter and country gentleman, which prevailed so extensively in all that region when Washington inhabited Mount Vernon, has passed utterly away. The whole surroundings of the estate are calculated to remind one of the English country seats which still remain, in some parts of England, much as they were two centuries ago. The quaint staircases, and odd little angular passages in the mansion, are thronged by fashionable tourists from the cities, who never fail to express their wonder that the Father of his Country lived in such a simple, unostentatious style.

Below Mount Vernon on the Virginia side one comes upon naked sandbluffs standing out into the stream here and there; on shad and herring fishing stations, where in spring time, when the herring shoals come in, hundreds of fishermen are busy; and upon forests, where in autumn the hickories and cedars, the oaks and the ashes, the chestnuts and the beeches clothe the hill-sides in brilliant colors. At Acquia Creek, a dreary and forlorn little place to-day, but an important military depot during the war, one may take the railroad for Fredericksburg. In the vicinity of Acquia Creek there were many Confederate batteries, which of course did their best to injure the Federal shipping on the Potomac in the early years of the war.

A journey by land from Mount Vernon to either Alexandria or Fredericksburg may be made along the main road, which extends through a wild country, and which those who have traversed it declare to be not only the worst road in any country, but probably much worse now than it was when Washington was wont to ride over it.

On the road from Mount Vernon to Fredericksburg one passes Pohick, where stands a ruined church, which the family of Washington attended until the close of the Revolution; and crosses a pretty river, called Occoquan, which empties into the Potomac near the headland known as High Point, upon which, during the fall after the battle of Bull Run, the Confederates established their nearest river battery to Washington.

Southward, on the Washington City, Virginia Midland and Great Southern railroad, is Clifton Station, twelve miles from the old Bull Run battle-field. This was a famous depot during the war for army supplies, and is now a prosperous summer resort, frequented by visitors from Northern cities. In Prince William county, on the same line of rail, is the flourishing village of Manassas. It is situated on the summit of a high table-land, twenty-seven miles from Alexandria, and commands a beautiful view of the surrounding country. Six miles to the right of it, in the direction of Fairfax, the first battle of Manassas was fought, and here and there a ruined earthwork marks the site of the old struggle.   In 1868 there was not a fence or a building on the spot where the town now stands, but since that time many Northern and Western people have flocked into it.   The centre of a prosperous county with ample facilities for transportation, with a fine free school system, and with the best of hematite iron ore in its vicinity, it can but have a prosperous future. Throughout this entire section the tide of battle raged during 1862 and 1863. Hooker and Ewell, Warren and Hill, marched and countermarched over the devastated country, which to-day is rapidly recovering from the shock of war.

In Fauquier county are situated the Warrenton White Sulphur Springs, where formerly a brilliant society annually gathered.   Warrenton, fifty miles from Alexandria, now receives many fashionable visitors yearly.   Nine miles from the town is the birthplace of Chief-Justice Marshall.   In Culpepper county stands the town of Culpepper, founded in 1759, and first named after Lord

The Potomac and Washington — Seen from Arlington, Virginia.

Fairfax, the original proprietor of the section.   The little town looks down upon the beautiful and vast extent of the Blue Ridge, has a handsome and costly court-house, and many prosperous manufactories, and is also the site of the annual fair of the Piedmont Agricultural Society, of which General Kemper, the present Governor of Virginia, was, for two years, the chief executive officer.   Near Mitchell's Station the battle known as that of Cedar Mountain was fought in August, 1862.   Magnetic iron ores and fine grass-lands are gradually attracting Northern immigration to the surroundings of the old battle-field.   From Culpepper the Washington City, Virginia Midland and Great Southern railroad runs through Gordonsville, Charlottesville and Lynchburg to Danville, four miles from the North Carolina line in Pittsylvania county, whence it connects with the Piedmont air line via Charlotte in North Carolina, to Atlanta in Georgia.

The railroad known as the Manassas Division, and running through the town of Manassas, through Warren, Shenandoah, and other counties in Northern Virginia, passes Front Royal, near which is the finest and most profitable vineyard in the whole South. The Northern visitor, while at Front Royal, has his attention directed to the exploits of General Stonewall Jackson, who, in 1862, in a severe battle near this town, drove General Banks out of the Shenandoah valley. At Rivington Station, the junction of the North and South forks of the Shenandoah river, much of the brown hematite and magnetic iron ore which comes down the river in flat-boats from the counties of Rockingham, Page and Warren, is received and exported. A joint-stock company of Northern capitalists, with a million dollars of capital stock, is now operating in this region.

The traveler along the romantic gaps of the Shenandoah passes the sites of the battles of Chester Gap, Cedar Creek and Front Royal, and, straying by the ruins of burned bridges and devastated farms, cannot but wonder that the Virginians of the section have so soon recovered their courage and shown a disposition to rebuild after the prostrating struggle. Five miles from Strasburg, the present western terminus of the "Manassas Division," Ashby's Confederate cavalry and Banks's infantry fought a sharp battle in May of 1862, and a little north of this, at Cedarville, that dashing and gallant West Virginian, McCausland, met, in a severe fight, part of General Phil Sheridan's forces. Shenandoah county, originally called Dunmore, after the Tory Lord of that name, but later more properly named after the beautiful and picturesque Shenandoah river, which wanders by cliff and through meadow within its limits, is extremely fertile. Strasburg was so named because its original settlers came from Germany. It will in due time be a place of great importance, and the Capon and Orkney Springs near it will give it a good tide of summer travel. One mile south of the town is Officers' Hill, where Early and Sheridan met in a tremendous fight in September of 1864, and in October of the same year severe battles were fought in the immediate vicinity. This region is one of the most beautiful in Virginia. The rugged and mighty slopes of the Massanuttan contain much delightful and wild scenery, and near Newmarket Station there is a beautiful cataract.

Along these lines of rail many fine bodies of land are offered to capitalists and actual settlers. Many of the lands are admirably adapted to the production of the grape; and the fine air, the beautiful springs of fresh water, the short and mild winters, the long and equable summers, offer superior attractions to the emigrant from England or from middle Europe.

The traveler along the Potomac will do well to scale the hill opposite Georgetown, in the District of Columbia, on which stands Arlington House. The famous mansion, once the residence of George Washington Parke Custis, one of the last survivors of the Washington family, stands more than two hundred feet above the Potomac; and from its massive portico one can look out over Washington, and can see the white dome of the National Capitol gleaming through dark green foliage. Arlington was, for many years before the late war, a part of the estate of General Robert E. Lee, but when that valiant soldier unsheathed his sword in the Confederate cause, the grand old mansion and the beautiful grounds about it were confiscated to Government use, and are now held on an arrear of taxes title. The ravages of war have destroyed many of the beauties of the parks and gardens. To-day, the fields of Arlington, which the proud leader of the Confederate hosts cherished as one of his favorite resorts, are covered with national cemeteries. Fifteen thousand graves, on the head-boards over many of which is written the word "Unknown," dot the slopes and lawns. Near the mansion is a short but heavy granite monument, on which is the following inscription:

> "Beneath this stone
> repose the bones of two thousand one hundred and eleven
> unknown soldiers, gathered after the war, from
> the fields of Bull Run and the route to the Rappahannock.
> Their remains could not be identified, but their names and deaths
> are recorded in the archives of the
> country, and its grateful citizens honor them
> as of their noble army of martyrs.
> May they rest in peace.
> Sept. A. D. 1866."

Thousands of negro soldiers and "contrabands" who died during the war, are also buried at Arlington. In the eastern division of the largest of the three cemeteries are monuments to the memory of George Washington Parke Custis and Mary his wife. Thousands of visitors yearly come and go, over the hills, under the oaks, and among the graves at Arlington; and now and then old soldiers, who for long years fought fiercely against each other in opposing ranks, pause in friendly converse by some grassy mound, beneath which sleeps an unknown and forgotten member of the great army that has passed into the silence and shadows beyond.

APPENDIX.

—

FACTS AND FIGURES CONCERNING THE EX-SLAVE STATES, AND DELAWARE AND THE DISTRICT OF COLUMBIA.

POPULATION.

Compiled from the United States Census of 1870.

STATES.	WHITES.	BLACKS.
Alabama	521,384	475,501
Arkansas	362,115	122,169
Delaware	102,221	22,794
Florida	96,057	91,689
Georgia	638,926	545,142
Kentucky	1,098,692	222,210
Louisiana	362,065	364,210
Maryland	605,497	175,391
Mississippi	382,896	444,201
Missouri	1,603,146	118,071
North Carolina	678,470	391,650
South Carolina	289,667	415,814
Tennessee	936,119	322,331
Texas	564,700	253,475
Virginia	712,089	512,841
West Virginia	424,033	17,980
District of Columbia	88,288	43,404
Totals	9,466,355	4,538,782

MANUFACTURES OF COTTON IN THE UNITED STATES.
NEW ENGLAND STATES.

STATES.	1860. RAW MATERIAL USED.		1870. RAW MATERIAL USED.	
	POUNDS.	VALUE.	POUNDS.	VALUE.
Maine	23,733,165	$3,319,335	25,887,771	$6,746,780
New Hampshire	51,002,324	7,128,196	41,469,719	12,318,867
Vermont..................	1,447,250	181,030	1,235,652	292,269
Massachusetts	134,012,759	17,214,592	130,654,040	37,371,599
Rhode Island..........	41,614,797	5,799,223	44,630,787	13,268,315
Connecticut	31,891,011	4,028,406	31,747,309	8,818,651
Total..................	283,701,306	$37,670,782	275,625,278	$78,816,482

MIDDLE STATES.

STATES.	POUNDS.	VALUE.	POUNDS.	VALUE.
New York..................	23,945,627	$3,061,105	24,783,351	$6,990,626
Pennsylvania	37,496,203	7,386,213	32,953,318	10,724,052
New Jersey................	9,094,649	1,165,435	7,920,035	1,964,758
Delaware	3,403,000	570,102	2,587,615	704,733
Maryland	12,880,119	1,698,413	12,693,647	3,409,426
District of Columbia.........	294,117	47,403	....	....
Total..................	87,113,715	$13,928,671	80,937,966	$23,793,595

WESTERN STATES.

STATES.	POUNDS.	VALUE.	POUNDS.	VALUE.
Ohio	3,192,500	$374,100	2,226,400	$493,740
Indiana...	1,813,944	229,925	2,070,318	542,875
Illinois....	95,000	11,930	857,000	177,525
Iowa	....	....	20,000	4,950
Utah	12,000	6,600	23,500	7,051
Missouri	990,000	110,000	2,196,600	481,745
Kentucky	1,826,000	214,755	1,584,625	375,048
Total..................	7,929,444	$946,710	8,908,443	$2,082,934

SOUTHERN STATES.

STATES.	POUNDS.	VALUE.	POUNDS.	VALUE.
Virginia	7,544,297	$811,187	4,255,383	$937,820
North Carolina	5,540,738	622,363	4,238,276	963,809
South Carolina	3,978,061	431,525	4,756,823	761,469
Georgia	13,907,904	1,466,375	10,921,176	2,504,758
Florida	200,000	23,000	....	....
Alabama..................	5,246,800	617,633	3,249,523	764,965
Louisiana	1,995,700	226,000	748,525	161,485
Texas	588,000	64,140	1,079,118	216,519
Mississippi	638,800	79,800	580,764	123,568
Arkansas	187,500	11,600	66,400	13,780
Tennessee......	4,072,710	384,548	2,872,582	595,789
Total..................	43,960,510	$4,739,371	32,768,570	$7,042,962
Total United States	422,704,975	$57,285,534	398,248,257	$111,735,973

STATISTICS OF THE MANUFACTURES OF COTTON IN THE UNITED STATES.

NEW ENGLAND STATES.

STATES.	1850. Value of Product.	1860. Value of Product.	1870. Value of Product.
Maine	$2,630,616	$6,235,623	$11,844,181
New Hampshire	8,861,749	13,699,994	16,999,672
Vermont	280,300	357,450	546,510
Massachusetts	21,394,401	38,004,255	59,493,153
Rhode Island	6,495,972	12,151,191	22,049,203
Connecticut	4,122,952	8,911,387	14,026,334
Total	$43,785,990	$79,359,900	$124,759,053

MIDDLE STATES.

STATES.	1850. Value of Product.	1860. Value of Product.	1870. Value of Product.
New York	$5,019,323	$6,676,878	$11,178,211
Pennsylvania	5,812,126	13,650,114	17,490,080
New Jersey	1,289,648	2,217,728	4,015,768
Delaware	538,439	941,703	1,060,898
Maryland	2,021,396	2,973,877	4,832,808
District of Columbia	100,000	74,400	....
Total	$14,780,932	$26,534,700	$38,587,765

WESTERN STATES.

STATES.	1850. Value of Product.	1860. Value of Product.	1870. Value of Product.
Ohio	$594,204	$723,500	$681,335
Indiana	86,660	344,350	778,047
Illinois	....	18,987	279,000
Iowa	....	....	7,000
Utah	....	10,000	16,803
Missouri	142,900	230,000	798,850
Kentucky	445,639	315,270	251,550
Total	$1,269,403	$1,642,107	$2,792,585

SOUTHERN STATES.

STATES.	1850. Value of Product.	1860. Value of Product.	1870. Value of Product.
Virginia	$1,446,109	$1,489,971	$1,435,800
North Carolina	985,411	1,046,047	1,345,052
South Carolina	842,440	713,050	1,529,930
Georgia	1,395,056	2,371,207	3,648,973
Florida	49,920	40,000	....
Alabama	398,585	1,040,147	1,088,767
Louisiana	....	466,500	251,550
Texas	....	80,695	374,598
Mississippi	22,000	176,328	234,445
Arkansas	17,360	23,000	22,362
Tennessee	508,481	698,122	941,542
Total	$5,665,362	$8,145,067	$10,873,019
Total United States	$65,501,687	$115,681,774	$177,022,422

COTTON TRADE OF THE UNITED STATES FOR FORTY-EIGHT YEARS.

YEARS ENDING AUGUST 31.	PRODUCTION.	CONSUMPTION.	EXPORTS.	AVERAGE NET WEIGHT PER BALE.	AVERAGE PRICE PER LB. IN NEW YORK.	AVERAGE PRICE PER LB. IN LIVER-POOL.
	BALES.	BALES.	BALES.	LBS.	CENTS.	PENCE.
1825–26	720,027	....	....	...	12.19	5.85
1826–27	975,231	149,516	854,000	331	9.29	5.79
1827–28	720,593	120,593	600,000	335	10.32	5.84
1828–29	870,415	118,853	740,000	341	9.88	5.32
1829–30	976,845	126,512	839,000	339	10.04	6.44
1830–31	1,038,847	182,142	773,000	341	9.71	5.72
1831–32	987,477	173,800	892,000	360	9.38	6.22
1832–33	1,070,438	194,412	867,000	350	12.32	7.87
1833–34	1,205,394	196,413	1,028,000	363	12.90	8.10
1834–35	1,254,328	216,888	1,023,500	367	17.45	9.13
1835–36	1,360,725	236,733	1,116,000	373	16.50	8.97
1836–37·	1,423,930	222,540	1,169,000	379	13.25	6.09
1837–38	1,801,497	246,063	1,575,000	379	10.14	6.28
1838–39	1,360,532	276,018	1,074,000	384	13.36	7.19
1839–40	2,177,835	295,193	1,876,000	383	8.92	5.42
1840–41	1,634,954	267,850	1,313,500	394	9.50	5.73
1841–42	1,683,574	267,850	1,465,500	397	7.85	4.86
1842–43	2,378,875	325,129	2,010,000	409	7.25	4.37
1843–44	2,030,409	346,750	1,629,500	412	7.73	4.71
1844–45	2,394,503	389,000	2,083,700	415	5.63	3.92
1845–46	3,100,537	422,600	1,666,700	411	7.87	4.80
1846–47	1,778,651	428,000	1,241,200	431	11.21	6.03
1847–48	2,439,786	616,044	1,858,000	417	8.03	3.93
1848–49	2,866,938	642,485	2,228,000	436	7.55	4.09
1849–50	2,233,718	613,498	1,590,200	429	12.34	7.10
1850–51	2,454,442	485,614	1,988,710	416	12.14	5.51
1851–52	3,126,310	689,603	2,443,646	428	31.9–50	5.05
1852–53	3,416,214	803,725	2,528,400	428	11.02	5.54
1853–54	3,074,979	737,236	2,319.148	430	10.97	5.31
1854–55	2,982,634	706,417	2,244,209	434	10.39	5.60
1855–56	3,665,557	770,739	2,954,606	420	10.30	6.22
1856–57	3,093,737	819,936	2,252,657	444	13.51	7.73
1857–58	3,257,339	595,562	2,590,455	442	12.23	6.91
1858–59	4,018,914	927,651	3,021,403	447	12.08	6.68
1859–60	4,861,292	978,043	3,774,173	461	11.00	5.97
1860–61	3,849,469	843,740	3,127,568	477	13.01	8.50
1861–62	....	....	....	...	31.29	18.37
1862–63	....	....	....	...	67.21	22.46
1863–64	....	....	....	...	101.50	27.17
1864–65	....	....	....	...	83.38	19.11
1865–66	2,269,316	666,100	1,554,664	441	43.20	15.30
1866–67	2,097,254	770,030	1,557,054	444	31.59	10.98
1867–68	2,519,554	906,636	1,655,816	445	24.85	10.52
1868–69	2,366,467	926,374	1,465,880	444	29.01	12.12
1869–70	3,122,551	865,160	2,206,480	440	23.98	9.89
1870–71	4,362,317	1,110,196	3,166,742	442	16.95	8.55
1871–72	3,014,351	1,237,330	1,957,314	443	20.48	10.78
1872–73	3,930,508	1,201,127	2,679,986	464	18.15	9.65

INDEX

Abingdon, Va., 571
Acadians: in Louisiana, 85
Agriculture: Alabama, 330–31; Arkansas, 280; Florida, 385, 402–406, 418; Georgia, 348, 371–72; Kentucky, 713–18, 724–25; Louisiana, 78–88, 297–302; Maryland, 738–39; Mississippi, 311, 317; Missouri, 253, 255; North Carolina, 466, 489; in Sandhill region of Georgia and South Carolina, 345–48; South Carolina, 346, 428, 431–37, 451; Tennessee, 548, 729, 732; Texas, 136, 145; Virginia, 565–66, 577–78, 580, 588, 591, 594–95, 632–34, 649–50, 656–57, 659; West Virginia, 688–92. *See also* Cattle, Cotton, Horses, Indigo, Oranges, Rice, Sheep, Sugar, Tobacco, Truck farming, Wheat
Aiken, S. C., 345–46
Alabama: area in square miles, 328; character of people, 340–41; cotton cultivation, 330–31; description of, 339–40; education, 342–43, 606; emigration of blacks from, 300; history of, 321–22, 328; ignorance of whites, 334; illiteracy, 342; manufacturing, 334–35; mineral resources of, 335–38; natural resources of, 328; politics, 332–33; property value in, 311, 330; railroads, 325, 330, 339; river system of, 329; timber, 311, 324, 329–30
Alabama State University, 312
Alamo, The, 131, 150, 163–66
Alcorn, James L. (1816–94): Mississippi governor and

senator, 315
Alcorn University, 316
Alcott, A. Bronson (1799–1888): influence on William T. Harris, 226
Alexander, Mr.: Kentucky horse-breeder, 716–17
Alexandria, Va., 797
Alleghany Mountains. *See* Mountains
Alligators: in Florida, 415
Almonaster, Don Andrés: and St. Louis Cathedral, New Orleans, 18
American Missionary Association, 596–601
Ames, Adelbert (1835–1933): Mississippi governor and senator, 315
Andry, Louis: leader of exiled Acadians, 85
Annapolis, Md., 770
Appalachian Mountains. *See* Mountains
Appleton, Mo., 191
Appomattox Court House, Va., 579–80
Archbishop's Palace, New Orleans, 31
Architecture: Baltimore, 758–59; Charleston, S. C., 446; New Orleans, 37, 62, 64–66; Texas, 150–55
Arkansas: agriculture, 280; area in acres, 283; blacks, 281–82; churches, 283; climate, 279; coal, 285; state debt, 282; education, 283–84; geographical description of, 278–79, 286; history of, 278; hot springs, 286; minerals, 280, 285; outlaws in, 280; politics, 284; population, 196; railroads, 280, 284; taxes, 282, 285; timber, 280, 286; violence in, 285
Arkansas River, 278, 279
Arlington Cemetery, 802

Arlington, Va., 801–802
Armstrong, Samuel C. (1839–93): founder of Hampton Normal Institute, 603–604
Army: in forts in Texas, 172–73
Asheville, N. C., 504–505
Ashland Estate, Lexington, Ky., 720
Asylums for blind, deaf and dumb, and insane: Austin, Tex., 127–28; Baltimore, 759–60; Columbia, S. C., 459; Jackson, Miss., 314; Knoxville, 548; Little Rock, 281, Louisville, 711; Milledgeville, Ga., 375; Staunton, Va., 657; Tuscaloosa, 312
Atchafalaya River, La., 85
Atlanta: description of, 350; hotels, 353; manufacturing in, 356; newspapers, 356; Opera House, 353; population, 356; railroads, 350
Atlanta University, 605–606
Attakapas prairie, La., 84
Augusta, Ga.: cotton factories, 346–48; description of, 347–49; history of, 349; railroads, 347
Austin, Moses (1761–1821), 164
Austin, Stephen F. (1793–1836): founder of Texas, 137, 164–65
Austin, Tex.: description of, 127; founding of, 131; insane asylum, 127–28; population, 128–29; Texas Military Institute, 128

Bald mountains, 487, 512
"Balize, The," La., 75
Baltimore: architecture, 758–59; art galleries, 756; Battle Monument, 758;

charitable institutions, 759–60; coal trade, 751; coffee trade, 751; commerce, 745–47, 751–55; description of, 748, 757–65; Druid Hill Park, 763; education, 765; Federal Hill, 755–56; history of, 734–35, 737; iron manufacturing and trade, 752–53; Locust Point, 745; newspapers, 765; parks, 763–64; railroads, 741, 748–51; as seaport, 744–47; sugar trade, 752; tobacco trade, 752; Washington Monument, 757

Baltimore and Ohio Railroad: history of, 741–44

Baptist Medical College, Richmond, Va., 638

Baton Rouge, La., 76–77

Baxter, Elisha (1827–99): Arkansas governor, 285

Beaufort, N. C., 467

Beaufort, S. C., 425–26, 428

Bee (tow-boat): and yellow fever in Memphis, 268

Belmont, August (1816–90): capitalist, and American Iron Mountain Company of St. Louis, 241

Berea College, Ky., 605

Berwick Bay, La., 86

Bienville, Jean Baptiste le Moyne, Sieur de (1680–1767): and colonial Louisiana, 18, 21, 22, 24, 78, 321–22, 326, 328

Big Tree: Kiowa Indian chief, 121

Birmingham, Ala., 336–38

Bissell, Mr.: South Carolina rice planter, 434

Black Mountains, N. C., 510–12

Blacks: in Alabama, 341–42; in Arkansas, 281–82; attitudes toward whites, 276, 297–304, 430, 453, 596; attitudes of whites concerning, 82, 89, 274, 291–92, 297, 372, 430, 452–53, 470, 599, 603–607, 712, 715, 731, 778–79, 782–85, 788, 794; as beggars, 45; carrying weapons, 275, 778; character of, 275, 276–77, 303–304, 778–79, 789; children in Louisiana, 23; colleges and normal schools for, 316, 343, 599–600, 603–07, 712,

769; as cotton thieves, 309–10; in cotton trade, 52–56; and crime, 120; description of in New Orleans, 34–35; dialect and speech of, 429, 553, 788–91; as a diminishing race, 33; education of and need for, 276–77, 574, 596–608; effects of Civil War on, 275, 598; emigration to the new cotton lands of the Southwest, 270–71, 275, 299–301, 740; employment opportunities for, 32; financial expenditures of, 132; free laborers and as farmers, 81, 104, 125–26, 270–77, 298–301, 305–306, 309–10, 435, 565; French-speaking in Louisiana, 29; in higher education, 462–63; housing, 46, 652; in Houston, Tex., 113; illiteracy of, 303; in Indian Territory, 212; as inferior, 33; influence on Southern speech, 785; injustice toward, 89, 372, 599, 715, 778–79; laziness, 33; life on plantations, 306–307; in Louisiana, 22–23, 34–35; mental capacity of, 607; military organizations, 355; on Mississippi River, 68–69, 72, 290–91; in Montgomery, Ala., 331–32; morality of, 276–77, 430, 779–80, 782; music, songs, and spirituals of, 608–20; in New Orleans, 23; as non-agricultural laborers, 30, 552–56, 580, 582; as officeholders, 97, 113, 281–85, 291–95, 314–16, 332–33, 420, 460–61, 580–81; in Petersburg, 580–87; on plantations, 81–82, 270–77, 297–310, 435; in politics, 33, 89–91, 94, 95, 97, 295–96, 300, 333, 369, 431, 453, 460–62, 580–81; and poll tax, 306; population growth, 793; in prewar South, 773; as property owners, 274, 427; religion, 430, 521–22, 583–87, 607–608, 618, 779–81; social organizations of, 267; in South Carolina, 427, 429–30, 452–53, 464; taxation of, 306; in Tennessee, 542; in Texas, 104, 132; as thieves,

72, 301; on trains, 783; in Virginia, 580; voters in Georgia, 354; in West Virginia, 678

Blacksburg, Va., 575

Black Warrior River, Ala., 313

Blair, James (1655–1743): founder of College of William and Mary, 622

Blue Ridge Mountains. *See* Mountains

Blue Ridge Springs, Va., 566

Boll-worms. *See* Cotton worms

Brackenridge, Mr.: San Antonio banker, 157

Brazos River, 136

Brenham, Tex., 135–36

Bristol, Va.-Tenn., 569

Brockmeyer, Henry C. (1828–1906): Prussian-born philosopher in St. Louis, 226

Brown, John (1800–59): and Harpers Ferry, Va., 768

Brown, Mr.: mayor of St. Louis, 250

Bullock, Rufus B. (1834–1907): Georgia governor, 351–53

Buncombe, Edward (d. 1777): North Carolina Revolutionary War patriot, 505

Butler, Benjamin F. (1818–93): and "contrabands," 596–97

Cabot, Sebastian (d. 1557): explorer for England, 379

Cadillac, Antoine de la Mothe (c. 1658–1730): French colonial governor, 21–22

Cahokia, Ill., 222

Calcasieu River, La., 88

Caldwell, Tod R. (1818–74): governor of North Carolina, 469

Calhoun, Mo., 188–89

Calvert, George (c. 1580–1632): projector of colony of Maryland, 733

Camden, Ark., 284

Canal Street, New Orleans, 60–62

Canton Company: trade and manufacturing suburb of Baltimore, 748

Cape Fear River, 471

Capital punishment: in Texas, 185

Carondelet, Francisco Luis
Hector (c. 1748–1807):
governor of Louisiana, 25
Carondelet: industrial section
of St. Louis, 234, 237–39,
244
Carpenter, R. B.: South
Carolina governor, 455
Cartersville, Ga., 357
Casey, J. F.: Collector of
Port of New Orleans, 91
Catholics: in Maryland, 734,
757–60; in New Orleans,
18–19; in St. Louis, 228–
29; the Spanish missions in
Texas, 147–56
Caton, Parson: North Caro-
lina mountaineer, 479–81
Cattle: Georgia, 372; Indian
Territory, 201; Kansas
City, Mo., 251; Kentucky,
718; Louisiana, 78, 84–85;
stampede, 171; Tennessee,
732; Texas, 167–72
Cave City, Ky., 699
Cemeteries: Arlington, 802;
Augusta, Ga., 349; Balti-
more, 758, 764; Charleston,
S. C., 445; Memphis, 265;
Monument Cemetery, La.,
72–73; Nashville, 729;
New Orleans, 36–37;
Petersburg, Va., 583;
Richmond, 630; Savannah,
368; Vicksburg, 288
Chalmette Battlefield, La.,
72–73
Charleston, S. C.: architec-
ture, 446; charitable
institutions, 464; churches,
444–46; College of, 464;
description of, 438, 439–44,
451; history of, 423–24,
440, 442; manufacturing in,
449–51; Military Academy,
464; Orphan House, 446;
politics, 447–49; taxes, 448
Charleston, W. Va., 688–89
Charlestown, W. Va., 768
Charlotte, N. C., 473, 514
Charlottesville, Va., 650–51
Chattahoochee River, 373
Chattanooga: commerce, 530;
history of, 530, 538–40;
railroads, 530–31
Chattanooga Valley, 529
Cherokee Indians: in Georgia, Alabama, Tennessee,
North Carolina, and re-
moval from, 527–28; in
Indian Territory, 197–99,
205

Cheyenne and Arapaho
Indians: in Indian Ter-
ritory, 197
Chickasaw Indians: in Indian
Territory, 197–98; in Loui-
siana, 23
Chihuahua: sector of San
Antonio, 163
Chisholm Trail, 170
Choctaw Indians: in Indian
Territory, 197–98; in
Louisiana, 23
Cholera: in Nashville,
Tenn., 726
Chouteau, R. Auguste (1749–
1829): co-founder of St.
Louis, 216–17
Christian Baptist College,
Harrodsburg, Ky., 716
Christiansburg, Va., 577
Churches: Arkansas, 283;
Baltimore, 757, 762;
Charleston, S. C., 444–46;
and education of blacks,
598–99; Galveston, 109;
Louisiana, 23; Louisville,
711; Mobile, 327; New
Orleans, 64–65; North
Carolina, 504; organized by
blacks, 608; St. Augustine,
Fla., 395–96; St. Louis,
247; Savannah, 369; South
Carolina, 451; Tennessee,
480; Texas, 151–53, 160–
61; Virginia, 629–30
Clairmont plantation: in
Louisiana, across from
Natchez, Miss., 273
Clarksville, Ga., 521, 522–23
Clarksville, Tex., 126
Clay, Henry (1777–1852):
home and grave in Ken-
tucky, 720
Clayton, Ga., 519–20
Clayton, Powell (1833–1914):
Arkansas governor and
senator, 284
Coahuila, State of (Mexico),
101, 165
Coal: Alabama, 335–36;
Arkansas, 285; Baltimore,
751; East Tennessee Val-
ley, 530–32, 547; Kentucky,
723–24; Missouri, 189;
West Virginia, 680, 682–86
Coffee imports: Baltimore,
751; Galveston, 106;
Mobile, 325
Coke, Richard (1829–97):
Democratic governor of
Texas, 130

Coligny, Gaspard de (1517–
72): and French coloniza-
tion efforts in South
Carolina, 423
Colleges, institutes, and
universities: Alcorn Uni-
versity, 316; Alabama State
University, 312; Atlanta
University, 605–606;
Christian Baptist College,
Harrodsburg, Ky., 716;
Baptist Medical College,
Richmond, Va., 638; Berea
College, 605; for blacks,
599–600, 603–607; Cumber-
land University, 731;
Davidson College, 470;
East Tennessee University,
548; Fairmont Normal
School, 640; Fisk Univer-
sity, 604–605; Hampden-
Sydney College, 557;
Hampton Normal and
Industrial Institute, 605;
Howard University, 608;
Johns Hopkins University,
761–62; Kentucky Univer-
sity, 720; King College,
569; Louisiana State Uni-
versity, 98; Louisiana,
University of, 62; Mary-
land State Agricultural
College, 739; Marshall
College, 641; Mary
Institute, St. Louis, 229;
Military Academy (The
Citadel), 464; Mississippi,
University of, 316; Mis-
souri, University of, 229;
mixed, 605; Nashville,
University of, 729; Oak-
land College, Miss., 316;
Peabody Institute, 757;
Richmond Institute, 638;
Presbyterian Female Col-
lege, Harrodsburg, Ky.,
716; Roanoke College, 557,
577; Shepherdstown Nor-
mal School, 640–41;
South, University of the
(Sewanee), 541–42;
South Carolina, University
of, 459; Storer College,
Va., 769; Straight Uni-
versity, 606; Synodical
Institute, Florence, Ala.,
340; Talladega College,
606; Texas Military
Institute, 128; Tougaloo
Normal School, 607;
Transylvania University,
720; Trinity College, 470;

Vanderbilt University, 728; Virginia Military Institute, 557, 662; Virginia Medical College, 638; Virginia State Agricultural and Mechanical College, 577; Virginia, University of, 653–55; Wake Forest College, 470; Washington and Lee College (University), 557, 663–65; Washington College, Tenn., 546; Washington University, 229; Wesleyan University, Florence, Ala., 340; West Liberty Normal School, 640; West Virginia, University of, 640; William and Mary College, 316. *See also* Education

Colorado River (of Texas), 184

Columbia, S. C.: description of, 458–59; State-House, 460

Columbus, Ga., 373

Columbus, Miss., 313

Comal River, Tex., 145

"Company of the Indies": and Louisiana, 22

Concordia Parish, La., 275

Confederate Peories: in Indian Territory, 197

Convict labor: in Texas, 119–20; in Nashville, 727. *See also* Jails, penitentiaries, and convicts

Cooper, Peter (1791–1883): inventor of the steam locomotive, 741–42

Coosa River, Ala., 329

Copper: Georgia, 525; North Carolina, 504; Tennessee, 549

Corinth, Miss., 311–12

Corwin, Thomas (1794–1865): Minister to Mexico, 172

Cos, Gen.: and siege of San Antonio, 165

Cotton: Alabama, 330–31; description of farming, 298; description of plants, 307; effects of Civil War on, 270–77; Georgia, 348, 366; harvesting, 308; Louisiana plantations, 270–74, 297–99; labor conditions, 270, 273; Mississippi, 311; North Carolina, 471; sharecropping, 273; South Carolina, 428, 517; statis-

tics on, in United States, 51–52; stealing of, 309–10; Texas, 110, 125; value of, 52–53; Virginia, 582; westward movement of cultivation, 270

Cotton factories (mills): Alabama, middle and northern regions of, 334–35; Augusta, Ga., 346–47; Charlotte, N. C., 473; Eureka, Tex., 115; Graniteville, S. C., 347; Houston, 110, 115; Nashville, Tenn., 728; New Orleans, 54; Petersburg, Va., 582; the Sandhill region of Georgia and South Carolina, 344–49

Cotton gin: description of, 308–309

Cotton markets and trade: Augusta, Ga., 348; Charleston, S. C., 439; Chattanooga, 530; Galveston, 104–105; growth of, 51–52; Memphis, 265–67; Mobile, 322–23; New Orleans, 50–55; Norfolk, 591; Savannah, 363–66; St. Louis, 231

Cotton press, 309

Cotton-seed oil: production of, 325

Cotton steamer: description of, 304

Cotton worms, 307–308

Council Grove, N. M., 194

Covington, Va., 668

Cox, Samuel S. (1824–89): New York congressman, in Jacksonville, 419

"Crackers": in Florida, 420–21; in Georgia, 372

Crawford, David, Jr.: railroad financier, 187

Creek Indians: in Indian Territory, 197–98

Creoles, 29–33

Crozat, Anthony: French merchant and slave trader to colonial Louisiana, 21

Culpepper, Va., 800

Cumberland, Md., 769

Cumberland River, Tenn., 728

Cumberland University, Tenn., 731

Cunningham, Ann Pamela (1816–75): and preservation of Mt. Vernon, 799

Cunningham, Mr.: mayor of Charleston, S. C., 448

Cunningham, "Uncle John":

postmaster at Fort Gibson, Indian Territory, 208

Dallas, Tex.: description of, 125; minerals, 125; wheat, 125

Dalton, Ga., 357

Davis, Edmund J. (1827–83): Texas governor, 122, 129–30

Davis, Jefferson (1808–89): house in Montgomery, 332; plantation, 290

Decatur, Ala., 340

Declouet, Paul L.: St. Martin Parish, La., planter, 87

Demopolis, Ala., 313

Denison, George: railroad financier and director, 187

Denison, Tex., 175–78, 181

De Soto, Hernando (c. 1500–42): and explorations, 243, 328, 379

Diehl, Conrad: head of School of Design in St. Louis, 228, 249

Diet, 182–84, 421, 791

Dodge, William E. (1805–83): financier and president of Houston and Texas Central Railroad, 115

Druid Hill Park, Baltimore, 763

"Dry Falls," N. C., 497–98

Dublin, Va., 476

Ducktown, Tenn., 549

Durell, Edward H. (1810–87): federal judge in Louisiana, 92

Eads, James B. (1820–87): and Mississippi River bridge at St. Louis, 234–35

East Tennessee University, 548

Edgefield, Tenn., 728

Education: Alabama, 342–43, 606; Arkansas, 283–84; Baltimore, 765; for blacks, 276–77, 316, 343, 462–63, 574, 596–600, 603–607; Florida, 382, 397, 420; Georgia, 355, 369–70, 374–75, 605–606; Indian Territory, 211–12; Kentucky, 605, 711–12, 723; Louisiana, 97–98, 606–607; Maryland, 770; Mississippi, 293–94, 316, 607; Missouri, 227–29; mixed schools, 601–602, 605; need for and progress of, 600–602; North Carolina, 470; South Carolina, 462–64; Tennessee, 267, 541–42, 547–48, 604–605, 728–29, 731; Texas, 134–35; Virginia, 557, 565–66, 574–75, 581–82, 604, 638, 646, 769; West Virginia, 640–41. *See also* Colleges, institutes, and universities

Eliot, William G. (1811–87): founder of Washington University, St. Louis, 229

Emigration: to the new cotton lands of the Southwest, 136, 270–71, 275, 299–301, 740, 774–75; from Georgia and Alabama, 366

Enterprise, Fla., 417

Essayons (dredge boat), 74–75

Estaing, Charles Hector, Comte d' (1729–94): French admiral, and American Revolution, 361

Eureka cotton mill, Tex., 115

Factories. *See* Manufacturing

Fairchild, Edward H. (1815–89): president of Berea College, 605

Fairmont Normal School, 640

Farragut, David G. (1801–70): and Battle of Mobile Bay, 326

Fayetteville, N. C., 473

Federal Hill, Baltimore, 755–56

Fenner, Thomas P.: director of Hampton Student Singers, 613

Fernandina, Fla., 376

Fishback, George W.: manager of St. Louis *Democrat,* 248

Fisk University, 604–605

Florence, Ala., 340

Florida: agriculture, 402–404, 405–406, 418; alligators, 415; area in square miles, 378; state constitution, 421; "crackers," 420–21; climate, 398–99; state debt, 419; description of, 378–79, 380, 417–18; education, 382, 397, 420; fertility of land, 405–406; early history of, 379–80; housing, 407; hotels, 382, 400, 408; immigration, efforts to encourage,

418; orange culture, 385, 402–404; politics, 419, 421; railroads, 419–20; taxes, 419; timber, 324, 379, 381, 383, 405, 410–11; water transportation, 413–14; wildlife, 384, 410, 411, 417

Forests. *See* Timber

Forsyth, John (1812–77): ex-diplomat, and editor of Mobile *Register,* 327

Fort Gibson, Indian Territory, 208

Fort Marion, St. Augustine, Fla., 394–95

Fort Riley, Kan., 195

Fort St. Philip canal, La., 77

Fort Scott, Kan., 191–92

Fort Smith, Ark., 283

Frankfort, Ky.: commerce, 715; description of, 714–15

Franklin, La., 87

Franklin, State of (Tenn.), 545

Fredericksburg, Va., 795–96

Freedmen. *See* Blacks

Freedmen's Bureau, 598, 604

French: and Louisiana, 17–27, 75, 78–79, 85–87; and Missouri, 215–19, 222; in New Orleans, 27–31, 36–49

French Broad River, N. C.–Tenn., 507–508, 543

French language: in New Orleans, 36

Froissart, Jean (c. 1337–1410?): French chronicler and poet, 43

Front Royal, Va., 801

Gallego flour mill, Richmond, Va., 631

Galveston: climate, 102; cotton trade, 51, 104–105; description of, 101–102, 106–109; exports and imports, 105–106; history of, 103; immigration, 105–106; slavery in, 103

Garret [Garrett], John W. (1820–84); president, Baltimore and Ohio Railroad, 743

George C. Wolf (river boat): and yellow fever in Memphis, 268

Georgia: agriculture, 348, 366, 371–72; and the American Revolution, 360–61; character of people, 371–72; 374; "crackers," 372; description of, 375–76, 520–25;

education, 355, 605–606; emigration from, 366; emigration of blacks, 300; history of, 528; illiteracy, 356; material assets and progress, 366–67; minerals, 519, 525–26; politics, 351–54; property value, 371; railroads, 352, 357, 363–64, 367; timber, 358

Germans: in Houston, 113; in New Braunfels, Tex., 144–45; in politics, 250; in San Antonio, 152–53, 158–60; in St. Louis, 222–29

Girard, Ga., 373

Gold: Georgia, 519; North Carolina, 491

Gordon, John B. (1832–1904): Confederate general and U. S. Senator from Georgia, 356

Gourgues, Dominique de (c. 1530–93): French adventurer on South Carolina coast, 380

Graham, Christopher: Kentucky pioneer and philanthropist, 698, 716

Grand Cote Island, La., 86

Grangers: and cotton trade, 276

Graniteville, S. C., 347

Grant, Ulysses S. (1822–85): and Chattanooga campaign, 540

Great Dismal Swamp, Va., 589

Great Republic (Mississippi River steamboat), 258–59

Greenbrier River, W. Va., 671, 678–79

Greenville, S. C., 517

Greeneville, Tenn.: and Andrew Johnson, 545

Gribault, Father: French priest in St. Louis, 229

Grow, Galusha A. (1822–1907): former Congressman, president of International and Great Northern Railroad, 115, 118, 137

Guerrero, Vincent (1782–1831): Mexican revolutionist and president, 164

Guyandotte, W. Va., 692

Hahn, Michael (1830–86): Louisiana Unionist governor, 90

Haines, Hiram: Alabama iron furnace engineer, 336

Hall, "Red": Denison, Tex., deputy-sheriff, 178–79
Hamilton, Andrew J. (1815–75): Texas provisional governor, 129
Hampden-Sydney College, 557
Hampton Normal and Agricultural Institute, 604
Hampton Student Singers, 613
Hancock, Winfield S.: military governor of Texas-Louisiana District, 129
Harper, Robert: founder of Harpers Ferry, Va., 767
Harpers Ferry, Va., 766–69
Harris, William T. (1835–1909): educator and philosopher in St. Louis, 225–27
Harrison, James (1803–70): president American Iron Mountain Company, St. Louis, 241
Harrisonburg, Va., 659
Harrodsburg, Ky., 716
Hart, Edmund H. (1839–98): pioneer Florida citrus fruit grower, 400–403, 413
Hayne, Paul Hamilton (1830–86): southern poet, 375
Hearne, Tex., 124
Hickory Nut Gap, Blue Ridge Mountains, 518–19
Hillsborough, N. C., 470
Holden, William W. (1818–92): North Carolina governor, 468–69
Hopkins, Johns (1795–1873): Baltimore merchant and philanthropist, 761–62
Hopkins, Mr.: North Carolina mountaineer, 483
Horse raising: Kentucky, 717–18; Tennessee, 732; Texas, 172
Hospitals: Baltimore, 761; New Orleans, 63–64. See also Asylums
Hotchkiss, Jedediah (1827–99): Virginia engineer and promoter of mineral resources and railroads, 684–86
Hotels: Charleston, S. C., Florida, 382, 400, 408; Georgia, 353, 519; Louisville, 697; Missouri, 190–91; New Orleans, 37; Texas, 183–84; Virginia, 567–68; White Sulphur

Springs, W. Va., 673. See also Springs and health resorts
Hot Springs, Ark., 285–86
Housing: for blacks, 46, 273, 281–82, 299, 303, 430–31, 542–43, 652; Florida, 400, 407; Indian Territory, 208; Kansas, 193–94; Little Rock, 281; Louisiana, 24, 28, 31, 61, 96; North Carolina, 496, 502; St. Louis, 222–23; Sandhill region, 346; Tennessee, 480; Texas, 145, 156, 161–63
Houston City cotton mill, 115
Houston, Samuel (1793–1863): early life, and career in Texas, 117–18, 131
Houston, Tex.: climate, 112–13; commerce and transportation, 112, 114–15; cotton mills, 110, 115; cotton trade, 104; description of, 111–13
Howard, Oliver O. (1830–1909): and Freedmen's Bureau, 598
Howard University, 608
Howell [Howells?], C. N.: army engineer, and Louisiana and Texas river and harbor improvements, 75, 108
Huntington, W. Va., 692
Huntsville, Ala., 340
Hurricane Island, Miss.: Davis brothers' plantation, 290
Hurricanes: in colonial Louisiana, 23

Iberville, Pierre le Moyne, Sieur de (1661–1706): and colonial Louisiana, 326, 328
Illiteracy and ignorance: Alabama, 334, 340; Arkansas, 283; Florida, 420; Georgia, 356; North Carolina, 470; among poor whites, 774–75; in the South, 602; Tennessee, 547, 730; Texas, 134
Immigration and immigrants: Alabama, 330–31; Arkansas, 271, 383; the cotton states, 792; Florida, 418; Georgia, 375; Italians, 792; Kentucky, 717; Louisiana, 33, 99, 271; the lower Mississippi Valley, 276; Mississippi, 316–17; Missouri, 219, 252–53; North Carolina, 468; South

Carolina, 451–52; Tennessee, 729–30; Texas, 99, 105, 133, 366, 792; Virginia, 552, 565, 641, 792
Indian agents, 198
Indian River, Fla., 417
Indians: in Alabama, Georgia, North Carolina, and Tennessee, 527–28; cattle raising among, 201; five civilized tribes, 198; food of, 202; clothing of, 209; government of, 198; Kansas, 194; Louisiana, 23, 293; marriage among, 203; Missouri, 217; missionaries and missions, 211–12, 528; in penitentiary, 120–21; population of tribes in Indian Territory, 197; religion, 202; removal from Southeast to Indian Territory, 200, 527–28; in Texas, 124–26, 138, 150–52, 169, 172–74; treaties with whites, 198
Indian Territory: area in acres, 197; description of, 196–97, 199, 205, 208, 212–14; education, 211–12; effect of Civil War on, 200–202; housing, 208; land sales, 198; lawlessness, 206–207; liquor laws and liquor, 209–10; railroads, 195–96, 204
Indian wars: in colonial Louisiana, 23
Indigo: in St. Augustine, Fla., 396; in South Carolina, 424
Industry. See Manufacturing
Institutes. See Education, and Colleges, institutes, and universities
Iron Mountain, Mo., 239, 240–42
Iron ore and processing (forges, furnaces, mills): Alabama, 239–40, 336–38; Baltimore, 751–53; Chattanooga, and vicinity, 532–35; Kentucky, 724; North Carolina, 491; Richmond, Va., 636–37; St. Louis, and vicinity, 237–44; southwest Virginia, 576; West Virginia, 686–87

Jackson, Andrew (1767–1845): and Battle of New

Orleans, 26–27; statue in Memphis, 264

Jackson, Miss.: description of, 314; newspapers, 316

Jackson Railroad: and cotton traffic, 54

Jackson Square, New Orleans, 21, 27

Jackson, Thomas J. (Stonewall) (1824–63): Valley campaigns, 660; grave of, 662

Jacksonville, Fla.: climate, 382; description of, 380–82; education, 382; history of, 382; hotels, 382

Jails, penitentiaries, and convicts: Arkansas, 281; Kentucky, 714–15; Mississippi, 314; Missouri, 256; Tennessee, 727; Texas, 107, 118–22

James River and Kanawha Canal, 690

Jamestown, Va., 621

Jasper, William (1750–79): Revolutionary War hero at Charleston and Savannah, 361

Jefferson, Tex., 124

Jefferson, Thomas (1743–1826): and Monticello, 651–52; and University of Virginia, 653–55

Jews: banished in colonial Louisiana, 23; in commerce, 274; in Jackson, Miss., 314

Jonathan's Creek, N. C., 486

Jones, Anson (1798–1858): last President of Republic of Texas, 132

Joplin, Mo., 243

Journal of Speculative Philosophy: founded by William T. Harris, 226–27

Jubilee Singers, Fisk University, 605, 612–13

Kanawha River, W. Va., 690–91

Kansas City, Mo.: cattle market and meat-packing industry, 251; history of, 251; population, 251

Kansas: corn granaries, 193; description of, 192–93; housing, 193–94; Indians, 194

Kant, Immanuel (1724–1804): influence of on William T. Harris, 226

"Kaw" Indians, 194

Kellogg, William Pitt (1830–1918): Louisiana governor, and his administration, 88, 91, 93, 95

Kemper, James L. (1823–95): Conservative governor of Virginia, 572, 644

Kennedy, Mr.: Texas rancher, 172

Kentucky: agriculture, 713–18, 724–25; Blue Grass region, 718; character of people, 698; coal, 723–24; description of, 699, 717–18; education, 605, 711–12, 723; iron ore and processing, 723–24; political history and politics, 721–23; population, 721; race-horses, 716–17; railroads, 709

Kentucky River, Ky., 713

Kentucky University, 720

Key, Francis Scott (1779–1843): and "The Star-Spangled Banner," 737

Key West, Fla., 418

Killebrew, Joseph B. (1831–1906): Secretary of Tennessee State Board of Agriculture, 730

Kimball, H. J.: Atlanta entrepreneur, 352–54

Kimball House, Atlanta, 353

Kimball-Ramsey-Pullman Sleeping-Car Company, 353

King College, Bristol, Tenn., 569

Kingsbury, Cyrus (1786–1870): missionary to Cherokees, 528

Knoxville, Tenn.: description and history of, 543–44, 546–47, 550

Ku Klux Klan: Alabama, 333; Georgia, 351; Kentucky, 706, 715, 722; Louisiana, 88; North Carolina, 493, 503; South Carolina, 454, 546–57, 515

La Bahia prairie, Tex., 136

Labor: Louisiana, 32, 273–79; Texas, 125–26. See also Blacks

Lafitte, Jean (c. 1780–1854): adventurer and outlaw on Texas and Louisiana coasts, 103

Lake Pontchartrain, La., 22, 59–60

Lamar, Mirabeau B. (1798–1859): President of Repub-lic of Texas, 131–32

La Motte, Mr.: and lead mine in Arkansas, 243

Land sales: in Indian Territory, 198

Laredito: Mexican quarter of San Antonio, 161–62

La Salle, Robert Cavelier, Sieur de (1643–87): in Louisiana and Texas, 24, 103, 149

Law, John (1671–1729): and the Mississippi Company in colonial Louisiana, 22, 328

Lawrence, Effingham: and life on his Louisiana plantation, 81

Lawson, Lt. Col.: commanding officer of Fort Gibson, Indian Territory, 210

Lead: in Missouri, 243–44

Lee, Robert E. (1807–70): and Washington College, 663–65

Lestrapes, André P.: St. Martin Parish, La., planter, 87

Levees: in Louisiana, 67–68, 73; along the Mississippi River, 260–63; in St. Louis, 221

Lewis, David P. (1820–84): Alabama governor, 333

Lexington, Ky., 718–20

Lexington, Va., 662–63

Libraries: Louisville, 697, 711; St. Louis, 249; the University of South Carolina, 462

Liguest, Laclede: French explorer and founder of St. Louis, 215–17

Limestone Gap, Indian Territory, 212

Lindsay, Robert B., Alabama governor, 333

Liquor, and consumption of: Arkansas, 177, 184; Indian Territory, 209; North Carolina, 478, 488; by Southerners, 778; Texas, 283; Virginia, 645

Little Rock, Ark.: blacks in, 281–82; description of, 281; housing, 281; manufacturing, 282; population, 281

Livingston, Robert R. (1746–1813): and Louisiana Purchase, 26

Lockwood, L. C.: and school for blacks in eastern Virginia, 597

Locust Point, Baltimore, 745–46

Lookout Mountain, Tenn., 529, 536–37

Louis XIV (1638–1715): and Louisiana, 21

Louis Phillippe (1773–1850): and Texas, 131

Louisiana: Acadians, 85; agriculture, 78–88, 273–75, 297–302; blacks in, 22–23, 34–35, 273–77, 297–301; burial customs and cemeteries, 36–37; cattle, 78, 84–85; churches, 23; climate, 21, 33, 78; commerce, 45–49; cotton culture and trade, 50–55, 273–75, 297–303; education, 62, 97–98, 606–607; effects of Civil War on, 32; emigration, 33; history, government, and customs in French and Spanish regimes, 17–18, 20–22, 24, 26–28; Kellogg legislature, 95; housing, 96; hurricanes, 23; immigration, 33; industries, 78; labor conditions and system, 28–29, 32, 275, 299, 301; levees, 67–68, 73; minerals, 88; oranges, 88; plantations, 23, 32, 80, 81, 273–75, 297–303; politics, 33, 88, 89–94; population of, 26; property values, 96; purchase by United States, 26; railroads, 76; early religious customs, 23; rice, 78; salt mining, 86, 88; sheep, 85; slaves and slave laws, 21, 23; social customs, 30–31; soil, 78; swamps, 70; taxes, 33, 93–94; Bayou Teche country, 85–88; timber, 84, 87–88, wheat, 78–79; "White League," 88, 96

Louisiana State University, 98

Louisiana, University of, 62

Louisville, Ky.: commerce, 707–708; public debt, 710; description of, 696–97, 710–11; education, 711–12; early history of, 698; hotels, 697; libraries, 697, 711; rail and water transportation, 708–709; tobacco market, 707

Lumber. See Timber

Lynchburg, Va.: description of, 552–53, 554–55, 560

McAllister, Gen.: designer of dredgeboat, 74

McComb, H. E.: founder of McComb City, Miss., 318

McDowell, Silas: North Carolina mountaineer, 494, 500

McEnery, John (1833–91): unrecognized Louisiana governor, 91

Macon, Ga., 374

Madison's Cave, Va., 658

Magee, Augustus W.: and 1813 Texas filibustering expedition, 154

Magnolia plantation, La.: and sugar making, 81–82

Mahone, William (1826–95): Virginia railroad developer and politician, 558–59

Malaria: in Virginia, 595

Mammoth Cave, Ky., 700–705

Manassas, Va., 799–800

Mandarin, Fla., 385–86

Manufacturing: Alabama, 334–35; Atlanta, 356; Charleston, S. C., 450–51; Charleston, W. Va., 689–90; Chattanooga and vicinity, 530–35; effect on social status of workers, 774; Kentucky, 708, 715; Little Rock, 282; Memphis, 268; Missouri, 238–45; Mobile, 325, 327; Natchez, absence of, 293; the Sandhill region, 344–47; the southern states, 792; Tennessee, 547–49; Texas, 109–10, 115, 124, 145; Virginia, 556–57, 571, 582, 631–38. See also Cotton factories, Iron, Sugar

Mardi Gras: in Mobile, 327; in New Orleans, 38–45

Marietta, Ga., 356

Marion, Va., 572, 575

Markets, street: in New Orleans, 46–49

Marriage: among blacks, 33, 277, 779–80, 782; of Indians, 203; interracial in Louisiana, 23

Marshall College, 641

Martinsburg, W. Va., 769

Mary Institute, St. Louis, 229

Maryland: agriculture, 738–39; commerce, 739; state debt, 770; description of, 738–40, 765, 768–69; history of, 733–38; minerals, 738; politics, 770; timber, 738; tobacco, 738–39; truck farming, 738

Maryland State Agricultural College, 739

Maverick cattle: origin of the name, 171

Medina, Battle of: in Texas Revolution, 154

Memphis and St. Louis Packet Company, 267

Memphis: carnival, 269; cemetery, 265; commerce, 267; cotton trade, 265–67; description of, 264; education, 267; manufacturing, 268; newspapers, 265; population, 265; railroads, 265–66; taxes, 267; yellow fever in, 265, 268–69

Menéndez de Avilés, Pedro (1519–74): founder of St. Augustine, 379–80, 390–91

Meridian, Miss., 312

Mexicans: in Texas, 132, 142–43, 148, 156, 161–63, 167

Miami: as a health resort, 399

Milam, Ben R. (1788–1835): hero of Texas Revolution, and San Antonio, 165

Military Academy, Charleston, S. C. (The Citadel), 464

Milledgeville, Ga., 375

Minerals: Alabama, 335–38; Arkansas, 280, 285; Georgia, 519, 525–26; Kentucky, 723–24; Louisiana, 86, 88; Maryland, 738–39, 751–53, 769–70; Missouri, 218, 237–245; North Carolina, 468, 488, 491; South Carolina, 449–50; Tennessee, 530–35, 547, 549–50; Texas, 124–126, 131, 147; Virginia, 575–76, 636–37, 648–49, 657; West Virginia, 680–92. See also Coal, Copper, Gold, Iron, Lead, Phosphates, Salt, and Sulphur

Missions: in Kansas, 192; in Texas, 150–56

Mission schools: for Indians, 211–12, 528

Mississippi: agriculture, 311, 317; area in square miles, 313; cotton production, 311; state debt, 315; description of, 317–18; dueling and violence in, 289; education, 316, 607; blacks in politics, 314–15; property values, 311; railroads, 292, 312–13,

317–18; taxes, 315; timber, 311, 317

Mississippi River: course, description of, 262, 288; crevasses, 261–62; flooding of, 260–61, 263; ice gorges, 232–33; in Louisiana, 59, 67–68, 73–75; mud lumps, 73–74; at New Orleans, 59; passes at mouth of, 73–75; "rocky chain" at St. Louis, 262; and traffic at St. Louis, 232–35; wildlife on, 70–71

Mississippi riverboat men: language and quaint expressions of, 233

Mississippi Valley Transportation Company: towboat company, 56

Missouri: agriculture, 253, 255; character of people, 190–91; small cities and towns, 188–90, 253–55; climate, 230; coal, 243–44; state debt, 219; description of, 252–54; education, 227–29; state fair, 247; Great Swamp, 254; early history of, 215–17; iron resources and processing, 237–45; lead, 243–44; politics, 256; population, 219; property value, 219, 255; navigable rivers, 219; timber, 253

Missouri River, 251

Missouri State University, 229

Mitchell, Elisha (1793–1857): geologist and explorer in North Carolina, 513–14

Mobile: churches, 327; commerce, 325; cotton trade, 322–23; description of, 322, 325–27; early history of, 321–22; Mardi Gras and secret societies, 327; population, 322; railroads, 323–25; prominent residents, 327

Mobile Bay: and Battle of, 326–27

Montgomery: economic conditions in, 331–32; history of, 331–32

Monticello, Va.: and Thomas Jefferson, 651–52

Moragné, Dr.: and orange culture in Palatka, Fla., 404

Morgan, Charles (1795–1878): shipping and railroad magnate, and the Morgan Line, 100–101

"Mountain House": and Mount Mitchell, N. C., 510–11

Mountains: Appalachian, 474–578, 666–92, passim; Alleghany, 329, 483, 512, 568; Bald, 487, 512; Black, 488, 510–12; Blue Ridge, 484–500, passim, 504, 511, 518–19, 563, 686; Ozark, 243, 279; Great Smoky, 482–85, 501, 525; in Texas, 101

Mount Vernon, 798–99

Mount Mitchell, N. C.: 510–14

Mumford, William B.: hanged by Gen. Butler in New Orleans, 66

Music, songs, and spirituals: of blacks, 608–20

Muskogee, Indian Territory, 206–207

Napoleon, Ark., 278

Napoleon I (1769–1821): and Louisiana, 20, 26

Nashville, Tenn., commerce, 727; cotton factories, 728; description of, 726, 729; schools and colleges, 728–29; railroads, and water transportation, 727–28

Natchez: Mississippi River steamboat, 304

Natchez Indians, 293

Natchez, Miss.: Brown's Garden, 293; description of, 292; education, 293–94; history of, 293; politics, 293; taxes, 295

Natural Bridge, Va., 561–62

Negroes. See Blacks

Neosho Valley, Kan., 193

New Braunfels, Tex., 144–45

New Iberia, La., 86

New Orleans: Battle of, 26–27; blacks in, 22–23; canals, 59; as capital of French Louisiana, 22; churches, 23; climate, 62–63; cotton trade, 50–55; public debt, and expenses, 94; description of, 18, 22–26, 28–30, 59–66; early fortification of, 25; Franco-Spanish heritage and influence on, 19–20, 25–26; French Quarter, 28–30; hospitals, 63–64; hotels, 37; housing, 24, 28, 31, 61; Lake Pontchartrain, 59; Mardi Gras, 38–45; markets, 46–49; population of,

24; street names, 23; coastwise trade, 57–58

New River, Va. and W. Va., 679–80

New Smyrna, Fla., 396

Newspapers: Atlanta, 356; Baltimore, 765; Galveston, 109, 134; Houston, 134; Jackson, Miss., 316; Louisville, 697–98; Memphis, 265; Mobile, 327; St. Augustine, 397; St. Louis, 224–25, 248–49; Texas, 134

Norfolk: commerce, 591–92; description of, 589–90, 592–93; early history of, 592; waterways and transportation, 590–91

Normal schools: for blacks, 599–607. See also Education, and Colleges, institutes, and universities

North Carolina: agriculture, 466, 489; area in square miles and acres, 466; climate, 471; copper, 504; cotton, 471; description of, 466–68, 488, 492–93, 504–505, 508–509; education, 470; effects of Civil War on, 468; minerals, 488, 491, 504; mountain region, 483–514; outer banks, 467; politics, 468–69; property values, 468; railroads, 467, 471, 505–507; timber, 472, 489; turpentine, 472–73

Notre Dame des Kahokias, Cahokia, Ill., 222

Oakes, James, (1826–1910): commander, Fort Riley, Kan., 195

Oakland College, Miss., 316

Oclawaha River, Fla., 408–11

Ogden, E. A., founder of Fort Riley, Kan., 195

Oglethorpe, James E. (1696–1785): founder and defender of Georgia, 359, 391–92

Ohio River: trip from Huntington to Louisville on, 693–96

Opera: New Orleans, 35–36; St. Louis, 225

Opothlehola: Creek chief in Indian Territory, 201

Oranges: Florida, 385, 402–404; Louisiana, 81, 86, 88

Osage Indians: in Indian Territory, 197; in Missouri, 217

Overland Transportation Company: stagecoach line in northeast Texas, 179
Overton, John (1766–1833): and Memphis, 264
Ozark Mountains, 243, 279

Packard, Stephen B.: U. S. marshal, Louisiana governor, 91
Palatka, Fla.: as a resort and center of orange culture, 400–404
Palmer, Benjamin M. (1818–1902): Presbyterian clergyman in New Orleans, 65
Parsons, Lewis E. (1817–95): Alabama Unionist governor, 332
Parsons, Kan., 192–93
Patton, Robert M. (1809–85): Alabama governor, 333
Peabody, George (1795–1869): banker and philanthropist, 757
Peabody Institute, Baltimore, 757
Peake, Mary A., black teacher in eastern Virginia, 597
Pea Ridge, Ark.: Battle of, 200
Pease, Elisha M. (1812–83): Texas governor, 129
Peigneur Lake, La., 86
Pensacola, Fla., 324
Petersburg, Va.: blacks in, 580–87; description of, 580, 582–83; education, 581–82; manufacturing and trade, 582; politics, 580
Petit Anse Island, La., 86
Phelps, John: president New Orleans Cotton Exchange, 53
Phosphates: in South Carolina, 450
Pierce, Thomas W.: railroad builder in Texas, 114
Pierpont, Francis H. (1814–99): governor of "restored" state of Virginia, 641
Pike, Albert (1809–91): Confederate general in Indian Territory and Arkansas, 200, 281
Pike, James S. (1811–82): and comments on South Carolina government, 464
Pilot Knob Iron Company:

near Iron Mountain, Mo., 242
Plantations: cotton, 270–77, 297–304, 318; rice, 429–37; sugar, 78–84
Plaquemine, La., 67
Police: Charleston, S. C., 448; Savannah, 369; Texas, 130
Politics: Alabama, 332–33; Arkansas, 284; blacks in, 33, 89–91, 94, 95, 97, 295–96, 300, 333, 369, 431, 453, 460–62, 580–81; black-white relations in, 793; Charleston, S. C., 446–49; Florida, 419, 421; Georgia, 351–54; Germans in, 250; Kentucky, 721–23; Louisiana, 33, 34, 88–94; Maryland, 770; Mississippi, 314–15; Missouri, 256; Natchez, Miss., 293; North Carolina, 468–69; Petersburg, Va., 580–81; San Antonio, 148; Savannah, 369; South Carolina, 454–58, 460–62; Tennessee, 547, 729–31; Texas, 129–31, 148; Virginia, 573–74, 640–44; West Virginia, 639–41
Poll tax: on blacks, 306
Ponce de León, Juan (1460–1521): in Florida, 379
Poor whites: Alabama, 334, 340; Arkansas, 283; Florida, 420–21; Georgia, 346, 356, 372; North Carolina, 467, 470; South Carolina, 515; Tennessee, 547, 730; South, in general, 602, 774–76, 786, 788–89; Texas, 99, 134, 181–84
Population: Arkansas, 196, 283; Asheville, N. C., 505; Atlanta, 356; Austin, 128–29; black, increase of, 793; Bristol, Va.-Tenn., 569; Chattanooga, 530; Columbus, Ga., 374; Denison, Tex., 175; Fort Smith, Ark., 283; Huntsville, Ala., 340; of tribes in Indian Territory, 197; Kansas City, Mo., 251; Kentucky, 721; Key West, 418; Knoxville, 546; Little Rock, 281; Louisiana, 26; Louisville, 698; Lynchburg, Va., 555; Macon, Ga., 374; Memphis, 265; Missouri, 219; of blacks in Missouri, 219;

Missouri and Kansas, 196; Mobile, 322; Nashville, 727; New Orleans, 24; of blacks in New Orleans, 23; New Braunfels, Tex., 144; Pensacola, 324; Raleigh, N. C., 469; Richmond, 631; St. Louis, 217–19, 255; of Germans in St. Louis, 224; Savannah, 369; black-white ratio in South Carolina, 427; Tennessee, 729; of blacks in Texas, 134; northern Texas, 124–25; Texas, 132, 134; Vicksburg, 289; Virginia, 645
Port Royal Island, S. C.: description of, 425; early French and English colonization efforts, 422–24
Pratte, Joseph: original owner of Iron Mountain, Mo., 240
Prentice, George D. (1802–70): Louisville journalist, 711
Press. See Newspapers
Pretorius, Mr.: St. Louis journalist, 224
Private schools: in St. Louis, 228–29; in Texas, 135. See also Education
Profanity: in Texas, 183–84
Property value: Alabama, 311, 330; Georgia, 371; Louisiana, 31–34, 276; Mississippi, 311; Missouri, 219, 255; North Carolina, 468; St. Louis, 250; Tennessee, 729–30; Texas, 133; Virginia, 565, 578, 644–45
Prostitution: in St. Louis, 250
Pulaski, Casimir (c. 1748–79): and siege of Savannah in American Revolution, 361

Quawpaw Indians: in Indian Territory, 197

Rabun Gap, Ga., 519
Race riots: in Louisiana, 90–93
Racehorses, in Kentucky, 716–18
Racial conflict: in Louisiana, 89–93, 95
Railroads: Alabama, 325, 330, 339; Arkansas, 280, 284; Atlanta, 350; Augusta, Ga., 347; Baltimore, 741, 748–51; blacks as passengers on, 783; effect on Southern

provincialism, 772; effect on towns in Missouri, 189–90; Florida, 419–20; Georgia, 352, 357, 367, Houston, Tex., 114–15; Indian Territory, 195–96, 204; Kentucky, 709; land grants for, 187; Louisiana, 76; Memphis, 265–66; Mississippi, 292, 312–13, 317–18; Mobile, 323–25; New Orleans, 56–57; North Carolina, 467, 471, 505–507; Richmond, Va., 647–48; St. Louis, 231; Savannah, Ga., 363–65; South Carolina, 425, 438–39, 449, 516–17; in the Southwest, 187–88, 195; Tennessee, 530–31, 727–28; Texas, and need for, 114–15, 132, 160, 173, 179; Virginia, 556, 558–59, 570, 647–48

Raleigh, N. C.: description and population of, 469

Raleigh, Sir Walter (1552?–1618): and early colonization efforts, 623–24

Read, Daniel (1805–78): president, University of Missouri, 229

Red Mountain, Ala., 336–38

Red River: removal of driftwood raft from, 310

Red River Iron Works, Ky., 724

Religion: of blacks, 521–22, 583–87, 607–608, 618, 779–81; of Indians, 202; in North Carolina and Tennessee mountains, 481

Religious holidays: in Louisiana, 23

Restaurants and dining places: New Orleans, 29–30; other cities, 791; Texas, 183–84

Reynolds, John (1713–88): colonial governor of Georgia, 360

Ribault, Jean (c. 1520–65): and French colonization efforts in Florida and South Carolina, 390–91, 423

Rice: Louisiana, 78; South Carolina, 432–37

Richardson, Willard (1802–75): Galveston newspaperman, 109

Richmond Institute, 638

Richmond, Va.: churches, 629–30; commerce and trade, 631–36; description of, 626–31; education, 638; Hollywood Cemetery, 630; manufacturing, 631, 635–38; tobacco factories and trade, 632–37; water power, 635

Roanoke College, 557, 577

Robert E. Lee: Mississippi River steamboat, 304–305

Rockbridge Alum Springs, Va., 661–62

Rockwood, Tenn., 533–34

Rolla, Mo., 229

Ross, John (1790–1866): Cherokee chief and leader, 200

Ross, William P., Cherokee chief, 200

Ross-Ridge Cherokee Indian feud, 200

Rousseau, Lovell H. (1818–69): military governor of Texas–Louisiana District, 130

Sac and Fox Indians: in Indian Territory, 197

St. Augustine, Fla.: churches, 395–96; climate, 393; description of, 387–89, 393; education, 397; effect of Civil War on, 397; early history of, 390–92; indigo culture, 396; newspaper, 397; as tourist attraction, 396–97

St. Charles, Mo., 254

Sainte Genevieve, Mo., 254

St. John's River, Fla., 381, 383–85, 416–17

St. Joseph, Mo., 253

St. Louis Cathedral, New Orleans, 18–19

St. Louis: auctions, 223; breweries, 225; Carondelet (industrial suburb), 234, 237–39, 244; churches, 247; commerce and trade, 230–32, 249; cotton trade, 231; description of, 217–22, 230, 246–48; education, 227–28; French influence, 222; Germans and German culture, 224–26; history of, 216–19; housing, 222–23; iron processing, 237–39, 244–45; libraries, 249; Merchant's Exchange, 230–31; Mississippi River bridge and construction of, 234–36; newspapers, 224–25, 248; opera, 225; parks and gardens, 246–47; study of philosophy in, 225–26; population, 217–19, 255; property value, 250; prostitution in, 250; railroads, 231; and river traffic, 232–34

St. Martin Parish, La., 87

St. Mary Parish, La., 87

Salcedo, Gen.: Spanish commander at San Antonio in 1813, p. 154

Salem, Va., 575, 577–78

Saloons: in Texas, 177, 184

Salt: Florida, 406; Louisiana, 86, 88; Virginia, 571; West Virginia, 689–90

Saltville, Va., 571

San Antonio, Tex.: The Alamo, 131, 150, 163–66; beer gardens, 158; description of, 141, 148–49, 155–63; Germans in, 152–53, 158–60; history of, 148–66, *passim;* missions, 150–52, 154, 156; plazas, 160–61

Sandhill region of Ga. and S. C.: agriculture, 345–48; climate, 345; manufacturing, 344–48; timber, 345

San Jacinto, Battle of, 117–18

San Jose Mission, 154–55

San Marcos River, 144

San Pedro Springs, San Antonio, 158

Santa Anna, Antonio López de (1794–1876): Mexican dictator, and Texas Revolution, 111, 118, 137, 165–66

Sargent, Winthrop (1753–1820): governor of Mississippi Territory, 322

Satanta: Kiowa chief, 120–21

Sauvolle, de la Villantray, Sieur de: acting governor of French Louisiana, 21, 24

Savannah, Ga.: climate, 362; cotton trade, 363–66; description of, 359, 361–63, 368–69; education, 369–70; early history of, 359–61; police, 369; blacks and politics, 369; population, 369; railroads and shipping, 363–65

Savannah River, 358

Sayle, William (d. 1671): governor of colonial Carolina, 423

Schools. *See* Education, and Colleges, institutes, and universities

Schumacher, Father: missionary to Osage Indians, 192

Schurz, Carl (1829–1906): comments on Louisiana politics, 92–93; in Missouri, 224–25

Scott, John G. (1819–92): developer of Iron Mountain, Mo., 242

Sears, Barnas (1802–80): agent of Peabody Fund, and work in southern education, 600–601, 658

Sedalia, Mo., 186

Seminole Indians: in Indian Territory, 197–99

Seneca Indians: in Indian Territory, 197

Sewanee, Tenn., 541–42

Sharecropping, 273. See also Blacks, free laborers and as farmers

Shawnee Indians: in Indian Territory, 197

Shaw's Botanical Gardens, St. Louis, 246

Sheep: Louisiana, 85; Tennessee, 732

Shelbyville, Ky., 715–16

Shenandoah Valley, Va., 656–60

Shepherdstown Normal School, 640–41

Sheridan, Philip H. (1831–88): as military governor of Texas–Louisiana District, 129

Sherman, Tex., 180–81

Shreveport, La., 76, 84

Silver Spring, Fla., 412–13

Slavery, and effects of: in Galveston, 103, 348; in Georgia, 346; in Kentucky, 694, 708, 717; in Louisiana, 23, 80, 87, 90; in Maryland, 749; in St. Louis, 218–19; in South Carolina, 427, 432–33; in the South generally, 773; in Texas, 125, 159, 182

Smith, William H. (1826–99): Alabama governor, 333

Somers, Robert (1822–91): British journalist, and observations on blacks in Alabama, 305–307

Songs. See Music, songs, and spirituals

South Carolina: churches, 451; cotton, 428, 517; state debt, 455–56; description of, 425–26, 451; education, 462–64; effects of Civil War in, 426–28, 431; early history of, 422–25; immigration, 452; land commission, 457; minerals, 449–50; politics, 446–49, 454–58, 460–62; black-white population ratio, 427; possibilities for economic and political progress, 464–65; railroads, 425, 438–39, 449, 516–17; rice, 432–37; slaves, importation of, 432–33; taxes, 432; timber, 439; truck farming, 451

South Carolina, University of, 459

Southerners, general characteristics and habits of: blacks, 778–91; whites, 771–78, 784–91

Speech and dialect: of blacks, 429, 542, 553, 785, 788–91; of whites, 183, 372, 415, 474, 477–83, 486, 491, 497, 784–89

Spotswood, Alexander (1676–1740): Virginia colonial governor, 622–23

Springs and health resorts: Arkansas, 285–86; Asheville, 505; Asheville-Greenville area, 518; Florida, 396–97, 408–13; North Carolina, 508; San Antonio, 157–58; Sandhill region, 345–46; Staunton, Va., 658; Tennessee, 541; Virginia, 566–68, 570, 575–78, 661–62, 667, 674–78; West Virginia, 670–75, 800

Stagecoach: in Texas, 140

State pride, 772–73, 776

Staunton, Va., 657–59

Stewart, Robert M. (1815–71): Missouri governor, 256

Stone Mountain, Ga., 356

Storer College, Va., 769

Stowe, Harriet Beecher (1811–96): winter home in Florida, 386

Straight University, 606

Sugar culture, processing, and trade: Baltimore, 752; Florida, 405–406; harvesting of cane, 82; Louisiana, 79–84; manufacture, 82–84; St. Louis, 249

Sulphur: in Louisiana, 88

Summers, E. H.: president New Orleans Cotton Exchange, 53

Summerville, Ga., 345

Swannanoa River, N. C., 509–10

Synodical Institute, Florence, Ala., 340

Tahlequah: capital of Indian Territory, 199

Talcot, Capt.: and survey of the mouths of the Mississippi River, 74

Tallulah Falls, Ga., 522–25

Tappan, Lewis (1788–1873): and American Missionary Association, 597

Taxes: Arkansas, 282, 285; on blacks, 306; Charleston, S. C., 448; Florida, 419; Louisiana, 33, 93–94; Memphis, 267; Mississippi, 315; Natchez, Miss., 295; South Carolina, 432; for support of public education in the South, 600–602; Tennessee, 731; Virginia, 565, 574–75, 644–46

Tennessee: agriculture, 548, 729, 732; character of people, 478, 480; copper, 549; state debt, 731; description of, 475–79, 482, 540, 731; education, 541–42, 547–48, 604–605, 731; history of, 529–30, 544–46; immigration, 729–30; minerals, 532–35, 547, 549–50; "moonshine" whiskey, 478; politics, 547, 729–31; property value, 729–30; railroads, 530–31; 727–28; timber, 547; tobacco, 732; wheat, 732

Tennessee River, 329, 339, 494, 543, 550–51

Texas: agriculture, 136, 145; architecture, 150–55; cattle and cattle stealing, 167–72; climate, 137–38, 184; clothing, 183; coastline, 100–101; convicts, jails, and penitentiary, 107, 118–22; cotton, 104–105, 110, 115, 125; state debt, 133; description of, 138–46, 155–56, 184–85; diet, 182–84; education, 109, 134–35; effects of Civil War on, 184; forts, 172–73; geographic sections, 147; Ger-

mans in, 113, 144–45, 158–60; history of, 131, 137, 149–50; hangings in, 185; horse raising, 172; housing, 145, 156, 161–63; immigration, 99, 105, 133, 366, 792; Indians, 124–26, 138, 150–52, 169–70, 172–74; labor, 125–26; public land, preemption, and Land Office, 132–33; manufacturing, 109–10, 115, 124, 145; Mexicans, 148, 156, 161–63, 167; minerals, 124–26, 131, 147; missions, 150–56; newspapers, 109, 134; people, character of, 181–82; plains, 100, 122–23; state police, 130; politics, 129–31, 148; population, 124–25, 132, 134, 196; ports, 108; profanity, 183; railroads, and need for, 114–15, 132, 160, 173, 179; old San Antonio road, 147–49; saloons, 177, 184; private schools, 135; slavery, and effects of, 103, 125, 159, 182, 348; social customs, 115; Spanish influence, 150, 153–54; speech and dialect, 183; stagecoach, 140; small towns, description of, 183–84; timber, 125; wheat, 110, 125; yellow fever, 102
Texas Almanac, 109
Texas Military Institute, 128
Thompson, Jeff: Louisiana State Engineer, 67
Throckmorton, James W. (1825–94): Texas governor, 129
Timber: Alabama, 311, 324, 329–30; Arkansas, 280, 286; Florida, 324, 379, 381, 383, 405, 410–11; Georgia, 358; Louisiana, 84, 87–88; Maryland, 738; Mississippi, 311, 317; Missouri, 253; North Carolina, 472, 489; the Sandhill region of Ga. and S. C., 345; South Carolina, 439; Tennessee, 547; Texas, 125; Virginia, 666; West Virginia, 666, 671, 689
Tobacco, culture, processing, and trade: Baltimore, 752; Louisville, 707; Maryland, 738–39; Richmond, 632–37; Tennessee, 732; Virginia, 556–57, 580, 582, 649–50,

656–57; West Virginia, 691
Toccoa Falls, Ga., 525
Tombigbee River, 313
Toombs, Robert A. (1810–85): and Georgia politics, 351–52
Tougaloo Normal School, 607
Transylvania University, 720
Travis, William B. (1809–36): commander at the Alamo, 166
Tredegar Iron Works, Richmond, Va., 636
Trinity College, N. C. (Duke University), 470
Truck farming: South Carolina, 451; Maryland, 738; Virginia, 591
Trudeau, Zenon: Spanish governor in upper Louisiana, 240
Tuckaseege River, N. C., 492–93
Turnbull, Andrew (c. 1718–92): and colony at New Smyrna, Fla., 396
Turpentine: in North Carolina, 472–73
Tuscaloosa, Ala., 312
Tuscumbia, Ala., 340
Twain, Mark (Clemens, Samuel L.) (1835–1910): and Mississippi River steamboats, 259

Universities. *See* Colleges, institutes, and universities, and Education

Vanderbilt University, 728
Vergennes, Charles Gravier, Comte de (1717–87): comment on Louisiana soil and climate, 78
Vick, Col.: Mississippi planter, 289
Vicksburg, Miss., 287–88
Vinita, Indian Territory, 204
Virginia: climate, in eastern section of, 388; colleges, 557, 577, 605, 638, 653–55, 663–65; cotton mills, 582; state debt, 645; description of, 561, 572, 576–78, 580, 588, 594, 648, 656, 659–61, 665–69, 795, 799; education, 565–66, 575–77, 581–82, 646; education for blacks, 599, 603–604; history of, 579–80, 623–25, 639–40, 641,

800–801; liquor consumption, 645; minerals, 575–76, 636–37, 648–49, 657; Peaks of Otter, 562–64; Piedmont region, 649–50; politics, 572–74, 640–44; property value, 565, 578, 644–45; railroads, 556, 558–59, 570, 647–48; salt, 571; springs and resort areas, 566–68, 570, 575–78, 661–62, 667, 674–78; taxes, 565, 574–75, 644–46; timber, 666; tobacco, 556–57, 580, 582, 632–37, 649–50, 656–57, 580; truck farming, 591; waterways and transportation, 590–91; wheat, 649, 657
Virginia Medical College, 638
Virginia Military Institute, 557, 662
Virginia State Agricultural and Mechanical College, 577
Vulcan Iron Works, St. Louis, 238

Waco, Tex., 125
Wake Forrest College, 470
Walhalla, S. C., 517
Walker, Gilbert C. (1832–85): Conservative governor of Virginia, 643
Warmoth, Henry C. (1842–1931): Republican governor of Louisiana, 90–91
Warm Springs, N. C., 508
Washington and Lee College (University), 557, 663–65
Washington College, Tenn., 546
Washington, George (1732–99): and Mount Vernon, 798
Washington Monument, Baltimore, 757
Washington University, St. Louis, 229
Watauga Association: in colonial North Carolina, 544–45
Waynesville, N. C., 486, 487–89
Weapons, 275, 777–78
Weatie (Waite), Stand: and Ross-Ridge Indian feud, 200
Webster, N. C., 492–93
Welaka, Fla., 416

Wells, J. Madison (1808–99) : Louisiana Unionist governor, 90

Wesley, John (1703–91) : in Savannah, Ga., 359

Wesleyan University, Florence, Ala., 340

Westcott, Dr.: of Tocoi, Fla., 400

West Liberty Normal School, 640

West Virginia: blacks, 678; coal, 680, 682–86; description of, 678–79, 681, 690–91; education, 640–41; history of, 639–41; iron, 686–87; minerals, 681–91; politics, 639–41; springs and resort areas, 670–75; timber, 666, 671, 689; tobacco, 691; wheat, 691

West Virginia, University of, 640

Weyer, Bernard: and Weyer's Cave, Va., 658

Wheat: Louisiana, 78–79; Tennessee, 732; Texas, 110, 125; Virginia, 649, 657; West Virginia, 691

White, George L. (1838–95) : conductor of Fisk "Jubilee Singers," 613

"White League": in Louisiana, 88, 96

White River, Ark., 278–79

Whiteside Mountain, N. C., 498–502

White Sulphur Springs, Warrenton, Va., 800

White Sulphur Springs, Greenbrier, W. Va., 670–75

Wilder, John T. (1830–1917) : iron and coal developer in Tennessee, 533

Wildlife: Florida, 410, 417; on Mississippi River, 70–71

Wilkins, F. B.: St. Martin Parish, La., planter, 87

William and Mary College, 622

Williamsburg, Va., 621–23

Wilmington, N. C.: commerce and trade, 472–73; description of, 471

Winchester, James (1752–1826) : and founding of Memphis, 264

Winchester, Va., 660

Wine, production of: in Aiken, S. C., 346

Worcester, Samuel A. (1798–1859) : missionary to Cherokees, 527–28

Wyandotte Indians: in Indian Territory, 197

Wytheville, Va., 575

Yellow Fever: Memphis, 265, 268–69; New Orleans, 62–63; Texas, 102

Yerger, E. M.: and murder of military mayor of Jackson, Miss., 316

Yorktown, Va., 623

Young, David: black Louisiana legislator, 295–96

DATE DUE

JUN 22 1990			

DEMCO 38-297